W9-AGC-972

Computer Networks

Fourth Edition

ISBN 0-13-066102-3

Other bestselling titles by Andrew S. Tanenbaum

Distributed Systems: Principles and Paradigms

This new book, co-authored with Maarten van Steen, covers both the principles and paradigms of modern distributed systems. In the first part, it covers the principles of communication, processes, naming, synchronization, consistency and replication, fault tolerance, and security in detail. Then in the second part, it goes into different paradigms used to build distributed systems, including object-based systems, distributed file systems, document-based systems, and coordination-based systems. Numerous examples are discussed at length.

Modern Operating Systems, 2nd edition

This comprehensive text covers the principles of modern operating systems in detail and illustrates them with numerous real-world examples. After an introductory chapter, the next five chapters deal with the basic concepts: processes and threads, deadlocks, memory management, input/output, and file systems. The next six chapters deal with more advanced material, including multimedia systems, multiple processor systems, security. Finally, two detailed case studies are given: UNIX/Linux and Windows 2000.

Structured Computer Organization, 4th edition

This widely-read classic, now in its fourth edition, provides the ideal introduction to computer architecture. It covers the topic in an easy-to-understand way, bottom up. There is a chapter on digital logic for beginners, followed by chapters on microarchitecture, the instruction set architecture level, operating systems, assembly language, and parallel computer architectures.

Operating Systems: Design and Implementation, 2nd edition

This popular text on operating systems, co-authored with Albert S. Woodhull, is the only book covering both the principles of operating systems and their application to a real system. All the traditional operating systems topics are covered in detail. In addition, the principles are carefully illustrated with MINIX, a free POSIX-based UNIX-like operating system for personal computers. Each book contains a free CD-ROM containing the complete MINIX system, including all the source code. The source code is listed in an appendix to the book and explained in detail in the text.

Computer Networks

Fourth Edition

Andrew S. Tanenbaum

Vrije Universiteit
Amsterdam, The Netherlands

Prentice Hall PTR
Upper Saddle River, NJ 07458
www.phptr.com

Library of Congress Cataloging-in-Publication Data

Tanenbaum, Andrew S.
Computer networks / Andrew S. Tanenbaum.--4th ed.
p. cm.
Includes bibliographical references.
ISBN 0-13-066102-3
1. Computer networks. I. Title.
TK5105.5 .T36 2002
004.6--dc21 2002029263

Editorial/production supervision: *Patti Guerrieri*
Cover design director: *Jerry Votta*
Cover designer: *Anthony Gemmellaro*
Cover design: *Andrew S. Tanenbaum*
Art director: *Gail Cocker-Bogusz*
Interior Design: *Andrew S. Tanenbaum*
Interior graphics: *Hadel Studio*
Typesetting: *Andrew S. Tanenbaum*
Manufacturing buyer: *Maura Zaldivar*
Executive editor: *Mary Franz*
Editorial assistant: *Noreen Regina*
Marketing manager: *Dan DePasquale*

Publishing as Prentice Hall PTR
Upper Saddle River, New Jersey 07458

Prentice Hall books are widely used by corporations and government agencies for training, marketing, and resale.

For information regarding corporate and government bulk discounts please contact:
Corporate and Government Sales (800) 382-3419 or corpsales@pearsontechgroup.com

ISBN 0130661023

Text printed in the United States on recyled paper at Courier Westford in Westford, Massachusetts.

10th Printing November 2006

Pearson Education LTD.
Pearson Education Australia PTY, Limited
Pearson Education Singapore, Pte. Ltd.
Pearson Education North Asia Ltd.
Pearson Education Canada, Ltd.
Pearson Educación de Mexico, S.A. de C.V.
Pearson Education — Japan
Pearson Education Malaysia, Pte. Ltd.

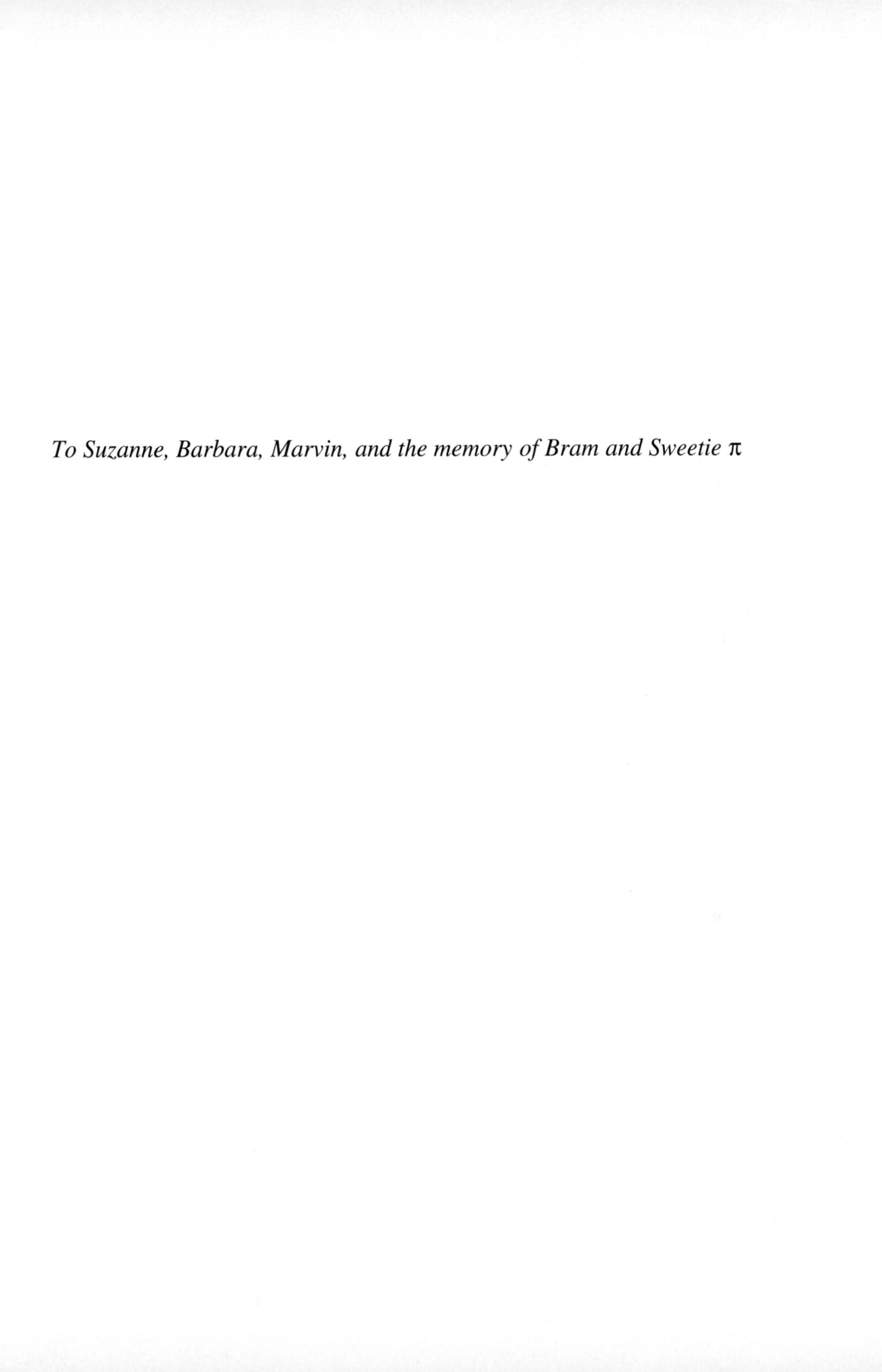

To Suzanne, Barbara, Marvin, and the memory of Bram and Sweetie π

CONTENTS

5 THE NETWORK LAYER 343

PREFACE

This book is now in its fourth edition. Each edition has corresponded to a different phase in the way computer networks were used. When the first edition appeared in 1980, networks were an academic curiosity. When the second edition appeared in 1988, networks were used by universities and large businesses. When the third edition appeared in 1996, computer networks, especially the Internet, had become a daily reality for millions of people. The new item in the fourth edition is the rapid growth of wireless networking in many forms.

The networking picture has changed radically since the third edition. In the mid-1990s, numerous kinds of LANs and WANs existed, along with multiple protocol stacks. By 2003, the only wired LAN in widespread use was Ethernet, and virtually all WANs were on the Internet. Accordingly, a large amount of material about these older networks has been removed.

However, new developments are also plentiful. The most important is the huge increase in wireless networks, including 802.11, wireless local loops, 2G and 3G cellular networks, Bluetooth, WAP, i-mode, and others. Accordingly, a large amount of material has been added on wireless networks. Another newly-important topic is security, so a whole chapter on it has been added.

Although Chap. 1 has the same introductory function as it did in the third edition, the contents have been revised and brought up to date. For example, introductions to the Internet, Ethernet, and wireless LANs are given there, along with some history and background. Home networking is also discussed briefly.

Chapter 2 has been reorganized somewhat. After a brief introduction to the principles of data communication, there are three major sections on transmission (guided media, wireless, and satellite), followed by three more on important examples (the public switched telephone system, the mobile telephone system, and cable television). Among the new topics covered in this chapter are ADSL, broadband wireless, wireless MANs, and Internet access over cable and DOCSIS.

Chapter 3 has always dealt with the fundamental principles of point-to-point protocols. These ideas are essentially timeless and have not changed for decades.

Accordingly, the series of detailed example protocols presented in this chapter is largely unchanged from the third edition.

In contrast, the MAC sublayer has been an area of great activity in recent years, so many changes are present in Chap. 4. The section on Ethernet has been expanded to include gigabit Ethernet. Completely new are major sections on wireless LANs, broadband wireless, Bluetooth, and data link layer switching, including MPLS.

Chapter 5 has also been updated, with the removal of all the ATM material and the addition of additional material on the Internet. Quality of service is now also a major topic, including discussions of integrated services and differentiated services. Wireless networks are also present here, with a discussion of routing in ad hoc networks. Other new topics include NAT and peer-to-peer networks.

Chap. 6 is still about the transport layer, but here, too, some changes have occurred. Among these is an example of socket programming. A one-page client and a one-page server are given in C and discussed. These programs, available on the book's Web site, can be compiled and run. Together they provide a primitive remote file or Web server available for experimentation. Other new topics include remote procedure call, RTP, and transaction/TCP.

Chap. 7, on the application layer, has been more sharply focused. After a short introduction to DNS, the rest of the chapter deals with just three topics: e-mail, the Web, and multimedia. But each topic is treated in great detail. The discussion of how the Web works is now over 60 pages, covering a vast array of topics, including static and dynamic Web pages, HTTP, CGI scripts, content delivery networks, cookies, and Web caching. Material is also present on how modern Web pages are written, including brief introductions to XML, XSL, XHTML, PHP, and more, all with examples that can be tested. The wireless Web is also discussed, focusing on i-mode and WAP. The multimedia material now includes MP3, streaming audio, Internet radio, and voice over IP.

Security has become so important that it has now been expanded to a complete chapter of over 100 pages. It covers both the principles of security (symmetric- and public-key algorithms, digital signatures, and X.509 certificates) and the applications of these principles (authentication, e-mail security, and Web security). The chapter is both broad (ranging from quantum cryptography to government censorship) and deep (e.g., how SHA-1 works in detail).

Chapter 9 contains an all-new list of suggested readings and a comprehensive bibliography of over 350 citations to the current literature. Over 200 of these are to papers and books written in 2000 or later.

Computer books are full of acronyms. This one is no exception. By the time you are finished reading this one, the following should ring a bell: ADSL, AES, AMPS, AODV, ARP, ATM, BGP, CDMA, CDN, CGI, CIDR, DCF, DES, DHCP, DMCA, FDM, FHSS, GPRS, GSM, HDLC, HFC, HTML, HTTP, ICMP, IMAP, ISP, ITU, LAN, LMDS, MAC, MACA, MIME, MPEG, MPLS, MTU, NAP, NAT, NSA, NTSC, OFDM, OSPF, PCF, PCM, PGP, PHP, PKI, POTS,

PPP, PSTN, QAM, QPSK, RED, RFC, RPC, RSA, RSVP, RTP, SSL, TCP, TDM, UDP, URL, UTP, VLAN, VPN, VSAT, WAN, WAP, WDMA, WEP, WWW, and XML But don't worry. Each will be carefully defined before it is used.

To help instructors using this book as a text for a course, the author has prepared various teaching aids, including

- A problem solutions manual.
- Files containing the figures in multiple formats.
- PowerPoint sheets for a course using the book.
- A simulator (written in C) for the example protocols of Chap. 3.
- A Web page with links to many tutorials, organizations, FAQs, etc.

The solutions manual is available directly from Prentice Hall (but **only** to instructors, not to students). All the other material is on the book's Web site:

http://www.prenhall.com/tanenbaum

From there, click on the book's cover.

Many people helped me during the course of the fourth edition. I would especially like to thank the following people: Ross Anderson, Elizabeth Belding-Royer, Steve Bellovin, Chatschik Bisdikian, Kees Bot, Scott Bradner, Jennifer Bray, Pat Cain, Ed Felten, Warwick Ford, Kevin Fu, Ron Fulle, Jim Geier, Mario Gerla, Natalie Giroux, Steve Hanna, Jeff Hayes, Amir Herzberg, Philip Homburg, Philipp Hoschka, David Green, Bart Jacobs, Frans Kaashoek, Steve Kent, Roger Kermode, Robert Kinicki, Shay Kutten, Rob Lanphier, Marcus Leech, Tom Maufer, Brent Miller, Shivakant Mishra, Thomas Nadeau, Shlomo Ovadia, Kaveh Pahlavan, Radia Perlman, Guillaume Pierre, Wayne Pleasant, Patrick Powell, Thomas Robertazzi, Medy Sanadidi, Christian Schmutzer, Henning Schulzrinne, Paul Sevinc, Mihail Sichitiu, Bernard Sklar, Ed Skoudis, Bob Strader, George Swallow, George Thiruvathukal, Peter Tomsu, Patrick Verkaik, Dave Vittali, Spyros Voulgaris, Jan-Mark Wams, Ruediger Weis, Bert Wijnen, Joseph Wilkes, Leendert van Doorn, and Maarten van Steen.

Special thanks go to Trudy Levine for proving that grandmothers can do a fine job of reviewing technical material. Shivakant Mishra thought of many challenging end-of-chapter problems. Andy Dornan suggested additional readings for Chap. 9. Jan Looyen provided essential hardware at a critical moment. Dr. F. de Nies did an expert cut-and-paste job right when it was needed. My editor at Prentice Hall, Mary Franz, provided me with more reading material than I had consumed in the previous 7 years and was helpful in numerous other ways as well.

Finally, we come to the most important people: Suzanne, Barbara, and Marvin. To Suzanne for her love, patience, and picnic lunches. To Barbara and Marvin for being fun and cheery all the time (except when complaining about awful college textbooks, thus keeping me on my toes). Thank you.

ANDREW S. TANENBAUM

1

INTRODUCTION

Each of the past three centuries has been dominated by a single technology. The 18th century was the era of the great mechanical systems accompanying the Industrial Revolution. The 19th century was the age of the steam engine. During the 20th century, the key technology was information gathering, processing, and distribution. Among other developments, we saw the installation of worldwide telephone networks, the invention of radio and television, the birth and unprecedented growth of the computer industry, and the launching of communication satellites.

As a result of rapid technological progress, these areas are rapidly converging and the differences between collecting, transporting, storing, and processing information are quickly disappearing. Organizations with hundreds of offices spread over a wide geographical area routinely expect to be able to examine the current status of even their most remote outpost at the push of a button. As our ability to gather, process, and distribute information grows, the demand for ever more sophisticated information processing grows even faster.

Although the computer industry is still young compared to other industries (e.g., automobiles and air transportation), computers have made spectacular progress in a short time. During the first two decades of their existence, computer systems were highly centralized, usually within a single large room. Not infrequently, this room had glass walls, through which visitors could gawk at the great electronic wonder inside. A medium-sized company or university might have had one or two computers, while large institutions had at most a few dozen. The idea that within twenty years equally powerful computers smaller than postage stamps would be mass produced by the millions was pure science fiction.

The merging of computers and communications has had a profound influence on the way computer systems are organized. The concept of the "computer center" as a room with a large computer to which users bring their work for processing is now totally obsolete. The old model of a single computer serving all of the organization's computational needs has been replaced by one in which a large number of separate but interconnected computers do the job. These systems are called **computer networks**. The design and organization of these networks are the subjects of this book.

Throughout the book we will use the term "computer network" to mean a collection of autonomous computers interconnected by a single technology. Two computers are said to be interconnected if they are able to exchange information. The connection need not be via a copper wire; fiber optics, microwaves, infrared, and communication satellites can also be used. Networks come in many sizes, shapes and forms, as we will see later. Although it may sound strange to some people, neither the Internet nor the World Wide Web is a computer network. By the end of this book, it should be clear why. The quick answer is: the Internet is not a single network but a network of networks and the Web is a distributed system that runs on top of the Internet.

There is considerable confusion in the literature between a computer network and a **distributed system**. The key distinction is that in a distributed system, a collection of independent computers appears to its users as a single coherent system. Usually, it has a single model or paradigm that it presents to the users. Often a layer of software on top of the operating system, called **middleware**, is responsible for implementing this model. A well-known example of a distributed system is the **World Wide Web**, in which everything looks like a document (Web page).

In a computer network, this coherence, model, and software are absent. Users are exposed to the actual machines, without any attempt by the system to make the machines look and act in a coherent way. If the machines have different hardware and different operating systems, that is fully visible to the users. If a user wants to run a program on a remote machine, he† has to log onto that machine and run it there.

In effect, a distributed system is a software system built on top of a network. The software gives it a high degree of cohesiveness and transparency. Thus, the distinction between a network and a distributed system lies with the software (especially the operating system), rather than with the hardware.

Nevertheless, there is considerable overlap between the two subjects. For example, both distributed systems and computer networks need to move files around. The difference lies in who invokes the movement, the system or the user.

† "He" should be read as "he or she" throughout this book.

Although this book primarily focuses on networks, many of the topics are also important in distributed systems. For more information about distributed systems, see (Tanenbaum and Van Steen, 2002).

1.1 USES OF COMPUTER NETWORKS

Before we start to examine the technical issues in detail, it is worth devoting some time to pointing out why people are interested in computer networks and what they can be used for. After all, if nobody were interested in computer networks, few of them would be built. We will start with traditional uses at companies and for individuals and then move on to recent developments regarding mobile users and home networking.

1.1.1 Business Applications

Many companies have a substantial number of computers. For example, a company may have separate computers to monitor production, keep track of inventories, and do the payroll. Initially, each of these computers may have worked in isolation from the others, but at some point, management may have decided to connect them to be able to extract and correlate information about the entire company.

Put in slightly more general form, the issue here is **resource sharing**, and the goal is to make all programs, equipment, and especially data available to anyone on the network without regard to the physical location of the resource and the user. An obvious and widespread example is having a group of office workers share a common printer. None of the individuals really needs a private printer, and a high-volume networked printer is often cheaper, faster, and easier to maintain than a large collection of individual printers.

However, probably even more important than sharing physical resources such as printers, scanners, and CD burners, is sharing information. Every large and medium-sized company and many small companies are vitally dependent on computerized information. Most companies have customer records, inventories, accounts receivable, financial statements, tax information, and much more online. If all of its computers went down, a bank could not last more than five minutes. A modern manufacturing plant, with a computer-controlled assembly line, would not last even that long. Even a small travel agency or three-person law firm is now highly dependent on computer networks for allowing employees to access relevant information and documents instantly.

For smaller companies, all the computers are likely to be in a single office or perhaps a single building, but for larger ones, the computers and employees may be scattered over dozens of offices and plants in many countries. Nevertheless, a sales person in New York might sometimes need access to a product inventory database in Singapore. In other words, the mere fact that a user happens to be 15,000 km away from his data should not prevent him from using the data as though they were local. This goal may be summarized by saying that it is an attempt to end the "tyranny of geography."

In the simplest of terms, one can imagine a company's information system as consisting of one or more databases and some number of employees who need to access them remotely. In this model, the data are stored on powerful computers called **servers**. Often these are centrally housed and maintained by a system administrator. In contrast, the employees have simpler machines, called **clients**, on their desks, with which they access remote data, for example, to include in spreadsheets they are constructing. (Sometimes we will refer to the human user of the client machine as the "client," but it should be clear from the context whether we mean the computer or its user.) The client and server machines are connected by a network, as illustrated in Fig. 1-1. Note that we have shown the network as a simple oval, without any detail. We will use this form when we mean a network in the abstract sense. When more detail is required, it will be provided.

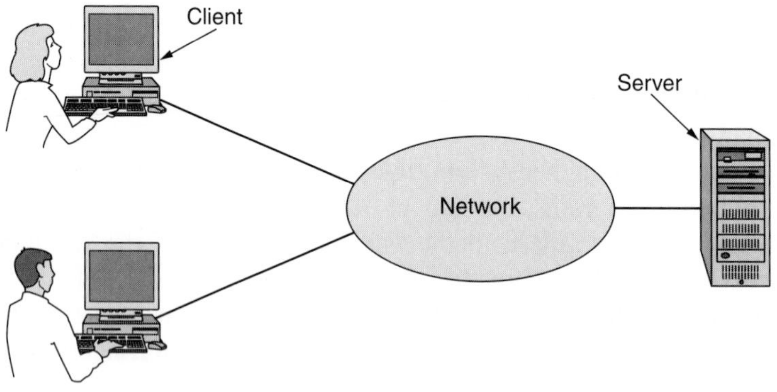

Figure 1-1. A network with two clients and one server.

This whole arrangement is called the **client-server model**. It is widely used and forms the basis of much network usage. It is applicable when the client and server are both in the same building (e.g., belong to the same company), but also when they are far apart. For example, when a person at home accesses a page on the World Wide Web, the same model is employed, with the remote Web server being the server and the user's personal computer being the client. Under most conditions, one server can handle a large number of clients.

If we look at the client-server model in detail, we see that two processes are involved, one on the client machine and one on the server machine. Communication takes the form of the client process sending a message over the network to the server process. The client process then waits for a reply message. When the server process gets the request, it performs the requested work or looks up the requested data and sends back a reply. These messages are shown in Fig. 1-2.

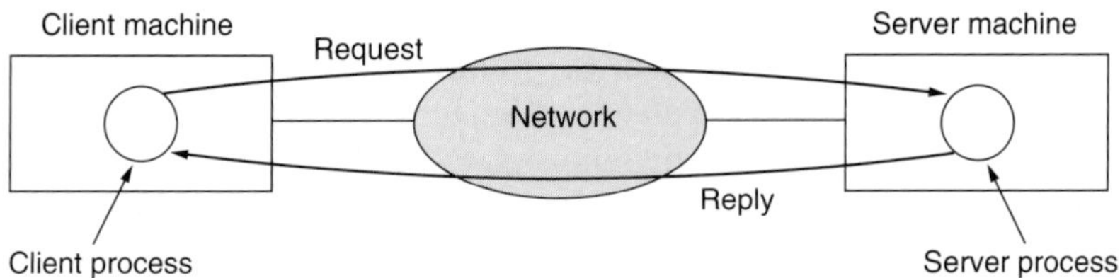

Figure 1-2. The client-server model involves requests and replies.

A second goal of setting up a computer network has to do with people rather than information or even computers. A computer network can provide a powerful **communication medium** among employees. Virtually every company that has two or more computers now has **e-mail** (**electronic mail**), which employees generally use for a great deal of daily communication. In fact, a common gripe around the water cooler is how much e-mail everyone has to deal with, much of it meaningless because bosses have discovered that they can send the same (often content-free) message to all their subordinates at the push of a button.

But e-mail is not the only form of improved communication made possible by computer networks. With a network, it is easy for two or more people who work far apart to write a report together. When one worker makes a change to an on-line document, the others can see the change immediately, instead of waiting several days for a letter. Such a speedup makes cooperation among far-flung groups of people easy where it previously had been impossible.

Yet another form of computer-assisted communication is videoconferencing. Using this technology, employees at distant locations can hold a meeting, seeing and hearing each other and even writing on a shared virtual blackboard. Videoconferencing is a powerful tool for eliminating the cost and time previously devoted to travel. It is sometimes said that communication and transportation are having a race, and whichever wins will make the other obsolete.

A third goal for increasingly many companies is doing business electronically with other companies, especially suppliers and customers. For example, manufacturers of automobiles, aircraft, and computers, among others, buy subsystems from a variety of suppliers and then assemble the parts. Using computer networks, manufacturers can place orders electronically as needed. Being able to place orders in real time (i.e., as needed) reduces the need for large inventories and enhances efficiency.

A fourth goal that is starting to become more important is doing business with consumers over the Internet. Airlines, bookstores, and music vendors have discovered that many customers like the convenience of shopping from home. Consequently, many companies provide catalogs of their goods and services on-line and take orders on-line. This sector is expected to grow quickly in the future. It is called **e-commerce** (**electronic commerce**).

1.1.2 Home Applications

In 1977, Ken Olsen was president of the Digital Equipment Corporation, then the number two computer vendor in the world (after IBM). When asked why Digital was not going after the personal computer market in a big way, he said: "There is no reason for any individual to have a computer in his home." History showed otherwise and Digital no longer exists. Why do people buy computers for home use? Initially, for word processing and games, but in recent years that picture has changed radically. Probably the biggest reason now is for Internet access. Some of the more popular uses of the Internet for home users are as follows:

1. Access to remote information.
2. Person-to-person communication.
3. Interactive entertainment.
4. Electronic commerce.

Access to remote information comes in many forms. It can be surfing the World Wide Web for information or just for fun. Information available includes the arts, business, cooking, government, health, history, hobbies, recreation, science, sports, travel, and many others. Fun comes in too many ways to mention, plus some ways that are better left unmentioned.

Many newspapers have gone on-line and can be personalized. For example, it is sometimes possible to tell a newspaper that you want everything about corrupt politicians, big fires, scandals involving celebrities, and epidemics, but no football, thank you. Sometimes it is even possible to have the selected articles downloaded to your hard disk while you sleep or printed on your printer just before breakfast. As this trend continues, it will cause massive unemployment among 12-year-old paperboys, but newspapers like it because distribution has always been the weakest link in the whole production chain.

The next step beyond newspapers (plus magazines and scientific journals) is the on-line digital library. Many professional organizations, such as the ACM (*www.acm.org*) and the IEEE Computer Society (*www.computer.org*), already have many journals and conference proceedings on-line. Other groups are following rapidly. Depending on the cost, size, and weight of book-sized notebook computers, printed books may become obsolete. Skeptics should take note of the effect the printing press had on the medieval illuminated manuscript.

All of the above applications involve interactions between a person and a remote database full of information. The second broad category of network use is person-to-person communication, basically the 21st century's answer to the 19th century's telephone. E-mail is already used on a daily basis by millions of people all over the world and its use is growing rapidly. It already routinely contains audio and video as well as text and pictures. Smell may take a while.

Any teenager worth his or her salt is addicted to **instant messaging**. This facility, derived from the UNIX *talk* program in use since around 1970, allows two people to type messages at each other in real time. A multiperson version of this idea is the **chat room**, in which a group of people can type messages for all to see.

Worldwide newsgroups, with discussions on every conceivable topic, are already commonplace among a select group of people, and this phenomenon will grow to include the population at large. These discussions, in which one person posts a message and all the other subscribers to the newsgroup can read it, run the gamut from humorous to impassioned. Unlike chat rooms, newsgroups are not real time and messages are saved so that when someone comes back from vacation, all messages that have been posted in the meanwhile are patiently waiting for reading.

Another type of person-to-person communication often goes by the name of **peer-to-peer** communication, to distinguish it from the client-server model (Parameswaran et al., 2001). In this form, individuals who form a loose group can communicate with others in the group, as shown in Fig. 1-3. Every person can, in principle, communicate with one or more other people; there is no fixed division into clients and servers.

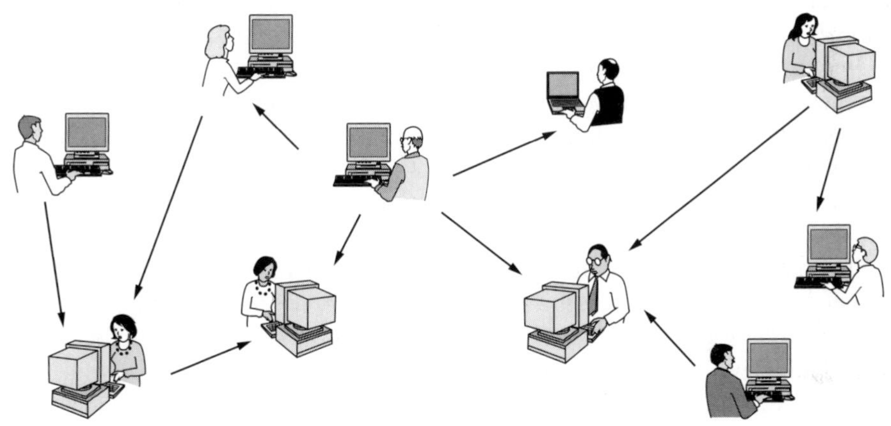

Figure 1-3. In a peer-to-peer system there are no fixed clients and servers.

Peer-to-peer communication really hit the big time around 2000 with a service called Napster, which at its peak had over 50 million music fans swapping music, in what was probably the biggest copyright infringement in all of recorded history (Lam and Tan, 2001; and Macedonia, 2000). The idea was fairly simple. Members registered the music they had on their hard disks in a central database maintained on the Napster server. If a member wanted a song, he checked the database to see who had it and went directly there to get it. By not actually keeping any music on its machines, Napster argued that it was not infringing anyone's copyright. The courts did not agree and shut it down.

However, the next generation of peer-to-peer systems eliminates the central database by having each user maintain his own database locally, as well as providing a list of other nearby people who are members of the system. A new user can then go to any existing member to see what he has and get a list of other members to inspect for more music and more names. This lookup process can be repeated indefinitely to build up a large local database of what is out there. It is an activity that would get tedious for people but is one at which computers excel.

Legal applications for peer-to-peer communication also exist. For example, fans sharing public domain music or sample tracks that new bands have released for publicity purposes, families sharing photos, movies, and genealogical information, and teenagers playing multiperson on-line games. In fact, one of the most popular Internet applications of all, e-mail, is inherently peer-to-peer. This form of communication is expected to grow considerably in the future.

Electronic crime is not restricted to copyright law. Another hot area is electronic gambling. Computers have been simulating things for decades. Why not simulate slot machines, roulette wheels, blackjack dealers, and more gambling equipment? Well, because it is illegal in a lot of places. The trouble is, gambling is legal in a lot of other places (England, for example) and casino owners there have grasped the potential for Internet gambling. What happens if the gambler and the casino are in different countries, with conflicting laws? Good question.

Other communication-oriented applications include using the Internet to carry telephone calls, video phone, and Internet radio, three rapidly growing areas. Another application is telelearning, meaning attending 8 A.M. classes without the inconvenience of having to get out of bed first. In the long run, the use of networks to enhance human-to-human communication may prove more important than any of the others.

Our third category is entertainment, which is a huge and growing industry. The killer application here (the one that may drive all the rest) is video on demand. A decade or so hence, it may be possible to select any movie or television program ever made, in any country, and have it displayed on your screen instantly. New films may become interactive, where the user is occasionally prompted for the story direction (should Macbeth murder Duncan or just bide his time?) with alternative scenarios provided for all cases. Live television may also become interactive, with the audience participating in quiz shows, choosing among contestants, and so on.

On the other hand, maybe the killer application will not be video on demand. Maybe it will be game playing. Already we have multiperson real-time simulation games, like hide-and-seek in a virtual dungeon, and flight simulators with the players on one team trying to shoot down the players on the opposing team. If games are played with goggles and three-dimensional real-time, photographic-quality moving images, we have a kind of worldwide shared virtual reality.

Our fourth category is electronic commerce in the broadest sense of the term. Home shopping is already popular and enables users to inspect the on-line catalogs of thousands of companies. Some of these catalogs will soon provide the ability to get an instant video on any product by just clicking on the product's name. After the customer buys a product electronically but cannot figure out how to use it, on-line technical support may be consulted.

Another area in which e-commerce is already happening is access to financial institutions. Many people already pay their bills, manage their bank accounts, and handle their investments electronically. This will surely grow as networks become more secure.

One area that virtually nobody foresaw is electronic flea markets (e-flea?). On-line auctions of second-hand goods have become a massive industry. Unlike traditional e-commerce, which follows the client-server model, on-line auctions are more of a peer-to-peer system, sort of consumer-to-consumer. Some of these forms of e-commerce have acquired cute little tags based on the fact that "to" and "2" are pronounced the same. The most popular ones are listed in Fig. 1-4.

Tag	Full name	Example
B2C	Business-to-consumer	Ordering books on-line
B2B	Business-to-business	Car manufacturer ordering tires from supplier
G2C	Government-to-consumer	Government distributing tax forms electronically
C2C	Consumer-to-consumer	Auctioning second-hand products on line
P2P	Peer-to-peer	File sharing

Figure 1-4. Some forms of e-commerce.

No doubt the range of uses of computer networks will grow rapidly in the future, and probably in ways no one can now foresee. After all, how many people in 1990 predicted that teenagers tediously typing short text messages on mobile phones while riding buses would be an immense money maker for telephone companies in 10 years? But short message service is very profitable.

Computer networks may become hugely important to people who are geographically challenged, giving them the same access to services as people living in the middle of a big city. Telelearning may radically affect education; universities may go national or international. Telemedicine is only now starting to catch on (e.g., remote patient monitoring) but may become much more important. But the killer application may be something mundane, like using the webcam in your refrigerator to see if you have to buy milk on the way home from work.

1.1.3 Mobile Users

Mobile computers, such as notebook computers and personal digital assistants (PDAs), are one of the fastest-growing segments of the computer industry. Many owners of these computers have desktop machines back at the office and want to be connected to their home base even when away from home or en route. Since having a wired connection is impossible in cars and airplanes, there is a lot of interest in wireless networks. In this section we will briefly look at some of the uses of wireless networks.

Why would anyone want one? A common reason is the portable office. People on the road often want to use their portable electronic equipment to send and receive telephone calls, faxes, and electronic mail, surf the Web, access remote files, and log on to remote machines. And they want to do this from anywhere on land, sea, or air. For example, at computer conferences these days, the organizers often set up a wireless network in the conference area. Anyone with a notebook computer and a wireless modem can just turn the computer on and be connected to the Internet, as though the computer were plugged into a wired network. Similarly, some universities have installed wireless networks on campus so students can sit under the trees and consult the library's card catalog or read their e-mail.

Wireless networks are of great value to fleets of trucks, taxis, delivery vehicles, and repairpersons for keeping in contact with home. For example, in many cities, taxi drivers are independent businessmen, rather than being employees of a taxi company. In some of these cities, the taxis have a display the driver can see. When a customer calls up, a central dispatcher types in the pickup and destination points. This information is displayed on the drivers' displays and a beep sounds. The first driver to hit a button on the display gets the call.

Wireless networks are also important to the military. If you have to be able to fight a war anywhere on earth on short notice, counting on using the local networking infrastructure is probably not a good idea. It is better to bring your own.

Although wireless networking and mobile computing are often related, they are not identical, as Fig. 1-5 shows. Here we see a distinction between **fixed wireless** and **mobile wireless**. Even notebook computers are sometimes wired. For example, if a traveler plugs a notebook computer into the telephone jack in a hotel room, he has mobility without a wireless network.

Wireless	Mobile	Applications
No	No	Desktop computers in offices
No	Yes	A notebook computer used in a hotel room
Yes	No	Networks in older, unwired buildings
Yes	Yes	Portable office; PDA for store inventory

Figure 1-5. Combinations of wireless networks and mobile computing.

On the other hand, some wireless computers are not mobile. An important example is a company that owns an older building lacking network cabling, and which wants to connect its computers. Installing a wireless network may require little more than buying a small box with some electronics, unpacking it, and plugging it in. This solution may be far cheaper than having workmen put in cable ducts to wire the building.

But of course, there are also the true mobile, wireless applications, ranging from the portable office to people walking around a store with a PDA doing inventory. At many busy airports, car rental return clerks work in the parking lot with wireless portable computers. They type in the license plate number of returning cars, and their portable, which has a built-in printer, calls the main computer, gets the rental information, and prints out the bill on the spot.

As wireless technology becomes more widespread, numerous other applications are likely to emerge. Let us take a quick look at some of the possibilities. Wireless parking meters have advantages for both users and city governments. The meters could accept credit or debit cards with instant verification over the wireless link. When a meter expires, it could check for the presence of a car (by bouncing a signal off it) and report the expiration to the police. It has been estimated that city governments in the U.S. alone could collect an additional $10 billion this way (Harte et al., 2000). Furthermore, better parking enforcement would help the environment, as drivers who knew their illegal parking was sure to be caught might use public transport instead.

Food, drink, and other vending machines are found everywhere. However, the food does not get into the machines by magic. Periodically, someone comes by with a truck to fill them. If the vending machines issued a wireless report once a day announcing their current inventories, the truck driver would know which machines needed servicing and how much of which product to bring. This information could lead to more efficient route planning. Of course, this information could be sent over a standard telephone line as well, but giving every vending machine a fixed telephone connection for one call a day is expensive on account of the fixed monthly charge.

Another area in which wireless could save money is utility meter reading. If electricity, gas, water, and other meters in people's homes were to report usage over a wireless network, there would be no need to send out meter readers. Similarly, wireless smoke detectors could call the fire department instead of making a big noise (which has little value if no one is home). As the cost of both the radio devices and the air time drops, more and more measurement and reporting will be done with wireless networks.

A whole different application area for wireless networks is the expected merger of cell phones and PDAs into tiny wireless computers. A first attempt was tiny wireless PDAs that could display stripped-down Web pages on their even tinier screens. This system, called **WAP 1.0** (**Wireless Application Protocol**) failed, mostly due to the microscopic screens, low bandwidth, and poor service. But newer devices and services will be better with WAP 2.0.

One area in which these devices may excel is called **m-commerce** (**mobile-commerce**) (Senn, 2000). The driving force behind this phenomenon consists of an amalgam of wireless PDA manufacturers and network operators who are trying hard to figure out how to get a piece of the e-commerce pie. One of their hopes is to use wireless PDAs for banking and shopping. One idea is to use the wireless

PDAs as a kind of electronic wallet, authorizing payments in stores, as a replacement for cash and credit cards. The charge then appears on the mobile phone bill. From the store's point of view, this scheme may save them most of the credit card company's fee, which can be several percent. Of course, this plan may backfire, since customers in a store might use their PDAs to check out competitors' prices before buying. Worse yet, telephone companies might offer PDAs with bar code readers that allow a customer to scan a product in a store and then instantaneously get a detailed report on where else it can be purchased and at what price.

Since the network operator knows where the user is, some services are intentionally location dependent. For example, it may be possible to ask for a nearby bookstore or Chinese restaurant. Mobile maps are another candidate. So are very local weather forecasts ("When is it going to stop raining in my backyard?"). No doubt many other applications appear as these devices become more widespread.

One huge thing that m-commerce has going for it is that mobile phone users are accustomed to paying for everything (in contrast to Internet users, who expect everything to be free). If an Internet Web site charged a fee to allow its customers to pay by credit card, there would be an immense howling noise from the users. If a mobile phone operator allowed people to pay for items in a store by using the phone and then tacked on a fee for this convenience, it would probably be accepted as normal. Time will tell.

A little further out in time are personal area networks and wearable computers. IBM has developed a watch that runs Linux (including the X11 windowing system) and has wireless connectivity to the Internet for sending and receiving e-mail (Narayanaswami et al., 2002). In the future, people may exchange business cards just by exposing their watches to each other. Wearable wireless computers may give people access to secure rooms the same way magnetic stripe cards do now (possibly in combination with a PIN code or biometric measurement). These watches may also be able to retrieve information relevant to the user's current location (e.g., local restaurants). The possibilities are endless.

Smart watches with radios have been part of our mental space since their appearance in the Dick Tracy comic strip in 1946. But smart dust? Researchers at Berkeley have packed a wireless computer into a cube 1 mm on edge (Warneke et al., 2001). Potential applications include tracking inventory, packages, and even small birds, rodents, and insects.

1.1.4 Social Issues

The widespread introduction of networking has introduced new social, ethical, and political problems. Let us just briefly mention a few of them; a thorough study would require a full book, at least. A popular feature of many networks are newsgroups or bulletin boards whereby people can exchange messages with like-minded individuals. As long as the subjects are restricted to technical topics or hobbies like gardening, not too many problems will arise.

The trouble comes when newsgroups are set up on topics that people actually care about, like politics, religion, or sex. Views posted to such groups may be deeply offensive to some people. Worse yet, they may not be politically correct. Furthermore, messages need not be limited to text. High-resolution color photographs and even short video clips can now easily be transmitted over computer networks. Some people take a live-and-let-live view, but others feel that posting certain material (e.g., attacks on particular countries or religions, pornography, etc.) is simply unacceptable and must be censored. Different countries have different and conflicting laws in this area. Thus, the debate rages.

People have sued network operators, claiming that they are responsible for the contents of what they carry, just as newspapers and magazines are. The inevitable response is that a network is like a telephone company or the post office and cannot be expected to police what its users say. Stronger yet, were network operators to censor messages, they would likely delete everything containing even the slightest possibility of them being sued, and thus violate their users' rights to free speech. It is probably safe to say that this debate will go on for a while.

Another fun area is employee rights versus employer rights. Many people read and write e-mail at work. Many employers have claimed the right to read and possibly censor employee messages, including messages sent from a home computer after work. Not all employees agree with this.

Even if employers have power over employees, does this relationship also govern universities and students? How about high schools and students? In 1994, Carnegie-Mellon University decided to turn off the incoming message stream for several newsgroups dealing with sex because the university felt the material was inappropriate for minors (i.e., those few students under 18). The fallout from this event took years to settle.

Another key topic is government versus citizen. The FBI has installed a system at many Internet service providers to snoop on all incoming and outgoing e-mail for nuggets of interest to it (Blaze and Bellovin, 2000; Sobel, 2001; and Zacks, 2001). The system was originally called **Carnivore** but bad publicity caused it to be renamed to the more innocent-sounding DCS1000. But its goal is still to spy on millions of people in the hope of finding information about illegal activities. Unfortunately, the Fourth Amendment to the U.S. Constitution prohibits government searches without a search warrant. Whether these 54 words, written in the 18th century, still carry any weight in the 21st century is a matter that may keep the courts busy until the 22nd century.

The government does not have a monopoly on threatening people's privacy. The private sector does its bit too. For example, small files called cookies that Web browsers store on users' computers allow companies to track users' activities in cyberspace and also may allow credit card numbers, social security numbers, and other confidential information to leak all over the Internet (Berghel, 2001).

Computer networks offer the potential for sending anonymous messages. In some situations, this capability may be desirable. For example, it provides a way for students, soldiers, employees, and citizens to blow the whistle on illegal behavior on the part of professors, officers, superiors, and politicians without fear of reprisals. On the other hand, in the United States and most other democracies, the law specifically permits an accused person the right to confront and challenge his accuser in court. Anonymous accusations cannot be used as evidence.

In short, computer networks, like the printing press 500 years ago, allow ordinary citizens to distribute their views in different ways and to different audiences than were previously possible. This new-found freedom brings with it many unsolved social, political, and moral issues.

Along with the good comes the bad. Life seems to be like that. The Internet makes it possible to find information quickly, but a lot of it is ill-informed, misleading, or downright wrong. The medical advice you plucked from the Internet may have come from a Nobel Prize winner or from a high school dropout. Computer networks have also introduced new kinds of antisocial and criminal behavior. Electronic junk mail (spam) has become a part of life because people have collected millions of e-mail addresses and sell them on CD-ROMs to would-be marketeers. E-mail messages containing active content (basically programs or macros that execute on the receiver's machine) can contain viruses that wreak havoc.

Identity theft is becoming a serious problem as thieves collect enough information about a victim to obtain get credit cards and other documents in the victim's name. Finally, being able to transmit music and video digitally has opened the door to massive copyright violations that are hard to catch and enforce.

A lot of these problems could be solved if the computer industry took computer security seriously. If all messages were encrypted and authenticated, it would be harder to commit mischief. This technology is well established and we will study it in detail in Chap. 8. The problem is that hardware and software vendors know that putting in security features costs money and their customers are not demanding such features. In addition, a substantial number of the problems are caused by buggy software, which occurs because vendors keep adding more and more features to their programs, which inevitably means more code and thus more bugs. A tax on new features might help, but that is probably a tough sell in some quarters. A refund for defective software might be nice, except it would bankrupt the entire software industry in the first year.

1.2 NETWORK HARDWARE

It is now time to turn our attention from the applications and social aspects of networking (the fun stuff) to the technical issues involved in network design (the work stuff). There is no generally accepted taxonomy into which all computer networks fit, but two dimensions stand out as important: transmission technology and scale. We will now examine each of these in turn.

Broadly speaking, there are two types of transmission technology that are in widespread use. They are as follows:

1. Broadcast links.
2. Point-to-point links.

Broadcast networks have a single communication channel that is shared by all the machines on the network. Short messages, called **packets** in certain contexts, sent by any machine are received by all the others. An address field within the packet specifies the intended recipient. Upon receiving a packet, a machine checks the address field. If the packet is intended for the receiving machine, that machine processes the packet; if the packet is intended for some other machine, it is just ignored.

As an analogy, consider someone standing at the end of a corridor with many rooms off it and shouting "Watson, come here. I want you." Although the packet may actually be received (heard) by many people, only Watson responds. The others just ignore it. Another analogy is an airport announcement asking all flight 644 passengers to report to gate 12 for immediate boarding.

Broadcast systems generally also allow the possibility of addressing a packet to *all* destinations by using a special code in the address field. When a packet with this code is transmitted, it is received and processed by every machine on the network. This mode of operation is called **broadcasting**. Some broadcast systems also support transmission to a subset of the machines, something known as **multicasting**. One possible scheme is to reserve one bit to indicate multicasting. The remaining $n - 1$ address bits can hold a group number. Each machine can "subscribe" to any or all of the groups. When a packet is sent to a certain group, it is delivered to all machines subscribing to that group.

In contrast, **point-to-point** networks consist of many connections between individual pairs of machines. To go from the source to the destination, a packet on this type of network may have to first visit one or more intermediate machines. Often multiple routes, of different lengths, are possible, so finding good ones is important in point-to-point networks. As a general rule (although there are many exceptions), smaller, geographically localized networks tend to use broadcasting, whereas larger networks usually are point-to-point. Point-to-point transmission with one sender and one receiver is sometimes called **unicasting**.

An alternative criterion for classifying networks is their scale. In Fig. 1-6 we classify multiple processor systems by their physical size. At the top are the **personal area networks**, networks that are meant for one person. For example, a wireless network connecting a computer with its mouse, keyboard, and printer is a personal area network. Also, a PDA that controls the user's hearing aid or pacemaker fits in this category. Beyond the personal area networks come longer-range networks. These can be divided into local, metropolitan, and wide area networks. Finally, the connection of two or more networks is called an internetwork.

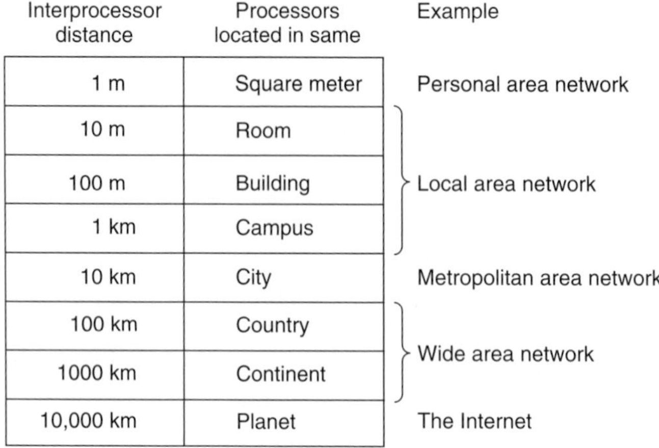

Interprocessor distance	Processors located in same	Example
1 m	Square meter	Personal area network
10 m	Room	Local area network
100 m	Building	
1 km	Campus	
10 km	City	Metropolitan area network
100 km	Country	Wide area network
1000 km	Continent	
10,000 km	Planet	The Internet

Figure 1-6. Classification of interconnected processors by scale.

The worldwide Internet is a well-known example of an internetwork. Distance is important as a classification metric because different techniques are used at different scales. In this book we will be concerned with networks at all these scales. Below we give a brief introduction to network hardware.

1.2.1 Local Area Networks

Local area networks, generally called **LANs**, are privately-owned networks within a single building or campus of up to a few kilometers in size. They are widely used to connect personal computers and workstations in company offices and factories to share resources (e.g., printers) and exchange information. LANs are distinguished from other kinds of networks by three characteristics: (1) their size, (2) their transmission technology, and (3) their topology.

LANs are restricted in size, which means that the worst-case transmission time is bounded and known in advance. Knowing this bound makes it possible to use certain kinds of designs that would not otherwise be possible. It also simplifies network management.

LANs may use a transmission technology consisting of a cable to which all the machines are attached, like the telephone company party lines once used in rural areas. Traditional LANs run at speeds of 10 Mbps to 100 Mbps, have low delay (microseconds or nanoseconds), and make very few errors. Newer LANs operate at up to 10 Gbps. In this book, we will adhere to tradition and measure line speeds in megabits/sec (1 Mbps is 1,000,000 bits/sec) and gigabits/sec (1 Gbps is 1,000,000,000 bits/sec).

Various topologies are possible for broadcast LANs. Figure 1-7 shows two of them. In a bus (i.e., a linear cable) network, at any instant at most one machine is the master and is allowed to transmit. All other machines are required to refrain from sending. An arbitration mechanism is needed to resolve conflicts when two or more machines want to transmit simultaneously. The arbitration mechanism may be centralized or distributed. IEEE 802.3, popularly called **Ethernet**, for example, is a bus-based broadcast network with decentralized control, usually operating at 10 Mbps to 10 Gbps. Computers on an Ethernet can transmit whenever they want to; if two or more packets collide, each computer just waits a random time and tries again later.

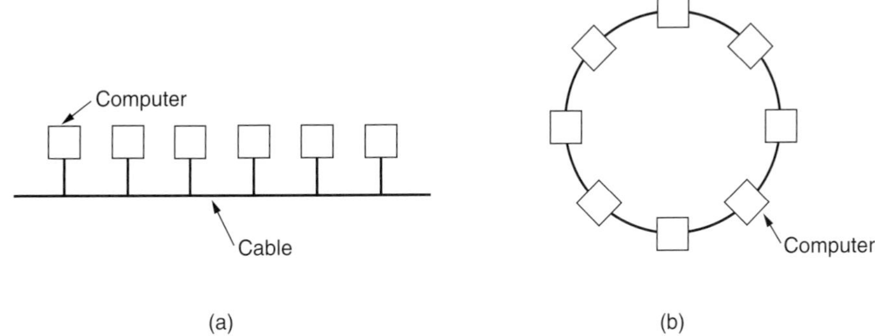

Figure 1-7. Two broadcast networks. (a) Bus. (b) Ring.

A second type of broadcast system is the ring. In a ring, each bit propagates around on its own, not waiting for the rest of the packet to which it belongs. Typically, each bit circumnavigates the entire ring in the time it takes to transmit a few bits, often before the complete packet has even been transmitted. As with all other broadcast systems, some rule is needed for arbitrating simultaneous accesses to the ring. Various methods, such as having the machines take turns, are in use. IEEE 802.5 (the IBM token ring), is a ring-based LAN operating at 4 and 16 Mbps. FDDI is another example of a ring network.

Broadcast networks can be further divided into static and dynamic, depending on how the channel is allocated. A typical static allocation would be to divide time into discrete intervals and use a round-robin algorithm, allowing each machine to broadcast only when its time slot comes up. Static allocation wastes channel capacity when a machine has nothing to say during its allocated slot, so most systems attempt to allocate the channel dynamically (i.e., on demand).

Dynamic allocation methods for a common channel are either centralized or decentralized. In the centralized channel allocation method, there is a single entity, for example, a bus arbitration unit, which determines who goes next. It might do this by accepting requests and making a decision according to some internal algorithm. In the decentralized channel allocation method, there is no central entity; each machine must decide for itself whether to transmit. You might think that this always leads to chaos, but it does not. Later we will study many algorithms designed to bring order out of the potential chaos.

1.2.2 Metropolitan Area Networks

A **metropolitan area network**, or **MAN**, covers a city. The best-known example of a MAN is the cable television network available in many cities. This system grew from earlier community antenna systems used in areas with poor over-the-air television reception. In these early systems, a large antenna was placed on top of a nearby hill and signal was then piped to the subscribers' houses.

At first, these were locally-designed, ad hoc systems. Then companies began jumping into the business, getting contracts from city governments to wire up an entire city. The next step was television programming and even entire channels designed for cable only. Often these channels were highly specialized, such as all news, all sports, all cooking, all gardening, and so on. But from their inception until the late 1990s, they were intended for television reception only.

Starting when the Internet attracted a mass audience, the cable TV network operators began to realize that with some changes to the system, they could provide two-way Internet service in unused parts of the spectrum. At that point, the cable TV system began to morph from a way to distribute television to a metropolitan area network. To a first approximation, a MAN might look something like the system shown in Fig. 1-8. In this figure we see both television signals and Internet being fed into the centralized **head end** for subsequent distribution to people's homes. We will come back to this subject in detail in Chap. 2.

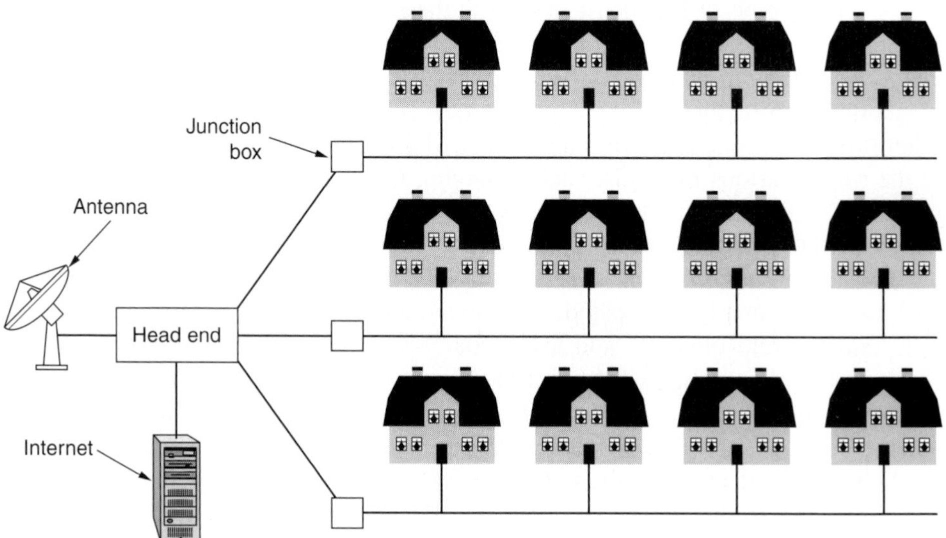

Figure 1-8. A metropolitan area network based on cable TV.

Cable television is not the only MAN. Recent developments in high-speed wireless Internet access resulted in another MAN, which has been standardized as IEEE 802.16. We will look at this area in Chap. 2.

1.2.3 Wide Area Networks

A **wide area network**, or **WAN**, spans a large geographical area, often a country or continent. It contains a collection of machines intended for running user (i.e., application) programs. We will follow traditional usage and call these machines **hosts**. The hosts are connected by a **communication subnet**, or just **subnet** for short. The hosts are owned by the customers (e.g., people's personal computers), whereas the communication subnet is typically owned and operated by a telephone company or Internet service provider. The job of the subnet is to carry messages from host to host, just as the telephone system carries words from speaker to listener. Separation of the pure communication aspects of the network (the subnet) from the application aspects (the hosts), greatly simplifies the complete network design.

In most wide area networks, the subnet consists of two distinct components: transmission lines and switching elements. **Transmission lines** move bits between machines. They can be made of copper wire, optical fiber, or even radio links. **Switching elements** are specialized computers that connect three or more transmission lines. When data arrive on an incoming line, the switching element must choose an outgoing line on which to forward them. These switching computers have been called by various names in the past; the name **router** is now most commonly used. Unfortunately, some people pronounce it "rooter" and others have it rhyme with "doubter." Determining the correct pronunciation will be left as an exercise for the reader. (Note: the perceived correct answer may depend on where you live.)

In this model, shown in Fig. 1-9, each host is frequently connected to a LAN on which a router is present, although in some cases a host can be connected directly to a router. The collection of communication lines and routers (but not the hosts) form the subnet.

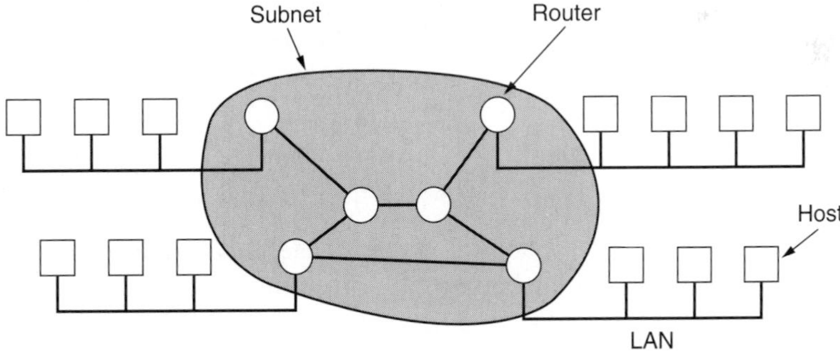

Figure 1-9. Relation between hosts on LANs and the subnet.

A short comment about the term "subnet" is in order here. Originally, its **only** meaning was the collection of routers and communication lines that moved packets from the source host to the destination host. However, some years later, it also acquired a second meaning in conjunction with network addressing (which we will discuss in Chap. 5). Unfortunately, no widely-used alternative exists for its initial meaning, so with some hesitation we will use it in both senses. From the context, it will always be clear which is meant.

In most WANs, the network contains numerous transmission lines, each one connecting a pair of routers. If two routers that do not share a transmission line wish to communicate, they must do this indirectly, via other routers. When a packet is sent from one router to another via one or more intermediate routers, the packet is received at each intermediate router in its entirety, stored there until the required output line is free, and then forwarded. A subnet organized according to this principle is called a **store-and-forward** or **packet-switched** subnet. Nearly all wide area networks (except those using satellites) have store-and-forward subnets. When the packets are small and all the same size, they are often called **cells**.

The principle of a packet-switched WAN is so important that it is worth devoting a few more words to it. Generally, when a process on some host has a message to be sent to a process on some other host, the sending host first cuts the message into packets, each one bearing its number in the sequence. These packets are then injected into the network one at a time in quick succession. The packets are transported individually over the network and deposited at the receiving host, where they are reassembled into the original message and delivered to the receiving process. A stream of packets resulting from some initial message is illustrated in Fig. 1-10.

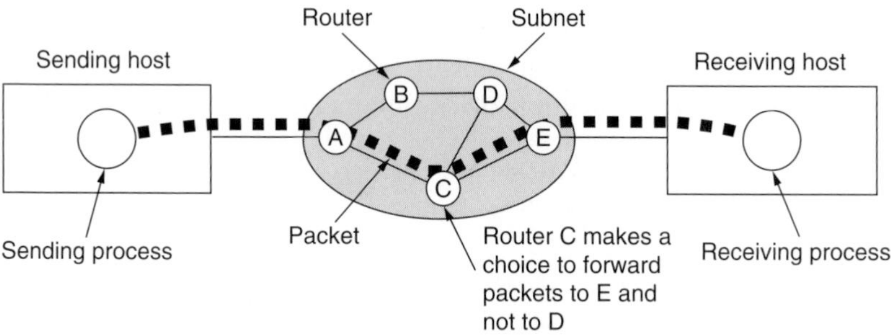

Figure 1-10. A stream of packets from sender to receiver.

In this figure, all the packets follow the route *ACE*, rather than *ABDE* or *ACDE*. In some networks all packets from a given message *must* follow the same route; in others each packet is routed separately. Of course, if *ACE* is the best route, all packets may be sent along it, even if each packet is individually routed.

Routing decisions are made locally. When a packet arrives at router *A*, it is up to *A* to decide if this packet should be sent on the line to *B* or the line to *C*. How *A* makes that decision is called the **routing algorithm**. Many of them exist. We will study some of them in detail in Chap. 5.

Not all WANs are packet switched. A second possibility for a WAN is a satellite system. Each router has an antenna through which it can send and receive. All routers can hear the output *from* the satellite, and in some cases they can also hear the upward transmissions of their fellow routers *to* the satellite as well. Sometimes the routers are connected to a substantial point-to-point subnet, with only some of them having a satellite antenna. Satellite networks are inherently broadcast and are most useful when the broadcast property is important.

1.2.4 Wireless Networks

Digital wireless communication is not a new idea. As early as 1901, the Italian physicist Guglielmo Marconi demonstrated a ship-to-shore wireless telegraph, using Morse Code (dots and dashes are binary, after all). Modern digital wireless systems have better performance, but the basic idea is the same.

To a first approximation, wireless networks can be divided into three main categories:

1. System interconnection.
2. Wireless LANs.
3. Wireless WANs.

System interconnection is all about interconnecting the components of a computer using short-range radio. Almost every computer has a monitor, keyboard, mouse, and printer connected to the main unit by cables. So many new users have a hard time plugging all the cables into the right little holes (even though they are usually color coded) that most computer vendors offer the option of sending a technician to the user's home to do it. Consequently, some companies got together to design a short-range wireless network called **Bluetooth** to connect these components without wires. Bluetooth also allows digital cameras, headsets, scanners, and other devices to connect to a computer by merely being brought within range. No cables, no driver installation, just put them down, turn them on, and they work. For many people, this ease of operation is a big plus.

In the simplest form, system interconnection networks use the master-slave paradigm of Fig. 1-11(a). The system unit is normally the master, talking to the mouse, keyboard, etc., as slaves. The master tells the slaves what addresses to use, when they can broadcast, how long they can transmit, what frequencies they can use, and so on. We will discuss Bluetooth in more detail in Chap. 4.

The next step up in wireless networking are the wireless LANs. These are systems in which every computer has a radio modem and antenna with which it can communicate with other systems. Often there is an antenna on the ceiling that the machines talk to, as shown in Fig. 1-11(b). However, if the systems are close enough, they can communicate directly with one another in a peer-to-peer configuration. Wireless LANs are becoming increasingly common in small offices and

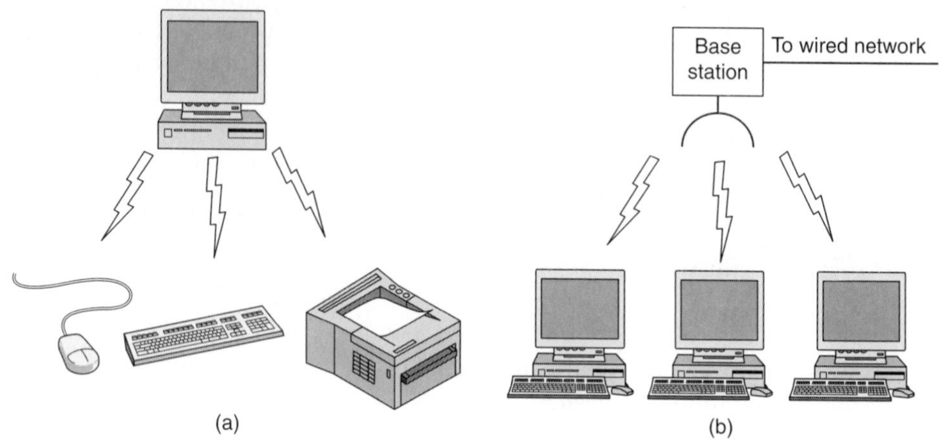

Figure 1-11. (a) Bluetooth configuration. (b) Wireless LAN.

homes, where installing Ethernet is considered too much trouble, as well as in older office buildings, company cafeterias, conference rooms, and other places. There is a standard for wireless LANs, called **IEEE 802.11**, which most systems implement and which is becoming very widespread. We will discuss it in Chap. 4.

The third kind of wireless network is used in wide area systems. The radio network used for cellular telephones is an example of a low-bandwidth wireless system. This system has already gone through three generations. The first generation was analog and for voice only. The second generation was digital and for voice only. The third generation is digital and is for both voice and data. In a certain sense, cellular wireless networks are like wireless LANs, except that the distances involved are much greater and the bit rates much lower. Wireless LANs can operate at rates up to about 50 Mbps over distances of tens of meters. Cellular systems operate below 1 Mbps, but the distance between the base station and the computer or telephone is measured in kilometers rather than in meters. We will have a lot to say about these networks in Chap. 2.

In addition to these low-speed networks, high-bandwidth wide area wireless networks are also being developed. The initial focus is high-speed wireless Internet access from homes and businesses, bypassing the telephone system. This service is often called local multipoint distribution service. We will study it later in the book. A standard for it, called IEEE 802.16, has also been developed. We will examine the standard in Chap. 4.

Almost all wireless networks hook up to the wired network at some point to provide access to files, databases, and the Internet. There are many ways these connections can be realized, depending on the circumstances. For example, in Fig. 1-12(a), we depict an airplane with a number of people using modems and seat-back telephones to call the office. Each call is independent of the other ones. A much more efficient option, however, is the flying LAN of Fig. 1-12(b). Here each seat comes equipped with an Ethernet connector into which passengers can plug their computers. A single router on the aircraft maintains a radio link with some router on the ground, changing routers as it flies along. This configuration is just a traditional LAN, except that its connection to the outside world happens to be a radio link instead of a hardwired line.

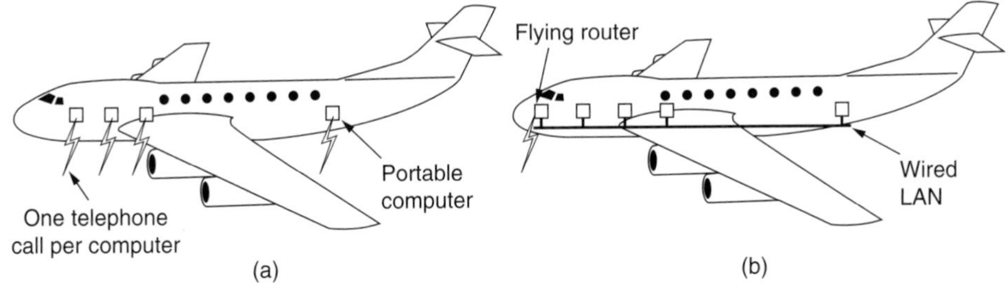

Figure 1-12. (a) Individual mobile computers. (b) A flying LAN.

Many people believe wireless is the wave of the future (e.g., Bi et al., 2001; Leeper, 2001; Varshey and Vetter, 2000) but at least one dissenting voice has been heard. Bob Metcalfe, the inventor of Ethernet, has written: "Mobile wireless computers are like mobile pipeless bathrooms—portapotties. They will be common on vehicles, and at construction sites, and rock concerts. My advice is to wire up your home and stay there" (Metcalfe, 1995). History may record this remark in the same category as IBM's chairman T.J. Watson's 1945 explanation of why IBM was not getting into the computer business: "Four or five computers should be enough for the entire world until the year 2000."

1.2.5 Home Networks

Home networking is on the horizon. The fundamental idea is that in the future most homes will be set up for networking. Every device in the home will be capable of communicating with every other device, and all of them will be accessible over the Internet. This is one of those visionary concepts that nobody asked for (like TV remote controls or mobile phones), but once they arrived nobody can imagine how they lived without them.

Many devices are capable of being networked. Some of the more obvious categories (with examples) are as follows:

1. Computers (desktop PC, notebook PC, PDA, shared peripherals).
2. Entertainment (TV, DVD, VCR, camcorder, camera, stereo, MP3).
3. Telecommunications (telephone, mobile telephone, intercom, fax).
4. Appliances (microwave, refrigerator, clock, furnace, airco, lights).
5. Telemetry (utility meter, smoke/burglar alarm, thermostat, babycam).

Home computer networking is already here in a limited way. Many homes already have a device to connect multiple computers to a fast Internet connection. Networked entertainment is not quite here, but as more and more music and movies can be downloaded from the Internet, there will be a demand to connect stereos and televisions to it. Also, people will want to share their own videos with friends and family, so the connection will need to go both ways. Telecommunications gear is already connected to the outside world, but soon it will be digital and go over the Internet. The average home probably has a dozen clocks (e.g., in appliances), all of which have to be reset twice a year when daylight saving time (summer time) comes and goes. If all the clocks were on the Internet, that resetting could be done automatically. Finally, remote monitoring of the home and its contents is a likely winner. Probably many parents would be willing to spend some money to monitor their sleeping babies on their PDAs when they are eating out, even with a rented teenager in the house. While one can imagine a separate network for each application area, integrating all of them into a single network is probably a better idea.

Home networking has some fundamentally different properties than other network types. First, the network and devices have to be easy to install. The author has installed numerous pieces of hardware and software on various computers over the years, with mixed results. A series of phone calls to the vendor's helpdesk typically resulted in answers like (1) Read the manual, (2) Reboot the computer, (3) Remove all hardware and software except ours and try again, (4) Download the newest driver from our Web site, and if all else fails, (5) Reformat the hard disk and then reinstall Windows from the CD-ROM. Telling the purchaser of an Internet refrigerator to download and install a new version of the refrigerator's operating system is not going to lead to happy customers. Computer users are accustomed to putting up with products that do not work; the car-, television-, and refrigerator-buying public is far less tolerant. They expect products to work for 100% from the word go.

Second, the network and devices have to be foolproof in operation. Air conditioners used to have one knob with four settings: OFF, LOW, MEDIUM, and HIGH. Now they have 30-page manuals. Once they are networked, expect the chapter on security alone to be 30 pages. This will be beyond the comprehension of virtually all the users.

Third, low price is essential for success. People will not pay a $50 premium for an Internet thermostat because few people regard monitoring their home temperature from work that important. For $5 extra, it might sell, though.

Fourth, the main application is likely to involve multimedia, so the network needs sufficient capacity. There is no market for Internet-connected televisions that show shaky movies at 320×240 pixel resolution and 10 frames/sec. Fast Ethernet, the workhorse in most offices, is not good enough for multimedia. Consequently, home networks will need better performance than that of existing office networks and at lower prices before they become mass market items.

Fifth, it must be possible to start out with one or two devices and expand the reach of the network gradually. This means no format wars. Telling consumers to buy peripherals with IEEE 1394 (FireWire) interfaces and a few years later retracting that and saying USB 2.0 is the interface-of-the-month is going to make consumers skittish. The network interface will have to remain stable for many years; the wiring (if any) will have to remain stable for decades.

Sixth, security and reliability will be very important. Losing a few files to an e-mail virus is one thing; having a burglar disarm your security system from his PDA and then plunder your house is something quite different.

An interesting question is whether home networks will be wired or wireless. Most homes already have six networks installed: electricity, telephone, cable television, water, gas, and sewer. Adding a seventh one during construction is not difficult, but retrofitting existing houses is expensive. Cost favors wireless networking, but security favors wired networking. The problem with wireless is that the radio waves they use are quite good at going through fences. Not everyone is overjoyed at the thought of having the neighbors piggybacking on their Internet connection and reading their e-mail on its way to the printer. In Chap. 8 we will study how encryption can be used to provide security, but in the context of a home network, security has to be foolproof, even with inexperienced users. This is easier said than done, even with highly sophisticated users.

In short, home networking offers many opportunities and challenges. Most of them relate to the need to be easy to manage, dependable, and secure, especially in the hands of nontechnical users, while at the same time delivering high performance at low cost.

1.2.6 Internetworks

Many networks exist in the world, often with different hardware and software. People connected to one network often want to communicate with people attached to a different one. The fulfillment of this desire requires that different, and frequently incompatible networks, be connected, sometimes by means of machines called **gateways** to make the connection and provide the necessary translation, both in terms of hardware and software. A collection of interconnected networks is called an **internetwork** or **internet**. These terms will be used in a generic sense, in contrast to the worldwide Internet (which is one specific internet), which we will always capitalize.

A common form of internet is a collection of LANs connected by a WAN. In fact, if we were to replace the label "subnet" in Fig. 1-9 by "WAN," nothing else in the figure would have to change. The only real technical distinction between a subnet and a WAN in this case is whether hosts are present. If the system within the gray area contains only routers, it is a subnet; if it contains both routers and hosts, it is a WAN. The real differences relate to ownership and use.

Subnets, networks, and internetworks are often confused. Subnet makes the most sense in the context of a wide area network, where it refers to the collection of routers and communication lines owned by the network operator. As an analogy, the telephone system consists of telephone switching offices connected to one another by high-speed lines, and to houses and businesses by low-speed lines. These lines and equipment, owned and managed by the telephone company, form the subnet of the telephone system. The telephones themselves (the hosts in this analogy) are not part of the subnet. The combination of a subnet and its hosts forms a network. In the case of a LAN, the cable and the hosts form the network. There really is no subnet.

An internetwork is formed when distinct networks are interconnected. In our view, connecting a LAN and a WAN or connecting two LANs forms an internetwork, but there is little agreement in the industry over terminology in this area. One rule of thumb is that if different organizations paid to construct different parts of the network and each maintains its part, we have an internetwork rather than a single network. Also, if the underlying technology is different in different parts (e.g., broadcast versus point-to-point), we probably have two networks.

1.3 NETWORK SOFTWARE

The first computer networks were designed with the hardware as the main concern and the software as an afterthought. This strategy no longer works. Network software is now highly structured. In the following sections we examine the software structuring technique in some detail. The method described here forms the keystone of the entire book and will occur repeatedly later on.

1.3.1 Protocol Hierarchies

To reduce their design complexity, most networks are organized as a stack of **layers** or **levels**, each one built upon the one below it. The number of layers, the name of each layer, the contents of each layer, and the function of each layer differ from network to network. The purpose of each layer is to offer certain services to the higher layers, shielding those layers from the details of how the offered services are actually implemented. In a sense, each layer is a kind of virtual machine, offering certain services to the layer above it.

This concept is actually a familiar one and used throughout computer science, where it is variously known as information hiding, abstract data types, data encapsulation, and object-oriented programming. The fundamental idea is that a particular piece of software (or hardware) provides a service to its users but keeps the details of its internal state and algorithms hidden from them.

Layer n on one machine carries on a conversation with layer n on another machine. The rules and conventions used in this conversation are collectively known as the layer n protocol. Basically, a **protocol** is an agreement between the communicating parties on how communication is to proceed. As an analogy, when a woman is introduced to a man, she may choose to stick out her hand. He, in turn, may decide either to shake it or kiss it, depending, for example, on whether she is an American lawyer at a business meeting or a European princess at a formal ball. Violating the protocol will make communication more difficult, if not completely impossible.

A five-layer network is illustrated in Fig. 1-13. The entities comprising the corresponding layers on different machines are called **peers**. The peers may be processes, hardware devices, or even human beings. In other words, it is the peers that communicate by using the protocol.

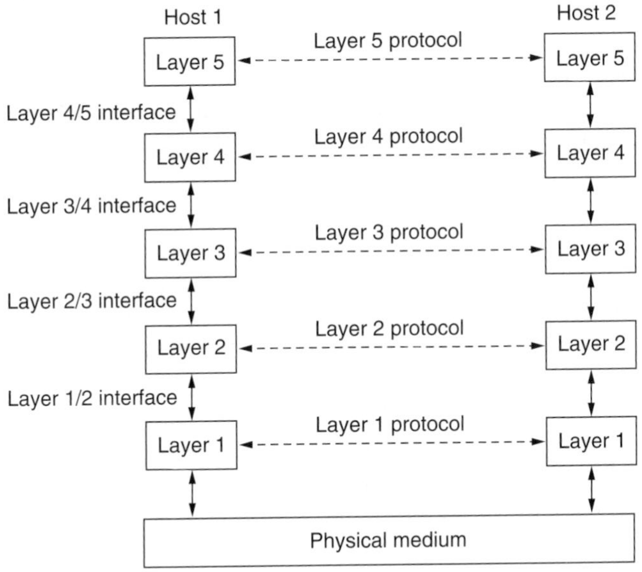

Figure 1-13. Layers, protocols, and interfaces.

In reality, no data are directly transferred from layer n on one machine to layer n on another machine. Instead, each layer passes data and control information to the layer immediately below it, until the lowest layer is reached. Below layer 1 is the **physical medium** through which actual communication occurs. In Fig. 1-13, virtual communication is shown by dotted lines and physical communication by solid lines.

Between each pair of adjacent layers is an **interface**. The interface defines which primitive operations and services the lower layer makes available to the upper one. When network designers decide how many layers to include in a network and what each one should do, one of the most important considerations is defining clean interfaces between the layers. Doing so, in turn, requires that each layer perform a specific collection of well-understood functions. In addition to minimizing the amount of information that must be passed between layers, clear-cut interfaces also make it simpler to replace the implementation of one layer with a completely different implementation (e.g., all the telephone lines are replaced by satellite channels) because all that is required of the new implementation is that it offer exactly the same set of services to its upstairs neighbor as the old implementation did. In fact, it is common that different hosts use different implementations.

A set of layers and protocols is called a **network architecture**. The specification of an architecture must contain enough information to allow an implementer to write the program or build the hardware for each layer so that it will correctly obey the appropriate protocol. Neither the details of the implementation nor the specification of the interfaces is part of the architecture because these are hidden away inside the machines and not visible from the outside. It is not even necessary that the interfaces on all machines in a network be the same, provided that each machine can correctly use all the protocols. A list of protocols used by a certain system, one protocol per layer, is called a **protocol stack**. The subjects of network architectures, protocol stacks, and the protocols themselves are the principal topics of this book.

An analogy may help explain the idea of multilayer communication. Imagine two philosophers (peer processes in layer 3), one of whom speaks Urdu and English and one of whom speaks Chinese and French. Since they have no common language, they each engage a translator (peer processes at layer 2), each of whom in turn contacts a secretary (peer processes in layer 1). Philosopher 1 wishes to convey his affection for *oryctolagus cuniculus* to his peer. To do so, he passes a message (in English) across the 2/3 interface to his translator, saying "I like rabbits," as illustrated in Fig. 1-14. The translators have agreed on a neutral language known to both of them, Dutch, so the message is converted to "Ik vind konijnen leuk." The choice of language is the layer 2 protocol and is up to the layer 2 peer processes.

The translator then gives the message to a secretary for transmission, by, for example, fax (the layer 1 protocol). When the message arrives, it is translated into French and passed across the 2/3 interface to philosopher 2. Note that each protocol is completely independent of the other ones as long as the interfaces are not changed. The translators can switch from Dutch to say, Finnish, at will, provided that they both agree, and neither changes his interface with either layer 1 or layer 3. Similarly, the secretaries can switch from fax to e-mail or telephone without disturbing (or even informing) the other layers. Each process may add some information intended only for its peer. This information is not passed upward to the layer above.

Now consider a more technical example: how to provide communication to the top layer of the five-layer network in Fig. 1-15. A message, M, is produced by an application process running in layer 5 and given to layer 4 for transmission.

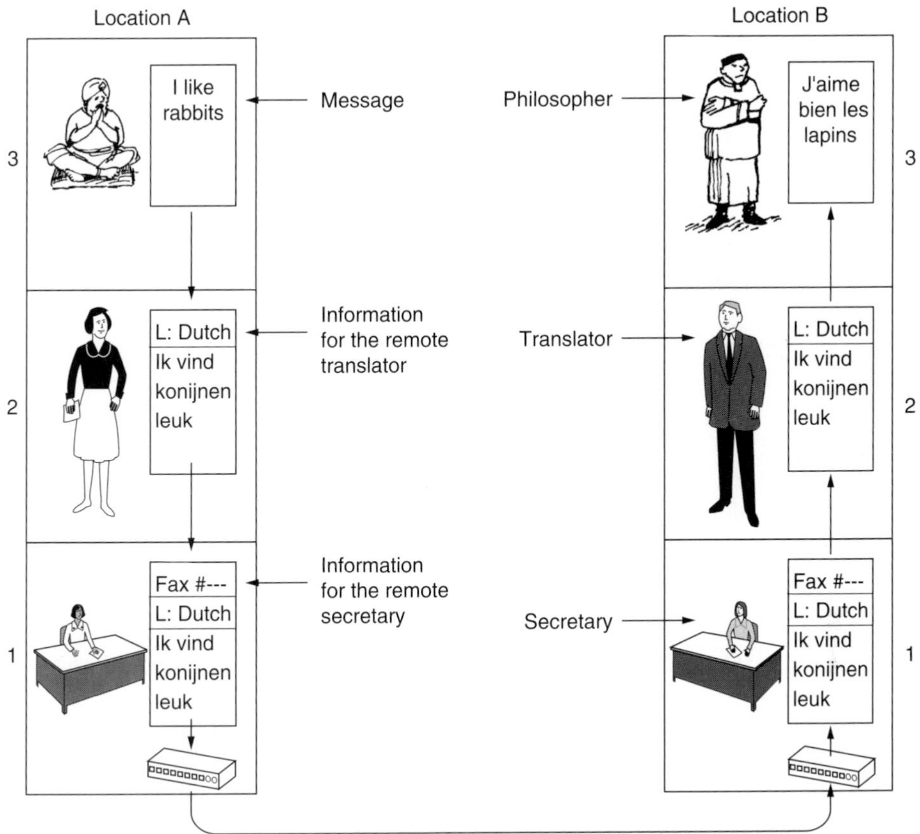

Figure 1-14. The philosopher-translator-secretary architecture.

Layer 4 puts a **header** in front of the message to identify the message and passes the result to layer 3. The header includes control information, such as sequence numbers, to allow layer 4 on the destination machine to deliver messages in the right order if the lower layers do not maintain sequence. In some layers, headers can also contain sizes, times, and other control fields.

In many networks, there is no limit to the size of messages transmitted in the layer 4 protocol, but there is nearly always a limit imposed by the layer 3 protocol. Consequently, layer 3 must break up the incoming messages into smaller units, packets, prepending a layer 3 header to each packet. In this example, M is split into two parts, M_1 and M_2.

Layer 3 decides which of the outgoing lines to use and passes the packets to layer 2. Layer 2 adds not only a header to each piece, but also a trailer, and gives the resulting unit to layer 1 for physical transmission. At the receiving machine the message moves upward, from layer to layer, with headers being stripped off as it progresses. None of the headers for layers below n are passed up to layer n.

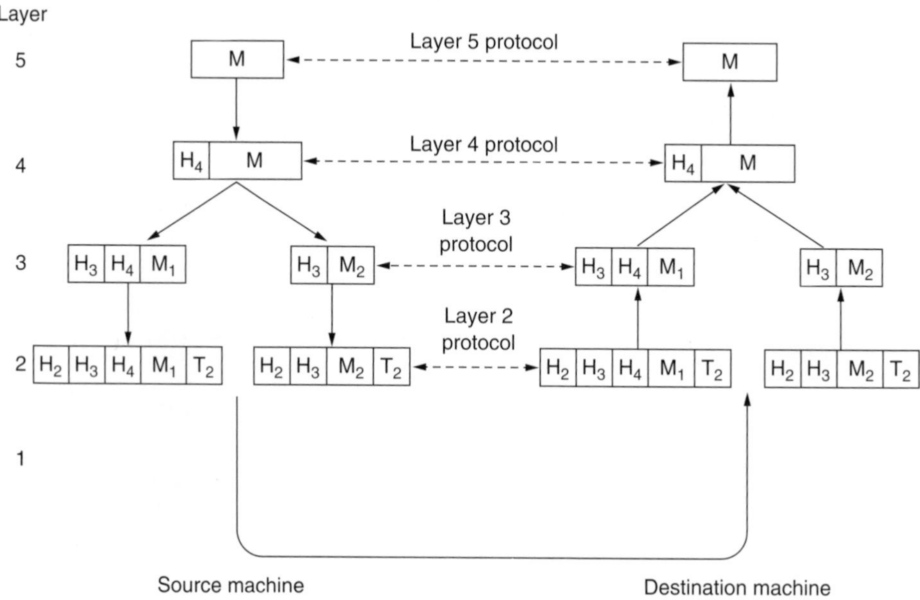

Figure 1-15. Example information flow supporting virtual communication in layer 5.

The important thing to understand about Fig. 1-15 is the relation between the virtual and actual communication and the difference between protocols and interfaces. The peer processes in layer 4, for example, conceptually think of their communication as being "horizontal," using the layer 4 protocol. Each one is likely to have a procedure called something like *SendToOtherSide* and *GetFromOtherSide*, even though these procedures actually communicate with lower layers across the 3/4 interface, not with the other side.

The peer process abstraction is crucial to all network design. Using it, the unmanageable task of designing the complete network can be broken into several smaller, manageable design problems, namely, the design of the individual layers.

Although Sec. 1.3 is called "Network Software," it is worth pointing out that the lower layers of a protocol hierarchy are frequently implemented in hardware or firmware. Nevertheless, complex protocol algorithms are involved, even if they are embedded (in whole or in part) in hardware.

1.3.2 Design Issues for the Layers

Some of the key design issues that occur in computer networks are present in several layers. Below, we will briefly mention some of the more important ones.

Every layer needs a mechanism for identifying senders and receivers. Since a network normally has many computers, some of which have multiple processes, a means is needed for a process on one machine to specify with whom it wants to talk. As a consequence of having multiple destinations, some form of **addressing** is needed in order to specify a specific destination.

Another set of design decisions concerns the rules for data transfer. In some systems, data only travel in one direction; in others, data can go both ways. The protocol must also determine how many logical channels the connection corresponds to and what their priorities are. Many networks provide at least two logical channels per connection, one for normal data and one for urgent data.

Error control is an important issue because physical communication circuits are not perfect. Many error-detecting and error-correcting codes are known, but both ends of the connection must agree on which one is being used. In addition, the receiver must have some way of telling the sender which messages have been correctly received and which have not.

Not all communication channels preserve the order of messages sent on them. To deal with a possible loss of sequencing, the protocol must make explicit provision for the receiver to allow the pieces to be reassembled properly. An obvious solution is to number the pieces, but this solution still leaves open the question of what should be done with pieces that arrive out of order.

An issue that occurs at every level is how to keep a fast sender from swamping a slow receiver with data. Various solutions have been proposed and will be discussed later. Some of them involve some kind of feedback from the receiver to the sender, either directly or indirectly, about the receiver's current situation. Others limit the sender to an agreed-on transmission rate. This subject is called **flow control**.

Another problem that must be solved at several levels is the inability of all processes to accept arbitrarily long messages. This property leads to mechanisms for disassembling, transmitting, and then reassembling messages. A related issue is the problem of what to do when processes insist on transmitting data in units that are so small that sending each one separately is inefficient. Here the solution is to gather several small messages heading toward a common destination into a single large message and dismember the large message at the other side.

When it is inconvenient or expensive to set up a separate connection for each pair of communicating processes, the underlying layer may decide to use the same connection for multiple, unrelated conversations. As long as this **multiplexing** and **demultiplexing** is done transparently, it can be used by any layer. Multiplexing is needed in the physical layer, for example, where all the traffic for all connections has to be sent over at most a few physical circuits.

When there are multiple paths between source and destination, a route must be chosen. Sometimes this decision must be split over two or more layers. For example, to send data from London to Rome, a high-level decision might have to be made to transit France or Germany based on their respective privacy laws. Then a low-level decision might have to made to select one of the available circuits based on the current traffic load. This topic is called **routing**.

1.3.3 Connection-Oriented and Connectionless Services

Layers can offer two different types of service to the layers above them: connection-oriented and connectionless. In this section we will look at these two types and examine the differences between them.

Connection-oriented service is modeled after the telephone system. To talk to someone, you pick up the phone, dial the number, talk, and then hang up. Similarly, to use a connection-oriented network service, the service user first establishes a connection, uses the connection, and then releases the connection. The essential aspect of a connection is that it acts like a tube: the sender pushes objects (bits) in at one end, and the receiver takes them out at the other end. In most cases the order is preserved so that the bits arrive in the order they were sent.

In some cases when a connection is established, the sender, receiver, and subnet conduct a **negotiation** about parameters to be used, such as maximum message size, quality of service required, and other issues. Typically, one side makes a proposal and the other side can accept it, reject it, or make a counterproposal.

In contrast, **connectionless service** is modeled after the postal system. Each message (letter) carries the full destination address, and each one is routed through the system independent of all the others. Normally, when two messages are sent to the same destination, the first one sent will be the first one to arrive. However, it is possible that the first one sent can be delayed so that the second one arrives first.

Each service can be characterized by a **quality of service**. Some services are reliable in the sense that they never lose data. Usually, a reliable service is implemented by having the receiver acknowledge the receipt of each message so the sender is sure that it arrived. The acknowledgement process introduces overhead and delays, which are often worth it but are sometimes undesirable.

A typical situation in which a reliable connection-oriented service is appropriate is file transfer. The owner of the file wants to be sure that all the bits arrive correctly and in the same order they were sent. Very few file transfer customers would prefer a service that occasionally scrambles or loses a few bits, even if it is much faster.

Reliable connection-oriented service has two minor variations: message sequences and byte streams. In the former variant, the message boundaries are preserved. When two 1024-byte messages are sent, they arrive as two distinct 1024-byte messages, never as one 2048-byte message. In the latter, the connection is simply a stream of bytes, with no message boundaries. When 2048 bytes arrive at the receiver, there is no way to tell if they were sent as one 2048-byte message, two 1024-byte messages, or 2048 1-byte messages. If the pages of a book are sent over a network to a phototypesetter as separate messages, it might be important to preserve the message boundaries. On the other hand, when a user logs into a remote server, a byte stream from the user's computer to the server is all that is needed. Message boundaries are not relevant.

As mentioned above, for some applications, the transit delays introduced by acknowledgements are unacceptable. One such application is digitized voice traffic. It is preferable for telephone users to hear a bit of noise on the line from time to time than to experience a delay waiting for acknowledgements. Similarly, when transmitting a video conference, having a few pixels wrong is no problem, but having the image jerk along as the flow stops to correct errors is irritating.

Not all applications require connections. For example, as electronic mail becomes more common, electronic junk is becoming more common too. The electronic junk-mail sender probably does not want to go to the trouble of setting up and later tearing down a connection just to send one item. Nor is 100 percent reliable delivery essential, especially if it costs more. All that is needed is a way to send a single message that has a high probability of arrival, but no guarantee. Unreliable (meaning not acknowledged) connectionless service is often called **datagram service**, in analogy with telegram service, which also does not return an acknowledgement to the sender.

In other situations, the convenience of not having to establish a connection to send one short message is desired, but reliability is essential. The **acknowledged datagram service** can be provided for these applications. It is like sending a registered letter and requesting a return receipt. When the receipt comes back, the sender is absolutely sure that the letter was delivered to the intended party and not lost along the way.

Still another service is the **request-reply service**. In this service the sender transmits a single datagram containing a request; the reply contains the answer. For example, a query to the local library asking where Uighur is spoken falls into this category. Request-reply is commonly used to implement communication in the client-server model: the client issues a request and the server responds to it. Figure 1-16 summarizes the types of services discussed above.

	Service	Example
Connection-oriented	Reliable message stream	Sequence of pages
	Reliable byte stream	Remote login
	Unreliable connection	Digitized voice
Connection-less	Unreliable datagram	Electronic junk mail
	Acknowledged datagram	Registered mail
	Request-reply	Database query

Figure 1-16. Six different types of service.

The concept of using unreliable communication may be confusing at first. After all, why would anyone actually prefer unreliable communication to reliable communication? First of all, reliable communication (in our sense, that is, acknowledged) may not be available. For example, Ethernet does not provide reliable communication. Packets can occasionally be damaged in transit. It is up to higher protocol levels to deal with this problem. Second, the delays inherent in providing a reliable service may be unacceptable, especially in real-time applications such as multimedia. For these reasons, both reliable and unreliable communication coexist.

1.3.4 Service Primitives

A service is formally specified by a set of **primitives** (operations) available to a user process to access the service. These primitives tell the service to perform some action or report on an action taken by a peer entity. If the protocol stack is located in the operating system, as it often is, the primitives are normally system calls. These calls cause a trap to kernel mode, which then turns control of the machine over to the operating system to send the necessary packets.

The set of primitives available depends on the nature of the service being provided. The primitives for connection-oriented service are different from those of connectionless service. As a minimal example of the service primitives that might be provided to implement a reliable byte stream in a client-server environment, consider the primitives listed in Fig. 1-17.

Primitive	Meaning
LISTEN	Block waiting for an incoming connection
CONNECT	Establish a connection with a waiting peer
RECEIVE	Block waiting for an incoming message
SEND	Send a message to the peer
DISCONNECT	Terminate a connection

Figure 1-17. Five service primitives for implementing a simple connection-oriented service.

These primitives might be used as follows. First, the server executes LISTEN to indicate that it is prepared to accept incoming connections. A common way to implement LISTEN is to make it a blocking system call. After executing the primitive, the server process is blocked until a request for connection appears.

Next, the client process executes CONNECT to establish a connection with the server. The CONNECT call needs to specify who to connect to, so it might have a parameter giving the server's address. The operating system then typically sends a packet to the peer asking it to connect, as shown by (1) in Fig. 1-18. The client process is suspended until there is a response. When the packet arrives at the server, it is processed by the operating system there. When the system sees that the packet is requesting a connection, it checks to see if there is a listener. If so, it does two things: unblocks the listener and sends back an acknowledgement (2). The arrival of this acknowledgement then releases the client. At this point the client and server are both running and they have a connection established. It is important to note that the acknowledgement (2) is generated by the protocol code itself, not in response to a user-level primitive. If a connection request arrives and there is no listener, the result is undefined. In some systems the packet may be queued for a short time in anticipation of a LISTEN.

The obvious analogy between this protocol and real life is a customer (client) calling a company's customer service manager. The service manager starts out by being near the telephone in case it rings. Then the client places the call. When the manager picks up the phone, the connection is established.

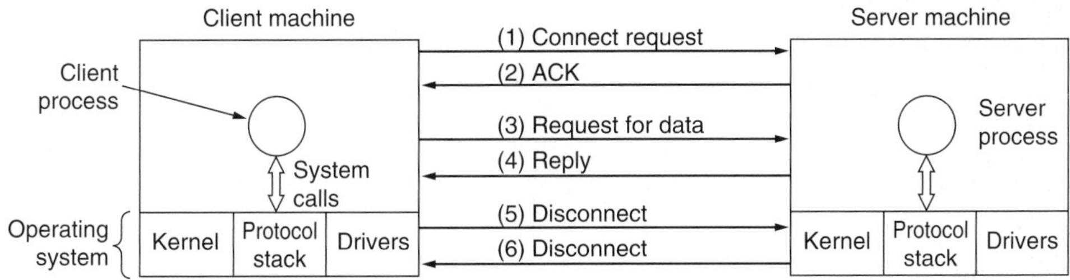

Figure 1-18. Packets sent in a simple client-server interaction on a connection-oriented network.

The next step is for the server to execute RECEIVE to prepare to accept the first request. Normally, the server does this immediately upon being released from the LISTEN, before the acknowledgement can get back to the client. The RECEIVE call blocks the server.

Then the client executes SEND to transmit its request (3) followed by the execution of RECEIVE to get the reply.

The arrival of the request packet at the server machine unblocks the server process so it can process the request. After it has done the work, it uses SEND to return the answer to the client (4). The arrival of this packet unblocks the client, which can now inspect the answer. If the client has additional requests, it can make them now. If it is done, it can use DISCONNECT to terminate the connection. Usually, an initial DISCONNECT is a blocking call, suspending the client and sending a packet to the server saying that the connection is no longer needed (5). When the server gets the packet, it also issues a DISCONNECT of its own, acknowledging the client and releasing the connection. When the server's packet (6) gets back to the client machine, the client process is released and the connection is broken. In a nutshell, this is how connection-oriented communication works.

Of course, life is not so simple. Many things can go wrong here. The timing can be wrong (e.g., the CONNECT is done before the LISTEN), packets can get lost, and much more. We will look at these issues in great detail later, but for the moment, Fig. 1-18 briefly summarizes how client-server communication might work over a connection-oriented network.

Given that six packets are required to complete this protocol, one might wonder why a connectionless protocol is not used instead. The answer is that in a perfect world it could be, in which case only two packets would be needed: one for the request and one for the reply. However, in the face of large messages in either direction (e.g., a megabyte file), transmission errors, and lost packets, the situation changes. If the reply consisted of hundreds of packets, some of which could be lost during transmission, how would the client know if some pieces were missing? How would the client know whether the last packet actually received was really the last packet sent? Suppose that the client wanted a second file. How could it tell packet 1 from the second file from a lost packet 1 from the first file that suddenly found its way to the client? In short, in the real world, a simple request-reply protocol over an unreliable network is often inadequate. In Chap. 3 we will study a variety of protocols in detail that overcome these and other problems. For the moment, suffice it to say that having a reliable, ordered byte stream between processes is sometimes very convenient.

1.3.5 The Relationship of Services to Protocols

Services and protocols are distinct concepts, although they are frequently confused. This distinction is so important, however, that we emphasize it again here. A *service* is a set of primitives (operations) that a layer provides to the layer above it. The service defines what operations the layer is prepared to perform on behalf of its users, but it says nothing at all about how these operations are implemented. A service relates to an interface between two layers, with the lower layer being the service provider and the upper layer being the service user.

A *protocol*, in contrast, is a set of rules governing the format and meaning of the packets, or messages that are exchanged by the peer entities within a layer. Entities use protocols to implement their service definitions. They are free to change their protocols at will, provided they do not change the service visible to their users. In this way, the service and the protocol are completely decoupled.

In other words, services relate to the interfaces between layers, as illustrated in Fig. 1-19. In contrast, protocols relate to the packets sent between peer entities on different machines. It is important not to confuse the two concepts.

An analogy with programming languages is worth making. A service is like an abstract data type or an object in an object-oriented language. It defines operations that can be performed on an object but does not specify how these operations are implemented. A protocol relates to the *implementation* of the service and as such is not visible to the user of the service.

Many older protocols did not distinguish the service from the protocol. In effect, a typical layer might have had a service primitive SEND PACKET with the

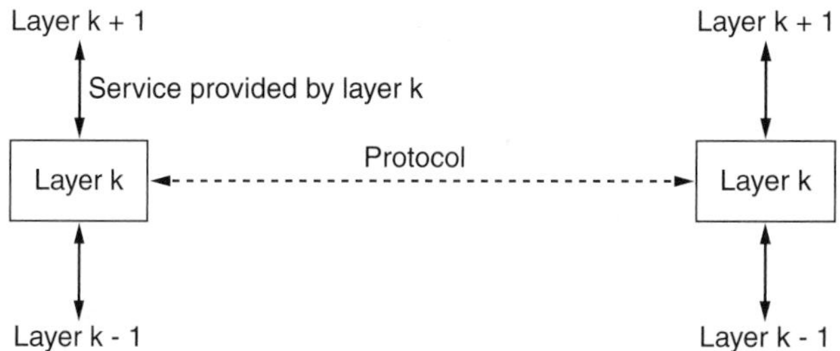

Figure 1-19. The relationship between a service and a protocol.

user providing a pointer to a fully assembled packet. This arrangement meant that all changes to the protocol were immediately visible to the users. Most network designers now regard such a design as a serious blunder.

1.4 REFERENCE MODELS

Now that we have discussed layered networks in the abstract, it is time to look at some examples. In the next two sections we will discuss two important network architectures, the OSI reference model and the TCP/IP reference model. Although the *protocols* associated with the OSI model are rarely used any more, the *model* itself is actually quite general and still valid, and the features discussed at each layer are still very important. The TCP/IP model has the opposite properties: the model itself is not of much use but the protocols are widely used. For this reason we will look at both of them in detail. Also, sometimes you can learn more from failures than from successes.

1.4.1 The OSI Reference Model

The OSI model (minus the physical medium) is shown in Fig. 1-20. This model is based on a proposal developed by the International Standards Organization (ISO) as a first step toward international standardization of the protocols used in the various layers (Day and Zimmermann, 1983). It was revised in 1995 (Day, 1995). The model is called the **ISO OSI (Open Systems Interconnection) Reference Model** because it deals with connecting open systems—that is, systems that are open for communication with other systems. We will just call it the OSI model for short.

The OSI model has seven layers. The principles that were applied to arrive at the seven layers can be briefly summarized as follows:

1. A layer should be created where a different abstraction is needed.
2. Each layer should perform a well-defined function.
3. The function of each layer should be chosen with an eye toward defining internationally standardized protocols.
4. The layer boundaries should be chosen to minimize the information flow across the interfaces.
5. The number of layers should be large enough that distinct functions need not be thrown together in the same layer out of necessity and small enough that the architecture does not become unwieldy.

Below we will discuss each layer of the model in turn, starting at the bottom layer. Note that the OSI model itself is not a network architecture because it does not specify the exact services and protocols to be used in each layer. It just tells what each layer should do. However, ISO has also produced standards for all the layers, although these are not part of the reference model itself. Each one has been published as a separate international standard.

The Physical Layer

The **physical layer** is concerned with transmitting raw bits over a communication channel. The design issues have to do with making sure that when one side sends a 1 bit, it is received by the other side as a 1 bit, not as a 0 bit. Typical questions here are how many volts should be used to represent a 1 and how many for a 0, how many nanoseconds a bit lasts, whether transmission may proceed simultaneously in both directions, how the initial connection is established and how it is torn down when both sides are finished, and how many pins the network connector has and what each pin is used for. The design issues here largely deal with mechanical, electrical, and timing interfaces, and the physical transmission medium, which lies below the physical layer.

The Data Link Layer

The main task of the **data link layer** is to transform a raw transmission facility into a line that appears free of undetected transmission errors to the network layer. It accomplishes this task by having the sender break up the input data into **data frames** (typically a few hundred or a few thousand bytes) and transmit the frames sequentially. If the service is reliable, the receiver confirms correct receipt of each frame by sending back an **acknowledgement frame**.

Another issue that arises in the data link layer (and most of the higher layers as well) is how to keep a fast transmitter from drowning a slow receiver in data. Some traffic regulation mechanism is often needed to let the transmitter know

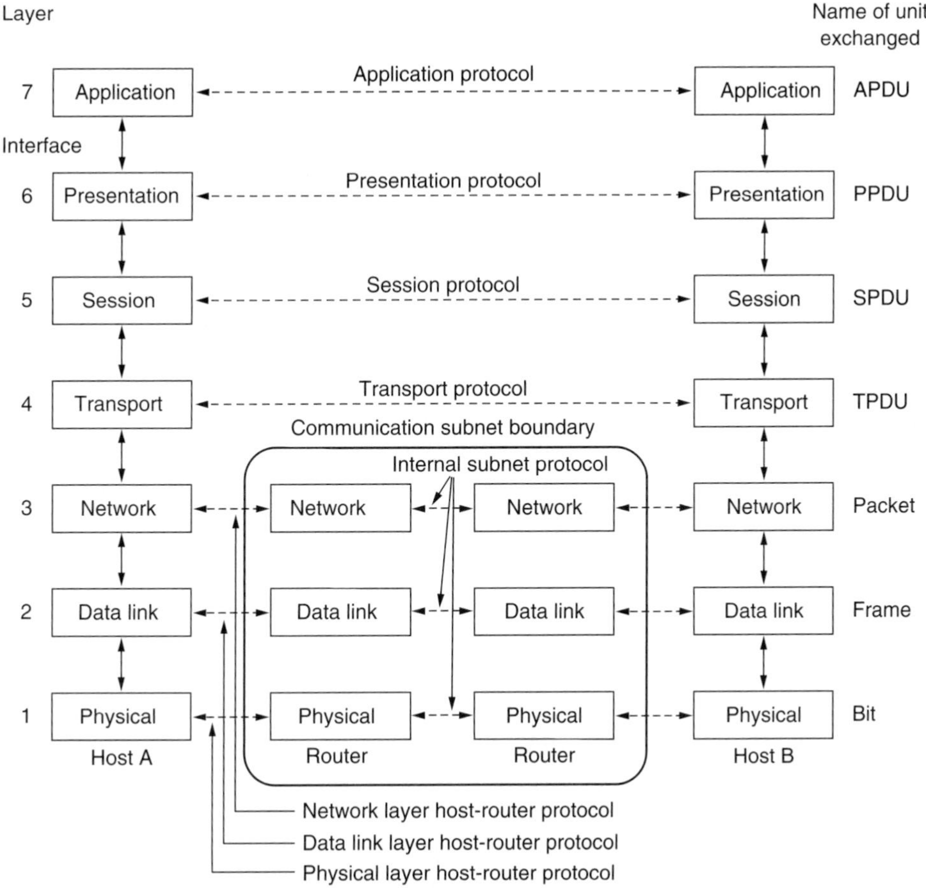

Figure 1-20. The OSI reference model.

how much buffer space the receiver has at the moment. Frequently, this flow regulation and the error handling are integrated.

Broadcast networks have an additional issue in the data link layer: how to control access to the shared channel. A special sublayer of the data link layer, the medium access control sublayer, deals with this problem.

The Network Layer

The **network layer** controls the operation of the subnet. A key design issue is determining how packets are routed from source to destination. Routes can be based on static tables that are "wired into" the network and rarely changed. They can also be determined at the start of each conversation, for example, a terminal session (e.g., a login to a remote machine). Finally, they can be highly dynamic, being determined anew for each packet, to reflect the current network load.

If too many packets are present in the subnet at the same time, they will get in one another's way, forming bottlenecks. The control of such congestion also belongs to the network layer. More generally, the quality of service provided (delay, transit time, jitter, etc.) is also a network layer issue.

When a packet has to travel from one network to another to get to its destination, many problems can arise. The addressing used by the second network may be different from the first one. The second one may not accept the packet at all because it is too large. The protocols may differ, and so on. It is up to the network layer to overcome all these problems to allow heterogeneous networks to be interconnected.

In broadcast networks, the routing problem is simple, so the network layer is often thin or even nonexistent.

The Transport Layer

The basic function of the **transport layer** is to accept data from above, split it up into smaller units if need be, pass these to the network layer, and ensure that the pieces all arrive correctly at the other end. Furthermore, all this must be done efficiently and in a way that isolates the upper layers from the inevitable changes in the hardware technology.

The transport layer also determines what type of service to provide to the session layer, and, ultimately, to the users of the network. The most popular type of transport connection is an error-free point-to-point channel that delivers messages or bytes in the order in which they were sent. However, other possible kinds of transport service are the transporting of isolated messages, with no guarantee about the order of delivery, and the broadcasting of messages to multiple destinations. The type of service is determined when the connection is established. (As an aside, an error-free channel is impossible to achieve; what people really mean by this term is that the error rate is low enough to ignore in practice.)

The transport layer is a true end-to-end layer, all the way from the source to the destination. In other words, a program on the source machine carries on a conversation with a similar program on the destination machine, using the message headers and control messages. In the lower layers, the protocols are between each machine and its immediate neighbors, and not between the ultimate source and destination machines, which may be separated by many routers. The difference between layers 1 through 3, which are chained, and layers 4 through 7, which are end-to-end, is illustrated in Fig. 1-20.

The Session Layer

The session layer allows users on different machines to establish **sessions** between them. Sessions offer various services, including **dialog control** (keeping track of whose turn it is to transmit), **token management** (preventing two parties from attempting the same critical operation at the same time), and **synchronization** (checkpointing long transmissions to allow them to continue from where they were after a crash).

The Presentation Layer

Unlike lower layers, which are mostly concerned with moving bits around, the **presentation layer** is concerned with the syntax and semantics of the information transmitted. In order to make it possible for computers with different data representations to communicate, the data structures to be exchanged can be defined in an abstract way, along with a standard encoding to be used "on the wire." The presentation layer manages these abstract data structures and allows higher-level data structures (e.g., banking records), to be defined and exchanged.

The Application Layer

The **application layer** contains a variety of protocols that are commonly needed by users. One widely-used application protocol is **HTTP** (**HyperText Transfer Protocol**), which is the basis for the World Wide Web. When a browser wants a Web page, it sends the name of the page it wants to the server using HTTP. The server then sends the page back. Other application protocols are used for file transfer, electronic mail, and network news.

1.4.2 The TCP/IP Reference Model

Let us now turn from the OSI reference model to the reference model used in the grandparent of all wide area computer networks, the ARPANET, and its successor, the worldwide Internet. Although we will give a brief history of the ARPANET later, it is useful to mention a few key aspects of it now. The ARPANET was a research network sponsored by the DoD (U.S. Department of Defense). It eventually connected hundreds of universities and government installations, using leased telephone lines. When satellite and radio networks were added later, the existing protocols had trouble interworking with them, so a new reference architecture was needed. Thus, the ability to connect multiple networks in a seamless way was one of the major design goals from the very beginning. This architecture later became known as the **TCP/IP Reference Model**, after its two primary protocols. It was first defined in (Cerf and Kahn, 1974). A later perspective is given in (Leiner et al., 1985). The design philosophy behind the model is discussed in (Clark, 1988).

Given the DoD's worry that some of its precious hosts, routers, and internetwork gateways might get blown to pieces at a moment's notice, another major goal was that the network be able to survive loss of subnet hardware, with existing conversations not being broken off. In other words, DoD wanted connections to remain intact as long as the source and destination machines were functioning, even if some of the machines or transmission lines in between were suddenly put out of operation. Furthermore, a flexible architecture was needed since applications with divergent requirements were envisioned, ranging from transferring files to real-time speech transmission.

The Internet Layer

All these requirements led to the choice of a packet-switching network based on a connectionless internetwork layer. This layer, called the **internet layer**, is the linchpin that holds the whole architecture together. Its job is to permit hosts to inject packets into any network and have them travel independently to the destination (potentially on a different network). They may even arrive in a different order than they were sent, in which case it is the job of higher layers to rearrange them, if in-order delivery is desired. Note that "internet" is used here in a generic sense, even though this layer is present in the Internet.

The analogy here is with the (snail) mail system. A person can drop a sequence of international letters into a mail box in one country, and with a little luck, most of them will be delivered to the correct address in the destination country. Probably the letters will travel through one or more international mail gateways along the way, but this is transparent to the users. Furthermore, that each country (i.e., each network) has its own stamps, preferred envelope sizes, and delivery rules is hidden from the users.

The internet layer defines an official packet format and protocol called **IP** (**Internet Protocol**). The job of the internet layer is to deliver IP packets where they are supposed to go. Packet routing is clearly the major issue here, as is avoiding congestion. For these reasons, it is reasonable to say that the TCP/IP internet layer is similar in functionality to the OSI network layer. Figure 1-21 shows this correspondence.

The Transport Layer

The layer above the internet layer in the TCP/IP model is now usually called the **transport layer**. It is designed to allow peer entities on the source and destination hosts to carry on a conversation, just as in the OSI transport layer. Two end-to-end transport protocols have been defined here. The first one, **TCP** (**Transmission Control Protocol**), is a reliable connection-oriented protocol that allows a byte stream originating on one machine to be delivered without error on any other machine in the internet. It fragments the incoming byte stream into discrete messages and passes each one on to the internet layer. At the destination, the receiving TCP process reassembles the received messages into the output stream. TCP also handles flow control to make sure a fast sender cannot swamp a slow receiver with more messages than it can handle.

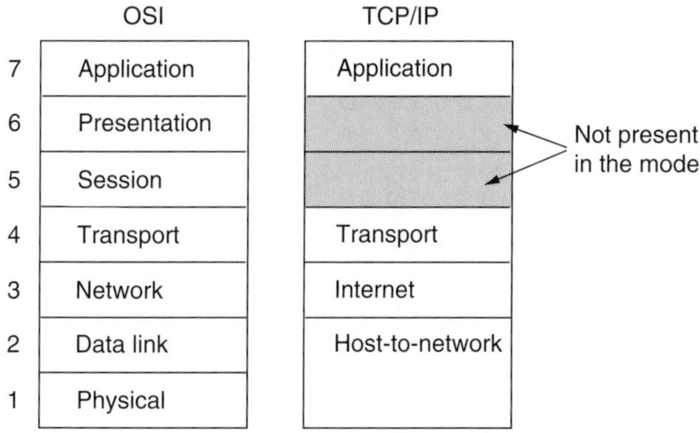

Figure 1-21. The TCP/IP reference model.

The second protocol in this layer, **UDP** (**User Datagram Protocol**), is an unreliable, connectionless protocol for applications that do not want TCP's sequencing or flow control and wish to provide their own. It is also widely used for one-shot, client-server-type request-reply queries and applications in which prompt delivery is more important than accurate delivery, such as transmitting speech or video. The relation of IP, TCP, and UDP is shown in Fig. 1-22. Since the model was developed, IP has been implemented on many other networks.

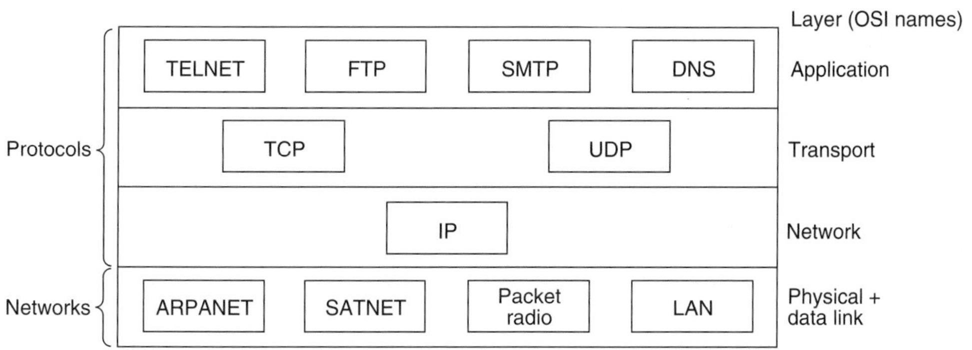

Figure 1-22. Protocols and networks in the TCP/IP model initially.

The Application Layer

The TCP/IP model does not have session or presentation layers. No need for them was perceived, so they were not included. Experience with the OSI model has proven this view correct: they are of little use to most applications.

On top of the transport layer is the **application layer**. It contains all the higher-level protocols. The early ones included virtual terminal (TELNET), file transfer (FTP), and electronic mail (SMTP), as shown in Fig. 1-22. The virtual terminal protocol allows a user on one machine to log onto a distant machine and work there. The file transfer protocol provides a way to move data efficiently from one machine to another. Electronic mail was originally just a kind of file transfer, but later a specialized protocol (SMTP) was developed for it. Many other protocols have been added to these over the years: the Domain Name System (DNS) for mapping host names onto their network addresses, NNTP, the protocol for moving USENET news articles around, and HTTP, the protocol for fetching pages on the World Wide Web, and many others.

The Host-to-Network Layer

Below the internet layer is a great void. The TCP/IP reference model does not really say much about what happens here, except to point out that the host has to connect to the network using some protocol so it can send IP packets to it. This protocol is not defined and varies from host to host and network to network. Books and papers about the TCP/IP model rarely discuss it.

1.4.3 A Comparison of the OSI and TCP/IP Reference Models

The OSI and TCP/IP reference models have much in common. Both are based on the concept of a stack of independent protocols. Also, the functionality of the layers is roughly similar. For example, in both models the layers up through and including the transport layer are there to provide an end-to-end, network-independent transport service to processes wishing to communicate. These layers form the transport provider. Again in both models, the layers above transport are application-oriented users of the transport service.

Despite these fundamental similarities, the two models also have many differences. In this section we will focus on the key differences between the two reference models. It is important to note that we are comparing the *reference models* here, not the corresponding *protocol stacks*. The protocols themselves will be discussed later. For an entire book comparing and contrasting TCP/IP and OSI, see (Piscitello and Chapin, 1993).

Three concepts are central to the OSI model:

1. Services.

2. Interfaces.

3. Protocols.

Probably the biggest contribution of the OSI model is to make the distinction between these three concepts explicit. Each layer performs some services for the layer above it. The *service* definition tells what the layer does, not how entities above it access it or how the layer works. It defines the layer's semantics.

A layer's *interface* tells the processes above it how to access it. It specifies what the parameters are and what results to expect. It, too, says nothing about how the layer works inside.

Finally, the peer *protocols* used in a layer are the layer's own business. It can use any protocols it wants to, as long as it gets the job done (i.e., provides the offered services). It can also change them at will without affecting software in higher layers.

These ideas fit very nicely with modern ideas about object-oriented programming. An object, like a layer, has a set of methods (operations) that processes outside the object can invoke. The semantics of these methods define the set of services that the object offers. The methods' parameters and results form the object's interface. The code internal to the object is its protocol and is not visible or of any concern outside the object.

The TCP/IP model did not originally clearly distinguish between service, interface, and protocol, although people have tried to retrofit it after the fact to make it more OSI-like. For example, the only real services offered by the internet layer are SEND IP PACKET and RECEIVE IP PACKET.

As a consequence, the protocols in the OSI model are better hidden than in the TCP/IP model and can be replaced relatively easily as the technology changes. Being able to make such changes is one of the main purposes of having layered protocols in the first place.

The OSI reference model was devised *before* the corresponding protocols were invented. This ordering means that the model was not biased toward one particular set of protocols, a fact that made it quite general. The downside of this ordering is that the designers did not have much experience with the subject and did not have a good idea of which functionality to put in which layer.

For example, the data link layer originally dealt only with point-to-point networks. When broadcast networks came around, a new sublayer had to be hacked into the model. When people started to build real networks using the OSI model and existing protocols, it was discovered that these networks did not match the required service specifications (wonder of wonders), so convergence sublayers had to be grafted onto the model to provide a place for papering over the differences. Finally, the committee originally expected that each country would have one network, run by the government and using the OSI protocols, so no thought was given to internetworking. To make a long story short, things did not turn out that way.

With TCP/IP the reverse was true: the protocols came first, and the model was really just a description of the existing protocols. There was no problem with the protocols fitting the model. They fit perfectly. The only trouble was that the *model* did not fit any other protocol stacks. Consequently, it was not especially useful for describing other, non-TCP/IP networks.

Turning from philosophical matters to more specific ones, an obvious difference between the two models is the number of layers: the OSI model has seven layers and the TCP/IP has four layers. Both have (inter)network, transport, and application layers, but the other layers are different.

Another difference is in the area of connectionless versus connection-oriented communication. The OSI model supports both connectionless and connection-oriented communication in the network layer, but only connection-oriented communication in the transport layer, where it counts (because the transport service is visible to the users). The TCP/IP model has only one mode in the network layer (connectionless) but supports both modes in the transport layer, giving the users a choice. This choice is especially important for simple request-response protocols.

1.4.4 A Critique of the OSI Model and Protocols

Neither the OSI model and its protocols nor the TCP/IP model and its protocols are perfect. Quite a bit of criticism can be, and has been, directed at both of them. In this section and the next one, we will look at some of these criticisms. We will begin with OSI and examine TCP/IP afterward.

At the time the second edition of this book was published (1989), it appeared to many experts in the field that the OSI model and its protocols were going to take over the world and push everything else out of their way. This did not happen. Why? A look back at some of the lessons may be useful. These lessons can be summarized as:

1. Bad timing.
2. Bad technology.
3. Bad implementations.
4. Bad politics.

Bad Timing

First let us look at reason one: bad timing. The time at which a standard is established is absolutely critical to its success. David Clark of M.I.T. has a theory of standards that he calls the *apocalypse of the two elephants*, which is illustrated in Fig. 1-23.

This figure shows the amount of activity surrounding a new subject. When the subject is first discovered, there is a burst of research activity in the form of discussions, papers, and meetings. After a while this activity subsides, corporations discover the subject, and the billion-dollar wave of investment hits.

It is essential that the standards be written in the trough in between the two "elephants." If the standards are written too early, before the research is finished, the subject may still be poorly understood; the result is bad standards. If they are written too late, so many companies may have already made major investments in

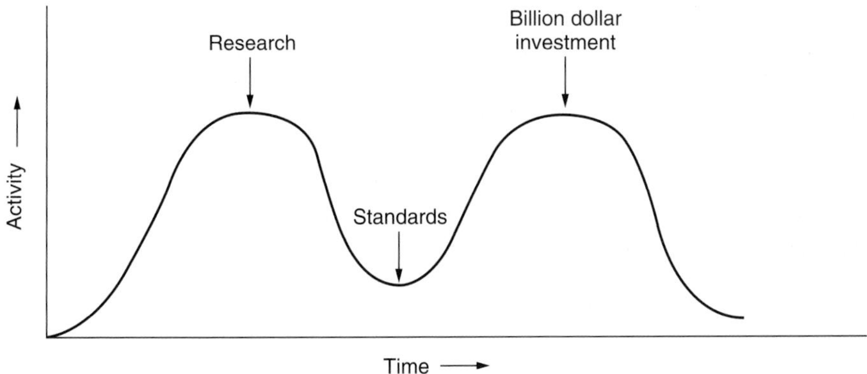

Figure 1-23. The apocalypse of the two elephants.

different ways of doing things that the standards are effectively ignored. If the interval between the two elephants is very short (because everyone is in a hurry to get started), the people developing the standards may get crushed.

It now appears that the standard OSI protocols got crushed. The competing TCP/IP protocols were already in widespread use by research universities by the time the OSI protocols appeared. While the billion-dollar wave of investment had not yet hit, the academic market was large enough that many vendors had begun cautiously offering TCP/IP products. When OSI came around, they did not want to support a second protocol stack until they were forced to, so there were no initial offerings. With every company waiting for every other company to go first, no company went first and OSI never happened.

Bad Technology

The second reason that OSI never caught on is that both the model and the protocols are flawed. The choice of seven layers was more political than technical, and two of the layers (session and presentation) are nearly empty, whereas two other ones (data link and network) are overfull.

The OSI model, along with the associated service definitions and protocols, is extraordinarily complex. When piled up, the printed standards occupy a significant fraction of a meter of paper. They are also difficult to implement and inefficient in operation. In this context, a riddle posed by Paul Mockapetris and cited in (Rose, 1993) comes to mind:

Q: What do you get when you cross a mobster with an international standard?
A: Someone who makes you an offer you can't understand.

In addition to being incomprehensible, another problem with OSI is that some functions, such as addressing, flow control, and error control, reappear again and again in each layer. Saltzer et al. (1984), for example, have pointed out that to be effective, error control must be done in the highest layer, so that repeating it over and over in each of the lower layers is often unnecessary and inefficient.

Bad Implementations

Given the enormous complexity of the model and the protocols, it will come as no surprise that the initial implementations were huge, unwieldy, and slow. Everyone who tried them got burned. It did not take long for people to associate "OSI" with "poor quality." Although the products improved in the course of time, the image stuck.

In contrast, one of the first implementations of TCP/IP was part of Berkeley UNIX and was quite good (not to mention, free). People began using it quickly, which led to a large user community, which led to improvements, which led to an even larger community. Here the spiral was upward instead of downward.

Bad Politics

On account of the initial implementation, many people, especially in academia, thought of TCP/IP as part of UNIX, and UNIX in the 1980s in academia was not unlike parenthood (then incorrectly called motherhood) and apple pie.

OSI, on the other hand, was widely thought to be the creature of the European telecommunication ministries, the European Community, and later the U.S. Government. This belief was only partly true, but the very idea of a bunch of government bureaucrats trying to shove a technically inferior standard down the throats of the poor researchers and programmers down in the trenches actually developing computer networks did not help much. Some people viewed this development in the same light as IBM announcing in the 1960s that PL/I was the language of the future, or DoD correcting this later by announcing that it was actually Ada.

1.4.5 A Critique of the TCP/IP Reference Model

The TCP/IP model and protocols have their problems too. First, the model does not clearly distinguish the concepts of service, interface, and protocol. Good software engineering practice requires differentiating between the specification and the implementation, something that OSI does very carefully, and TCP/IP does not. Consequently, the TCP/IP model is not much of a guide for designing new networks using new technologies.

Second, the TCP/IP model is not at all general and is poorly suited to describing any protocol stack other than TCP/IP. Trying to use the TCP/IP model to describe Bluetooth, for example, is completely impossible.

Third, the host-to-network layer is not really a layer at all in the normal sense of the term as used in the context of layered protocols. It is an interface (between the network and data link layers). The distinction between an interface and a layer is crucial, and one should not be sloppy about it.

Fourth, the TCP/IP model does not distinguish (or even mention) the physical and data link layers. These are completely different. The physical layer has to do with the transmission characteristics of copper wire, fiber optics, and wireless communication. The data link layer's job is to delimit the start and end of frames and get them from one side to the other with the desired degree of reliability. A proper model should include both as separate layers. The TCP/IP model does not do this.

Finally, although the IP and TCP protocols were carefully thought out and well implemented, many of the other protocols were ad hoc, generally produced by a couple of graduate students hacking away until they got tired. The protocol implementations were then distributed free, which resulted in their becoming widely used, deeply entrenched, and thus hard to replace. Some of them are a bit of an embarrassment now. The virtual terminal protocol, TELNET, for example, was designed for a ten-character per second mechanical Teletype terminal. It knows nothing of graphical user interfaces and mice. Nevertheless, 25 years later, it is still in widespread use.

In summary, despite its problems, the OSI *model* (minus the session and presentation layers) has proven to be exceptionally useful for discussing computer networks. In contrast, the OSI *protocols* have not become popular. The reverse is true of TCP/IP: the *model* is practically nonexistent, but the *protocols* are widely used. Since computer scientists like to have their cake and eat it, too, in this book we will use a modified OSI model but concentrate primarily on the TCP/IP and related protocols, as well as newer ones such as 802, SONET, and Bluetooth. In effect, we will use the hybrid model of Fig. 1-24 as the framework for this book.

5	Application layer
4	Transport layer
3	Network layer
2	Data link layer
1	Physical layer

Figure 1-24. The hybrid reference model to be used in this book.

1.5 EXAMPLE NETWORKS

The subject of computer networking covers many different kinds of networks, large and small, well known and less well known. They have different goals, scales, and technologies. In the following sections, we will look at some examples, to get an idea of the variety one finds in the area of computer networking.

We will start with the Internet, probably the best known network, and look at its history, evolution, and technology. Then we will consider ATM, which is often used within the core of large (telephone) networks. Technically, it is quite different from the Internet, contrasting nicely with it. Next we will introduce Ethernet, the dominant local area network. Finally, we will look at IEEE 802.11, the standard for wireless LANs.

1.5.1 The Internet

The Internet is not a network at all, but a vast collection of different networks that use certain common protocols and provide certain common services. It is an unusual system in that it was not planned by anyone and is not controlled by anyone. To better understand it, let us start from the beginning and see how it has developed and why. For a wonderful history of the Internet, John Naughton's (2000) book is highly recommended. It is one of those rare books that is not only fun to read, but also has 20 pages of *ibid.*'s and *op. cit.*'s for the serious historian. Some of the material below is based on this book.

Of course, countless technical books have been written about the Internet and its protocols as well. For more information, see, for example, (Maufer, 1999).

The ARPANET

The story begins in the late 1950s. At the height of the Cold War, the DoD wanted a command-and-control network that could survive a nuclear war. At that time, all military communications used the public telephone network, which was considered vulnerable. The reason for this belief can be gleaned from Fig. 1-25(a). Here the black dots represent telephone switching offices, each of which was connected to thousands of telephones. These switching offices were, in turn, connected to higher-level switching offices (toll offices), to form a national hierarchy with only a small amount of redundancy. The vulnerability of the system was that the destruction of a few key toll offices could fragment the system into many isolated islands.

Around 1960, the DoD awarded a contract to the RAND Corporation to find a solution. One of its employees, Paul Baran, came up with the highly distributed and fault-tolerant design of Fig. 1-25(b). Since the paths between any two switching offices were now much longer than analog signals could travel without distortion, Baran proposed using digital packet-switching technology throughout the system. Baran wrote several reports for the DoD describing his ideas in detail. Officials at the Pentagon liked the concept and asked AT&T, then the U.S. national telephone monopoly, to build a prototype. AT&T dismissed Baran's ideas out of hand. The biggest and richest corporation in the world was not about to allow some young whippersnapper tell it how to build a telephone system. They said Baran's network could not be built and the idea was killed.

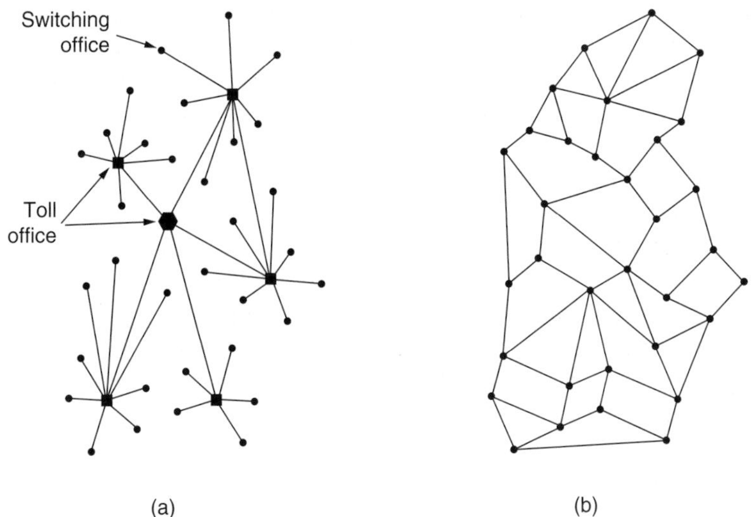

Figure 1-25. (a) Structure of the telephone system. (b) Baran's proposed distributed switching system.

Several years went by and still the DoD did not have a better command-and-control system. To understand what happened next, we have to go back to October 1957, when the Soviet Union beat the U.S. into space with the launch of the first artificial satellite, Sputnik. When President Eisenhower tried to find out who was asleep at the switch, he was appalled to find the Army, Navy, and Air Force squabbling over the Pentagon's research budget. His immediate response was to create a single defense research organization, **ARPA**, the **Advanced Research Projects Agency**. ARPA had no scientists or laboratories; in fact, it had nothing more than an office and a small (by Pentagon standards) budget. It did its work by issuing grants and contracts to universities and companies whose ideas looked promising to it.

For the first few years, ARPA tried to figure out what its mission should be, but in 1967, the attention of ARPA's then director, Larry Roberts, turned to networking. He contacted various experts to decide what to do. One of them, Wesley Clark, suggested building a packet-switched subnet, giving each host its own router, as illustrated in Fig. 1-10.

After some initial skepticism, Roberts bought the idea and presented a somewhat vague paper about it at the ACM SIGOPS Symposium on Operating System Principles held in Gatlinburg, Tennessee in late 1967 (Roberts, 1967). Much to Roberts' surprise, another paper at the conference described a similar system that had not only been designed but actually implemented under the direction of Donald Davies at the National Physical Laboratory in England. The NPL system was not a national system (it just connected several computers on the NPL campus), but it demonstrated that packet switching could be made to work. Furthermore, it cited Baran's now discarded earlier work. Roberts came away from Gatlinburg determined to build what later became known as the **ARPANET**.

The subnet would consist of minicomputers called **IMP**s (**Interface Message Processors**) connected by 56-kbps transmission lines. For high reliability, each IMP would be connected to at least two other IMPs. The subnet was to be a datagram subnet, so if some lines and IMPs were destroyed, messages could be automatically rerouted along alternative paths.

Each node of the network was to consist of an IMP and a host, in the same room, connected by a short wire. A host could send messages of up to 8063 bits to its IMP, which would then break these up into packets of at most 1008 bits and forward them independently toward the destination. Each packet was received in its entirety before being forwarded, so the subnet was the first electronic store-and-forward packet-switching network.

ARPA then put out a tender for building the subnet. Twelve companies bid for it. After evaluating all the proposals, ARPA selected BBN, a consulting firm in Cambridge, Massachusetts, and in December 1968, awarded it a contract to build the subnet and write the subnet software. BBN chose to use specially modified Honeywell DDP-316 minicomputers with 12K 16-bit words of core memory as the IMPs. The IMPs did not have disks, since moving parts were considered unreliable. The IMPs were interconnected by 56-kbps lines leased from telephone companies. Although 56 kbps is now the choice of teenagers who cannot afford ADSL or cable, it was then the best money could buy.

The software was split into two parts: subnet and host. The subnet software consisted of the IMP end of the host-IMP connection, the IMP-IMP protocol, and a source IMP to destination IMP protocol designed to improve reliability. The original ARPANET design is shown in Fig. 1-26.

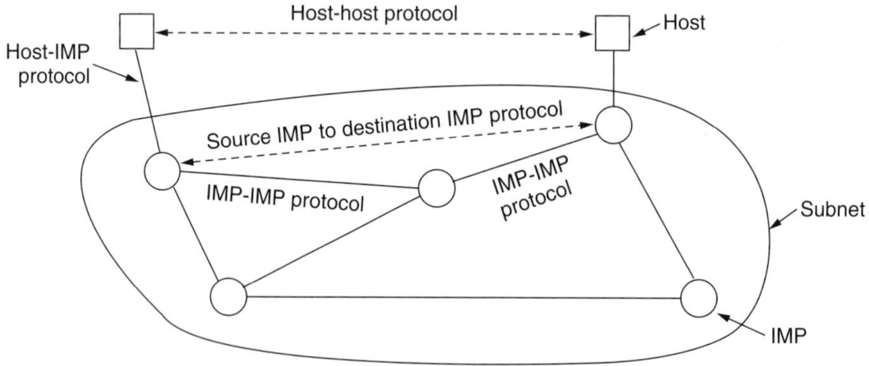

Figure 1-26. The original ARPANET design.

Outside the subnet, software was also needed, namely, the host end of the host-IMP connection, the host-host protocol, and the application software. It soon became clear that BBN felt that when it had accepted a message on a host-IMP wire and placed it on the host-IMP wire at the destination, its job was done.

Roberts had a problem: the hosts needed software too. To deal with it, he convened a meeting of network researchers, mostly graduate students, at Snowbird, Utah, in the summer of 1969. The graduate students expected some network expert to explain the grand design of the network and its software to them and then to assign each of them the job of writing part of it. They were astounded when there was no network expert and no grand design. They had to figure out what to do on their own.

Nevertheless, somehow an experimental network went on the air in December 1969 with four nodes: at UCLA, UCSB, SRI, and the University of Utah. These four were chosen because all had a large number of ARPA contracts, and all had different and completely incompatible host computers (just to make it more fun). The network grew quickly as more IMPs were delivered and installed; it soon spanned the United States. Figure 1-27 shows how rapidly the ARPANET grew in the first 3 years.

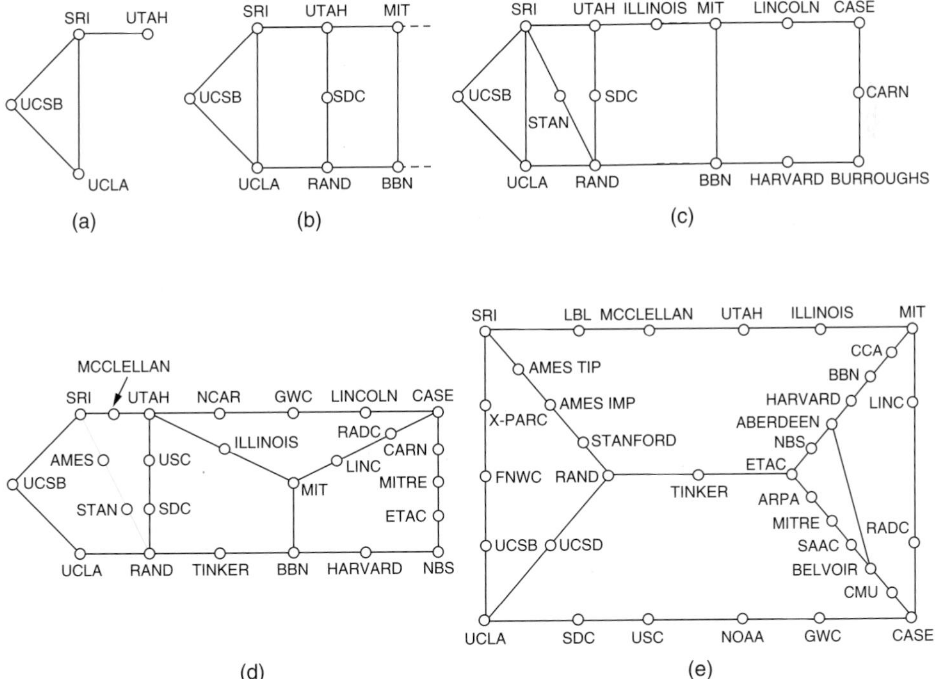

Figure 1-27. Growth of the ARPANET. (a) December 1969. (b) July 1970. (c) March 1971. (d) April 1972. (e) September 1972.

In addition to helping the fledgling ARPANET grow, ARPA also funded research on the use of satellite networks and mobile packet radio networks. In one now famous demonstration, a truck driving around in California used the packet radio network to send messages to SRI, which were then forwarded over the ARPANET to the East Coast, where they were shipped to University College in London over the satellite network. This allowed a researcher in the truck to use a computer in London while driving around in California.

This experiment also demonstrated that the existing ARPANET protocols were not suitable for running over multiple networks. This observation led to more research on protocols, culminating with the invention of the TCP/IP model and protocols (Cerf and Kahn, 1974). TCP/IP was specifically designed to handle communication over internetworks, something becoming increasingly important as more and more networks were being hooked up to the ARPANET.

To encourage adoption of these new protocols, ARPA awarded several contracts to BBN and the University of California at Berkeley to integrate them into Berkeley UNIX. Researchers at Berkeley developed a convenient program interface to the network (sockets) and wrote many application, utility, and management programs to make networking easier.

The timing was perfect. Many universities had just acquired a second or third VAX computer and a LAN to connect them, but they had no networking software. When 4.2BSD came along, with TCP/IP, sockets, and many network utilities, the complete package was adopted immediately. Furthermore, with TCP/IP, it was easy for the LANs to connect to the ARPANET, and many did.

During the 1980s, additional networks, especially LANs, were connected to the ARPANET. As the scale increased, finding hosts became increasingly expensive, so **DNS** (**Domain Name System**) was created to organize machines into domains and map host names onto IP addresses. Since then, DNS has become a generalized, distributed database system for storing a variety of information related to naming. We will study it in detail in Chap. 7.

NSFNET

By the late 1970s, NSF (the U.S. National Science Foundation) saw the enormous impact the ARPANET was having on university research, allowing scientists across the country to share data and collaborate on research projects. However, to get on the ARPANET, a university had to have a research contract with the DoD, which many did not have. NSF's response was to design a successor to the ARPANET that would be open to all university research groups. To have something concrete to start with, NSF decided to build a backbone network to connect its six supercomputer centers, in San Diego, Boulder, Champaign, Pittsburgh, Ithaca, and Princeton. Each supercomputer was given a little brother, consisting of an LSI-11 microcomputer called a **fuzzball**. The fuzzballs were connected with 56-kbps leased lines and formed the subnet, the same hardware technology as the ARPANET used. The software technology was different however: the fuzzballs spoke TCP/IP right from the start, making it the first TCP/IP WAN.

NSF also funded some (eventually about 20) regional networks that connected to the backbone to allow users at thousands of universities, research labs, libraries, and museums to access any of the supercomputers and to communicate with one another. The complete network, including the backbone and the regional networks, was called **NSFNET**. It connected to the ARPANET through a link between an IMP and a fuzzball in the Carnegie-Mellon machine room. The first NSFNET backbone is illustrated in Fig. 1-28.

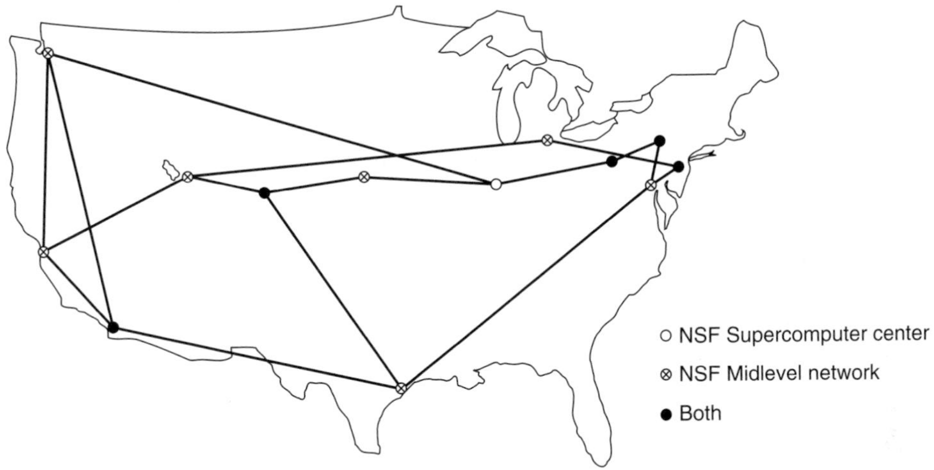

Figure 1-28. The NSFNET backbone in 1988.

NSFNET was an instantaneous success and was overloaded from the word go. NSF immediately began planning its successor and awarded a contract to the Michigan-based MERIT consortium to run it. Fiber optic channels at 448 kbps were leased from MCI (since merged with WorldCom) to provide the version 2 backbone. IBM PC-RTs were used as routers. This, too, was soon overwhelmed, and by 1990, the second backbone was upgraded to 1.5 Mbps.

As growth continued, NSF realized that the government could not continue financing networking forever. Furthermore, commercial organizations wanted to join but were forbidden by NSF's charter from using networks NSF paid for. Consequently, NSF encouraged MERIT, MCI, and IBM to form a nonprofit corporation, **ANS** (**Advanced Networks and Services**), as the first step along the road to commercialization. In 1990, ANS took over NSFNET and upgraded the 1.5-Mbps links to 45 Mbps to form **ANSNET**. This network operated for 5 years and was then sold to America Online. But by then, various companies were offering commercial IP service and it was clear the government should now get out of the networking business.

To ease the transition and make sure every regional network could communicate with every other regional network, NSF awarded contracts to four different network operators to establish a **NAP** (**Network Access Point**). These operators were PacBell (San Francisco), Ameritech (Chicago), MFS (Washington, D.C.), and Sprint (New York City, where for NAP purposes, Pennsauken, New Jersey counts as New York City). Every network operator that wanted to provide backbone service to the NSF regional networks had to connect to all the NAPs.

This arrangement meant that a packet originating on any regional network had a choice of backbone carriers to get from its NAP to the destination's NAP. Consequently, the backbone carriers were forced to compete for the regional networks' business on the basis of service and price, which was the idea, of course. As a result, the concept of a single default backbone was replaced by a commercially-driven competitive infrastructure. Many people like to criticize the Federal Government for not being innovative, but in the area of networking, it was DoD and NSF that created the infrastructure that formed the basis for the Internet and then handed it over to industry to operate.

During the 1990s, many other countries and regions also built national research networks, often patterned on the ARPANET and NSFNET. These included EuropaNET and EBONE in Europe, which started out with 2-Mbps lines and then upgraded to 34-Mbps lines. Eventually, the network infrastructure in Europe was handed over to industry as well.

Internet Usage

The number of networks, machines, and users connected to the ARPANET grew rapidly after TCP/IP became the only official protocol on January 1, 1983. When NSFNET and the ARPANET were interconnected, the growth became exponential. Many regional networks joined up, and connections were made to networks in Canada, Europe, and the Pacific.

Sometime in the mid-1980s, people began viewing the collection of networks as an internet, and later as the Internet, although there was no official dedication with some politician breaking a bottle of champagne over a fuzzball.

The glue that holds the Internet together is the TCP/IP reference model and TCP/IP protocol stack. TCP/IP makes universal service possible and can be compared to the adoption of standard gauge by the railroads in the 19th century or the adoption of common signaling protocols by all the telephone companies.

What does it actually mean to be on the Internet? Our definition is that a machine is on the Internet if it runs the TCP/IP protocol stack, has an IP address, and can send IP packets to all the other machines on the Internet. The mere ability to send and receive electronic mail is not enough, since e-mail is gatewayed to many networks outside the Internet. However, the issue is clouded somewhat by the fact that millions of personal computers can call up an Internet service provider using a modem, be assigned a temporary IP address, and send IP packets to other Internet hosts. It makes sense to regard such machines as being on the Internet for as long as they are connected to the service provider's router.

Traditionally (meaning 1970 to about 1990), the Internet and its predecessors had four main applications:

1. **E-mail**. The ability to compose, send, and receive electronic mail has been around since the early days of the ARPANET and is enormously popular. Many people get dozens of messages a day and consider it their primary way of interacting with the outside world, far outdistancing the telephone and snail mail. E-mail programs are available on virtually every kind of computer these days.

2. **News**. Newsgroups are specialized forums in which users with a common interest can exchange messages. Thousands of newsgroups exist, devoted to technical and nontechnical topics, including computers, science, recreation, and politics. Each newsgroup has its own etiquette, style, and customs, and woe betide anyone violating them.

3. **Remote login**. Using the telnet, rlogin, or ssh programs, users anywhere on the Internet can log on to any other machine on which they have an account.

4. **File transfer**. Using the FTP program, users can copy files from one machine on the Internet to another. Vast numbers of articles, databases, and other information are available this way.

Up until the early 1990s, the Internet was largely populated by academic, government, and industrial researchers. One new application, the **WWW** (**World Wide Web**) changed all that and brought millions of new, nonacademic users to the net. This application, invented by CERN physicist Tim Berners-Lee, did not change any of the underlying facilities but made them easier to use. Together with the Mosaic browser, written by Marc Andreessen at the National Center for Supercomputer Applications in Urbana, Illinois, the WWW made it possible for a site to set up a number of pages of information containing text, pictures, sound, and even video, with embedded links to other pages. By clicking on a link, the user is suddenly transported to the page pointed to by that link. For example, many companies have a home page with entries pointing to other pages for product information, price lists, sales, technical support, communication with employees, stockholder information, and more.

Numerous other kinds of pages have come into existence in a very short time, including maps, stock market tables, library card catalogs, recorded radio programs, and even a page pointing to the complete text of many books whose copyrights have expired (Mark Twain, Charles Dickens, etc.). Many people also have personal pages (home pages).

Much of this growth during the 1990s was fueled by companies called **ISPs** (**Internet Service Providers**). These are companies that offer individual users at home the ability to call up one of their machines and connect to the Internet, thus gaining access to e-mail, the WWW, and other Internet services. These companies signed up tens of millions of new users a year during the late 1990s, completely changing the character of the network from an academic and military playground to a public utility, much like the telephone system. The number of Internet users now is unknown, but is certainly hundreds of millions worldwide and will probably hit 1 billion fairly soon.

Architecture of the Internet

In this section we will attempt to give a brief overview of the Internet today. Due to the many mergers between telephone companies (telcos) and ISPs, the waters have become muddied and it is often hard to tell who is doing what. Consequently, this description will be of necessity somewhat simpler than reality. The big picture is shown in Fig. 1-29. Let us examine this figure piece by piece now.

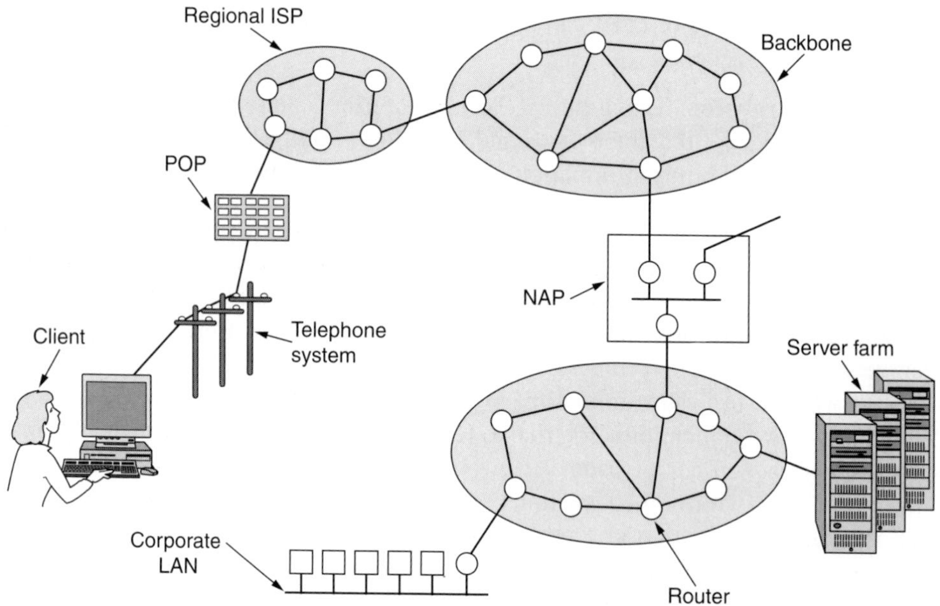

Figure 1-29. Overview of the Internet.

A good place to start is with a client at home. Let us assume our client calls his or her ISP over a dial-up telephone line, as shown in Fig. 1-29. The modem is a card within the PC that converts the digital signals the computer produces to analog signals that can pass unhindered over the telephone system. These signals are transferred to the ISP's **POP** (**Point of Presence**), where they are removed from the telephone system and injected into the ISP's regional network. From this point on, the system is fully digital and packet switched. If the ISP is the local telco, the POP will probably be located in the telephone switching office where the telephone wire from the client terminates. If the ISP is not the local telco, the POP may be a few switching offices down the road.

The ISP's regional network consists of interconnected routers in the various cities the ISP serves. If the packet is destined for a host served directly by the ISP, the packet is delivered to the host. Otherwise, it is handed over to the ISP's backbone operator.

At the top of the food chain are the major backbone operators, companies like AT&T and Sprint. They operate large international backbone networks, with thousands of routers connected by high-bandwidth fiber optics. Large corporations and hosting services that run server farms (machines that can serve thousands of Web pages per second) often connect directly to the backbone. Backbone operators encourage this direct connection by renting space in what are called **carrier hotels**, basically equipment racks in the same room as the router to allow short, fast connections between server farms and the backbone.

If a packet given to the backbone is destined for an ISP or company served by the backbone, it is sent to the closest router and handed off there. However, many backbones, of varying sizes, exist in the world, so a packet may have to go to a competing backbone. To allow packets to hop between backbones, all the major backbones connect at the NAPs discussed earlier. Basically, a NAP is a room full of routers, at least one per backbone. A LAN in the room connects all the routers, so packets can be forwarded from any backbone to any other backbone. In addition to being interconnected at NAPs, the larger backbones have numerous direct connections between their routers, a technique known as **private peering**. One of the many paradoxes of the Internet is that ISPs who publicly compete with one another for customers often privately cooperate to do private peering (Metz, 2001).

This ends our quick tour of the Internet. We will have a great deal to say about the individual components and their design, algorithms, and protocols in subsequent chapters. Also worth mentioning in passing is that some companies have interconnected all their existing internal networks, often using the same technology as the Internet. These **intranets** are typically accessible only within the company but otherwise work the same way as the Internet.

1.5.2 Connection-Oriented Networks: X.25, Frame Relay, and ATM

Since the beginning of networking, a war has been going on between the people who support connectionless (i.e., datagram) subnets and the people who support connection-oriented subnets. The main proponents of the connectionless subnets come from the ARPANET/Internet community. Remember that DoD's original desire in funding and building the ARPANET was to have a network that would continue functioning even after multiple direct hits by nuclear weapons wiped out numerous routers and transmission lines. Thus, fault tolerance was high on their priority list; billing customers was not. This approach led to a connectionless design in which every packet is routed independently of every other packet. As a consequence, if some routers go down during a session, no harm is done as long as the system can reconfigure itself dynamically so that subsequent packets can find some route to the destination, even if it is different from that which previous packets used.

The connection-oriented camp comes from the world of telephone companies. In the telephone system, a caller must dial the called party's number and wait for a connection before talking or sending data. This connection setup establishes a route through the telephone system that is maintained until the call is terminated. All words or packets follow the same route. If a line or switch on the path goes down, the call is aborted. This property is precisely what the DoD did not like about it.

Why do the telephone companies like it then? There are two reasons:

1. Quality of service.
2. Billing.

By setting up a connection in advance, the subnet can reserve resources such as buffer space and router CPU capacity. If an attempt is made to set up a call and insufficient resources are available, the call is rejected and the caller gets a kind of busy signal. In this way, once a connection has been set up, the connection will get good service. With a connectionless network, if too many packets arrive at the same router at the same moment, the router will choke and probably lose packets. The sender will eventually notice this and resend them, but the quality of service will be jerky and unsuitable for audio or video unless the network is very lightly loaded. Needless to say, providing adequate audio quality is something telephone companies care about very much, hence their preference for connections.

The second reason the telephone companies like connection-oriented service is that they are accustomed to charging for connect time. When you make a long distance call (or even a local call outside North America) you are charged by the minute. When networks came around, they just automatically gravitated toward a model in which charging by the minute was easy to do. If you have to set up a connection before sending data, that is when the billing clock starts running. If there is no connection, they cannot charge for it.

Ironically, maintaining billing records is very expensive. If a telephone company were to adopt a flat monthly rate with unlimited calling and no billing or record keeping, it would probably save a huge amount of money, despite the increased calling this policy would generate. Political, regulatory, and other factors weigh against doing this, however. Interestingly enough, flat rate service exists in other sectors. For example, cable TV is billed at a flat rate per month, no matter how many programs you watch. It could have been designed with pay-per-view as the basic concept, but it was not, due in part to the expense of billing (and given the quality of most television, the embarrassment factor cannot be totally discounted either). Also, many theme parks charge a daily admission fee for unlimited rides, in contrast to traveling carnivals, which charge by the ride.

That said, it should come as no surprise that all networks designed by the telephone industry have had connection-oriented subnets. What is perhaps surprising, is that the Internet is also drifting in that direction, in order to provide a better quality of service for audio and video, a subject we will return to in Chap. 5. But now let us examine some connection-oriented networks.

X.25 and Frame Relay

Our first example of a connection-oriented network is **X.25**, which was the first public data network. It was deployed in the 1970s at a time when telephone service was a monopoly everywhere and the telephone company in each country expected there to be one data network per country—theirs. To use X.25, a computer first established a connection to the remote computer, that is, placed a telephone call. This connection was given a connection number to be used in data transfer packets (because multiple connections could be open at the same time). Data packets were very simple, consisting of a 3-byte header and up to 128 bytes of data. The header consisted of a 12-bit connection number, a packet sequence number, an acknowledgement number, and a few miscellaneous bits. X.25 networks operated for about a decade with mixed success.

In the 1980s, the X.25 networks were largely replaced by a new kind of network called **frame relay**. The essence of frame relay is that it is a connection-oriented network with no error control and no flow control. Because it was connection-oriented, packets were delivered in order (if they were delivered at all). The properties of in-order delivery, no error control, and no flow control make frame relay akin to a wide area LAN. Its most important application is interconnecting LANs at multiple company offices. Frame relay enjoyed a modest success and is still in use in places today.

Asynchronous Transfer Mode

Yet another, and far more important, connection-oriented network is **ATM** (**Asynchronous Transfer Mode**). The reason for the somewhat strange name is that in the telephone system, most transmission is synchronous (closely tied to a clock), and ATM is not.

ATM was designed in the early 1990s and launched amid truly incredible hype (Ginsburg, 1996; Goralski, 1995; Ibe, 1997; Kim et al., 1994; and Stallings, 2000). ATM was going to solve all the world's networking and telecommunications problems by merging voice, data, cable television, telex, telegraph, carrier pigeon, tin cans connected by strings, tom-toms, smoke signals, and everything else into a single integrated system that could do everything for everyone. It did not happen. In large part, the problems were similar to those we described earlier concerning OSI, that is, bad timing, technology, implementation, and politics. Having just beaten back the telephone companies in round 1, many in the Internet community saw ATM as Internet versus the Telcos: the Sequel. But it really was not, and this time around even diehard datagram fanatics were aware that the Internet's quality of service left a lot to be desired. To make a long story short, ATM was much more successful than OSI, and it is now widely used deep within the telephone system, often for moving IP packets. Because it is now mostly used by carriers for internal transport, users are often unaware of its existence, but it is definitely alive and well.

ATM Virtual Circuits

Since ATM networks are connection-oriented, sending data requires first sending a packet to set up the connection. As the setup packet wends its way through the subnet, all the routers on the path make an entry in their internal tables noting the existence of the connection and reserving whatever resources are needed for it. Connections are often called **virtual circuits**, in analogy with the physical circuits used within the telephone system. Most ATM networks also support **permanent virtual circuits**, which are permanent connections between two (distant) hosts. They are similar to leased lines in the telephone world. Each connection, temporary or permanent, has a unique connection identifier. A virtual circuit is illustrated in Fig. 1-30.

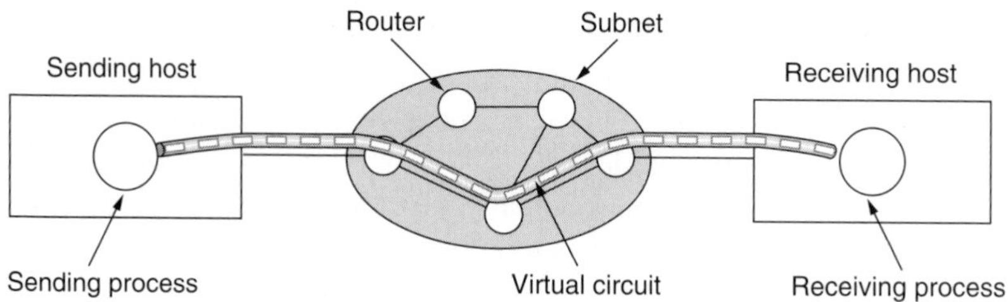

Figure 1-30. A virtual circuit.

Once a connection has been established, either side can begin transmitting data. The basic idea behind ATM is to transmit all information in small, fixed-size packets called **cells**. The cells are 53 bytes long, of which 5 bytes are header and 48 bytes are payload, as shown in Fig. 1-31. Part of the header is the connection identifier, so the sending and receiving hosts and all the intermediate routers can tell which cells belong to which connections. This information allows each router to know how to route each incoming cell. Cell routing is done in hardware, at high speed. In fact, the main argument for having fixed-size cells is that it is easy to build hardware routers to handle short, fixed-length cells. Variable-length

IP packets have to be routed by software, which is a slower process. Another plus of ATM is that the hardware can be set up to copy one incoming cell to multiple output lines, a property that is required for handling a television program that is being broadcast to many receivers. Finally, small cells do not block any line for very long, which makes guaranteeing quality of service easier.

All cells follow the same route to the destination. Cell delivery is not guaranteed, but their order is. If cells 1 and 2 are sent in that order, then if both arrive, they will arrive in that order, never first 2 then 1. But either or both of them can be lost along the way. It is up to higher protocol levels to recover from lost cells. Note that although this guarantee is not perfect, it is better than what the Internet provides. There packets can not only be lost, but delivered out of order as well. ATM, in contrast, guarantees never to deliver cells out of order.

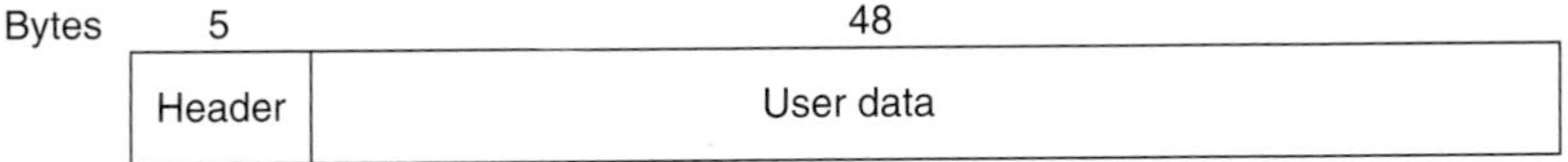

Figure 1-31. An ATM cell.

ATM networks are organized like traditional WANs, with lines and switches (routers). The most common speeds for ATM networks are 155 Mbps and 622 Mbps, although higher speeds are also supported. The 155-Mbps speed was chosen because this is about what is needed to transmit high definition television. The exact choice of 155.52 Mbps was made for compatibility with AT&T's SONET transmission system, something we will study in Chap. 2. The 622 Mbps speed was chosen so that four 155-Mbps channels could be sent over it.

The ATM Reference Model

ATM has its own reference model, different from the OSI model and also different from the TCP/IP model. This model is shown in Fig. 1-32. It consists of three layers, the physical, ATM, and ATM adaptation layers, plus whatever users want to put on top of that.

The physical layer deals with the physical medium: voltages, bit timing, and various other issues. ATM does not prescribe a particular set of rules but instead says that ATM cells can be sent on a wire or fiber by themselves, but they can also be packaged inside the payload of other carrier systems. In other words, ATM has been designed to be independent of the transmission medium.

The **ATM layer** deals with cells and cell transport. It defines the layout of a cell and tells what the header fields mean. It also deals with establishment and release of virtual circuits. Congestion control is also located here.

Because most applications do not want to work directly with cells (although some may), a layer above the ATM layer has been defined to allow users to send

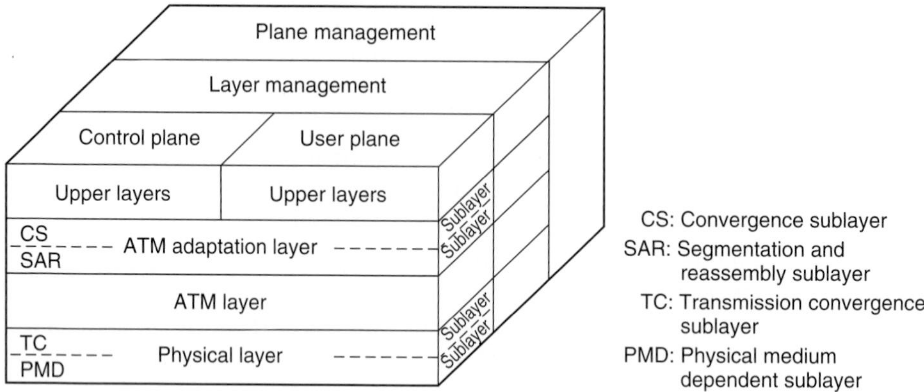

Figure 1-32. The ATM reference model.

packets larger than a cell. The ATM interface segments these packets, transmits the cells individually, and reassembles them at the other end. This layer is the **AAL** (**ATM Adaptation Layer**).

Unlike the earlier two-dimensional reference models, the ATM model is defined as being three-dimensional, as shown in Fig. 1-32. The **user plane** deals with data transport, flow control, error correction, and other user functions. In contrast, the **control plane** is concerned with connection management. The layer and plane management functions relate to resource management and interlayer coordination.

The physical and AAL layers are each divided into two sublayers, one at the bottom that does the work and a convergence sublayer on top that provides the proper interface to the layer above it. The functions of the layers and sublayers are given in Fig. 1-33.

The **PMD** (**Physical Medium Dependent**) sublayer interfaces to the actual cable. It moves the bits on and off and handles the bit timing. For different carriers and cables, this layer will be different.

The other sublayer of the physical layer is the **TC** (**Transmission Convergence**) sublayer. When cells are transmitted, the TC layer sends them as a string of bits to the PMD layer. Doing this is easy. At the other end, the TC sublayer gets a pure incoming bit stream from the PMD sublayer. Its job is to convert this bit stream into a cell stream for the ATM layer. It handles all the issues related to telling where cells begin and end in the bit stream. In the ATM model, this functionality is in the physical layer. In the OSI model and in pretty much all other networks, the job of framing, that is, turning a raw bit stream into a sequence of frames or cells, is the data link layer's task.

As we mentioned earlier, the ATM layer manages cells, including their generation and transport. Most of the interesting aspects of ATM are located here. It is a mixture of the OSI data link and network layers; it is not split into sublayers.

OSI layer	ATM layer	ATM sublayer	Functionality
3/4	AAL	CS	Providing the standard interface (convergence)
		SAR	Segmentation and reassembly
2/3	ATM		Flow control Cell header generation/extraction Virtual circuit/path management Cell multiplexing/demultiplexing
2	Physical	TC	Cell rate decoupling Header checksum generation and verification Cell generation Packing/unpacking cells from the enclosing envelope Frame generation
1		PMD	Bit timing Physical network access

Figure 1-33. The ATM layers and sublayers, and their functions.

The AAL layer is split into a **SAR** (**Segmentation And Reassembly**) sublayer and a **CS** (**Convergence Sublayer**). The lower sublayer breaks up packets into cells on the transmission side and puts them back together again at the destination. The upper sublayer makes it possible to have ATM systems offer different kinds of services to different applications (e.g., file transfer and video on demand have different requirements concerning error handling, timing, etc.).

As it is probably mostly downhill for ATM from now on, we will not discuss it further in this book. Nevertheless, since it has a substantial installed base, it will probably be around for at least a few more years. For more information about ATM, see (Dobrowski and Grise, 2001; and Gadecki and Heckart, 1997).

1.5.3 Ethernet

Both the Internet and ATM were designed for wide area networking. However, many companies, universities, and other organizations have large numbers of computers that must be connected. This need gave rise to the local area network. In this section we will say a little bit about the most popular LAN, Ethernet.

The story starts out in pristine Hawaii in the early 1970s. In this case, "pristine" can be interpreted as "not having a working telephone system." While not being interrupted by the phone all day long makes life more pleasant for vacationers, it did not make life more pleasant for researcher Norman Abramson and his colleagues at the University of Hawaii who were trying to connect users on remote islands to the main computer in Honolulu. Stringing their own cables under the Pacific Ocean was not in the cards, so they looked for a different solution.

The one they found was short-range radios. Each user terminal was equipped with a small radio having two frequencies: upstream (to the central computer) and downstream (from the central computer). When the user wanted to contact the computer, it just transmitted a packet containing the data in the upstream channel. If no one else was transmitting at that instant, the packet probably got through and was acknowledged on the downstream channel. If there was contention for the upstream channel, the terminal noticed the lack of acknowledgement and tried again. Since there was only one sender on the downstream channel (the central computer), there were never collisions there. This system, called ALOHANET, worked fairly well under conditions of low traffic but bogged down badly when the upstream traffic was heavy.

About the same time, a student named Bob Metcalfe got his bachelor's degree at M.I.T. and then moved up the river to get his Ph.D. at Harvard. During his studies, he was exposed to Abramson's work. He became so interested in it that after graduating from Harvard, he decided to spend the summer in Hawaii working with Abramson before starting work at Xerox PARC (Palo Alto Research Center). When he got to PARC, he saw that the researchers there had designed and built what would later be called personal computers. But the machines were isolated. Using his knowledge of Abramson's work, he, together with his colleague David Boggs, designed and implemented the first local area network (Metcalfe and Boggs, 1976).

They called the system **Ethernet** after the *luminiferous ether*, through which electromagnetic radiation was once thought to propagate. (When the 19th century British physicist James Clerk Maxwell discovered that electromagnetic radiation could be described by a wave equation, scientists assumed that space must be filled with some ethereal medium in which the radiation was propagating. Only after the famous Michelson-Morley experiment in 1887 did physicists discover that electromagnetic radiation could propagate in a vacuum.)

The transmission medium here was not a vacuum, but a thick coaxial cable (the ether) up to 2.5 km long (with repeaters every 500 meters). Up to 256 machines could be attached to the system via transceivers screwed onto the cable. A cable with multiple machines attached to it in parallel is called a **multidrop cable**. The system ran at 2.94 Mbps. A sketch of its architecture is given in Fig. 1-34. Ethernet had a major improvement over ALOHANET: before transmitting, a computer first listened to the cable to see if someone else was already transmitting. If so, the computer held back until the current transmission finished. Doing so avoided interfering with existing transmissions, giving a much higher efficiency. ALOHANET did not work like this because it was impossible for a terminal on one island to sense the transmission of a terminal on a distant island. With a single cable, this problem does not exist.

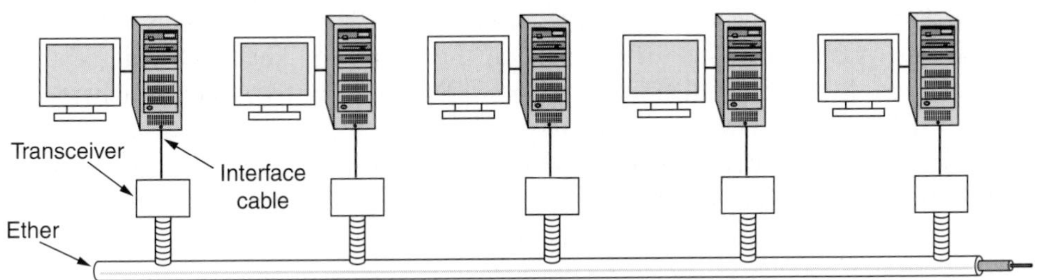

Figure 1-34. Architecture of the original Ethernet.

Despite the computer listening before transmitting, a problem still arises: what happens if two or more computers all wait until the current transmission completes and then all start at once? The solution is to have each computer listen during its own transmission and if it detects interference, jam the ether to alert all senders. Then back off and wait a random time before retrying. If a second collision happens, the random waiting time is doubled, and so on, to spread out the competing transmissions and give one of them a chance to go first.

The Xerox Ethernet was so successful that DEC, Intel, and Xerox drew up a standard in 1978 for a 10-Mbps Ethernet, called the **DIX standard**. With two minor changes, the DIX standard became the IEEE 802.3 standard in 1983.

Unfortunately for Xerox, it already had a history of making seminal inventions (such as the personal computer) and then failing to commercialize on them, a story told in *Fumbling the Future* (Smith and Alexander, 1988). When Xerox showed little interest in doing anything with Ethernet other than helping standardize it, Metcalfe formed his own company, 3Com, to sell Ethernet adapters for PCs. It has sold over 100 million of them.

Ethernet continued to develop and is still developing. New versions at 100 Mbps, 1000 Mbps, and still higher have come out. Also the cabling has improved, and switching and other features have been added. We will discuss Ethernet in detail in Chap. 4.

In passing, it is worth mentioning that Ethernet (IEEE 802.3) is not the only LAN standard. The committee also standardized a token bus (802.4) and a token ring (802.5). The need for three more-or-less incompatible standards has little to do with technology and everything to do with politics. At the time of standardization, General Motors was pushing a LAN in which the topology was the same as Ethernet (a linear cable) but computers took turns in transmitting by passing a short packet called a **token** from computer to computer. A computer could only send if it possessed the token, thus avoiding collisions. General Motors announced that this scheme was essential for manufacturing cars and was not prepared to budge from this position. This announcement notwithstanding, 802.4 has basically vanished from sight.

Similarly, IBM had its own favorite: its proprietary token ring. The token was passed around the ring and whichever computer held the token was allowed to transmit before putting the token back on the ring. Unlike 802.4, this scheme, standardized as 802.5, is still in use at some IBM sites, but virtually nowhere outside of IBM sites. However, work is progressing on a gigabit version (802.5v), but it seems unlikely that it will ever catch up with Ethernet. In short, there was a war between Ethernet, token bus, and token ring, and Ethernet won, mostly because it was there first and the challengers were not as good.

1.5.4 Wireless LANs: 802.11

Almost as soon as notebook computers appeared, many people had a dream of walking into an office and magically having their notebook computer be connected to the Internet. Consequently, various groups began working on ways to accomplish this goal. The most practical approach is to equip both the office and the notebook computers with short-range radio transmitters and receivers to allow them to communicate. This work rapidly led to wireless LANs being marketed by a variety of companies.

The trouble was that no two of them were compatible. This proliferation of standards meant that a computer equipped with a brand *X* radio would not work in a room equipped with a brand *Y* base station. Finally, the industry decided that a wireless LAN standard might be a good idea, so the IEEE committee that standardized the wired LANs was given the task of drawing up a wireless LAN standard. The standard it came up with was named 802.11. A common slang name for it is **WiFi**. It is an important standard and deserves respect, so we will call it by its proper name, 802.11.

The proposed standard had to work in two modes:

1. In the presence of a base station.
2. In the absence of a base station.

In the former case, all communication was to go through the base station, called an **access point** in 802.11 terminology. In the latter case, the computers would just send to one another directly. This mode is now sometimes called **ad hoc networking**. A typical example is two or more people sitting down together in a room not equipped with a wireless LAN and having their computers just communicate directly. The two modes are illustrated in Fig. 1-35.

The first decision was the easiest: what to call it. All the other LAN standards had numbers like 802.1, 802.2, 802.3, up to 802.10, so the wireless LAN standard was dubbed 802.11. The rest was harder.

In particular, some of the many challenges that had to be met were: finding a suitable frequency band that was available, preferably worldwide; dealing with the fact that radio signals have a finite range; ensuring that users' privacy was

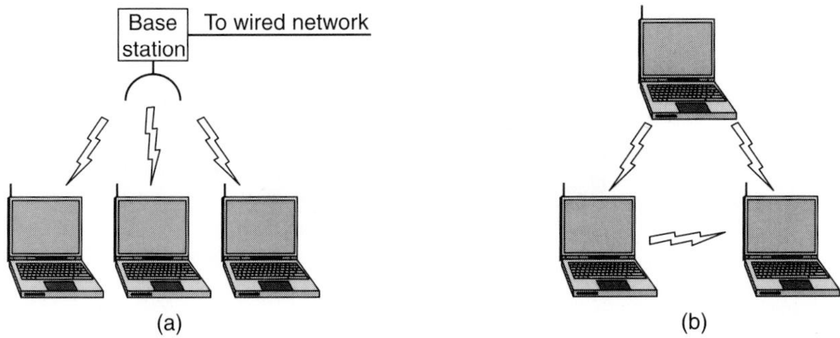

Figure 1-35. (a) Wireless networking with a base station. (b) Ad hoc networking.

maintained; taking limited battery life into account; worrying about human safety (do radio waves cause cancer?); understanding the implications of computer mobility; and finally, building a system with enough bandwidth to be economically viable.

At the time the standardization process started (mid-1990s), Ethernet had already come to dominate local area networking, so the committee decided to make 802.11 compatible with Ethernet above the data link layer. In particular, it should be possible to send an IP packet over the wireless LAN the same way a wired computer sent an IP packet over Ethernet. Nevertheless, in the physical and data link layers, several inherent differences with Ethernet exist and had to be dealt with by the standard.

First, a computer on Ethernet always listens to the ether before transmitting. Only if the ether is idle does the computer begin transmitting. With wireless LANs, that idea does not work so well. To see why, examine Fig. 1-36. Suppose that computer *A* is transmitting to computer *B*, but the radio range of *A*'s transmitter is too short to reach computer *C*. If *C* wants to transmit to *B* it can listen to the ether before starting, but the fact that it does not hear anything does not mean that its transmission will succeed. The 802.11 standard had to solve this problem.

The second problem that had to be solved is that a radio signal can be reflected off solid objects, so it may be received multiple times (along multiple paths). This interference results in what is called **multipath fading**.

The third problem is that a great deal of software is not aware of mobility. For example, many word processors have a list of printers that users can choose from to print a file. When the computer on which the word processor runs is taken into a new environment, the built-in list of printers becomes invalid.

The fourth problem is that if a notebook computer is moved away from the ceiling-mounted base station it is using and into the range of a different base station, some way of handing it off is needed. Although this problem occurs with cellular telephones, it does not occur with Ethernet and needed to be solved. In

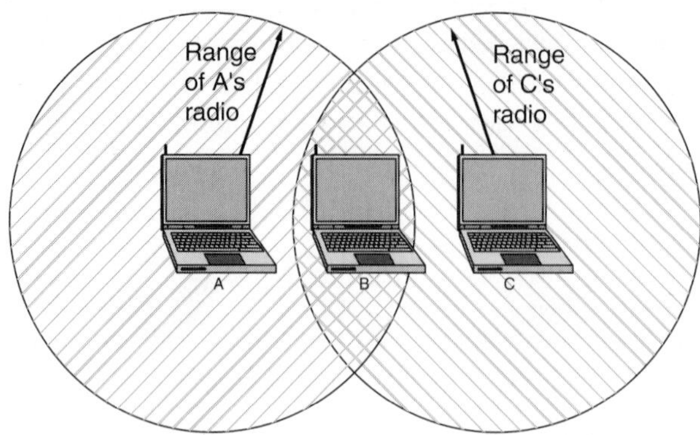

Figure 1-36. The range of a single radio may not cover the entire system.

particular, the network envisioned consists of multiple cells, each with its own base station, but with the base stations connected by Ethernet, as shown in Fig. 1-37. From the outside, the entire system should look like a single Ethernet. The connection between the 802.11 system and the outside world is called a **portal**.

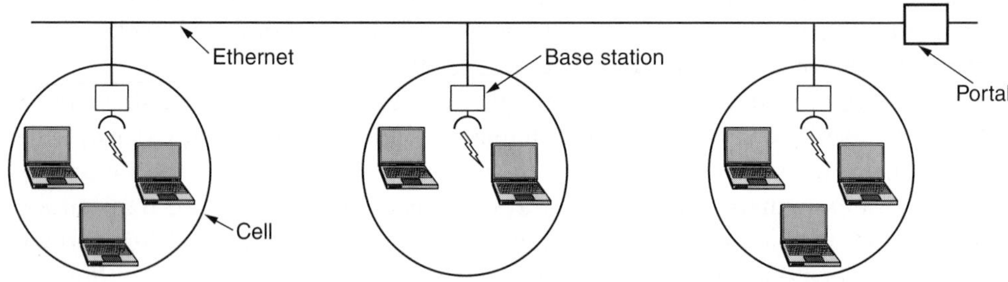

Figure 1-37. A multicell 802.11 network.

After some work, the committee came up with a standard in 1997 that addressed these and other concerns. The wireless LAN it described ran at either 1 Mbps or 2 Mbps. Almost immediately, people complained that it was too slow, so work began on faster standards. A split developed within the committee, resulting in two new standards in 1999. The 802.11a standard uses a wider frequency band and runs at speeds up to 54 Mbps. The 802.11b standard uses the same frequency band as 802.11, but uses a different modulation technique to achieve 11 Mbps. Some people see this as psychologically important since 11 Mbps is faster than the original wired Ethernet. It is likely that the original 1-Mbps 802.11 will die off quickly, but it is not yet clear which of the new standards will win out.

To make matters even more complicated than they already were, the 802 committee has come up with yet another variant, 802.11g, which uses the modulation technique of 802.11a but the frequency band of 802.11b. We will come back to 802.11 in detail in Chap. 4.

That 802.11 is going to cause a revolution in computing and Internet access is now beyond any doubt. Airports, train stations, hotels, shopping malls, and universities are rapidly installing it. Even upscale coffee shops are installing 802.11 so that the assembled yuppies can surf the Web while drinking their lattes. It is likely that 802.11 will do to the Internet what notebook computers did to computing: make it mobile.

1.6 NETWORK STANDARDIZATION

Many network vendors and suppliers exist, each with its own ideas of how things should be done. Without coordination, there would be complete chaos, and users would get nothing done. The only way out is to agree on some network standards.

Not only do standards allow different computers to communicate, but they also increase the market for products adhering to the standard. A larger market leads to mass production, economies of scale in manufacturing, VLSI implementations, and other benefits that decrease price and further increase acceptance. In the following sections we will take a quick look at the important, but little-known, world of international standardization.

Standards fall into two categories: de facto and de jure. **De facto** (Latin for "from the fact") standards are those that have just happened, without any formal plan. The IBM PC and its successors are de facto standards for small-office and home computers because dozens of manufacturers chose to copy IBM's machines very closely. Similarly, UNIX is the de facto standard for operating systems in university computer science departments.

De jure (Latin for "by law") standards, in contrast, are formal, legal standards adopted by some authorized standardization body. International standardization authorities are generally divided into two classes: those established by treaty among national governments, and those comprising voluntary, nontreaty organizations. In the area of computer network standards, there are several organizations of each type, which are discussed below.

1.6.1 Who's Who in the Telecommunications World

The legal status of the world's telephone companies varies considerably from country to country. At one extreme is the United States, which has 1500 separate, privately owned telephone companies. Before it was broken up in 1984, AT&T, at that time the world's largest corporation, completely dominated the scene. It provided telephone service to about 80 percent of America's telephones, spread throughout half of its geographical area, with all the other companies combined servicing the remaining (mostly rural) customers. Since the breakup, AT&T continues to provide long-distance service, although now in competition with other companies. The seven Regional Bell Operating Companies that were split off from AT&T and numerous independents provide local and cellular telephone service. Due to frequent mergers and other changes, the industry is in a constant state of flux.

Companies in the United States that provide communication services to the public are called **common carriers**. Their offerings and prices are described by a document called a **tariff**, which must be approved by the Federal Communications Commission for the interstate and international traffic and by the state public utilities commissions for intrastate traffic.

At the other extreme are countries in which the national government has a complete monopoly on all communication, including the mail, telegraph, telephone, and often, radio and television. Most of the world falls in this category. In some cases the telecommunication authority is a nationalized company, and in others it is simply a branch of the government, usually known as the **PTT** (**Post, Telegraph & Telephone** administration). Worldwide, the trend is toward liberalization and competition and away from government monopoly. Most European countries have now (partially) privatized their PTTs, but elsewhere the process is still slowly gaining steam.

With all these different suppliers of services, there is clearly a need to provide compatibility on a worldwide scale to ensure that people (and computers) in one country can call their counterparts in another one. Actually, this need has existed for a long time. In 1865, representatives from many European governments met to form the predecessor to today's **ITU** (**International Telecommunication Union**). Its job was standardizing international telecommunications, which in those days meant telegraphy. Even then it was clear that if half the countries used Morse code and the other half used some other code, there was going to be a problem. When the telephone was put into international service, ITU took over the job of standardizing telephony (pronounced te-LEF-ony) as well. In 1947, ITU became an agency of the United Nations.

ITU has three main sectors:

1. Radiocommunications Sector (ITU-R).

2. Telecommunications Standardization Sector (ITU-T).

3. Development Sector (ITU-D).

ITU-R is concerned with allocating radio frequencies worldwide to the competing interest groups. We will focus primarily on ITU-T, which is concerned with telephone and data communication systems. From 1956 to 1993, ITU-T was known as **CCITT**, an acronym for its French name: Comité Consultatif International Télégraphique et Téléphonique. On March 1, 1993, CCITT was reorganized to make it less bureaucratic and renamed to reflect its new role. Both ITU-T and

CCITT issued recommendations in the area of telephone and data communications. One still frequently runs into CCITT recommendations, such as CCITT X.25, although since 1993 recommendations bear the ITU-T label.

ITU-T has four classes of members:

1. National governments.
2. Sector members.
3. Associate members.
4. Regulatory agencies.

ITU-T has about 200 governmental members, including almost every member of the United Nations. Since the United States does not have a PTT, somebody else had to represent it in ITU-T. This task fell to the State Department, probably on the grounds that ITU-T had to do with foreign countries, the State Department's specialty. There are approximately 500 sector members, including telephone companies (e.g., AT&T, Vodafone, WorldCom), telecom equipment manufacturers (e.g., Cisco, Nokia, Nortel), computer vendors (e.g., Compaq, Sun, Toshiba), chip manufacturers (e.g., Intel, Motorola, TI), media companies (e.g., AOL Time Warner, CBS, Sony), and other interested companies (e.g., Boeing, Samsung, Xerox). Various nonprofit scientific organizations and industry consortia are also sector members (e.g., IFIP and IATA). Associate members are smaller organizations that are interested in a particular Study Group. Regulatory agencies are the folks who watch over the telecom business, such as the U.S. Federal Communications Commission.

ITU-T's task is to make technical recommendations about telephone, telegraph, and data communication interfaces. These often become internationally recognized standards, for example, V.24 (also known as EIA RS-232 in the United States), which specifies the placement and meaning of the various pins on the connector used by most asynchronous terminals and external modems.

It should be noted that ITU-T recommendations are technically only suggestions that governments can adopt or ignore, as they wish (because governments are like 13-year-old boys—they do not take kindly to being given orders). In practice, a country that wishes to adopt a telephone standard different from that used by the rest of the world is free to do so, but at the price of cutting itself off from everyone else. This might work for North Korea, but elsewhere it would be a real problem. The fiction of calling ITU-T standards "recommendations" was and is necessary to keep nationalist forces in many countries placated.

The real work of ITU-T is done in its 14 Study Groups, often as large as 400 people. There are currently 14 Study Groups, covering topics ranging from telephone billing to multimedia services. In order to make it possible to get anything at all done, the Study Groups are divided into Working Parties, which are in turn divided into Expert Teams, which are in turn divided into ad hoc groups. Once a bureaucracy, always a bureaucracy.

Despite all this, ITU-T actually gets things done. Since its inception, it has produced close to 3000 recommendations occupying about 60,000 pages of paper. Many of these are widely used in practice. For example, the popular V.90 56-kbps modem standard is an ITU recommendation.

As telecommunications completes the transition started in the 1980s from being entirely national to being entirely global, standards will become increasingly important, and more and more organizations will want to become involved in setting them. For more information about ITU, see (Irmer, 1994).

1.6.2 Who's Who in the International Standards World

International standards are produced and published by **ISO** (**International Standards Organization**†), a voluntary nontreaty organization founded in 1946. Its members are the national standards organizations of the 89 member countries. These members include ANSI (U.S.), BSI (Great Britain), AFNOR (France), DIN (Germany), and 85 others.

ISO issues standards on a truly vast number of subjects, ranging from nuts and bolts (literally) to telephone pole coatings [not to mention cocoa beans (ISO 2451), fishing nets (ISO 1530), women's underwear (ISO 4416) and quite a few other subjects one might not think were subject to standardization]. Over 13,000 standards have been issued, including the OSI standards. ISO has almost 200 Technical Committees, numbered in the order of their creation, each dealing with a specific subject. TC1 deals with the nuts and bolts (standardizing screw thread pitches). TC97 deals with computers and information processing. Each TC has subcommittees (SCs) divided into working groups (WGs).

The real work is done largely in the WGs by over 100,000 volunteers worldwide. Many of these "volunteers" are assigned to work on ISO matters by their employers, whose products are being standardized. Others are government officials keen on having their country's way of doing things become the international standard. Academic experts also are active in many of the WGs.

On issues of telecommunication standards, ISO and ITU-T often cooperate (ISO is a member of ITU-T) to avoid the irony of two official and mutually incompatible international standards.

The U.S. representative in ISO is **ANSI** (**American National Standards Institute**), which despite its name, is a private, nongovernmental, nonprofit organization. Its members are manufacturers, common carriers, and other interested parties. ANSI standards are frequently adopted by ISO as international standards.

The procedure used by ISO for adopting standards has been designed to achieve as broad a consensus as possible. The process begins when one of the

† For the purist, ISO's true name is the International Organization for Standardization.

national standards organizations feels the need for an international standard in some area. A working group is then formed to come up with a **CD** (**Committee Draft**). The CD is then circulated to all the member bodies, which get 6 months to criticize it. If a substantial majority approves, a revised document, called a **DIS** (**Draft International Standard**) is produced and circulated for comments and voting. Based on the results of this round, the final text of the **IS** (**International Standard**) is prepared, approved, and published. In areas of great controversy, a CD or DIS may have to go through several versions before acquiring enough votes, and the whole process can take years.

NIST (**National Institute of Standards and Technology**) is part of the U.S. Department of Commerce. It used to be the National Bureau of Standards. It issues standards that are mandatory for purchases made by the U.S. Government, except for those of the Department of Defense, which has its own standards.

Another major player in the standards world is **IEEE** (**Institute of Electrical and Electronics Engineers**), the largest professional organization in the world. In addition to publishing scores of journals and running hundreds of conferences each year, IEEE has a standardization group that develops standards in the area of electrical engineering and computing. IEEE's 802 committee has standardized many kinds of LANs. We will study some of its output later in this book. The actual work is done by a collection of working groups, which are listed in Fig. 1-38. The success rate of the various 802 working groups has been low; having an 802.x number is no guarantee of success. But the impact of the success stories (especially 802.3 and 802.11) has been enormous.

1.6.3 Who's Who in the Internet Standards World

The worldwide Internet has its own standardization mechanisms, very different from those of ITU-T and ISO. The difference can be crudely summed up by saying that the people who come to ITU or ISO standardization meetings wear suits. The people who come to Internet standardization meetings wear jeans (except when they meet in San Diego, when they wear shorts and T-shirts).

ITU-T and ISO meetings are populated by corporate officials and government civil servants for whom standardization is their job. They regard standardization as a Good Thing and devote their lives to it. Internet people, on the other hand, prefer anarchy as a matter of principle. However, with hundreds of millions of people all doing their own thing, little communication can occur. Thus, standards, however regrettable, are sometimes needed.

When the ARPANET was set up, DoD created an informal committee to oversee it. In 1983, the committee was renamed the **IAB** (**Internet Activities Board**) and was given a slighter broader mission, namely, to keep the researchers involved with the ARPANET and the Internet pointed more-or-less in the same direction, an activity not unlike herding cats. The meaning of the acronym "IAB" was later changed to **Internet Architecture Board**.

Number	Topic
802.1	Overview and architecture of LANs
802.2 ↓	Logical link control
802.3 *	Ethernet
802.4 ↓	Token bus (was briefly used in manufacturing plants)
802.5	Token ring (IBM's entry into the LAN world)
802.6 ↓	Dual queue dual bus (early metropolitan area network)
802.7 ↓	Technical advisory group on broadband technologies
802.8 †	Technical advisory group on fiber optic technologies
802.9 ↓	Isochronous LANs (for real-time applications)
802.10 ↓	Virtual LANs and security
802.11 *	Wireless LANs
802.12 ↓	Demand priority (Hewlett-Packard's AnyLAN)
802.13	Unlucky number. Nobody wanted it
802.14 ↓	Cable modems (defunct: an industry consortium got there first)
802.15 *	Personal area networks (Bluetooth)
802.16 *	Broadband wireless
802.17	Resilient packet ring

Figure 1-38. The 802 working groups. The important ones are marked with *. The ones marked with ↓ are hibernating. The one marked with † gave up and disbanded itself.

Each of the approximately ten members of the IAB headed a task force on some issue of importance. The IAB met several times a year to discuss results and to give feedback to the DoD and NSF, which were providing most of the funding at this time. When a standard was needed (e.g., a new routing algorithm), the IAB members would thrash it out and then announce the change so the graduate students who were the heart of the software effort could implement it. Communication was done by a series of technical reports called **RFCs** (**Request For Comments**). RFCs are stored on-line and can be fetched by anyone interested in them from *www.ietf.org/rfc*. They are numbered in chronological order of creation. Over 3000 now exist. We will refer to many RFCs in this book.

By 1989, the Internet had grown so large that this highly informal style no longer worked. Many vendors by then offered TCP/IP products and did not want to change them just because ten researchers had thought of a better idea. In the summer of 1989, the IAB was reorganized again. The researchers were moved to the **IRTF** (**Internet Research Task Force**), which was made subsidiary to IAB, along with the **IETF** (**Internet Engineering Task Force**). The IAB was repopulated with people representing a broader range of organizations than just the research community. It was initially a self-perpetuating group, with members serving for a 2-year term and new members being appointed by the old ones. Later, the **Internet Society** was created, populated by people interested in the Internet. The Internet Society is thus in a sense comparable to ACM or IEEE. It is governed by elected trustees who appoint the IAB members.

The idea of this split was to have the IRTF concentrate on long-term research while the IETF dealt with short-term engineering issues. The IETF was divided up into working groups, each with a specific problem to solve. The chairmen of these working groups initially met as a steering committee to direct the engineering effort. The working group topics include new applications, user information, OSI integration, routing and addressing, security, network management, and standards. Eventually, so many working groups were formed (more than 70) that they were grouped into areas and the area chairmen met as the steering committee.

In addition, a more formal standardization process was adopted, patterned after ISOs. To become a **Proposed Standard**, the basic idea must be completely explained in an RFC and have sufficient interest in the community to warrant consideration. To advance to the **Draft Standard** stage, a working implementation must have been rigorously tested by at least two independent sites for at least 4 months. If the IAB is convinced that the idea is sound and the software works, it can declare the RFC to be an Internet Standard. Some Internet Standards have become DoD standards (MIL-STD), making them mandatory for DoD suppliers. David Clark once made a now-famous remark about Internet standardization consisting of "rough consensus and running code."

1.7 METRIC UNITS

To avoid any confusion, it is worth stating explicitly that in this book, as in computer science in general, metric units are used instead of traditional English units (the furlong-stone-fortnight system). The principal metric prefixes are listed in Fig. 1-39. The prefixes are typically abbreviated by their first letters, with the units greater than 1 capitalized (KB, MB, etc.). One exception (for historical reasons) is kbps for kilobits/sec. Thus, a 1-Mbps communication line transmits 10^6 bits/sec and a 100 psec (or 100 ps) clock ticks every 10^{-10} seconds. Since milli and micro both begin with the letter "m," a choice had to be made. Normally, "m" is for milli and "μ" (the Greek letter mu) is for micro.

It is also worth pointing out that for measuring memory, disk, file, and database sizes, in common industry practice, the units have slightly different meanings. There, kilo means 2^{10} (1024) rather than 10^3 (1000) because memories are always a power of two. Thus, a 1-KB memory contains 1024 bytes, not 1000 bytes. Similarly, a 1-MB memory contains 2^{20} (1,048,576) bytes, a 1-GB memory contains 2^{30} (1,073,741,824) bytes, and a 1-TB database contains 2^{40}

Exp.	Explicit	Prefix	Exp.	Explicit	Prefix
10^{-3}	0.001	milli	10^{3}	1,000	Kilo
10^{-6}	0.000001	micro	10^{6}	1,000,000	Mega
10^{-9}	0.000000001	nano	10^{9}	1,000,000,000	Giga
10^{-12}	0.000000000001	pico	10^{12}	1,000,000,000,000	Tera
10^{-15}	0.000000000000001	femto	10^{15}	1,000,000,000,000,000	Peta
10^{-18}	0.0000000000000000001	atto	10^{18}	1,000,000,000,000,000,000	Exa
10^{-21}	0.0000000000000000000001	zepto	10^{21}	1,000,000,000,000,000,000,000	Zetta
10^{-24}	0.0000000000000000000000001	yocto	10^{24}	1,000,000,000,000,000,000,000,000	Yotta

Figure 1-39. The principal metric prefixes.

(1,099,511,627,776) bytes. However, a 1-kbps communication line transmits 1000 bits per second and a 10-Mbps LAN runs at 10,000,000 bits/sec because these speeds are not powers of two. Unfortunately, many people tend to mix up these two systems, especially for disk sizes. To avoid ambiguity, in this book, we will use the symbols KB, MB, and GB for 2^{10}, 2^{20}, and 2^{30} bytes, respectively, and the symbols kbps, Mbps, and Gbps for 10^{3}, 10^{6}, and 10^{9} bits/sec, respectively.

1.8 OUTLINE OF THE REST OF THE BOOK

This book discusses both the principles and practice of computer networking. Most chapters start with a discussion of the relevant principles, followed by a number of examples that illustrate these principles. These examples are usually taken from the Internet and wireless networks since these are both important and very different. Other examples will be given where relevant.

The book is structured according to the hybrid model of Fig. 1-24. Starting with Chap. 2, we begin working our way up the protocol hierarchy beginning at the bottom. The second chapter provides some background in the field of data communication. It covers wired, wireless, and satellite transmission systems. This material is concerned with the physical layer, although we cover only the architectural rather than the hardware aspects. Several examples of the physical layer, such as the public switched telephone network, mobile telephones, and the cable television network are also discussed.

Chapter 3 discusses the data link layer and its protocols by means of a number of increasingly complex examples. The analysis of these protocols is also covered. After that, some important real-world protocols are discussed, including HDLC (used in low- and medium-speed networks) and PPP (used in the Internet).

Chapter 4 concerns the medium access sublayer, which is part of the data link layer. The basic question it deals with is how to determine who may use the network next when the network consists of a single shared channel, as in most LANs and some satellite networks. Many examples are given from the areas of wired LANs, wireless LANs (especially Ethernet), wireless MANs, Bluetooth, and satellite networks. Bridges and data link switches, which are used to connect LANs, are also discussed here.

Chapter 5 deals with the network layer, especially routing, with many routing algorithms, both static and dynamic, being covered. Even with good routing algorithms though, if more traffic is offered than the network can handle, congestion can develop, so we discuss congestion and how to prevent it. Even better than just preventing congestion is guaranteeing a certain quality of service. We will discuss that topic as well here. Connecting heterogeneous networks to form internetworks leads to numerous problems that are discussed here. The network layer in the Internet is given extensive coverage.

Chapter 6 deals with the transport layer. Much of the emphasis is on connection-oriented protocols, since many applications need these. An example transport service and its implementation are discussed in detail. The actual code is given for this simple example to show how it could be implemented. Both Internet transport protocols, UDP and TCP, are covered in detail, as are their performance issues. Issues concerning wireless networks are also covered.

Chapter 7 deals with the application layer, its protocols and applications. The first topic is DNS, which is the Internet's telephone book. Next comes e-mail, including a discussion of its protocols. Then we move onto the Web, with detailed discussions of the static content, dynamic content, what happens on the client side, what happens on the server side, protocols, performance, the wireless Web, and more. Finally, we examine networked multimedia, including streaming audio, Internet radio, and video on demand.

Chapter 8 is about network security. This topic has aspects that relate to all layers, so it is easiest to treat it after all the layers have been thoroughly explained. The chapter starts with an introduction to cryptography. Later, it shows how cryptography can be used to secure communication, e-mail, and the Web. The book ends with a discussion of some areas in which security hits privacy, freedom of speech, censorship, and other social issues collide head on.

Chapter 9 contains an annotated list of suggested readings arranged by chapter. It is intended to help those readers who would like to pursue their study of networking further. The chapter also has an alphabetical bibliography of all references cited in this book.

The author's Web site at Prentice Hall:

http://www.prenhall.com/tanenbaum

has a page with links to many tutorials, FAQs, companies, industry consortia, professional organizations, standards organizations, technologies, papers, and more.

1.9 SUMMARY

Computer networks can be used for numerous services, both for companies and for individuals. For companies, networks of personal computers using shared servers often provide access to corporate information. Typically they follow the client-server model, with client workstations on employee desktops accessing powerful servers in the machine room. For individuals, networks offer access to a variety of information and entertainment resources. Individuals often access the Internet by calling up an ISP using a modem, although increasingly many people have a fixed connection at home. An up-and-coming area is wireless networking with new applications such as mobile e-mail access and m-commerce.

Roughly speaking, networks can be divided up into LANs, MANs, WANs, and internetworks, with their own characteristics, technologies, speeds, and niches. LANs cover a building and operate at high speeds. MANs cover a city, for example, the cable television system, which is now used by many people to access the Internet. WANs cover a country or continent. LANs and MANs are unswitched (i.e., do not have routers); WANs are switched. Wireless networks are becoming extremely popular, especially wireless LANs. Networks can be interconnected to form internetworks.

Network software consists of protocols, which are rules by which processes communicate. Protocols are either connectionless or connection-oriented. Most networks support protocol hierarchies, with each layer providing services to the layers above it and insulating them from the details of the protocols used in the lower layers. Protocol stacks are typically based either on the OSI model or on the TCP/IP model. Both have network, transport, and application layers, but they differ on the other layers. Design issues include multiplexing, flow control, error control, and others. Much of this book deals with protocols and their design.

Networks provide services to their users. These services can be connection-oriented or connectionless. In some networks, connectionless service is provided in one layer and connection-oriented service is provided in the layer above it.

Well-known networks include the Internet, ATM networks, Ethernet, and the IEEE 802.11 wireless LAN. The Internet evolved from the ARPANET, to which other networks were added to form an internetwork. The present Internet is actually a collection of many thousands of networks, rather than a single network. What characterizes it is the use of the TCP/IP protocol stack throughout. ATM is widely used inside the telephone system for long-haul data traffic. Ethernet is the most popular LAN and is present in most large companies and universities. Finally, wireless LANs at surprisingly high speeds (up to 54 Mbps) are beginning to be widely deployed.

To have multiple computers talk to each other requires a large amount of standardization, both in the hardware and software. Organizations such as the ITU-T, ISO, IEEE, and IAB manage different parts of the standardization process.

PROBLEMS

1. Imagine that you have trained your St. Bernard, Bernie, to carry a box of three 8mm tapes instead of a flask of brandy. (When your disk fills up, you consider that an emergency.) These tapes each contain 7 gigabytes. The dog can travel to your side, wherever you may be, at 18 km/hour. For what range of distances does Bernie have a higher data rate than a transmission line whose data rate (excluding overhead) is 150 Mbps?

2. An alternative to a LAN is simply a big timesharing system with terminals for all users. Give two advantages of a client-server system using a LAN.

3. The performance of a client-server system is influenced by two network factors: the bandwidth of the network (how many bits/sec it can transport) and the latency (how many seconds it takes for the first bit to get from the client to the server). Give an example of a network that exhibits high bandwidth and high latency. Then give an example of one with low bandwidth and low latency.

4. Besides bandwidth and latency, what other parameter is needed to give a good characterization of the quality of service offered by a network used for digitized voice traffic?

5. A factor in the delay of a store-and-forward packet-switching system is how long it takes to store and forward a packet through a switch. If switching time is 10 μsec, is this likely to be a major factor in the response of a client-server system where the client is in New York and the server is in California? Assume the propagation speed in copper and fiber to be 2/3 the speed of light in vacuum.

6. A client-server system uses a satellite network, with the satellite at a height of 40,000 km. What is the best-case delay in response to a request?

7. In the future, when everyone has a home terminal connected to a computer network, instant public referendums on important pending legislation will become possible. Ultimately, existing legislatures could be eliminated, to let the will of the people be expressed directly. The positive aspects of such a direct democracy are fairly obvious; discuss some of the negative aspects.

8. A collection of five routers is to be connected in a point-to-point subnet. Between each pair of routers, the designers may put a high-speed line, a medium-speed line, a low-speed line, or no line. If it takes 100 ms of computer time to generate and inspect each topology, how long will it take to inspect all of them?

9. A group of $2^n - 1$ routers are interconnected in a centralized binary tree, with a router at each tree node. Router i communicates with router j by sending a message to the root of the tree. The root then sends the message back down to j. Derive an approximate expression for the mean number of hops per message for large n, assuming that all router pairs are equally likely.

10. A disadvantage of a broadcast subnet is the capacity wasted when multiple hosts attempt to access the channel at the same time. As a simplistic example, suppose that

time is divided into discrete slots, with each of the n hosts attempting to use the channel with probability p during each slot. What fraction of the slots are wasted due to collisions?

11. What are two reasons for using layered protocols?

12. The president of the Specialty Paint Corp. gets the idea to work with a local beer brewer to produce an invisible beer can (as an anti-litter measure). The president tells her legal department to look into it, and they in turn ask engineering for help. As a result, the chief engineer calls his counterpart at the other company to discuss the technical aspects of the project. The engineers then report back to their respective legal departments, which then confer by telephone to arrange the legal aspects. Finally, the two corporate presidents discuss the financial side of the deal. Is this an example of a multilayer protocol in the sense of the OSI model?

13. What is the principal difference between connectionless communication and connection-oriented communication?

14. Two networks each provide reliable connection-oriented service. One of them offers a reliable byte stream and the other offers a reliable message stream. Are these identical? If so, why is the distinction made? If not, give an example of how they differ.

15. What does "negotiation" mean when discussing network protocols? Give an example.

16. In Fig. 1-19, a service is shown. Are any other services implicit in this figure? If so, where? If not, why not?

17. In some networks, the data link layer handles transmission errors by requesting damaged frames to be retransmitted. If the probability of a frame's being damaged is p, what is the mean number of transmissions required to send a frame? Assume that acknowledgements are never lost.

18. Which of the OSI layers handles each of the following:
(a) Dividing the transmitted bit stream into frames.
(b) Determining which route through the subnet to use.

19. If the unit exchanged at the data link level is called a frame and the unit exchanged at the network level is called a packet, do frames encapsulate packets or do packets encapsulate frames? Explain your answer.

20. A system has an n-layer protocol hierarchy. Applications generate messages of length M bytes. At each of the layers, an h-byte header is added. What fraction of the network bandwidth is filled with headers?

21. List two ways in which the OSI reference model and the TCP/IP reference model are the same. Now list two ways in which they differ.

22. What is the main difference between TCP and UDP?

23. The subnet of Fig. 1-25(b) was designed to withstand a nuclear war. How many bombs would it take to partition the nodes into two disconnected sets? Assume that any bomb wipes out a node and all of the links connected to it.

24. The Internet is roughly doubling in size every 18 months. Although no one really knows for sure, one estimate put the number of hosts on it at 100 million in 2001. Use these data to compute the expected number of Internet hosts in the year 2010. Do you believe this? Explain why or why not.

25. When a file is transferred between two computers, two acknowledgement strategies are possible. In the first one, the file is chopped up into packets, which are individually acknowledged by the receiver, but the file transfer as a whole is not acknowledged. In the second one, the packets are not acknowledged individually, but the entire file is acknowledged when it arrives. Discuss these two approaches.

26. Why does ATM use small, fixed-length cells?

27. How long was a bit on the original 802.3 standard in meters? Use a transmission speed of 10 Mbps and assume the propagation speed in coax is 2/3 the speed of light in vacuum.

28. An image is 1024×768 pixels with 3 bytes/pixel. Assume the image is uncompressed. How long does it take to transmit it over a 56-kbps modem channel? Over a 1-Mbps cable modem? Over a 10-Mbps Ethernet? Over 100-Mbps Ethernet?

29. Ethernet and wireless networks have some similarities and some differences. One property of Ethernet is that only one frame at a time can be transmitted on an Ethernet. Does 802.11 share this property with Ethernet? Discuss your answer.

30. Wireless networks are easy to install, which makes them inexpensive since installation costs usually far overshadow equipment costs. Nevertheless, they also have some disadvantages. Name two of them.

31. List two advantages and two disadvantages of having international standards for network protocols.

32. When a system has a permanent part and a removable part (such as a CD-ROM drive and the CD-ROM), it is important that the system be standardized, so that different companies can make both the permanent and removable parts and everything still works together. Give three examples outside the computer industry where such international standards exist. Now give three areas outside the computer industry where they do not exist.

33. Make a list of activities that you do every day in which computer networks are used. How would your life be altered if these networks were suddenly switched off?

34. Find out what networks are used at your school or place of work. Describe the network types, topologies, and switching methods used there.

35. The *ping* program allows you to send a test packet to a given location and see how long it takes to get there and back. Try using *ping* to see how long it takes to get from your location to several known locations. From thes data, plot the one-way transit time over the Internet as a function of distance. It is best to use universities since the location of their servers is known very accurately. For example, *berkeley.edu* is in Berkeley, California, *mit.edu* is in Cambridge, Massachusetts, *vu.nl* is in Amsterdam, The Netherlands, *www.usyd.edu.au* is in Sydney, Australia, and *www.uct.ac.za* is in Cape Town, South Africa.

36. Go to IETF's Web site, *www.ietf.org*, to see what they are doing. Pick a project you like and write a half-page report on the problem and the proposed solution.

37. Standardization is very important in the network world. ITU and ISO are the main official standardization organizations. Go to their Web sites, *www.itu.org* and *www.iso.org*, respectively, and learn about their standardization work. Write a short report about the kinds of things they have standardized.

38. The Internet is made up of a large number of networks. Their arrangement determines the topology of the Internet. A considerable amount of information about the Internet topology is available on line. Use a search engine to find out more about the Internet topology and write a short report summarizing your findings.

2

THE PHYSICAL LAYER

In this chapter we will look at the lowest layer depicted in the hierarchy of Fig. 1-24. It defines the mechanical, electrical, and timing interfaces to the network. We will begin with a theoretical analysis of data transmission, only to discover that Mother (Parent?) Nature puts some limits on what can be sent over a channel.

Then we will cover three kinds of transmission media: guided (copper wire and fiber optics), wireless (terrestrial radio), and satellite. This material will provide background information on the key transmission technologies used in modern networks.

The remainder of the chapter will be devoted to three examples of communication systems used in practice for wide area computer networks: the (fixed) telephone system, the mobile phone system, and the cable television system. All three use fiber optics in the backbone, but they are organized differently and use different technologies for the last mile.

2.1 THE THEORETICAL BASIS FOR DATA COMMUNICATION

Information can be transmitted on wires by varying some physical property such as voltage or current. By representing the value of this voltage or current as a single-valued function of time, $f(t)$, we can model the behavior of the signal and analyze it mathematically. This analysis is the subject of the following sections.

2.1.1 Fourier Analysis

In the early 19th century, the French mathematician Jean-Baptiste Fourier proved that any reasonably behaved periodic function, $g(t)$ with period T can be constructed as the sum of a (possibly infinite) number of sines and cosines:

$$g(t) = \frac{1}{2}c + \sum_{n=1}^{\infty} a_n \sin(2\pi nft) + \sum_{n=1}^{\infty} b_n \cos(2\pi nft) \qquad (2\text{-}1)$$

where $f = 1/T$ is the fundamental frequency, a_n and b_n are the sine and cosine amplitudes of the nth **harmonics** (terms), and c is a constant. Such a decomposition is called a **Fourier series**. From the Fourier series, the function can be reconstructed; that is, if the period, T, is known and the amplitudes are given, the original function of time can be found by performing the sums of Eq. (2-1).

A data signal that has a finite duration (which all of them do) can be handled by just imagining that it repeats the entire pattern over and over forever (i.e., the interval from T to $2T$ is the same as from 0 to T, etc.).

The a_n amplitudes can be computed for any given $g(t)$ by multiplying both sides of Eq. (2-1) by $\sin(2\pi kft)$ and then integrating from 0 to T. Since

$$\int_0^T \sin(2\pi kft)\sin(2\pi nft)\,dt = \begin{cases} 0 \text{ for } k \neq n \\ T/2 \text{ for } k = n \end{cases}$$

only one term of the summation survives: a_n. The b_n summation vanishes completely. Similarly, by multiplying Eq. (2-1) by $\cos(2\pi kft)$ and integrating between 0 and T, we can derive b_n. By just integrating both sides of the equation as it stands, we can find c. The results of performing these operations are as follows:

$$a_n = \frac{2}{T}\int_0^T g(t)\sin(2\pi nft)\,dt \qquad b_n = \frac{2}{T}\int_0^T g(t)\cos(2\pi nft)\,dt \qquad c = \frac{2}{T}\int_0^T g(t)\,dt$$

2.1.2 Bandwidth-Limited Signals

To see what all this has to do with data communication, let us consider a specific example: the transmission of the ASCII character "b" encoded in an 8-bit byte. The bit pattern that is to be transmitted is 01100010. The left-hand part of Fig. 2-1(a) shows the voltage output by the transmitting computer. The Fourier analysis of this signal yields the coefficients:

$$a_n = \frac{1}{\pi n}[\cos(\pi n/4) - \cos(3\pi n/4) + \cos(6\pi n/4) - \cos(7\pi n/4)]$$

$$b_n = \frac{1}{\pi n}[\sin(3\pi n/4) - \sin(\pi n/4) + \sin(7\pi n/4) - \sin(6\pi n/4)]$$

$$c = 3/4$$

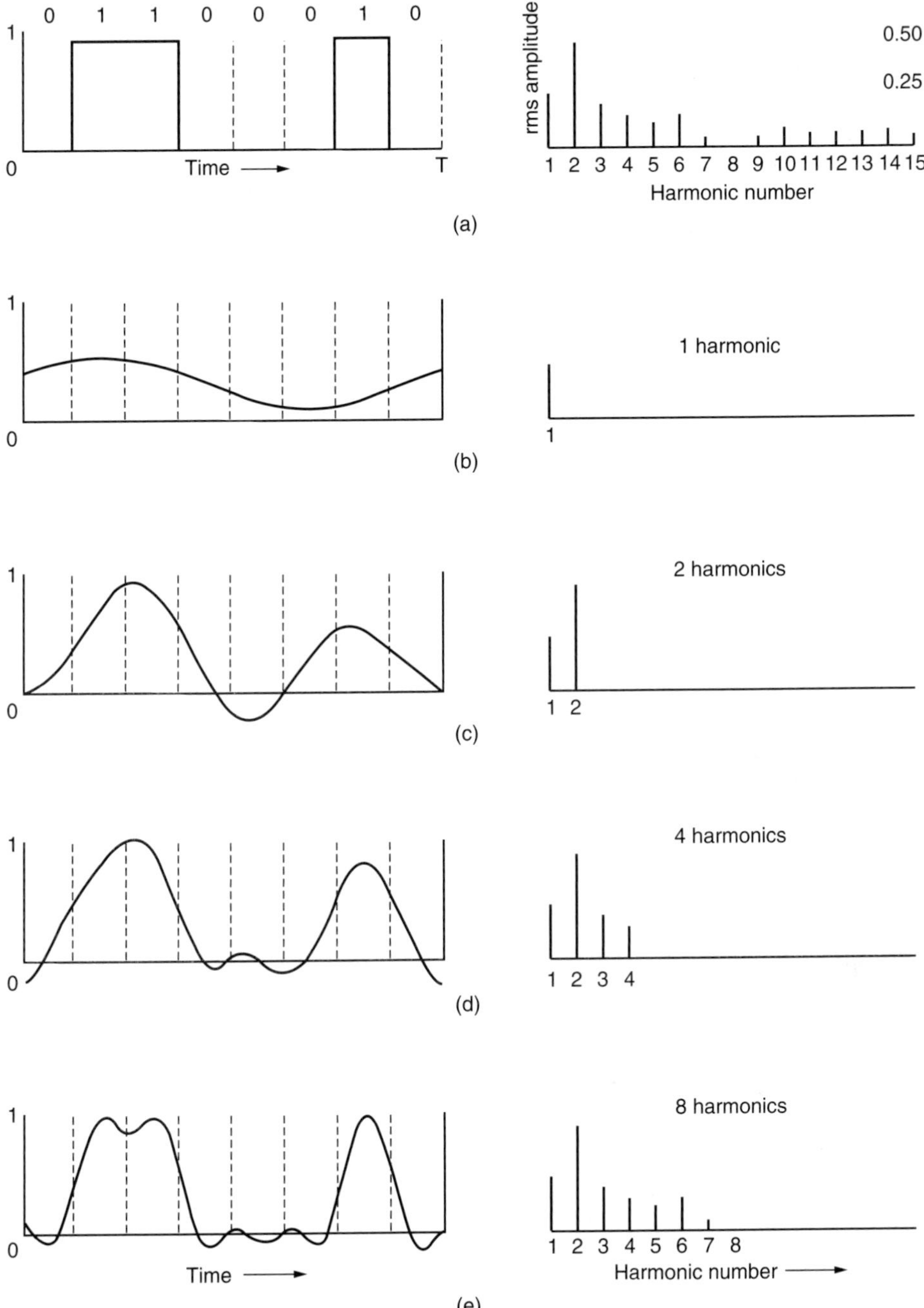

Figure 2-1. (a) A binary signal and its root-mean-square Fourier amplitudes. (b)-(e) Successive approximations to the original signal.

The root-mean-square amplitudes, $\sqrt{a_n^2 + b_n^2}$, for the first few terms are shown on the right-hand side of Fig. 2-1(a). These values are of interest because their squares are proportional to the energy transmitted at the corresponding frequency.

No transmission facility can transmit signals without losing some power in the process. If all the Fourier components were equally diminished, the resulting signal would be reduced in amplitude but not distorted [i.e., it would have the same nice squared-off shape as Fig. 2-1(a)]. Unfortunately, all transmission facilities diminish different Fourier components by different amounts, thus introducing distortion. Usually, the amplitudes are transmitted undiminished from 0 up to some frequency f_c [measured in cycles/sec or Hertz (Hz)] with all frequencies above this cutoff frequency attenuated. The range of frequencies transmitted without being strongly attenuated is called the **bandwidth**. In practice, the cutoff is not really sharp, so often the quoted bandwidth is from 0 to the frequency at which half the power gets through.

The bandwidth is a physical property of the transmission medium and usually depends on the construction, thickness, and length of the medium. In some cases a filter is introduced into the circuit to limit the amount of bandwidth available to each customer. For example, a telephone wire may have a bandwidth of 1 MHz for short distances, but telephone companies add a filter restricting each customer to about 3100 Hz. This bandwidth is adequate for intelligible speech and improves system-wide efficiency by limiting resource usage by customers.

Now let us consider how the signal of Fig. 2-1(a) would look if the bandwidth were so low that only the lowest frequencies were transmitted [i.e., if the function were being approximated by the first few terms of Eq. (2-1)]. Figure 2-1(b) shows the signal that results from a channel that allows only the first harmonic (the fundamental, f) to pass through. Similarly, Fig. 2-1(c)-(e) show the spectra and reconstructed functions for higher-bandwidth channels.

Given a bit rate of b bits/sec, the time required to send 8 bits (for example) 1 bit at a time is $8/b$ sec, so the frequency of the first harmonic is $b/8$ Hz. An ordinary telephone line, often called a **voice-grade line**, has an artificially-introduced cutoff frequency just above 3000 Hz. This restriction means that the number of the highest harmonic passed through is roughly $3000/(b/8)$ or $24{,}000/b$, (the cutoff is not sharp).

For some data rates, the numbers work out as shown in Fig. 2-2. From these numbers, it is clear that trying to send at 9600 bps over a voice-grade telephone line will transform Fig. 2-1(a) into something looking like Fig. 2-1(c), making accurate reception of the original binary bit stream tricky. It should be obvious that at data rates much higher than 38.4 kbps, there is no hope at all for *binary* signals, even if the transmission facility is completely noiseless. In other words, limiting the bandwidth limits the data rate, even for perfect channels. However, sophisticated coding schemes that make use of several voltage levels do exist and can achieve higher data rates. We will discuss these later in this chapter.

Bps	T (msec)	First harmonic (Hz)	# Harmonics sent
300	26.67	37.5	80
600	13.33	75	40
1200	6.67	150	20
2400	3.33	300	10
4800	1.67	600	5
9600	0.83	1200	2
19200	0.42	2400	1
38400	0.21	4800	0

Figure 2-2. Relation between data rate and harmonics.

2.1.3 The Maximum Data Rate of a Channel

As early as 1924, an AT&T engineer, Henry Nyquist, realized that even a perfect channel has a finite transmission capacity. He derived an equation expressing the maximum data rate for a finite bandwidth noiseless channel. In 1948, Claude Shannon carried Nyquist's work further and extended it to the case of a channel subject to random (that is, thermodynamic) noise (Shannon, 1948). We will just briefly summarize their now classical results here.

Nyquist proved that if an arbitrary signal has been run through a low-pass filter of bandwidth H, the filtered signal can be completely reconstructed by making only $2H$ (exact) samples per second. Sampling the line faster than $2H$ times per second is pointless because the higher frequency components that such sampling could recover have already been filtered out. If the signal consists of V discrete levels, Nyquist's theorem states:

$$\text{maximum data rate} = 2H \log_2 V \text{ bits/sec}$$

For example, a noiseless 3-kHz channel cannot transmit binary (i.e., two-level) signals at a rate exceeding 6000 bps.

So far we have considered only noiseless channels. If random noise is present, the situation deteriorates rapidly. And there is always random (thermal) noise present due to the motion of the molecules in the system. The amount of thermal noise present is measured by the ratio of the signal power to the noise power, called the **signal-to-noise ratio**. If we denote the signal power by S and the noise power by N, the signal-to-noise ratio is S/N. Usually, the ratio itself is not quoted; instead, the quantity $10 \log_{10} S/N$ is given. These units are called **decibels** (dB). An S/N ratio of 10 is 10 dB, a ratio of 100 is 20 dB, a ratio of 1000 is 30 dB, and so on. The manufacturers of stereo amplifiers often characterize the bandwidth (frequency range) over which their product is linear by giving the 3-dB frequency on each end. These are the points at which the amplification factor has been approximately halved (because $\log_{10}3 \approx 0.5$).

Shannon's major result is that the maximum data rate of a noisy channel whose bandwidth is H Hz, and whose signal-to-noise ratio is S/N, is given by

$$\text{maximum number of bits/sec} = H \log_2 (1 + S/N)$$

For example, a channel of 3000-Hz bandwidth with a signal to thermal noise ratio of 30 dB (typical parameters of the analog part of the telephone system) can never transmit much more than 30,000 bps, no matter how many or how few signal levels are used and no matter how often or how infrequently samples are taken. Shannon's result was derived from information-theory arguments and applies to any channel subject to thermal noise. Counterexamples should be treated in the same category as perpetual motion machines. It should be noted that this is only an upper bound and real systems rarely achieve it.

2.2 GUIDED TRANSMISSION MEDIA

The purpose of the physical layer is to transport a raw bit stream from one machine to another. Various physical media can be used for the actual transmission. Each one has its own niche in terms of bandwidth, delay, cost, and ease of installation and maintenance. Media are roughly grouped into guided media, such as copper wire and fiber optics, and unguided media, such as radio and lasers through the air. We will look at all of these in the following sections.

2.2.1 Magnetic Media

One of the most common ways to transport data from one computer to another is to write them onto magnetic tape or removable media (e.g., recordable DVDs), physically transport the tape or disks to the destination machine, and read them back in again. Although this method is not as sophisticated as using a geosynchronous communication satellite, it is often more cost effective, especially for applications in which high bandwidth or cost per bit transported is the key factor.

A simple calculation will make this point clear. An industry standard Ultrium tape can hold 200 gigabytes. A box $60 \times 60 \times 60$ cm can hold about 1000 of these tapes, for a total capacity of 200 terabytes, or 1600 terabits (1.6 petabits). A box of tapes can be delivered anywhere in the United States in 24 hours by Federal Express and other companies. The effective bandwidth of this transmission is 1600 terabits/86,400 sec, or 19 Gbps. If the destination is only an hour away by road, the bandwidth is increased to over 400 Gbps. No computer network can even approach this.

For a bank with many gigabytes of data to be backed up daily on a second machine (so the bank can continue to function even in the face of a major flood or earthquake), it is likely that no other transmission technology can even begin to approach magnetic tape for performance. Of course, networks are getting faster, but tape densities are increasing, too.

If we now look at cost, we get a similar picture. The cost of an Ultrium tape is around $40 when bought in bulk. A tape can be reused at least ten times, so the tape cost is maybe $4000 per box per usage. Add to this another $1000 for shipping (probably much less), and we have a cost of roughly $5000 to ship 200 TB. This amounts to shipping a gigabyte for under 3 cents. No network can beat that. The moral of the story is:

Never underestimate the bandwidth of a station wagon full of tapes hurtling down the highway

2.2.2 Twisted Pair

Although the bandwidth characteristics of magnetic tape are excellent, the delay characteristics are poor. Transmission time is measured in minutes or hours, not milliseconds. For many applications an on-line connection is needed. One of the oldest and still most common transmission media is **twisted pair**. A twisted pair consists of two insulated copper wires, typically about 1 mm thick. The wires are twisted together in a helical form, just like a DNA molecule. Twisting is done because two parallel wires constitute a fine antenna. When the wires are twisted, the waves from different twists cancel out, so the wire radiates less effectively.

The most common application of the twisted pair is the telephone system. Nearly all telephones are connected to the telephone company (telco) office by a twisted pair. Twisted pairs can run several kilometers without amplification, but for longer distances, repeaters are needed. When many twisted pairs run in parallel for a substantial distance, such as all the wires coming from an apartment building to the telephone company office, they are bundled together and encased in a protective sheath. The pairs in these bundles would interfere with one another if it were not for the twisting. In parts of the world where telephone lines run on poles above ground, it is common to see bundles several centimeters in diameter.

Twisted pairs can be used for transmitting either analog or digital signals. The bandwidth depends on the thickness of the wire and the distance traveled, but several megabits/sec can be achieved for a few kilometers in many cases. Due to their adequate performance and low cost, twisted pairs are widely used and are likely to remain so for years to come.

Twisted pair cabling comes in several varieties, two of which are important for computer networks. **Category 3** twisted pairs consist of two insulated wires gently twisted together. Four such pairs are typically grouped in a plastic sheath to protect the wires and keep them together. Prior to about 1988, most office buildings had one category 3 cable running from a central **wiring closet** on each floor into each office. This scheme allowed up to four regular telephones or two multiline telephones in each office to connect to the telephone company equipment in the wiring closet.

Starting around 1988, the more advanced **category 5** twisted pairs were introduced. They are similar to category 3 pairs, but with more twists per centimeter, which results in less crosstalk and a better-quality signal over longer distances, making them more suitable for high-speed computer communication. Up-and-coming categories are 6 and 7, which are capable of handling signals with bandwidths of 250 MHz and 600 MHz, respectively (versus a mere 16 MHz and 100 MHz for categories 3 and 5, respectively).

All of these wiring types are often referred to as **UTP** (**Unshielded Twisted Pair**), to contrast them with the bulky, expensive, shielded twisted pair cables IBM introduced in the early 1980s, but which have not proven popular outside of IBM installations. Twisted pair cabling is illustrated in Fig. 2-3.

Figure 2-3. (a) Category 3 UTP. (b) Category 5 UTP.

2.2.3 Coaxial Cable

Another common transmission medium is the **coaxial cable** (known to its many friends as just "coax" and pronounced "co-ax"). It has better shielding than twisted pairs, so it can span longer distances at higher speeds. Two kinds of coaxial cable are widely used. One kind, 50-ohm cable, is commonly used when it is intended for digital transmission from the start. The other kind, 75-ohm cable, is commonly used for analog transmission and cable television but is becoming more important with the advent of Internet over cable. This distinction is based on historical, rather than technical, factors (e.g., early dipole antennas had an impedance of 300 ohms, and it was easy to use existing 4:1 impedance matching transformers).

A coaxial cable consists of a stiff copper wire as the core, surrounded by an insulating material. The insulator is encased by a cylindrical conductor, often as a closely-woven braided mesh. The outer conductor is covered in a protective plastic sheath. A cutaway view of a coaxial cable is shown in Fig. 2-4.

The construction and shielding of the coaxial cable give it a good combination of high bandwidth and excellent noise immunity. The bandwidth possible depends on the cable quality, length, and signal-to-noise ratio of the data signal. Modern cables have a bandwidth of close to 1 GHz. Coaxial cables used to be widely used within the telephone system for long-distance lines but have now largely been replaced by fiber optics on long-haul routes. Coax is still widely used for cable television and metropolitan area networks, however.

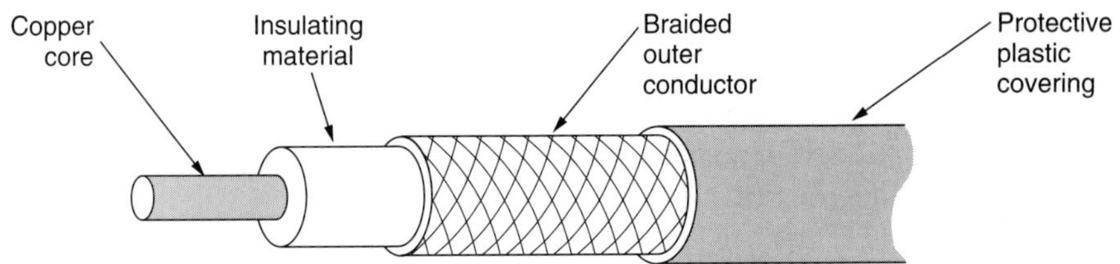

Figure 2-4. A coaxial cable.

2.2.4 Fiber Optics

Many people in the computer industry take enormous pride in how fast computer technology is improving. The original (1981) IBM PC ran at a clock speed of 4.77 MHz. Twenty years later, PCs could run at 2 GHz, a gain of a factor of 20 per decade. Not too bad.

In the same period, wide area data communication went from 56 kbps (the ARPANET) to 1 Gbps (modern optical communication), a gain of more than a factor of 125 per decade, while at the same time the error rate went from 10^{-5} per bit to almost zero.

Furthermore, single CPUs are beginning to approach physical limits, such as speed of light and heat dissipation problems. In contrast, with *current* fiber technology, the achievable bandwidth is certainly in excess of 50,000 Gbps (50 Tbps) and many people are looking very hard for better technologies and materials. The current practical signaling limit of about 10 Gbps is due to our inability to convert between electrical and optical signals any faster, although in the laboratory, 100 Gbps has been achieved on a single fiber.

In the race between computing and communication, communication won. The full implications of essentially infinite bandwidth (although not at zero cost) have not yet sunk in to a generation of computer scientists and engineers taught to think in terms of the low Nyquist and Shannon limits imposed by copper wire. The new conventional wisdom should be that all computers are hopelessly slow and that networks should try to avoid computation at all costs, no matter how much bandwidth that wastes. In this section we will study fiber optics to see how that transmission technology works.

An optical transmission system has three key components: the light source, the transmission medium, and the detector. Conventionally, a pulse of light indicates a 1 bit and the absence of light indicates a 0 bit. The transmission medium is an ultra-thin fiber of glass. The detector generates an electrical pulse when light falls on it. By attaching a light source to one end of an optical fiber and a detector to the other, we have a unidirectional data transmission system that accepts an electrical signal, converts and transmits it by light pulses, and then reconverts the output to an electrical signal at the receiving end.

This transmission system would leak light and be useless in practice except for an interesting principle of physics. When a light ray passes from one medium to another, for example, from fused silica to air, the ray is refracted (bent) at the silica/air boundary, as shown in Fig. 2-5(a). Here we see a light ray incident on the boundary at an angle α_1 emerging at an angle β_1. The amount of refraction depends on the properties of the two media (in particular, their indices of refraction). For angles of incidence above a certain critical value, the light is refracted back into the silica; none of it escapes into the air. Thus, a light ray incident at or above the critical angle is trapped inside the fiber, as shown in Fig. 2-5(b), and can propagate for many kilometers with virtually no loss.

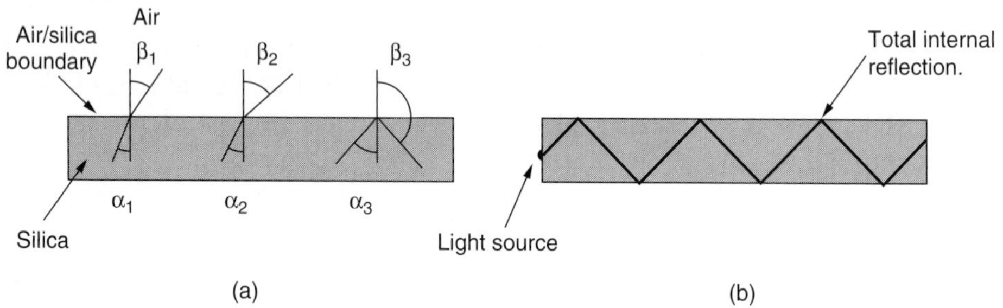

Figure 2-5. (a) Three examples of a light ray from inside a silica fiber impinging on the air/silica boundary at different angles. (b) Light trapped by total internal reflection.

The sketch of Fig. 2-5(b) shows only one trapped ray, but since any light ray incident on the boundary above the critical angle will be reflected internally, many different rays will be bouncing around at different angles. Each ray is said to have a different **mode**, so a fiber having this property is called a **multimode fiber**.

However, if the fiber's diameter is reduced to a few wavelengths of light, the fiber acts like a wave guide, and the light can propagate only in a straight line, without bouncing, yielding a **single-mode fiber**. Single-mode fibers are more expensive but are widely used for longer distances. Currently available single-mode fibers can transmit data at 50 Gbps for 100 km without amplification. Even higher data rates have been achieved in the laboratory for shorter distances.

Transmission of Light through Fiber

Optical fibers are made of glass, which, in turn, is made from sand, an inexpensive raw material available in unlimited amounts. Glassmaking was known to the ancient Egyptians, but their glass had to be no more than 1 mm thick or the light could not shine through. Glass transparent enough to be useful for windows was developed during the Renaissance. The glass used for modern optical fibers is so transparent that if the oceans were full of it instead of water, the seabed would be as visible from the surface as the ground is from an airplane on a clear day.

The attenuation of light through glass depends on the wavelength of the light (as well as on some physical properties of the glass). For the kind of glass used in fibers, the attenuation is shown in Fig. 2-6 in decibels per linear kilometer of fiber. The attenuation in decibels is given by the formula

$$\text{Attenuation in decibels} = 10 \log_{10} \frac{\text{transmitted power}}{\text{received power}}$$

For example, a factor of two loss gives an attenuation of $10 \log_{10} 2 = 3$ dB. The figure shows the near infrared part of the spectrum, which is what is used in practice. Visible light has slightly shorter wavelengths, from 0.4 to 0.7 microns (1 micron is 10^{-6} meters). The true metric purist would refer to these wavelengths as 400 nm to 700 nm, but we will stick with traditional usage.

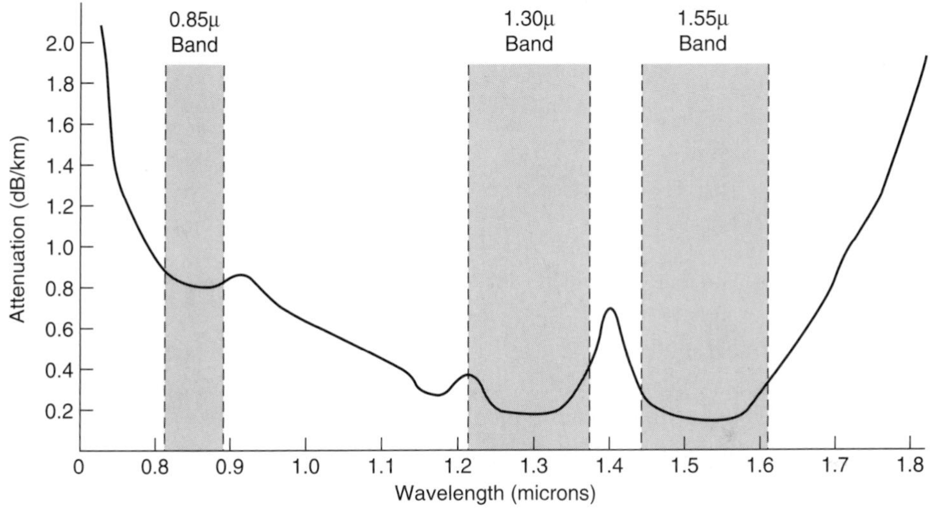

Figure 2-6. Attenuation of light through fiber in the infrared region.

Three wavelength bands are used for optical communication. They are centered at 0.85, 1.30, and 1.55 microns, respectively. The last two have good attenuation properties (less than 5 percent loss per kilometer). The 0.85 micron band has higher attenuation, but at that wavelength the lasers and electronics can be made from the same material (gallium arsenide). All three bands are 25,000 to 30,000 GHz wide.

Light pulses sent down a fiber spread out in length as they propagate. This spreading is called **chromatic dispersion**. The amount of it is wavelength dependent. One way to keep these spread-out pulses from overlapping is to increase the distance between them, but this can be done only by reducing the signaling rate. Fortunately, it has been discovered that by making the pulses in a special shape related to the reciprocal of the hyperbolic cosine, nearly all the dispersion effects cancel out, and it is possible to send pulses for thousands of kilometers without appreciable shape distortion. These pulses are called **solitons**. A considerable amount of research is going on to take solitons out of the lab and into the field.

Fiber Cables

Fiber optic cables are similar to coax, except without the braid. Figure 2-7(a) shows a single fiber viewed from the side. At the center is the glass core through which the light propagates. In multimode fibers, the core is typically 50 microns in diameter, about the thickness of a human hair. In single-mode fibers, the core is 8 to 10 microns.

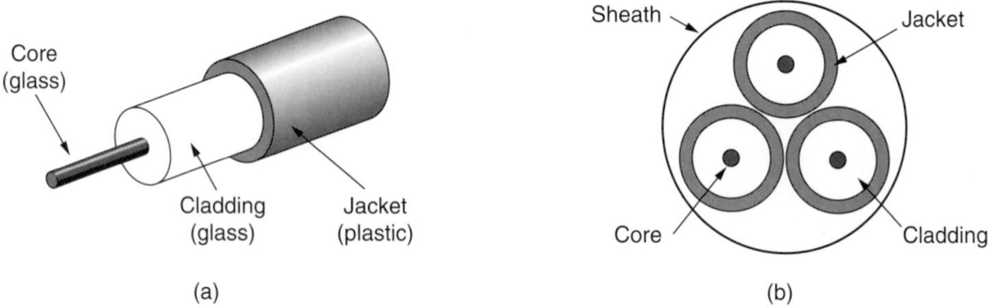

Figure 2-7. (a) Side view of a single fiber. (b) End view of a sheath with three fibers.

The core is surrounded by a glass cladding with a lower index of refraction than the core, to keep all the light in the core. Next comes a thin plastic jacket to protect the cladding. Fibers are typically grouped in bundles, protected by an outer sheath. Figure 2-7(b) shows a sheath with three fibers.

Terrestrial fiber sheaths are normally laid in the ground within a meter of the surface, where they are occasionally subject to attacks by backhoes or gophers. Near the shore, transoceanic fiber sheaths are buried in trenches by a kind of seaplow. In deep water, they just lie on the bottom, where they can be snagged by fishing trawlers or attacked by giant squid.

Fibers can be connected in three different ways. First, they can terminate in connectors and be plugged into fiber sockets. Connectors lose about 10 to 20 percent of the light, but they make it easy to reconfigure systems.

Second, they can be spliced mechanically. Mechanical splices just lay the two carefully-cut ends next to each other in a special sleeve and clamp them in place. Alignment can be improved by passing light through the junction and then making small adjustments to maximize the signal. Mechanical splices take trained personnel about 5 minutes and result in a 10 percent light loss.

Third, two pieces of fiber can be fused (melted) to form a solid connection. A fusion splice is almost as good as a single drawn fiber, but even here, a small amount of attenuation occurs.

For all three kinds of splices, reflections can occur at the point of the splice, and the reflected energy can interfere with the signal.

Two kinds of light sources are typically used to do the signaling, LEDs (Light Emitting Diodes) and semiconductor lasers. They have different properties, as shown in Fig. 2-8. They can be tuned in wavelength by inserting Fabry-Perot or Mach-Zehnder interferometers between the source and the fiber. Fabry-Perot interferometers are simple resonant cavities consisting of two parallel mirrors. The light is incident perpendicular to the mirrors. The length of the cavity selects out those wavelengths that fit inside an integral number of times. Mach-Zehnder interferometers separate the light into two beams. The two beams travel slightly different distances. They are recombined at the end and are in phase for only certain wavelengths.

Item	LED	Semiconductor laser
Data rate	Low	High
Fiber type	Multimode	Multimode or single mode
Distance	Short	Long
Lifetime	Long life	Short life
Temperature sensitivity	Minor	Substantial
Cost	Low cost	Expensive

Figure 2-8. A comparison of semiconductor diodes and LEDs as light sources.

The receiving end of an optical fiber consists of a photodiode, which gives off an electrical pulse when struck by light. The typical response time of a photodiode is 1 nsec, which limits data rates to about 1 Gbps. Thermal noise is also an issue, so a pulse of light must carry enough energy to be detected. By making the pulses powerful enough, the error rate can be made arbitrarily small.

Fiber Optic Networks

Fiber optics can be used for LANs as well as for long-haul transmission, although tapping into it is more complex than connecting to an Ethernet. One way around the problem is to realize that a ring network is really just a collection of point-to-point links, as shown in Fig. 2-9. The interface at each computer passes the light pulse stream through to the next link and also serves as a T junction to allow the computer to send and accept messages.

Two types of interfaces are used. A passive interface consists of two taps fused onto the main fiber. One tap has an LED or laser diode at the end of it (for transmitting), and the other has a photodiode (for receiving). The tap itself is

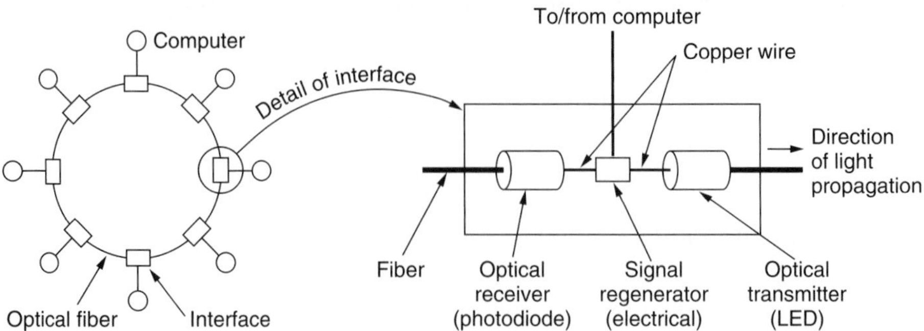

Figure 2-9. A fiber optic ring with active repeaters.

completely passive and is thus extremely reliable because a broken LED or photodiode does not break the ring. It just takes one computer off-line.

The other interface type, shown in Fig. 2-9, is the **active repeater**. The incoming light is converted to an electrical signal, regenerated to full strength if it has been weakened, and retransmitted as light. The interface with the computer is an ordinary copper wire that comes into the signal regenerator. Purely optical repeaters are now being used, too. These devices do not require the optical to electrical to optical conversions, which means they can operate at extremely high bandwidths.

If an active repeater fails, the ring is broken and the network goes down. On the other hand, since the signal is regenerated at each interface, the individual computer-to-computer links can be kilometers long, with virtually no limit on the total size of the ring. The passive interfaces lose light at each junction, so the number of computers and total ring length are greatly restricted.

A ring topology is not the only way to build a LAN using fiber optics. It is also possible to have hardware broadcasting by using the **passive star** construction of Fig. 2-10. In this design, each interface has a fiber running from its transmitter to a silica cylinder, with the incoming fibers fused to one end of the cylinder. Similarly, fibers fused to the other end of the cylinder are run to each of the receivers. Whenever an interface emits a light pulse, it is diffused inside the passive star to illuminate all the receivers, thus achieving broadcast. In effect, the passive star combines all the incoming signals and transmits the merged result on all lines. Since the incoming energy is divided among all the outgoing lines, the number of nodes in the network is limited by the sensitivity of the photodiodes.

Comparison of Fiber Optics and Copper Wire

It is instructive to compare fiber to copper. Fiber has many advantages. To start with, it can handle much higher bandwidths than copper. This alone would require its use in high-end networks. Due to the low attenuation, repeaters are

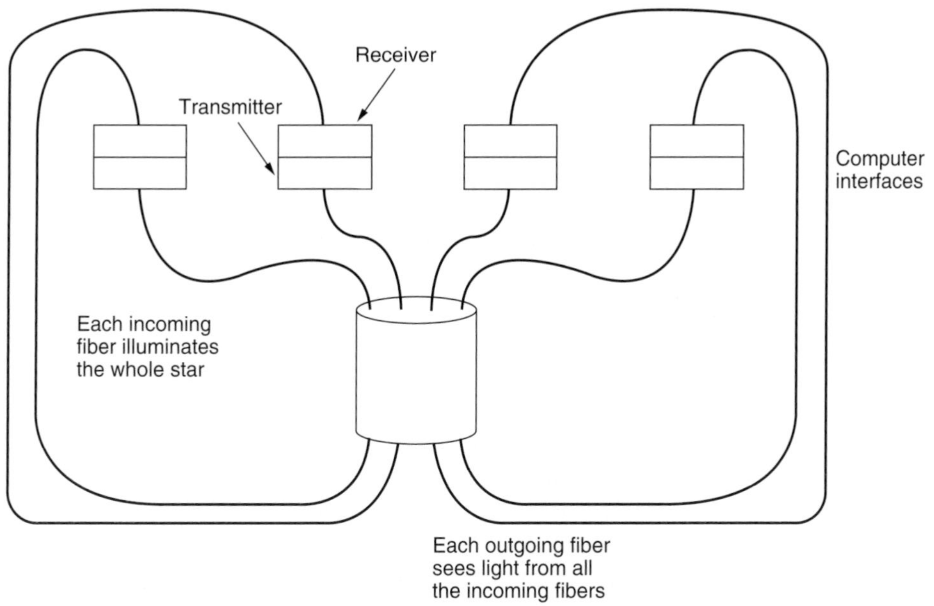

Figure 2-10. A passive star connection in a fiber optics network.

needed only about every 50 km on long lines, versus about every 5 km for copper, a substantial cost saving. Fiber also has the advantage of not being affected by power surges, electromagnetic interference, or power failures. Nor is it affected by corrosive chemicals in the air, making it ideal for harsh factory environments.

Oddly enough, telephone companies like fiber for a different reason: it is thin and lightweight. Many existing cable ducts are completely full, so there is no room to add new capacity. Removing all the copper and replacing it by fiber empties the ducts, and the copper has excellent resale value to copper refiners who see it as very high grade ore. Also, fiber is much lighter than copper. One thousand twisted pairs 1 km long weigh 8000 kg. Two fibers have more capacity and weigh only 100 kg, which greatly reduces the need for expensive mechanical support systems that must be maintained. For new routes, fiber wins hands down due to its much lower installation cost.

Finally, fibers do not leak light and are quite difficult to tap. These properties gives fiber excellent security against potential wiretappers.

On the downside, fiber is a less familiar technology requiring skills not all engineers have, and fibers can be damaged easily by being bent too much. Since optical transmission is inherently unidirectional, two-way communication requires either two fibers or two frequency bands on one fiber. Finally, fiber interfaces cost more than electrical interfaces. Nevertheless, the future of all fixed data communication for distances of more than a few meters is clearly with fiber. For a discussion of all aspects of fiber optics and their networks, see (Hecht, 2001).

2.3 WIRELESS TRANSMISSION

Our age has given rise to information junkies: people who need to be on-line all the time. For these mobile users, twisted pair, coax, and fiber optics are of no use. They need to get their hits of data for their laptop, notebook, shirt pocket, palmtop, or wristwatch computers without being tethered to the terrestrial communication infrastructure. For these users, wireless communication is the answer. In the following sections, we will look at wireless communication in general, as it has many other important applications besides providing connectivity to users who want to surf the Web from the beach.

Some people believe that the future holds only two kinds of communication: fiber and wireless. All fixed (i.e., nonmobile) computers, telephones, faxes, and so on will use fiber, and all mobile ones will use wireless.

Wireless has advantages for even fixed devices in some circumstances. For example, if running a fiber to a building is difficult due to the terrain (mountains, jungles, swamps, etc.), wireless may be better. It is noteworthy that modern wireless digital communication began in the Hawaiian Islands, where large chunks of Pacific Ocean separated the users and the telephone system was inadequate.

2.3.1 The Electromagnetic Spectrum

When electrons move, they create electromagnetic waves that can propagate through space (even in a vacuum). These waves were predicted by the British physicist James Clerk Maxwell in 1865 and first observed by the German physicist Heinrich Hertz in 1887. The number of oscillations per second of a wave is called its **frequency**, f, and is measured in **Hz** (in honor of Heinrich Hertz). The distance between two consecutive maxima (or minima) is called the **wavelength**, which is universally designated by the Greek letter λ (lambda).

When an antenna of the appropriate size is attached to an electrical circuit, the electromagnetic waves can be broadcast efficiently and received by a receiver some distance away. All wireless communication is based on this principle.

In vacuum, all electromagnetic waves travel at the same speed, no matter what their frequency. This speed, usually called the **speed of light**, c, is approximately 3×10^8 m/sec, or about 1 foot (30 cm) per nanosecond. (A case could be made for redefining the foot as the distance light travels in a vacuum in 1 nsec rather than basing it on the shoe size of some long-dead king.) In copper or fiber the speed slows to about 2/3 of this value and becomes slightly frequency dependent. The speed of light is the ultimate speed limit. No object or signal can ever move faster than it.

The fundamental relation between f, λ, and c (in vacuum) is

$$\lambda f = c \tag{2-2}$$

Since c is a constant, if we know f, we can find λ, and vice versa. As a rule of thumb, when λ is in meters and f is in MHz, $\lambda f \approx 300$. For example, 100-MHz waves are about 3 meters long, 1000-MHz waves are 0.3-meters long, and 0.1-meter waves have a frequency of 3000 MHz.

The electromagnetic spectrum is shown in Fig. 2-11. The radio, microwave, infrared, and visible light portions of the spectrum can all be used for transmitting information by modulating the amplitude, frequency, or phase of the waves. Ultraviolet light, X-rays, and gamma rays would be even better, due to their higher frequencies, but they are hard to produce and modulate, do not propagate well through buildings, and are dangerous to living things. The bands listed at the bottom of Fig. 2-11 are the official ITU names and are based on the wavelengths, so the LF band goes from 1 km to 10 km (approximately 30 kHz to 300 kHz). The terms LF, MF, and HF refer to low, medium, and high frequency, respectively. Clearly, when the names were assigned, nobody expected to go above 10 MHz, so the higher bands were later named the Very, Ultra, Super, Extremely, and Tremendously High Frequency bands. Beyond that there are no names, but Incredibly, Astonishingly, and Prodigiously high frequency (IHF, AHF, and PHF) would sound nice.

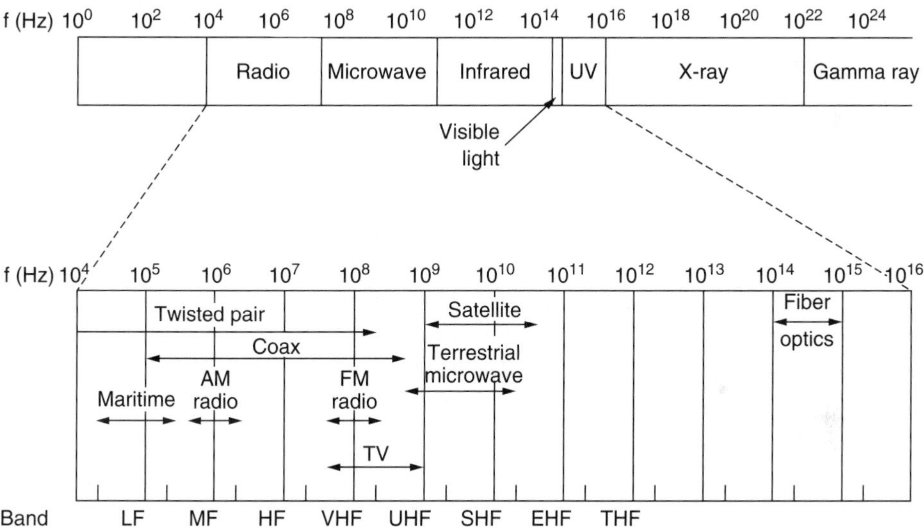

Figure 2-11. The electromagnetic spectrum and its uses for communication.

The amount of information that an electromagnetic wave can carry is related to its bandwidth. With current technology, it is possible to encode a few bits per Hertz at low frequencies, but often as many as 8 at high frequencies, so a coaxial cable with a 750 MHz bandwidth can carry several gigabits/sec. From Fig. 2-11 it should now be obvious why networking people like fiber optics so much.

If we solve Eq. (2-2) for f and differentiate with respect to λ, we get

$$\frac{df}{d\lambda} = -\frac{c}{\lambda^2}$$

If we now go to finite differences instead of differentials and only look at absolute values, we get

$$\Delta f = \frac{c\Delta\lambda}{\lambda^2} \tag{2-3}$$

Thus, given the width of a wavelength band, $\Delta\lambda$, we can compute the corresponding frequency band, Δf, and from that the data rate the band can produce. The wider the band, the higher the data rate. As an example, consider the 1.30-micron band of Fig. 2-6. Here we have $\lambda = 1.3 \times 10^{-6}$ and $\Delta\lambda = 0.17 \times 10^{-6}$, so Δf is about 30 THz. At, say, 8 bits/Hz, we get 240 Tbps.

Most transmissions use a narrow frequency band (i.e., $\Delta f/f \ll 1$) to get the best reception (many watts/Hz). However, in some cases, a wide band is used, with two variations. In **frequency hopping spread spectrum**, the transmitter hops from frequency to frequency hundreds of times per second. It is popular for military communication because it makes transmissions hard to detect and next to impossible to jam. It also offers good resistance to multipath fading because the direct signal always arrives at the receiver first. Reflected signals follow a longer path and arrive later. By then the receiver may have changed frequency and no longer accepts signals on the previous frequency, thus eliminating interference between the direct and reflected signals. In recent years, this technique has also been applied commercially—both 802.11 and Bluetooth use it, for example.

As a curious footnote, the technique was co-invented by the Austrian-born sex goddess Hedy Lamarr, the first woman to appear nude in a motion picture (the 1933 Czech film *Extase*). Her first husband was an armaments manufacturer who told her how easy it was to block the radio signals then used to control torpedos. When she discovered that he was selling weapons to Hitler, she was horrified, disguised herself as a maid to escape him, and fled to Hollywood to continue her career as a movie actress. In her spare time, she invented frequency hopping to help the Allied war effort. Her scheme used 88 frequencies, the number of keys (and frequencies) on the piano. For their invention, she and her friend, the musical composer George Antheil, received U.S. patent 2,292,387. However, they were unable to convince the U.S. Navy that their invention had any practical use and never received any royalties. Only years after the patent expired did it become popular.

The other form of spread spectrum, **direct sequence spread spectrum**, which spreads the signal over a wide frequency band, is also gaining popularity in the commercial world. In particular, some second-generation mobile phones use it, and it will become dominant with the third generation, thanks to its good spectral efficiency, noise immunity, and other properties. Some wireless LANs also use it. We will come back to spread spectrum later in this chapter. For a fascinating and detailed history of spread spectrum communication, see (Scholtz, 1982).

For the moment, we will assume that all transmissions use a narrow frequency band. We will now discuss how the various parts of the electromagnetic spectrum of Fig. 2-11 are used, starting with radio.

2.3.2 Radio Transmission

Radio waves are easy to generate, can travel long distances, and can penetrate buildings easily, so they are widely used for communication, both indoors and outdoors. Radio waves also are omnidirectional, meaning that they travel in all directions from the source, so the transmitter and receiver do not have to be carefully aligned physically.

Sometimes omnidirectional radio is good, but sometimes it is bad. In the 1970s, General Motors decided to equip all its new Cadillacs with computer-controlled antilock brakes. When the driver stepped on the brake pedal, the computer pulsed the brakes on and off instead of locking them on hard. One fine day an Ohio Highway Patrolman began using his new mobile radio to call headquarters, and suddenly the Cadillac next to him began behaving like a bucking bronco. When the officer pulled the car over, the driver claimed that he had done nothing and that the car had gone crazy.

Eventually, a pattern began to emerge: Cadillacs would sometimes go berserk, but only on major highways in Ohio and then only when the Highway Patrol was watching. For a long, long time General Motors could not understand why Cadillacs worked fine in all the other states and also on minor roads in Ohio. Only after much searching did they discover that the Cadillac's wiring made a fine antenna for the frequency used by the Ohio Highway Patrol's new radio system.

The properties of radio waves are frequency dependent. At low frequencies, radio waves pass through obstacles well, but the power falls off sharply with distance from the source, roughly as $1/r^2$ in air. At high frequencies, radio waves tend to travel in straight lines and bounce off obstacles. They are also absorbed by rain. At all frequencies, radio waves are subject to interference from motors and other electrical equipment.

Due to radio's ability to travel long distances, interference between users is a problem. For this reason, all governments tightly license the use of radio transmitters, with one exception, discussed below.

In the VLF, LF, and MF bands, radio waves follow the ground, as illustrated in Fig. 2-12(a). These waves can be detected for perhaps 1000 km at the lower frequencies, less at the higher ones. AM radio broadcasting uses the MF band, which is why the ground waves from Boston AM radio stations cannot be heard easily in New York. Radio waves in these bands pass through buildings easily, which is why portable radios work indoors. The main problem with using these bands for data communication is their low bandwidth [see Eq. (2-3)].

In the HF and VHF bands, the ground waves tend to be absorbed by the earth. However, the waves that reach the ionosphere, a layer of charged particles circling the earth at a height of 100 to 500 km, are refracted by it and sent back to earth, as shown in Fig. 2-12(b). Under certain atmospheric conditions, the signals can bounce several times. Amateur radio operators (hams) use these bands to talk long distance. The military also communicate in the HF and VHF bands.

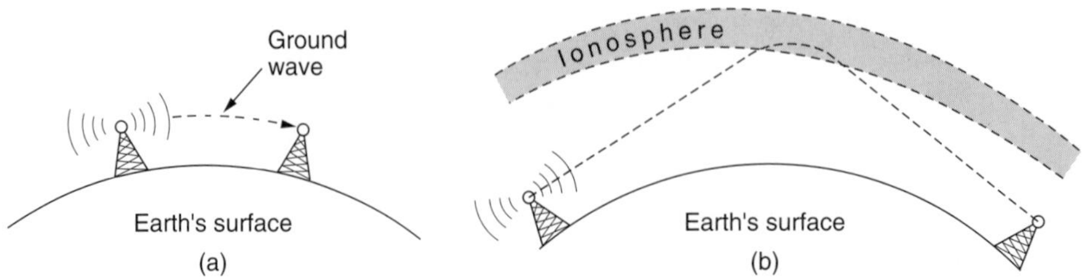

Figure 2-12. (a) In the VLF, LF, and MF bands, radio waves follow the curvature of the earth. (b) In the HF band, they bounce off the ionosphere.

2.3.3 Microwave Transmission

Above 100 MHz, the waves travel in nearly straight lines and can therefore be narrowly focused. Concentrating all the energy into a small beam by means of a parabolic antenna (like the familiar satellite TV dish) gives a much higher signal-to-noise ratio, but the transmitting and receiving antennas must be accurately aligned with each other. In addition, this directionality allows multiple transmitters lined up in a row to communicate with multiple receivers in a row without interference, provided some minimum spacing rules are observed. Before fiber optics, for decades these microwaves formed the heart of the long-distance telephone transmission system. In fact, MCI, one of AT&T's first competitors after it was deregulated, built its entire system with microwave communications going from tower to tower tens of kilometers apart. Even the company's name reflected this (MCI stood for Microwave Communications, Inc.). MCI has since gone over to fiber and merged with WorldCom.

Since the microwaves travel in a straight line, if the towers are too far apart, the earth will get in the way (think about a San Francisco to Amsterdam link). Consequently, repeaters are needed periodically. The higher the towers are, the farther apart they can be. The distance between repeaters goes up very roughly with the square root of the tower height. For 100-meter-high towers, repeaters can be spaced 80 km apart.

Unlike radio waves at lower frequencies, microwaves do not pass through buildings well. In addition, even though the beam may be well focused at the transmitter, there is still some divergence in space. Some waves may be refracted off low-lying atmospheric layers and may take slightly longer to arrive than the direct waves. The delayed waves may arrive out of phase with the direct wave and thus cancel the signal. This effect is called **multipath fading** and is often a serious problem. It is weather and frequency dependent. Some operators keep 10 percent of their channels idle as spares to switch on when multipath fading wipes out some frequency band temporarily.

The demand for more and more spectrum drives operators to yet higher frequencies. Bands up to 10 GHz are now in routine use, but at about 4 GHz a new problem sets in: absorption by water. These waves are only a few centimeters long and are absorbed by rain. This effect would be fine if one were planning to build a huge outdoor microwave oven for roasting passing birds, but for communication, it is a severe problem. As with multipath fading, the only solution is to shut off links that are being rained on and route around them.

In summary, microwave communication is so widely used for long-distance telephone communication, mobile phones, television distribution, and other uses that a severe shortage of spectrum has developed. It has several significant advantages over fiber. The main one is that no right of way is needed, and by buying a small plot of ground every 50 km and putting a microwave tower on it, one can bypass the telephone system and communicate directly. This is how MCI managed to get started as a new long-distance telephone company so quickly. (Sprint went a completely different route: it was formed by the Southern Pacific Railroad, which already owned a large amount of right of way and just buried fiber next to the tracks.)

Microwave is also relatively inexpensive. Putting up two simple towers (may be just big poles with four guy wires) and putting antennas on each one may be cheaper than burying 50 km of fiber through a congested urban area or up over a mountain, and it may also be cheaper than leasing the telephone company's fiber, especially if the telephone company has not yet even fully paid for the copper it ripped out when it put in the fiber.

The Politics of the Electromagnetic Spectrum

To prevent total chaos, there are national and international agreements about who gets to use which frequencies. Since everyone wants a higher data rate, everyone wants more spectrum. National governments allocate spectrum for AM and FM radio, television, and mobile phones, as well as for telephone companies, police, maritime, navigation, military, government, and many other competing users. Worldwide, an agency of ITU-R (WARC) tries to coordinate this allocation so devices that work in multiple countries can be manufactured. However, countries are not bound by ITU-R's recommendations, and the FCC (Federal Communication Commission), which does the allocation for the United States, has occasionally rejected ITU-R's recommendations (usually because they required some politically-powerful group giving up some piece of the spectrum).

Even when a piece of spectrum has been allocated to some use, such as mobile phones, there is the additional issue of which carrier is allowed to use which frequencies. Three algorithms were widely used in the past. The oldest algorithm, often called the **beauty contest**, requires each carrier to explain why its proposal serves the public interest best. Government officials then decide which of the nice stories they enjoy most. Having some government official award property worth billions of dollars to his favorite company often leads to bribery, corruption, nepotism, and worse. Furthermore, even a scrupulously honest government official who thought that a foreign company could do a better job than any of the national companies would have a lot of explaining to do.

This observation led to algorithm 2, holding a lottery among the interested companies. The problem with that idea is that companies with no interest in using the spectrum can enter the lottery. If, say, a fast food restaurant or shoe store chain wins, it can resell the spectrum to a carrier at a huge profit and with no risk.

Bestowing huge windfalls on alert, but otherwise random, companies has been severely criticized by many, which led to algorithm 3: auctioning off the bandwidth to the highest bidder. When England auctioned off the frequencies needed for third-generation mobile systems in 2000, they expected to get about $4 billion. They actually received about $40 billion because the carriers got into a feeding frenzy, scared to death of missing the mobile boat. This event switched on nearby governments' greedy bits and inspired them to hold their own auctions. It worked, but it also left some of the carriers with so much debt that they are close to bankruptcy. Even in the best cases, it will take many years to recoup the licensing fee.

A completely different approach to allocating frequencies is to not allocate them at all. Just let everyone transmit at will but regulate the power used so that stations have such a short range they do not interfere with each other. Accordingly, most governments have set aside some frequency bands, called the **ISM** (**Industrial, Scientific, Medical**) bands for unlicensed usage. Garage door openers, cordless phones, radio-controlled toys, wireless mice, and numerous other wireless household devices use the ISM bands. To minimize interference between these uncoordinated devices, the FCC mandates that all devices in the ISM bands use spread spectrum techniques. Similar rules apply in other countries

The location of the ISM bands varies somewhat from country to country. In the United States, for example, devices whose power is under 1 watt can use the bands shown in Fig. 2-13 without requiring a FCC license. The 900-MHz band works best, but it is crowded and not available worldwide. The 2.4-GHz band is available in most countries, but it is subject to interference from microwave ovens and radar installations. Bluetooth and some of the 802.11 wireless LANs operate in this band. The 5.7-GHz band is new and relatively undeveloped, so equipment for it is expensive, but since 802.11a uses it, it will quickly become more popular.

2.3.4 Infrared and Millimeter Waves

Unguided infrared and millimeter waves are widely used for short-range communication. The remote controls used on televisions, VCRs, and stereos all use infrared communication. They are relatively directional, cheap, and easy to build

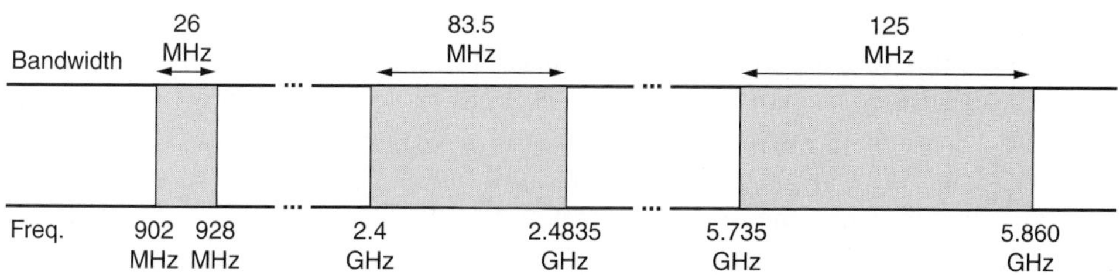

Figure 2-13. The ISM bands in the United States.

but have a major drawback: they do not pass through solid objects (try standing between your remote control and your television and see if it still works). In general, as we go from long-wave radio toward visible light, the waves behave more and more like light and less and less like radio.

On the other hand, the fact that infrared waves do not pass through solid walls well is also a plus. It means that an infrared system in one room of a building will not interfere with a similar system in adjacent rooms or buildings: you cannot control your neighbor's television with your remote control. Furthermore, security of infrared systems against eavesdropping is better than that of radio systems precisely for this reason. Therefore, no government license is needed to operate an infrared system, in contrast to radio systems, which must be licensed outside the ISM bands. Infrared communication has a limited use on the desktop, for example, connecting notebook computers and printers, but it is not a major player in the communication game.

2.3.5 Lightwave Transmission

Unguided optical signaling has been in use for centuries. Paul Revere used binary optical signaling from the Old North Church just prior to his famous ride. A more modern application is to connect the LANs in two buildings via lasers mounted on their rooftops. Coherent optical signaling using lasers is inherently unidirectional, so each building needs its own laser and its own photodetector. This scheme offers very high bandwidth and very low cost. It is also relatively easy to install and, unlike microwave, does not require an FCC license.

The laser's strength, a very narrow beam, is also its weakness here. Aiming a laser beam 1-mm wide at a target the size of a pin head 500 meters away requires the marksmanship of a latter-day Annie Oakley. Usually, lenses are put into the system to defocus the beam slightly.

A disadvantage is that laser beams cannot penetrate rain or thick fog, but they normally work well on sunny days. However, the author once attended a conference at a modern hotel in Europe at which the conference organizers thoughtfully provided a room full of terminals for the attendees to read their e-mail during boring presentations. Since the local PTT was unwilling to install a large number of telephone lines for just 3 days, the organizers put a laser on the roof and aimed it at their university's computer science building a few kilometers away. They tested it the night before the conference and it worked perfectly. At 9 a.m. the next morning, on a bright sunny day, the link failed completely and stayed down all day. That evening, the organizers tested it again very carefully, and once again it worked absolutely perfectly. The pattern repeated itself for two more days consistently.

After the conference, the organizers discovered the problem. Heat from the sun during the daytime caused convection currents to rise up from the roof of the building, as shown in Fig. 2-14. This turbulent air diverted the beam and made it dance around the detector. Atmospheric "seeing" like this makes the stars twinkle (which is why astronomers put their telescopes on the tops of mountains—to get above as much of the atmosphere as possible). It is also responsible for shimmering roads on a hot day and the wavy images seen when one looks out above a hot radiator.

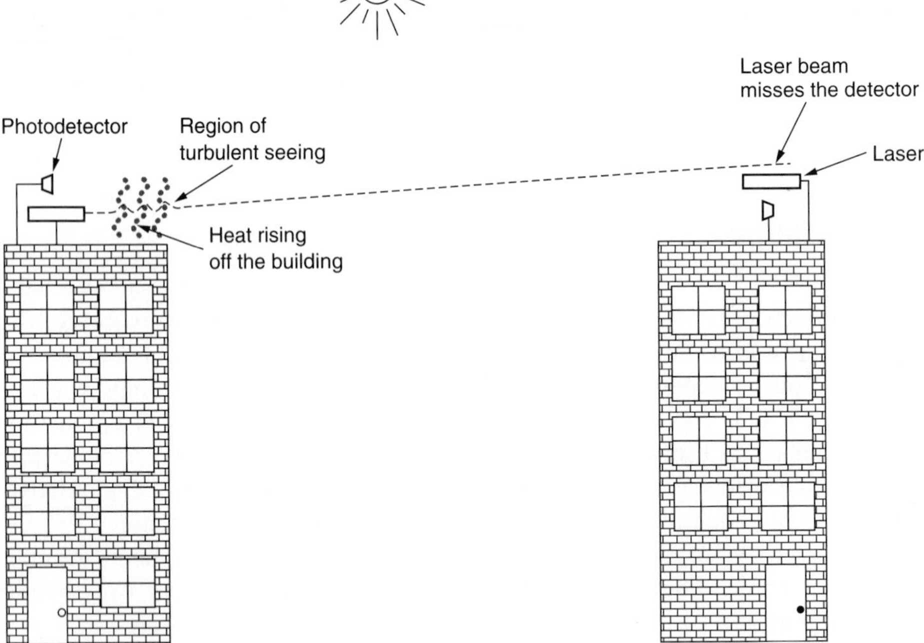

Figure 2-14. Convection currents can interfere with laser communication systems. A bidirectional system with two lasers is pictured here.

2.4 COMMUNICATION SATELLITES

In the 1950s and early 1960s, people tried to set up communication systems by bouncing signals off metallized weather balloons. Unfortunately, the received signals were too weak to be of any practical use. Then the U.S. Navy noticed a kind of permanent weather balloon in the sky—the moon—and built an operational system for ship-to-shore communication by bouncing signals off it.

Further progress in the celestial communication field had to wait until the first communication satellite was launched. The key difference between an artificial satellite and a real one is that the artificial one can amplify the signals before sending them back, turning a strange curiosity into a powerful communication system.

Communication satellites have some interesting properties that make them attractive for many applications. In its simplest form, a communication satellite can be thought of as a big microwave repeater in the sky. It contains several **transponders**, each of which listens to some portion of the spectrum, amplifies the incoming signal, and then rebroadcasts it at another frequency to avoid interference with the incoming signal. The downward beams can be broad, covering a substantial fraction of the earth's surface, or narrow, covering an area only hundreds of kilometers in diameter. This mode of operation is known as a **bent pipe**.

According to Kepler's law, the orbital period of a satellite varies as the radius of the orbit to the 3/2 power. The higher the satellite, the longer the period. Near the surface of the earth, the period is about 90 minutes. Consequently, low-orbit satellites pass out of view fairly quickly, so many of them are needed to provide continuous coverage. At an altitude of about 35,800 km, the period is 24 hours. At an altitude of 384,000 km, the period is about one month, as anyone who has observed the moon regularly can testify.

A satellite's period is important, but it is not the only issue in determining where to place it. Another issue is the presence of the Van Allen belts, layers of highly charged particles trapped by the earth's magnetic field. Any satellite flying within them would be destroyed fairly quickly by the highly-energetic charged particles trapped there by the earth's magnetic field. These factors lead to three regions in which satellites can be placed safely. These regions and some of their properties are illustrated in Fig. 2-15. Below we will briefly describe the satellites that inhabit each of these regions.

2.4.1 Geostationary Satellites

In 1945, the science fiction writer Arthur C. Clarke calculated that a satellite at an altitude of 35,800 km in a circular equatorial orbit would appear to remain motionless in the sky. so it would not need to be tracked (Clarke, 1945). He went on to describe a complete communication system that used these (manned)

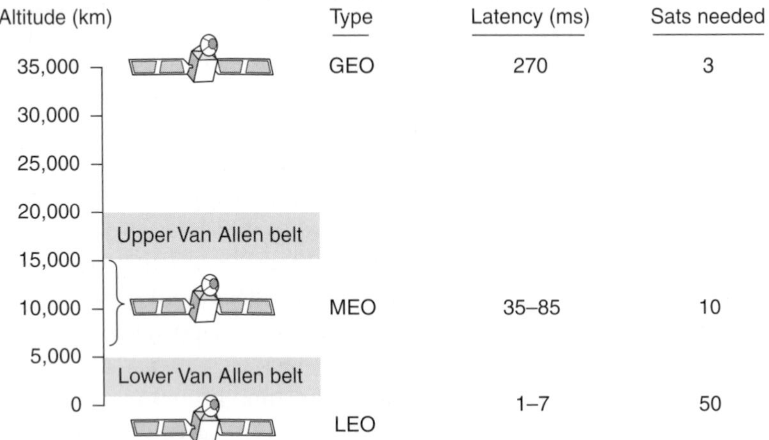

Figure 2-15. Communication satellites and some of their properties, including altitude above the earth, round-trip delay time, and number of satellites needed for global coverage.

geostationary satellites, including the orbits, solar panels, radio frequencies, and launch procedures. Unfortunately, he concluded that satellites were impractical due to the impossibility of putting power-hungry, fragile, vacuum tube amplifiers into orbit, so he never pursued this idea further, although he wrote some science fiction stories about it.

The invention of the transistor changed all that, and the first artificial communication satellite, Telstar, was launched in July 1962. Since then, communication satellites have become a multibillion dollar business and the only aspect of outer space that has become highly profitable. These high-flying satellites are often called **GEO** (**Geostationary Earth Orbit**) satellites.

With current technology, it is unwise to have geostationary satellites spaced much closer than 2 degrees in the 360-degree equatorial plane, to avoid interference. With a spacing of 2 degrees, there can only be 360/2 = 180 of these satellites in the sky at once. However, each transponder can use multiple frequencies and polarizations to increase the available bandwidth.

To prevent total chaos in the sky, orbit slot allocation is done by ITU. This process is highly political, with countries barely out of the stone age demanding "their" orbit slots (for the purpose of leasing them to the highest bidder). Other countries, however, maintain that national property rights do not extend up to the moon and that no country has a legal right to the orbit slots above its territory. To add to the fight, commercial telecommunication is not the only application. Television broadcasters, governments, and the military also want a piece of the orbiting pie.

Modern satellites can be quite large, weighing up to 4000 kg and consuming several kilowatts of electric power produced by the solar panels. The effects of solar, lunar, and planetary gravity tend to move them away from their assigned orbit slots and orientations, an effect countered by on-board rocket motors. This fine-tuning activity is called **station keeping**. However, when the fuel for the motors has been exhausted, typically in about 10 years, the satellite drifts and tumbles helplessly, so it has to be turned off. Eventually, the orbit decays and the satellite reenters the atmosphere and burns up or occasionally crashes to earth.

Orbit slots are not the only bone of contention. Frequencies are, too, because the downlink transmissions interfere with existing microwave users. Consequently, ITU has allocated certain frequency bands to satellite users. The main ones are listed in Fig. 2-16. The C band was the first to be designated for commercial satellite traffic. Two frequency ranges are assigned in it, the lower one for downlink traffic (from the satellite) and the upper one for uplink traffic (to the satellite). To allow traffic to go both ways at the same time, two channels are required, one going each way. These bands are already overcrowded because they are also used by the common carriers for terrestrial microwave links. The L and S bands were added by international agreement in 2000. However, they are narrow and crowded.

Band	Downlink	Uplink	Bandwidth	Problems
L	1.5 GHz	1.6 GHz	15 MHz	Low bandwidth; crowded
S	1.9 GHz	2.2 GHz	70 MHz	Low bandwidth; crowded
C	4.0 GHz	6.0 GHz	500 MHz	Terrestrial interference
Ku	11 GHz	14 GHz	500 MHz	Rain
Ka	20 GHz	30 GHz	3500 MHz	Rain, equipment cost

Figure 2-16. The principal satellite bands.

The next highest band available to commercial telecommunication carriers is the Ku (K under) band. This band is not (yet) congested, and at these frequencies, satellites can be spaced as close as 1 degree. However, another problem exists: rain. Water is an excellent absorber of these short microwaves. Fortunately, heavy storms are usually localized, so using several widely separated ground stations instead of just one circumvents the problem but at the price of extra antennas, extra cables, and extra electronics to enable rapid switching between stations. Bandwidth has also been allocated in the Ka (K above) band for commercial satellite traffic, but the equipment needed to use it is still expensive. In addition to these commercial bands, many government and military bands also exist.

A modern satellite has around 40 transponders, each with an 80-MHz bandwidth. Usually, each transponder operates as a bent pipe, but recent satellites have some on-board processing capacity, allowing more sophisticated operation. In the earliest satellites, the division of the transponders into channels was static: the bandwidth was simply split up into fixed frequency bands. Nowadays, each transponder beam is divided into time slots, with various users taking turns. We will study these two techniques (frequency division multiplexing and time division multiplexing) in detail later in this chapter.

The first geostationary satellites had a single spatial beam that illuminated about 1/3 of the earth's surface, called its **footprint**. With the enormous decline in the price, size, and power requirements of microelectronics, a much more sophisticated broadcasting strategy has become possible. Each satellite is equipped with multiple antennas and multiple transponders. Each downward beam can be focused on a small geographical area, so multiple upward and downward transmissions can take place simultaneously. Typically, these so-called **spot beams** are elliptically shaped, and can be as small as a few hundred km in diameter. A communication satellite for the United States typically has one wide beam for the contiguous 48 states, plus spot beams for Alaska and Hawaii.

A new development in the communication satellite world is the development of low-cost microstations, sometimes called **VSATs (Very Small Aperture Terminals)** (Abramson, 2000). These tiny terminals have 1-meter or smaller antennas (versus 10 m for a standard GEO antenna) and can put out about 1 watt of power. The uplink is generally good for 19.2 kbps, but the downlink is more often 512 kbps or more. Direct broadcast satellite television uses this technology for one-way transmission.

In many VSAT systems, the microstations do not have enough power to communicate directly with one another (via the satellite, of course). Instead, a special ground station, the **hub**, with a large, high-gain antenna is needed to relay traffic between VSATs, as shown in Fig. 2-17. In this mode of operation, either the sender or the receiver has a large antenna and a powerful amplifier. The trade-off is a longer delay in return for having cheaper end-user stations.

VSATs have great potential in rural areas. It is not widely appreciated, but over half the world's population lives over an hour's walk from the nearest telephone. Stringing telephone wires to thousands of small villages is far beyond the budgets of most Third World governments, but installing 1-meter VSAT dishes powered by solar cells is often feasible. VSATs provide the technology that will wire the world.

Communication satellites have several properties that are radically different from terrestrial point-to-point links. To begin with, even though signals to and from a satellite travel at the speed of light (nearly 300,000 km/sec), the long round-trip distance introduces a substantial delay for GEO satellites. Depending on the distance between the user and the ground station, and the elevation of the satellite above the horizon, the end-to-end transit time is between 250 and 300 msec. A typical value is 270 msec (540 msec for a VSAT system with a hub).

For comparison purposes, terrestrial microwave links have a propagation delay of roughly 3 μsec/km, and coaxial cable or fiber optic links have a delay of approximately 5 μsec/km. The latter is slower than the former because electromagnetic signals travel faster in air than in solid materials.

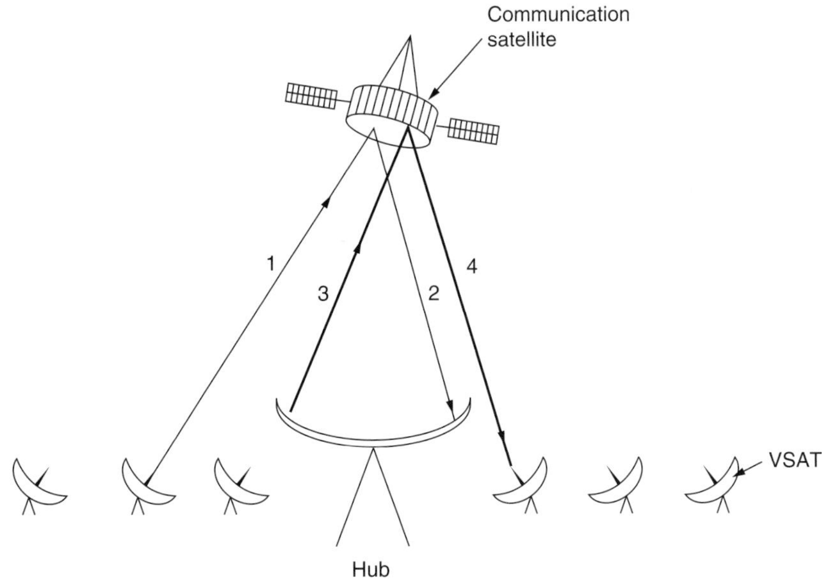

Figure 2-17. VSATs using a hub.

Another important property of satellites is that they are inherently broadcast media. It does not cost more to send a message to thousands of stations within a transponder's footprint than it does to send to one. For some applications, this property is very useful. For example, one could imagine a satellite broadcasting popular Web pages to the caches of a large number of computers spread over a wide area. Even when broadcasting can be simulated with point-to-point lines, satellite broadcasting may be much cheaper. On the other hand, from a security and privacy point of view, satellites are a complete disaster: everybody can hear everything. Encryption is essential when security is required.

Satellites also have the property that the cost of transmitting a message is independent of the distance traversed. A call across the ocean costs no more to service than a call across the street. Satellites also have excellent error rates and can be deployed almost instantly, a major consideration for military communication.

2.4.2 Medium-Earth Orbit Satellites

At much lower altitudes, between the two Van Allen belts, we find the **MEO** (**Medium-Earth Orbit**) satellites. As viewed from the earth, these drift slowly in longitude, taking something like 6 hours to circle the earth. Accordingly, they must be tracked as they move through the sky. Because they are lower than the GEOs, they have a smaller footprint on the ground and require less powerful transmitters to reach them. Currently they are not used for telecommunications, so we will not examine them further here. The 24 **GPS** (**Global Positioning System**) satellites orbiting at about 18,000 km are examples of MEO satellites.

2.4.3 Low-Earth Orbit Satellites

Moving down in altitude, we come to the **LEO** (**Low-Earth Orbit**) satellites. Due to their rapid motion, large numbers of them are needed for a complete system. On the other hand, because the satellites are so close to the earth, the ground stations do not need much power, and the round-trip delay is only a few milliseconds. In this section we will examine three examples, two aimed at voice communication and one aimed at Internet service.

Iridium

As mentioned above, for the first 30 years of the satellite era, low-orbit satellites were rarely used because they zip into and out of view so quickly. In 1990, Motorola broke new ground by filing an application with the FCC asking for permission to launch 77 low-orbit satellites for the Iridium project (element 77 is iridium). The plan was later revised to use only 66 satellites, so the project should have been renamed Dysprosium (element 66), but that probably sounded too much like a disease. The idea was that as soon as one satellite went out of view, another would replace it. This proposal set off a feeding frenzy among other communication companies. All of a sudden, everyone wanted to launch a chain of low-orbit satellites.

After seven years of cobbling together partners and financing, the partners launched the Iridium satellites in 1997. Communication service began in November 1998. Unfortunately, the commercial demand for large, heavy satellite telephones was negligible because the mobile phone network had grown spectacularly since 1990. As a consequence, Iridium was not profitable and was forced into bankruptcy in August 1999 in one of the most spectacular corporate fiascos in history. The satellites and other assets (worth $5 billion) were subsequently purchased by an investor for $25 million at a kind of extraterrestrial garage sale. The Iridium service was restarted in March 2001.

Iridium's business was (and is) providing worldwide telecommunication service using hand-held devices that communicate directly with the Iridium satellites. It provides voice, data, paging, fax, and navigation service everywhere on land, sea, and air. Customers include the maritime, aviation, and oil exploration industries, as well as people traveling in parts of the world lacking a telecommunications infrastructure (e.g., deserts, mountains, jungles, and some Third World countries).

The Iridium satellites are positioned at an altitude of 750 km, in circular polar orbits. They are arranged in north-south necklaces, with one satellite every 32 degrees of latitude. With six satellite necklaces, the entire earth is covered, as suggested by Fig. 2-18(a). People not knowing much about chemistry can think of this arrangement as a very, very big dysprosium atom, with the earth as the nucleus and the satellites as the electrons.

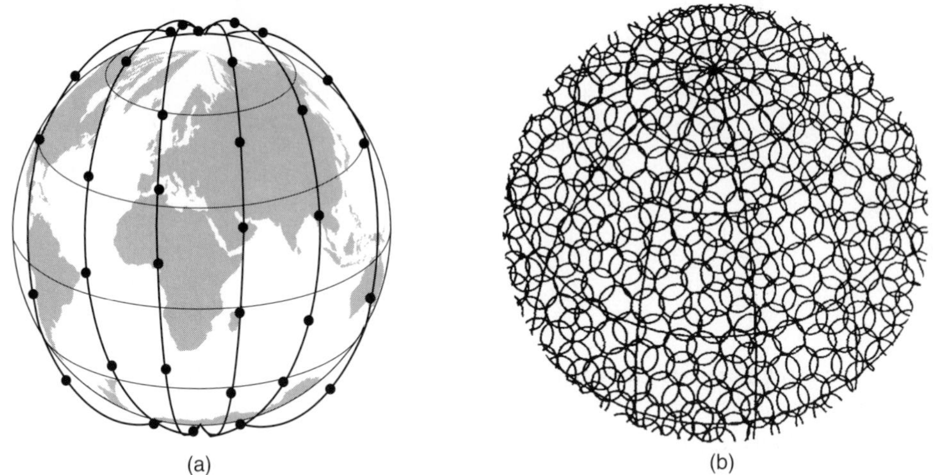

Figure 2-18. (a) The Iridium satellites form six necklaces around the earth. (b) 1628 moving cells cover the earth.

Each satellite has a maximum of 48 cells (spot beams), with a total of 1628 cells over the surface of the earth, as shown in Fig. 2-18(b). Each satellite has a capacity of 3840 channels, or 253,440 in all. Some of these are used for paging and navigation, while others are used for data and voice.

An interesting property of Iridium is that communication between distant customers takes place in space, with one satellite relaying data to the next one, as illustrated in Fig. 2-19(a). Here we see a caller at the North Pole contacting a satellite directly overhead. The call is relayed via other satellites and finally sent down to the callee at the South Pole.

Globalstar

An alternative design to Iridium is Globalstar. It is based on 48 LEO satellites but uses a different switching scheme than that of Iridium. Whereas Iridium relays calls from satellite to satellite, which requires sophisticated switching equipment in the satellites, Globalstar uses a traditional bent-pipe design. The call originating at the North Pole in Fig. 2-19(b) is sent back to earth and picked up by the large ground station at Santa's Workshop. The call is then routed via a terrestrial network to the ground station nearest the callee and delivered by a bent-pipe connection as shown. The advantage of this scheme is that it puts much

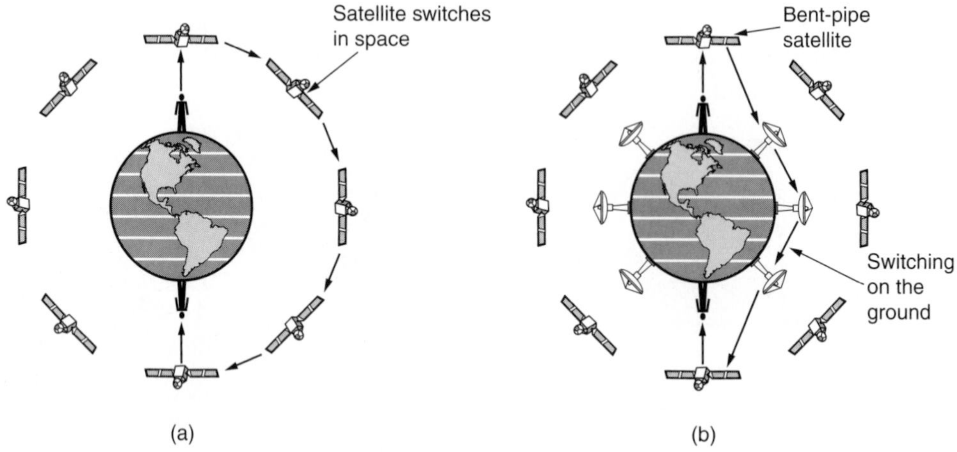

Figure 2-19. (a) Relaying in space. (b) Relaying on the ground.

of the complexity on the ground, where it is easier to manage. Also, the use of large ground station antennas that can put out a powerful signal and receive a weak one means that lower-powered telephones can be used. After all, the telephone puts out only a few milliwatts of power, so the signal that gets back to the ground station is fairly weak, even after having been amplified by the satellite.

Teledesic

Iridium is targeted at telephone users located in odd places. Our next example, **Teledesic**, is targeted at bandwidth-hungry Internet users all over the world. It was conceived in 1990 by mobile phone pioneer Craig McCaw and Microsoft founder Bill Gates, who was unhappy with the snail's pace at which the world's telephone companies were providing high bandwidth to computer users. The goal of the Teledesic system is to provide millions of concurrent Internet users with an uplink of as much as 100 Mbps and a downlink of up to 720 Mbps using a small, fixed, VSAT-type antenna, completely bypassing the telephone system. To telephone companies, this is pie-in-the-sky.

The original design was for a system consisting of 288 small-footprint satellites arranged in 12 planes just below the lower Van Allen belt at an altitude of 1350 km. This was later changed to 30 satellites with larger footprints. Transmission occurs in the relatively uncrowded and high-bandwidth Ka band. The system is packet-switched in space, with each satellite capable of routing packets to its neighboring satellites. When a user needs bandwidth to send packets, it is requested and assigned dynamically in about 50 msec. The system is scheduled to go live in 2005 if all goes as planned.

2.4.4 Satellites versus Fiber

A comparison between satellite communication and terrestrial communication is instructive. As recently as 20 years ago, a case could be made that the future of communication lay with communication satellites. After all, the telephone system had changed little in the past 100 years and showed no signs of changing in the next 100 years. This glacial movement was caused in no small part by the regulatory environment in which the telephone companies were expected to provide good voice service at reasonable prices (which they did), and in return got a guaranteed profit on their investment. For people with data to transmit, 1200-bps modems were available. That was pretty much all there was.

The introduction of competition in 1984 in the United States and somewhat later in Europe changed all that radically. Telephone companies began replacing their long-haul networks with fiber and introduced high-bandwidth services like ADSL (Asymmetric Digital Subscriber Line). They also stopped their long-time practice of charging artificially-high prices to long-distance users to subsidize local service.

All of a sudden, terrestrial fiber connections looked like the long-term winner. Nevertheless, communication satellites have some major niche markets that fiber does not (and, sometimes, cannot) address. We will now look at a few of these.

First, while a single fiber has, in principle, more potential bandwidth than all the satellites ever launched, this bandwidth is not available to most users. The fibers that are now being installed are used within the telephone system to handle many long distance calls at once, not to provide individual users with high bandwidth. With satellites, it is practical for a user to erect an antenna on the roof of the building and completely bypass the telephone system to get high bandwidth. Teledesic is based on this idea.

A second niche is for mobile communication. Many people nowadays want to communicate while jogging, driving, sailing, and flying. Terrestrial fiber optic links are of no use to them, but satellite links potentially are. It is possible, however, that a combination of cellular radio and fiber will do an adequate job for most users (but probably not for those airborne or at sea).

A third niche is for situations in which broadcasting is essential. A message sent by satellite can be received by thousands of ground stations at once. For example, an organization transmitting a stream of stock, bond, or commodity prices to thousands of dealers might find a satellite system to be much cheaper than simulating broadcasting on the ground.

A fourth niche is for communication in places with hostile terrain or a poorly developed terrestrial infrastructure. Indonesia, for example, has its own satellite for domestic telephone traffic. Launching one satellite was cheaper than stringing thousands of undersea cables among the 13,677 islands in the archipelago.

A fifth niche market for satellites is to cover areas where obtaining the right of way for laying fiber is difficult or unduly expensive.

Sixth, when rapid deployment is critical, as in military communication systems in time of war, satellites win easily.

In short, it looks like the mainstream communication of the future will be terrestrial fiber optics combined with cellular radio, but for some specialized uses, satellites are better. However, there is one caveat that applies to all of this: economics. Although fiber offers more bandwidth, it is certainly possible that terrestrial and satellite communication will compete aggressively on price. If advances in technology radically reduce the cost of deploying a satellite (e.g., some future space shuttle can toss out dozens of satellites on one launch) or low-orbit satellites catch on in a big way, it is not certain that fiber will win in all markets.

2.5 THE PUBLIC SWITCHED TELEPHONE NETWORK

When two computers owned by the same company or organization and located close to each other need to communicate, it is often easiest just to run a cable between them. LANs work this way. However, when the distances are large or there are many computers or the cables have to pass through a public road or other public right of way, the costs of running private cables are usually prohibitive. Furthermore, in just about every country in the world, stringing private transmission lines across (or underneath) public property is also illegal. Consequently, the network designers must rely on the existing telecommunication facilities.

These facilities, especially the **PSTN** (**Public Switched Telephone Network**), were usually designed many years ago, with a completely different goal in mind: transmitting the human voice in a more-or-less recognizable form. Their suitability for use in computer-computer communication is often marginal at best, but the situation is rapidly changing with the introduction of fiber optics and digital technology. In any event, the telephone system is so tightly intertwined with (wide area) computer networks, that it is worth devoting some time to studying it.

To see the order of magnitude of the problem, let us make a rough but illustrative comparison of the properties of a typical computer-computer connection via a local cable and via a dial-up telephone line. A cable running between two computers can transfer data at 10^9 bps, maybe more. In contrast, a dial-up line has a maximum data rate of 56 kbps, a difference of a factor of almost 20,000. That is the difference between a duck waddling leisurely through the grass and a rocket to the moon. If the dial-up line is replaced by an ADSL connection, there is still a factor of 1000–2000 difference.

The trouble, of course, is that computer systems designers are used to working with computer systems and when suddenly confronted with another system whose performance (from their point of view) is 3 or 4 orders of magnitude worse, they, not surprising, devoted much time and effort to trying to figure out how to use it efficiently. In the following sections we will describe the telephone system and show how it works. For additional information about the innards of the telephone system see (Bellamy, 2000).

2.5.1 Structure of the Telephone System

Soon after Alexander Graham Bell patented the telephone in 1876 (just a few hours ahead of his rival, Elisha Gray), there was an enormous demand for his new invention. The initial market was for the sale of telephones, which came in pairs. It was up to the customer to string a single wire between them. The electrons returned through the earth. If a telephone owner wanted to talk to *n* other telephone owners, separate wires had to be strung to all *n* houses. Within a year, the cities were covered with wires passing over houses and trees in a wild jumble. It became immediately obvious that the model of connecting every telephone to every other telephone, as shown in Fig. 2-20(a), was not going to work.

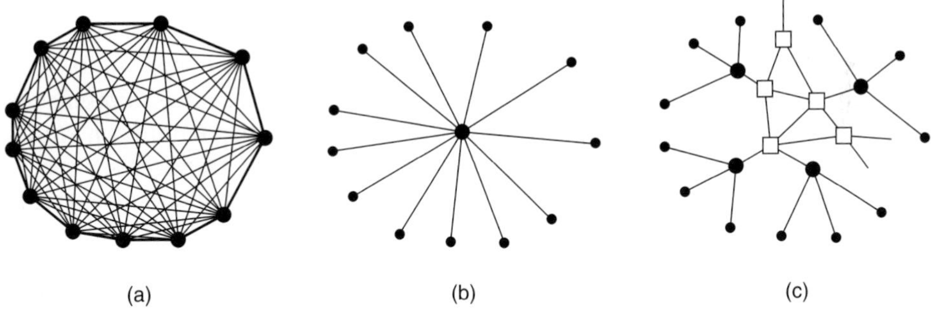

Figure 2-20. (a) Fully-interconnected network. (b) Centralized switch. (c) Two-level hierarchy.

To his credit, Bell saw this and formed the Bell Telephone Company, which opened its first switching office (in New Haven, Connecticut) in 1878. The company ran a wire to each customer's house or office. To make a call, the customer would crank the phone to make a ringing sound in the telephone company office to attract the attention of an operator, who would then manually connect the caller to the callee by using a jumper cable. The model of a single switching office is illustrated in Fig. 2-20(b).

Pretty soon, Bell System switching offices were springing up everywhere and people wanted to make long-distance calls between cities, so the Bell system began to connect the switching offices. The original problem soon returned: to connect every switching office to every other switching office by means of a wire between them quickly became unmanageable, so second-level switching offices were invented. After a while, multiple second-level offices were needed, as illustrated in Fig. 2-20(c). Eventually, the hierarchy grew to five levels.

By 1890, the three major parts of the telephone system were in place: the switching offices, the wires between the customers and the switching offices (by now balanced, insulated, twisted pairs instead of open wires with an earth return), and the long-distance connections between the switching offices. While there have been improvements in all three areas since then, the basic Bell System model has remained essentially intact for over 100 years. For a short technical history of the telephone system, see (Hawley, 1991).

Prior to the 1984 breakup of AT&T, the telephone system was organized as a highly-redundant, multilevel hierarchy. The following description is highly simplified but gives the essential flavor nevertheless. Each telephone has two copper wires coming out of it that go directly to the telephone company's nearest **end office** (also called a **local central office**). The distance is typically 1 to 10 km, being shorter in cities than in rural areas. In the United States alone there are about 22,000 end offices. The two-wire connections between each subscriber's telephone and the end office are known in the trade as the **local loop**. If the world's local loops were stretched out end to end, they would extend to the moon and back 1000 times.

At one time, 80 percent of AT&T's capital value was the copper in the local loops. AT&T was then, in effect, the world's largest copper mine. Fortunately, this fact was not widely known in the investment community. Had it been known, some corporate raider might have bought AT&T, terminated all telephone service in the United States, ripped out all the wire, and sold the wire to a copper refiner to get a quick payback.

If a subscriber attached to a given end office calls another subscriber attached to the same end office, the switching mechanism within the office sets up a direct electrical connection between the two local loops. This connection remains intact for the duration of the call.

If the called telephone is attached to another end office, a different procedure has to be used. Each end office has a number of outgoing lines to one or more nearby switching centers, called **toll offices** (or if they are within the same local area, **tandem offices**). These lines are called **toll connecting trunks**. If both the caller's and callee's end offices happen to have a toll connecting trunk to the same toll office (a likely occurrence if they are relatively close by), the connection may be established within the toll office. A telephone network consisting only of telephones (the small dots), end offices (the large dots), and toll offices (the squares) is shown in Fig. 2-20(c).

If the caller and callee do not have a toll office in common, the path will have to be established somewhere higher up in the hierarchy. Primary, sectional, and regional offices form a network by which the toll offices are connected. The toll, primary, sectional, and regional exchanges communicate with each other via high-bandwidth **intertoll trunks** (also called **interoffice trunks**). The number of different kinds of switching centers and their topology (e.g., can two sectional offices have a direct connection or must they go through a regional office?) varies from country to country depending on the country's telephone density. Figure 2-21 shows how a medium-distance connection might be routed.

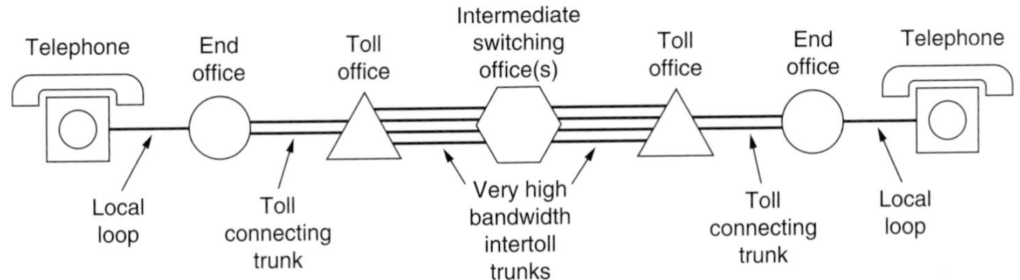

Figure 2-21. A typical circuit route for a medium-distance call.

A variety of transmission media are used for telecommunication. Local loops consist of category 3 twisted pairs nowadays, although in the early days of telephony, uninsulated wires spaced 25 cm apart on telephone poles were common. Between switching offices, coaxial cables, microwaves, and especially fiber optics are widely used.

In the past, transmission throughout the telephone system was analog, with the actual voice signal being transmitted as an electrical voltage from source to destination. With the advent of fiber optics, digital electronics, and computers, all the trunks and switches are now digital, leaving the local loop as the last piece of analog technology in the system. Digital transmission is preferred because it is not necessary to accurately reproduce an analog waveform after it has passed through many amplifiers on a long call. Being able to correctly distinguish a 0 from a 1 is enough. This property makes digital transmission more reliable than analog. It is also cheaper and easier to maintain.

In summary, the telephone system consists of three major components:

1. Local loops (analog twisted pairs going into houses and businesses).
2. Trunks (digital fiber optics connecting the switching offices).
3. Switching offices (where calls are moved from one trunk to another).

After a short digression on the politics of telephones, we will come back to each of these three components in some detail. The local loops provide everyone access to the whole system, so they are critical. Unfortunately, they are also the weakest link in the system. For the long-haul trunks, the main issue is how to collect multiple calls together and send them out over the same fiber. This subject is called multiplexing, and we will study three different ways to do it. Finally, there are two fundamentally different ways of doing switching; we will look at both.

2.5.2 The Politics of Telephones

For decades prior to 1984, the Bell System provided both local and long distance service throughout most of the United States. In the 1970s, the U.S. Federal Government came to believe that this was an illegal monopoly and sued to break it up. The government won, and on January 1, 1984, AT&T was broken up into AT&T Long Lines, 23 **BOC**s (**Bell Operating Companies**), and a few other pieces. The 23 BOCs were grouped into seven regional BOCs (RBOCs) to make them economically viable. The entire nature of telecommunication in the United States was changed overnight by court order (*not* by an act of Congress).

The exact details of the divestiture were described in the so-called **MFJ** (**Modified Final Judgment**, an oxymoron if ever there was one—if the judgment could be modified, it clearly was not final). This event led to increased competition, better service, and lower long distance prices to consumers and businesses. However, prices for local service rose as the cross subsidies from long-distance calling were eliminated and local service had to become self supporting. Many other countries have now introduced competition along similar lines.

To make it clear who could do what, the United States was divided up into 164 **LATA**s (**Local Access and Transport Areas**). Very roughly, a LATA is about as big as the area covered by one area code. Within a LATA, there was one **LEC** (**Local Exchange Carrier**) that had a monopoly on traditional telephone service within its area. The most important LECs were the BOCs, although some LATAs contained one or more of the 1500 independent telephone companies operating as LECs.

All inter-LATA traffic was handled by a different kind of company, an **IXC** (**IntereXchange Carrier**). Originally, AT&T Long Lines was the only serious IXC, but now WorldCom and Sprint are well-established competitors in the IXC business. One of the concerns at the breakup was to ensure that all the IXCs would be treated equally in terms of line quality, tariffs, and the number of digits their customers would have to dial to use them. The way this is handled is illustrated in Fig. 2-22. Here we see three example LATAs, each with several end offices. LATAs 2 and 3 also have a small hierarchy with tandem offices (intra-LATA toll offices).

Any IXC that wishes to handle calls originating in a LATA can build a switching office called a **POP** (**Point of Presence**) there. The LEC is required to connect each IXC to every end office, either directly, as in LATAs 1 and 3, or indirectly, as in LATA 2. Furthermore, the terms of the connection, both technical and financial, must be identical for all IXCs. In this way, a subscriber in, say, LATA 1, can choose which IXC to use for calling subscribers in LATA 3.

As part of the MFJ, the IXCs were forbidden to offer local telephone service and the LECs were forbidden to offer inter-LATA telephone service, although both were free to enter any other business, such as operating fried chicken restaurants. In 1984, that was a fairly unambiguous statement. Unfortunately, technol-

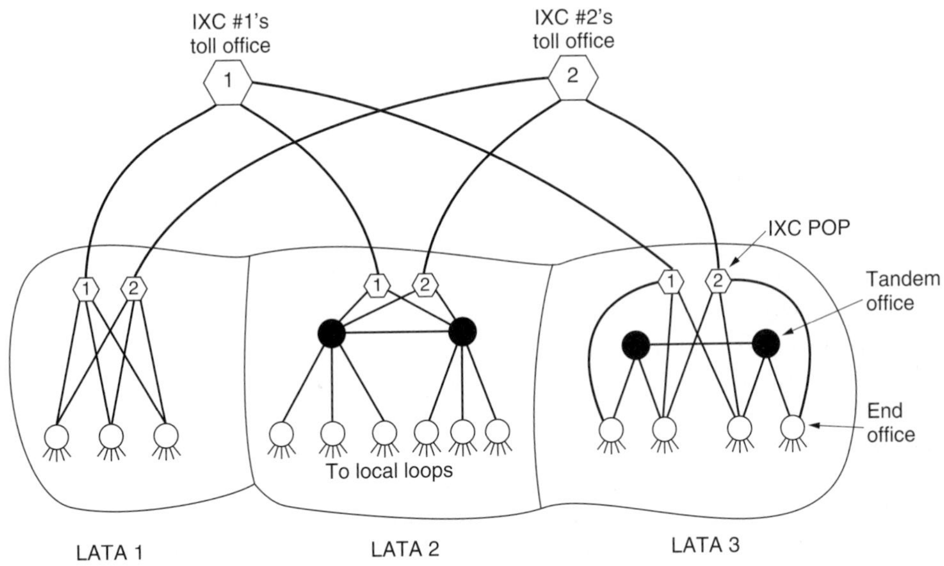

Figure 2-22. The relationship of LATAs, LECs, and IXCs. All the circles are LEC switching offices. Each hexagon belongs to the IXC whose number is in it.

ogy has a funny way of making the law obsolete. Neither cable television nor mobile phones were covered by the agreement. As cable television went from one way to two way and mobile phones exploded in popularity, both LECs and IXCs began buying up or merging with cable and mobile operators.

By 1995, Congress saw that trying to maintain a distinction between the various kinds of companies was no longer tenable and drafted a bill to allow cable TV companies, local telephone companies, long-distance carriers, and mobile operators to enter one another's businesses. The idea was that any company could then offer its customers a single integrated package containing cable TV, telephone, and information services and that different companies would compete on service and price. The bill was enacted into law in February 1996. As a result, some BOCs became IXCs and some other companies, such as cable television operators, began offering local telephone service in competition with the LECs.

One interesting property of the 1996 law is the requirement that LECs implement local number portability. This means that a customer can change local telephone companies without having to get a new telephone number. This provision removes a huge hurdle for many people and makes them much more inclined to switch LECs, thus increasing competition. As a result, the U.S. telecommunications landscape is currently undergoing a radical restructuring. Again, many other countries are starting to follow suit. Often other countries wait to see how this kind of experiment works out in the U.S. If it works well, they do the same thing; if it works badly, they try something else.

2.5.3 The Local Loop: Modems, ADSL, and Wireless

It is now time to start our detailed study of how the telephone system works. The main parts of the system are illustrated in Fig. 2-23. Here we see the local loops, the trunks, and the toll offices and end offices, both of which contain switching equipment that switches calls. An end office has up to 10,000 local loops (in the U.S. and other large countries). In fact, until recently, the area code + exchange indicated the end office, so (212) 601-xxxx was a specific end office with 10,000 subscribers, numbered 0000 through 9999. With the advent of competition for local service, this system was no longer tenable because multiple companies wanted to own the end office code. Also, the number of codes was basically used up, so complex mapping schemes had to be introduced.

Let us begin with the part that most people are familiar with: the two-wire local loop coming from a telephone company end office into houses and small businesses. The local loop is also frequently referred to as the "last mile," although the length can be up to several miles. It has used analog signaling for over 100 years and is likely to continue doing so for some years to come, due to the high cost of converting to digital. Nevertheless, even in this last bastion of analog transmission, change is taking place. In this section we will study the traditional local loop and the new developments taking place here, with particular emphasis on data communication from home computers.

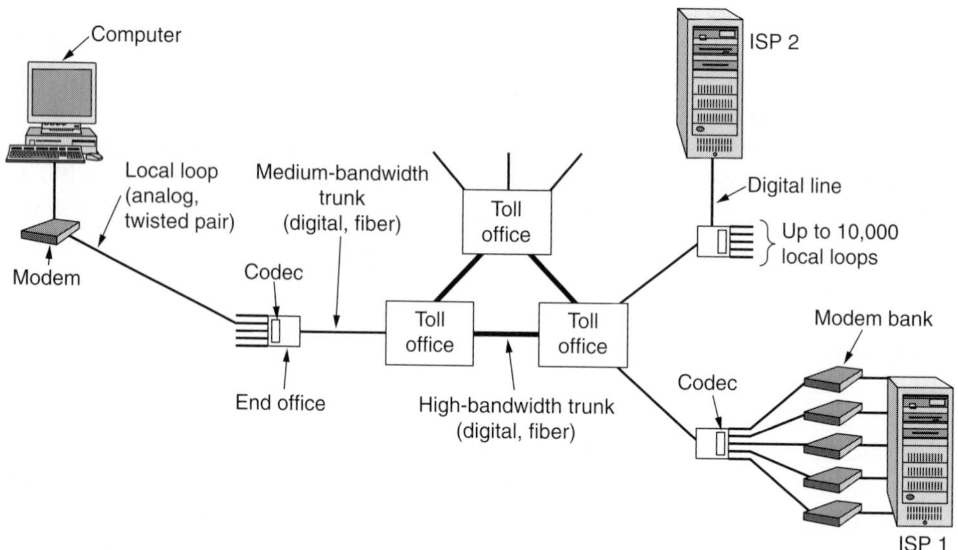

Figure 2-23. The use of both analog and digital transmission for a computer to computer call. Conversion is done by the modems and codecs.

When a computer wishes to send digital data over an analog dial-up line, the data must first be converted to analog form for transmission over the local loop.

This conversion is done by a device called a modem, something we will study shortly. At the telephone company end office the data are converted to digital form for transmission over the long-haul trunks.

If the other end is a computer with a modem, the reverse conversion—digital to analog—is needed to traverse the local loop at the destination. This arrangement is shown in Fig. 2-23 for ISP 1 (Internet Service Provider), which has a bank of modems, each connected to a different local loop. This ISP can handle as many connections as it has modems (assuming its server or servers have enough computing power). This arrangement was the normal one until 56-kbps modems appeared, for reasons that will become apparent shortly.

Analog signaling consists of varying a voltage with time to represent an information stream. If transmission media were perfect, the receiver would receive exactly the same signal that the transmitter sent. Unfortunately, media are not perfect, so the received signal is not the same as the transmitted signal. For digital data, this difference can lead to errors.

Transmission lines suffer from three major problems: attenuation, delay distortion, and noise. **Attenuation** is the loss of energy as the signal propagates outward. The loss is expressed in decibels per kilometer. The amount of energy lost depends on the frequency. To see the effect of this frequency dependence, imagine a signal not as a simple waveform, but as a series of Fourier components. Each component is attenuated by a different amount, which results in a different Fourier spectrum at the receiver.

To make things worse, the different Fourier components also propagate at different speeds in the wire. This speed difference leads to **distortion** of the signal received at the other end.

Another problem is **noise**, which is unwanted energy from sources other than the transmitter. Thermal noise is caused by the random motion of the electrons in a wire and is unavoidable. Crosstalk is caused by inductive coupling between two wires that are close to each other. Sometimes when talking on the telephone, you can hear another conversation in the background. That is crosstalk. Finally, there is impulse noise, caused by spikes on the power line or other causes. For digital data, impulse noise can wipe out one or more bits.

Modems

Due to the problems just discussed, especially the fact that both attenuation and propagation speed are frequency dependent, it is undesirable to have a wide range of frequencies in the signal. Unfortunately, the square waves used in digital signals have a wide frequency spectrum and thus are subject to strong attenuation and delay distortion. These effects make baseband (DC) signaling unsuitable except at slow speeds and over short distances.

To get around the problems associated with DC signaling, especially on telephone lines, AC signaling is used. A continuous tone in the 1000 to 2000-Hz range, called a **sine wave carrier**, is introduced. Its amplitude, frequency, or phase can be modulated to transmit information. In **amplitude modulation**, two different amplitudes are used to represent 0 and 1, respectively. In **frequency modulation**, also known as **frequency shift keying**, two (or more) different tones are used. (The term **keying** is also widely used in the industry as a synonym for modulation.) In the simplest form of **phase modulation**, the carrier wave is systematically shifted 0 or 180 degrees at uniformly spaced intervals. A better scheme is to use shifts of 45, 135, 225, or 315 degrees to transmit 2 bits of information per time interval. Also, always requiring a phase shift at the end of every time interval, makes it is easier for the receiver to recognize the boundaries of the time intervals.

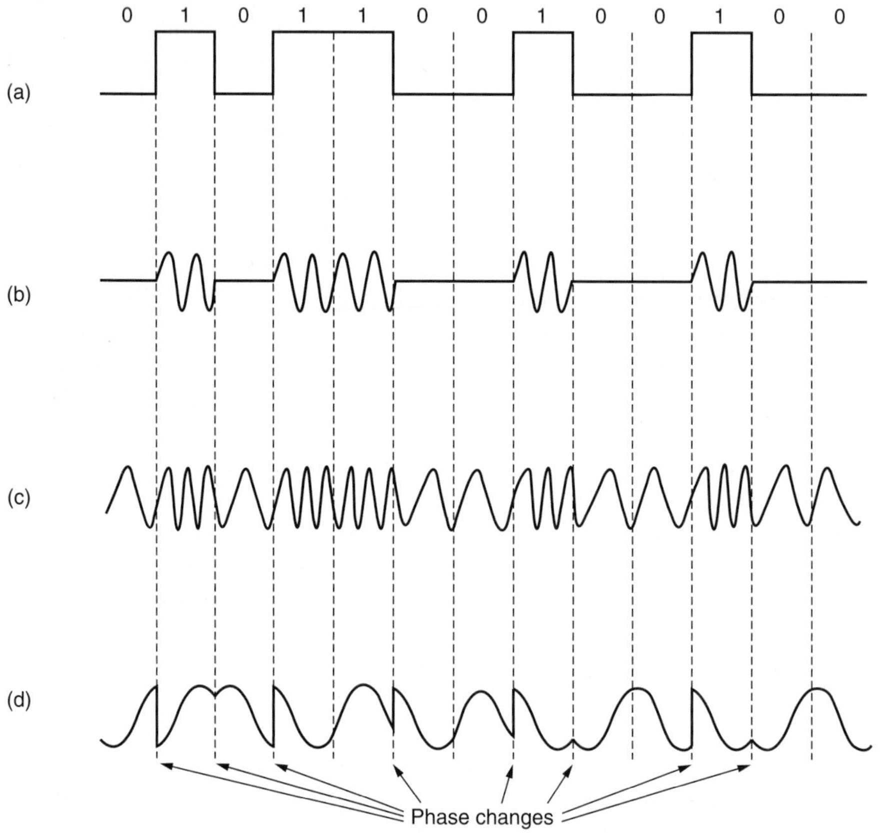

Figure 2-24. (a) A binary signal. (b) Amplitude modulation. (c) Frequency modulation. (d) Phase modulation.

Figure 2-24 illustrates the three forms of modulation. In Fig. 2-24(a) one of the amplitudes is nonzero and one is zero. In Fig. 2-24(b) two frequencies are used. In Fig. 2-24(c) a phase shift is either present or absent at each bit boundary.

A device that accepts a serial stream of bits as input and produces a carrier modulated by one (or more) of these methods (or vice versa) is called a **modem** (for modulator-demodulator). The modem is inserted between the (digital) computer and the (analog) telephone system.

To go to higher and higher speeds, it is not possible to just keep increasing the sampling rate. The Nyquist theorem says that even with a perfect 3000-Hz line (which a dial-up telephone is decidedly not), there is no point in sampling faster than 6000 Hz. In practice, most modems sample 2400 times/sec and focus on getting more bits per sample.

The number of samples per second is measured in **baud**. During each baud, one **symbol** is sent. Thus, an *n*-baud line transmits *n* symbols/sec. For example, a 2400-baud line sends one symbol about every 416.667 μsec. If the symbol consists of 0 volts for a logical 0 and 1 volt for a logical 1, the bit rate is 2400 bps. If, however, the voltages 0, 1, 2, and 3 volts are used, every symbol consists of 2 bits, so a 2400-baud line can transmit 2400 symbols/sec at a data rate of 4800 bps. Similarly, with four possible phase shifts, there are also 2 bits/symbol, so again here the bit rate is twice the baud rate. The latter technique is widely used and called **QPSK** (**Quadrature Phase Shift Keying**).

The concepts of bandwidth, baud, symbol, and bit rate are commonly confused, so let us restate them here. The bandwidth of a medium is the range of frequencies that pass through it with minimum attenuation. It is a physical property of the medium (usually from 0 to some maximum frequency) and measured in Hz. The baud rate is the number of samples/sec made. Each sample sends one piece of information, that is, one symbol. The baud rate and symbol rate are thus the same. The modulation technique (e.g., QPSK) determines the number of bits/symbol. The bit rate is the amount of information sent over the channel and is equal to the number of symbols/sec times the number of bits/symbol.

All advanced modems use a combination of modulation techniques to transmit multiple bits per baud. Often multiple amplitudes and multiple phase shifts are combined to transmit several bits/symbol. In Fig. 2-25(a), we see dots at 45, 135, 225, and 315 degrees with constant amplitude (distance from the origin). The phase of a dot is indicated by the angle a line from it to the origin makes with the positive x-axis. Fig. 2-25(a) has four valid combinations and can be used to transmit 2 bits per symbol. It is QPSK.

In Fig. 2-25(b) we see a different modulation scheme, in which four amplitudes and four phases are used, for a total of 16 different combinations. This modulation scheme can be used to transmit 4 bits per symbol. It is called **QAM-16** (**Quadrature Amplitude Modulation**). Sometimes the term **16-QAM** is used instead. QAM-16 can be used, for example, to transmit 9600 bps over a 2400-baud line.

Figure 2-25(c) is yet another modulation scheme involving amplitude and phase. It allows 64 different combinations, so 6 bits can be transmitted per symbol. It is called **QAM-64**. Higher-order QAMs also are used.

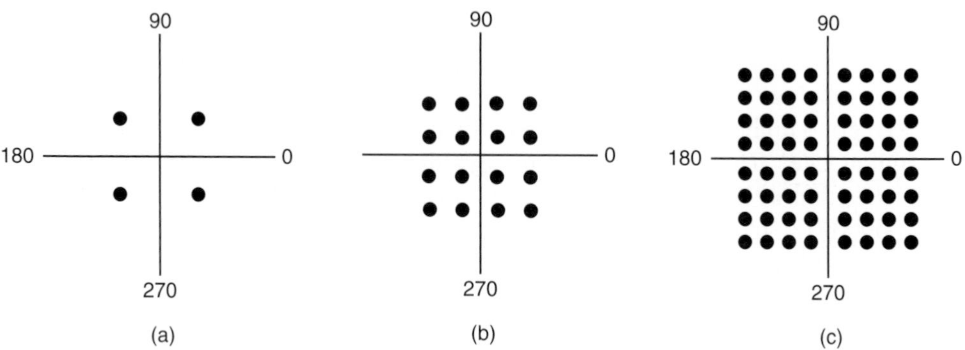

Figure 2-25. (a) QPSK. (b) QAM-16. (c) QAM-64.

Diagrams such as those of Fig. 2-25, which show the legal combinations of amplitude and phase, are called **constellation diagrams**. Each high-speed modem standard has its own constellation pattern and can talk only to other modems that use the same one (although most modems can emulate all the slower ones).

With many points in the constellation pattern, even a small amount of noise in the detected amplitude or phase can result in an error and, potentially, many bad bits. To reduce the chance of an error, standards for the higher speeds modems do error correction by adding extra bits to each sample. The schemes are known as **TCM** (**Trellis Coded Modulation**). Thus, for example, the V.32 modem standard uses 32 constellation points to transmit 4 data bits and 1 parity bit per symbol at 2400 baud to achieve 9600 bps with error correction. Its constellation pattern is shown in Fig. 2-26(a). The decision to "rotate" around the origin by 45 degrees was done for engineering reasons; the rotated and unrotated constellations have the same information capacity.

The next step above 9600 bps is 14,400 bps. It is called **V.32 bis**. This speed is achieved by transmitting 6 data bits and 1 parity bit per sample at 2400 baud. Its constellation pattern has 128 points when QAM-128 is used and is shown in Fig. 2-26(b). Fax modems use this speed to transmit pages that have been scanned in as bit maps. QAM-256 is not used in any standard telephone modems, but it is used on cable networks, as we shall see.

The next telephone modem after V.32 bis is **V.34**, which runs at 28,800 bps at 2400 baud with 12 data bits/symbol. The final modem in this series is **V.34 bis** which uses 14 data bits/symbol at 2400 baud to achieve 33,600 bps.

To increase the effective data rate further, many modems compress the data before transmitting it, to get an effective data rate higher than 33,600 bps. On the other hand, nearly all modems test the line before starting to transmit user data, and if they find the quality lacking, cut back to a speed lower than the rated maximum. Thus, the *effective* modem speed observed by the user can be lower, equal to, or higher than the official rating.

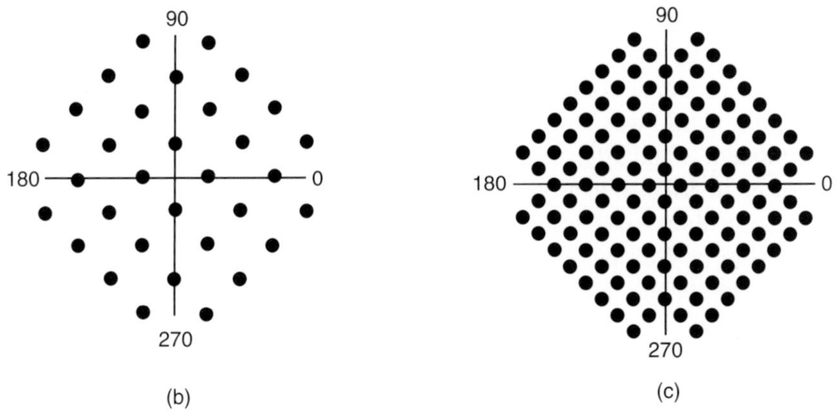

Figure 2-26. (a) V.32 for 9600 bps. (b) V32 bis for 14,400 bps.

All modern modems allow traffic in both directions at the same time (by using different frequencies for different directions). A connection that allows traffic in both directions simultaneously is called **full duplex**. A two-lane road is full duplex. A connection that allows traffic either way, but only one way at a time is called **half duplex**. A single railroad track is half duplex. A connection that allows traffic only one way is called **simplex**. A one-way street is simplex. Another example of a simplex connection is an optical fiber with a laser on one end and a light detector on the other end.

The reason that standard modems stop at 33,600 is that the Shannon limit for the telephone system is about 35 kbps, so going faster than this would violate the laws of physics (department of thermodynamics). To find out whether 56-kbps modems are theoretically possible, stay tuned.

But why is the theoretical limit 35 kbps? It has to do with the average length of the local loops and the quality of these lines. The 35 kbps is determined by the average length of the local loops. In Fig. 2-23, a call originating at the computer on the left and terminating at ISP 1 goes over two local loops as an analog signal, once at the source and once at the destination. Each of these adds noise to the signal. If we could get rid of one of these local loops, the maximum rate would be doubled.

ISP 2 does precisely that. It has a pure digital feed from the nearest end office. The digital signal used on the trunks is fed directly to ISP 2, eliminating the codecs, modems, and analog transmission on its end. Thus, when one end of the connection is purely digital, as it is with most ISPs now, the maximum data rate can be as high as 70 kbps. Between two home users with modems and analog lines, the maximum is 33.6 kbps.

The reason that 56 kbps modems are in use has to do with the Nyquist theorem. The telephone channel is about 4000 Hz wide (including the guard bands).

The maximum number of independent samples per second is thus 8000. The number of bits per sample in the U.S. is 8, one of which is used for control purposes, allowing 56,000 bit/sec of user data. In Europe, all 8 bits are available to users, so 64,000-bit/sec modems could have been used, but to get international agreement on a standard, 56,000 was chosen.

This modem standard is called **V.90**. It provides for a 33.6-kbps upstream channel (user to ISP), but a 56 kbps downstream channel (ISP to user) because there is usually more data transport from the ISP to the user than the other way (e.g., requesting a Web page takes only a few bytes, but the actual page could be megabytes). In theory, an upstream channel wider than 33.6 kbps would have been possible, but since many local loops are too noisy for even 33.6 kbps, it was decided to allocate more of the bandwidth to the downstream channel to increase the chances of it actually working at 56 kbps.

The next step beyond V.90 is **V.92**. These modems are capable of 48 kbps on the upstream channel if the line can handle it. They also determine the appropriate speed to use in about half of the usual 30 seconds required by older modems. Finally, they allow an incoming telephone call to interrupt an Internet session, provided that the line has call waiting service.

Digital Subscriber Lines

When the telephone industry finally got to 56 kbps, it patted itself on the back for a job well done. Meanwhile, the cable TV industry was offering speeds up to 10 Mbps on shared cables, and satellite companies were planning to offer upward of 50 Mbps. As Internet access became an increasingly important part of their business, the telephone companies (LECs) began to realize they needed a more competitive product. Their answer was to start offering new digital services over the local loop. Services with more bandwidth than standard telephone service are sometimes called **broadband**, although the term really is more of a marketing concept than a specific technical concept.

Initially, there were many overlapping offerings, all under the general name of **xDSL** (**Digital Subscriber Line**), for various x. Below we will discuss these but primarily focus on what is probably going to become the most popular of these services, **ADSL** (**Asymmetric DSL**). Since ADSL is still being developed and not all the standards are fully in place, some of the details given below may change in time, but the basic picture should remain valid. For more information about ADSL, see (Summers, 1999; and Vetter et al., 2000).

The reason that modems are so slow is that telephones were invented for carrying the human voice and the entire system has been carefully optimized for this purpose. Data have always been stepchildren. At the point where each local loop terminates in the end office, the wire runs through a filter that attenuates all frequencies below 300 Hz and above 3400 Hz. The cutoff is not sharp—300 Hz and 3400 Hz are the 3 dB points—so the bandwidth is usually quoted as 4000 Hz even though the distance between the 3 dB points is 3100 Hz. Data are thus also restricted to this narrow band.

The trick that makes xDSL work is that when a customer subscribes to it, the incoming line is connected to a different kind of switch, one that does not have this filter, thus making the entire capacity of the local loop available. The limiting factor then becomes the physics of the local loop, not the artificial 3100 Hz bandwidth created by the filter.

Unfortunately, the capacity of the local loop depends on several factors, including its length, thickness, and general quality. A plot of the potential bandwidth as a function of distance is given in Fig. 2-27. This figure assumes that all the other factors are optimal (new wires, modest bundles, etc.).

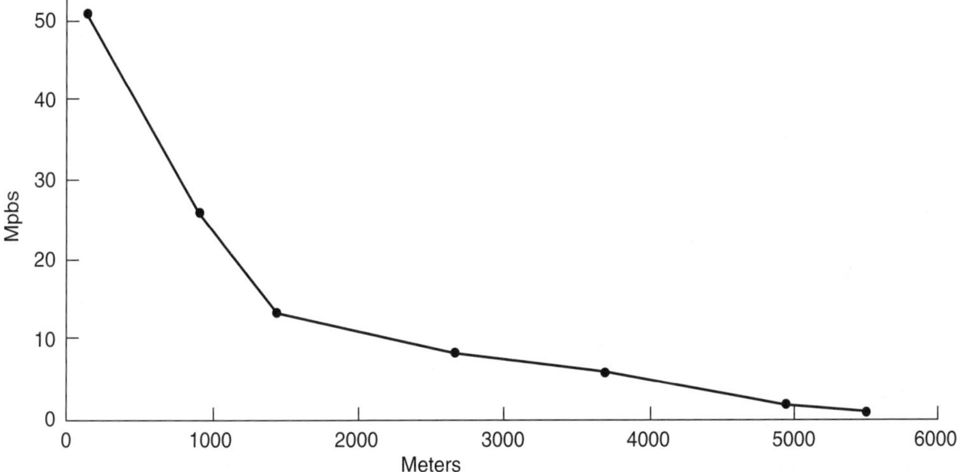

Figure 2-27. Bandwidth versus distance over category 3 UTP for DSL.

The implication of this figure creates a problem for the telephone company. When it picks a speed to offer, it is simultaneously picking a radius from its end offices beyond which the service cannot be offered. This means that when distant customers try to sign up for the service, they may be told "Thanks a lot for your interest, but you live 100 meters too far from the nearest end office to get the service. Could you please move?" The lower the chosen speed, the larger the radius and the more customers covered. But the lower the speed, the less attractive the service and the fewer the people who will be willing to pay for it. This is where business meets technology. (One potential solution is building mini end offices out in the neighborhoods, but that is an expensive proposition.)

The xDSL services have all been designed with certain goals in mind. First, the services must work over the existing category 3 twisted pair local loops. Second, they must not affect customers' existing telephones and fax machines. Third, they must be much faster than 56 kbps. Fourth, they should be always on, with just a monthly charge but no per-minute charge.

The initial ADSL offering was from AT&T and worked by dividing the spectrum available on the local loop, which is about 1.1 MHz, into three frequency bands: **POTS** (**Plain Old Telephone Service**) upstream (user to end office) and downstream (end office to user). The technique of having multiple frequency bands is called frequency division multiplexing; we will study it in detail in a later section. Subsequent offerings from other providers have taken a different approach, and it appears this one is likely to win out, so we will describe it below.

The alternative approach, called **DMT** (**Discrete MultiTone**), is illustrated in Fig. 2-28. In effect, what it does is divide the available 1.1 MHz spectrum on the local loop into 256 independent channels of 4312.5 Hz each. Channel 0 is used for POTS. Channels 1–5 are not used, to keep the voice signal and data signals from interfering with each other. Of the remaining 250 channels, one is used for upstream control and one is used for downstream control. The rest are available for user data.

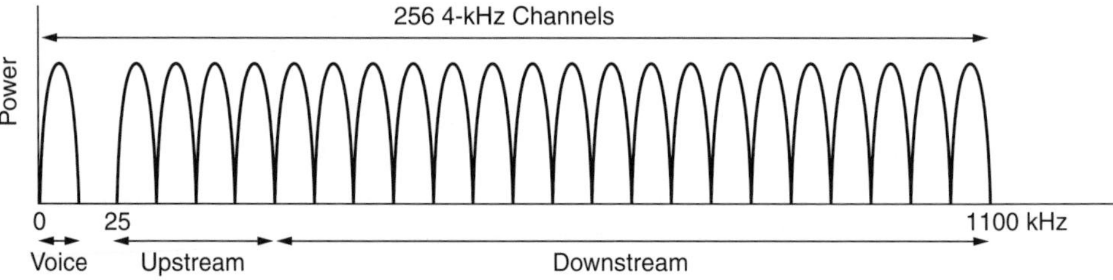

Figure 2-28. Operation of ADSL using discrete multitone modulation.

In principle, each of the remaining channels can be used for a full-duplex data stream, but harmonics, crosstalk, and other effects keep practical systems well below the theoretical limit. It is up to the provider to determine how many channels are used for upstream and how many for downstream. A 50–50 mix of upstream and downstream is technically possible, but most providers allocate something like 80%–90% of the bandwidth to the downstream channel since most users download more data than they upload. This choice gives rise to the "A" in ADSL. A common split is 32 channels for upstream and the rest downstream. It is also possible to have a few of the highest upstream channels be bidirectional for increased bandwidth, although making this optimization requires adding a special circuit to cancel echoes.

The ADSL standard (ANSI T1.413 and ITU G.992.1) allows speeds of as much as 8 Mbps downstream and 1 Mbps upstream. However, few providers offer this speed. Typically, providers offer 512 kbps downstream and 64 kbps upstream (standard service) and 1 Mbps downstream and 256 kbps upstream (premium service).

Within each channel, a modulation scheme similar to V.34 is used, although the sampling rate is 4000 baud instead of 2400 baud. The line quality in each channel is constantly monitored and the data rate adjusted continuously as needed, so different channels may have different data rates. The actual data are sent with QAM modulation, with up to 15 bits per baud, using a constellation diagram analogous to that of Fig. 2-25(b). With, for example, 224 downstream channels and 15 bits/baud at 4000 baud, the downstream bandwidth is 13.44 Mbps. In practice, the signal-to-noise ratio is never good enough to achieve this rate, but 8 Mbps is possible on short runs over high-quality loops, which is why the standard goes up this far.

A typical ADSL arrangement is shown in Fig. 2-29. In this scheme, a telephone company technician must install a **NID** (**Network Interface Device**) on the customer's premises. This small plastic box marks the end of the telephone company's property and the start of the customer's property. Close to the NID (or sometimes combined with it) is a **splitter**, an analog filter that separates the 0-4000 Hz band used by POTS from the data. The POTS signal is routed to the existing telephone or fax machine, and the data signal is routed to an ADSL modem. The ADSL modem is actually a digital signal processor that has been set up to act as 250 QAM modems operating in parallel at different frequencies. Since most current ADSL modems are external, the computer must be connected to it at high speed. Usually, this is done by putting an Ethernet card in the computer and operating a very short two-node Ethernet containing only the computer and ADSL modem. Occasionally the USB port is used instead of Ethernet. In the future, internal ADSL modem cards will no doubt become available.

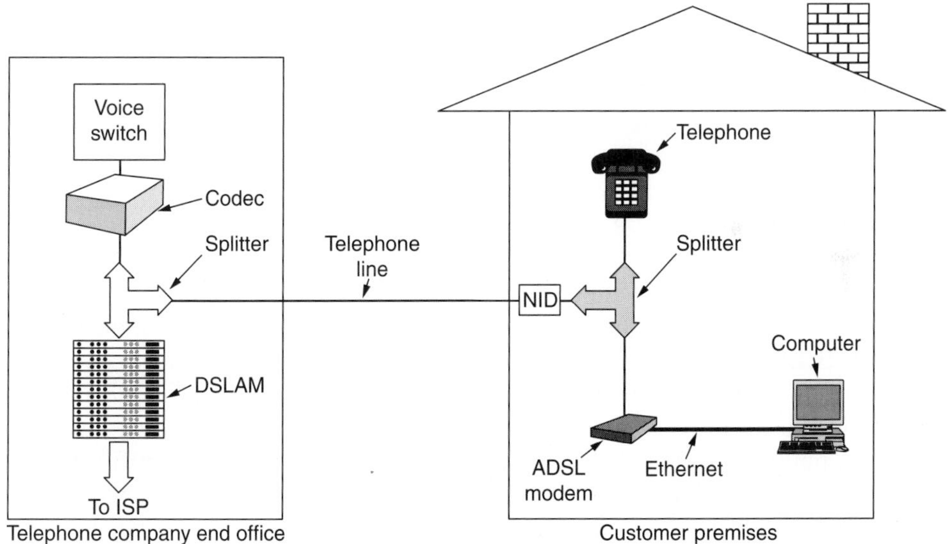

Figure 2-29. A typical ADSL equipment configuration.

At the other end of the wire, on the end office side, a corresponding splitter is installed. Here the voice portion of the signal is filtered out and sent to the normal voice switch. The signal above 26 kHz is routed to a new kind of device called a **DSLAM** (**Digital Subscriber Line Access Multiplexer**), which contains the same kind of digital signal processor as the ADSL modem. Once the digital signal has been recovered into a bit stream, packets are formed and sent off to the ISP.

This complete separation between the voice system and ADSL makes it relatively easy for a telephone company to deploy ADSL. All that is needed is buying a DSLAM and splitter and attaching the ADSL subscribers to the splitter. Other high-bandwidth services (e.g., ISDN) require much greater changes to the existing switching equipment.

One disadvantage of the design of Fig. 2-29 is the presence of the NID and splitter on the customer premises. Installing these can only be done by a telephone company technician, necessitating an expensive "truck roll" (i.e., sending a technician to the customer's premises). Therefore, an alternative splitterless design has also been standardized. It is informally called G.lite but the ITU standard number is G.992.2. It is the same as Fig. 2-29 but without the splitter. The existing telephone line is used as is. The only difference is that a microfilter has to be inserted into each telephone jack between the telephone or ADSL modem and the wire. The microfilter for the telephone is a low-pass filter eliminating frequencies above 3400 Hz; the microfilter for the ADSL modem is a high-pass filter eliminating frequencies below 26 kHz. However this system is not as reliable as having a splitter, so G.lite can be used only up to 1.5 Mbps (versus 8 Mbps for ADSL with a splitter). G.lite still requires a splitter in the end office, however, but that installation does not require thousands of truck rolls.

ADSL is just a physical layer standard. What runs on top of it depends on the carrier. Often the choice is ATM due to ATM's ability to manage quality of service and the fact that many telephone companies run ATM in the core network.

Wireless Local Loops

Since 1996 in the U.S. and a bit later in other countries, companies that wish to compete with the entrenched local telephone company (the former monopolist), called an **ILEC** (**Incumbent LEC**), are free to do so. The most likely candidates are long-distance telephone companies (IXCs). Any IXC wishing to get into the local phone business in some city must do the following things. First, it must buy or lease a building for its first end office in that city. Second, it must fill the end office with telephone switches and other equipment, all of which are available as off-the-shelf products from various vendors. Third, it must run a fiber between the end office and its nearest toll office so the new local customers will have access to its national network. Fourth, it must acquire customers, typically by advertising better service or lower prices than those of the ILEC.

Then the hard part begins. Suppose that some customers actually show up. How is the new local phone company, called a **CLEC** (**Competitive LEC**) going to connect customer telephones and computers to its shiny new end office? Buying the necessary rights of way and stringing wires or fibers is prohibitively expensive. Many CLECs have discovered a cheaper alternative to the traditional twisted-pair local loop: the **WLL** (**Wireless Local Loop**).

In a certain sense, a fixed telephone using a wireless local loop is a bit like a mobile phone, but there are three crucial technical differences. First, the wireless local loop customer often wants high-speed Internet connectivity, often at speeds at least equal to ADSL. Second, the new customer probably does not mind having a CLEC technician install a large directional antenna on his roof pointed at the CLEC's end office. Third, the user does not move, eliminating all the problems with mobility and cell handoff that we will study later in this chapter. And thus a new industry is born: **fixed wireless** (local telephone and Internet service run by CLECs over wireless local loops).

Although WLLs began serious operation in 1998, we first have to go back to 1969 to see the origin. In that year the FCC allocated two television channels (at 6 MHz each) for instructional television at 2.1 GHz. In subsequent years, 31 more channels were added at 2.5 GHz for a total of 198 MHz.

Instructional television never took off and in 1998, the FCC took the frequencies back and allocated them to two-way radio. They were immediately seized upon for wireless local loops. At these frequencies, the microwaves are 10–12 cm long. They have a range of about 50 km and can penetrate vegetation and rain moderately well. The 198 MHz of new spectrum was immediately put to use for wireless local loops as a service called **MMDS** (**Multichannel Multipoint Distribution Service**). MMDS can be regarded as a MAN (Metropolitan Area Network), as can its cousin LMDS (discussed below).

The big advantage of this service is that the technology is well established and the equipment is readily available. The disadvantage is that the total bandwidth available is modest and must be shared by many users over a fairly large geographic area.

The low bandwidth of MMDS led to interest in millimeter waves as an alternative. At frequencies of 28–31 GHz in the U.S. and 40 GHz in Europe, no frequencies were allocated because it is difficult to build silicon integrated circuits that operate so fast. That problem was solved with the invention of gallium arsenide integrated circuits, opening up millimeter bands for radio communication. The FCC responded to the demand by allocating 1.3 GHz to a new wireless local loop service called **LMDS** (**Local Multipoint Distribution Service**). This allocation is the single largest chunk of bandwidth ever allocated by the FCC for any one use. A similar chunk is being allocated in Europe, but at 40 GHz.

The operation of LMDS is shown in Fig. 2-30. Here a tower is shown with multiple antennas on it, each pointing in a different direction. Since millimeter waves are highly directional, each antenna defines a sector, independent of the other ones. At this frequency, the range is 2–5 km, which means that many towers are needed to cover a city.

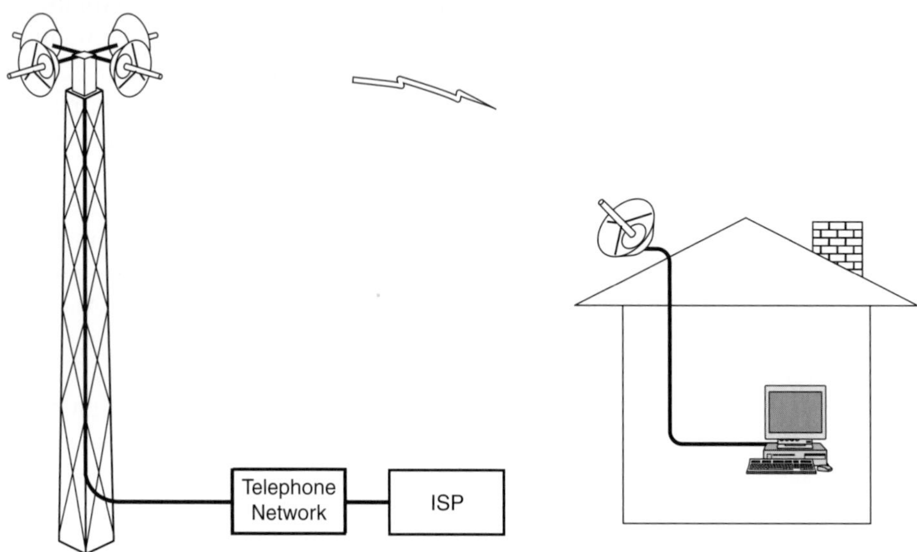

Figure 2-30. Architecture of an LMDS system.

Like ADSL, LMDS uses an asymmetric bandwidth allocation favoring the downstream channel. With current technology, each sector can have 36 Gbps downstream and 1 Mbps upstream, shared among all the users in that sector. If each active user downloads three 5-KB pages per minute, the user is occupying an average of 2000 bps of spectrum, which allows a maximum of 18,000 active users per sector. To keep the delay reasonable, no more than 9000 active users should be supported, though. With four sectors, as shown in Fig. 2-30, an active user population of 36,000 could be supported. Assuming that one in three customers is on line during peak periods, a single tower with four antennas could serve 100,000 people within a 5-km radius of the tower. These calculations have been done by many potential CLECs, some of whom have concluded that for a modest investment in millimeter-wave towers, they can get into the local telephone and Internet business and offer users data rates comparable to cable TV and at a lower price.

LMDS has a few problems, however. For one thing, millimeter waves propagate in straight lines, so there must be a clear line of sight between the roof top antennas and the tower. For another, leaves absorb these waves well, so the tower must be high enough to avoid having trees in the line of sight. And what may have looked like a clear line of sight in December may not be clear in July when the trees are full of leaves. Rain also absorbs these waves. To some extent, errors introduced by rain can be compensated for with error correcting codes or turning up the power when it is raining. Nevertheless, LMDS service is more likely to be rolled out first in dry climates, say, in Arizona rather than in Seattle.

Wireless local loops are not likely to catch on unless there are standards, to encourage equipment vendors to produce products and to ensure that customers can change CLECs without having to buy new equipment. To provide this standardization, IEEE set up a committee called 802.16 to draw up a standard for LMDS. The 802.16 standard was published in April 2002. IEEE calls 802.16 a **wireless MAN**.

IEEE 802.16 was designed for digital telephony, Internet access, connection of two remote LANs, television and radio broadcasting, and other uses. We will look at it in more detail in Chap. 4.

2.5.4 Trunks and Multiplexing

Economies of scale play an important role in the telephone system. It costs essentially the same amount of money to install and maintain a high-bandwidth trunk as a low-bandwidth trunk between two switching offices (i.e., the costs come from having to dig the trench and not from the copper wire or optical fiber). Consequently, telephone companies have developed elaborate schemes for multiplexing many conversations over a single physical trunk. These multiplexing schemes can be divided into two basic categories: **FDM** (**Frequency Division Multiplexing**) and **TDM** (**Time Division Multiplexing**). In FDM, the frequency spectrum is divided into frequency bands, with each user having exclusive possession of some band. In TDM, the users take turns (in a round-robin fashion), each one periodically getting the entire bandwidth for a little burst of time.

AM radio broadcasting provides illustrations of both kinds of multiplexing. The allocated spectrum is about 1 MHz, roughly 500 to 1500 kHz. Different frequencies are allocated to different logical channels (stations), each operating in a portion of the spectrum, with the interchannel separation great enough to prevent interference. This system is an example of frequency division multiplexing. In addition (in some countries), the individual stations have two logical subchannels: music and advertising. These two alternate in time on the same frequency, first a burst of music, then a burst of advertising, then more music, and so on. This situation is time division multiplexing.

Below we will examine frequency division multiplexing. After that we will see how FDM can be applied to fiber optics (wavelength division multiplexing). Then we will turn to TDM, and end with an advanced TDM system used for fiber optics (SONET).

Frequency Division Multiplexing

Figure 2-31 shows how three voice-grade telephone channels are multiplexed using FDM. Filters limit the usable bandwidth to about 3100 Hz per voice-grade channel. When many channels are multiplexed together, 4000 Hz is allocated to each channel to keep them well separated. First the voice channels are raised in frequency, each by a different amount. Then they can be combined because no two channels now occupy the same portion of the spectrum. Notice that even though there are gaps (guard bands) between the channels, there is some overlap between adjacent channels because the filters do not have sharp edges. This overlap means that a strong spike at the edge of one channel will be felt in the adjacent one as nonthermal noise.

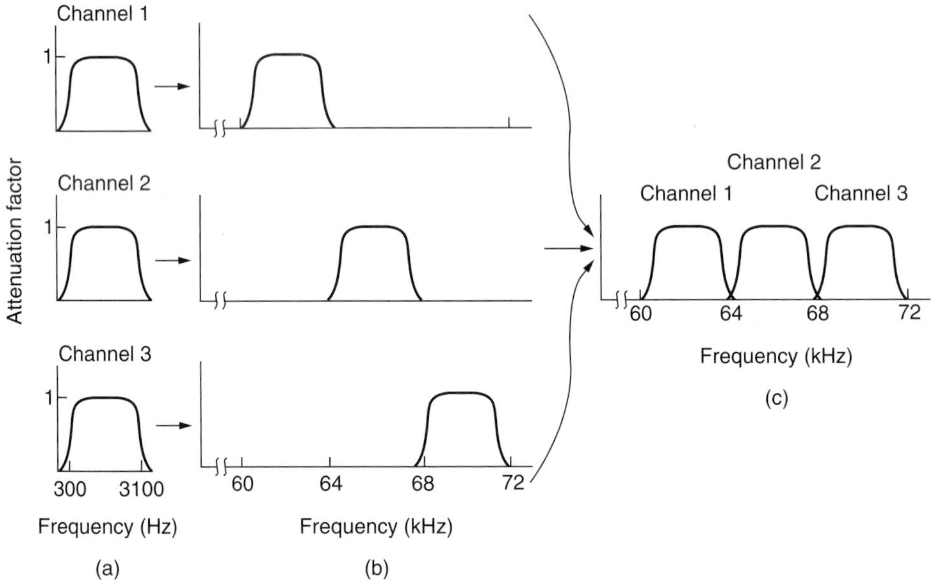

Figure 2-31. Frequency division multiplexing. (a) The original bandwidths. (b) The bandwidths raised in frequency. (c) The multiplexed channel.

The FDM schemes used around the world are to some degree standardized. A widespread standard is twelve 4000-Hz voice channels multiplexed into the 60 to 108 kHz band. This unit is called a **group.** The 12-kHz to 60-kHz band is sometimes used for another group. Many carriers offer a 48- to 56-kbps leased line service to customers, based on the group. Five groups (60 voice channels) can be multiplexed to form a **supergroup**. The next unit is the **mastergroup**, which is five supergroups (CCITT standard) or ten supergroups (Bell system). Other standards of up to 230,000 voice channels also exist.

Wavelength Division Multiplexing

For fiber optic channels, a variation of frequency division multiplexing is used. It is called **WDM (Wavelength Division Multiplexing)**. The basic principle of WDM on fibers is depicted in Fig. 2-32. Here four fibers come together at an optical combiner, each with its energy present at a different wavelength. The four beams are combined onto a single shared fiber for transmission to a distant destination. At the far end, the beam is split up over as many fibers as there were on the input side. Each output fiber contains a short, specially-constructed core that filters out all but one wavelength. The resulting signals can be routed to their destination or recombined in different ways for additional multiplexed transport.

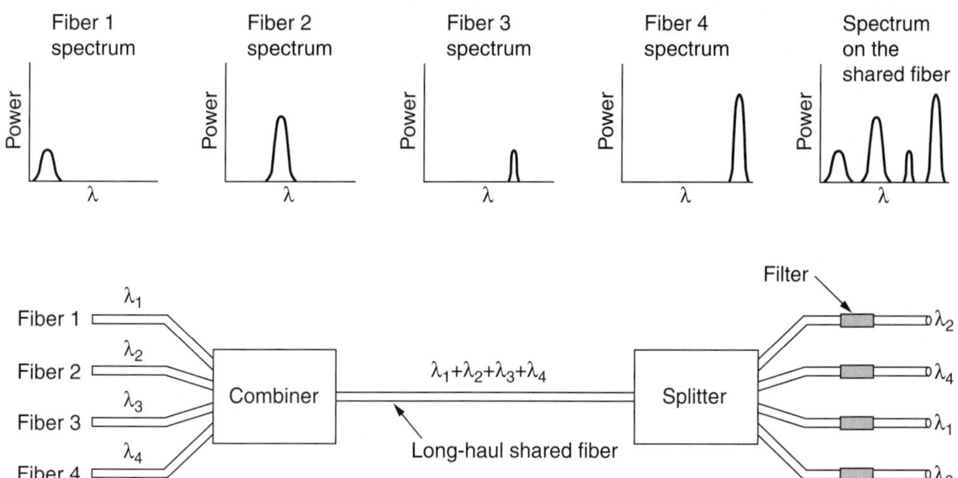

Figure 2-32. Wavelength division multiplexing.

There is really nothing new here. This is just frequency division multiplexing at very high frequencies. As long as each channel has its own frequency (i.e., wavelength) range and all the ranges are disjoint, they can be multiplexed together on the long-haul fiber. The only difference with electrical FDM is that an optical system using a diffraction grating is completely passive and thus highly reliable.

WDM technology has been progressing at a rate that puts computer technology to shame. WDM was invented around 1990. The first commercial systems had eight channels of 2.5 Gbps per channel. By 1998, systems with 40 channels of 2.5 Gbps were on the market. By 2001, there were products with 96 channels of 10 Gbps, for a total of 960 Gbps. This is enough bandwidth to transmit 30 full-length movies per second (in MPEG-2). Systems with 200 channels are already working in the laboratory. When the number of channels is very large and the wavelengths are spaced close together, for example, 0.1 nm, the system is often referred to as **DWDM** (**Dense WDM**).

It should be noted that the reason WDM is popular is that the energy on a single fiber is typically only a few gigahertz wide because it is currently impossible to convert between electrical and optical media any faster. By running many channels in parallel on different wavelengths, the aggregate bandwidth is increased linearly with the number of channels. Since the bandwidth of a single fiber band is about 25,000 GHz (see Fig. 2-6), there is theoretically room for 2500 10-Gbps channels even at 1 bit/Hz (and higher rates are also possible).

Another new development is all optical amplifiers. Previously, every 100 km it was necessary to split up all the channels and convert each one to an electrical signal for amplification separately before reconverting to optical and combining them. Nowadays, all optical amplifiers can regenerate the entire signal once every 1000 km without the need for multiple opto-electrical conversions.

In the example of Fig. 2-32, we have a fixed wavelength system. Bits from input fiber 1 go to output fiber 3, bits from input fiber 2 go to output fiber 1, etc. However, it is also possible to build WDM systems that are switched. In such a device, the output filters are tunable using Fabry-Perot or Mach-Zehnder interferometers. For more information about WDM and its application to Internet packet switching, see (Elmirghani and Mouftah, 2000; Hunter and Andonovic, 2000; and Listani et al., 2001).

Time Division Multiplexing

WDM technology is wonderful, but there is still a lot of copper wire in the telephone system, so let us turn back to it for a while. Although FDM is still used over copper wires or microwave channels, it requires analog circuitry and is not amenable to being done by a computer. In contrast, TDM can be handled entirely by digital electronics, so it has become far more widespread in recent years. Unfortunately, it can only be used for digital data. Since the local loops produce analog signals, a conversion is needed from analog to digital in the end office, where all the individual local loops come together to be combined onto outgoing trunks.

We will now look at how multiple analog voice signals are digitized and combined onto a single outgoing digital trunk. Computer data sent over a modem are also analog, so the following description also applies to them. The analog signals are digitized in the end office by a device called a **codec** (coder-decoder), producing a series of 8-bit numbers. The codec makes 8000 samples per second (125 μsec/sample) because the Nyquist theorem says that this is sufficient to capture all the information from the 4-kHz telephone channel bandwidth. At a lower sampling rate, information would be lost; at a higher one, no extra information would be gained. This technique is called **PCM** (**Pulse Code Modulation**). PCM forms the heart of the modern telephone system. As a consequence, virtually all time intervals within the telephone system are multiples of 125 μsec.

When digital transmission began emerging as a feasible technology, CCITT was unable to reach agreement on an international standard for PCM. Consequently, a variety of incompatible schemes are now in use in different countries around the world.

The method used in North America and Japan is the **T1** carrier, depicted in Fig. 2-33. (Technically speaking, the format is called DS1 and the carrier is called T1, but following widespread industry tradition, we will not make that subtle distinction here.) The T1 carrier consists of 24 voice channels multiplexed together. Usually, the analog signals are sampled on a round-robin basis with the resulting analog stream being fed to the codec rather than having 24 separate codecs and then merging the digital output. Each of the 24 channels, in turn, gets to insert 8 bits into the output stream. Seven bits are data and one is for control, yielding $7 \times 8000 = 56{,}000$ bps of data, and $1 \times 8000 = 8000$ bps of signaling information per channel.

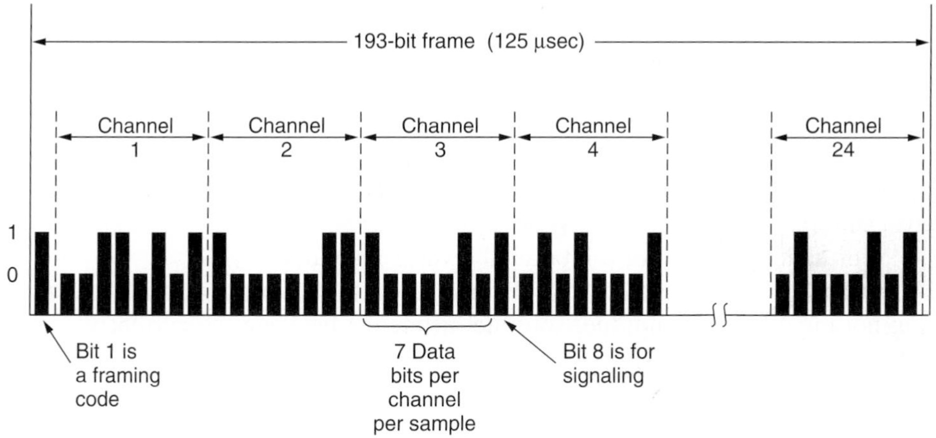

Figure 2-33. The T1 carrier (1.544 Mbps).

A frame consists of $24 \times 8 = 192$ bits plus one extra bit for framing, yielding 193 bits every 125 μsec. This gives a gross data rate of 1.544 Mbps. The 193rd bit is used for frame synchronization. It takes on the pattern 0101010101 . . . . Normally, the receiver keeps checking this bit to make sure that it has not lost synchronization. If it does get out of sync, the receiver can scan for this pattern to get resynchronized. Analog customers cannot generate the bit pattern at all because it corresponds to a sine wave at 4000 Hz, which would be filtered out. Digital customers can, of course, generate this pattern, but the odds are against its being present when the frame slips. When a T1 system is being used entirely for data, only 23 of the channels are used for data. The 24th one is used for a special synchronization pattern, to allow faster recovery in the event that the frame slips.

When CCITT finally did reach agreement, they felt that 8000 bps of signaling information was far too much, so its 1.544-Mbps standard is based on an 8- rather than a 7-bit data item; that is, the analog signal is quantized into 256 rather than 128 discrete levels. Two (incompatible) variations are provided. In **common-channel signaling**, the extra bit (which is attached onto the rear rather than the front of the 193-bit frame) takes on the values 10101010 . . . in the odd frames and contains signaling information for all the channels in the even frames.

In the other variation, **channel-associated signaling**, each channel has its own private signaling subchannel. A private subchannel is arranged by allocating one of the eight user bits in every sixth frame for signaling purposes, so five out of six samples are 8 bits wide, and the other one is only 7 bits wide. CCITT also recommended a PCM carrier at 2.048 Mbps called **E1**. This carrier has 32 8-bit data samples packed into the basic 125-μsec frame. Thirty of the channels are used for information and two are used for signaling. Each group of four frames provides 64 signaling bits, half of which are used for channel-associated signaling and half of which are used for frame synchronization or are reserved for each country to use as it wishes. Outside North America and Japan, the 2.048-Mbps E1 carrier is used instead of T1.

Once the voice signal has been digitized, it is tempting to try to use statistical techniques to reduce the number of bits needed per channel. These techniques are appropriate not only for encoding speech, but for the digitization of any analog signal. All of the compaction methods are based on the principle that the signal changes relatively slowly compared to the sampling frequency, so that much of the information in the 7- or 8-bit digital level is redundant.

One method, called **differential pulse code modulation**, consists of outputting not the digitized amplitude, but the difference between the current value and the previous one. Since jumps of ±16 or more on a scale of 128 are unlikely, 5 bits should suffice instead of 7. If the signal does occasionally jump wildly, the encoding logic may require several sampling periods to "catch up." For speech, the error introduced can be ignored.

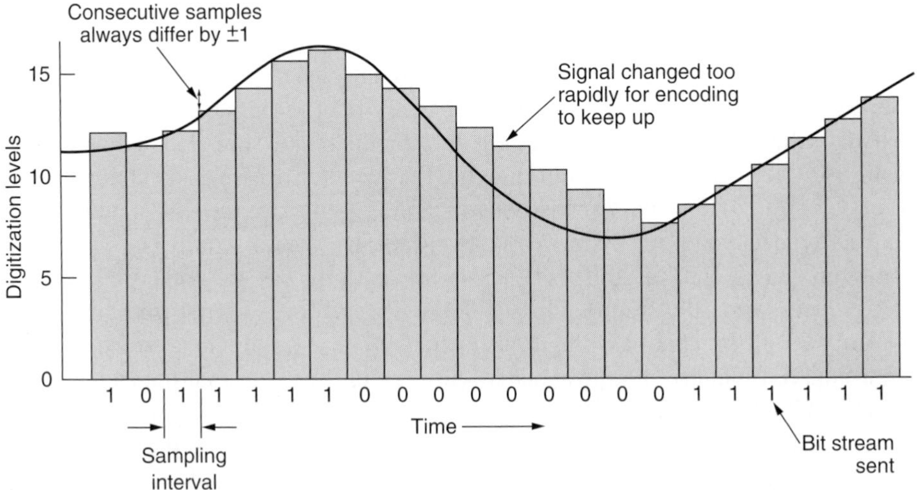

Figure 2-34. Delta modulation.

A variation of this compaction method requires each sampled value to differ from its predecessor by either +1 or −1. Under these conditions, a single bit can be transmitted, telling whether the new sample is above or below the previous one.

This technique, called **delta modulation**, is illustrated in Fig. 2-34. Like all compaction techniques that assume small level changes between consecutive samples, delta encoding can get into trouble if the signal changes too fast, as shown in the figure. When this happens, information is lost.

An improvement to differential PCM is to extrapolate the previous few values to predict the next value and then to encode the difference between the actual signal and the predicted one. The transmitter and receiver must use the same prediction algorithm, of course. Such schemes are called **predictive encoding**. They are useful because they reduce the size of the numbers to be encoded, hence the number of bits to be sent.

Time division multiplexing allows multiple T1 carriers to be multiplexed into higher-order carriers. Figure 2-35 shows how this can be done. At the left we see four T1 channels being multiplexed onto one T2 channel. The multiplexing at T2 and above is done bit for bit, rather than byte for byte with the 24 voice channels that make up a T1 frame. Four T1 streams at 1.544 Mbps should generate 6.176 Mbps, but T2 is actually 6.312 Mbps. The extra bits are used for framing and recovery in case the carrier slips. T1 and T3 are widely used by customers, whereas T2 and T4 are only used within the telephone system itself, so they are not well known.

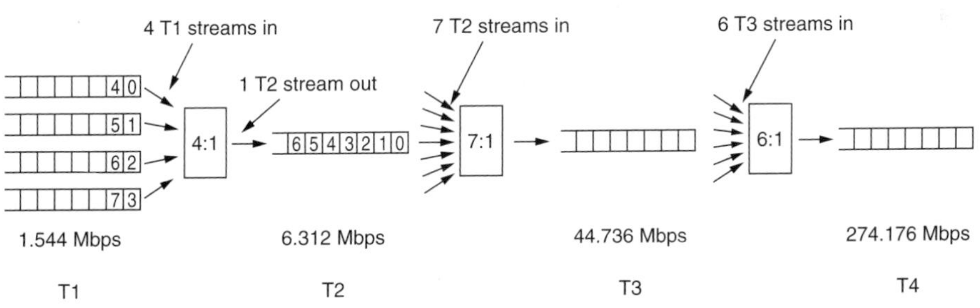

Figure 2-35. Multiplexing T1 streams onto higher carriers.

At the next level, seven T2 streams are combined bitwise to form a T3 stream. Then six T3 streams are joined to form a T4 stream. At each step a small amount of overhead is added for framing and recovery in case the synchronization between sender and receiver is lost.

Just as there is little agreement on the basic carrier between the United States and the rest of the world, there is equally little agreement on how it is to be multiplexed into higher-bandwidth carriers. The U.S. scheme of stepping up by 4, 7, and 6 did not strike everyone else as the way to go, so the CCITT standard calls for multiplexing four streams onto one stream at each level. Also, the framing and recovery data are different between the U.S. and CCITT standards. The CCITT hierarchy for 32, 128, 512, 2048, and 8192 channels runs at speeds of 2.048, 8.848, 34.304, 139.264, and 565.148 Mbps.

SONET/SDH

In the early days of fiber optics, every telephone company had its own proprietary optical TDM system. After AT&T was broken up in 1984, local telephone companies had to connect to multiple long-distance carriers, all with different optical TDM systems, so the need for standardization became obvious. In 1985, Bellcore, the RBOCs research arm, began working on a standard, called **SONET** (**Synchronous Optical NETwork**). Later, CCITT joined the effort, which resulted in a SONET standard and a set of parallel CCITT recommendations (G.707, G.708, and G.709) in 1989. The CCITT recommendations are called **SDH** (**Synchronous Digital Hierarchy**) but differ from SONET only in minor ways. Virtually all the long-distance telephone traffic in the United States, and much of it elsewhere, now uses trunks running SONET in the physical layer. For additional information about SONET, see (Bellamy, 2000; Goralski, 2000; and Shepard, 2001).

The SONET design had four major goals. First and foremost, SONET had to make it possible for different carriers to interwork. Achieving this goal required defining a common signaling standard with respect to wavelength, timing, framing structure, and other issues.

Second, some means was needed to unify the U.S., European, and Japanese digital systems, all of which were based on 64-kbps PCM channels, but all of which combined them in different (and incompatible) ways.

Third, SONET had to provide a way to multiplex multiple digital channels. At the time SONET was devised, the highest-speed digital carrier actually used widely in the United States was T3, at 44.736 Mbps. T4 was defined, but not used much, and nothing was even defined above T4 speed. Part of SONET's mission was to continue the hierarchy to gigabits/sec and beyond. A standard way to multiplex slower channels into one SONET channel was also needed.

Fourth, SONET had to provide support for operations, administration, and maintenance (OAM). Previous systems did not do this very well.

An early decision was to make SONET a traditional TDM system, with the entire bandwidth of the fiber devoted to one channel containing time slots for the various subchannels. As such, SONET is a synchronous system. It is controlled by a master clock with an accuracy of about 1 part in 10^9. Bits on a SONET line are sent out at extremely precise intervals, controlled by the master clock. When cell switching was later proposed to be the basis of ATM, the fact that it permitted irregular cell arrivals got it labeled as *Asynchronous* Transfer Mode to contrast it to the synchronous operation of SONET. With SONET, the sender and receiver are tied to a common clock; with ATM they are not.

The basic SONET frame is a block of 810 bytes put out every 125 μsec. Since SONET is synchronous, frames are emitted whether or not there are any useful data to send. Having 8000 frames/sec exactly matches the sampling rate of the PCM channels used in all digital telephony systems.

The 810-byte SONET frames are best described as a rectangle of bytes, 90 columns wide by 9 rows high. Thus, $8 \times 810 = 6480$ bits are transmitted 8000 times per second, for a gross data rate of 51.84 Mbps. This is the basic SONET channel, called **STS-1** (**Synchronous Transport Signal-1**). All SONET trunks are a multiple of STS-1.

The first three columns of each frame are reserved for system management information, as illustrated in Fig. 2-36. The first three rows contain the section overhead; the next six contain the line overhead. The section overhead is generated and checked at the start and end of each section, whereas the line overhead is generated and checked at the start and end of each line.

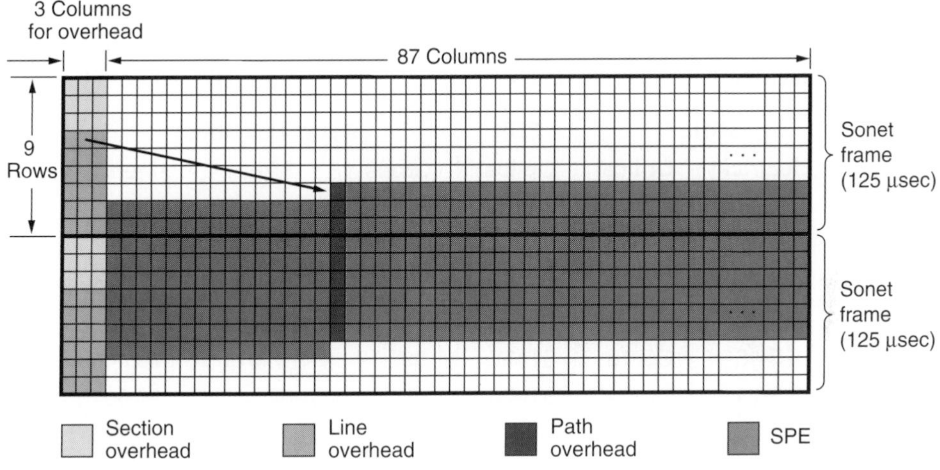

Figure 2-36. Two back-to-back SONET frames.

A SONET transmitter sends back-to-back 810-byte frames, without gaps between them, even when there are no data (in which case it sends dummy data). From the receiver's point of view, all it sees is a continuous bit stream, so how does it know where each frame begins? The answer is that the first two bytes of each frame contain a fixed pattern that the receiver searches for. If it finds this pattern in the same place in a large number of consecutive frames, it assumes that it is in sync with the sender. In theory, a user could insert this pattern into the payload in a regular way, but in practice it cannot be done due to the multiplexing of multiple users into the same frame and other reasons.

The remaining 87 columns hold $87 \times 9 \times 8 \times 8000 = 50.112$ Mbps of user data. However, the user data, called the **SPE** (**Synchronous Payload Envelope**), do not always begin in row 1, column 4. The SPE can begin anywhere within the frame. A pointer to the first byte is contained in the first row of the line overhead. The first column of the SPE is the path overhead (i.e., header for the end-to-end path sublayer protocol).

The ability to allow the SPE to begin anywhere within the SONET frame and even to span two frames, as shown in Fig. 2-36, gives added flexibility to the system. For example, if a payload arrives at the source while a dummy SONET frame is being constructed, it can be inserted into the current frame instead of being held until the start of the next one.

The SONET multiplexing hierarchy is shown in Fig. 2-37. Rates from STS-1 to STS-192 have been defined. The optical carrier corresponding to STS-*n* is called OC-*n* but is bit for bit the same except for a certain bit reordering needed for synchronization. The SDH names are different, and they start at OC-3 because CCITT-based systems do not have a rate near 51.84 Mbps. The OC-9 carrier is present because it closely matches the speed of a major high-speed trunk used in Japan. OC-18 and OC-36 are used in Japan. The gross data rate includes all the overhead. The SPE data rate excludes the line and section overhead. The user data rate excludes all overhead and counts only the 86 payload columns.

SONET		SDH	Data rate (Mbps)		
Electrical	**Optical**	**Optical**	**Gross**	**SPE**	**User**
STS-1	OC-1		51.84	50.112	49.536
STS-3	OC-3	STM-1	155.52	150.336	148.608
STS-9	OC-9	STM-3	466.56	451.008	445.824
STS-12	OC-12	STM-4	622.08	601.344	594.432
STS-18	OC-18	STM-6	933.12	902.016	891.648
STS-24	OC-24	STM-8	1244.16	1202.688	1188.864
STS-36	OC-36	STM-12	1866.24	1804.032	1783.296
STS-48	OC-48	STM-16	2488.32	2405.376	2377.728
STS-192	OC-192	STM-64	9953.28	9621.504	9510.912

Figure 2-37. SONET and SDH multiplex rates.

As an aside, when a carrier, such as OC-3, is not multiplexed, but carries the data from only a single source, the letter *c* (for concatenated) is appended to the designation, so OC-3 indicates a 155.52-Mbps carrier consisting of three separate OC-1 carriers, but OC-3c indicates a data stream from a single source at 155.52 Mbps. The three OC-1 streams within an OC-3c stream are interleaved by column, first column 1 from stream 1, then column 1 from stream 2, then column 1 from stream 3, followed by column 2 from stream 1, and so on, leading to a frame 270 columns wide and 9 rows deep.

2.5.5 Switching

From the point of view of the average telephone engineer, the phone system is divided into two principal parts: outside plant (the local loops and trunks, since they are physically outside the switching offices) and inside plant (the switches), which are inside the switching offices. We have just looked at the outside plant. Now it is time to examine the inside plant.

Two different switching techniques are used nowadays: circuit switching and packet switching. We will give a brief introduction to each of them below. Then we will go into circuit switching in detail because that is how the telephone system works. We will study packet switching in detail in subsequent chapters.

Circuit Switching

When you or your computer places a telephone call, the switching equipment within the telephone system seeks out a physical path all the way from your telephone to the receiver's telephone. This technique is called **circuit switching** and is shown schematically in Fig. 2-38(a). Each of the six rectangles represents a carrier switching office (end office, toll office, etc.). In this example, each office has three incoming lines and three outgoing lines. When a call passes through a switching office, a physical connection is (conceptually) established between the line on which the call came in and one of the output lines, as shown by the dotted lines.

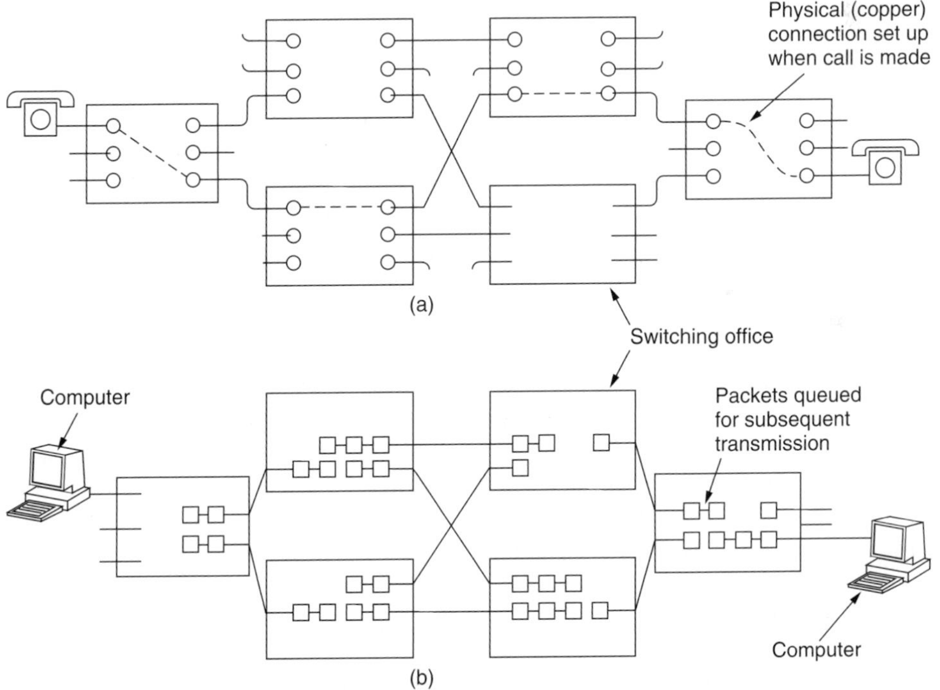

Figure 2-38. (a) Circuit switching. (b) Packet switching.

In the early days of the telephone, the connection was made by the operator plugging a jumper cable into the input and output sockets. In fact, a surprising little story is associated with the invention of automatic circuit switching equipment. It was invented by a 19th century Missouri undertaker named Almon B. Strowger. Shortly after the telephone was invented, when someone died, one of the survivors would call the town operator and say "Please connect me to an undertaker." Unfortunately for Mr. Strowger, there were two undertakers in his town, and the other one's wife was the town telephone operator. He quickly saw that either he was going to have to invent automatic telephone switching equipment or he was going to go out of business. He chose the first option. For nearly 100 years, the circuit-switching equipment used worldwide was known as Strowger gear. (History does not record whether the now-unemployed switchboard operator got a job as an information operator, answering questions such as "What is the phone number of an undertaker?")

The model shown in Fig. 2-39(a) is highly simplified, of course, because parts of the physical path between the two telephones may, in fact, be microwave or fiber links onto which thousands of calls are multiplexed. Nevertheless, the basic idea is valid: once a call has been set up, a dedicated path between both ends exists and will continue to exist until the call is finished.

The alternative to circuit switching is packet switching, shown in Fig. 2-38(b). With this technology, individual packets are sent as need be, with no dedicated path being set up in advance. It is up to each packet to find its way to the destination on its own.

An important property of circuit switching is the need to set up an end-to-end path *before* any data can be sent. The elapsed time between the end of dialing and the start of ringing can easily be 10 sec, more on long-distance or international calls. During this time interval, the telephone system is hunting for a path, as shown in Fig. 2-39(a). Note that before data transmission can even begin, the call request signal must propagate all the way to the destination and be acknowledged. For many computer applications (e.g., point-of-sale credit verification), long setup times are undesirable.

As a consequence of the reserved path between the calling parties, once the setup has been completed, the only delay for data is the propagation time for the electromagnetic signal, about 5 msec per 1000 km. Also as a consequence of the established path, there is no danger of congestion—that is, once the call has been put through, you never get busy signals. Of course, you might get one before the connection has been established due to lack of switching or trunk capacity.

Message Switching

An alternative switching strategy is **message switching**, illustrated in Fig. 2-39(b). When this form of switching is used, no physical path is established in advance between sender and receiver. Instead, when the sender has a block of

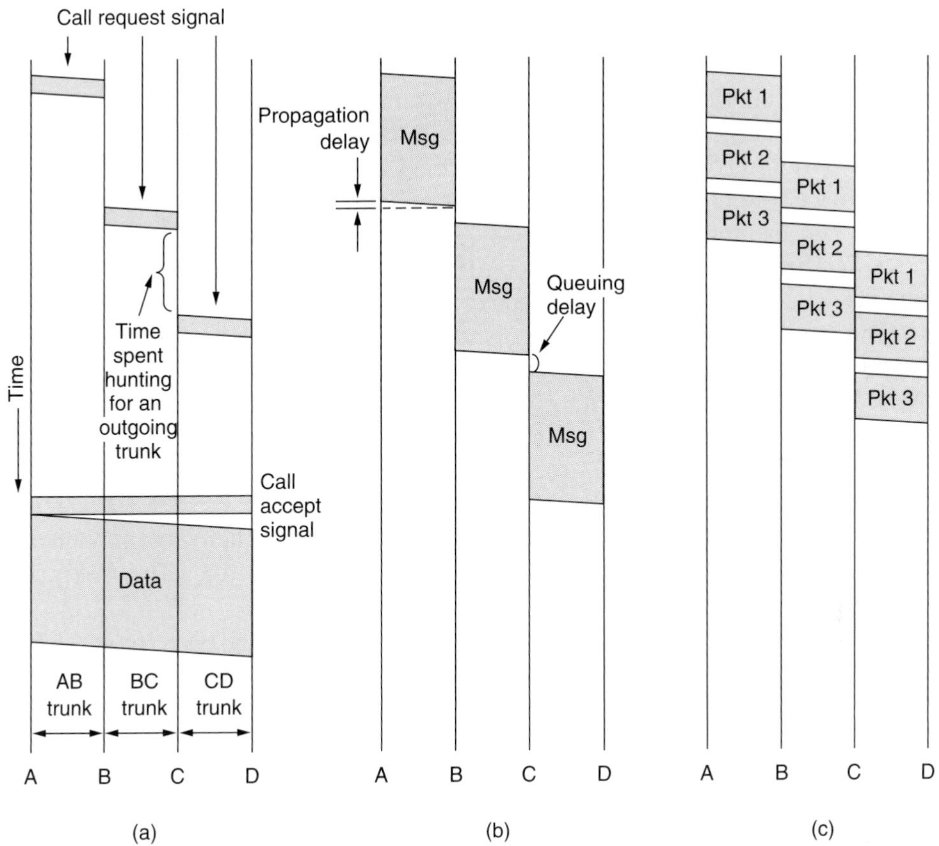

Figure 2-39. Timing of events in (a) circuit switching, (b) message switching, (c) packet switching.

data to be sent, it is stored in the first switching office (i.e., router) and then forwarded later, one hop at a time. Each block is received in its entirety, inspected for errors, and then retransmitted. A network using this technique is called a **store-and-forward** network, as mentioned in Chap. 1.

The first electromechanical telecommunication systems used message switching, namely, for telegrams. The message was punched on paper tape (off-line) at the sending office, and then read in and transmitted over a communication line to the next office along the way, where it was punched out on paper tape. An operator there tore the tape off and read it in on one of the many tape readers, one reader per outgoing trunk. Such a switching office was called a **torn tape office**. Paper tape is long gone and message switching is not used any more, so we will not discuss it further in this book.

Packet Switching

With message switching, there is no limit at all on block size, which means that routers (in a modern system) must have disks to buffer long blocks. It also means that a single block can tie up a router-router line for minutes, rendering message switching useless for interactive traffic. To get around these problems, **packet switching** was invented, as described in Chap. 1. Packet-switching networks place a tight upper limit on block size, allowing packets to be buffered in router main memory instead of on disk. By making sure that no user can monopolize any transmission line very long (milliseconds), packet-switching networks are well suited for handling interactive traffic. A further advantage of packet switching over message switching is shown in Fig. 2-39(b) and (c): the first packet of a multipacket message can be forwarded before the second one has fully arrived, reducing delay and improving throughput. For these reasons, computer networks are usually packet switched, occasionally circuit switched, but never message switched.

Circuit switching and packet switching differ in many respects. To start with, circuit switching requires that a circuit be set up end to end before communication begins. Packet switching does not require any advance setup. The first packet can just be sent as soon as it is available.

The result of the connection setup with circuit switching is the reservation of bandwidth all the way from the sender to the receiver. All packets follow this path. Among other properties, having all packets follow the same path means that they cannot arrive out of order. With packet switching there is no path, so different packets can follow different paths, depending on network conditions at the time they are sent. They may arrive out of order.

Packet switching is more fault tolerant than circuit switching. In fact, that is why it was invented. If a switch goes down, all of the circuits using it are terminated and no more traffic can be sent on any of them. With packet switching, packets can be routed around dead switches.

Setting up a path in advance also opens up the possibility of reserving bandwidth in advance. If bandwidth is reserved, then when a packet arrives, it can be sent out immediately over the reserved bandwidth. With packet switching, no bandwidth is reserved, so packets may have to wait their turn to be forwarded.

Having bandwidth reserved in advance means that no congestion can occur when a packet shows up (unless more packets show up than expected). On the other hand, when an attempt is made to establish a circuit, the attempt can fail due to congestion. Thus, congestion can occur at different times with circuit switching (at setup time) and packet switching (when packets are sent).

If a circuit has been reserved for a particular user and there is no traffic to send, the bandwidth of that circuit is wasted. It cannot be used for other traffic. Packet switching does not waste bandwidth and thus is more efficient from a system-wide perspective. Understanding this trade-off is crucial for comprehending the difference between circuit switching and packet switching. The trade-off is between guaranteed service and wasting resources versus not guaranteeing service and not wasting resources.

Packet switching uses store-and-forward transmission. A packet is accumulated in a router's memory, then sent on to the next router. With circuit switching, the bits just flow through the wire continuously. The store-and-forward technique adds delay.

Another difference is that circuit switching is completely transparent. The sender and receiver can use any bit rate, format, or framing method they want to. The carrier does not know or care. With packet switching, the carrier determines the basic parameters. A rough analogy is a road versus a railroad. In the former, the user determines the size, speed, and nature of the vehicle; in the latter, the carrier does. It is this transparency that allows voice, data, and fax to coexist within the phone system.

A final difference between circuit and packet switching is the charging algorithm. With circuit switching, charging has historically been based on distance and time. For mobile phones, distance usually does not play a role, except for international calls, and time plays only a minor role (e.g., a calling plan with 2000 free minutes costs more than one with 1000 free minutes and sometimes night or weekend calls are cheaper than normal). With packet switching, connect time is not an issue, but the volume of traffic sometimes is. For home users, ISPs usually charge a flat monthly rate because it is less work for them and their customers can understand this model easily, but backbone carriers charge regional networks based on the volume of their traffic. The differences are summarized in Fig. 2-40.

Item	Circuit switched	Packet switched
Call setup	Required	Not needed
Dedicated physical path	Yes	No
Each packet follows the same route	Yes	No
Packets arrive in order	Yes	No
Is a switch crash fatal	Yes	No
Bandwidth available	Fixed	Dynamic
Time of possible congestion	At setup time	On every packet
Potentially wasted bandwidth	Yes	No
Store-and-forward transmission	No	Yes
Transparency	Yes	No
Charging	Per minute	Per packet

Figure 2-40. A comparison of circuit-switched and packet-switched networks.

Both circuit switching and packet switching are important enough that we will come back to them shortly and describe the various technologies used in detail.

2.6 THE MOBILE TELEPHONE SYSTEM

The traditional telephone system (even if it some day gets multigigabit end-to-end fiber) will still not be able to satisfy a growing group of users: people on the go. People now expect to make phone calls from airplanes, cars, swimming pools, and while jogging in the park. Within a few years they will also expect to send e-mail and surf the Web from all these locations and more. Consequently, there is a tremendous amount of interest in wireless telephony. In the following sections we will study this topic in some detail.

Wireless telephones come in two basic varieties: cordless phones and mobile phones (sometimes called **cell phones**). **Cordless phones** are devices consisting of a base station and a handset sold as a set for use within the home. These are never used for networking, so we will not examine them further. Instead we will concentrate on the mobile system, which is used for wide area voice and data communication.

Mobile phones have gone through three distinct generations, with different technologies:

1. Analog voice.
2. Digital voice.
3. Digital voice and data (Internet, e-mail, etc.).

Although most of our discussion will be about the technology of these systems, it is interesting to note how political and tiny marketing decisions can have a huge impact. The first mobile system was devised in the U.S. by AT&T and mandated for the whole country by the FCC. As a result, the entire U.S. had a single (analog) system and a mobile phone purchased in California also worked in New York. In contrast, when mobile came to Europe, every country devised its own system, which resulted in a fiasco.

Europe learned from its mistake and when digital came around, the government-run PTTs got together and standardized on a single system (GSM), so any European mobile phone will work anywhere in Europe. By then, the U.S. had decided that government should not be in the standardization business, so it left digital to the marketplace. This decision resulted in different equipment manufacturers producing different kinds of mobile phones. As a consequence, the U.S. now has two major incompatible digital mobile phone systems in operation (plus one minor one).

Despite an initial lead by the U.S., mobile phone ownership and usage in Europe is now far greater than in the U.S. Having a single system for all of Europe is part of the reason, but there is more. A second area where the U.S. and Europe differed is in the humble matter of phone numbers. In the U.S. mobile phones are mixed in with regular (fixed) telephones. Thus, there is no way for a caller to see if, say, (212) 234-5678 is a fixed telephone (cheap or free call) or a mobile phone (expensive call). To keep people from getting nervous about using the telephone, the telephone companies decided to make the mobile phone owner pay for incoming calls. As a consequence, many people hesitated to buy a mobile phone for fear of running up a big bill by just receiving calls. In Europe, mobile phones have a special area code (analogous to 800 and 900 numbers) so they are instantly recognizable. Consequently, the usual rule of "caller pays" also applies to mobile phones in Europe (except for international calls where costs are split).

A third issue that has had a large impact on adoption is the widespread use of prepaid mobile phones in Europe (up to 75% in some areas). These can be purchased in many stores with no more formality than buying a radio. You pay and you go. They are preloaded with, for example, 20 or 50 euro and can be recharged (using a secret PIN code) when the balance drops to zero. As a consequence, practically every teenager and many small children in Europe have (usually prepaid) mobile phones so their parents can locate them, without the danger of the child running up a huge bill. If the mobile phone is used only occasionally, its use is essentially free since there is no monthly charge or charge for incoming calls.

2.6.1 First-Generation Mobile Phones: Analog Voice

Enough about the politics and marketing aspects of mobile phones. Now let us look at the technology, starting with the earliest system. Mobile radiotelephones were used sporadically for maritime and military communication during the early decades of the 20th century. In 1946, the first system for car-based telephones was set up in St. Louis. This system used a single large transmitter on top of a tall building and had a single channel, used for both sending and receiving. To talk, the user had to push a button that enabled the transmitter and disabled the receiver. Such systems, known as **push-to-talk systems**, were installed in several cities beginning in the late 1950s. CB-radio, taxis, and police cars on television programs often use this technology.

In the 1960s, **IMTS** (**Improved Mobile Telephone System**) was installed. It, too, used a high-powered (200-watt) transmitter, on top of a hill, but now had two frequencies, one for sending and one for receiving, so the push-to-talk button was no longer needed. Since all communication from the mobile telephones went inbound on a different channel than the outbound signals, the mobile users could not hear each other (unlike the push-to-talk system used in taxis).

IMTS supported 23 channels spread out from 150 MHz to 450 MHz. Due to the small number of channels, users often had to wait a long time before getting a dial tone. Also, due to the large power of the hilltop transmitter, adjacent systems had to be several hundred kilometers apart to avoid interference. All in all, the limited capacity made the system impractical.

Advanced Mobile Phone System

All that changed with **AMPS** (**Advanced Mobile Phone System**), invented by Bell Labs and first installed in the United States in 1982. It was also used in England, where it was called TACS, and in Japan, where it was called MCS-L1. Although no longer state of the art, we will look at it in some detail because many of its fundamental properties have been directly inherited by its digital successor, D-AMPS, in order to achieve backward compatibility.

In all mobile phone systems, a geographic region is divided up into **cells**, which is why the devices are sometimes called cell phones. In AMPS, the cells are typically 10 to 20 km across; in digital systems, the cells are smaller. Each cell uses some set of frequencies not used by any of its neighbors. The key idea that gives cellular systems far more capacity than previous systems is the use of relatively small cells and the reuse of transmission frequencies in nearby (but not adjacent) cells. Whereas an IMTS system 100 km across can have one call on each frequency, an AMPS system might have 100 10-km cells in the same area and be able to have 10 to 15 calls on each frequency, in widely separated cells. Thus, the cellular design increases the system capacity by at least an order of magnitude, more as the cells get smaller. Furthermore, smaller cells mean that less power is needed, which leads to smaller and cheaper transmitters and handsets. Hand-held telephones put out 0.6 watts; transmitters in cars are 3 watts, the maximum allowed by the FCC.

The idea of frequency reuse is illustrated in Fig. 2-41(a). The cells are normally roughly circular, but they are easier to model as hexagons. In Fig. 2-41(a), the cells are all the same size. They are grouped in units of seven cells. Each letter indicates a group of frequencies. Notice that for each frequency set, there is a buffer about two cells wide where that frequency is not reused, providing for good separation and low interference.

Finding locations high in the air to place base station antennas is a major issue. This problem has led some telecommunication carriers to forge alliances with the Roman Catholic Church, since the latter owns a substantial number of exalted potential antenna sites worldwide, all conveniently under a single management.

In an area where the number of users has grown to the point that the system is overloaded, the power is reduced, and the overloaded cells are split into smaller **microcells** to permit more frequency reuse, as shown in Fig. 2-41(b). Telephone companies sometimes create temporary microcells, using portable towers with satellite links at sporting events, rock concerts, and other places where large numbers of mobile users congregate for a few hours. How big the cells should be is a complex matter, which is treated in (Hac, 1995).

At the center of each cell is a base station to which all the telephones in the cell transmit. The base station consists of a computer and transmitter/receiver connected to an antenna. In a small system, all the base stations are connected to

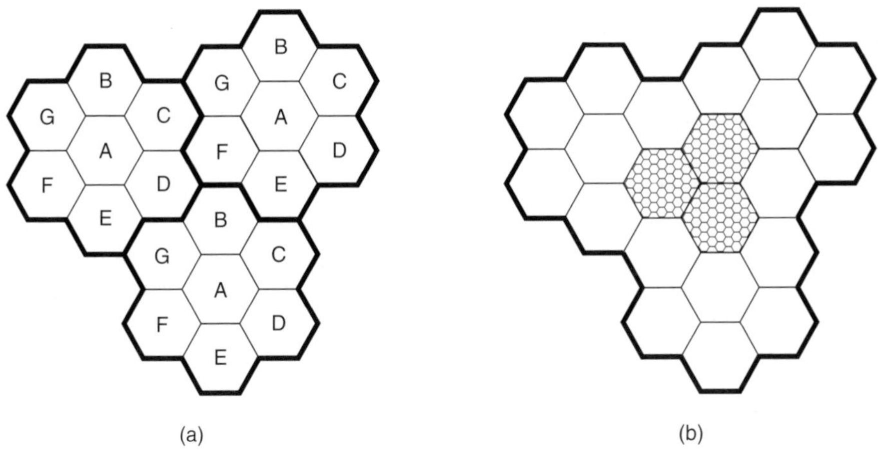

Figure 2-41. (a) Frequencies are not reused in adjacent cells. (b) To add more users, smaller cells can be used.

a single device called an **MTSO** (**Mobile Telephone Switching Office**) or **MSC** (**Mobile Switching Center**). In a larger one, several MTSOs may be needed, all of which are connected to a second-level MTSO, and so on. The MTSOs are essentially end offices as in the telephone system, and are, in fact, connected to at least one telephone system end office. The MTSOs communicate with the base stations, each other, and the PSTN using a packet-switching network.

At any instant, each mobile telephone is logically in one specific cell and under the control of that cell's base station. When a mobile telephone physically leaves a cell, its base station notices the telephone's signal fading away and asks all the surrounding base stations how much power they are getting from it. The base station then transfers ownership to the cell getting the strongest signal, that is, the cell where the telephone is now located. The telephone is then informed of its new boss, and if a call is in progress, it will be asked to switch to a new channel (because the old one is not reused in any of the adjacent cells). This process, called **handoff**, takes about 300 msec. Channel assignment is done by the MTSO, the nerve center of the system. The base stations are really just radio relays.

Handoffs can be done in two ways. In a **soft handoff**, the telephone is acquired by the new base station before the previous one signs off. In this way there is no loss of continuity. The downside here is that the telephone needs to be able to tune to two frequencies at the same time (the old one and the new one). Neither first nor second generation devices can do this.

In a **hard handoff**, the old base station drops the telephone before the new one acquires it. If the new one is unable to acquire it (e.g., because there is no available frequency), the call is disconnected abruptly. Users tend to notice this, but it is inevitable occasionally with the current design.

Channels

The AMPS system uses 832 full-duplex channels, each consisting of a pair of simplex channels. There are 832 simplex transmission channels from 824 to 849 MHz and 832 simplex receive channels from 869 to 894 MHz. Each of these simplex channels is 30 kHz wide. Thus, AMPS uses FDM to separate the channels.

In the 800-MHz band, radio waves are about 40 cm long and travel in straight lines. They are absorbed by trees and plants and bounce off the ground and buildings. It is possible that a signal sent by a mobile telephone will reach the base station by the direct path, but also slightly later after bouncing off the ground or a building. This may lead to an echo or signal distortion (multipath fading). Sometimes, it is even possible to hear a distant conversation that has bounced several times.

The 832 channels are divided into four categories:

1. Control (base to mobile) to manage the system.
2. Paging (base to mobile) to alert mobile users to calls for them.
3. Access (bidirectional) for call setup and channel assignment.
4. Data (bidirectional) for voice, fax, or data.

Twenty-one of the channels are reserved for control, and these are wired into a PROM in each telephone. Since the same frequencies cannot be reused in nearby cells, the actual number of voice channels available per cell is much smaller than 832, typically about 45.

Call Management

Each mobile telephone in AMPS has a 32-bit serial number and a 10-digit telephone number in its PROM. The telephone number is represented as a 3-digit area code in 10 bits, and a 7-digit subscriber number in 24 bits. When a phone is switched on, it scans a preprogrammed list of 21 control channels to find the most powerful signal.

The phone then broadcasts its 32-bit serial number and 34-bit telephone number. Like all the control information in AMPS, this packet is sent in digital form, multiple times, and with an error-correcting code, even though the voice channels themselves are analog.

When the base station hears the announcement, it tells the MTSO, which records the existence of its new customer and also informs the customer's home MTSO of his current location. During normal operation, the mobile telephone reregisters about once every 15 minutes.

To make a call, a mobile user switches on the phone, enters the number to be called on the keypad, and hits the SEND button. The phone then transmits the number to be called and its own identity on the access channel. If a collision occurs there, it tries again later. When the base station gets the request, it informs the MTSO. If the caller is a customer of the MTSO's company (or one of its partners), the MTSO looks for an idle channel for the call. If one is found, the channel number is sent back on the control channel. The mobile phone then automatically switches to the selected voice channel and waits until the called party picks up the phone.

Incoming calls work differently. To start with, all idle phones continuously listen to the paging channel to detect messages directed at them. When a call is placed to a mobile phone (either from a fixed phone or another mobile phone), a packet is sent to the callee's home MTSO to find out where it is. A packet is then sent to the base station in its current cell, which then sends a broadcast on the paging channel of the form "Unit 14, are you there?" The called phone then responds with "Yes" on the access channel. The base then says something like: "Unit 14, call for you on channel 3." At this point, the called phone switches to channel 3 and starts making ringing sounds (or playing some melody the owner was given as a birthday present).

2.6.2 Second-Generation Mobile Phones: Digital Voice

The first generation of mobile phones was analog; the second generation was digital. Just as there was no worldwide standardization during the first generation, there was also no standardization during the second, either. Four systems are in use now: D-AMPS, GSM, CDMA, and PDC. Below we will discuss the first three. PDC is used only in Japan and is basically D-AMPS modified for backward compatibility with the first-generation Japanese analog system. The name **PCS** (**Personal Communications Services**) is sometimes used in the marketing literature to indicate a second-generation (i.e., digital) system. Originally it meant a mobile phone using the 1900 MHz band, but that distinction is rarely made now.

D-AMPS—The Digital Advanced Mobile Phone System

The second generation of the AMPS systems is **D-AMPS** and is fully digital. It is described in International Standard IS-54 and its successor IS-136. D-AMPS was carefully designed to co-exist with AMPS so that both first- and second-generation mobile phones could operate simultaneously in the same cell. In particular, D-AMPS uses the same 30 kHz channels as AMPS and at the same frequencies so that one channel can be analog and the adjacent ones can be digital. Depending on the mix of phones in a cell, the cell's MTSO determines which channels are analog and which are digital, and it can change channel types dynamically as the mix of phones in a cell changes.

When D-AMPS was introduced as a service, a new frequency band was made available to handle the expected increased load. The upstream channels were in the 1850–1910 MHz range, and the corresponding downstream channels were in the 1930–1990 MHz range, again in pairs, as in AMPS. In this band, the waves are 16 cm long, so a standard ¼-wave antenna is only 4 cm long, leading to smaller phones. However, many D-AMPS phones can use both the 850-MHz and 1900-MHz bands to get a wider range of available channels.

On a D-AMPS mobile phone, the voice signal picked up by the microphone is digitized and compressed using a model that is more sophisticated than the delta modulation and predictive encoding schemes we studied earlier. Compression takes into account detailed properties of the human vocal system to get the bandwidth from the standard 56-kbps PCM encoding to 8 kbps or less. The compression is done by a circuit called a **vocoder** (Bellamy, 2000). The compression is done in the telephone, rather than in the base station or end office, to reduce the number of bits sent over the air link. With fixed telephony, there is no benefit to having compression done in the telephone, since reducing the traffic over the local loop does not increase system capacity at all.

With mobile telephony there is a huge gain from doing digitization and compression in the handset, so much so that in D-AMPS, three users can share a single frequency pair using time division multiplexing. Each frequency pair supports 25 frames/sec of 40 msec each. Each frame is divided into six time slots of 6.67 msec each, as illustrated in Fig. 2-42(a) for the lowest frequency pair.

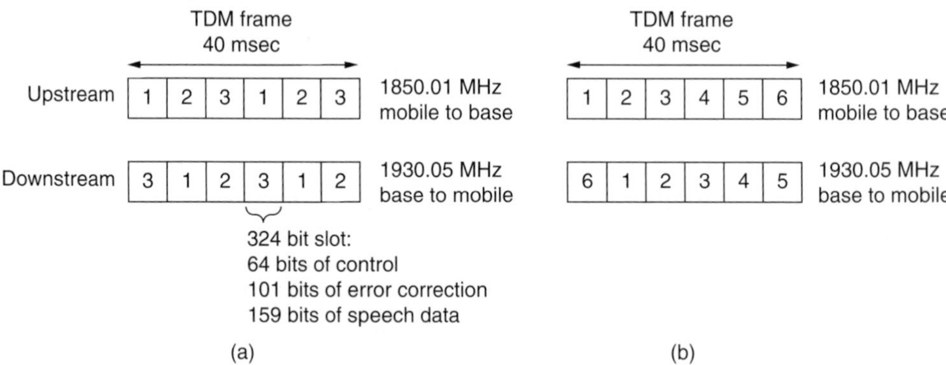

Figure 2-42. (a) A D-AMPS channel with three users. (b) A D-AMPS channel with six users.

Each frame holds three users who take turns using the upstream and downstream links. During slot 1 of Fig. 2-42(a), for example, user 1 may transmit to the base station and user 3 is receiving from the base station. Each slot is 324 bits long, of which 64 bits are used for guard times, synchronization, and control purposes, leaving 260 bits for the user payload. Of the payload bits, 101 are used for error correction over the noisy air link, so ultimately only 159 bits are left for compressed speech. With 50 slots/sec, the bandwidth available for compressed speech is just under 8 kbps, 1/7 of the standard PCM bandwidth.

Using better compression algorithms, it is possible to get the speech down to 4 kbps, in which case six users can be stuffed into a frame, as illustrated in Fig. 2-42(b). From the operator's perspective, being able to squeeze three to six times as many D-AMPS users into the same spectrum as one AMPS user is a huge win and explains much of the popularity of PCS. Of course, the quality of speech at 4 kbps is not comparable to what can be achieved at 56 kbps, but few PCS operators advertise their hi-fi sound quality. It should also be clear that for data, an 8 kbps channel is not even as good as an ancient 9600-bps modem.

The control structure of D-AMPS is fairly complicated. Briefly summarized, groups of 16 frames form a superframe, with certain control information present in each superframe a limited number of times. Six main control channels are used: system configuration, real-time and nonreal-time control, paging, access response, and short messages. But conceptually, it works like AMPS. When a mobile is switched on, it makes contact with the base station to announce itself and then listens on a control channel for incoming calls. Having picked up a new mobile, the MTSO informs the user's home base where he is, so calls can be routed correctly.

One difference between AMPS and D-AMPS is how handoff is handled. In AMPS, the MTSO manages it completely without help from the mobile devices. As can be seen from Fig. 2-42, in D-AMPS, 1/3 of the time a mobile is neither sending nor receiving. It uses these idle slots to measure the line quality. When it discovers that the signal is waning, it complains to the MTSO, which can then break the connection, at which time the mobile can try to tune to a stronger signal from another base station. As in AMPS, it still takes about 300 msec to do the handoff. This technique is called **MAHO** (**Mobile Assisted HandOff**).

GSM—The Global System for Mobile Communications

D-AMPS is widely used in the U.S. and (in modified form) in Japan. Virtually everywhere else in the world, a system called **GSM** (**Global System for Mobile communications**) is used, and it is even starting to be used in the U.S. on a limited scale. To a first approximation, GSM is similar to D-AMPS. Both are cellular systems. In both systems, frequency division multiplexing is used, with each mobile transmitting on one frequency and receiving on a higher frequency (80 MHz higher for D-AMPS, 55 MHz higher for GSM). Also in both systems, a single frequency pair is split by time-division multiplexing into time slots shared by multiple mobiles. However, the GSM channels are much wider than the AMPS channels (200 kHz versus 30 kHz) and hold relatively few additional users (8 versus 3), giving GSM a much higher data rate per user than D-AMPS.

Below we will briefly discuss some of the main properties of GSM. However, the printed GSM standard is over 5000 [sic] pages long. A large fraction of this material relates to engineering aspects of the system, especially the design of receivers to handle multipath signal propagation, and synchronizing transmitters and receivers. None of this will be even mentioned below.

Each frequency band is 200 kHz wide, as shown in Fig. 2-43. A GSM system has 124 pairs of simplex channels. Each simplex channel is 200 kHz wide and supports eight separate connections on it, using time division multiplexing. Each currently active station is assigned one time slot on one channel pair. Theoretically, 992 channels can be supported in each cell, but many of them are not available, to avoid frequency conflicts with neighboring cells. In Fig. 2-43, the eight shaded time slots all belong to the same connection, four of them in each direction. Transmitting and receiving does not happen in the same time slot because the GSM radios cannot transmit and receive at the same time and it takes time to switch from one to the other. If the mobile station assigned to 890.4/935.4 MHz and time slot 2 wanted to transmit to the base station, it would use the lower four shaded slots (and the ones following them in time), putting some data in each slot until all the data had been sent.

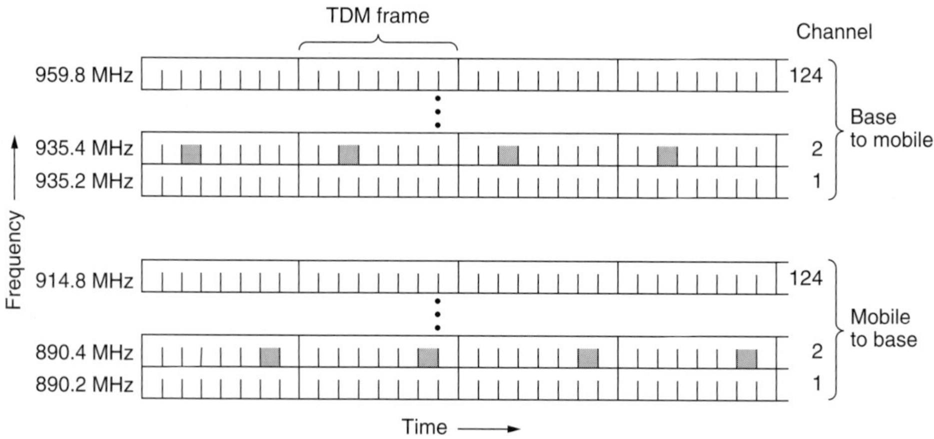

Figure 2-43. GSM uses 124 frequency channels, each of which uses an eight-slot TDM system.

The TDM slots shown in Fig. 2-43 are part of a complex framing hierarchy. Each TDM slot has a specific structure, and groups of TDM slots form multiframes, also with a specific structure. A simplified version of this hierarchy is shown in Fig. 2-44. Here we can see that each TDM slot consists of a 148-bit data frame that occupies the channel for 577 μsec (including a 30-μsec guard time after each slot). Each data frame starts and ends with three 0 bits, for frame delineation purposes. It also contains two 57-bit *Information* fields, each one having a control bit that indicates whether the following *Information* field is for voice or data. Between the *Information* fields is a 26-bit *Sync* (training) field that is used by the receiver to synchronize to the sender's frame boundaries.

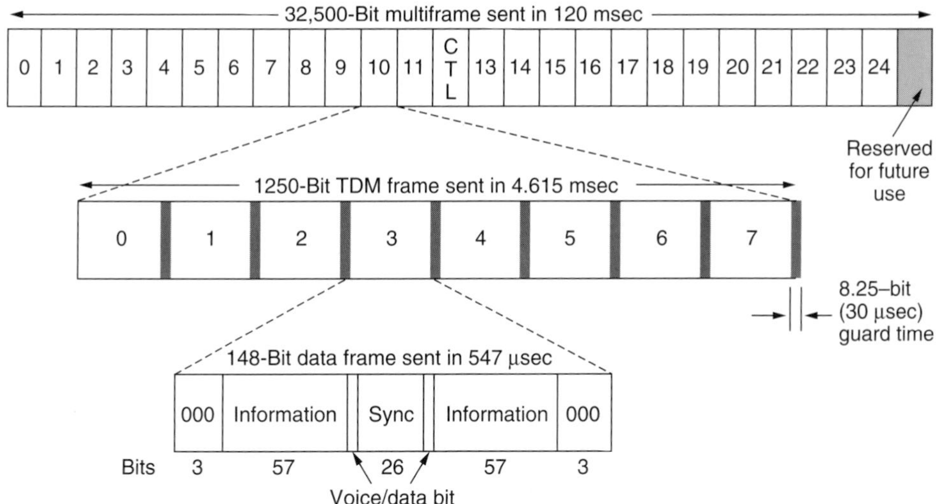

Figure 2-44. A portion of the GSM framing structure.

A data frame is transmitted in 547 μsec, but a transmitter is only allowed to send one data frame every 4.615 msec, since it is sharing the channel with seven other stations. The gross rate of each channel is 270,833 bps, divided among eight users. This gives 33.854 kbps gross, more than double D-AMPS' 324 bits 50 times per second for 16.2 kbps. However, as with AMPS, the overhead eats up a large fraction of the bandwidth, ultimately leaving 24.7 kbps worth of payload per user before error correction. After error correction, 13 kbps is left for speech, giving substantially better voice quality than D-AMPS (at the cost of correspondingly more bandwidth).

As can be seen from Fig. 2-44, eight data frames make up a TDM frame and 26 TDM frames make up a 120-msec multiframe. Of the 26 TDM frames in a multiframe, slot 12 is used for control and slot 25 is reserved for future use, so only 24 are available for user traffic.

However, in addition to the 26-slot multiframe shown in Fig. 2-44, a 51-slot multiframe (not shown) is also used. Some of these slots are used to hold several control channels used to manage the system. The **broadcast control channel** is a continuous stream of output from the base station containing the base station's identity and the channel status. All mobile stations monitor their signal strength to see when they have moved into a new cell.

The **dedicated control channel** is used for location updating, registration, and call setup. In particular, each base station maintains a database of mobile stations currently under its jurisdiction. Information needed to maintain this database is sent on the dedicated control channel.

Finally, there is the **common control channel**, which is split up into three logical subchannels. The first of these subchannels is the **paging channel**, which the base station uses to announce incoming calls. Each mobile station monitors it continuously to watch for calls it should answer. The second is the **random access channel**, which allows users to request a slot on the dedicated control channel. If two requests collide, they are garbled and have to be retried later. Using the dedicated control channel slot, the station can set up a call. The assigned slot is announced on the third subchannel, the **access grant channel**.

CDMA—Code Division Multiple Access

D-AMPS and GSM are fairly conventional systems. They use both FDM and TDM to divide the spectrum into channels and the channels into time slots. However, there is a third kid on the block, **CDMA** (**Code Division Multiple Access**), which works completely differently. When CDMA was first proposed, the industry gave it approximately the same reaction that Columbus first got from Queen Isabella when he proposed reaching India by sailing in the wrong direction. However, through the persistence of a single company, Qualcomm, CDMA has matured to the point where it is not only acceptable, it is now viewed as the best technical solution around and the basis for the third-generation mobile systems. It is also widely used in the U.S. in second-generation mobile systems, competing head-on with D-AMPS. For example, Sprint PCS uses CDMA, whereas AT&T Wireless uses D-AMPS. CDMA is described in International Standard IS-95 and is sometimes referred to by that name. The brand name **cdmaOne** is also used.

CDMA is completely different from AMPS, D-AMPS, and GSM. Instead of dividing the allowed frequency range into a few hundred narrow channels, CDMA allows each station to transmit over the entire frequency spectrum all the time. Multiple simultaneous transmissions are separated using coding theory. CDMA also relaxes the assumption that colliding frames are totally garbled. Instead, it assumes that multiple signals add linearly.

Before getting into the algorithm, let us consider an analogy: an airport lounge with many pairs of people conversing. TDM is comparable to all the people being in the middle of the room but taking turns speaking. FDM is comparable to the people being in widely separated clumps, each clump holding its own conversation at the same time as, but still independent of, the others. CDMA is comparable to everybody being in the middle of the room talking at once, but with each pair in a different language. The French-speaking couple just hones in on the French, rejecting everything that is not French as noise. Thus, the key to CDMA is to be able to extract the desired signal while rejecting everything else as random noise. A somewhat simplified description of CDMA follows.

In CDMA, each bit time is subdivided into m short intervals called **chips**. Typically, there are 64 or 128 chips per bit, but in the example given below we will use 8 chips/bit for simplicity.

Each station is assigned a unique m-bit code called a **chip sequence**. To transmit a 1 bit, a station sends its chip sequence. To transmit a 0 bit, it sends the one's complement of its chip sequence. No other patterns are permitted. Thus, for $m = 8$, if station A is assigned the chip sequence 00011011, it sends a 1 bit by sending 00011011 and a 0 bit by sending 11100100.

Increasing the amount of information to be sent from b bits/sec to mb chips/sec can only be done if the bandwidth available is increased by a factor of m, making CDMA a form of spread spectrum communication (assuming no changes in the modulation or encoding techniques). If we have a 1-MHz band available for 100 stations, with FDM each one would have 10 kHz and could send at 10 kbps (assuming 1 bit per Hz). With CDMA, each station uses the full 1 MHz, so the chip rate is 1 megachip per second. With fewer than 100 chips per bit, the effective bandwidth per station is higher for CDMA than FDM, and the channel allocation problem is also solved.

For pedagogical purposes, it is more convenient to use a bipolar notation, with binary 0 being −1 and binary 1 being +1. We will show chip sequences in parentheses, so a 1 bit for station A now becomes (−1 −1 −1 +1 +1 −1 +1 +1). In Fig. 2-45(a) we show the binary chip sequences assigned to four example stations. In Fig. 2-45(b) we show them in our bipolar notation.

(a)	(b)
A: 0 0 0 1 1 0 1 1	A: (−1 −1 −1 +1 +1 −1 +1 +1)
B: 0 0 1 0 1 1 1 0	B: (−1 −1 +1 −1 +1 +1 +1 −1)
C: 0 1 0 1 1 1 0 0	C: (−1 +1 −1 +1 +1 +1 −1 −1)
D: 0 1 0 0 0 0 1 0	D: (−1 +1 −1 −1 −1 −1 +1 −1)

Six examples:

− − 1 −	**C**	S_1 = (−1 +1 −1 +1 +1 +1 −1 −1)
− 1 1 −	**B** + **C**	S_2 = (−2 0 0 0 +2 +2 0 −2)
1 0 − −	**A** + $\overline{\mathbf{B}}$	S_3 = (0 0 −2 +2 0 −2 0 +2)
1 0 1 −	**A** + $\overline{\mathbf{B}}$ + **C**	S_4 = (−1 +1 −3 +3 +1 −1 −1 +1)
1 1 1 1	**A** + **B** + **C** + **D**	S_5 = (−4 0 −2 0 +2 0 +2 −2)
1 1 0 1	**A** + **B** + $\overline{\mathbf{C}}$ + **D**	S_6 = (−2 −2 0 −2 0 −2 +4 0)

(c)

S_1 • C = (1 +1 +1 +1 +1 +1 +1 +1)/8 = 1
S_2 • C = (2 +0 +0 +0 +2 +2 +0 +2)/8 = 1
S_3 • C = (0 +0 +2 +2 +0 −2 +0 −2)/8 = 0
S_4 • C = (1 +1 +3 +3 +1 −1 +1 −1)/8 = 1
S_5 • C = (4 +0 +2 +0 +2 +0 −2 +2)/8 = 1
S_6 • C = (2 −2 +0 −2 +0 −2 −4 +0)/8 = −1

(d)

Figure 2-45. (a) Binary chip sequences for four stations. (b) Bipolar chip sequences. (c) Six examples of transmissions. (d) Recovery of station C's signal.

Each station has its own unique chip sequence. Let us use the symbol **S** to indicate the m-chip vector for station S, and $\overline{\mathbf{S}}$ for its negation. All chip sequences are pairwise **orthogonal**, by which we mean that the normalized inner product of any two distinct chip sequences, **S** and **T** (written as **S•T**), is 0. It is known how to generate such orthogonal chip sequences using a method known as **Walsh codes**. In mathematical terms, orthogonality of the chip sequences can be expressed as follows:

$$\mathbf{S} \bullet \mathbf{T} \equiv \frac{1}{m} \sum_{i=1}^{m} S_i T_i = 0 \tag{2-4}$$

In plain English, as many pairs are the same as are different. This orthogonality property will prove crucial later on. Note that if **S•T** = 0, then $\mathbf{S} \bullet \overline{\mathbf{T}}$ is also 0. The normalized inner product of any chip sequence with itself is 1:

$$\mathbf{S} \bullet \mathbf{S} = \frac{1}{m} \sum_{i=1}^{m} S_i S_i = \frac{1}{m} \sum_{i=1}^{m} S_i^2 = \frac{1}{m} \sum_{i=1}^{m} (\pm 1)^2 = 1$$

This follows because each of the m terms in the inner product is 1, so the sum is m. Also note that $\mathbf{S} \bullet \overline{\mathbf{S}} = -1$.

During each bit time, a station can transmit a 1 by sending its chip sequence, it can transmit a 0 by sending the negative of its chip sequence, or it can be silent and transmit nothing. For the moment, we assume that all stations are synchronized in time, so all chip sequences begin at the same instant.

When two or more stations transmit simultaneously, their bipolar signals add linearly. For example, if in one chip period three stations output +1 and one station outputs −1, the result is +2. One can think of this as adding voltages: three stations outputting +1 volts and 1 station outputting −1 volts gives 2 volts.

In Fig. 2-45(c) we see six examples of one or more stations transmitting at the same time. In the first example, C transmits a 1 bit, so we just get C's chip sequence. In the second example, both B and C transmit 1 bits, so we get the sum of their bipolar chip sequences, namely:

$$(-1\ -1\ +1\ -1\ +1\ +1\ +1\ -1) + (-1\ +1\ -1\ +1\ +1\ +1\ -1\ -1) = (-2\ \ 0\ \ 0\ \ 0\ +2\ +2\ \ 0\ -2)$$

In the third example, station A sends a 1 and station B sends a 0. The others are silent. In the fourth example, A and C send a 1 bit while B sends a 0 bit. In the fifth example, all four stations send a 1 bit. Finally, in the last example, A, B, and D send a 1 bit, while C sends a 0 bit. Note that each of the six sequences S_1 through S_6 given in Fig. 2-45(c) represents only one bit time.

To recover the bit stream of an individual station, the receiver must know that station's chip sequence in advance. It does the recovery by computing the normalized inner product of the received chip sequence (the linear sum of all the stations that transmitted) and the chip sequence of the station whose bit stream it is trying to recover. If the received chip sequence is **S** and the receiver is trying to listen to a station whose chip sequence is **C**, it just computes the normalized inner product, **S•C**.

To see why this works, just imagine that two stations, *A* and *C*, both transmit a 1 bit at the same time that *B* transmits a 0 bit. The receiver sees the sum, $\mathbf{S} = \mathbf{A} + \overline{\mathbf{B}} + \mathbf{C}$ and computes

$$\mathbf{S} \bullet \mathbf{C} = (\mathbf{A} + \overline{\mathbf{B}} + \mathbf{C}) \bullet \mathbf{C} = \mathbf{A} \bullet \mathbf{C} + \overline{\mathbf{B}} \bullet \mathbf{C} + \mathbf{C} \bullet \mathbf{C} = 0 + 0 + 1 = 1$$

The first two terms vanish because all pairs of chip sequences have been carefully chosen to be orthogonal, as shown in Eq. (2-4). Now it should be clear why this property must be imposed on the chip sequences.

An alternative way of thinking about this situation is to imagine that the three chip sequences all came in separately, rather than summed. Then, the receiver would compute the inner product with each one separately and add the results. Due to the orthogonality property, all the inner products except $\mathbf{C} \bullet \mathbf{C}$ would be 0. Adding them and then doing the inner product is in fact the same as doing the inner products and then adding those.

To make the decoding process more concrete, let us consider the six examples of Fig. 2-45(c) again as illustrated in Fig. 2-45(d). Suppose that the receiver is interested in extracting the bit sent by station *C* from each of the six sums S_1 through S_6. It calculates the bit by summing the pairwise products of the received **S** and the **C** vector of Fig. 2-45(b) and then taking 1/8 of the result (since $m = 8$ here). As shown, the correct bit is decoded each time. It is just like speaking French.

In an ideal, noiseless CDMA system, the capacity (i.e., number of stations) can be made arbitrarily large, just as the capacity of a noiseless Nyquist channel can be made arbitrarily large by using more and more bits per sample. In practice, physical limitations reduce the capacity considerably. First, we have assumed that all the chips are synchronized in time. In reality, such synchronization is impossible. What can be done is that the sender and receiver synchronize by having the sender transmit a predefined chip sequence that is long enough for the receiver to lock onto. All the other (unsynchronized) transmissions are then seen as random noise. If there are not too many of them, however, the basic decoding algorithm still works fairly well. A large body of theory exists relating the superposition of chip sequences to noise level (Pickholtz et al., 1982). As one might expect, the longer the chip sequence, the higher the probability of detecting it correctly in the presence of noise. For extra reliability, the bit sequence can use an error-correcting code. Chip sequences never use error-correcting codes.

An implicit assumption in our discussion is that the power levels of all stations are the same as perceived by the receiver. CDMA is typically used for wireless systems with a fixed base station and many mobile stations at varying distances from it. The power levels received at the base station depend on how far away the transmitters are. A good heuristic here is for each mobile station to transmit to the base station at the inverse of the power level it receives from the base station. In other words, a mobile station receiving a weak signal from the will use more power than one getting a strong signal. The base station can also give explicit commands to the mobile stations to increase or decrease their transmission power.

We have also assumed that the receiver knows who the sender is. In principle, given enough computing capacity, the receiver can listen to all the senders at once by running the decoding algorithm for each of them in parallel. In real life, suffice it to say that this is easier said than done. CDMA also has many other complicating factors that have been glossed over in this brief introduction. Nevertheless, CDMA is a clever scheme that is being rapidly introduced for wireless mobile communication. It normally operates in a band of 1.25 MHz (versus 30 kHz for D-AMPS and 200 kHz for GSM), but it supports many more users in that band than either of the other systems. In practice, the bandwidth available to each user is at least as good as GSM and often much better.

Engineers who want to gain a very deep understanding of CDMA should read (Lee and Miller, 1998). An alternative spreading scheme, in which the spreading is over time rather than frequency, is described in (Crespo et al., 1995). Yet another scheme is described in (Sari et al., 2000). All of these references require quite a bit of background in communication engineering.

2.6.3 Third-Generation Mobile Phones: Digital Voice and Data

What is the future of mobile telephony? Let us take a quick look. A number of factors are driving the industry. First, data traffic already exceeds voice traffic on the fixed network and is growing exponentially, whereas voice traffic is essentially flat. Many industry experts expect data traffic to dominate voice on mobile devices as well soon. Second, the telephone, entertainment, and computer industries have all gone digital and are rapidly converging. Many people are drooling over a lightweight, portable device that acts as a telephone, CD player, DVD player, e-mail terminal, Web interface, gaming machine, word processor, and more, all with worldwide wireless connectivity to the Internet at high bandwidth. This device and how to connect it is what third generation mobile telephony is all about. For more information, see (Huber et al., 2000; and Sarikaya, 2000).

Back in 1992, ITU tried to get a bit more specific about this dream and issued a blueprint for getting there called **IMT-2000**, where IMT stood for **International Mobile Telecommunications**. The number 2000 stood for three things: (1) the year it was supposed to go into service, (2) the frequency it was supposed to operate at (in MHz), and (3) the bandwidth the service should have (in kHz).

It did not make it on any of the three counts. Nothing was implemented by 2000. ITU recommended that all governments reserve spectrum at 2 GHz so devices could roam seamlessly from country to country. China reserved the required bandwidth but nobody else did. Finally, it was recognized that 2 Mbps is not currently feasible for users who are *too* mobile (due to the difficulty of performing handoffs quickly enough). More realistic is 2 Mbps for stationary indoor users (which will compete head-on with ADSL), 384 kbps for people walking, and 144 kbps for connections in cars. Nevertheless, the whole area of **3G**, as it is called, is one great cauldron of activity. The third generation may be a bit less than originally hoped for and a bit late, but it will surely happen.

The basic services that the IMT-2000 network is supposed to provide to its users are:

1. High-quality voice transmission.
2. Messaging (replacing e-mail, fax, SMS, chat, etc.).
3. Multimedia (playing music, viewing videos, films, television, etc.).
4. Internet access (Web surfing, including pages with audio and video).

Additional services might be video conferencing, telepresence, group game playing, and m-commerce (waving your telephone at the cashier to pay in a store). Furthermore, all these services are supposed to be available worldwide (with automatic connection via a satellite when no terrestrial network can be located), instantly (always on), and with quality-of-service guarantees.

ITU envisioned a single worldwide technology for IMT-2000, so that manufacturers could build a single device that could be sold and used anywhere in the world (like CD players and computers and unlike mobile phones and televisions). Having a single technology would also make life much simpler for network operators and would encourage more people to use the services. Format wars, such as the Betamax versus VHS battle when videorecorders first came out, are not good for business.

Several proposals were made, and after some winnowing, it came down to two main ones. The first one, **W-CDMA** (**Wideband CDMA**), was proposed by Ericsson. This system uses direct sequence spread spectrum of the type we described above. It runs in a 5 MHz bandwidth and has been designed to interwork with GSM networks although it is not backward compatible with GSM. It does, however, have the property that a caller can leave a W-CDMA cell and enter a GSM cell without losing the call. This system was pushed hard by the European Union, which called it **UMTS** (**Universal Mobile Telecommunications System**).

The other contender was **CDMA2000**, proposed by Qualcomm. It, too, is a direct sequence spread spectrum design, basically an extension of IS-95 and backward compatible with it. It also uses a 5-MHz bandwidth, but it has not been designed to interwork with GSM and cannot hand off calls to a GSM cell (or a D-AMPS cell, for that matter). Other technical differences with W-CDMA include a different chip rate, different frame time, different spectrum used, and a different way to do time synchronization.

If the Ericsson and Qualcomm engineers were put in a room and told to come to a common design, they probably could. After all, the basic principle behind both systems is CDMA in a 5 MHz channel and nobody is willing to die for his preferred chip rate. The trouble is that the real problem is not engineering, but politics (as usual). Europe wanted a system that interworked with GSM; the U.S. wanted a system that was compatible with one already widely deployed in the U.S. (IS-95). Each side also supported its local company (Ericsson is based in Sweden; Qualcomm is in California). Finally, Ericsson and Qualcomm were involved in numerous lawsuits over their respective CDMA patents.

In March 1999, the two companies settled the lawsuits when Ericsson agreed to buy Qualcomm's infrastructure. They also agreed to a single 3G standard, but one with multiple incompatible options, which to a large extent just papers over the technical differences. These disputes notwithstanding, 3G devices and services are likely to start appearing in the coming years.

Much has been written about 3G systems, most of it praising it as the greatest thing since sliced bread. Some references are (Collins and Smith, 2001; De Vriendt et al., 2002; Harte et al., 2002; Lu, 2002; and Sarikaya, 2000). However, some dissenters think that the industry is pointed in the wrong direction (Garber, 2002; and Goodman, 2000).

While waiting for the fighting over 3G to stop, some operators are gingerly taking a cautious small step in the direction of 3G by going to what is sometimes called **2.5G**, although 2.1G might be more accurate. One such system is **EDGE** (**Enhanced Data rates for GSM Evolution**), which is just GSM with more bits per baud. The trouble is, more bits per baud also means more errors per baud, so EDGE has nine different schemes for modulation and error correction, differing on how much of the bandwidth is devoted to fixing the errors introduced by the higher speed.

Another 2.5G scheme is **GPRS** (**General Packet Radio Service**), which is an overlay packet network on top of D-AMPS or GSM. It allows mobile stations to send and receive IP packets in a cell running a voice system. When GPRS is in operation, some time slots on some frequencies are reserved for packet traffic. The number and location of the time slots can be dynamically managed by the base station, depending on the ratio of voice to data traffic in the cell.

The available time slots are divided into several logical channels, used for different purposes. The base station determines which logical channels are mapped onto which time slots. One logical channel is for downloading packets from the base station to some mobile station, with each packet indicating who it is destined for. To send an IP packet, a mobile station requests one or more time slots by sending a request to the base station. If the request arrives without damage, the base station announces the frequency and time slots allocated to the mobile for sending the packet. Once the packet has arrived at the base station, it is transferred to the Internet by a wired connection. Since GPRS is just an overlay over the existing voice system, it is at best a stop-gap measure until 3G arrives.

Even though 3G networks are not fully deployed yet, some researchers regard 3G as a done deal and thus not interesting any more. These people are already working on 4G systems (Berezdivin et al., 2002; Guo and Chaskar, 2002; Huang and Zhuang, 2002; Kellerer et al., 2002; and Misra et al., 2002). Some of the proposed features of 4G systems include high bandwidth, ubiquity (connectivity everywhere), seamless integration with wired networks and especially IP, adaptive resource and spectrum management, software radios, and high quality of service for multimedia.

Then on the other hand, so many 802.11 wireless LAN access points are being set up all over the place, that some people think 3G is not only not a done deal, it is doomed. In this vision, people will just wander from one 802.11 access point to another to stay connected. To say the industry is in a state of enormous flux is a huge understatement. Check back in about 5 years to see what happens.

2.7 CABLE TELEVISION

We have now studied both the fixed and wireless telephone systems in a fair amount of detail. Both will clearly play a major role in future networks. However, an alternative available for fixed networking is now becoming a major player: cable television networks. Many people already get their telephone and Internet service over the cable, and the cable operators are actively working to increase their market share. In the following sections we will look at cable television as a networking system in more detail and contrast it with the telephone systems we have just studied. For more information about cable, see (Laubach et al., 2001; Louis, 2002; Ovadia, 2001; and Smith, 2002).

2.7.1 Community Antenna Television

Cable television was conceived in the late 1940s as a way to provide better reception to people living in rural or mountainous areas. The system initially consisted of a big antenna on top of a hill to pluck the television signal out of the air, an amplifier, called the **head end**, to strengthen it, and a coaxial cable to deliver it to people's houses, as illustrated in Fig. 2-46.

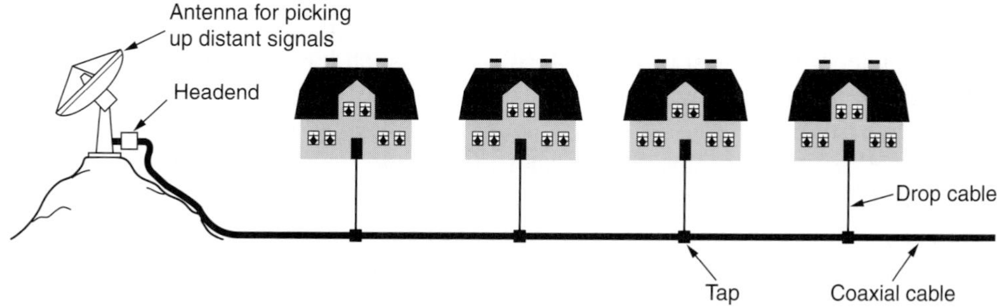

Figure 2-46. An early cable television system.

In the early years, cable television was called **Community Antenna Television**. It was very much a mom-and-pop operation; anyone handy with electronics could set up a service for his town, and the users would chip in to pay the costs. As the number of subscribers grew, additional cables were spliced onto the original cable and amplifiers were added as needed. Transmission was one way, from the headend to the users. By 1970, thousands of independent systems existed.

In 1974, Time, Inc., started a new channel, Home Box Office, with new content (movies) and distributed only on cable. Other cable-only channels followed with news, sports, cooking, and many other topics. This development gave rise to two changes in the industry. First, large corporations began buying up existing cable systems and laying new cable to acquire new subscribers. Second, there was now a need to connect multiple systems, often in distant cities, in order to distribute the new cable channels. The cable companies began to lay cable between their cities to connect them all into a single system. This pattern was analogous to what happened in the telephone industry 80 years earlier with the connection of previously isolated end offices to make long distance calling possible.

2.7.2 Internet over Cable

Over the course of the years the cable system grew and the cables between the various cities were replaced by high-bandwidth fiber, similar to what was happening in the telephone system. A system with fiber for the long-haul runs and coaxial cable to the houses is called an **HFC** (**Hybrid Fiber Coax**) system. The electro-optical converters that interface between the optical and electrical parts of the system are called **fiber nodes**. Because the bandwidth of fiber is so much more than that of coax, a fiber node can feed multiple coaxial cables. Part of a modern HFC system is shown in Fig. 2-47(a).

In recent years, many cable operators have decided to get into the Internet access business, and often the telephony business as well. However, technical differences between the cable plant and telephone plant have an effect on what has to be done to achieve these goals. For one thing, all the one-way amplifiers in the system have to be replaced by two-way amplifiers.

However, there is another difference between the HFC system of Fig. 2-47(a) and the telephone system of Fig. 2-47(b) that is much harder to remove. Down in the neighborhoods, a single cable is shared by many houses, whereas in the telephone system, every house has its own private local loop. When used for television broadcasting, this sharing does not play a role. All the programs are broadcast on the cable and it does not matter whether there are 10 viewers or 10,000 viewers. When the same cable is used for Internet access, it matters a lot if there are 10 users or 10,000. If one user decides to download a very large file, that bandwidth is potentially being taken away from other users. The more users, the more competition for bandwidth. The telephone system does not have this particular property: downloading a large file over an ADSL line does not reduce your

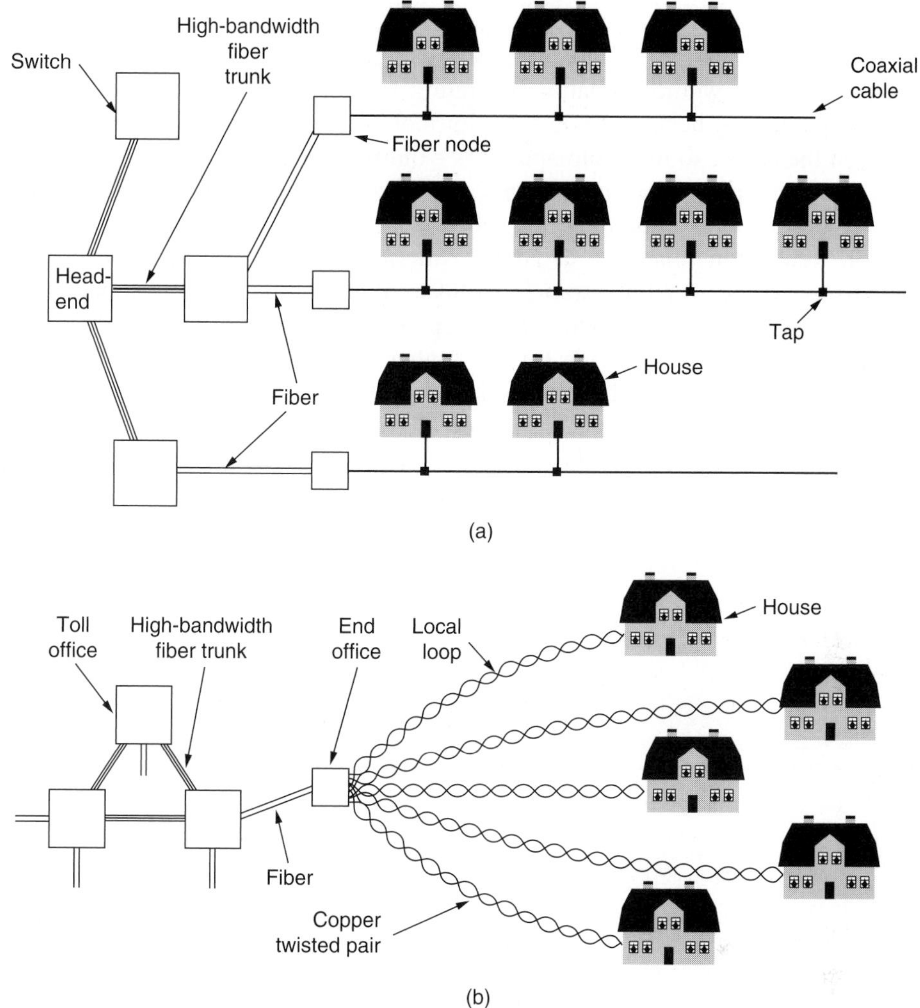

Figure 2-47. (a) Cable television. (b) The fixed telephone system.

neighbor's bandwidth. On the other hand, the bandwidth of coax is much higher than that of twisted pairs.

The way the cable industry has tackled this problem is to split up long cables and connect each one directly to a fiber node. The bandwidth from the headend to each fiber node is effectively infinite, so as long as there are not too many subscribers on each cable segment, the amount of traffic is manageable. Typical cables nowadays have 500–2000 houses, but as more and more people subscribe to Internet over cable, the load may become too much, requiring more splitting and more fiber nodes.

2.7.3 Spectrum Allocation

Throwing off all the TV channels and using the cable infrastructure strictly for Internet access would probably generate a fair number of irate customers, so cable companies are hesitant to do this. Furthermore, most cities heavily regulate what is on the cable, so the cable operators would not be allowed to do this even if they really wanted to. As a consequence, they needed to find a way to have television and Internet coexist on the same cable.

Cable television channels in North America normally occupy the 54–550 MHz region (except for FM radio from 88 to 108 MHz). These channels are 6 MHz wide, including guard bands. In Europe the low end is usually 65 MHz and the channels are 6–8 MHz wide for the higher resolution required by PAL and SECAM but otherwise the allocation scheme is similar. The low part of the band is not used. Modern cables can also operate well above 550 MHz, often to 750 MHz or more. The solution chosen was to introduce upstream channels in the 5–42 MHz band (slightly higher in Europe) and use the frequencies at the high end for the downstream. The cable spectrum is illustrated in Fig. 2-48.

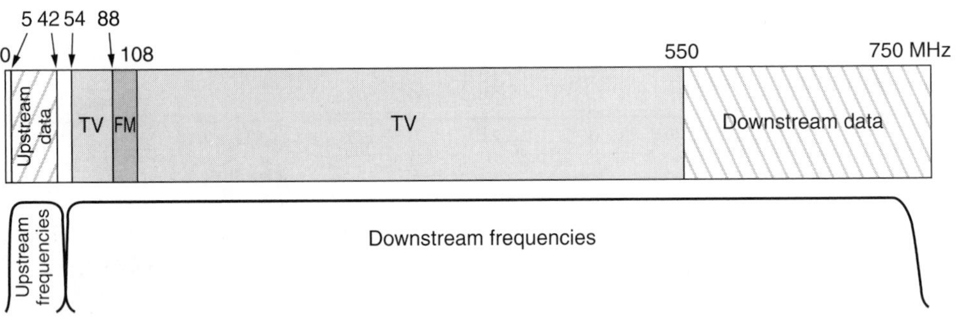

Figure 2-48. Frequency allocation in a typical cable TV system used for Internet access.

Note that since the television signals are all downstream, it is possible to use upstream amplifiers that work only in the 5–42 MHz region and downstream amplifiers that work only at 54 MHz and up, as shown in the figure. Thus, we get an asymmetry in the upstream and downstream bandwidths because more spectrum is available above television than below it. On the other hand, most of the traffic is likely to be downstream, so cable operators are not unhappy with this fact of life. As we saw earlier, telephone companies usually offer an asymmetric DSL service, even though they have no technical reason for doing so.

Long coaxial cables are not any better for transmitting digital signals than are long local loops, so analog modulation is needed here, too. The usual scheme is to take each 6 MHz or 8 MHz downstream channel and modulate it with QAM-64 or, if the cable quality is exceptionally good, QAM-256. With a 6 MHz channel and QAM-64, we get about 36 Mbps. When the overhead is subtracted, the net payload is about 27 Mbps. With QAM-256, the net payload is about 39 Mbps. The European values are 1/3 larger.

For upstream, even QAM-64 does not work well. There is too much noise from terrestrial microwaves, CB radios, and other sources, so a more conservative scheme—QPSK—is used. This method (shown in Fig. 2-25) yields 2 bits per baud instead of the 6 or 8 bits QAM provides on the downstream channels. Consequently, the asymmetry between upstream bandwidth and downstream bandwidth is much more than suggested by Fig. 2-48.

In addition to upgrading the amplifiers, the operator has to upgrade the headend, too, from a dumb amplifier to an intelligent digital computer system with a high-bandwidth fiber interface to an ISP. Often the name gets upgraded as well, from "headend" to **CMTS** (**Cable Modem Termination System**). In the following text, we will refrain from doing a name upgrade and stick with the traditional "headend."

2.7.4 Cable Modems

Internet access requires a cable modem, a device that has two interfaces on it: one to the computer and one to the cable network. In the early years of cable Internet, each operator had a proprietary cable modem, which was installed by a cable company technician. However, it soon became apparent that an open standard would create a competitive cable modem market and drive down prices, thus encouraging use of the service. Furthermore, having the customers buy cable modems in stores and install them themselves (as they do with V.9x telephone modems) would eliminate the dreaded truck rolls.

Consequently, the larger cable operators teamed up with a company called CableLabs to produce a cable modem standard and to test products for compliance. This standard, called **DOCSIS** (**Data Over Cable Service Interface Specification**) is just starting to replace proprietary modems. The European version is called **EuroDOCSIS**. Not all cable operators like the idea of a standard, however, since many of them were making good money leasing their modems to their captive customers. An open standard with dozens of manufacturers selling cable modems in stores ends this lucrative practice.

The modem-to-computer interface is straightforward. It is normally 10-Mbps Ethernet (or occasionally USB) at present. In the future, the entire modem might be a small card plugged into the computer, just as with V.9x internal modems.

The other end is more complicated. A large part of the standard deals with radio engineering, a subject that is far beyond the scope of this book. The only part worth mentioning here is that cable modems, like ADSL modems, are always on. They make a connection when turned on and maintain that connection as long as they are powered up because cable operators do not charge for connect time.

To better understand how they work, let us see what happens when a cable modem is plugged in and powered up. The modem scans the downstream channels looking for a special packet periodically put out by the headend to provide system parameters to modems that have just come on-line. Upon finding this packet, the new modem announces its presence on one of the upstream channels. The headend responds by assigning the modem to its upstream and downstream channels. These assignments can be changed later if the headend deems it necessary to balance the load.

The modem then determines its distance from the headend by sending it a special packet and seeing how long it takes to get the response. This process is called **ranging**. It is important for the modem to know its distance to accommodate the way the upstream channels operate and to get the timing right. They are divided in time in **minislots**. Each upstream packet must fit in one or more consecutive minislots. The headend announces the start of a new round of minislots periodically, but the starting gun is not heard at all modems simultaneously due to the propagation time down the cable. By knowing how far it is from the headend, each modem can compute how long ago the first minislot really started. Minislot length is network dependent. A typical payload is 8 bytes.

During initialization, the headend also assigns each modem to a minislot to use for requesting upstream bandwidth. As a rule, multiple modems will be assigned the same minislot, which leads to contention. When a computer wants to send a packet, it transfers the packet to the modem, which then requests the necessary number of minislots for it. If the request is accepted, the headend puts an acknowledgement on the downstream channel telling the modem which minislots have been reserved for its packet. The packet is then sent, starting in the minislot allocated to it. Additional packets can be requested using a field in the header.

On the other hand, if there is contention for the request minislot, there will be no acknowledgement and the modem just waits a random time and tries again. After each successive failure, the randomization time is doubled. (For readers already somewhat familiar with networking, this algorithm is just slotted ALOHA with binary exponential backoff. Ethernet cannot be used on cable because stations cannot sense the medium. We will come back to these issues in Chap. 4.)

The downstream channels are managed differently from the upstream channels. For one thing, there is only one sender (the headend) so there is no contention and no need for minislots, which is actually just time division statistical multiplexing. For another, the traffic downstream is usually much larger than upstream, so a fixed packet size of 204 bytes is used. Part of that is a Reed-Solomon error-correcting code and some other overhead, leaving a user payload of 184 bytes. These numbers were chosen for compatibility with digital television using MPEG-2, so the TV and downstream data channels are formatted the same way. Logically, the connections are as depicted in Fig. 2-49.

Getting back to modem initialization, once the modem has completed ranging and gotten its upstream channel, downstream channel, and minislot assignments,

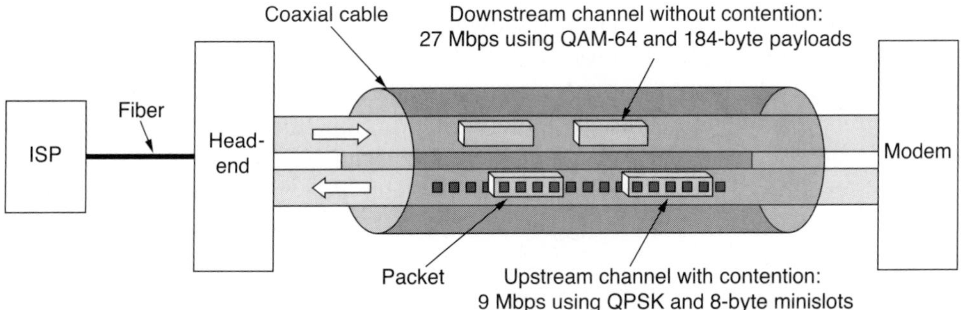

Figure 2-49. Typical details of the upstream and downstream channels in North America.

it is free to start sending packets. The first packet it sends is one to the ISP requesting an IP address, which is dynamically assigned using a protocol called DHCP, which we will study in Chap. 5. It also requests and gets an accurate time of day from the headend.

The next step involves security. Since cable is a shared medium, anybody who wants to go to the trouble to do so can read all the traffic going past him. To prevent everyone from snooping on their neighbors (literally), all traffic is encrypted in both directions. Part of the initialization procedure involves establishing encryption keys. At first one might think that having two strangers, the headend and the modem, establish a secret key in broad daylight with thousands of people watching would be impossible. Turns out it is not, but we have to wait until Chap. 8 to explain how (the short answer: use the Diffie-Hellman algorithm).

Finally, the modem has to log in and provide its unique identifier over the secure channel. At this point the initialization is complete. The user can now log in to the ISP and get to work.

There is much more to be said about cable modems. Some relevant references are (Adams and Dulchinos, 2001; Donaldson and Jones, 2001; and Dutta-Roy, 2001).

2.7.5 ADSL versus Cable

Which is better, ADSL or cable? That is like asking which operating system is better. Or which language is better. Or which religion. Which answer you get depends on whom you ask. Let us compare ADSL and cable on a few points. Both use fiber in the backbone, but they differ on the edge. Cable uses coax; ADSL uses twisted pair. The theoretical carrying capacity of coax is hundreds of times more than twisted pair. However, the full capacity of the cable is not available for data users because much of the cable's bandwidth is wasted on useless stuff such as television programs.

In practice, it is hard to generalize about effective capacity. ADSL providers give specific statements about the bandwidth (e.g., 1 Mbps downstream, 256 kbps upstream) and generally achieve about 80% of it consistently. Cable providers do not make any claims because the effective capacity depends on how many people are currently active on the user's cable segment. Sometimes it may be better than ADSL and sometimes it may be worse. What can be annoying, though, is the unpredictability. Having great service one minute does not guarantee great service the next minute since the biggest bandwidth hog in town may have just turned on his computer.

As an ADSL system acquires more users, their increasing numbers have little effect on existing users, since each user has a dedicated connection. With cable, as more subscribers sign up for Internet service, performance for existing users will drop. The only cure is for the cable operator to split busy cables and connect each one to a fiber node directly. Doing so costs time and money, so there are business pressures to avoid it.

As an aside, we have already studied another system with a shared channel like cable: the mobile telephone system. Here, too, a group of users, we could call them cellmates, share a fixed amount of bandwidth. Normally, it is rigidly divided in fixed chunks among the active users by FDM and TDM because voice traffic is fairly smooth. But for data traffic, this rigid division is very inefficient because data users are frequently idle, in which case their reserved bandwidth is wasted. Nevertheless, in this respect, cable access is more like the mobile phone system than it is like the fixed system.

Availability is an issue on which ADSL and cable differ. Everyone has a telephone, but not all users are close enough to their end office to get ADSL. On the other hand, not everyone has cable, but if you do have cable and the company provides Internet access, you can get it. Distance to the fiber node or headend is not an issue. It is also worth noting that since cable started out as a television distribution medium, few businesses have it.

Being a point-to-point medium, ADSL is inherently more secure than cable. Any cable user can easily read all the packets going down the cable. For this reason, any decent cable provider will encrypt all traffic in both directions. Nevertheless, having your neighbor get your encrypted messages is still less secure than having him not get anything at all.

The telephone system is generally more reliable than cable. For example, it has backup power and continues to work normally even during a power outage. With cable, if the power to any amplifier along the chain fails, all downstream users are cut off instantly.

Finally, most ADSL providers offer a choice of ISPs. Sometimes they are even required to do so by law. This is not always the case with cable operators.

The conclusion is that ADSL and cable are much more alike than they are different. They offer comparable service and, as competition between them heats up, probably comparable prices.

2.8 SUMMARY

The physical layer is the basis of all networks. Nature imposes two fundamental limits on all channels, and these determine their bandwidth. These limits are the Nyquist limit, which deals with noiseless channels, and the Shannon limit, which deals with noisy channels.

Transmission media can be guided or unguided. The principal guided media are twisted pair, coaxial cable, and fiber optics. Unguided media include radio, microwaves, infrared, and lasers through the air. An up-and-coming transmission system is satellite communication, especially LEO systems.

A key element in most wide area networks is the telephone system. Its main components are the local loops, trunks, and switches. Local loops are analog, twisted pair circuits, which require modems for transmitting digital data. ADSL offers speeds up to 50 Mbps by dividing the local loop into many virtual channels and modulating each one separately. Wireless local loops are another new development to watch, especially LMDS.

Trunks are digital, and can be multiplexed in several ways, including FDM, TDM, and WDM. Both circuit switching and packet switching are important.

For mobile applications, the fixed telephone system is not suitable. Mobile phones are currently in widespread use for voice and will soon be in widespread use for data. The first generation was analog, dominated by AMPS. The second generation was digital, with D-AMPS, GSM, and CDMA the major options. The third generation will be digital and based on broadband CDMA.

An alternative system for network access is the cable television system, which has gradually evolved from a community antenna to hybrid fiber coax. Potentially, it offers very high bandwidth, but the actual bandwidth available in practice depends heavily on the number of other users currently active and what they are doing.

PROBLEMS

1. Compute the Fourier coefficients for the function $f(t) = t \quad (0 \le t \le 1)$.

2. A noiseless 4-kHz channel is sampled every 1 msec. What is the maximum data rate?

3. Television channels are 6 MHz wide. How many bits/sec can be sent if four-level digital signals are used? Assume a noiseless channel.

4. If a binary signal is sent over a 3-kHz channel whose signal-to-noise ratio is 20 dB, what is the maximum achievable data rate?

5. What signal-to-noise ratio is needed to put a T1 carrier on a 50-kHz line?

6. What is the difference between a passive star and an active repeater in a fiber network?

7. How much bandwidth is there in 0.1 micron of spectrum at a wavelength of 1 micron?

8. It is desired to send a sequence of computer screen images over an optical fiber. The screen is 480×640 pixels, each pixel being 24 bits. There are 60 screen images per second. How much bandwidth is needed, and how many microns of wavelength are needed for this band at 1.30 microns?

9. Is the Nyquist theorem true for optical fiber or only for copper wire?

10. In Fig. 2-6 the lefthand band is narrower than the others. Why?

11. Radio antennas often work best when the diameter of the antenna is equal to the wavelength of the radio wave. Reasonable antennas range from 1 cm to 5 meters in diameter. What frequency range does this cover?

12. Multipath fading is maximized when the two beams arrive 180 degrees out of phase. How much of a path difference is required to maximize the fading for a 50-km-long 1-GHz microwave link?

13. A laser beam 1 mm wide is aimed at a detector 1 mm wide 100 m away on the roof of a building. How much of an angular diversion (in degrees) does the laser have to have before it misses the detector?

14. The 66 low-orbit satellites in the Iridium project are divided into six necklaces around the earth. At the altitude they are using, the period is 90 minutes. What is the average interval for handoffs for a stationary transmitter?

15. Consider a satellite at the altitude of geostationary satellites but whose orbital plane is inclined to the equatorial plane by an angle ϕ. To a stationary user on the earth's surface at north latitude ϕ, does this satellite appear motionless in the sky? If not, describe its motion.

16. How many end office codes were there pre-1984, when each end office was named by its three-digit area code and the first three digits of the local number? Area codes started with a digit in the range 2–9, had a 0 or 1 as the second digit, and ended with any digit. The first two digits of a local number were always in the range 2–9. The third digit could be any digit.

17. Using *only* the data given in the text, what is the maximum number of telephones that the existing U.S. system can support without changing the numbering plan or adding additional equipment? Could this number of telephones actually be achieved? For purposes of this problem, a computer or fax machine counts as a telephone. Assume there is only one device per subscriber line.

18. A simple telephone system consists of two end offices and a single toll office to which each end office is connected by a 1-MHz full-duplex trunk. The average telephone is used to make four calls per 8-hour workday. The mean call duration is 6 min. Ten percent of the calls are long-distance (i.e., pass through the toll office). What is the maximum number of telephones an end office can support? (Assume 4 kHz per circuit.)

19. A regional telephone company has 10 million subscribers. Each of their telephones is connected to a central office by a copper twisted pair. The average length of these twisted pairs is 10 km. How much is the copper in the local loops worth? Assume that the cross section of each strand is a circle 1 mm in diameter, the density of copper is 9.0 grams/cm^3, and that copper sells for 3 dollars per kilogram.

20. Is an oil pipeline a simplex system, a half-duplex system, a full-duplex system, or none of the above?

21. The cost of a fast microprocessor has dropped to the point where it is now possible to put one in each modem. How does that affect the handling of telephone line errors?

22. A modem constellation diagram similar to Fig. 2-25 has data points at the following coordinates: (1, 1), (1, −1), (−1, 1), and (−1, −1). How many bps can a modem with these parameters achieve at 1200 baud?

23. A modem constellation diagram similar to Fig. 2-25 has data points at (0, 1) and (0, 2). Does the modem use phase modulation or amplitude modulation?

24. In a constellation diagram, all the points lie on a circle centered on the origin. What kind of modulation is being used?

25. How many frequencies does a full-duplex QAM-64 modem use?

26. An ADSL system using DMT allocates 3/4 of the available data channels to the downstream link. It uses QAM-64 modulation on each channel. What is the capacity of the downstream link?

27. In the four-sector LMDS example of Fig. 2-30, each sector has its own 36-Mbps channel. According to queueing theory, if the channel is 50% loaded, the queueing time will be equal to the download time. Under these conditions, how long does it take to download a 5-KB Web page? How long does it take to download the page over a 1-Mbps ADSL line? Over a 56-kbps modem?

28. Ten signals, each requiring 4000 Hz, are multiplexed on to a single channel using FDM. How much minimum bandwidth is required for the multiplexed channel? Assume that the guard bands are 400 Hz wide.

29. Why has the PCM sampling time been set at 125 μsec?

30. What is the percent overhead on a T1 carrier; that is, what percent of the 1.544 Mbps are not delivered to the end user?

31. Compare the maximum data rate of a noiseless 4-kHz channel using
(a) Analog encoding (e.g., QPSK) with 2 bits per sample.
(b) The T1 PCM system.

32. If a T1 carrier system slips and loses track of where it is, it tries to resynchronize using the 1st bit in each frame. How many frames will have to be inspected on average to resynchronize with a probability of 0.001 of being wrong?

33. What is the difference, if any, between the demodulator part of a modem and the coder part of a codec? (After all, both convert analog signals to digital ones.)

34. A signal is transmitted digitally over a 4-kHz noiseless channel with one sample every 125 μsec. How many bits per second are actually sent for each of these encoding methods?
(a) CCITT 2.048 Mbps standard.
(b) DPCM with a 4-bit relative signal value.
(c) Delta modulation.

35. A pure sine wave of amplitude A is encoded using delta modulation, with x samples/sec. An output of +1 corresponds to a signal change of $+A/8$, and an output signal of −1 corresponds to a signal change of $-A/8$. What is the highest frequency that can be tracked without cumulative error?

36. SONET clocks have a drift rate of about 1 part in 10^9. How long does it take for the drift to equal the width of 1 bit? What are the implications of this calculation?

37. In Fig. 2-37, the user data rate for OC-3 is stated to be 148.608 Mbps. Show how this number can be derived from the SONET OC-3 parameters.

38. To accommodate lower data rates than STS-1, SONET has a system of virtual tributaries (VT). A VT is a partial payload that can be inserted into an STS-1 frame and combined with other partial payloads to fill the data frame. VT1.5 uses 3 columns, VT2 uses 4 columns, VT3 uses 6 columns, and VT6 uses 12 columns of an STS-1 frame. Which VT can accommodate
(a) A DS-1 service (1.544 Mbps)?
(b) European CEPT-1 service (2.048 Mbps)?
(c) A DS-2 service (6.312 Mbps)?

39. What is the essential difference between message switching and packet switching?

40. What is the available user bandwidth in an OC-12c connection?

41. Three packet-switching networks each contain n nodes. The first network has a star topology with a central switch, the second is a (bidirectional) ring, and the third is fully interconnected, with a wire from every node to every other node. What are the best-, average-, and-worst case transmission paths in hops?

42. Compare the delay in sending an x-bit message over a k-hop path in a circuit-switched network and in a (lightly loaded) packet-switched network. The circuit setup time is s sec, the propagation delay is d sec per hop, the packet size is p bits, and the data rate is b bps. Under what conditions does the packet network have a lower delay?

43. Suppose that x bits of user data are to be transmitted over a k-hop path in a packet-switched network as a series of packets, each containing p data bits and h header bits, with $x \gg p + h$. The bit rate of the lines is b bps and the propagation delay is negligible. What value of p minimizes the total delay?

44. In a typical mobile phone system with hexagonal cells, it is forbidden to reuse a frequency band in an adjacent cell. If 840 frequencies are available, how many can be used in a given cell?

45. The actual layout of cells is seldom as regular that as shown in Fig. 2-41. Even the shapes of individual cells are typically irregular. Give a possible reason why this might be.

46. Make a rough estimate of the number of PCS microcells 100 m in diameter it would take to cover San Francisco (120 square km).

47. Sometimes when a mobile user crosses the boundary from one cell to another, the current call is abruptly terminated, even though all transmitters and receivers are functioning perfectly. Why?

48. D-AMPS has appreciably worse speech quality than GSM. Is this due to the requirement that D-AMPS be backward compatible with AMPS, whereas GSM had no such constraint? If not, what is the cause?

49. Calculate the maximum number of users that D-AMPS can support simultaneously within a single cell. Do the same calculation for GSM. Explain the difference.

50. Suppose that *A*, *B*, and *C* are simultaneously transmitting 0 bits, using a CDMA system with the chip sequences of Fig. 2-45(b). What is the resulting chip sequence?

51. In the discussion about orthogonality of CDMA chip sequences, it was stated that if $\mathbf{S} \bullet \mathbf{T} = 0$ then $\mathbf{S} \bullet \overline{\mathbf{T}}$ is also 0. Prove this.

52. Consider a different way of looking at the orthogonality property of CDMA chip sequences. Each bit in a pair of sequences can match or not match. Express the orthogonality property in terms of matches and mismatches.

53. A CDMA receiver gets the following chips: (−1 +1 −3 +1 −1 −3 +1 +1). Assuming the chip sequences defined in Fig. 2-45(b), which stations transmitted, and which bits did each one send?

54. At the low end, the telephone system is star shaped, with all the local loops in a neighborhood converging on an end office. In contrast, cable television consists of a single long cable snaking its way past all the houses in the same neighborhood. Suppose that a future TV cable were 10 Gbps fiber instead of copper. Could it be used to simulate the telephone model of everybody having their own private line to the end office? If so, how many one-telephone houses could be hooked up to a single fiber?

55. A cable TV system has 100 commercial channels, all of them alternating programs with advertising. Is this more like TDM or like FDM?

56. A cable company decides to provide Internet access over cable in a neighborhood consisting of 5000 houses. The company uses a coaxial cable and spectrum allocation allowing 100 Mbps downstream bandwidth per cable. To attract customers, the company decides to guarantee at least 2 Mbps downstream bandwidth to each house at any time. Describe what the cable company needs to do to provide this guarantee.

57. Using the spectral allocation shown in Fig. 2-48 and the information given in the text, how many Mbps does a cable system allocate to upstream and how many to downstream?

58. How fast can a cable user receive data if the network is otherwise idle?

59. Multiplexing STS-1 multiple data streams, called tributaries, plays an important role in SONET. A 3:1 multiplexer multiplexes three input STS-1 tributaries onto one output STS-3 stream. This multiplexing is done byte for byte, that is, the first three output bytes are the first bytes of tributaries 1, 2, and 3, respectively. The next three output bytes are the second bytes of tributaries 1, 2, and 3, respectively, and so on. Write a program that simulates this 3:1 multiplexer. Your program should consist of five processes. The main process creates four processes, one each for the three STS-1 tributaries and one for the multiplexer. Each tributary process reads in an STS-1 frame from an input file as a sequence of 810 bytes. They send their frames (byte by byte) to the multiplexer process. The multiplexer process receives these bytes and outputs an STS-3 frame (byte by byte) by writing it on standard output. Use pipes for communication among processes.

3

THE DATA LINK LAYER

In this chapter we will study the design principles for layer 2, the data link layer. This study deals with the algorithms for achieving reliable, efficient communication between two adjacent machines at the data link layer. By adjacent, we mean that the two machines are connected by a communication channel that acts conceptually like a wire (e.g., a coaxial cable, telephone line, or point-to-point wireless channel). The essential property of a channel that makes it "wire-like" is that the bits are delivered in exactly the same order in which they are sent.

At first you might think this problem is so trivial that there is no software to study—machine *A* just puts the bits on the wire, and machine *B* just takes them off. Unfortunately, communication circuits make errors occasionally. Furthermore, they have only a finite data rate, and there is a nonzero propagation delay between the time a bit is sent and the time it is received. These limitations have important implications for the efficiency of the data transfer. The protocols used for communications must take all these factors into consideration. These protocols are the subject of this chapter.

After an introduction to the key design issues present in the data link layer, we will start our study of its protocols by looking at the nature of errors, their causes, and how they can be detected and corrected. Then we will study a series of increasingly complex protocols, each one solving more and more of the problems present in this layer. Finally, we will conclude with an examination of protocol modeling and correctness and give some examples of data link protocols.

3.1 DATA LINK LAYER DESIGN ISSUES

The data link layer has a number of specific functions it can carry out. These functions include

1. Providing a well-defined service interface to the network layer.
2. Dealing with transmission errors.
3. Regulating the flow of data so that slow receivers are not swamped by fast senders.

To accomplish these goals, the data link layer takes the packets it gets from the network layer and encapsulates them into **frames** for transmission. Each frame contains a frame header, a payload field for holding the packet, and a frame trailer, as illustrated in Fig. 3-1. Frame management forms the heart of what the data link layer does. In the following sections we will examine all the above-mentioned issues in detail.

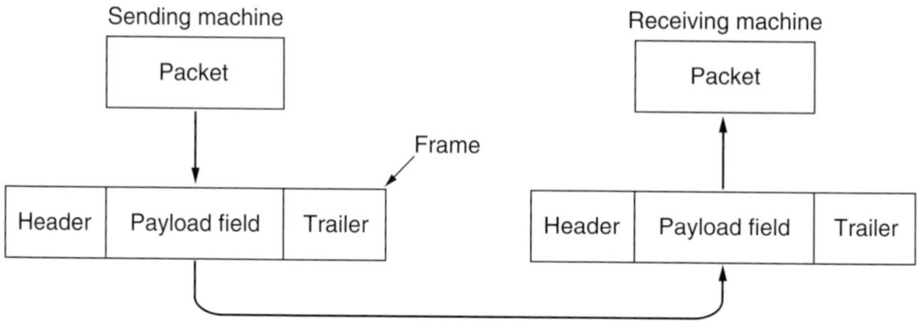

Figure 3-1. Relationship between packets and frames.

Although this chapter is explicitly about the data link layer and the data link protocols, many of the principles we will study here, such as error control and flow control, are found in transport and other protocols as well. In fact, in many networks, these functions are found only in the upper layers and not in the data link layer. However, no matter where they are found, the principles are pretty much the same, so it does not really matter where we study them. In the data link layer they often show up in their simplest and purest forms, making this a good place to examine them in detail.

3.1.1 Services Provided to the Network Layer

The function of the data link layer is to provide services to the network layer. The principal service is transferring data from the network layer on the source machine to the network layer on the destination machine. On the source machine is an entity, call it a process, in the network layer that hands some bits to the data link layer for transmission to the destination. The job of the data link layer is to transmit the bits to the destination machine so they can be handed over to the network layer there, as shown in Fig. 3-2(a). The actual transmission follows the path of Fig. 3-2(b), but it is easier to think in terms of two data link layer processes communicating using a data link protocol. For this reason, we will implicitly use the model of Fig. 3-2(a) throughout this chapter.

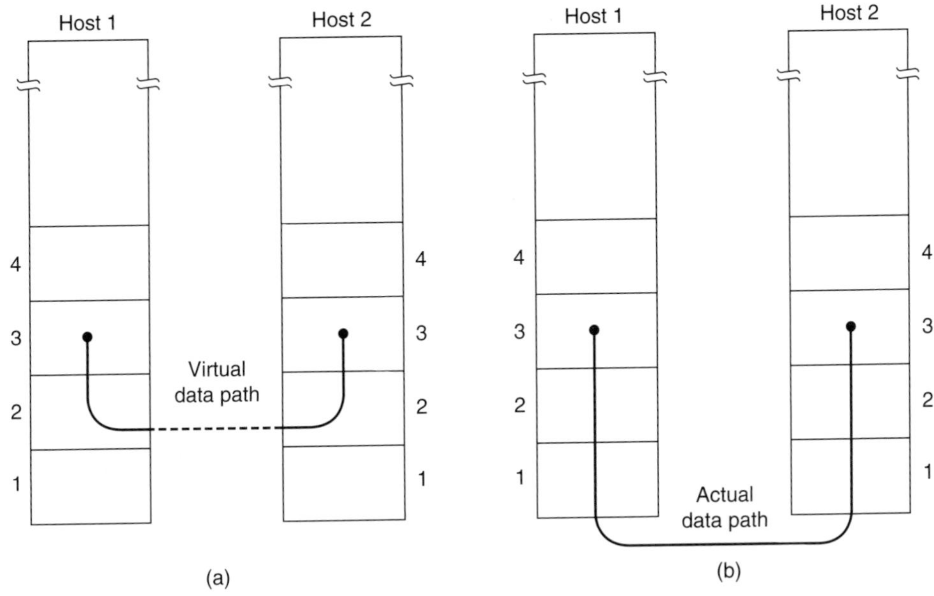

Figure 3-2. (a) Virtual communication. (b) Actual communication.

The data link layer can be designed to offer various services. The actual services offered can vary from system to system. Three reasonable possibilities that are commonly provided are

1. Unacknowledged connectionless service.
2. Acknowledged connectionless service.
3. Acknowledged connection-oriented service.

Let us consider each of these in turn.

Unacknowledged connectionless service consists of having the source machine send independent frames to the destination machine without having the destination machine acknowledge them. No logical connection is established beforehand or released afterward. If a frame is lost due to noise on the line, no attempt is made to detect the loss or recover from it in the data link layer. This class of service is appropriate when the error rate is very low so that recovery is left to higher layers. It is also appropriate for real-time traffic, such as voice, in which late data are worse than bad data. Most LANs use unacknowledged connectionless service in the data link layer.

The next step up in terms of reliability is acknowledged connectionless service. When this service is offered, there are still no logical connections used, but each frame sent is individually acknowledged. In this way, the sender knows whether a frame has arrived correctly. If it has not arrived within a specified time interval, it can be sent again. This service is useful over unreliable channels, such as wireless systems.

It is perhaps worth emphasizing that providing acknowledgements in the data link layer is just an optimization, never a requirement. The network layer can always send a packet and wait for it to be acknowledged. If the acknowledgement is not forthcoming before the timer expires, the sender can just send the entire message again. The trouble with this strategy is that frames usually have a strict maximum length imposed by the hardware and network layer packets do not. If the average packet is broken up into, say, 10 frames, and 20 percent of all frames are lost, it may take a very long time for the packet to get through. If individual frames are acknowledged and retransmitted, entire packets get through much faster. On reliable channels, such as fiber, the overhead of a heavyweight data link protocol may be unnecessary, but on wireless channels, with their inherent unreliability, it is well worth the cost.

Getting back to our services, the most sophisticated service the data link layer can provide to the network layer is connection-oriented service. With this service, the source and destination machines establish a connection before any data are transferred. Each frame sent over the connection is numbered, and the data link layer guarantees that each frame sent is indeed received. Furthermore, it guarantees that each frame is received exactly once and that all frames are received in the right order. With connectionless service, in contrast, it is conceivable that a lost acknowledgement causes a packet to be sent several times and thus received several times. Connection-oriented service, in contrast, provides the network layer processes with the equivalent of a reliable bit stream.

When connection-oriented service is used, transfers go through three distinct phases. In the first phase, the connection is established by having both sides initialize variables and counters needed to keep track of which frames have been received and which ones have not. In the second phase, one or more frames are actually transmitted. In the third and final phase, the connection is released, freeing up the variables, buffers, and other resources used to maintain the connection.

Consider a typical example: a WAN subnet consisting of routers connected by point-to-point leased telephone lines. When a frame arrives at a router, the hardware checks it for errors (using techniques we will study late in this chapter), then passes the frame to the data link layer software (which might be embedded in a chip on the network interface board). The data link layer software checks to see if this is the frame expected, and if so, gives the packet contained in the payload field to the routing software. The routing software then chooses the appropriate outgoing line and passes the packet back down to the data link layer software, which then transmits it. The flow over two routers is shown in Fig. 3-3.

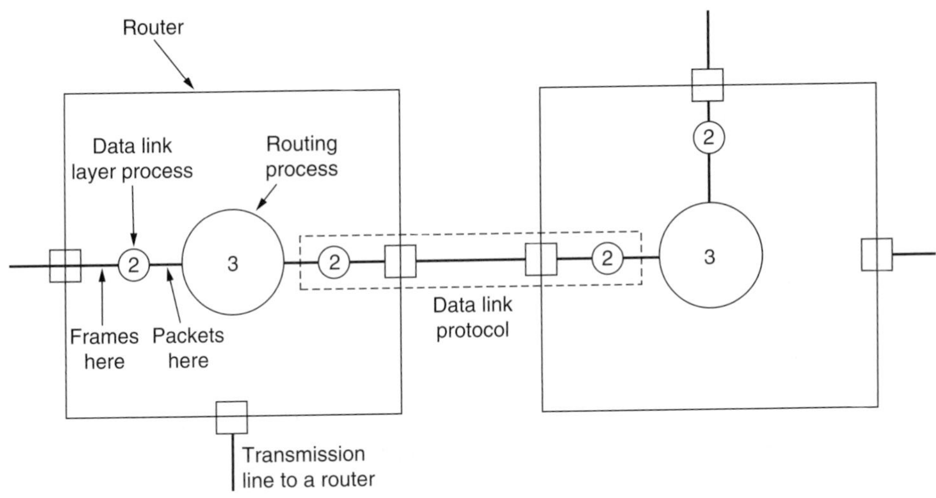

Figure 3-3. Placement of the data link protocol.

The routing code frequently wants the job done right, that is, with reliable, sequenced connections on each of the point-to-point lines. It does not want to be bothered too often with packets that got lost on the way. It is up to the data link protocol, shown in the dotted rectangle, to make unreliable communication lines look perfect or, at least, fairly good. As an aside, although we have shown multiple copies of the data link layer software in each router, in fact, one copy handles all the lines, with different tables and data structures for each one.

3.1.2 Framing

To provide service to the network layer, the data link layer must use the service provided to it by the physical layer. What the physical layer does is accept a raw bit stream and attempt to deliver it to the destination. This bit stream is not guaranteed to be error free. The number of bits received may be less than, equal to, or more than the number of bits transmitted, and they may have different values. It is up to the data link layer to detect and, if necessary, correct errors.

The usual approach is for the data link layer to break the bit stream up into discrete frames and compute the checksum for each frame. (Checksum algorithms will be discussed later in this chapter.) When a frame arrives at the destination, the checksum is recomputed. If the newly-computed checksum is different from the one contained in the frame, the data link layer knows that an error has occurred and takes steps to deal with it (e.g., discarding the bad frame and possibly also sending back an error report).

Breaking the bit stream up into frames is more difficult than it at first appears. One way to achieve this framing is to insert time gaps between frames, much like the spaces between words in ordinary text. However, networks rarely make any guarantees about timing, so it is possible these gaps might be squeezed out or other gaps might be inserted during transmission.

Since it is too risky to count on timing to mark the start and end of each frame, other methods have been devised. In this section we will look at four methods:

1. Character count.
2. Flag bytes with byte stuffing.
3. Starting and ending flags, with bit stuffing.
4. Physical layer coding violations.

The first framing method uses a field in the header to specify the number of characters in the frame. When the data link layer at the destination sees the character count, it knows how many characters follow and hence where the end of the frame is. This technique is shown in Fig. 3-4(a) for four frames of sizes 5, 5, 8, and 8 characters, respectively.

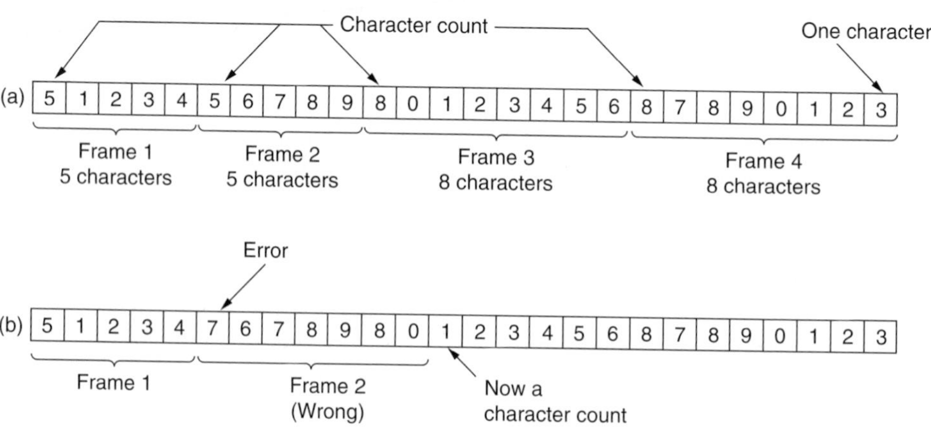

Figure 3-4. A character stream. (a) Without errors. (b) With one error.

The trouble with this algorithm is that the count can be garbled by a transmission error. For example, if the character count of 5 in the second frame of Fig. 3-4(b) becomes a 7, the destination will get out of synchronization and will be unable to locate the start of the next frame. Even if the checksum is incorrect so the destination knows that the frame is bad, it still has no way of telling where the next frame starts. Sending a frame back to the source asking for a retransmission does not help either, since the destination does not know how many characters to skip over to get to the start of the retransmission. For this reason, the character count method is rarely used anymore.

The second framing method gets around the problem of resynchronization after an error by having each frame start and end with special bytes. In the past, the starting and ending bytes were different, but in recent years most protocols have used the same byte, called a **flag byte**, as both the starting and ending delimiter, as shown in Fig. 3-5(a) as FLAG. In this way, if the receiver ever loses synchronization, it can just search for the flag byte to find the end of the current frame. Two consecutive flag bytes indicate the end of one frame and start of the next one.

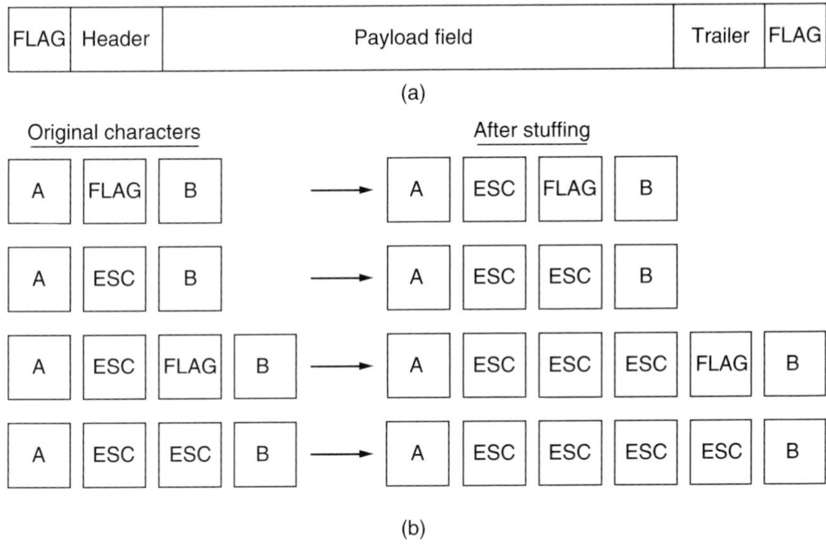

Figure 3-5. (a) A frame delimited by flag bytes. (b) Four examples of byte sequences before and after byte stuffing.

A serious problem occurs with this method when binary data, such as object programs or floating-point numbers, are being transmitted. It may easily happen that the flag byte's bit pattern occurs in the data. This situation will usually interfere with the framing. One way to solve this problem is to have the sender's data link layer insert a special escape byte (ESC) just before each "accidental" flag byte in the data. The data link layer on the receiving end removes the escape byte before the data are given to the network layer. This technique is called **byte stuffing** or **character stuffing**. Thus, a framing flag byte can be distinguished from one in the data by the absence or presence of an escape byte before it.

Of course, the next question is: What happens if an escape byte occurs in the middle of the data? The answer is that it, too, is stuffed with an escape byte. Thus, any single escape byte is part of an escape sequence, whereas a doubled one indicates that a single escape occurred naturally in the data. Some examples are shown in Fig. 3-5(b). In all cases, the byte sequence delivered after destuffing is exactly the same as the original byte sequence.

The byte-stuffing scheme depicted in Fig. 3-5 is a slight simplification of the one used in the PPP protocol that most home computers use to communicate with their Internet service provider. We will discuss PPP later in this chapter.

A major disadvantage of using this framing method is that it is closely tied to the use of 8-bit characters. Not all character codes use 8-bit characters. For example. UNICODE uses 16-bit characters, As networks developed, the disadvantages of embedding the character code length in the framing mechanism became more and more obvious, so a new technique had to be developed to allow arbitrary sized characters.

The new technique allows data frames to contain an arbitrary number of bits and allows character codes with an arbitrary number of bits per character. It works like this. Each frame begins and ends with a special bit pattern, 01111110 (in fact, a flag byte). Whenever the sender's data link layer encounters five consecutive 1s in the data, it automatically stuffs a 0 bit into the outgoing bit stream. This **bit stuffing** is analogous to byte stuffing, in which an escape byte is stuffed into the outgoing character stream before a flag byte in the data.

When the receiver sees five consecutive incoming 1 bits, followed by a 0 bit, it automatically destuffs (i.e., deletes) the 0 bit. Just as byte stuffing is completely transparent to the network layer in both computers, so is bit stuffing. If the user data contain the flag pattern, 01111110, this flag is transmitted as 011111010 but stored in the receiver's memory as 01111110. Figure 3-6 gives an example of bit stuffing.

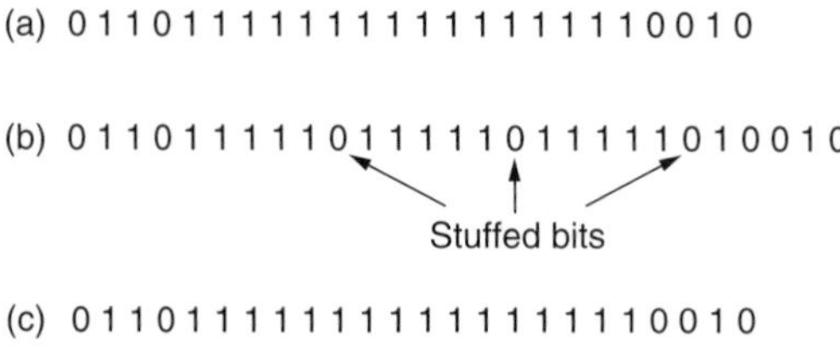

Figure 3-6. Bit stuffing. (a) The original data. (b) The data as they appear on the line. (c) The data as they are stored in the receiver's memory after destuffing.

With bit stuffing, the boundary between two frames can be unambiguously recognized by the flag pattern. Thus, if the receiver loses track of where it is, all it has to do is scan the input for flag sequences, since they can only occur at frame boundaries and never within the data.

The last method of framing is only applicable to networks in which the encoding on the physical medium contains some redundancy. For example, some LANs encode 1 bit of data by using 2 physical bits. Normally, a 1 bit is a high-low pair and a 0 bit is a low-high pair. The scheme means that every data bit has a transition in the middle, making it easy for the receiver to locate the bit boundaries. The combinations high-high and low-low are not used for data but are used for delimiting frames in some protocols.

As a final note on framing, many data link protocols use a combination of a character count with one of the other methods for extra safety. When a frame arrives, the count field is used to locate the end of the frame. Only if the appropriate delimiter is present at that position and the checksum is correct is the frame accepted as valid. Otherwise, the input stream is scanned for the next delimiter.

3.1.3 Error Control

Having solved the problem of marking the start and end of each frame, we come to the next problem: how to make sure all frames are eventually delivered to the network layer at the destination and in the proper order. Suppose that the sender just kept outputting frames without regard to whether they were arriving properly. This might be fine for unacknowledged connectionless service, but would most certainly not be fine for reliable, connection-oriented service.

The usual way to ensure reliable delivery is to provide the sender with some feedback about what is happening at the other end of the line. Typically, the protocol calls for the receiver to send back special control frames bearing positive or negative acknowledgements about the incoming frames. If the sender receives a positive acknowledgement about a frame, it knows the frame has arrived safely. On the other hand, a negative acknowledgement means that something has gone wrong, and the frame must be transmitted again.

An additional complication comes from the possibility that hardware troubles may cause a frame to vanish completely (e.g., in a noise burst). In this case, the receiver will not react at all, since it has no reason to react. It should be clear that a protocol in which the sender transmits a frame and then waits for an acknowledgement, positive or negative, will hang forever if a frame is ever lost due to, for example, malfunctioning hardware.

This possibility is dealt with by introducing timers into the data link layer. When the sender transmits a frame, it generally also starts a timer. The timer is set to expire after an interval long enough for the frame to reach the destination, be processed there, and have the acknowledgement propagate back to the sender. Normally, the frame will be correctly received and the acknowledgement will get back before the timer runs out, in which case the timer will be canceled.

However, if either the frame or the acknowledgement is lost, the timer will go off, alerting the sender to a potential problem. The obvious solution is to just transmit the frame again. However, when frames may be transmitted multiple times there is a danger that the receiver will accept the same frame two or more times and pass it to the network layer more than once. To prevent this from happening, it is generally necessary to assign sequence numbers to outgoing frames, so that the receiver can distinguish retransmissions from originals.

The whole issue of managing the timers and sequence numbers so as to ensure that each frame is ultimately passed to the network layer at the destination exactly once, no more and no less, is an important part of the data link layer's duties. Later in this chapter, we will look at a series of increasingly sophisticated examples to see how this management is done.

3.1.4 Flow Control

Another important design issue that occurs in the data link layer (and higher layers as well) is what to do with a sender that systematically wants to transmit frames faster than the receiver can accept them. This situation can easily occur when the sender is running on a fast (or lightly loaded) computer and the receiver is running on a slow (or heavily loaded) machine. The sender keeps pumping the frames out at a high rate until the receiver is completely swamped. Even if the transmission is error free, at a certain point the receiver will simply be unable to handle the frames as they arrive and will start to lose some. Clearly, something has to be done to prevent this situation.

Two approaches are commonly used. In the first one, **feedback-based flow control**, the receiver sends back information to the sender giving it permission to send more data or at least telling the sender how the receiver is doing. In the second one, **rate-based flow control**, the protocol has a built-in mechanism that limits the rate at which senders may transmit data, without using feedback from the receiver. In this chapter we will study feedback-based flow control schemes because rate-based schemes are never used in the data link layer. We will look at rate-based schemes in Chap. 5.

Various feedback-based flow control schemes are known, but most of them use the same basic principle. The protocol contains well-defined rules about when a sender may transmit the next frame. These rules often prohibit frames from being sent until the receiver has granted permission, either implicitly or explicitly. For example, when a connection is set up, the receiver might say: "You may send me n frames now, but after they have been sent, do not send any more until I have told you to continue." We will examine the details shortly.

3.2 ERROR DETECTION AND CORRECTION

As we saw in Chap. 2, the telephone system has three parts: the switches, the interoffice trunks, and the local loops. The first two are now almost entirely digital in most developed countries. The local loops are still analog twisted copper pairs and will continue to be so for years due to the enormous expense of replacing them. While errors are rare on the digital part, they are still common on the local loops. Furthermore, wireless communication is becoming more common, and the error rates here are orders of magnitude worse than on the interoffice fiber trunks. The conclusion is: transmission errors are going to be with us for many years to come. We have to learn how to deal with them.

As a result of the physical processes that generate them, errors on some media (e.g., radio) tend to come in bursts rather than singly. Having the errors come in bursts has both advantages and disadvantages over isolated single-bit errors. On the advantage side, computer data are always sent in blocks of bits. Suppose that the block size is 1000 bits and the error rate is 0.001 per bit. If errors were independent, most blocks would contain an error. If the errors came in bursts of 100 however, only one or two blocks in 100 would be affected, on average. The disadvantage of burst errors is that they are much harder to correct than are isolated errors.

3.2.1 Error-Correcting Codes

Network designers have developed two basic strategies for dealing with errors. One way is to include enough redundant information along with each block of data sent, to enable the receiver to deduce what the transmitted data must have been. The other way is to include only enough redundancy to allow the receiver to deduce that an error occurred, but not which error, and have it request a retransmission. The former strategy uses **error-correcting codes** and the latter uses **error-detecting codes**. The use of error-correcting codes is often referred to as **forward error correction**.

Each of these techniques occupies a different ecological niche. On channels that are highly reliable, such as fiber, it is cheaper to use an error detecting code and just retransmit the occasional block found to be faulty. However, on channels such as wireless links that make many errors, it is better to add enough redundancy to each block for the receiver to be able to figure out what the original block was, rather than relying on a retransmission, which itself may be in error.

To understand how errors can be handled, it is necessary to look closely at what an error really is. Normally, a frame consists of m data (i.e., message) bits and r redundant, or check, bits. Let the total length be n (i.e., $n = m + r$). An n-bit unit containing data and check bits is often referred to as an n-bit **codeword**.

Given any two codewords, say, 10001001 and 10110001, it is possible to determine how many corresponding bits differ. In this case, 3 bits differ. To determine how many bits differ, just exclusive OR the two codewords and count the number of 1 bits in the result, for example:

```
10001001
10110001
--------
00111000
```

The number of bit positions in which two codewords differ is called the **Hamming distance** (Hamming, 1950). Its significance is that if two codewords are a

Hamming distance d apart, it will require d single-bit errors to convert one into the other.

In most data transmission applications, all 2^m possible data messages are legal, but due to the way the check bits are computed, not all of the 2^n possible codewords are used. Given the algorithm for computing the check bits, it is possible to construct a complete list of the legal codewords, and from this list find the two codewords whose Hamming distance is minimum. This distance is the Hamming distance of the complete code.

The error-detecting and error-correcting properties of a code depend on its Hamming distance. To detect d errors, you need a distance $d + 1$ code because with such a code there is no way that d single-bit errors can change a valid codeword into another valid codeword. When the receiver sees an invalid codeword, it can tell that a transmission error has occurred. Similarly, to correct d errors, you need a distance $2d + 1$ code because that way the legal codewords are so far apart that even with d changes, the original codeword is still closer than any other codeword, so it can be uniquely determined.

As a simple example of an error-detecting code, consider a code in which a single **parity bit** is appended to the data. The parity bit is chosen so that the number of 1 bits in the codeword is even (or odd). For example, when 1011010 is sent in even parity, a bit is added to the end to make it 10110100. With odd parity 1011010 becomes 10110101. A code with a single parity bit has a distance 2, since any single-bit error produces a codeword with the wrong parity. It can be used to detect single errors.

As a simple example of an error-correcting code, consider a code with only four valid codewords:

0000000000, 0000011111, 1111100000, and 1111111111

This code has a distance 5, which means that it can correct double errors. If the codeword 0000000111 arrives, the receiver knows that the original must have been 0000011111. If, however, a triple error changes 0000000000 into 0000000111, the error will not be corrected properly.

Imagine that we want to design a code with m message bits and r check bits that will allow all single errors to be corrected. Each of the 2^m legal messages has n illegal codewords at a distance 1 from it. These are formed by systematically inverting each of the n bits in the n-bit codeword formed from it. Thus, each of the 2^m legal messages requires $n + 1$ bit patterns dedicated to it. Since the total number of bit patterns is 2^n, we must have $(n + 1)2^m \leq 2^n$. Using $n = m + r$, this requirement becomes $(m + r + 1) \leq 2^r$. Given m, this puts a lower limit on the number of check bits needed to correct single errors.

This theoretical lower limit can, in fact, be achieved using a method due to Hamming (1950). The bits of the codeword are numbered consecutively, starting with bit 1 at the left end, bit 2 to its immediate right, and so on. The bits that are powers of 2 (1, 2, 4, 8, 16, etc.) are check bits. The rest (3, 5, 6, 7, 9, etc.) are filled up with the m data bits. Each check bit forces the parity of some collection of bits, including itself, to be even (or odd). A bit may be included in several parity computations. To see which check bits the data bit in position k contributes to, rewrite k as a sum of powers of 2. For example, $11 = 1 + 2 + 8$ and $29 = 1 + 4 + 8 + 16$. A bit is checked by just those check bits occurring in its expansion (e.g., bit 11 is checked by bits 1, 2, and 8).

When a codeword arrives, the receiver initializes a counter to zero. It then examines each check bit, k ($k = 1, 2, 4, 8, \ldots$), to see if it has the correct parity. If not, the receiver adds k to the counter. If the counter is zero after all the check bits have been examined (i.e., if they were all correct), the codeword is accepted as valid. If the counter is nonzero, it contains the number of the incorrect bit. For example, if check bits 1, 2, and 8 are in error, the inverted bit is 11, because it is the only one checked by bits 1, 2, and 8. Figure 3-7 shows some 7-bit ASCII characters encoded as 11-bit codewords using a Hamming code. Remember that the data are found in bit positions 3, 5, 6, 7, 9, 10, and 11.

Char.	ASCII	Check bits
H	1001000	00110010000
a	1100001	10111001001
m	1101101	11101010101
m	1101101	11101010101
i	1101001	01101011001
n	1101110	01101010110
g	1100111	01111001111
	0100000	10011000000
c	1100011	11111000011
o	1101111	10101011111
d	1100100	11111001100
e	1100101	00111000101

Order of bit transmission

Figure 3-7. Use of a Hamming code to correct burst errors.

Hamming codes can only correct single errors. However, there is a trick that can be used to permit Hamming codes to correct burst errors. A sequence of k consecutive codewords are arranged as a matrix, one codeword per row. Normally, the data would be transmitted one codeword at a time, from left to right. To correct burst errors, the data should be transmitted one column at a time, starting with the leftmost column. When all k bits have been sent, the second column is sent, and so on, as indicated in Fig. 3-7. When the frame arrives at the receiver, the matrix is reconstructed, one column at a time. If a burst error of length k occurs, at most 1 bit in each of the k codewords will have been affected, but the Hamming code can correct one error per codeword, so the entire block can be restored. This method uses kr check bits to make blocks of km data bits immune to a single burst error of length k or less.

3.2.2 Error-Detecting Codes

Error-correcting codes are widely used on wireless links, which are notoriously noisy and error prone when compared to copper wire or optical fibers. Without error-correcting codes, it would be hard to get anything through. However, over copper wire or fiber, the error rate is much lower, so error detection and retransmission is usually more efficient there for dealing with the occasional error.

As a simple example, consider a channel on which errors are isolated and the error rate is 10^{-6} per bit. Let the block size be 1000 bits. To provide error correction for 1000-bit blocks, 10 check bits are needed; a megabit of data would require 10,000 check bits. To merely detect a block with a single 1-bit error, one parity bit per block will suffice. Once every 1000 blocks, an extra block (1001 bits) will have to be transmitted. The total overhead for the error detection + retransmission method is only 2001 bits per megabit of data, versus 10,000 bits for a Hamming code.

If a single parity bit is added to a block and the block is badly garbled by a long burst error, the probability that the error will be detected is only 0.5, which is hardly acceptable. The odds can be improved considerably if each block to be sent is regarded as a rectangular matrix n bits wide and k bits high, as described above. A parity bit is computed separately for each column and affixed to the matrix as the last row. The matrix is then transmitted one row at a time. When the block arrives, the receiver checks all the parity bits. If any one of them is wrong, the receiver requests a retransmission of the block. Additional retransmissions are requested as needed until an entire block is received without any parity errors.

This method can detect a single burst of length n, since only 1 bit per column will be changed. A burst of length $n + 1$ will pass undetected, however, if the first bit is inverted, the last bit is inverted, and all the other bits are correct. (A burst error does not imply that all the bits are wrong; it just implies that at least the first and last are wrong.) If the block is badly garbled by a long burst or by multiple shorter bursts, the probability that any of the n columns will have the correct parity, by accident, is 0.5, so the probability of a bad block being accepted when it should not be is 2^{-n}.

Although the above scheme may sometimes be adequate, in practice, another method is in widespread use: the **polynomial code**, also known as a **CRC** (**Cyclic Redundancy Check**). Polynomial codes are based upon treating bit strings as representations of polynomials with coefficients of 0 and 1 only. A k-bit frame is regarded as the coefficient list for a polynomial with k terms, ranging from x^{k-1} to x^0. Such a polynomial is said to be of degree $k - 1$. The high-order (leftmost) bit is the coefficient of x^{k-1}; the next bit is the coefficient of x^{k-2}, and so on. For example, 110001 has 6 bits and thus represents a six-term polynomial with coefficients 1, 1, 0, 0, 0, and 1: $x^5 + x^4 + x^0$.

Polynomial arithmetic is done modulo 2, according to the rules of algebraic field theory. There are no carries for addition or borrows for subtraction. Both addition and subtraction are identical to exclusive OR. For example:

$$\begin{array}{r} 10011011 \\ +\ 11001010 \\ \hline 01010001 \end{array} \qquad \begin{array}{r} 00110011 \\ +\ 11001101 \\ \hline 11111110 \end{array} \qquad \begin{array}{r} 11110000 \\ -\ 10100110 \\ \hline 01010110 \end{array} \qquad \begin{array}{r} 01010101 \\ -\ 10101111 \\ \hline 11111010 \end{array}$$

Long division is carried out the same way as it is in binary except that the subtraction is done modulo 2, as above. A divisor is said "to go into" a dividend if the dividend has as many bits as the divisor.

When the polynomial code method is employed, the sender and receiver must agree upon a **generator polynomial**, $G(x)$, in advance. Both the high- and low-order bits of the generator must be 1. To compute the **checksum** for some frame with m bits, corresponding to the polynomial $M(x)$, the frame must be longer than the generator polynomial. The idea is to append a checksum to the end of the frame in such a way that the polynomial represented by the checksummed frame is divisible by $G(x)$. When the receiver gets the checksummed frame, it tries dividing it by $G(x)$. If there is a remainder, there has been a transmission error.

The algorithm for computing the checksum is as follows:

1. Let r be the degree of $G(x)$. Append r zero bits to the low-order end of the frame so it now contains $m + r$ bits and corresponds to the polynomial $x^r M(x)$.
2. Divide the bit string corresponding to $G(x)$ into the bit string corresponding to $x^r M(x)$, using modulo 2 division.
3. Subtract the remainder (which is always r or fewer bits) from the bit string corresponding to $x^r M(x)$ using modulo 2 subtraction. The result is the checksummed frame to be transmitted. Call its polynomial $T(x)$.

Figure 3-8 illustrates the calculation for a frame 1101011011 using the generator $G(x) = x^4 + x + 1$.

It should be clear that $T(x)$ is divisible (modulo 2) by $G(x)$. In any division problem, if you diminish the dividend by the remainder, what is left over is divisible by the divisor. For example, in base 10, if you divide 210,278 by 10,941, the remainder is 2399. By subtracting 2399 from 210,278, what is left over (207,879) is divisible by 10,941.

Now let us analyze the power of this method. What kinds of errors will be detected? Imagine that a transmission error occurs, so that instead of the bit string for $T(x)$ arriving, $T(x) + E(x)$ arrives. Each 1 bit in $E(x)$ corresponds to a bit that has been inverted. If there are k 1 bits in $E(x)$, k single-bit errors have occurred. A single burst error is characterized by an initial 1, a mixture of 0s and 1s, and a final 1, with all other bits being 0.

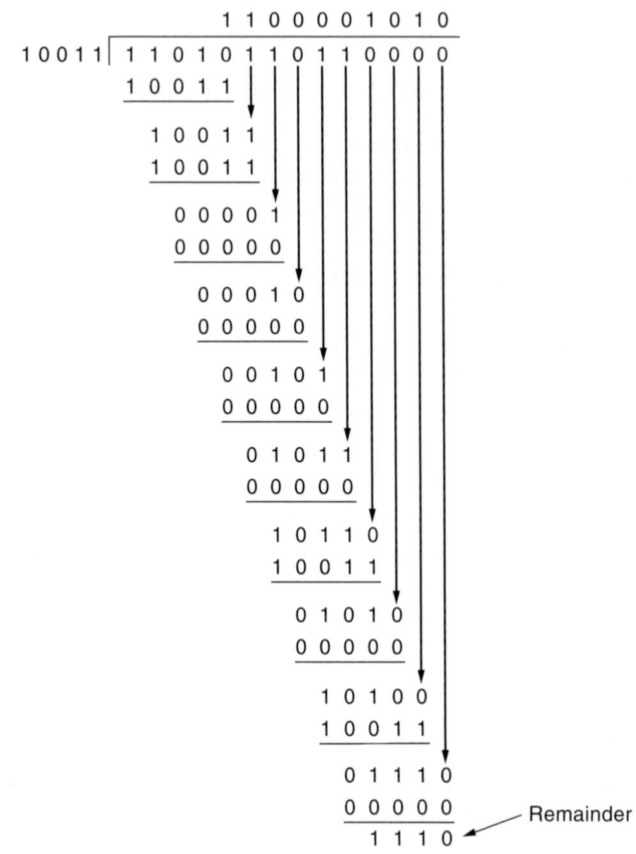

Figure 3-8. Calculation of the polynomial code checksum.

Upon receiving the checksummed frame, the receiver divides it by $G(x)$; that is, it computes $[T(x)+E(x)]/G(x)$. $T(x)/G(x)$ is 0, so the result of the computation is simply $E(x)/G(x)$. Those errors that happen to correspond to polynomials containing $G(x)$ as a factor will slip by; all other errors will be caught.

If there has been a single-bit error, $E(x)=x^i$, where i determines which bit is in error. If $G(x)$ contains two or more terms, it will never divide $E(x)$, so all single-bit errors will be detected.

If there have been two isolated single-bit errors, $E(x) = x^i + x^j$, where $i > j$. Alternatively, this can be written as $E(x) = x^j(x^{i-j} + 1)$. If we assume that $G(x)$ is not divisible by x, a sufficient condition for all double errors to be detected is that $G(x)$ does not divide $x^k + 1$ for any k up to the maximum value of $i - j$ (i.e., up to the maximum frame length). Simple, low-degree polynomials that give protection to long frames are known. For example, $x^{15} + x^{14} + 1$ will not divide $x^k + 1$ for any value of k below 32,768.

If there are an odd number of bits in error, $E(X)$ contains an odd number of terms (e.g., $x^5 + x^2 + 1$, but not $x^2 + 1$). Interestingly, no polynomial with an odd number of terms has $x + 1$ as a factor in the modulo 2 system. By making $x + 1$ a factor of $G(x)$, we can catch all errors consisting of an odd number of inverted bits.

To see that no polynomial with an odd number of terms is divisible by $x + 1$, assume that $E(x)$ has an odd number of terms and is divisible by $x + 1$. Factor $E(x)$ into $(x + 1)\ Q(x)$. Now evaluate $E(1) = (1 + 1)Q(1)$. Since $1 + 1 = 0$ (modulo 2), $E(1)$ must be zero. If $E(x)$ has an odd number of terms, substituting 1 for x everywhere will always yield 1 as the result. Thus, no polynomial with an odd number of terms is divisible by $x + 1$.

Finally, and most importantly, a polynomial code with r check bits will detect all burst errors of length $\le r$. A burst error of length k can be represented by $x^i(x^{k-1} + \ldots + 1)$, where i determines how far from the right-hand end of the received frame the burst is located. If $G(x)$ contains an x^0 term, it will not have x^i as a factor, so if the degree of the parenthesized expression is less than the degree of $G(x)$, the remainder can never be zero.

If the burst length is $r + 1$, the remainder of the division by $G(x)$ will be zero if and only if the burst is identical to $G(x)$. By definition of a burst, the first and last bits must be 1, so whether it matches depends on the $r - 1$ intermediate bits. If all combinations are regarded as equally likely, the probability of such an incorrect frame being accepted as valid is $\frac{1}{2}^{r-1}$.

It can also be shown that when an error burst longer than $r + 1$ bits occurs or when several shorter bursts occur, the probability of a bad frame getting through unnoticed is $\frac{1}{2}^r$, assuming that all bit patterns are equally likely.

Certain polynomials have become international standards. The one used in IEEE 802 is

$$x^{32} + x^{26} + x^{23} + x^{22} + x^{16} + x^{12} + x^{11} + x^{10} + x^8 + x^7 + x^5 + x^4 + x^2 + x^1 + 1$$

Among other desirable properties, it has the property that it detects all bursts of length 32 or less and all bursts affecting an odd number of bits.

Although the calculation required to compute the checksum may seem complicated, Peterson and Brown (1961) have shown that a simple shift register circuit can be constructed to compute and verify the checksums in hardware. In practice, this hardware is nearly always used. Virtually all LANs use it and point-to-point lines do, too, in some cases.

For decades, it has been assumed that frames to be checksummed contain random bits. All analyses of checksum algorithms have been made under this assumption. Inspection of real data has shown this assumption to be quite wrong. As a consequence, under some circumstances, undetected errors are much more common than had been previously thought (Partridge et al., 1995).

3.3 ELEMENTARY DATA LINK PROTOCOLS

To introduce the subject of protocols, we will begin by looking at three protocols of increasing complexity. For interested readers, a simulator for these and subsequent protocols is available via the Web (see the preface). Before we look at the protocols, it is useful to make explicit some of the assumptions underlying the model of communication. To start with, we assume that in the physical layer, data link layer, and network layer are independent processes that communicate by passing messages back and forth. In many cases, the physical and data link layer processes will be running on a processor inside a special network I/O chip and the network layer code will be running on the main CPU. However, other implementations are also possible (e.g., three processes inside a single I/O chip; or the physical and data link layers as procedures called by the network layer process). In any event, treating the three layers as separate processes makes the discussion conceptually cleaner and also serves to emphasize the independence of the layers.

Another key assumption is that machine *A* wants to send a long stream of data to machine *B*, using a reliable, connection-oriented service. Later, we will consider the case where *B* also wants to send data to *A* simultaneously. *A* is assumed to have an infinite supply of data ready to send and never has to wait for data to be produced. Instead, when *A*'s data link layer asks for data, the network layer is always able to comply immediately. (This restriction, too, will be dropped later.)

We also assume that machines do not crash. That is, these protocols deal with communication errors, but not the problems caused by computers crashing and rebooting.

As far as the data link layer is concerned, the packet passed across the interface to it from the network layer is pure data, whose every bit is to be delivered to the destination's network layer. The fact that the destination's network layer may interpret part of the packet as a header is of no concern to the data link layer.

When the data link layer accepts a packet, it encapsulates the packet in a frame by adding a data link header and trailer to it (see Fig. 3-1). Thus, a frame consists of an embedded packet, some control information (in the header), and a checksum (in the trailer). The frame is then transmitted to the data link layer on the other machine. We will assume that there exist suitable library procedures *to_physical_layer* to send a frame and *from_physical_layer* to receive a frame. The transmitting hardware computes and appends the checksum (thus creating the trailer), so that the datalink layer software need not worry about it. The polynomial algorithm discussed earlier in this chapter might be used, for example.

Initially, the receiver has nothing to do. It just sits around waiting for something to happen. In the example protocols of this chapter we will indicate that the data link layer is waiting for something to happen by the procedure call *wait_for_event(&event)*. This procedure only returns when something has happened (e.g., a frame has arrived). Upon return, the variable *event* tells what happened. The set of possible events differs for the various protocols to be described and will be defined separately for each protocol. Note that in a more realistic situation, the data link layer will not sit in a tight loop waiting for an event, as we have suggested, but will receive an interrupt, which will cause it to stop whatever it was doing and go handle the incoming frame. Nevertheless, for simplicity we will ignore all the details of parallel activity within the data link layer and assume that it is dedicated full time to handling just our one channel.

When a frame arrives at the receiver, the hardware computes the checksum. If the checksum is incorrect (i.e., there was a transmission error), the data link layer is so informed (*event* = *cksum_err*). If the inbound frame arrived undamaged, the data link layer is also informed (*event* = *frame_arrival*) so that it can acquire the frame for inspection using *from_physical_layer*. As soon as the receiving data link layer has acquired an undamaged frame, it checks the control information in the header, and if everything is all right, passes the packet portion to the network layer. Under no circumstances is a frame header ever given to a network layer.

There is a good reason why the network layer must never be given any part of the frame header: to keep the network and data link protocols completely separate. As long as the network layer knows nothing at all about the data link protocol or the frame format, these things can be changed without requiring changes to the network layer's software. Providing a rigid interface between network layer and data link layer greatly simplifies the software design because communication protocols in different layers can evolve independently.

Figure 3-9 shows some declarations (in C) common to many of the protocols to be discussed later. Five data structures are defined there: *boolean*, *seq_nr*, *packet*, *frame_kind*, and *frame*. A *boolean* is an enumerated type and can take on the values *true* and *false*. A *seq_nr* is a small integer used to number the frames so that we can tell them apart. These sequence numbers run from 0 up to and including *MAX_SEQ*, which is defined in each protocol needing it. A *packet* is the unit of information exchanged between the network layer and the data link layer on the same machine, or between network layer peers. In our model it always contains *MAX_PKT* bytes, but more realistically it would be of variable length.

A *frame* is composed of four fields: *kind*, *seq*, *ack*, and *info*, the first three of which contain control information and the last of which may contain actual data to be transferred. These control fields are collectively called the **frame header**.

```
#define MAX_PKT 1024                                  /* determines packet size in bytes */

typedef enum {false, true} boolean;                   /* boolean type */
typedef unsigned int seq_nr;                          /* sequence or ack numbers */
typedef struct {unsigned char data[MAX_PKT];} packet;/*   packet definition */
typedef enum {data, ack, nak} frame_kind;             /* frame_kind definition */

typedef struct {                                      /* frames are transported in this layer */
  frame_kind kind;                                    /* what kind of a frame is it? */
  seq_nr seq;                                         /* sequence number */
  seq_nr ack;                                         /* acknowledgement number */
  packet info;                                        /* the network layer packet */
} frame;

/* Wait for an event to happen; return its type in event. */
void wait_for_event(event_type *event);

/* Fetch a packet from the network layer for transmission on the channel. */
void from_network_layer(packet *p);

/* Deliver information from an inbound frame to the network layer. */
void to_network_layer(packet *p);

/* Go get an inbound frame from the physical layer and copy it to r. */
void from_physical_layer(frame *r);

/* Pass the frame to the physical layer for transmission. */
void to_physical_layer(frame *s);

/* Start the clock running and enable the timeout event. */
void start_timer(seq_nr k);

/* Stop the clock and disable the timeout event. */
void stop_timer(seq_nr k);

/* Start an auxiliary timer and enable the ack_timeout event. */
void start_ack_timer(void);

/* Stop the auxiliary timer and disable the ack_timeout event. */
void stop_ack_timer(void);

/* Allow the network layer to cause a network_layer_ready event. */
void enable_network_layer(void);

/* Forbid the network layer from causing a network_layer_ready event. */
void disable_network_layer(void);

/* Macro inc is expanded in-line: Increment k circularly. */
#define inc(k) if (k < MAX_SEQ) k = k + 1; else k = 0
```

Figure 3-9. Some definitions needed in the protocols to follow. These definitions are located in the file *protocol.h*.

The *kind* field tells whether there are any data in the frame, because some of the protocols distinguish frames containing only control information from those containing data as well. The *seq* and *ack* fields are used for sequence numbers and acknowledgements, respectively; their use will be described in more detail later. The *info* field of a data frame contains a single packet; the *info* field of a control frame is not used. A more realistic implementation would use a variable-length *info* field, omitting it altogether for control frames.

Again, it is important to realize the relationship between a packet and a frame. The network layer builds a packet by taking a message from the transport layer and adding the network layer header to it. This packet is passed to the data link layer for inclusion in the *info* field of an outgoing frame. When the frame arrives at the destination, the data link layer extracts the packet from the frame and passes the packet to the network layer. In this manner, the network layer can act as though machines can exchange packets directly.

A number of procedures are also listed in Fig. 3-9. These are library routines whose details are implementation dependent and whose inner workings will not concern us further here. The procedure *wait_for_event* sits in a tight loop waiting for something to happen, as mentioned earlier. The procedures *to_network_layer* and *from_network_layer* are used by the data link layer to pass packets to the network layer and accept packets from the network layer, respectively. Note that *from_physical_layer* and *to_physical_layer* pass frames between the data link layer and physical layer. On the other hand, the procedures *to_network_layer* and *from_network_layer* pass packets between the data link layer and network layer. In other words, *to_network_layer* and *from_network_layer* deal with the interface between layers 2 and 3, whereas *from_physical_layer* and *to_physical_layer* deal with the interface between layers 1 and 2.

In most of the protocols, we assume that the channel is unreliable and loses entire frames upon occasion. To be able to recover from such calamities, the sending data link layer must start an internal timer or clock whenever it sends a frame. If no reply has been received within a certain predetermined time interval, the clock times out and the data link layer receives an interrupt signal.

In our protocols this is handled by allowing the procedure *wait_for_event* to return *event* = *timeout*. The procedures *start_timer* and *stop_timer* turn the timer on and off, respectively. Timeouts are possible only when the timer is running. It is explicitly permitted to call *start_timer* while the timer is running; such a call simply resets the clock to cause the next timeout after a full timer interval has elapsed (unless it is reset or turned off in the meanwhile).

The procedures *start_ack_timer* and *stop_ack_timer* control an auxiliary timer used to generate acknowledgements under certain conditions.

The procedures *enable_network_layer* and *disable_network_layer* are used in the more sophisticated protocols, where we no longer assume that the network layer always has packets to send. When the data link layer enables the network layer, the network layer is then permitted to interrupt when it has a packet to be sent. We indicate this with *event = network_layer_ready*. When a network layer is disabled, it may not cause such events. By being careful about when it enables and disables its network layer, the data link layer can prevent the network layer from swamping it with packets for which it has no buffer space.

Frame sequence numbers are always in the range 0 to *MAX_SEQ* (inclusive), where *MAX_SEQ* is different for the different protocols. It is frequently necessary to advance a sequence number by 1 circularly (i.e., *MAX_SEQ* is followed by 0). The macro *inc* performs this incrementing. It has been defined as a macro because it is used in-line within the critical path. As we will see later, the factor limiting network performance is often protocol processing, so defining simple operations like this as macros does not affect the readability of the code but does improve performance. Also, since *MAX_SEQ* will have different values in different protocols, by making it a macro, it becomes possible to include all the protocols in the same binary without conflict. This ability is useful for the simulator.

The declarations of Fig. 3-9 are part of each of the protocols to follow. To save space and to provide a convenient reference, they have been extracted and listed together, but conceptually they should be merged with the protocols themselves. In C, this merging is done by putting the definitions in a special header file, in this case *protocol.h*, and using the #include facility of the C preprocessor to include them in the protocol files.

3.3.1 An Unrestricted Simplex Protocol

As an initial example we will consider a protocol that is as simple as it can be. Data are transmitted in one direction only. Both the transmitting and receiving network layers are always ready. Processing time can be ignored. Infinite buffer space is available. And best of all, the communication channel between the data link layers never damages or loses frames. This thoroughly unrealistic protocol, which we will nickname "utopia," is shown in Fig. 3-10.

The protocol consists of two distinct procedures, a sender and a receiver. The sender runs in the data link layer of the source machine, and the receiver runs in the data link layer of the destination machine. No sequence numbers or acknowledgements are used here, so *MAX_SEQ* is not needed. The only event type possible is *frame_arrival* (i.e., the arrival of an undamaged frame).

The sender is in an infinite while loop just pumping data out onto the line as fast as it can. The body of the loop consists of three actions: go fetch a packet from the (always obliging) network layer, construct an outbound frame using the variable *s*, and send the frame on its way. Only the *info* field of the frame is used by this protocol, because the other fields have to do with error and flow control and there are no errors or flow control restrictions here.

The receiver is equally simple. Initially, it waits for something to happen, the only possibility being the arrival of an undamaged frame. Eventually, the frame

```
/* Protocol 1 (utopia) provides for data transmission in one direction only, from
   sender to receiver. The communication channel is assumed to be error free
   and the receiver is assumed to be able to process all the input infinitely quickly.
   Consequently, the sender just sits in a loop pumping data out onto the line as
   fast as it can. */

typedef enum {frame_arrival} event_type;
#include "protocol.h"

void sender1(void)
{
 frame s;                            /* buffer for an outbound frame */
 packet buffer;                      /* buffer for an outbound packet */

 while (true) {
     from_network_layer(&buffer);    /* go get something to send */
     s.info = buffer;                /* copy it into s for transmission */
     to_physical_layer(&s);          /* send it on its way */
 }                                   /* Tomorrow, and tomorrow, and tomorrow,
                                        Creeps in this petty pace from day to day
                                        To the last syllable of recorded time.
                                           - Macbeth, V, v */
}


void receiver1(void)
{
 frame r;
 event_type event;                   /* filled in by wait, but not used here */

 while (true) {
     wait_for_event(&event);         /* only possibility is frame_arrival */
     from_physical_layer(&r);        /* go get the inbound frame */
     to_network_layer(&r.info);      /* pass the data to the network layer */
 }
}
```

Figure 3-10. An unrestricted simplex protocol.

arrives and the procedure *wait_for_event* returns, with *event* set to *frame_arrival* (which is ignored anyway). The call to *from_physical_layer* removes the newly arrived frame from the hardware buffer and puts it in the variable *r*, where the receiver code can get at it. Finally, the data portion is passed on to the network layer, and the data link layer settles back to wait for the next frame, effectively suspending itself until the frame arrives.

3.3.2 A Simplex Stop-and-Wait Protocol

Now we will drop the most unrealistic restriction used in protocol 1: the ability of the receiving network layer to process incoming data infinitely quickly (or equivalently, the presence in the receiving data link layer of an infinite amount of buffer space in which to store all incoming frames while they are waiting their respective turns). The communication channel is still assumed to be error free however, and the data traffic is still simplex.

The main problem we have to deal with here is how to prevent the sender from flooding the receiver with data faster than the latter is able to process them. In essence, if the receiver requires a time Δt to execute *from_physical_layer* plus *to_network_layer*, the sender must transmit at an average rate less than one frame per time Δt. Moreover, if we assume that no automatic buffering and queueing are done within the receiver's hardware, the sender must never transmit a new frame until the old one has been fetched by *from_physical_layer*, lest the new one overwrite the old one.

In certain restricted circumstances (e.g., synchronous transmission and a receiving data link layer fully dedicated to processing the one input line), it might be possible for the sender to simply insert a delay into protocol 1 to slow it down sufficiently to keep from swamping the receiver. However, more usually, each data link layer will have several lines to attend to, and the time interval between a frame arriving and its being processed may vary considerably. If the network designers can calculate the worst-case behavior of the receiver, they can program the sender to transmit so slowly that even if every frame suffers the maximum delay, there will be no overruns. The trouble with this approach is that it is too conservative. It leads to a bandwidth utilization that is far below the optimum, unless the best and worst cases are almost the same (i.e., the variation in the data link layer's reaction time is small).

A more general solution to this dilemma is to have the receiver provide feedback to the sender. After having passed a packet to its network layer, the receiver sends a little dummy frame back to the sender which, in effect, gives the sender permission to transmit the next frame. After having sent a frame, the sender is required by the protocol to bide its time until the little dummy (i.e., acknowledgement) frame arrives. Using feedback from the receiver to let the sender know when it may send more data is an example of the flow control mentioned earlier.

Protocols in which the sender sends one frame and then waits for an acknowledgement before proceeding are called **stop-and-wait**. Figure 3-11 gives an example of a simplex stop-and-wait protocol.

Although data traffic in this example is simplex, going only from the sender to the receiver, frames do travel in both directions. Consequently, the communication channel between the two data link layers needs to be capable of bidirectional information transfer. However, this protocol entails a strict alternation of flow: first the sender sends a frame, then the receiver sends a frame, then the sender

```
/* Protocol 2 (stop-and-wait) also provides for a one-directional flow of data from
   sender to receiver. The communication channel is once again assumed to be error
   free, as in protocol 1. However, this time, the receiver has only a finite buffer
   capacity and a finite processing speed, so the protocol must explicitly prevent
   the sender from flooding the receiver with data faster than it can be handled. */

typedef enum {frame_arrival} event_type;
#include "protocol.h"

void sender2(void)
{
  frame s;                              /* buffer for an outbound frame */
  packet buffer;                        /* buffer for an outbound packet */
  event_type event;                     /* frame_arrival is the only possibility */

  while (true) {
      from_network_layer(&buffer);      /* go get something to send */
      s.info = buffer;                  /* copy it into s for transmission */
      to_physical_layer(&s);            /* bye-bye little frame */
      wait_for_event(&event);           /* do not proceed until given the go ahead */
  }
}

void receiver2(void)
{
  frame r, s;                           /* buffers for frames */
  event_type event;                     /* frame_arrival is the only possibility */
  while (true) {
      wait_for_event(&event);           /* only possibility is frame_arrival */
      from_physical_layer(&r);          /* go get the inbound frame */
      to_network_layer(&r.info);        /* pass the data to the network layer */
      to_physical_layer(&s);            /* send a dummy frame to awaken sender */
  }
}
```

Figure 3-11. A simplex stop-and-wait protocol.

sends another frame, then the receiver sends another one, and so on. A half-duplex physical channel would suffice here.

As in protocol 1, the sender starts out by fetching a packet from the network layer, using it to construct a frame, and sending it on its way. But now, unlike in protocol 1, the sender must wait until an acknowledgement frame arrives before looping back and fetching the next packet from the network layer. The sending data link layer need not even inspect the incoming frame: there is only one possibility. The incoming frame is always an acknowledgement.

The only difference between *receiver1* and *receiver2* is that after delivering a packet to the network layer, *receiver2* sends an acknowledgement frame back to the sender before entering the wait loop again. Because only the arrival of the frame back at the sender is important, not its contents, the receiver need not put any particular information in it.

3.3.3 A Simplex Protocol for a Noisy Channel

Now let us consider the normal situation of a communication channel that makes errors. Frames may be either damaged or lost completely. However, we assume that if a frame is damaged in transit, the receiver hardware will detect this when it computes the checksum. If the frame is damaged in such a way that the checksum is nevertheless correct, an unlikely occurrence, this protocol (and all other protocols) can fail (i.e., deliver an incorrect packet to the network layer).

At first glance it might seem that a variation of protocol 2 would work: adding a timer. The sender could send a frame, but the receiver would only send an acknowledgement frame if the data were correctly received. If a damaged frame arrived at the receiver, it would be discarded. After a while the sender would time out and send the frame again. This process would be repeated until the frame finally arrived intact.

The above scheme has a fatal flaw in it. Think about the problem and try to discover what might go wrong before reading further.

To see what might go wrong, remember that it is the task of the data link layer processes to provide error-free, transparent communication between network layer processes. The network layer on machine *A* gives a series of packets to its data link layer, which must ensure that an identical series of packets are delivered to the network layer on machine *B* by its data link layer. In particular, the network layer on *B* has no way of knowing that a packet has been lost or duplicated, so the data link layer must guarantee that no combination of transmission errors, however unlikely, can cause a duplicate packet to be delivered to a network layer.

Consider the following scenario:

1. The network layer on *A* gives packet 1 to its data link layer. The packet is correctly received at *B* and passed to the network layer on *B*. *B* sends an acknowledgement frame back to *A*.

2. The acknowledgement frame gets lost completely. It just never arrives at all. Life would be a great deal simpler if the channel mangled and lost only data frames and not control frames, but sad to say, the channel is not very discriminating.

3. The data link layer on *A* eventually times out. Not having received an acknowledgement, it (incorrectly) assumes that its data frame was lost or damaged and sends the frame containing packet 1 again.

4. The duplicate frame also arrives at the data link layer on B perfectly and is unwittingly passed to the network layer there. If A is sending a file to B, part of the file will be duplicated (i.e., the copy of the file made by B will be incorrect and the error will not have been detected). In other words, the protocol will fail.

Clearly, what is needed is some way for the receiver to be able to distinguish a frame that it is seeing for the first time from a retransmission. The obvious way to achieve this is to have the sender put a sequence number in the header of each frame it sends. Then the receiver can check the sequence number of each arriving frame to see if it is a new frame or a duplicate to be discarded.

Since a small frame header is desirable, the question arises: What is the minimum number of bits needed for the sequence number? The only ambiguity in this protocol is between a frame, m, and its direct successor, $m + 1$. If frame m is lost or damaged, the receiver will not acknowledge it, so the sender will keep trying to send it. Once it has been correctly received, the receiver will send an acknowledgement to the sender. It is here that the potential trouble crops up. Depending upon whether the acknowledgement frame gets back to the sender correctly or not, the sender may try to send m or $m + 1$.

The event that triggers the sender to start sending frame $m + 2$ is the arrival of an acknowledgement for frame $m + 1$. But this implies that m has been correctly received, and furthermore that its acknowledgement has also been correctly received by the sender (otherwise, the sender would not have begun with $m + 1$, let alone $m + 2$). As a consequence, the only ambiguity is between a frame and its immediate predecessor or successor, not between the predecessor and successor themselves.

A 1-bit sequence number (0 or 1) is therefore sufficient. At each instant of time, the receiver expects a particular sequence number next. Any arriving frame containing the wrong sequence number is rejected as a duplicate. When a frame containing the correct sequence number arrives, it is accepted and passed to the network layer. Then the expected sequence number is incremented modulo 2 (i.e., 0 becomes 1 and 1 becomes 0).

An example of this kind of protocol is shown in Fig. 3-12. Protocols in which the sender waits for a positive acknowledgement before advancing to the next data item are often called **PAR** (**Positive Acknowledgement with Retransmission**) or **ARQ** (**Automatic Repeat reQuest**). Like protocol 2, this one also transmits data only in one direction.

Protocol 3 differs from its predecessors in that both sender and receiver have a variable whose value is remembered while the data link layer is in the wait state. The sender remembers the sequence number of the next frame to send in *next_frame_to_send*; the receiver remembers the sequence number of the next frame expected in *frame_expected*. Each protocol has a short initialization phase before entering the infinite loop.

```
/* Protocol 3 (par) allows unidirectional data flow over an unreliable channel. */

#define MAX_SEQ 1                           /* must be 1 for protocol 3 */
typedef enum {frame_arrival, cksum_err, timeout} event_type;
#include "protocol.h"

void sender3(void)
{
 seq_nr next_frame_to_send;                 /* seq number of next outgoing frame */
 frame s;                                   /* scratch variable */
 packet buffer;                             /* buffer for an outbound packet */
 event_type event;

 next_frame_to_send = 0;                    /* initialize outbound sequence numbers */
 from_network_layer(&buffer);               /* fetch first packet */
 while (true) {
     s.info = buffer;                       /* construct a frame for transmission */
     s.seq = next_frame_to_send;            /* insert sequence number in frame */
     to_physical_layer(&s);                 /* send it on its way */
     start_timer(s.seq);                    /* if answer takes too long, time out */
     wait_for_event(&event);                /* frame_arrival, cksum_err, timeout */
     if (event == frame_arrival) {
           from_physical_layer(&s);         /* get the acknowledgement */
           if (s.ack == next_frame_to_send) {
                 stop_timer(s.ack);         /* turn the timer off */
                 from_network_layer(&buffer); /* get the next one to send */
                 inc(next_frame_to_send);   /* invert next_frame_to_send */
           }
     }
 }
}

void receiver3(void)
{
 seq_nr frame_expected;
 frame r, s;
 event_type event;

 frame_expected = 0;
 while (true) {
     wait_for_event(&event);                /* possibilities: frame_arrival, cksum_err */
     if (event == frame_arrival) {          /* a valid frame has arrived. */
           from_physical_layer(&r);         /* go get the newly arrived frame */
           if (r.seq == frame_expected) {   /* this is what we have been waiting for. */
                 to_network_layer(&r.info); /* pass the data to the network layer */
                 inc(frame_expected);       /* next time expect the other sequence nr */
           }
           s.ack = 1 – frame_expected;      /* tell which frame is being acked */
           to_physical_layer(&s);           /* send acknowledgement */
     }
 }
}
```

Figure 3-12. A positive acknowledgement with retransmission protocol.

After transmitting a frame, the sender starts the timer running. If it was already running, it will be reset to allow another full timer interval. The time interval should be chosen to allow enough time for the frame to get to the receiver, for the receiver to process it in the worst case, and for the acknowledgement frame to propagate back to the sender. Only when that time interval has elapsed is it safe to assume that either the transmitted frame or its acknowledgement has been lost, and to send a duplicate. If the timeout interval is set too short, the sender will transmit unnecessary frames. While these extra frames will not affect the correctness of the protocol, they will hurt performance.

After transmitting a frame and starting the timer, the sender waits for something exciting to happen. Only three possibilities exist: an acknowledgement frame arrives undamaged, a damaged acknowledgement frame staggers in, or the timer expires. If a valid acknowledgement comes in, the sender fetches the next packet from its network layer and puts it in the buffer, overwriting the previous packet. It also advances the sequence number. If a damaged frame arrives or no frame at all arrives, neither the buffer nor the sequence number is changed so that a duplicate can be sent.

When a valid frame arrives at the receiver, its sequence number is checked to see if it is a duplicate. If not, it is accepted, passed to the network layer, and an acknowledgement is generated. Duplicates and damaged frames are not passed to the network layer.

3.4 SLIDING WINDOW PROTOCOLS

In the previous protocols, data frames were transmitted in one direction only. In most practical situations, there is a need for transmitting data in both directions. One way of achieving full-duplex data transmission is to have two separate communication channels and use each one for simplex data traffic (in different directions). If this is done, we have two separate physical circuits, each with a "forward" channel (for data) and a "reverse" channel (for acknowledgements). In both cases the bandwidth of the reverse channel is almost entirely wasted. In effect, the user is paying for two circuits but using only the capacity of one.

A better idea is to use the same circuit for data in both directions. After all, in protocols 2 and 3 it was already being used to transmit frames both ways, and the reverse channel has the same capacity as the forward channel. In this model the data frames from *A* to *B* are intermixed with the acknowledgement frames from *A* to *B*. By looking at the *kind* field in the header of an incoming frame, the receiver can tell whether the frame is data or acknowledgement.

Although interleaving data and control frames on the same circuit is an improvement over having two separate physical circuits, yet another improvement is possible. When a data frame arrives, instead of immediately sending a separate control frame, the receiver restrains itself and waits until the network layer passes it the next packet. The acknowledgement is attached to the outgoing data frame (using the *ack* field in the frame header). In effect, the acknowledgement gets a free ride on the next outgoing data frame. The technique of temporarily delaying outgoing acknowledgements so that they can be hooked onto the next outgoing data frame is known as **piggybacking**.

The principal advantage of using piggybacking over having distinct acknowledgement frames is a better use of the available channel bandwidth. The *ack* field in the frame header costs only a few bits, whereas a separate frame would need a header, the acknowledgement, and a checksum. In addition, fewer frames sent means fewer "frame arrival" interrupts, and perhaps fewer buffers in the receiver, depending on how the receiver's software is organized. In the next protocol to be examined, the piggyback field costs only 1 bit in the frame header. It rarely costs more than a few bits.

However, piggybacking introduces a complication not present with separate acknowledgements. How long should the data link layer wait for a packet onto which to piggyback the acknowledgement? If the data link layer waits longer than the sender's timeout period, the frame will be retransmitted, defeating the whole purpose of having acknowledgements. If the data link layer were an oracle and could foretell the future, it would know when the next network layer packet was going to come in and could decide either to wait for it or send a separate acknowledgement immediately, depending on how long the projected wait was going to be. Of course, the data link layer cannot foretell the future, so it must resort to some ad hoc scheme, such as waiting a fixed number of milliseconds. If a new packet arrives quickly, the acknowledgement is piggybacked onto it; otherwise, if no new packet has arrived by the end of this time period, the data link layer just sends a separate acknowledgement frame.

The next three protocols are bidirectional protocols that belong to a class called **sliding window** protocols. The three differ among themselves in terms of efficiency, complexity, and buffer requirements, as discussed later. In these, as in all sliding window protocols, each outbound frame contains a sequence number, ranging from 0 up to some maximum. The maximum is usually $2^n - 1$ so the sequence number fits exactly in an n-bit field. The stop-and-wait sliding window protocol uses $n = 1$, restricting the sequence numbers to 0 and 1, but more sophisticated versions can use arbitrary n.

The essence of all sliding window protocols is that at any instant of time, the sender maintains a set of sequence numbers corresponding to frames it is permitted to send. These frames are said to fall within the **sending window**. Similarly, the receiver also maintains a **receiving window** corresponding to the set of frames it is permitted to accept. The sender's window and the receiver's window need not have the same lower and upper limits or even have the same size. In some protocols they are fixed in size, but in others they can grow or shrink over the course of time as frames are sent and received.

Although these protocols give the data link layer more freedom about the order in which it may send and receive frames, we have definitely not dropped the requirement that the protocol must deliver packets to the destination network layer in the same order they were passed to the data link layer on the sending machine. Nor have we changed the requirement that the physical communication channel is "wire-like," that is, it must deliver all frames in the order sent.

The sequence numbers within the sender's window represent frames that have been sent or can be sent but are as yet not acknowledged. Whenever a new packet arrives from the network layer, it is given the next highest sequence number, and the upper edge of the window is advanced by one. When an acknowledgement comes in, the lower edge is advanced by one. In this way the window continuously maintains a list of unacknowledged frames. Figure 3-13 shows an example.

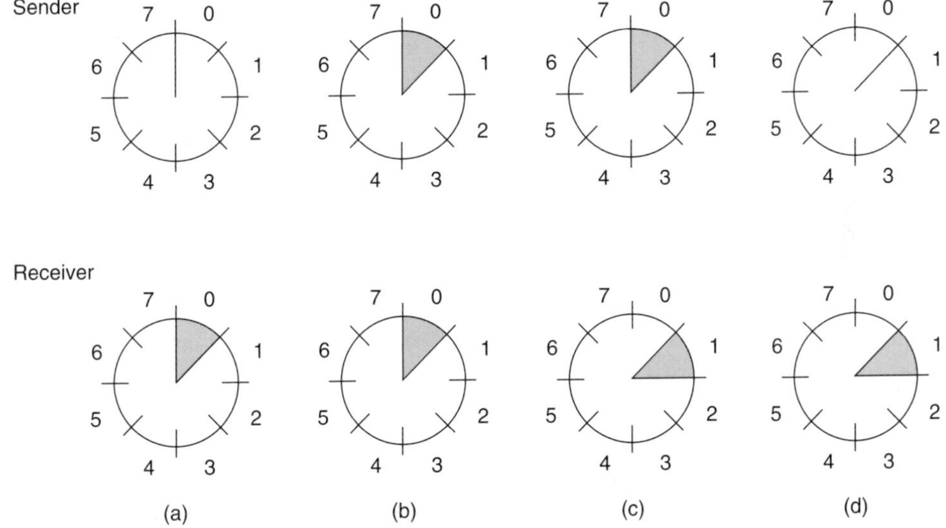

Figure 3-13. A sliding window of size 1, with a 3-bit sequence number. (a) Initially. (b) After the first frame has been sent. (c) After the first frame has been received. (d) After the first acknowledgement has been received.

Since frames currently within the sender's window may ultimately be lost or damaged in transit, the sender must keep all these frames in its memory for possible retransmission. Thus, if the maximum window size is n, the sender needs n buffers to hold the unacknowledged frames. If the window ever grows to its maximum size, the sending data link layer must forcibly shut off the network layer until another buffer becomes free.

The receiving data link layer's window corresponds to the frames it may accept. Any frame falling outside the window is discarded without comment. When a frame whose sequence number is equal to the lower edge of the window is received, it is passed to the network layer, an acknowledgement is generated, and the window is rotated by one. Unlike the sender's window, the receiver's window always remains at its initial size. Note that a window size of 1 means that the data link layer only accepts frames in order, but for larger windows this is not so. The network layer, in contrast, is always fed data in the proper order, regardless of the data link layer's window size.

Figure 3-13 shows an example with a maximum window size of 1. Initially, no frames are outstanding, so the lower and upper edges of the sender's window are equal, but as time goes on, the situation progresses as shown.

3.4.1 A One-Bit Sliding Window Protocol

Before tackling the general case, let us first examine a sliding window protocol with a maximum window size of 1. Such a protocol uses stop-and-wait since the sender transmits a frame and waits for its acknowledgement before sending the next one.

Figure 3-14 depicts such a protocol. Like the others, it starts out by defining some variables. *Next_frame_to_send* tells which frame the sender is trying to send. Similarly, *frame_expected* tells which frame the receiver is expecting. In both cases, 0 and 1 are the only possibilities.

Under normal circumstances, one of the two data link layers goes first and transmits the first frame. In other words, only one of the data link layer programs should contain the *to_physical_layer* and *start_timer* procedure calls outside the main loop. In the event that both data link layers start off simultaneously, a peculiar situation arises, as discussed later. The starting machine fetches the first packet from its network layer, builds a frame from it, and sends it. When this (or any) frame arrives, the receiving data link layer checks to see if it is a duplicate, just as in protocol 3. If the frame is the one expected, it is passed to the network layer and the receiver's window is slid up.

The acknowledgement field contains the number of the last frame received without error. If this number agrees with the sequence number of the frame the sender is trying to send, the sender knows it is done with the frame stored in *buffer* and can fetch the next packet from its network layer. If the sequence number disagrees, it must continue trying to send the same frame. Whenever a frame is received, a frame is also sent back.

Now let us examine protocol 4 to see how resilient it is to pathological scenarios. Assume that computer *A* is trying to send its frame 0 to computer *B* and that *B* is trying to send its frame 0 to *A*. Suppose that *A* sends a frame to *B*, but *A*'s timeout interval is a little too short. Consequently, *A* may time out repeatedly, sending a series of identical frames, all with $seq = 0$ and $ack = 1$.

When the first valid frame arrives at computer *B*, it will be accepted and *frame_expected* will be set to 1. All the subsequent frames will be rejected because *B* is now expecting frames with sequence number 1, not 0. Furthermore,

```
/* Protocol 4 (sliding window) is bidirectional. */

#define MAX_SEQ 1                               /* must be 1 for protocol 4 */
typedef enum {frame_arrival, cksum_err, timeout} event_type;
#include "protocol.h"

void protocol4 (void)
{
  seq_nr next_frame_to_send;                    /* 0 or 1 only */
  seq_nr frame_expected;                        /* 0 or 1 only */
  frame r, s;                                   /* scratch variables */
  packet buffer;                                /* current packet being sent */
  event_type event;

  next_frame_to_send = 0;                       /* next frame on the outbound stream */
  frame_expected = 0;                           /* frame expected next */
  from_network_layer(&buffer);                  /* fetch a packet from the network layer */
  s.info = buffer;                              /* prepare to send the initial frame */
  s.seq = next_frame_to_send;                   /* insert sequence number into frame */
  s.ack = 1 – frame_expected;                   /* piggybacked ack */
  to_physical_layer(&s);                        /* transmit the frame */
  start_timer(s.seq);                           /* start the timer running */

  while (true) {
     wait_for_event(&event);                    /* frame_arrival, cksum_err, or timeout */
     if (event == frame_arrival) {              /* a frame has arrived undamaged. */
          from_physical_layer(&r);              /* go get it */

          if (r.seq == frame_expected) {        /* handle inbound frame stream. */
               to_network_layer(&r.info);       /* pass packet to network layer */
               inc(frame_expected);             /* invert seq number expected next */
          }

          if (r.ack == next_frame_to_send) {    /* handle outbound frame stream. */
               stop_timer(r.ack);               /* turn the timer off */
               from_network_layer(&buffer);     /* fetch new pkt from network layer */
               inc(next_frame_to_send);         /* invert sender's sequence number */
          }
     }
     s.info = buffer;                           /* construct outbound frame */
     s.seq = next_frame_to_send;                /* insert sequence number into it */
     s.ack = 1 – frame_expected;                /* seq number of last received frame */
     to_physical_layer(&s);                     /* transmit a frame */
     start_timer(s.seq);                        /* start the timer running */
  }
}
```

Figure 3-14. A 1-bit sliding window protocol.

since all the duplicates have *ack* = 1 and *B* is still waiting for an acknowledgement of 0, *B* will not fetch a new packet from its network layer.

After every rejected duplicate comes in, *B* sends *A* a frame containing *seq* = 0 and *ack* = 0. Eventually, one of these arrives correctly at *A*, causing *A* to begin sending the next packet. No combination of lost frames or premature timeouts can cause the protocol to deliver duplicate packets to either network layer, to skip a packet, or to deadlock.

However, a peculiar situation arises if both sides simultaneously send an initial packet. This synchronization difficulty is illustrated by Fig. 3-15. In part (a), the normal operation of the protocol is shown. In (b) the peculiarity is illustrated. If *B* waits for *A*'s first frame before sending one of its own, the sequence is as shown in (a), and every frame is accepted. However, if *A* and *B* simultaneously initiate communication, their first frames cross, and the data link layers then get into situation (b). In (a) each frame arrival brings a new packet for the network layer; there are no duplicates. In (b) half of the frames contain duplicates, even though there are no transmission errors. Similar situations can occur as a result of premature timeouts, even when one side clearly starts first. In fact, if multiple premature timeouts occur, frames may be sent three or more times.

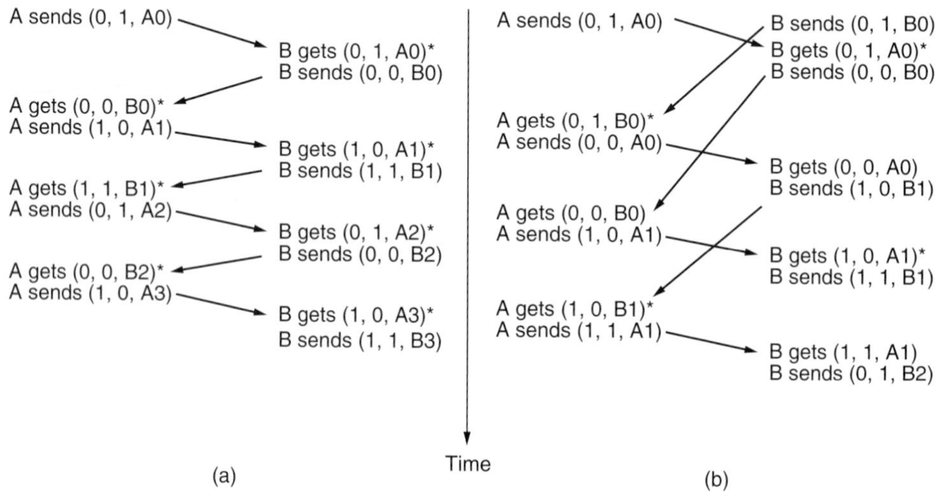

Figure 3-15. Two scenarios for protocol 4. (a) Normal case. (b) Abnormal case. The notation is (seq, ack, packet number). An asterisk indicates where a network layer accepts a packet.

3.4.2 A Protocol Using Go Back N

Until now we have made the tacit assumption that the transmission time required for a frame to arrive at the receiver plus the transmission time for the acknowledgement to come back is negligible. Sometimes this assumption is clearly false. In these situations the long round-trip time can have important implications for the efficiency of the bandwidth utilization. As an example, consider a 50-kbps satellite channel with a 500-msec round-trip propagation delay. Let us imagine trying to use protocol 4 to send 1000-bit frames via the satellite. At $t = 0$ the sender starts sending the first frame. At $t = 20$ msec the frame has been completely sent. Not until $t = 270$ msec has the frame fully arrived at the receiver, and not until $t = 520$ msec has the acknowledgement arrived back at the sender, under the best of circumstances (no waiting in the receiver and a short acknowledgement frame). This means that the sender was blocked during 500/520 or 96 percent of the time. In other words, only 4 percent of the available bandwidth was used. Clearly, the combination of a long transit time, high bandwidth, and short frame length is disastrous in terms of efficiency.

The problem described above can be viewed as a consequence of the rule requiring a sender to wait for an acknowledgement before sending another frame. If we relax that restriction, much better efficiency can be achieved. Basically, the solution lies in allowing the sender to transmit up to w frames before blocking, instead of just 1. With an appropriate choice of w the sender will be able to continuously transmit frames for a time equal to the round-trip transit time without filling up the window. In the example above, w should be at least 26. The sender begins sending frame 0 as before. By the time it has finished sending 26 frames, at $t = 520$, the acknowledgement for frame 0 will have just arrived. Thereafter, acknowledgements arrive every 20 msec, so the sender always gets permission to continue just when it needs it. At all times, 25 or 26 unacknowledged frames are outstanding. Put in other terms, the sender's maximum window size is 26.

The need for a large window on the sending side occurs whenever the product of bandwidth × round-trip-delay is large. If the bandwidth is high, even for a moderate delay, the sender will exhaust its window quickly unless it has a large window. If the delay is high (e.g., on a geostationary satellite channel), the sender will exhaust its window even for a moderate bandwidth. The product of these two factors basically tells what the capacity of the pipe is, and the sender needs the ability to fill it without stopping in order to operate at peak efficiency.

This technique is known as **pipelining**. If the channel capacity is b bits/sec, the frame size l bits, and the round-trip propagation time R sec, the time required to transmit a single frame is l/b sec. After the last bit of a data frame has been sent, there is a delay of $R/2$ before that bit arrives at the receiver and another delay of at least $R/2$ for the acknowledgement to come back, for a total delay of R. In stop-and-wait the line is busy for l/b and idle for R, giving

$$\text{line utilization} = l/(l + bR)$$

If $l < bR$, the efficiency will be less than 50 percent. Since there is always a nonzero delay for the acknowledgement to propagate back, pipelining can, in principle, be used to keep the line busy during this interval, but if the interval is small, the additional complexity is not worth the trouble.

Pipelining frames over an unreliable communication channel raises some serious issues. First, what happens if a frame in the middle of a long stream is damaged or lost? Large numbers of succeeding frames will arrive at the receiver before the sender even finds out that anything is wrong. When a damaged frame arrives at the receiver, it obviously should be discarded, but what should the receiver do with all the correct frames following it? Remember that the receiving data link layer is obligated to hand packets to the network layer in sequence. In Fig. 3-16 we see the effects of pipelining on error recovery. We will now examine it in some detail.

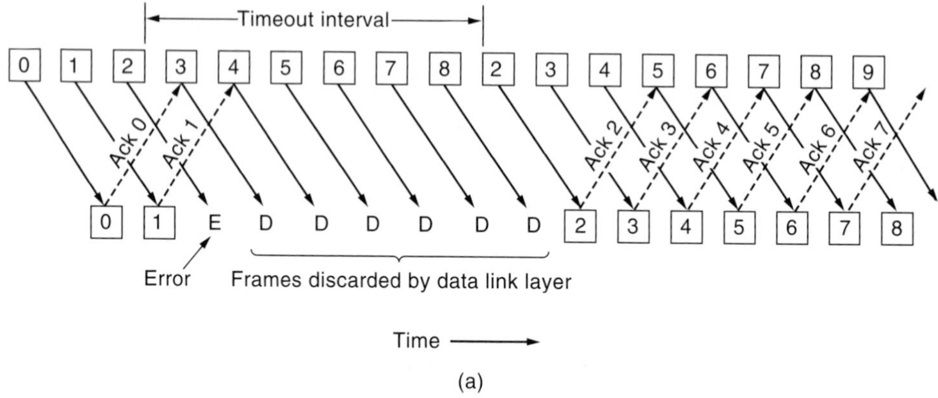

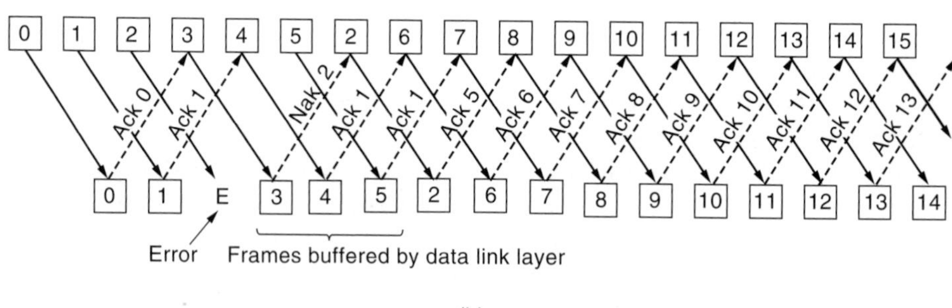

Figure 3-16. Pipelining and error recovery. Effect of an error when (a) receiver's window size is 1 and (b) receiver's window size is large.

Two basic approaches are available for dealing with errors in the presence of pipelining. One way, called **go back n**, is for the receiver simply to discard all subsequent frames, sending no acknowledgements for the discarded frames. This strategy corresponds to a receive window of size 1. In other words, the data link layer refuses to accept any frame except the next one it must give to the network layer. If the sender's window fills up before the timer runs out, the pipeline will begin to empty. Eventually, the sender will time out and retransmit all unacknowledged frames in order, starting with the damaged or lost one. This approach can waste a lot of bandwidth if the error rate is high.

In Fig. 3-16(a) we see go back n for the case in which the receiver's window is large. Frames 0 and 1 are correctly received and acknowledged. Frame 2, however, is damaged or lost. The sender, unaware of this problem, continues to send frames until the timer for frame 2 expires. Then it backs up to frame 2 and starts all over with it, sending 2, 3, 4, etc. all over again.

The other general strategy for handling errors when frames are pipelined is called **selective repeat**. When it is used, a bad frame that is received is discarded, but good frames received after it are buffered. When the sender times out, only the oldest unacknowledged frame is retransmitted. If that frame arrives correctly, the receiver can deliver to the network layer, in sequence, all the frames it has buffered. Selective repeat is often combined with having the receiver send a negative acknowledgement (NAK) when it detects an error, for example, when it receives a checksum error or a frame out of sequence. NAKs stimulate retransmission before the corresponding timer expires and thus improve performance.

In Fig. 3-16(b), frames 0 and 1 are again correctly received and acknowledged and frame 2 is lost. When frame 3 arrives at the receiver, the data link layer there notices that is has missed a frame, so it sends back a NAK for 2 but buffers 3. When frames 4 and 5 arrive, they, too, are buffered by the data link layer instead of being passed to the network layer. Eventually, the NAK 2 gets back to the sender, which immediately resends frame 2. When that arrives, the data link layer now has 2, 3, 4, and 5 and can pass all of them to the network layer in the correct order. It can also acknowledge all frames up to and including 5, as shown in the figure. If the NAK should get lost, eventually the sender will time out for frame 2 and send it (and only it) of its own accord, but that may be a quite a while later. In effect, the NAK speeds up the retransmission of one specific frame.

Selective repeat corresponds to a receiver window larger than 1. Any frame within the window may be accepted and buffered until all the preceding ones have been passed to the network layer. This approach can require large amounts of data link layer memory if the window is large.

These two alternative approaches are trade-offs between bandwidth and data link layer buffer space. Depending on which resource is scarcer, one or the other can be used. Figure 3-17 shows a pipelining protocol in which the receiving data link layer only accepts frames in order; frames following an error are discarded. In this protocol, for the first time we have dropped the assumption that the network layer always has an infinite supply of packets to send. When the network layer has a packet it wants to send, it can cause a *network_layer_ready* event to happen. However, to enforce the flow control rule of no more than *MAX_SEQ* unacknowledged frames outstanding at any time, the data link layer must be able to keep the network layer from bothering it with more work. The library procedures *enable_network_layer* and *disable_network_layer* do this job.

```
/* Protocol 5 (go back n) allows multiple outstanding frames. The sender may transmit up
   to MAX_SEQ frames without waiting for an ack. In addition, unlike in the previous
   protocols, the network layer is not assumed to have a new packet all the time. Instead,
   the network layer causes a network_layer_ready event when there is a packet to send. */

#define MAX_SEQ 7                          /* should be 2^n - 1 */
typedef enum {frame_arrival, cksum_err, timeout, network_layer_ready} event_type;
#include "protocol.h"

static boolean between(seq_nr a, seq_nr b, seq_nr c)
{
/* Return true if a <=b < c circularly; false otherwise. */
  if (((a <= b) && (b < c)) || ((c < a) && (a <= b)) || ((b < c) && (c < a)))
      return(true);
    else
      return(false);
}

static void send_data(seq_nr frame_nr, seq_nr frame_expected, packet buffer[ ])
{
/* Construct and send a data frame. */
  frame s;                                 /* scratch variable */

  s.info = buffer[frame_nr];               /* insert packet into frame */
  s.seq = frame_nr;                        /* insert sequence number into frame */
  s.ack = (frame_expected + MAX_SEQ) % (MAX_SEQ + 1);/* piggyback ack */
  to_physical_layer(&s);                   /* transmit the frame */
  start_timer(frame_nr);                   /* start the timer running */
}

void protocol5(void)
{
  seq_nr next_frame_to_send;               /* MAX_SEQ > 1; used for outbound stream */
  seq_nr ack_expected;                     /* oldest frame as yet unacknowledged */
  seq_nr frame_expected;                   /* next frame expected on inbound stream */
  frame r;                                 /* scratch variable */
  packet buffer[MAX_SEQ + 1];              /* buffers for the outbound stream */
  seq_nr nbuffered;                        /* # output buffers currently in use */
  seq_nr i;                                /* used to index into the buffer array */
  event_type event;

  enable_network_layer();                  /* allow network_layer_ready events */
  ack_expected = 0;                        /* next ack expected inbound */
  next_frame_to_send = 0;                  /* next frame going out */
  frame_expected = 0;                      /* number of frame expected inbound */
  nbuffered = 0;                           /* initially no packets are buffered */
```

```
while (true) {
  wait_for_event(&event);                /* four possibilities: see event_type above */

  switch(event) {
    case network_layer_ready:            /* the network layer has a packet to send */
         /* Accept, save, and transmit a new frame. */
         from_network_layer(&buffer[next_frame_to_send]); /* fetch new packet */
         nbuffered = nbuffered + 1;      /* expand the sender's window */
         send_data(next_frame_to_send, frame_expected, buffer);/* transmit the frame */
         inc(next_frame_to_send);        /* advance sender's upper window edge */
         break;

    case frame_arrival:                  /* a data or control frame has arrived */
         from_physical_layer(&r);        /* get incoming frame from physical layer */

         if (r.seq == frame_expected) {
              /* Frames are accepted only in order. */
              to_network_layer(&r.info); /* pass packet to network layer */
              inc(frame_expected);       /* advance lower edge of receiver's window */
         }

         /* Ack n implies n - 1, n - 2, etc.  Check for this. */
         while (between(ack_expected, r.ack, next_frame_to_send)) {
              /* Handle piggybacked ack. */
              nbuffered = nbuffered - 1; /* one frame fewer buffered */
              stop_timer(ack_expected); /* frame arrived intact; stop timer */
              inc(ack_expected);         /* contract sender's window */
         }
         break;

    case cksum_err: break;               /* just ignore bad frames */

    case timeout:                        /* trouble; retransmit all outstanding frames */
         next_frame_to_send = ack_expected;    /* start retransmitting here */
         for (i = 1; i <= nbuffered; i++) {
              send_data(next_frame_to_send, frame_expected, buffer);/* resend frame */
              inc(next_frame_to_send);  /* prepare to send the next one */
         }

  }

  if (nbuffered < MAX_SEQ)
         enable_network_layer();
  else
         disable_network_layer();
 }
}
```

Figure 3-17. A sliding window protocol using go back n.

Note that a maximum of *MAX_SEQ* frames and not *MAX_SEQ* + 1 frames may be outstanding at any instant, even though there are *MAX_SEQ* + 1 distinct sequence numbers: 0, 1, 2, . . . , *MAX_SEQ*. To see why this restriction is required, consider the following scenario with *MAX_SEQ* = 7.

1. The sender sends frames 0 through 7.
2. A piggybacked acknowledgement for frame 7 eventually comes back to the sender.
3. The sender sends another eight frames, again with sequence numbers 0 through 7.
4. Now another piggybacked acknowledgement for frame 7 comes in.

The question is this: Did all eight frames belonging to the second batch arrive successfully, or did all eight get lost (counting discards following an error as lost)? In both cases the receiver would be sending frame 7 as the acknowledgement. The sender has no way of telling. For this reason the maximum number of outstanding frames must be restricted to *MAX_SEQ*.

Although protocol 5 does not buffer the frames arriving after an error, it does not escape the problem of buffering altogether. Since a sender may have to retransmit all the unacknowledged frames at a future time, it must hang on to all transmitted frames until it knows for sure that they have been accepted by the receiver. When an acknowledgement comes in for frame n, frames $n - 1$, $n - 2$, and so on are also automatically acknowledged. This property is especially important when some of the previous acknowledgement-bearing frames were lost or garbled. Whenever any acknowledgement comes in, the data link layer checks to see if any buffers can now be released. If buffers can be released (i.e., there is some room available in the window), a previously blocked network layer can now be allowed to cause more *network_layer_ready* events.

For this protocol, we assume that there is always reverse traffic on which to piggyback acknowledgements. If there is not, no acknowledgements can be sent. Protocol 4 does not need this assumption since it sends back one frame every time it receives a frame, even if it has just already sent that frame. In the next protocol we will solve the problem of one-way traffic in an elegant way.

Because protocol 5 has multiple outstanding frames, it logically needs multiple timers, one per outstanding frame. Each frame times out independently of all the other ones. All of these timers can easily be simulated in software, using a single hardware clock that causes interrupts periodically. The pending timeouts form a linked list, with each node of the list telling the number of clock ticks until the timer expires, the frame being timed, and a pointer to the next node.

As an illustration of how the timers could be implemented, consider the example of Fig. 3-18(a). Assume that the clock ticks once every 100 msec. Initially, the real time is 10:00:00.0; three timeouts are pending, at 10:00:00.5, 10:00:01.3,

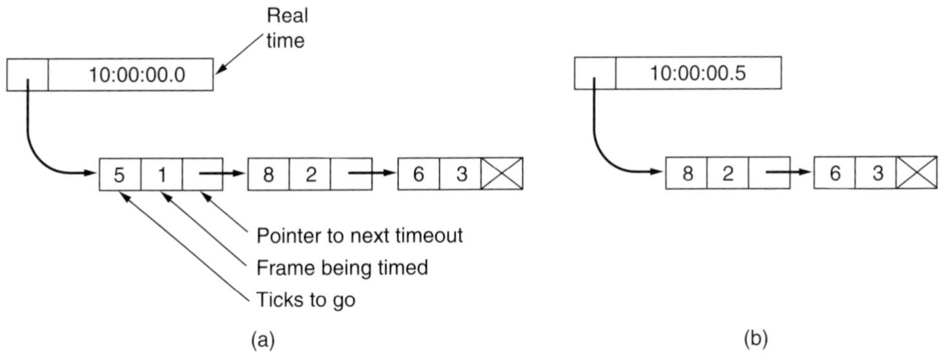

Figure 3-18. Simulation of multiple timers in software.

and 10:00:01.9. Every time the hardware clock ticks, the real time is updated and the tick counter at the head of the list is decremented. When the tick counter becomes zero, a timeout is caused and the node is removed from the list, as shown in Fig. 3-18(b). Although this organization requires the list to be scanned when *start_timer* or *stop_timer* is called, it does not require much work per tick. In protocol 5, both of these routines have been given a parameter, indicating which frame is to be timed.

3.4.3 A Protocol Using Selective Repeat

Protocol 5 works well if errors are rare, but if the line is poor, it wastes a lot of bandwidth on retransmitted frames. An alternative strategy for handling errors is to allow the receiver to accept and buffer the frames following a damaged or lost one. Such a protocol does not discard frames merely because an earlier frame was damaged or lost.

In this protocol, both sender and receiver maintain a window of acceptable sequence numbers. The sender's window size starts out at 0 and grows to some predefined maximum, *MAX_SEQ*. The receiver's window, in contrast, is always fixed in size and equal to *MAX_SEQ*. The receiver has a buffer reserved for each sequence number within its fixed window. Associated with each buffer is a bit (*arrived*) telling whether the buffer is full or empty. Whenever a frame arrives, its sequence number is checked by the function *between* to see if it falls within the window. If so and if it has not already been received, it is accepted and stored. This action is taken without regard to whether or not it contains the next packet expected by the network layer. Of course, it must be kept within the data link layer and not passed to the network layer until all the lower-numbered frames have already been delivered to the network layer in the correct order. A protocol using this algorithm is given in Fig. 3-19.

```
/* Protocol 6 (selective repeat) accepts frames out of order but passes packets to the
   network layer in order. Associated with each outstanding frame is a timer. When the timer
   expires, only that frame is retransmitted, not all the outstanding frames, as in protocol 5. */

#define MAX_SEQ 7                                /* should be 2^n - 1 */
#define NR_BUFS ((MAX_SEQ + 1)/2)
typedef enum {frame_arrival, cksum_err, timeout, network_layer_ready, ack_timeout} event_type;
#include "protocol.h"
boolean no_nak = true;                           /* no nak has been sent yet */
seq_nr oldest_frame = MAX_SEQ + 1;               /* initial value is only for the simulator */

static boolean between(seq_nr a, seq_nr b, seq_nr c)
{
/* Same as between in protocol5, but shorter and more obscure. */
  return ((a <= b) && (b < c)) || ((c < a) && (a <= b)) || ((b < c) && (c < a));
}

static void send_frame(frame_kind fk, seq_nr frame_nr, seq_nr frame_expected, packet buffer[ ])
{
/* Construct and send a data, ack, or nak frame. */
  frame s;                                       /* scratch variable */

  s.kind = fk;                                   /* kind == data, ack, or nak */
  if (fk == data) s.info = buffer[frame_nr % NR_BUFS];
  s.seq = frame_nr;                              /* only meaningful for data frames */
  s.ack = (frame_expected + MAX_SEQ) % (MAX_SEQ + 1);
  if (fk == nak) no_nak = false;                 /* one nak per frame, please */
  to_physical_layer(&s);                         /* transmit the frame */
  if (fk == data) start_timer(frame_nr % NR_BUFS);
  stop_ack_timer();                              /* no need for separate ack frame */
}

void protocol6(void)
{
  seq_nr ack_expected;                           /* lower edge of sender's window */
  seq_nr next_frame_to_send;                     /* upper edge of sender's window + 1 */
  seq_nr frame_expected;                         /* lower edge of receiver's window */
  seq_nr too_far;                                /* upper edge of receiver's window + 1 */
  int i;                                         /* index into buffer pool */
  frame r;                                       /* scratch variable */
  packet out_buf[NR_BUFS];                       /* buffers for the outbound stream */
  packet in_buf[NR_BUFS];                        /* buffers for the inbound stream */
  boolean arrived[NR_BUFS];                      /* inbound bit map */
  seq_nr nbuffered;                              /* how many output buffers currently used */
  event_type event;

  enable_network_layer();                        /* initialize */
  ack_expected = 0;                              /* next ack expected on the inbound stream */
  next_frame_to_send = 0;                        /* number of next outgoing frame */
  frame_expected = 0;
  too_far = NR_BUFS;
  nbuffered = 0;                                 /* initially no packets are buffered */
  for (i = 0; i < NR_BUFS; i++) arrived[i] = false;
```

```
 while (true) {
   wait_for_event(&event);                    /* five possibilities: see event_type above */
   switch(event) {
     case network_layer_ready:                /* accept, save, and transmit a new frame */
          nbuffered = nbuffered + 1;          /* expand the window */
          from_network_layer(&out_buf[next_frame_to_send % NR_BUFS]); /* fetch new packet */
          send_frame(data, next_frame_to_send, frame_expected, out_buf);/* transmit the frame */
          inc(next_frame_to_send);            /* advance upper window edge */
          break;

     case frame_arrival:                      /* a data or control frame has arrived */
          from_physical_layer(&r);            /* fetch incoming frame from physical layer */
          if (r.kind == data) {
               /* An undamaged frame has arrived. */
               if ((r.seq != frame_expected) && no_nak)
                  send_frame(nak, 0, frame_expected, out_buf); else start_ack_timer();
               if (between(frame_expected,r.seq,too_far) && (arrived[r.seq%NR_BUFS]==false)) {
                    /* Frames may be accepted in any order. */
                    arrived[r.seq % NR_BUFS] = true;     /* mark buffer as full */
                    in_buf[r.seq % NR_BUFS] = r.info;     /* insert data into buffer */
                    while (arrived[frame_expected % NR_BUFS]) {
                         /* Pass frames and advance window. */
                         to_network_layer(&in_buf[frame_expected % NR_BUFS]);
                         no_nak = true;
                         arrived[frame_expected % NR_BUFS] = false;
                         inc(frame_expected);    /* advance lower edge of receiver's window */
                         inc(too_far);           /* advance upper edge of receiver's window */
                         start_ack_timer();      /* to see if a separate ack is needed */
                    }
               }
          }
          if((r.kind==nak) && between(ack_expected,(r.ack+1)%(MAX_SEQ+1),next_frame_to_send))
               send_frame(data, (r.ack+1) % (MAX_SEQ + 1), frame_expected, out_buf);

          while (between(ack_expected, r.ack, next_frame_to_send)) {
               nbuffered = nbuffered - 1;          /* handle piggybacked ack */
               stop_timer(ack_expected % NR_BUFS);    /* frame arrived intact */
               inc(ack_expected);                  /* advance lower edge of sender's window */
          }
          break;

     case cksum_err:
          if (no_nak) send_frame(nak, 0, frame_expected, out_buf); /* damaged frame */
          break;

     case timeout:
          send_frame(data, oldest_frame, frame_expected, out_buf); /* we timed out */
          break;

     case ack_timeout:
          send_frame(ack,0,frame_expected, out_buf);     /* ack timer expired; send ack */
   }
   if (nbuffered < NR_BUFS) enable_network_layer(); else disable_network_layer();
 }
}
```

Figure 3-19. A sliding window protocol using selective repeat.

Nonsequential receive introduces certain problems not present in protocols in which frames are only accepted in order. We can illustrate the trouble most easily with an example. Suppose that we have a 3-bit sequence number, so that the sender is permitted to transmit up to seven frames before being required to wait for an acknowledgement. Initially, the sender's and receiver's windows are as shown in Fig. 3-20(a). The sender now transmits frames 0 through 6. The receiver's window allows it to accept any frame with sequence number between 0 and 6 inclusive. All seven frames arrive correctly, so the receiver acknowledges them and advances its window to allow receipt of 7, 0, 1, 2, 3, 4, or 5, as shown in Fig. 3-20(b). All seven buffers are marked empty.

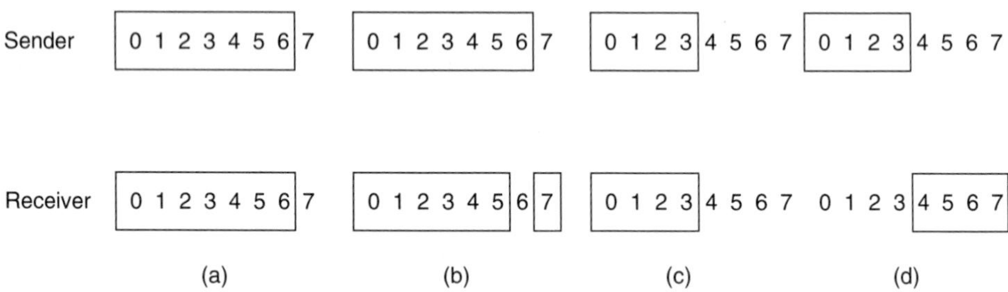

Figure 3-20. (a) Initial situation with a window of size seven. (b) After seven frames have been sent and received but not acknowledged. (c) Initial situation with a window size of four. (d) After four frames have been sent and received but not acknowledged.

It is at this point that disaster strikes in the form of a lightning bolt hitting the telephone pole and wiping out all the acknowledgements. The sender eventually times out and retransmits frame 0. When this frame arrives at the receiver, a check is made to see if it falls within the receiver's window. Unfortunately, in Fig. 3-20(b) frame 0 is within the new window, so it will be accepted. The receiver sends a piggybacked acknowledgement for frame 6, since 0 through 6 have been received.

The sender is happy to learn that all its transmitted frames did actually arrive correctly, so it advances its window and immediately sends frames 7, 0, 1, 2, 3, 4, and 5. Frame 7 will be accepted by the receiver and its packet will be passed directly to the network layer. Immediately thereafter, the receiving data link layer checks to see if it has a valid frame 0 already, discovers that it does, and passes the embedded packet to the network layer. Consequently, the network layer gets an incorrect packet, and the protocol fails.

The essence of the problem is that after the receiver advanced its window, the new range of valid sequence numbers overlapped the old one. Consequently, the following batch of frames might be either duplicates (if all the acknowledgements were lost) or new ones (if all the acknowledgements were received). The poor receiver has no way of distinguishing these two cases.

The way out of this dilemma lies in making sure that after the receiver has advanced its window, there is no overlap with the original window. To ensure that there is no overlap, the maximum window size should be at most half the range of the sequence numbers, as is done in Fig. 3-20(c) and Fig. 3-20(d). For example, if 4 bits are used for sequence numbers, these will range from 0 to 15. Only eight unacknowledged frames should be outstanding at any instant. That way, if the receiver has just accepted frames 0 through 7 and advanced its window to permit acceptance of frames 8 through 15, it can unambiguously tell if subsequent frames are retransmissions (0 through 7) or new ones (8 through 15). In general, the window size for protocol 6 will be (*MAX_SEQ* + 1)/2. Thus, for 3-bit sequence numbers, the window size is four.

An interesting question is: How many buffers must the receiver have? Under no conditions will it ever accept frames whose sequence numbers are below the lower edge of the window or frames whose sequence numbers are above the upper edge of the window. Consequently, the number of buffers needed is equal to the window size, not to the range of sequence numbers. In the above example of a 4-bit sequence number, eight buffers, numbered 0 through 7, are needed. When frame i arrives, it is put in buffer i mod 8. Notice that although i and $(i + 8)$ mod 8 are "competing" for the same buffer, they are never within the window at the same time, because that would imply a window size of at least 9.

For the same reason, the number of timers needed is equal to the number of buffers, not to the size of the sequence space. Effectively, a timer is associated with each buffer. When the timer runs out, the contents of the buffer are retransmitted.

In protocol 5, there is an implicit assumption that the channel is heavily loaded. When a frame arrives, no acknowledgement is sent immediately. Instead, the acknowledgement is piggybacked onto the next outgoing data frame. If the reverse traffic is light, the acknowledgement will be held up for a long period of time. If there is a lot of traffic in one direction and no traffic in the other direction, only *MAX_SEQ* packets are sent, and then the protocol blocks, which is why we had to assume there was always some reverse traffic.

In protocol 6 this problem is fixed. After an in-sequence data frame arrives, an auxiliary timer is started by *start_ack_timer*. If no reverse traffic has presented itself before this timer expires, a separate acknowledgement frame is sent. An interrupt due to the auxiliary timer is called an *ack_timeout* event. With this arrangement, one-directional traffic flow is now possible because the lack of reverse data frames onto which acknowledgements can be piggybacked is no longer an obstacle. Only one auxiliary timer exists, and if *start_ack_timer* is called while the timer is running, it is reset to a full acknowledgement timeout interval.

It is essential that the timeout associated with the auxiliary timer be appreciably shorter than the timer used for timing out data frames. This condition is required to make sure a correctly received frame is acknowledged early enough that the frame's retransmission timer does not expire and retransmit the frame.

Protocol 6 uses a more efficient strategy than protocol 5 for dealing with errors. Whenever the receiver has reason to suspect that an error has occurred, it sends a negative acknowledgement (NAK) frame back to the sender. Such a frame is a request for retransmission of the frame specified in the NAK. There are two cases when the receiver should be suspicious: a damaged frame has arrived or a frame other than the expected one arrived (potential lost frame). To avoid making multiple requests for retransmission of the same lost frame, the receiver should keep track of whether a NAK has already been sent for a given frame. The variable *no_nak* in protocol 6 is true if no NAK has been sent yet for *frame_expected*. If the NAK gets mangled or lost, no real harm is done, since the sender will eventually time out and retransmit the missing frame anyway. If the wrong frame arrives after a NAK has been sent and lost, *no_nak* will be true and the auxiliary timer will be started. When it expires, an ACK will be sent to resynchronize the sender to the receiver's current status.

In some situations, the time required for a frame to propagate to the destination, be processed there, and have the acknowledgement come back is (nearly) constant. In these situations, the sender can adjust its timer to be just slightly larger than the normal time interval expected between sending a frame and receiving its acknowledgement. However, if this time is highly variable, the sender is faced with the choice of either setting the interval to a small value (and risking unnecessary retransmissions), or setting it to a large value (and going idle for a long period after an error).

Both choices waste bandwidth. If the reverse traffic is sporadic, the time before acknowledgement will be irregular, being shorter when there is reverse traffic and longer when there is not. Variable processing time within the receiver can also be a problem here. In general, whenever the standard deviation of the acknowledgement interval is small compared to the interval itself, the timer can be set "tight" and NAKs are not useful. Otherwise the timer must be set "loose," to avoid unnecessary retransmissions, but NAKs can appreciably speed up retransmission of lost or damaged frames.

Closely related to the matter of timeouts and NAKs is the question of determining which frame caused a timeout. In protocol 5, it is always *ack_expected*, because it is always the oldest. In protocol 6, there is no trivial way to determine who timed out. Suppose that frames 0 through 4 have been transmitted, meaning that the list of outstanding frames is 01234, in order from oldest to youngest. Now imagine that 0 times out, 5 (a new frame) is transmitted, 1 times out, 2 times out, and 6 (another new frame) is transmitted. At this point the list of outstanding frames is 3405126, from oldest to youngest. If all inbound traffic (i.e., acknowledgement-bearing frames) is lost for a while, the seven outstanding frames will time out in that order.

To keep the example from getting even more complicated than it already is, we have not shown the timer administration. Instead, we just assume that the variable *oldest_frame* is set upon timeout to indicate which frame timed out.

3.5 PROTOCOL VERIFICATION

Realistic protocols and the programs that implement them are often quite complicated. Consequently, much research has been done trying to find formal, mathematical techniques for specifying and verifying protocols. In the following sections we will look at some models and techniques. Although we are looking at them in the context of the data link layer, they are also applicable to other layers.

3.5.1 Finite State Machine Models

A key concept used in many protocol models is the **finite state machine**. With this technique, each **protocol machine** (i.e., sender or receiver) is always in a specific state at every instant of time. Its state consists of all the values of its variables, including the program counter.

In most cases, a large number of states can be grouped for purposes of analysis. For example, considering the receiver in protocol 3, we could abstract out from all the possible states two important ones: waiting for frame 0 or waiting for frame 1. All other states can be thought of as transient, just steps on the way to one of the main states. Typically, the states are chosen to be those instants that the protocol machine is waiting for the next event to happen [i.e., executing the procedure call *wait*(*event*) in our examples]. At this point the state of the protocol machine is completely determined by the states of its variables. The number of states is then 2^n, where n is the number of bits needed to represent all the variables combined.

The state of the complete system is the combination of all the states of the two protocol machines and the channel. The state of the channel is determined by its contents. Using protocol 3 again as an example, the channel has four possible states: a 0 frame or a 1 frame moving from sender to receiver, an acknowledgement frame going the other way, or an empty channel. If we model the sender and receiver as each having two states, the complete system has 16 distinct states.

A word about the channel state is in order. The concept of a frame being "on the channel" is an abstraction, of course. What we really mean is that a frame has possibly been received, but not yet processed at the destination. A frame remains "on the channel" until the protocol machine executes *FromPhysicalLayer* and processes it.

From each state, there are zero or more possible **transitions** to other states. Transitions occur when some event happens. For a protocol machine, a transition might occur when a frame is sent, when a frame arrives, when a timer expires, when an interrupt occurs, etc. For the channel, typical events are insertion of a new frame onto the channel by a protocol machine, delivery of a frame to a protocol machine, or loss of a frame due to noise. Given a complete description of the protocol machines and the channel characteristics, it is possible to draw a directed graph showing all the states as nodes and all the transitions as directed arcs.

One particular state is designated as the **initial state**. This state corresponds to the description of the system when it starts running, or at some convenient starting place shortly thereafter. From the initial state, some, perhaps all, of the other states can be reached by a sequence of transitions. Using well-known techniques from graph theory (e.g., computing the transitive closure of a graph), it is possible to determine which states are reachable and which are not. This technique is called **reachability analysis** (Lin et al., 1987). This analysis can be helpful in determining whether a protocol is correct.

Formally, a finite state machine model of a protocol can be regarded as a quadruple (S, M, I, T), where:

S is the set of states the processes and channel can be in.

M is the set of frames that can be exchanged over the channel.

I is the set of initial states of the processes.

T is the set of transitions between states.

At the beginning of time, all processes are in their initial states. Then events begin to happen, such as frames becoming available for transmission or timers going off. Each event may cause one of the processes or the channel to take an action and switch to a new state. By carefully enumerating each possible successor to each state, one can build the reachability graph and analyze the protocol.

Reachability analysis can be used to detect a variety of errors in the protocol specification. For example, if it is possible for a certain frame to occur in a certain state and the finite state machine does not say what action should be taken, the specification is in error (incompleteness). If there exists a set of states from which no exit can be made and from which no progress can be made (i.e., no correct frames can be received any more), we have another error (deadlock). A less serious error is protocol specification that tells how to handle an event in a state in which the event cannot occur (extraneous transition). Other errors can also be detected.

As an example of a finite state machine model, consider Fig. 3-21(a). This graph corresponds to protocol 3 as described above: each protocol machine has two states and the channel has four states. A total of 16 states exist, not all of them reachable from the initial one. The unreachable ones are not shown in the figure. Checksum errors are also ignored here for simplicity.

Each state is labeled by three characters, SRC, where S is 0 or 1, corresponding to the frame the sender is trying to send; R is also 0 or 1, corresponding to the frame the receiver expects, and C is 0, 1, A, or empty (–), corresponding to the state of the channel. In this example the initial state has been chosen as (000). In other words, the sender has just sent frame 0, the receiver expects frame 0, and frame 0 is currently on the channel.

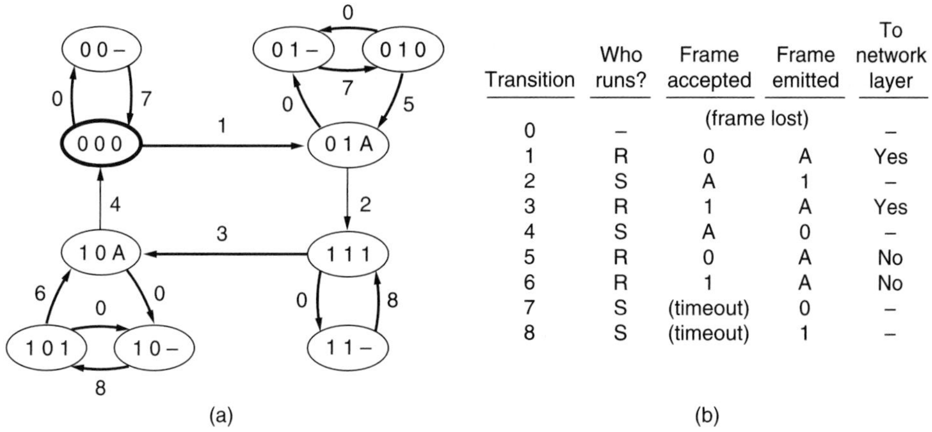

Transition	Who runs?	Frame accepted	Frame emitted	To network layer
0	–	(frame lost)		–
1	R	0	A	Yes
2	S	A	1	–
3	R	1	A	Yes
4	S	A	0	–
5	R	0	A	No
6	R	1	A	No
7	S	(timeout)	0	–
8	S	(timeout)	1	–

Figure 3-21. (a) State diagram for protocol 3. (b) Transitions.

Nine kinds of transitions are shown in Fig. 3-21. Transition 0 consists of the channel losing its contents. Transition 1 consists of the channel correctly delivering packet 0 to the receiver, with the receiver then changing its state to expect frame 1 and emitting an acknowledgement. Transition 1 also corresponds to the receiver delivering packet 0 to the network layer. The other transitions are listed in Fig. 3-21(b). The arrival of a frame with a checksum error has not been shown because it does not change the state (in protocol 3).

During normal operation, transitions 1, 2, 3, and 4 are repeated in order over and over. In each cycle, two packets are delivered, bringing the sender back to the initial state of trying to send a new frame with sequence number 0. If the channel loses frame 0, it makes a transition from state (000) to state (00–). Eventually, the sender times out (transition 7) and the system moves back to (000). The loss of an acknowledgement is more complicated, requiring two transitions, 7 and 5, or 8 and 6, to repair the damage.

One of the properties that a protocol with a 1-bit sequence number must have is that no matter what sequence of events happens, the receiver never delivers two odd packets without an intervening even packet, and vice versa. From the graph of Fig. 3-21 we see that this requirement can be stated more formally as "there must not exist any paths from the initial state on which two occurrences of transition 1 occur without an occurrence of transition 3 between them, or vice versa." From the figure it can be seen that the protocol is correct in this respect.

A similar requirement is that there not exist any paths on which the sender changes state twice (e.g., from 0 to 1 and back to 0) while the receiver state remains constant. Were such a path to exist, then in the corresponding sequence of events, two frames would be irretrievably lost without the receiver noticing. The packet sequence delivered would have an undetected gap of two packets in it.

Yet another important property of a protocol is the absence of deadlocks. A **deadlock** is a situation in which the protocol can make no more forward progress (i.e., deliver packets to the network layer) no matter what sequence of events happens. In terms of the graph model, a deadlock is characterized by the existence of a subset of states that is reachable from the initial state and that has two properties:

1. There is no transition out of the subset.
2. There are no transitions in the subset that cause forward progress.

Once in the deadlock situation, the protocol remains there forever. Again, it is easy to see from the graph that protocol 3 does not suffer from deadlocks.

3.5.2 Petri Net Models

The finite state machine is not the only technique for formally specifying protocols. In this section we will describe a completely different technique, the **Petri net** (Danthine, 1980). A Petri net has four basic elements: places, transitions, arcs, and tokens. A **place** represents a state which (part of) the system may be in. Figure 3-22 shows a Petri net with two places, *A* and *B*, both shown as circles. The system is currently in state *A*, indicated by the **token** (heavy dot) in place *A*. A **transition** is indicated by a horizontal or vertical bar. Each transition has zero or more **input arcs** coming from its input places, and zero or more **output arcs**, going to its output places.

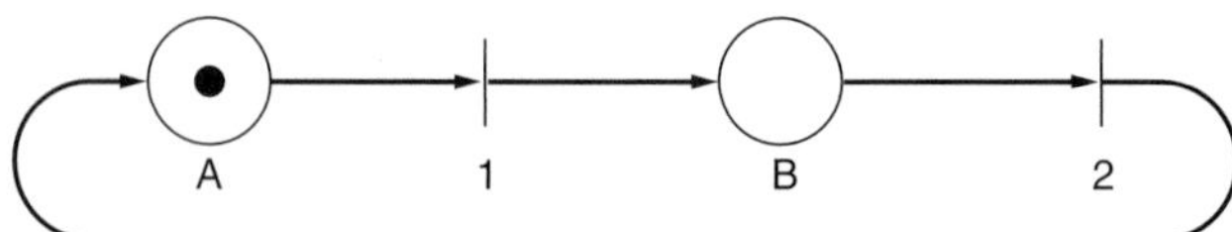

Figure 3-22. A Petri net with two places and two transitions.

A transition is **enabled** if there is at least one input token in each of its input places. Any enabled transition may **fire** at will, removing one token from each input place and depositing a token in each output place. If the number of input arcs and output arcs differs, tokens will not be conserved. If two or more transitions are enabled, any one of them may fire. The choice of a transition to fire is indeterminate, which is why Petri nets are useful for modeling protocols. The Petri net of Fig. 3-22 is deterministic and can be used to model any two-phase process (e.g., the behavior of a baby: eat, sleep, eat, sleep, and so on). As with all modeling tools, unnecessary detail is suppressed.

Figure 3-23 gives the Petri net model of Fig. 3-12. Unlike the finite state machine model, there are no composite states here; the sender's state, channel state,

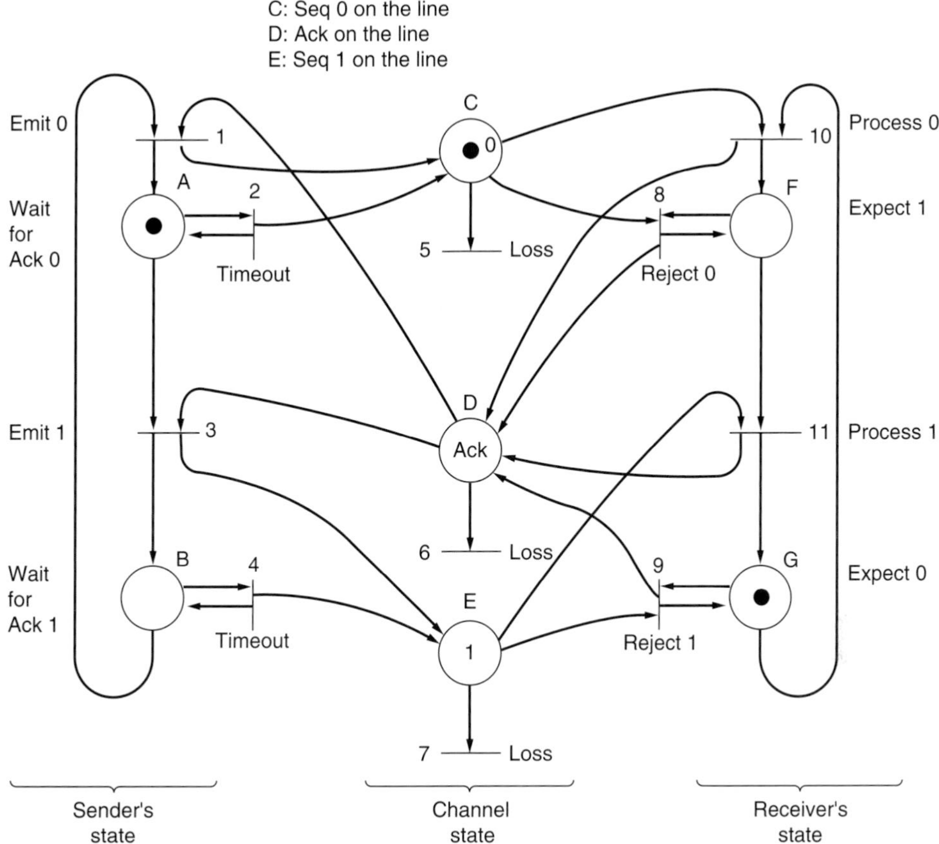

Figure 3-23. A Petri net model for protocol 3.

and receiver's state are represented separately. Transitions 1 and 2 correspond to transmission of frame 0 by the sender, normally, and on a timeout respectively. Transitions 3 and 4 are analogous for frame 1. Transitions 5, 6, and 7 correspond to the loss of frame 0, an acknowledgement, and frame 1, respectively. Transitions 8 and 9 occur when a data frame with the wrong sequence number arrives at the receiver. Transitions 10 and 11 represent the arrival at the receiver of the next frame in sequence and its delivery to the network layer.

Petri nets can be used to detect protocol failures in a way similar to the use of finite state machines. For example, if some firing sequence included transition 10 twice without transition 11 intervening, the protocol would be incorrect. The concept of a deadlock in a Petri net is similar to its finite state machine counterpart.

Petri nets can be represented in convenient algebraic form resembling a grammar. Each transition contributes one rule to the grammar. Each rule specifies the input and output places of the transition. Since Fig. 3-23 has 11 transitions, its grammar has 11 rules, numbered 1–11, each one corresponding to the transition with the same number. The grammar for the Petri net of Fig. 3-23 is as follows:

1: BD → AC
2: A → A
3: AD → BE
4: B → B
5: C →
6: D →
7: E →
8: CF → DF
9: EG → DG
10: CG → DF
11: EF → DG

It is interesting to note how we have managed to reduce a complex protocol to 11 simple grammar rules that can easily be manipulated by a computer program.

The current state of the Petri net is represented as an unordered collection of places, each place represented in the collection as many times as it has tokens. Any rule, all of whose left-hand side places are present can be fired, removing those places from the current state, and adding its output places to the current state. The marking of Fig. 3-23 is *ACG*, (i.e., *A*, *C*, and *G* each have one token). Consequently, rules 2, 5, and 10 are all enabled and any of them can be applied, leading to a new state (possibly with the same marking as the original one). In contrast, rule 3 ($AD \rightarrow BE$) cannot be applied because *D* is not marked.

3.6 EXAMPLE DATA LINK PROTOCOLS

In the following sections we will examine several widely-used data link protocols. The first one, HDLC, is a classical bit-oriented protocol whose variants have been in use for decades in many applications. The second one, PPP, is the data link protocol used to connect home computers to the Internet.

3.6.1 HDLC—High-Level Data Link Control

In this section we will examine a group of closely related protocols that are a bit old but are still heavily used. They are all derived from the data link protocol first used in the IBM mainframe world: **SDLC** (**Synchronous Data Link Control**) protocol. After developing SDLC, IBM submitted it to ANSI and ISO for acceptance as U.S. and international standards, respectively. ANSI modified it to become **ADCCP** (**Advanced Data Communication Control Procedure**), and ISO modified it to become **HDLC** (**High-level Data Link Control**). CCITT then adopted and modified HDLC for its **LAP** (**Link Access Procedure**) as part of the X.25 network interface standard but later modified it again to **LAPB**, to make it more compatible with a later version of HDLC. The nice thing about standards is that you have so many to choose from. Furthermore, if you do not like any of them, you can just wait for next year's model.

These protocols are based on the same principles. All are bit oriented, and all use bit stuffing for data transparency. They differ only in minor, but nevertheless irritating, ways. The discussion of bit-oriented protocols that follows is intended as a general introduction. For the specific details of any one protocol, please consult the appropriate definition.

All the bit-oriented protocols use the frame structure shown in Fig. 3-24. The *Address* field is primarily of importance on lines with multiple terminals, where it is used to identify one of the terminals. For point-to-point lines, it is sometimes used to distinguish commands from responses.

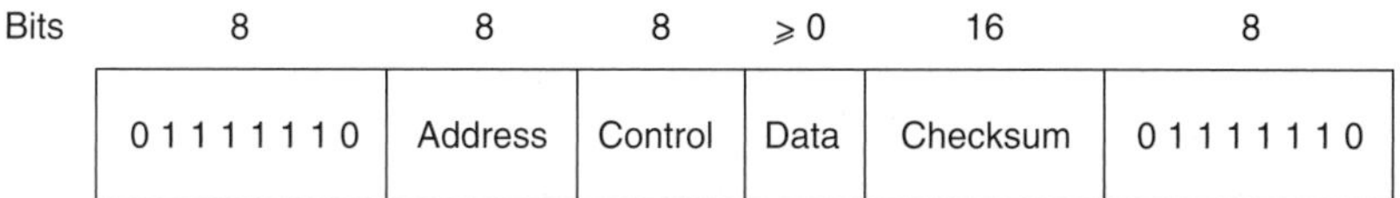

Figure 3-24. Frame format for bit-oriented protocols.

The *Control* field is used for sequence numbers, acknowledgements, and other purposes, as discussed below.

The *Data* field may contain any information. It may be arbitrarily long, although the efficiency of the checksum falls off with increasing frame length due to the greater probability of multiple burst errors.

The *Checksum* field is a cyclic redundancy code using the technique we examined in Sec. 3-2.2.

The frame is delimited with another flag sequence (01111110). On idle point-to-point lines, flag sequences are transmitted continuously. The minimum frame contains three fields and totals 32 bits, excluding the flags on either end.

There are three kinds of frames: **Information**, **Supervisory**, and **Unnumbered**. The contents of the *Control* field for these three kinds are shown in Fig. 3-25. The protocol uses a sliding window, with a 3-bit sequence number. Up to seven unacknowledged frames may be outstanding at any instant. The *Seq* field in Fig. 3-25(a) is the frame sequence number. The *Next* field is a piggybacked acknowledgement. However, all the protocols adhere to the convention that instead of piggybacking the number of the last frame received correctly, they use the number of the first frame not yet received (i.e., the next frame expected). The choice of using the last frame received or the next frame expected is arbitrary; it does not matter which convention is used, provided that it is used consistently.

The *P/F* bit stands for *Poll/Final*. It is used when a computer (or concentrator) is polling a group of terminals. When used as *P*, the computer is inviting the terminal to send data. All the frames sent by the terminal, except the final one, have the *P/F* bit set to *P*. The final one is set to *F*.

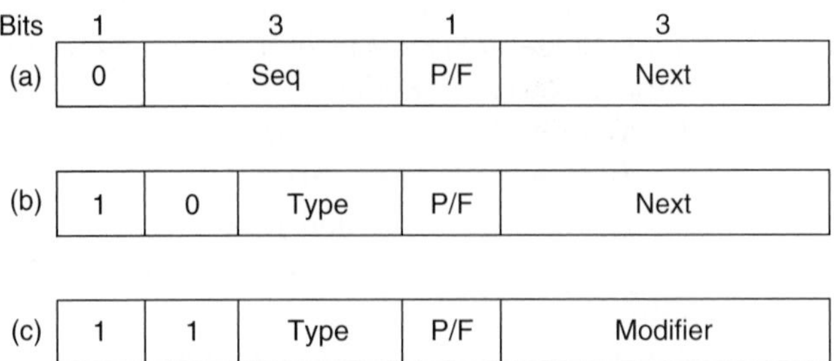

Figure 3-25. Control field of (a) an information frame, (b) a supervisory frame, (c) an unnumbered frame.

In some of the protocols, the *P/F* bit is used to force the other machine to send a Supervisory frame immediately rather than waiting for reverse traffic onto which to piggyback the window information. The bit also has some minor uses in connection with the Unnumbered frames.

The various kinds of Supervisory frames are distinguished by the *Type* field. Type 0 is an acknowledgement frame (officially called RECEIVE READY) used to indicate the next frame expected. This frame is used when there is no reverse traffic to use for piggybacking.

Type 1 is a negative acknowledgement frame (officially called REJECT). It is used to indicate that a transmission error has been detected. The *Next* field indicates the first frame in sequence not received correctly (i.e., the frame to be retransmitted). The sender is required to retransmit all outstanding frames starting at *Next*. This strategy is similar to our protocol 5 rather than our protocol 6.

Type 2 is RECEIVE NOT READY. It acknowledges all frames up to but not including *Next*, just as RECEIVE READY does, but it tells the sender to stop sending. RECEIVE NOT READY is intended to signal certain temporary problems with the receiver, such as a shortage of buffers, and not as an alternative to the sliding window flow control. When the condition has been repaired, the receiver sends a RECEIVE READY, REJECT, or certain control frames.

Type 3 is the SELECTIVE REJECT. It calls for retransmission of only the frame specified. In this sense it is like our protocol 6 rather than 5 and is therefore most useful when the sender's window size is half the sequence space size, or less. Thus, if a receiver wishes to buffer out-of-sequence frames for potential future use, it can force the retransmission of any specific frame using Selective Reject. HDLC and ADCCP allow this frame type, but SDLC and LAPB do not allow it (i.e., there is no Selective Reject), and type 3 frames are undefined.

The third class of frame is the Unnumbered frame. It is sometimes used for control purposes but can also carry data when unreliable connectionless service is called for. The various bit-oriented protocols differ considerably here, in contrast with the other two kinds, where they are nearly identical. Five bits are available to indicate the frame type, but not all 32 possibilities are used.

All the protocols provide a command, DISC (DISConnect), that allows a machine to announce that it is going down (e.g., for preventive maintenance). They also have a command that allows a machine that has just come back on-line to announce its presence and force all the sequence numbers back to zero. This command is called SNRM (Set Normal Response Mode). Unfortunately, "Normal Response Mode" is anything but normal. It is an unbalanced (i.e., asymmetric) mode in which one end of the line is the master and the other the slave. SNRM dates from a time when data communication meant a dumb terminal talking to a big host computer, which clearly is asymmetric. To make the protocol more suitable when the two partners are equals, HDLC and LAPB have an additional command, SABM (Set Asynchronous Balanced Mode), which resets the line and declares both parties to be equals. They also have commands SABME and SNRME, which are the same as SABM and SNRM, respectively, except that they enable an extended frame format that uses 7-bit sequence numbers instead of 3-bit sequence numbers.

A third command provided by all the protocols is FRMR (FRaMe Reject), used to indicate that a frame with a correct checksum but impossible semantics arrived. Examples of impossible semantics are a type 3 Supervisory frame in LAPB, a frame shorter than 32 bits, an illegal control frame, and an acknowledgement of a frame that was outside the window, etc. FRMR frames contain a 24-bit data field telling what was wrong with the frame. The data include the control field of the bad frame, the window parameters, and a collection of bits used to signal specific errors.

Control frames can be lost or damaged, just like data frames, so they must be acknowledged too. A special control frame, called UA (Unnumbered Acknowledgement), is provided for this purpose. Since only one control frame may be outstanding, there is never any ambiguity about which control frame is being acknowledged.

The remaining control frames deal with initialization, polling, and status reporting. There is also a control frame that may contain arbitrary information, UI (Unnumbered Information). These data are not passed to the network layer but are for the receiving data link layer itself.

Despite its widespread use, HDLC is far from perfect. A discussion of a variety of problems associated with it can be found in (Fiorini et al., 1994).

3.6.2 The Data Link Layer in the Internet

The Internet consists of individual machines (hosts and routers) and the communication infrastructure that connects them. Within a single building, LANs are widely used for interconnection, but most of the wide area infrastructure is built up from point-to-point leased lines. In Chap. 4, we will look at LANs; here we will examine the data link protocols used on point-to-point lines in the Internet.

In practice, point-to-point communication is primarily used in two situations. First, thousands of organizations have one or more LANs, each with some number of hosts (personal computers, user workstations, servers, and so on) along with a router (or a bridge, which is functionally similar). Often, the routers are interconnected by a backbone LAN. Typically, all connections to the outside world go through one or two routers that have point-to-point leased lines to distant routers. It is these routers and their leased lines that make up the communication subnets on which the Internet is built.

The second situation in which point-to-point lines play a major role in the Internet is the millions of individuals who have home connections to the Internet using modems and dial-up telephone lines. Usually, what happens is that the user's home PC calls up an Internet service provider's router and then acts like a full-blown Internet host. This method of operation is no different from having a leased line between the PC and the router, except that the connection is terminated when the user ends the session. A home PC calling an Internet service provider is illustrated in Fig. 3-26. The modem is shown external to the computer to emphasize its role, but modern computers have internal modems.

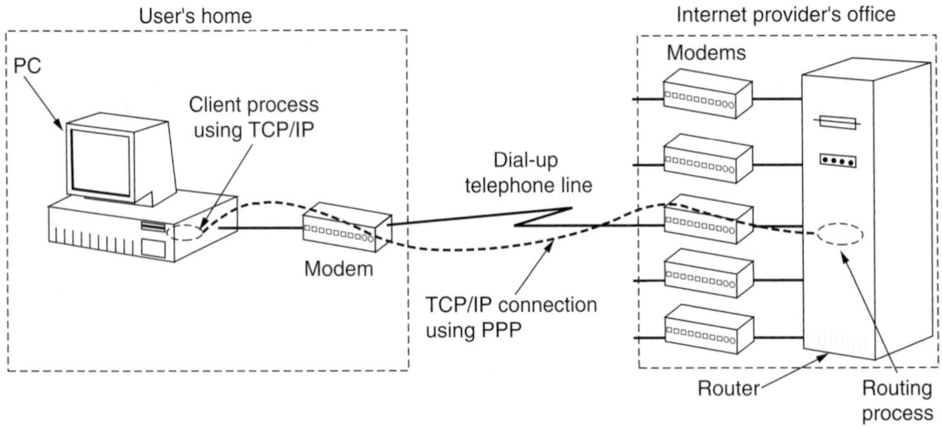

Figure 3-26. A home personal computer acting as an Internet host.

For both the router-router leased line connection and the dial-up host-router connection, some point-to-point data link protocol is required on the line for framing, error control, and the other data link layer functions we have studied in this chapter. The one used in the Internet is called PPP. We will now examine it.

PPP—The Point-to-Point Protocol

The Internet needs a point-to-point protocol for a variety of purposes, including router-to-router traffic and home user-to-ISP traffic. This protocol is **PPP** (**Point-to-Point Protocol**), which is defined in RFC 1661 and further elaborated on in several other RFCs (e.g., RFCs 1662 and 1663). PPP handles error detection, supports multiple protocols, allows IP addresses to be negotiated at connection time, permits authentication, and has many other features.

PPP provides three features:

1. A framing method that unambiguously delineates the end of one frame and the start of the next one. The frame format also handles error detection.

2. A link control protocol for bringing lines up, testing them, negotiating options, and bringing them down again gracefully when they are no longer needed. This protocol is called **LCP** (**Link Control Protocol**). It supports synchronous and asynchronous circuits and byte-oriented and bit-oriented encodings.

3. A way to negotiate network-layer options in a way that is independent of the network layer protocol to be used. The method chosen is to have a different **NCP** (**Network Control Protocol**) for each network layer supported.

To see how these pieces fit together, let us consider the typical scenario of a home user calling up an Internet service provider to make a home PC a temporary Internet host. The PC first calls the provider's router via a modem. After the router's modem has answered the phone and established a physical connection, the PC sends the router a series of LCP packets in the payload field of one or more PPP frames. These packets and their responses select the PPP parameters to be used.

Once the parameters have been agreed upon, a series of NCP packets are sent to configure the network layer. Typically, the PC wants to run a TCP/IP protocol stack, so it needs an IP address. There are not enough IP addresses to go around, so normally each Internet provider gets a block of them and then dynamically assigns one to each newly attached PC for the duration of its login session. If a provider owns n IP addresses, it can have up to n machines logged in simultaneously, but its total customer base may be many times that. The NCP for IP assigns the IP address.

At this point, the PC is now an Internet host and can send and receive IP packets, just as hardwired hosts can. When the user is finished, NCP tears down the network layer connection and frees up the IP address. Then LCP shuts down the data link layer connection. Finally, the computer tells the modem to hang up the phone, releasing the physical layer connection.

The PPP frame format was chosen to closely resemble the HDLC frame format, since there was no reason to reinvent the wheel. The major difference between PPP and HDLC is that PPP is character oriented rather than bit oriented. In particular, PPP uses byte stuffing on dial-up modem lines, so all frames are an integral number of bytes. It is not possible to send a frame consisting of 30.25

bytes, as it is with HDLC. Not only can PPP frames be sent over dial-up telephone lines, but they can also be sent over SONET or true bit-oriented HDLC lines (e.g., for router-router connections). The PPP frame format is shown in Fig. 3-27.

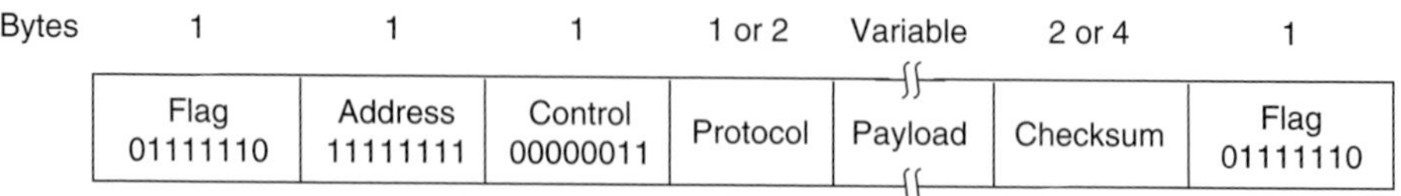

Figure 3-27. The PPP full frame format for unnumbered mode operation.

All PPP frames begin with the standard HDLC flag byte (01111110), which is byte stuffed if it occurs within the payload field. Next comes the *Address* field, which is always set to the binary value 11111111 to indicate that all stations are to accept the frame. Using this value avoids the issue of having to assign data link addresses.

The *Address* field is followed by the *Control* field, the default value of which is 00000011. This value indicates an unnumbered frame. In other words, PPP does not provide reliable transmission using sequence numbers and acknowledgements as the default. In noisy environments, such as wireless networks, reliable transmission using numbered mode can be used. The exact details are defined in RFC 1663, but in practice it is rarely used.

Since the *Address* and *Control* fields are always constant in the default configuration, LCP provides the necessary mechanism for the two parties to negotiate an option to just omit them altogether and save 2 bytes per frame.

The fourth PPP field is the *Protocol* field. Its job is to tell what kind of packet is in the *Payload* field. Codes are defined for LCP, NCP, IP, IPX, AppleTalk, and other protocols. Protocols starting with a 0 bit are network layer protocols such as IP, IPX, OSI CLNP, XNS. Those starting with a 1 bit are used to negotiate other protocols. These include LCP and a different NCP for each network layer protocol supported. The default size of the *Protocol* field is 2 bytes, but it can be negotiated down to 1 byte using LCP.

The *Payload* field is variable length, up to some negotiated maximum. If the length is not negotiated using LCP during line setup, a default length of 1500 bytes is used. Padding may follow the payload if need be.

After the *Payload* field comes the *Checksum* field, which is normally 2 bytes, but a 4-byte checksum can be negotiated.

In summary, PPP is a multiprotocol framing mechanism suitable for use over modems, HDLC bit-serial lines, SONET, and other physical layers. It supports error detection, option negotiation, header compression, and, optionally, reliable transmission using an HDLC-type frame format.

Let us now turn from the PPP frame format to the way lines are brought up and down. The (simplified) diagram of Fig. 3-28 shows the phases that a line goes through when it is brought up, used, and taken down again. This sequence applies both to modem connections and to router-router connections.

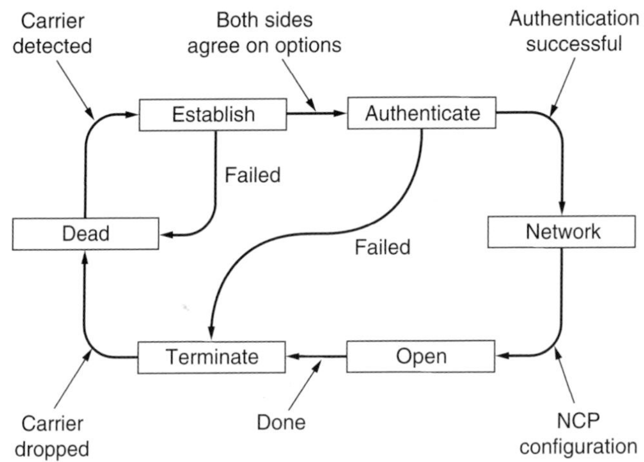

Figure 3-28. A simplified phase diagram for bringing a line up and down.

The protocol starts with the line in the *DEAD* state, which means that no physical layer carrier is present and no physical layer connection exists. After physical connection is established, the line moves to *ESTABLISH*. At that point LCP option negotiation begins, which, if successful, leads to *AUTHENTICATE*. Now the two parties can check on each other's identities if desired. When the *NETWORK* phase is entered, the appropriate NCP protocol is invoked to configure the network layer. If the configuration is successful, *OPEN* is reached and data transport can take place. When data transport is finished, the line moves into the *TERMINATE* phase, and from there, back to *DEAD* when the carrier is dropped.

LCP negotiates data link protocol options during the *ESTABLISH* phase. The LCP protocol is not actually concerned with the options themselves, but with the mechanism for negotiation. It provides a way for the initiating process to make a proposal and for the responding process to accept or reject it, in whole or in part. It also provides a way for the two processes to test the line quality to see if they consider it good enough to set up a connection. Finally, the LCP protocol also allows lines to be taken down when they are no longer needed.

Eleven types of LCP frames are defined in RFC 1661. These are listed in Fig. 3-29. The four *Configure-* types allow the initiator (I) to propose option values and the responder (R) to accept or reject them. In the latter case, the responder can make an alternative proposal or announce that it is not willing to negotiate certain options at all. The options being negotiated and their proposed values are part of the LCP frames.

The *Terminate-* codes shut a line down when it is no longer needed. The *Code-reject* and *Protocol-reject* codes indicate that the responder got something

Name	Direction	Description
Configure-request	I → R	List of proposed options and values
Configure-ack	I ← R	All options are accepted
Configure-nak	I ← R	Some options are not accepted
Configure-reject	I ← R	Some options are not negotiable
Terminate-request	I → R	Request to shut the line down
Terminate-ack	I ← R	OK, line shut down
Code-reject	I ← R	Unknown request received
Protocol-reject	I ← R	Unknown protocol requested
Echo-request	I → R	Please send this frame back
Echo-reply	I ← R	Here is the frame back
Discard-request	I → R	Just discard this frame (for testing)

Figure 3-29. The LCP frame types.

that it does not understand. This situation could mean that an undetected transmission error has occurred, but more likely it means that the initiator and responder are running different versions of the LCP protocol. The *Echo-* types are used to test the line quality. Finally, *Discard-request* help debugging. If either end is having trouble getting bits onto the wire, the programmer can use this type for testing. If it manages to get through, the receiver just throws it away, rather than taking some other action that might confuse the person doing the testing.

The options that can be negotiated include setting the maximum payload size for data frames, enabling authentication and choosing a protocol to use, enabling line-quality monitoring during normal operation, and selecting various header compression options.

There is little to say about the NCP protocols in a general way. Each one is specific to some network layer protocol and allows configuration requests to be made that are specific to that protocol. For IP, for example, dynamic address assignment is the most important possibility.

3.7 SUMMARY

The task of the data link layer is to convert the raw bit stream offered by the physical layer into a stream of frames for use by the network layer. Various framing methods are used, including character count, byte stuffing, and bit stuffing. Data link protocols can provide error control to retransmit damaged or lost frames. To prevent a fast sender from overrunning a slow receiver, the data link protocol can also provide flow control. The sliding window mechanism is widely used to integrate error control and flow control in a convenient way.

Sliding window protocols can be categorized by the size of the sender's window and the size of the receiver's window. When both are equal to 1, the protocol is stop-and-wait. When the sender's window is greater than 1, for example, to prevent the sender from blocking on a circuit with a long propagation delay, the receiver can be programmed either to discard all frames other than the next one in sequence or to buffer out-of-order frames until they are needed.

We examined a series of protocols in this chapter. Protocol 1 is designed for an error-free environment in which the receiver can handle any flow sent to it. Protocol 2 still assumes an error-free environment but introduces flow control. Protocol 3 handles errors by introducing sequence numbers and using the stop-and-wait algorithm. Protocol 4 allows bidirectional communication and introduces the concept of piggybacking. Protocol 5 uses a sliding window protocol with go back n. Finally, protocol 6 uses selective repeat and negative acknowledgements.

Protocols can be modeled using various techniques to help demonstrate their correctness (or lack thereof). Finite state machine models and Petri net models are commonly used for this purpose.

Many networks use one of the bit-oriented protocols—SDLC, HDLC, ADCCP, or LAPB—at the data link level. All of these protocols use flag bytes to delimit frames, and bit stuffing to prevent flag bytes from occurring in the data. All of them also use a sliding window for flow control. The Internet uses PPP as the primary data link protocol over point-to-point lines.

PROBLEMS

1. An upper-layer packet is split into 10 frames, each of which has an 80 percent chance of arriving undamaged. If no error control is done by the data link protocol, how many times must the message be sent on average to get the entire thing through?

2. The following character encoding is used in a data link protocol:
A: 01000111; B: 11100011; FLAG: 01111110; ESC: 11100000
Show the bit sequence transmitted (in binary) for the four-character frame: A B ESC FLAG when each of the following framing methods are used:
(a) Character count.
(b) Flag bytes with byte stuffing.
(c) Starting and ending flag bytes, with bit stuffing.

3. The following data fragment occurs in the middle of a data stream for which the byte-stuffing algorithm described in the text is used: A B ESC C ESC FLAG FLAG D. What is the output after stuffing?

4. One of your classmates, Scrooge, has pointed out that it is wasteful to end each frame with a flag byte and then begin the next one with a second flag byte. One flag byte could do the job as well, and a byte saved is a byte earned. Do you agree?

5. A bit string, 0111101111101111110, needs to be transmitted at the data link layer. What is the string actually transmitted after bit stuffing?

6. When bit stuffing is used, is it possible for the loss, insertion, or modification of a single bit to cause an error not detected by the checksum? If not, why not? If so, how? Does the checksum length play a role here?

7. Can you think of any circumstances under which an open-loop protocol, (e.g., a Hamming code) might be preferable to the feedback-type protocols discussed throughout this chapter?

8. To provide more reliability than a single parity bit can give, an error-detecting coding scheme uses one parity bit for checking all the odd-numbered bits and a second parity bit for all the even-numbered bits. What is the Hamming distance of this code?

9. Sixteen-bit messages are transmitted using a Hamming code. How many check bits are needed to ensure that the receiver can detect and correct single bit errors? Show the bit pattern transmitted for the message 1101001100110101. Assume that even parity is used in the Hamming code.

10. An 8-bit byte with binary value 10101111 is to be encoded using an even-parity Hamming code. What is the binary value after encoding?

11. A 12-bit Hamming code whose hexadecimal value is 0xE4F arrives at a receiver. What was the original value in hexadecimal? Assume that not more than 1 bit is in error.

12. One way of detecting errors is to transmit data as a block of n rows of k bits per row and adding parity bits to each row and each column. The lower-right corner is a parity bit that checks its row and its column. Will this scheme detect all single errors? Double errors? Triple errors?

13. A block of bits with n rows and k columns uses horizontal and vertical parity bits for error detection. Suppose that exactly 4 bits are inverted due to transmission errors. Derive an expression for the probability that the error will be undetected.

14. What is the remainder obtained by dividing $x^7 + x^5 + 1$ by the generator polynomial $x^3 + 1$?

15. A bit stream 10011101 is transmitted using the standard CRC method described in the text. The generator polynomial is $x^3 + 1$. Show the actual bit string transmitted. Suppose the third bit from the left is inverted during transmission. Show that this error is detected at the receiver's end.

16. Data link protocols almost always put the CRC in a trailer rather than in a header. Why?

17. A channel has a bit rate of 4 kbps and a propagation delay of 20 msec. For what range of frame sizes does stop-and-wait give an efficiency of at least 50 percent?

18. A 3000-km-long T1 trunk is used to transmit 64-byte frames using protocol 5. If the propagation speed is 6 μsec/km, how many bits should the sequence numbers be?

19. In protocol 3, is it possible that the sender starts the timer when it is already running? If so, how might this occur? If not, why is it impossible?

20. Imagine a sliding window protocol using so many bits for sequence numbers that wraparound never occurs. What relations must hold among the four window edges and the window size, which is constant and the same for both the sender and the receiver.

21. If the procedure *between* in protocol 5 checked for the condition $a \le b \le c$ instead of the condition $a \le b < c$, would that have any effect on the protocol's correctness or efficiency? Explain your answer.

22. In protocol 6, when a data frame arrives, a check is made to see if the sequence number differs from the one expected and *no_nak* is true. If both conditions hold, a NAK is sent. Otherwise, the auxiliary timer is started. Suppose that the else clause were omitted. Would this change affect the protocol's correctness?

23. Suppose that the three-statement while loop near the end of protocol 6 were removed from the code. Would this affect the correctness of the protocol or just the performance? Explain your answer.

24. Suppose that the case for checksum errors were removed from the switch statement of protocol 6. How would this change affect the operation of the protocol?

25. In protocol 6 the code for *frame_arrival* has a section used for NAKs. This section is invoked if the incoming frame is a NAK and another condition is met. Give a scenario where the presence of this other condition is essential.

26. Imagine that you are writing the data link layer software for a line used to send data to you, but not from you. The other end uses HDLC, with a 3-bit sequence number and a window size of seven frames. You would like to buffer as many out-of-sequence frames as possible to enhance efficiency, but you are not allowed to modify the software on the sending side. Is it possible to have a receiver window greater than 1, and still guarantee that the protocol will never fail? If so, what is the largest window that can be safely used?

27. Consider the operation of protocol 6 over a 1-Mbps error-free line. The maximum frame size is 1000 bits. New packets are generated 1 second apart. The timeout interval is 10 msec. If the special acknowledgement timer were eliminated, unnecessary timeouts would occur. How many times would the average message be transmitted?

28. In protocol 6, $MAX\_SEQ = 2^n - 1$. While this condition is obviously desirable to make efficient use of header bits, we have not demonstrated that it is essential. Does the protocol work correctly for $MAX\_SEQ = 4$, for example?

29. Frames of 1000 bits are sent over a 1-Mbps channel using a geostationary satellite whose propagation time from the earth is 270 msec. Acknowledgements are always piggybacked onto data frames. The headers are very short. Three-bit sequence numbers are used. What is the maximum achievable channel utilization for
(a) Stop-and-wait.
(b) Protocol 5.
(c) Protocol 6.

30. Compute the fraction of the bandwidth that is wasted on overhead (headers and retransmissions) for protocol 6 on a heavily-loaded 50-kbps satellite channel with data frames consisting of 40 header and 3960 data bits. Assume that the signal propagation time from the earth to the satellite is 270 msec. ACK frames never occur. NAK frames are 40 bits. The error rate for data frames is 1 percent, and the error rate for NAK frames is negligible. The sequence numbers are 8 bits.

31. Consider an error-free 64-kbps satellite channel used to send 512-byte data frames in one direction, with very short acknowledgements coming back the other way. What is the maximum throughput for window sizes of 1, 7, 15, and 127? The earth-satellite propagation time is 270 msec.

32. A 100-km-long cable runs at the T1 data rate. The propagation speed in the cable is 2/3 the speed of light in vacuum. How many bits fit in the cable?

33. Suppose that we model protocol 4 using the finite state machine model. How many states exist for each machine? How many states exist for the communication channel? How many states exist for the complete system (two machines and the channel)? Ignore the checksum errors.

34. Give the firing sequence for the Petri net of Fig. 3-23 corresponding to the state sequence (000), (01A), (01—), (010), (01A) in Fig. 3-21. Explain in words what the sequence represents.

35. Given the transition rules $AC \rightarrow B$, $B \rightarrow AC$, $CD \rightarrow E$, and $E \rightarrow CD$, draw the Petri net described. From the Petri net, draw the finite state graph reachable from the initial state *ACD*. What well-known concept do these transition rules model?

36. PPP is based closely on HDLC, which uses bit stuffing to prevent accidental flag bytes within the payload from causing confusion. Give at least one reason why PPP uses byte stuffing instead.

37. What is the minimum overhead to send an IP packet using PPP? Count only the overhead introduced by PPP itself, not the IP header overhead.

38. The goal of this lab exercise is to implement an error detection mechanism using the standard CRC algorithm described in the text. Write two programs, generator and verifier. The generator program reads from standard input an n-bit message as a string of 0s and 1s as a line of ASCII text. The second line is the k-bit polynomial, also in ASCII. It outputs to standard output a line of ASCII text with $n + k$ 0s and 1s representing the message to be transmitted. Then it outputs the polynomial, just as it read it in. The verifier program reads in the output of the generator program and outputs a message indicating whether it is correct or not. Finally, write a program, alter, that inverts one bit on the first line depending on its argument (the bit number counting the leftmost bit as 1) but copies the rest of the two lines correctly. By typing:

```
generator <file | verifier
```

you should see that the message is correct, but by typing

```
generator <file | alter arg | verifier
```

you should get the error message.

39. Write a program to simulate the behavior of a Petri net. The program should read in the transition rules as well as a list of states corresponding to the network link layer issuing a new packet or accepting a new packet. From the initial state, also read in, the program should pick enabled transitions at random and fire them, checking to see if a host ever accepts 2 packets without the other host emitting a new one in between.

4

THE MEDIUM ACCESS CONTROL SUBLAYER

As we pointed out in Chap. 1, networks can be divided into two categories: those using point-to-point connections and those using broadcast channels. This chapter deals with broadcast networks and their protocols.

In any broadcast network, the key issue is how to determine who gets to use the channel when there is competition for it. To make this point clearer, consider a conference call in which six people, on six different telephones, are all connected so that each one can hear and talk to all the others. It is very likely that when one of them stops speaking, two or more will start talking at once, leading to chaos. In a face-to-face meeting, chaos is avoided by external means, for example, at a meeting, people raise their hands to request permission to speak. When only a single channel is available, determining who should go next is much harder. Many protocols for solving the problem are known and form the contents of this chapter. In the literature, broadcast channels are sometimes referred to as **multiaccess channels** or **random access channels**.

The protocols used to determine who goes next on a multiaccess channel belong to a sublayer of the data link layer called the **MAC** (**Medium Access Control**) sublayer. The MAC sublayer is especially important in LANs, many of which use a multiaccess channel as the basis for communication. WANs, in contrast, use point-to-point links, except for satellite networks. Because multiaccess channels and LANs are so closely related, in this chapter we will discuss LANs in general, including a few issues that are not strictly part of the MAC sublayer.

Technically, the MAC sublayer is the bottom part of the data link layer, so logically we should have studied it before examining all the point-to-point protocols in Chap. 3. Nevertheless, for most people, understanding protocols involving multiple parties is easier after two-party protocols are well understood. For that reason we have deviated slightly from a strict bottom-up order of presentation.

4.1 THE CHANNEL ALLOCATION PROBLEM

The central theme of this chapter is how to allocate a single broadcast channel among competing users. We will first look at static and dynamic schemes in general. Then we will examine a number of specific algorithms.

4.1.1 Static Channel Allocation in LANs and MANs

The traditional way of allocating a single channel, such as a telephone trunk, among multiple competing users is Frequency Division Multiplexing (FDM). If there are N users, the bandwidth is divided into N equal-sized portions (see Fig. 2-31), each user being assigned one portion. Since each user has a private frequency band, there is no interference between users. When there is only a small and constant number of users, each of which has a heavy (buffered) load of traffic (e.g., carriers' switching offices), FDM is a simple and efficient allocation mechanism.

However, when the number of senders is large and continuously varying or the traffic is bursty, FDM presents some problems. If the spectrum is cut up into N regions and fewer than N users are currently interested in communicating, a large piece of valuable spectrum will be wasted. If more than N users want to communicate, some of them will be denied permission for lack of bandwidth, even if some of the users who have been assigned a frequency band hardly ever transmit or receive anything.

However, even assuming that the number of users could somehow be held constant at N, dividing the single available channel into static subchannels is inherently inefficient. The basic problem is that when some users are quiescent, their bandwidth is simply lost. They are not using it, and no one else is allowed to use it either. Furthermore, in most computer systems, data traffic is extremely bursty (peak traffic to mean traffic ratios of 1000:1 are common). Consequently, most of the channels will be idle most of the time.

The poor performance of static FDM can easily be seen from a simple queueing theory calculation. Let us start with the mean time delay, T, for a channel of capacity C bps, with an arrival rate of λ frames/sec, each frame having a length drawn from an exponential probability density function with mean $1/\mu$ bits/frame.

With these parameters the arrival rate is λ frames/sec and the service rate is μC frames/sec. From queueing theory it can be shown that for Poisson arrival and service times,

$$T = \frac{1}{\mu C - \lambda}$$

For example, if C is 100 Mbps, the mean frame length, $1/\mu$, is 10,000 bits, and the frame arrival rate, λ, is 5000 frames/sec, then $T = 200$ μsec. Note that if we ignored the queueing delay and just asked how long it takes to send a 10,000 bit frame on a 100-Mbps network, we would get the (incorrect) answer of 100 μsec. That result only holds when there is no contention for the channel.

Now let us divide the single channel into N independent subchannels, each with capacity C/N bps. The mean input rate on each of the subchannels will now be λ/N. Recomputing T we get

$$T_{\mathrm{FDM}} = \frac{1}{\mu(C/N) - (\lambda/N)} = \frac{N}{\mu C - \lambda} = NT \qquad \text{(4-1)}$$

The mean delay using FDM is N times worse than if all the frames were somehow magically arranged orderly in a big central queue.

Precisely the same arguments that apply to FDM also apply to time division multiplexing (TDM). Each user is statically allocated every Nth time slot. If a user does not use the allocated slot, it just lies fallow. The same holds if we split up the networks physically. Using our previous example again, if we were to replace the 100-Mbps network with 10 networks of 10 Mbps each and statically allocate each user to one of them, the mean delay would jump from 200 μsec to 2 msec.

Since none of the traditional static channel allocation methods work well with bursty traffic, we will now explore dynamic methods.

4.1.2 Dynamic Channel Allocation in LANs and MANs

Before we get into the first of the many channel allocation methods to be discussed in this chapter, it is worthwhile carefully formulating the allocation problem. Underlying all the work done in this area are five key assumptions, described below.

1. **Station Model**. The model consists of N independent **stations** (e.g., computers, telephones, or personal communicators), each with a program or user that generates frames for transmission. Stations are sometimes called **terminals**. The probability of a frame being generated in an interval of length Δt is $\lambda \Delta t$, where λ is a constant (the arrival rate of new frames). Once a frame has been generated, the station is blocked and does nothing until the frame has been successfully transmitted.

2. **Single Channel Assumption**. A single channel is available for all communication. All stations can transmit on it and all can receive from it. As far as the hardware is concerned, all stations are equivalent, although protocol software may assign priorities to them.

3. **Collision Assumption**. If two frames are transmitted simultaneously, they overlap in time and the resulting signal is garbled. This event is called a **collision**. All stations can detect collisions. A collided frame must be transmitted again later. There are no errors other than those generated by collisions.

4a. **Continuous Time**. Frame transmission can begin at any instant. There is no master clock dividing time into discrete intervals.

4b. **Slotted Time**. Time is divided into discrete intervals (slots). Frame transmissions always begin at the start of a slot. A slot may contain 0, 1, or more frames, corresponding to an idle slot, a successful transmission, or a collision, respectively.

5a. **Carrier Sense**. Stations can tell if the channel is in use before trying to use it. If the channel is sensed as busy, no station will attempt to use it until it goes idle.

5b. **No Carrier Sense**. Stations cannot sense the channel before trying to use it. They just go ahead and transmit. Only later can they determine whether the transmission was successful.

Some discussion of these assumptions is in order. The first one says that stations are independent and that work is generated at a constant rate. It also implicitly assumes that each station only has one program or user, so while the station is blocked, no new work is generated. More sophisticated models allow multiprogrammed stations that can generate work while a station is blocked, but the analysis of these stations is much more complex.

The single channel assumption is the heart of the model. There are no external ways to communicate. Stations cannot raise their hands to request that the teacher call on them.

The collision assumption is also basic, although in some systems (notably spread spectrum), this assumption is relaxed, with surprising results. Also, some LANs, such as token rings, pass a special token from station to station, possession of which allows the current holder to transmit a frame. But in the coming sections we will stick to the single channel with contention and collisions model.

Two alternative assumptions about time are possible. Either it is continuous (4a) or it is slotted (4b). Some systems use one and some systems use the other, so we will discuss and analyze both. For a given system, only one of them holds.

Similarly, a network can either have carrier sensing (5a) or not have it (5b). LANs generally have carrier sense. However, wireless networks cannot use it effectively because not every station may be within radio range of every other station. Stations on wired carrier sense networks can terminate their transmission prematurely if they discover that it is colliding with another transmission. Collision detection is rarely done on wireless networks, for engineering reasons. Note that the word "carrier" in this sense refers to an electrical signal on the cable and has nothing to do with the common carriers (e.g., telephone companies) that date back to the Pony Express days.

4.2 MULTIPLE ACCESS PROTOCOLS

Many algorithms for allocating a multiple access channel are known. In the following sections we will study a small sample of the more interesting ones and give some examples of their use.

4.2.1 ALOHA

In the 1970s, Norman Abramson and his colleagues at the University of Hawaii devised a new and elegant method to solve the channel allocation problem. Their work has been extended by many researchers since then (Abramson, 1985). Although Abramson's work, called the ALOHA system, used ground-based radio broadcasting, the basic idea is applicable to any system in which uncoordinated users are competing for the use of a single shared channel.

We will discuss two versions of ALOHA here: pure and slotted. They differ with respect to whether time is divided into discrete slots into which all frames must fit. Pure ALOHA does not require global time synchronization; slotted ALOHA does.

Pure ALOHA

The basic idea of an ALOHA system is simple: let users transmit whenever they have data to be sent. There will be collisions, of course, and the colliding frames will be damaged. However, due to the feedback property of broadcasting, a sender can always find out whether its frame was destroyed by listening to the channel, the same way other users do. With a LAN, the feedback is immediate; with a satellite, there is a delay of 270 msec before the sender knows if the transmission was successful. If listening while transmitting is not possible for some reason, acknowledgements are needed. If the frame was destroyed, the sender just waits a random amount of time and sends it again. The waiting time must be random or the same frames will collide over and over, in lockstep. Systems in which multiple users share a common channel in a way that can lead to conflicts are widely known as **contention** systems.

A sketch of frame generation in an ALOHA system is given in Fig. 4-1. We have made the frames all the same length because the throughput of ALOHA systems is maximized by having a uniform frame size rather than by allowing variable length frames.

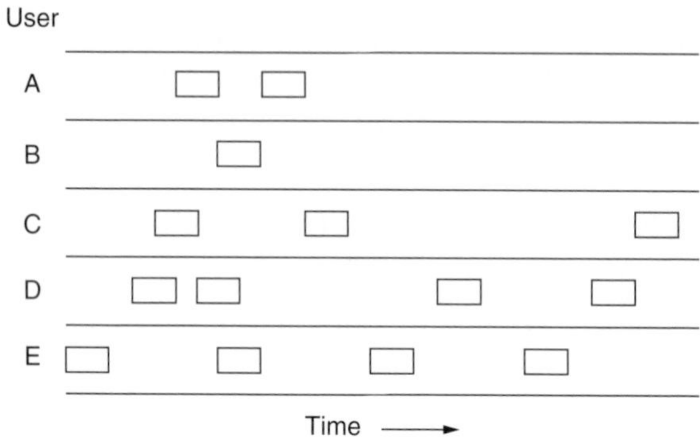

Figure 4-1. In pure ALOHA, frames are transmitted at completely arbitrary times.

Whenever two frames try to occupy the channel at the same time, there will be a collision and both will be garbled. If the first bit of a new frame overlaps with just the last bit of a frame almost finished, both frames will be totally destroyed and both will have to be retransmitted later. The checksum cannot (and should not) distinguish between a total loss and a near miss. Bad is bad.

An interesting question is: What is the efficiency of an ALOHA channel? In other words, what fraction of all transmitted frames escape collisions under these chaotic circumstances? Let us first consider an infinite collection of interactive users sitting at their computers (stations). A user is always in one of two states: typing or waiting. Initially, all users are in the typing state. When a line is finished, the user stops typing, waiting for a response. The station then transmits a frame containing the line and checks the channel to see if it was successful. If so, the user sees the reply and goes back to typing. If not, the user continues to wait and the frame is retransmitted over and over until it has been successfully sent.

Let the "frame time" denote the amount of time needed to transmit the standard, fixed-length frame (i.e., the frame length divided by the bit rate). At this point we assume that the infinite population of users generates new frames according to a Poisson distribution with mean N frames per frame time. (The infinite-population assumption is needed to ensure that N does not decrease as users become blocked.) If $N > 1$, the user community is generating frames at a higher rate than the channel can handle, and nearly every frame will suffer a collision. For reasonable throughput we would expect $0 < N < 1$.

In addition to the new frames, the stations also generate retransmissions of frames that previously suffered collisions. Let us further assume that the probability of k transmission attempts per frame time, old and new combined, is also

Poisson, with mean G per frame time. Clearly, $G \geq N$. At low load (i.e., $N \approx 0$), there will be few collisions, hence few retransmissions, so $G \approx N$. At high load there will be many collisions, so $G > N$. Under all loads, the throughput, S, is just the offered load, G, times the probability, P_0, of a transmission succeeding—that is, $S = GP_0$, where P_0 is the probability that a frame does not suffer a collision.

A frame will not suffer a collision if no other frames are sent within one frame time of its start, as shown in Fig. 4-2. Under what conditions will the shaded frame arrive undamaged? Let t be the time required to send a frame. If any other user has generated a frame between time t_0 and $t_0 + t$, the end of that frame will collide with the beginning of the shaded one. In fact, the shaded frame's fate was already sealed even before the first bit was sent, but since in pure ALOHA a station does not listen to the channel before transmitting, it has no way of knowing that another frame was already underway. Similarly, any other frame started between $t_0 + t$ and $t_0 + 2t$ will bump into the end of the shaded frame.

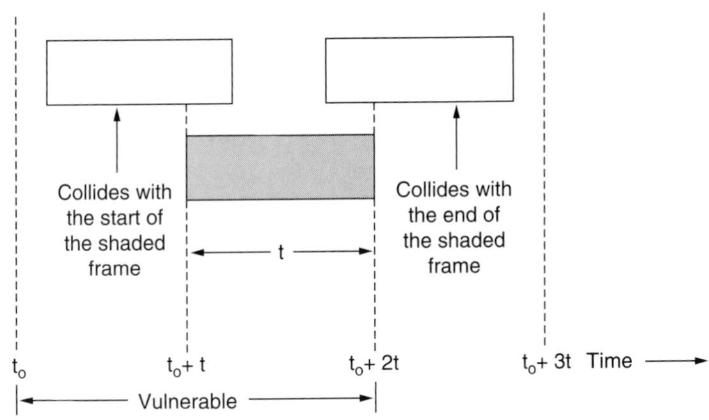

Figure 4-2. Vulnerable period for the shaded frame.

The probability that k frames are generated during a given frame time is given by the Poisson distribution:

$$\Pr[k] = \frac{G^k e^{-G}}{k!} \tag{4-2}$$

so the probability of zero frames is just e^{-G}. In an interval two frame times long, the mean number of frames generated is $2G$. The probability of no other traffic being initiated during the entire vulnerable period is thus given by $P_0 = e^{-2G}$. Using $S = GP_0$, we get

$$S = Ge^{-2G}$$

The relation between the offered traffic and the throughput is shown in Fig. 4-3. The maximum throughput occurs at $G = 0.5$, with $S = 1/2e$, which is about 0.184. In other words, the best we can hope for is a channel utilization of

18 percent. This result is not very encouraging, but with everyone transmitting at will, we could hardly have expected a 100 percent success rate.

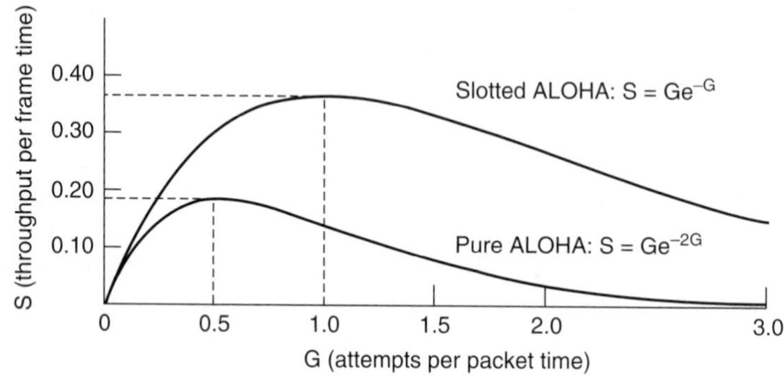

Figure 4-3. Throughput versus offered traffic for ALOHA systems.

Slotted ALOHA

In 1972, Roberts published a method for doubling the capacity of an ALOHA system (Roberts, 1972). His proposal was to divide time into discrete intervals, each interval corresponding to one frame. This approach requires the users to agree on slot boundaries. One way to achieve synchronization would be to have one special station emit a pip at the start of each interval, like a clock.

In Roberts' method, which has come to be known as **slotted ALOHA**, in contrast to Abramson's **pure ALOHA**, a computer is not permitted to send whenever a carriage return is typed. Instead, it is required to wait for the beginning of the next slot. Thus, the continuous pure ALOHA is turned into a discrete one. Since the vulnerable period is now halved, the probability of no other traffic during the same slot as our test frame is e^{-G} which leads to

$$S = Ge^{-G} \tag{4-3}$$

As you can see from Fig. 4-3, slotted ALOHA peaks at $G = 1$, with a throughput of $S = 1/e$ or about 0.368, twice that of pure ALOHA. If the system is operating at $G = 1$, the probability of an empty slot is 0.368 (from Eq. 4-2). The best we can hope for using slotted ALOHA is 37 percent of the slots empty, 37 percent successes, and 26 percent collisions. Operating at higher values of G reduces the number of empties but increases the number of collisions exponentially. To see how this rapid growth of collisions with G comes about, consider the transmission of a test frame. The probability that it will avoid a collision is e^{-G}, the probability that all the other users are silent in that slot. The probability of a collision is then just $1 - e^{-G}$. The probability of a transmission requiring exactly k attempts, (i.e., $k - 1$ collisions followed by one success) is

$$P_k = e^{-G}(1 - e^{-G})^{k-1}$$

The expected number of transmissions, E, per carriage return typed is then

$$E = \sum_{k=1}^{\infty} kP_k = \sum_{k=1}^{\infty} ke^{-G}(1 - e^{-G})^{k-1} = e^G$$

As a result of the exponential dependence of E upon G, small increases in the channel load can drastically reduce its performance.

Slotted Aloha is important for a reason that may not be initially obvious. It was devised in the 1970s, used in a few early experimental systems, then almost forgotten. When Internet access over the cable was invented, all of a sudden there was a problem of how to allocate a shared channel among multiple competing users, and slotted Aloha was pulled out of the garbage can to save the day. It has often happened that protocols that are perfectly valid fall into disuse for political reasons (e.g., some big company wants everyone to do things its way), but years later some clever person realizes that a long-discarded protocol solves his current problem. For this reason, in this chapter we will study a number of elegant protocols that are not currently in widespread use, but might easily be used in future applications, provided that enough network designers are aware of them. Of course, we will also study many protocols that are in current use as well.

4.2.2 Carrier Sense Multiple Access Protocols

With slotted ALOHA the best channel utilization that can be achieved is $1/e$. This is hardly surprising, since with stations transmitting at will, without paying attention to what the other stations are doing, there are bound to be many collisions. In local area networks, however, it is possible for stations to detect what other stations are doing, and adapt their behavior accordingly. These networks can achieve a much better utilization than $1/e$. In this section we will discuss some protocols for improving performance.

Protocols in which stations listen for a carrier (i.e., a transmission) and act accordingly are called **carrier sense protocols**. A number of them have been proposed. Kleinrock and Tobagi (1975) have analyzed several such protocols in detail. Below we will mention several versions of the carrier sense protocols.

Persistent and Nonpersistent CSMA

The first carrier sense protocol that we will study here is called **1-persistent CSMA** (Carrier Sense Multiple Access). When a station has data to send, it first listens to the channel to see if anyone else is transmitting at that moment. If the channel is busy, the station waits until it becomes idle. When the station detects an idle channel, it transmits a frame. If a collision occurs, the station waits a random amount of time and starts all over again. The protocol is called 1-persistent because the station transmits with a probability of 1 when it finds the channel idle.

The propagation delay has an important effect on the performance of the protocol. There is a small chance that just after a station begins sending, another station will become ready to send and sense the channel. If the first station's signal has not yet reached the second one, the latter will sense an idle channel and will also begin sending, resulting in a collision. The longer the propagation delay, the more important this effect becomes, and the worse the performance of the protocol.

Even if the propagation delay is zero, there will still be collisions. If two stations become ready in the middle of a third station's transmission, both will wait politely until the transmission ends and then both will begin transmitting exactly simultaneously, resulting in a collision. If they were not so impatient, there would be fewer collisions. Even so, this protocol is far better than pure ALOHA because both stations have the decency to desist from interfering with the third station's frame. Intuitively, this approach will lead to a higher performance than pure ALOHA. Exactly the same holds for slotted ALOHA.

A second carrier sense protocol is **nonpersistent CSMA**. In this protocol, a conscious attempt is made to be less greedy than in the previous one. Before sending, a station senses the channel. If no one else is sending, the station begins doing so itself. However, if the channel is already in use, the station does not continually sense it for the purpose of seizing it immediately upon detecting the end of the previous transmission. Instead, it waits a random period of time and then repeats the algorithm. Consequently, this algorithm leads to better channel utilization but longer delays than 1-persistent CSMA.

The last protocol is **p-persistent CSMA**. It applies to slotted channels and works as follows. When a station becomes ready to send, it senses the channel. If it is idle, it transmits with a probability p. With a probability $q = 1 - p$, it defers until the next slot. If that slot is also idle, it either transmits or defers again, with probabilities p and q. This process is repeated until either the frame has been transmitted or another station has begun transmitting. In the latter case, the unlucky station acts as if there had been a collision (i.e., it waits a random time and starts again). If the station initially senses the channel busy, it waits until the next slot and applies the above algorithm. Figure 4-4 shows the computed throughput versus offered traffic for all three protocols, as well as for pure and slotted ALOHA.

CSMA with Collision Detection

Persistent and nonpersistent CSMA protocols are clearly an improvement over ALOHA because they ensure that no station begins to transmit when it senses the channel busy. Another improvement is for stations to abort their trans-

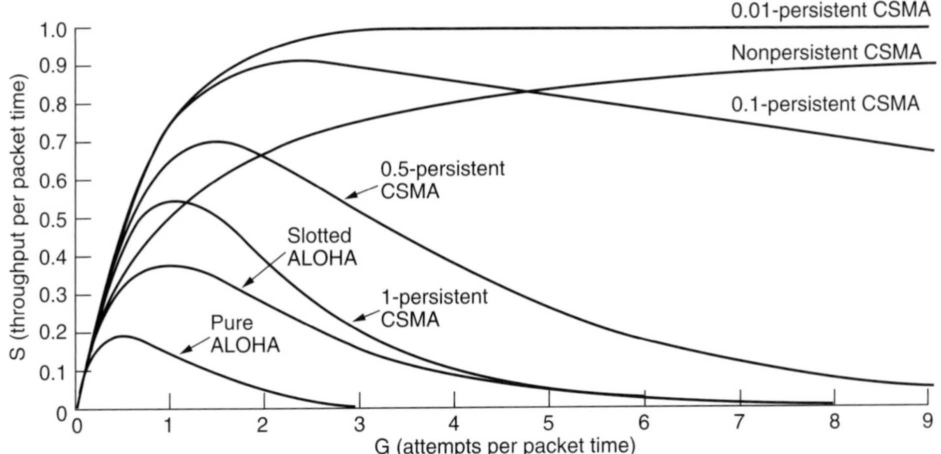

Figure 4-4. Comparison of the channel utilization versus load for various random access protocols.

missions as soon as they detect a collision. In other words, if two stations sense the channel to be idle and begin transmitting simultaneously, they will both detect the collision almost immediately. Rather than finish transmitting their frames, which are irretrievably garbled anyway, they should abruptly stop transmitting as soon as the collision is detected. Quickly terminating damaged frames saves time and bandwidth. This protocol, known as **CSMA/CD** (**CSMA with Collision Detection**) is widely used on LANs in the MAC sublayer. In particular, it is the basis of the popular Ethernet LAN, so it is worth devoting some time to looking at it in detail.

CSMA/CD, as well as many other LAN protocols, uses the conceptual model of Fig. 4-5. At the point marked t_0, a station has finished transmitting its frame. Any other station having a frame to send may now attempt to do so. If two or more stations decide to transmit simultaneously, there will be a collision. Collisions can be detected by looking at the power or pulse width of the received signal and comparing it to the transmitted signal.

After a station detects a collision, it aborts its transmission, waits a random period of time, and then tries again, assuming that no other station has started transmitting in the meantime. Therefore, our model for CSMA/CD will consist of alternating contention and transmission periods, with idle periods occurring when all stations are quiet (e.g., for lack of work).

Now let us look closely at the details of the contention algorithm. Suppose that two stations both begin transmitting at exactly time t_0. How long will it take them to realize that there has been a collision? The answer to this question is vital to determining the length of the contention period and hence what the delay and throughput will be. The minimum time to detect the collision is then just the time it takes the signal to propagate from one station to the other.

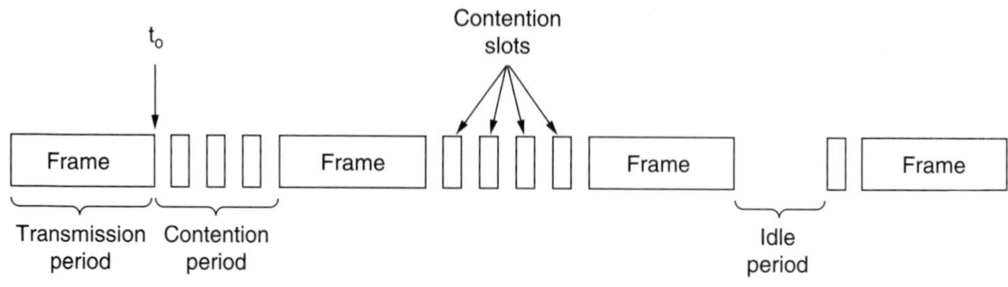

Figure 4-5. CSMA/CD can be in one of three states: contention, transmission, or idle.

Based on this reasoning, you might think that a station not hearing a collision for a time equal to the full cable propagation time after starting its transmission could be sure it had seized the cable. By "seized," we mean that all other stations knew it was transmitting and would not interfere. This conclusion is wrong. Consider the following worst-case scenario. Let the time for a signal to propagate between the two farthest stations be τ. At t_0, one station begins transmitting. At $\tau - \varepsilon$, an instant before the signal arrives at the most distant station, that station also begins transmitting. Of course, it detects the collision almost instantly and stops, but the little noise burst caused by the collision does not get back to the original station until time $2\tau - \varepsilon$. In other words, in the worst case a station cannot be sure that it has seized the channel until it has transmitted for 2τ without hearing a collision. For this reason we will model the contention interval as a slotted ALOHA system with slot width 2τ. On a 1-km long coaxial cable, $\tau \approx 5$ μsec. For simplicity we will assume that each slot contains just 1 bit. Once the channel has been seized, a station can transmit at any rate it wants to, of course, not just at 1 bit per 2τ sec.

It is important to realize that collision detection is an *analog* process. The station's hardware must listen to the cable while it is transmitting. If what it reads back is different from what it is putting out, it knows that a collision is occurring. The implication is that the signal encoding must allow collisions to be detected (e.g., a collision of two 0-volt signals may well be impossible to detect). For this reason, special encoding is commonly used.

It is also worth noting that a sending station must continually monitor the channel, listening for noise bursts that might indicate a collision. For this reason, CSMA/CD with a single channel is inherently a half-duplex system. It is impossible for a station to transmit and receive frames at the same time because the receiving logic is in use, looking for collisions during every transmission.

To avoid any misunderstanding, it is worth noting that no MAC-sublayer protocol guarantees reliable delivery. Even in the absence of collisions, the receiver may not have copied the frame correctly for various reasons (e.g., lack of buffer space or a missed interrupt).

4.2.3 Collision-Free Protocols

Although collisions do not occur with CSMA/CD once a station has unambiguously captured the channel, they can still occur during the contention period. These collisions adversely affect the system performance, especially when the cable is long (i.e., large τ) and the frames are short. And CSMA/CD is not universally applicable. In this section, we will examine some protocols that resolve the contention for the channel without any collisions at all, not even during the contention period. Most of these are not currently used in major systems, but in a rapidly changing field, having some protocols with excellent properties available for future systems is often a good thing.

In the protocols to be described, we assume that there are exactly N stations, each with a unique address from 0 to $N - 1$ "wired" into it. It does not matter that some stations may be inactive part of the time. We also assume that propagation delay is negligible. The basic question remains: Which station gets the channel after a successful transmission? We continue using the model of Fig. 4-5 with its discrete contention slots.

A Bit-Map Protocol

In our first collision-free protocol, the **basic bit-map method**, each contention period consists of exactly N slots. If station 0 has a frame to send, it transmits a 1 bit during the zeroth slot. No other station is allowed to transmit during this slot. Regardless of what station 0 does, station 1 gets the opportunity to transmit a 1 during slot 1, but only if it has a frame queued. In general, station j may announce that it has a frame to send by inserting a 1 bit into slot j. After all N slots have passed by, each station has complete knowledge of which stations wish to transmit. At that point, they begin transmitting in numerical order (see Fig. 4-6).

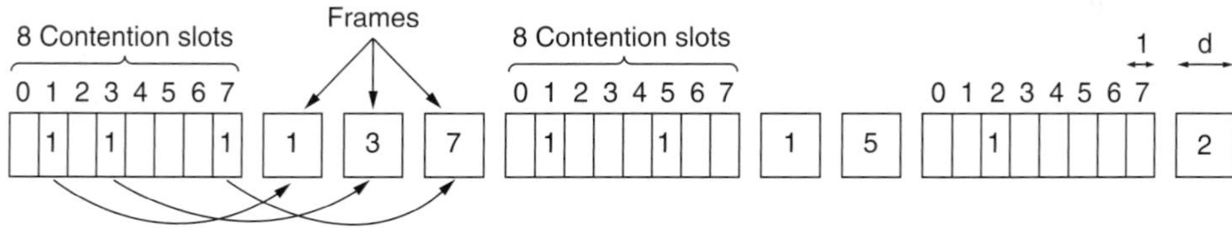

Figure 4-6. The basic bit-map protocol.

Since everyone agrees on who goes next, there will never be any collisions. After the last ready station has transmitted its frame, an event all stations can easily monitor, another N bit contention period is begun. If a station becomes ready just after its bit slot has passed by, it is out of luck and must remain silent until every station has had a chance and the bit map has come around again. Protocols like this in which the desire to transmit is broadcast before the actual transmission are called **reservation protocols**.

Let us briefly analyze the performance of this protocol. For convenience, we will measure time in units of the contention bit slot, with data frames consisting of d time units. Under conditions of low load, the bit map will simply be repeated over and over, for lack of data frames.

Consider the situation from the point of view of a low-numbered station, such as 0 or 1. Typically, when it becomes ready to send, the "current" slot will be somewhere in the middle of the bit map. On average, the station will have to wait $N/2$ slots for the current scan to finish and another full N slots for the following scan to run to completion before it may begin transmitting.

The prospects for high-numbered stations are brighter. Generally, these will only have to wait half a scan ($N/2$ bit slots) before starting to transmit. High-numbered stations rarely have to wait for the next scan. Since low-numbered stations must wait on average $1.5N$ slots and high-numbered stations must wait on average $0.5N$ slots, the mean for all stations is N slots. The channel efficiency at low load is easy to compute. The overhead per frame is N bits, and the amount of data is d bits, for an efficiency of $d/(N + d)$.

At high load, when all the stations have something to send all the time, the N bit contention period is prorated over N frames, yielding an overhead of only 1 bit per frame, or an efficiency of $d/(d + 1)$. The mean delay for a frame is equal to the sum of the time it queues inside its station, plus an additional $N(d + 1)/2$ once it gets to the head of its internal queue.

Binary Countdown

A problem with the basic bit-map protocol is that the overhead is 1 bit per station, so it does not scale well to networks with thousands of stations. We can do better than that by using binary station addresses. A station wanting to use the channel now broadcasts its address as a binary bit string, starting with the high-order bit. All addresses are assumed to be the same length. The bits in each address position from different stations are BOOLEAN ORed together. We will call this protocol **binary countdown**. It was used in Datakit (Fraser, 1987). It implicitly assumes that the transmission delays are negligible so that all stations see asserted bits essentially instantaneously.

To avoid conflicts, an arbitration rule must be applied: as soon as a station sees that a high-order bit position that is 0 in its address has been overwritten with a 1, it gives up. For example, if stations 0010, 0100, 1001, and 1010 are all trying to get the channel, in the first bit time the stations transmit 0, 0, 1, and 1, respectively. These are ORed together to form a 1. Stations 0010 and 0100 see the 1 and know that a higher-numbered station is competing for the channel, so they give up for the current round. Stations 1001 and 1010 continue.

The next bit is 0, and both stations continue. The next bit is 1, so station 1001 gives up. The winner is station 1010 because it has the highest address. After winning the bidding, it may now transmit a frame, after which another bidding cycle starts. The protocol is illustrated in Fig. 4-7. It has the property that higher-numbered stations have a higher priority than lower-numbered stations, which may be either good or bad, depending on the context.

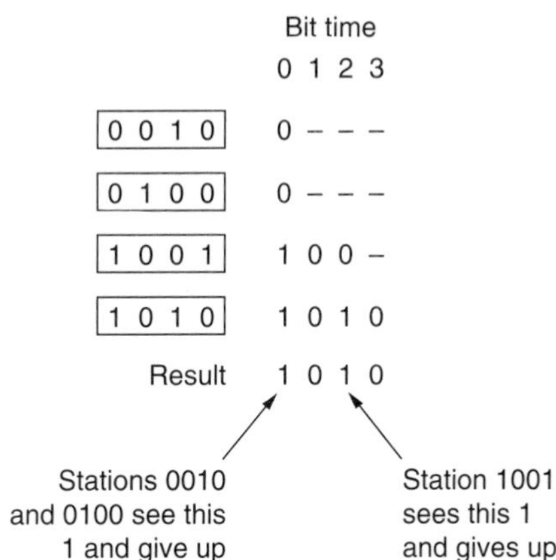

Figure 4-7. The binary countdown protocol. A dash indicates silence.

The channel efficiency of this method is $d/(d + \log_2 N)$. If, however, the frame format has been cleverly chosen so that the sender's address is the first field in the frame, even these $\log_2 N$ bits are not wasted, and the efficiency is 100 percent.

Mok and Ward (1979) have described a variation of binary countdown using a parallel rather than a serial interface. They also suggest using virtual station numbers, with the virtual station numbers from 0 up to and including the successful station being circularly permuted after each transmission, in order to give higher priority to stations that have been silent unusually long. For example, if stations *C*, *H*, *D*, *A*, *G*, *B*, *E*, *F* have priorities 7, 6, 5, 4, 3, 2, 1, and 0, respectively, then a successful transmission by *D* puts it at the end of the list, giving a priority order of *C*, *H*, *A*, *G*, *B*, *E*, *F*, *D*. Thus, *C* remains virtual station 7, but *A* moves up from 4 to 5 and *D* drops from 5 to 0. Station *D* will now only be able to acquire the channel if no other station wants it.

Binary countdown is an example of a simple, elegant, and efficient protocol that is waiting to be rediscovered. Hopefully, it will find a new home some day.

4.2.4 Limited-Contention Protocols

We have now considered two basic strategies for channel acquisition in a cable network: contention, as in CSMA, and collision-free methods. Each strategy can be rated as to how well it does with respect to the two important performance measures, delay at low load and channel efficiency at high load. Under conditions of light load, contention (i.e., pure or slotted ALOHA) is preferable due to its low delay. As the load increases, contention becomes increasingly less attractive, because the overhead associated with channel arbitration becomes greater. Just the reverse is true for the collision-free protocols. At low load, they have high delay, but as the load increases, the channel efficiency improves rather than gets worse as it does for contention protocols.

Obviously, it would be nice if we could combine the best properties of the contention and collision-free protocols, arriving at a new protocol that used contention at low load to provide low delay, but used a collision-free technique at high load to provide good channel efficiency. Such protocols, which we will call **limited-contention protocols**, do, in fact, exist, and will conclude our study of carrier sense networks.

Up to now the only contention protocols we have studied have been symmetric, that is, each station attempts to acquire the channel with some probability, p, with all stations using the same p. Interestingly enough, the overall system performance can sometimes be improved by using a protocol that assigns different probabilities to different stations.

Before looking at the asymmetric protocols, let us quickly review the performance of the symmetric case. Suppose that k stations are contending for channel access. Each has a probability p of transmitting during each slot. The probability that some station successfully acquires the channel during a given slot is then $kp(1-p)^{k-1}$. To find the optimal value of p, we differentiate with respect to p, set the result to zero, and solve for p. Doing so, we find that the best value of p is $1/k$. Substituting $p = 1/k$, we get

$$\Pr[\text{success with optimal } p] = \left[\frac{k-1}{k}\right]^{k-1} \tag{4-4}$$

This probability is plotted in Fig. 4-8. For small numbers of stations, the chances of success are good, but as soon as the number of stations reaches even five, the probability has dropped close to its asymptotic value of $1/e$.

From Fig. 4-8, it is fairly obvious that the probability of some station acquiring the channel can be increased only by decreasing the amount of competition. The limited-contention protocols do precisely that. They first divide the stations into (not necessarily disjoint) groups. Only the members of group 0 are permitted to compete for slot 0. If one of them succeeds, it acquires the channel and transmits its frame. If the slot lies fallow or if there is a collision, the members of group 1 contend for slot 1, etc. By making an appropriate division of stations into groups, the amount of contention for each slot can be reduced, thus operating each slot near the left end of Fig. 4-8.

The trick is how to assign stations to slots. Before looking at the general case, let us consider some special cases. At one extreme, each group has but one mem-

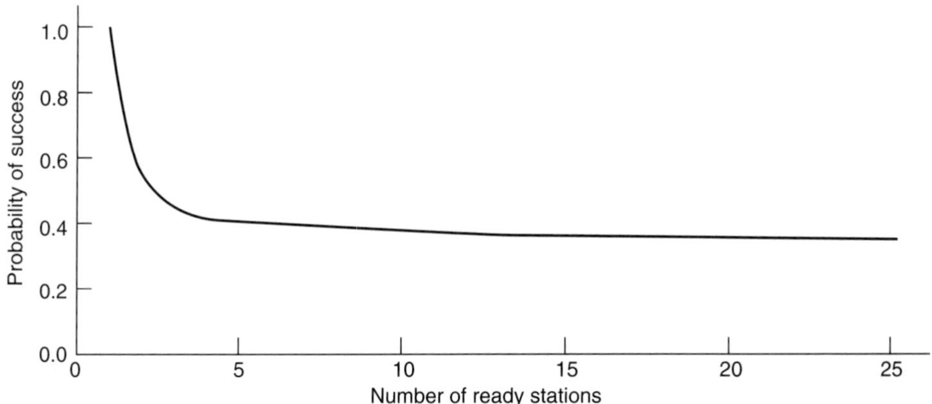

Figure 4-8. Acquisition probability for a symmetric contention channel.

ber. Such an assignment guarantees that there will never be collisions because at most one station is contending for any given slot. We have seen such protocols before (e.g., binary countdown). The next special case is to assign two stations per group. The probability that both will try to transmit during a slot is p^2, which for small p is negligible. As more and more stations are assigned to the same slot, the probability of a collision grows, but the length of the bit-map scan needed to give everyone a chance shrinks. The limiting case is a single group containing all stations (i.e., slotted ALOHA). What we need is a way to assign stations to slots dynamically, with many stations per slot when the load is low and few (or even just one) station per slot when the load is high.

The Adaptive Tree Walk Protocol

One particularly simple way of performing the necessary assignment is to use the algorithm devised by the U.S. Army for testing soldiers for syphilis during World War II (Dorfman, 1943). In short, the Army took a blood sample from N soldiers. A portion of each sample was poured into a single test tube. This mixed sample was then tested for antibodies. If none were found, all the soldiers in the group were declared healthy. If antibodies were present, two new mixed samples were prepared, one from soldiers 1 through $N/2$ and one from the rest. The process was repeated recursively until the infected soldiers were determined.

For the computerized version of this algorithm (Capetanakis, 1979), it is convenient to think of the stations as the leaves of a binary tree, as illustrated in Fig. 4-9. In the first contention slot following a successful frame transmission, slot 0, all stations are permitted to try to acquire the channel. If one of them does so, fine. If there is a collision, then during slot 1 only those stations falling under node 2 in the tree may compete. If one of them acquires the channel, the slot following the frame is reserved for those stations under node 3. If, on the other hand, two or more stations under node 2 want to transmit, there will be a collision during slot 1, in which case it is node 4's turn during slot 2.

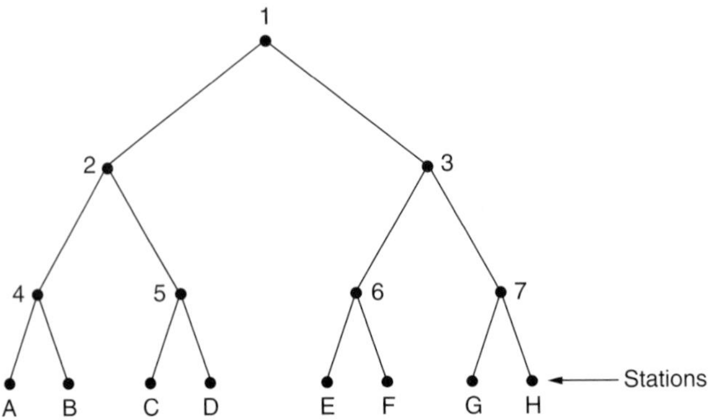

Figure 4-9. The tree for eight stations.

In essence, if a collision occurs during slot 0, the entire tree is searched, depth first, to locate all ready stations. Each bit slot is associated with some particular node in the tree. If a collision occurs, the search continues recursively with the node's left and right children. If a bit slot is idle or if only one station transmits in it, the searching of its node can stop because all ready stations have been located. (Were there more than one, there would have been a collision.)

When the load on the system is heavy, it is hardly worth the effort to dedicate slot 0 to node 1, because that makes sense only in the unlikely event that precisely one station has a frame to send. Similarly, one could argue that nodes 2 and 3 should be skipped as well for the same reason. Put in more general terms, at what level in the tree should the search begin? Clearly, the heavier the load, the farther down the tree the search should begin. We will assume that each station has a good estimate of the number of ready stations, q, for example, from monitoring recent traffic.

To proceed, let us number the levels of the tree from the top, with node 1 in Fig. 4-9 at level 0, nodes 2 and 3 at level 1, etc. Notice that each node at level i has a fraction 2^{-i} of the stations below it. If the q ready stations are uniformly distributed, the expected number of them below a specific node at level i is just $2^{-i}q$. Intuitively, we would expect the optimal level to begin searching the tree as the one at which the mean number of contending stations per slot is 1, that is, the level at which $2^{-i}q = 1$. Solving this equation, we find that $i = \log_2 q$.

Numerous improvements to the basic algorithm have been discovered and are discussed in some detail by Bertsekas and Gallager (1992). For example, consider the case of stations G and H being the only ones wanting to transmit. At node 1 a collision will occur, so 2 will be tried and discovered idle. It is pointless to probe node 3 since it is guaranteed to have a collision (we know that two or more stations under 1 are ready and none of them are under 2, so they must all be under 3). The probe of 3 can be skipped and 6 tried next. When this probe also turns up nothing, 7 can be skipped and node *G* tried next.

4.2.5 Wavelength Division Multiple Access Protocols

A different approach to channel allocation is to divide the channel into subchannels using FDM, TDM, or both, and dynamically allocate them as needed. Schemes like this are commonly used on fiber optic LANs to permit different conversations to use different wavelengths (i.e., frequencies) at the same time. In this section we will examine one such protocol (Humblet et al., 1992).

A simple way to build an all-optical LAN is to use a passive star coupler (see Fig. 2-10). In effect, two fibers from each station are fused to a glass cylinder. One fiber is for output to the cylinder and one is for input from the cylinder. Light output by any station illuminates the cylinder and can be detected by all the other stations. Passive stars can handle hundreds of stations.

To allow multiple transmissions at the same time, the spectrum is divided into channels (wavelength bands), as shown in Fig. 2-32. In this protocol, **WDMA** (**Wavelength Division Multiple Access**), each station is assigned two channels. A narrow channel is provided as a control channel to signal the station, and a wide channel is provided so the station can output data frames.

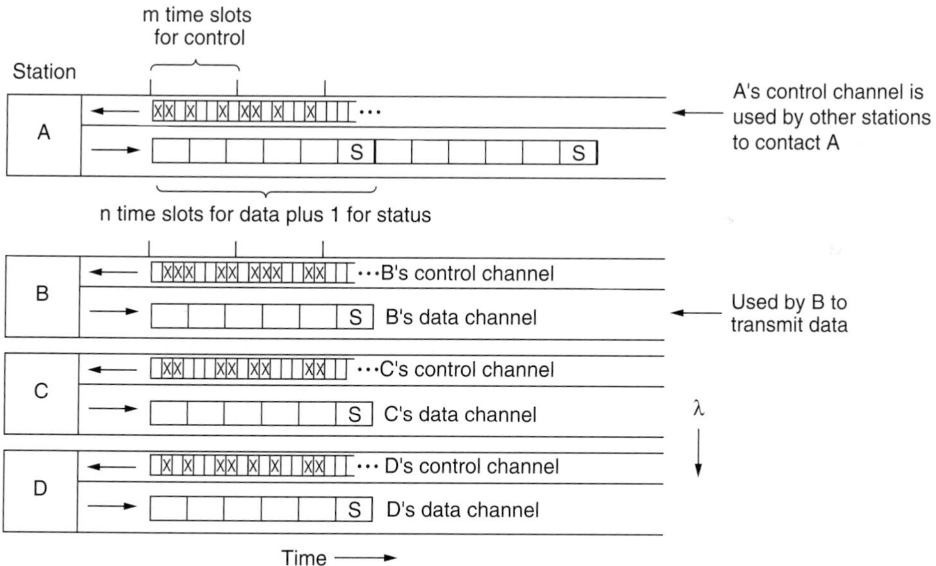

Figure 4-10. Wavelength division multiple access.

Each channel is divided into groups of time slots, as shown in Fig. 4-10. Let us call the number of slots in the control channel m and the number of slots in the data channel $n + 1$, where n of these are for data and the last one is used by the station to report on its status (mainly, which slots on both channels are free). On both channels, the sequence of slots repeats endlessly, with slot 0 being marked in a special way so latecomers can detect it. All channels are synchronized by a single global clock.

The protocol supports three traffic classes : (1) constant data rate connection-oriented traffic, such as uncompressed video, (2) variable data rate connection-oriented traffic, such as file transfer, and (3) datagram traffic, such as UDP packets. For the two connection-oriented protocols, the idea is that for *A* to communicate with *B*, it must first insert a CONNECTION REQUEST frame in a free slot on *B*'s control channel. If *B* accepts, communication can take place on *A*'s data channel.

Each station has two transmitters and two receivers, as follows:

1. A fixed-wavelength receiver for listening to its own control channel.
2. A tunable transmitter for sending on other stations' control channels.
3. A fixed-wavelength transmitter for outputting data frames.
4. A tunable receiver for selecting a data transmitter to listen to.

In other words, every station listens to its own control channel for incoming requests but has to tune to the transmitter's wavelength to get the data. Wavelength tuning is done by a Fabry-Perot or Mach-Zehnder interferometer that filters out all wavelengths except the desired wavelength band.

Let us now consider how station *A* sets up a class 2 communication channel with station *B* for, say, file transfer. First, *A* tunes its data receiver to *B*'s data channel and waits for the status slot. This slot tells which control slots are currently assigned and which are free. In Fig. 4-10, for example, we see that of *B*'s eight control slots, 0, 4, and 5 are free. The rest are occupied (indicated by crosses).

A picks one of the free control slots, say, 4, and inserts its CONNECTION REQUEST message there. Since *B* constantly monitors its control channel, it sees the request and grants it by assigning slot 4 to *A*. This assignment is announced in the status slot of *B*'s data channel. When *A* sees the announcement, it knows it has a unidirectional connection. If *A* asked for a two-way connection, *B* now repeats the same algorithm with *A*.

It is possible that at the same time *A* tried to grab *B*'s control slot 4, *C* did the same thing. Neither will get it, and both will notice the failure by monitoring the status slot in *B*'s control channel. They now each wait a random amount of time and try again later.

At this point, each party has a conflict-free way to send short control messages to the other one. To perform the file transfer, *A* now sends *B* a control message saying, for example, "Please watch my next data output slot 3. There is a data frame for you in it." When B gets the control message, it tunes its receiver to A's output channel to read the data frame. Depending on the higher-layer protocol, B can use the same mechanism to send back an acknowledgement if it wishes.

Note that a problem arises if both A and C have connections to B and each of them suddenly tells B to look at slot 3. B will pick one of these requests at random, and the other transmission will be lost.

For constant rate traffic, a variation of this protocol is used. When A asks for a connection, it simultaneously says something like: Is it all right if I send you a frame in every occurrence of slot 3? If B is able to accept (i.e., has no previous commitment for slot 3), a guaranteed bandwidth connection is established. If not, A can try again with a different proposal, depending on which output slots it has free.

Class 3 (datagram) traffic uses still another variation. Instead of writing a CONNECTION REQUEST message into the control slot it just found (4), it writes a DATA FOR YOU IN SLOT 3 message. If B is free during the next data slot 3, the transmission will succeed. Otherwise, the data frame is lost. In this manner, no connections are ever needed.

Several variants of the protocol are possible. For example, instead of each station having its own control channel, a single control channel can be shared by all stations. Each station is assigned a block of slots in each group, effectively multiplexing multiple virtual channels onto one physical one.

It is also possible to make do with a single tunable transmitter and a single tunable receiver per station by having each station's channel be divided into m control slots followed by $n + 1$ data slots. The disadvantage here is that senders have to wait longer to capture a control slot and consecutive data frames are farther apart because some control information is in the way.

Numerous other WDMA protocols have been proposed and implemented, differing in various details. Some have only one control channel; others have multiple control channels. Some take propagation delay into account; others do not. Some make tuning time an explicit part of the model; others ignore it. The protocols also differ in terms of processing complexity, throughput, and scalability. When a large number of frequencies are being used, the system is sometimes called **DWDM** (**Dense Wavelength Division Multiplexing**). For more information see (Bogineni et al., 1993; Chen, 1994; Goralski, 2001; Kartalopoulos, 1999; and Levine and Akyildiz, 1995).

4.2.6 Wireless LAN Protocols

As the number of mobile computing and communication devices grows, so does the demand to connect them to the outside world. Even the very first mobile telephones had the ability to connect to other telephones. The first portable computers did not have this capability, but soon afterward, modems became commonplace on notebook computers. To go on-line, these computers had to be plugged into a telephone wall socket. Requiring a wired connection to the fixed network meant that the computers were portable, but not mobile.

To achieve true mobility, notebook computers need to use radio (or infrared) signals for communication. In this manner, dedicated users can read and send e-mail while hiking or boating. A system of notebook computers that communicate by radio can be regarded as a wireless LAN, as we discussed in Sec. 1.5.4. These LANs have somewhat different properties than conventional LANs and require special MAC sublayer protocols. In this section we will examine some of these protocols. More information about wireless LANs can be found in (Geier, 2002; and O'Hara and Petrick, 1999).

A common configuration for a wireless LAN is an office building with base stations (also called access points) strategically placed around the building. All the base stations are wired together using copper or fiber. If the transmission power of the base stations and notebooks is adjusted to have a range of 3 or 4 meters, then each room becomes a single cell and the entire building becomes a large cellular system, as in the traditional cellular telephony systems we studied in Chap. 2. Unlike cellular telephone systems, each cell has only one channel, covering the entire available bandwidth and covering all the stations in its cell. Typically, its bandwidth is 11 to 54 Mbps.

In our discussions below, we will make the simplifying assumption that all radio transmitters have some fixed range. When a receiver is within range of two active transmitters, the resulting signal will generally be garbled and useless, in other words, we will not consider CDMA-type systems further in this discussion. It is important to realize that in some wireless LANs, not all stations are within range of one another, which leads to a variety of complications. Furthermore, for indoor wireless LANs, the presence of walls between stations can have a major impact on the effective range of each station.

A naive approach to using a wireless LAN might be to try CSMA: just listen for other transmissions and only transmit if no one else is doing so. The trouble is, this protocol is not really appropriate because what matters is interference at the receiver, not at the sender. To see the nature of the problem, consider Fig. 4-11, where four wireless stations are illustrated. For our purposes, it does not matter which are base stations and which are notebooks. The radio range is such that *A* and *B* are within each other's range and can potentially interfere with one another. *C* can also potentially interfere with both *B* and *D*, but not with *A*.

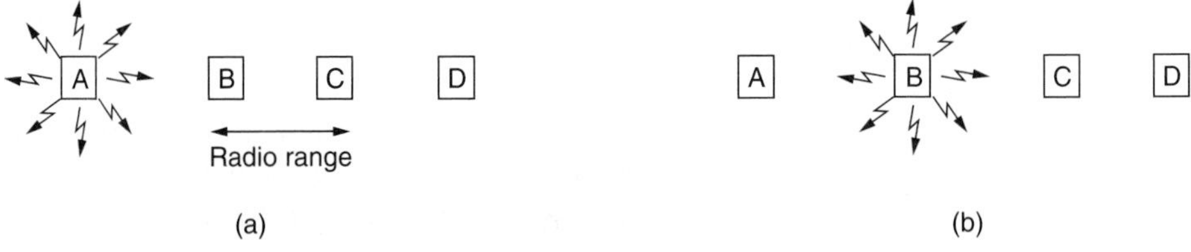

Figure 4-11. A wireless LAN. (a) *A* transmitting. (b) *B* transmitting.

First consider what happens when *A* is transmitting to *B*, as depicted in Fig. 4-11(a). If *C* senses the medium, it will not hear *A* because *A* is out of range, and thus falsely conclude that it can transmit to *B*. If *C* does start transmitting, it will interfere at *B*, wiping out the frame from *A*. The problem of a station not being able to detect a potential competitor for the medium because the competitor is too far away is called the **hidden station problem**.

Now let us consider the reverse situation: *B* transmitting to *A*, as shown in Fig. 4-11(b). If *C* senses the medium, it will hear an ongoing transmission and falsely conclude that it may not send to *D*, when in fact such a transmission would cause bad reception only in the zone between *B* and *C*, where neither of the intended receivers is located. This is called the **exposed station problem**.

The problem is that before starting a transmission, a station really wants to know whether there is activity around the receiver. CSMA merely tells it whether there is activity around the station sensing the carrier. With a wire, all signals propagate to all stations so only one transmission can take place at once anywhere in the system. In a system based on short-range radio waves, multiple transmissions can occur simultaneously if they all have different destinations and these destinations are out of range of one another.

Another way to think about this problem is to imagine an office building in which every employee has a wireless notebook computer. Suppose that Linda wants to send a message to Milton. Linda's computer senses the local environment and, detecting no activity, starts sending. However, there may still be a collision in Milton's office because a third party may currently be sending to him from a location so far from Linda that her computer could not detect it.

MACA and MACAW

An early protocol designed for wireless LANs is **MACA** (**Multiple Access with Collision Avoidance**) (Karn, 1990). The basic idea behind it is for the sender to stimulate the receiver into outputting a short frame, so stations nearby can detect this transmission and avoid transmitting for the duration of the upcoming (large) data frame. MACA is illustrated in Fig. 4-12.

Let us now consider how *A* sends a frame to *B*. *A* starts by sending an **RTS** (**Request To Send**) frame to *B*, as shown in Fig. 4-12(a). This short frame (30 bytes) contains the length of the data frame that will eventually follow. Then *B* replies with a **CTS** (**Clear to Send**) frame, as shown in Fig. 4-12(b). The CTS frame contains the data length (copied from the RTS frame). Upon receipt of the CTS frame, *A* begins transmission.

Now let us see how stations overhearing either of these frames react. Any station hearing the RTS is clearly close to *A* and must remain silent long enough for the CTS to be transmitted back to *A* without conflict. Any station hearing the CTS is clearly close to *B* and must remain silent during the upcoming data transmission, whose length it can tell by examining the CTS frame.

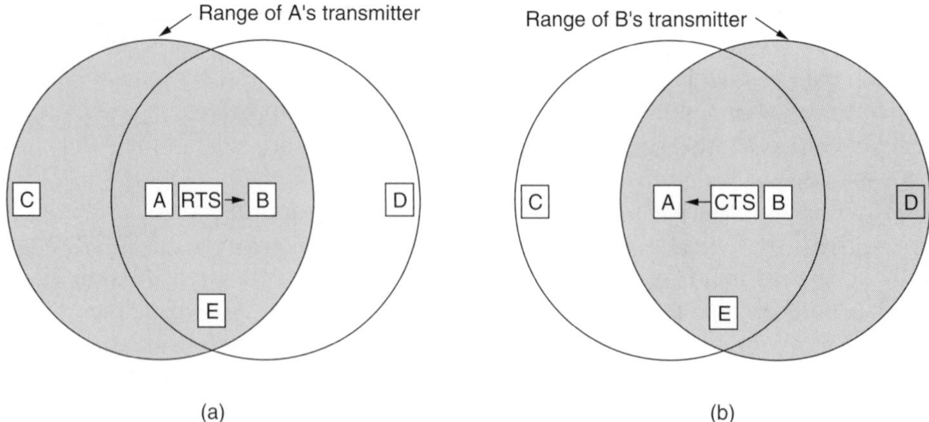

Figure 4-12. The MACA protocol. (a) *A* sending an RTS to *B*. (b) *B* responding with a CTS to *A*.

In Fig. 4-12, *C* is within range of *A* but not within range of *B*. Therefore, it hears the RTS from *A* but not the CTS from *B*. As long as it does not interfere with the CTS, it is free to transmit while the data frame is being sent. In contrast, *D* is within range of *B* but not *A*. It does not hear the RTS but does hear the CTS. Hearing the CTS tips it off that it is close to a station that is about to receive a frame, so it defers sending anything until that frame is expected to be finished. Station *E* hears both control messages and, like *D*, must be silent until the data frame is complete.

Despite these precautions, collisions can still occur. For example, *B* and *C* could both send RTS frames to *A* at the same time. These will collide and be lost. In the event of a collision, an unsuccessful transmitter (i.e., one that does not hear a CTS within the expected time interval) waits a random amount of time and tries again later. The algorithm used is binary exponential backoff, which we will study when we come to Ethernet.

Based on simulation studies of MACA, Bharghavan et al. (1994) fine tuned MACA to improve its performance and renamed their new protocol **MACAW** (**MACA for Wireless**). To start with, they noticed that without data link layer acknowledgements, lost frames were not retransmitted until the transport layer noticed their absence, much later. They solved this problem by introducing an ACK frame after each successful data frame. They also observed that CSMA has some use, namely, to keep a station from transmitting an RTS at the same time another nearby station is also doing so to the same destination, so carrier sensing was added. In addition, they decided to run the backoff algorithm separately for each data stream (source-destination pair), rather than for each station. This change improves the fairness of the protocol. Finally, they added a mechanism for stations to exchange information about congestion and a way to make the backoff algorithm react less violently to temporary problems, to improve system performance.

4.3 ETHERNET

We have now finished our general discussion of channel allocation protocols in the abstract, so it is time to see how these principles apply to real systems, in particular, LANs. As discussed in Sec. 1.5.3, the IEEE has standardized a number of local area networks and metropolitan area networks under the name of IEEE 802. A few have survived but many have not, as we saw in Fig. 1-38. Some people who believe in reincarnation think that Charles Darwin came back as a member of the IEEE Standards Association to weed out the unfit. The most important of the survivors are 802.3 (Ethernet) and 802.11 (wireless LAN). With 802.15 (Bluetooth) and 802.16 (wireless MAN), it is too early to tell. Please consult the 5th edition of this book to find out. Both 802.3 and 802.11 have different physical layers and different MAC sublayers but converge on the same logical link control sublayer (defined in 802.2), so they have the same interface to the network layer.

We introduced Ethernet in Sec. 1.5.3 and will not repeat that material here. Instead we will focus on the technical details of Ethernet, the protocols, and recent developments in high-speed (gigabit) Ethernet. Since Ethernet and IEEE 802.3 are identical except for two minor differences that we will discuss shortly, many people use the terms "Ethernet" and "IEEE 802.3" interchangeably, and we will do so, too. For more information about Ethernet, see (Breyer and Riley, 1999 ; Seifert, 1998; and Spurgeon, 2000).

4.3.1 Ethernet Cabling

Since the name "Ethernet" refers to the cable (the ether), let us start our discussion there. Four types of cabling are commonly used, as shown in Fig. 4-13.

Name	Cable	Max. seg.	Nodes/seg.	Advantages
10Base5	Thick coax	500 m	100	Original cable; now obsolete
10Base2	Thin coax	185 m	30	No hub needed
10Base-T	Twisted pair	100 m	1024	Cheapest system
10Base-F	Fiber optics	2000 m	1024	Best between buildings

Figure 4-13. The most common kinds of Ethernet cabling.

Historically, **10Base5** cabling, popularly called **thick Ethernet,** came first. It resembles a yellow garden hose, with markings every 2.5 meters to show where the taps go. (The 802.3 standard does not actually *require* the cable to be yellow, but it does *suggest* it.) Connections to it are generally made using **vampire taps**, in which a pin is *very* carefully forced halfway into the coaxial cable's core. The notation 10Base5 means that it operates at 10 Mbps, uses baseband signaling, and can support segments of up to 500 meters. The first number is the speed in Mbps.

Then comes the word "Base" (or sometimes "BASE") to indicate baseband transmission. There used to be a broadband variant, 10Broad36, but it never caught on in the marketplace and has since vanished. Finally, if the medium is coax, its length is given rounded to units of 100 m after "Base."

Historically, the second cable type was **10Base2**, or **thin Ethernet,** which, in contrast to the garden-hose-like thick Ethernet, bends easily. Connections to it are made using industry-standard BNC connectors to form T junctions, rather than using vampire taps. BNC connectors are easier to use and more reliable. Thin Ethernet is much cheaper and easier to install, but it can run for only 185 meters per segment, each of which can handle only 30 machines.

Detecting cable breaks, excessive length, bad taps, or loose connectors can be a major problem with both media. For this reason, techniques have been developed to track them down. Basically, a pulse of known shape is injected into the cable. If the pulse hits an obstacle or the end of the cable, an echo will be generated and sent back. By carefully timing the interval between sending the pulse and receiving the echo, it is possible to localize the origin of the echo. This technique is called **time domain reflectometry**.

The problems associated with finding cable breaks drove systems toward a different kind of wiring pattern, in which all stations have a cable running to a central **hub** in which they are all connected electrically (as if they were soldered together). Usually, these wires are telephone company twisted pairs, since most office buildings are already wired this way, and normally plenty of spare pairs are available. This scheme is called **10Base-T**. Hubs do not buffer incoming traffic. We will discuss an improved version of this idea (switches), which do buffer incoming traffic later in this chapter.

These three wiring schemes are illustrated in Fig. 4-14. For 10Base5, a **transceiver** is clamped securely around the cable so that its tap makes contact with the inner core. The transceiver contains the electronics that handle carrier detection and collision detection. When a collision is detected, the transceiver also puts a special invalid signal on the cable to ensure that all other transceivers also realize that a collision has occurred.

With 10Base5, a **transceiver cable** or **drop cable** connects the transceiver to an interface board in the computer. The transceiver cable may be up to 50 meters long and contains five individually shielded twisted pairs. Two of the pairs are for data in and data out, respectively. Two more are for control signals in and out. The fifth pair, which is not always used, allows the computer to power the transceiver electronics. Some transceivers allow up to eight nearby computers to be attached to them, to reduce the number of transceivers needed.

The transceiver cable terminates on an interface board inside the computer. The interface board contains a controller chip that transmits frames to, and receives frames from, the transceiver. The controller is responsible for assembling the data into the proper frame format, as well as computing checksums on outgoing frames and verifying them on incoming frames. Some controller chips also

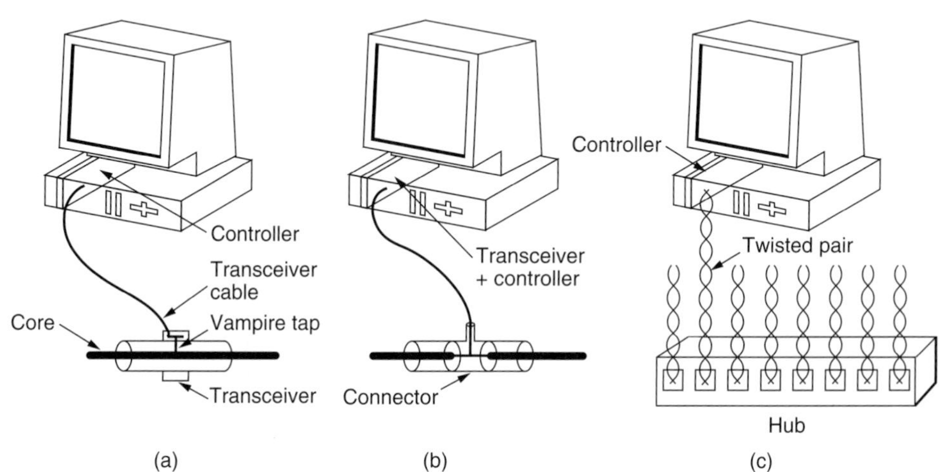

Figure 4-14. Three kinds of Ethernet cabling. (a) 10Base5. (b) 10Base2. (c) 10Base-T.

manage a pool of buffers for incoming frames, a queue of buffers to be transmitted, direct memory transfers with the host computers, and other aspects of network management.

With 10Base2, the connection to the cable is just a passive BNC T-junction connector. The transceiver electronics are on the controller board, and each station always has its own transceiver.

With 10Base-T, there is no shared cable at all, just the hub (a box full of electronics) to which each station is connected by a dedicated (i.e., not shared) cable. Adding or removing a station is simpler in this configuration, and cable breaks can be detected easily. The disadvantage of 10Base-T is that the maximum cable run from the hub is only 100 meters, maybe 200 meters if very high quality category 5 twisted pairs are used. Nevertheless, 10Base-T quickly became dominant due to its use of existing wiring and the ease of maintenance that it offers. A faster version of 10Base-T (100Base-T) will be discussed later in this chapter.

A fourth cabling option for Ethernet is **10Base-F**, which uses fiber optics. This alternative is expensive due to the cost of the connectors and terminators, but it has excellent noise immunity and is the method of choice when running between buildings or widely-separated hubs. Runs of up to km are allowed. It also offers good security since wiretapping fiber is much more difficult than wiretapping copper wire.

Figure 4-15 shows different ways of wiring a building. In Fig. 4-15(a), a single cable is snaked from room to room, with each station tapping into it at the nearest point. In Fig. 4-15(b), a vertical spine runs from the basement to the roof, with horizontal cables on each floor connected to the spine by special amplifiers (repeaters). In some buildings, the horizontal cables are thin and the backbone is thick. The most general topology is the tree, as in Fig. 4-15(c), because a network with two paths between some pairs of stations would suffer from interference between the two signals.

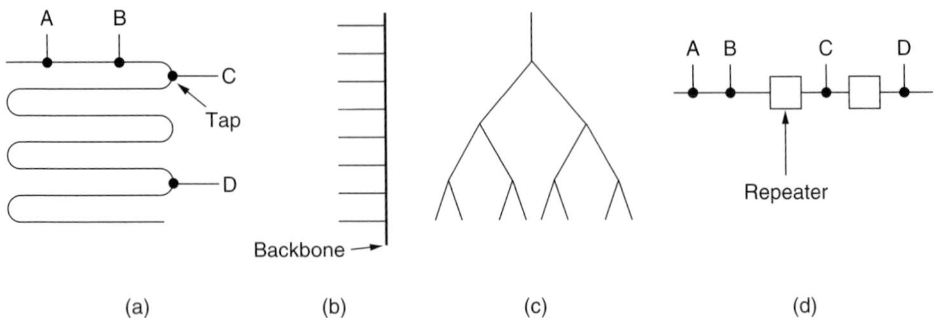

Figure 4-15. Cable topologies. (a) Linear. (b) Spine. (c) Tree. (d) Segmented.

Each version of Ethernet has a maximum cable length per segment. To allow larger networks, multiple cables can be connected by **repeaters**, as shown in Fig. 4-15(d). A repeater is a physical layer device. It receives, amplifies (regenerates), and retransmits signals in both directions. As far as the software is concerned, a series of cable segments connected by repeaters is no different from a single cable (except for some delay introduced by the repeaters). A system may contain multiple cable segments and multiple repeaters, but no two transceivers may be more than 2.5 km apart and no path between any two transceivers may traverse more than four repeaters.

4.3.2 Manchester Encoding

None of the versions of Ethernet uses straight binary encoding with 0 volts for a 0 bit and 5 volts for a 1 bit because it leads to ambiguities. If one station sends the bit string 0001000, others might falsely interpret it as 10000000 or 01000000 because they cannot tell the difference between an idle sender (0 volts) and a 0 bit (0 volts). This problem can be solved by using +1 volts for a 1 and −1 volts for a 0, but there is still the problem of a receiver sampling the signal at a slightly different frequency than the sender used to generate it. Different clock speeds can cause the receiver and sender to get out of synchronization about where the bit boundaries are, especially after a long run of consecutive 0s or a long run of consecutive 1s.

What is needed is a way for receivers to unambiguously determine the start, end, or middle of each bit without reference to an external clock. Two such approaches are called **Manchester encoding** and **differential Manchester encoding**. With Manchester encoding, each bit period is divided into two equal intervals. A binary 1 bit is sent by having the voltage set high during the first interval and low in the second one. A binary 0 is just the reverse: first low and then high.

This scheme ensures that every bit period has a transition in the middle, making it easy for the receiver to synchronize with the sender. A disadvantage of Manchester encoding is that it requires twice as much bandwidth as straight binary encoding because the pulses are half the width. For example, to send data at 10 Mbps, the signal has to change 20 million times/sec. Manchester encoding is shown in Fig. 4-16(b).

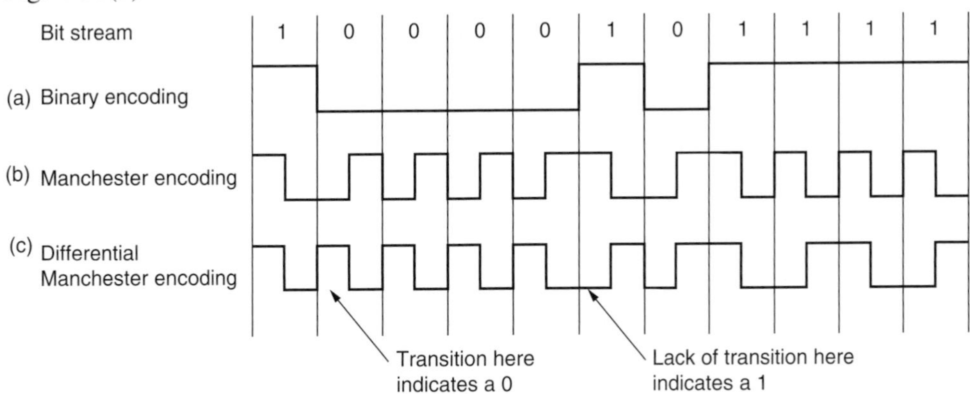

Figure 4-16. (a) Binary encoding. (b) Manchester encoding. (c) Differential Manchester encoding.

Differential Manchester encoding, shown in Fig. 4-16(c), is a variation of basic Manchester encoding. In it, a 1 bit is indicated by the absence of a transition at the start of the interval. A 0 bit is indicated by the presence of a transition at the start of the interval. In both cases, there is a transition in the middle as well. The differential scheme requires more complex equipment but offers better noise immunity. All Ethernet systems use Manchester encoding due to its simplicity. The high signal is +0.85 volts and the low signal is −0.85 volts, giving a DC value of 0 volts. Ethernet does not use differential Manchester encoding, but other LANs (e.g., the 802.5 token ring) do use it.

4.3.3 The Ethernet MAC Sublayer Protocol

The original DIX (DEC, Intel, Xerox) frame structure is shown in Fig. 4-17(a). Each frame starts with a *Preamble* of 8 bytes, each containing the bit pattern 10101010. The Manchester encoding of this pattern produces a 10-MHz square wave for 6.4 μsec to allow the receiver's clock to synchronize with the sender's. They are required to stay synchronized for the rest of the frame, using the Manchester encoding to keep track of the bit boundaries.

The frame contains two addresses, one for the destination and one for the source. The standard allows 2-byte and 6-byte addresses, but the parameters defined for the 10-Mbps baseband standard use only the 6-byte addresses. The high-order bit of the destination address is a 0 for ordinary addresses and 1 for

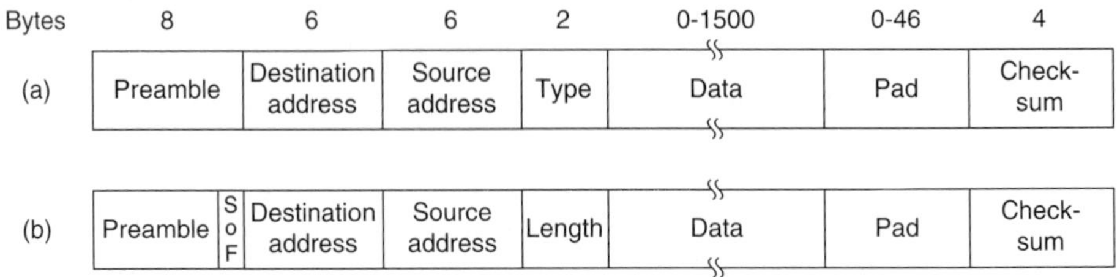

Figure 4-17. Frame formats. (a) DIX Ethernet. (b) IEEE 802.3.

group addresses. Group addresses allow multiple stations to listen to a single address. When a frame is sent to a group address, all the stations in the group receive it. Sending to a group of stations is called **multicast**. The address consisting of all 1 bits is reserved for **broadcast**. A frame containing all 1s in the destination field is accepted by all stations on the network. The difference between multicast and broadcast is important enough to warrant repeating. A multicast frame is sent to a selected group of stations on the Ethernet; a broadcast frame is sent to all stations on the Ethernet. Multicast is more selective, but involves group management. Broadcasting is coarser but does not require any group management.

Another interesting feature of the addressing is the use of bit 46 (adjacent to the high-order bit) to distinguish local from global addresses. Local addresses are assigned by each network administrator and have no significance outside the local network. Global addresses, in contrast, are assigned centrally by IEEE to ensure that no two stations anywhere in the world have the same global address. With $48 - 2 = 46$ bits available, there are about 7×10^{13} global addresses. The idea is that any station can uniquely address any other station by just giving the right 48-bit number. It is up to the network layer to figure out how to locate the destination.

Next comes the *Type* field, which tells the receiver what to do with the frame. Multiple network-layer protocols may be in use at the same time on the same machine, so when an Ethernet frame arrives, the kernel has to know which one to hand the frame to. The *Type* field specifies which process to give the frame to.

Next come the data, up to 1500 bytes. This limit was chosen somewhat arbitrarily at the time the DIX standard was cast in stone, mostly based on the fact that a transceiver needs enough RAM to hold an entire frame and RAM was expensive in 1978. A larger upper limit would have meant more RAM, hence a more expensive transceiver.

In addition to there being a maximum frame length, there is also a minimum frame length. While a data field of 0 bytes is sometimes useful, it causes a problem. When a transceiver detects a collision, it truncates the current frame, which means that stray bits and pieces of frames appear on the cable all the time. To make it easier to distinguish valid frames from garbage, Ethernet requires that valid frames must be at least 64 bytes long, from destination address to checksum, including both. If the data portion of a frame is less than 46 bytes, the *Pad* field is used to fill out the frame to the minimum size.

Another (and more important) reason for having a minimum length frame is to prevent a station from completing the transmission of a short frame before the first bit has even reached the far end of the cable, where it may collide with another frame. This problem is illustrated in Fig. 4-18. At time 0, station *A*, at one end of the network, sends off a frame. Let us call the propagation time for this frame to reach the other end τ. Just before the frame gets to the other end (i.e., at time $\tau - \varepsilon$), the most distant station, *B*, starts transmitting. When *B* detects that it is receiving more power than it is putting out, it knows that a collision has occurred, so it aborts its transmission and generates a 48-bit noise burst to warn all other stations. In other words, it jams the ether to make sure the sender does not miss the collision. At about time 2τ, the sender sees the noise burst and aborts its transmission, too. It then waits a random time before trying again.

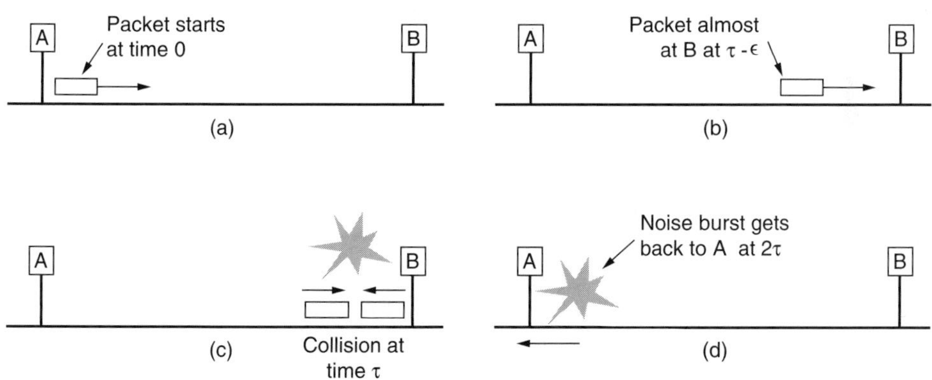

Figure 4-18. Collision detection can take as long as 2τ.

If a station tries to transmit a very short frame, it is conceivable that a collision occurs, but the transmission completes before the noise burst gets back at 2τ. The sender will then incorrectly conclude that the frame was successfully sent. To prevent this situation from occurring, all frames must take more than 2τ to send so that the transmission is still taking place when the noise burst gets back to the sender. For a 10-Mbps LAN with a maximum length of 2500 meters and four repeaters (from the 802.3 specification), the round-trip time (including time to propagate through the four repeaters) has been determined to be nearly 50 μsec in the worst case, including the time to pass through the repeaters, which is most certainly not zero. Therefore, the minimum frame must take at least this long to transmit. At 10 Mbps, a bit takes 100 nsec, so 500 bits is the smallest frame that is guaranteed to work. To add some margin of safety, this number was rounded up to 512 bits or 64 bytes. Frames with fewer than 64 bytes are padded out to 64 bytes with the *Pad* field.

As the network speed goes up, the minimum frame length must go up or the maximum cable length must come down, proportionally. For a 2500-meter LAN operating at 1 Gbps, the minimum frame size would have to be 6400 bytes. Alternatively, the minimum frame size could be 640 bytes and the maximum distance between any two stations 250 meters. These restrictions are becoming increasingly painful as we move toward multigigabit networks.

The final Ethernet field is the *Checksum*. It is effectively a 32-bit hash code of the data. If some data bits are erroneously received (due to noise on the cable), the checksum will almost certainly be wrong and the error will be detected. The checksum algorithm is a cyclic redundancy check (CRC) of the kind discussed in Chap. 3. It just does error detection, not forward error correction.

When IEEE standardized Ethernet, the committee made two changes to the DIX format, as shown in Fig. 4-17(b). The first one was to reduce the preamble to 7 bytes and use the last byte for a *Start of Frame* delimiter, for compatibility with 802.4 and 802.5. The second one was to change the *Type* field into a *Length* field. Of course, now there was no way for the receiver to figure out what to do with an incoming frame, but that problem was handled by the addition of a small header to the data portion itself to provide this information. We will discuss the format of the data portion when we come to logical link control later in this chapter.

Unfortunately, by the time 802.3 was published, so much hardware and software for DIX Ethernet was already in use that few manufacturers and users were enthusiastic about converting the *Type* field into a *Length* field. In 1997 IEEE threw in the towel and said that both ways were fine with it. Fortunately, all the *Type* fields in use before 1997 were greater than 1500. Consequently, any number there less than or equal to 1500 can be interpreted as *Length*, and any number greater than 1500 can be interpreted as *Type*. Now IEEE can maintain that everyone is using its standard and everybody else can keep on doing what they were already doing without feeling guilty about it.

4.3.4 The Binary Exponential Backoff Algorithm

Let us now see how randomization is done when a collision occurs. The model is that of Fig. 4-5. After a collision, time is divided into discrete slots whose length is equal to the worst-case round-trip propagation time on the ether (2τ). To accommodate the longest path allowed by Ethernet, the slot time has been set to 512 bit times, or 51.2 μsec as mentioned above.

After the first collision, each station waits either 0 or 1 slot times before trying again. If two stations collide and each one picks the same random number, they will collide again. After the second collision, each one picks either 0, 1, 2, or 3 at random and waits that number of slot times. If a third collision occurs (the probability of this happening is 0.25), then the next time the number of slots to wait is chosen at random from the interval 0 to $2^3 - 1$.

In general, after i collisions, a random number between 0 and $2^i - 1$ is chosen, and that number of slots is skipped. However, after ten collisions have been reached, the randomization interval is frozen at a maximum of 1023 slots. After 16 collisions, the controller throws in the towel and reports failure back to the computer. Further recovery is up to higher layers.

This algorithm, called **binary exponential backoff**, was chosen to dynamically adapt to the number of stations trying to send. If the randomization interval for all collisions was 1023, the chance of two stations colliding for a second time would be negligible, but the average wait after a collision would be hundreds of slot times, introducing significant delay. On the other hand, if each station always delayed for either zero or one slots, then if 100 stations ever tried to send at once, they would collide over and over until 99 of them picked 1 and the remaining station picked 0. This might take years. By having the randomization interval grow exponentially as more and more consecutive collisions occur, the algorithm ensures a low delay when only a few stations collide but also ensures that the collision is resolved in a reasonable interval when many stations collide. Truncating the backoff at 1023 keeps the bound from growing too large.

As described so far, CSMA/CD provides no acknowledgements. Since the mere absence of collisions does not guarantee that bits were not garbled by noise spikes on the cable, for reliable communication the destination must verify the checksum, and if correct, send back an acknowledgement frame to the source. Normally, this acknowledgement would be just another frame as far as the protocol is concerned and would have to fight for channel time just like a data frame. However, a simple modification to the contention algorithm would allow speedy confirmation of frame receipt (Tokoro and Tamaru, 1977). All that would be needed is to reserve the first contention slot following successful transmission for the destination station. Unfortunately, the standard does not provide for this possibility.

4.3.5 Ethernet Performance

Now let us briefly examine the performance of Ethernet under conditions of heavy and constant load, that is, k stations always ready to transmit. A rigorous analysis of the binary exponential backoff algorithm is complicated. Instead, we will follow Metcalfe and Boggs (1976) and assume a constant retransmission probability in each slot. If each station transmits during a contention slot with probability p, the probability A that some station acquires the channel in that slot is

$$A = kp(1-p)^{k-1} \tag{4-5}$$

A is maximized when $p = 1/k$, with $A \rightarrow 1/e$ as $k \rightarrow \infty$. The probability that the contention interval has exactly j slots in it is $A(1-A)^{j-1}$, so the mean number of slots per contention is given by

$$\sum_{j=0}^{\infty} jA(1-A)^{j-1} = \frac{1}{A}$$

Since each slot has a duration 2τ, the mean contention interval, w, is $2\tau/A$. Assuming optimal p, the mean number of contention slots is never more than e, so w is at most $2\tau e \approx 5.4\tau$.

If the mean frame takes P sec to transmit, when many stations have frames to send,

$$\text{Channel efficiency} = \frac{P}{P + 2\tau/A} \tag{4-6}$$

Here we see where the maximum cable distance between any two stations enters into the performance figures, giving rise to topologies other than that of Fig. 4-15(a). The longer the cable, the longer the contention interval. This observation is why the Ethernet standard specifies a maximum cable length.

It is instructive to formulate Eq. (4-6) in terms of the frame length, F, the network bandwidth, B, the cable length, L, and the speed of signal propagation, c, for the optimal case of e contention slots per frame. With $P = F/B$, Eq. (4-6) becomes

$$\text{Channel efficiency} = \frac{1}{1 + 2BLe/cF} \tag{4-7}$$

When the second term in the denominator is large, network efficiency will be low. More specifically, increasing network bandwidth or distance (the BL product) reduces efficiency for a given frame size. Unfortunately, much research on network hardware is aimed precisely at increasing this product. People want high bandwidth over long distances (fiber optic MANs, for example), which suggests that Ethernet implemented in this manner may not be the best system for these applications. We will see other ways of implementing Ethernet when we come to switched Ethernet later in this chapter.

In Fig. 4-19, the channel efficiency is plotted versus number of ready stations for $2\tau = 51.2$ μsec and a data rate of 10 Mbps, using Eq. (4-7). With a 64-byte slot time, it is not surprising that 64-byte frames are not efficient. On the other hand, with 1024-byte frames and an asymptotic value of e 64-byte slots per contention interval, the contention period is 174 bytes long and the efficiency is 0.85.

To determine the mean number of stations ready to transmit under conditions of high load, we can use the following (crude) observation. Each frame ties up the channel for one contention period and one frame transmission time, for a total of $P + w$ sec. The number of frames per second is therefore $1/(P + w)$. If each station generates frames at a mean rate of λ frames/sec, then when the system is

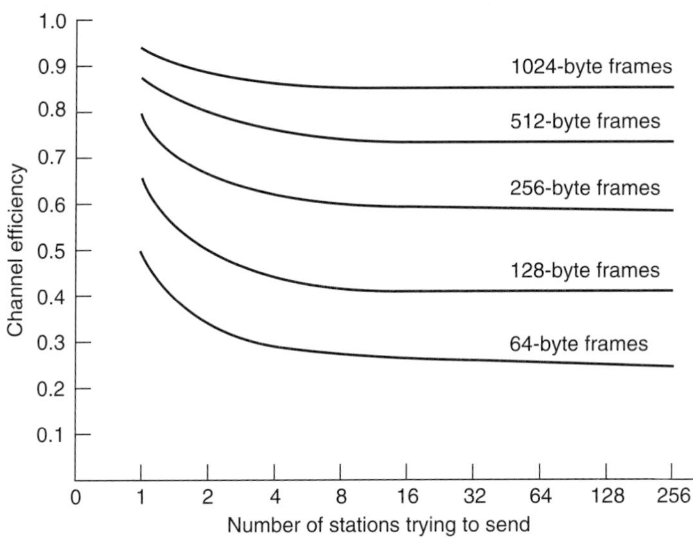

Figure 4-19. Efficiency of Ethernet at 10 Mbps with 512-bit slot times.

in state k, the total input rate of all unblocked stations combined is $k\lambda$ frames/sec. Since in equilibrium the input and output rates must be identical, we can equate these two expressions and solve for k. (Notice that w is a function of k.) A more sophisticated analysis is given in (Bertsekas and Gallager, 1992).

It is probably worth mentioning that there has been a large amount of theoretical performance analysis of Ethernet (and other networks). Virtually all of this work has assumed that traffic is Poisson. As researchers have begun looking at real data, it now appears that network traffic is rarely Poisson, but self-similar (Paxson and Floyd, 1994; and Willinger et al., 1995). What this means is that averaging over long periods of time does not smooth out the traffic. The average number of frames in each minute of an hour has as much variance as the average number of frames in each second of a minute. The consequence of this discovery is that most models of network traffic do not apply to the real world and should be taken with a grain (or better yet, a metric ton) of salt.

4.3.6 Switched Ethernet

As more and more stations are added to an Ethernet, the traffic will go up. Eventually, the LAN will saturate. One way out is to go to a higher speed, say, from 10 Mbps to 100 Mbps. But with the growth of multimedia, even a 100-Mbps or 1-Gbps Ethernet can become saturated.

Fortunately, there is an additional way to deal with increased load: switched Ethernet, as shown in Fig. 4-20. The heart of this system is a **switch** containing a high-speed backplane and room for typically 4 to 32 plug-in line cards, each containing one to eight connectors. Most often, each connector has a 10Base-T twisted pair connection to a single host computer.

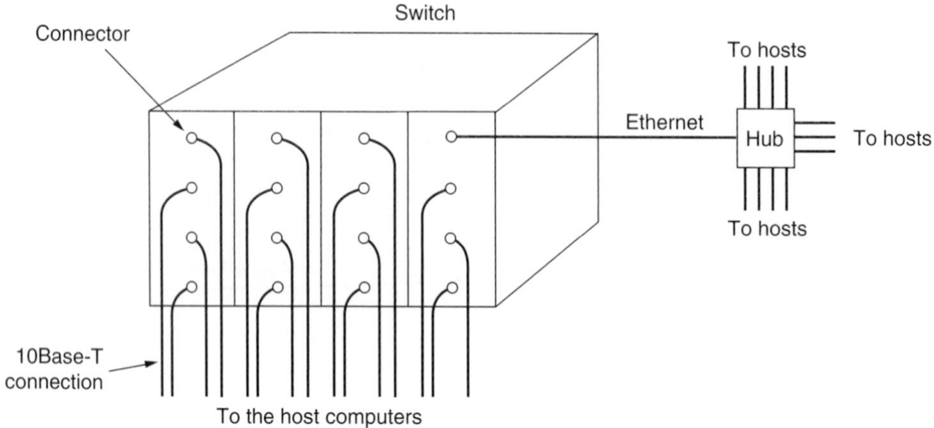

Figure 4-20. A simple example of switched Ethernet.

When a station wants to transmit an Ethernet frame, it outputs a standard frame to the switch. The plug-in card getting the frame may check to see if it is destined for one of the other stations connected to the same card. If so, the frame is copied there. If not, the frame is sent over the high-speed backplane to the destination station's card. The backplane typically runs at many Gbps, using a proprietary protocol.

What happens if two machines attached to the same plug-in card transmit frames at the same time? It depends on how the card has been constructed. One possibility is for all the ports on the card to be wired together to form a local on-card LAN. Collisions on this on-card LAN will be detected and handled the same as any other collisions on a CSMA/CD network—with retransmissions using the binary exponential backoff algorithm. With this kind of plug-in card, only one transmission per card is possible at any instant, but all the cards can be transmitting in parallel. With this design, each card forms its own **collision domain**, independent of the others. With only one station per collision domain, collisions are impossible and performance is improved.

With the other kind of plug-in card, each input port is buffered, so incoming frames are stored in the card's on-board RAM as they arrive. This design allows all input ports to receive (and transmit) frames at the same time, for parallel, full-duplex operation, something not possible with CSMA/CD on a single channel. Once a frame has been completely received, the card can then check to see if the frame is destined for another port on the same card or for a distant port. In the former case, it can be transmitted directly to the destination. In the latter case, it must be transmitted over the backplane to the proper card. With this design, each port is a separate collision domain, so collisions do not occur. The total system throughput can often be increased by an order of magnitude over 10Base5, which has a single collision domain for the entire system.

Since the switch just expects standard Ethernet frames on each input port, it is possible to use some of the ports as concentrators. In Fig. 4-20, the port in the upper-right corner is connected not to a single station, but to a 12-port hub. As frames arrive at the hub, they contend for the ether in the usual way, including collisions and binary backoff. Successful frames make it to the switch and are treated there like any other incoming frames: they are switched to the correct output line over the high-speed backplane. Hubs are cheaper than switches, but due to falling switch prices, they are rapidly becoming obsolete. Nevertheless, legacy hubs still exist.

4.3.7 Fast Ethernet

At first, 10 Mbps seemed like heaven, just as 1200-bps modems seemed like heaven to the early users of 300-bps acoustic modems. But the novelty wore off quickly. As a kind of corollary to Parkinson's Law ("Work expands to fill the time available for its completion"), it seemed that data expanded to fill the bandwidth available for their transmission. To pump up the speed, various industry groups proposed two new ring-based optical LANs. One was called **FDDI** (**Fiber Distributed Data Interface**) and the other was called **Fibre Channel**†. To make a long story short, while both were used as backbone networks, neither one made the breakthrough to the desktop. In both cases, the station management was too complicated, which led to complex chips and high prices. The lesson that should have been learned here was KISS (Keep It Simple, Stupid).

In any event, the failure of the optical LANs to catch fire left a gap for garden-variety Ethernet at speeds above 10 Mbps. Many installations needed more bandwidth and thus had numerous 10-Mbps LANs connected by a maze of repeaters, bridges, routers, and gateways, although to the network managers it sometimes felt that they were being held together by bubble gum and chicken wire.

It was in this environment that IEEE reconvened the 802.3 committee in 1992 with instructions to come up with a faster LAN. One proposal was to keep 802.3 exactly as it was, but just make it go faster. Another proposal was to redo it totally to give it lots of new features, such as real-time traffic and digitized voice, but just keep the old name (for marketing reasons). After some wrangling, the committee decided to keep 802.3 the way it was, but just make it go faster. The people behind the losing proposal did what any computer-industry people would have done under these circumstances—they stomped off and formed their own committee and standardized their LAN anyway (eventually as 802.12). It flopped miserably.

† It is called "fibre channel" and not "fiber channel" because the document editor was British.

The 802.3 committee decided to go with a souped-up Ethernet for three primary reasons:

1. The need to be backward compatible with existing Ethernet LANs.
2. The fear that a new protocol might have unforeseen problems.
3. The desire to get the job done before the technology changed.

The work was done quickly (by standards committees' norms), and the result, **802.3u**, was officially approved by IEEE in June 1995. Technically, 802.3u is not a new standard, but an addendum to the existing 802.3 standard (to emphasize its backward compatibility). Since practically everyone calls it **fast Ethernet**, rather than 802.3u, we will do that, too.

The basic idea behind fast Ethernet was simple: keep all the old frame formats, interfaces, and procedural rules, but just reduce the bit time from 100 nsec to 10 nsec. Technically, it would have been possible to copy either 10Base-5 or 10Base-2 and still detect collisions on time by just reducing the maximum cable length by a factor of ten. However, the advantages of 10Base-T wiring were so overwhelming that fast Ethernet is based entirely on this design. Thus, all fast Ethernet systems use hubs and switches; multidrop cables with vampire taps or BNC connectors are not permitted.

Nevertheless, some choices still had to be made, the most important being which wire types to support. One contender was category 3 twisted pair. The argument for it was that practically every office in the Western world has at least four category 3 (or better) twisted pairs running from it to a telephone wiring closet within 100 meters. Sometimes two such cables exist. Thus, using category 3 twisted pair would make it possible to wire up desktop computers using fast Ethernet without having to rewire the building, an enormous advantage for many organizations.

The main disadvantage of category 3 twisted pair is its inability to carry 200 megabaud signals (100 Mbps with Manchester encoding) 100 meters, the maximum computer-to-hub distance specified for 10Base-T (see Fig. 4-13). In contrast, category 5 twisted pair wiring can handle 100 meters easily, and fiber can go much farther. The compromise chosen was to allow all three possibilities, as shown in Fig. 4-21, but to pep up the category 3 solution to give it the additional carrying capacity needed.

Name	Cable	Max. segment	Advantages
100Base-T4	Twisted pair	100 m	Uses category 3 UTP
100Base-TX	Twisted pair	100 m	Full duplex at 100 Mbps (Cat 5 UTP)
100Base-FX	Fiber optics	2000 m	Full duplex at 100 Mbps; long runs

Figure 4-21. The original fast Ethernet cabling.

The category 3 UTP scheme, called **100Base-T4**, uses a signaling speed of 25 MHz, only 25 percent faster than standard Ethernet's 20 MHz (remember that Manchester encoding, as shown in Fig. 4-16, requires two clock periods for each of the 10 million bits each second). However, to achieve the necessary bandwidth, 100Base-T4 requires four twisted pairs. Since standard telephone wiring for decades has had four twisted pairs per cable, most offices are able to handle this. Of course, it means giving up your office telephone, but that is surely a small price to pay for faster e-mail.

Of the four twisted pairs, one is always to the hub, one is always from the hub, and the other two are switchable to the current transmission direction. To get the necessary bandwidth, Manchester encoding is not used, but with modern clocks and such short distances, it is no longer needed. In addition, ternary signals are sent, so that during a single clock period the wire can contain a 0, a 1, or a 2. With three twisted pairs going in the forward direction and ternary signaling, any one of 27 possible symbols can be transmitted, making it possible to send 4 bits with some redundancy. Transmitting 4 bits in each of the 25 million clock cycles per second gives the necessary 100 Mbps. In addition, there is always a 33.3-Mbps reverse channel using the remaining twisted pair. This scheme, known as **8B/6T** (8 bits map to 6 trits), is not likely to win any prizes for elegance, but it works with the existing wiring plant.

For category 5 wiring, the design, **100Base-TX**, is simpler because the wires can handle clock rates of 125 MHz. Only two twisted pairs per station are used, one to the hub and one from it. Straight binary coding is not used; instead a scheme called **4B/5B** is used at 125 MHz. It is taken from FDDI and compatible with it. Every group of five clock periods, each containing one of two signal values, yields 32 combinations. Sixteen of these combinations are used to transmit the four bit groups 0000, 0001, 0010, ..., 1111. Some of the remaining 16 are used for control purposes such as marking frame boundaries. The combinations used have been carefully chosen to provide enough transitions to maintain clock synchronization. The 100Base-TX system is full duplex; stations can transmit at 100 Mbps and receive at 100 Mbps at the same time. Often 100Base-TX and 100Base-T4 are collectively referred to as **100Base-T**.

The last option, **100Base-FX**, uses two strands of multimode fiber, one for each direction, so it, too, is full duplex with 100 Mbps in each direction. In addition, the distance between a station and the hub can be up to 2 km.

In response to popular demand, in 1997 the 802 committee added a new cabling type, 100Base-T2, allowing fast Ethernet to run over two pairs of existing category 3 wiring. However, a sophisticated digital signal processor is needed to handle the encoding scheme required, making this option fairly expensive. So far, it is rarely used due to its complexity, cost, and the fact that many office buildings have already been rewired with category 5 UTP.

Two kinds of interconnection devices are possible with 100Base-T: hubs and switches, as shown in Fig. 4-20. In a hub, all the incoming lines (or at least all the lines arriving at one plug-in card) are logically connected, forming a single collision domain. All the standard rules, including the binary exponential backoff algorithm, apply, so the system works just like old-fashioned Ethernet. In particular, only one station at a time can be transmitting. In other words, hubs require half-duplex communication.

In a switch, each incoming frame is buffered on a plug-in line card and passed over a high-speed backplane from the source card to the destination card if need be. The backplane has not been standardized, nor does it need to be, since it is entirely hidden deep inside the switch. If past experience is any guide, switch vendors will compete vigorously to produce ever faster backplanes in order to improve system throughput. Because 100Base-FX cables are too long for the normal Ethernet collision algorithm, they must be connected to switches, so each one is a collision domain unto itself. Hubs are not permitted with 100Base-FX.

As a final note, virtually all switches can handle a mix of 10-Mbps and 100-Mbps stations, to make upgrading easier. As a site acquires more and more 100-Mbps workstations, all it has to do is buy the necessary number of new line cards and insert them into the switch. In fact, the standard itself provides a way for two stations to automatically negotiate the optimum speed (10 or 100 Mbps) and duplexity (half or full). Most fast Ethernet products use this feature to autoconfigure themselves.

4.3.8 Gigabit Ethernet

The ink was barely dry on the fast Ethernet standard when the 802 committee began working on a yet faster Ethernet (1995). It was quickly dubbed **gigabit Ethernet** and was ratified by IEEE in 1998 under the name 802.3z. This identifier suggests that gigabit Ethernet is going to be the end of the line unless somebody quickly invents a new letter after z. Below we will discuss some of the key features of gigabit Ethernet. More information can be found in (Seifert, 1998).

The 802.3z committee's goals were essentially the same as the 802.3u committee's goals: make Ethernet go 10 times faster yet remain backward compatible with all existing Ethernet standards. In particular, gigabit Ethernet had to offer unacknowledged datagram service with both unicast and multicast, use the same 48-bit addressing scheme already in use, and maintain the same frame format, including the minimum and maximum frame sizes. The final standard met all these goals.

All configurations of gigabit Ethernet are point-to-point rather than multidrop as in the original 10 Mbps standard, now honored as **classic Ethernet**. In the simplest gigabit Ethernet configuration, illustrated in Fig. 4-22(a), two computers are directly connected to each other. The more common case, however, is having a switch or a hub connected to multiple computers and possibly additional switches or hubs, as shown in Fig. 4-22(b). In both configurations each individual Ethernet cable has exactly two devices on it, no more and no fewer.

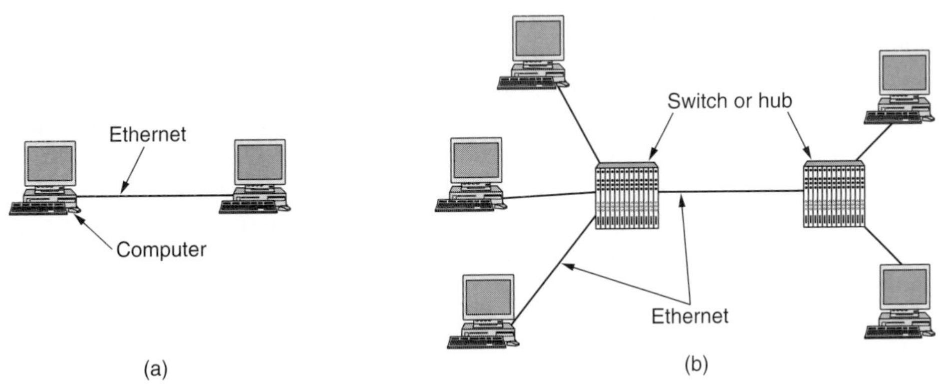

Figure 4-22. (a) A two-station Ethernet. (b) A multistation Ethernet.

Gigabit Ethernet supports two different modes of operation: full-duplex mode and half-duplex mode. The "normal" mode is full-duplex mode, which allows traffic in both directions at the same time. This mode is used when there is a central switch connected to computers (or other switches) on the periphery. In this configuration, all lines are buffered so each computer and switch is free to send frames whenever it wants to. The sender does not have to sense the channel to see if anybody else is using it because contention is impossible. On the line between a computer and a switch, the computer is the only possible sender on that line to the switch and the transmission succeeds even if the switch is currently sending a frame to the computer (because the line is full duplex). Since no contention is possible, the CSMA/CD protocol is not used, so the maximum length of the cable is determined by signal strength issues rather than by how long it takes for a noise burst to propagate back to the sender in the worst case. Switches are free to mix and match speeds. Autoconfiguration is supported just as in fast Ethernet.

The other mode of operation, half-duplex, is used when the computers are connected to a hub rather than a switch. A hub does not buffer incoming frames. Instead, it electrically connects all the lines internally, simulating the multidrop cable used in classic Ethernet. In this mode, collisions are possible, so the standard CSMA/CD protocol is required. Because a minimum (i.e., 64-byte) frame can now be transmitted 100 times faster than in classic Ethernet, the maximum distance is 100 times less, or 25 meters, to maintain the essential property that the sender is still transmitting when the noise burst gets back to it, even in the worst case. With a 2500-meter-long cable, the sender of a 64-byte frame at 1 Gbps would be long done before the frame got even a tenth of the way to the other end, let alone to the end and back.

The 802.3z committee considered a radius of 25 meters to be unacceptable and added two features to the standard to increase the radius. The first feature, called **carrier extension**, essentially tells the hardware to add its own padding after the normal frame to extend the frame to 512 bytes. Since this padding is added by the sending hardware and removed by the receiving hardware, the software is unaware of it, meaning that no changes are needed to existing software. Of course, using 512 bytes worth of bandwidth to transmit 46 bytes of user data (the payload of a 64-byte frame) has a line efficiency of 9%.

The second feature, called **frame bursting**, allows a sender to transmit a concatenated sequence of multiple frames in a single transmission. If the total burst is less than 512 bytes, the hardware pads it again. If enough frames are waiting for transmission, this scheme is highly efficient and preferred over carrier extension. These new features extend the radius of the network to 200 meters, which is probably enough for most offices.

In all fairness, it is hard to imagine an organization going to the trouble of buying and installing gigabit Ethernet cards to get high performance and then connecting the computers with a hub to simulate classic Ethernet with all its collisions. While hubs are somewhat cheaper than switches, gigabit Ethernet interface cards are still relatively expensive. To then economize by buying a cheap hub and slash the performance of the new system is foolish. Still, backward compatibility is sacred in the computer industry, so the 802.3z committee was required to put it in.

Gigabit Ethernet supports both copper and fiber cabling, as listed in Fig. 4-23. Signaling at or near 1 Gbps over fiber means that the light source has to be turned on and off in under 1 nsec. LEDs simply cannot operate this fast, so lasers are required. Two wavelengths are permitted: 0.85 microns (Short) and 1.3 microns (Long). Lasers at 0.85 microns are cheaper but do not work on single-mode fiber.

Name	Cable	Max. segment	Advantages
1000Base-SX	Fiber optics	550 m	Multimode fiber (50, 62.5 microns)
1000Base-LX	Fiber optics	5000 m	Single (10 μ) or multimode (50, 62.5 μ)
1000Base-CX	2 Pairs of STP	25 m	Shielded twisted pair
1000Base-T	4 Pairs of UTP	100 m	Standard category 5 UTP

Figure 4-23. Gigabit Ethernet cabling.

Three fiber diameters are permitted: 10, 50, and 62.5 microns. The first is for single mode and the last two are for multimode. Not all six combinations are allowed, however, and the maximum distance depends on the combination used. The numbers given in Fig. 4-23 are for the best case. In particular, 5000 meters is only achievable with 1.3 micron lasers operating over 10 micron fiber in single mode, but this is the best choice for campus backbones and is expected to be popular, despite its being the most expensive choice.

The 1000Base-CX option uses short shielded copper cables. Its problem is that it is competing with high-performance fiber from above and cheap UTP from below. It is unlikely to be used much, if at all.

The last option is bundles of four category 5 UTP wires working together. Because so much of this wiring is already installed, it is likely to be the poor man's gigabit Ethernet.

Gigabit Ethernet uses new encoding rules on the fibers. Manchester encoding at 1 Gbps would require a 2 Gbaud signal, which was considered too difficult and also too wasteful of bandwidth. Instead a new scheme, called **8B/10B**, was chosen, based on fibre channel. Each 8-bit byte is encoded on the fiber as 10 bits, hence the name 8B/10B. Since there are 1024 possible output codewords for each input byte, some leeway was available in choosing which codewords to allow. The following two rules were used in making the choices:

1. No codeword may have more than four identical bits in a row.
2. No codeword may have more than six 0s or six 1s.

These choices were made to keep enough transitions in the stream to make sure the receiver stays in sync with the sender and also to keep the number of 0s and 1s on the fiber as close to equal as possible. In addition, many input bytes have two possible codewords assigned to them. When the encoder has a choice of codewords, it always chooses the codeword that moves in the direction of equalizing the number of 0s and 1s transmitted so far. This emphasis of balancing 0s and 1s is needed to keep the DC component of the signal as low as possible to allow it to pass through transformers unmodified. While computer scientists are not fond of having the properties of transformers dictate their coding schemes, life is like that sometimes.

Gigabit Ethernets using 1000Base-T use a different encoding scheme since clocking data onto copper wire in 1 nsec is too difficult. This solution uses four category 5 twisted pairs to allow four symbols to be transmitted in parallel. Each symbol is encoded using one of five voltage levels. This scheme allows a single symbol to encode 00, 01, 10, 11, or a special value for control purposes. Thus, there are 2 data bits per twisted pair or 8 data bits per clock cycle. The clock runs at 125 MHz, allowing 1-Gbps operation. The reason for allowing five voltage levels instead of four is to have combinations left over for framing and control purposes.

A speed of 1 Gbps is quite fast. For example, if a receiver is busy with some other task for even 1 msec and does not empty the input buffer on some line, up to 1953 frames may have accumulated there in that 1 ms gap. Also, when a computer on a gigabit Ethernet is shipping data down the line to a computer on a classic Ethernet, buffer overruns are very likely. As a consequence of these two observations, gigabit Ethernet supports flow control (as does fast Ethernet, although the two are different).

The flow control consists of one end sending a special control frame to the other end telling it to pause for some period of time. Control frames are normal Ethernet frames containing a type of 0x8808. The first two bytes of the data field give the command; succeeding bytes provide the parameters, if any. For flow control, PAUSE frames are used, with the parameter telling how long to pause, in units of the minimum frame time. For gigabit Ethernet, the time unit is 512 nsec, allowing for pauses as long as 33.6 msec.

As soon as gigabit Ethernet was standardized, the 802 committee got bored and wanted to get back to work. IEEE told them to start on 10-gigabit Ethernet. After searching hard for a letter to follow z, they abandoned that approach and went over to two-letter suffixes. They got to work and that standard was approved by IEEE in 2002 as 802.3ae. Can 100-gigabit Ethernet be far behind?

4.3.9 IEEE 802.2: Logical Link Control

It is now perhaps time to step back and compare what we have learned in this chapter with what we studied in the previous one. In Chap. 3, we saw how two machines could communicate reliably over an unreliable line by using various data link protocols. These protocols provided error control (using acknowledgements) and flow control (using a sliding window).

In contrast, in this chapter, we have not said a word about reliable communication. All that Ethernet and the other 802 protocols offer is a best-efforts datagram service. Sometimes, this service is adequate. For example, for transporting IP packets, no guarantees are required or even expected. An IP packet can just be inserted into an 802 payload field and sent on its way. If it gets lost, so be it.

Nevertheless, there are also systems in which an error-controlled, flow-controlled data link protocol is desired. IEEE has defined one that can run on top of Ethernet and the other 802 protocols. In addition, this protocol, called **LLC** (**Logical Link Control**), hides the differences between the various kinds of 802 networks by providing a single format and interface to the network layer. This format, interface, and protocol are all closely based on the HDLC protocol we studied in Chap. 3. LLC forms the upper half of the data link layer, with the MAC sublayer below it, as shown in Fig. 4-24.

Typical usage of LLC is as follows. The network layer on the sending machine passes a packet to LLC, using the LLC access primitives. The LLC sublayer then adds an LLC header, containing sequence and acknowledgement numbers. The resulting structure is then inserted into the payload field of an 802 frame and transmitted. At the receiver, the reverse process takes place.

LLC provides three service options: unreliable datagram service, acknowledged datagram service, and reliable connection-oriented service. The LLC header contains three fields: a destination access point, a source access point, and a control field. The access points tell which process the frame came from and where it is to be delivered, replacing the DIX *Type* field. The control field contains sequence and acknowledgement numbers, very much in the style of HDLC (see Fig. 3-24), but not identical to it. These fields are primarily used when a re-

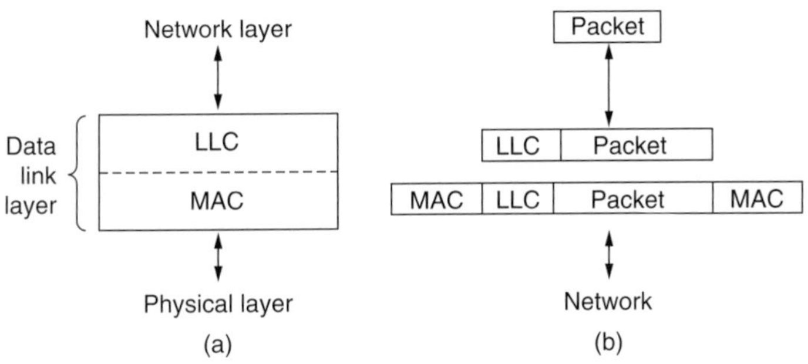

Figure 4-24. (a) Position of LLC. (b) Protocol formats.

liable connection is needed at the data link level, in which case protocols similar to the ones discussed in Chap. 3 would be used. For the Internet, best-efforts attempts to deliver IP packets is sufficient, so no acknowledgements at the LLC level are required.

4.3.10 Retrospective on Ethernet

Ethernet has been around for over 20 years and has no serious competitors in sight, so it is likely to be around for many years to come. Few CPU architectures, operating systems, or programming languages have been king of the mountain for two decades going on three. Clearly, Ethernet did something right. What?

Probably the main reason for its longevity is that Ethernet is simple and flexible. In practice, simple translates into reliable, cheap, and easy to maintain. Once the vampire taps were replaced by BNC connectors, failures became extremely rare. People hesitate to replace something that works perfectly all the time, especially when they know that an awful lot of things in the computer industry work very poorly, so that many so-called "upgrades" are appreciably worse than what they replaced.

Simple also translates into cheap. Thin Ethernet and twisted pair wiring is relatively inexpensive. The interface cards are also low cost. Only when hubs and switches were introduced were substantial investments required, but by the time they were in the picture, Ethernet was already well established.

Ethernet is easy to maintain. There is no software to install (other than the drivers) and there are no configuration tables to manage (and get wrong). Also, adding new hosts is as simple as just plugging them in.

Another point is that Ethernet interworks easily with TCP/IP, which has become dominant. IP is a connectionless protocol, so it fits perfectly with Ethernet, which is also connectionless. IP fits much less well with ATM, which is connection oriented. This mismatch definitely hurt ATM's chances.

Lastly, Ethernet has been able to evolve in certain crucial ways. Speeds have gone up by several orders of magnitude and hubs and switches have been introduced, but these changes have not required changing the software. When a network salesman shows up at a large installation and says: "I have this fantastic new network for you. All you have to do is throw out all your hardware and rewrite all your software," he has a problem. FDDI, Fibre Channel, and ATM were all faster than Ethernet when introduced, but they were incompatible with Ethernet, far more complex, and harder to manage. Eventually, Ethernet caught up with them in terms of speed, so they had no advantages left and quietly died off except for ATM's use deep within the core of the telephone system.

4.4 WIRELESS LANS

Although Ethernet is widely used, it is about to get some competition. Wireless LANs are increasingly popular, and more and more office buildings, airports, and other public places are being outfitted with them. Wireless LANs can operate in one of two configurations, as we saw in Fig. 1-35: with a base station and without a base station. Consequently, the 802.11 LAN standard takes this into account and makes provision for both arrangements, as we will see shortly.

We gave some background information on 802.11 in Sec. 1.5.4. Now is the time to take a closer look at the technology. In the following sections we will look at the protocol stack, physical layer radio transmission techniques, MAC sublayer protocol, frame structure, and services. For more information about 802.11, see (Crow et al., 1997; Geier, 2002; Heegard et al., 2001; Kapp, 2002; O'Hara and Petrick, 1999; and Severance, 1999). To hear the truth from the mouth of the horse, consult the published 802.11 standard itself.

4.4.1 The 802.11 Protocol Stack

The protocols used by all the 802 variants, including Ethernet, have a certain commonality of structure. A partial view of the 802.11 protocol stack is given in Fig. 4-25. The physical layer corresponds to the OSI physical layer fairly well, but the data link layer in all the 802 protocols is split into two or more sublayers. In 802.11, the MAC (Medium Access Control) sublayer determines how the channel is allocated, that is, who gets to transmit next. Above it is the LLC (Logical Link Control) sublayer, whose job it is to hide the differences between the different 802 variants and make them indistinguishable as far as the network layer is concerned. We studied the LLC when examining Ethernet earlier in this chapter and will not repeat that material here.

The 1997 802.11 standard specifies three transmission techniques allowed in the physical layer. The infrared method uses much the same technology as television remote controls do. The other two use short-range radio, using techniques

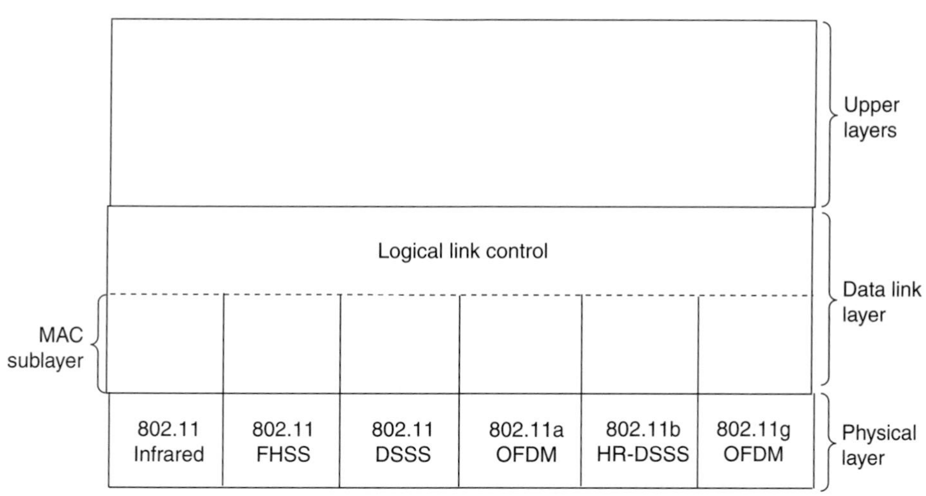

Figure 4-25. Part of the 802.11 protocol stack.

called FHSS and DSSS. Both of these use a part of the spectrum that does not require licensing (the 2.4-GHz ISM band). Radio-controlled garage door openers also use this piece of the spectrum, so your notebook computer may find itself in competition with your garage door. Cordless telephones and microwave ovens also use this band. All of these techniques operate at 1 or 2 Mbps and at low enough power that they do not conflict too much. In 1999, two new techniques were introduced to achieve higher bandwidth. These are called OFDM and HR-DSSS. They operate at up to 54 Mbps and 11 Mbps, respectively. In 2001, a second OFDM modulation was introduced, but in a different frequency band from the first one. Now we will examine each of them briefly. Technically, these belong to the physical layer and should have been examined in Chapter 2, but since they are so closely tied to LANs in general and the 802.11 MAC sublayer, we treat them here instead.

4.4.2 The 802.11 Physical Layer

Each of the five permitted transmission techniques makes it possible to send a MAC frame from one station to another. They differ, however, in the technology used and speeds achievable. A detailed discussion of these technologies is far beyond the scope of this book, but a few words on each one, along with some of the key words, may provide interested readers with terms to search for on the Internet or elsewhere for more information.

The infrared option uses diffused (i.e., not line of sight) transmission at 0.85 or 0.95 microns. Two speeds are permitted: 1 Mbps and 2 Mbps. At 1 Mbps, an encoding scheme is used in which a group of 4 bits is encoded as a 16-bit codeword containing fifteen 0s and a single 1, using what is called **Gray code**. This code has the property that a small error in time synchronization leads to only a single bit error in the output. At 2 Mbps, the encoding takes 2 bits and produces a 4-bit codeword, also with only a single 1, that is one of 0001, 0010, 0100, or 1000. Infrared signals cannot penetrate walls, so cells in different rooms are well isolated from each other. Nevertheless, due to the low bandwidth (and the fact that sunlight swamps infrared signals), this is not a popular option.

FHSS (**Frequency Hopping Spread Spectrum**) uses 79 channels, each 1-MHz wide, starting at the low end of the 2.4-GHz ISM band. A pseudorandom number generator is used to produce the sequence of frequencies hopped to. As long as all stations use the same seed to the pseudorandom number generator and stay synchronized in time, they will hop to the same frequencies simultaneously. The amount of time spent at each frequency, the **dwell time**, is an adjustable parameter, but must be less than 400 msec. FHSS' randomization provides a fair way to allocate spectrum in the unregulated ISM band. It also provides a modicum of security since an intruder who does not know the hopping sequence or dwell time cannot eavesdrop on transmissions. Over longer distances, multipath fading can be an issue, and FHSS offers good resistance to it. It is also relatively insensitive to radio interference, which makes it popular for building-to-building links. Its main disadvantage is its low bandwidth.

The third modulation method, **DSSS** (**Direct Sequence Spread Spectrum**), is also restricted to 1 or 2 Mbps. The scheme used has some similarities to the CDMA system we examined in Sec. 2.6.2, but differs in other ways. Each bit is transmitted as 11 chips, using what is called a **Barker sequence**. It uses phase shift modulation at 1 Mbaud, transmitting 1 bit per baud when operating at 1 Mbps and 2 bits per baud when operating at 2 Mbps. For years, the FCC required all wireless communications equipment operating in the ISM bands in the U.S. to use spread spectrum, but in May 2002, that rule was dropped as new technologies emerged.

The first of the high-speed wireless LANs, **802.11a**, uses **OFDM** (**Orthogonal Frequency Division Multiplexing**) to deliver up to 54 Mbps in the wider 5-GHz ISM band. As the term FDM suggests, different frequencies are used—52 of them, 48 for data and 4 for synchronization—not unlike ADSL. Since transmissions are present on multiple frequencies at the same time, this technique is considered a form of spread spectrum, but different from both CDMA and FHSS. Splitting the signal into many narrow bands has some key advantages over using a single wide band, including better immunity to narrowband interference and the possibility of using noncontiguous bands. A complex encoding system is used, based on phase-shift modulation for speeds up to 18 Mbps and on QAM above that. At 54 Mbps, 216 data bits are encoded into 288-bit symbols. Part of the motivation for OFDM is compatibility with the European HiperLAN/2 system (Doufexi et al., 2002). The technique has a good spectrum efficiency in terms of bits/Hz and good immunity to multipath fading.

Next, we come to **HR-DSSS (High Rate Direct Sequence Spread Spectrum)**, another spread spectrum technique, which uses 11 million chips/sec to achieve 11 Mbps in the 2.4-GHz band. It is called **802.11b** but is not a follow-up to 802.11a. In fact, its standard was approved first and it got to market first. Data rates supported by 802.11b are 1, 2, 5.5, and 11 Mbps. The two slow rates run at 1 Mbaud, with 1 and 2 bits per baud, respectively, using phase shift modulation (for compatibility with DSSS). The two faster rates run at 1.375 Mbaud, with 4 and 8 bits per baud, respectively, using **Walsh/Hadamard** codes. The data rate may be dynamically adapted during operation to achieve the optimum speed possible under current conditions of load and noise. In practice, the operating speed of 802.11b is nearly always 11 Mbps. Although 802.11b is slower than 802.11a, its range is about 7 times greater, which is more important in many situations.

An enhanced version of 802.11b, **802.11g**, was approved by IEEE in November 2001 after much politicking about whose patented technology it would use. It uses the OFDM modulation method of 802.11a but operates in the narrow 2.4-GHz ISM band along with 802.11b. In theory it can operate at up to 54 MBps. It is not yet clear whether this speed will be realized in practice. What it does mean is that the 802.11 committee has produced three different high-speed wireless LANs: 802.11a, 802.11b, and 802.11g (not to mention three low-speed wireless LANs). One can legitimately ask if this is a good thing for a standards committee to do. Maybe three was their lucky number.

4.4.3 The 802.11 MAC Sublayer Protocol

Let us now return from the land of electrical engineering to the land of computer science. The 802.11 MAC sublayer protocol is quite different from that of Ethernet due to the inherent complexity of the wireless environment compared to that of a wired system. With Ethernet, a station just waits until the ether goes silent and starts transmitting. If it does not receive a noise burst back within the first 64 bytes, the frame has almost assuredly been delivered correctly. With wireless, this situation does not hold.

To start with, there is the hidden station problem mentioned earlier and illustrated again in Fig. 4-26(a). Since not all stations are within radio range of each other, transmissions going on in one part of a cell may not be received elsewhere in the same cell. In this example, station *C* is transmitting to station *B*. If *A* senses the channel, it will not hear anything and falsely conclude that it may now start transmitting to *B*.

In addition, there is the inverse problem, the exposed station problem, illustrated in Fig. 4-26(b). Here *B* wants to send to *C* so it listens to the channel. When it hears a transmission, it falsely concludes that it may not send to *C*, even

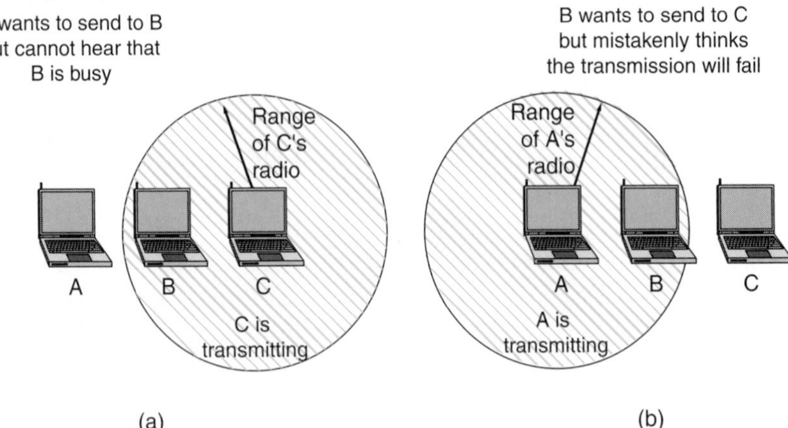

Figure 4-26. (a) The hidden station problem. (b) The exposed station problem.

though *A* may be transmitting to *D* (not shown). In addition, most radios are half duplex, meaning that they cannot transmit and listen for noise bursts at the same time on a single frequency. As a result of these problems, 802.11 does not use CSMA/CD, as Ethernet does.

To deal with this problem, 802.11 supports two modes of operation. The first, called **DCF** (**Distributed Coordination Function**), does not use any kind of central control (in that respect, similar to Ethernet). The other, called **PCF** (**Point Coordination Function**), uses the base station to control all activity in its cell. All implementations must support DCF but PCF is optional. We will now discuss these two modes in turn.

When DCF is employed, 802.11 uses a protocol called **CSMA/CA** (**CSMA with Collision Avoidance**). In this protocol, both physical channel sensing and virtual channel sensing are used. Two methods of operation are supported by CSMA/CA. In the first method, when a station wants to transmit, it senses the channel. If it is idle, it just starts transmitting. It does not sense the channel while transmitting but emits its entire frame, which may well be destroyed at the receiver due to interference there. If the channel is busy, the sender defers until it goes idle and then starts transmitting. If a collision occurs, the colliding stations wait a random time, using the Ethernet binary exponential backoff algorithm, and then try again later.

The other mode of CSMA/CA operation is based on MACAW and uses virtual channel sensing, as illustrated in Fig. 4-27. In this example, *A* wants to send to *B*. C is a station within range of *A* (and possibly within range of *B*, but that does not matter). *D* is a station within range of *B* but not within range of *A*.

The protocol starts when *A* decides it wants to send data to *B*. It begins by sending an RTS frame to *B* to request permission to send it a frame. When *B* receives this request, it may decide to grant permission, in which case it sends a

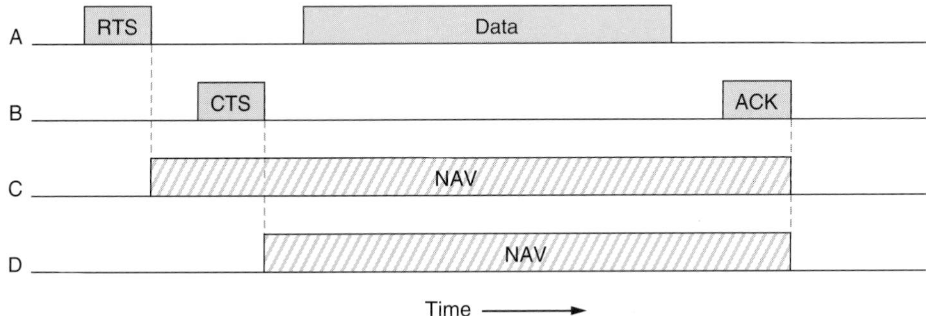

Figure 4-27. The use of virtual channel sensing using CSMA/CA.

CTS frame back. Upon receipt of the CTS, *A* now sends its frame and starts an ACK timer. Upon correct receipt of the data frame, *B* responds with an ACK frame, terminating the exchange. If *A*'s ACK timer expires before the ACK gets back to it, the whole protocol is run again.

Now let us consider this exchange from the viewpoints of *C* and *D*. *C* is within range of *A*, so it may receive the RTS frame. If it does, it realizes that someone is going to send data soon, so for the good of all it desists from transmitting anything until the exchange is completed. From the information provided in the RTS request, it can estimate how long the sequence will take, including the final ACK, so it asserts a kind of virtual channel busy for itself, indicated by **NAV** (**Network Allocation Vector**) in Fig. 4-27. *D* does not hear the RTS, but it does hear the CTS, so it also asserts the *NAV* signal for itself. Note that the *NAV* signals are not transmitted; they are just internal reminders to keep quiet for a certain period of time.

In contrast to wired networks, wireless networks are noisy and unreliable, in no small part due to microwave ovens, which also use the unlicensed ISM bands. As a consequence, the probability of a frame making it through successfully decreases with frame length. If the probability of any bit being in error is p, then the probability of an n-bit frame being received entirely correctly is $(1 - p)^n$. For example, for $p = 10^{-4}$, the probability of receiving a full Ethernet frame (12,144 bits) correctly is less than 30%. If $p = 10^{-5}$, about one frame in 9 will be damaged. Even if $p = 10^{-6}$, over 1% of the frames will be damaged, which amounts to almost a dozen per second, and more if frames shorter than the maximum are used. In summary, if a frame is too long, it has very little chance of getting through undamaged and will probably have to be retransmitted.

To deal with the problem of noisy channels, 802.11 allows frames to be fragmented into smaller pieces, each with its own checksum. The fragments are individually numbered and acknowledged using a stop-and-wait protocol (i.e., the sender may not transmit fragment $k + 1$ until it has received the acknowledgment for fragment k). Once the channel has been acquired using RTS and CTS, multiple fragments can be sent in a row, as shown in Fig. 4-28. sequence of fragments is called a **fragment burst**.

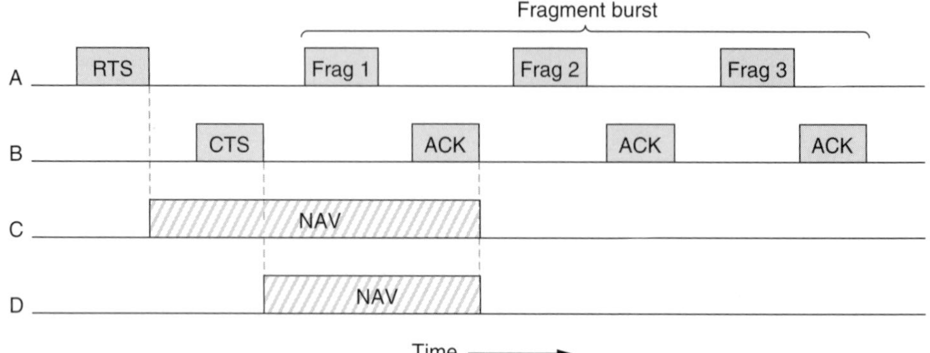

Figure 4-28. A fragment burst.

Fragmentation increases the throughput by restricting retransmissions to the bad fragments rather than the entire frame. The fragment size is not fixed by the standard but is a parameter of each cell and can be adjusted by the base station. The NAV mechanism keeps other stations quiet only until the next acknowledgement, but another mechanism (described below) is used to allow a whole fragment burst to be sent without interference.

All of the above discussion applies to the 802.11 DCF mode. In this mode, there is no central control, and stations compete for air time, just as they do with Ethernet. The other allowed mode is PCF, in which the base station polls the other stations, asking them if they have any frames to send. Since transmission order is completely controlled by the base station in PCF mode, no collisions ever occur. The standard prescribes the mechanism for polling, but not the polling frequency, polling order, or even whether all stations need to get equal service.

The basic mechanism is for the base station to broadcast a **beacon frame** periodically (10 to 100 times per second). The beacon frame contains system parameters, such as hopping sequences and dwell times (for FHSS), clock synchronization, etc. It also invites new stations to sign up for polling service. Once a station has signed up for polling service at a certain rate, it is effectively guaranteed a certain fraction of the bandwidth, thus making it possible to give quality-of-service guarantees.

Battery life is always an issue with mobile wireless devices, so 802.11 pays attention to the issue of power management. In particular, the base station can direct a mobile station to go into sleep state until explicitly awakened by the base station or the user. Having told a station to go to sleep, however, means that the base station has the responsibility for buffering any frames directed at it while the mobile station is asleep. These can be collected later.

PCF and DCF can coexist within one cell. At first it might seem impossible to have central control and distributed control operating at the same time, but

802.11 provides a way to achieve this goal. It works by carefully defining the interframe time interval. After a frame has been sent, a certain amount of dead time is required before any station may send a frame. Four different intervals are defined, each for a specific purpose. The four intervals are depicted in Fig. 4-29.

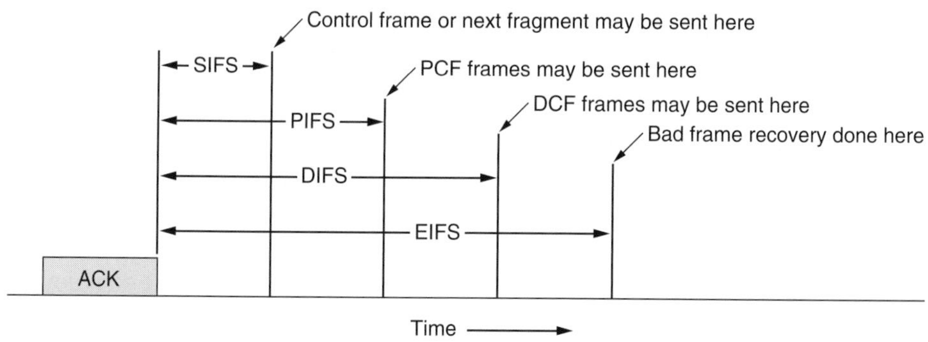

Figure 4-29. Interframe spacing in 802.11

The shortest interval is **SIFS (Short InterFrame Spacing)**. It is used to allow the parties in a single dialog the chance to go first. This includes letting the receiver send a CTS to respond to an RTS, letting the receiver send an ACK for a fragment or full data frame, and letting the sender of a fragment burst transmit the next fragment without having to send an RTS again.

There is always exactly one station that is entitled to respond after a SIFS interval. If it fails to make use of its chance and a time **PIFS (PCF InterFrame Spacing)** elapses, the base station may send a beacon frame or poll frame. This mechanism allows a station sending a data frame or fragment sequence to finish its frame without anyone else getting in the way, but gives the base station a chance to grab the channel when the previous sender is done without having to compete with eager users.

If the base station has nothing to say and a time **DIFS (DCF InterFrame Spacing)** elapses, any station may attempt to acquire the channel to send a new frame. The usual contention rules apply, and binary exponential backoff may be needed if a collision occurs.

The last time interval, **EIFS (Extended InterFrame Spacing)**, is used only by a station that has just received a bad or unknown frame to report the bad frame. The idea of giving this event the lowest priority is that since the receiver may have no idea of what is going on, it should wait a substantial time to avoid interfering with an ongoing dialog between two stations.

4.4.4 The 802.11 Frame Structure

The 802.11 standard defines three different classes of frames on the wire: data, control, and management. Each of these has a header with a variety of fields used within the MAC sublayer. In addition, there are some headers used by the physical layer but these mostly deal with the modulation techniques used, so we will not discuss them here.

The format of the data frame is shown in Fig. 4-30. First comes the *Frame Control* field. It itself has 11 subfields. The first of these is the *Protocol version*, which allows two versions of the protocol to operate at the same time in the same cell. Then come the *Type* (data, control, or management) and *Subtype* fields (e.g., RTS or CTS). The *To DS* and *From DS* bits indicate the frame is going to or coming from the intercell distribution system (e.g., Ethernet). The *MF* bit means that more fragments will follow. The *Retry* bit marks a retransmission of a frame sent earlier. The *Power management* bit is used by the base station to put the receiver into sleep state or take it out of sleep state. The *More* bit indicates that the sender has additional frames for the receiver. The *W* bit specifies that the frame body has been encrypted using the **WEP** (**Wired Equivalent Privacy**) algorithm. Finally, the *O* bit tells the receiver that a sequence of frames with this bit on must be processed strictly in order.

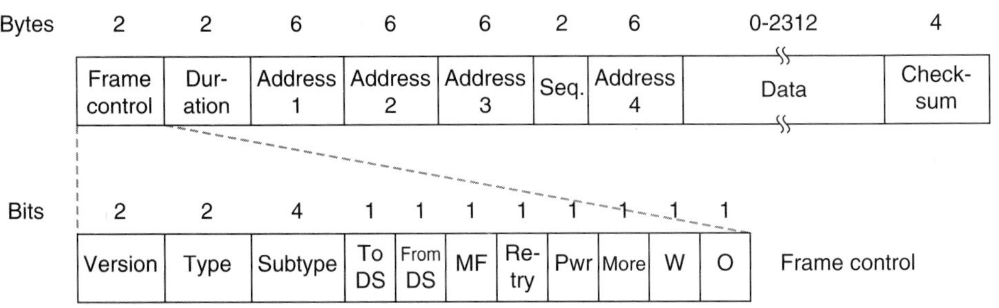

Figure 4-30. The 802.11 data frame.

The second field of the data frame, the *Duration* field, tells how long the frame and its acknowledgement will occupy the channel. This field is also present in the control frames and is how other stations manage the NAV mechanism. The frame header contains four addresses, all in standard IEEE 802 format. The source and destination are obviously needed, but what are the other two for? Remember that frames may enter or leave a cell via a base station. The other two addresses are used for the source and destination base stations for intercell traffic.

The *Sequence* field allows fragments to be numbered. Of the 16 bits available, 12 identify the frame and 4 identify the fragment. The *Data* field contains the payload, up to 2312 bytes, followed by the usual *Checksum*.

Management frames have a format similar to that of data frames, except without one of the base station addresses, because management frames are restricted to a single cell. Control frames are shorter still, having only one or two addresses, no *Data* field, and no *Sequence* field. The key information here is in the *Subtype* field, usually RTS, CTS, or ACK.

4.4.5 Services

The 802.11 standard states that each conformant wireless LAN must provide nine services. These services are divided into two categories: five distribution services and four station services. The distribution services relate to managing cell membership and interacting with stations outside the cell. In contrast, the station services relate to activity within a single cell.

The five distribution services are provided by the base stations and deal with station mobility as they enter and leave cells, attaching themselves to and detaching themselves from base stations. They are as follows.

1. **Association**. This service is used by mobile stations to connect themselves to base stations. Typically, it is used just after a station moves within the radio range of the base station. Upon arrival, it announces its identity and capabilities. The capabilities include the data rates supported, need for PCF services (i.e., polling), and power management requirements. The base station may accept or reject the mobile station. If the mobile station is accepted, it must then authenticate itself.

2. **Disassociation**. Either the station or the base station may disassociate, thus breaking the relationship. A station should use this service before shutting down or leaving, but the base station may also use it before going down for maintenance.

3. **Reassociation**. A station may change its preferred base station using this service. This facility is useful for mobile stations moving from one cell to another. If it is used correctly, no data will be lost as a consequence of the handover. (But 802.11, like Ethernet, is just a best-efforts service.)

4. **Distribution**. This service determines how to route frames sent to the base station. If the destination is local to the base station, the frames can be sent out directly over the air. Otherwise, they will have to be forwarded over the wired network.

5. **Integration**. If a frame needs to be sent through a non-802.11 network with a different addressing scheme or frame format, this service handles the translation from the 802.11 format to the format required by the destination network.

The remaining four services are intracell (i.e., relate to actions within a single cell). They are used after association has taken place and are as follows.

1. **Authentication**. Because wireless communication can easily be sent or received by unauthorized stations, a station must authenticate itself before it is permitted to send data. After a mobile station has been associated by the base station (i.e., accepted into its cell), the base station sends a special challenge frame to it to see if the mobile station knows the secret key (password) that has been assigned to it. It proves its knowledge of the secret key by encrypting the challenge frame and sending it back to the base station. If the result is correct, the mobile is fully enrolled in the cell. In the initial standard, the base station does not have to prove its identity to the mobile station, but work to repair this defect in the standard is underway.

2. **Deauthentication**. When a previously authenticated station wants to leave the network, it is deauthenticated. After deauthentication, it may no longer use the network.

3. **Privacy**. For information sent over a wireless LAN to be kept confidential, it must be encrypted. This service manages the encryption and decryption. The encryption algorithm specified is RC4, invented by Ronald Rivest of M.I.T.

4. **Data delivery**. Finally, data transmission is what it is all about, so 802.11 naturally provides a way to transmit and receive data. Since 802.11 is modeled on Ethernet and transmission over Ethernet is not guaranteed to be 100% reliable, transmission over 802.11 is not guaranteed to be reliable either. Higher layers must deal with detecting and correcting errors.

An 802.11 cell has some parameters that can be inspected and, in some cases, adjusted. They relate to encryption, timeout intervals, data rates, beacon frequency, and so on.

Wireless LANs based on 802.11 are starting to be deployed in office buildings, airports, hotels, restaurants, and campuses around the world. Rapid growth is expected. For some experience about the widespread deployment of 802.11 at CMU, see (Hills, 2001).

4.5 BROADBAND WIRELESS

We have been indoors too long. Let us now go outside and see if any interesting networking is going on there. It turns out that quite a bit is going on there, and some of it has to do with the so-called last mile. With the deregulation of the telephone system in many countries, competitors to the entrenched telephone company are now often allowed to offer local voice and high-speed Internet service.

There is certainly plenty of demand. The problem is that running fiber, coax, or even category 5 twisted pair to millions of homes and businesses is prohibitively expensive. What is a competitor to do?

The answer is broadband wireless. Erecting a big antenna on a hill just outside of town and installing antennas directed at it on customers' roofs is much easier and cheaper than digging trenches and stringing cables. Thus, competing telecommunication companies have a great interest in providing a multimegabit wireless communication service for voice, Internet, movies on demand, etc. As we saw in Fig. 2-30, LMDS was invented for this purpose. However, until recently, every carrier devised its own system. This lack of standards meant that hardware and software could not be mass produced, which kept prices high and acceptance low.

Many people in the industry realized that having a broadband wireless standard was the key element missing, so IEEE was asked to form a committee composed of people from key companies and academia to draw up the standard. The next number available in the 802 numbering space was **802.16**, so the standard got this number. Work was started in July 1999, and the final standard was approved in April 2002. Officially the standard is called "Air Interface for Fixed Broadband Wireless Access Systems." However, some people prefer to call it a **wireless MAN (Metropolitan Area Network)** or a **wireless local loop**. We regard all these terms as interchangeable.

Like some of the other 802 standards, 802.16 was heavily influenced by the OSI model, including the (sub)layers, terminology, service primitives, and more. Unfortunately, also like OSI, it is fairly complicated. In the following sections we will give a brief description of some of the highlights of 802.16, but this treatment is far from complete and leaves out many details. For additional information about broadband wireless in general, see (Bolcskei et al., 2001; and Webb, 2001). For information about 802.16 in particular, see (Eklund et al., 2002).

4.5.1 Comparison of 802.11 with 802.16

At this point you may be thinking: Why devise a new standard? Why not just use 802.11? There are some very good reasons for not using 802.11, primarily because 802.11 and 802.16 solve different problems. Before getting into the technology of 802.16, it is probably worthwhile saying a few words about why a new standard is needed at all.

The environments in which 802.11 and 802.16 operate are similar in some ways, primarily in that they were designed to provide high-bandwidth wireless communications. But they also differ in some major ways. To start with, 802.16 provides service to buildings, and buildings are not mobile. They do not migrate from cell to cell often. Much of 802.11 deals with mobility, and none of that is relevant here. Next, buildings can have more than one computer in them, a complication that does not occur when the end station is a single notebook computer.

Because building owners are generally willing to spend much more money for communication gear than are notebook owners, better radios are available. This difference means that 802.16 can use full-duplex communication, something 802.11 avoids to keep the cost of the radios low.

Because 802.16 runs over part of a city, the distances involved can be several kilometers, which means that the perceived power at the base station can vary widely from station to station. This variation affects the signal-to-noise ratio, which, in, turn, dictates multiple modulation schemes. Also, open communication over a city means that security and privacy are essential and mandatory.

Furthermore, each cell is likely to have many more users than will a typical 802.11 cell, and these users are expected to use more bandwidth than will a typical 802.11 user. After all it is rare for a company to invite 50 employees to show up in a room with their laptops to see if they can saturate the 802.11 wireless network by watching 50 separate movies at once. For this reason, more spectrum is needed than the ISM bands can provide, forcing 802.16 to operate in the much higher 10-to-66 GHz frequency range, the only place unused spectrum is still available.

But these millimeter waves have different physical properties than the longer waves in the ISM bands, which in turn requires a completely different physical layer. One property that millimeter waves have is that they are strongly absorbed by water (especially rain, but to some extent also by snow, hail, and with a bit of bad luck, heavy fog). Consequently, error handling is more important than in an indoor environment. Millimeter waves can be focused into directional beams (802.11 is omnidirectional), so choices made in 802.11 relating to multipath propagation are moot here.

Another issue is quality of service. While 802.11 provides some support for real-time traffic (using PCF mode), it was not really designed for telephony and heavy-duty multimedia usage. In contrast, 802.16 is expected to support these applications completely because it is intended for residential as well as business use.

In short, 802.11 was designed to be mobile Ethernet, whereas 802.16 was designed to be wireless, but stationary, cable television. These differences are so big that the resulting standards are very different as they try to optimize different things.

A very brief comparison with the cellular phone system is also worthwhile. With mobile phones, we are talking about narrow-band, voice-oriented, low-powered, mobile stations that communicate using medium-length microwaves. Nobody watches high-resolution, two-hour movies on GSM mobile phones (yet). Even UMTS has little hope of changing this situation. In short, the wireless MAN world is far more demanding than is the mobile phone world, so a completely different system is needed. Whether 802.16 could be used for mobile devices in the future is an interesting question. It was not optimized for them, but the possibility is there. For the moment it is focused on fixed wireless.

4.5.2 The 802.16 Protocol Stack

The 802.16 protocol stack is illustrated in Fig. 4-31. The general structure is similar to that of the other 802 networks, but with more sublayers. The bottom sublayer deals with transmission. Traditional narrow-band radio is used with conventional modulation schemes. Above the physical transmission layer comes a convergence sublayer to hide the different technologies from the data link layer. Actually, 802.11 has something like this too, only the committee chose not to formalize it with an OSI-type name.

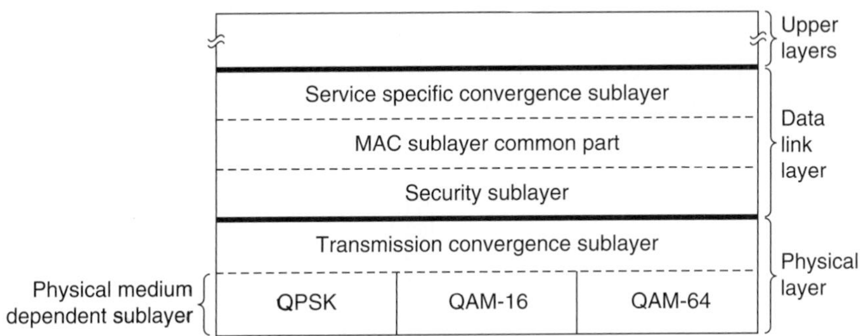

Figure 4-31. The 802.16 protocol stack.

Although we have not shown them in the figure, work is already underway to add two new physical layer protocols. The 802.16a standard will support OFDM in the 2-to-11 GHz frequency range. The 802.16b standard will operate in the 5-GHz ISM band. Both of these are attempts to move closer to 802.11.

The data link layer consists of three sublayers. The bottom one deals with privacy and security, which is far more crucial for public outdoor networks than for private indoor networks. It manages encryption, decryption, and key management.

Next comes the MAC sublayer common part. This is where the main protocols, such as channel management, are located. The model is that the base station controls the system. It can schedule the downstream (i.e., base to subscriber) channels very efficiently and plays a major role in managing the upstream (i.e., subscriber to base) channels as well. An unusual feature of the MAC sublayer is that, unlike those of the other 802 networks, it is completely connection oriented, in order to provide quality-of-service guarantees for telephony and multimedia communication.

The service-specific convergence sublayer takes the place of the logical link sublayer in the other 802 protocols. Its function is to interface to the network layer. A complication here is that 802.16 was designed to integrate seamlessly with both datagram protocols (e.g., PPP, IP, and Ethernet) and ATM. The problem is that packet protocols are connectionless and ATM is connection oriented.

This means that every ATM connection has to map onto an 802.16 connection, in principle a straightforward matter. But onto which 802.16 connection should an incoming IP packet be mapped? That problem is dealt with in this sublayer.

4.5.3 The 802.16 Physical Layer

As mentioned above, broadband wireless needs a lot of spectrum, and the only place to find it is in the 10-to-66 GHz range. These millimeter waves have an interesting property that longer microwaves do not: they travel in straight lines, unlike sound but similar to light. As a consequence, the base station can have multiple antennas, each pointing at a different sector of the surrounding terrain, as shown in Fig. 4-32. Each sector has its own users and is fairly independent of the adjoining ones, something not true of cellular radio, which is omnidirectional.

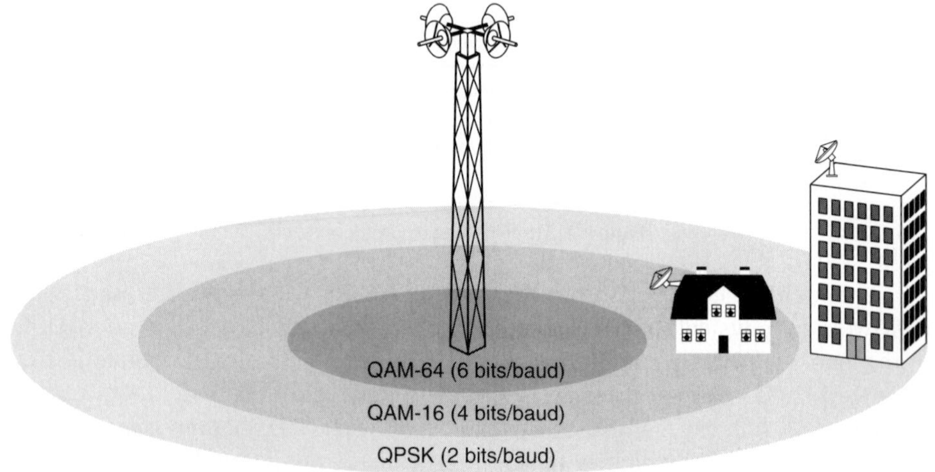

Figure 4-32. The 802.16 transmission environment.

Because signal strength in the millimeter band falls off sharply with distance from the base station, the signal-to-noise ratio also drops with distance from the base station. For this reason, 802.16 employs three different modulation schemes, depending on how far the subscriber station is from the base station. For close-in subscribers, QAM-64 is used, with 6 bits/baud. For medium-distance subscribers, QAM-16 is used, with 4 bits/baud. For distant subscribers, QPSK is used, with 2 bits/baud. For example, for a typical value of 25 MHz worth of spectrum, QAM-64 gives 150 Mbps, QAM-16 gives 100 Mbps, and QPSK gives 50 Mbps. In other words, the farther the subscriber is from the base station, the lower the data rate (similar to what we saw with ADSL in Fig. 2-27). The constellation diagrams for these three modulation techniques were shown in Fig. 2-25.

Given the goal of producing a broadband system, and subject to the above physical constraints, the 802.16 designers worked hard to use the available spectrum efficiently. One thing they did not like was the way GSM and DAMPS work. Both of those use different but equal frequency bands for upstream and downstream traffic. For voice, traffic is probably symmetric for the most part, but for Internet access, there is often more downstream traffic than upstream traffic. Consequently, 802.16 provides a more flexible way to allocate the bandwidth. Two schemes are used, **FDD** (**Frequency Division Duplexing**) and **TDD** (**Time Division Duplexing**). The latter is illustrated in Fig. 4-33. Here the base station periodically sends out frames. Each frame contains time slots. The first ones are for downstream traffic. Then comes a guard time used by the stations to switch direction. Finally, we have slots for upstream traffic. The number of time slots devoted to each direction can be changed dynamically to match the bandwidth in each direction to the traffic.

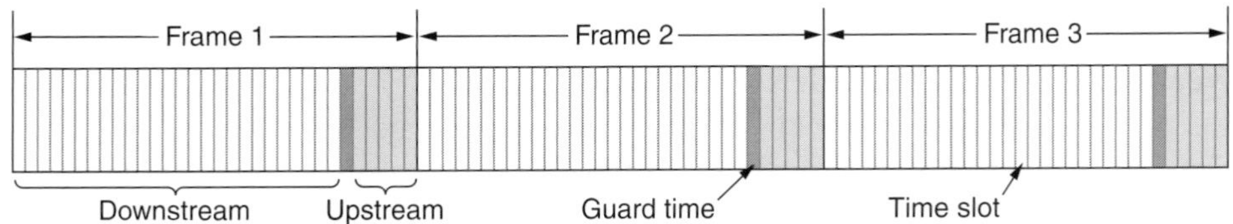

Figure 4-33. Frames and time slots for time division duplexing.

Downstream traffic is mapped onto time slots by the base station. The base station is completely in control for this direction. Upstream traffic is more complex and depends on the quality of service required. We will come to slot allocation when we discuss the MAC sublayer below.

Another interesting feature of the physical layer is its ability to pack multiple MAC frames back-to back in a single physical transmission. The feature enhances spectral efficiency by reducing the number of preambles and physical layer headers needed.

Also noteworthy is the use of Hamming codes to do forward error correction in the physical layer. Nearly all other networks simply rely on checksums to detect errors and request retransmission when frames are received in error. But in the wide area broadband environment, so many transmission errors are expected that error correction is employed in the physical layer, in addition to checksums in the higher layers. The net effect of the error correction is to make the channel look better than it really is (in the same way that CD-ROMs appear to be very reliable, but only because more than half the total bits are devoted to error correction in the physical layer).

4.5.4 The 802.16 MAC Sublayer Protocol

The data link layer is divided into three sublayers, as we saw in Fig. 4-31. Since we will not study cryptography until Chap. 8, it is difficult to explain now how the security sublayer works. Suffice it to say that encryption is used to keep secret all data transmitted. Only the frame payloads are encrypted; the headers are not. This property means that a snooper can see who is talking to whom but cannot tell what they are saying to each other.

If you already know something about cryptography, here comes a one-paragraph explanation of the security sublayer. If you know nothing about cryptography, you are not likely to find the next paragraph terribly enlightening (but you might consider rereading it after finishing Chap. 8).

At the time a subscriber connects to a base station, they perform mutual authentication with RSA public-key cryptography using X.509 certificates. The payloads themselves are encrypted using a symmetric-key system, either DES with cipher block chaining or triple DES with two keys. AES (Rijndael) is likely to be added soon. Integrity checking uses SHA-1. Now that was not so bad, was it?

Let us now look at the MAC sublayer common part. MAC frames occupy an integral number of physical layer time slots. Each frame is composed of subframes, the first two of which are the downstream and upstream maps. These maps tell what is in which time slot and which time slots are free. The downstream map also contains various system parameters to inform new stations as they come on-line.

The downstream channel is fairly straightforward. The base station simply decides what to put in which subframe. The upstream channel is more complicated since there are competing uncoordinated subscribers that need access to it. Its allocation is tied closely to the quality-of-service issue. Four classes of service are defined as follows:

1. Constant bit rate service.
2. Real-time variable bit rate service.
3. Non-real-time variable bit rate service.
4. Best-efforts service.

All service in 802.16 is connection-oriented, and each connection gets one of the above classes of service, determined when the connection is set up. This design is very different from that of 802.11 or Ethernet, which have no connections in the MAC sublayer.

Constant bit rate service is intended for transmitting uncompressed voice such as on a T1 channel. This service needs to send a predetermined amount of data at predetermined time intervals. It is accommodated by dedicating certain time slots to each connection of this type. Once the bandwidth has been allocated, the time slots are available automatically, without the need to ask for each one.

Real-time variable bit rate service is for compressed multimedia and other soft real-time applications in which the amount of bandwidth needed each instant may vary. It is accommodated by the base station polling the subscriber at a fixed interval to ask how much bandwidth is needed this time.

Non-real-time variable bit rate service is for heavy transmissions that are not real time, such as large file transfers. For this service the base station polls the subscriber often, but not at rigidly-prescribed time intervals. A constant bit rate customer can set a bit in one of its frames requesting a poll in order to send additional (variable bit rate) traffic.

If a station does not respond to a poll k times in a row, the base station puts it into a multicast group and takes away its personal poll. Instead, when the multicast group is polled, any of the stations in it can respond, contending for service. In this way, stations with little traffic do not waste valuable polls.

Finally, best-efforts service is for everything else. No polling is done and the subscriber must contend for bandwidth with other best-efforts subscribers. Requests for bandwidth are done in time slots marked in the upstream map as available for contention. If a request is successful, its success will be noted in the next downstream map. If it is not successful, unsuccessful subscribers have to try again later. To minimize collisions, the Ethernet binary exponential backoff algorithm is used.

The standard defines two forms of bandwidth allocation: per station and per connection. In the former case, the subscriber station aggregates the needs of all the users in the building and makes collective requests for them. When it is granted bandwidth, it doles out that bandwidth to its users as it sees fit. In the latter case, the base station manages each connection directly.

4.5.5 The 802.16 Frame Structure

All MAC frames begin with a generic header. The header is followed by an optional payload and an optional checksum (CRC), as illustrated in Fig. 4-34. The payload is not needed in control frames, for example, those requesting channel slots. The checksum is (surprisingly) also optional due to the error correction in the physical layer and the fact that no attempt is ever made to retransmit real-time frames. If no retransmissions will be attempted, why even bother with a checksum?

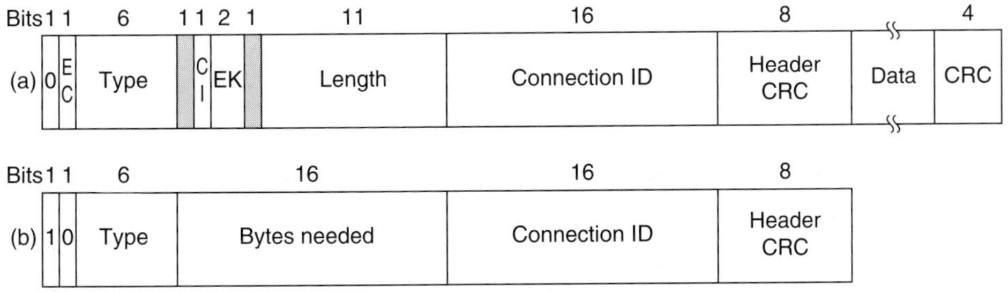

Figure 4-34. (a) A generic frame. (b) A bandwidth request frame.

A quick rundown of the header fields of Fig. 4-34(a) is as follows. The *EC* bit tells whether the payload is encrypted. The *Type* field identifies the frame type, mostly telling whether packing and fragmentation are present. The *CI* field indicates the presence or absence of the final checksum. The *EK* field tells which of the encryption keys is being used (if any). The *Length* field gives the complete length of the frame, including the header. The *Connection identifier* tells which connection this frame belongs to. Finally, the *HeaderCRC* field is a checksum over the header only, using the polynomial $x^8 + x^2 + x + 1$.

A second header type, for frames that request bandwidth, is shown in Fig. 4-34(b). It starts with a 1 bit instead of a 0 bit and is similar to the generic header except that the second and third bytes form a 16-bit number telling how much bandwidth is needed to carry the specified number of bytes. Bandwidth request frames do not carry a payload or full-frame CRC.

A great deal more could be said about 802.16, but this is not the place to say it. For more information, please consult the standard itself.

4.6 BLUETOOTH

In 1994, the L. M. Ericsson company became interested in connecting its mobile phones to other devices (e.g., PDAs) without cables. Together with four other companies (IBM, Intel, Nokia, and Toshiba), it formed a SIG (Special Interest Group, i.e., consortium) to develop a wireless standard for interconnecting computing and communication devices and accessories using short-range, low-power, inexpensive wireless radios. The project was named **Bluetooth**, after Harald Blaatand (Bluetooth) II (940-981), a Viking king who unified (i.e., conquered) Denmark and Norway, also without cables.

Although the original idea was just to get rid of the cables between devices, it soon began to expand in scope and encroach on the area of wireless LANs. While this move makes the standard more useful, it also creates some competition for mindshare with 802.11. To make matters worse, the two systems also interfere with each other electrically. It is also worth noting that Hewlett-Packard introduced an infrared network for connecting computer peripherals without wires some years ago, but it never really caught on in a big way.

Undaunted by all this, in July 1999 the Bluetooth SIG issued a 1500-page specification of V1.0. Shortly thereafter, the IEEE standards group looking at wireless personal area networks, 802.15, adopted the Bluetooth document as a basis and began hacking on it. While it might seem strange to standardize something that already had a very detailed specification and no incompatible implementations that needed to be harmonized, history shows that having an open standard managed by a neutral body such as the IEEE often promotes the use of a technology. To be a bit more precise, it should be noted that the Bluetooth specification is for a complete system, from the physical layer to the application layer.

The IEEE 802.15 committee is standardizing only the physical and data link layers; the rest of the protocol stack falls outside its charter.

Even though IEEE approved the first PAN standard, 802.15.1, in 2002, the Bluetooth SIG is still active busy with improvements. Although the Bluetooth SIG and IEEE versions are not identical, it is hoped that they will soon converge to a single standard.

4.6.1 Bluetooth Architecture

Let us start our study of the Bluetooth system with a quick overview of what it contains and what it is intended to do. The basic unit of a Bluetooth system is a **piconet**, which consists of a master node and up to seven active slave nodes within a distance of 10 meters. Multiple piconets can exist in the same (large) room and can even be connected via a bridge node, as shown in Fig. 4-35. An interconnected collection of piconets is called a **scatternet**.

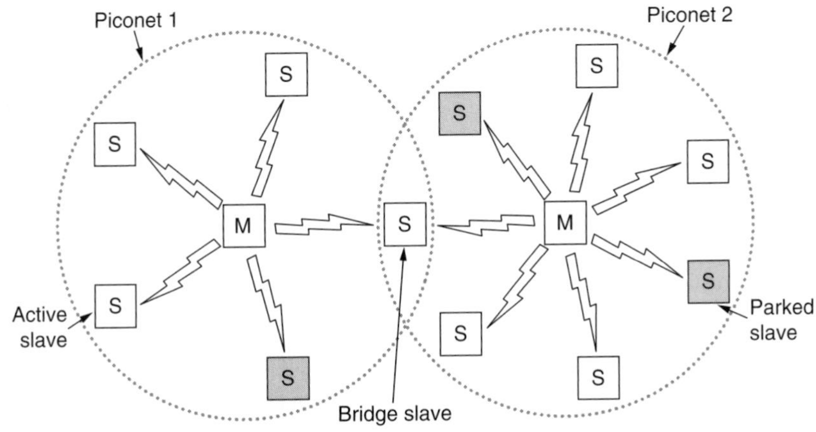

Figure 4-35. Two piconets can be connected to form a scatternet.

In addition to the seven active slave nodes in a piconet, there can be up to 255 parked nodes in the net. These are devices that the master has switched to a low-power state to reduce the drain on their batteries. In parked state, a device cannot do anything except respond to an activation or beacon signal from the master. There are also two intermediate power states, hold and sniff, but these will not concern us here.

The reason for the master/slave design is that the designers intended to facilitate the implementation of complete Bluetooth chips for under $5. The consequence of this decision is that the slaves are fairly dumb, basically just doing whatever the master tells them to do. At its heart, a piconet is a centralized TDM system, with the master controlling the clock and determining which device gets to communicate in which time slot. All communication is between the master and a slave; direct slave-slave communication is not possible.

4.6.2 Bluetooth Applications

Most network protocols just provide channels between communicating entities and let applications designers figure out what they want to use them for. For example, 802.11 does not specify whether users should use their notebook computers for reading e-mail, surfing the Web, or something else. In contrast, the Bluetooth V1.1 specification names 13 specific applications to be supported and provides different protocol stacks for each one. Unfortunately, this approach leads to a very large amount of complexity, which we will omit here. The 13 applications, which are called **profiles**, are listed in Fig. 4-36. By looking at them briefly now, we may see more clearly what the Bluetooth SIG is trying to accomplish.

Name	Description
Generic access	Procedures for link management
Service discovery	Protocol for discovering offered services
Serial port	Replacement for a serial port cable
Generic object exchange	Defines client-server relationship for object movement
LAN access	Protocol between a mobile computer and a fixed LAN
Dial-up networking	Allows a notebook computer to call via a mobile phone
Fax	Allows a mobile fax machine to talk to a mobile phone
Cordless telephony	Connects a handset and its local base station
Intercom	Digital walkie-talkie
Headset	Allows hands-free voice communication
Object push	Provides a way to exchange simple objects
File transfer	Provides a more general file transfer facility
Synchronization	Permits a PDA to synchronize with another computer

Figure 4-36. The Bluetooth profiles.

The generic access profile is not really an application, but rather the basis upon which the real applications are built. Its main job is to provide a way to establish and maintain secure links (channels) between the master and the slaves. Also relatively generic is the service discovery profile, which is used by devices to discover what services other devices have to offer. All Bluetooth devices are expected to implement these two profiles. The remaining ones are optional.

The serial port profile is a transport protocol that most of the remaining profiles use. It emulates a serial line and is especially useful for legacy applications that expect a serial line.

The generic object exchange profile defines a client-server relationship for moving data around. Clients initiate operations, but a slave can be either a client or a server. Like the serial port profile, it is a building block for other profiles.

The next group of three profiles is for networking. The LAN access profile allows a Bluetooth device to connect to a fixed network. This profile is a direct competitor to 802.11. The dial-up networking profile was the original motivation for the whole project. It allows a notebook computer to connect to a mobile phone containing a built-in modem without wires. The fax profile is similar to dial-up networking, except that it allows wireless fax machines to send and receive faxes using mobile phones without a wire between the two.

The next three profiles are for telephony. The cordless telephony profile provides a way to connect the handset of a cordless telephone to the base station. Currently, most cordless telephones cannot also be used as mobile phones, but in the future, cordless and mobile phones may merge. The intercom profile allows two telephones to connect as walkie-talkies. Finally, the headset profile provides hands-free voice communication between the headset and its base station, for example, for hands-free telephony while driving a car.

The remaining three profiles are for actually exchanging objects between two wireless devices. These could be business cards, pictures, or data files. The synchronization profile, in particular, is intended for loading data into a PDA or notebook computer when it leaves home and collecting data from it when it returns.

Was it really necessary to spell out all these applications in detail and provide different protocol stacks for each one? Probably not, but there were a number of different working groups that devised different parts of the standard, and each one just focused on its specific problem and generated its own profile. Think of this as Conway's law in action. (In the April 1968 issue of *Datamation* magazine, Melvin Conway observed that if you assign *n* people to write a compiler, you will get an *n*-pass compiler, or more generally, the software structure mirrors the structure of the group that produced it.) It would probably have been possible to get away with two protocol stacks instead of 13, one for file transfer and one for streaming real-time communication.

4.6.3 The Bluetooth Protocol Stack

The Bluetooth standard has many protocols grouped loosely into layers. The layer structure does not follow the OSI model, the TCP/IP model, the 802 model, or any other known model. However, IEEE is working on modifying Bluetooth to shoehorn it into the 802 model better. The basic Bluetooth protocol architecture as modified by the 802 committee is shown in Fig. 4-37.

The bottom layer is the physical radio layer, which corresponds fairly well to the physical layer in the OSI and 802 models. It deals with radio transmission and modulation. Many of the concerns here have to do with the goal of making the system inexpensive so that it can become a mass market item.

The baseband layer is somewhat analogous to the MAC sublayer but also includes elements of the physical layer. It deals with how the master controls time slots and how these slots are grouped into frames.

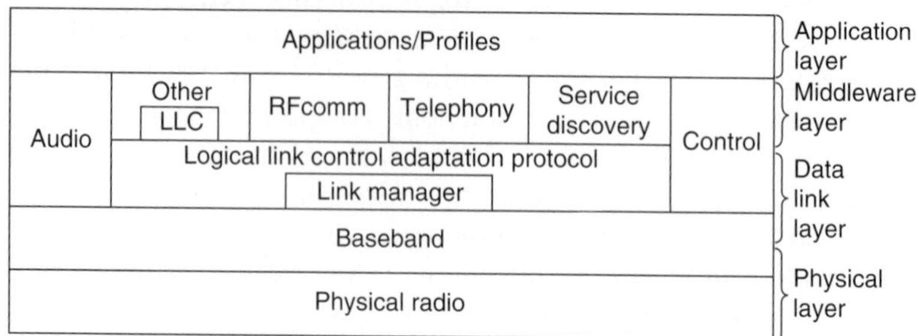

Figure 4-37. The 802.15 version of the Bluetooth protocol architecture.

Next comes a layer with a group of somewhat related protocols. The link manager handles the establishment of logical channels between devices, including power management, authentication, and quality of service. The logical link control adaptation protocol (often called L2CAP) shields the upper layers from the details of transmission. It is analogous to the standard 802 LLC sublayer, but technically different from it. As the names suggest, the audio and control protocols deal with audio and control, respectively. The applications can get at them directly, without having to go through the L2CAP protocol.

The next layer up is the middleware layer, which contains a mix of different protocols. The 802 LLC was inserted here by IEEE for compatibility with its other 802 networks. The RFcomm, telephony, and service discovery protocols are native. RFcomm (Radio Frequency communication) is the protocol that emulates the standard serial port found on PCs for connecting the keyboard, mouse, and modem, among other devices. It has been designed to allow legacy devices to use it easily. The telephony protocol is a real-time protocol used for the three speech-oriented profiles. It also manages call setup and termination. Finally, the service discovery protocol is used to locate services within the network.

The top layer is where the applications and profiles are located. They make use of the protocols in lower layers to get their work done. Each application has its own dedicated subset of the protocols. Specific devices, such as a headset, usually contain only those protocols needed by that application and no others.

In the following sections we will examine the three lowest layers of the Bluetooth protocol stack since these roughly correspond to the physical and MAC sublayers.

4.6.4 The Bluetooth Radio Layer

The radio layer moves the bits from master to slave, or vice versa. It is a low-power system with a range of 10 meters operating in the 2.4-GHz ISM band. The band is divided into 79 channels of 1 MHz each. Modulation is frequency shift keying, with 1 bit per Hz giving a gross data rate of 1 Mbps, but much of this spectrum is consumed by overhead. To allocate the channels fairly, frequency hopping spread spectrum is used with 1600 hops/sec and a dwell time of 625 μsec. All the nodes in a piconet hop simultaneously, with the master dictating the hop sequence.

Because both 802.11 and Bluetooth operate in the 2.4-GHz ISM band on the same 79 channels, they interfere with each other. Since Bluetooth hops far faster than 802.11, it is far more likely that a Bluetooth device will ruin 802.11 transmissions than the other way around. Since 802.11 and 802.15 are both IEEE standards, IEEE is looking for a solution to this problem, but it is not so easy to find since both systems use the ISM band for the same reason: no license is required there. The 802.11a standard uses the other (5 GHz) ISM band, but it has a much shorter range than 802.11b (due to the physics of radio waves), so using 802.11a is not a perfect solution for all cases. Some companies have solved the problem by banning Bluetooth altogether. A market-based solution is for the network with more power (politically and economically, not electrically) to demand that the weaker party modify its standard to stop interfering with it. Some thoughts on this matter are given in (Lansford et al., 2001).

4.6.5 The Bluetooth Baseband Layer

The baseband layer is the closest thing Bluetooth has to a MAC sublayer. It turns the raw bit stream into frames and defines some key formats. In the simplest form, the master in each piconet defines a series of 625 μsec time slots, with the master's transmissions starting in the even slots and the slaves' transmissions starting in the odd ones. This is traditional time division multiplexing, with the master getting half the slots and the slaves sharing the other half. Frames can be 1, 3, or 5 slots long.

The frequency hopping timing allows a settling time of 250–260 μsec per hop to allow the radio circuits to become stable. Faster settling is possible, but only at higher cost. For a single-slot frame, after settling, 366 of the 625 bits are left over. Of these, 126 are for an access code and the header, leaving 240 bits for data. When five slots are strung together, only one settling period is needed and a slightly shorter settling period is used, so of the $5 \times 625 = 3125$ bits in five time slots, 2781 are available to the baseband layer. Thus, longer frames are much more efficient than single-slot frames.

Each frame is transmitted over a logical channel, called a **link**, between the master and a slave. Two kinds of links exist. The first is the **ACL** (**Asynchronous Connection-Less**) link, which is used for packet-switched data available at irregular intervals. These data come from the L2CAP layer on the sending side and are delivered to the L2CAP layer on the receiving side. ACL traffic is delivered on a best-efforts basis. No guarantees are given. Frames can be lost and may have to be retransmitted. A slave may have only one ACL link to its master.

The other is the **SCO** (**Synchronous Connection Oriented**) link, for real-time data, such as telephone connections. This type of channel is allocated a fixed slot in each direction. Due to the time-critical nature of SCO links, frames sent over them are never retransmitted. Instead, forward error correction can be used to provide high reliability. A slave may have up to three SCO links with its master. Each SCO link can transmit one 64,000 bps PCM audio channel.

4.6.6 The Bluetooth L2CAP Layer

The L2CAP layer has three major functions. First, it accepts packets of up to 64 KB from the upper layers and breaks them into frames for transmission. At the far end, the frames are reassembled into packets again.

Second, it handles the multiplexing and demultiplexing of multiple packet sources. When a packet has been reassembled, the L2CAP layer determines which upper-layer protocol to hand it to, for example, RFcomm or telephony.

Third, L2CAP handles the quality of service requirements, both when links are established and during normal operation. Also negotiated at setup time is the maximum payload size allowed, to prevent a large-packet device from drowning a small-packet device. This feature is needed because not all devices can handle the 64-KB maximum packet.

4.6.7 The Bluetooth Frame Structure

There are several frame formats, the most important of which is shown in Fig. 4-38. It begins with an access code that usually identifies the master so that slaves within radio range of two masters can tell which traffic is for them. Next comes a 54-bit header containing typical MAC sublayer fields. Then comes the data field, of up to 2744 bits (for a five-slot transmission). For a single time slot, the format is the same except that the data field is 240 bits.

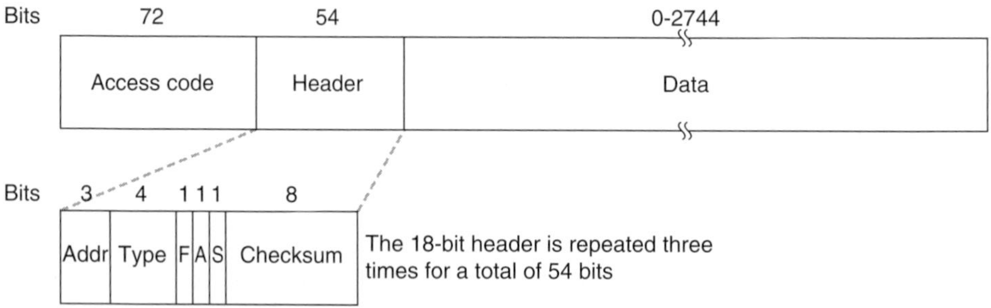

Figure 4-38. A typical Bluetooth data frame.

Let us take a quick look at the header. The *Address* field identifies which of the eight active devices the frame is intended for. The *Type* field identifies the frame type (ACL, SCO, poll, or null), the type of error correction used in the data field, and how many slots long the frame is. The *Flow* bit is asserted by a slave when its buffer is full and cannot receive any more data. This is a primitive form of flow control. The *Acknowledgement* bit is used to piggyback an ACK onto a frame. The *Sequence* bit is used to number the frames to detect retransmissions. The protocol is stop-and-wait, so 1 bit is enough. Then comes the 8-bit header *Checksum*. The entire 18-bit header is repeated three times to form the 54-bit header shown in Fig. 4-38. On the receiving side, a simple circuit examines all three copies of each bit. If all three are the same, the bit is accepted. If not, the majority opinion wins. Thus, 54 bits of transmission capacity are used to send 10 bits of header. The reason is that to reliably send data in a noisy environment using cheap, low-powered (2.5 mW) devices with little computing capacity, a great deal of redundancy is needed.

Various formats are used for the data field for ACL frames. The SCO frames are simpler though: the data field is always 240 bits. Three variants are defined, permitting 80, 160, or 240 bits of actual payload, with the rest being used for error correction. In the most reliable version (80-bit payload), the contents are just repeated three times, the same as the header.

Since the slave may use only the odd slots, it gets 800 slots/sec, just as the master does. With an 80-bit payload, the channel capacity from the slave is 64,000 bps and the channel capacity from the master is also 64,000 bps, exactly enough for a single full-duplex PCM voice channel (which is why a hop rate of 1600 hops/sec was chosen). These numbers mean that a full-duplex voice channel with 64,000 bps in each direction using the most reliable format completely saturates the piconet despite a raw bandwidth of 1 Mbps. For the least reliable variant (240 bits/slot with no redundancy at this level), three full-duplex voice channels can be supported at once, which is why a maximum of three SCO links is permitted per slave.

There is much more to be said about Bluetooth, but no more space to say it here. For more information, see (Bhagwat, 2001; Bisdikian, 2001; Bray and Sturman, 2002; Haartsen, 2000; Johansson et al., 2001; Miller and Bisdikian, 2001; and Sairam et al., 2002).

4.7 DATA LINK LAYER SWITCHING

Many organizations have multiple LANs and wish to connect them. LANs can be connected by devices called **bridges**, which operate in the data link layer. Bridges examine the data layer link addresses to do routing. Since they are not supposed to examine the payload field of the frames they route, they can transport IPv4 (used in the Internet now), IPv6 (will be used in the Internet in the future), AppleTalk, ATM, OSI, or any other kinds of packets. In contrast, *routers* examine the addresses in packets and route based on them. Although this seems like a clear division between bridges and routers, some modern developments, such as the advent of switched Ethernet, have muddied the waters, as we will see later. In the following sections we will look at bridges and switches, especially for connecting different 802 LANs. For a comprehensive treatment of bridges, switches, and related topics, see (Perlman, 2000).

Before getting into the technology of bridges, it is worthwhile taking a look at some common situations in which bridges are used. We will mention six reasons why a single organization may end up with multiple LANs.

First, many university and corporate departments have their own LANs, primarily to connect their own personal computers, workstations, and servers. Since the goals of the various departments differ, different departments choose different LANs, without regard to what other departments are doing. Sooner or later, there is a need for interaction, so bridges are needed. In this example, multiple LANs came into existence due to the autonomy of their owners.

Second, the organization may be geographically spread over several buildings separated by considerable distances. It may be cheaper to have separate LANs in each building and connect them with bridges and laser links than to run a single cable over the entire site.

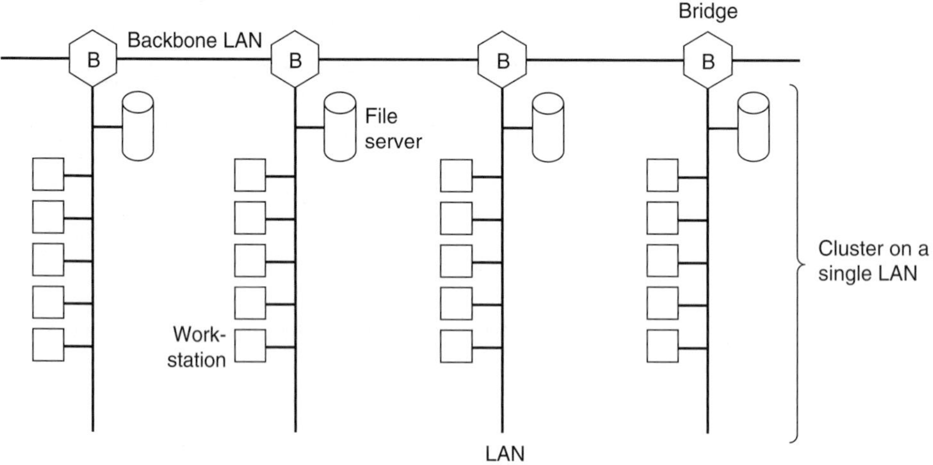

Figure 4-39. Multiple LANs connected by a backbone to handle a total load higher than the capacity of a single LAN.

Third, it may be necessary to split what is logically a single LAN into separate LANs to accommodate the load. At many universities, for example, thousands of workstations are available for student and faculty computing. Files are normally kept on file server machines and are downloaded to users' machines upon request. The enormous scale of this system precludes putting all the workstations on a single LAN—the total bandwidth needed is far too high. Instead, multiple LANs connected by bridges are used, as shown in Fig. 4-39. Each LAN contains a cluster of workstations with its own file server so that most traffic is restricted to a single LAN and does not add load to the backbone.

It is worth noting that although we usually draw LANs as multidrop cables as in Fig. 4-39 (the classic look), they are more often implemented with hubs or especially switches nowadays. However, a long multidrop cable with multiple machines plugged into it and a hub with the machines connected inside the hub are functionally identical. In both cases, all the machines belong to the same collision domain, and all use the CSMA/CD protocol to send frames. Switched LANs are different, however, as we saw before and will see again shortly.

Fourth, in some situations, a single LAN would be adequate in terms of the load, but the physical distance between the most distant machines is too great (e.g., more than 2.5 km for Ethernet). Even if laying the cable is easy to do, the network would not work due to the excessively long round-trip delay. The only solution is to partition the LAN and install bridges between the segments. Using bridges, the total physical distance covered can be increased.

Fifth, there is the matter of reliability. On a single LAN, a defective node that keeps outputting a continuous stream of garbage can cripple the LAN. Bridges can be inserted at critical places, like fire doors in a building, to prevent a single node that has gone berserk from bringing down the entire system. Unlike a repeater, which just copies whatever it sees, a bridge can be programmed to exercise some discretion about what it forwards and what it does not forward.

Sixth, and last, bridges can contribute to the organization's security. Most LAN interfaces have a **promiscuous mode**, in which *all* frames are given to the computer, not just those addressed to it. Spies and busybodies love this feature. By inserting bridges at various places and being careful not to forward sensitive traffic, a system administrator can isolate parts of the network so that its traffic cannot escape and fall into the wrong hands.

Ideally, bridges should be fully transparent, meaning it should be possible to move a machine from one cable segment to another without changing any hardware, software, or configuration tables. Also, it should be possible for machines on any segment to communicate with machines on any other segment without regard to the types of LANs being used on the two segments or on segments in between them. This goal is sometimes achieved, but not always.

4.7.1 Bridges from 802.x to 802.y

Having seen why bridges are needed, let us now turn to the question of how they work. Figure 4-40 illustrates the operation of a simple two-port bridge. Host *A* on a wireless (802.11) LAN has a packet to send to a fixed host, *B*, on an (802.3) Ethernet to which the wireless LAN is connected. The packet descends into the LLC sublayer and acquires an LLC header (shown in black in the figure). Then it passes into the MAC sublayer and an 802.11 header is prepended to it (also a trailer, not shown in the figure). This unit goes out over the air and is

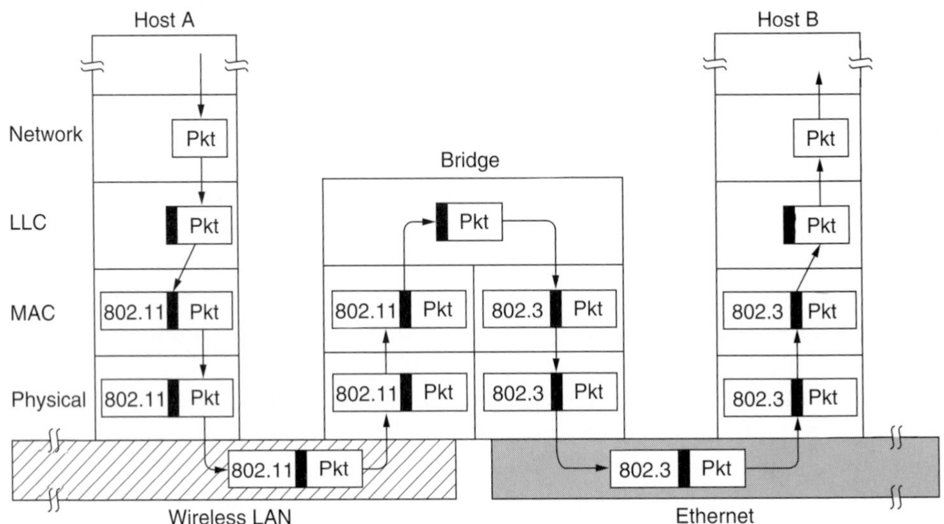

Figure 4-40. Operation of a LAN bridge from 802.11 to 802.3.

picked up by the base station, which sees that it needs to go to the fixed Ethernet. When it hits the bridge connecting the 802.11 network to the 802.3 network, it starts in the physical layer and works its way upward. In the MAC sublayer in the bridge, the 802.11 header is stripped off. The bare packet (with LLC header) is then handed off to the LLC sublayer in the bridge. In this example, the packet is destined for an 802.3 LAN, so it works its way down the 802.3 side of the bridge and off it goes on the Ethernet. Note that a bridge connecting k different LANs will have k different MAC sublayers and k different physical layers, one for each type.

So far it looks like moving a frame from one LAN to another is easy. Such is not the case. In this section we will point out some of the difficulties that one encounters when trying to build a bridge between the various 802 LANs (and MANs). We will focus on 802.3, 802.11, and 802.16, but there are others as well, each with its unique problems.

To start with, each of the LANs uses a different frame format (see Fig. 4-41). Unlike the differences between Ethernet, token bus, and token ring, which were due to history and big corporate egos, here the differences are to some extent legitimate. For example, the *Duration* field in 802.11 is there due to the MACAW protocol and makes no sense in Ethernet. As a result, any copying between different LANs requires reformatting, which takes CPU time, requires a new checksum calculation, and introduces the possibility of undetected errors due to bad bits in the bridge's memory.

A second problem is that interconnected LANs do not necessarily run at the same data rate. When forwarding a long run of back-to-back frames from a fast

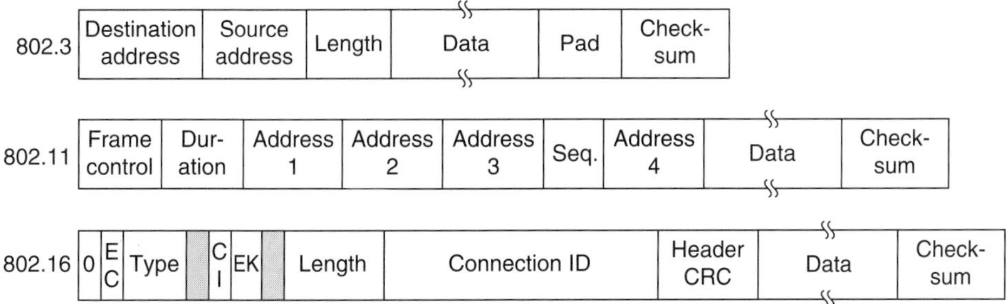

Figure 4-41. The IEEE 802 frame formats. The drawing is not to scale.

LAN to a slower one, the bridge will not be able to get rid of the frames as fast as they come in. For example, if a gigabit Ethernet is pouring bits into an 11-Mbps 802.11b LAN at top speed, the bridge will have to buffer them, hoping not to run out of memory. Bridges that connect three or more LANs have a similar problem when several LANs are trying to feed the same output LAN at the same time even if all the LANs run at the same speed.

A third problem, and potentially the most serious of all, is that different 802 LANs have different maximum frame lengths. An obvious problem arises when a long frame must be forwarded onto a LAN that cannot accept it. Splitting the frame into pieces is out of the question in this layer. All the protocols assume that frames either arrive or they do not. There is no provision for reassembling frames out of smaller units. This is not to say that such protocols could not be devised. They could be and have been. It is just that no data link protocols provide this feature, so bridges must keep their hands off the frame payload. Basically, there is no solution. Frames that are too large to be forwarded must be discarded. So much for transparency.

Another point is security. Both 802.11 and 802.16 support encryption in the data link layer. Ethernet does not. This means that the various encryption services available to the wireless networks are lost when traffic passes over an Ethernet. Worse yet, if a wireless station uses data link layer encryption, there will be no way to decrypt it when it arrives over an Ethernet. If the wireless station does not use encryption, its traffic will be exposed over the air link. Either way there is a problem.

One solution to the security problem is to do encryption in a higher layer, but then the 802.11 station has to know whether it is talking to another station on an 802.11 network (meaning use data link layer encryption) or not (meaning do not use it). Forcing the station to make a choice destroys transparency.

A final point is quality of service. Both 802.11 and 802.16 provide it in various forms, the former using PCF mode and the latter using constant bit rate connections. Ethernet has no concept of quality of service, so traffic from either of the others will lose its quality of service when passing over an Ethernet.

4.7.2 Local Internetworking

The previous section dealt with the problems encountered in connecting two different IEEE 802 LANs via a single bridge. However, in large organizations with many LANs, just interconnecting them all raises a variety of issues, even if they are all just Ethernet. Ideally, it should be possible to go out and buy bridges designed to the IEEE standard, plug the connectors into the bridges, and everything should work perfectly, instantly. There should be no hardware changes required, no software changes required, no setting of address switches, no downloading of routing tables or parameters, nothing. Just plug in the cables and walk away. Furthermore, the operation of the existing LANs should not be affected by the bridges at all. In other words, the bridges should be completely transparent (invisible to all the hardware and software). Surprisingly enough, this is actually possible. Let us now take a look at how this magic is accomplished.

In its simplest form, a transparent bridge operates in promiscuous mode, accepting every frame transmitted on all the LANs to which it is attached. As an example, consider the configuration of Fig. 4-42. Bridge B1 is connected to LANs 1 and 2, and bridge B2 is connected to LANs 2, 3, and 4. A frame arriving at bridge B1 on LAN 1 destined for *A* can be discarded immediately, because it is already on the correct LAN, but a frame arriving on LAN 1 for *C* or *F* must be forwarded.

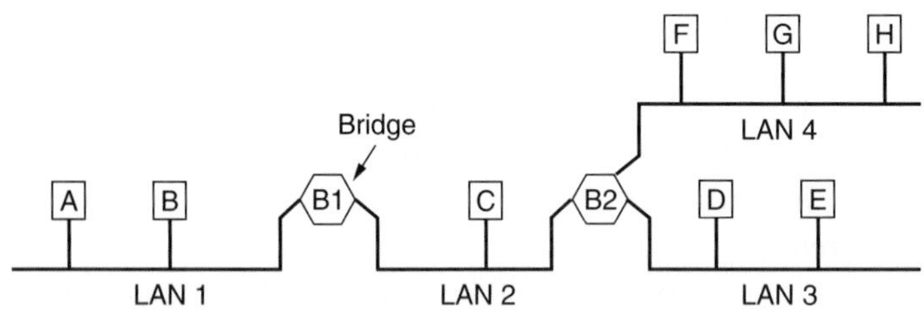

Figure 4-42. A configuration with four LANs and two bridges.

When a frame arrives, a bridge must decide whether to discard or forward it, and if the latter, on which LAN to put the frame. This decision is made by looking up the destination address in a big (hash) table inside the bridge. The table can list each possible destination and tell which output line (LAN) it belongs on. For example, B2's table would list *A* as belonging to LAN 2, since all B2 has to know is which LAN to put frames for *A* on. That, in fact, more forwarding happens later is not of interest to it.

When the bridges are first plugged in, all the hash tables are empty. None of the bridges know where any of the destinations are, so they use a flooding algorithm: every incoming frame for an unknown destination is output on all the LANs to which the bridge is connected except the one it arrived on. As time goes on, the bridges learn where destinations are, as described below. Once a destination is known, frames destined for it are put on only the proper LAN and are not flooded.

The algorithm used by the transparent bridges is **backward learning**. As mentioned above, the bridges operate in promiscuous mode, so they see every frame sent on any of their LANs. By looking at the source address, they can tell which machine is accessible on which LAN. For example, if bridge B1 in Fig. 4-42 sees a frame on LAN 2 coming from *C*, it knows that *C* must be reachable via LAN 2, so it makes an entry in its hash table noting that frames going to *C* should use LAN 2. Any subsequent frame addressed to *C* coming in on LAN 1 will be forwarded, but a frame for *C* coming in on LAN 2 will be discarded.

The topology can change as machines and bridges are powered up and down and moved around. To handle dynamic topologies, whenever a hash table entry is made, the arrival time of the frame is noted in the entry. Whenever a frame whose source is already in the table arrives, its entry is updated with the current time. Thus, the time associated with every entry tells the last time a frame from that machine was seen.

Periodically, a process in the bridge scans the hash table and purges all entries more than a few minutes old. In this way, if a computer is unplugged from its LAN, moved around the building, and plugged in again somewhere else, within a few minutes it will be back in normal operation, without any manual intervention. This algorithm also means that if a machine is quiet for a few minutes, any traffic sent to it will have to be flooded until it next sends a frame itself.

The routing procedure for an incoming frame depends on the LAN it arrives on (the source LAN) and the LAN its destination is on (the destination LAN), as follows:

1. If destination and source LANs are the same, discard the frame.
2. If the destination and source LANs are different, forward the frame.
3. If the destination LAN is unknown, use flooding.

As each frame arrives, this algorithm must be applied. Special-purpose VLSI chips do the lookup and update the table entry, all in a few microseconds.

4.7.3 Spanning Tree Bridges

To increase reliability, some sites use two or more bridges in parallel between pairs of LANs, as shown in Fig. 4-43. This arrangement, however, also introduces some additional problems because it creates loops in the topology.

A simple example of these problems can be seen by observing how a frame, *F*, with unknown destination is handled in Fig. 4-43. Each bridge, following the normal rules for handling unknown destinations, uses flooding, which in this example just means copying it to LAN 2. Shortly thereafter, bridge 1 sees F_2, a

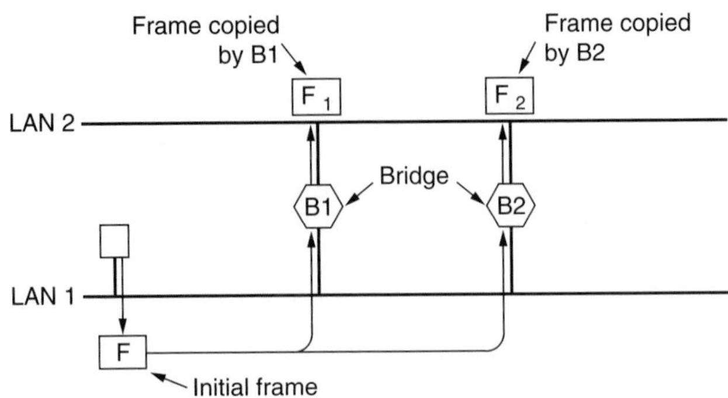

Figure 4-43. Two parallel transparent bridges.

frame with an unknown destination, which it copies to LAN 1, generating F_3 (not shown). Similarly, bridge 2 copies F_1 to LAN 1 generating F_4 (also not shown). Bridge 1 now forwards F_4 and bridge 2 copies F_3. This cycle goes on forever.

The solution to this difficulty is for the bridges to communicate with each other and overlay the actual topology with a spanning tree that reaches every LAN. In effect, some potential connections between LANs are ignored in the interest of constructing a fictitious loop-free topology. For example, in Fig. 4-44(a) we see nine LANs interconnected by ten bridges. This configuration can be abstracted into a graph with the LANs as the nodes. An arc connects any two LANs that are connected by a bridge. The graph can be reduced to a spanning tree by dropping the arcs shown as dotted lines in Fig. 4-44(b). Using this spanning tree, there is exactly one path from every LAN to every other LAN. Once the bridges have agreed on the spanning tree, all forwarding between LANs follows the spanning tree. Since there is a unique path from each source to each destination, loops are impossible.

To build the spanning tree, first the bridges have to choose one bridge to be the root of the tree. They make this choice by having each one broadcast its serial number, installed by the manufacturer and guaranteed to be unique worldwide. The bridge with the lowest serial number becomes the root. Next, a tree of shortest paths from the root to every bridge and LAN is constructed. This tree is the spanning tree. If a bridge or LAN fails, a new one is computed.

The result of this algorithm is that a unique path is established from every LAN to the root and thus to every other LAN. Although the tree spans all the LANs, not all the bridges are necessarily present in the tree (to prevent loops). Even after the spanning tree has been established, the algorithm continues to run during normal operation in order to automatically detect topology changes and update the tree. The distributed algorithm used for constructing the spanning tree was invented by Radia Perlman and is described in detail in (Perlman, 2000). It is standardized in IEEE 802.1D.

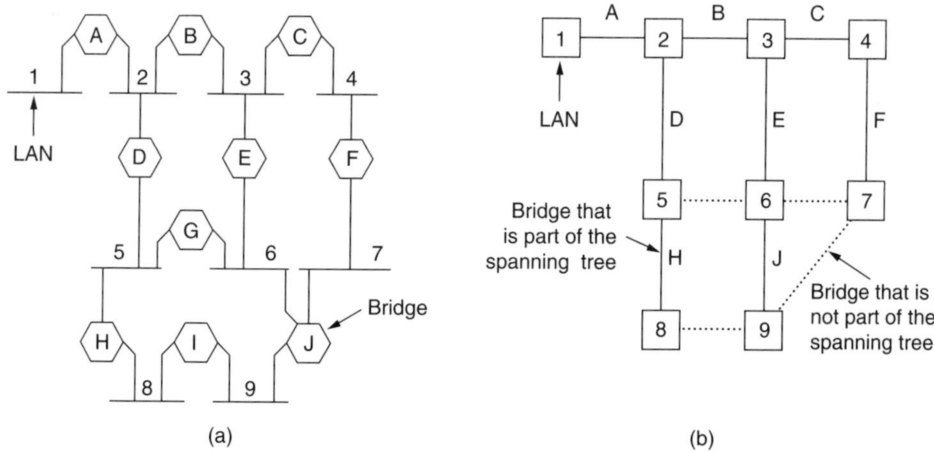

Figure 4-44. (a) Interconnected LANs. (b) A spanning tree covering the LANs. The dotted lines are not part of the spanning tree.

4.7.4 Remote Bridges

A common use of bridges is to connect two (or more) distant LANs. For example, a company might have plants in several cities, each with its own LAN. Ideally, all the LANs should be interconnected, so the complete system acts like one large LAN.

This goal can be achieved by putting a bridge on each LAN and connecting the bridges pairwise with point-to-point lines (e.g., lines leased from a telephone company). A simple system, with three LANs, is illustrated in Fig. 4-45. The usual routing algorithms apply here. The simplest way to see this is to regard the three point-to-point lines as hostless LANs. Then we have a normal system of six LANS interconnected by four bridges. Nothing in what we have studied so far says that a LAN must have hosts on it.

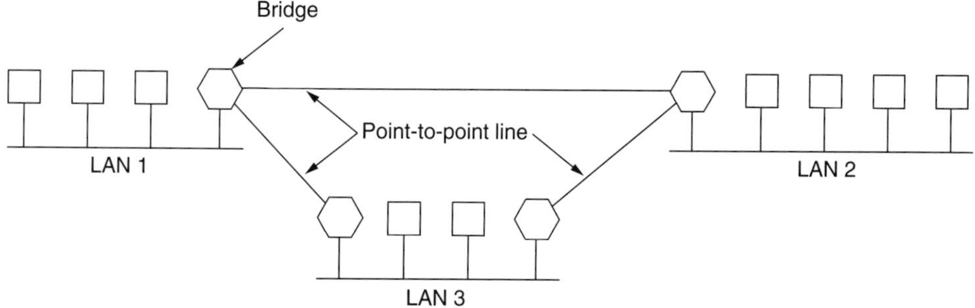

Figure 4-45. Remote bridges can be used to interconnect distant LANs.

Various protocols can be used on the point-to-point lines. One possibility is to choose some standard point-to-point data link protocol such as PPP, putting complete MAC frames in the payload field. This strategy works best if all the LANs are identical, and the only problem is getting frames to the correct LAN. Another option is to strip off the MAC header and trailer at the source bridge and put what is left in the payload field of the point-to-point protocol. A new MAC header and trailer can then be generated at the destination bridge. A disadvantage of this approach is that the checksum that arrives at the destination host is not the one computed by the source host, so errors caused by bad bits in a bridge's memory may not be detected.

4.7.5 Repeaters, Hubs, Bridges, Switches, Routers, and Gateways

So far in this book we have looked at a variety of ways to get frames and packets from one cable segment to another. We have mentioned repeaters, bridges, switches, hubs, routers, and gateways. All of these devices are in common use, but they all differ in subtle and not-so-subtle ways. Since there are so many of them, it is probably worth taking a look at them together to see what the similarities and differences are.

To start with, these devices operate in different layers, as illustrated in Fig. 4-46(a). The layer matters because different devices use different pieces of information to decide how to switch. In a typical scenario, the user generates some data to be sent to a remote machine. Those data are passed to the transport layer, which then adds a header, for example, a TCP header, and passes the resulting unit down to the network layer. The network layer adds its own header to form a network layer packet, for example, an IP packet. In Fig. 4-46(b) we see the IP packet shaded in gray. Then the packet goes to the data link layer, which adds its own header and checksum (CRC) and gives the resulting frame to the physical layer for transmission, for example, over a LAN.

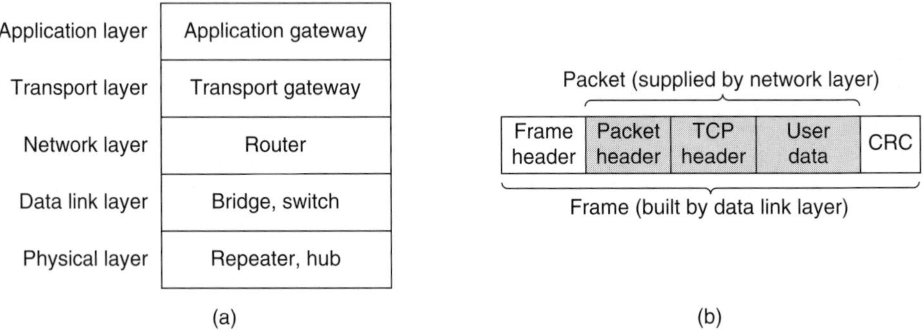

Figure 4-46. (a) Which device is in which layer. (b) Frames, packets, and headers.

Now let us look at the switching devices and see how they relate to the packets and frames. At the bottom, in the physical layer, we find the repeaters. These are analog devices that are connected to two cable segments. A signal appearing on one of them is amplified and put out on the other. Repeaters do not understand frames, packets, or headers. They understand volts. Classic Ethernet, for example, was designed to allow four repeaters, in order to extend the maximum cable length from 500 meters to 2500 meters.

Next we come to the hubs. A hub has a number of input lines that it joins electrically. Frames arriving on any of the lines are sent out on all the others. If two frames arrive at the same time, they will collide, just as on a coaxial cable. In other words, the entire hub forms a single collision domain. All the lines coming into a hub must operate at the same speed. Hubs differ from repeaters in that they do not (usually) amplify the incoming signals and are designed to hold multiple line cards each with multiple inputs, but the differences are slight. Like repeaters, hubs do not examine the 802 addresses or use them in any way. A hub is shown in Fig. 4-47(a).

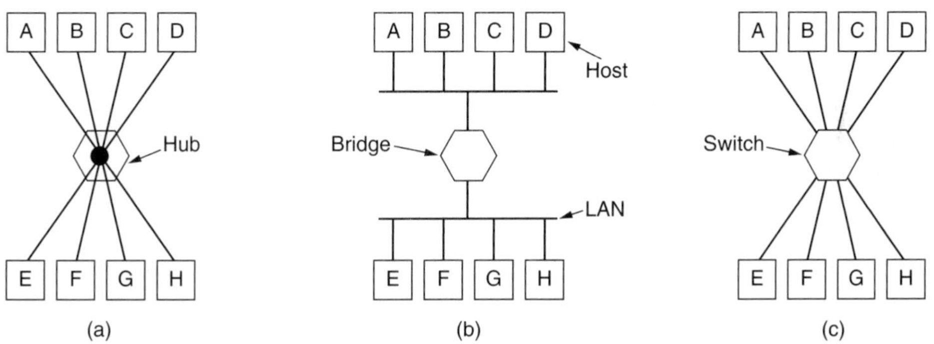

Figure 4-47. (a) A hub. (b) A bridge. (c) A switch.

Now let us move up to the data link layer where we find bridges and switches. We just studied bridges at some length. A bridge connects two or more LANs, as shown in Fig. 4-47(b). When a frame arrives, software in the bridge extracts the destination address from the frame header and looks it up in a table to see where to send the frame. For Ethernet, this address is the 48-bit destination address shown in Fig. 4-17. Like a hub, a modern bridge has line cards, usually for four or eight input lines of a certain type. A line card for Ethernet cannot handle, say, token ring frames, because it does not know where to find the destination address in the frame header. However, a bridge may have line cards for different network types and different speeds. With a bridge, each line is its own collision domain, in contrast to a hub.

Switches are similar to bridges in that both route on frame addresses. In fact, many people uses the terms interchangeably. The main difference is that a switch is most often used to connect individual computers, as shown in Fig. 4-47(c). As a consequence, when host *A* in Fig. 4-47(b) wants to send a frame to host *B*, the bridge gets the frame but just discards it. In contrast, in Fig. 4-47(c), the switch must actively forward the frame from *A* to *B* because there is no other way for the frame to get there. Since each switch port usually goes to a single computer, switches must have space for many more line cards than do bridges intended to connect only LANs. Each line card provides buffer space for frames arriving on its ports. Since each port is its own collision domain, switches never lose frames to collisions. However, if frames come in faster than they can be retransmitted, the switch may run out of buffer space and have to start discarding frames.

To alleviate this problem slightly, modern switches start forwarding frames as soon as the destination header field has come in, but before the rest of the frame has arrived (provided the output line is available, of course). These switches do not use store-and-forward switching. Sometimes they are referred to as **cut-through switches**. Usually, cut-through is handled entirely in hardware, whereas bridges traditionally contained an actual CPU that did store-and-forward switching in software. But since all modern bridges and switches contain special integrated circuits for switching, the difference between a switch and bridge is more a marketing issue than a technical one.

So far we have seen repeaters and hubs, which are quite similar, as well as bridges and switches, which are also very similar to each other. Now we move up to routers, which are different from all of the above. When a packet comes into a router, the frame header and trailer are stripped off and the packet located in the frame's payload field (shaded in Fig. 4-46) is passed to the routing software. This software uses the packet header to choose an output line. For an IP packet, the packet header will contain a 32-bit (IPv4) or 128-bit (IPv6) address, but not a 48-bit 802 address. The routing software does not see the frame addresses and does not even know whether the packet came in on a LAN or a point-to-point line. We will study routers and routing in Chap. 5.

Up another layer we find transport gateways. These connect two computers that use different connection-oriented transport protocols. For example, suppose a computer using the connection-oriented TCP/IP protocol needs to talk to a computer using the connection-oriented ATM transport protocol. The transport gateway can copy the packets from one connection to the other, reformatting them as need be.

Finally, application gateways understand the format and contents of the data and translate messages from one format to another. An e-mail gateway could translate Internet messages into SMS messages for mobile phones, for example.

4.7.6 Virtual LANs

In the early days of local area networking, thick yellow cables snaked through the cable ducts of many office buildings. Every computer they passed was plugged in. Often there were many cables, which were connected to a central backbone (as in Fig. 4-39) or to a central hub. No thought was given to which computer belonged on which LAN. All the people in adjacent offices were put on the same LAN whether they belonged together or not. Geography trumped logic.

With the advent of 10Base-T and hubs in the 1990s, all that changed. Buildings were rewired (at considerable expense) to rip out all the yellow garden hoses and install twisted pairs from every office to central wiring closets at the end of each corridor or in a central machine room, as illustrated in Fig. 4-48. If the Vice President in Charge of Wiring was a visionary, category 5 twisted pairs were installed; if he was a bean counter, the existing (category 3) telephone wiring was used (only to be replaced a few years later when fast Ethernet emerged).

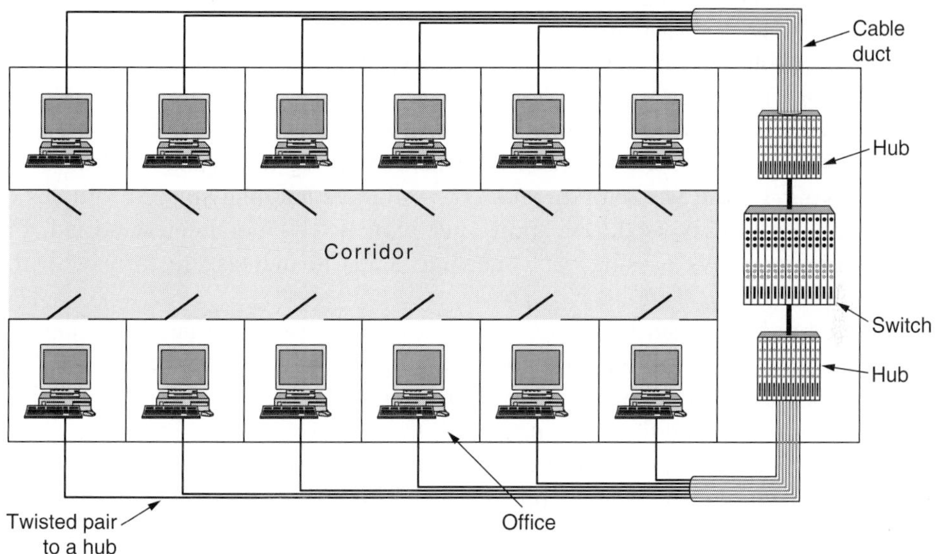

Figure 4-48. A building with centralized wiring using hubs and a switch.

With hubbed (and later, switched) Ethernet, it was often possible to configure LANs logically rather than physically. If a company wants *k* LANs, it buys *k* hubs. By carefully choosing which connectors to plug into which hubs, the occupants of a LAN can be chosen in a way that makes organizational sense, without too much regard to geography. Of course, if two people in the same department work in different buildings, they are probably going to be on different hubs and thus different LANs. Nevertheless, the situation is a lot better than having LAN membership entirely based on geography.

Does it matter who is on which LAN? After all, in virtually all organizations, all the LANs are interconnected. In short, yes, it often matters. Network administrators like to group users on LANs to reflect the organizational structure rather than the physical layout of the building for a variety of reasons. One issue is security. Any network interface can be put in promiscuous mode, copying all the traffic that comes down the pipe. Many departments, such as research, patents, and accounting, have information that they do not want passed outside their department. In such a situation, putting all the people in a department on a single LAN and not letting any of that traffic off the LAN makes sense. Management does not like hearing that such an arrangement is impossible unless all the people in each department are located in adjacent offices with no interlopers.

A second issue is load. Some LANs are more heavily used than others and it may be desirable to separate them at times. For example, if the folks in research are running all kinds of nifty experiments that sometimes get out of hand and saturate their LAN, the folks in accounting may not be enthusiastic about donating some of their capacity to help out.

A third issue is broadcasting. Most LANs support broadcasting, and many upper-layer protocols use this feature extensively. For example, when a user wants to send a packet to an IP address *x*, how does it know which MAC address to put in the frame? We will study this question in Chap. 5, but briefly summarized, the answer is that it broadcasts a frame containing the question: Who owns IP address *x*? Then it waits for an answer. And there are many more examples of where broadcasting is used. As more and more LANs get interconnected, the number of broadcasts passing each machine tends to increase linearly with the number of machines.

Related to broadcasts is the problem that once in a while a network interface will break down and begin generating an endless stream of broadcast frames. The result of this **broadcast storm** is that (1) the entire LAN capacity is occupied by these frames, and (2) all the machines on all the interconnected LANs are crippled just processing and discarding all the frames being broadcast.

At first it might appear that broadcast storms could be limited in scope by separating the LANs with bridges or switches, but if the goal is to achieve transparency (i.e., a machine can be moved to a different LAN across the bridge without anyone noticing it), then bridges have to forward broadcast frames.

Having seen why companies might want multiple LANs with restricted scope, let us get back to the problem of decoupling the logical topology from the physical topology. Suppose that a user gets shifted within the company from one department to another without changing offices or changes offices without changing departments. With hubbed wiring, moving the user to the correct LAN means having the network administrator walk down to the wiring closet and pull the connector for the user's machine from one hub and put it into a new hub.

In many companies, organizational changes occur all the time, meaning that system administrators spend a lot of time pulling out plugs and pushing them back in somewhere else. Also, in some cases, the change cannot be made at all because the twisted pair from the user's machine is too far from the correct hub (e.g., in the wrong building).

In response to user requests for more flexibility, network vendors began working on a way to rewire buildings entirely in software. The resulting concept is called a **VLAN (Virtual LAN)** and has even been standardized by the 802 committee. It is now being deployed in many organizations. Let us now take a look at it. For additional information about VLANs, see (Breyer and Riley, 1999; and Seifert, 2000).

VLANs are based on specially-designed VLAN-aware switches, although they may also have some hubs on the periphery, as in Fig. 4-48. To set up a VLAN-based network, the network administrator decides how many VLANs there will be, which computers will be on which VLAN, and what the VLANs will be called. Often the VLANs are (informally) named by colors, since it is then possible to print color diagrams showing the physical layout of the machines, with the members of the red LAN in red, members of the green LAN in green, and so on. In this way, both the physical and logical layouts are visible in a single view.

As an example, consider the four LANs of Fig. 4-49(a), in which eight of the machines belong to the G (gray) VLAN and seven of them belong to the W (white) VLAN. The four physical LANs are connected by two bridges, *B1* and *B2*. If centralized twisted pair wiring is used, there might also be four hubs (not shown), but logically a multidrop cable and a hub are the same thing. Drawing it this way just makes the figure a little less cluttered. Also, the term "bridge" tends to be used nowadays mostly when there are multiple machines on each port, as in this figure, but otherwise, "bridge" and "switch" are essentially interchangeable. Fig. 4-49(b) shows the same machines and same VLANs using switches with a single computer on each port.

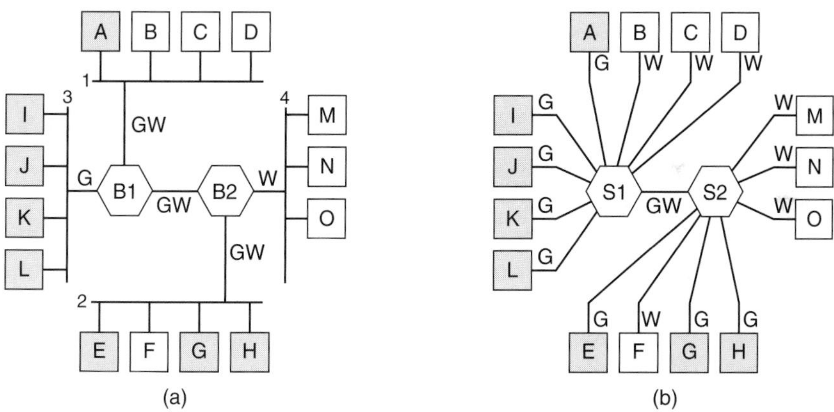

Figure 4-49. (a) Four physical LANs organized into two VLANs, gray and white, by two bridges. (b) The same 15 machines organized into two VLANs by switches.

To make the VLANs function correctly, configuration tables have to be set up in the bridges or switches. These tables tell which VLANs are accessible via which ports (lines). When a frame comes in from, say, the gray VLAN, it must be forwarded on all the ports marked G. This holds for ordinary (i.e., unicast) traffic as well as for multicast and broadcast traffic.

Note that a port may be labeled with multiple VLAN colors. We see this most clearly in Fig. 4-49(a). Suppose that machine *A* broadcasts a frame. Bridge *B1* receives the frame and sees that it came from a machine on the gray VLAN, so it forwards it on all ports labeled G (except the incoming port). Since *B1* has only two other ports and both of them are labeled G, the frame is sent to both of them.

At *B2* the story is different. Here the bridge knows that there are no gray machines on LAN 4, so the frame is not forwarded there. It goes only to LAN 2. If one of the users on LAN 4 should change departments and be moved to the gray VLAN, then the tables inside *B2* have to be updated to relabel that port as GW instead of W. If machine *F* goes gray, then the port to LAN 2 has to be changed to G instead of GW.

Now let us imagine that all the machines on both LAN 2 and LAN 4 become gray. Then not only do *B2*'s ports to LAN 2 and LAN 4 get marked G, but *B1*'s port to *B2* also has to change from GW to G since white frames arriving at *B1* from LANs 1 and 3 no longer have to be forwarded to *B2*. In Fig. 4-49(b) the same situation holds, only here all the ports that go to a single machine are labeled with a single color because only one VLAN is out there.

So far we have assumed that bridges and switches somehow know what color an incoming frame is. How do they know this? Three methods are in use, as follows:

1. Every port is assigned a VLAN color.

2. Every MAC address is assigned a VLAN color.

3. Every layer 3 protocol or IP address is assigned a VLAN color.

In the first method, each port is labeled with VLAN color. However, this method only works if all machines on a port belong to the same VLAN. In Fig. 4-49(a), this property holds for *B1* for the port to LAN 3 but not for the port to LAN 1.

In the second method, the bridge or switch has a table listing the 48-bit MAC address of each machine connected to it along with the VLAN that machine is on. Under these conditions, it is possible to mix VLANs on a physical LAN, as in LAN 1 in Fig. 4-49(a). When a frame arrives, all the bridge or switch has to do is to extract the MAC address and look it up in a table to see which VLAN the frame came from.

The third method is for the bridge or switch to examine the payload field of the frame, for example, to classify all IP machines as belonging to one VLAN and all AppleTalk machines as belonging to another. For the former, the IP address can also be used to identify the machine. This strategy is most useful when many machines are notebook computers that can be docked in any one of several places. Since each docking station has its own MAC address, just knowing which docking station was used does not say anything about which VLAN the notebook is on.

The only problem with this approach is that it violates the most fundamental rule of networking: independence of the layers. It is none of the data link layer's business what is in the payload field. It should not be examining the payload and certainly not be making decisions based on the contents. A consequence of using this approach is that a change to the layer 3 protocol (for example, an upgrade from IPv4 to IPv6) suddenly causes the switches to fail. Unfortunately, switches that work this way are on the market.

Of course, there is nothing wrong with routing based on IP addresses—nearly all of Chap. 5 is devoted to IP routing—but mixing the layers is looking for trouble. A switch vendor might pooh-pooh this argument saying that its switches understand both IPv4 and IPv6, so everything is fine. But what happens when IPv7 happens? The vendor would probably say: Buy new switches, is that so bad?

The IEEE 802.1Q Standard

Some more thought on this subject reveals that what actually matters is the VLAN of the frame itself, not the VLAN of the sending machine. If there were some way to identify the VLAN in the frame header, then the need to inspect the payload would vanish. For a new LAN, such as 802.11 or 802.16, it would have been easy enough to just add a VLAN field in the header. In fact, the *Connection Identifier* field in 802.16 is somewhat similar in spirit to a VLAN identifier. But what to do about Ethernet, which is the dominant LAN, and does not have any spare fields lying around for the VLAN identifier?

The IEEE 802 committee had this problem thrown into its lap in 1995. After much discussion, it did the unthinkable and changed the Ethernet header. The new format was published in IEEE standard **802.1Q**, issued in 1998. The new format contains a VLAN tag; we will examine it shortly. Not surprisingly, changing something as well established as the Ethernet header is not entirely trivial. A few questions that come to mind are:

1. Need we throw out several hundred million existing Ethernet cards?
2. If not, who generates the new fields?
3. What happens to frames that are already the maximum size?

Of course, the 802 committee was (only too painfully) aware of these problems and had to come up with solutions, which it did.

The key to the solution is to realize that the VLAN fields are only actually used by the bridges and switches and not by the user machines. Thus in Fig. 4-49, it is not really essential that they are present on the lines going out to the end stations as long as they are on the line between the bridges or switches. Thus, to use VLANs, the bridges or switches have to be VLAN aware, but that was already a requirement. Now we are only introducing the additional requirement that they are 802.1Q aware, which new ones already are.

As to throwing out all existing Ethernet cards, the answer is no. Remember that the 802.3 committee could not even get people to change the *Type* field into a *Length* field. You can imagine the reaction to an announcement that all existing Ethernet cards had to be thrown out. However, as new Ethernet cards come on the market, the hope is that they will be 802.1Q compliant and correctly fill in the VLAN fields.

So if the originator does not generate the VLAN fields, who does? The answer is that the first VLAN-aware bridge or switch to touch a frame adds them and the last one down the road removes them. But how does it know which frame belongs to which VLAN? Well, the first bridge or switch could assign a VLAN number to a port, look at the MAC address, or (heaven forbid) examine the payload. Until Ethernet cards are all 802.1Q compliant, we are kind of back where we started. The real hope here is that all gigabit Ethernet cards will be 802.1Q compliant from the start and that as people upgrade to gigabit Ethernet, 802.1Q will be introduced automatically. As to the problem of frames longer than 1518 bytes, 802.1Q just raised the limit to 1522 bytes.

During the transition process, many installations will have some legacy machines (typically classic or fast Ethernet) that are not VLAN aware and others (typically gigabit Ethernet) that are. This situation is illustrated in Fig. 4-50, where the shaded symbols are VLAN aware and the empty ones are not. For simplicity, we assume that all the switches are VLAN aware. If this is not the case, the first VLAN-aware switch can add the tags based on MAC or IP addresses.

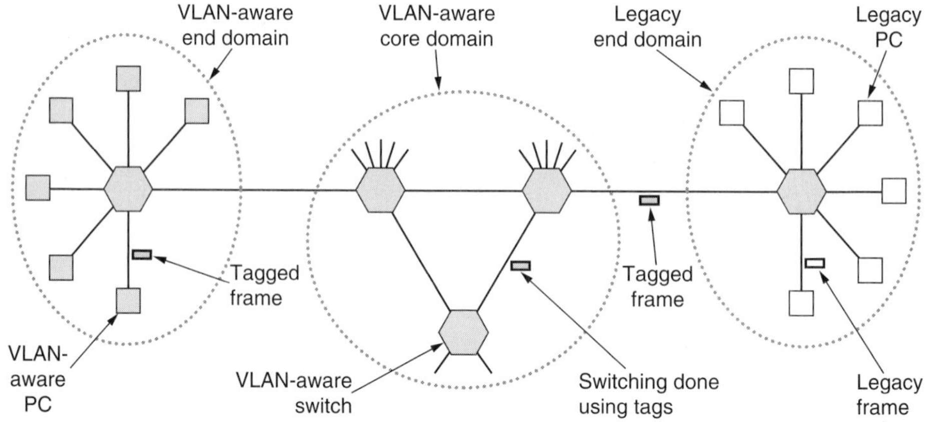

Figure 4-50. Transition from legacy Ethernet to VLAN-aware Ethernet. The shaded symbols are VLAN aware. The empty ones are not.

In this figure, VLAN-aware Ethernet cards generate tagged (i.e., 802.1Q) frames directly, and further switching uses these tags. To do this switching, the switches have to know which VLANs are reachable on each port, just as before. Knowing that a frame belongs to the gray VLAN does not help much until the switch knows which ports connect to machines on the gray VLAN. Thus, the switch needs a table indexed by VLAN telling which ports to use and whether they are VLAN aware or legacy.

When a legacy PC sends a frame to a VLAN-aware switch, the switch builds a new tagged frame based on its knowledge of the sender's VLAN (using the port, MAC address, or IP address). From that point on, it no longer matters that the sender was a legacy machine. Similarly, a switch that needs to deliver a tagged frame to a legacy machine has to reformat the frame in the legacy format before delivering it.

Now let us take a look at the 802.1Q frame format. It is shown in Fig. 4-51. The only change is the addition of a pair of 2-byte fields. The first one is the *VLAN protocol ID*. It always has the value 0x8100. Since this number is greater than 1500, all Ethernet cards interpret it as a type rather than a length. What a legacy card does with such a frame is moot since such frames are not supposed to be sent to legacy cards.

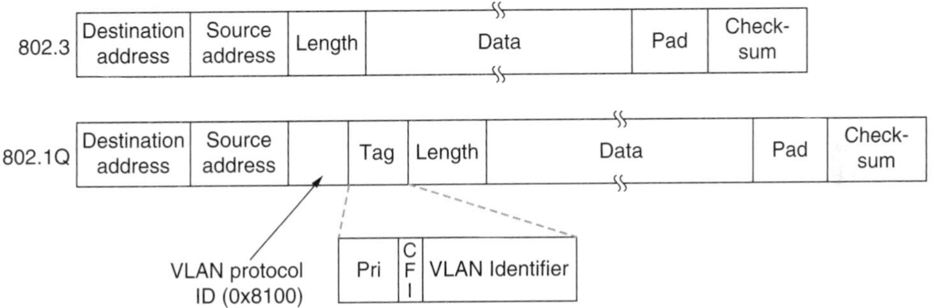

Figure 4-51. The 802.3 (legacy) and 802.1Q Ethernet frame formats.

The second 2-byte field contains three subfields. The main one is the *VLAN identifier*, occupying the low-order 12 bits. This is what the whole thing is about—which VLAN does the frame belong to? The 3-bit *Priority* field has nothing to do with VLANs at all, but since changing the Ethernet header is a once-in-a-decade event taking three years and featuring a hundred people, why not put in some other good things while you are at it? This field makes it possible to distinguish hard real-time traffic from soft real-time traffic from time-insensitive traffic in order to provide better quality of service over Ethernet. It is needed for voice over Ethernet (although in all fairness, IP has had a similar field for a quarter of a century and nobody ever used it).

The last bit, *CFI* (*Canonical Format Indicator*) should have been called the *CEI* (*Corporate Ego Indicator*). It was originally intended to indicate little-endian MAC addresses versus big-endian MAC addresses, but that use got lost in other controversies. Its presence now indicates that the payload contains a freeze-dried 802.5 frame that is hoping to find another 802.5 LAN at the destination while being carried by Ethernet in between. This whole arrangement, of course, has nothing whatsoever to do with VLANs. But standards' committee politics is not unlike regular politics: if you vote for my bit, I will vote for your bit.

As we mentioned above, when a tagged frame arrives at a VLAN-aware switch, the switch uses the VLAN ID as an index into a table to find out which ports to send it on. But where does the table come from? If it is manually constructed, we are back to square zero: manual configuration of bridges. The beauty of the transparent bridge is that it is plug-and-play and does not require any manual configuration. It would be a terrible shame to lose that property. Fortunately, VLAN-aware bridges can also autoconfigure themselves based on observing the tags that come by. If a frame tagged as VLAN 4 comes in on port 3, then apparently some machine on port 3 is on VLAN 4. The 802.1Q standard explains how to build the tables dynamically, mostly by referencing appropriate portions of Perlman's algorithm standardized in 802.1D.

Before leaving the subject of VLAN routing, it is worth making one last observation. Many people in the Internet and Ethernet worlds are fanatically in favor of connectionless networking and violently opposed to anything smacking of connections in the data link or network layers. Yet VLANs introduce something that is surprisingly similar to a connection. To use VLANs properly, each frame carries a new special identifier that is used as an index into a table inside the switch to look up where the frame is supposed to be sent. That is precisely what happens in connection-oriented networks. In connectionless networks, it is the destination address that is used for routing, not some kind of connection identifier. We will see more of this creeping connectionism in Chap. 5.

4.8 SUMMARY

Some networks have a single channel that is used for all communication. In these networks, the key design issue is the allocation of this channel among the competing stations wishing to use it. Numerous channel allocation algorithms have been devised. A summary of some of the more important channel allocation methods is given in Fig. 4-52.

The simplest allocation schemes are FDM and TDM. These are efficient when the number of stations is small and fixed and the traffic is continuous. Both are widely used under these circumstances, for example, for dividing up the bandwidth on telephone trunks.

When the number of stations is large and variable or the traffic is fairly bursty, FDM and TDM are poor choices. The ALOHA protocol, with and without slotting, has been proposed as an alternative. ALOHA and its many variants and derivatives have been widely discussed, analyzed, and used in real systems.

When the state of the channel can be sensed, stations can avoid starting a transmission while another station is transmitting. This technique, carrier sensing, has led to a variety of protocols that can be used on LANs and MANs.

Method	Description
FDM	Dedicate a frequency band to each station
WDM	A dynamic FDM scheme for fiber
TDM	Dedicate a time slot to each station
Pure ALOHA	Unsynchronized transmission at any instant
Slotted ALOHA	Random transmission in well-defined time slots
1-persistent CSMA	Standard carrier sense multiple access
Nonpersistent CSMA	Random delay when channel is sensed busy
P-persistent CSMA	CSMA, but with a probability of p of persisting
CSMA/CD	CSMA, but abort on detecting a collision
Bit map	Round-robin scheduling using a bit map
Binary countdown	Highest-numbered ready station goes next
Tree walk	Reduced contention by selective enabling
MACA, MACAW	Wireless LAN protocols
Ethernet	CSMA/CD with binary exponential backoff
FHSS	Frequency hopping spread spectrum
DSSS	Direct sequence spread spectrum
CSMA/CA	Carrier sense multiple access with collision avoidance

Figure 4-52. Channel allocation methods and systems for a common channel.

A class of protocols that eliminates contention altogether, or at least reduce it considerably, is well known. Binary countdown completely eliminates contention. The tree walk protocol reduces it by dynamically dividing the stations into two disjoint groups, one of which is permitted to transmit and one of which is not. It tries to make the division in such a way that only one station that is ready to send is permitted to do so.

Wireless LANs have their own problems and solutions. The biggest problem is caused by hidden stations, so CSMA does not work. One class of solutions, typified by MACA and MACAW, attempts to stimulate transmissions around the destination, to make CSMA work better. Frequency hopping spread spectrum and direct sequence spread spectrum are also used. IEEE 802.11 combines CSMA and MACAW to produce CSMA/CA.

Ethernet is the dominant form of local area networking. It uses CSMA/CD for channel allocation. Older versions used a cable that snaked from machine to machine, but now twisted pairs to hubs and switches are most common. Speeds have risen from 10 Mbps to 1 Gbps and are still rising.

Wireless LANs are becoming common, with 802.11 dominating the field. Its physical layer allows five different transmission modes, including infrared, various spread spectrum schemes, and a multichannel FDM system. It can operate with a base station in each cell, but it can also operate without one. The protocol is a variant of MACAW, with virtual carrier sensing.

Wireless MANs are starting to appear. These are broadband systems that use radio to replace the last mile on telephone connections. Traditional narrowband modulation techniques are used. Quality of service is important, with the 802.16 standard defining four classes (constant bit rate, two variable bit rate, and one best efforts).

The Bluetooth system is also wireless but aimed more at the desktop, for connecting headsets and other peripherals to computers without wires. It is also intended to connect peripherals, such as fax machines, to mobile telephones. Like 801.11, it uses frequency hopping spread spectrum in the ISM band. Due to the expected noise level of many environments and need for real-time interaction, elaborate forward error correction is built into its various protocols.

With so many different LANs, a way is needed to interconnect them all. Bridges and switches are used for this purpose. The spanning tree algorithm is used to build plug-and-play bridges. A new development in the LAN interconnection world is the VLAN, which separates the logical topology of the LANs from their physical topology. A new format for Ethernet frames (802.1Q) has been introduced to ease the introduction of VLANs into organizations.

PROBLEMS

1. For this problem, use a formula from this chapter, but first state the formula. Frames arrive randomly at a 100-Mbps channel for transmission. If the channel is busy when a frame arrives, it waits its turn in a queue. Frame length is exponentially distributed with a mean of 10,000 bits/frame. For each of the following frame arrival rates, give the delay experienced by the average frame, including both queueing time and transmission time.
(a) 90 frames/sec.
(b) 900 frames/sec.
(c) 9000 frames/sec.

2. A group of N stations share a 56-kbps pure ALOHA channel. Each station outputs a 1000-bit frame on an average of once every 100 sec, even if the previous one has not yet been sent (e.g., the stations can buffer outgoing frames). What is the maximum value of N?

3. Consider the delay of pure ALOHA versus slotted ALOHA at low load. Which one is less? Explain your answer.

4. Ten thousand airline reservation stations are competing for the use of a single slotted ALOHA channel. The average station makes 18 requests/hour. A slot is 125 μsec. What is the approximate total channel load?

5. A large population of ALOHA users manages to generate 50 requests/sec, including both originals and retransmissions. Time is slotted in units of 40 msec.
(a) What is the chance of success on the first attempt?
(b) What is the probability of exactly k collisions and then a success?
(c) What is the expected number of transmission attempts needed?

6. Measurements of a slotted ALOHA channel with an infinite number of users show that 10 percent of the slots are idle.
(a) What is the channel load, G?
(b) What is the throughput?
(c) Is the channel underloaded or overloaded?

7. In an infinite-population slotted ALOHA system, the mean number of slots a station waits between a collision and its retransmission is 4. Plot the delay versus throughput curve for this system.

8. How long does a station, s, have to wait in the worst case before it can start transmitting its frame over a LAN that uses
(a) the basic bit-map protocol?
(b) Mok and Ward's protocol with permuting virtual station numbers?

9. A LAN uses Mok and Ward's version of binary countdown. At a certain instant, the ten stations have the virtual station numbers 8, 2, 4, 5, 1, 7, 3, 6, 9, and 0. The next three stations to send are 4, 3, and 9, in that order. What are the new virtual station numbers after all three have finished their transmissions?

10. Sixteen stations, numbered 1 through 16, are contending for the use of a shared channel by using the adaptive tree walk protocol. If all the stations whose addresses are prime numbers suddenly become ready at once, how many bit slots are needed to resolve the contention?

11. A collection of 2^n stations uses the adaptive tree walk protocol to arbitrate access to a shared cable. At a certain instant, two of them become ready. What are the minimum, maximum, and mean number of slots to walk the tree if $2^n \gg 1$?

12. The wireless LANs that we studied used protocols such as MACA instead of using CSMA/CD. Under what conditions, if any, would it be possible to use CSMA/CD instead?

13. What properties do the WDMA and GSM channel access protocols have in common? See Chap. 2 for GSM.

14. Six stations, A through F, communicate using the MACA protocol. Is it possible that two transmissions take place simultaneously? Explain your answer.

15. A seven-story office building has 15 adjacent offices per floor. Each office contains a wall socket for a terminal in the front wall, so the sockets form a rectangular grid in the vertical plane, with a separation of 4 m between sockets, both horizontally and vertically. Assuming that it is feasible to run a straight cable between any pair of sockets, horizontally, vertically, or diagonally, how many meters of cable are needed to connect all sockets using
(a) a star configuration with a single router in the middle?
(b) an 802.3 LAN?

16. What is the baud rate of the standard 10-Mbps Ethernet?

17. Sketch the Manchester encoding for the bit stream: 0001110101.

18. Sketch the differential Manchester encoding for the bit stream of the previous problem. Assume the line is initially in the low state.

19. A 1-km-long, 10-Mbps CSMA/CD LAN (not 802.3) has a propagation speed of 200 m/μsec. Repeaters are not allowed in this system. Data frames are 256 bits long, including 32 bits of header, checksum, and other overhead. The first bit slot after a successful transmission is reserved for the receiver to capture the channel in order to send a 32-bit acknowledgement frame. What is the effective data rate, excluding overhead, assuming that there are no collisions?

20. Two CSMA/CD stations are each trying to transmit long (multiframe) files. After each frame is sent, they contend for the channel, using the binary exponential backoff algorithm. What is the probability that the contention ends on round *k*, and what is the mean number of rounds per contention period?

21. Consider building a CSMA/CD network running at 1 Gbps over a 1-km cable with no repeaters. The signal speed in the cable is 200,000 km/sec. What is the minimum frame size?

22. An IP packet to be transmitted by Ethernet is 60 bytes long, including all its headers. If LLC is not in use, is padding needed in the Ethernet frame, and if so, how many bytes?

23. Ethernet frames must be at least 64 bytes long to ensure that the transmitter is still going in the event of a collision at the far end of the cable. Fast Ethernet has the same 64-byte minimum frame size but can get the bits out ten times faster. How is it possible to maintain the same minimum frame size?

24. Some books quote the maximum size of an Ethernet frame as 1518 bytes instead of 1500 bytes. Are they wrong? Explain your answer.

25. The 1000Base-SX specification states that the clock shall run at 1250 MHz, even though gigabit Ethernet is only supposed to deliver 1 Gbps. Is this higher speed to provide for an extra margin of safety? If not, what is going on here?

26. How many frames per second can gigabit Ethernet handle? Think carefully and take into account all the relevant cases. *Hint*: the fact that it is *gigabit* Ethernet matters.

27. Name two networks that allow frames to be packed back-to-back. Why is this feature worth having?

28. In Fig. 4-27, four stations, *A*, *B*, *C*, and *D*, are shown. Which of the last two stations do you think is closest to *A* and why?

29. Suppose that an 11-Mbps 802.11b LAN is transmitting 64-byte frames back-to-back over a radio channel with a bit error rate of 10^{-7}. How many frames per second will be damaged on average?

30. An 802.16 network has a channel width of 20 MHz. How many bits/sec can be sent to a subscriber station?

31. IEEE 802.16 supports four service classes. Which service class is the best choice for sending uncompressed video?

32. Give two reasons why networks might use an error-correcting code instead of error detection and retransmission.

33. From Fig. 4-35, we see that a Bluetooth device can be in two piconets at the same time. Is there any reason why one device cannot be the master in both of them at the same time?

34. Figure 4-25 shows several physical layer protocols. Which of these is closest to the Bluetooth physical layer protocol? What is the biggest difference between the two?

35. Bluetooth supports two types of links between a master and a slave. What are they and what is each one used for?

36. Beacon frames in the frequency hopping spread spectrum variant of 802.11 contain the dwell time. Do you think the analogous beacon frames in Bluetooth also contain the dwell time? Discuss your answer.

37. Consider the interconnected LANs showns in Fig. 4-44. Assume that hosts *a* and *b* are on LAN 1, *c* is on LAN 2, and *d* is on LAN 8. Initially, hash tables in all bridges are empty and the spanning tree shown in Fig 4-44(b) is used. Show how the hash tables of different bridges change after each of the following events happen in sequence, first (a) then (b) and so on.
(a) *a* sends to *d*.
(b) *c* sends to *a*.
(c) *d* sends to *c*.
(d) *d* moves to LAN 6.
(e) *d* sends to *a*.

38. One consequence of using a spanning tree to forward frames in an extended LAN is that some bridges may not participate at all in forwarding frames. Identify three such bridges in Fig. 4-44. Is there any reason for keeping these bridges, even though they are not used for forwarding?

39. Imagine that a switch has line cards for four input lines. It frequently happens that a frame arriving on one of the lines has to exit on another line on the same card. What choices is the switch designer faced with as a result of this situation?

40. A switch designed for use with fast Ethernet has a backplane that can move 10 Gbps. How many frames/sec can it handle in the worst case?

41. Consider the network of Fig. 4-49(a). If machine *J* were to suddenly become white, would any changes be needed to the labeling? If so, what?

42. Briefly describe the difference between store-and-forward and cut-through switches.

43. Store-and-forward switches have an advantage over cut-through switches with respect to damaged frames. Explain what it is.

44. To make VLANs work, configuration tables are needed in the switches and bridges. What if the VLANs of Fig. 4-49(a) use hubs rather than multidrop cables? Do the hubs need configuration tables, too? Why or why not?

45. In Fig. 4-50 the switch in the legacy end domain on the right is a VLAN-aware switch. Would it be possible to use a legacy switch there? If so, how would that work? If not, why not?

46. Write a program to simulate the behavior of the CSMA/CD protocol over Ethernet when there are *N* stations ready to transmit while a frame is being transmitted. Your program should report the times when each station successfully starts sending its frame. Assume that a clock tick occurs once every slot time (51.2 microseconds) and a collision detection and sending of jamming sequence takes one slot time. All frames are the maximum length allowed.

5

THE NETWORK LAYER

The network layer is concerned with getting packets from the source all the way to the destination. Getting to the destination may require making many hops at intermediate routers along the way. This function clearly contrasts with that of the data link layer, which has the more modest goal of just moving frames from one end of a wire to the other. Thus, the network layer is the lowest layer that deals with end-to-end transmission.

To achieve its goals, the network layer must know about the topology of the communication subnet (i.e., the set of all routers) and choose appropriate paths through it. It must also take care to choose routes to avoid overloading some of the communication lines and routers while leaving others idle. Finally, when the source and destination are in different networks, new problems occur. It is up to the network layer to deal with them. In this chapter we will study all these issues and illustrate them, primarily using the Internet and its network layer protocol, IP, although wireless networks will also be addressed.

5.1 NETWORK LAYER DESIGN ISSUES

In the following sections we will provide an introduction to some of the issues that the designers of the network layer must grapple with. These issues include the service provided to the transport layer and the internal design of the subnet.

5.1.1 Store-and-Forward Packet Switching

But before starting to explain the details of the network layer, it is probably worth restating the context in which the network layer protocols operate. This context can be seen in Fig. 5-1. The major components of the system are the carrier's equipment (routers connected by transmission lines), shown inside the shaded oval, and the customers' equipment, shown outside the oval. Host *H1* is directly connected to one of the carrier's routers, *A*, by a leased line. In contrast, *H2* is on a LAN with a router, *F*, owned and operated by the customer. This router also has a leased line to the carrier's equipment. We have shown *F* as being outside the oval because it does not belong to the carrier, but in terms of construction, software, and protocols, it is probably no different from the carrier's routers. Whether it belongs to the subnet is arguable, but for the purposes of this chapter, routers on customer premises are considered part of the subnet because they run the same algorithms as the carrier's routers (and our main concern here is algorithms).

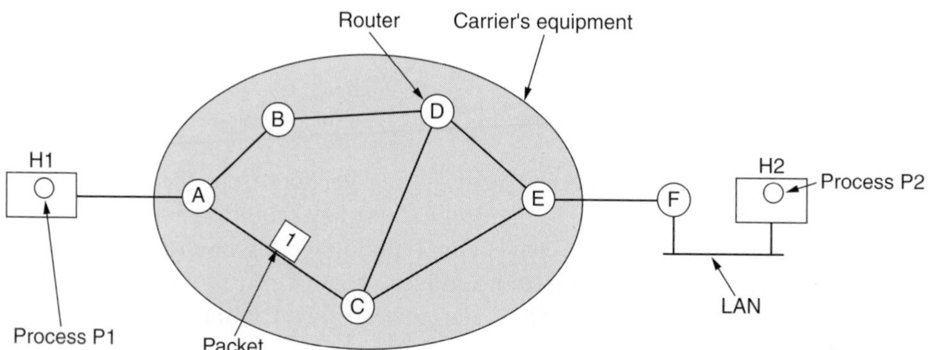

Figure 5-1. The environment of the network layer protocols.

This equipment is used as follows. A host with a packet to send transmits it to the nearest router, either on its own LAN or over a point-to-point link to the carrier. The packet is stored there until it has fully arrived so the checksum can be verified. Then it is forwarded to the next router along the path until it reaches the destination host, where it is delivered. This mechanism is store-and-forward packet switching, as we have seen in previous chapters.

5.1.2 Services Provided to the Transport Layer

The network layer provides services to the transport layer at the network layer/transport layer interface. An important question is what kind of services the network layer provides to the transport layer. The network layer services have been designed with the following goals in mind.

1. The services should be independent of the router technology.
2. The transport layer should be shielded from the number, type, and topology of the routers present.
3. The network addresses made available to the transport layer should use a uniform numbering plan, even across LANs and WANs.

Given these goals, the designers of the network layer have a lot of freedom in writing detailed specifications of the services to be offered to the transport layer. This freedom often degenerates into a raging battle between two warring factions. The discussion centers on whether the network layer should provide connection-oriented service or connectionless service.

One camp (represented by the Internet community) argues that the routers' job is moving packets around and nothing else. In their view (based on 30 years of actual experience with a real, working computer network), the subnet is inherently unreliable, no matter how it is designed. Therefore, the hosts should accept the fact that the network is unreliable and do error control (i.e., error detection and correction) and flow control themselves.

This viewpoint leads quickly to the conclusion that the network service should be connectionless, with primitives SEND PACKET and RECEIVE PACKET and little else. In particular, no packet ordering and flow control should be done, because the hosts are going to do that anyway, and there is usually little to be gained by doing it twice. Furthermore, each packet must carry the full destination address, because each packet sent is carried independently of its predecessors, if any.

The other camp (represented by the telephone companies) argues that the subnet should provide a reliable, connection-oriented service. They claim that 100 years of successful experience with the worldwide telephone system is an excellent guide. In this view, quality of service is the dominant factor, and without connections in the subnet, quality of service is very difficult to achieve, especially for real-time traffic such as voice and video.

These two camps are best exemplified by the Internet and ATM. The Internet offers connectionless network-layer service; ATM networks offer connection-oriented network-layer service. However, it is interesting to note that as quality-of-service guarantees are becoming more and more important, the Internet is evolving. In particular, it is starting to acquire properties normally associated with connection-oriented service, as we will see later. Actually, we got an inkling of this evolution during our study of VLANs in Chap. 4.

5.1.3 Implementation of Connectionless Service

Having looked at the two classes of service the network layer can provide to its users, it is time to see how this layer works inside. Two different organizations are possible, depending on the type of service offered. If connectionless service is offered, packets are injected into the subnet individually and routed independently of each other. No advance setup is needed. In this context, the packets are frequently called **datagrams** (in analogy with telegrams) and the subnet is called a **datagram subnet**. If connection-oriented service is used, a path from the source router to the destination router must be established before any data packets can be sent. This connection is called a **VC** (**virtual circuit**), in analogy with the physical circuits set up by the telephone system, and the subnet is called a **virtual-circuit subnet**. In this section we will examine datagram subnets; in the next one we will examine virtual-circuit subnets.

Let us now see how a datagram subnet works. Suppose that the process *P1* in Fig. 5-2 has a long message for *P2*. It hands the message to the transport layer with instructions to deliver it to process *P2* on host *H2*. The transport layer code runs on *H1*, typically within the operating system. It prepends a transport header to the front of the message and hands the result to the network layer, probably just another procedure within the operating system.

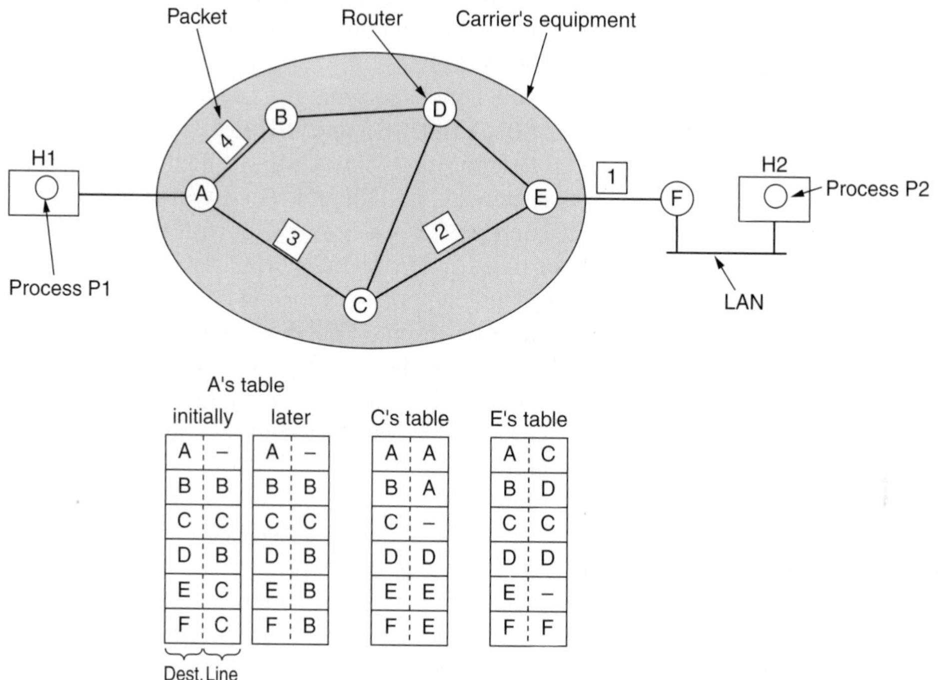

Dest.	A's table initially	A's table later	C's table	E's table
A	–	–	A	C
B	B	B	A	D
C	C	C	–	C
D	B	B	D	D
E	C	B	E	–
F	C	B	E	F

Figure 5-2. Routing within a datagram subnet.

Let us assume that the message is four times longer than the maximum packet size, so the network layer has to break it into four packets, 1, 2, 3, and 4 and sends each of them in turn to router *A* using some point-to-point protocol, for example, PPP. At this point the carrier takes over. Every router has an internal table telling it where to send packets for each possible destination. Each table entry is a pair consisting of a destination and the outgoing line to use for that destination. Only directly-connected lines can be used. For example, in Fig. 5-2, *A* has only two outgoing lines—to *B* and *C*—so every incoming packet must be sent to one of these routers, even if the ultimate destination is some other router. *A*'s initial routing table is shown in the figure under the label "initially."

As they arrived at *A*, packets 1, 2, and 3 were stored briefly (to verify their checksums). Then each was forwarded to *C* according to *A*'s table. Packet 1 was then forwarded to *E* and then to *F*. When it got to *F*, it was encapsulated in a data link layer frame and sent to *H2* over the LAN. Packets 2 and 3 follow the same route.

However, something different happened to packet 4. When it got to *A* it was sent to router *B*, even though it is also destined for *F*. For some reason, *A* decided to send packet 4 via a different route than that of the first three. Perhaps it learned of a traffic jam somewhere along the *ACE* path and updated its routing table, as shown under the label "later." The algorithm that manages the tables and makes the routing decisions is called the **routing algorithm**. Routing algorithms are one of the main things we will study in this chapter.

5.1.4 Implementation of Connection-Oriented Service

For connection-oriented service, we need a virtual-circuit subnet. Let us see how that works. The idea behind virtual circuits is to avoid having to choose a new route for every packet sent, as in Fig. 5-2. Instead, when a connection is established, a route from the source machine to the destination machine is chosen as part of the connection setup and stored in tables inside the routers. That route is used for all traffic flowing over the connection, exactly the same way that the telephone system works. When the connection is released, the virtual circuit is also terminated. With connection-oriented service, each packet carries an identifier telling which virtual circuit it belongs to.

As an example, consider the situation of Fig. 5-3. Here, host *H1* has established connection 1 with host *H2*. It is remembered as the first entry in each of the routing tables. The first line of *A*'s table says that if a packet bearing connection identifier 1 comes in from *H1*, it is to be sent to router *C* and given connection identifier 1. Similarly, the first entry at *C* routes the packet to *E*, also with connection identifier 1.

Now let us consider what happens if *H3* also wants to establish a connection to *H2*. It chooses connection identifier 1 (because it is initiating the connection and this is its only connection) and tells the subnet to establish the virtual circuit. This leads to the second row in the tables. Note that we have a conflict here because although *A* can easily distinguish connection 1 packets from *H1* from connection 1 packets from *H3*, *C* cannot do this. For this reason, *A* assigns a different

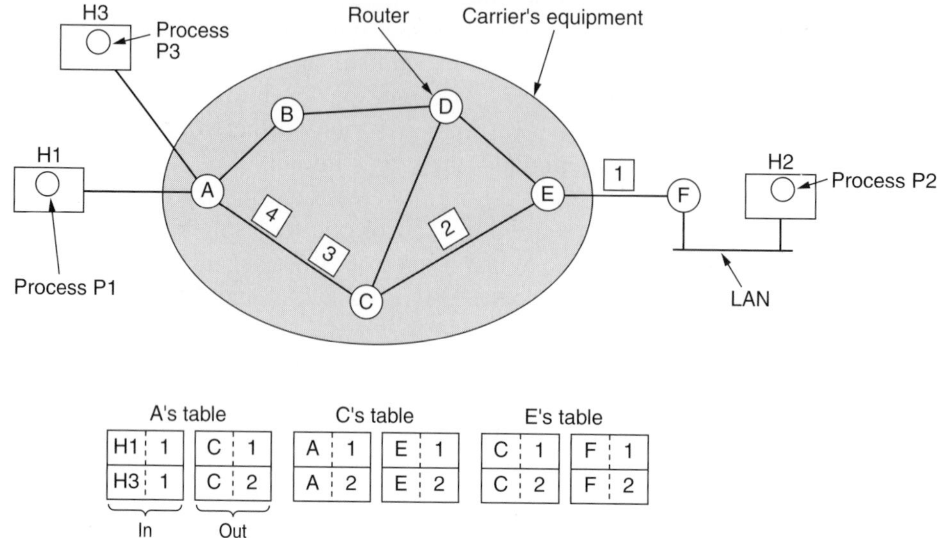

A's table		C's table		E's table	
H1 ⁞ 1	C ⁞ 1	A ⁞ 1	E ⁞ 1	C ⁞ 1	F ⁞ 1
H3 ⁞ 1	C ⁞ 2	A ⁞ 2	E ⁞ 2	C ⁞ 2	F ⁞ 2
In	Out				

Figure 5-3. Routing within a virtual-circuit subnet.

connection identifier to the outgoing traffic for the second connection. Avoiding conflicts of this kind is why routers need the ability to replace connection identifiers in outgoing packets. In some contexts, this is called label switching.

5.1.5 Comparison of Virtual-Circuit and Datagram Subnets

Both virtual circuits and datagrams have their supporters and their detractors. We will now attempt to summarize the arguments both ways. The major issues are listed in Fig. 5-4, although purists could probably find a counterexample for everything in the figure.

Inside the subnet, several trade-offs exist between virtual circuits and datagrams. One trade-off is between router memory space and bandwidth. Virtual circuits allow packets to contain circuit numbers instead of full destination addresses. If the packets tend to be fairly short, a full destination address in every packet may represent a significant amount of overhead and hence, wasted bandwidth. The price paid for using virtual circuits internally is the table space within the routers. Depending upon the relative cost of communication circuits versus router memory, one or the other may be cheaper.

Another trade-off is setup time versus address parsing time. Using virtual circuits requires a setup phase, which takes time and consumes resources. However, figuring out what to do with a data packet in a virtual-circuit subnet is easy: the router just uses the circuit number to index into a table to find out where the pac-

Issue	Datagram subnet	Virtual-circuit subnet
Circuit setup	Not needed	Required
Addressing	Each packet contains the full source and destination address	Each packet contains a short VC number
State information	Routers do not hold state information about connections	Each VC requires router table space per connection
Routing	Each packet is routed independently	Route chosen when VC is set up; all packets follow it
Effect of router failures	None, except for packets lost during the crash	All VCs that passed through the failed router are terminated
Quality of service	Difficult	Easy if enough resources can be allocated in advance for each VC
Congestion control	Difficult	Easy if enough resources can be allocated in advance for each VC

Figure 5-4. Comparison of datagram and virtual-circuit subnets.

ket goes. In a datagram subnet, a more complicated lookup procedure is required to locate the entry for the destination.

Yet another issue is the amount of table space required in router memory. A datagram subnet needs to have an entry for every possible destination, whereas a virtual-circuit subnet just needs an entry for each virtual circuit. However, this advantage is somewhat illusory since connection setup packets have to be routed too, and they use destination addresses, the same as datagrams do.

Virtual circuits have some advantages in guaranteeing quality of service and avoiding congestion within the subnet because resources (e.g., buffers, bandwidth, and CPU cycles) can be reserved in advance, when the connection is established. Once the packets start arriving, the necessary bandwidth and router capacity will be there. With a datagram subnet, congestion avoidance is more difficult.

For transaction processing systems (e.g., stores calling up to verify credit card purchases), the overhead required to set up and clear a virtual circuit may easily dwarf the use of the circuit. If the majority of the traffic is expected to be of this kind, the use of virtual circuits inside the subnet makes little sense. On the other hand, permanent virtual circuits, which are set up manually and last for months or years, may be useful here.

Virtual circuits also have a vulnerability problem. If a router crashes and loses its memory, even if it comes back up a second later, all the virtual circuits passing through it will have to be aborted. In contrast, if a datagram router goes down, only those users whose packets were queued in the router at the time will suffer, and maybe not even all those, depending upon whether they have already been acknowledged. The loss of a communication line is fatal to virtual circuits using it but can be easily compensated for if datagrams are used. Datagrams also allow the routers to balance the traffic throughout the subnet, since routes can be changed partway through a long sequence of packet transmissions.

5.2 ROUTING ALGORITHMS

The main function of the network layer is routing packets from the source machine to the destination machine. In most subnets, packets will require multiple hops to make the journey. The only notable exception is for broadcast networks, but even here routing is an issue if the source and destination are not on the same network. The algorithms that choose the routes and the data structures that they use are a major area of network layer design.

The **routing algorithm** is that part of the network layer software responsible for deciding which output line an incoming packet should be transmitted on. If the subnet uses datagrams internally, this decision must be made anew for every arriving data packet since the best route may have changed since last time. If the subnet uses virtual circuits internally, routing decisions are made only when a new virtual circuit is being set up. Thereafter, data packets just follow the previously-established route. The latter case is sometimes called **session routing** because a route remains in force for an entire user session (e.g., a login session at a terminal or a file transfer).

It is sometimes useful to make a distinction between routing, which is making the decision which routes to use, and forwarding, which is what happens when a packet arrives. One can think of a router as having two processes inside it. One of them handles each packet as it arrives, looking up the outgoing line to use for it in the routing tables. This process is **forwarding**. The other process is responsible for filling in and updating the routing tables. That is where the routing algorithm comes into play.

Regardless of whether routes are chosen independently for each packet or only when new connections are established, certain properties are desirable in a routing algorithm: correctness, simplicity, robustness, stability, fairness, and optimality. Correctness and simplicity hardly require comment, but the need for robustness may be less obvious at first. Once a major network comes on the air, it may be expected to run continuously for years without systemwide failures. During that period there will be hardware and software failures of all kinds. Hosts, routers, and lines will fail repeatedly, and the topology will change many times. The routing algorithm should be able to cope with changes in the topology and traffic without requiring all jobs in all hosts to be aborted and the network to be rebooted every time some router crashes.

Stability is also an important goal for the routing algorithm. There exist routing algorithms that never converge to equilibrium, no matter how long they run. A stable algorithm reaches equilibrium and stays there. Fairness and optimality may sound obvious—surely no reasonable person would oppose them—but as it turns out, they are often contradictory goals. As a simple example of this conflict, look at Fig. 5-5. Suppose that there is enough traffic between A and A', between B and B', and between C and C' to saturate the horizontal links. To maximize the total flow, the X to X' traffic should be shut off altogether. Unfortunately, X and X' may not see it that way. Evidently, some compromise between global efficiency and fairness to individual connections is needed.

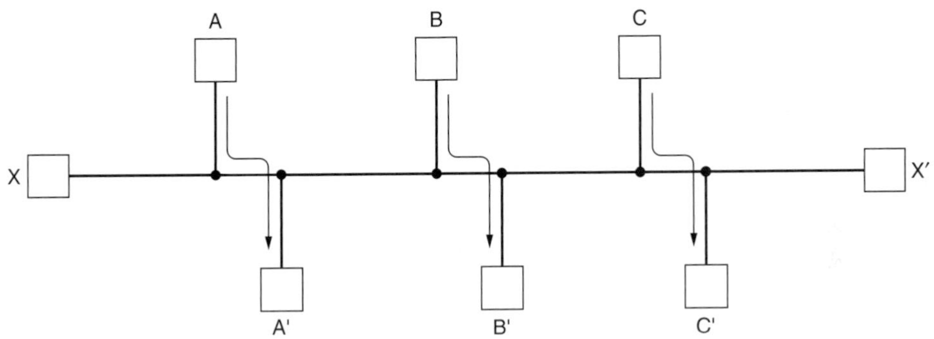

Figure 5-5. Conflict between fairness and optimality.

Before we can even attempt to find trade-offs between fairness and optimality, we must decide what it is we seek to optimize. Minimizing mean packet delay is an obvious candidate, but so is maximizing total network throughput. Furthermore, these two goals are also in conflict, since operating any queueing system near capacity implies a long queueing delay. As a compromise, many networks attempt to minimize the number of hops a packet must make, because reducing the number of hops tends to improve the delay and also reduce the amount of bandwidth consumed, which tends to improve the throughput as well.

Routing algorithms can be grouped into two major classes: nonadaptive and adaptive. **Nonadaptive algorithms** do not base their routing decisions on measurements or estimates of the current traffic and topology. Instead, the choice of the route to use to get from I to J (for all I and J) is computed in advance, off-line, and downloaded to the routers when the network is booted. This procedure is sometimes called **static routing**.

Adaptive algorithms, in contrast, change their routing decisions to reflect changes in the topology, and usually the traffic as well. Adaptive algorithms differ in where they get their information (e.g., locally, from adjacent routers, or from all routers), when they change the routes (e.g., every ΔT sec, when the load changes or when the topology changes), and what metric is used for optimization (e.g., distance, number of hops, or estimated transit time). In the following sections we will discuss a variety of routing algorithms, both static and dynamic.

5.2.1 The Optimality Principle

Before we get into specific algorithms, it may be helpful to note that one can make a general statement about optimal routes without regard to network topology or traffic. This statement is known as the **optimality principle**. It states that if router J is on the optimal path from router I to router K, then the optimal path from J to K also falls along the same route. To see this, call the part of the route from I to J r_1 and the rest of the route r_2. If a route better than r_2 existed from J to K, it could be concatenated with r_1 to improve the route from I to K, contradicting our statement that $r_1 r_2$ is optimal.

As a direct consequence of the optimality principle, we can see that the set of optimal routes from all sources to a given destination form a tree rooted at the destination. Such a tree is called a **sink tree** and is illustrated in Fig. 5-6, where the distance metric is the number of hops. Note that a sink tree is not necessarily unique; other trees with the same path lengths may exist. The goal of all routing algorithms is to discover and use the sink trees for all routers.

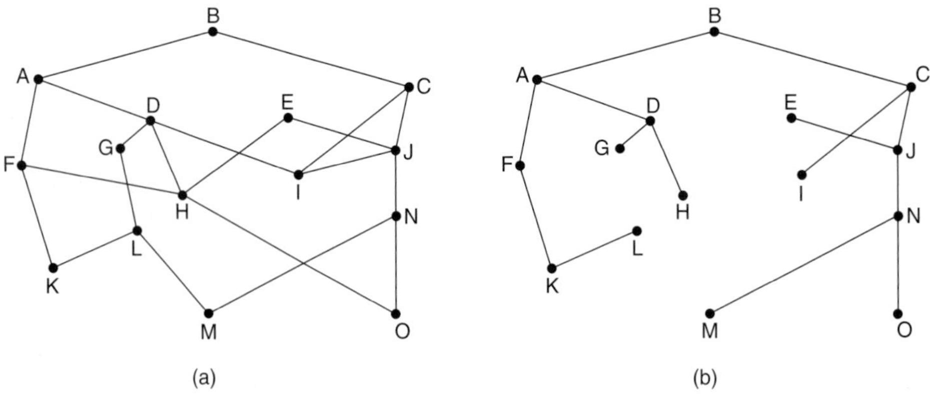

Figure 5-6. (a) A subnet. (b) A sink tree for router B.

Since a sink tree is indeed a tree, it does not contain any loops, so each packet will be delivered within a finite and bounded number of hops. In practice, life is not quite this easy. Links and routers can go down and come back up during operation, so different routers may have different ideas about the current topology. Also, we have quietly finessed the issue of whether each router has to individually acquire the information on which to base its sink tree computation or whether this information is collected by some other means. We will come back to these issues shortly. Nevertheless, the optimality principle and the sink tree provide a benchmark against which other routing algorithms can be measured.

5.2.2 Shortest Path Routing

Let us begin our study of feasible routing algorithms with a technique that is widely used in many forms because it is simple and easy to understand. The idea is to build a graph of the subnet, with each node of the graph representing a router and each arc of the graph representing a communication line (often called a link). To choose a route between a given pair of routers, the algorithm just finds the shortest path between them on the graph.

The concept of a **shortest path** deserves some explanation. One way of measuring path length is the number of hops. Using this metric, the paths *ABC* and *ABE* in Fig. 5-7 are equally long. Another metric is the geographic distance in kilometers, in which case *ABC* is clearly much longer than *ABE* (assuming the figure is drawn to scale).

However, many other metrics besides hops and physical distance are also possible. For example, each arc could be labeled with the mean queueing and transmission delay for some standard test packet as determined by hourly test runs. With this graph labeling, the shortest path is the fastest path rather than the path with the fewest arcs or kilometers.

In the general case, the labels on the arcs could be computed as a function of the distance, bandwidth, average traffic, communication cost, mean queue length, measured delay, and other factors. By changing the weighting function, the algorithm would then compute the "shortest" path measured according to any one of a number of criteria or to a combination of criteria.

Several algorithms for computing the shortest path between two nodes of a graph are known. This one is due to Dijkstra (1959). Each node is labeled (in parentheses) with its distance from the source node along the best known path. Initially, no paths are known, so all nodes are labeled with infinity. As the algorithm proceeds and paths are found, the labels may change, reflecting better paths. A label may be either tentative or permanent. Initially, all labels are tentative. When it is discovered that a label represents the shortest possible path from the source to that node, it is made permanent and never changed thereafter.

To illustrate how the labeling algorithm works, look at the weighted, undirected graph of Fig. 5-7(a), where the weights represent, for example, distance. We want to find the shortest path from *A* to *D*. We start out by marking node *A* as permanent, indicated by a filled-in circle. Then we examine, in turn, each of the nodes adjacent to *A* (the working node), relabeling each one with the distance to *A*. Whenever a node is relabeled, we also label it with the node from which the probe was made so that we can reconstruct the final path later. Having examined each of the nodes adjacent to *A*, we examine all the tentatively labeled nodes in

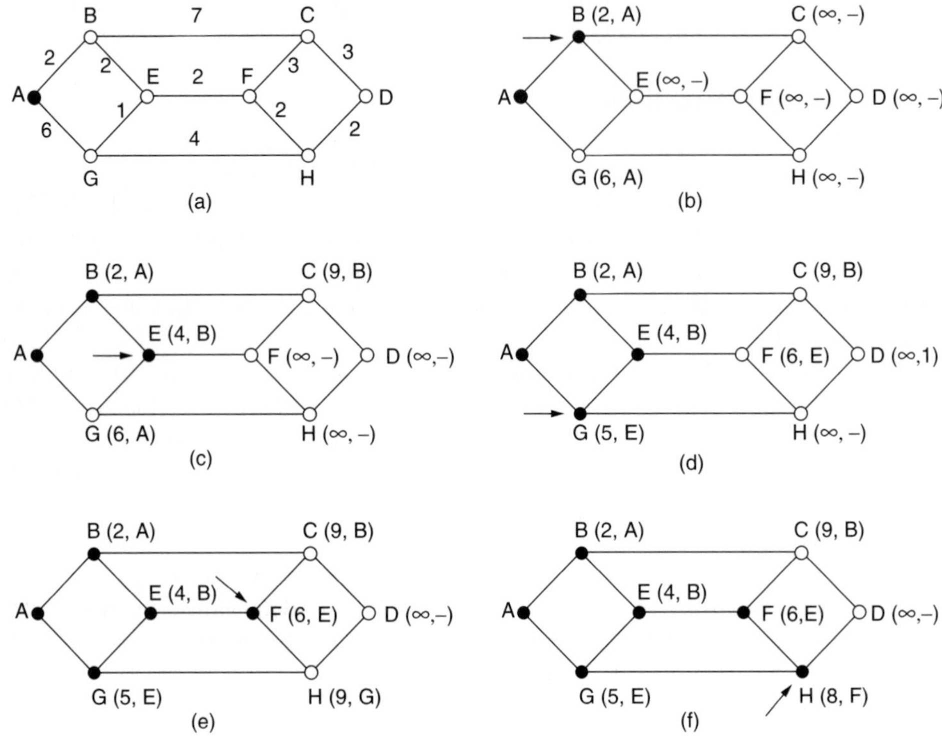

Figure 5-7. The first five steps used in computing the shortest path from *A* to *D*. The arrows indicate the working node.

the whole graph and make the one with the smallest label permanent, as shown in Fig. 5-7(b). This one becomes the new working node.

We now start at *B* and examine all nodes adjacent to it. If the sum of the label on *B* and the distance from *B* to the node being considered is less than the label on that node, we have a shorter path, so the node is relabeled.

After all the nodes adjacent to the working node have been inspected and the tentative labels changed if possible, the entire graph is searched for the tentatively-labeled node with the smallest value. This node is made permanent and becomes the working node for the next round. Figure 5-7 shows the first five steps of the algorithm.

To see why the algorithm works, look at Fig. 5-7(c). At that point we have just made *E* permanent. Suppose that there were a shorter path than *ABE*, say *AXYZE*. There are two possibilities: either node *Z* has already been made permanent, or it has not been. If it has, then *E* has already been probed (on the round following the one when *Z* was made permanent), so the *AXYZE* path has not escaped our attention and thus cannot be a shorter path.

Now consider the case where Z is still tentatively labeled. Either the label at Z is greater than or equal to that at E, in which case $AXYZE$ cannot be a shorter path than ABE, or it is less than that of E, in which case Z and not E will become permanent first, allowing E to be probed from Z.

This algorithm is given in Fig. 5-8. The global variables n and *dist* describe the graph and are initialized before *shortest_path* is called. The only difference between the program and the algorithm described above is that in Fig. 5-8, we compute the shortest path starting at the terminal node, t, rather than at the source node, s. Since the shortest path from t to s in an undirected graph is the same as the shortest path from s to t, it does not matter at which end we begin (unless there are several shortest paths, in which case reversing the search might discover a different one). The reason for searching backward is that each node is labeled with its predecessor rather than its successor. When the final path is copied into the output variable, *path*, the path is thus reversed. By reversing the search, the two effects cancel, and the answer is produced in the correct order.

5.2.3 Flooding

Another static algorithm is **flooding**, in which every incoming packet is sent out on every outgoing line except the one it arrived on. Flooding obviously generates vast numbers of duplicate packets, in fact, an infinite number unless some measures are taken to damp the process. One such measure is to have a hop counter contained in the header of each packet, which is decremented at each hop, with the packet being discarded when the counter reaches zero. Ideally, the hop counter should be initialized to the length of the path from source to destination. If the sender does not know how long the path is, it can initialize the counter to the worst case, namely, the full diameter of the subnet.

An alternative technique for damming the flood is to keep track of which packets have been flooded, to avoid sending them out a second time.
achieve this goal is to have the source router put a sequence number in each packet it receives from its hosts. Each router then needs a list per source router telling which sequence numbers originating at that source have already been seen. If an incoming packet is on the list, it is not flooded.

To prevent the list from growing without bound, each list should be augmented by a counter, k, meaning that all sequence numbers through k have been seen. When a packet comes in, it is easy to check if the packet is a duplicate; if so, it is discarded. Furthermore, the full list below k is not needed, since k effectively summarizes it.

A variation of flooding that is slightly more practical is **selective flooding**. In this algorithm the routers do not send every incoming packet out on every line, only on those lines that are going approximately in the right direction. There is usually little point in sending a westbound packet on an eastbound line unless the topology is extremely peculiar and the router is sure of this fact.

```
#define MAX_NODES 1024                    /* maximum number of nodes */
#define INFINITY 1000000000               /* a number larger than every maximum path */
int n, dist[MAX_NODES][MAX_NODES];/* dist[i][j] is the distance from i to j */

void shortest_path(int s, int t, int path[])
{ struct state {                          /* the path being worked on */
      int predecessor;                    /* previous node */
      int length;                         /* length from source to this node */
      enum {permanent, tentative} label; /* label state */
  } state[MAX_NODES];

  int i, k, min;
  struct state *p;

  for (p = &state[0]; p < &state[n]; p++) { /* initialize state */
      p->predecessor = -1;
      p->length = INFINITY;
      p->label = tentative;
  }
  state[t].length = 0; state[t].label = permanent;
  k = t;                                  /* k is the initial working node */
  do {                                    /* Is there a better path from k? */
      for (i = 0; i < n; i++)             /* this graph has n nodes */
           if (dist[k][i] != 0 && state[i].label == tentative) {
                 if (state[k].length + dist[k][i] < state[i].length) {
                      state[i].predecessor = k;
                      state[i].length = state[k].length + dist[k][i];
                 }
           }

      /* Find the tentatively labeled node with the smallest label. */
      k = 0; min = INFINITY;
      for (i = 0; i < n; i++)
           if (state[i].label == tentative && state[i].length < min) {
                 min = state[i].length;
                 k = i;
           }
      state[k].label = permanent;
  } while (k != s);

  /* Copy the path into the output array. */
  i = 0; k = s;
  do {path[i++] = k; k = state[k].predecessor; } while (k >= 0);
}
```

Figure 5-8. Dijkstra's algorithm to compute the shortest path through a graph.

Flooding is not practical in most applications, but it does have some uses. For example, in military applications, where large numbers of routers may be blown to bits at any instant, the tremendous robustness of flooding is highly desirable. In distributed database applications, it is sometimes necessary to update all the databases concurrently, in which case flooding can be useful. In wireless networks, all messages transmitted by a station can be received by all other stations within its radio range, which is, in fact, flooding, and some algorithms utilize this property. A fourth possible use of flooding is as a metric against which other routing algorithms can be compared. Flooding always chooses the shortest path because it chooses every possible path in parallel. Consequently, no other algorithm can produce a shorter delay (if we ignore the overhead generated by the flooding process itself).

5.2.4 Distance Vector Routing

Modern computer networks generally use dynamic routing algorithms rather than the static ones described above because static algorithms do not take the current network load into account. Two dynamic algorithms in particular, distance vector routing and link state routing, are the most popular. In this section we will look at the former algorithm. In the following section we will study the latter algorithm.

Distance vector routing algorithms operate by having each router maintain a table (i.e, a vector) giving the best known distance to each destination and which line to use to get there. These tables are updated by exchanging information with the neighbors.

The distance vector routing algorithm is sometimes called by other names, most commonly the distributed **Bellman-Ford** routing algorithm and the **Ford-Fulkerson** algorithm, after the researchers who developed it (Bellman, 1957; and Ford and Fulkerson, 1962). It was the original ARPANET routing algorithm and was also used in the Internet under the name RIP.

In distance vector routing, each router maintains a routing table indexed by, and containing one entry for, each router in the subnet. This entry contains two parts: the preferred outgoing line to use for that destination and an estimate of the time or distance to that destination. The metric used might be number of hops, time delay in milliseconds, total number of packets queued along the path, or something similar.

The router is assumed to know the "distance" to each of its neighbors. If the metric is hops, the distance is just one hop. If the metric is queue length, the router simply examines each queue. If the metric is delay, the router can measure it directly with special ECHO packets that the receiver just timestamps and sends back as fast as it can.

As an example, assume that delay is used as a metric and that the router knows the delay to each of its neighbors. Once every T msec each router sends to each neighbor a list of its estimated delays to each destination. It also receives a similar list from each neighbor. Imagine that one of these tables has just come in from neighbor X, with X_i being X's estimate of how long it takes to get to router i. If the router knows that the delay to X is m msec, it also knows that it can reach router i via X in $X_i + m$ msec. By performing this calculation for each neighbor, a router can find out which estimate seems the best and use that estimate and the corresponding line in its new routing table. Note that the old routing table is not used in the calculation.

This updating process is illustrated in Fig. 5-9. Part (a) shows a subnet. The first four columns of part (b) show the delay vectors received from the neighbors of router *J*. *A* claims to have a 12-msec delay to *B*, a 25-msec delay to *C*, a 40-msec delay to *D*, etc. Suppose that *J* has measured or estimated its delay to its neighbors, *A*, *I*, *H*, and *K* as 8, 10, 12, and 6 msec, respectively.

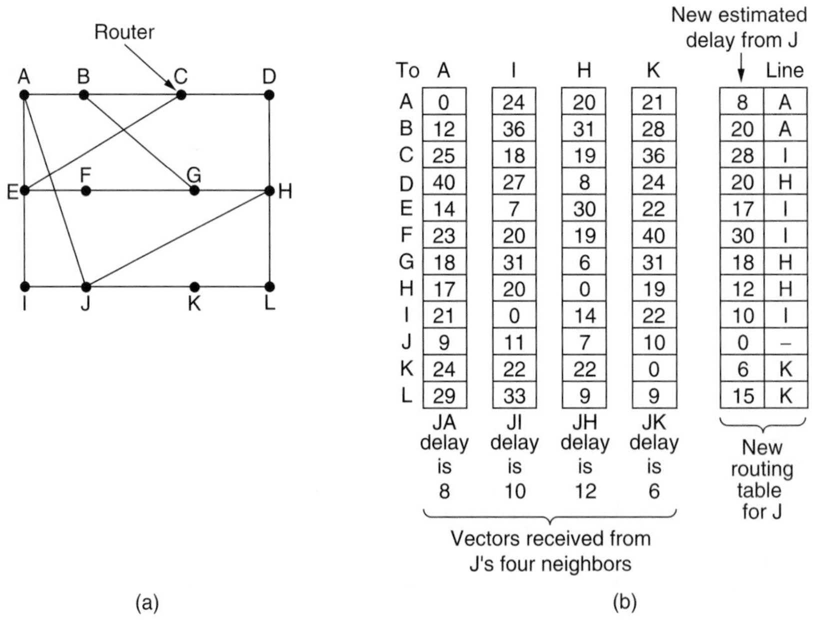

To	A	I	H	K	New estimated delay from J	Line
A	0	24	20	21	8	A
B	12	36	31	28	20	A
C	25	18	19	36	28	I
D	40	27	8	24	20	H
E	14	7	30	22	17	I
F	23	20	19	40	30	I
G	18	31	6	31	18	H
H	17	20	0	19	12	H
I	21	0	14	22	10	I
J	9	11	7	10	0	–
K	24	22	22	0	6	K
L	29	33	9	9	15	K

Figure 5-9. (a) A subnet. (b) Input from *A*, *I*, *H*, *K*, and the new routing table for *J*.

Consider how *J* computes its new route to router *G*. It knows that it can get to *A* in 8 msec, and *A* claims to be able to get to *G* in 18 msec, so *J* knows it can count on a delay of 26 msec to *G* if it forwards packets bound for *G* to *A*. Similarly, it computes the delay to *G* via *I*, *H*, and *K* as 41 (31 + 10), 18 (6 + 12), and 37 (31 + 6) msec, respectively. The best of these values is 18, so it makes an entry in its routing table that the delay to *G* is 18 msec and that the route to use is via *H*. The same calculation is performed for all the other destinations, with the new routing table shown in the last column of the figure.

The Count-to-Infinity Problem

Distance vector routing works in theory but has a serious drawback in practice: although it converges to the correct answer, it may do so slowly. In particular, it reacts rapidly to good news, but leisurely to bad news. Consider a router whose best route to destination *X* is large. If on the next exchange neighbor *A* suddenly reports a short delay to *X*, the router just switches over to using the line to *A* to send traffic to *X*. In one vector exchange, the good news is processed.

To see how fast good news propagates, consider the five-node (linear) subnet of Fig. 5-10, where the delay metric is the number of hops. Suppose *A* is down initially and all the other routers know this. In other words, they have all recorded the delay to *A* as infinity.

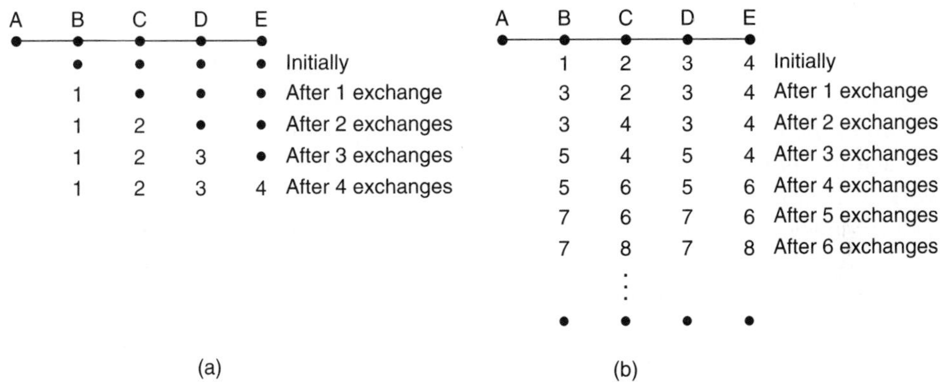

Figure 5-10. The count-to-infinity problem.

When *A* comes up, the other routers learn about it via the vector exchanges. For simplicity we will assume that there is a gigantic gong somewhere that is struck periodically to initiate a vector exchange at all routers simultaneously. At the time of the first exchange, *B* learns that its left neighbor has zero delay to *A*. *B* now makes an entry in its routing table that *A* is one hop away to the left. All the other routers still think that *A* is down. At this point, the routing table entries for *A* are as shown in the second row of Fig. 5-10(a). On the next exchange, *C* learns that *B* has a path of length 1 to *A*, so it updates its routing table to indicate a path of length 2, but *D* and *E* do not hear the good news until later. Clearly, the good news is spreading at the rate of one hop per exchange. In a subnet whose longest path is of length *N* hops, within *N* exchanges everyone will know about newly-revived lines and routers.

Now let us consider the situation of Fig. 5-10(b), in which all the lines and routers are initially up. Routers *B*, *C*, *D*, and *E* have distances to *A* of 1, 2, 3, and 4, respectively. Suddenly *A* goes down, or alternatively, the line between *A* and *B* is cut, which is effectively the same thing from *B*'s point of view.

At the first packet exchange, *B* does not hear anything from *A*. Fortunately, *C* says: Do not worry; I have a path to *A* of length 2. Little does *B* know that *C*'s path runs through *B* itself. For all *B* knows, *C* might have ten lines all with separate paths to *A* of length 2. As a result, *B* thinks it can reach *A* via *C*, with a path length of 3. *D* and *E* do not update their entries for *A* on the first exchange.

On the second exchange, *C* notices that each of its neighbors claims to have a path to *A* of length 3. It picks one of the them at random and makes its new distance to *A* 4, as shown in the third row of Fig. 5-10(b). Subsequent exchanges produce the history shown in the rest of Fig. 5-10(b).

From this figure, it should be clear why bad news travels slowly: no router ever has a value more than one higher than the minimum of all its neighbors. Gradually, all routers work their way up to infinity, but the number of exchanges required depends on the numerical value used for infinity. For this reason, it is wise to set infinity to the longest path plus 1. If the metric is time delay, there is no well-defined upper bound, so a high value is needed to prevent a path with a long delay from being treated as down. Not entirely surprisingly, this problem is known as the **count-to-infinity** problem. There have been a few attempts to solve it (such as split horizon with poisoned reverse in RFC 1058), but none of these work well in general. The core of the problem is that when *X* tells *Y* that it has a path somewhere, *Y* has no way of knowing whether it itself is on the path.

5.2.5 Link State Routing

Distance vector routing was used in the ARPANET until 1979, when it was replaced by link state routing. Two primary problems caused its demise. First, since the delay metric was queue length, it did not take line bandwidth into account when choosing routes. Initially, all the lines were 56 kbps, so line bandwidth was not an issue, but after some lines had been upgraded to 230 kbps and others to 1.544 Mbps, not taking bandwidth into account was a major problem. Of course, it would have been possible to change the delay metric to factor in line bandwidth, but a second problem also existed, namely, the algorithm often took too long to converge (the count-to-infinity problem). For these reasons, it was replaced by an entirely new algorithm, now called **link state routing**. Variants of link state routing are now widely used.

The idea behind link state routing is simple and can be stated as five parts. Each router must do the following:

1. Discover its neighbors and learn their network addresses.
2. Measure the delay or cost to each of its neighbors.
3. Construct a packet telling all it has just learned.
4. Send this packet to all other routers.
5. Compute the shortest path to every other router.

In effect, the complete topology and all delays are experimentally measured and distributed to every router. Then Dijkstra's algorithm can be run to find the shortest path to every other router. Below we will consider each of these five steps in more detail.

Learning about the Neighbors

When a router is booted, its first task is to learn who its neighbors are. It accomplishes this goal by sending a special HELLO packet on each point-to-point line. The router on the other end is expected to send back a reply telling who it is. These names must be globally unique because when a distant router later hears that three routers are all connected to *F*, it is essential that it can determine whether all three mean the same *F*.

When two or more routers are connected by a LAN, the situation is slightly more complicated. Fig. 5-11(a) illustrates a LAN to which three routers, *A*, *C*, and *F*, are directly connected. Each of these routers is connected to one or more additional routers, as shown.

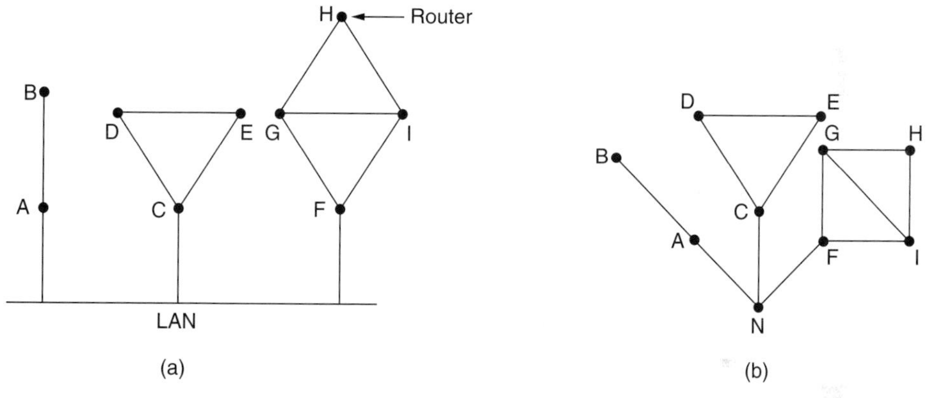

Figure 5-11. (a) Nine routers and a LAN. (b) A graph model of (a).

One way to model the LAN is to consider it as a node itself, as shown in Fig. 5-11(b). Here we have introduced a new, artificial node, *N*, to which *A*, *C*, and *F* are connected. The fact that it is possible to go from *A* to *C* on the LAN is represented by the path *ANC* here.

Measuring Line Cost

The link state routing algorithm requires each router to know, or at least have a reasonable estimate of, the delay to each of its neighbors. The most direct way to determine this delay is to send over the line a special ECHO packet that the other side is required to send back immediately. By measuring the round-trip time and dividing it by two, the sending router can get a reasonable estimate of the delay. For even better results, the test can be conducted several times, and the average used. Of course, this method implicitly assumes the delays are symmetric, which may not always be the case.

An interesting issue is whether to take the load into account when measuring the delay. To factor the load in, the round-trip timer must be started when the ECHO packet is queued. To ignore the load, the timer should be started when the ECHO packet reaches the front of the queue.

Arguments can be made both ways. Including traffic-induced delays in the measurements means that when a router has a choice between two lines with the same bandwidth, one of which is heavily loaded all the time and one of which is not, the router will regard the route over the unloaded line as a shorter path. This choice will result in better performance.

Unfortunately, there is also an argument against including the load in the delay calculation. Consider the subnet of Fig. 5-12, which is divided into two parts, East and West, connected by two lines, *CF* and *EI*.

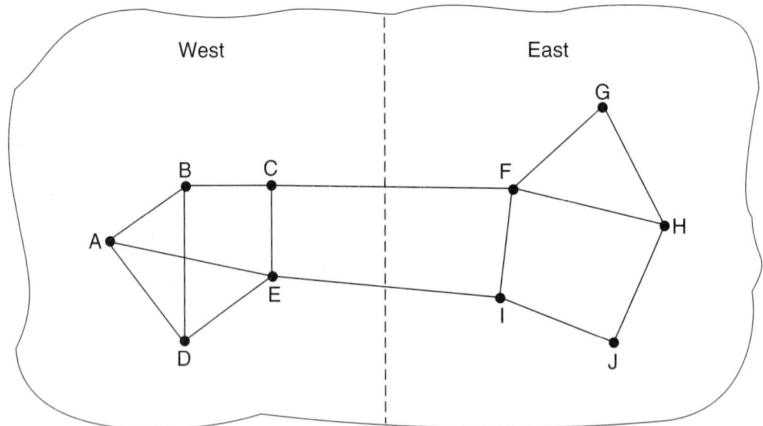

Figure 5-12. A subnet in which the East and West parts are connected by two lines.

Suppose that most of the traffic between East and West is using line *CF*, and as a result, this line is heavily loaded with long delays. Including queueing delay in the shortest path calculation will make *EI* more attractive. After the new routing tables have been installed, most of the East-West traffic will now go over *EI*, overloading this line. Consequently, in the next update, *CF* will appear to be the shortest path. As a result, the routing tables may oscillate wildly, leading to erratic routing and many potential problems. If load is ignored and only bandwidth is considered, this problem does not occur. Alternatively, the load can be spread over both lines, but this solution does not fully utilize the best path. Nevertheless, to avoid oscillations in the choice of best path, it may be wise to distribute the load over multiple lines, with some known fraction going over each line.

Building Link State Packets

Once the information needed for the exchange has been collected, the next step is for each router to build a packet containing all the data. The packet starts with the identity of the sender, followed by a sequence number and age (to be described later), and a list of neighbors. For each neighbor, the delay to that neighbor is given. An example subnet is given in Fig. 5-13(a) with delays shown as labels on the lines. The corresponding link state packets for all six routers are shown in Fig. 5-13(b).

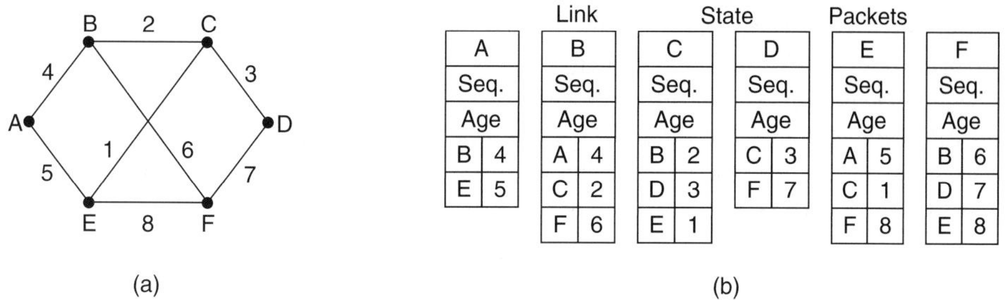

Figure 5-13. (a) A subnet. (b) The link state packets for this subnet.

Building the link state packets is easy. The hard part is determining when to build them. One possibility is to build them periodically, that is, at regular intervals. Another possibility is to build them when some significant event occurs, such as a line or neighbor going down or coming back up again or changing its properties appreciably.

Distributing the Link State Packets

The trickiest part of the algorithm is distributing the link state packets reliably. As the packets are distributed and installed, the routers getting the first ones will change their routes. Consequently, the different routers may be using different versions of the topology, which can lead to inconsistencies, loops, unreachable machines, and other problems.

First we will describe the basic distribution algorithm. Later we will give some refinements. The fundamental idea is to use flooding to distribute the link state packets. To keep the flood in check, each packet contains a sequence number that is incremented for each new packet sent. Routers keep track of all the (source router, sequence) pairs they see. When a new link state packet comes in, it is checked against the list of packets already seen. If it is new, it is forwarded on all lines except the one it arrived on. If it is a duplicate, it is discarded. If a packet with a sequence number lower than the highest one seen so far ever arrives, it is rejected as being obsolete since the router has more recent data.

This algorithm has a few problems, but they are manageable. First, if the sequence numbers wrap around, confusion will reign. The solution here is to use a 32-bit sequence number. With one link state packet per second, it would take 137 years to wrap around, so this possibility can be ignored.

Second, if a router ever crashes, it will lose track of its sequence number. If it starts again at 0, the next packet will be rejected as a duplicate.

Third, if a sequence number is ever corrupted and 65,540 is received instead of 4 (a 1-bit error), packets 5 through 65,540 will be rejected as obsolete, since the current sequence number is thought to be 65,540.

The solution to all these problems is to include the age of each packet after the sequence number and decrement it once per second. When the age hits zero, the information from that router is discarded. Normally, a new packet comes in, say, every 10 sec, so router information only times out when a router is down (or six consecutive packets have been lost, an unlikely event). The *Age* field is also decremented by each router during the initial flooding process, to make sure no packet can get lost and live for an indefinite period of time (a packet whose age is zero is discarded).

Some refinements to this algorithm make it more robust. When a link state packet comes in to a router for flooding, it is not queued for transmission immediately. Instead it is first put in a holding area to wait a short while. If another link state packet from the same source comes in before the first packet is transmitted, their sequence numbers are compared. If they are equal, the duplicate is discarded. If they are different, the older one is thrown out. To guard against errors on the router-router lines, all link state packets are acknowledged. When a line goes idle, the holding area is scanned in round-robin order to select a packet or acknowledgement to send.

The data structure used by router *B* for the subnet shown in Fig. 5-13(a) is depicted in Fig. 5-14. Each row here corresponds to a recently-arrived, but as yet not fully-processed, link state packet. The table records where the packet originated, its sequence number and age, and the data. In addition, there are send and acknowledgement flags for each of *B*'s three lines (to *A*, *C*, and *F*, respectively). The send flags mean that the packet must be sent on the indicated line. The acknowledgement flags mean that it must be acknowledged there.

In Fig. 5-14, the link state packet from *A* arrives directly, so it must be sent to *C* and *F* and acknowledged to *A*, as indicated by the flag bits. Similarly, the packet from *F* has to be forwarded to *A* and *C* and acknowledged to *F*.

However, the situation with the third packet, from *E*, is different. It arrived twice, once via *EAB* and once via *EFB*. Consequently, it has to be sent only to *C* but acknowledged to both *A* and *F*, as indicated by the bits.

If a duplicate arrives while the original is still in the buffer, bits have to be changed. For example, if a copy of *C*'s state arrives from *F* before the fourth entry in the table has been forwarded, the six bits will be changed to 100011 to indicate that the packet must be acknowledged to *F* but not sent there.

Source	Seq.	Age	Send flags A	Send flags C	Send flags F	ACK flags A	ACK flags C	ACK flags F	Data
A	21	60	0	1	1	1	0	0	
F	21	60	1	1	0	0	0	1	
E	21	59	0	1	0	1	0	1	
C	20	60	1	0	1	0	1	0	
D	21	59	1	0	0	0	1	1	

Figure 5-14. The packet buffer for router *B* in Fig. 5-13.

Computing the New Routes

Once a router has accumulated a full set of link state packets, it can construct the entire subnet graph because every link is represented. Every link is, in fact, represented twice, once for each direction. The two values can be averaged or used separately.

Now Dijkstra's algorithm can be run locally to construct the shortest path to all possible destinations. The results of this algorithm can be installed in the routing tables, and normal operation resumed.

For a subnet with n routers, each of which has k neighbors, the memory required to store the input data is proportional to kn. For large subnets, this can be a problem. Also, the computation time can be an issue. Nevertheless, in many practical situations, link state routing works well.

However, problems with the hardware or software can wreak havoc with this algorithm (also with other ones). For example, if a router claims to have a line it does not have or forgets a line it does have, the subnet graph will be incorrect. If a router fails to forward packets or corrupts them while forwarding them, trouble will arise. Finally, if it runs out of memory or does the routing calculation wrong, bad things will happen. As the subnet grows into the range of tens or hundreds of thousands of nodes, the probability of some router failing occasionally becomes nonnegligible. The trick is to try to arrange to limit the damage when the inevitable happens. Perlman (1988) discusses these problems and their solutions in detail.

Link state routing is widely used in actual networks, so a few words about some example protocols using it are in order. The OSPF protocol, which is widely used in the Internet, uses a link state algorithm. We will describe OSPF in Sec. 5.6.4.

Another link state protocol is **IS-IS** (**Intermediate System-Intermediate System**), which was designed for DECnet and later adopted by ISO for use with its connectionless network layer protocol, CLNP. Since then it has been modified to handle other protocols as well, most notably, IP. IS-IS is used in some Internet backbones (including the old NSFNET backbone) and in some digital cellular systems such as CDPD. Novell NetWare uses a minor variant of IS-IS (NLSP) for routing IPX packets.

Basically IS-IS distributes a picture of the router topology, from which the shortest paths are computed. Each router announces, in its link state information, which network layer addresses it can reach directly. These addresses can be IP, IPX, AppleTalk, or any other addresses. IS-IS can even support multiple network layer protocols at the same time.

Many of the innovations designed for IS-IS were adopted by OSPF (OSPF was designed several years after IS-IS). These include a self-stabilizing method of flooding link state updates, the concept of a designated router on a LAN, and the method of computing and supporting path splitting and multiple metrics. As a consequence, there is very little difference between IS-IS and OSPF. The most important difference is that IS-IS is encoded in such a way that it is easy and natural to simultaneously carry information about multiple network layer protocols, a feature OSPF does not have. This advantage is especially valuable in large multiprotocol environments.

5.2.6 Hierarchical Routing

As networks grow in size, the router routing tables grow proportionally. Not only is router memory consumed by ever-increasing tables, but more CPU time is needed to scan them and more bandwidth is needed to send status reports about them. At a certain point the network may grow to the point where it is no longer feasible for every router to have an entry for every other router, so the routing will have to be done hierarchically, as it is in the telephone network.

When hierarchical routing is used, the routers are divided into what we will call **regions**, with each router knowing all the details about how to route packets to destinations within its own region, but knowing nothing about the internal structure of other regions. When different networks are interconnected, it is natural to regard each one as a separate region in order to free the routers in one network from having to know the topological structure of the other ones.

For huge networks, a two-level hierarchy may be insufficient; it may be necessary to group the regions into clusters, the clusters into zones, the zones into groups, and so on, until we run out of names for aggregations. As an example of a multilevel hierarchy, consider how a packet might be routed from Berkeley, California, to Malindi, Kenya. The Berkeley router would know the detailed topology within California but would send all out-of-state traffic to the Los Angeles router. The Los Angeles router would be able to route traffic to other domestic routers but would send foreign traffic to New York. The New York router would be programmed to direct all traffic to the router in the destination country responsible for handling foreign traffic, say, in Nairobi. Finally, the packet would work its way down the tree in Kenya until it got to Malindi.

Figure 5-15 gives a quantitative example of routing in a two-level hierarchy with five regions. The full routing table for router *1A* has 17 entries, as shown in Fig. 5-15(b). When routing is done hierarchically, as in Fig. 5-15(c), there are entries for all the local routers as before, but all other regions have been condensed into a single router, so all traffic for region 2 goes via the *1B*–*2A* line, but the rest of the remote traffic goes via the *1C*–*3B* line. Hierarchical routing has reduced the table from 17 to 7 entries. As the ratio of the number of regions to the number of routers per region grows, the savings in table space increase.

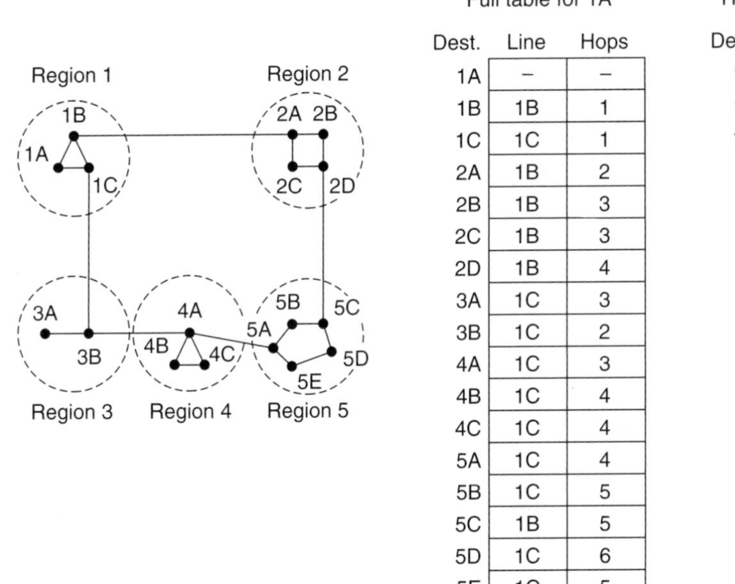

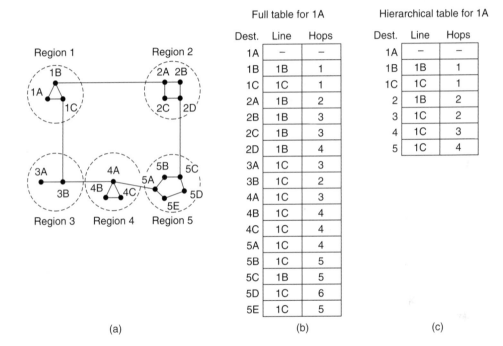

Full table for 1A

Dest.	Line	Hops
1A	–	–
1B	1B	1
1C	1C	1
2A	1B	2
2B	1B	3
2C	1B	3
2D	1B	4
3A	1C	3
3B	1C	2
4A	1C	3
4B	1C	4
4C	1C	4
5A	1C	4
5B	1C	5
5C	1B	5
5D	1C	6
5E	1C	5

(b)

Hierarchical table for 1A

Dest.	Line	Hops
1A	–	–
1B	1B	1
1C	1C	1
2	1B	2
3	1C	2
4	1C	3
5	1C	4

(c)

Figure 5-15. Hierarchical routing.

Unfortunately, these gains in space are not free. There is a penalty to be paid, and this penalty is in the form of increased path length. For example, the best route from *1A* to *5C* is via region 2, but with hierarchical routing all traffic to region 5 goes via region 3, because that is better for most destinations in region 5.

When a single network becomes very large, an interesting question is: How many levels should the hierarchy have? For example, consider a subnet with 720 routers. If there is no hierarchy, each router needs 720 routing table entries. If the subnet is partitioned into 24 regions of 30 routers each, each router needs 30 local entries plus 23 remote entries for a total of 53 entries. If a three-level hierarchy is chosen, with eight clusters, each containing 9 regions of 10 routers, each router needs 10 entries for local routers, 8 entries for routing to other regions within its own cluster, and 7 entries for distant clusters, for a total of 25 entries. Kamoun and Kleinrock (1979) discovered that the optimal number of levels for an N router subnet is $\ln N$, requiring a total of $e \ln N$ entries per router. They have also shown that the increase in effective mean path length caused by hierarchical routing is sufficiently small that it is usually acceptable.

5.2.7 Broadcast Routing

In some applications, hosts need to send messages to many or all other hosts. For example, a service distributing weather reports, stock market updates, or live radio programs might work best by broadcasting to all machines and letting those that are interested read the data. Sending a packet to all destinations simultaneously is called **broadcasting**; various methods have been proposed for doing it.

One broadcasting method that requires no special features from the subnet is for the source to simply send a distinct packet to each destination. Not only is the method wasteful of bandwidth, but it also requires the source to have a complete list of all destinations. In practice this may be the only possibility, but it is the least desirable of the methods.

Flooding is another obvious candidate. Although flooding is ill-suited for ordinary point-to-point communication, for broadcasting it might rate serious consideration, especially if none of the methods described below are applicable. The problem with flooding as a broadcast technique is the same problem it has as a point-to-point routing algorithm: it generates too many packets and consumes too much bandwidth.

A third algorithm is **multidestination routing**. If this method is used, each packet contains either a list of destinations or a bit map indicating the desired destinations. When a packet arrives at a router, the router checks all the destinations to determine the set of output lines that will be needed. (An output line is needed if it is the best route to at least one of the destinations.) The router generates a new copy of the packet for each output line to be used and includes in each packet only those destinations that are to use the line. In effect, the destination set is partitioned among the output lines. After a sufficient number of hops, each packet will carry only one destination and can be treated as a normal packet. Multidestination routing is like separately addressed packets, except that when several packets must follow the same route, one of them pays full fare and the rest ride free.

A fourth broadcast algorithm makes explicit use of the sink tree for the router initiating the broadcast—or any other convenient spanning tree for that matter. A **spanning tree** is a subset of the subnet that includes all the routers but contains no loops. If each router knows which of its lines belong to the spanning tree, it can copy an incoming broadcast packet onto all the spanning tree lines except the one it arrived on. This method makes excellent use of bandwidth, generating the absolute minimum number of packets necessary to do the job. The only problem is that each router must have knowledge of some spanning tree for the method to be applicable. Sometimes this information is available (e.g., with link state routing) but sometimes it is not (e.g., with distance vector routing).

Our last broadcast algorithm is an attempt to approximate the behavior of the previous one, even when the routers do not know anything at all about spanning trees. The idea, called **reverse path forwarding**, is remarkably simple once it has been pointed out. When a broadcast packet arrives at a router, the router checks to see if the packet arrived on the line that is normally used for sending packets *to* the source of the broadcast. If so, there is an excellent chance that the broadcast packet itself followed the best route from the router and is therefore the first copy to arrive at the router. This being the case, the router forwards copies of it onto all lines except the one it arrived on. If, however, the broadcast packet arrived on a line other than the preferred one for reaching the source, the packet is discarded as a likely duplicate.

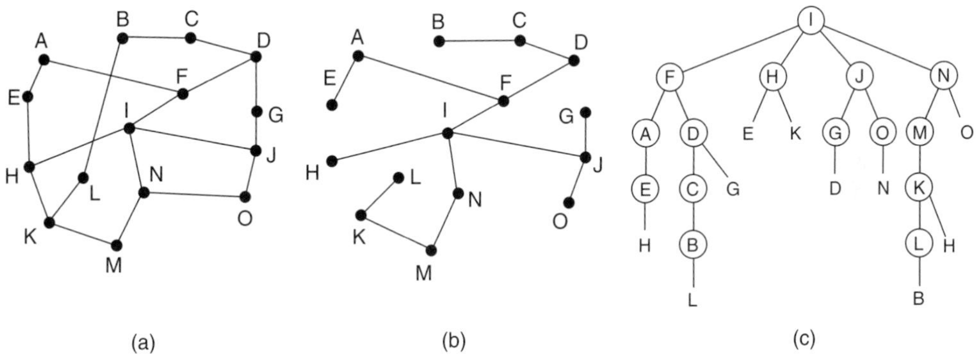

Figure 5-16. Reverse path forwarding. (a) A subnet. (b) A sink tree. (c) The tree built by reverse path forwarding.

An example of reverse path forwarding is shown in Fig. 5-16. Part (a) shows a subnet, part (b) shows a sink tree for router *I* of that subnet, and part (c) shows how the reverse path algorithm works. On the first hop, *I* sends packets to *F*, *H*, *J*, and *N*, as indicated by the second row of the tree. Each of these packets arrives on the preferred path to *I* (assuming that the preferred path falls along the sink tree) and is so indicated by a circle around the letter. On the second hop, eight packets are generated, two by each of the routers that received a packet on the first hop. As it turns out, all eight of these arrive at previously unvisited routers, and five of these arrive along the preferred line. Of the six packets generated on the third hop, only three arrive on the preferred path (at *C*, *E*, and *K*); the others are duplicates. After five hops and 24 packets, the broadcasting terminates, compared with four hops and 14 packets had the sink tree been followed exactly.

The principal advantage of reverse path forwarding is that it is both reasonably efficient and easy to implement. It does not require routers to know about spanning trees, nor does it have the overhead of a destination list or bit map in each broadcast packet as does multidestination addressing. Nor does it require any special mechanism to stop the process, as flooding does (either a hop counter in each packet and a priori knowledge of the subnet diameter, or a list of packets already seen per source).

5.2.8 Multicast Routing

Some applications require that widely-separated processes work together in groups, for example, a group of processes implementing a distributed database system. In these situations, it is frequently necessary for one process to send a message to all the other members of the group. If the group is small, it can just send each other member a point-to-point message. If the group is large, this strategy is expensive. Sometimes broadcasting can be used, but using broadcasting to inform 1000 machines on a million-node network is inefficient because most receivers are not interested in the message (or worse yet, they are definitely interested but are not supposed to see it). Thus, we need a way to send messages to well-defined groups that are numerically large in size but small compared to the network as a whole.

Sending a message to such a group is called **multicasting**, and its routing algorithm is called **multicast routing**. In this section we will describe one way of doing multicast routing. For additional information, see (Chu et al., 2000; Costa et al. 2001; Kasera et al., 2000; Madruga and Garcia-Luna-Aceves, 2001; Zhang and Ryu, 2001).

Multicasting requires group management. Some way is needed to create and destroy groups, and to allow processes to join and leave groups. How these tasks are accomplished is not of concern to the routing algorithm. What is of concern is that when a process joins a group, it informs its host of this fact. It is important that routers know which of their hosts belong to which groups. Either hosts must inform their routers about changes in group membership, or routers must query their hosts periodically. Either way, routers learn about which of their hosts are in which groups. Routers tell their neighbors, so the information propagates through the subnet.

To do multicast routing, each router computes a spanning tree covering all other routers. For example, in Fig. 5-17(a) we have two groups, 1 and 2. Some routers are attached to hosts that belong to one or both of these groups, as indicated in the figure. A spanning tree for the leftmost router is shown in Fig. 5-17(b).

When a process sends a multicast packet to a group, the first router examines its spanning tree and prunes it, removing all lines that do not lead to hosts that are members of the group. In our example, Fig. 5-17(c) shows the pruned spanning tree for group 1. Similarly, Fig. 5-17(d) shows the pruned spanning tree for group 2. Multicast packets are forwarded only along the appropriate spanning tree.

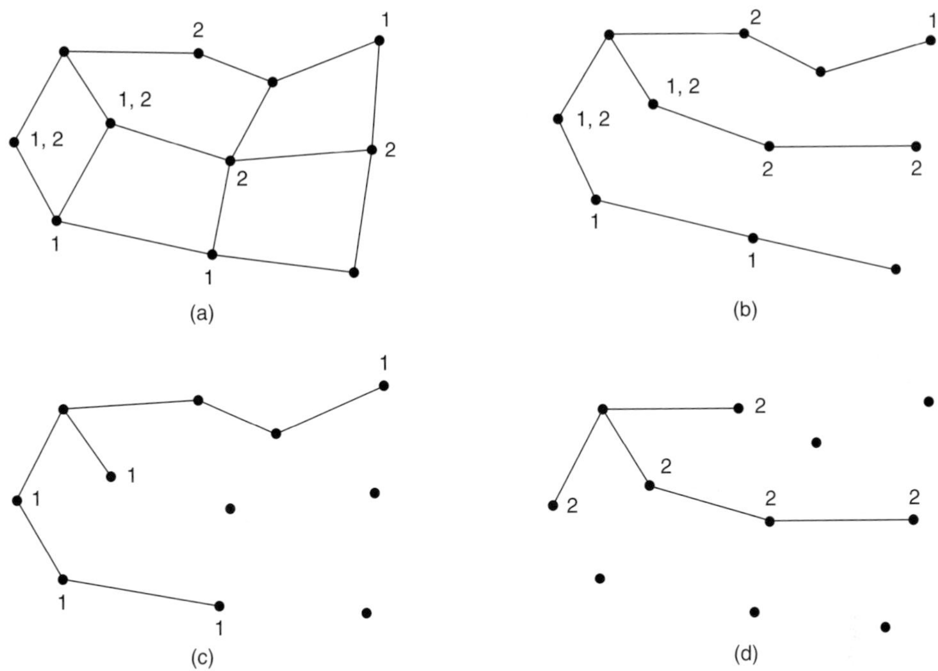

Figure 5-17. (a) A network. (b) A spanning tree for the leftmost router. (c) A multicast tree for group 1. (d) A multicast tree for group 2.

Various ways of pruning the spanning tree are possible. The simplest one can be used if link state routing is used and each router is aware of the complete topology, including which hosts belong to which groups. Then the spanning tree can be pruned, starting at the end of each path, working toward the root, and removing all routers that do not belong to the group in question.

With distance vector routing, a different pruning strategy can be followed. The basic algorithm is reverse path forwarding. However, whenever a router with no hosts interested in a particular group and no connections to other routers receives a multicast message for that group, it responds with a PRUNE message, telling the sender not to send it any more multicasts for that group. When a router with no group members among its own hosts has received such messages on all its lines, it, too, can respond with a PRUNE message. In this way, the subnet is recursively pruned.

One potential disadvantage of this algorithm is that it scales poorly to large networks. Suppose that a network has *n* groups, each with an average of *m* members. For each group, *m* pruned spanning trees must be stored, for a total of *mn* trees. When many large groups exist, considerable storage is needed to store all the trees.

An alternative design uses **core-based trees** (Ballardie et al., 1993). Here, a single spanning tree per group is computed, with the root (the core) near the middle of the group. To send a multicast message, a host sends it to the core, which then does the multicast along the spanning tree. Although this tree will not be optimal for all sources, the reduction in storage costs from *m* trees to one tree per group is a major saving.

5.2.9 Routing for Mobile Hosts

Millions of people have portable computers nowadays, and they generally want to read their e-mail and access their normal file systems wherever in the world they may be. These mobile hosts introduce a new complication: to route a packet to a mobile host, the network first has to find it. The subject of incorporating mobile hosts into a network is very young, but in this section we will sketch some of the issues and give a possible solution.

The model of the world that network designers typically use is shown in Fig. 5-18. Here we have a WAN consisting of routers and hosts. Connected to the WAN are LANs, MANs, and wireless cells of the type we studied in Chap. 2.

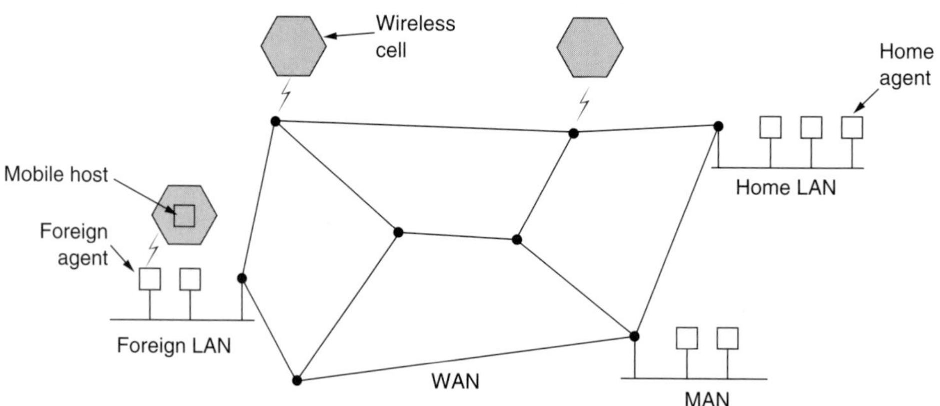

Figure 5-18. A WAN to which LANs, MANs, and wireless cells are attached.

Hosts that never move are said to be stationary. They are connected to the network by copper wires or fiber optics. In contrast, we can distinguish two other kinds of hosts. Migratory hosts are basically stationary hosts who move from one fixed site to another from time to time but use the network only when they are physically connected to it. Roaming hosts actually compute on the run and want to maintain their connections as they move around. We will use the term **mobile hosts** to mean either of the latter two categories, that is, all hosts that are away from home and still want to be connected.

All hosts are assumed to have a permanent **home location** that never changes. Hosts also have a permanent home address that can be used to determine their home locations, analogous to the way the telephone number 1-212-5551212 indicates the United States (country code 1) and Manhattan (212). The routing goal in systems with mobile hosts is to make it possible to send packets to mobile hosts using their home addresses and have the packets efficiently reach them wherever they may be. The trick, of course, is to find them.

In the model of Fig. 5-18, the world is divided up (geographically) into small units. Let us call them areas, where an area is typically a LAN or wireless cell. Each area has one or more **foreign agents**, which are processes that keep track of all mobile hosts visiting the area. In addition, each area has a **home agent**, which keeps track of hosts whose home is in the area, but who are currently visiting another area.

When a new host enters an area, either by connecting to it (e.g., plugging into the LAN) or just wandering into the cell, his computer must register itself with the foreign agent there. The registration procedure typically works like this:

1. Periodically, each foreign agent broadcasts a packet announcing its existence and address. A newly-arrived mobile host may wait for one of these messages, but if none arrives quickly enough, the mobile host can broadcast a packet saying: Are there any foreign agents around?

2. The mobile host registers with the foreign agent, giving its home address, current data link layer address, and some security information.

3. The foreign agent contacts the mobile host's home agent and says: One of your hosts is over here. The message from the foreign agent to the home agent contains the foreign agent's network address. It also includes the security information to convince the home agent that the mobile host is really there.

4. The home agent examines the security information, which contains a timestamp, to prove that it was generated within the past few seconds. If it is happy, it tells the foreign agent to proceed.

5. When the foreign agent gets the acknowledgement from the home agent, it makes an entry in its tables and informs the mobile host that it is now registered.

Ideally, when a host leaves an area, that, too, should be announced to allow deregistration, but many users abruptly turn off their computers when done.

When a packet is sent to a mobile host, it is routed to the host's home LAN because that is what the address says should be done, as illustrated in step 1 of Fig. 5-19. Here the sender, in the northwest city of Seattle, wants to send a packet to a host normally across the United States in New York. Packets sent to the mobile host on its home LAN in New York are intercepted by the home agent there. The home agent then looks up the mobile host's new (temporary) location and finds the address of the foreign agent handling the mobile host, in Los Angeles.

The home agent then does two things. First, it encapsulates the packet in the payload field of an outer packet and sends the latter to the foreign agent (step 2 in Fig. 5-19). This mechanism is called tunneling; we will look at it in more detail later. After getting the encapsulated packet, the foreign agent removes the original packet from the payload field and sends it to the mobile host as a data link frame.

Second, the home agent tells the sender to henceforth send packets to the mobile host by encapsulating them in the payload of packets explicitly addressed to the foreign agent instead of just sending them to the mobile host's home address (step 3). Subsequent packets can now be routed directly to the host via the foreign agent (step 4), bypassing the home location entirely.

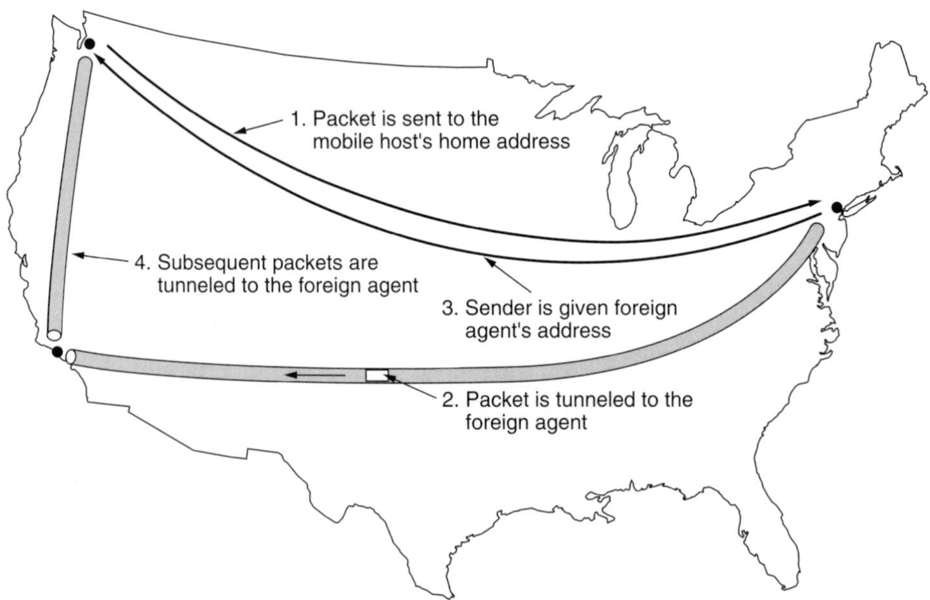

Figure 5-19. Packet routing for mobile hosts.

The various schemes that have been proposed differ in several ways. First, there is the issue of how much of this protocol is carried out by the routers and how much by the hosts, and in the latter case, by which layer in the hosts. Second, in a few schemes, routers along the way record mapped addresses so they can intercept and redirect traffic even before it gets to the home location. Third, in some schemes each visitor is given a unique temporary address; in others, the temporary address refers to an agent that handles traffic for all visitors.

Fourth, the schemes differ in how they actually manage to arrange for packets that are addressed to one destination to be delivered to a different one. One choice is changing the destination address and just retransmitting the modified packet. Alternatively, the whole packet, home address and all, can be encapsulated inside the payload of another packet sent to the temporary address. Finally, the schemes differ in their security aspects. In general, when a host or router gets a message of the form "Starting right now, please send all of Stephany's mail to me," it might have a couple of questions about whom it was talking to and whether this is a good idea. Several mobile host protocols are discussed and compared in (Hac and Guo, 2000; Perkins, 1998a; Snoeren and Balakrishnan, 2000; Solomon, 1998; and Wang and Chen, 2001).

5.2.10 Routing in Ad Hoc Networks

We have now seen how to do routing when the hosts are mobile but the routers are fixed. An even more extreme case is one in which the routers themselves are mobile. Among the possibilities are:

1. Military vehicles on a battlefield with no existing infrastructure.
2. A fleet of ships at sea.
3. Emergency workers at an earthquake that destroyed the infrastructure.
4. A gathering of people with notebook computers in an area lacking 802.11.

In all these cases, and others, each node consists of a router and a host, usually on the same computer. Networks of nodes that just happen to be near each other are called **ad hoc networks** or **MANETs** (**Mobile Ad hoc NETworks**). Let us now examine them briefly. More information can be found in (Perkins, 2001).

What makes ad hoc networks different from wired networks is that all the usual rules about fixed topologies, fixed and known neighbors, fixed relationship between IP address and location, and more are suddenly tossed out the window. Routers can come and go or appear in new places at the drop of a bit. With a wired network, if a router has a valid path to some destination, that path continues to be valid indefinitely (barring a failure somewhere in the system). With an ad hoc network, the topology may be changing all the time, so desirability and even validity of paths can change spontaneously, without warning. Needless to say, these circumstances make routing in ad hoc networks quite different from routing in their fixed counterparts.

A variety of routing algorithms for ad hoc networks have been proposed. One of the more interesting ones is the **AODV** (**Ad hoc On-demand Distance Vector**) routing algorithm (Perkins and Royer, 1999). It is a distant relative of the Bellman-Ford distance vector algorithm but adapted to work in a mobile environment and takes into account the limited bandwidth and low battery life found in this environment. Another unusual characteristic is that it is an on-demand algorithm, that is, it determines a route to some destination only when somebody wants to send a packet to that destination. Let us now see what that means.

Route Discovery

At any instant of time, an ad hoc network can be described by a graph of the nodes (routers + hosts). Two nodes are connected (i.e., have an arc between them in the graph) if they can communicate directly using their radios. Since one of the two may have a more powerful transmitter than the other, it is possible that *A* is connected to *B* but *B* is not connected to *A*. However, for simplicity, we will assume all connections are symmetric. It should also be noted that the mere fact that two nodes are within radio range of each other does not mean that they are connected. There may be buildings, hills, or other obstacles that block their communication.

To describe the algorithm, consider the ad hoc network of Fig. 5-20, in which a process at node *A* wants to send a packet to node *I*. The AODV algorithm maintains a table at each node, keyed by destination, giving information about that destination, including which neighbor to send packets to in order to reach the destination. Suppose that *A* looks in its table and does not find an entry for *I*. It now has to discover a route to *I*. This property of discovering routes only when they are needed is what makes this algorithm "on demand."

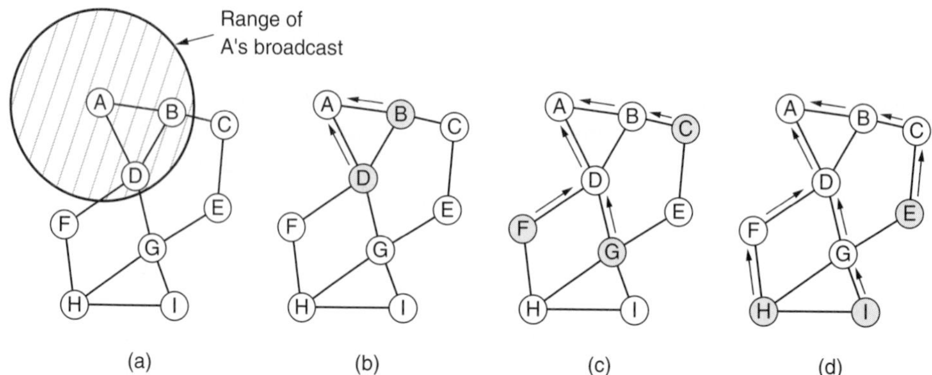

Figure 5-20. (a) Range of *A*'s broadcast. (b) After *B* and *D* have received *A*'s broadcast. (c) After *C*, *F*, and *G* have received *A*'s broadcast. (d) After *E*, *H*, and *I* have received *A*'s broadcast. The shaded nodes are new recipients. The arrows show the possible reverse routes.

To locate *I*, *A* constructs a special ROUTE REQUEST packet and broadcasts it. The packet reaches *B* and *D*, as illustrated in Fig. 5-20(a). In fact, the reason *B* and *D* are connected to *A* in the graph is that they can receive communication from *A*. *F*, for example, is not shown with an arc to *A* because it cannot receive *A*'s radio signal. Thus, *F* is not connected to *A*.

The format of the ROUTE REQUEST packet is shown in Fig. 5-21. It contains the source and destination addresses, typically their IP addresses, which identify who is looking for whom. It also contains a *Request ID*, which is a local counter maintained separately by each node and incremented each time a ROUTE REQUEST is broadcast. Together, the *Source address* and *Request ID* fields uniquely identify the ROUTE REQUEST packet to allow nodes to discard any duplicates they may receive.

Source address	Request ID	Destination address	Source sequence #	Dest. sequence #	Hop count

Figure 5-21. Format of a ROUTE REQUEST packet.

In addition to the *Request ID* counter, each node also maintains a second sequence counter incremented whenever a ROUTE REQUEST is sent (or a reply to someone else's ROUTE REQUEST). It functions a little bit like a clock and is used to tell new routes from old routes. The fourth field of Fig. 5-21 is *A*'s sequence counter; the fifth field is the most recent value of *I*'s sequence number that *A* has seen (0 if it has never seen it). The use of these fields will become clear shortly. The final field, *Hop count*, will keep track of how many hops the packet has made. It is initialized to 0.

When a ROUTE REQUEST packet arrives at a node (*B* and *D* in this case), it is processed in the following steps.

1. The (*Source address*, *Request ID*) pair is looked up in a local history table to see if this request has already been seen and processed. If it is a duplicate, it is discarded and processing stops. If it is not a duplicate, the pair is entered into the history table so future duplicates can be rejected, and processing continues.

2. The receiver looks up the destination in its route table. If a fresh route to the destination is known, a ROUTE REPLY packet is sent back to the source telling it how to get to the destination (basically: Use me). Fresh means that the *Destination sequence number* stored in the routing table is greater than or equal to the *Destination sequence number* in the ROUTE REQUEST packet. If it is less, the stored route is older than the previous route the source had for the destination, so step 3 is executed.

3. Since the receiver does not know a fresh route to the destination, it increments the *Hop count* field and rebroadcasts the ROUTE REQUEST packet. It also extracts the data from the packet and stores it as a new entry in its reverse route table. This information will be

used to construct the reverse route so that the reply can get back to the source later. The arrows in Fig. 5-20 are used for building the reverse route. A timer is also started for the newly-made reverse route entry. If it expires, the entry is deleted.

Neither *B* nor *D* knows where *I* is, so each of them creates a reverse route entry pointing back to *A*, as shown by the arrows in Fig. 5-20, and broadcasts the packet with *Hop count* set to 1. The broadcast from *B* reaches *C* and *D*. *C* makes an entry for it in its reverse route table and rebroadcasts it. In contrast, *D* rejects it as a duplicate. Similarly, *D*'s broadcast is rejected by *B*. However, *D*'s broadcast is accepted by *F* and *G* and stored, as shown in Fig. 5-20(c). After *E*, *H*, and *I* receive the broadcast, the ROUTE REQUEST finally reaches a destination that knows where *I* is, namely, *I* itself, as illustrated in Fig. 5-20(d). Note that although we have shown the broadcasts in three discrete steps here, the broadcasts from different nodes are not coordinated in any way.

In response to the incoming request, *I* builds a ROUTE REPLY packet, as shown in Fig. 5-22. The *Source address*, *Destination address*, and *Hop count* are copied from the incoming request, but the *Destination sequence number* taken from its counter in memory. The *Hop count* field is set to 0. The *Lifetime* field controls how long the route is valid. This packet is unicast to the node that the ROUTE REQUEST packet came from, in this case, *G*. It then follows the reverse path to *D* and finally to *A*. At each node, *Hop count* is incremented so the node can see how far from the destination (*I*) it is.

Source address	Destination address	Destination sequence #	Hop count	Lifetime

Figure 5-22. Format of a ROUTE REPLY packet.

At each intermediate node on the way back, the packet is inspected. It is entered into the local routing table as a route to *I* if one or more of the following three conditions are met:

1. No route to *I* is known.
2. The sequence number for *I* in the ROUTE REPLY packet is greater than the value in the routing table.
3. The sequence numbers are equal but the new route is shorter.

In this way, all the nodes on the reverse route learn the route to *I* for free, as a byproduct of *A*'s route discovery. Nodes that got the original REQUEST ROUTE packet but were not on the reverse path (*B*, *C*, *E*, *F*, and *H* in this example) discard the reverse route table entry when the associated timer expires.

In a large network, the algorithm generates many broadcasts, even for destinations that are close by. The number of broadcasts can be reduced as follows. The

IP packet's *Time to live* is initialized by the sender to the expected diameter of the network and decremented on each hop. If it hits 0, the packet is discarded instead of being broadcast.

The discovery process is then modified as follows. To locate a destination, the sender broadcasts a ROUTE REQUEST packet with *Time to live* set to 1. If no response comes back within a reasonable time, another one is sent, this time with *Time to live* set to 2. Subsequent attempts use 3, 4, 5, etc. In this way, the search is first attempted locally, then in increasingly wider rings.

Route Maintenance

Because nodes can move or be switched off, the topology can change spontaneously. For example, in Fig. 5-20, if *G* is switched off, *A* will not realize that the route it was using to *I* (*ADGI*) is no longer valid. The algorithm needs to be able to deal with this. Periodically, each node broadcasts a *Hello* message. Each of its neighbors is expected to respond to it. If no response is forthcoming, the broadcaster knows that that neighbor has moved out of range and is no longer connected to it. Similarly, if it tries to send a packet to a neighbor that does not respond, it learns that the neighbor is no longer available.

This information is used to purge routes that no longer work. For each possible destination, each node, *N*, keeps track of its neighbors that have fed it a packet for that destination during the last ΔT seconds. These are called *N*'s **active neighbors** for that destination. *N* does this by having a routing table keyed by destination and containing the outgoing node to use to reach the destination, the hop count to the destination, the most recent destination sequence number, and the list of active neighbors for that destination. A possible routing table for node *D* in our example topology is shown in Fig. 5-23(a).

Dest.	Next hop	Distance	Active neighbors	Other fields
A	A	1	F, G	
B	B	1	F, G	
C	B	2	F	
E	G	2		
F	F	1	A, B	
G	G	1	A, B	
H	F	2	A, B	
I	G	2	A, B	

(a)

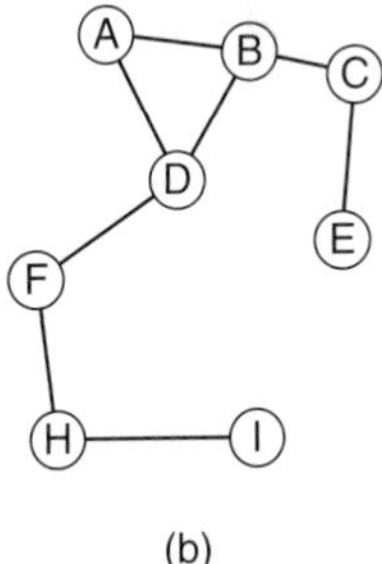

(b)

Figure 5-23. (a) *D*'s routing table before *G* goes down. (b) The graph after *G* has gone down.

When any of *N*'s neighbors becomes unreachable, it checks its routing table to see which destinations have routes using the now-gone neighbor. For each of these routes, the active neighbors are informed that their route via *N* is now invalid and must be purged from their routing tables. The active neighbors then tell their active neighbors, and so on, recursively, until all routes depending on the now-gone node are purged from all routing tables.

As an example of route maintenance, consider our previous example, but now with *G* suddenly switched off. The changed topology is illustrated in Fig. 5-23(b). When *D* discovers that *G* is gone, it looks at its routing table and sees that *G* was used on routes to *E*, *G*, and *I*. The union of the active neighbors for these destinations is the set {*A*, *B*}. In other words, *A* and *B* depend on *G* for some of their routes, so they have to be informed that these routes no longer work. *D* tells them by sending them packets that cause them to update their own routing tables accordingly. *D* also purges the entries for *E*, *G*, and *I* from its routing table.

It may not have been obvious from our description, but a critical difference between AODV and Bellman-Ford is that nodes do not send out periodic broadcasts containing their entire routing table. This difference saves both bandwidth and battery life.

AODV is also capable of doing broadcast and multicast routing. For details, consult (Perkins and Royer, 2001). Ad hoc routing is a red-hot research area. A great deal has been published on the topic. A few of the papers include (Chen et al., 2002; Hu and Johnson, 2001; Li et al., 2001; Raju and Garcia-Luna-Aceves, 2001; Ramanathan and Redi, 2002; Royer and Toh, 1999; Spohn and Garcia-Luna-Aceves, 2001; Tseng et al., 2001; and Zadeh et al., 2002).

5.2.11 Node Lookup in Peer-to-Peer Networks

A relatively new phenomenon is peer-to-peer networks, in which a large number of people, usually with permanent wired connections to the Internet, are in contact to share resources. The first widespread application of peer-to-peer technology was for mass crime: 50 million Napster users were exchanging copyrighted songs without the copyright owners' permission until Napster was shut down by the courts amid great controversy. Nevertheless, peer-to-peer technology has many interesting and legal uses. It also has something similar to a routing problem, although it is not quite the same as the ones we have studied so far. Nevertheless, it is worth a quick look.

What makes peer-to-peer systems interesting is that they are totally distributed. All nodes are symmetric and there is no central control or hierarchy. In a typical peer-to-peer system the users each have some information that may be of interest to other users. This information may be free software, (public domain) music, photographs, and so on. If there are large numbers of users, they will not know each other and will not know where to find what they are looking for. One solution is a big central database, but this may not be feasible for some reason (e.g., nobody is willing to host and maintain it). Thus, the problem comes down to how a user finds a node that contains what he is looking for in the absence of a centralized database or even a centralized index.

Let us assume that each user has one or more data items such as songs, photographs, programs, files, and so on that other users might want to read. Each item has an ASCII string naming it. A potential user knows just the ASCII string and wants to find out if one or more people have copies and, if so, what their IP addresses are.

As an example, consider a distributed genealogical database. Each genealogist has some on-line records for his or her ancestors and relatives, possibly with photos, audio, or even video clips of the person. Multiple people may have the same great grandfather, so an ancestor may have records at multiple nodes. The name of the record is the person's name in some canonical form. At some point, a genealogist discovers his great grandfather's will in an archive, in which the great grandfather bequeaths his gold pocket watch to his nephew. The genealogist now knows the nephew's name and wants to find out if any other genealogist has a record for him. How, without a central database, do we find out who, if anyone, has records?

Various algorithms have been proposed to solve this problem. The one we will examine is Chord (Dabek et al., 2001a; and Stoica et al., 2001). A simplified explanation of how it works is as follows. The Chord system consists of n participating users, each of whom may have some stored records and each of whom is prepared to store bits and pieces of the index for use by other users. Each user node has an IP address that can be hashed to an m-bit number using a hash function, *hash*. Chord uses SHA-1 for *hash*. SHA-1 is used in cryptography; we will look at it in Chap. 8. For now, it is just a function that takes a variable-length byte string as argument and produces a highly-random 160-bit number. Thus, we can convert any IP address to a 160-bit number called the **node identifier**.

Conceptually, all the 2^{160} node identifiers are arranged in ascending order in a big circle. Some of them correspond to participating nodes, but most of them do not. In Fig. 5-24(a) we show the node identifier circle for $m = 5$ (just ignore the arcs in the middle for the moment). In this example, the nodes with identifiers 1, 4, 7, 12, 15, 20, and 27 correspond to actual nodes and are shaded in the figure; the rest do not exist.

Let us now define the function $successor(k)$ as the node identifier of the first actual node following k around the circle clockwise. For example, $successor(6) = 7$, $successor(8) = 12$, and $successor(22) = 27$.

The names of the records (song names, ancestors' names, and so on) are also hashed with *hash* (i.e., SHA-1) to generate a 160-bit number, called the **key**. Thus, to convert *name* (the ASCII name of the record) to its key, we use $key = hash(name)$. This computation is just a local procedure call to *hash*. If a person holding a genealogical record for *name* wants to make it available to everyone, he first builds a tuple consisting of (*name*, *my-IP-address*) and then asks $successor(hash(name))$ to store the tuple. If multiple records (at different

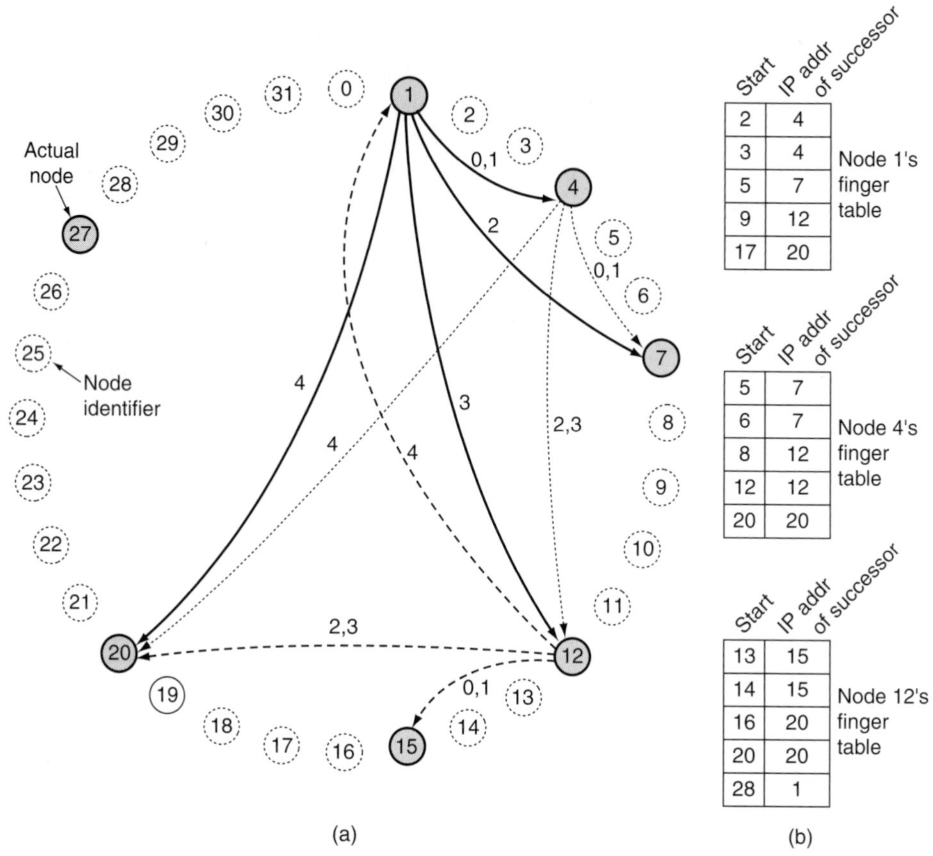

Node 1's finger table

Start	IP addr of successor
2	4
3	4
5	7
9	12
17	20

Node 4's finger table

Start	IP addr of successor
5	7
6	7
8	12
12	12
20	20

Node 12's finger table

Start	IP addr of successor
13	15
14	15
16	20
20	20
28	1

Figure 5-24. (a) A set of 32 node identifiers arranged in a circle. The shaded ones correspond to actual machines. The arcs show the fingers from nodes 1, 4, and 12. The labels on the arcs are the table indices. (b) Examples of the finger tables.

nodes) exist for this name, their tuple will all be stored at the same node. In this way, the index is distributed over the nodes at random. For fault tolerance, *p* different hash functions could be used to store each tuple at *p* nodes, but we will not consider that further here.

If some user later wants to look up *name*, he hashes it to get *key* and then uses *successor*(*key*) to find the IP address of the node storing its index tuples. The first step is easy; the second one is not. To make it possible to find the IP address of the node corresponding to a certain key, each node must maintain certain administrative data structures. One of these is the IP address of its successor node along the node identifier circle. For example, in Fig. 5-24, node 4's successor is 7 and node 7's successor is 12.

Lookup can now proceed as follows. The requesting node sends a packet to its successor containing its IP address and the key it is looking for. The packet is propagated around the ring until it locates the successor to the node identifier being sought. That node checks to see if it has any information matching the key, and if so, returns it directly to the requesting node, whose IP address it has.

As a first optimization, each node could hold the IP addresses of both its successor and its predecessor, so that queries could be sent either clockwise or counterclockwise, depending on which path is thought to be shorter. For example, node 7 in Fig. 5-24 could go clockwise to find node identifier 10 but counterclockwise to find node identifier 3.

Even with two choices of direction, linearly searching all the nodes is very inefficient in a large peer-to-peer system since the mean number of nodes required per search is $n/2$. To greatly speed up the search, each node also maintains what Chord calls a **finger table**. The finger table has m entries, indexed by 0 through $m - 1$, each one pointing to a different actual node. Each of the entries has two fields: *start* and the IP address of $successor(start)$, as shown for three example nodes in Fig. 5-24(b). The values of the fields for entry i at node k are:

$$start = k + 2^i \ \ (modulo\, 2^m)$$
$$\text{IP address of } \ successor(start\,[i\,])$$

Note that each node stores the IP addresses of a relatively small number of nodes and that most of these are fairly close by in terms of node identifier.

Using the finger table, the lookup of *key* at node k proceeds as follows. If *key* falls between k and $successor(k)$, then the node holding information about *key* is $successor(k)$ and the search terminates. Otherwise, the finger table is searched to find the entry whose *start* field is the closest predecessor of *key*. A request is then sent directly to the IP address in that finger table entry to ask it to continue the search. Since it is closer to *key* but still below it, chances are good that it will be able to return the answer with only a small number of additional queries. In fact, since every lookup halves the remaining distance to the target, it can be shown that the average number of lookups is $\log_2 n$.

As a first example, consider looking up $key = 3$ at node 1. Since node 1 knows that 3 lies between it and its successor, 4, the desired node is 4 and the search terminates, returning node 4's IP address.

As a second example, consider looking up $key = 14$ at node 1. Since 14 does not lie between 1 and 4, the finger table is consulted. The closest predecessor to 14 is 9, so the request is forwarded to the IP address of 9's entry, namely, that of node 12. Node 12 sees that 14 falls between it and its successor (15), so it returns the IP address of node 15.

As a third example, consider looking up $key = 16$ at node 1. Again a query is sent to node 12, but this time node 12 does not know the answer itself. It looks for the node most closely preceding 16 and finds 14, which yields the IP address of node 15. A query is then sent there. Node 15 observes that 16 lies between it and its successor (20), so it returns the IP address of 20 to the caller, which works its way back to node 1.

Since nodes join and leave all the time, Chord needs a way to handle these operations. We assume that when the system began operation it was small enough that the nodes could just exchange information directly to build the first circle and finger tables. After that an automated procedure is needed, as follows. When a new node, r, wants to join, it must contact some existing node and ask it to look up the IP address of $successor(r)$ for it. The new node then asks $successor(r)$ for its predecessor. The new node then asks both of these to insert r in between them in the circle. For example, if 24 in Fig. 5-24 wants to join, it asks any node to look up $successor(24)$, which is 27. Then it asks 27 for its predecessor (20). After it tells both of those about its existence, 20 uses 24 as its successor and 27 uses 24 as its predecessor. In addition, node 27 hands over those keys in the range 21–24, which now belong to 24. At this point, 24 is fully inserted.

However, many finger tables are now wrong. To correct them, every node runs a background process that periodically recomputes each finger by calling *successor*. When one of these queries hits a new node, the corresponding finger entry is updated.

When a node leaves gracefully, it hands its keys over to its successor and informs its predecessor of its departure so the predecessor can link to the departing node's successor. When a node crashes, a problem arises because its predecessor no longer has a valid successor. To alleviate this problem, each node keeps track not only of its direct successor but also its s direct successors, to allow it to skip over up to $s - 1$ consecutive failed nodes and reconnect the circle.

Chord has been used to construct a distributed file system (Dabek et al., 2001b) and other applications, and research is ongoing. A different peer-to-peer system, Pastry, and its applications are described in (Rowstron and Druschel, 2001a; and Rowstron and Druschel, 2001b). A third peer-to-peer system, Freenet, is discussed in (Clarke et al., 2002). A fourth system of this type is described in (Ratnasamy et al., 2001).

5.3 CONGESTION CONTROL ALGORITHMS

When too many packets are present in (a part of) the subnet, performance degrades. This situation is called **congestion**. Figure 5-25 depicts the symptom. When the number of packets dumped into the subnet by the hosts is within its carrying capacity, they are all delivered (except for a few that are afflicted with transmission errors) and the number delivered is proportional to the number sent. However, as traffic increases too far, the routers are no longer able to cope and they begin losing packets. This tends to make matters worse. At very high traffic, performance collapses completely and almost no packets are delivered.

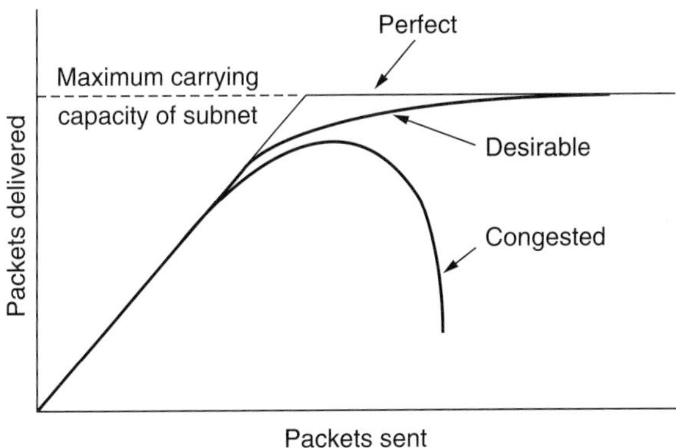

Figure 5-25. When too much traffic is offered, congestion sets in and performance degrades sharply.

Congestion can be brought on by several factors. If all of a sudden, streams of packets begin arriving on three or four input lines and all need the same output line, a queue will build up. If there is insufficient memory to hold all of them, packets will be lost. Adding more memory may help up to a point, but Nagle (1987) discovered that if routers have an infinite amount of memory, congestion gets worse, not better, because by the time packets get to the front of the queue, they have already timed out (repeatedly) and duplicates have been sent. All these packets will be dutifully forwarded to the next router, increasing the load all the way to the destination.

Slow processors can also cause congestion. If the routers' CPUs are slow at performing the bookkeeping tasks required of them (queueing buffers, updating tables, etc.), queues can build up, even though there is excess line capacity. Similarly, low-bandwidth lines can also cause congestion. Upgrading the lines but not changing the processors, or vice versa, often helps a little, but frequently just shifts the bottleneck. Also, upgrading part, but not all, of the system, often just moves the bottleneck somewhere else. The real problem is frequently a mismatch between parts of the system. This problem will persist until all the components are in balance.

It is worth explicitly pointing out the difference between congestion control and flow control, as the relationship is subtle. Congestion control has to do with making sure the subnet is able to carry the offered traffic. It is a global issue, involving the behavior of all the hosts, all the routers, the store-and-forwarding processing within the routers, and all the other factors that tend to diminish the carrying capacity of the subnet.

Flow control, in contrast, relates to the point-to-point traffic between a given sender and a given receiver. Its job is to make sure that a fast sender cannot continually transmit data faster than the receiver is able to absorb it. Flow control frequently involves some direct feedback from the receiver to the sender to tell the sender how things are doing at the other end.

To see the difference between these two concepts, consider a fiber optic network with a capacity of 1000 gigabits/sec on which a supercomputer is trying to transfer a file to a personal computer at 1 Gbps. Although there is no congestion (the network itself is not in trouble), flow control is needed to force the supercomputer to stop frequently to give the personal computer a chance to breathe.

At the other extreme, consider a store-and-forward network with 1-Mbps lines and 1000 large computers, half of which are trying to transfer files at 100 kbps to the other half. Here the problem is not that of fast senders overpowering slow receivers, but that the total offered traffic exceeds what the network can handle.

The reason congestion control and flow control are often confused is that some congestion control algorithms operate by sending messages back to the various sources telling them to slow down when the network gets into trouble. Thus, a host can get a "slow down" message either because the receiver cannot handle the load or because the network cannot handle it. We will come back to this point later.

We will start our study of congestion control by looking at a general model for dealing with it. Then we will look at broad approaches to preventing it in the first place. After that, we will look at various dynamic algorithms for coping with it once it has set in.

5.3.1 General Principles of Congestion Control

Many problems in complex systems, such as computer networks, can be viewed from a control theory point of view. This approach leads to dividing all solutions into two groups: open loop and closed loop. Open loop solutions attempt to solve the problem by good design, in essence, to make sure it does not occur in the first place. Once the system is up and running, midcourse corrections are not made.

Tools for doing open-loop control include deciding when to accept new traffic, deciding when to discard packets and which ones, and making scheduling decisions at various points in the network. All of these have in common the fact that they make decisions without regard to the current state of the network.

In contrast, closed loop solutions are based on the concept of a feedback loop. This approach has three parts when applied to congestion control:

1. Monitor the system to detect when and where congestion occurs.

2. Pass this information to places where action can be taken.

3. Adjust system operation to correct the problem.

A variety of metrics can be used to monitor the subnet for congestion. Chief among these are the percentage of all packets discarded for lack of buffer space, the average queue lengths, the number of packets that time out and are retransmitted, the average packet delay, and the standard deviation of packet delay. In all cases, rising numbers indicate growing congestion.

The second step in the feedback loop is to transfer the information about the congestion from the point where it is detected to the point where something can be done about it. The obvious way is for the router detecting the congestion to send a packet to the traffic source or sources, announcing the problem. Of course, these extra packets increase the load at precisely the moment that more load is not needed, namely, when the subnet is congested.

However, other possibilities also exist. For example, a bit or field can be reserved in every packet for routers to fill in whenever congestion gets above some threshold level. When a router detects this congested state, it fills in the field in all outgoing packets, to warn the neighbors.

Still another approach is to have hosts or routers periodically send probe packets out to explicitly ask about congestion. This information can then be used to route traffic around problem areas. Some radio stations have helicopters flying around their cities to report on road congestion to make it possible for their mobile listeners to route their packets (cars) around hot spots.

In all feedback schemes, the hope is that knowledge of congestion will cause the hosts to take appropriate action to reduce the congestion. For a scheme to work correctly, the time scale must be adjusted carefully. If every time two packets arrive in a row, a router yells STOP and every time a router is idle for 20 μsec, it yells GO, the system will oscillate wildly and never converge. On the other hand, if it waits 30 minutes to make sure before saying anything, the congestion control mechanism will react too sluggishly to be of any real use. To work well, some kind of averaging is needed, but getting the time constant right is a nontrivial matter.

Many congestion control algorithms are known. To provide a way to organize them in a sensible way, Yang and Reddy (1995) have developed a taxonomy for congestion control algorithms. They begin by dividing all algorithms into open loop or closed loop, as described above. They further divide the open loop algorithms into ones that act at the source versus ones that act at the destination. The closed loop algorithms are also divided into two subcategories: explicit feedback versus implicit feedback. In explicit feedback algorithms, packets are sent back from the point of congestion to warn the source. In implicit algorithms, the source deduces the existence of congestion by making local observations, such as the time needed for acknowledgements to come back.

The presence of congestion means that the load is (temporarily) greater than the resources (in part of the system) can handle. Two solutions come to mind: increase the resources or decrease the load. For example, the subnet may start using dial-up telephone lines to temporarily increase the bandwidth between certain points. On satellite systems, increasing transmission power often gives higher bandwidth. Splitting traffic over multiple routes instead of always using the best one may also effectively increase the bandwidth. Finally, spare routers that are normally used only as backups (to make the system fault tolerant) can be put on-line to give more capacity when serious congestion appears.

However, sometimes it is not possible to increase the capacity, or it has already been increased to the limit. The only way then to beat back the congestion is to decrease the load. Several ways exist to reduce the load, including denying service to some users, degrading service to some or all users, and having users schedule their demands in a more predictable way.

Some of these methods, which we will study shortly, can best be applied to virtual circuits. For subnets that use virtual circuits internally, these methods can be used at the network layer. For datagram subnets, they can nevertheless sometimes be used on transport layer connections. In this chapter, we will focus on their use in the network layer. In the next one, we will see what can be done at the transport layer to manage congestion.

5.3.2 Congestion Prevention Policies

Let us begin our study of methods to control congestion by looking at open loop systems. These systems are designed to minimize congestion in the first place, rather than letting it happen and reacting after the fact. They try to achieve their goal by using appropriate policies at various levels. In Fig. 5-26 we see different data link, network, and transport policies that can affect congestion (Jain, 1990).

Layer	Policies
Transport	• Retransmission policy • Out-of-order caching policy • Acknowledgement policy • Flow control policy • Timeout determination
Network	• Virtual circuits versus datagram inside the subnet • Packet queueing and service policy • Packet discard policy • Routing algorithm • Packet lifetime management
Data link	• Retransmission policy • Out-of-order caching policy • Acknowledgement policy • Flow control policy

Figure 5-26. Policies that affect congestion.

Let us start at the data link layer and work our way upward. The retransmission policy is concerned with how fast a sender times out and what it transmits upon timeout. A jumpy sender that times out quickly and retransmits all outstanding packets using go back n will put a heavier load on the system than will a leisurely sender that uses selective repeat. Closely related to this is the buffering policy. If receivers routinely discard all out-of-order packets, these packets will have to be transmitted again later, creating extra load. With respect to congestion control, selective repeat is clearly better than go back n.

Acknowledgement policy also affects congestion. If each packet is acknowledged immediately, the acknowledgement packets generate extra traffic. However, if acknowledgements are saved up to piggyback onto reverse traffic, extra timeouts and retransmissions may result. A tight flow control scheme (e.g., a small window) reduces the data rate and thus helps fight congestion.

At the network layer, the choice between using virtual circuits and using datagrams affects congestion since many congestion control algorithms work only with virtual-circuit subnets. Packet queueing and service policy relates to whether routers have one queue per input line, one queue per output line, or both. It also relates to the order in which packets are processed (e.g., round robin or priority based). Discard policy is the rule telling which packet is dropped when there is no space. A good policy can help alleviate congestion and a bad one can make it worse.

A good routing algorithm can help avoid congestion by spreading the traffic over all the lines, whereas a bad one can send too much traffic over already congested lines. Finally, packet lifetime management deals with how long a packet may live before being discarded. If it is too long, lost packets may clog up the works for a long time, but if it is too short, packets may sometimes time out before reaching their destination, thus inducing retransmissions.

In the transport layer, the same issues occur as in the data link layer, but in addition, determining the timeout interval is harder because the transit time across the network is less predictable than the transit time over a wire between two routers. If the timeout interval is too short, extra packets will be sent unnecessarily. If it is too long, congestion will be reduced but the response time will suffer whenever a packet is lost.

5.3.3 Congestion Control in Virtual-Circuit Subnets

The congestion control methods described above are basically open loop: they try to prevent congestion from occurring in the first place, rather than dealing with it after the fact. In this section we will describe some approaches to dynamically controlling congestion in virtual-circuit subnets. In the next two, we will look at techniques that can be used in any subnet.

One technique that is widely used to keep congestion that has already started from getting worse is **admission control**. The idea is simple: once congestion has been signaled, no more virtual circuits are set up until the problem has gone away. Thus, attempts to set up new transport layer connections fail. Letting more people in just makes matters worse. While this approach is crude, it is simple and easy to carry out. In the telephone system, when a switch gets overloaded, it also practices admission control by not giving dial tones.

An alternative approach is to allow new virtual circuits but carefully route all new virtual circuits around problem areas. For example, consider the subnet of Fig. 5-27(a), in which two routers are congested, as indicated.

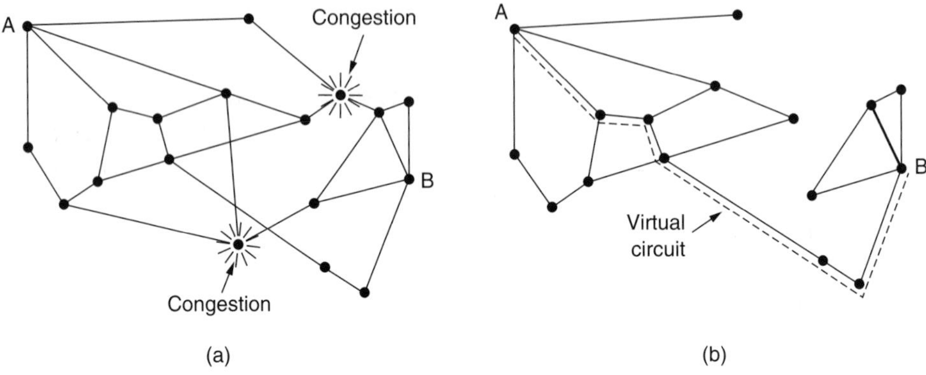

Figure 5-27. (a) A congested subnet. (b) A redrawn subnet that eliminates the congestion. A virtual circuit from *A* to *B* is also shown.

Suppose that a host attached to router *A* wants to set up a connection to a host attached to router *B*. Normally, this connection would pass through one of the congested routers. To avoid this situation, we can redraw the subnet as shown in Fig. 5-27(b), omitting the congested routers and all of their lines. The dashed line shows a possible route for the virtual circuit that avoids the congested routers.

Another strategy relating to virtual circuits is to negotiate an agreement between the host and subnet when a virtual circuit is set up. This agreement normally specifies the volume and shape of the traffic, quality of service required, and other parameters. To keep its part of the agreement, the subnet will typically reserve resources along the path when the circuit is set up. These resources can include table and buffer space in the routers and bandwidth on the lines. In this way, congestion is unlikely to occur on the new virtual circuits because all the necessary resources are guaranteed to be available.

This kind of reservation can be done all the time as standard operating procedure or only when the subnet is congested. A disadvantage of doing it all the time is that it tends to waste resources. If six virtual circuits that might use 1 Mbps all pass through the same physical 6-Mbps line, the line has to be marked as full, even though it may rarely happen that all six virtual circuits are transmitting full blast at the same time. Consequently, the price of the congestion control is unused (i.e., wasted) bandwidth in the normal case.

5.3.4 Congestion Control in Datagram Subnets

Let us now turn to some approaches that can be used in datagram subnets (and also in virtual-circuit subnets). Each router can easily monitor the utilization of its output lines and other resources. For example, it can associate with each line a real variable, u, whose value, between 0.0 and 1.0, reflects the recent utilization of that line. To maintain a good estimate of u, a sample of the instantaneous line utilization, f (either 0 or 1), can be made periodically and u updated according to

$$u_{\text{new}} = au_{\text{old}} + (1 - a)f$$

where the constant a determines how fast the router forgets recent history.

Whenever u moves above the threshold, the output line enters a "warning" state. Each newly-arriving packet is checked to see if its output line is in warning state. If it is, some action is taken. The action taken can be one of several alternatives, which we will now discuss.

The Warning Bit

The old DECNET architecture signaled the warning state by setting a special bit in the packet's header. So does frame relay. When the packet arrived at its destination, the transport entity copied the bit into the next acknowledgement sent back to the source. The source then cut back on traffic.

As long as the router was in the warning state, it continued to set the warning bit, which meant that the source continued to get acknowledgements with it set. The source monitored the fraction of acknowledgements with the bit set and adjusted its transmission rate accordingly. As long as the warning bits continued to flow in, the source continued to decrease its transmission rate. When they slowed to a trickle, it increased its transmission rate. Note that since every router along the path could set the warning bit, traffic increased only when no router was in trouble.

Choke Packets

The previous congestion control algorithm is fairly subtle. It uses a roundabout means to tell the source to slow down. Why not just tell it directly? In this approach, the router sends a **choke packet** back to the source host, giving it the destination found in the packet. The original packet is tagged (a header bit is turned on) so that it will not generate any more choke packets farther along the path and is then forwarded in the usual way.

When the source host gets the choke packet, it is required to reduce the traffic sent to the specified destination by X percent. Since other packets aimed at the same destination are probably already under way and will generate yet more choke packets, the host should ignore choke packets referring to that destination for a fixed time interval. After that period has expired, the host listens for more choke packets for another interval. If one arrives, the line is still congested, so the host reduces the flow still more and begins ignoring choke packets again. If no choke packets arrive during the listening period, the host may increase the flow again. The feedback implicit in this protocol can help prevent congestion yet not throttle any flow unless trouble occurs.

Hosts can reduce traffic by adjusting their policy parameters, for example, their window size. Typically, the first choke packet causes the data rate to be reduced to 0.50 of its previous rate, the next one causes a reduction to 0.25, and so on. Increases are done in smaller increments to prevent congestion from reoccurring quickly.

Several variations on this congestion control algorithm have been proposed. For one, the routers can maintain several thresholds. Depending on which threshold has been crossed, the choke packet can contain a mild warning, a stern warning, or an ultimatum.

Another variation is to use queue lengths or buffer utilization instead of line utilization as the trigger signal. The same exponential weighting can be used with this metric as with *u*, of course.

Hop-by-Hop Choke Packets

At high speeds or over long distances, sending a choke packet to the source hosts does not work well because the reaction is so slow. Consider, for example, a host in San Francisco (router *A* in Fig. 5-28) that is sending traffic to a host in New York (router *D* in Fig. 5-28) at 155 Mbps. If the New York host begins to run out of buffers, it will take about 30 msec for a choke packet to get back to San Francisco to tell it to slow down. The choke packet propagation is shown as the second, third, and fourth steps in Fig. 5-28(a). In those 30 msec, another 4.6 megabits will have been sent. Even if the host in San Francisco completely shuts down immediately, the 4.6 megabits in the pipe will continue to pour in and have to be dealt with. Only in the seventh diagram in Fig. 5-28(a) will the New York router notice a slower flow.

An alternative approach is to have the choke packet take effect at every hop it passes through, as shown in the sequence of Fig. 5-28(b). Here, as soon as the choke packet reaches *F*, *F* is required to reduce the flow to *D*. Doing so will require *F* to devote more buffers to the flow, since the source is still sending away at full blast, but it gives *D* immediate relief, like a headache remedy in a television commercial. In the next step, the choke packet reaches *E*, which tells *E* to reduce the flow to *F*. This action puts a greater demand on *E*'s buffers but gives *F* immediate relief. Finally, the choke packet reaches *A* and the flow genuinely slows down.

The net effect of this hop-by-hop scheme is to provide quick relief at the point of congestion at the price of using up more buffers upstream. In this way, con-

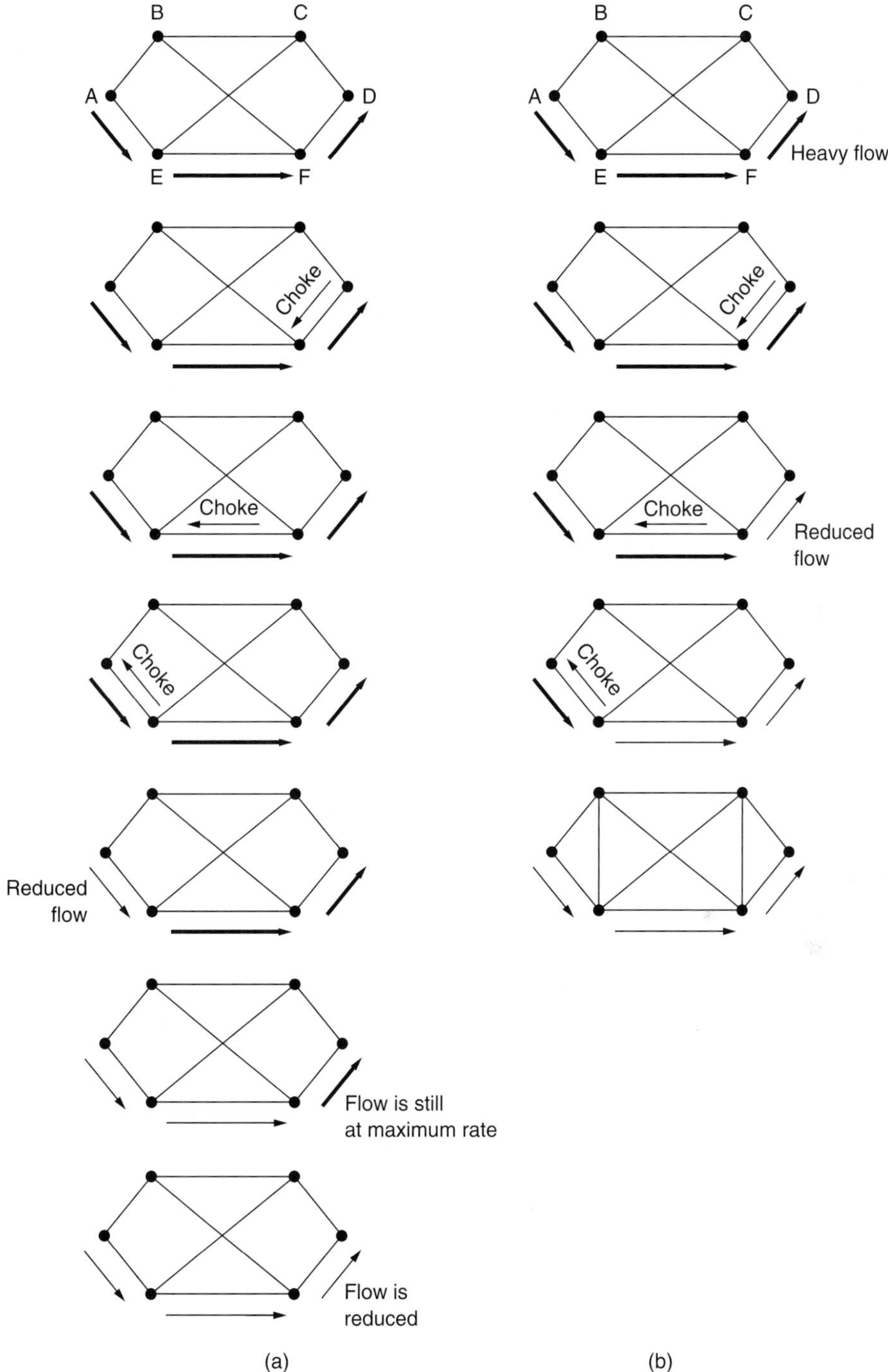

Figure 5-28. (a) A choke packet that affects only the source. (b) A choke packet that affects each hop it passes through.

gestion can be nipped in the bud without losing any packets. The idea is discussed in detail and simulation results are given in (Mishra and Kanakia, 1992).

5.3.5 Load Shedding

When none of the above methods make the congestion disappear, routers can bring out the heavy artillery: load shedding. **Load shedding** is a fancy way of saying that when routers are being inundated by packets that they cannot handle, they just throw them away. The term comes from the world of electrical power generation, where it refers to the practice of utilities intentionally blacking out certain areas to save the entire grid from collapsing on hot summer days when the demand for electricity greatly exceeds the supply.

A router drowning in packets can just pick packets at random to drop, but usually it can do better than that. Which packet to discard may depend on the applications running. For file transfer, an old packet is worth more than a new one because dropping packet 6 and keeping packets 7 through 10 will cause a gap at the receiver that may force packets 6 through 10 to be retransmitted (if the receiver routinely discards out-of-order packets). In a 12-packet file, dropping 6 may require 7 through 12 to be retransmitted, whereas dropping 10 may require only 10 through 12 to be retransmitted. In contrast, for multimedia, a new packet is more important than an old one. The former policy (old is better than new) is often called **wine** and the latter (new is better than old) is often called **milk**.

A step above this in intelligence requires cooperation from the senders. For many applications, some packets are more important than others. For example, certain algorithms for compressing video periodically transmit an entire frame and then send subsequent frames as differences from the last full frame. In this case, dropping a packet that is part of a difference is preferable to dropping one that is part of a full frame. As another example, consider transmitting a document containing ASCII text and pictures. Losing a line of pixels in some image is far less damaging than losing a line of readable text.

To implement an intelligent discard policy, applications must mark their packets in priority classes to indicate how important they are. If they do this, then when packets have to be discarded, routers can first drop packets from the lowest class, then the next lowest class, and so on. Of course, unless there is some significant incentive to mark packets as anything other than VERY IMPORTANT—NEVER, EVER DISCARD, nobody will do it.

The incentive might be in the form of money, with the low-priority packets being cheaper to send than the high-priority ones. Alternatively, senders might be allowed to send high-priority packets under conditions of light load, but as the load increased they would be discarded, thus encouraging the users to stop sending them.

Another option is to allow hosts to exceed the limits specified in the agreement negotiated when the virtual circuit was set up (e.g., use a higher bandwidth than allowed), but subject to the condition that all excess traffic be marked as low priority. Such a strategy is actually not a bad idea, because it makes more efficient use of idle resources, allowing hosts to use them as long as nobody else is interested, but without establishing a right to them when times get tough.

Random Early Detection

It is well known that dealing with congestion after it is first detected is more effective than letting it gum up the works and then trying to deal with it. This observation leads to the idea of discarding packets before all the buffer space is really exhausted. A popular algorithm for doing this is called **RED** (**Random Early Detection**) (Floyd and Jacobson, 1993). In some transport protocols (including TCP), the response to lost packets is for the source to slow down. The reasoning behind this logic is that TCP was designed for wired networks and wired networks are very reliable, so lost packets are mostly due to buffer overruns rather than transmission errors. This fact can be exploited to help reduce congestion.

By having routers drop packets before the situation has become hopeless (hence the "early" in the name), the idea is that there is time for action to be taken before it is too late. To determine when to start discarding, routers maintain a running average of their queue lengths. When the average queue length on some line exceeds a threshold, the line is said to be congested and action is taken.

Since the router probably cannot tell which source is causing most of the trouble, picking a packet at random from the queue that triggered the action is probably as good as it can do.

How should the router tell the source about the problem? One way is to send it a choke packet, as we have described. A problem with that approach is that it puts even more load on the already congested network. A different strategy is to just discard the selected packet and not report it. The source will eventually notice the lack of acknowledgement and take action. Since it knows that lost packets are generally caused by congestion and discards, it will respond by slowing down instead of trying harder. This implicit form of feedback only works when sources respond to lost packets by slowing down their transmission rate. In wireless networks, where most losses are due to noise on the air link, this approach cannot be used.

5.3.6 Jitter Control

For applications such as audio and video streaming, it does not matter much if the packets take 20 msec or 30 msec to be delivered, as long as the transit time is constant. The variation (i.e., standard deviation) in the packet arrival times is called **jitter**. High jitter, for example, having some packets taking 20 msec and others taking 30 msec to arrive will give an uneven quality to the sound or movie. Jitter is illustrated in Fig. 5-29. In contrast, an agreement that 99 percent of the packets be delivered with a delay in the range of 24.5 msec to 25.5 msec might be acceptable.

The range chosen must be feasible, of course. It must take into account the speed-of-light transit time and the minimum delay through the routers and perhaps leave a little slack for some inevitable delays.

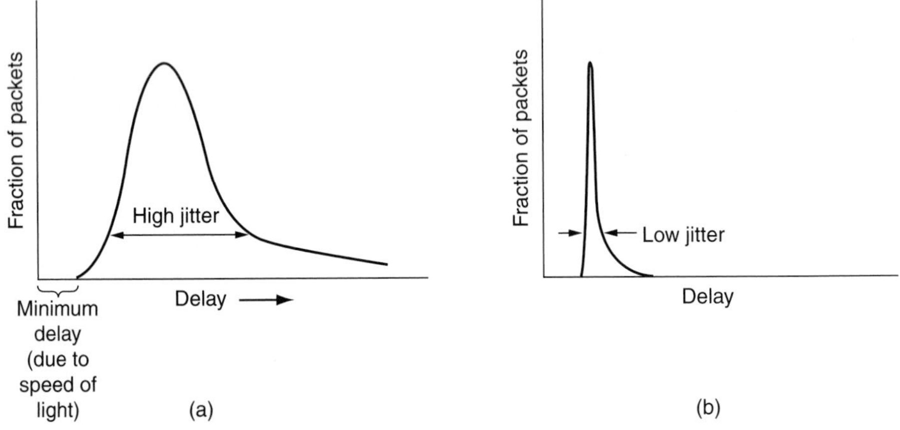

Figure 5-29. (a) High jitter. (b) Low jitter.

The jitter can be bounded by computing the expected transit time for each hop along the path. When a packet arrives at a router, the router checks to see how much the packet is behind or ahead of its schedule. This information is stored in the packet and updated at each hop. If the packet is ahead of schedule, it is held just long enough to get it back on schedule. If it is behind schedule, the router tries to get it out the door quickly.

In fact, the algorithm for determining which of several packets competing for an output line should go next can always choose the packet furthest behind in its schedule. In this way, packets that are ahead of schedule get slowed down and packets that are behind schedule get speeded up, in both cases reducing the amount of jitter.

In some applications, such as video on demand, jitter can be eliminated by buffering at the receiver and then fetching data for display from the buffer instead of from the network in real time. However, for other applications, especially those that require real-time interaction between people such as Internet telephony and videoconferencing, the delay inherent in buffering is not acceptable.

Congestion control is an active area of research. The state-of-the-art is summarized in (Gevros et al., 2001).

5.4 QUALITY OF SERVICE

The techniques we looked at in the previous sections are designed to reduce congestion and improve network performance. However, with the growth of multimedia networking, often these ad hoc measures are not enough. Serious attempts at guaranteeing quality of service through network and protocol design are needed. In the following sections we will continue our study of network performance, but now with a sharper focus on ways to provide a quality of service matched to application needs. It should be stated at the start, however, that many of these ideas are in flux and are subject to change.

5.4.1 Requirements

A stream of packets from a source to a destination is called a **flow**. In a connection-oriented network, all the packets belonging to a flow follow the same route; in a connectionless network, they may follow different routes. The needs of each flow can be characterized by four primary parameters: reliability, delay, jitter, and bandwidth. Together these determine the **QoS** (**Quality of Service**) the flow requires. Several common applications and the stringency of their requirements are listed in Fig. 5-30.

Application	Reliability	Delay	Jitter	Bandwidth
E-mail	High	Low	Low	Low
File transfer	High	Low	Low	Medium
Web access	High	Medium	Low	Medium
Remote login	High	Medium	Medium	Low
Audio on demand	Low	Low	High	Medium
Video on demand	Low	Low	High	High
Telephony	Low	High	High	Low
Videoconferencing	Low	High	High	High

Figure 5-30. How stringent the quality-of-service requirements are.

The first four applications have stringent requirements on reliability. No bits may be delivered incorrectly. This goal is usually achieved by checksumming each packet and verifying the checksum at the destination. If a packet is damaged in transit, it is not acknowledged and will be retransmitted eventually. This strategy gives high reliability. The four final (audio/video) applications can tolerate errors, so no checksums are computed or verified.

File transfer applications, including e-mail and video, are not delay sensitive. If all packets are delayed uniformly by a few seconds, no harm is done. Interactive applications, such as Web surfing and remote login, are more delay sensitive.

Real-time applications, such as telephony and videoconferencing have strict delay requirements. If all the words in a telephone call are each delayed by exactly 2.000 seconds, the users will find the connection unacceptable. On the other hand, playing audio or video files from a server does not require low delay.

The first three applications are not sensitive to the packets arriving with irregular time intervals between them. Remote login is somewhat sensitive to that, since characters on the screen will appear in little bursts if the connection suffers much jitter. Video and especially audio are extremely sensitive to jitter. If a user is watching a video over the network and the frames are all delayed by exactly 2.000 seconds, no harm is done. But if the transmission time varies randomly between 1 and 2 seconds, the result will be terrible. For audio, a jitter of even a few milliseconds is clearly audible.

Finally, the applications differ in their bandwidth needs, with e-mail and remote login not needing much, but video in all forms needing a great deal.

ATM networks classify flows in four broad categories with respect to their QoS demands as follows:

1. Constant bit rate (e.g., telephony).
2. Real-time variable bit rate (e.g., compressed videoconferencing).
3. Non-real-time variable bit rate (e.g., watching a movie over the Internet).
4. Available bit rate (e.g., file transfer).

These categories are also useful for other purposes and other networks. Constant bit rate is an attempt to simulate a wire by providing a uniform bandwidth and a uniform delay. Variable bit rate occurs when video is compressed, some frames compressing more than others. Thus, sending a frame with a lot of detail in it may require sending many bits whereas sending a shot of a white wall may compress extremely well. Available bit rate is for applications, such as e-mail, that are not sensitive to delay or jitter.

5.4.2 Techniques for Achieving Good Quality of Service

Now that we know something about QoS requirements, how do we achieve them? Well, to start with, there is no magic bullet. No single technique provides efficient, dependable QoS in an optimum way. Instead, a variety of techniques have been developed, with practical solutions often combining multiple techniques. We will now examine some of the techniques system designers use to achieve QoS.

Overprovisioning

An easy solution is to provide so much router capacity, buffer space, and bandwidth that the packets just fly through easily. The trouble with this solution is that it is expensive. As time goes on and designers have a better idea of how much is enough, this technique may even become practical. To some extent, the telephone system is overprovisioned. It is rare to pick up a telephone and not get a dial tone instantly. There is simply so much capacity available there that demand can always be met.

Buffering

Flows can be buffered on the receiving side before being delivered. Buffering them does not affect the reliability or bandwidth, and increases the delay, but it smooths out the jitter. For audio and video on demand, jitter is the main problem, so this technique helps a lot.

We saw the difference between high jitter and low jitter in Fig. 5-29. In Fig. 5-31 we see a stream of packets being delivered with substantial jitter. Packet 1 is sent from the server at $t = 0$ sec and arrives at the client at $t = 1$ sec. Packet 2 undergoes more delay and takes 2 sec to arrive. As the packets arrive, they are buffered on the client machine.

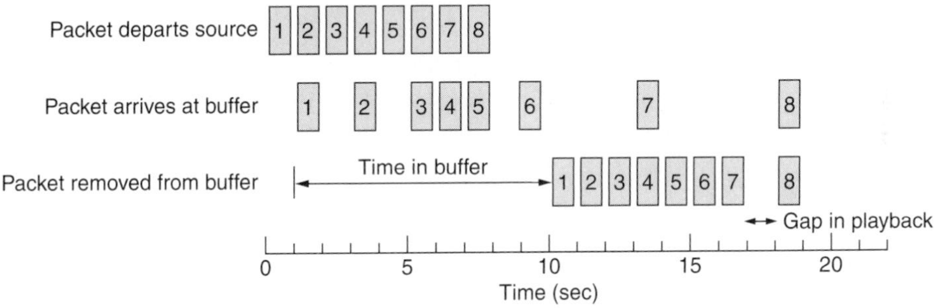

Figure 5-31. Smoothing the output stream by buffering packets.

At $t = 10$ sec, playback begins. At this time, packets 1 through 6 have been buffered so that they can be removed from the buffer at uniform intervals for smooth play. Unfortunately, packet 8 has been delayed so much that it is not available when its play slot comes up, so playback must stop until it arrives, creating an annoying gap in the music or movie. This problem can be alleviated by delaying the starting time even more, although doing so also requires a larger buffer. Commercial Web sites that contain streaming audio or video all use players that buffer for about 10 seconds before starting to play.

Traffic Shaping

In the above example, the source outputs the packets with a uniform spacing between them, but in other cases, they may be emitted irregularly, which may cause congestion to occur in the network. Nonuniform output is common if the server is handling many streams at once, and it also allows other actions, such as fast forward and rewind, user authentication, and so on. Also, the approach we used here (buffering) is not always possible, for example, with videoconferencing. However, if something could be done to make the server (and hosts in general) transmit at a uniform rate, quality of service would be better. We will now examine a technique, **traffic shaping**, which smooths out the traffic on the server side, rather than on the client side.

Traffic shaping is about regulating the average *rate* (and burstiness) of data transmission. In contrast, the sliding window protocols we studied earlier limit the amount of data in transit at once, not the rate at which it is sent. When a connection is set up, the user and the subnet (i.e., the customer and the carrier) agree on a certain traffic pattern (i.e., shape) for that circuit. Sometimes this is called a **service level agreement**. As long as the customer fulfills her part of the bargain and only sends packets according to the agreed-on contract, the carrier promises to deliver them all in a timely fashion. Traffic shaping reduces congestion and thus helps the carrier live up to its promise. Such agreements are not so important for file transfers but are of great importance for real-time data, such as audio and video connections, which have stringent quality-of-service requirements.

In effect, with traffic shaping the customer says to the carrier: My transmission pattern will look like this; can you handle it? If the carrier agrees, the issue arises of how the carrier can tell if the customer is following the agreement and what to do if the customer is not. Monitoring a traffic flow is called **traffic policing**. Agreeing to a traffic shape and policing it afterward are easier with virtual-circuit subnets than with datagram subnets. However, even with datagram subnets, the same ideas can be applied to transport layer connections.

The Leaky Bucket Algorithm

Imagine a bucket with a small hole in the bottom, as illustrated in Fig. 5-32(a). No matter the rate at which water enters the bucket, the outflow is at a constant rate, ρ, when there is any water in the bucket and zero when the bucket is empty. Also, once the bucket is full, any additional water entering it spills over the sides and is lost (i.e., does not appear in the output stream under the hole).

The same idea can be applied to packets, as shown in Fig. 5-32(b). Conceptually, each host is connected to the network by an interface containing a leaky bucket, that is, a finite internal queue. If a packet arrives at the queue when it is full, the packet is discarded. In other words, if one or more processes within the host try to send a packet when the maximum number is already queued, the new packet is unceremoniously discarded. This arrangement can be built into the hardware interface or simulated by the host operating system. It was first proposed by Turner (1986) and is called the **leaky bucket algorithm**. In fact, it is nothing other than a single-server queueing system with constant service time.

The host is allowed to put one packet per clock tick onto the network. Again, this can be enforced by the interface card or by the operating system. This mech-

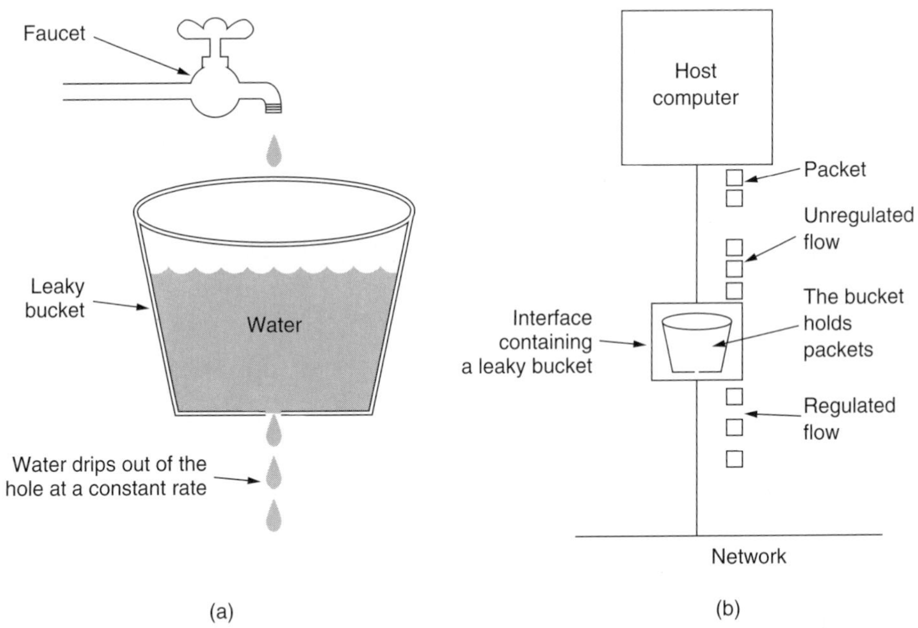

Figure 5-32. (a) A leaky bucket with water. (b) A leaky bucket with packets.

anism turns an uneven flow of packets from the user processes inside the host into an even flow of packets onto the network, smoothing out bursts and greatly reducing the chances of congestion.

When the packets are all the same size (e.g., ATM cells), this algorithm can be used as described. However, when variable-sized packets are being used, it is often better to allow a fixed number of bytes per tick, rather than just one packet. Thus, if the rule is 1024 bytes per tick, a single 1024-byte packet can be admitted on a tick, two 512-byte packets, four 256-byte packets, and so on. If the residual byte count is too low, the next packet must wait until the next tick.

Implementing the original leaky bucket algorithm is easy. The leaky bucket consists of a finite queue. When a packet arrives, if there is room on the queue it is appended to the queue; otherwise, it is discarded. At every clock tick, one packet is transmitted (unless the queue is empty).

The byte-counting leaky bucket is implemented almost the same way. At each tick, a counter is initialized to n. If the first packet on the queue has fewer bytes than the current value of the counter, it is transmitted, and the counter is decremented by that number of bytes. Additional packets may also be sent, as long as the counter is high enough. When the counter drops below the length of the next packet on the queue, transmission stops until the next tick, at which time the residual byte count is reset and the flow can continue.

As an example of a leaky bucket, imagine that a computer can produce data at 25 million bytes/sec (200 Mbps) and that the network also runs at this speed. However, the routers can accept this data rate only for short intervals (basically, until their buffers fill up). For long intervals, they work best at rates not exceeding 2 million bytes/sec. Now suppose data comes in 1-million-byte bursts, one 40-msec burst every second. To reduce the average rate to 2 MB/sec, we could use a leaky bucket with $\rho = 2$ MB/sec and a capacity, C, of 1 MB. This means that bursts of up to 1 MB can be handled without data loss and that such bursts are spread out over 500 msec, no matter how fast they come in.

In Fig. 5-33(a) we see the input to the leaky bucket running at 25 MB/sec for 40 msec. In Fig. 5-33(b) we see the output draining out at a uniform rate of 2 MB/sec for 500 msec.

The Token Bucket Algorithm

The leaky bucket algorithm enforces a rigid output pattern at the average rate, no matter how bursty the traffic is. For many applications, it is better to allow the output to speed up somewhat when large bursts arrive, so a more flexible algorithm is needed, preferably one that never loses data. One such algorithm is the **token bucket algorithm**. In this algorithm, the leaky bucket holds tokens, generated by a clock at the rate of one token every ΔT sec. In Fig. 5-34(a) we see a bucket holding three tokens, with five packets waiting to be transmitted. For a packet to be transmitted, it must capture and destroy one token. In Fig. 5-34(b) we see that three of the five packets have gotten through, but the other two are stuck waiting for two more tokens to be generated.

The token bucket algorithm provides a different kind of traffic shaping than that of the leaky bucket algorithm. The leaky bucket algorithm does not allow idle hosts to save up permission to send large bursts later. The token bucket algorithm does allow saving, up to the maximum size of the bucket, n. This property means that bursts of up to n packets can be sent at once, allowing some burstiness in the output stream and giving faster response to sudden bursts of input.

Another difference between the two algorithms is that the token bucket algorithm throws away tokens (i.e., transmission capacity) when the bucket fills up but never discards packets. In contrast, the leaky bucket algorithm discards packets when the bucket fills up.

Here, too, a minor variant is possible, in which each token represents the right to send not one packet, but k bytes. A packet can only be transmitted if enough tokens are available to cover its length in bytes. Fractional tokens are kept for future use.

The leaky bucket and token bucket algorithms can also be used to smooth traffic between routers, as well as to regulate host output as in our examples. However, one clear difference is that a token bucket regulating a host can make

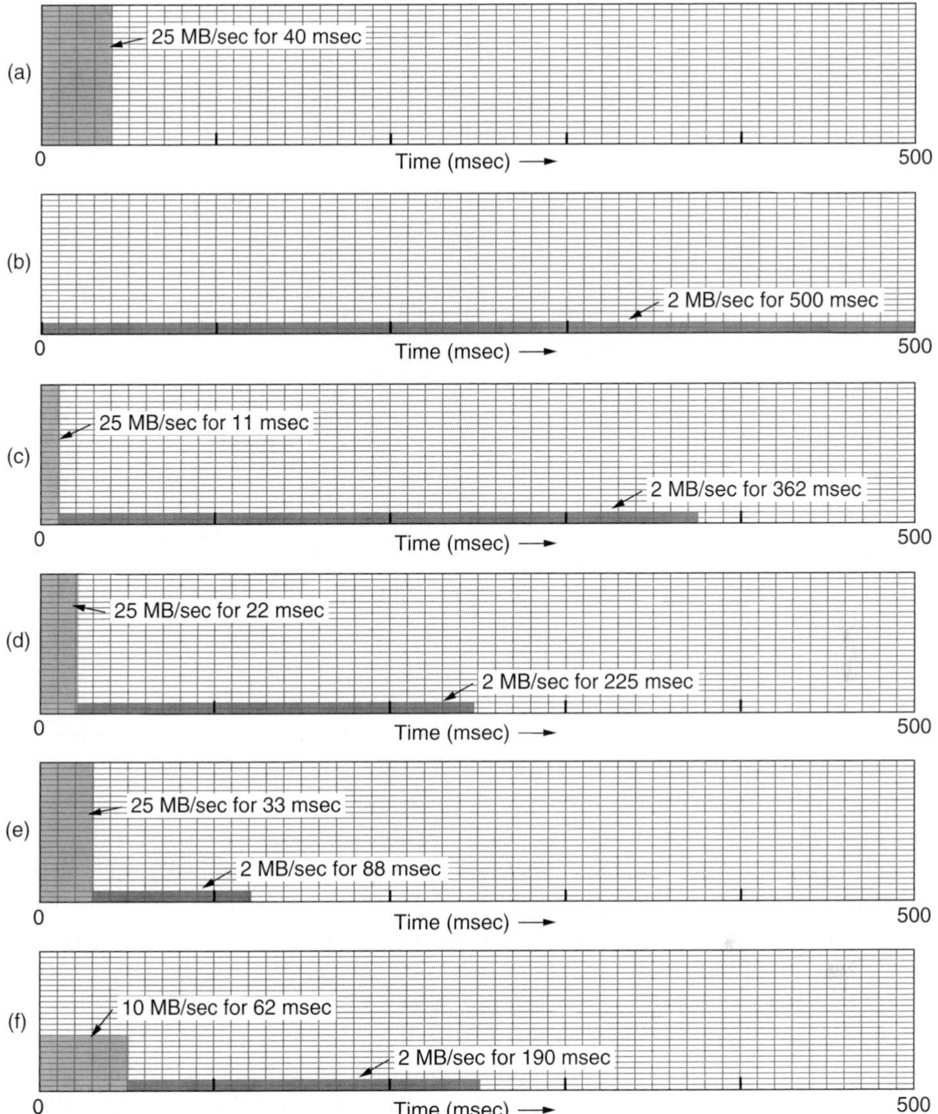

Figure 5-33. (a) Input to a leaky bucket. (b) Output from a leaky bucket. Output from a token bucket with capacities of (c) 250 KB, (d) 500 KB, and (e) 750 KB. (f) Output from a 500KB token bucket feeding a 10-MB/sec leaky bucket.

the host stop sending when the rules say it must. Telling a router to stop sending while its input keeps pouring in may result in lost data.

The implementation of the basic token bucket algorithm is just a variable that counts tokens. The counter is incremented by one every ΔT and decremented by one whenever a packet is sent. When the counter hits zero, no packets may be

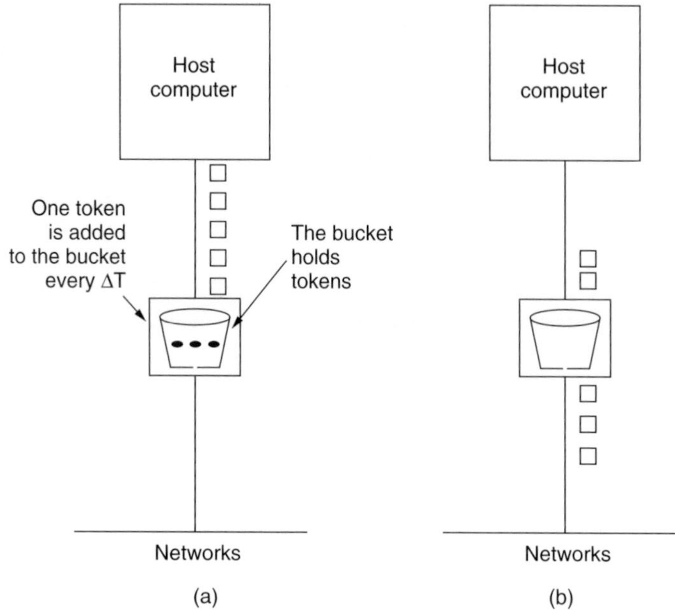

Figure 5-34. The token bucket algorithm. (a) Before. (b) After.

sent. In the byte-count variant, the counter is incremented by k bytes every ΔT and decremented by the length of each packet sent.

Essentially what the token bucket does is allow bursts, but up to a regulated maximum length. Look at Fig. 5-33(c) for example. Here we have a token bucket with a capacity of 250 KB. Tokens arrive at a rate allowing output at 2 MB/sec. Assuming the token bucket is full when the 1-MB burst arrives, the bucket can drain at the full 25 MB/sec for about 11 msec. Then it has to cut back to 2 MB/sec until the entire input burst has been sent.

Calculating the length of the maximum rate burst is slightly tricky. It is not just 1 MB divided by 25 MB/sec because while the burst is being output, more tokens arrive. If we call the burst length S sec, the token bucket capacity C bytes, the token arrival rate ρ bytes/sec, and the maximum output rate M bytes/sec, we see that an output burst contains a maximum of $C + \rho S$ bytes. We also know that the number of bytes in a maximum-speed burst of length S seconds is MS. Hence we have

$$C + \rho S = MS$$

We can solve this equation to get $S = C/(M - \rho)$. For our parameters of $C = 250$ KB, $M = 25$ MB/sec, and $\rho = 2$ MB/sec, we get a burst time of about 11 msec. Figure 5-33(d) and Fig. 5-33(e) show the token bucket for capacities of 500 KB and 750 KB, respectively.

A potential problem with the token bucket algorithm is that it allows large bursts again, even though the maximum burst interval can be regulated by careful selection of ρ and *M*. It is frequently desirable to reduce the peak rate, but without going back to the low value of the original leaky bucket.

One way to get smoother traffic is to insert a leaky bucket after the token bucket. The rate of the leaky bucket should be higher than the token bucket's ρ but lower than the maximum rate of the network. Figure 5-33(f) shows the output for a 500-KB token bucket followed by a 10-MB/sec leaky bucket.

Policing all these schemes can be a bit tricky. Essentially, the network has to simulate the algorithm and make sure that no more packets or bytes are being sent than are permitted. Nevertheless, these tools provide ways to shape the network traffic into more manageable forms to assist meeting quality-of-service requirements.

Resource Reservation

Being able to regulate the shape of the offered traffic is a good start to guaranteeing the quality of service. However, effectively using this information implicitly means requiring all the packets of a flow to follow the same route. Spraying them over routers at random makes it hard to guarantee anything. As a consequence, something similar to a virtual circuit has to be set up from the source to the destination, and all the packets that belong to the flow must follow this route.

Once we have a specific route for a flow, it becomes possible to reserve resources along that route to make sure the needed capacity is available. Three different kinds of resources can potentially be reserved:

1. Bandwidth.
2. Buffer space.
3. CPU cycles.

The first one, bandwidth, is the most obvious. If a flow requires 1 Mbps and the outgoing line has a capacity of 2 Mbps, trying to direct three flows through that line is not going to work. Thus, reserving bandwidth means not oversubscribing any output line.

A second resource that is often in short supply is buffer space. When a packet arrives, it is usually deposited on the network interface card by the hardware itself. The router software then has to copy it to a buffer in RAM and queue that buffer for transmission on the chosen outgoing line. If no buffer is available, the packet has to be discarded since there is no place to put it. For a good quality of service, some buffers can be reserved for a specific flow so that flow does not have to compete for buffers with other flows. There will always be a buffer available when the flow needs one, up to some maximum.

Finally, CPU cycles are also a scarce resource. It takes router CPU time to process a packet, so a router can process only a certain number of packets per second. Making sure that the CPU is not overloaded is needed to ensure timely processing of each packet.

At first glance, it might appear that if it takes, say, 1 μsec to process a packet, a router can process 1 million packets/sec. This observation is not true because there will always be idle periods due to statistical fluctuations in the load. If the CPU needs every single cycle to get its work done, losing even a few cycles due to occasional idleness creates a backlog it can never get rid of.

However, even with a load slightly below the theoretical capacity, queues can build up and delays can occur. Consider a situation in which packets arrive at random with a mean arrival rate of λ packets/sec. The CPU time required by each one is also random, with a mean processing capacity of μ packets/sec. Under the assumption that both the arrival and service distributions are Poisson distributions, it can be proven using queueing theory that the mean delay experienced by a packet, T, is

$$T = \frac{1}{\mu} \times \frac{1}{1 - \lambda/\mu} = \frac{1}{\mu} \times \frac{1}{1 - \rho}$$

where $\rho = \lambda/\mu$ is the CPU utilization. The first factor, $1/\mu$, is what the service time would be in the absence of competition. The second factor is the slowdown due to competition with other flows. For example, if $\lambda = 950{,}000$ packets/sec and $\mu = 1{,}000{,}000$ packets/sec, then $\rho = 0.95$ and the mean delay experienced by each packet will be 20 μsec instead of 1 μsec. This time accounts for both the queueing time and the service time, as can be seen when the load is very low ($\lambda/\mu \approx 0$). If there are, say, 30 routers along the flow's route, queueing delay alone will account for 600 μsec of delay.

Admission Control

Now we are at the point where the incoming traffic from some flow is well shaped and can potentially follow a single route in which capacity can be reserved in advance on the routers along the path. When such a flow is offered to a router, it has to decide, based on its capacity and how many commitments it has already made for other flows, whether to admit or reject the flow.

The decision to accept or reject a flow is not a simple matter of comparing the (bandwidth, buffers, cycles) requested by the flow with the router's excess capacity in those three dimensions. It is a little more complicated than that. To start with, although some applications may know about their bandwidth requirements, few know about buffers or CPU cycles, so at the minimum, a different way is needed to describe flows. Next, some applications are far more tolerant of an occasional missed deadline than others. Finally, some applications may be willing to haggle about the flow parameters and others may not. For example, a movie viewer that normally runs at 30 frames/sec may be willing to drop back to 25 frames/sec if there is not enough free bandwidth to support 30 frames/sec. Similarly, the number of pixels per frame, audio bandwidth, and other properties may be adjustable.

Because many parties may be involved in the flow negotiation (the sender, the receiver, and all the routers along the path between them), flows must be described accurately in terms of specific parameters that can be negotiated. A set of such parameters is called a **flow specification**. Typically, the sender (e.g., the video server) produces a flow specification proposing the parameters it would like to use. As the specification propagates along the route, each router examines it and modifies the parameters as need be. The modifications can only reduce the flow, not increase it (e.g., a lower data rate, not a higher one). When it gets to the other end, the parameters can be established.

As an example of what can be in a flow specification, consider the example of Fig. 5-35, which is based on RFCs 2210 and 2211. It has five parameters, the first of which, the *Token bucket rate*, is the number of bytes per second that are put into the bucket. This is the maximum sustained rate the sender may transmit, averaged over a long time interval.

Parameter	Unit
Token bucket rate	Bytes/sec
Token bucket size	Bytes
Peak data rate	Bytes/sec
Minimum packet size	Bytes
Maximum packet size	Bytes

Figure 5-35. An example flow specification.

The second parameter is the size of the bucket in bytes. If, for example, the *Token bucket rate* is 1 Mbps and the *Token bucket size* is 500 KB, the bucket can fill continuously for 4 sec before it fills up (in the absence of any transmissions). Any tokens sent after that are lost.

The third parameter, the *Peak data rate*, is the maximum tolerated transmission rate, even for brief time intervals. The sender must never exceed this rate.

The last two parameters specify the minimum and maximum packet sizes, including the transport and network layer headers (e.g., TCP and IP). The minimum size is important because processing each packet takes some fixed time, no matter how short. A router may be prepared to handle 10,000 packets/sec of 1 KB each, but not be prepared to handle 100,000 packets/sec of 50 bytes each, even though this represents a lower data rate. The maximum packet size is important due to internal network limitations that may not be exceeded. For example, if part of the path goes over an Ethernet, the maximum packet size will be restricted to no more than 1500 bytes no matter what the rest of the network can handle.

An interesting question is how a router turns a flow specification into a set of specific resource reservations. That mapping is implementation specific and is not standardized. Suppose that a router can process 100,000 packets/sec. If it is offered a flow of 1 MB/sec with minimum and maximum packet sizes of 512 bytes, the router can calculate that it might get 2048 packets/sec from that flow. In that case, it must reserve 2% of its CPU for that flow, preferably more to avoid long queueing delays. If a router's policy is never to allocate more than 50% of its CPU (which implies a factor of two delay, and it is already 49% full, then this flow must be rejected. Similar calculations are needed for the other resources.

The tighter the flow specification, the more useful it is to the routers. If a flow specification states that it needs a *Token bucket rate* of 5 MB/sec but packets can vary from 50 bytes to 1500 bytes, then the packet rate will vary from about 3500 packets/sec to 105,000 packets/sec. The router may panic at the latter number and reject the flow, whereas with a minimum packet size of 1000 bytes, the 5 MB/sec flow might have been accepted.

Proportional Routing

Most routing algorithms try to find the best path for each destination and send all traffic to that destination over the best path. A different approach that has been proposed to provide a higher quality of service is to split the traffic for each destination over multiple paths. Since routers generally do not have a complete overview of network-wide traffic, the only feasible way to split traffic over multiple routes is to use locally-available information. A simple method is to divide the traffic equally or in proportion to the capacity of the outgoing links. However, more sophisticated algorithms are also available (Nelakuditi and Zhang, 2002).

Packet Scheduling

If a router is handling multiple flows, there is a danger that one flow will hog too much of its capacity and starve all the other flows. Processing packets in the order of their arrival means that an aggressive sender can capture most of the capacity of the routers its packets traverse, reducing the quality of service for others. To thwart such attempts, various packet scheduling algorithms have been devised (Bhatti and Crowcroft, 2000).

One of the first ones was the **fair queueing** algorithm (Nagle, 1987). The essence of the algorithm is that routers have separate queues for each output line, one for each flow. When a line becomes idle, the router scans the queues round robin, taking the first packet on the next queue. In this way, with n hosts competing for a given output line, each host gets to send one out of every n packets. Sending more packets will not improve this fraction.

Although a start, the algorithm has a problem: it gives more bandwidth to hosts that use large packets than to hosts that use small packets. Demers et al.

(1990) suggested an improvement in which the round robin is done in such a way as to simulate a byte-by-byte round robin, instead of a packet-by-packet round robin. In effect, it scans the queues repeatedly, byte-for-byte, until it finds the tick on which each packet will be finished. The packets are then sorted in order of their finishing and sent in that order. The algorithm is illustrated in Fig. 5-36.

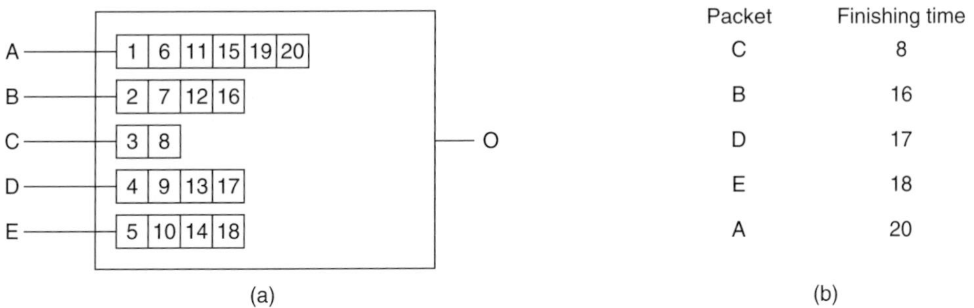

Figure 5-36. (a) A router with five packets queued for line *O*. (b) Finishing times for the five packets.

In Fig. 5-36(a) we see packets of length 2 to 6 bytes. At (virtual) clock tick 1, the first byte of the packet on line *A* is sent. Then goes the first byte of the packet on line *B*, and so on. The first packet to finish is *C*, after eight ticks. The sorted order is given in Fig. 5-36(b). In the absence of new arrivals, the packets will be sent in the order listed, from *C* to *A*.

One problem with this algorithm is that it gives all hosts the same priority. In many situations, it is desirable to give video servers more bandwidth than regular file servers so that they can be given two or more bytes per tick. This modified algorithm is called **weighted fair queueing** and is widely used. Sometimes the weight is equal to the number of flows coming out of a machine, so each process gets equal bandwidth. An efficient implementation of the algorithm is discussed in (Shreedhar and Varghese, 1995). Increasingly, the actual forwarding of packets through a router or switch is being done in hardware (Elhanany et al., 2001).

5.4.3 Integrated Services

Between 1995 and 1997, IETF put a lot of effort into devising an architecture for streaming multimedia. This work resulted in over two dozen RFCs, starting with RFCs 2205–2210. The generic name for this work is **flow-based algorithms** or **integrated services**. It was aimed at both unicast and multicast applications. An example of the former is a single user streaming a video clip from a news site. An example of the latter is a collection of digital television stations broadcasting their programs as streams of IP packets to many receivers at various locations. Below we will concentrate on multicast, since unicast is a special case of multicast.

In many multicast applications, groups can change membership dynamically, for example, as people enter a video conference and then get bored and switch to a soap opera or the croquet channel. Under these conditions, the approach of having the senders reserve bandwidth in advance does not work well, since it would require each sender to track all entries and exits of its audience. For a system designed to transmit television with millions of subscribers, it would not work at all.

RSVP—The Resource reSerVation Protocol

The main IETF protocol for the integrated services architecture is **RSVP**. It is described in RFC 2205 and others. This protocol is used for making the reservations; other protocols are used for sending the data. RSVP allows multiple senders to transmit to multiple groups of receivers, permits individual receivers to switch channels freely, and optimizes bandwidth use while at the same time eliminating congestion.

In its simplest form, the protocol uses multicast routing using spanning trees, as discussed earlier. Each group is assigned a group address. To send to a group, a sender puts the group's address in its packets. The standard multicast routing algorithm then builds a spanning tree covering all group members. The routing algorithm is not part of RSVP. The only difference from normal multicasting is a little extra information that is multicast to the group periodically to tell the routers along the tree to maintain certain data structures in their memories.

As an example, consider the network of Fig. 5-37(a). Hosts 1 and 2 are multicast senders, and hosts 3, 4, and 5 are multicast receivers. In this example, the senders and receivers are disjoint, but in general, the two sets may overlap. The multicast trees for hosts 1 and 2 are shown in Fig. 5-37(b) and Fig. 5-37(c), respectively.

To get better reception and eliminate congestion, any of the receivers in a group can send a reservation message up the tree to the sender. The message is propagated using the reverse path forwarding algorithm discussed earlier. At each hop, the router notes the reservation and reserves the necessary bandwidth. If insufficient bandwidth is available, it reports back failure. By the time the message gets back to the source, bandwidth has been reserved all the way from the sender to the receiver making the reservation request along the spanning tree.

An example of such a reservation is shown in Fig. 5-38(a). Here host 3 has requested a channel to host 1. Once it has been established, packets can flow from 1 to 3 without congestion. Now consider what happens if host 3 next reserves a channel to the other sender, host 2, so the user can watch two television programs at once. A second path is reserved, as illustrated in Fig. 5-38(b). Note that two separate channels are needed from host 3 to router E because two independent streams are being transmitted.

Finally, in Fig. 5-38(c), host 5 decides to watch the program being transmitted by host 1 and also makes a reservation. First, dedicated bandwidth is reserved as

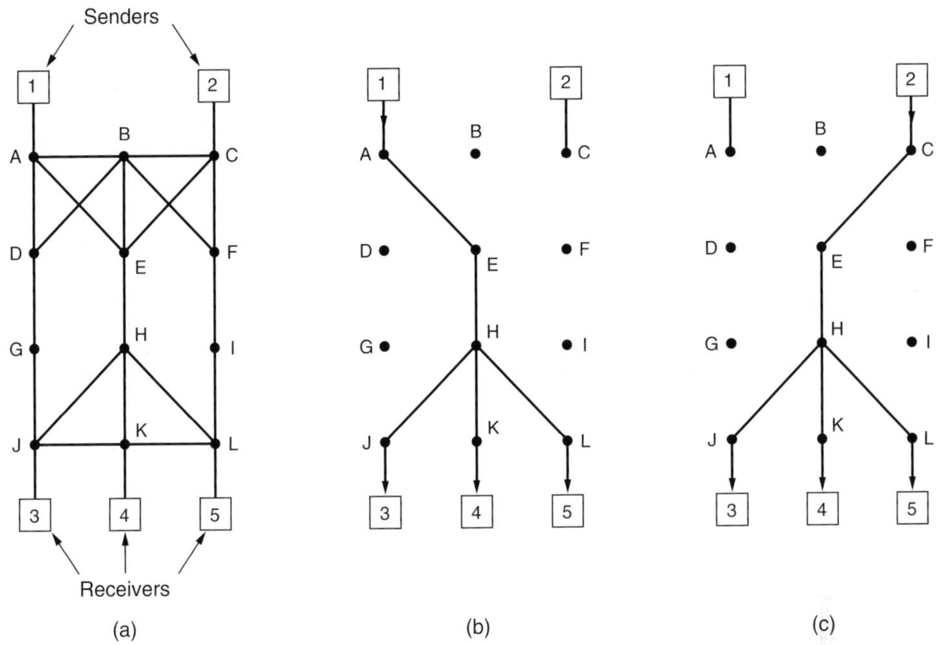

Figure 5-37. (a) A network. (b) The multicast spanning tree for host 1. (c) The multicast spanning tree for host 2.

far as router *H*. However, this router sees that it already has a feed from host 1, so if the necessary bandwidth has already been reserved, it does not have to reserve any more. Note that hosts 3 and 5 might have asked for different amounts of bandwidth (e.g., 3 has a black-and-white television set, so it does not want the color information), so the capacity reserved must be large enough to satisfy the greediest receiver.

When making a reservation, a receiver can (optionally) specify one or more sources that it wants to receive from. It can also specify whether these choices are fixed for the duration of the reservation or whether the receiver wants to keep open the option of changing sources later. The routers use this information to optimize bandwidth planning. In particular, two receivers are only set up to share a path if they both agree not to change sources later on.

The reason for this strategy in the fully dynamic case is that reserved bandwidth is decoupled from the choice of source. Once a receiver has reserved bandwidth, it can switch to another source and keep that portion of the existing path that is valid for the new source. If host 2 is transmitting several video streams, for example, host 3 may switch between them at will without changing its reservation: the routers do not care what program the receiver is watching.

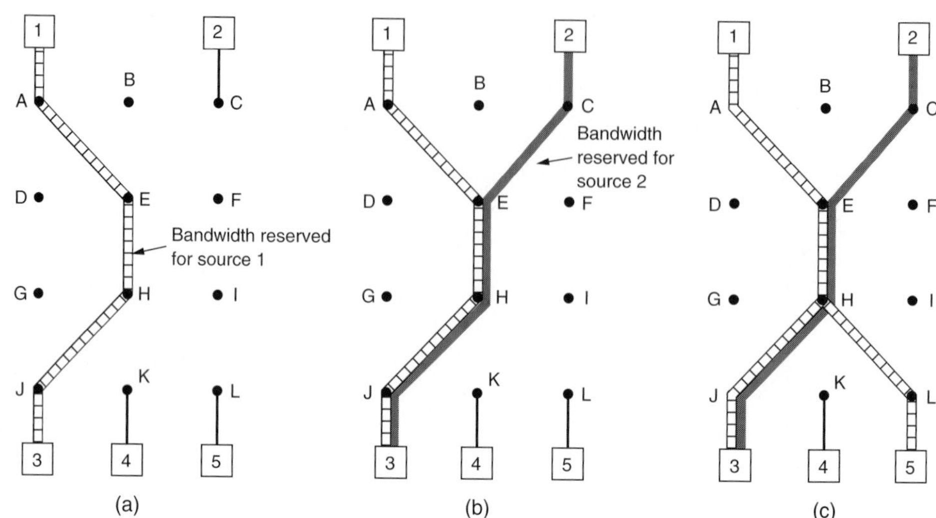

Figure 5-38. (a) Host 3 requests a channel to host 1. (b) Host 3 then requests a second channel, to host 2. (c) Host 5 requests a channel to host 1.

5.4.4 Differentiated Services

Flow-based algorithms have the potential to offer good quality of service to one or more flows because they reserve whatever resources are needed along the route. However, they also have a downside. They require an advance setup to establish each flow, something that does not scale well when there are thousands or millions of flows. Also, they maintain internal per-flow state in the routers, making them vulnerable to router crashes. Finally, the changes required to the router code are substantial and involve complex router-to-router exchanges for setting up the flows. As a consequence, few implementations of RSVP or anything like it exist yet.

For these reasons, IETF has also devised a simpler approach to quality of service, one that can be largely implemented locally in each router without advance setup and without having the whole path involved. This approach is known as **class-based** (as opposed to flow-based) quality of service. IETF has standardized an architecture for it, called **differentiated services**, which is described in RFCs 2474, 2475, and numerous others. We will now describe it.

Differentiated services (DS) can be offered by a set of routers forming an administrative domain (e.g., an ISP or a telco). The administration defines a set of service classes with corresponding forwarding rules. If a customer signs up for DS, customer packets entering the domain may carry a *Type of Service* field in them, with better service provided to some classes (e.g., premium service) than to others. Traffic within a class may be required to conform to some specific shape, such as a leaky bucket with some specified drain rate. An operator with a nose for business might charge extra for each premium packet transported or might allow up to *N* premium packets per month for a fixed additional monthly fee. Note that this scheme requires no advance setup, no resource reservation, and no time-consuming end-to-end negotiation for each flow, as with integrated services. This makes DS relatively easy to implement.

Class-based service also occurs in other industries. For example, package delivery companies often offer overnight, two-day, and three-day service. Airlines offer first class, business class, and cattle class service. Long-distance trains often have multiple service classes. Even the Paris subway has two service classes. For packets, the classes may differ in terms of delay, jitter, and probability of being discarded in the event of congestion, among other possibilities (but probably not roomier Ethernet frames).

To make the difference between flow-based quality of service and class-based quality of service clearer, consider an example: Internet telephony. With a flow-based scheme, each telephone call gets its own resources and guarantees. With a class-based scheme, all the telephone calls together get the resources reserved for the class telephony. These resources cannot be taken away by packets from the file transfer class or other classes, but no telephone call gets any private resources reserved for it alone.

Expedited Forwarding

The choice of service classes is up to each operator, but since packets are often forwarded between subnets run by different operators, IETF is working on defining network-independent service classes. The simplest class is **expedited forwarding**, so let us start with that one. It is described in RFC 3246.

The idea behind expedited forwarding is very simple. Two classes of service are available: regular and expedited. The vast majority of the traffic is expected to be regular, but a small fraction of the packets are expedited. The expedited packets should be able to transit the subnet as though no other packets were present. A symbolic representation of this "two-tube" system is given in Fig. 5-39. Note that there is still just one physical line. The two logical pipes shown in the figure represent a way to reserve bandwidth, not a second physical line.

One way to implement this strategy is to program the routers to have two output queues for each outgoing line, one for expedited packets and one for regular packets. When a packet arrives, it is queued accordingly. Packet scheduling should use something like weighted fair queueing. For example, if 10% of the traffic is expedited and 90% is regular, 20% of the bandwidth could be dedicated to expedited traffic and the rest to regular traffic. Doing so would give the expedited traffic twice as much bandwidth as it needs in order to provide low delay for it. This allocation can be achieved by transmitting one expedited packet for every four regular packets (assuming the size distribution for both classes is

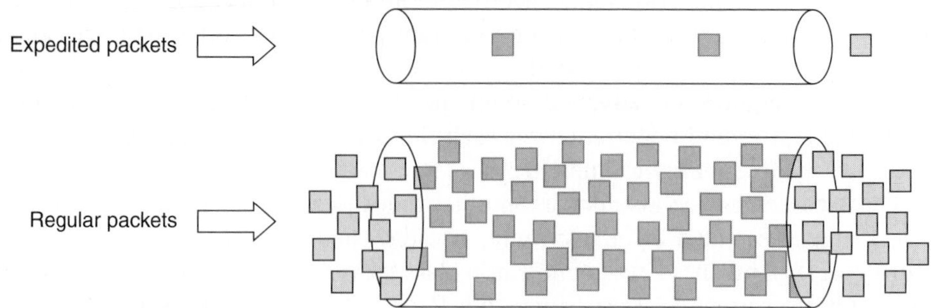

Figure 5-39. Expedited packets experience a traffic-free network.

similar). In this way, it is hoped that expedited packets see an unloaded subnet, even when there is, in fact, a heavy load.

Assured Forwarding

A somewhat more elaborate scheme for managing the service classes is called **assured forwarding**. It is described in RFC 2597. It specifies that there shall be four priority classes, each class having its own resources. In addition, it defines three discard probabilities for packets that are undergoing congestion: low, medium, and high. Taken together, these two factors define 12 service classes.

Figure 5-40 shows one way packets might be processed under assured forwarding. Step 1 is to classify the packets into one of the four priority classes. This step might be done on the sending host (as shown in the figure) or in the ingress (first) router. The advantage of doing classification on the sending host is that more information is available about which packets belong to which flows there.

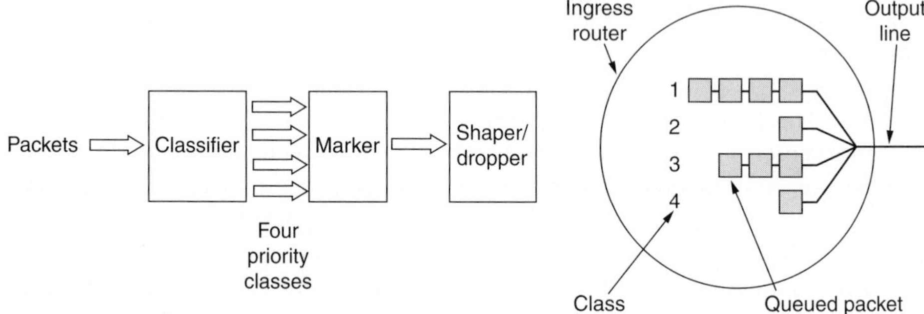

Figure 5-40. A possible implementation of the data flow for assured forwarding.

Step 2 is to mark the packets according to their class. A header field is needed for this purpose. Fortunately, an 8-bit *Type of service* field is available in the

IP header, as we will see shortly. RFC 2597 specifies that six of these bits are to be used for the service class, leaving coding room for historical service classes and future ones.

Step 3 is to pass the packets through a shaper/dropper filter that may delay or drop some of them to shape the four streams into acceptable forms, for example, by using leaky or token buckets. If there are too many packets, some of them may be discarded here, by discard category. More elaborate schemes involving metering or feedback are also possible.

In this example, these three steps are performed on the sending host, so the output stream is now fed into the ingress router. It is worth noting that these steps may be performed by special networking software or even the operating system, to avoid having to change existing applications.

5.4.5 Label Switching and MPLS

While IETF was working out integrated services and differentiated services, several router vendors were working on better forwarding methods. This work focused on adding a label in front of each packet and doing the routing based on the label rather than on the destination address. Making the label an index into an internal table makes finding the correct output line becomes just a matter of table lookup. Using this technique, routing can be done very quickly and any necessary resources can be reserved along the path.

Of course, labeling flows this way comes perilously close to virtual circuits. X.25, ATM, frame relay, and all other networks with a virtual-circuit subnet also put a label (i.e., virtual-circuit identifier) in each packet, look it up in a table, and route based on the table entry. Despite the fact that many people in the Internet community have an intense dislike for connection-oriented networking, the idea seems to keep coming back, this time to provide fast routing and quality of service. However, there are essential differences between the way the Internet handles route construction and the way connection-oriented networks do it, so the technique is certainly not traditional circuit switching.

This "new" switching idea goes by various (proprietary) names, including **label switching** and **tag switching**. Eventually, IETF began to standardize the idea under the name **MPLS** (**MultiProtocol Label Switching**). We will call it MPLS below. It is described in RFC 3031 and many other RFCs.

As an aside, some people make a distinction between *routing* and *switching*. Routing is the process of looking up a destination address in a table to find where to send it. In contrast, switching uses a label taken from the packet as an index into a forwarding table. These definitions are far from universal, however.

The first problem is where to put the label. Since IP packets were not designed for virtual circuits, there is no field available for virtual-circuit numbers within the IP header. For this reason, a new MPLS header had to be added in front of the IP header. On a router-to-router line using PPP as the framing protocol, the frame format, including the PPP, MPLS, IP, and TCP headers, is as shown in Fig. 5-41. In a sense, MPLS is thus layer 2.5.

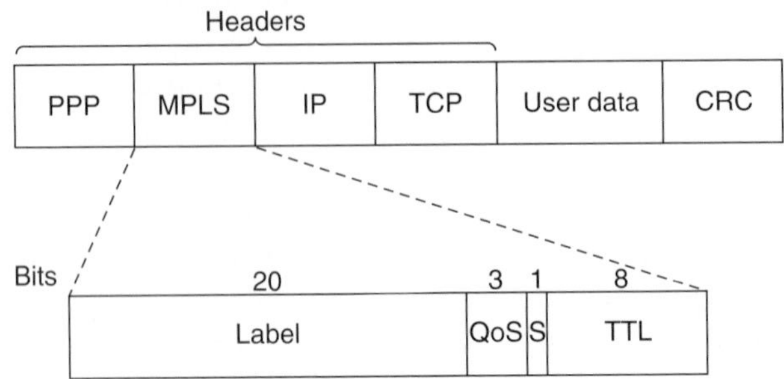

Figure 5-41. Transmitting a TCP segment using IP, MPLS, and PPP.

The generic MPLS header has four fields, the most important of which is the *Label* field, which holds the index. The *QoS* field indicates the class of service. The *S* field relates to stacking multiple labels in hierarchical networks (discussed below). If it hits 0, the packet is discarded. This feature prevents infinite looping in the case of routing instability.

Because the MPLS headers are not part of the network layer packet or the data link layer frame, MPLS is to a large extent independent of both layers. Among other things, this property means it is possible to build MPLS switches that can forward both IP packets and ATM cells, depending on what shows up. This feature is where the "multiprotocol" in the name MPLS came from.

When an MPLS-enhanced packet (or cell) arrives at an MPLS-capable router, the label is used as an index into a table to determine the outgoing line to use and also the new label to use. This label swapping is used in all virtual-circuit subnets because labels have only local significance and two different routers can feed unrelated packets with the same label into another router for transmission on the same outgoing line. To be distinguishable at the other end, labels have to be remapped at every hop. We saw this mechanism in action in Fig. 5-3. MPLS uses the same technique.

One difference from traditional virtual circuits is the level of aggregation. It is certainly possible for each flow to have its own set of labels through the subnet. However, it is more common for routers to group multiple flows that end at a particular router or LAN and use a single label for them. The flows that are grouped together under a single label are said to belong to the same **FEC** (**Forwarding Equivalence Class**). This class covers not only where the packets are going, but also their service class (in the differentiated services sense) because all their packets are treated the same way for forwarding purposes.

With traditional virtual-circuit routing, it is not possible to group several distinct paths with different end points onto the same virtual-circuit identifier because there would be no way to distinguish them at the final destination. With MPLS, the packets still contain their final destination address, in addition to the label, so that at the end of the labeled route the label header can be removed and forwarding can continue the usual way, using the network layer destination address.

One major difference between MPLS and conventional VC designs is how the forwarding table is constructed. In traditional virtual-circuit networks, when a user wants to establish a connection, a setup packet is launched into the network to create the path and make the forwarding table entries. MPLS does not work that way because there is no setup phase for each connection (because that would break too much existing Internet software).

Instead, there are two ways for the forwarding table entries to be created. In the **data-driven** approach, when a packet arrives, the first router it hits contacts the router downstream where the packet has to go and asks it to generate a label for the flow. This method is applied recursively. Effectively, this is on-demand virtual-circuit creation.

The protocols that do this spreading are very careful to avoid loops. They often use a technique called **colored threads**. The backward propagation of an FEC can be compared to pulling a uniquely colored thread back into the subnet. If a router ever sees a color it already has, it knows there is a loop and takes remedial action. The data-driven approach is primarily used on networks in which the underlying transport is ATM (such as much of the telephone system).

The other way, used on networks not based on ATM, is the **control-driven** approach. It has several variants. One of these works like this. When a router is booted, it checks to see for which routes it is the final destination (e.g., which hosts are on its LAN). It then creates one or more FECs for them, allocates a label for each one, and passes the labels to its neighbors. They, in turn, enter the labels in their forwarding tables and send new labels to their neighbors, until all the routers have acquired the path. Resources can also be reserved as the path is constructed to guarantee an appropriate quality of service.

MPLS can operate at multiple levels at once. At the highest level, each carrier can be regarded as a kind of metarouter, with there being a path through the metarouters from source to destination. This path can use MPLS. However, within each carrier's network, MPLS can also be used, leading to a second level of labeling. In fact, a packet may carry an entire stack of labels with it. The *S* bit in Fig. 5-41 allows a router removing a label to know if there are any additional labels left. It is set to 1 for the bottom label and 0 for all the other labels. In practice, this facility is mostly used to implement virtual private networks and recursive tunnels.

Although the basic ideas behind MPLS are straightforward, the details are extremely complicated, with many variations and optimizations, so we will not pursue this topic further. For more information, see (Davie and Rekhter, 2000; Lin et al., 2002; Pepelnjak and Guichard, 2001; and Wang, 2001).

5.5 INTERNETWORKING

Until now, we have implicitly assumed that there is a single homogeneous network, with each machine using the same protocol in each layer. Unfortunately, this assumption is wildly optimistic. Many different networks exist, including LANs, MANs, and WANs. Numerous protocols are in widespread use in every layer. In the following sections we will take a careful look at the issues that arise when two or more networks are connected to form an **internet**.

Considerable controversy exists about the question of whether today's abundance of network types is a temporary condition that will go away as soon as everyone realizes how wonderful [fill in your favorite network] is or whether it is an inevitable, but permanent, feature of the world that is here to stay. Having different networks invariably means having different protocols.

We believe that a variety of different networks (and thus protocols) will always be around, for the following reasons. First of all, the installed base of different networks is large. Nearly all personal computers run TCP/IP. Many large businesses have mainframes running IBM's SNA. A substantial number of telephone companies operate ATM networks. Some personal computer LANs still use Novell NCP/IPX or AppleTalk. Finally, wireless is an up-and-coming area with a variety of protocols. This trend will continue for years due to legacy problems, new technology, and the fact that not all vendors perceive it in their interest for their customers to be able to easily migrate to another vendor's system.

Second, as computers and networks get cheaper, the place where decisions get made moves downward in organizations. Many companies have a policy to the effect that purchases costing over a million dollars have to be approved by top management, purchases costing over 100,000 dollars have to be approved by middle management, but purchases under 100,000 dollars can be made by department heads without any higher approval. This can easily lead to the engineering department installing UNIX workstations running TCP/IP and the marketing department installing Macs with AppleTalk.

Third, different networks (e.g., ATM and wireless) have radically different technology, so it should not be surprising that as new hardware developments occur, new software will be created to fit the new hardware. For example, the average home now is like the average office ten years ago: it is full of computers that do not talk to one another. In the future, it may be commonplace for the telephone, the television set, and other appliances all to be networked together so that they can be controlled remotely. This new technology will undoubtedly bring new networks and new protocols.

As an example of how different networks might be connected, consider the example of Fig. 5-42. Here we see a corporate network with multiple locations tied together by a wide area ATM network. At one of the locations, an FDDI optical backbone is used to connect an Ethernet, an 802.11 wireless LAN, and the corporate data center's SNA mainframe network.

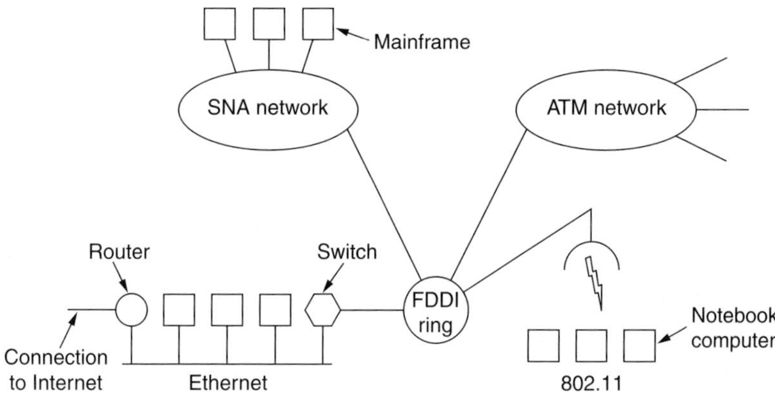

Figure 5-42. A collection of interconnected networks.

The purpose of interconnecting all these networks is to allow users on any of them to communicate with users on all the other ones and also to allow users on any of them to access data on any of them. Accomplishing this goal means sending packets from one network to another. Since networks often differ in important ways, getting packets from one network to another is not always so easy, as we will now see.

5.5.1 How Networks Differ

Networks can differ in many ways. Some of the differences, such as different modulation techniques or frame formats, are in the physical and data link layers, These differences will not concern us here. Instead, in Fig. 5-43 we list some of the differences that can occur in the network layer. It is papering over these differences that makes internetworking more difficult than operating within a single network.

When packets sent by a source on one network must transit one or more foreign networks before reaching the destination network (which also may be different from the source network), many problems can occur at the interfaces between networks. To start with, when packets from a connection-oriented network must transit a connectionless one, they may be reordered, something the sender does not expect and the receiver is not prepared to deal with. Protocol conversions will often be needed, which can be difficult if the required functionality cannot be expressed. Address conversions will also be needed, which may require some kind of directory system. Passing multicast packets through a network that does not support multicasting requires generating separate packets for each destination.

The differing maximum packet sizes used by different networks can be a major nuisance. How do you pass an 8000-byte packet through a network whose

Item	Some Possibilities
Service offered	Connection oriented versus connectionless
Protocols	IP, IPX, SNA, ATM, MPLS, AppleTalk, etc.
Addressing	Flat (802) versus hierarchical (IP)
Multicasting	Present or absent (also broadcasting)
Packet size	Every network has its own maximum
Quality of service	Present or absent; many different kinds
Error handling	Reliable, ordered, and unordered delivery
Flow control	Sliding window, rate control, other, or none
Congestion control	Leaky bucket, token bucket, RED, choke packets, etc.
Security	Privacy rules, encryption, etc.
Parameters	Different timeouts, flow specifications, etc.
Accounting	By connect time, by packet, by byte, or not at all

Figure 5-43. Some of the many ways networks can differ.

maximum size is 1500 bytes? Differing qualities of service is an issue when a packet that has real-time delivery constraints passes through a network that does not offer any real-time guarantees.

Error, flow, and congestion control often differ among different networks. If the source and destination both expect all packets to be delivered in sequence without error but an intermediate network just discards packets whenever it smells congestion on the horizon, many applications will break. Also, if packets can wander around aimlessly for a while and then suddenly emerge and be delivered, trouble will occur if this behavior was not anticipated and dealt with. Different security mechanisms, parameter settings, and accounting rules, and even national privacy laws also can cause problems.

5.5.2 How Networks Can Be Connected

Networks can be interconnected by different devices, as we saw in Chap 4. Let us briefly review that material. In the physical layer, networks can be connected by repeaters or hubs, which just move the bits from one network to an identical network. These are mostly analog devices and do not understand anything about digital protocols (they just regenerate signals).

One layer up we find bridges and switches, which operate at the data link layer. They can accept frames, examine the MAC addresses, and forward the frames to a different network while doing minor protocol translation in the process, for example, from Ethernet to FDDI or to 802.11.

In the network layer, we have routers that can connect two networks. If two networks have dissimilar network layers, the router may be able to translate between the packet formats, although packet translation is now increasingly rare. A router that can handle multiple protocols is called a **multiprotocol router**.

In the transport layer we find transport gateways, which can interface between two transport connections. For example, a transport gateway could allow packets to flow between a TCP network and an SNA network, which has a different transport protocol, by essentially gluing a TCP connection to an SNA connection.

Finally, in the application layer, application gateways translate message semantics. As an example, gateways between Internet e-mail (RFC 822) and X.400 e-mail must parse the e-mail messages and change various header fields.

In this chapter we will focus on internetworking in the network layer. To see how that differs from switching in the data link layer, examine Fig. 5-44. In Fig. 5-44(a), the source machine, *S*, wants to send a packet to the destination machine, *D*. These machines are on different Ethernets, connected by a switch. *S* encapsulates the packet in a frame and sends it on its way. The frame arrives at the switch, which then determines that the frame has to go to LAN 2 by looking at its MAC address. The switch just removes the frame from LAN 1 and deposits it on LAN 2.

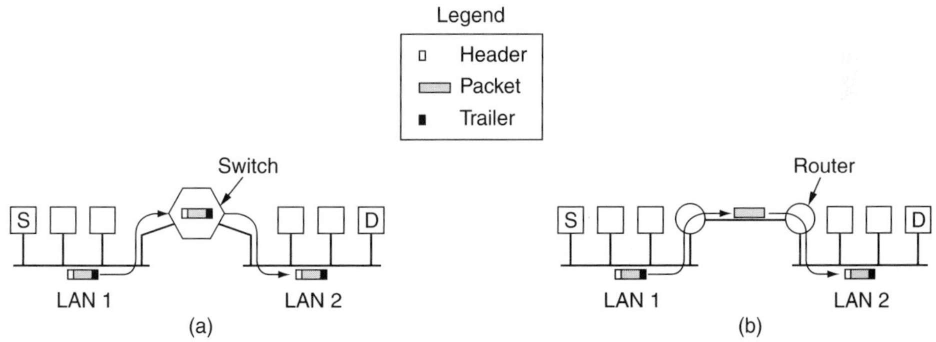

Figure 5-44. (a) Two Ethernets connected by a switch. (b) Two Ethernets connected by routers.

Now let us consider the same situation but with the two Ethernets connected by a pair of routers instead of a switch. The routers are connected by a point-to-point line, possibly a leased line thousands of kilometers long. Now the frame is picked up by the router and the packet removed from the frame's data field. The router examines the address in the packet (e.g., an IP address) and looks up this address in its routing table. Based on this address, it decides to send the packet to the remote router, potentially encapsulated in a different kind of frame, depending on the line protocol. At the far end, the packet is put into the data field of an Ethernet frame and deposited onto LAN 2.

An essential difference between the switched (or bridged) case and the routed case is this. With a switch (or bridge), the entire frame is transported on the basis of its MAC address. With a router, the packet is extracted from the frame and the address in the packet is used for deciding where to send it. Switches do not have to understand the network layer protocol being used to switch packets. Routers do.

5.5.3 Concatenated Virtual Circuits

Two styles of internetworking are possible: a connection-oriented concatenation of virtual-circuit subnets, and a datagram internet style. We will now examine these in turn, but first a word of caution. In the past, most (public) networks were connection oriented (and frame relay, SNA, 802.16, and ATM still are). Then with the rapid acceptance of the Internet, datagrams became fashionable. However, it would be a mistake to think that datagrams are forever. In this business, the only thing that is forever is change. With the growing importance of multimedia networking, it is likely that connection-orientation will make a comeback in one form or another since it is easier to guarantee quality of service with connections than without them. Therefore, we will devote some space to connection-oriented networking below

In the concatenated virtual-circuit model, shown in Fig. 5-45, a connection to a host in a distant network is set up in a way similar to the way connections are normally established. The subnet sees that the destination is remote and builds a virtual circuit to the router nearest the destination network. Then it constructs a virtual circuit from that router to an external **gateway** (multiprotocol router). This gateway records the existence of the virtual circuit in its tables and proceeds to build another virtual circuit to a router in the next subnet. This process continues until the destination host has been reached.

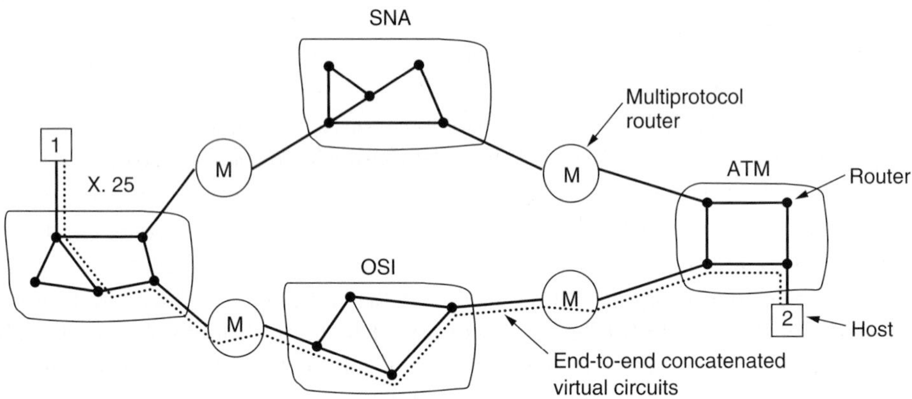

Figure 5-45. Internetworking using concatenated virtual circuits.

Once data packets begin flowing along the path, each gateway relays incoming packets, converting between packet formats and virtual-circuit numbers as needed. Clearly, all data packets must traverse the same sequence of gateways. Consequently, packets in a flow are never reordered by the network.

The essential feature of this approach is that a sequence of virtual circuits is set up from the source through one or more gateways to the destination. Each gateway maintains tables telling which virtual circuits pass through it, where they are to be routed, and what the new virtual-circuit number is.

This scheme works best when all the networks have roughly the same properties. For example, if all of them guarantee reliable delivery of network layer packets, then barring a crash somewhere along the route, the flow from source to destination will also be reliable. Similarly, if none of them guarantee reliable delivery, then the concatenation of the virtual circuits is not reliable either. On the other hand, if the source machine is on a network that does guarantee reliable delivery but one of the intermediate networks can lose packets, the concatenation has fundamentally changed the nature of the service.

Concatenated virtual circuits are also common in the transport layer. In particular, it is possible to build a bit pipe using, say, SNA, which terminates in a gateway, and have a TCP connection go from the gateway to the next gateway. In this manner, an end-to-end virtual circuit can be built spanning different networks and protocols.

5.5.4 Connectionless Internetworking

The alternative internetwork model is the datagram model, shown in Fig. 5-46. In this model, the only service the network layer offers to the transport layer is the ability to inject datagrams into the subnet and hope for the best. There is no notion of a virtual circuit at all in the network layer, let alone a concatenation of them. This model does not require all packets belonging to one connection to traverse the same sequence of gateways. In Fig. 5-46 datagrams from host 1 to host 2 are shown taking different routes through the internetwork. A routing decision is made separately for each packet, possibly depending on the traffic at the moment the packet is sent. This strategy can use multiple routes and thus achieve a higher bandwidth than the concatenated virtual-circuit model. On the other hand, there is no guarantee that the packets arrive at the destination in order, assuming that they arrive at all.

The model of Fig. 5-46 is not quite as simple as it looks. For one thing, if each network has its own network layer protocol, it is not possible for a packet from one network to transit another one. One could imagine the multiprotocol routers actually trying to translate from one format to another, but unless the two formats are close relatives with the same information fields, such conversions will always be incomplete and often doomed to failure. For this reason, conversion is rarely attempted.

A second, and more serious, problem is addressing. Imagine a simple case: a host on the Internet is trying to send an IP packet to a host on an adjoining SNA network. The IP and SNA addresses are different. One would need a mapping

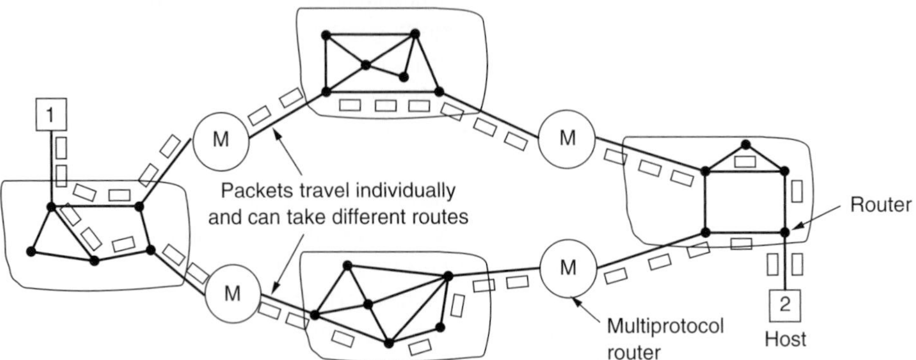

Figure 5-46. A connectionless internet.

between IP and SNA addresses in both directions. Furthermore, the concept of what is addressable is different. In IP, hosts (actually, interface cards) have addresses. In SNA, entities other than hosts (e.g., hardware devices) can also have addresses. At best, someone would have to maintain a database mapping everything to everything to the extent possible, but it would constantly be a source of trouble.

Another idea is to design a universal ''internet'' packet and have all routers recognize it. This approach is, in fact, what IP is—a packet designed to be carried through many networks. Of course, it may turn out that IPv4 (the current Internet protocol) drives all other formats out of the market, IPv6 (the future Internet protocol) does not catch on, and nothing new is ever invented, but history suggests otherwise. Getting everybody to agree to a single format is difficult when companies perceive it to their commercial advantage to have a proprietary format that they control.

Let us now briefly recap the two ways internetworking can be approached. The concatenated virtual-circuit model has essentially the same advantages as using virtual circuits within a single subnet: buffers can be reserved in advance, sequencing can be guaranteed, short headers can be used, and the troubles caused by delayed duplicate packets can be avoided.

It also has the same disadvantages: table space required in the routers for each open connection, no alternate routing to avoid congested areas, and vulnerability to router failures along the path. It also has the disadvantage of being difficult, if not impossible, to implement if one of the networks involved is an unreliable datagram network.

The properties of the datagram approach to internetworking are pretty much the same as those of datagram subnets: more potential for congestion, but also more potential for adapting to it, robustness in the face of router failures, and longer headers needed. Various adaptive routing algorithms are possible in an internet, just as they are within a single datagram network.

A major advantage of the datagram approach to internetworking is that it can be used over subnets that do not use virtual circuits inside. Many LANs, mobile networks (e.g., aircraft and naval fleets), and even some WANs fall into this category. When an internet includes one of these, serious problems occur if the internetworking strategy is based on virtual circuits.

5.5.5 Tunneling

Handling the general case of making two different networks interwork is exceedingly difficult. However, there is a common special case that is manageable. This case is where the source and destination hosts are on the same type of network, but there is a different network in between. As an example, think of an international bank with a TCP/IP-based Ethernet in Paris, a TCP/IP-based Ethernet in London, and a non-IP wide area network (e.g., ATM) in between, as shown in Fig. 5-47.

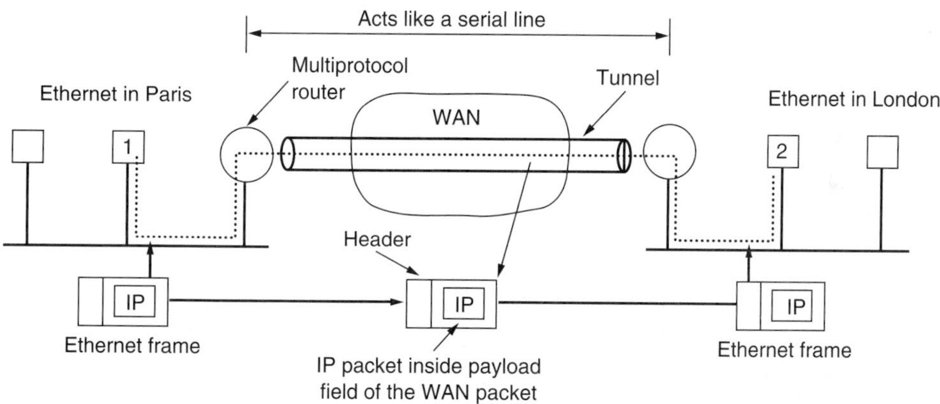

Figure 5-47. Tunneling a packet from Paris to London.

The solution to this problem is a technique called **tunneling**. To send an IP packet to host 2, host 1 constructs the packet containing the IP address of host 2, inserts it into an Ethernet frame addressed to the Paris multiprotocol router, and puts it on the Ethernet. When the multiprotocol router gets the frame, it removes the IP packet, inserts it in the payload field of the WAN network layer packet, and addresses the latter to the WAN address of the London multiprotocol router. When it gets there, the London router removes the IP packet and sends it to host 2 inside an Ethernet frame.

The WAN can be seen as a big tunnel extending from one multiprotocol router to the other. The IP packet just travels from one end of the tunnel to the other, snug in its nice box. It does not have to worry about dealing with the WAN at all. Neither do the hosts on either Ethernet. Only the multiprotocol router has to understand IP and WAN packets. In effect, the entire distance from the middle of one multiprotocol router to the middle of the other acts like a serial line.

An analogy may make tunneling clearer. Consider a person driving her car from Paris to London. Within France, the car moves under its own power, but when it hits the English Channel, it is loaded into a high-speed train and transported to England through the Chunnel (cars are not permitted to drive through the Chunnel). Effectively, the car is being carried as freight, as depicted in Fig. 5-48. At the far end, the car is let loose on the English roads and once again continues to move under its own power. Tunneling of packets through a foreign network works the same way.

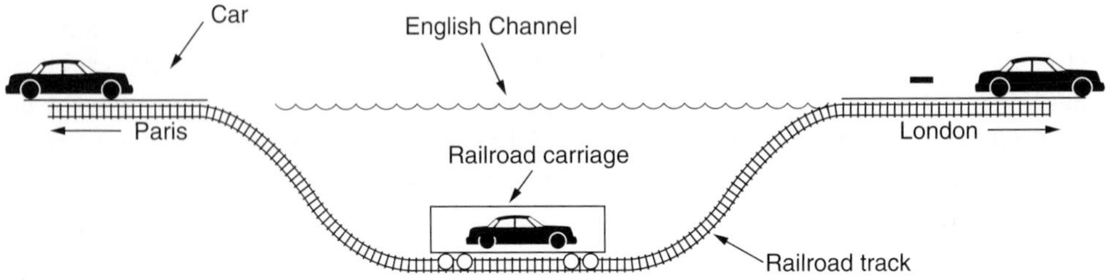

Figure 5-48. Tunneling a car from France to England.

5.5.6 Internetwork Routing

Routing through an internetwork is similar to routing within a single subnet, but with some added complications. Consider, for example, the internetwork of Fig. 5-49(a) in which five networks are connected by six (possibly multiprotocol) routers. Making a graph model of this situation is complicated by the fact that every router can directly access (i.e., send packets to) every other router connected to any network to which it is connected. For example, *B* in Fig. 5-49(a) can directly access *A* and *C* via network 2 and also *D* via network 3. This leads to the graph of Fig. 5-49(b).

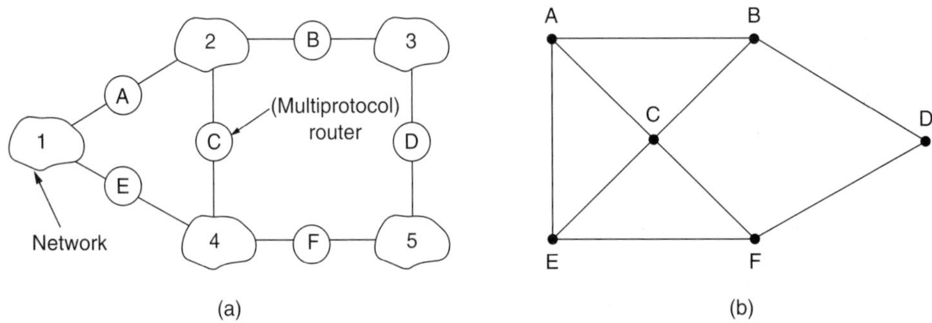

Figure 5-49. (a) An internetwork. (b) A graph of the internetwork.

Once the graph has been constructed, known routing algorithms, such as the distance vector and link state algorithms, can be applied to the set of multiprotocol routers. This gives a two-level routing algorithm: within each network an **interior gateway protocol** is used, but between the networks, an **exterior gateway protocol** is used ("gateway" is an older term for "router"). In fact, since each network is independent, they may all use different algorithms. Because each network in an internetwork is independent of all the others, it is often referred to as an **Autonomous System** (**AS**).

A typical internet packet starts out on its LAN addressed to the local multiprotocol router (in the MAC layer header). After it gets there, the network layer code decides which multiprotocol router to forward the packet to, using its own routing tables. If that router can be reached using the packet's native network protocol, the packet is forwarded there directly. Otherwise it is tunneled there, encapsulated in the protocol required by the intervening network. This process is repeated until the packet reaches the destination network.

One of the differences between internetwork routing and intranetwork routing is that internetwork routing may require crossing international boundaries. Various laws suddenly come into play, such as Sweden's strict privacy laws about exporting personal data about Swedish citizens from Sweden. Another example is the Canadian law saying that data traffic originating in Canada and ending in Canada may not leave the country. This law means that traffic from Windsor, Ontario to Vancouver may not be routed via nearby Detroit, even if that route is the fastest and cheapest.

Another difference between interior and exterior routing is the cost. Within a single network, a single charging algorithm normally applies. However, different networks may be under different managements, and one route may be less expensive than another. Similarly, the quality of service offered by different networks may be different, and this may be a reason to choose one route over another.

5.5.7 Fragmentation

Each network imposes some maximum size on its packets. These limits have various causes, among them:

1. Hardware (e.g., the size of an Ethernet frame).
2. Operating system (e.g., all buffers are 512 bytes).
3. Protocols (e.g., the number of bits in the packet length field).
4. Compliance with some (inter)national standard.
5. Desire to reduce error-induced retransmissions to some level.
6. Desire to prevent one packet from occupying the channel too long.

The result of all these factors is that the network designers are not free to choose any maximum packet size they wish. Maximum payloads range from 48 bytes (ATM cells) to 65,515 bytes (IP packets), although the payload size in higher layers is often larger.

An obvious problem appears when a large packet wants to travel through a network whose maximum packet size is too small. One solution is to make sure the problem does not occur in the first place. In other words, the internet should use a routing algorithm that avoids sending packets through networks that cannot handle them. However, this solution is no solution at all. What happens if the original source packet is too large to be handled by the destination network? The routing algorithm can hardly bypass the destination.

Basically, the only solution to the problem is to allow gateways to break up packets into **fragments**, sending each fragment as a separate internet packet. However, as every parent of a small child knows, converting a large object into small fragments is considerably easier than the reverse process. (Physicists have even given this effect a name: the second law of thermodynamics.) Packet-switching networks, too, have trouble putting the fragments back together again.

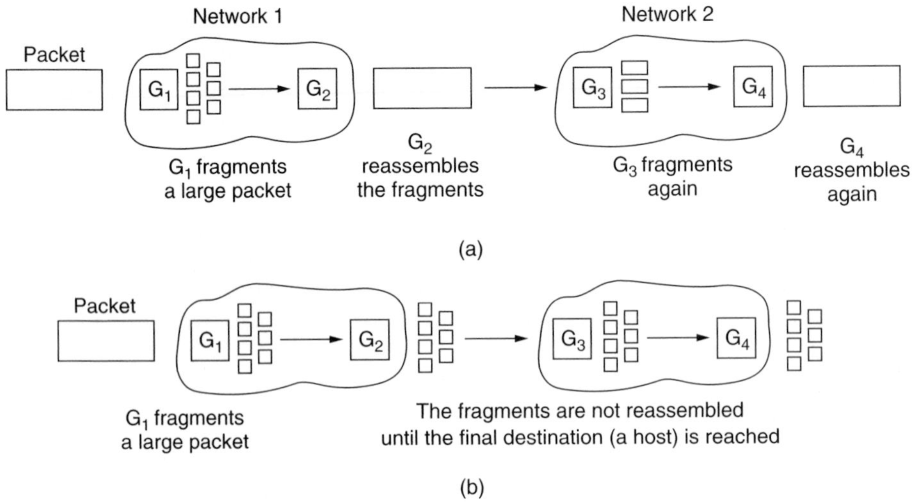

Figure 5-50. (a) Transparent fragmentation. (b) Nontransparent fragmentation.

Two opposing strategies exist for recombining the fragments back into the original packet. The first strategy is to make fragmentation caused by a "small-packet" network transparent to any subsequent networks through which the packet must pass on its way to the ultimate destination. This option is shown in Fig. 5-50(a). In this approach, the small-packet network has gateways (most likely, specialized routers) that interface to other networks. When an oversized packet arrives at a gateway, the gateway breaks it up into fragments. Each fragment is addressed to the same exit gateway, where the pieces are recombined. In this way passage through the small-packet network has been made transparent. Subsequent networks are not even aware that fragmentation has occurred. ATM networks, for example, have special hardware to provide transparent fragmentation of packets into cells and then reassembly of cells into packets. In the ATM world, fragmentation is called segmentation; the concept is the same, but some of the details are different.

Transparent fragmentation is straightforward but has some problems. For one thing, the exit gateway must know when it has received all the pieces, so either a count field or an "end of packet" bit must be provided. For another thing, all packets must exit via the same gateway. By not allowing some fragments to follow one route to the ultimate destination and other fragments a disjoint route, some performance may be lost. A last problem is the overhead required to repeatedly reassemble and then refragment a large packet passing through a series of small-packet networks. ATM requires transparent fragmentation.

The other fragmentation strategy is to refrain from recombining fragments at any intermediate gateways. Once a packet has been fragmented, each fragment is treated as though it were an original packet. All fragments are passed through the exit gateway (or gateways), as shown in Fig. 5-50(b). Recombination occurs only at the destination host. IP works this way.

Nontransparent fragmentation also has some problems. For example, it requires *every* host to be able to do reassembly. Yet another problem is that when a large packet is fragmented, the total overhead increases because each fragment must have a header. Whereas in the first method this overhead disappears as soon as the small-packet network is exited, in this method the overhead remains for the rest of the journey. An advantage of nontransparent fragmentation, however, is that multiple exit gateways can now be used and higher performance can be achieved. Of course, if the concatenated virtual-circuit model is being used, this advantage is of no use.

When a packet is fragmented, the fragments must be numbered in such a way that the original data stream can be reconstructed. One way of numbering the fragments is to use a tree. If packet 0 must be split up, the pieces are called 0.0, 0.1, 0.2, etc. If these fragments themselves must be fragmented later on, the pieces are numbered 0.0.0, 0.0.1, 0.0.2, . . . , 0.1.0, 0.1.1, 0.1.2, etc. If enough fields have been reserved in the header for the worst case and no duplicates are generated anywhere, this scheme is sufficient to ensure that all the pieces can be correctly reassembled at the destination, no matter what order they arrive in.

However, if even one network loses or discards packets, end-to-end retransmissions are needed, with unfortunate effects for the numbering system. Suppose that a 1024-bit packet is initially fragmented into four equal-sized fragments, 0.0, 0.1, 0.2, and 0.3. Fragment 0.1 is lost, but the other parts arrive at the destination. Eventually, the source times out and retransmits the original packet again. Only this time Murphy's law strikes and the route taken passes through a network with a 512-bit limit, so two fragments are generated. When the new fragment 0.1 arrives at the destination, the receiver will think that all four pieces are now accounted for and reconstruct the packet incorrectly.

A completely different (and better) numbering system is for the internetwork protocol to define an elementary fragment size small enough that the elementary fragment can pass through every network. When a packet is fragmented, all the pieces are equal to the elementary fragment size except the last one, which may be shorter. An internet packet may contain several fragments, for efficiency reasons. The internet header must provide the original packet number and the number of the (first) elementary fragment contained in the packet. As usual, there must also be a bit indicating that the last elementary fragment contained within the internet packet is the last one of the original packet.

This approach requires two sequence fields in the internet header: the original packet number and the fragment number. There is clearly a trade-off between the size of the elementary fragment and the number of bits in the fragment number. Because the elementary fragment size is presumed to be acceptable to every network, subsequent fragmentation of an internet packet containing several fragments causes no problem. The ultimate limit here is to have the elementary fragment be a single bit or byte, with the fragment number then being the bit or byte offset within the original packet, as shown in Fig. 5-51.

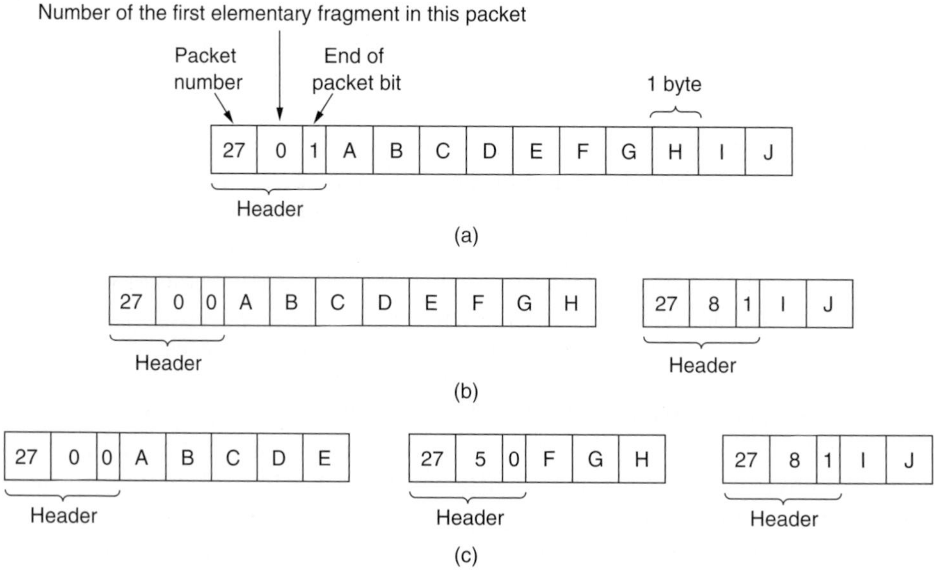

Figure 5-51. Fragmentation when the elementary data size is 1 byte. (a) Original packet, containing 10 data bytes. (b) Fragments after passing through a network with maximum packet size of 8 payload bytes plus header. (c) Fragments after passing through a size 5 gateway.

Some internet protocols take this method even further and consider the entire transmission on a virtual circuit to be one giant packet, so that each fragment contains the absolute byte number of the first byte within the fragment.

5.6 THE NETWORK LAYER IN THE INTERNET

Before getting into the specifics of the network layer in the Internet, it is worth taking at look at the principles that drove its design in the past and made it the success that it is today. All too often, nowadays, people seem to have forgotten them. These principles are enumerated and discussed in RFC 1958, which is well worth reading (and should be mandatory for all protocol designers—with a final exam at the end). This RFC draws heavily on ideas found in (Clark, 1988; and Saltzer et al., 1984). We will now summarize what we consider to be the top 10 principles (from most important to least important).

1. **Make sure it works.** Do not finalize the design or standard until multiple prototypes have successfully communicated with each other. All too often designers first write a 1000-page standard, get it approved, then discover it is deeply flawed and does not work. Then they write version 1.1 of the standard. This is not the way to go.

2. **Keep it simple.** When in doubt, use the simplest solution. William of Occam stated this principle (Occam's razor) in the 14th century. Put in modern terms: fight features. If a feature is not absolutely essential, leave it out, especially if the same effect can be achieved by combining other features.

3. **Make clear choices.** If there are several ways of doing the same thing, choose one. Having two or more ways to do the same thing is looking for trouble. Standards often have multiple options or modes or parameters because several powerful parties insist that their way is best. Designers should strongly resist this tendency. Just say no.

4. **Exploit modularity.** This principle leads directly to the idea of having protocol stacks, each of whose layers is independent of all the other ones. In this way, if circumstances that require one module or layer to be changed, the other ones will not be affected.

5. **Expect heterogeneity.** Different types of hardware, transmission facilities, and applications will occur on any large network. To handle them, the network design must be simple, general, and flexible.

6. **Avoid static options and parameters.** If parameters are unavoidable (e.g., maximum packet size), it is best to have the sender and receiver negotiate a value than defining fixed choices.

7. **Look for a good design; it need not be perfect.** Often the designers have a good design but it cannot handle some weird special case. Rather than messing up the design, the designers should go with the good design and put the burden of working around it on the people with the strange requirements.

8. **Be strict when sending and tolerant when receiving.** In other words, only send packets that rigorously comply with the standards, but expect incoming packets that may not be fully conformant and try to deal with them.

9. **Think about scalability.** If the system is to handle millions of hosts and billions of users effectively, no centralized databases of any kind are tolerable and load must be spread as evenly as possible over the available resources.

10. **Consider performance and cost.** If a network has poor performance or outrageous costs, nobody will use it.

Let us now leave the general principles and start looking at the details of the Internet's network layer. At the network layer, the Internet can be viewed as a collection of subnetworks or **Autonomous Systems** (**ASes**) that are interconnected. There is no real structure, but several major backbones exist. These are constructed from high-bandwidth lines and fast routers. Attached to the backbones are regional (midlevel) networks, and attached to these regional networks are the LANs at many universities, companies, and Internet service providers. A sketch of this quasi-hierarchical organization is given in Fig. 5-52.

The glue that holds the whole Internet together is the network layer protocol, **IP** (**Internet Protocol**). Unlike most older network layer protocols, it was designed from the beginning with internetworking in mind. A good way to think of the network layer is this. Its job is to provide a best-efforts (i.e., not guaranteed) way to transport datagrams from source to destination, without regard to whether these machines are on the same network or whether there are other networks in between them.

Communication in the Internet works as follows. The transport layer takes data streams and breaks them up into datagrams. In theory, datagrams can be up to 64 Kbytes each, but in practice they are usually not more than 1500 bytes (so they fit in one Ethernet frame). Each datagram is transmitted through the Internet, possibly being fragmented into smaller units as it goes. When all the pieces finally get to the destination machine, they are reassembled by the network layer into the original datagram. This datagram is then handed to the transport layer, which inserts it into the receiving process' input stream. As can be seen from Fig. 5-52, a packet originating at host 1 has to traverse six networks to get to host 2. In practice, it is often much more than six.

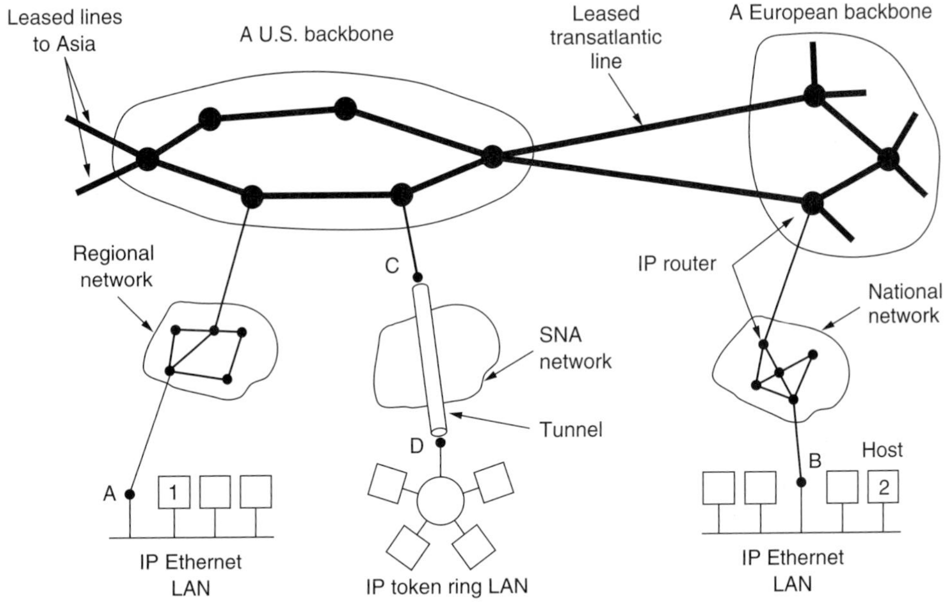

Figure 5-52. The Internet is an interconnected collection of many networks.

5.6.1 The IP Protocol

An appropriate place to start our study of the network layer in the Internet is the format of the IP datagrams themselves. An IP datagram consists of a header part and a text part. The header has a 20-byte fixed part and a variable length optional part. The header format is shown in Fig. 5-53. It is transmitted in big-endian order: from left to right, with the high-order bit of the *Version* field going first. (The SPARC is big endian; the Pentium is little-endian.) On little endian machines, software conversion is required on both transmission and reception.

The *Version* field keeps track of which version of the protocol the datagram belongs to. By including the version in each datagram, it becomes possible to have the transition between versions take years, with some machines running the old version and others running the new one. Currently a transition between IPv4 and IPv6 is going on, has already taken years, and is by no means close to being finished (Durand, 2001; Wiljakka, 2002; and Waddington and Chang, 2002). Some people even think it will never happen (Weiser, 2001). As an aside on numbering, IPv5 was an experimental real-time stream protocol that was never widely used.

Since the header length is not constant, a field in the header, *IHL*, is provided to tell how long the header is, in 32-bit words. The minimum value is 5, which applies when no options are present. The maximum value of this 4-bit field is 15,

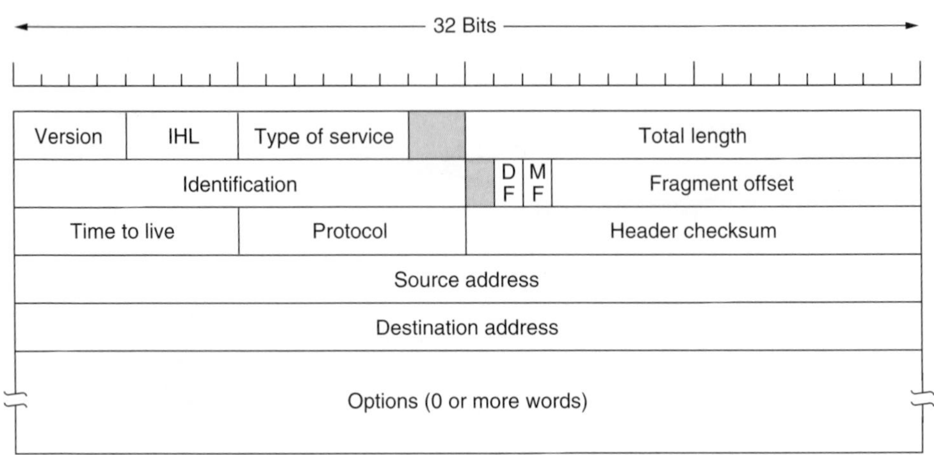

Figure 5-53. The IPv4 (Internet Protocol) header.

which limits the header to 60 bytes, and thus the *Options* field to 40 bytes. For some options, such as one that records the route a packet has taken, 40 bytes is far too small, making that option useless.

The *Type of service* field is one of the few fields that has changed its meaning (slightly) over the years. It was and is still intended to distinguish between different classes of service. Various combinations of reliability and speed are possible. For digitized voice, fast delivery beats accurate delivery. For file transfer, error-free transmission is more important than fast transmission.

Originally, the 6-bit field contained (from left to right), a three-bit *Precedence* field and three flags, *D*, *T*, and *R*. The *Precedence* field was a priority, from 0 (normal) to 7 (network control packet). The three flag bits allowed the host to specify what it cared most about from the set {Delay, Throughput, Reliability}. In theory, these fields allow routers to make choices between, for example, a satellite link with high throughput and high delay or a leased line with low throughput and low delay. In practice, current routers often ignore the *Type of service* field altogether.

Eventually, IETF threw in the towel and changed the field slightly to accommodate differentiated services. Six of the bits are used to indicate which of the service classes discussed earlier each packet belongs to. These classes include the four queueing priorities, three discard probabilities, and the historical classes.

The *Total length* includes everything in the datagram—both header and data. The maximum length is 65,535 bytes. At present, this upper limit is tolerable, but with future gigabit networks, larger datagrams may be needed.

The *Identification* field is needed to allow the destination host to determine which datagram a newly arrived fragment belongs to. All the fragments of a datagram contain the same *Identification* value.

Next comes an unused bit and then two 1-bit fields. *DF* stands for Don't Fragment. It is an order to the routers not to fragment the datagram because the destination is incapable of putting the pieces back together again. For example, when a computer boots, its ROM might ask for a memory image to be sent to it as a single datagram. By marking the datagram with the *DF* bit, the sender knows it will arrive in one piece, even if this means that the datagram must avoid a small-packet network on the best path and take a suboptimal route. All machines are required to accept fragments of 576 bytes or less.

MF stands for More Fragments. All fragments except the last one have this bit set. It is needed to know when all fragments of a datagram have arrived.

The *Fragment offset* tells where in the current datagram this fragment belongs. All fragments except the last one in a datagram must be a multiple of 8 bytes, the elementary fragment unit. Since 13 bits are provided, there is a maximum of 8192 fragments per datagram, giving a maximum datagram length of 65,536 bytes, one more than the *Total length* field.

The *Time to live* field is a counter used to limit packet lifetimes. It is supposed to count time in seconds, allowing a maximum lifetime of 255 sec. It must be decremented on each hop and is supposed to be decremented multiple times when queued for a long time in a router. In practice, it just counts hops. When it hits zero, the packet is discarded and a warning packet is sent back to the source host. This feature prevents datagrams from wandering around forever, something that otherwise might happen if the routing tables ever become corrupted.

When the network layer has assembled a complete datagram, it needs to know what to do with it. The *Protocol* field tells it which transport process to give it to. TCP is one possibility, but so are UDP and some others. The numbering of protocols is global across the entire Internet. Protocols and other assigned numbers were formerly listed in RFC 1700, but nowadays they are contained in an on-line data base located at *www.iana.org*.

The *Header checksum* verifies the header only. Such a checksum is useful for detecting errors generated by bad memory words inside a router. The algorithm is to add up all the 16-bit halfwords as they arrive, using one's complement arithmetic and then take the one's complement of the result. For purposes of this algorithm, the *Header checksum* is assumed to be zero upon arrival. This algorithm is more robust than using a normal add. Note that the *Header checksum* must be recomputed at each hop because at least one field always changes (the *Time to live* field), but tricks can be used to speed up the computation.

The *Source address* and *Destination address* indicate the network number and host number. We will discuss Internet addresses in the next section. The *Options* field was designed to provide an escape to allow subsequent versions of the protocol to include information not present in the original design, to permit experimenters to try out new ideas, and to avoid allocating header bits to information that is rarely needed. The options are variable length. Each begins with a 1-byte code identifying the option. Some options are followed by a 1-byte option length field, and then one or more data bytes. The *Options* field is padded out to a multiple of four bytes. Originally, five options were defined, as listed in Fig. 5-54, but since then some new ones have been added. The current complete list is now maintained on-line at *www.iana.org/assignments/ip-parameters*.

Option	Description
Security	Specifies how secret the datagram is
Strict source routing	Gives the complete path to be followed
Loose source routing	Gives a list of routers not to be missed
Record route	Makes each router append its IP address
Timestamp	Makes each router append its address and timestamp

Figure 5-54. Some of the IP options.

The *Security* option tells how secret the information is. In theory, a military router might use this field to specify not to route through certain countries the military considers to be "bad guys." In practice, all routers ignore it, so its only practical function is to help spies find the good stuff more easily.

The *Strict source routing* option gives the complete path from source to destination as a sequence of IP addresses. The datagram is required to follow that exact route. It is most useful for system managers to send emergency packets when the routing tables are corrupted, or for making timing measurements.

The *Loose source routing* option requires the packet to traverse the list of routers specified, and in the order specified, but it is allowed to pass through other routers on the way. Normally, this option would only provide a few routers, to force a particular path. For example, to force a packet from London to Sydney to go west instead of east, this option might specify routers in New York, Los Angeles, and Honolulu. This option is most useful when political or economic considerations dictate passing through or avoiding certain countries.

The *Record route* option tells the routers along the path to append their IP address to the option field. This allows system managers to track down bugs in the routing algorithms ("Why are packets from Houston to Dallas visiting Tokyo first?"). When the ARPANET was first set up, no packet ever passed through more than nine routers, so 40 bytes of option was ample. As mentioned above, now it is too small.

Finally, the *Timestamp* option is like the *Record route* option, except that in addition to recording its 32-bit IP address, each router also records a 32-bit timestamp. This option, too, is mostly for debugging routing algorithms.

5.6.2 IP Addresses

Every host and router on the Internet has an IP address, which encodes its network number and host number. The combination is unique: in principle, no two machines on the Internet have the same IP address. All IP addresses are 32 bits long and are used in the *Source address* and *Destination address* fields of IP packets. It is important to note that an IP address does not actually refer to a host. It really refers to a network interface, so if a host is on two networks, it must have two IP addresses. However, in practice, most hosts are on one network and thus have one IP address.

For several decades, IP addresses were divided into the five categories listed in Fig. 5-55. This allocation has come to be called **classful addressing**. It is no longer used, but references to it in the literature are still common. We will discuss the replacement of classful addressing shortly.

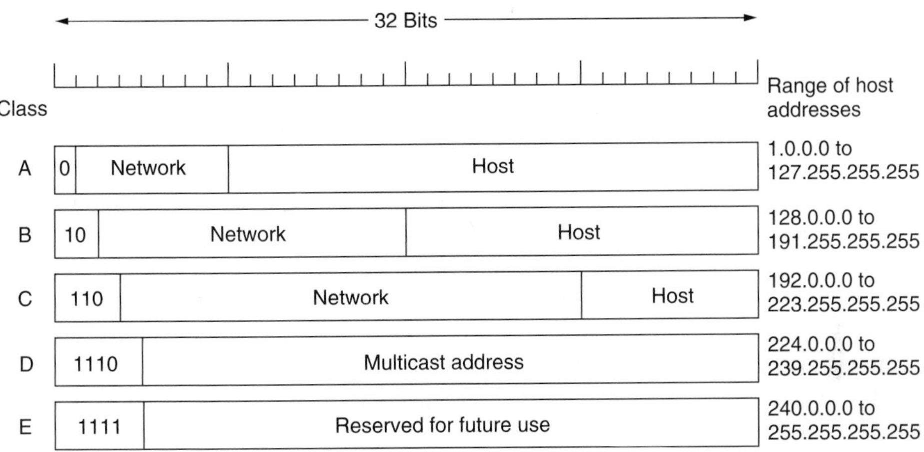

Figure 5-55. IP address formats.

The class A, B, C, and D formats allow for up to 128 networks with 16 million hosts each, 16,384 networks with up to 64K hosts, and 2 million networks (e.g., LANs) with up to 256 hosts each (although a few of these are special). Also supported is multicast, in which a datagram is directed to multiple hosts. Addresses beginning with 1111 are reserved for future use. Over 500,000 networks are now connected to the Internet, and the number grows every year. Network numbers are managed by a nonprofit corporation called **ICANN** (**Internet Corporation for Assigned Names and Numbers**) to avoid conflicts. In turn, ICANN has delegated parts of the address space to various regional authorities, which then dole out IP addresses to ISPs and other companies.

Network addresses, which are 32-bit numbers, are usually written in **dotted decimal notation**. In this format, each of the 4 bytes is written in decimal, from 0 to 255. For example, the 32-bit hexadecimal address C0290614 is written as 192.41.6.20. The lowest IP address is 0.0.0.0 and the highest is 255.255.255.255.

The values 0 and −1 (all 1s) have special meanings, as shown in Fig. 5-56. The value 0 means this network or this host. The value of −1 is used as a broadcast address to mean all hosts on the indicated network.

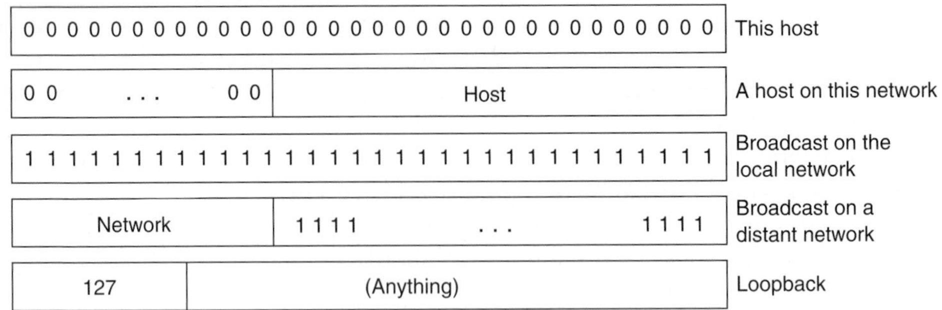

Figure 5-56. Special IP addresses.

The IP address 0.0.0.0 is used by hosts when they are being booted. IP addresses with 0 as network number refer to the current network. These addresses allow machines to refer to their own network without knowing its number (but they have to know its class to know how many 0s to include). The address consisting of all 1s allows broadcasting on the local network, typically a LAN. The addresses with a proper network number and all 1s in the host field allow machines to send broadcast packets to distant LANs anywhere in the Internet (although many network administrators disable this feature). Finally, all addresses of the form 127.*xx*.*yy*.*zz* are reserved for loopback testing. Packets sent to that address are not put out onto the wire; they are processed locally and treated as incoming packets. This allows packets to be sent to the local network without the sender knowing its number.

Subnets

As we have seen, all the hosts in a network must have the same network number. This property of IP addressing can cause problems as networks grow. For example, consider a university that started out with one class B network used by the Computer Science Dept. for the computers on its Ethernet. A year later, the Electrical Engineering Dept. wanted to get on the Internet, so they bought a repeater to extend the CS Ethernet to their building. As time went on, many other departments acquired computers and the limit of four repeaters per Ethernet was quickly reached. A different organization was required.

Getting a second network address would be hard to do since network addresses are scarce and the university already had enough addresses for over 60,000 hosts. The problem is the rule that a single class A, B, or C address refers to one network, not to a collection of LANs. As more and more organizations ran into this situation, a small change was made to the addressing system to deal with it.

The solution is to allow a network to be split into several parts for internal use but still act like a single network to the outside world. A typical campus network nowadays might look like that of Fig. 5-57, with a main router connected to an ISP or regional network and numerous Ethernets spread around campus in different departments. Each of the Ethernets has its own router connected to the main router (possibly via a backbone LAN, but the nature of the interrouter connection is not relevant here).

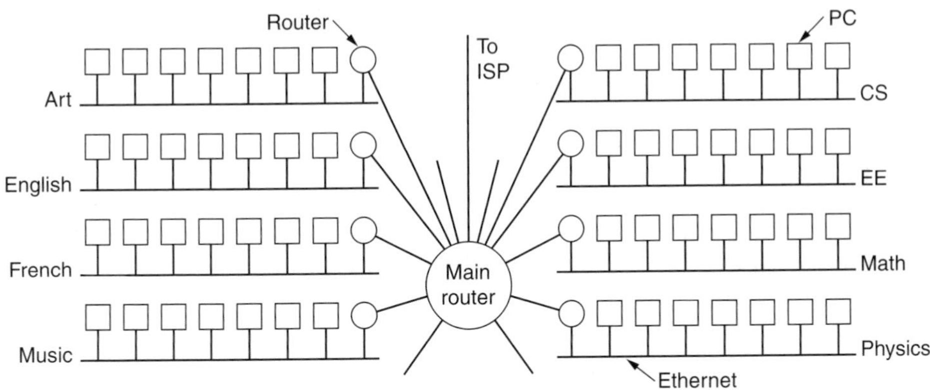

Figure 5-57. A campus network consisting of LANs for various departments.

In the Internet literature, the parts of the network (in this case, Ethernets) are called **subnets**. As we mentioned in Chap. 1, this usage conflicts with "subnet" to mean the set of all routers and communication lines in a network. Hopefully, it will be clear from the context which meaning is intended. In this section and the next one, the new definition will be the one used exclusively.

When a packet comes into the main router, how does it know which subnet (Ethernet) to give it to? One way would be to have a table with 65,536 entries in the main router telling which router to use for each host on campus. This idea would work, but it would require a very large table in the main router and a lot of manual maintenance as hosts were added, moved, or taken out of service.

Instead, a different scheme was invented. Basically, instead of having a single class B address with 14 bits for the network number and 16 bits for the host number, some bits are taken away from the host number to create a subnet number. For example, if the university has 35 departments, it could use a 6-bit subnet number and a 10-bit host number, allowing for up to 64 Ethernets, each with a maximum of 1022 hosts (0 and −1 are not available, as mentioned earlier). This split could be changed later if it turns out to be the wrong one.

To implement subnetting, the main router needs a **subnet mask** that indicates the split between network + subnet number and host, as shown in Fig. 5-58. Subnet masks are also written in dotted decimal notation, with the addition of a slash followed by the number of bits in the network + subnet part. For the example of Fig. 5-58, the subnet mask can be written as 255.255.252.0. An alternative notation is /22 to indicate that the subnet mask is 22 bits long.

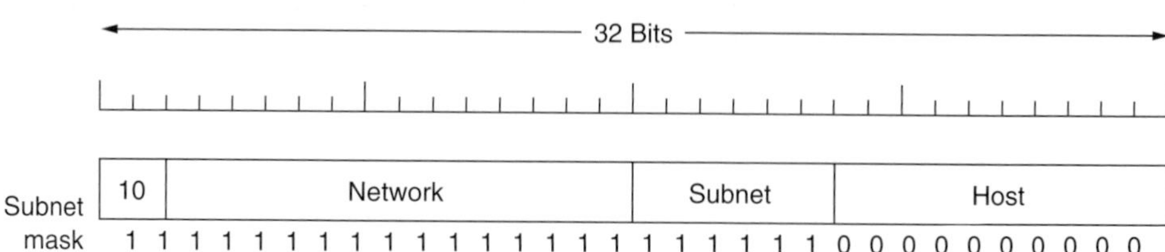

Figure 5-58. A class B network subnetted into 64 subnets.

Outside the network, the subnetting is not visible, so allocating a new subnet does not require contacting ICANN or changing any external databases. In this example, the first subnet might use IP addresses starting at 130.50.4.1; the second subnet might start at 130.50.8.1; the third subnet might start at 130.50.12.1; and so on. To see why the subnets are counting by fours, note that the corresponding binary addresses are as follows:

```
Subnet 1: 10000010  00110010  000001|00  00000001
Subnet 2: 10000010  00110010  000010|00  00000001
Subnet 3: 10000010  00110010  000011|00  00000001
```

Here the vertical bar (|) shows the boundary between the subnet number and the host number. To its left is the 6-bit subnet number; to its right is the 10-bit host number.

To see how subnets work, it is necessary to explain how IP packets are processed at a router. Each router has a table listing some number of (network, 0) IP addresses and some number of (this-network, host) IP addresses. The first kind tells how to get to distant networks. The second kind tells how to get to local hosts. Associated with each table is the network interface to use to reach the destination, and certain other information.

When an IP packet arrives, its destination address is looked up in the routing table. If the packet is for a distant network, it is forwarded to the next router on the interface given in the table. If it is a local host (e.g., on the router's LAN), it is sent directly to the destination. If the network is not present, the packet is forwarded to a default router with more extensive tables. This algorithm means that each router only has to keep track of other networks and local hosts, not (network, host) pairs, greatly reducing the size of the routing table.

When subnetting is introduced, the routing tables are changed, adding entries of the form (this-network, subnet, 0) and (this-network, this-subnet, host). Thus, a router on subnet *k* knows how to get to all the other subnets and also how to get to all the hosts on subnet *k*. It does not have to know the details about hosts on other subnets. In fact, all that needs to be changed is to have each router do a Boolean AND with the network's subnet mask to get rid of the host number and look up the resulting address in its tables (after determining which network class it is).

For example, a packet addressed to 130.50.15.6 and arriving at the main router is ANDed with the subnet mask 255.255.252.0/22 to give the address 130.50.12.0. This address is looked up in the routing tables to find out which output line to use to get to the router for subnet 3. Subnetting thus reduces router table space by creating a three-level hierarchy consisting of network, subnet, and host.

CIDR—Classless InterDomain Routing

IP has been in heavy use for decades. It has worked extremely well, as demonstrated by the exponential growth of the Internet. Unfortunately, IP is rapidly becoming a victim of its own popularity: it is running out of addresses. This looming disaster has sparked a great deal of discussion and controversy within the Internet community about what to do about it. In this section we will describe both the problem and several proposed solutions.

Back in 1987, a few visionaries predicted that some day the Internet might grow to 100,000 networks. Most experts pooh-poohed this as being decades in the future, if ever. The 100,000th network was connected in 1996. The problem, as mentioned above, is that the Internet is rapidly running out of IP addresses. In principle, over 2 billion addresses exist, but the practice of organizing the address space by classes (see Fig. 5-55) wastes millions of them. In particular, the real villain is the class B network. For most organizations, a class A network, with 16 million addresses is too big, and a class C network, with 256 addresses is too small. A class B network, with 65,536, is just right. In Internet folklore, this situation is known as the **three bears problem** (as in *Goldilocks and the Three Bears*).

In reality, a class B address is far too large for most organizations. Studies have shown that more than half of all class B networks have fewer than 50 hosts. A class C network would have done the job, but no doubt every organization that asked for a class B address thought that one day it would outgrow the 8-bit host field. In retrospect, it might have been better to have had class C networks use 10 bits instead of eight for the host number, allowing 1022 hosts per network. Had this been the case, most organizations would have probably settled for a class C network, and there would have been half a million of them (versus only 16,384 class B networks).

It is hard to fault the Internet designers for not having provided more (and smaller) class B addresses. At the time the decision was made to create the three classes, the Internet was a research network connecting the major research universities in the U.S. (plus a very small number of companies and military sites doing networking research). No one then perceived the Internet as becoming a mass market communication system rivaling the telephone network. At the time, someone no doubt said: "The U.S. has about 2000 colleges and universities. Even if all of them connect to the Internet and many universities in other countries join, too, we are never going to hit 16,000 since there are not that many universities in the whole world. Furthermore, having the host number be an integral number of bytes speeds up packet processing.''

However, if the split had allocated 20 bits to the class B network number, another problem would have emerged: the routing table explosion. From the point of view of the routers, the IP address space is a two-level hierarchy, with network numbers and host numbers. Routers do not have to know about all the hosts, but they do have to know about all the networks. If half a million class C networks were in use, every router in the entire Internet would need a table with half a million entries, one per network, telling which line to use to get to that network, as well as providing other information.

The actual physical storage of half a million entry tables is probably doable, although expensive for critical routers that keep the tables in static RAM on I/O boards. A more serious problem is that the complexity of various algorithms relating to management of the tables grows faster than linear. Worse yet, much of the existing router software and firmware was designed at a time when the Internet had 1000 connected networks and 10,000 networks seemed decades away. Design choices made then often are far from optimal now.

In addition, various routing algorithms require each router to transmit its tables periodically (e.g., distance vector protocols). The larger the tables, the more likely it is that some parts will get lost underway, leading to incomplete data at the other end and possibly routing instabilities.

The routing table problem could have been solved by going to a deeper hierarchy. For example, having each IP address contain a country, state/province, city, network, and host field might work. Then each router would only need to know how to get to each country, the states or provinces in its own country, the cities in its state or province, and the networks in its city. Unfortunately, this solution would require considerably more than 32 bits for IP addresses and would use addresses inefficiently (Liechtenstein would have as many bits as the United States).

In short, some solutions solve one problem but create a new one. The solution that was implemented and that gave the Internet a bit of extra breathing room is **CIDR** (**Classless InterDomain Routing**). The basic idea behind CIDR, which is described in RFC 1519, is to allocate the remaining IP addresses in variable-sized blocks, without regard to the classes. If a site needs, say, 2000 addresses, it is given a block of 2048 addresses on a 2048-byte boundary.

Dropping the classes makes forwarding more complicated. In the old classful system, forwarding worked like this. When a packet arrived at a router, a copy of the IP address was shifted right 28 bits to yield a 4-bit class number. A 16-way branch then sorted packets into A, B, C, and D (if supported), with eight of the cases for class A, four of the cases for class B, two of the cases for class C, and one each for D and E. The code for each class then masked off the 8-, 16-, or 24-bit network number and right aligned it in a 32-bit word. The network number was then looked up in the A, B, or C table, usually by indexing for A and B networks and hashing for C networks. Once the entry was found, the outgoing line could be looked up and the packet forwarded.

With CIDR, this simple algorithm no longer works. Instead, each routing table entry is extended by giving it a 32-bit mask. Thus, there is now a single routing table for all networks consisting of an array of (IP address, subnet mask, outgoing line) triples. When a packet comes in, its destination IP address is first extracted. Then (conceptually) the routing table is scanned entry by entry, masking the destination address and comparing it to the table entry looking for a match. It is possible that multiple entries (with different subnet mask lengths) match, in which case the longest mask is used. Thus, if there is a match for a /20 mask and a /24 mask, the /24 entry is used.

Complex algorithms have been devised to speed up the address matching process (Ruiz-Sanchez et al., 2001). Commercial routers use custom VLSI chips with these algorithms embedded in hardware.

To make the forwarding algorithm easier to understand, let us consider an example in which millions of addresses are available starting at 194.24.0.0. Suppose that Cambridge University needs 2048 addresses and is assigned the addresses 194.24.0.0 through 194.24.7.255, along with mask 255.255.248.0. Next, Oxford University asks for 4096 addresses. Since a block of 4096 addresses must lie on a 4096-byte boundary, they cannot be given addresses starting at 194.24.8.0. Instead, they get 194.24.16.0 through 194.24.31.255 along with subnet mask 255.255.240.0. Now the University of Edinburgh asks for 1024 addresses and is assigned addresses 194.24.8.0 through 194.24.11.255 and mask 255.255.252.0. These assignments are summarized in Fig. 5-59.

University	First address	Last address	How many	Written as
Cambridge	194.24.0.0	194.24.7.255	2048	194.24.0.0/21
Edinburgh	194.24.8.0	194.24.11.255	1024	194.24.8.0/22
(Available)	194.24.12.0	194.24.15.255	1024	194.24.12/22
Oxford	194.24.16.0	194.24.31.255	4096	194.24.16.0/20

Figure 5-59. A set of IP address assignments.

The routing tables all over the world are now updated with the three assigned entries. Each entry contains a base address and a subnet mask. These entries (in binary) are:

```
   Address                                   Mask
C: 11000010 00011000 00000000 00000000    11111111 11111111 11111000 00000000
E: 11000010 00011000 00001000 00000000    11111111 11111111 11111100 00000000
O: 11000010 00011000 00010000 00000000    11111111 11111111 11110000 00000000
```

Now consider what happens when a packet comes in addressed to 194.24.17.4, which in binary is represented as the following 32-bit string

11000010 00011000 00010001 00000100

First it is Boolean ANDed with the Cambridge mask to get

11000010 00011000 00010000 00000000

This value does not match the Cambridge base address, so the original address is next ANDed with the Edinburgh mask to get

11000010 00011000 00010000 00000000

This value does not match the Edinburgh base address, so Oxford is tried next, yielding

11000010 00011000 00010000 00000000

This value does match the Oxford base. If no longer matches are found farther down the table, the Oxford entry is used and the packet is sent along the line named in it.

Now let us look at these three universities from the point of view of a router in Omaha, Nebraska, that has only four outgoing lines: Minneapolis, New York, Dallas, and Denver. When the router software there gets the three new entries, it notices that it can combine all three entries into a single **aggregate entry** 194.24.0.0/19 with a binary address and submask as follows:

11000010 0000000 00000000 00000000   11111111 11111111 11100000 00000000

This entry sends all packets destined for any of the three universities to New York. By aggregating the three entries, the Omaha router has reduced its table size by two entries.

If New York has a single line to London for all U.K. traffic, it can use an aggregated entry as well. However, if it has separate lines for London and Edinburgh, then it has to have three separate entries. Aggregation is heavily used throughout the Internet to reduce the size of the router tables.

As a final note on this example, the aggregate route entry in Omaha also sends packets for the unassigned addresses to New York. As long as the addresses are truly unassigned, this does not matter because they are not supposed to occur. However, if they are later assigned to a company in California, an additional entry, 194.24.12.0/22, will be needed to deal with them.

NAT—Network Address Translation

IP addresses are scarce. An ISP might have a /16 (formerly class B) address, giving it 65,534 host numbers. If it has more customers than that, it has a problem. For home customers with dial-up connections, one way around the problem is to dynamically assign an IP address to a computer when it calls up and logs in and take the IP address back when the session ends. In this way, a single /16 address can handle up to 65,534 active users, which is probably good enough for an ISP with several hundred thousand customers. When the session is terminated, the IP address is reassigned to another caller. While this strategy works well for an ISP with a moderate number of home users, it fails for ISPs that primarily serve business customers.

The problem is that business customers expect to be on-line continuously during business hours. Both small businesses, such as three-person travel agencies, and large corporations have multiple computers connected by a LAN. Some computers are employee PCs; others may be Web servers. Generally, there is a router on the LAN that is connected to the ISP by a leased line to provide continuous connectivity. This arrangement means that each computer must have its own IP address all day long. In effect, the total number of computers owned by all its business customers combined cannot exceed the number of IP addresses the ISP has. For a /16 address, this limits the total number of computers to 65,534. For an ISP with tens of thousands of business customers, this limit will quickly be exceeded.

To make matters worse, more and more home users are subscribing to ADSL or Internet over cable. Two of the features of these services are (1) the user gets a permanent IP address and (2) there is no connect charge (just a monthly flat rate charge), so many ADSL and cable users just stay logged in permanently. This development just adds to the shortage of IP addresses. Assigning IP addresses on-the-fly as is done with dial-up users is of no use because the number of IP addresses in use at any one instant may be many times the number the ISP owns.

And just to make it a bit more complicated, many ADSL and cable users have two or more computers at home, often one for each family member, and they all want to be on-line all the time using the single IP address their ISP has given them. The solution here is to connect all the PCs via a LAN and put a router on it. From the ISP's point of view, the family is now the same as a small business with a handful of computers. Welcome to Jones, Inc.

The problem of running out of IP addresses is not a theoretical problem that might occur at some point in the distant future. It is happening right here and right now. The long-term solution is for the whole Internet to migrate to IPv6, which has 128-bit addresses. This transition is slowly occurring, but it will be years before the process is complete. As a consequence, some people felt that a quick fix was needed for the short term. This quick fix came in the form of **NAT** (**Network Address Translation**), which is described in RFC 3022 and which we will summarize below. For additional information, see (Dutcher, 2001).

The basic idea behind NAT is to assign each company a single IP address (or at most, a small number of them) for Internet traffic. *Within* the company, every computer gets a unique IP address, which is used for routing intramural traffic. However, when a packet exits the company and goes to the ISP, an address translation takes place. To make this scheme possible, three ranges of IP addresses have been declared as private. Companies may use them internally as they wish.

The only rule is that no packets containing these addresses may appear on the Internet itself. The three reserved ranges are:

```
10.0.0.0    – 10.255.255.255/8     (16,777,216 hosts)
172.16.0.0  – 172.31.255.255/12    (1,048,576 hosts)
192.168.0.0 – 192.168.255.255/16   (65,536 hosts)
```

The first range provides for 16,777,216 addresses (except for 0 and −1, as usual) and is the usual choice of most companies, even if they do not need so many addresses.

The operation of NAT is shown in Fig. 5-60. Within the company premises, every machine has a unique address of the form 10.*x*.*y*.*z*. However, when a packet leaves the company premises, it passes through a **NAT box** that converts the internal IP source address, 10.0.0.1 in the figure, to the company's true IP address, 198.60.42.12 in this example. The NAT box is often combined in a single device with a firewall, which provides security by carefully controlling what goes into the company and what comes out. We will study firewalls in Chap. 8. It is also possible to integrate the NAT box into the company's router.

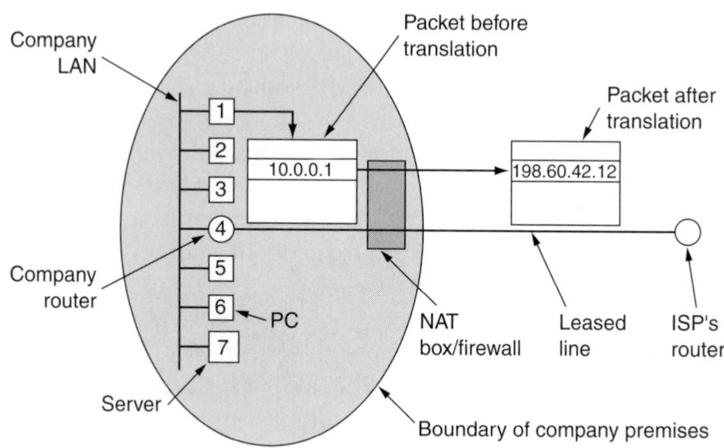

Figure 5-60. Placement and operation of a NAT box.

So far we have glossed over one tiny little detail: when the reply comes back (e.g., from a Web server), it is naturally addressed to 198.60.42.12, so how does the NAT box know which address to replace it with? Herein lies the problem with NAT. If there were a spare field in the IP header, that field could be used to keep track of who the real sender was, but only 1 bit is still unused. In principle, a new option could be created to hold the true source address, but doing so would require changing the IP code on all the machines on the entire Internet to handle the new option. This is not a promising alternative for a quick fix.

What actually happened is as follows. The NAT designers observed that most IP packets carry either TCP or UDP payloads. When we study TCP and UDP in Chap. 6, we will see that both of these have headers containing a source port and a destination port. Below we will just discuss TCP ports, but exactly the same story holds for UDP ports. The ports are 16-bit integers that indicate where the TCP connection begins and ends. These ports provide the field needed to make NAT work.

When a process wants to establish a TCP connection with a remote process, it attaches itself to an unused TCP port on its own machine. This is called the **source port** and tells the TCP code where to send incoming packets belonging to this connection. The process also supplies a **destination port** to tell who to give the packets to on the remote side. Ports 0–1023 are reserved for well-known services. For example, port 80 is the port used by Web servers, so remote clients can locate them. Each outgoing TCP message contains both a source port and a destination port. Together, these ports serve to identify the processes using the connection on both ends.

An analogy may make the use of ports clearer. Imagine a company with a single main telephone number. When people call the main number, they reach an operator who asks which extension they want and then puts them through to that extension. The main number is analogous to the company's IP address and the extensions on both ends are analogous to the ports. Ports are an extra 16-bits of addressing that identify which process gets which incoming packet.

Using the *Source port* field, we can solve our mapping problem. Whenever an outgoing packet enters the NAT box, the 10.*x*.*y*.*z* source address is replaced by the company's true IP address. In addition, the TCP *Source port* field is replaced by an index into the NAT box's 65,536-entry translation table. This table entry contains the original IP address and the original source port. Finally, both the IP and TCP header checksums are recomputed and inserted into the packet. It is necessary to replace the *Source port* because connections from machines 10.0.0.1 and 10.0.0.2 may both happen to use port 5000, for example, so the *Source port* alone is not enough to identify the sending process.

When a packet arrives at the NAT box from the ISP, the *Source port* in the TCP header is extracted and used as an index into the NAT box's mapping table. From the entry located, the internal IP address and original TCP *Source port* are extracted and inserted into the packet. Then both the IP and TCP checksums are recomputed and inserted into the packet. The packet is then passed to the company router for normal delivery using the 10.*x*.*y*.*z* address.

NAT can also be used to alleviate the IP shortage for ADSL and cable users. When the ISP assigns each user an address, it uses 10.*x*.*y*.*z* addresses. When packets from user machines exit the ISP and enter the main Internet, they pass through a NAT box that translates them to the ISP's true Internet address. On the way back, packets undergo the reverse mapping. In this respect, to the rest of the Internet, the ISP and its home ADSL/cable users just looks like a big company.

Although this scheme sort of solves the problem, many people in the IP community regard it as an abomination-on-the-face-of-the-earth. Briefly summarized, here are some of the objections. First, NAT violates the architectural model of IP, which states that every IP address uniquely identifies a single machine worldwide. The whole software structure of the Internet is built on this fact. With NAT, thousands of machines may (and do) use address 10.0.0.1.

Second, NAT changes the Internet from a connectionless network to a kind of connection-oriented network. The problem is that the NAT box must maintain information (the mapping) for each connection passing through it. Having the network maintain connection state is a property of connection-oriented networks, not connectionless ones. If the NAT box crashes and its mapping table is lost, all its TCP connections are destroyed. In the absence of NAT, router crashes have no effect on TCP. The sending process just times out within a few seconds and retransmits all unacknowledged packets. With NAT, the Internet becomes as vulnerable as a circuit-switched network.

Third, NAT violates the most fundamental rule of protocol layering: layer k may not make any assumptions about what layer $k + 1$ has put into the payload field. This basic principle is there to keep the layers independent. If TCP is later upgraded to TCP-2, with a different header layout (e.g., 32-bit ports), NAT will fail. The whole idea of layered protocols is to ensure that changes in one layer do not require changes in other layers. NAT destroys this independence.

Fourth, processes on the Internet are not required to use TCP or UDP. If a user on machine *A* decides to use some new transport protocol to talk to a user on machine *B* (for example, for a multimedia application), introduction of a NAT box will cause the application to fail because the NAT box will not be able to locate the TCP *Source port* correctly.

Fifth, some applications insert IP addresses in the body of the text. The receiver then extracts these addresses and uses them. Since NAT knows nothing about these addresses, it cannot replace them, so any attempt to use them on the remote side will fail. **FTP**, the standard **File Transfer Protocol** works this way and can fail in the presence of NAT unless special precautions are taken. Similarly, the H.323 Internet telephony protocol (which we will study in Chap. 7) has this property and can fail in the presence of NAT. It may be possible to patch NAT to work with H.323, but having to patch the code in the NAT box every time a new application comes along is not a good idea.

Sixth, since the TCP *Source port* field is 16 bits, at most 65,536 machines can be mapped onto an IP address. Actually, the number is slightly less because the first 4096 ports are reserved for special uses. However, if multiple IP addresses are available, each one can handle up to 61,440 machines.

These and other problems with NAT are discussed in RFC 2993. In general, the opponents of NAT say that by fixing the problem of insufficient IP addresses with a temporary and ugly hack, the pressure to implement the real solution, that is, the transition to IPv6, is reduced, and this is a bad thing.

5.6.3 Internet Control Protocols

In addition to IP, which is used for data transfer, the Internet has several control protocols used in the network layer, including ICMP, ARP, RARP, BOOTP, and DHCP. In this section we will look at each of these in turn.

The Internet Control Message Protocol

The operation of the Internet is monitored closely by the routers. When something unexpected occurs, the event is reported by the **ICMP** (**Internet Control Message Protocol**), which is also used to test the Internet. About a dozen types of ICMP messages are defined. The most important ones are listed in Fig. 5-61. Each ICMP message type is encapsulated in an IP packet.

Message type	Description
Destination unreachable	Packet could not be delivered
Time exceeded	Time to live field hit 0
Parameter problem	Invalid header field
Source quench	Choke packet
Redirect	Teach a router about geography
Echo	Ask a machine if it is alive
Echo reply	Yes, I am alive
Timestamp request	Same as Echo request, but with timestamp
Timestamp reply	Same as Echo reply, but with timestamp

Figure 5-61. The principal ICMP message types.

The DESTINATION UNREACHABLE message is used when the subnet or a router cannot locate the destination or when a packet with the *DF* bit cannot be delivered because a "small-packet" network stands in the way.

The TIME EXCEEDED message is sent when a packet is dropped because its counter has reached zero. This event is a symptom that packets are looping, that there is enormous congestion, or that the timer values are being set too low.

The PARAMETER PROBLEM message indicates that an illegal value has been detected in a header field. This problem indicates a bug in the sending host's IP software or possibly in the software of a router transited.

The SOURCE QUENCH message was formerly used to throttle hosts that were sending too many packets. When a host received this message, it was expected to slow down. It is rarely used any more because when congestion occurs, these packets tend to add more fuel to the fire. Congestion control in the Internet is now done largely in the transport layer; we will study it in detail in Chap. 6.

The REDIRECT message is used when a router notices that a packet seems to be routed wrong. It is used by the router to tell the sending host about the probable error.

The ECHO and ECHO REPLY messages are used to see if a given destination is reachable and alive. Upon receiving the ECHO message, the destination is expected to send an ECHO REPLY message back. The TIMESTAMP REQUEST and TIMESTAMP REPLY messages are similar, except that the arrival time of the message and the departure time of the reply are recorded in the reply. This facility is used to measure network performance.

In addition to these messages, others have been defined. The on-line list is now kept at *www.iana.org/assignments/icmp-parameters*.

ARP—The Address Resolution Protocol

Although every machine on the Internet has one (or more) IP addresses, these cannot actually be used for sending packets because the data link layer hardware does not understand Internet addresses. Nowadays, most hosts at companies and universities are attached to a LAN by an interface board that only understands LAN addresses. For example, every Ethernet board ever manufactured comes equipped with a 48-bit Ethernet address. Manufacturers of Ethernet boards request a block of addresses from a central authority to ensure that no two boards have the same address (to avoid conflicts should the two boards ever appear on the same LAN). The boards send and receive frames based on 48-bit Ethernet addresses. They know nothing at all about 32-bit IP addresses.

The question now arises: How do IP addresses get mapped onto data link layer addresses, such as Ethernet? To explain how this works, let us use the example of Fig. 5-62, in which a small university with several class C (now called /24) networks is illustrated. Here we have two Ethernets, one in the Computer Science Dept., with IP address 192.31.65.0 and one in Electrical Engineering, with IP address 192.31.63.0. These are connected by a campus backbone ring (e.g., FDDI) with IP address 192.31.60.0. Each machine on an Ethernet has a unique Ethernet address, labeled *E1* through *E6*, and each machine on the FDDI ring has an FDDI address, labeled *F1* through *F3*.

Let us start out by seeing how a user on host 1 sends a packet to a user on host 2. Let us assume the sender knows the name of the intended receiver, possibly something like *mary@eagle.cs.uni.edu*. The first step is to find the IP address for host 2, known as *eagle.cs.uni.edu*. This lookup is performed by the Domain Name System, which we will study in Chap. 7. For the moment, we will just assume that DNS returns the IP address for host 2 (192.31.65.5).

The upper layer software on host 1 now builds a packet with 192.31.65.5 in the *Destination address* field and gives it to the IP software to transmit. The IP software can look at the address and see that the destination is on its own network,

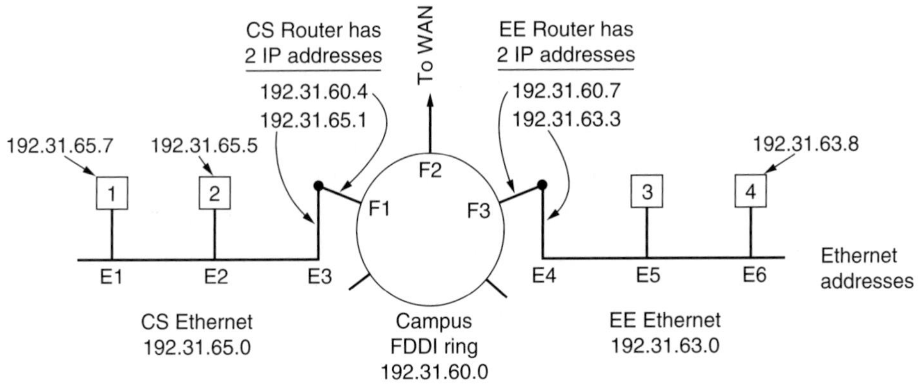

Figure 5-62. Three interconnected /24 networks: two Ethernets and an FDDI ring.

but it needs some way to find the destination's Ethernet address. One solution is to have a configuration file somewhere in the system that maps IP addresses onto Ethernet addresses. While this solution is certainly possible, for organizations with thousands of machines, keeping all these files up to date is an error-prone, time-consuming job.

A better solution is for host 1 to output a broadcast packet onto the Ethernet asking: Who owns IP address 192.31.65.5? The broadcast will arrive at every machine on Ethernet 192.31.65.0, and each one will check its IP address. Host 2 alone will respond with its Ethernet address (*E2*). In this way host 1 learns that IP address 192.31.65.5 is on the host with Ethernet address *E2*. The protocol used for asking this question and getting the reply is called **ARP** (**Address Resolution Protocol**). Almost every machine on the Internet runs it. ARP is defined in RFC 826.

The advantage of using ARP over configuration files is the simplicity. The system manager does not have to do much except assign each machine an IP address and decide about subnet masks. ARP does the rest.

At this point, the IP software on host 1 builds an Ethernet frame addressed to *E2*, puts the IP packet (addressed to 192.31.65.5) in the payload field, and dumps it onto the Ethernet. The Ethernet board of host 2 detects this frame, recognizes it as a frame for itself, scoops it up, and causes an interrupt. The Ethernet driver extracts the IP packet from the payload and passes it to the IP software, which sees that it is correctly addressed and processes it.

Various optimizations are possible to make ARP work more efficiently. To start with, once a machine has run ARP, it caches the result in case it needs to contact the same machine shortly. Next time it will find the mapping in its own cache, thus eliminating the need for a second broadcast. In many cases host 2 will need to send back a reply, forcing it, too, to run ARP to determine the sender's

Ethernet address. This ARP broadcast can be avoided by having host 1 include its IP-to-Ethernet mapping in the ARP packet. When the ARP broadcast arrives at host 2, the pair (192.31.65.7, E1) is entered into host 2's ARP cache for future use. In fact, all machines on the Ethernet can enter this mapping into their ARP caches.

Yet another optimization is to have every machine broadcast its mapping when it boots. This broadcast is generally done in the form of an ARP looking for its own IP address. There should not be a response, but a side effect of the broadcast is to make an entry in everyone's ARP cache. If a response does (unexpectedly) arrive, two machines have been assigned the same IP address. The new one should inform the system manager and not boot.

To allow mappings to change, for example, when an Ethernet board breaks and is replaced with a new one (and thus a new Ethernet address), entries in the ARP cache should time out after a few minutes.

Now let us look at Fig. 5-62 again, only this time host 1 wants to send a packet to host 4 (192.31.63.8). Using ARP will fail because host 4 will not see the broadcast (routers do not forward Ethernet-level broadcasts). There are two solutions. First, the CS router could be configured to respond to ARP requests for network 192.31.63.0 (and possibly other local networks). In this case, host 1 will make an ARP cache entry of (192.31.63.8, E3) and happily send all traffic for host 4 to the local router. This solution is called **proxy ARP**. The second solution is to have host 1 immediately see that the destination is on a remote network and just send all such traffic to a default Ethernet address that handles all remote traffic, in this case *E3*. This solution does not require having the CS router know which remote networks it is serving.

Either way, what happens is that host 1 packs the IP packet into the payload field of an Ethernet frame addressed to *E3*. When the CS router gets the Ethernet frame, it removes the IP packet from the payload field and looks up the IP address in its routing tables. It discovers that packets for network 192.31.63.0 are supposed to go to router 192.31.60.7. If it does not already know the FDDI address of 192.31.60.7, it broadcasts an ARP packet onto the ring and learns that its ring address is *F3*. It then inserts the packet into the payload field of an FDDI frame addressed to *F3* and puts it on the ring.

At the EE router, the FDDI driver removes the packet from the payload field and gives it to the IP software, which sees that it needs to send the packet to 192.31.63.8. If this IP address is not in its ARP cache, it broadcasts an ARP request on the EE Ethernet and learns that the destination address is *E6*, so it builds an Ethernet frame addressed to *E6*, puts the packet in the payload field, and sends it over the Ethernet. When the Ethernet frame arrives at host 4, the packet is extracted from the frame and passed to the IP software for processing.

Going from host 1 to a distant network over a WAN works essentially the same way, except that this time the CS router's tables tell it to use the WAN router whose FDDI address is *F2*.

RARP, BOOTP, and DHCP

ARP solves the problem of finding out which Ethernet address corresponds to a given IP address. Sometimes the reverse problem has to be solved: Given an Ethernet address, what is the corresponding IP address? In particular, this problem occurs when a diskless workstation is booted. Such a machine will normally get the binary image of its operating system from a remote file server. But how does it learn its IP address?

The first solution devised was to use **RARP** (**Reverse Address Resolution Protocol**) (defined in RFC 903). This protocol allows a newly-booted workstation to broadcast its Ethernet address and say: My 48-bit Ethernet address is 14.04.05.18.01.25. Does anyone out there know my IP address? The RARP server sees this request, looks up the Ethernet address in its configuration files, and sends back the corresponding IP address.

Using RARP is better than embedding an IP address in the memory image because it allows the same image to be used on all machines. If the IP address were buried inside the image, each workstation would need its own image.

A disadvantage of RARP is that it uses a destination address of all 1s (limited broadcasting) to reach the RARP server. However, such broadcasts are not forwarded by routers, so a RARP server is needed on each network. To get around this problem, an alternative bootstrap protocol called **BOOTP** was invented. Unlike RARP, BOOTP uses UDP messages, which are forwarded over routers. It also provides a diskless workstation with additional information, including the IP address of the file server holding the memory image, the IP address of the default router, and the subnet mask to use. BOOTP is described in RFCs 951, 1048, and 1084.

A serious problem with BOOTP is that it requires manual configuration of tables mapping IP address to Ethernet address. When a new host is added to a LAN, it cannot use BOOTP until an administrator has assigned it an IP address and entered its (Ethernet address, IP address) into the BOOTP configuration tables by hand. To eliminate this error-prone step, BOOTP was extended and given a new name: **DHCP** (**Dynamic Host Configuration Protocol**). DHCP allows both manual IP address assignment and automatic assignment. It is described in RFCs 2131 and 2132. In most systems, it has largely replaced RARP and BOOTP.

Like RARP and BOOTP, DHCP is based on the idea of a special server that assigns IP addresses to hosts asking for one. This server need not be on the same LAN as the requesting host. Since the DHCP server may not be reachable by broadcasting, a **DHCP relay agent** is needed on each LAN, as shown in Fig. 5-63.

To find its IP address, a newly-booted machine broadcasts a DHCP DISCOVER packet. The DHCP relay agent on its LAN intercepts all DHCP broadcasts. When it finds a DHCP DISCOVER packet, it sends the packet as a unicast

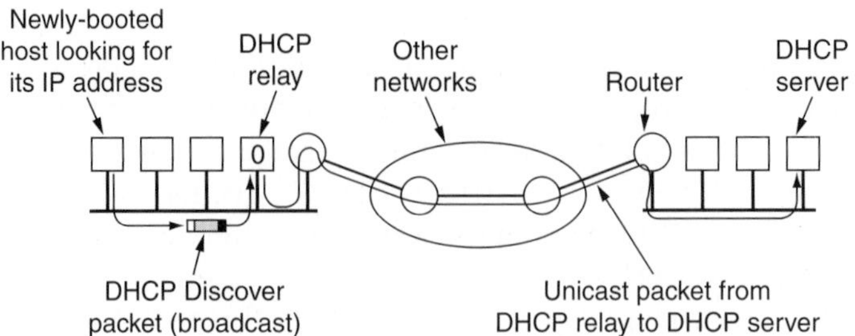

Figure 5-63. Operation of DHCP.

packet to the DHCP server, possibly on a distant network. The only piece of information the relay agent needs is the IP address of the DHCP server.

An issue that arises with automatic assignment of IP addresses from a pool is how long an IP address should be allocated. If a host leaves the network and does not return its IP address to the DHCP server, that address will be permanently lost. After a period of time, many addresses may be lost. To prevent that from happening, IP address assignment may be for a fixed period of time, a technique called **leasing**. Just before the lease expires, the host must ask the DHCP for a renewal. If it fails to make a request or the request is denied, the host may no longer use the IP address it was given earlier.

5.6.4 OSPF—The Interior Gateway Routing Protocol

We have now finished our study of Internet control protocols. It is time to move on the next topic: routing in the Internet. As we mentioned earlier, the Internet is made up of a large number of autonomous systems. Each AS is operated by a different organization and can use its own routing algorithm inside. For example, the internal networks of companies *X*, *Y*, and *Z* are usually seen as three ASes if all three are on the Internet. All three may use different routing algorithms internally. Nevertheless, having standards, even for internal routing, simplifies the implementation at the boundaries between ASes and allows reuse of code. In this section we will study routing within an AS. In the next one, we will look at routing between ASes. A routing algorithm within an AS is called an **interior gateway protocol**; an algorithm for routing between ASes is called an **exterior gateway protocol**.

The original Internet interior gateway protocol was a distance vector protocol (RIP) based on the Bellman-Ford algorithm inherited from the ARPANET. It worked well in small systems, but less well as ASes got larger. It also suffered from the count-to-infinity problem and generally slow convergence, so it was replaced in May 1979 by a link state protocol. In 1988, the Internet Engineering

Task Force began work on a successor. That successor, called **OSPF** (**Open Shortest Path First**), became a standard in 1990. Most router vendors now support it, and it has become the main interior gateway protocol. Below we will give a sketch of how OSPF works. For the complete story, see RFC 2328.

Given the long experience with other routing protocols, the group designing the new protocol had a long list of requirements that had to be met. First, the algorithm had to be published in the open literature, hence the "O" in OSPF. A proprietary solution owned by one company would not do. Second, the new protocol had to support a variety of distance metrics, including physical distance, delay, and so on. Third, it had to be a dynamic algorithm, one that adapted to changes in the topology automatically and quickly.

Fourth, and new for OSPF, it had to support routing based on type of service. The new protocol had to be able to route real-time traffic one way and other traffic a different way. The IP protocol has a *Type of Service* field, but no existing routing protocol used it. This field was included in OSPF but still nobody used it, and it was eventually removed.

Fifth, and related to the above, the new protocol had to do load balancing, splitting the load over multiple lines. Most previous protocols sent all packets over the best route. The second-best route was not used at all. In many cases, splitting the load over multiple lines gives better performance.

Sixth, support for hierarchical systems was needed. By 1988, the Internet had grown so large that no router could be expected to know the entire topology. The new routing protocol had to be designed so that no router would have to.

Seventh, some modicum of security was required to prevent fun-loving students from spoofing routers by sending them false routing information. Finally, provision was needed for dealing with routers that were connected to the Internet via a tunnel. Previous protocols did not handle this well.

OSPF supports three kinds of connections and networks:

1. Point-to-point lines between exactly two routers.
2. Multiaccess networks with broadcasting (e.g., most LANs).
3. Multiaccess networks without broadcasting (e.g., most packet-switched WANs).

A **multiaccess** network is one that can have multiple routers on it, each of which can directly communicate with all the others. All LANs and WANs have this property. Figure 5-64(a) shows an AS containing all three kinds of networks. Note that hosts do not generally play a role in OSPF.

OSPF operates by abstracting the collection of actual networks, routers, and lines into a directed graph in which each arc is assigned a cost (distance, delay, etc.). It then computes the shortest path based on the weights on the arcs. A serial connection between two routers is represented by a pair of arcs, one in each

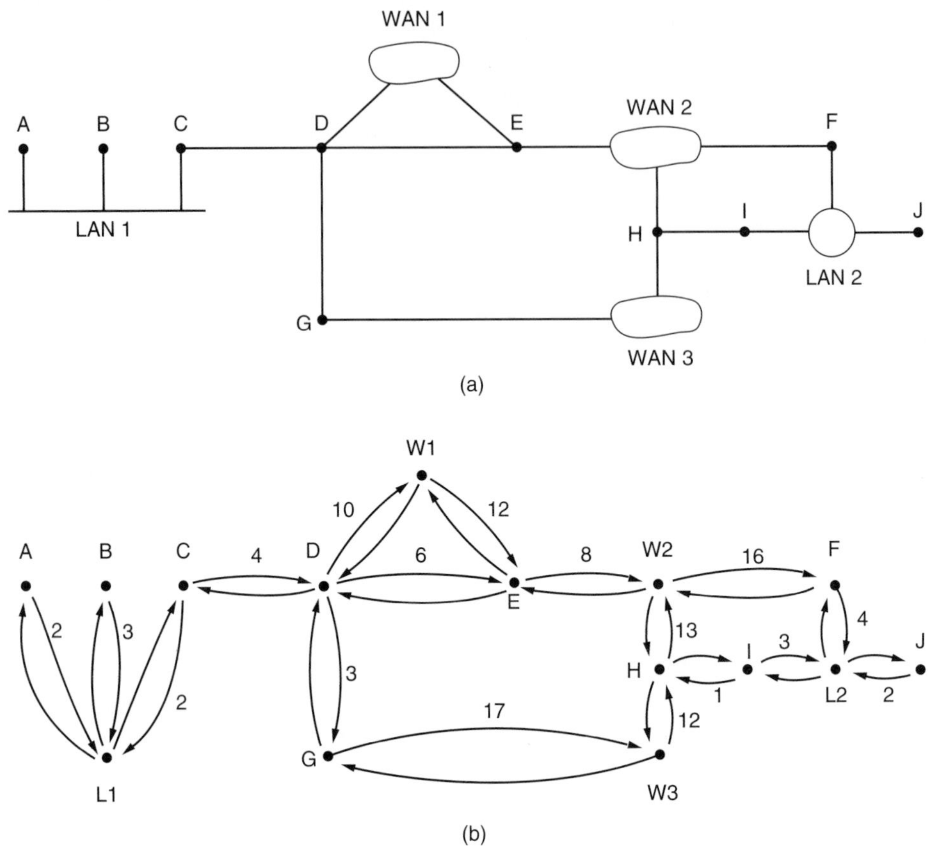

Figure 5-64. (a) An autonomous system. (b) A graph representation of (a).

direction. Their weights may be different. A multiaccess network is represented by a node for the network itself plus a node for each router. The arcs from the network node to the routers have weight 0 and are omitted from the graph.

Figure 5-64(b) shows the graph representation of the network of Fig. 5-64(a). Weights are symmetric, unless marked otherwise. What OSPF fundamentally does is represent the actual network as a graph like this and then compute the shortest path from every router to every other router.

Many of the ASes in the Internet are themselves large and nontrivial to manage. OSPF allows them to be divided into numbered **areas**, where an area is a network or a set of contiguous networks. Areas do not overlap but need not be exhaustive, that is, some routers may belong to no area. An area is a generalization of a subnet. Outside an area, its topology and details are not visible.

Every AS has a **backbone** area, called area 0. All areas are connected to the backbone, possibly by tunnels, so it is possible to go from any area in the AS to any other area in the AS via the backbone. A tunnel is represented in the graph as an arc and has a cost. Each router that is connected to two or more areas is part of the backbone. As with other areas, the topology of the backbone is not visible outside the backbone.

Within an area, each router has the same link state database and runs the same shortest path algorithm. Its main job is to calculate the shortest path from itself to every other router in the area, including the router that is connected to the backbone, of which there must be at least one. A router that connects to two areas needs the databases for both areas and must run the shortest path algorithm for each one separately.

During normal operation, three kinds of routes may be needed: intra-area, interarea, and inter-AS. Intra-area routes are the easiest, since the source router already knows the shortest path to the destination router. Interarea routing always proceeds in three steps: go from the source to the backbone; go across the backbone to the destination area; go to the destination. This algorithm forces a star configuration on OSPF with the backbone being the hub and the other areas being spokes. Packets are routed from source to destination "as is." They are not encapsulated or tunneled, unless going to an area whose only connection to the backbone is a tunnel. Figure 5-65 shows part of the Internet with ASes and areas.

OSPF distinguishes four classes of routers:

1. Internal routers are wholly within one area.
2. Area border routers connect two or more areas.
3. Backbone routers are on the backbone.
4. AS boundary routers talk to routers in other ASes.

These classes are allowed to overlap. For example, all the border routers are automatically part of the backbone. In addition, a router that is in the backbone but not part of any other area is also an internal router. Examples of all four classes of routers are illustrated in Fig. 5-65.

When a router boots, it sends HELLO messages on all of its point-to-point lines and multicasts them on LANs to the group consisting of all the other routers. On WANs, it needs some configuration information to know who to contact. From the responses, each router learns who its neighbors are. Routers on the same LAN are all neighbors.

OSPF works by exchanging information between adjacent routers, which is not the same as between neighboring routers. In particular, it is inefficient to have every router on a LAN talk to every other router on the LAN. To avoid this situation, one router is elected as the **designated router**. It is said to be **adjacent** to all the other routers on its LAN, and exchanges information with them. Neighboring routers that are not adjacent do not exchange information with each other. A backup designated router is always kept up to date to ease the transition should the primary designated router crash and need to replaced immediately.

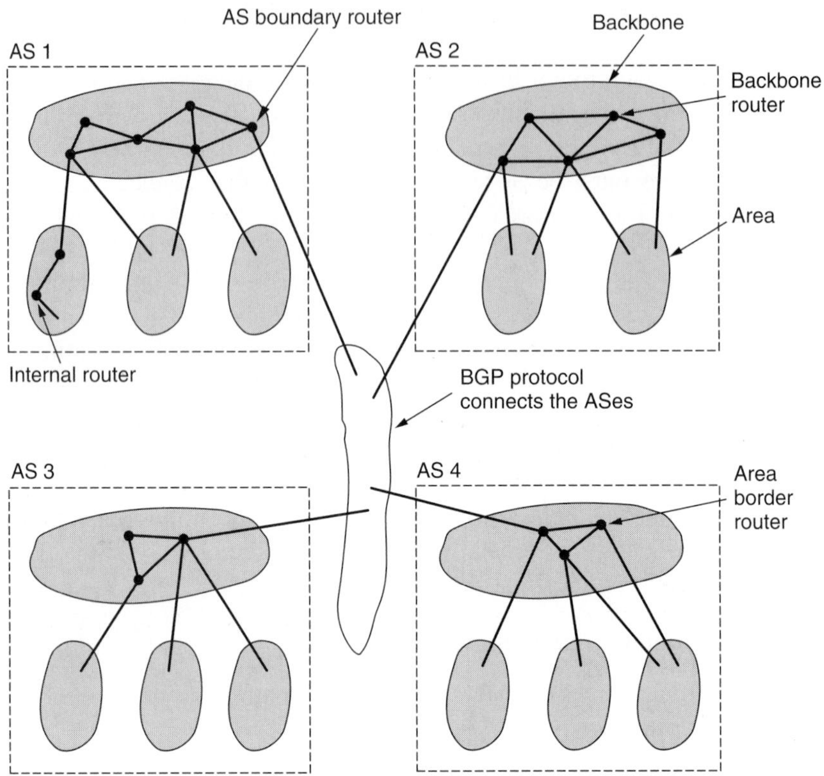

Figure 5-65. The relation between ASes, backbones, and areas in OSPF.

During normal operation, each router periodically floods LINK STATE UPDATE messages to each of its adjacent routers. This message gives its state and provides the costs used in the topological database. The flooding messages are acknowledged, to make them reliable. Each message has a sequence number, so a router can see whether an incoming LINK STATE UPDATE is older or newer than what it currently has. Routers also send these messages when a line goes up or down or its cost changes.

DATABASE DESCRIPTION messages give the sequence numbers of all the link state entries currently held by the sender. By comparing its own values with those of the sender, the receiver can determine who has the most recent values. These messages are used when a line is brought up.

Either partner can request link state information from the other one by using LINK STATE REQUEST messages. The result of this algorithm is that each pair of adjacent routers checks to see who has the most recent data, and new information is spread throughout the area this way. All these messages are sent as raw IP packets. The five kinds of messages are summarized in Fig. 5-66.

Message type	Description
Hello	Used to discover who the neighbors are
Link state update	Provides the sender's costs to its neighbors
Link state ack	Acknowledges link state update
Database description	Announces which updates the sender has
Link state request	Requests information from the partner

Figure 5-66. The five types of OSPF messages.

Finally, we can put all the pieces together. Using flooding, each router informs all the other routers in its area of its neighbors and costs. This information allows each router to construct the graph for its area(s) and compute the shortest path. The backbone area does this too. In addition, the backbone routers accept information from the area border routers in order to compute the best route from each backbone router to every other router. This information is propagated back to the area border routers, which advertise it within their areas. Using this information, a router about to send an interarea packet can select the best exit router to the backbone.

5.6.5 BGP—The Exterior Gateway Routing Protocol

Within a single AS, the recommended routing protocol is OSPF (although it is certainly not the only one in use). Between ASes, a different protocol, **BGP** (**Border Gateway Protocol**), is used. A different protocol is needed between ASes because the goals of an interior gateway protocol and an exterior gateway protocol are not the same. All an interior gateway protocol has to do is move packets as efficiently as possible from the source to the destination. It does not have to worry about politics.

Exterior gateway protocol routers have to worry about politics a great deal (Metz, 2001). For example, a corporate AS might want the ability to send packets to any Internet site and receive packets from any Internet site. However, it might be unwilling to carry transit packets originating in a foreign AS and ending in a different foreign AS, even if its own AS was on the shortest path between the two foreign ASes ("That's their problem, not ours"). On the other hand, it might be willing to carry transit traffic for its neighbors or even for specific other ASes that paid it for this service. Telephone companies, for example, might be happy to act as a carrier for their customers, but not for others. Exterior gateway protocols in general, and BGP in particular, have been designed to allow many kinds of routing policies to be enforced in the interAS traffic.

Typical policies involve political, security, or economic considerations. A few examples of routing constraints are:

1. No transit traffic through certain ASes.
2. Never put Iraq on a route starting at the Pentagon.
3. Do not use the United States to get from British Columbia to Ontario.
4. Only transit Albania if there is no alternative to the destination.
5. Traffic starting or ending at IBM should not transit Microsoft.

Policies are typically manually configured into each BGP router (or included using some kind of script). They are not part of the protocol itself.

From the point of view of a BGP router, the world consists of ASes and the lines connecting them. Two ASes are considered connected if there is a line between a border router in each one. Given BGP's special interest in transit traffic, networks are grouped into one of three categories. The first category is the **stub networks**, which have only one connection to the BGP graph. These cannot be used for transit traffic because there is no one on the other side. Then come the **multiconnected networks**. These could be used for transit traffic, except that they refuse. Finally, there are the **transit networks**, such as backbones, which are willing to handle third-party packets, possibly with some restrictions, and usually for pay.

Pairs of BGP routers communicate with each other by establishing TCP connections. Operating this way provides reliable communication and hides all the details of the network being passed through.

BGP is fundamentally a distance vector protocol, but quite different from most others such as RIP. Instead of maintaining just the cost to each destination, each BGP router keeps track of the path used. Similarly, instead of periodically giving each neighbor its estimated cost to each possible destination, each BGP router tells its neighbors the exact path it is using.

As an example, consider the BGP routers shown in Fig. 5-67(a). In particular, consider *F*'s routing table. Suppose that it uses the path *FGCD* to get to *D*. When the neighbors give it routing information, they provide their complete paths, as shown in Fig. 5-67(b) (for simplicity, only destination *D* is shown here).

After all the paths come in from the neighbors, *F* examines them to see which is the best. It quickly discards the paths from *I* and *E*, since these paths pass through *F* itself. The choice is then between using *B* and *G*. Every BGP router contains a module that examines routes to a given destination and scores them, returning a number for the "distance" to that destination for each route. Any route violating a policy constraint automatically gets a score of infinity. The router then adopts the route with the shortest distance. The scoring function is not part of the BGP protocol and can be any function the system managers want.

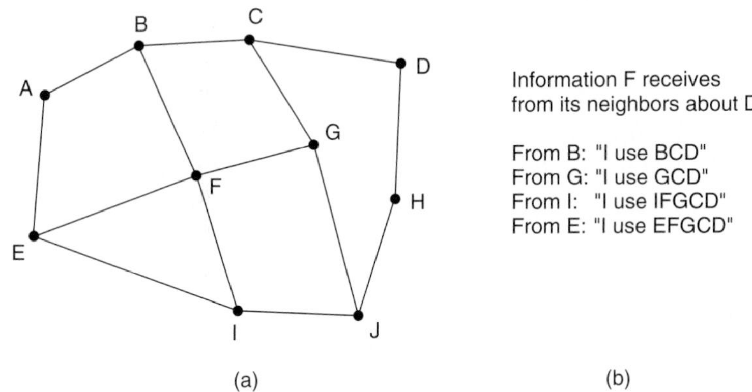

Figure 5-67. (a) A set of BGP routers. (b) Information sent to *F*.

BGP easily solves the count-to-infinity problem that plagues other distance vector routing algorithms. For example, suppose *G* crashes or the line *FG* goes down. *F* then receives routes from its three remaining neighbors. These routes are *BCD*, *IFGCD*, and *EFGCD*. It can immediately see that the two latter routes are pointless, since they pass through *F* itself, so it chooses *FBCD* as its new route. Other distance vector algorithms often make the wrong choice because they cannot tell which of their neighbors have independent routes to the destination and which do not. The definition of BGP is in RFCs 1771 to 1774.

5.6.6 Internet Multicasting

Normal IP communication is between one sender and one receiver. However, for some applications it is useful for a process to be able to send to a large number of receivers simultaneously. Examples are updating replicated, distributed databases, transmitting stock quotes to multiple brokers, and handling digital conference (i.e., multiparty) telephone calls.

IP supports multicasting, using class D addresses. Each class D address identifies a group of hosts. Twenty-eight bits are available for identifying groups, so over 250 million groups can exist at the same time. When a process sends a packet to a class D address, a best-efforts attempt is made to deliver it to all the members of the group addressed, but no guarantees are given. Some members may not get the packet.

Two kinds of group addresses are supported: permanent addresses and temporary ones. A permanent group is always there and does not have to be set up. Each permanent group has a permanent group address. Some examples of permanent group addresses are:

224.0.0.1 All systems on a LAN
224.0.0.2 All routers on a LAN
224.0.0.5 All OSPF routers on a LAN
224.0.0.6 All designated OSPF routers on a LAN

Temporary groups must be created before they can be used. A process can ask its host to join a specific group. It can also ask its host to leave the group. When the last process on a host leaves a group, that group is no longer present on the host. Each host keeps track of which groups its processes currently belong to.

Multicasting is implemented by special multicast routers, which may or may not be colocated with the standard routers. About once a minute, each multicast router sends a hardware (i.e., data link layer) multicast to the hosts on its LAN (address 224.0.0.1) asking them to report back on the groups their processes currently belong to. Each host sends back responses for all the class D addresses it is interested in.

These query and response packets use a protocol called **IGMP** (**Internet Group Management Protocol**), which is vaguely analogous to ICMP. It has only two kinds of packets: query and response, each with a simple, fixed format containing some control information in the first word of the payload field and a class D address in the second word. It is described in RFC 1112.

Multicast routing is done using spanning trees. Each multicast router exchanges information with its neighbors, using a modified distance vector protocol in order for each one to construct a spanning tree per group covering all group members. Various optimizations are used to prune the tree to eliminate routers and networks not interested in particular groups. The protocol makes heavy use of tunneling to avoid bothering nodes not in a spanning tree.

5.6.7 Mobile IP

Many users of the Internet have portable computers and want to stay connected to the Internet when they visit a distant Internet site and even on the road in between. Unfortunately, the IP addressing system makes working far from home easier said than done. In this section we will examine the problem and the solution. A more detailed description is given in (Perkins, 1998a).

The real villain is the addressing scheme itself. Every IP address contains a network number and a host number. For example, consider the machine with IP address 160.80.40.20/16. The 160.80 gives the network number (8272 in decimal); the 40.20 is the host number (10260 in decimal). Routers all over the world have routing tables telling which line to use to get to network 160.80. Whenever a packet comes in with a destination IP address of the form 160.80.xxx.yyy, it goes out on that line.

If all of a sudden, the machine with that address is carted off to some distant site, the packets for it will continue to be routed to its home LAN (or router). The owner will no longer get e-mail, and so on. Giving the machine a new IP address corresponding to its new location is unattractive because large numbers of people, programs, and databases would have to be informed of the change.

Another approach is to have the routers use complete IP addresses for routing, instead of just the network. However, this strategy would require each router to have millions of table entries, at astronomical cost to the Internet.

When people began demanding the ability to connect their notebook computers to the Internet wherever they were, IETF set up a Working Group to find a solution. The Working Group quickly formulated a number of goals considered desirable in any solution. The major ones were:

1. Each mobile host must be able to use its home IP address anywhere.
2. Software changes to the fixed hosts were not permitted.
3. Changes to the router software and tables were not permitted.
4. Most packets for mobile hosts should not make detours on the way.
5. No overhead should be incurred when a mobile host is at home.

The solution chosen was the one described in Sec. 5.2.8. To review it briefly, every site that wants to allow its users to roam has to create a home agent. Every site that wants to allow visitors has to create a foreign agent. When a mobile host shows up at a foreign site, it contacts the foreign host there and registers. The foreign host then contacts the user's home agent and gives it a **care-of address**, normally the foreign agent's own IP address.

When a packet arrives at the user's home LAN, it comes in at some router attached to the LAN. The router then tries to locate the host in the usual way, by broadcasting an ARP packet asking, for example: What is the Ethernet address of 160.80.40.20? The home agent responds to this query by giving its own Ethernet address. The router then sends packets for 160.80.40.20 to the home agent. It, in turn, tunnels them to the care-of address by encapsulating them in the payload field of an IP packet addressed to the foreign agent. The foreign agent then decapsulates and delivers them to the data link address of the mobile host. In addition, the home agent gives the care-of address to the sender, so future packets can be tunneled directly to the foreign agent. This solution meets all the requirements stated above.

One small detail is probably worth mentioning. At the time the mobile host moves, the router probably has its (soon-to-be-invalid) Ethernet address cached. Replacing that Ethernet address with the home agent's is done by a trick called **gratuitous ARP**. This is a special, unsolicited message to the router that causes it to replace a specific cache entry, in this case, that of the mobile host about to leave. When the mobile host returns later, the same trick is used to update the router's cache again.

Nothing in the design prevents a mobile host from being its own foreign agent, but that approach only works if the mobile host (in its capacity as foreign agent) is logically connected to the Internet at its current site. Also, the mobile host must be able to acquire a (temporary) care-of IP address to use. That IP address must belong to the LAN to which it is currently attached.

The IETF solution for mobile hosts solves a number of other problems not mentioned so far. For example, how are agents located? The solution is for each agent to periodically broadcast its address and the type of services it is willing to provide (e.g., home, foreign, or both). When a mobile host arrives somewhere, it can just listen for these broadcasts, called **advertisements**. Alternatively, it can broadcast a packet announcing its arrival and hope that the local foreign agent responds to it.

Another problem that had to be solved is what to do about impolite mobile hosts that leave without saying goodbye. The solution is to make registration valid only for a fixed time interval. If it is not refreshed periodically, it times out, so the foreign host can clear its tables.

Yet another issue is security. When a home agent gets a message asking it to please forward all of Roberta's packets to some IP address, it had better not comply unless it is convinced that Roberta is the source of this request, and not somebody trying to impersonate her. Cryptographic authentication protocols are used for this purpose. We will study such protocols in Chap. 8.

A final point addressed by the Working Group relates to levels of mobility. Imagine an airplane with an on-board Ethernet used by the navigation and avionics computers. On this Ethernet is a standard router that talks to the wired Internet on the ground over a radio link. One fine day, some clever marketing executive gets the idea to install Ethernet connectors in all the arm rests so passengers with mobile computers can also plug in.

Now we have two levels of mobility: the aircraft's own computers, which are stationary with respect to the Ethernet, and the passengers' computers, which are mobile with respect to it. In addition, the on-board router is mobile with respect to routers on the ground. Being mobile with respect to a system that is itself mobile can be handled using recursive tunneling.

5.6.8 IPv6

While CIDR and NAT may buy a few more years' time, everyone realizes that the days of IP in its current form (IPv4) are numbered. In addition to these technical problems, another issue looms in the background. In its early years, the Internet was largely used by universities, high-tech industry, and the U.S. Government (especially the Dept. of Defense). With the explosion of interest in the Internet starting in the mid-1990s, it began to be used by a different group of people, especially people with different requirements. For one thing, numerous people with wireless portables use it to keep in contact with their home bases. For another, with the impending convergence of the computer, communication, and entertainment industries, it may not be that long before every telephone and television set in the world is an Internet node, producing a billion machines being used audio and video on demand. Under these circumstances, it became apparent that IP had to evolve and become more flexible.

Seeing these problems on the horizon, in 1990, IETF started work on a new version of IP, one which would never run out of addresses, would solve a variety of other problems, and be more flexible and efficient as well. Its major goals were:

1. Support billions of hosts, even with inefficient address space allocation.
2. Reduce the size of the routing tables.
3. Simplify the protocol, to allow routers to process packets faster.
4. Provide better security (authentication and privacy) than current IP.
5. Pay more attention to type of service, particularly for real-time data.
6. Aid multicasting by allowing scopes to be specified.
7. Make it possible for a host to roam without changing its address.
8. Allow the protocol to evolve in the future.
9. Permit the old and new protocols to coexist for years.

To develop a protocol that met all these requirements, IETF issued a call for proposals and discussion in RFC 1550. Twenty-one responses were received, not all of them full proposals. By December 1992, seven serious proposals were on the table. They ranged from making minor patches to IP, to throwing it out altogether and replacing with a completely different protocol.

One proposal was to run TCP over CLNP, which, with its 160-bit addresses would have provided enough address space forever and would have unified two major network layer protocols. However, many people felt that this would have been an admission that something in the OSI world was actually done right, a statement considered Politically Incorrect in Internet circles. CLNP was patterned closely on IP, so the two are not really that different. In fact, the protocol ultimately chosen differs from IP far more than CLNP does. Another strike against CLNP was its poor support for service types, something required to transmit multimedia efficiently.

Three of the better proposals were published in *IEEE Network* (Deering, 1993; Francis, 1993; and Katz and Ford, 1993). After much discussion, revision, and jockeying for position, a modified combined version of the Deering and Francis proposals, by now called **SIPP** (**Simple Internet Protocol Plus**) was selected and given the designation **IPv6.**

IPv6 meets the goals fairly well. It maintains the good features of IP, discards or deemphasizes the bad ones, and adds new ones where needed. In general, IPv6 is not compatible with IPv4, but it is compatible with the other auxiliary Internet protocols, including TCP, UDP, ICMP, IGMP, OSPF, BGP, and DNS, sometimes with small modifications being required (mostly to deal with longer addresses). The main features of IPv6 are discussed below. More information about it can be found in RFCs 2460 through 2466.

First and foremost, IPv6 has longer addresses than IPv4. They are 16 bytes long, which solves the problem that IPv6 set out to solve: provide an effectively unlimited supply of Internet addresses. We will have more to say about addresses shortly.

The second major improvement of IPv6 is the simplification of the header. It contains only seven fields (versus 13 in IPv4). This change allows routers to process packets faster and thus improve throughput and delay. We will discuss the header shortly, too.

The third major improvement was better support for options. This change was essential with the new header because fields that previously were required are now optional. In addition, the way options are represented is different, making it simple for routers to skip over options not intended for them. This feature speeds up packet processing time.

A fourth area in which IPv6 represents a big advance is in security. IETF had its fill of newspaper stories about precocious 12-year-olds using their personal computers to break into banks and military bases all over the Internet. There was a strong feeling that something had to be done to improve security. Authentication and privacy are key features of the new IP. These were later retrofitted to IPv4, however, so in the area of security the differences are not so great any more.

Finally, more attention has been paid to quality of service. Various half-hearted efforts have been made in the past, but now with the growth of multimedia on the Internet, the sense of urgency is greater.

The Main IPv6 Header

The IPv6 header is shown in Fig. 5-68. The *Version* field is always 6 for IPv6 (and 4 for IPv4). During the transition period from IPv4, which will probably take a decade, routers will be able to examine this field to tell what kind of packet they have. As an aside, making this test wastes a few instructions in the critical path, so many implementations are likely to try to avoid it by using some field in the data link header to distinguish IPv4 packets from IPv6 packets. In this way, packets can be passed to the correct network layer handler directly. However, having the data link layer be aware of network packet types completely violates the design principle that each layer should not be aware of the meaning of the bits given to it from the layer above. The discussions between the "Do it right" and "Make it fast" camps will no doubt be lengthy and vigorous.

The *Traffic class* field is used to distinguish between packets with different real-time delivery requirements. A field designed for this purpose has been in IP

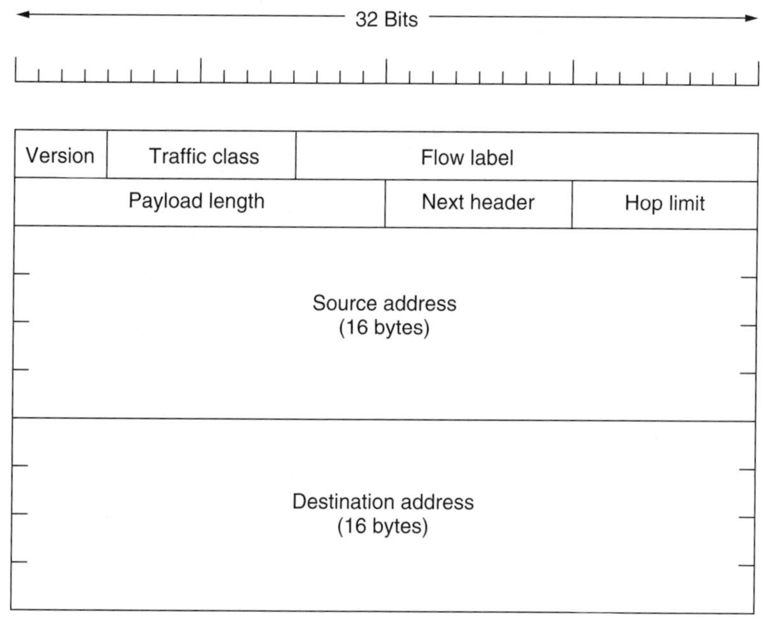

Figure 5-68. The IPv6 fixed header (required).

since the beginning, but it has been only sporadically implemented by routers. Experiments are now underway to determine how best it can be used for multimedia delivery.

The *Flow label* field is also still experimental but will be used to allow a source and destination to set up a pseudoconnection with particular properties and requirements. For example, a stream of packets from one process on a certain source host to a certain process on a certain destination host might have stringent delay requirements and thus need reserved bandwidth. The flow can be set up in advance and given an identifier. When a packet with a nonzero *Flow label* shows up, all the routers can look it up in internal tables to see what kind of special treatment it requires. In effect, flows are an attempt to have it both ways: the flexibility of a datagram subnet and the guarantees of a virtual-circuit subnet.

Each flow is designated by the source address, destination address, and flow number, so many flows may be active at the same time between a given pair of IP addresses. Also, in this way, even if two flows coming from different hosts but with the same flow label pass through the same router, the router will be able to tell them apart using the source and destination addresses. It is expected that flow labels will be chosen randomly, rather than assigned sequentially starting at 1, so routers as expected to hash them.

The *Payload length* field tells how many bytes follow the 40-byte header of Fig. 5-68. The name was changed from the IPv4 *Total length* field because the meaning was changed slightly: the 40 header bytes are no longer counted as part of the length (as they used to be).

The *Next header* field lets the cat out of the bag. The reason the header could be simplified is that there can be additional (optional) extension headers. This field tells which of the (currently) six extension headers, if any, follow this one. If this header is the last IP header, the *Next header* field tells which transport protocol handler (e.g., TCP, UDP) to pass the packet to.

The *Hop limit* field is used to keep packets from living forever. It is, in practice, the same as the *Time to live* field in IPv4, namely, a field that is decremented on each hop. In theory, in IPv4 it was a time in seconds, but no router used it that way, so the name was changed to reflect the way it is actually used.

Next come the *Source address* and *Destination address* fields. Deering's original proposal, SIP, used 8-byte addresses, but during the review process many people felt that with 8-byte addresses IPv6 would run out of addresses within a few decades, whereas with 16-byte addresses it would never run out. Other people argued that 16 bytes was overkill, whereas still others favored using 20-byte addresses to be compatible with the OSI datagram protocol. Still another faction wanted variable-sized addresses. After much debate, it was decided that fixed-length 16-byte addresses were the best compromise.

A new notation has been devised for writing 16-byte addresses. They are written as eight groups of four hexadecimal digits with colons between the groups, like this:

8000:0000:0000:0000:0123:4567:89AB:CDEF

Since many addresses will have many zeros inside them, three optimizations have been authorized. First, leading zeros within a group can be omitted, so 0123 can be written as 123. Second, one or more groups of 16 zero bits can be replaced by a pair of colons. Thus, the above address now becomes

8000::123:4567:89AB:CDEF

Finally, IPv4 addresses can be written as a pair of colons and an old dotted decimal number, for example

::192.31.20.46

Perhaps it is unnecessary to be so explicit about it, but there are a lot of 16-byte addresses. Specifically, there are 2^{128} of them, which is approximately 3×10^{38}. If the entire earth, land and water, were covered with computers, IPv6 would allow 7×10^{23} IP addresses per square meter. Students of chemistry will notice that this number is larger than Avogadro's number. While it was not the intention to give every molecule on the surface of the earth its own IP address, we are not that far off.

In practice, the address space will not be used efficiently, just as the telephone number address space is not (the area code for Manhattan, 212, is nearly full, but that for Wyoming, 307, is nearly empty). In RFC 3194, Durand and Huitema calculated that, using the allocation of telephone numbers as a guide, even in the most pessimistic scenario there will still be well over 1000 IP addresses per square meter of the entire earth's surface (land and water). In any likely scenario, there will be trillions of them per square meter. In short, it seems unlikely that we will run out in the foreseeable future.

It is instructive to compare the IPv4 header (Fig. 5-53) with the IPv6 header (Fig. 5-68) to see what has been left out in IPv6. The *IHL* field is gone because the IPv6 header has a fixed length. The *Protocol* field was taken out because the *Next header* field tells what follows the last IP header (e.g., a UDP or TCP segment).

All the fields relating to fragmentation were removed because IPv6 takes a different approach to fragmentation. To start with, all IPv6-conformant hosts are expected to dynamically determine the datagram size to use. This rule makes fragmentation less likely to occur in the first place. Also, the minimum has been raised from 576 to 1280 to allow 1024 bytes of data and many headers. In addition, when a host sends an IPv6 packet that is too large, instead of fragmenting it, the router that is unable to forward it sends back an error message. This message tells the host to break up all future packets to that destination. Having the host send packets that are the right size in the first place is ultimately much more efficient than having the routers fragment them on the fly.

Finally, the *Checksum* field is gone because calculating it greatly reduces performance. With the reliable networks now used, combined with the fact that the data link layer and transport layers normally have their own checksums, the value of yet another checksum was not worth the performance price it extracted. Removing all these features has resulted in a lean and mean network layer protocol. Thus, the goal of IPv6—a fast, yet flexible, protocol with plenty of address space—has been met by this design.

Extension Headers

Some of the missing IPv4 fields are occasionally still needed, so IPv6 has introduced the concept of an (optional) **extension header**. These headers can be supplied to provide extra information, but encoded in an efficient way. Six kinds of extension headers are defined at present, as listed in Fig. 5-69. Each one is optional, but if more than one is present, they must appear directly after the fixed header, and preferably in the order listed.

Some of the headers have a fixed format; others contain a variable number of variable-length fields. For these, each item is encoded as a (Type, Length, Value) tuple. The *Type* is a 1-byte field telling which option this is. The *Type* values have been chosen so that the first 2 bits tell routers that do not know how to process the option what to do. The choices are: skip the option; discard the packet; discard the packet and send back an ICMP packet; and the same as the previous

Extension header	Description
Hop-by-hop options	Miscellaneous information for routers
Destination options	Additional information for the destination
Routing	Loose list of routers to visit
Fragmentation	Management of datagram fragments
Authentication	Verification of the sender's identity
Encrypted security payload	Information about the encrypted contents

Figure 5-69. IPv6 extension headers.

one, except do not send ICMP packets for multicast addresses (to prevent one bad multicast packet from generating millions of ICMP reports).

The *Length* is also a 1-byte field. It tells how long the value is (0 to 255 bytes). The *Value* is any information required, up to 255 bytes.

The hop-by-hop header is used for information that all routers along the path must examine. So far, one option has been defined: support of datagrams exceeding 64K. The format of this header is shown in Fig. 5-70. When it is used, the *Payload length* field in the fixed header is set to zero.

Next header	0	194	4
Jumbo payload length			

Figure 5-70. The hop-by-hop extension header for large datagrams (jumbograms).

As with all extension headers, this one starts out with a byte telling what kind of header comes next. This byte is followed by one telling how long the hop-by-hop header is in bytes, excluding the first 8 bytes, which are mandatory. All extensions begin this way.

The next 2 bytes indicate that this option defines the datagram size (code 194) and that the size is a 4-byte number. The last 4 bytes give the size of the datagram. Sizes less than 65,536 bytes are not permitted and will result in the first router discarding the packet and sending back an ICMP error message. Datagrams using this header extension are called **jumbograms**. The use of jumbograms is important for supercomputer applications that must transfer gigabytes of data efficiently across the Internet.

The destination options header is intended for fields that need only be interpreted at the destination host. In the initial version of IPv6, the only options defined are null options for padding this header out to a multiple of 8 bytes, so initially it will not be used. It was included to make sure that new routing and host software can handle it, in case someone thinks of a destination option some day.

The routing header lists one or more routers that must be visited on the way to the destination. It is very similar to the IPv4 loose source routing in that all addresses listed must be visited in order, but other routers not listed may be visited in between. The format of the routing header is shown in Fig. 5-71.

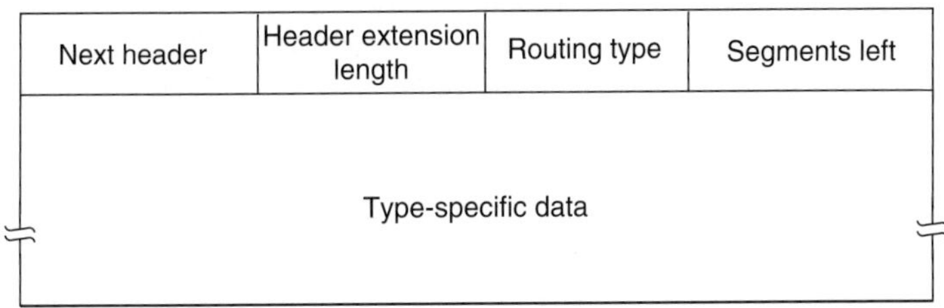

Figure 5-71. The extension header for routing.

The first 4 bytes of the routing extension header contain four 1-byte integers. The *Next header* and *Header entension length* fields were described above. The *Routing type* field gives the format of the rest of the header. Type 0 says that a reserved 32-bit word follows the first word, followed by some number of IPv6 addresses. Other types may be invented in the future as needed. Finally, the *Segments left* field keeps track of how many of the addresses in the list have not yet been visited. It is decremented every time one is visited. When it hits 0, the packet is on its own with no more guidance about what route to follow. Usually at this point it is so close to the destination that the best route is obvious.

The fragment header deals with fragmentation similarly to the way IPv4 does. The header holds the datagram identifier, fragment number, and a bit telling whether more fragments will follow. In IPv6, unlike in IPv4, only the source host can fragment a packet. Routers along the way may not do this. Although this change is a major philosophical break with the past, it simplifies the routers' work and makes routing go faster. As mentioned above, if a router is confronted with a packet that is too big, it discards the packet and sends an ICMP packet back to the source. This information allows the source host to fragment the packet into smaller pieces using this header and try again.

The authentication header provides a mechanism by which the receiver of a packet can be sure of who sent it. The encrypted security payload makes it possible to encrypt the contents of a packet so that only the intended recipient can read it. These headers use cryptographic techniques to accomplish their missions.

Controversies

Given the open design process and the strongly-held opinions of many of the people involved, it should come as no surprise that many choices made for IPv6 were highly controversial, to say the least. We will summarize a few of these briefly below. For all the gory details, see the RFCs.

We have already mentioned the argument about the address length. The result was a compromise: 16-byte fixed-length addresses.

Another fight developed over the length of the *Hop limit* field. One camp felt strongly that limiting the maximum number of hops to 255 (implicit in using an 8-bit field) was a gross mistake. After all, paths of 32 hops are common now, and 10 years from now much longer paths may be common. These people argued that using a huge address size was farsighted but using a tiny hop count was short-sighted. In their view, the greatest sin a computer scientist can commit is to provide too few bits somewhere.

The response was that arguments could be made to increase every field, leading to a bloated header. Also, the function of the *Hop limit* field is to keep packets from wandering around for a long time and 65,535 hops is far too long. Finally, as the Internet grows, more and more long-distance links will be built, making it possible to get from any country to any other country in half a dozen hops at most. If it takes more than 125 hops to get from the source and destination to their respective international gateways, something is wrong with the national backbones. The 8-bitters won this one.

Another hot potato was the maximum packet size. The supercomputer community wanted packets in excess of 64 KB. When a supercomputer gets started transferring, it really means business and does not want to be interrupted every 64 KB. The argument against large packets is that if a 1-MB packet hits a 1.5-Mbps T1 line, that packet will tie the line up for over 5 seconds, producing a very noticeable delay for interactive users sharing the line. A compromise was reached here: normal packets are limited to 64 KB, but the hop-by-hop extension header can be used to permit jumbograms.

A third hot topic was removing the IPv4 checksum. Some people likened this move to removing the brakes from a car. Doing so makes the car lighter so it can go faster, but if an unexpected event happens, you have a problem.

The argument against checksums was that any application that really cares about data integrity has to have a transport layer checksum anyway, so having another one in IP (in addition to the data link layer checksum) is overkill. Furthermore, experience showed that computing the IP checksum was a major expense in IPv4. The antichecksum camp won this one, and IPv6 does not have a checksum.

Mobile hosts were also a point of contention. If a portable computer flies halfway around the world, can it continue operating at the destination with the same IPv6 address, or does it have to use a scheme with home agents and foreign agents? Mobile hosts also introduce asymmetries into the routing system. It may well be the case that a small mobile computer can easily hear the powerful signal put out by a large stationary router, but the stationary router cannot hear the feeble signal put out by the mobile host. Consequently, some people wanted to build explicit support for mobile hosts into IPv6. That effort failed when no consensus could be found for any specific proposal.

Probably the biggest battle was about security. Everyone agreed it was essential, The war was about where and how. First where. The argument for putting it in the network layer is that it then becomes a standard service that all applications can use without any advance planning. The argument against it is that really secure applications generally want nothing less than end-to-end encryption, where the source application does the encryption and the destination application undoes it. With anything less, the user is at the mercy of potentially buggy network layer implementations over which he has no control. The response to this argument is that these applications can just refrain from using the IP security features and do the job themselves. The rejoinder to that is that the people who do not trust the network to do it right, do not want to pay the price of slow, bulky IP implementations that have this capability, even if it is disabled.

Another aspect of where to put security relates to the fact that many (but not all) countries have stringent export laws concerning cryptography. Some, notably France and Iraq, also restrict its use domestically, so that people cannot have secrets from the police. As a result, any IP implementation that used a cryptographic system strong enough to be of much value could not be exported from the United States (and many other countries) to customers worldwide. Having to maintain two sets of software, one for domestic use and one for export, is something most computer vendors vigorously oppose.

One point on which there was no controversy is that no one expects the IPv4 Internet to be turned off on a Sunday morning and come back up as an IPv6 Internet Monday morning. Instead, isolated "islands" of IPv6 will be converted, initially communicating via tunnels. As the IPv6 islands grow, they will merge into bigger islands. Eventually, all the islands will merge, and the Internet will be fully converted. Given the massive investment in IPv4 routers currently deployed, the conversion process will probably take a decade. For this reason, an enormous amount of effort has gone into making sure that this transition will be as painless as possible. For more information about IPv6, see (Loshin, 1999).

5.7 SUMMARY

The network layer provides services to the transport layer. It can be based on either virtual circuits or datagrams. In both cases, its main job is routing packets from the source to the destination. In virtual-circuit subnets, a routing decision is made when the virtual circuit is set up. In datagram subnets, it is made on every packet.

Many routing algorithms are used in computer networks. Static algorithms include shortest path routing and flooding. Dynamic algorithms include distance vector routing and link state routing. Most actual networks use one of these. Other important routing topics are hierarchical routing, routing for mobile hosts, broadcast routing, multicast routing, and routing in peer-to-peer networks.

Subnets can easily become congested, increasing the delay and lowering the throughput for packets. Network designers attempt to avoid congestion by proper design. Techniques include retransmission policy, caching, flow control, and more. If congestion does occur, it must be dealt with. Choke packets can be sent back, load can be shed, and other methods applied.

The next step beyond just dealing with congestion is to actually try to achieve a promised quality of service. The methods that can be used for this include buffering at the client, traffic shaping, resource reservation, and admission control. Approaches that have been designed for good quality of service include integrated services (including RSVP), differentiated services, and MPLS.

Networks differ in various ways, so when multiple networks are interconnected problems can occur. Sometimes the problems can be finessed by tunneling a packet through a hostile network, but if the source and destination networks are different, this approach fails. When different networks have different maximum packet sizes, fragmentation may be called for.

The Internet has a rich variety of protocols related to the network layer. These include the data transport protocol, IP, but also the control protocols ICMP, ARP, and RARP, and the routing protocols OSPF and BGP. The Internet is rapidly running out of IP addresses, so a new version of IP, IPv6, has been developed.

PROBLEMS

1. Give two example computer applications for which connection-oriented service is appropriate. Now give two examples for which connectionless service is best.

2. Are there any circumstances when connection-oriented service will (or at least should) deliver packets out of order? Explain.

3. Datagram subnets route each packet as a separate unit, independent of all others. Virtual-circuit subnets do not have to do this, since each data packet follows a predetermined route. Does this observation mean that virtual-circuit subnets do not need the capability to route isolated packets from an arbitrary source to an arbitrary destination? Explain your answer.

4. Give three examples of protocol parameters that might be negotiated when a connection is set up.

5. Consider the following design problem concerning implementation of virtual-circuit service. If virtual circuits are used internal to the subnet, each data packet must have a 3-byte header and each router must tie up 8 bytes of storage for circuit identification. If datagrams are used internally, 15-byte headers are needed but no router table space is required. Transmission capacity costs 1 cent per 10^6 bytes, per hop. Very fast router memory can be purchased for 1 cent per byte and is depreciated over two years, assuming a 40-hour business week. The statistically average session runs for 1000

sec, in which time 200 packets are transmitted. The mean packet requires four hops. Which implementation is cheaper, and by how much?

6. Assuming that all routers and hosts are working properly and that all software in both is free of all errors, is there any chance, however small, that a packet will be delivered to the wrong destination?

7. Consider the network of Fig. 5-7, but ignore the weights on the lines. Suppose that it uses flooding as the routing algorithm. If a packet sent by *A* to *D* has a maximum hop count of 3, list all the routes it will take. Also tell how many hops worth of bandwidth it consumes.

8. Give a simple heuristic for finding two paths through a network from a given source to a given destination that can survive the loss of any communication line (assuming two such paths exist). The routers are considered reliable enough, so it is not necessary to worry about the possibility of router crashes.

9. Consider the subnet of Fig. 5-13(a). Distance vector routing is used, and the following vectors have just come in to router *C*: from *B*: (5, 0, 8, 12, 6, 2); from *D*: (16, 12, 6, 0, 9, 10); and from *E*: (7, 6, 3, 9, 0, 4). The measured delays to *B*, *D*, and *E*, are 6, 3, and 5, respectively. What is *C*'s new routing table? Give both the outgoing line to use and the expected delay.

10. If delays are recorded as 8-bit numbers in a 50-router network, and delay vectors are exchanged twice a second, how much bandwidth per (full-duplex) line is chewed up by the distributed routing algorithm? Assume that each router has three lines to other routers.

11. In Fig. 5-14 the Boolean OR of the two sets of ACF bits are 111 in every row. Is this just an accident here, or does it hold for all subnets under all circumstances?

12. For hierarchical routing with 4800 routers, what region and cluster sizes should be chosen to minimize the size of the routing table for a three-layer hierarchy? A good starting place is the hypothesis that a solution with *k* clusters of *k* regions of *k* routers is close to optimal, which means that *k* is about the cube root of 4800 (around 16). Use trial and error to check out combinations where all three parameters are in the general vicinity of 16.

13. In the text it was stated that when a mobile host is not at home, packets sent to its home LAN are intercepted by its home agent on that LAN. For an IP network on an 802.3 LAN, how does the home agent accomplish this interception?

14. Looking at the subnet of Fig. 5-6, how many packets are generated by a broadcast from *B*, using
(a) reverse path forwarding?
(b) the sink tree?

15. Consider the network of Fig. 5-16(a). Imagine that one new line is added, between *F* and *G*, but the sink tree of Fig. 5-16(b) remains unchanged. What changes occur to Fig. 5-16(c)?

16. Compute a multicast spanning tree for router *C* in the following subnet for a group with members at routers *A*, *B*, *C*, *D*, *E*, *F*, *I*, and *K*.

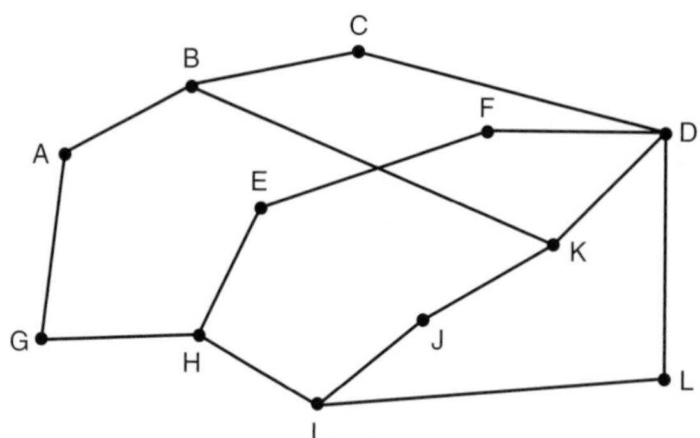

17. In Fig. 5-20, do nodes *H* or *I* ever broadcast on the lookup shown starting at *A*?

18. Suppose that node *B* in Fig. 5-20 has just rebooted and has no routing information in its tables. It suddenly needs a route to *H*. It sends out broadcasts with *TTL* set to 1, 2, 3, and so on. How many rounds does it take to find a route?

19. In the simplest version of the Chord algorithm for peer-to-peer lookup, searches do not use the finger table. Instead, they are linear around the circle, in either direction. Can a node accurately predict which direction it should search? Discuss your answer.

20. Consider the Chord circle of Fig. 5-24. Suppose that node 10 suddenly goes on line. Does this affect node 1's finger table, and if so, how?

21. As a possible congestion control mechanism in a subnet using virtual circuits internally, a router could refrain from acknowledging a received packet until (1) it knows its last transmission along the virtual circuit was received successfully and (2) it has a free buffer. For simplicity, assume that the routers use a stop-and-wait protocol and that each virtual circuit has one buffer dedicated to it for each direction of traffic. If it takes *T* sec to transmit a packet (data or acknowledgement) and there are *n* routers on the path, what is the rate at which packets are delivered to the destination host? Assume that transmission errors are rare and that the host-router connection is infinitely fast.

22. A datagram subnet allows routers to drop packets whenever they need to. The probability of a router discarding a packet is *p*. Consider the case of a source host connected to the source router, which is connected to the destination router, and then to the destination host. If either of the routers discards a packet, the source host eventually times out and tries again. If both host-router and router-router lines are counted as hops, what is the mean number of
(a) hops a packet makes per transmission?
(b) transmissions a packet makes?
(c) hops required per received packet?

23. Describe two major differences between the warning bit method and the RED method.

24. Give an argument why the leaky bucket algorithm should allow just one packet per tick, independent of how large the packet is.

25. The byte-counting variant of the leaky bucket algorithm is used in a particular system. The rule is that one 1024-byte packet, or two 512-byte packets, etc., may be sent on each tick. Give a serious restriction of this system that was not mentioned in the text.

26. An ATM network uses a token bucket scheme for traffic shaping. A new token is put into the bucket every 5 μsec. Each token is good for one cell, which contains 48 bytes of data. What is the maximum sustainable data rate?

27. A computer on a 6-Mbps network is regulated by a token bucket. The token bucket is filled at a rate of 1 Mbps. It is initially filled to capacity with 8 megabits. How long can the computer transmit at the full 6 Mbps?

28. Imagine a flow specification that has a maximum packet size of 1000 bytes, a token bucket rate of 10 million bytes/sec, a token bucket size of 1 million bytes, and a maximum transmission rate of 50 million bytes/sec. How long can a burst at maximum speed last?

29. The network of Fig. 5-37 uses RSVP with multicast trees for hosts 1 and 2 as shown. Suppose that host 3 requests a channel of bandwidth 2 MB/sec for a flow from host 1 and another channel of bandwidth 1 MB/sec for a flow from host 2. At the same time, host 4 requests a channel of bandwidth 2 MB/sec for a flow from host 1 and host 5 requests a channel of bandwidth 1 MB/sec for a flow from host 2. How much total bandwidth will be reserved for these requests at routers *A*, *B*, *C*, *E*, *H*, *J*, *K*, and *L*?

30. The CPU in a router can process 2 million packets/sec. The load offered to it is 1.5 million packets/sec. If a route from source to destination contains 10 routers, how much time is spent being queued and serviced by the CPUs?

31. Consider the user of differentiated services with expedited forwarding. Is there a guarantee that expedited packets experience a shorter delay than regular packets? Why or why not?

32. Is fragmentation needed in concatenated virtual-circuit internets or only in datagram systems?

33. Tunneling through a concatenated virtual-circuit subnet is straightforward: the multiprotocol router at one end just sets up a virtual circuit to the other end and passes packets through it. Can tunneling also be used in datagram subnets? If so, how?

34. Suppose that host *A* is connected to a router *R*1, *R*1 is connected to another router, *R*2, and *R*2 is connected to host *B*. Suppose that a TCP message that contains 900 bytes of data and 20 bytes of TCP header is passed to the IP code at host *A* for delivery to *B*. Show the *Total length, Identification*, *DF*, *MF*, and *Fragment offset* fields of the IP header in each packet transmitted over the three links. Assume that link *A-R1* can support a maximum frame size of 1024 bytes including a 14-byte frame header, link *R1-R2* can support a maximum frame size of 512 bytes, including an 8-byte frame header, and link *R2-B* can support a maximum frame size of 512 bytes including a 12-byte frame header.

35. A router is blasting out IP packets whose total length (data plus header) is 1024 bytes. Assuming that packets live for 10 sec, what is the maximum line speed the router can operate at without danger of cycling through the IP datagram ID number space?

36. An IP datagram using the *Strict source routing* option has to be fragmented. Do you think the option is copied into each fragment, or is it sufficient to just put it in the first fragment? Explain your answer.

37. Suppose that instead of using 16 bits for the network part of a class B address originally, 20 bits had been used. How many class B networks would there have been?

38. Convert the IP address whose hexadecimal representation is C22F1582 to dotted decimal notation.

39. A network on the Internet has a subnet mask of 255.255.240.0. What is the maximum number of hosts it can handle?

40. A large number of consecutive IP address are available starting at 198.16.0.0. Suppose that four organizations, *A*, *B*, *C*, and *D*, request 4000, 2000, 4000, and 8000 addresses, respectively, and in that order. For each of these, give the first IP address assigned, the last IP address assigned, and the mask in the *w.x.y.z/s* notation.

41. A router has just received the following new IP addresses: 57.6.96.0/21, 57.6.104.0/21, 57.6.112.0/21, and 57.6.120.0/21. If all of them use the same outgoing line, can they be aggregated? If so, to what? If not, why not?

42. The set of IP addresses from 29.18.0.0 to 19.18.128.255 has been aggregated to 29.18.0.0/17. However, there is a gap of 1024 unassigned addresses from 29.18.60.0 to 29.18.63.255 that are now suddenly assigned to a host using a different outgoing line. Is it now necessary to split up the aggregate address into its constituent blocks, add the new block to the table, and then see if any reaggregation is possible? If not, what can be done instead?

43. A router has the following (CIDR) entries in its routing table:

Address/mask	Next hop
135.46.56.0/22	Interface 0
135.46.60.0/22	Interface 1
192.53.40.0/23	Router 1
default	Router 2

For each of the following IP addresses, what does the router do if a packet with that address arrives?

(a) 135.46.63.10
(b) 135.46.57.14
(c) 135.46.52.2
(d) 192.53.40.7
(e) 192.53.56.7

44. Many companies have a policy of having two (or more) routers connecting the company to the Internet to provide some redundancy in case one of them goes down. Is this policy still possible with NAT? Explain your answer.

45. You have just explained the ARP protocol to a friend. When you are all done, he says: “I’ve got it. ARP provides a service to the network layer, so it is part of the data link layer.” What do you say to him?

46. ARP and RARP both map addresses from one space to another. In this respect, they are similar. However, their implementations are fundamentally different. In what major way do they differ?

47. Describe a way to reassemble IP fragments at the destination.

48. Most IP datagram reassembly algorithms have a timer to avoid having a lost fragment tie up reassembly buffers forever. Suppose that a datagram is fragmented into four fragments. The first three fragments arrive, but the last one is delayed. Eventually, the timer goes off and the three fragments in the receiver's memory are discarded. A little later, the last fragment stumbles in. What should be done with it?

49. In both IP and ATM, the checksum covers only the header and not the data. Why do you suppose this design was chosen?

50. A person who lives in Boston travels to Minneapolis, taking her portable computer with her. To her surprise, the LAN at her destination in Minneapolis is a wireless IP LAN, so she does not have to plug in. Is it still necessary to go through the entire business with home agents and foreign agents to make e-mail and other traffic arrive correctly?

51. IPv6 uses 16-byte addresses. If a block of 1 million addresses is allocated every picosecond, how long will the addresses last?

52. The *Protocol* field used in the IPv4 header is not present in the fixed IPv6 header. Why not?

53. When the IPv6 protocol is introduced, does the ARP protocol have to be changed? If so, are the changes conceptual or technical?

54. Write a program to simulate routing using flooding. Each packet should contain a counter that is decremented on each hop. When the counter gets to zero, the packet is discarded. Time is discrete, with each line handling one packet per time interval. Make three versions of the program: all lines are flooded, all lines except the input line are flooded, and only the (statically chosen) best k lines are flooded. Compare flooding with deterministic routing ($k = 1$) in terms of both delay and the bandwidth used.

55. Write a program that simulates a computer network using discrete time. The first packet on each router queue makes one hop per time interval. Each router has only a finite number of buffers. If a packet arrives and there is no room for it, it is discarded and not retransmitted. Instead, there is an end-to-end protocol, complete with timeouts and acknowledgement packets, that eventually regenerates the packet from the source router. Plot the throughput of the network as a function of the end-to-end timeout interval, parameterized by error rate.

56. Write a function to do forwarding in an IP router. The procedure has one parameter, an IP address. It also has access to a global table consisting of an array of triples. Each triple contains three integers: an IP address, a subnet mask, and the outline line to use. The function looks up the IP address in the table using CIDR and returns the line to use as its value.

57. Use the *traceroute* (UNIX) or *tracert* (Windows) programs to trace the route from your computer to various universities on other continents. Make a list of transoceanic links you have discovered. Some sites to try are

www.berkeley.edu (California)
www.mit.edu (Massachusetts)
www.vu.nl (Amsterdam)
www.ucl.ac.uk (London)
www.usyd.edu.au (Sydney)
www.u-tokyo.ac.jp (Tokyo)
www.uct.ac.za (Cape Town)

6

THE TRANSPORT LAYER

The transport layer is not just another layer. It is the heart of the whole protocol hierarchy. Its task is to provide reliable, cost-effective data transport from the source machine to the destination machine, independently of the physical network or networks currently in use. Without the transport layer, the whole concept of layered protocols would make little sense. In this chapter we will study the transport layer in detail, including its services, design, protocols, and performance.

6.1 THE TRANSPORT SERVICE

In the following sections we will provide an introduction to the transport service. We look at what kind of service is provided to the application layer. To make the issue of transport service more concrete, we will examine two sets of transport layer primitives. First comes a simple (but hypothetical) one to show the basic ideas. Then comes the interface commonly used in the Internet.

6.1.1 Services Provided to the Upper Layers

The ultimate goal of the transport layer is to provide efficient, reliable, and cost-effective service to its users, normally processes in the application layer. To achieve this goal, the transport layer makes use of the services provided by the network layer. The hardware and/or software within the transport layer that does the work is called the **transport entity**. The transport entity can be located in the operating system kernel, in a separate user process, in a library package bound into network applications, or conceivably on the network interface card. The (logical) relationship of the network, transport, and application layers is illustrated in Fig. 6-1.

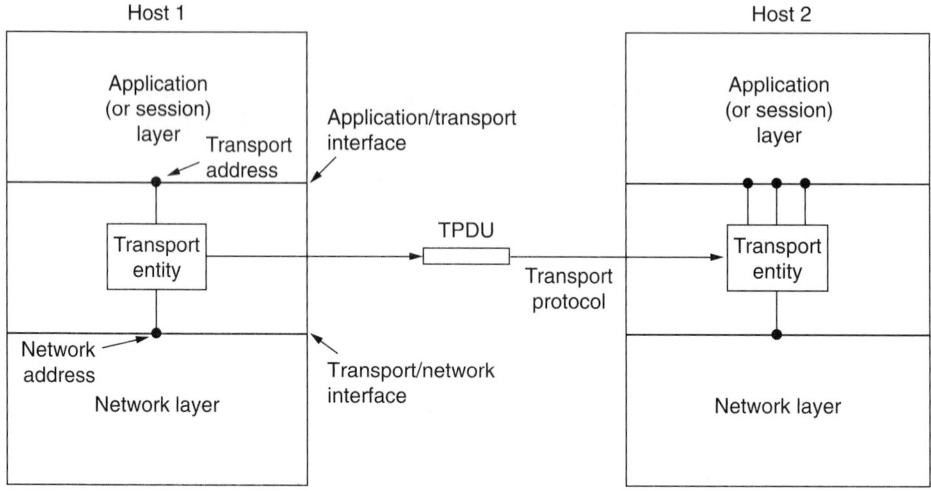

Figure 6-1. The network, transport, and application layers.

Just as there are two types of network service, connection-oriented and connectionless, there are also two types of transport service. The connection-oriented transport service is similar to the connection-oriented network service in many ways. In both cases, connections have three phases: establishment, data transfer, and release. Addressing and flow control are also similar in both layers. Furthermore, the connectionless transport service is also very similar to the connectionless network service.

The obvious question is then this: If the transport layer service is so similar to the network layer service, why are there two distinct layers? Why is one layer not adequate? The answer is subtle, but crucial, and goes back to Fig. 1-9. The transport code runs entirely on the users' machines, but the network layer mostly runs on the routers, which are operated by the carrier (at least for a wide area network). What happens if the network layer offers inadequate service? Suppose that it frequently loses packets? What happens if routers crash from time to time?

Problems occur, that's what. The users have no real control over the network layer, so they cannot solve the problem of poor service by using better routers or putting more error handling in the data link layer. The only possibility is to put on top of the network layer another layer that improves the quality of the service. If, in a connection-oriented subnet, a transport entity is informed halfway through a long transmission that its network connection has been abruptly terminated, with no indication of what has happened to the data currently in transit, it can set up a new network connection to the remote transport entity. Using this new network connection, it can send a query to its peer asking which data arrived and which did not, and then pick up from where it left off.

In essence, the existence of the transport layer makes it possible for the transport service to be more reliable than the underlying network service. Lost packets and mangled data can be detected and compensated for by the transport layer. Furthermore, the transport service primitives can be implemented as calls to library procedures in order to make them independent of the network service primitives. The network service calls may vary considerably from network to network (e.g., connectionless LAN service may be quite different from connection-oriented WAN service). By hiding the network service behind a set of transport service primitives, changing the network service merely requires replacing one set of library procedures by another one that does the same thing with a different underlying service.

Thanks to the transport layer, application programmers can write code according to a standard set of primitives and have these programs work on a wide variety of networks, without having to worry about dealing with different subnet interfaces and unreliable transmission. If all real networks were flawless and all had the same service primitives and were guaranteed never, ever to change, the transport layer might not be needed. However, in the real world it fulfills the key function of isolating the upper layers from the technology, design, and imperfections of the subnet.

For this reason, many people have traditionally made a distinction between layers 1 through 4 on the one hand and layer(s) above 4 on the other. The bottom four layers can be seen as the **transport service provider**, whereas the upper layer(s) are the **transport service user**. This distinction of provider versus user has a considerable impact on the design of the layers and puts the transport layer in a key position, since it forms the major boundary between the provider and user of the reliable data transmission service.

6.1.2 Transport Service Primitives

To allow users to access the transport service, the transport layer must provide some operations to application programs, that is, a transport service interface. Each transport service has its own interface. In this section, we will first examine a simple (hypothetical) transport service and its interface to see the bare essentials. In the following section we will look at a real example.

The transport service is similar to the network service, but there are also some important differences. The main difference is that the network service is intended to model the service offered by real networks, warts and all. Real networks can lose packets, so the network service is generally unreliable.

The (connection-oriented) transport service, in contrast, is reliable. Of course, real networks are not error-free, but that is precisely the purpose of the transport layer—to provide a reliable service on top of an unreliable network.

As an example, consider two processes connected by pipes in UNIX. They assume the connection between them is perfect. They do not want to know about acknowledgements, lost packets, congestion, or anything like that. What they want is a 100 percent reliable connection. Process *A* puts data into one end of the pipe, and process *B* takes it out of the other. This is what the connection-oriented transport service is all about—hiding the imperfections of the network service so that user processes can just assume the existence of an error-free bit stream.

As an aside, the transport layer can also provide unreliable (datagram) service. However, there is relatively little to say about that, so we will mainly concentrate on the connection-oriented transport service in this chapter. Nevertheless, there are some applications, such as client-server computing and streaming multimedia, which benefit from connectionless transport, so we will say a little bit about it later on.

A second difference between the network service and transport service is whom the services are intended for. The network service is used only by the transport entities. Few users write their own transport entities, and thus few users or programs ever see the bare network service. In contrast, many programs (and thus programmers) see the transport primitives. Consequently, the transport service must be convenient and easy to use.

To get an idea of what a transport service might be like, consider the five primitives listed in Fig. 6-2. This transport interface is truly bare bones, but it gives the essential flavor of what a connection-oriented transport interface has to do. It allows application programs to establish, use, and then release connections, which is sufficient for many applications.

Primitive	Packet sent	Meaning
LISTEN	(none)	Block until some process tries to connect
CONNECT	CONNECTION REQ.	Actively attempt to establish a connection
SEND	DATA	Send information
RECEIVE	(none)	Block until a DATA packet arrives
DISCONNECT	DISCONNECTION REQ.	This side wants to release the connection

Figure 6-2. The primitives for a simple transport service.

To see how these primitives might be used, consider an application with a server and a number of remote clients. To start with, the server executes a LISTEN primitive, typically by calling a library procedure that makes a system call to block the server until a client turns up. When a client wants to talk to the server, it executes a CONNECT primitive. The transport entity carries out this primitive by blocking the caller and sending a packet to the server. Encapsulated in the payload of this packet is a transport layer message for the server's transport entity.

A quick note on terminology is now in order. For lack of a better term, we will reluctantly use the somewhat ungainly acronym **TPDU** (**Transport Protocol Data Unit**) for messages sent from transport entity to transport entity. Thus, TPDUs (exchanged by the transport layer) are contained in packets (exchanged by the network layer). In turn, packets are contained in frames (exchanged by the data link layer). When a frame arrives, the data link layer processes the frame header and passes the contents of the frame payload field up to the network entity. The network entity processes the packet header and passes the contents of the packet payload up to the transport entity. This nesting is illustrated in Fig. 6-3.

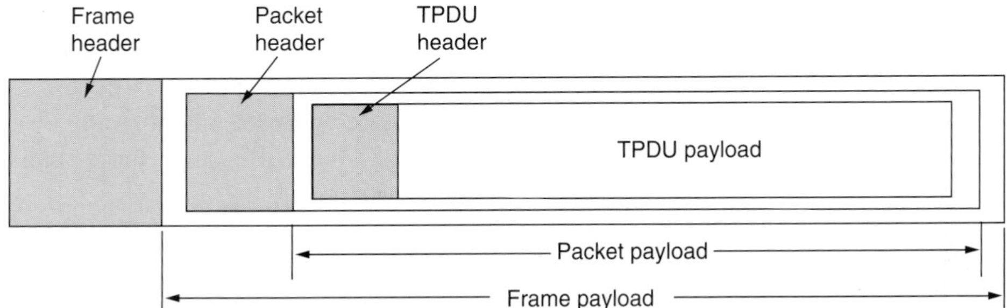

Figure 6-3. Nesting of TPDUs, packets, and frames.

Getting back to our client-server example, the client's CONNECT call causes a CONNECTION REQUEST TPDU to be sent to the server. When it arrives, the transport entity checks to see that the server is blocked on a LISTEN (i.e., is interested in handling requests). It then unblocks the server and sends a CONNECTION ACCEPTED TPDU back to the client. When this TPDU arrives, the client is unblocked and the connection is established.

Data can now be exchanged using the SEND and RECEIVE primitives. In the simplest form, either party can do a (blocking) RECEIVE to wait for the other party to do a SEND. When the TPDU arrives, the receiver is unblocked. It can then process the TPDU and send a reply. As long as both sides can keep track of whose turn it is to send, this scheme works fine.

Note that at the transport layer, even a simple unidirectional data exchange is more complicated than at the network layer. Every data packet sent will also be acknowledged (eventually). The packets bearing control TPDUs are also acknowledged, implicitly or explicitly. These acknowledgements are managed by the transport entities, using the network layer protocol, and are not visible to the transport users. Similarly, the transport entities will need to worry about timers and retransmissions. None of this machinery is visible to the transport users. To the transport users, a connection is a reliable bit pipe: one user stuffs bits in and they magically appear at the other end. This ability to hide complexity is the reason that layered protocols are such a powerful tool.

When a connection is no longer needed, it must be released to free up table space within the two transport entities. Disconnection has two variants: asymmetric and symmetric. In the asymmetric variant, either transport user can issue a DISCONNECT primitive, which results in a DISCONNECT TPDU being sent to the remote transport entity. Upon arrival, the connection is released.

In the symmetric variant, each direction is closed separately, independently of the other one. When one side does a DISCONNECT, that means it has no more data to send but it is still willing to accept data from its partner. In this model, a connection is released when both sides have done a DISCONNECT.

A state diagram for connection establishment and release for these simple primitives is given in Fig. 6-4. Each transition is triggered by some event, either a primitive executed by the local transport user or an incoming packet. For simplicity, we assume here that each TPDU is separately acknowledged. We also assume that a symmetric disconnection model is used, with the client going first. Please note that this model is quite unsophisticated. We will look at more realistic models later on.

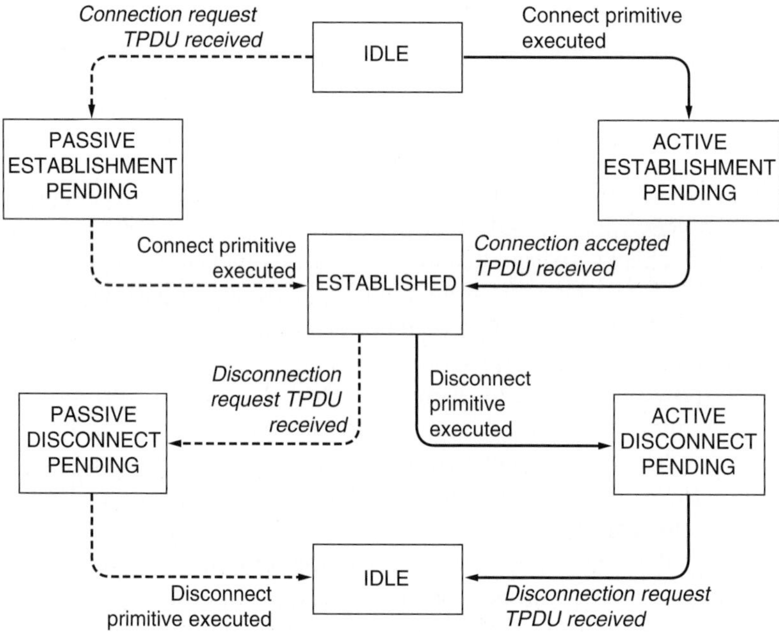

Figure 6-4. A state diagram for a simple connection management scheme. Transitions labeled in italics are caused by packet arrivals. The solid lines show the client's state sequence. The dashed lines show the server's state sequence.

6.1.3 Berkeley Sockets

Let us now briefly inspect another set of transport primitives, the socket primitives used in Berkeley UNIX for TCP. These primitives are widely used for Internet programming. They are listed in Fig. 6-5. Roughly speaking, they follow the model of our first example but offer more features and flexibility. We will not look at the corresponding TPDUs here. That discussion will have to wait until we study TCP later in this chapter.

Primitive	Meaning
SOCKET	Create a new communication end point
BIND	Attach a local address to a socket
LISTEN	Announce willingness to accept connections; give queue size
ACCEPT	Block the caller until a connection attempt arrives
CONNECT	Actively attempt to establish a connection
SEND	Send some data over the connection
RECEIVE	Receive some data from the connection
CLOSE	Release the connection

Figure 6-5. The socket primitives for TCP.

The first four primitives in the list are executed in that order by servers. The SOCKET primitive creates a new end point and allocates table space for it within the transport entity. The parameters of the call specify the addressing format to be used, the type of service desired (e.g., reliable byte stream), and the protocol. A successful SOCKET call returns an ordinary file descriptor for use in succeeding calls, the same way an OPEN call does.

Newly-created sockets do not have network addresses. These are assigned using the BIND primitive. Once a server has bound an address to a socket, remote clients can connect to it. The reason for not having the SOCKET call create an address directly is that some processes care about their address (e.g., they have been using the same address for years and everyone knows this address), whereas others do not care.

Next comes the LISTEN call, which allocates space to queue incoming calls for the case that several clients try to connect at the same time. In contrast to LISTEN in our first example, in the socket model LISTEN is not a blocking call.

To block waiting for an incoming connection, the server executes an ACCEPT primitive. When a TPDU asking for a connection arrives, the transport entity creates a new socket with the same properties as the original one and returns a file descriptor for it. The server can then fork off a process or thread to handle the connection on the new socket and go back to waiting for the next connection on the original socket. ACCEPT returns a normal file descriptor, which can be used for reading and writing in the standard way, the same as for files.

Now let us look at the client side. Here, too, a socket must first be created using the SOCKET primitive, but BIND is not required since the address used does not matter to the server. The CONNECT primitive blocks the caller and actively starts the connection process. When it completes (i.e., when the appropriate TPDU is received from the server), the client process is unblocked and the connection is established. Both sides can now use SEND and RECV to transmit and receive data over the full-duplex connection. The standard UNIX READ and WRITE system calls can also be used if none of the special options of SEND and RECV are required.

Connection release with sockets is symmetric. When both sides have executed a CLOSE primitive, the connection is released.

6.1.4 An Example of Socket Programming: An Internet File Server

As an example of how the socket calls are used, consider the client and server code of Fig. 6-6. Here we have a very primitive Internet file server along with an example client that uses it. The code has many limitations (discussed below), but in principle the server code can be compiled and run on any UNIX system connected to the Internet. The client code can then be compiled and run on any other UNIX machine on the Internet, anywhere in the world. The client code can be executed with appropriate parameters to fetch any file to which the server has access on its machine. The file is written to standard output, which, of course, can be redirected to a file or pipe.

Let us look at the server code first. It starts out by including some standard headers, the last three of which contain the main Internet-related definitions and data structures. Next comes a definition of *SERVER_PORT* as 12345. This number was chosen arbitrarily. Any number between 1024 and 65535 will work just as well as long as it is not in use by some other process. Of course, the client and server have to use the same port. If this server ever becomes a worldwide hit (unlikely, given how primitive it is), it will be assigned a permanent port below 1024 and appear on *www.iana.org*.

The next two lines in the server define two constants needed. The first one determines the chunk size used for the file transfer. The second one determines how many pending connections can be held before additional ones are discarded upon arrival.

After the declarations of local variables, the server code begins. It starts out by initializing a data structure that will hold the server's IP address. This data structure will soon be bound to the server's socket. The call to *memset* sets the data structure to all 0s. The three assignments following it fill in three of its fields. The last of these contains the server's port. The functions *htonl* and *htons* have to do with converting values to a standard format so the code runs correctly on both big-endian machines (e.g., the SPARC) and little-endian machines (e.g., the Pentium). Their exact semantics are not relevant here.

Next the server creates a socket and checks for errors (indicated by $s < 0$). In a production version of the code, the error message could be a trifle more explanatory. The call to *setsockopt* is needed to allow the port to be reused so the server can run indefinitely, fielding request after request. Now the IP address is bound to the socket and a check is made to see if the call to *bind* succeeded. The final step in the initialization is the call to *listen* to announce the server's willingness to accept incoming calls and tell the system to hold up to *QUEUE_SIZE* of them in case new requests arrive while the server is still processing the current one. If the queue is full and additional requests arrive, they are quietly discarded.

At this point the server enters its main loop, which it never leaves. The only way to stop it is to kill it from outside. The call to *accept* blocks the server until some client tries to establish a connection with it. If the *accept* call succeeds, it returns a file descriptor that can be used for reading and writing, analogous to how file descriptors can be used to read and write from pipes. However, unlike pipes, which are unidirectional, sockets are bidirectional, so *sa* (socket address) can be used for reading from the connection and also for writing to it.

After the connection is established, the server reads the file name from it. If the name is not yet available, the server blocks waiting for it. After getting the file name, the server opens the file and then enters a loop that alternately reads blocks from the file and writes them to the socket until the entire file has been copied. Then the server closes the file and the connection and waits for the next connection to show up. It repeats this loop forever.

Now let us look at the client code. To understand how it works, it is necessary to understand how it is invoked. Assuming it is called *client*, a typical call is

```
client flits.cs.vu.nl /usr/tom/filename >f
```

This call only works if the server is already running on *flits.cs.vu.nl* and the file */usr/tom/filename* exists and the server has read access to it. If the call is successful, the file is transferred over the Internet and written to *f*, after which the client program exits. Since the server continues after a transfer, the client can be started again and again to get other files.

The client code starts with some includes and declarations. Execution begins by checking to see if it has been called with the right number of arguments (*argc* = 3 means the program name plus two arguments). Note that *argv* [1] contains the server's name (e.g., *flits.cs.vu.nl*) and is converted to an IP address by *gethostbyname*. This function uses DNS to look up the name. We will study DNS in Chap. 7.

Next a socket is created and initialized. After that, the client attempts to establish a TCP connection to the server, using *connect*. If the server is up and running on the named machine and attached to *SERVER_PORT* and is either idle or has room in its *listen* queue, the connection will (eventually) be established. Using the connection, the client sends the name of the file by writing on the socket. The number of bytes sent is one larger than the name proper since the 0-byte terminating the name must also be sent to tell the server where the name ends.

```
/* This page contains a client program that can request a file from the server program
 * on the next page. The server responds by sending the whole file.
 */

#include <sys/types.h>
#include <sys/socket.h>
#include <netinet/in.h>
#include <netdb.h>

#define SERVER_PORT 12345                /* arbitrary, but client & server must agree */
#define BUF_SIZE 4096                    /* block transfer size */

int main(int argc, char **argv)
{
  int c, s, bytes;
  char buf[BUF_SIZE];                    /* buffer for incoming file */
  struct hostent *h;                     /* info about server */
  struct sockaddr_in channel;            /* holds IP address */

  if (argc != 3) fatal("Usage: client server-name file-name");
  h = gethostbyname(argv[1]);            /* look up host's IP address */
  if (!h) fatal("gethostbyname failed");

  s = socket(PF_INET, SOCK_STREAM, IPPROTO_TCP);
  if (s <0) fatal("socket");
  memset(&channel, 0, sizeof(channel));
  channel.sin_family= AF_INET;
  memcpy(&channel.sin_addr.s_addr, h->h_addr, h->h_length);
  channel.sin_port= htons(SERVER_PORT);

  c = connect(s, (struct sockaddr *) &channel, sizeof(channel));
  if (c < 0) fatal("connect failed");

  /* Connection is now established. Send file name including 0 byte at end. */
  write(s, argv[2], strlen(argv[2])+1);

  /* Go get the file and write it to standard output. */
  while (1) {
      bytes = read(s, buf, BUF_SIZE);    /* read from socket */
      if (bytes <= 0) exit(0);           /* check for end of file */
      write(1, buf, bytes);              /* write to standard output */
  }
}

fatal(char *string)
{
  printf("%s\n", string);
  exit(1);
}
```

Figure 6-6. Client code using sockets. The server code is on the next page.

```
#include <sys/types.h>                      /* This is the server code */
#include <sys/fcntl.h>
#include <sys/socket.h>
#include <netinet/in.h>
#include <netdb.h>

#define SERVER_PORT 12345                   /* arbitrary, but client & server must agree */
#define BUF_SIZE 4096                       /* block transfer size */
#define QUEUE_SIZE 10

int main(int argc, char *argv[])
{
 int s, b, l, fd, sa, bytes, on = 1;
 char buf[BUF_SIZE];                        /* buffer for outgoing file */
 struct sockaddr_in channel;                /* holds IP address */

 /* Build address structure to bind to socket. */
 memset(&channel, 0, sizeof(channel));      /* zero channel */
 channel.sin_family = AF_INET;
 channel.sin_addr.s_addr = htonl(INADDR_ANY);
 channel.sin_port = htons(SERVER_PORT);

 /* Passive open. Wait for connection. */
 s = socket(AF_INET, SOCK_STREAM, IPPROTO_TCP);    /* create socket */
 if (s < 0) fatal("socket failed");
 setsockopt(s, SOL_SOCKET, SO_REUSEADDR, (char *) &on, sizeof(on));

 b = bind(s, (struct sockaddr *) &channel, sizeof(channel));
 if (b < 0) fatal("bind failed");

 l = listen(s, QUEUE_SIZE);                 /* specify queue size */
 if (l < 0) fatal("listen failed");

 /* Socket is now set up and bound. Wait for connection and process it. */
 while (1) {
     sa = accept(s, 0, 0);                  /* block for connection request */
     if (sa < 0) fatal("accept failed");

     read(sa, buf, BUF_SIZE);               /* read file name from socket */

     /* Get and return the file. */
     fd = open(buf, O_RDONLY);              /* open the file to be sent back */
     if (fd < 0) fatal("open failed");

     while (1) {
          bytes = read(fd, buf, BUF_SIZE); /* read from file */
          if (bytes <= 0) break;            /* check for end of file */
          write(sa, buf, bytes);            /* write bytes to socket */
     }
     close(fd);                             /* close file */
     close(sa);                             /* close connection */
 }
}
```

Now the client enters a loop, reading the file block by block from the socket and copying it to standard output. When it is done, it just exits.

The procedure *fatal* prints an error message and exits. The server needs the same procedure, but it was omitted due to lack of space on the page. Since the client and server are compiled separately and normally run on different computers, they cannot share the code of *fatal*.

These two programs (as well as other material related to this book) can be fetched from the book's Web site

http://www.prenhall.com/tanenbaum

by clicking on the Web Site link next to the photo of the cover. They can be downloaded and compiled on any UNIX system (e.g., Solaris, BSD, Linux) by

```
cc –o client client.c –lsocket –lnsl
cc –o server server.c –lsocket –lnsl
```

The server is started by just typing

```
server
```

The client needs two arguments, as discussed above. A Windows version is also available on the Web site.

Just for the record, this server is not the last word in serverdom. Its error checking is meager and its error reporting is mediocre. It has clearly never heard about security, and using bare UNIX system calls is not the last word in platform independence. It also makes some assumptions that are technically illegal, such as assuming the file name fits in the buffer and is transmitted atomically. Since it handles all requests strictly sequentially (because it has only a single thread), its performance is poor. These shortcomings notwithstanding, it is a complete, working Internet file server. In the exercises, the reader is invited to improve it. For more information about programming with sockets, see (Stevens, 1997).

6.2 ELEMENTS OF TRANSPORT PROTOCOLS

The transport service is implemented by a **transport protocol** used between the two transport entities. In some ways, transport protocols resemble the data link protocols we studied in detail in Chap. 3. Both have to deal with error control, sequencing, and flow control, among other issues.

However, significant differences between the two also exist. These differences are due to major dissimilarities between the environments in which the two protocols operate, as shown in Fig. 6-7. At the data link layer, two routers communicate directly via a physical channel, whereas at the transport layer, this physical channel is replaced by the entire subnet. This difference has many important implications for the protocols, as we shall see in this chapter.

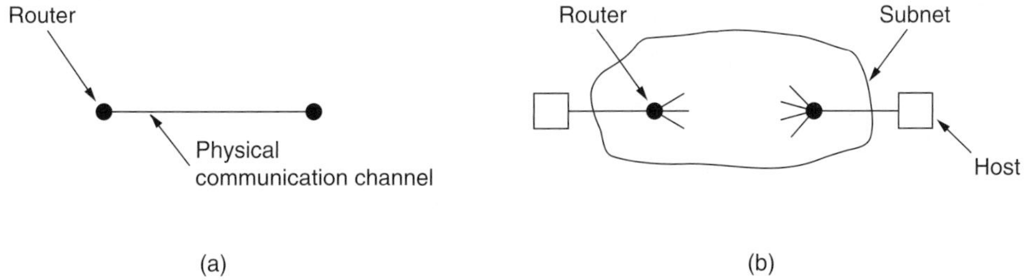

Figure 6-7. (a) Environment of the data link layer. (b) Environment of the transport layer.

For one thing, in the data link layer, it is not necessary for a router to specify which router it wants to talk to—each outgoing line uniquely specifies a particular router. In the transport layer, explicit addressing of destinations is required.

For another thing, the process of establishing a connection over the wire of Fig. 6-7(a) is simple: the other end is always there (unless it has crashed, in which case it is not there). Either way, there is not much to do. In the transport layer, initial connection establishment is more complicated, as we will see.

Another, exceedingly annoying, difference between the data link layer and the transport layer is the potential existence of storage capacity in the subnet. When a router sends a frame, it may arrive or be lost, but it cannot bounce around for a while, go into hiding in a far corner of the world, and then suddenly emerge at an inopportune moment 30 sec later. If the subnet uses datagrams and adaptive routing inside, there is a nonnegligible probability that a packet may be stored for a number of seconds and then delivered later. The consequences of the subnet's ability to store packets can sometimes be disastrous and can require the use of special protocols.

A final difference between the data link and transport layers is one of amount rather than of kind. Buffering and flow control are needed in both layers, but the presence of a large and dynamically varying number of connections in the transport layer may require a different approach than we used in the data link layer. In Chap. 3, some of the protocols allocate a fixed number of buffers to each line, so that when a frame arrives a buffer is always available. In the transport layer, the larger number of connections that must be managed make the idea of dedicating many buffers to each one less attractive. In the following sections, we will examine all of these important issues and others.

6.2.1 Addressing

When an application (e.g., a user) process wishes to set up a connection to a remote application process, it must specify which one to connect to. (Connectionless transport has the same problem: To whom should each message be sent?) The method normally used is to define transport addresses to which processes can listen for connection requests. In the Internet, these end points are called **ports**. In ATM networks, they are called **AAL-SAPs**. We will use the generic term **TSAP**, (**Transport Service Access Point**). The analogous end points in the network layer (i.e., network layer addresses) are then called **NSAPs**. IP addresses are examples of NSAPs.

Figure 6-8 illustrates the relationship between the NSAP, TSAP and transport connection. Application processes, both clients and servers, can attach themselves to a TSAP to establish a connection to a remote TSAP. These connections run through NSAPs on each host, as shown. The purpose of having TSAPs is that in some networks, each computer has a single NSAP, so some way is needed to distinguish multiple transport end points that share that NSAP.

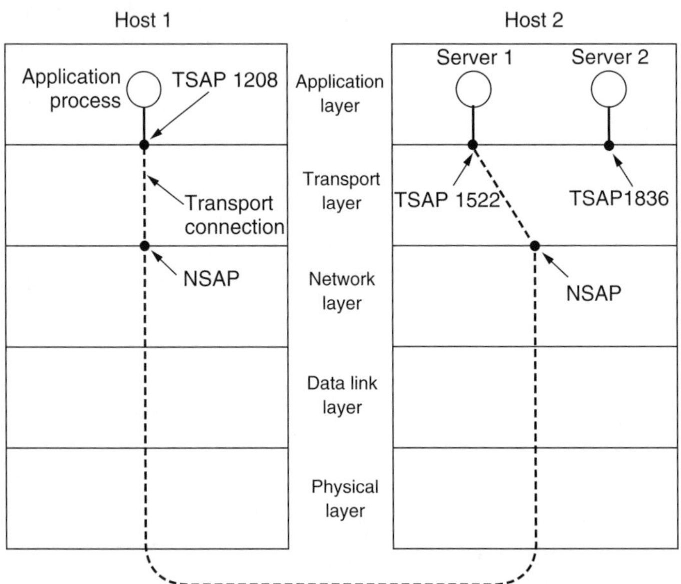

Figure 6-8. TSAPs, NSAPs, and transport connections.

A possible scenario for a transport connection is as follows.

1. A time of day server process on host 2 attaches itself to TSAP 1522 to wait for an incoming call. How a process attaches itself to a TSAP is outside the networking model and depends entirely on the local operating system. A call such as our LISTEN might be used, for example.

2. An application process on host 1 wants to find out the time-of-day, so it issues a CONNECT request specifying TSAP 1208 as the source and TSAP 1522 as the destination. This action ultimately results in a

transport connection being established between the application process on host 1 and server 1 on host 2.

3. The application process then sends over a request for the time.

4. The time server process responds with the current time.

5. The transport connection is then released.

Note that there may well be other servers on host 2 that are attached to other TSAPs and waiting for incoming connections that arrive over the same NSAP.

The picture painted above is fine, except we have swept one little problem under the rug: How does the user process on host 1 know that the time-of-day server is attached to TSAP 1522? One possibility is that the time-of-day server has been attaching itself to TSAP 1522 for years and gradually all the network users have learned this. In this model, services have stable TSAP addresses that are listed in files in well-known places, such as the */etc/services* file on UNIX systems, which lists which servers are permanently attached to which ports.

While stable TSAP addresses work for a small number of key services that never change (e.g. the Web server), user processes, in general, often want to talk to other user processes that only exist for a short time and do not have a TSAP address that is known in advance. Furthermore, if there are potentially many server processes, most of which are rarely used, it is wasteful to have each of them active and listening to a stable TSAP address all day long. In short, a better scheme is needed.

One such scheme is shown in Fig. 6-9 in a simplified form. It is known as the **initial connection protocol**. Instead of every conceivable server listening at a well-known TSAP, each machine that wishes to offer services to remote users has a special **process server** that acts as a proxy for less heavily used servers. It listens to a set of ports at the same time, waiting for a connection request. Potential users of a service begin by doing a CONNECT request, specifying the TSAP address of the service they want. If no server is waiting for them, they get a connection to the process server, as shown in Fig. 6-9(a).

After it gets the incoming request, the process server spawns the requested server, allowing it to inherit the existing connection with the user. The new server then does the requested work, while the process server goes back to listening for new requests, as shown in Fig. 6-9(b).

While the initial connection protocol works fine for those servers that can be created as they are needed, there are many situations in which services do exist independently of the process server. A file server, for example, needs to run on special hardware (a machine with a disk) and cannot just be created on-the-fly when someone wants to talk to it.

To handle this situation, an alternative scheme is often used. In this model, there exists a special process called a **name server** or sometimes a **directory server**. To find the TSAP address corresponding to a given service name, such as

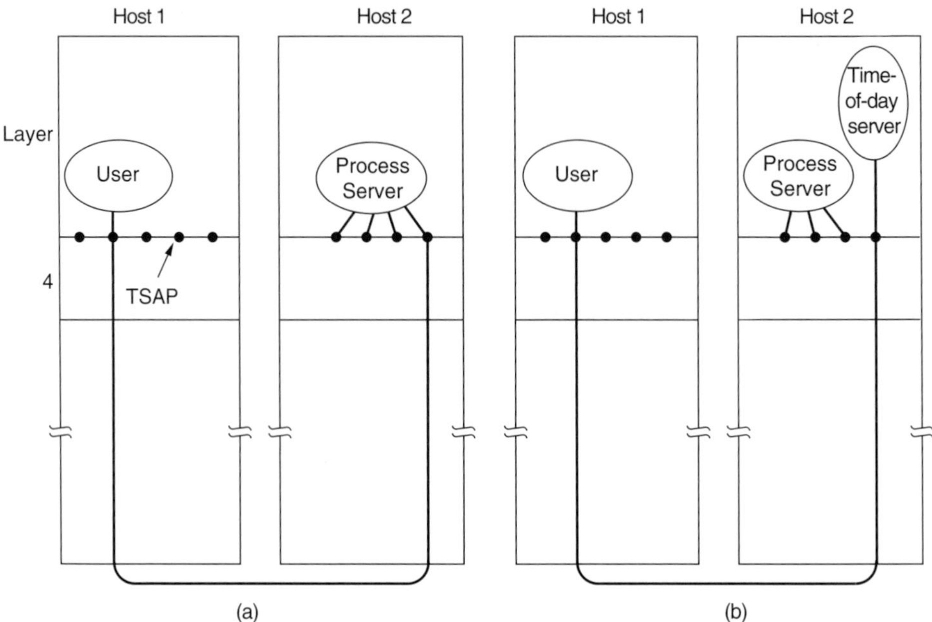

Figure 6-9. How a user process in host 1 establishes a connection with a time-of-day server in host 2.

"time of day," a user sets up a connection to the name server (which listens to a well-known TSAP). The user then sends a message specifying the service name, and the name server sends back the TSAP address. Then the user releases the connection with the name server and establishes a new one with the desired service.

In this model, when a new service is created, it must register itself with the name server, giving both its service name (typically, an ASCII string) and its TSAP. The name server records this information in its internal database so that when queries come in later, it will know the answers.

The function of the name server is analogous to the directory assistance operator in the telephone system—it provides a mapping of names onto numbers. Just as in the telephone system, it is essential that the address of the well-known TSAP used by the name server (or the process server in the initial connection protocol) is indeed well known. If you do not know the number of the information operator, you cannot call the information operator to find it out. If you think the number you dial for information is obvious, try it in a foreign country sometime.

6.2.2 Connection Establishment

Establishing a connection sounds easy, but it is actually surprisingly tricky. At first glance, it would seem sufficient for one transport entity to just send a CONNECTION REQUEST TPDU to the destination and wait for a CONNECTION

ACCEPTED reply. The problem occurs when the network can lose, store, and duplicate packets. This behavior causes serious complications.

Imagine a subnet that is so congested that acknowledgements hardly ever get back in time and each packet times out and is retransmitted two or three times. Suppose that the subnet uses datagrams inside and that every packet follows a different route. Some of the packets might get stuck in a traffic jam inside the subnet and take a long time to arrive, that is, they are stored in the subnet and pop out much later.

The worst possible nightmare is as follows. A user establishes a connection with a bank, sends messages telling the bank to transfer a large amount of money to the account of a not-entirely-trustworthy person, and then releases the connection. Unfortunately, each packet in the scenario is duplicated and stored in the subnet. After the connection has been released, all the packets pop out of the subnet and arrive at the destination in order, asking the bank to establish a new connection, transfer money (again), and release the connection. The bank has no way of telling that these are duplicates. It must assume that this is a second, independent transaction, and transfers the money again. For the remainder of this section we will study the problem of delayed duplicates, with special emphasis on algorithms for establishing connections in a reliable way, so that nightmares like the one above cannot happen.

The crux of the problem is the existence of delayed duplicates. It can be attacked in various ways, none of them very satisfactory. One way is to use throw-away transport addresses. In this approach, each time a transport address is needed, a new one is generated. When a connection is released, the address is discarded and never used again. This strategy makes the process server model of Fig. 6-9 impossible.

Another possibility is to give each connection a connection identifier (i.e., a sequence number incremented for each connection established) chosen by the initiating party and put in each TPDU, including the one requesting the connection. After each connection is released, each transport entity could update a table listing obsolete connections as (peer transport entity, connection identifier) pairs. Whenever a connection request comes in, it could be checked against the table, to see if it belonged to a previously-released connection.

Unfortunately, this scheme has a basic flaw: it requires each transport entity to maintain a certain amount of history information indefinitely. If a machine crashes and loses its memory, it will no longer know which connection identifiers have already been used.

Instead, we need to take a different tack. Rather than allowing packets to live forever within the subnet, we must devise a mechanism to kill off aged packets that are still hobbling about. If we can ensure that no packet lives longer than some known time, the problem becomes somewhat more manageable.

Packet lifetime can be restricted to a known maximum using one (or more) of the following techniques:

1. Restricted subnet design.
2. Putting a hop counter in each packet.
3. Timestamping each packet.

The first method includes any method that prevents packets from looping, combined with some way of bounding congestion delay over the (now known) longest possible path. The second method consists of having the hop count initialized to some appropriate value and decremented each time the packet is forwarded. The network protocol simply discards any packet whose hop counter becomes zero. The third method requires each packet to bear the time it was created, with the routers agreeing to discard any packet older than some agreed-upon time. This latter method requires the router clocks to be synchronized, which itself is a nontrivial task unless synchronization is achieved external to the network, for example by using GPS or some radio station that broadcasts the precise time periodically.

In practice, we will need to guarantee not only that a packet is dead, but also that all acknowledgements to it are also dead, so we will now introduce T, which is some small multiple of the true maximum packet lifetime. The multiple is protocol dependent and simply has the effect of making T longer. If we wait a time T after a packet has been sent, we can be sure that all traces of it are now gone and that neither it nor its acknowledgements will suddenly appear out of the blue to complicate matters.

With packet lifetimes bounded, it is possible to devise a foolproof way to establish connections safely. The method described below is due to Tomlinson (1975). It solves the problem but introduces some peculiarities of its own. The method was further refined by Sunshine and Dalal (1978). Variants of it are widely used in practice, including in TCP.

To get around the problem of a machine losing all memory of where it was after a crash, Tomlinson proposed equipping each host with a time-of-day clock. The clocks at different hosts need not be synchronized. Each clock is assumed to take the form of a binary counter that increments itself at uniform intervals. Furthermore, the number of bits in the counter must equal or exceed the number of bits in the sequence numbers. Last, and most important, the clock is assumed to continue running even if the host goes down.

The basic idea is to ensure that two identically numbered TPDUs are never outstanding at the same time. When a connection is set up, the low-order k bits of the clock are used as the initial sequence number (also k bits). Thus, unlike our protocols of Chap. 3, each connection starts numbering its TPDUs with a different initial sequence number. The sequence space should be so large that by the time sequence numbers wrap around, old TPDUs with the same sequence number are long gone. This linear relation between time and initial sequence numbers is shown in Fig. 6-10.

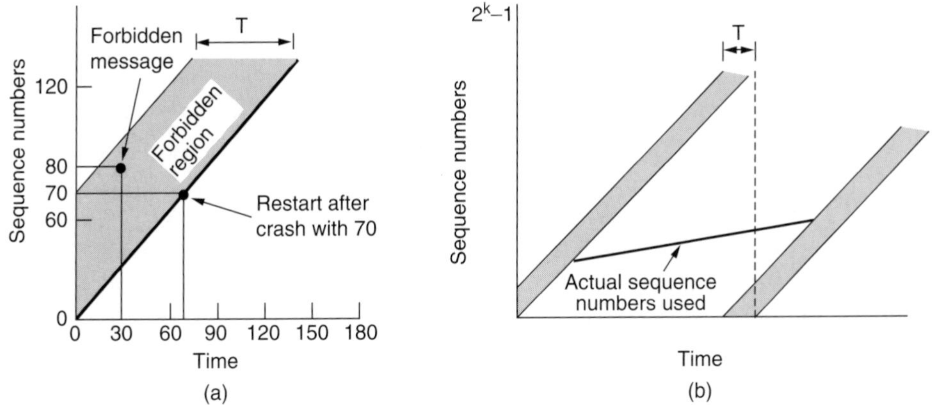

Figure 6-10. (a) TPDUs may not enter the forbidden region. (b) The resynchronization problem.

Once both transport entities have agreed on the initial sequence number, any sliding window protocol can be used for data flow control. In reality, the initial sequence number curve (shown by the heavy line) is not linear, but a staircase, since the clock advances in discrete steps. For simplicity we will ignore this detail.

A problem occurs when a host crashes. When it comes up again, its transport entity does not know where it was in the sequence space. One solution is to require transport entities to be idle for T sec after a recovery to let all old TPDUs die off. However, in a complex internetwork, T may be large, so this strategy is unattractive.

To avoid requiring T sec of dead time after a crash, it is necessary to introduce a new restriction on the use of sequence numbers. We can best see the need for this restriction by means of an example. Let T, the maximum packet lifetime, be 60 sec and let the clock tick once per second. As shown by the heavy line in Fig. 6-10(a), the initial sequence number for a connection opened at time x will be x. Imagine that at $t = 30$ sec, an ordinary data TPDU being sent on (a previously opened) connection 5 is given sequence number 80. Call this TPDU X. Immediately after sending TPDU X, the host crashes and then quickly restarts. At $t = 60$, it begins reopening connections 0 through 4. At $t = 70$, it reopens connection 5, using initial sequence number 70 as required. Within the next 15 sec it sends data TPDUs 70 through 80. Thus, at $t = 85$ a new TPDU with sequence number 80 and connection 5 has been injected into the subnet. Unfortunately, TPDU X still exists. If it should arrive at the receiver before the new TPDU 80, TPDU X will be accepted and the correct TPDU 80 will be rejected as a duplicate.

To prevent such problems, we must prevent sequence numbers from being used (i.e., assigned to new TPDUs) for a time T before their potential use as initial sequence numbers. The illegal combinations of time and sequence number are shown as the **forbidden region** in Fig. 6-10(a). Before sending any TPDU on any connection, the transport entity must read the clock and check to see that it is not in the forbidden region.

The protocol can get itself into trouble in two distinct ways. If a host sends too much data too fast on a newly-opened connection, the actual sequence number versus time curve may rise more steeply than the initial sequence number versus time curve. This means that the maximum data rate on any connection is one TPDU per clock tick. It also means that the transport entity must wait until the clock ticks before opening a new connection after a crash restart, lest the same number be used twice. Both of these points argue in favor of a short clock tick (a few μsec or less).

Unfortunately, entering the forbidden region from underneath by sending too fast is not the only way to get into trouble. From Fig. 6-10(b), we see that at any data rate less than the clock rate, the curve of actual sequence numbers used versus time will eventually run into the forbidden region from the left. The greater the slope of the actual sequence number curve, the longer this event will be delayed. As we stated above, just before sending every TPDU, the transport entity must check to see if it is about to enter the forbidden region, and if so, either delay the TPDU for T sec or resynchronize the sequence numbers.

The clock-based method solves the delayed duplicate problem for data TPDUs, but for this method to be useful, a connection must first be established. Since control TPDUs may also be delayed, there is a potential problem in getting both sides to agree on the initial sequence number. Suppose, for example, that connections are established by having host 1 send a CONNECTION REQUEST TPDU containing the proposed initial sequence number and destination port number to a remote peer, host 2. The receiver, host 2, then acknowledges this request by sending a CONNECTION ACCEPTED TPDU back. If the CONNECTION REQUEST TPDU is lost but a delayed duplicate CONNECTION REQUEST suddenly shows up at host 2, the connection will be established incorrectly.

To solve this problem, Tomlinson (1975) introduced the **three-way handshake**. This establishment protocol does not require both sides to begin sending with the same sequence number, so it can be used with synchronization methods other than the global clock method. The normal setup procedure when host 1 initiates is shown in Fig. 6-11(a). Host 1 chooses a sequence number, x, and sends a CONNECTION REQUEST TPDU containing it to host 2. Host 2 replies with an ACK TPDU acknowledging x and announcing its own initial sequence number, y. Finally, host 1 acknowledges host 2's choice of an initial sequence number in the first data TPDU that it sends.

Now let us see how the three-way handshake works in the presence of delayed duplicate control TPDUs. In Fig. 6-11(b), the first TPDU is a delayed duplicate CONNECTION REQUEST from an old connection. This TPDU arrives at host 2 without host 1's knowledge. Host 2 reacts to this TPDU by sending host 1 an

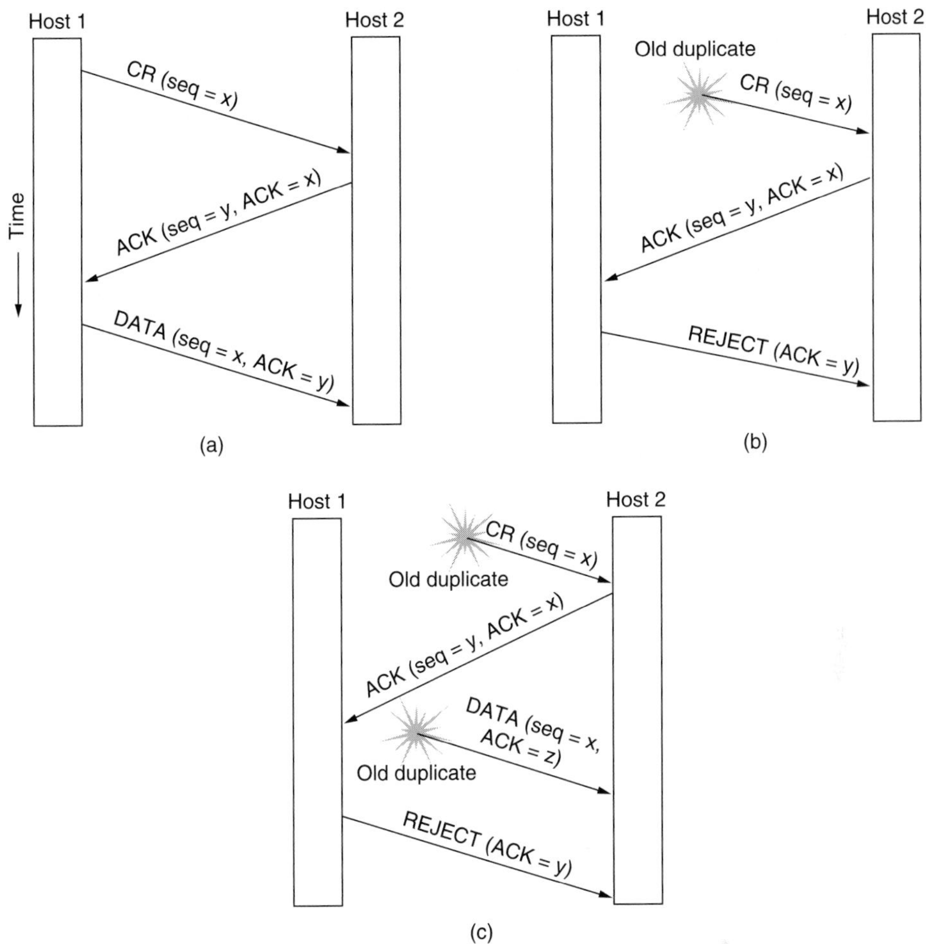

Figure 6-11. Three protocol scenarios for establishing a connection using a three-way handshake. CR denotes CONNECTION REQUEST. (a) Normal operation. (b) Old duplicate CONNECTION REQUEST appearing out of nowhere. (c) Duplicate CONNECTION REQUEST and duplicate ACK.

ACK TPDU, in effect asking for verification that host 1 was indeed trying to set up a new connection. When host 1 rejects host 2's attempt to establish a connection, host 2 realizes that it was tricked by a delayed duplicate and abandons the connection. In this way, a delayed duplicate does no damage.

The worst case is when both a delayed CONNECTION REQUEST and an ACK are floating around in the subnet. This case is shown in Fig. 6-11(c). As in the previous example, host 2 gets a delayed CONNECTION REQUEST and replies to it. At this point it is crucial to realize that host 2 has proposed using *y* as the initial sequence number for host 2 to host 1 traffic, knowing full well that no TPDUs containing sequence number y or acknowledgements to y are still in existence. When the second delayed TPDU arrives at host 2, the fact that z has been acknowledged rather than y tells host 2 that this, too, is an old duplicate. The important thing to realize here is that there is no combination of old TPDUs that can cause the protocol to fail and have a connection set up by accident when no one wants it.

6.2.3 Connection Release

Releasing a connection is easier than establishing one. Nevertheless, there are more pitfalls than one might expect. As we mentioned earlier, there are two styles of terminating a connection: asymmetric release and symmetric release. Asymmetric release is the way the telephone system works: when one party hangs up, the connection is broken. Symmetric release treats the connection as two separate unidirectional connections and requires each one to be released separately.

Asymmetric release is abrupt and may result in data loss. Consider the scenario of Fig. 6-12. After the connection is established, host 1 sends a TPDU that arrives properly at host 2. Then host 1 sends another TPDU. Unfortunately, host 2 issues a DISCONNECT before the second TPDU arrives. The result is that the connection is released and data are lost.

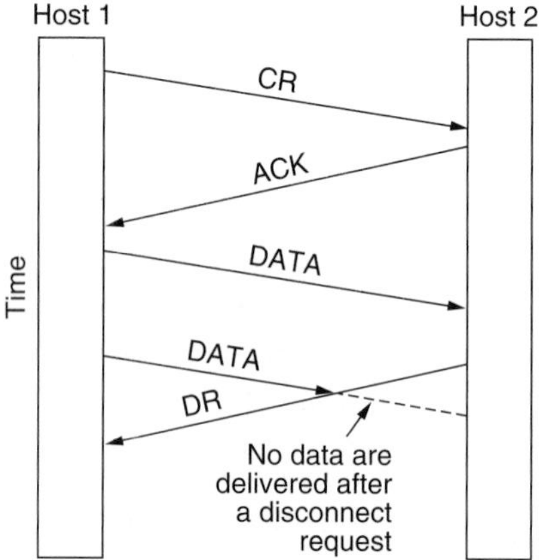

Figure 6-12. Abrupt disconnection with loss of data.

Clearly, a more sophisticated release protocol is needed to avoid data loss. One way is to use symmetric release, in which each direction is released independently of the other one. Here, a host can continue to receive data even after it has sent a DISCONNECT TPDU.

Symmetric release does the job when each process has a fixed amount of data to send and clearly knows when it has sent it. In other situations, determining that all the work has been done and the connection should be terminated is not so obvious. One can envision a protocol in which host 1 says: I am done. Are you done too? If host 2 responds: I am done too. Goodbye, the connection can be safely released.

Unfortunately, this protocol does not always work. There is a famous problem that illustrates this issue. It is called the **two-army problem**. Imagine that a white army is encamped in a valley, as shown in Fig. 6-13. On both of the surrounding hillsides are blue armies. The white army is larger than either of the blue armies alone, but together the blue armies are larger than the white army. If either blue army attacks by itself, it will be defeated, but if the two blue armies attack simultaneously, they will be victorious.

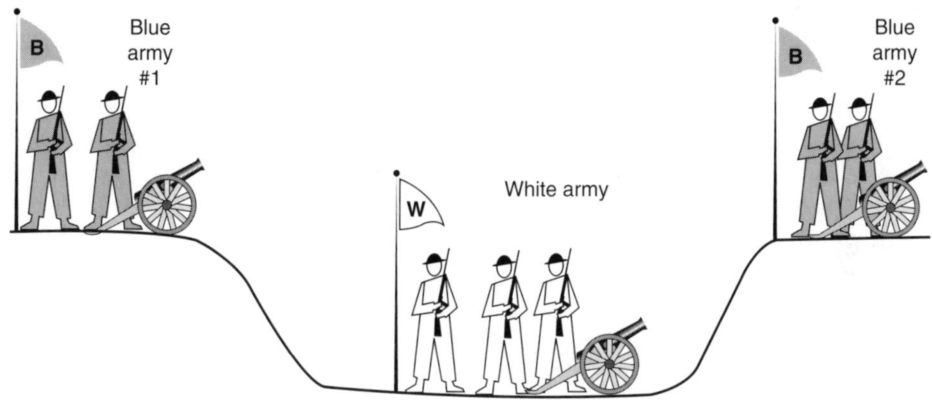

Figure 6-13. The two-army problem.

The blue armies want to synchronize their attacks. However, their only communication medium is to send messengers on foot down into the valley, where they might be captured and the message lost (i.e., they have to use an unreliable communication channel). The question is: Does a protocol exist that allows the blue armies to win?

Suppose that the commander of blue army #1 sends a message reading: "I propose we attack at dawn on March 29. How about it?" Now suppose that the message arrives, the commander of blue army #2 agrees, and his reply gets safely back to blue army #1. Will the attack happen? Probably not, because commander #2 does not know if his reply got through. If it did not, blue army #1 will not attack, so it would be foolish for him to charge into battle.

Now let us improve the protocol by making it a three-way handshake. The initiator of the original proposal must acknowledge the response. Assuming no messages are lost, blue army #2 will get the acknowledgement, but the commander of blue army #1 will now hesitate. After all, he does not know if his acknowledgement got through, and if it did not, he knows that blue army #2 will not attack. We could now make a four-way handshake protocol, but that does not help either.

In fact, it can be proven that no protocol exists that works. Suppose that some protocol did exist. Either the last message of the protocol is essential or it is not. If it is not, remove it (and any other unessential messages) until we are left with a protocol in which every message is essential. What happens if the final message does not get through? We just said that it was essential, so if it is lost, the attack does not take place. Since the sender of the final message can never be sure of its arrival, he will not risk attacking. Worse yet, the other blue army knows this, so it will not attack either.

To see the relevance of the two-army problem to releasing connections, just substitute "disconnect" for "attack." If neither side is prepared to disconnect until it is convinced that the other side is prepared to disconnect too, the disconnection will never happen.

In practice, one is usually prepared to take more risks when releasing connections than when attacking white armies, so the situation is not entirely hopeless. Figure 6-14 illustrates four scenarios of releasing using a three-way handshake. While this protocol is not infallible, it is usually adequate.

In Fig. 6-14(a), we see the normal case in which one of the users sends a DR (DISCONNECTION REQUEST) TPDU to initiate the connection release. When it arrives, the recipient sends back a DR TPDU, too, and starts a timer, just in case its DR is lost. When this DR arrives, the original sender sends back an ACK TPDU and releases the connection. Finally, when the ACK TPDU arrives, the receiver also releases the connection. Releasing a connection means that the transport entity removes the information about the connection from its table of currently open connections and signals the connection's owner (the transport user) somehow. This action is different from a transport user issuing a DISCONNECT primitive.

If the final ACK TPDU is lost, as shown in Fig. 6-14(b), the situation is saved by the timer. When the timer expires, the connection is released anyway.

Now consider the case of the second DR being lost. The user initiating the disconnection will not receive the expected response, will time out, and will start all over again. In Fig. 6-14(c) we see how this works, assuming that the second time no TPDUs are lost and all TPDUs are delivered correctly and on time.

Our last scenario, Fig. 6-14(d), is the same as Fig. 6-14(c) except that now we assume all the repeated attempts to retransmit the DR also fail due to lost TPDUs. After *N* retries, the sender just gives up and releases the connection. Meanwhile, the receiver times out and also exits.

While this protocol usually suffices, in theory it can fail if the initial DR and *N* retransmissions are all lost. The sender will give up and release the connection, while the other side knows nothing at all about the attempts to disconnect and is still fully active. This situation results in a half-open connection.

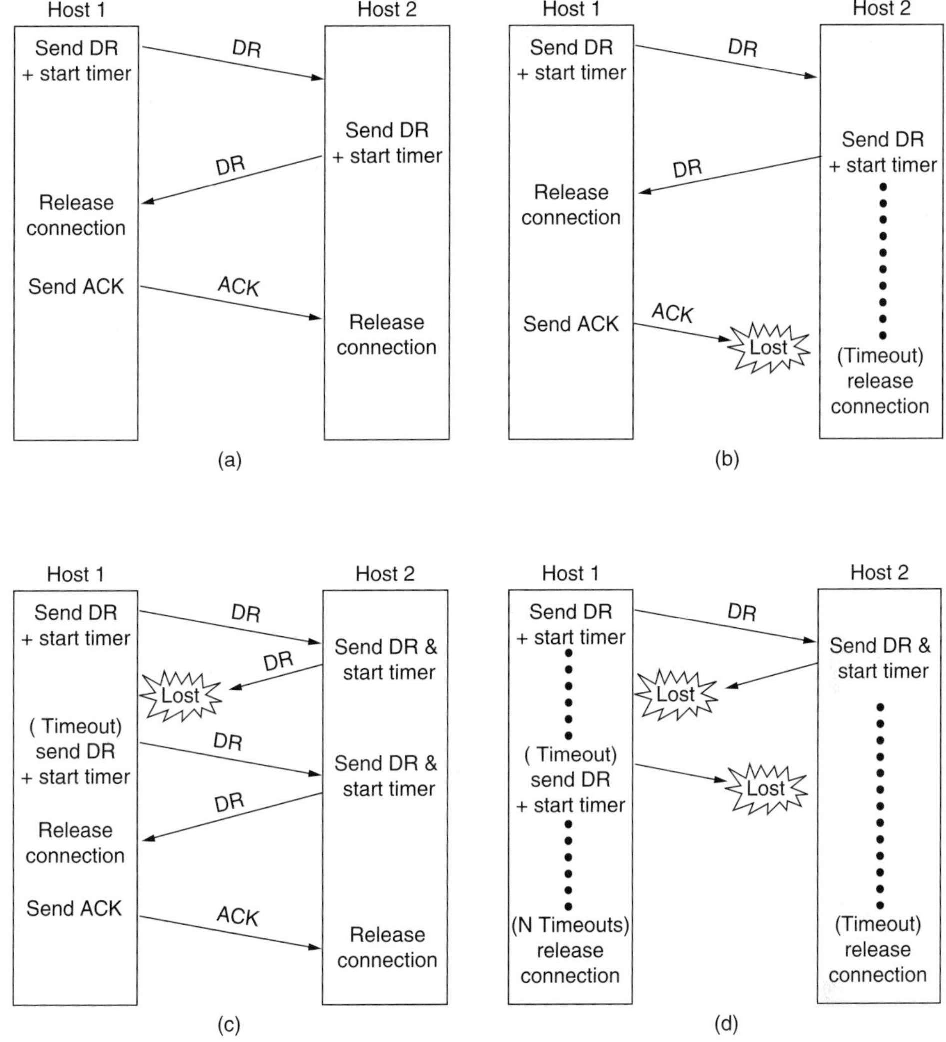

Figure 6-14. Four protocol scenarios for releasing a connection. (a) Normal case of three-way handshake. (b) Final ACK lost. (c) Response lost. (d) Response lost and subsequent DRs lost.

We could have avoided this problem by not allowing the sender to give up after *N* retries but forcing it to go on forever until it gets a response. However, if the other side is allowed to time out, then the sender will indeed go on forever, because no response will ever be forthcoming. If we do not allow the receiving side to time out, then the protocol hangs in Fig. 6-14(d).

One way to kill off half-open connections is to have a rule saying that if no TPDUs have arrived for a certain number of seconds, the connection is then automatically disconnected. That way, if one side ever disconnects, the other side will detect the lack of activity and also disconnect. Of course, if this rule is introduced, it is necessary for each transport entity to have a timer that is stopped and then restarted whenever a TPDU is sent. If this timer expires, a dummy TPDU is transmitted, just to keep the other side from disconnecting. On the other hand, if the automatic disconnect rule is used and too many dummy TPDUs in a row are lost on an otherwise idle connection, first one side, then the other side will automatically disconnect.

We will not belabor this point any more, but by now it should be clear that releasing a connection without data loss is not nearly as simple as it at first appears.

6.2.4 Flow Control and Buffering

Having examined connection establishment and release in some detail, let us now look at how connections are managed while they are in use. One of the key issues has come up before: flow control. In some ways the flow control problem in the transport layer is the same as in the data link layer, but in other ways it is different. The basic similarity is that in both layers a sliding window or other scheme is needed on each connection to keep a fast transmitter from overrunning a slow receiver. The main difference is that a router usually has relatively few lines, whereas a host may have numerous connections. This difference makes it impractical to implement the data link buffering strategy in the transport layer.

In the data link protocols of Chap. 3, frames were buffered at both the sending router and at the receiving router. In protocol 6, for example, both sender and receiver are required to dedicate $MAX\_SEQ + 1$ buffers to each line, half for input and half for output. For a host with a maximum of, say, 64 connections, and a 4-bit sequence number, this protocol would require 1024 buffers.

In the data link layer, the sending side must buffer outgoing frames because they might have to be retransmitted. If the subnet provides datagram service, the sending transport entity must also buffer, and for the same reason. If the receiver knows that the sender buffers all TPDUs until they are acknowledged, the receiver may or may not dedicate specific buffers to specific connections, as it sees fit. The receiver may, for example, maintain a single buffer pool shared by all connections. When a TPDU comes in, an attempt is made to dynamically acquire a new buffer. If one is available, the TPDU is accepted; otherwise, it is discarded. Since the sender is prepared to retransmit TPDUs lost by the subnet, no harm is done by having the receiver drop TPDUs, although some resources are wasted. The sender just keeps trying until it gets an acknowledgement.

In summary, if the network service is unreliable, the sender must buffer all TPDUs sent, just as in the data link layer. However, with reliable network service, other trade-offs become possible. In particular, if the sender knows that the receiver always has buffer space, it need not retain copies of the TPDUs it sends. However, if the receiver cannot guarantee that every incoming TPDU will be accepted, the sender will have to buffer anyway. In the latter case, the sender cannot trust the network layer's acknowledgement, because the acknowledgement means only that the TPDU arrived, not that it was accepted. We will come back to this important point later.

Even if the receiver has agreed to do the buffering, there still remains the question of the buffer size. If most TPDUs are nearly the same size, it is natural to organize the buffers as a pool of identically-sized buffers, with one TPDU per buffer, as in Fig. 6-15(a). However, if there is wide variation in TPDU size, from a few characters typed at a terminal to thousands of characters from file transfers, a pool of fixed-sized buffers presents problems. If the buffer size is chosen equal to the largest possible TPDU, space will be wasted whenever a short TPDU arrives. If the buffer size is chosen less than the maximum TPDU size, multiple buffers will be needed for long TPDUs, with the attendant complexity.

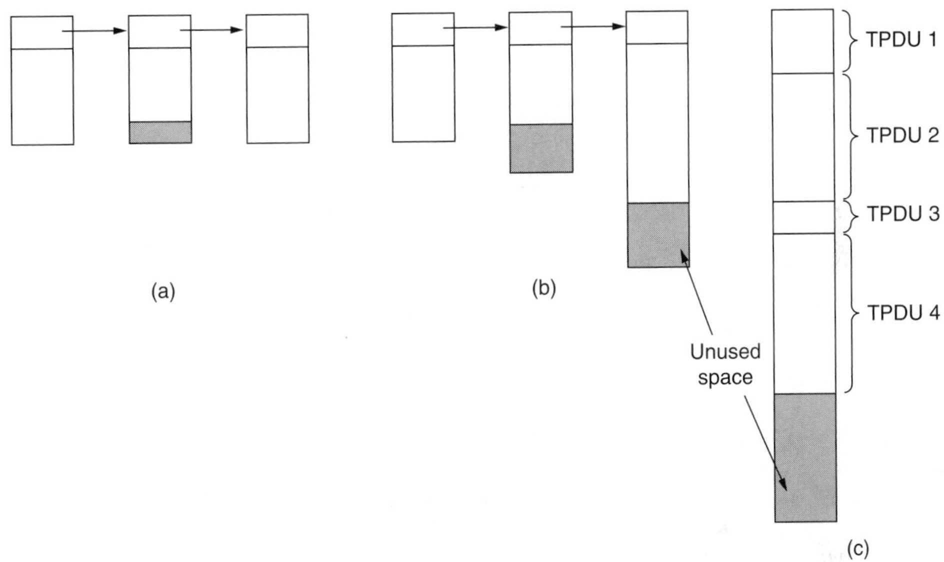

Figure 6-15. (a) Chained fixed-size buffers. (b) Chained variable-sized buffers. (c) One large circular buffer per connection.

Another approach to the buffer size problem is to use variable-sized buffers, as in Fig. 6-15(b). The advantage here is better memory utilization, at the price of more complicated buffer management. A third possibility is to dedicate a single large circular buffer per connection, as in Fig. 6-15(c). This system also makes good use of memory, provided that all connections are heavily loaded, but is poor if some connections are lightly loaded.

The optimum trade-off between source buffering and destination buffering depends on the type of traffic carried by the connection. For low-bandwidth bursty traffic, such as that produced by an interactive terminal, it is better not to dedicate any buffers, but rather to acquire them dynamically at both ends. Since the sender cannot be sure the receiver will be able to acquire a buffer, the sender must retain a copy of the TPDU until it is acknowledged. On the other hand, for file transfer and other high-bandwidth traffic, it is better if the receiver does dedicate a full window of buffers, to allow the data to flow at maximum speed. Thus, for low-bandwidth bursty traffic, it is better to buffer at the sender, and for high-bandwidth smooth traffic, it is better to buffer at the receiver.

As connections are opened and closed and as the traffic pattern changes, the sender and receiver need to dynamically adjust their buffer allocations. Consequently, the transport protocol should allow a sending host to request buffer space at the other end. Buffers could be allocated per connection, or collectively, for all the connections running between the two hosts. Alternatively, the receiver, knowing its buffer situation (but not knowing the offered traffic) could tell the sender "I have reserved *X* buffers for you." If the number of open connections should increase, it may be necessary for an allocation to be reduced, so the protocol should provide for this possibility.

A reasonably general way to manage dynamic buffer allocation is to decouple the buffering from the acknowledgements, in contrast to the sliding window protocols of Chap. 3. Dynamic buffer management means, in effect, a variable-sized window. Initially, the sender requests a certain number of buffers, based on its perceived needs. The receiver then grants as many of these as it can afford. Every time the sender transmits a TPDU, it must decrement its allocation, stopping altogether when the allocation reaches zero. The receiver then separately piggybacks both acknowledgements and buffer allocations onto the reverse traffic.

Figure 6-16 shows an example of how dynamic window management might work in a datagram subnet with 4-bit sequence numbers. Assume that buffer allocation information travels in separate TPDUs, as shown, and is not piggybacked onto reverse traffic. Initially, *A* wants eight buffers, but is granted only four of these. It then sends three TPDUs, of which the third is lost. TPDU 6 acknowledges receipt of all TPDUs up to and including sequence number 1, thus allowing *A* to release those buffers, and furthermore informs *A* that it has permission to send three more TPDUs starting beyond 1 (i.e., TPDUs 2, 3, and 4). *A* knows that it has already sent number 2, so it thinks that it may send TPDUs 3 and 4, which it proceeds to do. At this point it is blocked and must wait for more buffer allocation. Timeout-induced retransmissions (line 9), however, may occur while blocked, since they use buffers that have already been allocated. In line 10, *B* acknowledges receipt of all TPDUs up to and including 4 but refuses to let *A* continue. Such a situation is impossible with the fixed window protocols of Chap. 3. The next TPDU from *B* to *A* allocates another buffer and allows *A* to continue.

Potential problems with buffer allocation schemes of this kind can arise in datagram networks if control TPDUs can get lost. Look at line 16. *B* has now allocated more buffers to *A*, but the allocation TPDU was lost. Since control TPDUs are not sequenced or timed out, *A* is now deadlocked. To prevent this sit-

	A	Message	B	Comments
1	→	< request 8 buffers>	→	A wants 8 buffers
2	←	<ack = 15, buf = 4>	←	B grants messages 0-3 only
3	→	<seq = 0, data = m0>	→	A has 3 buffers left now
4	→	<seq = 1, data = m1>	→	A has 2 buffers left now
5	→	<seq = 2, data = m2>	• • •	Message lost but A thinks it has 1 left
6	←	<ack = 1, buf = 3>	←	B acknowledges 0 and 1, permits 2-4
7	→	<seq = 3, data = m3>	→	A has 1 buffer left
8	→	<seq = 4, data = m4>	→	A has 0 buffers left, and must stop
9	→	<seq = 2, data = m2>	→	A times out and retransmits
10	←	<ack = 4, buf = 0>	←	Everything acknowledged, but A still blocked
11	←	<ack = 4, buf = 1>	←	A may now send 5
12	←	<ack = 4, buf = 2>	←	B found a new buffer somewhere
13	→	<seq = 5, data = m5>	→	A has 1 buffer left
14	→	<seq = 6, data = m6>	→	A is now blocked again
15	←	<ack = 6, buf = 0>	←	A is still blocked
16	• • •	<ack = 6, buf = 4>	←	Potential deadlock

Figure 6-16. Dynamic buffer allocation. The arrows show the direction of transmission. An ellipsis (...) indicates a lost TPDU.

uation, each host should periodically send control TPDUs giving the acknowledgement and buffer status on each connection. That way, the deadlock will be broken, sooner or later.

Until now we have tacitly assumed that the only limit imposed on the sender's data rate is the amount of buffer space available in the receiver. As memory prices continue to fall dramatically, it may become feasible to equip hosts with so much memory that lack of buffers is rarely, if ever, a problem.

When buffer space no longer limits the maximum flow, another bottleneck will appear: the carrying capacity of the subnet. If adjacent routers can exchange at most x packets/sec and there are k disjoint paths between a pair of hosts, there is no way that those hosts can exchange more than kx TPDUs/sec, no matter how much buffer space is available at each end. If the sender pushes too hard (i.e., sends more than kx TPDUs/sec), the subnet will become congested because it will be unable to deliver TPDUs as fast as they are coming in.

What is needed is a mechanism based on the subnet's carrying capacity rather than on the receiver's buffering capacity. Clearly, the flow control mechanism must be applied at the sender to prevent it from having too many unacknowledged TPDUs outstanding at once. Belsnes (1975) proposed using a sliding window flow control scheme in which the sender dynamically adjusts the window size to match the network's carrying capacity. If the network can handle c TPDUs/sec and the cycle time (including transmission, propagation, queueing, processing at the receiver, and return of the acknowledgement) is r, then the sender's window should be cr. With a window of this size the sender normally operates with the pipeline full. Any small decrease in network performance will cause it to block.

In order to adjust the window size periodically, the sender could monitor both parameters and then compute the desired window size. The carrying capacity can be determined by simply counting the number of TPDUs acknowledged during some time period and then dividing by the time period. During the measurement, the sender should send as fast as it can, to make sure that the network's carrying capacity, and not the low input rate, is the factor limiting the acknowledgement rate. The time required for a transmitted TPDU to be acknowledged can be measured exactly and a running mean maintained. Since the network capacity available to any given flow varies in time, the window size should be adjusted frequently, to track changes in the carrying capacity. As we will see later, the Internet uses a similar scheme.

6.2.5 Multiplexing

Multiplexing several conversations onto connections, virtual circuits, and physical links plays a role in several layers of the network architecture. In the transport layer the need for multiplexing can arise in a number of ways. For example, if only one network address is available on a host, all transport connections on that machine have to use it. When a TPDU comes in, some way is needed to tell which process to give it to. This situation, called **upward multiplexing**, is shown in Fig. 6-17(a). In this figure, four distinct transport connections all use the same network connection (e.g., IP address) to the remote host.

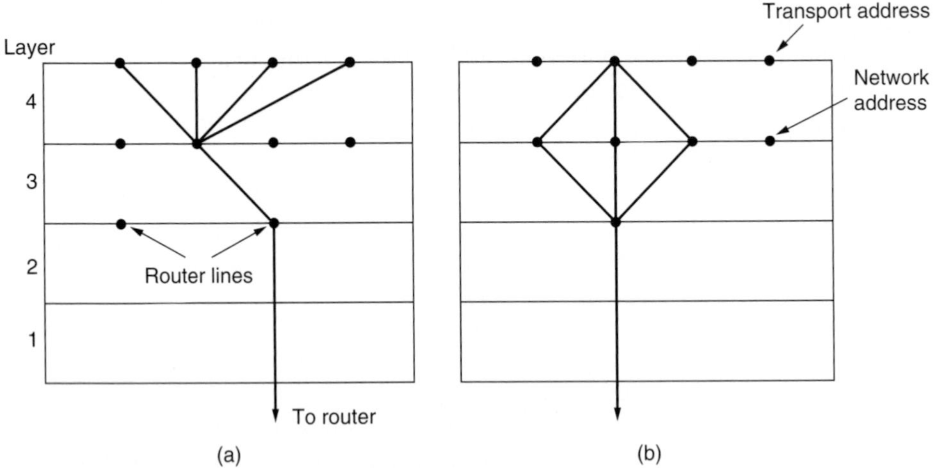

Figure 6-17. (a) Upward multiplexing. (b) Downward multiplexing.

Multiplexing can also be useful in the transport layer for another reason. Suppose, for example, that a subnet uses virtual circuits internally and imposes a maximum data rate on each one. If a user needs more bandwidth than one virtual circuit can provide, a way out is to open multiple network connections and distribute the traffic among them on a round-robin basis, as indicated in Fig. 6-17(b). This modus operandi is called **downward multiplexing**. With *k* network connections open, the effective bandwidth is increased by a factor of *k*. A common example of downward multiplexing occurs with home users who have an ISDN line. This line provides for two separate connections of 64 kbps each. Using both of them to call an Internet provider and dividing the traffic over both lines makes it possible to achieve an effective bandwidth of 128 kbps.

6.2.6 Crash Recovery

If hosts and routers are subject to crashes, recovery from these crashes becomes an issue. If the transport entity is entirely within the hosts, recovery from network and router crashes is straightforward. If the network layer provides datagram service, the transport entities expect lost TPDUs all the time and know how to cope with them. If the network layer provides connection-oriented service, then loss of a virtual circuit is handled by establishing a new one and then probing the remote transport entity to ask it which TPDUs it has received and which ones it has not received. The latter ones can be retransmitted.

A more troublesome problem is how to recover from host crashes. In particular, it may be desirable for clients to be able to continue working when servers crash and then quickly reboot. To illustrate the difficulty, let us assume that one host, the client, is sending a long file to another host, the file server, using a simple stop-and-wait protocol. The transport layer on the server simply passes the incoming TPDUs to the transport user, one by one. Partway through the transmission, the server crashes. When it comes back up, its tables are reinitialized, so it no longer knows precisely where it was.

In an attempt to recover its previous status, the server might send a broadcast TPDU to all other hosts, announcing that it had just crashed and requesting that its clients inform it of the status of all open connections. Each client can be in one of two states: one TPDU outstanding, *S1*, or no TPDUs outstanding, *S0*. Based on only this state information, the client must decide whether to retransmit the most recent TPDU.

At first glance it would seem obvious: the client should retransmit only if and only if it has an unacknowledged TPDU outstanding (i.e., is in state *S1*) when it learns of the crash. However, a closer inspection reveals difficulties with this naive approach. Consider, for example, the situation in which the server's transport entity first sends an acknowledgement, and then, when the acknowledgement has been sent, writes to the application process. Writing a TPDU onto the output stream and sending an acknowledgement are two distinct events that cannot be done simultaneously. If a crash occurs after the acknowledgement has been sent but before the write has been done, the client will receive the acknowledgement and thus be in state *S0* when the crash recovery announcement arrives. The client will therefore not retransmit, (incorrectly) thinking that the TPDU has arrived. This decision by the client leads to a missing TPDU.

At this point you may be thinking: "That problem can be solved easily. All you have to do is reprogram the transport entity to first do the write and then send the acknowledgement." Try again. Imagine that the write has been done but the crash occurs before the acknowledgement can be sent. The client will be in state *S1* and thus retransmit, leading to an undetected duplicate TPDU in the output stream to the server application process.

No matter how the client and server are programmed, there are always situations where the protocol fails to recover properly. The server can be programmed in one of two ways: acknowledge first or write first. The client can be programmed in one of four ways: always retransmit the last TPDU, never retransmit the last TPDU, retransmit only in state *S0*, or retransmit only in state *S1*. This gives eight combinations, but as we shall see, for each combination there is some set of events that makes the protocol fail.

Three events are possible at the server: sending an acknowledgement (*A*), writing to the output process (*W*), and crashing (*C*). The three events can occur in six different orderings: *AC*(*W*), *AWC*, *C*(*AW*), *C*(*WA*), *WAC*, and *WC*(*A*), where the parentheses are used to indicate that neither *A* nor *W* can follow *C* (i.e., once it has crashed, it has crashed). Figure 6-18 shows all eight combinations of client and server strategy and the valid event sequences for each one. Notice that for each strategy there is some sequence of events that causes the protocol to fail. For example, if the client always retransmits, the *AWC* event will generate an undetected duplicate, even though the other two events work properly.

Making the protocol more elaborate does not help. Even if the client and server exchange several TPDUs before the server attempts to write, so that the client knows exactly what is about to happen, the client has no way of knowing whether a crash occurred just before or just after the write. The conclusion is inescapable: under our ground rules of no simultaneous events, host crash and recovery cannot be made transparent to higher layers.

Put in more general terms, this result can be restated as recovery from a layer N crash can only be done by layer $N + 1$, and then only if the higher layer retains enough status information. As mentioned above, the transport layer can recover from failures in the network layer, provided that each end of a connection keeps track of where it is.

This problem gets us into the issue of what a so-called end-to-end acknowledgement really means. In principle, the transport protocol is end-to-end and not chained like the lower layers. Now consider the case of a user entering requests for transactions against a remote database. Suppose that the remote transport entity is programmed to first pass TPDUs to the next layer up and then acknowl-

Strategy used by sending host	Strategy used by receiving host: First ACK, then write			First write, then ACK		
	AC(W)	AWC	C(AW)	C(WA)	W AC	WC(A)
Always retransmit	OK	DUP	OK	OK	DUP	DUP
Never retransmit	LOST	OK	LOST	LOST	OK	OK
Retransmit in S0	OK	DUP	LOST	LOST	DUP	OK
Retransmit in S1	LOST	OK	OK	OK	OK	DUP

OK = Protocol functions correctly
DUP = Protocol generates a duplicate message
LOST = Protocol loses a message

Figure 6-18. Different combinations of client and server strategy.

edge. Even in this case, the receipt of an acknowledgement back at the user's machine does not necessarily mean that the remote host stayed up long enough to actually update the database. A truly end-to-end acknowledgement, whose receipt means that the work has actually been done and lack thereof means that it has not, is probably impossible to achieve. This point is discussed in more detail by Saltzer et al. (1984).

6.3 A SIMPLE TRANSPORT PROTOCOL

To make the ideas discussed so far more concrete, in this section we will study an example transport layer in detail. The abstract service primitives we will use are the connection-oriented primitives of Fig. 6-2. The choice of these connection-oriented primitives makes the example similar to (but simpler than) the popular TCP protocol.

6.3.1 The Example Service Primitives

Our first problem is how to express these transport primitives concretely. CONNECT is easy: we will just have a library procedure *connect* that can be called with the appropriate parameters necessary to establish a connection. The parameters are the local and remote TSAPs. During the call, the caller is blocked (i.e., suspended) while the transport entity tries to set up the connection. If the connection succeeds, the caller is unblocked and can start transmitting data.

When a process wants to be able to accept incoming calls, it calls *listen*, specifying a particular TSAP to listen to. The process then blocks until some remote process attempts to establish a connection to its TSAP.

Note that this model is highly asymmetric. One side is passive, executing a *listen* and waiting until something happens. The other side is active and initiates the connection. An interesting question arises of what to do if the active side begins first. One strategy is to have the connection attempt fail if there is no listener at the remote TSAP. Another strategy is to have the initiator block (possibly forever) until a listener appears.

A compromise, used in our example, is to hold the connection request at the receiving end for a certain time interval. If a process on that host calls *listen* before the timer goes off, the connection is established; otherwise, it is rejected and the caller is unblocked and given an error return.

To release a connection, we will use a procedure *disconnect*. When both sides have disconnected, the connection is released. In other words, we are using a symmetric disconnection model.

Data transmission has precisely the same problem as connection establishment: sending is active but receiving is passive. We will use the same solution for data transmission as for connection establishment: an active call *send* that transmits data and a passive call *receive* that blocks until a TPDU arrives.

Our concrete service definition therefore consists of five primitives: CONNECT, LISTEN, DISCONNECT, SEND, and RECEIVE. Each primitive corresponds exactly to a library procedure that executes the primitive. The parameters for the service primitives and library procedures are as follows:

```
connum = LISTEN(local)
connum = CONNECT(local, remote)
status  = SEND(connum, buffer, bytes)
status  = RECEIVE(connum, buffer, bytes)
status  = DISCONNECT(connum)
```

The LISTEN primitive announces the caller's willingness to accept connection requests directed at the indicated TSAP. The user of the primitive is blocked until an attempt is made to connect to it. There is no timeout.

The CONNECT primitive takes two parameters, a local TSAP (i.e., transport address), *local*, and a remote TSAP, *remote*, and tries to establish a transport connection between the two. If it succeeds, it returns in *connum* a nonnegative number used to identify the connection on subsequent calls. If it fails, the reason for failure is put in *connum* as a negative number. In our simple model, each TSAP may participate in only one transport connection, so a possible reason for failure is that one of the transport addresses is currently in use. Some other reasons are remote host down, illegal local address, and illegal remote address.

The SEND primitive transmits the contents of the buffer as a message on the indicated transport connection, in several units if need be. Possible errors, returned in *status*, are no connection, illegal buffer address, or negative count.

The RECEIVE primitive indicates the caller's desire to accept data. The size of the incoming message is placed in *bytes*. If the remote process has released the connection or the buffer address is illegal (e.g., outside the user's program), *status* is set to an error code indicating the nature of the problem.

The DISCONNECT primitive terminates a transport connection. The parameter *connum* tells which one. Possible errors are *connum* belongs to another process or *connum* is not a valid connection identifier. The error code, or 0 for success, is returned in *status*.

6.3.2 The Example Transport Entity

Before looking at the code of the example transport entity, please be sure you realize that this example is analogous to the early examples presented in Chap. 3: it is more for pedagogical purposes than a serious proposal. Many of the technical details (such as extensive error checking) that would be needed in a production system have been omitted here for the sake of simplicity.

The transport layer makes use of the network service primitives to send and receive TPDUs. For this example, we need to choose network service primitives to use. One choice would have been unreliable datagram service. To keep the example simple, we have not made that choice. With unreliable datagram service, the transport code would have been large and complex, mostly dealing with lost and delayed packets. Furthermore, most of these ideas have already been discussed at length in Chap. 3.

Instead, we have chosen to use a connection-oriented, reliable network service. This way we can focus on transport issues that do not occur in the lower layers. These include connection establishment, connection release, and credit management, among others. A simple transport service built on top of an ATM network might look something like this.

In general, the transport entity may be part of the host's operating system, or it may be a package of library routines running within the user's address space. For simplicity, our example has been programmed as though it were a library package, but the changes needed to make it part of the operating system are minimal (primarily how user buffers are accessed).

It is worth noting, however, that in this example, the "transport entity" is not really a separate entity at all, but part of the user process. In particular, when the user executes a primitive that blocks, such as LISTEN, the entire transport entity blocks as well. While this design is fine for a host with only a single-user process, on a host with multiple users, it would be more natural to have the transport entity be a separate process, distinct from all the user processes.

The interface to the network layer is via the procedures *to_net* and *from_net* (not shown). Each has six parameters. First comes the connection identifier, which maps one-to-one onto network virtual circuits. Next come the *Q* and *M* bits, which, when set to 1, indicate control message and that more data from this message follows in the next packet, respectively. After that we have the packet type, chosen from the set of six packet types listed in Fig. 6-19. Finally, we have a pointer to the data itself, and an integer giving the number of bytes of data.

Network packet	Meaning
CALL REQUEST	Sent to establish a connection
CALL ACCEPTED	Response to CALL REQUEST
CLEAR REQUEST	Sent to release a connection
CLEAR CONFIRMATION	Response to CLEAR REQUEST
DATA	Used to transport data
CREDIT	Control packet for managing the window

Figure 6-19. The network layer packets used in our example.

On calls to *to_net*, the transport entity fills in all the parameters for the network layer to read; on calls to *from_net*, the network layer dismembers an incoming packet for the transport entity. By passing information as procedure parameters rather than passing the actual outgoing or incoming packet itself, the transport layer is shielded from the details of the network layer protocol. If the transport entity should attempt to send a packet when the underlying virtual circuit's sliding window is full, it is suspended within *to_net* until there is room in the window. This mechanism is entirely transparent to the transport entity and is controlled by the network layer using commands analogous to the *enable_transport_layer* and *disable_transport_layer* commands used in the protocols of Chap. 3. The management of the packet layer window is also done by the network layer.

In addition to this transparent suspension mechanism, explicit *sleep* and *wakeup* procedures (not shown) are also called by the transport entity. The procedure *sleep* is called when the transport entity is logically blocked waiting for an external event to happen, generally the arrival of a packet. After *sleep* has been called, the transport entity (and the user process, of course) stop executing.

The actual code of the transport entity is shown in Fig. 6-20. Each connection is always in one of seven states, as follows:

1. IDLE—Connection not established yet.
2. WAITING—CONNECT has been executed and CALL REQUEST sent.
3. QUEUED—A CALL REQUEST has arrived; no LISTEN yet.
4. ESTABLISHED—The connection has been established.
5. SENDING—The user is waiting for permission to send a packet.
6. RECEIVING—A RECEIVE has been done.
7. DISCONNECTING—A DISCONNECT has been done locally.

Transitions between states can occur when any of the following events occur: a primitive is executed, a packet arrives, or the timer expires.

The procedures shown in Fig. 6-20 are of two types. Most are directly callable by user programs. *Packet_arrival* and *clock* are different, however. They are spontaneously triggered by external events: the arrival of a packet and the clock ticking, respectively. In effect, they are interrupt routines. We will assume that they are never invoked while a transport entity procedure is running. Only when the user process is sleeping or executing outside the transport entity may they be called. This property is crucial to the correct functioning of the code.

The existence of the Q (Qualifier) bit in the packet header allows us to avoid the overhead of a transport protocol header. Ordinary data messages are sent as data packets with $Q = 0$. Transport protocol control messages, of which there is only one (CREDIT) in our example, are sent as data packets with $Q = 1$. These control messages are detected and processed by the receiving transport entity.

The main data structure used by the transport entity is the array *conn*, which has one record for each potential connection. The record maintains the state of the connection, including the transport addresses at either end, the number of messages sent and received on the connection, the current state, the user buffer pointer, the number of bytes of the current messages sent or received so far, a bit indicating that the remote user has issued a DISCONNECT, a timer, and a permission counter used to enable sending of messages. Not all of these fields are used in our simple example, but a complete transport entity would need all of them, and perhaps more. Each *conn* entry is assumed initialized to the *IDLE* state.

When the user calls CONNECT, the network layer is instructed to send a CALL REQUEST packet to the remote machine, and the user is put to sleep. When the CALL REQUEST packet arrives at the other side, the transport entity is interrupted to run *packet_arrival* to check whether the local user is listening on the specified address. If so, a CALL ACCEPTED packet is sent back and the remote user is awakened; if not, the CALL REQUEST is queued for *TIMEOUT* clock ticks. If a LISTEN is done within this period, the connection is established; otherwise, it times out and is rejected with a CLEAR REQUEST packet lest it block forever.

Although we have eliminated the transport protocol header, we still need a way to keep track of which packet belongs to which transport connection, since multiple connections may exist simultaneously. The simplest approach is to use the network layer virtual circuit number as the transport connection number. Furthermore, the virtual circuit number can also be used as the index into the *conn* array. When a packet comes in on network layer virtual circuit k, it belongs to transport connection k, whose state is in the record *conn*[k]. For connections initiated at a host, the connection number is chosen by the originating transport entity. For incoming calls, the network layer makes the choice, choosing any unused virtual circuit number.

To avoid having to provide and manage buffers within the transport entity, here we use a flow control mechanism different from the normal sliding window.

```
#define MAX_CONN 32                        /* max number of simultaneous connections */
#define MAX_MSG_SIZE 8192                  /* largest message in bytes */
#define MAX_PKT_SIZE 512                   /* largest packet in bytes */
#define TIMEOUT 20
#define CRED 1
#define OK 0

#define ERR_FULL -1
#define ERR_REJECT -2
#define ERR_CLOSED -3
#define LOW_ERR -3

typedef int transport_address;
typedef enum {CALL_REQ,CALL_ACC,CLEAR_REQ,CLEAR_CONF,DATA_PKT,CREDIT} pkt_type;
typedef enum {IDLE,WAITING,QUEUED,ESTABLISHED,SENDING,RECEIVING,DISCONN} cstate;

/* Global variables. */
transport_address listen_address;          /* local address being listened to */
int listen_conn;                           /* connection identifier for listen */
unsigned char data[MAX_PKT_SIZE];          /* scratch area for packet data */

struct conn {
  transport_address local_address, remote_address;
  cstate state;                            /* state of this connection */
  unsigned char *user_buf_addr;            /* pointer to receive buffer */
  int byte_count;                          /* send/receive count */
  int clr_req_received;                    /* set when CLEAR_REQ packet received */
  int timer;                               /* used to time out CALL_REQ packets */
  int credits;                             /* number of messages that may be sent */
} conn[MAX_CONN + 1];                      /* slot 0 is not used */

void sleep(void);                          /* prototypes */
void wakeup(void);
void to_net(int cid, int q, int m, pkt_type pt, unsigned char *p, int bytes);
void from_net(int *cid, int *q, int *m, pkt_type *pt, unsigned char *p, int *bytes);

int listen(transport_address t)
{ /* User wants to listen for a connection. See if CALL_REQ has already arrived. */
  int i, found = 0;

  for (i = 1; i <= MAX_CONN; i++)          /* search the table for CALL_REQ */
     if (conn[i].state == QUEUED && conn[i].local_address == t) {
          found = i;
          break;
     }

  if (found == 0) {
     /* No CALL_REQ is waiting. Go to sleep until arrival or timeout. */
     listen_address = t; sleep(); i = listen_conn ;
  }
  conn[i].state = ESTABLISHED;             /* connection is ESTABLISHED */
  conn[i].timer = 0;                       /* timer is not used */
```

```
  listen_conn = 0;                          /* 0 is assumed to be an invalid address */
  to_net(i, 0, 0, CALL_ACC, data, 0);       /* tell net to accept connection */
  return(i);                                /* return connection identifier */
}

int connect(transport_address l, transport_address r)
{ /* User wants to connect to a remote process;  send CALL_REQ packet. */
  int i;
  struct conn *cptr;

  data[0] = r;   data[1] = l;               /* CALL_REQ packet needs these */
  i = MAX_CONN;                             /* search table backward */
  while (conn[i].state != IDLE && i > 1) i = i – 1;
  if (conn[i].state == IDLE) {
      /* Make a table entry that CALL_REQ has been sent. */
      cptr = &conn[i];
      cptr->local_address = l; cptr->remote_address = r;
      cptr->state = WAITING; cptr->clr_req_received = 0;
      cptr->credits = 0; cptr->timer = 0;
      to_net(i, 0, 0, CALL_REQ, data, 2);
      sleep();                              /* wait for CALL_ACC or CLEAR_REQ */
      if (cptr->state == ESTABLISHED) return(i);
      if (cptr->clr_req_received) {
            /* Other side refused call. */
            cptr->state = IDLE;             /* back to IDLE state */
            to_net(i, 0, 0, CLEAR_CONF, data, 0);
            return(ERR_REJECT);
      }
  } else return(ERR_FULL);                  /* reject CONNECT: no table space */
}

int send(int cid, unsigned char bufptr[], int bytes)
{ /* User wants to send a message. */
  int i, count, m;
  struct conn *cptr = &conn[cid];

  /* Enter SENDING state. */
  cptr->state = SENDING;
  cptr->byte_count = 0;                     /* # bytes sent so far this message */
  if (cptr->clr_req_received == 0 && cptr->credits == 0) sleep();
  if (cptr->clr_req_received == 0) {
      /* Credit available; split message into packets if need be. */
      do {
            if (bytes – cptr->byte_count > MAX_PKT_SIZE) {/* multipacket message */
                  count = MAX_PKT_SIZE;  m = 1;  /* more packets later */
            } else {                        /* single packet message */
                  count = bytes – cptr->byte_count;  m = 0;    /* last pkt of this message */
            }
            for (i = 0; i < count; i++) data[i] = bufptr[cptr->byte_count + i];
            to_net(cid, 0, m, DATA_PKT, data, count);  /* send 1 packet */
            cptr->byte_count = cptr->byte_count + count;      /* increment bytes sent so far */
      } while (cptr->byte_count < bytes);           /* loop until whole message sent */
```

```
      cptr->credits−−;                        /* each message uses up one credit */
      cptr->state = ESTABLISHED;
      return(OK);
  } else {
      cptr->state = ESTABLISHED;
      return(ERR_CLOSED);                     /* send failed: peer wants to disconnect */
  }
}

int receive(int cid, unsigned char bufptr[], int *bytes)
{ /* User is prepared to receive a message. */
  struct conn *cptr = &conn[cid];

  if (cptr->clr_req_received == 0) {
      /* Connection still established; try to receive. */
      cptr->state = RECEIVING;
      cptr->user_buf_addr = bufptr;
      cptr->byte_count = 0;
      data[0] = CRED;
      data[1] = 1;
      to_net(cid, 1, 0, CREDIT, data, 2);     /* send credit */
      sleep();                                /* block awaiting data */
      *bytes = cptr->byte_count;
  }
  cptr->state = ESTABLISHED;
  return(cptr->clr_req_received ? ERR_CLOSED : OK);
}

int disconnect(int cid)
{ /* User wants to release a connection. */
  struct conn *cptr = &conn[cid];

  if (cptr->clr_req_received) {               /* other side initiated termination */
      cptr->state = IDLE;                     /* connection is now released */
      to_net(cid, 0, 0, CLEAR_CONF, data, 0);
  } else {                                    /* we initiated termination */
      cptr->state = DISCONN;                  /* not released until other side agrees */
      to_net(cid, 0, 0, CLEAR_REQ, data, 0);
  }
  return(OK);
}

void packet_arrival(void)
{ /* A packet has arrived, get and process it. */
  int cid;                                    /* connection on which packet arrived */
  int count, i, q, m;
  pkt_type ptype;   /* CALL_REQ,CALL_ACC,CLEAR_REQ,CLEAR_CONF,DATA_PKT,CREDIT */
  unsigned char data[MAX_PKT_SIZE];           /* data portion of the incoming packet */
  struct conn *cptr;

  from_net(&cid, &q, &m, &ptype, data, &count);   /* go get it */
  cptr = &conn[cid];
```

```
  switch (ptype) {
    case CALL_REQ:                       /* remote user wants to establish connection */
      cptr->local_address = data[0]; cptr->remote_address = data[1];
      if (cptr->local_address == listen_address) {
           listen_conn = cid; cptr->state = ESTABLISHED; wakeup();
      } else {
           cptr->state = QUEUED; cptr->timer = TIMEOUT;
      }
      cptr->clr_req_received = 0;  cptr->credits = 0;
      break;

    case CALL_ACC:                       /* remote user has accepted our CALL_REQ */
      cptr->state = ESTABLISHED;
      wakeup();
      break;

    case CLEAR_REQ:                      /* remote user wants to disconnect or reject call */
      cptr->clr_req_received = 1;
      if (cptr->state == DISCONN) cptr->state = IDLE; /* clear collision */
      if (cptr->state == WAITING || cptr->state == RECEIVING || cptr->state == SENDING) wakeup();
      break;

    case CLEAR_CONF:                     /* remote user agrees to disconnect */
      cptr->state = IDLE;
      break;

    case CREDIT:                         /* remote user is waiting for data */
      cptr->credits += data[1];
      if (cptr->state == SENDING) wakeup();
      break;

    case DATA_PKT:                       /* remote user has sent data */
      for (i = 0; i < count; i++) cptr->user_buf_addr[cptr->byte_count + i] = data[i];
      cptr->byte_count += count;
      if (m == 0 ) wakeup();
  }
}

void clock(void)
{ /* The clock has ticked, check for timeouts of queued connect requests. */
  int i;
  struct conn *cptr;

  for (i = 1; i <= MAX_CONN; i++) {
       cptr = &conn[i];
       if (cptr->timer > 0) {            /* timer was running */
            cptr->timer--;
            if (cptr->timer == 0) {      /* timer has now expired */
                 cptr->state = IDLE;
                 to_net(i, 0, 0, CLEAR_REQ, data, 0);
            }
       }
  }
}
```

Figure 6-20. An example transport entity.

When a user calls RECEIVE, a special **credit message** is sent to the transport entity on the sending machine and is recorded in the *conn* array. When SEND is called, the transport entity checks to see if a credit has arrived on the specified connection. If so, the message is sent (in multiple packets if need be) and the credit decremented; if not, the transport entity puts itself to sleep until a credit arrives. This mechanism guarantees that no message is ever sent unless the other side has already done a RECEIVE. As a result, whenever a message arrives, there is guaranteed to be a buffer available into which the message can be put. The scheme can easily be generalized to allow receivers to provide multiple buffers and request multiple messages.

You should keep the simplicity of Fig. 6-20 in mind. A realistic transport entity would normally check all user-supplied parameters for validity, handle recovery from network layer crashes, deal with call collisions, and support a more general transport service including such facilities as interrupts, datagrams, and nonblocking versions of the SEND and RECEIVE primitives.

6.3.3 The Example as a Finite State Machine

Writing a transport entity is difficult and exacting work, especially for more realistic protocols. To reduce the chance of making an error, it is often useful to represent the state of the protocol as a finite state machine.

We have already seen that our example protocol has seven states per connection. It is also possible to isolate 12 events that can move a connection from one state to another. Five of these events are the five service primitives. Another six are the arrivals of the six legal packet types. The last one is the expiration of the timer. Figure 6-21 shows the main protocol actions in matrix form. The columns are the states and the rows are the 12 events.

Each entry in the matrix (i.e., the finite state machine) of Fig. 6-21 has up to three fields: a predicate, an action, and a new state. The predicate indicates under which conditions the action is taken. For example, in the upper-left entry, if a LISTEN is executed and there is no more table space (predicate *P1*), the LISTEN fails and the state does not change. On the other hand, if a CALL REQUEST packet has already arrived for the transport address being listened to (predicate *P2*), the connection is established immediately. Another possibility is that *P2* is false, that is, no CALL REQUEST has come in, in which case the connection remains in the *IDLE* state, awaiting a CALL REQUEST packet.

It is worth pointing out that the choice of states to use in the matrix is not entirely fixed by the protocol itself. In this example, there is no state *LISTENING*, which might have been a reasonable thing to have following a LISTEN. There is no *LISTENING* state because a state is associated with a connection record entry, and no connection record is created by LISTEN. Why not? Because we have decided to use the network layer virtual circuit numbers as the connection identifi-

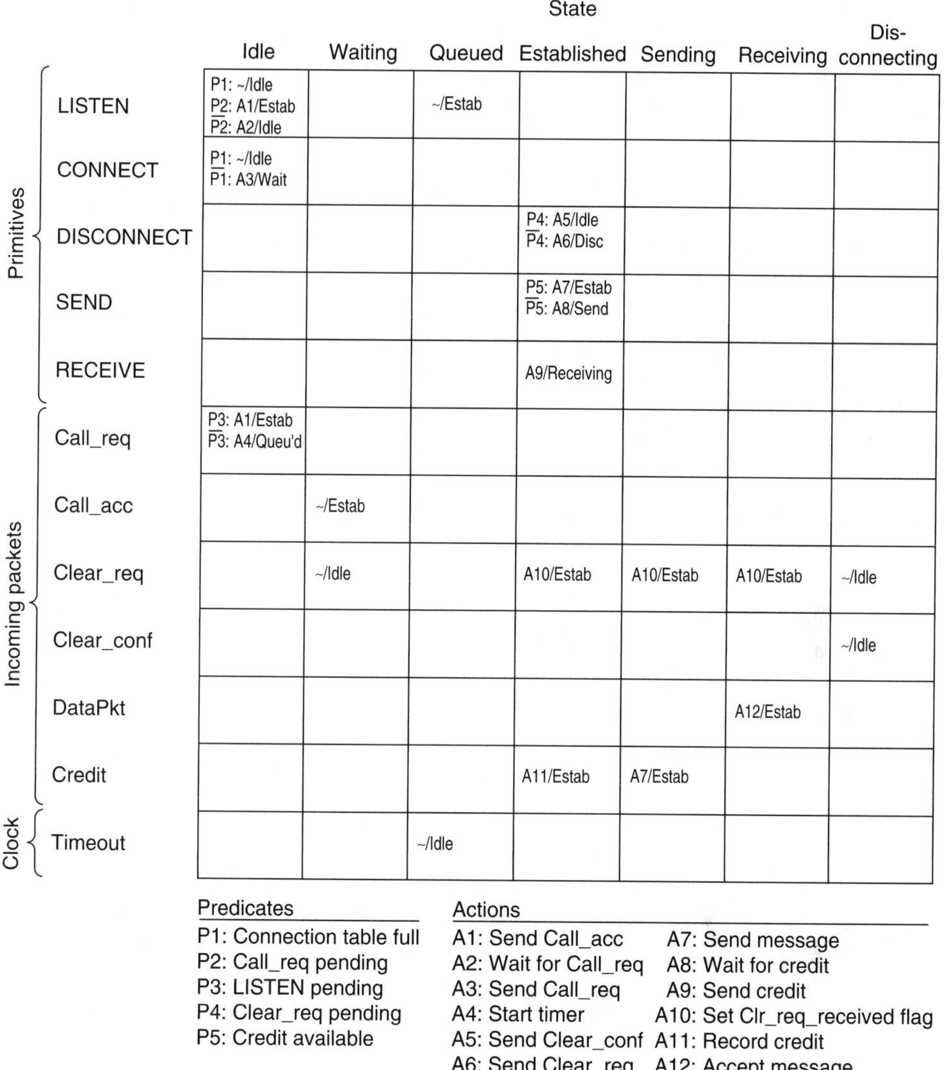

		State						
		Idle	Waiting	Queued	Established	Sending	Receiving	Dis-connecting
Primitives	LISTEN	P1: ~/Idle P2: A1/Estab $\overline{P2}$: A2/Idle		~/Estab				
	CONNECT	P1: ~/Idle $\overline{P1}$: A3/Wait						
	DISCONNECT				P4: A5/Idle $\overline{P4}$: A6/Disc			
	SEND				P5: A7/Estab $\overline{P5}$: A8/Send			
	RECEIVE				A9/Receiving			
Incoming packets	Call_req	P3: A1/Estab $\overline{P3}$: A4/Queu'd						
	Call_acc		~/Estab					
	Clear_req		~/Idle		A10/Estab	A10/Estab	A10/Estab	~/Idle
	Clear_conf							~/Idle
	DataPkt						A12/Estab	
	Credit				A11/Estab	A7/Estab		
Clock	Timeout			~/Idle				

Figure 6-21. The example protocol as a finite state machine. Each entry has an optional predicate, an optional action, and the new state. The tilde indicates that no major action is taken. An overbar above a predicate indicates the negation of the predicate. Blank entries correspond to impossible or invalid events.

ers, and for a LISTEN, the virtual circuit number is ultimately chosen by the network layer when the CALL REQUEST packet arrives.

The actions *A1* through *A12* are the major actions, such as sending packets and starting timers. Not all the minor actions, such as initializing the fields of a connection record, are listed. If an action involves waking up a sleeping process, the actions following the wakeup also count. For example, if a CALL REQUEST packet comes in and a process was asleep waiting for it, the transmission of the CALL ACCEPT packet following the wakeup counts as part of the action for CALL REQUEST. After each action is performed, the connection may move to a new state, as shown in Fig. 6-21.

The advantage of representing the protocol as a matrix is threefold. First, in this form it is much easier for the programmer to systematically check each combination of state and event to see if an action is required. In production implementations, some of the combinations would be used for error handling. In Fig. 6-21 no distinction is made between impossible situations and illegal ones. For example, if a connection is in *waiting* state, the DISCONNECT event is impossible because the user is blocked and cannot execute any primitives at all. On the other hand, in *sending* state, data packets are not expected because no credit has been issued. The arrival of a data packet is a protocol error.

The second advantage of the matrix representation of the protocol is in implementing it. One could envision a two-dimensional array in which element $a[i][j]$ was a pointer or index to the procedure that handled the occurrence of event i when in state j. One possible implementation is to write the transport entity as a short loop, waiting for an event at the top of the loop. When an event happens, the relevant connection is located and its state is extracted. With the event and state now known, the transport entity just indexes into the array a and calls the proper procedure. This approach gives a much more regular and systematic design than our transport entity.

The third advantage of the finite state machine approach is for protocol description. In some standards documents, the protocols are given as finite state machines of the type of Fig. 6-21. Going from this kind of description to a working transport entity is much easier if the transport entity is also driven by a finite state machine based on the one in the standard.

The primary disadvantage of the finite state machine approach is that it may be more difficult to understand than the straight programming example we used initially. However, this problem may be partially solved by drawing the finite state machine as a graph, as is done in Fig. 6-22.

6.4 THE INTERNET TRANSPORT PROTOCOLS: UDP

The Internet has two main protocols in the transport layer, a connectionless protocol and a connection-oriented one. In the following sections we will study both of them. The connectionless protocol is UDP. The connection-oriented protocol is TCP. Because UDP is basically just IP with a short header added, we will start with it. We will also look at two applications of UDP.

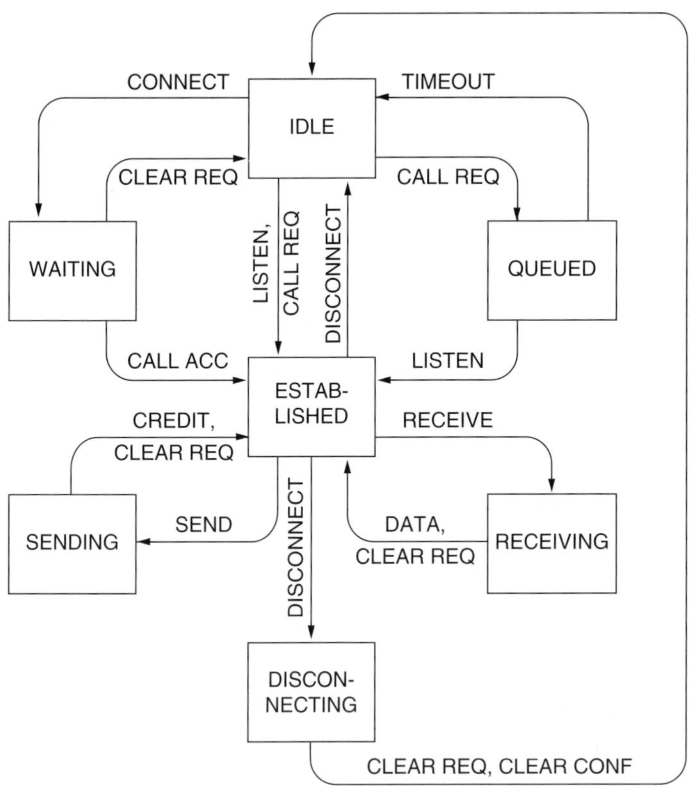

Figure 6-22. The example protocol in graphical form. Transitions that leave the connection state unchanged have been omitted for simplicity.

6.4.1 Introduction to UDP

The Internet protocol suite supports a connectionless transport protocol, **UDP** (**User Datagram Protocol**). UDP provides a way for applications to send encapsulated IP datagrams and send them without having to establish a connection. UDP is described in RFC 768.

UDP transmits **segments** consisting of an 8-byte header followed by the payload. The header is shown in Fig. 6-23. The two ports serve to identify the end points within the source and destination machines. When a UDP packet arrives, its payload is handed to the process attached to the destination port. This attachment occurs when BIND primitive or something similar is used, as we saw in Fig. 6-6 for TCP (the binding process is the same for UDP). In fact, the main value of having UDP over just using raw IP is the addition of the source and destination ports. Without the port fields, the transport layer would not know what to do with the packet. With them, it delivers segments correctly.

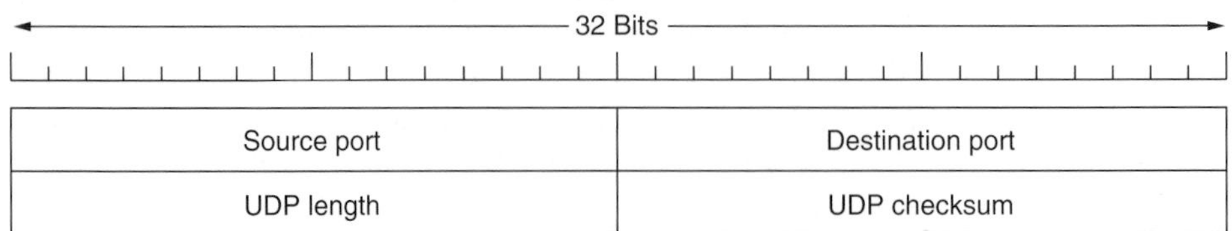

Figure 6-23. The UDP header.

The source port is primarily needed when a reply must be sent back to the source. By copying the *source port* field from the incoming segment into the *destination port* field of the outgoing segment, the process sending the reply can specify which process on the sending machine is to get it.

The *UDP length* field includes the 8-byte header and the data. The *UDP checksum* is optional and stored as 0 if not computed (a true computed 0 is stored as all 1s). Turning it off is foolish unless the quality of the data does not matter (e.g., digitized speech).

It is probably worth mentioning explicitly some of the things that UDP does *not* do. It does not do flow control, error control, or retransmission upon receipt of a bad segment. All of that is up to the user processes. What it does do is provide an interface to the IP protocol with the added feature of demultiplexing multiple processes using the ports. That is all it does. For applications that need to have precise control over the packet flow, error control, or timing, UDP provides just what the doctor ordered.

One area where UDP is especially useful is in client-server situations. Often, the client sends a short request to the server and expects a short reply back. If either the request or reply is lost, the client can just time out and try again. Not only is the code simple, but fewer messages are required (one in each direction) than with a protocol requiring an initial setup.

An application that uses UDP this way is DNS (the Domain Name System), which we will study in Chap. 7. In brief, a program that needs to look up the IP address of some host name, for example, *www.cs.berkeley.edu*, can send a UDP packet containing the host name to a DNS server. The server replies with a UDP packet containing the host's IP address. No setup is needed in advance and no release is needed afterward. Just two messages go over the network.

6.4.2 Remote Procedure Call

In a certain sense, sending a message to a remote host and getting a reply back is a lot like making a function call in a programming language. In both cases you start with one or more parameters and you get back a result. This observation has led people to try to arrange request-reply interactions on networks to be cast in the form of procedure calls. Such an arrangement makes network applications much easier to program and more familiar to deal with. For example, just imagine a procedure named *get_IP_address* (*host_name*) that works by sending a UDP packet to a DNS server and waiting for the reply, timing out and trying again if one is not forthcoming quickly enough. In this way, all the details of networking can be hidden from the programmer.

The key work in this area was done by Birrell and Nelson (1984). In a nutshell, what Birrell and Nelson suggested was allowing programs to call procedures located on remote hosts. When a process on machine 1 calls a procedure on machine 2, the calling process on 1 is suspended and execution of the called procedure takes place on 2. Information can be transported from the caller to the callee in the parameters and can come back in the procedure result. No message passing is visible to the programmer. This technique is known as **RPC** (**Remote Procedure Call**) and has become the basis for many networking applications. Traditionally, the calling procedure is known as the client and the called procedure is known as the server, and we will use those names here too.

The idea behind RPC is to make a remote procedure call look as much as possible like a local one. In the simplest form, to call a remote procedure, the client program must be bound with a small library procedure, called the **client stub**, that represents the server procedure in the client's address space. Similarly, the server is bound with a procedure called the **server stub**. These procedures hide the fact that the procedure call from the client to the server is not local.

The actual steps in making an RPC are shown in Fig. 6-24. Step 1 is the client calling the client stub. This call is a local procedure call, with the parameters pushed onto the stack in the normal way. Step 2 is the client stub packing the parameters into a message and making a system call to send the message. Packing the parameters is called **marshaling**. Step 3 is the kernel sending the message from the client machine to the server machine. Step 4 is the kernel passing the incoming packet to the server stub. Finally, step 5 is the server stub calling the server procedure with the unmarshaled parameters. The reply traces the same path in the other direction.

The key item to note here is that the client procedure, written by the user, just makes a normal (i.e., local) procedure call to the client stub, which has the same name as the server procedure. Since the client procedure and client stub are in the same address space, the parameters are passed in the usual way. Similarly, the server procedure is called by a procedure in its address space with the parameters it expects. To the server procedure, nothing is unusual. In this way, instead of I/O being done on sockets, network communication is done by faking a normal procedure call.

Despite the conceptual elegance of RPC, there are a few snakes hiding under the grass. A big one is the use of pointer parameters. Normally, passing a pointer to a procedure is not a problem. The called procedure can use the pointer in the same way the caller can because both procedures live in the same virtual address

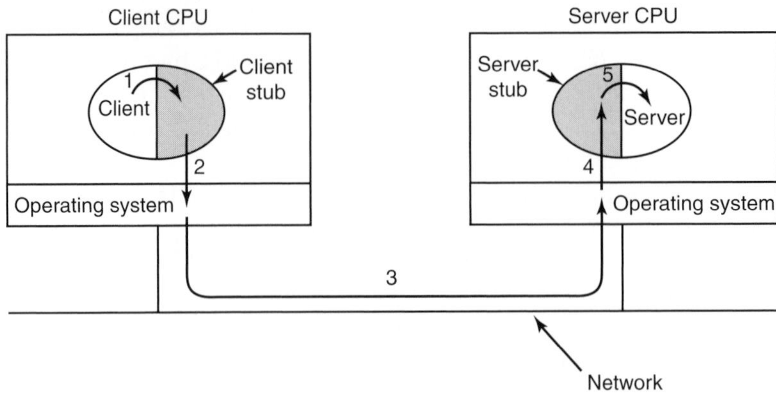

Figure 6-24. Steps in making a remote procedure call. The stubs are shaded.

space. With RPC, passing pointers is impossible because the client and server are in different address spaces.

In some cases, tricks can be used to make it possible to pass pointers. Suppose that the first parameter is a pointer to an integer, *k*. The client stub can marshal *k* and send it along to the server. The server stub then creates a pointer to *k* and passes it to the server procedure, just as it expects. When the server procedure returns control to the server stub, the latter sends *k* back to the client where the new *k* is copied over the old one, just in case the server changed it. In effect, the standard calling sequence of call-by-reference has been replaced by copy-restore. Unfortunately, this trick does not always work, for example, if the pointer points to a graph or other complex data structure. For this reason, some restrictions must be placed on parameters to procedures called remotely.

A second problem is that in weakly-typed languages, like C, it is perfectly legal to write a procedure that computes the inner product of two vectors (arrays), without specifying how large either one is. Each could be terminated by a special value known only to the calling and called procedure. Under these circumstances, it is essentially impossible for the client stub to marshal the parameters: it has no way of determining how large they are.

A third problem is that it is not always possible to deduce the types of the parameters, not even from a formal specification or the code itself. An example is *printf*, which may have any number of parameters (at least one), and the parameters can be an arbitrary mixture of integers, shorts, longs, characters, strings, floating-point numbers of various lengths, and other types. Trying to call *printf* as a remote procedure would be practically impossible because C is so permissive. However, a rule saying that RPC can be used provided that you do not program in C (or C++) would not be popular.

A fourth problem relates to the use of global variables. Normally, the calling and called procedure can communicate by using global variables, in addition to communicating via parameters. If the called procedure is now moved to a remote machine, the code will fail because the global variables are no longer shared.

These problems are not meant to suggest that RPC is hopeless. In fact, it is widely used, but some restrictions are needed to make it work well in practice.

Of course, RPC need not use UDP packets, but RPC and UDP are a good fit and UDP is commonly used for RPC. However, when the parameters or results may be larger than the maximum UDP packet or when the operation requested is not idempotent (i.e., cannot be repeated safely, such as when incrementing a counter), it may be necessary to set up a TCP connection and send the request over it rather than use UDP.

6.4.3 The Real-Time Transport Protocol

Client-server RPC is one area in which UDP is widely used. Another one is real-time multimedia applications. In particular, as Internet radio, Internet telephony, music-on-demand, videoconferencing, video-on-demand, and other multimedia applications became more commonplace, people discovered that each application was reinventing more or less the same real-time transport protocol. It gradually became clear that having a generic real-time transport protocol for multiple applications would be a good idea. Thus was **RTP** (**Real-time Transport Protocol**) born. It is described in RFC 1889 and is now in widespread use.

The position of RTP in the protocol stack is somewhat strange. It was decided to put RTP in user space and have it (normally) run over UDP. It operates as follows. The multimedia application consists of multiple audio, video, text, and possibly other streams. These are fed into the RTP library, which is in user space along with the application. This library then multiplexes the streams and encodes them in RTP packets, which it then stuffs into a socket. At the other end of the socket (in the operating system kernel), UDP packets are generated and embedded in IP packets. If the computer is on an Ethernet, the IP packets are then put in Ethernet frames for transmission. The protocol stack for this situation is shown in Fig. 6-25(a). The packet nesting is shown in Fig. 6-25(b).

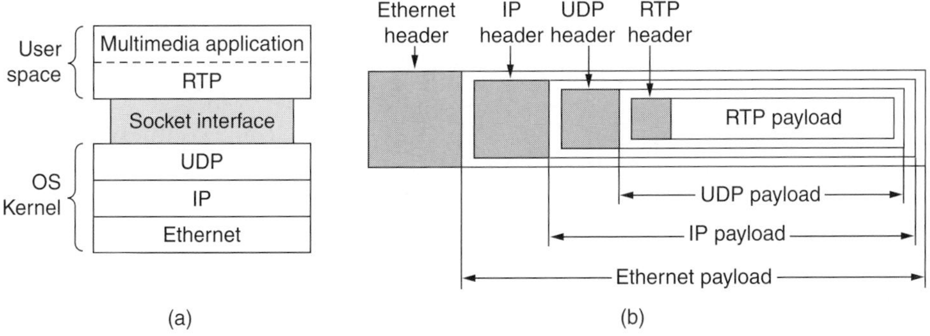

Figure 6-25. (a) The position of RTP in the protocol stack. (b) Packet nesting.

As a consequence of this design, it is a little hard to say which layer RTP is in. Since it runs in user space and is linked to the application program, it certainly looks like an application protocol. On the other hand, it is a generic, application-independent protocol that just provides transport facilities, so it also looks like a transport protocol. Probably the best description is that it is a transport protocol that is implemented in the application layer.

The basic function of RTP is to multiplex several real-time data streams onto a single stream of UDP packets. The UDP stream can be sent to a single destination (unicasting) or to multiple destinations (multicasting). Because RTP just uses normal UDP, its packets are not treated specially by the routers unless some normal IP quality-of-service features are enabled. In particular, there are no special guarantees about delivery, jitter, etc.

Each packet sent in an RTP stream is given a number one higher than its predecessor. This numbering allows the destination to determine if any packets are missing. If a packet is missing, the best action for the destination to take is to approximate the missing value by interpolation. Retransmission is not a practical option since the retransmitted packet would probably arrive too late to be useful. As a consequence, RTP has no flow control, no error control, no acknowledgements, and no mechanism to request retransmissions.

Each RTP payload may contain multiple samples, and they may be coded any way that the application wants. To allow for interworking, RTP defines several profiles (e.g., a single audio stream), and for each profile, multiple encoding formats may be allowed. For example, a single audio stream may be encoded as 8-bit PCM samples at 8 kHz, delta encoding, predictive encoding, GSM encoding, MP3, and so on. RTP provides a header field in which the source can specify the encoding but is otherwise not involved in how encoding is done.

Another facility many real-time applications need is timestamping. The idea here is to allow the source to associate a timestamp with the first sample in each packet. The timestamps are relative to the start of the stream, so only the differences between timestamps are significant. The absolute values have no meaning. This mechanism allows the destination to do a small amount of buffering and play each sample the right number of milliseconds after the start of the stream, independently of when the packet containing the sample arrived. Not only does timestamping reduce the effects of jitter, but it also allows multiple streams to be synchronized with each other. For example, a digital television program might have a video stream and two audio streams. The two audio streams could be for stereo broadcasts or for handling films with an original language soundtrack and a soundtrack dubbed into the local language, giving the viewer a choice. Each stream comes from a different physical device, but if they are timestamped from a single counter, they can be played back synchronously, even if the streams are transmitted somewhat erratically.

The RTP header is illustrated in Fig. 6-26. It consists of three 32-bit words and potentially some extensions. The first word contains the *Version* field, which is already at 2. Let us hope this version is very close to the ultimate version since there is only one code point left (although 3 could be defined as meaning that the real version was in an extension word).

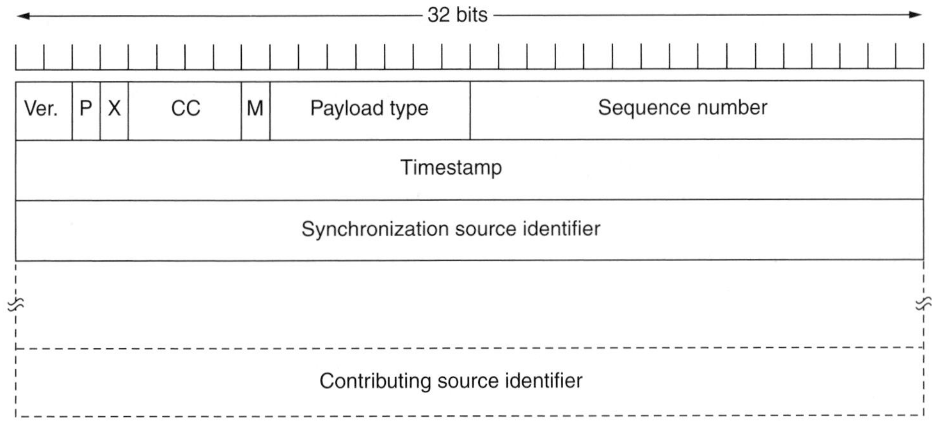

Figure 6-26. The RTP header.

The *P* bit indicates that the packet has been padded to a multiple of 4 bytes. The last padding byte tells how many bytes were added. The *X* bit indicates that an extension header is present. The format and meaning of the extension header are not defined. The only thing that is defined is that the first word of the extension gives the length. This is an escape hatch for any unforeseen requirements.

The *CC* field tells how many contributing sources are present, from 0 to 15 (see below). The *M* bit is an application-specific marker bit. It can be used to mark the start of a video frame, the start of a word in an audio channel, or something else that the application understands. The *Payload type* field tells which encoding algorithm has been used (e.g., uncompressed 8-bit audio, MP3, etc.). Since every packet carries this field, the encoding can change during transmission. The *Sequence number* is just a counter that is incremented on each RTP packet sent. It is used to detect lost packets.

The timestamp is produced by the stream's source to note when the first sample in the packet was made. This value can help reduce jitter at the receiver by decoupling the playback from the packet arrival time. The *Synchronization source identifier* tells which stream the packet belongs to. It is the method used to multiplex and demultiplex multiple data streams onto a single stream of UDP packets. Finally, the *Contributing source identifiers*, if any, are used when mixers are present in the studio. In that case, the mixer is the synchronizing source, and the streams being mixed are listed here.

RTP has a little sister protocol (little sibling protocol?) called **RTCP** (**Real-time Transport Control Protocol**). It handles feedback, synchronization, and the user interface but does not transport any data. The first function can be used to provide feedback on delay, jitter, bandwidth, congestion, and other network properties to the sources. This information can be used by the encoding process to increase the data rate (and give better quality) when the network is functioning well and to cut back the data rate when there is trouble in the network. By providing continuous feedback, the encoding algorithms can be continuously adapted to provide the best quality possible under the current circumstances. For example, if the bandwidth increases or decreases during the transmission, the encoding may switch from MP3 to 8-bit PCM to delta encoding as required. The *Payload type* field is used to tell the destination what encoding algorithm is used for the current packet, making it possible to vary it on demand.

RTCP also handles interstream synchronization. The problem is that different streams may use different clocks, with different granularities and different drift rates. RTCP can be used to keep them in sync.

Finally, RTCP provides a way for naming the various sources (e.g., in ASCII text). This information can be displayed on the receiver's screen to indicate who is talking at the moment.

More information about RTP can be found in (Perkins, 2002).

6.5 THE INTERNET TRANSPORT PROTOCOLS: TCP

UDP is a simple protocol and it has some niche uses, such as client-server interactions and multimedia, but for most Internet applications, reliable, sequenced delivery is needed. UDP cannot provide this, so another protocol is required. It is called TCP and is the main workhorse of the Internet. Let us now study it in detail.

6.5.1 Introduction to TCP

TCP (**Transmission Control Protocol**) was specifically designed to provide a reliable end-to-end byte stream over an unreliable internetwork. An internetwork differs from a single network because different parts may have wildly different topologies, bandwidths, delays, packet sizes, and other parameters. TCP was designed to dynamically adapt to properties of the internetwork and to be robust in the face of many kinds of failures.

TCP was formally defined in RFC 793. As time went on, various errors and inconsistencies were detected, and the requirements were changed in some areas. These clarifications and some bug fixes are detailed in RFC 1122. Extensions are given in RFC 1323.

Each machine supporting TCP has a TCP transport entity, either a library procedure, a user process, or part of the kernel. In all cases, it manages TCP streams and interfaces to the IP layer. A TCP entity accepts user data streams from local processes, breaks them up into pieces not exceeding 64 KB (in practice, often

1460 data bytes in order to fit in a single Ethernet frame with the IP and TCP headers), and sends each piece as a separate IP datagram. When datagrams containing TCP data arrive at a machine, they are given to the TCP entity, which reconstructs the original byte streams. For simplicity, we will sometimes use just "TCP" to mean the TCP transport entity (a piece of software) or the TCP protocol (a set of rules). From the context it will be clear which is meant. For example, in "The user gives TCP the data," the TCP transport entity is clearly intended.

The IP layer gives no guarantee that datagrams will be delivered properly, so it is up to TCP to time out and retransmit them as need be. Datagrams that do arrive may well do so in the wrong order; it is also up to TCP to reassemble them into messages in the proper sequence. In short, TCP must furnish the reliability that most users want and that IP does not provide.

6.5.2 The TCP Service Model

TCP service is obtained by both the sender and receiver creating end points, called sockets, as discussed in Sec. 6.1.3. Each socket has a socket number (address) consisting of the IP address of the host and a 16-bit number local to that host, called a **port**. A port is the TCP name for a TSAP. For TCP service to be obtained, a connection must be explicitly established between a socket on the sending machine and a socket on the receiving machine. The socket calls are listed in Fig. 6-5.

A socket may be used for multiple connections at the same time. In other words, two or more connections may terminate at the same socket. Connections are identified by the socket identifiers at both ends, that is, (*socket1*, *socket2*). No virtual circuit numbers or other identifiers are used.

Port numbers below 1024 are called **well-known ports** and are reserved for standard services. For example, any process wishing to establish a connection to a host to transfer a file using FTP can connect to the destination host's port 21 to contact its FTP daemon. The list of well-known ports is given at *www.iana.org*. Over 300 have been assigned. A few of the better known ones are listed in Fig. 6-27.

It would certainly be possible to have the FTP daemon attach itself to port 21 at boot time, the telnet daemon to attach itself to port 23 at boot time, and so on. However, doing so would clutter up memory with daemons that were idle most of the time. Instead, what is generally done is to have a single daemon, called **inetd** (**Internet daemon**) in UNIX, attach itself to multiple ports and wait for the first incoming connection. When that occurs, inetd forks off a new process and executes the appropriate daemon in it, letting that daemon handle the request. In this way, the daemons other than inetd are only active when there is work for them to do. Inetd learns which ports it is to use from a configuration file. Consequently, the system administrator can set up the system to have permanent daemons on the busiest ports (e.g., port 80) and inetd on the rest.

Port	Protocol	Use
21	FTP	File transfer
23	Telnet	Remote login
25	SMTP	E-mail
69	TFTP	Trivial file transfer protocol
79	Finger	Lookup information about a user
80	HTTP	World Wide Web
110	POP-3	Remote e-mail access
119	NNTP	USENET news

Figure 6-27. Some assigned ports.

All TCP connections are full duplex and point-to-point. Full duplex means that traffic can go in both directions at the same time. Point-to-point means that each connection has exactly two end points. TCP does not support multicasting or broadcasting.

A TCP connection is a byte stream, not a message stream. Message boundaries are not preserved end to end. For example, if the sending process does four 512-byte writes to a TCP stream, these data may be delivered to the receiving process as four 512-byte chunks, two 1024-byte chunks, one 2048-byte chunk (see Fig. 6-28), or some other way. There is no way for the receiver to detect the unit(s) in which the data were written.

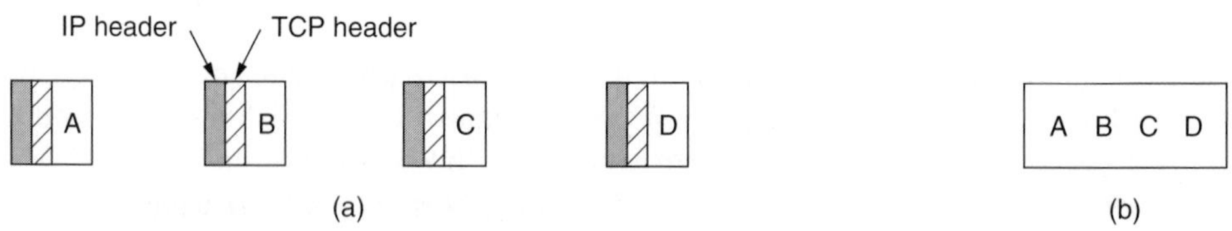

Figure 6-28. (a) Four 512-byte segments sent as separate IP datagrams. (b) The 2048 bytes of data delivered to the application in a single READ call.

Files in UNIX have this property too. The reader of a file cannot tell whether the file was written a block at a time, a byte at a time, or all in one blow. As with a UNIX file, the TCP software has no idea of what the bytes mean and no interest in finding out. A byte is just a byte.

When an application passes data to TCP, TCP may send it immediately or buffer it (in order to collect a larger amount to send at once), at its discretion. However, sometimes, the application really wants the data to be sent immediately. For example, suppose a user is logged in to a remote machine. After a command line has been finished and the carriage return typed, it is essential that the line be shipped off to the remote machine immediately and not buffered until the next line comes in. To force data out, applications can use the PUSH flag, which tells TCP not to delay the transmission.

Some early applications used the PUSH flag as a kind of marker to delineate messages boundaries. While this trick sometimes works, it sometimes fails since not all implementations of TCP pass the PUSH flag to the application on the receiving side. Furthermore, if additional PUSHes come in before the first one has been transmitted (e.g., because the output line is busy), TCP is free to collect all the PUSHed data into a single IP datagram, with no separation between the various pieces.

One last feature of the TCP service that is worth mentioning here is **urgent data**. When an interactive user hits the DEL or CTRL-C key to break off a remote computation that has already begun, the sending application puts some control information in the data stream and gives it to TCP along with the URGENT flag. This event causes TCP to stop accumulating data and transmit everything it has for that connection immediately.

When the urgent data are received at the destination, the receiving application is interrupted (e.g., given a signal in UNIX terms) so it can stop whatever it was doing and read the data stream to find the urgent data. The end of the urgent data is marked so the application knows when it is over. The start of the urgent data is not marked. It is up to the application to figure that out. This scheme basically provides a crude signaling mechanism and leaves everything else up to the application.

6.5.3 The TCP Protocol

In this section we will give a general overview of the TCP protocol. In the next one we will go over the protocol header, field by field.

A key feature of TCP, and one which dominates the protocol design, is that every byte on a TCP connection has its own 32-bit sequence number. When the Internet began, the lines between routers were mostly 56-kbps leased lines, so a host blasting away at full speed took over 1 week to cycle through the sequence numbers. At modern network speeds, the sequence numbers can be consumed at an alarming rate, as we will see later. Separate 32-bit sequence numbers are used for acknowledgements and for the window mechanism, as discussed below.

The sending and receiving TCP entities exchange data in the form of segments. A **TCP segment** consists of a fixed 20-byte header (plus an optional part) followed by zero or more data bytes. The TCP software decides how big segments should be. It can accumulate data from several writes into one segment or can split data from one write over multiple segments. Two limits restrict the segment size. First, each segment, including the TCP header, must fit in the 65,515-byte IP payload. Second, each network has a **maximum transfer unit**, or **MTU**, and each segment must fit in the MTU. In practice, the MTU is generally 1500 bytes (the Ethernet payload size) and thus defines the upper bound on segment size.

The basic protocol used by TCP entities is the sliding window protocol. When a sender transmits a segment, it also starts a timer. When the segment arrives at the destination, the receiving TCP entity sends back a segment (with data if any exist, otherwise without data) bearing an acknowledgement number equal to the next sequence number it expects to receive. If the sender's timer goes off before the acknowledgement is received, the sender transmits the segment again.

Although this protocol sounds simple, there are a number of sometimes subtle ins and outs, which we will cover below. Segments can arrive out of order, so bytes 3072–4095 can arrive but cannot be acknowledged because bytes 2048–-3071 have not turned up yet. Segments can also be delayed so long in transit that the sender times out and retransmits them. The retransmissions may include different byte ranges than the original transmission, requiring a careful administration to keep track of which bytes have been correctly received so far. However, since each byte in the stream has its own unique offset, it can be done.

TCP must be prepared to deal with these problems and solve them in an efficient way. A considerable amount of effort has gone into optimizing the performance of TCP streams, even in the face of network problems. A number of the algorithms used by many TCP implementations will be discussed below.

6.5.4 The TCP Segment Header

Figure 6-29 shows the layout of a TCP segment. Every segment begins with a fixed-format, 20-byte header. The fixed header may be followed by header options. After the options, if any, up to $65,535 - 20 - 20 = 65,495$ data bytes may follow, where the first 20 refer to the IP header and the second to the TCP header. Segments without any data are legal and are commonly used for acknowledgements and control messages.

Let us dissect the TCP header field by field. The *Source port* and *Destination port* fields identify the local end points of the connection. The well-known ports are defined at *www.iana.org* but each host can allocate the others as it wishes. A port plus its host's IP address forms a 48-bit unique end point. The source and destination end points together identify the connection.

The *Sequence number* and *Acknowledgement number* fields perform their usual functions. Note that the latter specifies the next byte expected, not the last byte correctly received. Both are 32 bits long because every byte of data is numbered in a TCP stream.

The *TCP header length* tells how many 32-bit words are contained in the TCP header. This information is needed because the *Options* field is of variable length, so the header is, too. Technically, this field really indicates the start of the data

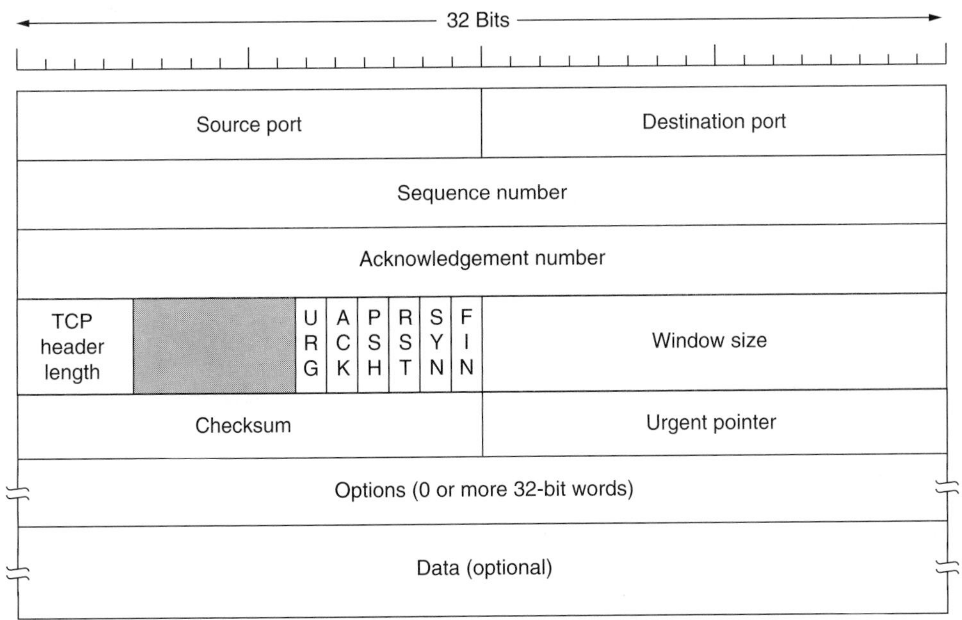

Figure 6-29. The TCP header.

within the segment, measured in 32-bit words, but that number is just the header length in words, so the effect is the same.

Next comes a 6-bit field that is not used. The fact that this field has survived intact for over a quarter of a century is testimony to how well thought out TCP is. Lesser protocols would have needed it to fix bugs in the original design.

Now come six 1-bit flags. *URG* is set to 1 if the *Urgent pointer* is in use. The *Urgent pointer* is used to indicate a byte offset from the current sequence number at which urgent data are to be found. This facility is in lieu of interrupt messages. As we mentioned above, this facility is a bare-bones way of allowing the sender to signal the receiver without getting TCP itself involved in the reason for the interrupt.

The *ACK* bit is set to 1 to indicate that the *Acknowledgement number* is valid. If *ACK* is 0, the segment does not contain an acknowledgement so the *Acknowledgement number* field is ignored.

The *PSH* bit indicates PUSHed data. The receiver is hereby kindly requested to deliver the data to the application upon arrival and not buffer it until a full buffer has been received (which it might otherwise do for efficiency).

The *RST* bit is used to reset a connection that has become confused due to a host crash or some other reason. It is also used to reject an invalid segment or refuse an attempt to open a connection. In general, if you get a segment with the *RST* bit on, you have a problem on your hands.

The *SYN* bit is used to establish connections. The connection request has *SYN* = 1 and *ACK* = 0 to indicate that the piggyback acknowledgement field is not in use. The connection reply does bear an acknowledgement, so it has *SYN* = 1 and *ACK* = 1. In essence the *SYN* bit is used to denote CONNECTION REQUEST and CONNECTION ACCEPTED, with the *ACK* bit used to distinguish between those two possibilities.

The *FIN* bit is used to release a connection. It specifies that the sender has no more data to transmit. However, after closing a connection, the closing process may continue to receive data indefinitely. Both *SYN* and *FIN* segments have sequence numbers and are thus guaranteed to be processed in the correct order.

Flow control in TCP is handled using a variable-sized sliding window. The *Window size* field tells how many bytes may be sent starting at the byte acknowledged. A *Window size* field of 0 is legal and says that the bytes up to and including *Acknowledgement number* – 1 have been received, but that the receiver is currently badly in need of a rest and would like no more data for the moment, thank you. The receiver can later grant permission to send by transmitting a segment with the same *Acknowledgement number* and a nonzero *Window size* field.

In the protocols of Chap. 3, acknowledgements of frames received and permission to send new frames were tied together. This was a consequence of a fixed window size for each protocol. In TCP, acknowledgements and permission to send additional data are completely decoupled. In effect, a receiver can say: I have received bytes up through *k* but I do not want any more just now. This decoupling (in fact, a variable-sized window) gives additional flexibility. We will study it in detail below.

A *Checksum* is also provided for extra reliability. It checksums the header, the data, and the conceptual pseudoheader shown in Fig. 6-30. When performing this computation, the TCP *Checksum* field is set to zero and the data field is padded out with an additional zero byte if its length is an odd number. The checksum algorithm is simply to add up all the 16-bit words in one's complement and then to take the one's complement of the sum. As a consequence, when the receiver performs the calculation on the entire segment, including the *Checksum* field, the result should be 0.

The pseudoheader contains the 32-bit IP addresses of the source and destination machines, the protocol number for TCP (6), and the byte count for the TCP segment (including the header). Including the pseudoheader in the TCP checksum computation helps detect misdelivered packets, but including it also violates the protocol hierarchy since the IP addresses in it belong to the IP layer, not to the TCP layer. UDP uses the same pseudoheader for its checksum.

The *Options* field provides a way to add extra facilities not covered by the regular header. The most important option is the one that allows each host to specify the maximum TCP payload it is willing to accept. Using large segments is more efficient than using small ones because the 20-byte header can then be amortized over more data, but small hosts may not be able to handle big segments.

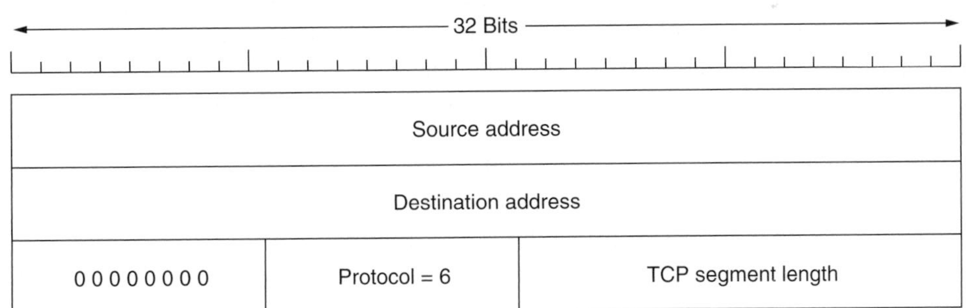

Figure 6-30. The pseudoheader included in the TCP checksum.

During connection setup, each side can announce its maximum and see its partner's. If a host does not use this option, it defaults to a 536-byte payload. All Internet hosts are required to accept TCP segments of 536 + 20 = 556 bytes. The maximum segment size in the two directions need not be the same.

For lines with high bandwidth, high delay, or both, the 64-KB window is often a problem. On a T3 line (44.736 Mbps), it takes only 12 msec to output a full 64-KB window. If the round-trip propagation delay is 50 msec (which is typical for a transcontinental fiber), the sender will be idle 3/4 of the time waiting for acknowledgements. On a satellite connection, the situation is even worse. A larger window size would allow the sender to keep pumping data out, but using the 16-bit *Window size* field, there is no way to express such a size. In RFC 1323, a *Window scale* option was proposed, allowing the sender and receiver to negotiate a window scale factor. This number allows both sides to shift the *Window size* field up to 14 bits to the left, thus allowing windows of up to 2^{30} bytes. Most TCP implementations now support this option.

Another option proposed by RFC 1106 and now widely implemented is the use of the selective repeat instead of go back n protocol. If the receiver gets one bad segment and then a large number of good ones, the normal TCP protocol will eventually time out and retransmit all the unacknowledged segments, including all those that were received correctly (i.e., the go back n protocol). RFC 1106 introduced NAKs to allow the receiver to ask for a specific segment (or segments). After it gets these, it can acknowledge all the buffered data, thus reducing the amount of data retransmitted.

6.5.5 TCP Connection Establishment

Connections are established in TCP by means of the three-way handshake discussed in Sec. 6.2.2. To establish a connection, one side, say, the server, passively waits for an incoming connection by executing the LISTEN and ACCEPT primitives, either specifying a specific source or nobody in particular.

The other side, say, the client, executes a CONNECT primitive, specifying the IP address and port to which it wants to connect, the maximum TCP segment size it is willing to accept, and optionally some user data (e.g., a password). The CONNECT primitive sends a TCP segment with the *SYN* bit on and *ACK* bit off and waits for a response.

When this segment arrives at the destination, the TCP entity there checks to see if there is a process that has done a LISTEN on the port given in the *Destination port* field. If not, it sends a reply with the *RST* bit on to reject the connection.

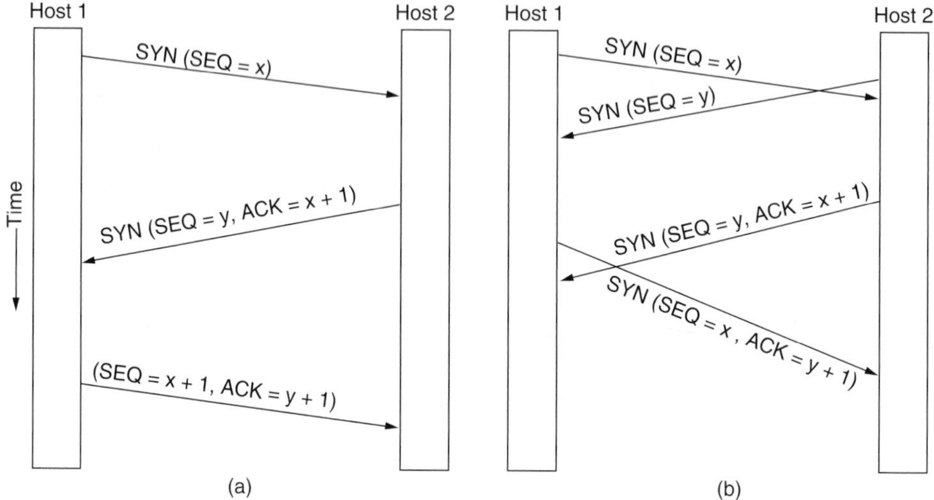

Figure 6-31. (a) TCP connection establishment in the normal case. (b) Call collision.

If some process is listening to the port, that process is given the incoming TCP segment. It can then either accept or reject the connection. If it accepts, an acknowledgement segment is sent back. The sequence of TCP segments sent in the normal case is shown in Fig. 6-31(a). Note that a *SYN* segment consumes 1 byte of sequence space so that it can be acknowledged unambiguously.

In the event that two hosts simultaneously attempt to establish a connection between the same two sockets, the sequence of events is as illustrated in Fig. 6-31(b). The result of these events is that just one connection is established, not two because connections are identified by their end points. If the first setup results in a connection identified by (x, y) and the second one does too, only one table entry is made, namely, for (x, y).

The initial sequence number on a connection is not 0 for the reasons we discussed earlier. A clock-based scheme is used, with a clock tick every 4 μsec. For additional safety, when a host crashes, it may not reboot for the maximum packet lifetime to make sure that no packets from previous connections are still roaming around the Internet somewhere.

6.5.6 TCP Connection Release

Although TCP connections are full duplex, to understand how connections are released it is best to think of them as a pair of simplex connections. Each simplex connection is released independently of its sibling. To release a connection, either party can send a TCP segment with the *FIN* bit set, which means that it has no more data to transmit. When the *FIN* is acknowledged, that direction is shut down for new data. Data may continue to flow indefinitely in the other direction, however. When both directions have been shut down, the connection is released. Normally, four TCP segments are needed to release a connection, one *FIN* and one *ACK* for each direction. However, it is possible for the first *ACK* and the second *FIN* to be contained in the same segment, reducing the total count to three.

Just as with telephone calls in which both people say goodbye and hang up the phone simultaneously, both ends of a TCP connection may send *FIN* segments at the same time. These are each acknowledged in the usual way, and the connection is shut down. There is, in fact, no essential difference between the two hosts releasing sequentially or simultaneously.

To avoid the two-army problem, timers are used. If a response to a *FIN* is not forthcoming within two maximum packet lifetimes, the sender of the *FIN* releases the connection. The other side will eventually notice that nobody seems to be listening to it any more and will time out as well. While this solution is not perfect, given the fact that a perfect solution is theoretically impossible, it will have to do. In practice, problems rarely arise.

6.5.7 TCP Connection Management Modeling

The steps required to establish and release connections can be represented in a finite state machine with the 11 states listed in Fig. 6-32. In each state, certain events are legal. When a legal event happens, some action may be taken. If some other event happens, an error is reported.

Each connection starts in the *CLOSED* state. It leaves that state when it does either a passive open (LISTEN), or an active open (CONNECT). If the other side does the opposite one, a connection is established and the state becomes *ESTABLISHED*. Connection release can be initiated by either side. When it is complete, the state returns to *CLOSED*.

The finite state machine itself is shown in Fig. 6-33. The common case of a client actively connecting to a passive server is shown with heavy lines—solid for the client, dotted for the server. The lightface lines are unusual event sequences. Each line in Fig. 6-33 is marked by an *event/action* pair. The event can either be a user-initiated system call (CONNECT, LISTEN, SEND, or CLOSE), a segment arrival (*SYN*, *FIN*, *ACK*, or *RST*), or, in one case, a timeout of twice the maximum packet lifetime. The action is the sending of a control segment (*SYN*, *FIN*, or *RST*) or nothing, indicated by —. Comments are shown in parentheses.

State	Description
CLOSED	No connection is active or pending
LISTEN	The server is waiting for an incoming call
SYN RCVD	A connection request has arrived; wait for ACK
SYN SENT	The application has started to open a connection
ESTABLISHED	The normal data transfer state
FIN WAIT 1	The application has said it is finished
FIN WAIT 2	The other side has agreed to release
TIMED WAIT	Wait for all packets to die off
CLOSING	Both sides have tried to close simultaneously
CLOSE WAIT	The other side has initiated a release
LAST ACK	Wait for all packets to die off

Figure 6-32. The states used in the TCP connection management finite state machine.

One can best understand the diagram by first following the path of a client (the heavy solid line), then later following the path of a server (the heavy dashed line). When an application program on the client machine issues a CONNECT request, the local TCP entity creates a connection record, marks it as being in the *SYN SENT* state, and sends a *SYN* segment. Note that many connections may be open (or being opened) at the same time on behalf of multiple applications, so the state is per connection and recorded in the connection record. When the *SYN+ACK* arrives, TCP sends the final *ACK* of the three-way handshake and switches into the *ESTABLISHED* state. Data can now be sent and received.

When an application is finished, it executes a CLOSE primitive, which causes the local TCP entity to send a *FIN* segment and wait for the corresponding *ACK* (dashed box marked active close). When the *ACK* arrives, a transition is made to state *FIN WAIT 2* and one direction of the connection is now closed. When the other side closes, too, a *FIN* comes in, which is acknowledged. Now both sides are closed, but TCP waits a time equal to the maximum packet lifetime to guarantee that all packets from the connection have died off, just in case the acknowledgement was lost. When the timer goes off, TCP deletes the connection record.

Now let us examine connection management from the server's viewpoint. The server does a LISTEN and settles down to see who turns up. When a *SYN* comes in, it is acknowledged and the server goes to the *SYN RCVD* state. When the server's *SYN* is itself acknowledged, the three-way handshake is complete and the server goes to the *ESTABLISHED* state. Data transfer can now occur.

When the client is done, it does a CLOSE, which causes a *FIN* to arrive at the server (dashed box marked passive close). The server is then signaled. When it, too, does a CLOSE, a *FIN* is sent to the client. When the client's acknowledgement shows up, the server releases the connection and deletes the connection record.

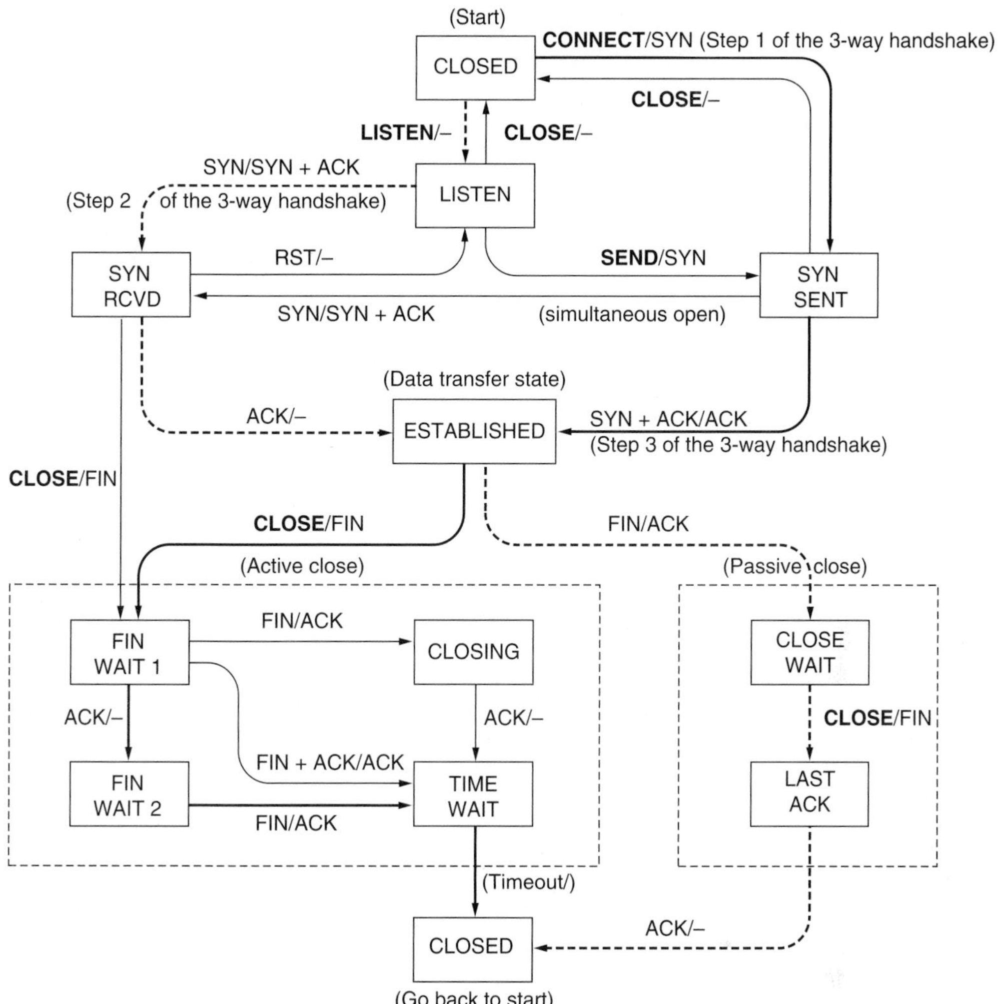

Figure 6-33. TCP connection management finite state machine. The heavy solid line is the normal path for a client. The heavy dashed line is the normal path for a server. The light lines are unusual events. Each transition is labeled by the event causing it and the action resulting from it, separated by a slash.

6.5.8 TCP Transmission Policy

As mentioned earlier, window management in TCP is not directly tied to acknowledgements as it is in most data link protocols. For example, suppose the receiver has a 4096-byte buffer, as shown in Fig. 6-34. If the sender transmits a 2048-byte segment that is correctly received, the receiver will acknowledge the segment. However, since it now has only 2048 bytes of buffer space (until the application removes some data from the buffer), it will advertise a window of 2048 starting at the next byte expected.

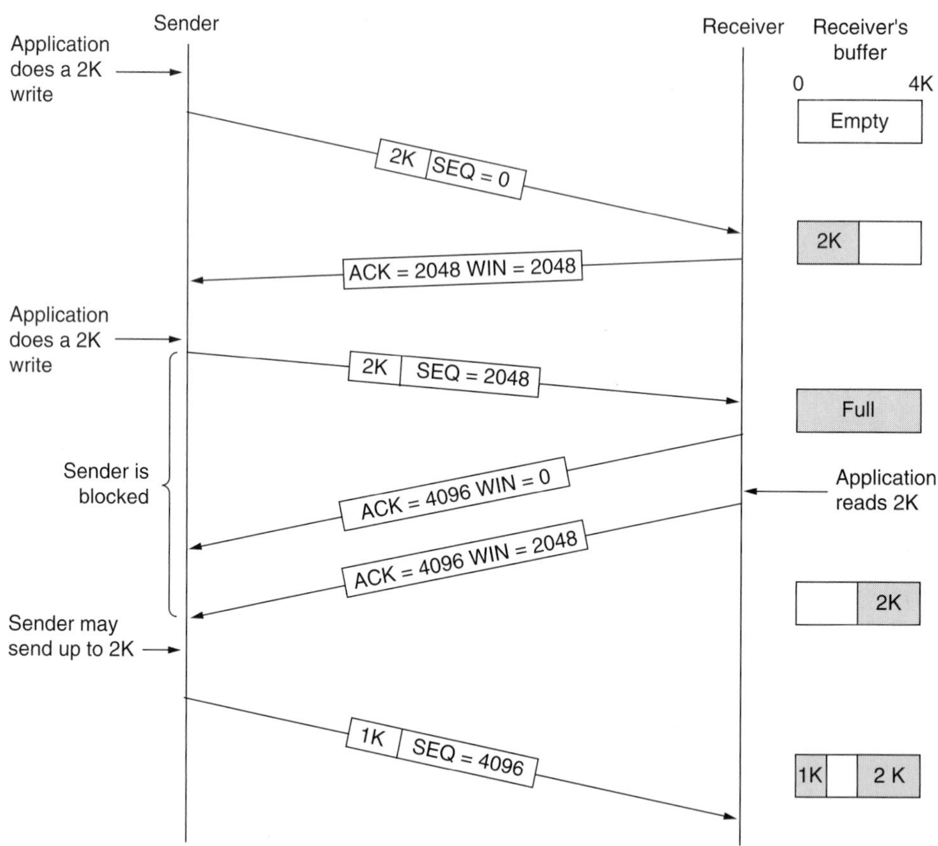

Figure 6-34. Window management in TCP.

Now the sender transmits another 2048 bytes, which are acknowledged, but the advertised window is 0. The sender must stop until the application process on the receiving host has removed some data from the buffer, at which time TCP can advertise a larger window.

When the window is 0, the sender may not normally send segments, with two exceptions. First, urgent data may be sent, for example, to allow the user to kill the process running on the remote machine. Second, the sender may send a 1-byte segment to make the receiver reannounce the next byte expected and window size. The TCP standard explicitly provides this option to prevent deadlock if a window announcement ever gets lost.

Senders are not required to transmit data as soon as they come in from the application. Neither are receivers required to send acknowledgements as soon as possible. For example, in Fig. 6-34, when the first 2 KB of data came in, TCP, knowing that it had a 4-KB window available, would have been completely correct in just buffering the data until another 2 KB came in, to be able to transmit a segment with a 4-KB payload. This freedom can be exploited to improve performance.

Consider a telnet connection to an interactive editor that reacts on every keystroke. In the worst case, when a character arrives at the sending TCP entity, TCP creates a 21-byte TCP segment, which it gives to IP to send as a 41-byte IP datagram. At the receiving side, TCP immediately sends a 40-byte acknowledgement (20 bytes of TCP header and 20 bytes of IP header). Later, when the editor has read the byte, TCP sends a window update, moving the window 1 byte to the right. This packet is also 40 bytes. Finally, when the editor has processed the character, it echoes the character as a 41-byte packet. In all, 162 bytes of bandwidth are used and four segments are sent for each character typed. When bandwidth is scarce, this method of doing business is not desirable.

One approach that many TCP implementations use to optimize this situation is to delay acknowledgements and window updates for 500 msec in the hope of acquiring some data on which to hitch a free ride. Assuming the editor echoes within 500 msec, only one 41-byte packet now need be sent back to the remote user, cutting the packet count and bandwidth usage in half.

Although this rule reduces the load placed on the network by the receiver, the sender is still operating inefficiently by sending 41-byte packets containing 1 byte of data. A way to reduce this usage is known as **Nagle's algorithm** (Nagle, 1984). What Nagle suggested is simple: when data come into the sender one byte at a time, just send the first byte and buffer all the rest until the outstanding byte is acknowledged. Then send all the buffered characters in one TCP segment and start buffering again until they are all acknowledged. If the user is typing quickly and the network is slow, a substantial number of characters may go in each segment, greatly reducing the bandwidth used. The algorithm additionally allows a new packet to be sent if enough data have trickled in to fill half the window or a maximum segment.

Nagle's algorithm is widely used by TCP implementations, but there are times when it is better to disable it. In particular, when an X Windows application is being run over the Internet, mouse movements have to be sent to the remote computer. (The X Window system is the windowing system used on most UNIX systems.) Gathering them up to send in bursts makes the mouse cursor move erratically, which makes for unhappy users.

Another problem that can degrade TCP performance is the **silly window syndrome** (Clark, 1982). This problem occurs when data are passed to the sending TCP entity in large blocks, but an interactive application on the receiving side reads data 1 byte at a time. To see the problem, look at Fig. 6-35. Initially, the

TCP buffer on the receiving side is full and the sender knows this (i.e., has a window of size 0). Then the interactive application reads one character from the TCP stream. This action makes the receiving TCP happy, so it sends a window update to the sender saying that it is all right to send 1 byte. The sender obliges and sends 1 byte. The buffer is now full, so the receiver acknowledges the 1-byte segment but sets the window to 0. This behavior can go on forever.

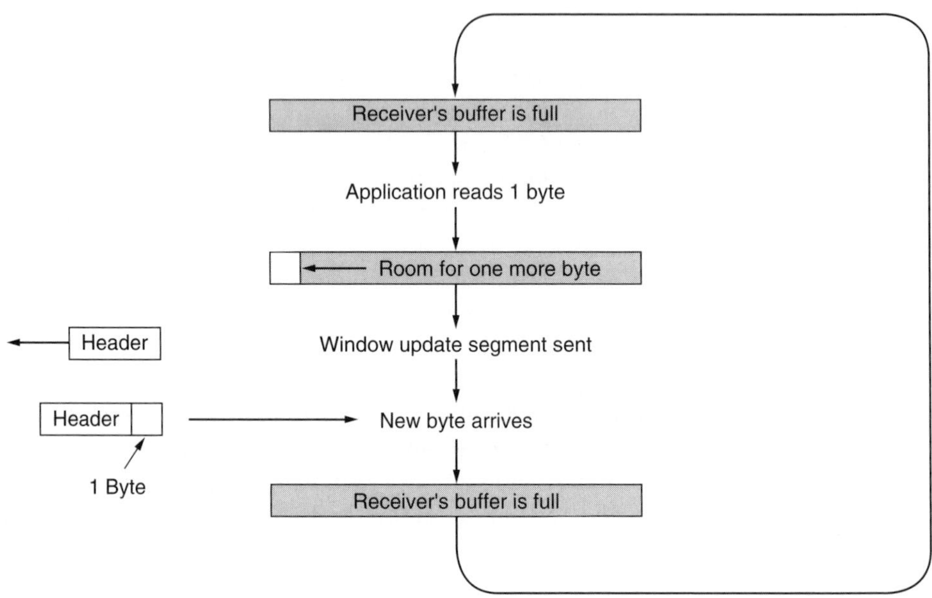

Figure 6-35. Silly window syndrome.

Clark's solution is to prevent the receiver from sending a window update for 1 byte. Instead it is forced to wait until it has a decent amount of space available and advertise that instead. Specifically, the receiver should not send a window update until it can handle the maximum segment size it advertised when the connection was established or until its buffer is half empty, whichever is smaller.

Furthermore, the sender can also help by not sending tiny segments. Instead, it should try to wait until it has accumulated enough space in the window to send a full segment or at least one containing half of the receiver's buffer size (which it must estimate from the pattern of window updates it has received in the past).

Nagle's algorithm and Clark's solution to the silly window syndrome are complementary. Nagle was trying to solve the problem caused by the sending application delivering data to TCP a byte at a time. Clark was trying to solve the problem of the receiving application sucking the data up from TCP a byte at a time. Both solutions are valid and can work together. The goal is for the sender not to send small segments and the receiver not to ask for them.

The receiving TCP can go further in improving performance than just doing window updates in large units. Like the sending TCP, it can also buffer data, so it can block a READ request from the application until it has a large chunk of data to provide. Doing this reduces the number of calls to TCP, and hence the overhead. Of course, it also increases the response time, but for noninteractive applications like file transfer, efficiency may be more important than response time to individual requests.

Another receiver issue is what to do with out-of-order segments. They can be kept or discarded, at the receiver's discretion. Of course, acknowledgements can be sent only when all the data up to the byte acknowledged have been received. If the receiver gets segments 0, 1, 2, 4, 5, 6, and 7, it can acknowledge everything up to and including the last byte in segment 2. When the sender times out, it then retransmits segment 3. If the receiver has buffered segments 4 through 7, upon receipt of segment 3 it can acknowledge all bytes up to the end of segment 7.

6.5.9 TCP Congestion Control

When the load offered to any network is more than it can handle, congestion builds up. The Internet is no exception. In this section we will discuss algorithms that have been developed over the past quarter of a century to deal with congestion. Although the network layer also tries to manage congestion, most of the heavy lifting is done by TCP because the real solution to congestion is to slow down the data rate.

In theory, congestion can be dealt with by employing a principle borrowed from physics: the law of conservation of packets. The idea is to refrain from injecting a new packet into the network until an old one leaves (i.e., is delivered). TCP attempts to achieve this goal by dynamically manipulating the window size.

The first step in managing congestion is detecting it. In the old days, detecting congestion was difficult. A timeout caused by a lost packet could have been caused by either (1) noise on a transmission line or (2) packet discard at a congested router. Telling the difference was difficult.

Nowadays, packet loss due to transmission errors is relatively rare because most long-haul trunks are fiber (although wireless networks are a different story). Consequently, most transmission timeouts on the Internet are due to congestion. All the Internet TCP algorithms assume that timeouts are caused by congestion and monitor timeouts for signs of trouble the way miners watch their canaries.

Before discussing how TCP reacts to congestion, let us first describe what it does to try to prevent congestion from occurring in the first place. When a connection is established, a suitable window size has to be chosen. The receiver can specify a window based on its buffer size. If the sender sticks to this window size, problems will not occur due to buffer overflow at the receiving end, but they may still occur due to internal congestion within the network.

In Fig. 6-36, we see this problem illustrated hydraulically. In Fig. 6-36(a), we see a thick pipe leading to a small-capacity receiver. As long as the sender does not send more water than the bucket can contain, no water will be lost. In Fig. 6-36(b), the limiting factor is not the bucket capacity, but the internal carrying capacity of the network. If too much water comes in too fast, it will back up and some will be lost (in this case by overflowing the funnel).

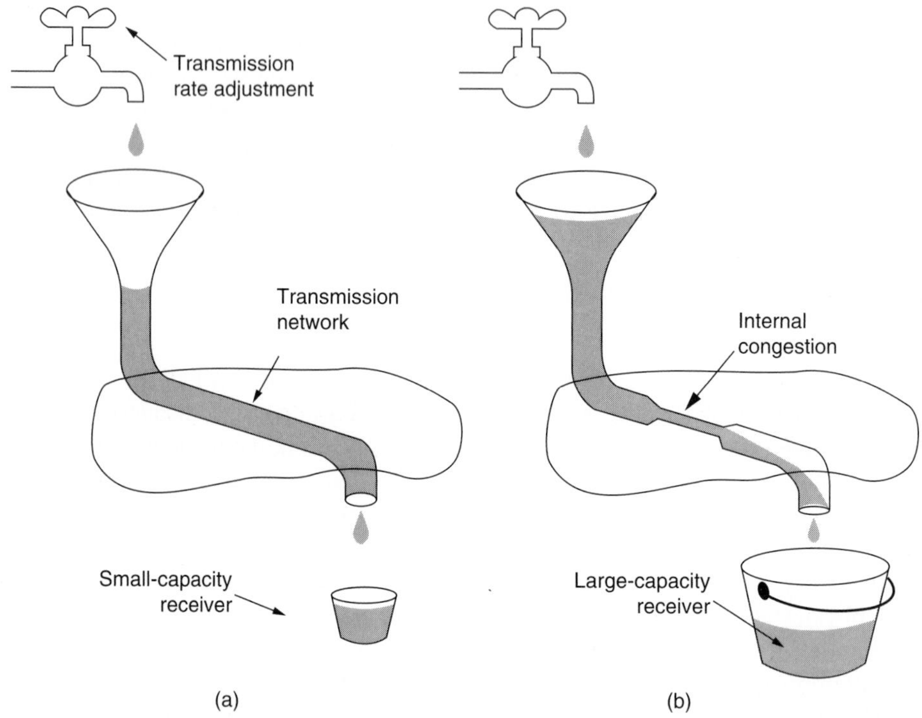

Figure 6-36. (a) A fast network feeding a low-capacity receiver. (b) A slow network feeding a high-capacity receiver.

The Internet solution is to realize that two potential problems exist—network capacity and receiver capacity—and to deal with each of them separately. To do so, each sender maintains two windows: the window the receiver has granted and a second window, the **congestion window**. Each reflects the number of bytes the sender may transmit. The number of bytes that may be sent is the minimum of the two windows. Thus, the effective window is the minimum of what the sender thinks is all right and what the receiver thinks is all right. If the receiver says "Send 8 KB" but the sender knows that bursts of more than 4 KB clog the network, it sends 4 KB. On the other hand, if the receiver says "Send 8 KB" and the sender knows that bursts of up to 32 KB get through effortlessly, it sends the full 8 KB requested.

When a connection is established, the sender initializes the congestion window to the size of the maximum segment in use on the connection. It then sends one maximum segment. If this segment is acknowledged before the timer goes off, it adds one segment's worth of bytes to the congestion window to make it two maximum size segments and sends two segments. As each of these segments is acknowledged, the congestion window is increased by one maximum segment size. When the congestion window is *n* segments, if all *n* are acknowledged on time, the congestion window is increased by the byte count corresponding to *n* segments. In effect, each burst acknowledged doubles the congestion window.

The congestion window keeps growing exponentially until either a timeout occurs or the receiver's window is reached. The idea is that if bursts of size, say, 1024, 2048, and 4096 bytes work fine but a burst of 8192 bytes gives a timeout, the congestion window should be set to 4096 to avoid congestion. As long as the congestion window remains at 4096, no bursts longer than that will be sent, no matter how much window space the receiver grants. This algorithm is called **slow start**, but it is not slow at all (Jacobson, 1988). It is exponential. All TCP implementations are required to support it.

Now let us look at the Internet congestion control algorithm. It uses a third parameter, the **threshold**, initially 64 KB, in addition to the receiver and congestion windows. When a timeout occurs, the threshold is set to half of the current congestion window, and the congestion window is reset to one maximum segment. Slow start is then used to determine what the network can handle, except that exponential growth stops when the threshold is hit. From that point on, successful transmissions grow the congestion window linearly (by one maximum segment for each burst) instead of one per segment. In effect, this algorithm is guessing that it is probably acceptable to cut the congestion window in half, and then it gradually works its way up from there.

As an illustration of how the congestion algorithm works, see Fig. 6-37. The maximum segment size here is 1024 bytes. Initially, the congestion window was 64 KB, but a timeout occurred, so the threshold is set to 32 KB and the congestion window to 1 KB for transmission 0 here. The congestion window then grows exponentially until it hits the threshold (32 KB). Starting then, it grows linearly.

Transmission 13 is unlucky (it should have known) and a timeout occurs. The threshold is set to half the current window (by now 40 KB, so half is 20 KB), and slow start is initiated all over again. When the acknowledgements from transmission 14 start coming in, the first four each double the congestion window, but after that, growth becomes linear again.

If no more timeouts occur, the congestion window will continue to grow up to the size of the receiver's window. At that point, it will stop growing and remain constant as long as there are no more timeouts and the receiver's window does not change size. As an aside, if an ICMP SOURCE QUENCH packet comes in and is passed to TCP, this event is treated the same way as a timeout. An alternative (and more recent approach) is described in RFC 3168.

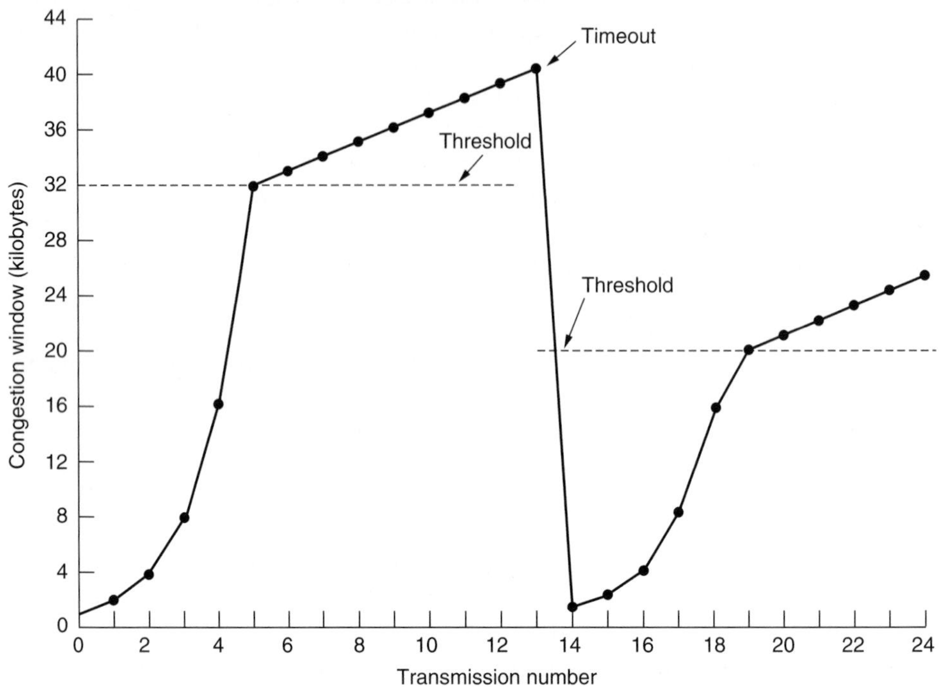

Figure 6-37. An example of the Internet congestion algorithm.

6.5.10 TCP Timer Management

TCP uses multiple timers (at least conceptually) to do its work. The most important of these is the **retransmission timer**. When a segment is sent, a retransmission timer is started. If the segment is acknowledged before the timer expires, the timer is stopped. If, on the other hand, the timer goes off before the acknowledgement comes in, the segment is retransmitted (and the timer started again). The question that arises is: How long should the timeout interval be?

This problem is much more difficult in the Internet transport layer than in the generic data link protocols of Chap. 3. In the latter case, the expected delay is highly predictable (i.e., has a low variance), so the timer can be set to go off just slightly after the acknowledgement is expected, as shown in Fig. 6-38(a). Since acknowledgements are rarely delayed in the data link layer (due to lack of congestion), the absence of an acknowledgement at the expected time generally means either the frame or the acknowledgement has been lost.

TCP is faced with a radically different environment. The probability density function for the time it takes for a TCP acknowledgement to come back looks more like Fig. 6-38(b) than Fig. 6-38(a). Determining the round-trip time to the destination is tricky. Even when it is known, deciding on the timeout interval is

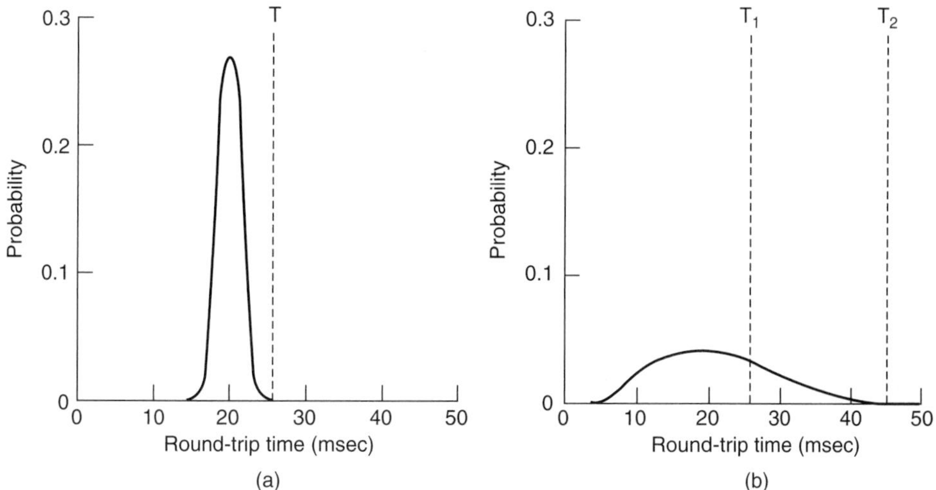

Figure 6-38. (a) Probability density of acknowledgement arrival times in the data link layer. (b) Probability density of acknowledgement arrival times for TCP.

also difficult. If the timeout is set too short, say, T_1 in Fig. 6-38(b), unnecessary retransmissions will occur, clogging the Internet with useless packets. If it is set too long, (e.g., T_2), performance will suffer due to the long retransmission delay whenever a packet is lost. Furthermore, the mean and variance of the acknowledgement arrival distribution can change rapidly within a few seconds as congestion builds up or is resolved.

The solution is to use a highly dynamic algorithm that constantly adjusts the timeout interval, based on continuous measurements of network performance. The algorithm generally used by TCP is due to Jacobson (1988) and works as follows. For each connection, TCP maintains a variable, *RTT*, that is the best current estimate of the round-trip time to the destination in question. When a segment is sent, a timer is started, both to see how long the acknowledgement takes and to trigger a retransmission if it takes too long. If the acknowledgement gets back before the timer expires, TCP measures how long the acknowledgement took, say, *M*. It then updates *RTT* according to the formula

$$RTT = \alpha RTT + (1 - \alpha)M$$

where α is a smoothing factor that determines how much weight is given to the old value. Typically $\alpha = 7/8$.

Even given a good value of *RTT*, choosing a suitable retransmission timeout is a nontrivial matter. Normally, TCP uses βRTT, but the trick is choosing β. In the initial implementations, β was always 2, but experience showed that a constant value was inflexible because it failed to respond when the variance went up.

In 1988, Jacobson proposed making β roughly proportional to the standard deviation of the acknowledgement arrival time probability density function so that a large variance means a large β, and vice versa. In particular, he suggested using the *mean deviation* as a cheap estimator of the *standard deviation*. His algorithm requires keeping track of another smoothed variable, D, the deviation. Whenever an acknowledgement comes in, the difference between the expected and observed values, $|RTT - M|$, is computed. A smoothed value of this is maintained in D by the formula

$$D = \alpha D + (1 - \alpha)\ |RTT - M|$$

where α may or may not be the same value used to smooth RTT. While D is not exactly the same as the standard deviation, it is good enough and Jacobson showed how it could be computed using only integer adds, subtracts, and shifts—a big plus. Most TCP implementations now use this algorithm and set the timeout interval to

$$\text{Timeout} = RTT + 4 \times D$$

The choice of the factor 4 is somewhat arbitrary, but it has two advantages. First, multiplication by 4 can be done with a single shift. Second, it minimizes unnecessary timeouts and retransmissions because less than 1 percent of all packets come in more than four standard deviations late. (Actually, Jacobson initially said to use 2, but later work has shown that 4 gives better performance.)

One problem that occurs with the dynamic estimation of RTT is what to do when a segment times out and is sent again. When the acknowledgement comes in, it is unclear whether the acknowledgement refers to the first transmission or a later one. Guessing wrong can seriously contaminate the estimate of RTT. Phil Karn discovered this problem the hard way. He is an amateur radio enthusiast interested in transmitting TCP/IP packets by ham radio, a notoriously unreliable medium (on a good day, half the packets get through). He made a simple proposal: do not update RTT on any segments that have been retransmitted. Instead, the timeout is doubled on each failure until the segments get through the first time. This fix is called **Karn's algorithm**. Most TCP implementations use it.

The retransmission timer is not the only timer TCP uses. A second timer is the **persistence timer**. It is designed to prevent the following deadlock. The receiver sends an acknowledgement with a window size of 0, telling the sender to wait. Later, the receiver updates the window, but the packet with the update is lost. Now both the sender and the receiver are waiting for each other to do something. When the persistence timer goes off, the sender transmits a probe to the receiver. The response to the probe gives the window size. If it is still zero, the persistence timer is set again and the cycle repeats. If it is nonzero, data can now be sent.

A third timer that some implementations use is the **keepalive timer**. When a connection has been idle for a long time, the keepalive timer may go off to cause one side to check whether the other side is still there. If it fails to respond, the connection is terminated. This feature is controversial because it adds overhead and may terminate an otherwise healthy connection due to a transient network partition.

The last timer used on each TCP connection is the one used in the *TIMED WAIT* state while closing. It runs for twice the maximum packet lifetime to make sure that when a connection is closed, all packets created by it have died off.

6.5.11 Wireless TCP and UDP

In theory, transport protocols should be independent of the technology of the underlying network layer. In particular, TCP should not care whether IP is running over fiber or over radio. In practice, it does matter because most TCP implementations have been carefully optimized based on assumptions that are true for wired networks but that fail for wireless networks. Ignoring the properties of wireless transmission can lead to a TCP implementation that is logically correct but has horrendous performance.

The principal problem is the congestion control algorithm. Nearly all TCP implementations nowadays assume that timeouts are caused by congestion, not by lost packets. Consequently, when a timer goes off, TCP slows down and sends less vigorously (e.g., Jacobson's slow start algorithm). The idea behind this approach is to reduce the network load and thus alleviate the congestion.

Unfortunately, wireless transmission links are highly unreliable. They lose packets all the time. The proper approach to dealing with lost packets is to send them again, and as quickly as possible. Slowing down just makes matters worse. If, say, 20 percent of all packets are lost, then when the sender transmits 100 packets/sec, the throughput is 80 packets/sec. If the sender slows down to 50 packets/sec, the throughput drops to 40 packets/sec.

In effect, when a packet is lost on a wired network, the sender should slow down. When one is lost on a wireless network, the sender should try harder. When the sender does not know what the network is, it is difficult to make the correct decision.

Frequently, the path from sender to receiver is heterogeneous. The first 1000 km might be over a wired network, but the last 1 km might be wireless. Now making the correct decision on a timeout is even harder, since it matters where the problem occurred. A solution proposed by Bakne and Badrinath (1995), **indirect TCP**, is to split the TCP connection into two separate connections, as shown in Fig. 6-39. The first connection goes from the sender to the base station. The second one goes from the base station to the receiver. The base station simply copies packets between the connections in both directions.

The advantage of this scheme is that both connections are now homogeneous. Timeouts on the first connection can slow the sender down, whereas timeouts on the second one can speed it up. Other parameters can also be tuned separately for

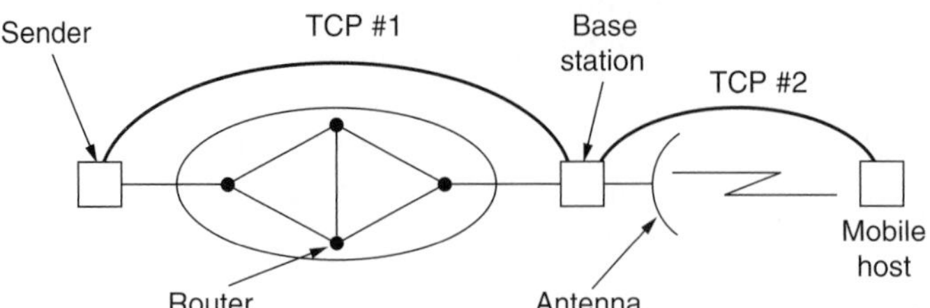

Figure 6-39. Splitting a TCP connection into two connections.

the two connections. The disadvantage of the scheme is that it violates the semantics of TCP. Since each part of the connection is a full TCP connection, the base station acknowledges each TCP segment in the usual way. Only now, receipt of an acknowledgement by the sender does not mean that the receiver got the segment, only that the base station got it.

A different solution, due to Balakrishnan et al. (1995), does not break the semantics of TCP. It works by making several small modifications to the network layer code in the base station. One of the changes is the addition of a snooping agent that observes and caches TCP segments going out to the mobile host and acknowledgements coming back from it. When the snooping agent sees a TCP segment going out to the mobile host but does not see an acknowledgement coming back before its (relatively short) timer goes off, it just retransmits that segment, without telling the source that it is doing so. It also retransmits when it sees duplicate acknowledgements from the mobile host go by, invariably meaning that the mobile host has missed something. Duplicate acknowledgements are discarded on the spot, to avoid having the source misinterpret them as congestion.

One disadvantage of this transparency, however, is that if the wireless link is very lossy, the source may time out waiting for an acknowledgement and invoke the congestion control algorithm. With indirect TCP, the congestion control algorithm will never be started unless there really is congestion in the wired part of the network.

The Balakrishnan et al. paper also has a solution to the problem of lost segments originating at the mobile host. When the base station notices a gap in the inbound sequence numbers, it generates a request for a selective repeat of the missing bytes by using a TCP option.

Using these fixes, the wireless link is made more reliable in both directions, without the source knowing about it and without changing the TCP semantics.

While UDP does not suffer from the same problems as TCP, wireless communication also introduces difficulties for it. The main trouble is that programs use UDP expecting it to be highly reliable. They know that no guarantees are given, but they still expect it to be near perfect. In a wireless environment, UDP will be far from perfect. For programs that can recover from lost UDP messages but only at considerable cost, suddenly going from an environment where messages theoretically can be lost but rarely are, to one in which they are constantly being lost can result in a performance disaster.

Wireless communication also affects areas other than just performance. For example, how does a mobile host find a local printer to connect to, rather than use its home printer? Somewhat related to this is how to get the WWW page for the local cell, even if its name is not known. Also, WWW page designers tend to assume lots of bandwidth is available. Putting a large logo on every page becomes counterproductive if it is going to take 10 sec to transmit over a slow wireless link every time the page is referenced, irritating the users no end.

As wireless networking becomes more common, the problems of running TCP over it become more acute. Additional work in this area is reported in (Barakat et al., 2000; Ghani and Dixit, 1999; Huston, 2001; and Xylomenos et al., 2001).

6.5.12 Transactional TCP

Earlier in this chapter we looked at remote procedure call as a way to implement client-server systems. If both the request and reply are small enough to fit into single packets and the operation is idempotent, UDP can simply be used, However, if these conditions are not met, using UDP is less attractive. For example, if the reply can be quite large, then the pieces must be sequenced and a mechanism must be devised to retransmit lost pieces. In effect, the application is required to reinvent TCP.

Clearly, that is unattractive, but using TCP itself is also unattractive. The problem is the efficiency. The normal sequence of packets for doing an RPC over TCP is shown in Fig. 6-40(a). Nine packets are required in the best case.

The nine packets are as follows:

1. The client sends a *SYN* packet to establish a connection.
2. The server sends an *ACK* packet to acknowledge the SYN packet.
3. The client completes the three-way handshake.
4. The client sends the actual request.
5. The client sends a *FIN* packet to indicate that it is done sending.
6. The server acknowledges the request and the *FIN*.
7. The server sends the reply back to the client.
8. The server sends a FIN packet to indicate that it is also done.
9. The client acknowledges the server's *FIN*.

Note that this is the best case. In the worst case, the client's request and *FIN* are acknowledged separately, as are the server's reply and *FIN*.

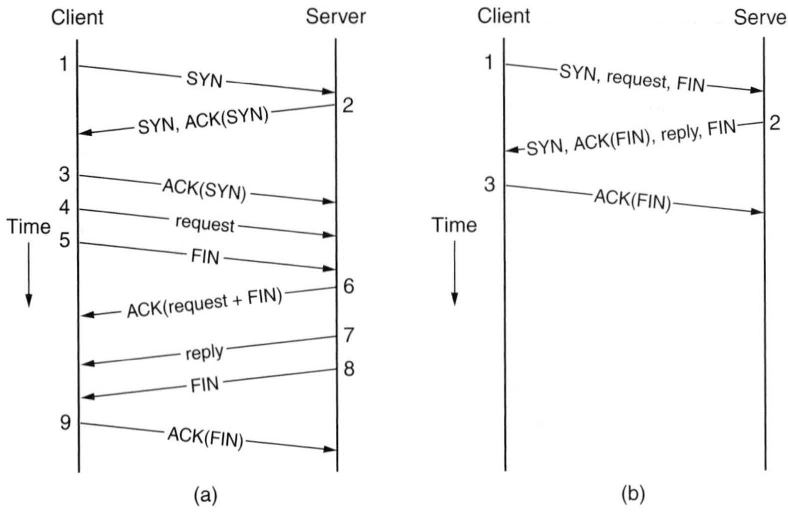

Figure 6-40. (a) RPC using normal TCP. (b) RPC using T/TCP.

The question quickly arises of whether there is some way to combine the efficiency of RPC using UDP (just two messages) with the reliability of TCP. The answer is: Almost. It can be done with an experimental TCP variant called **T/TCP** (**Transactional TCP**), which is described in RFCs 1379 and 1644.

The central idea here is to modify the standard connection setup sequence slightly to allow the transfer of data during setup. The T/TCP protocol is illustrated in Fig. 6-40(b). The client's first packet contains the *SYN* bit, the request itself, and the *FIN*. In effect it says: I want to establish a connection, here is the data, and I am done.

When the server gets the request, it looks up or computes the reply, and chooses how to respond. If the reply fits in one packet, it gives the reply of Fig. 6-40(b), which says: I acknowledge your *FIN*, here is the answer, and I am done. The client then acknowledges the server's *FIN* and the protocol terminates in three messages.

However, if the result is larger than 1 packet, the server also has the option of not turning on the *FIN* bit, in which case it can send multiple packets before closing its direction.

It is probably worth mentioning that T/TCP is not the only proposed improvement to TCP. Another proposal is **SCTP** (**Stream Control Transmission Protocol**). Its features include message boundary preservation, multiple delivery modes (e.g., unordered delivery), multihoming (backup destinations), and selective acknowledgements (Stewart and Metz, 2001). However, whenever someone proposes changing something that has worked so well for so long, there is always a huge battle between the "Users are demanding more features" and "If it ain't broken, don't fix it" camps.

6.6 PERFORMANCE ISSUES

Performance issues are very important in computer networks. When hundreds or thousands of computers are interconnected, complex interactions, with unforeseen consequences, are common. Frequently, this complexity leads to poor performance and no one knows why. In the following sections, we will examine many issues related to network performance to see what kinds of problems exist and what can be done about them.

Unfortunately, understanding network performance is more an art than a science. There is little underlying theory that is actually of any use in practice. The best we can do is give rules of thumb gained from hard experience and present examples taken from the real world. We have intentionally delayed this discussion until we studied the transport layer in TCP in order to be able to use TCP as an example in various places.

The transport layer is not the only place performance issues arise. We saw some of them in the network layer in the previous chapter. Nevertheless, the network layer tends to be largely concerned with routing and congestion control. The broader, system-oriented issues tend to be transport related, so this chapter is an appropriate place to examine them.

In the next five sections, we will look at five aspects of network performance:

1. Performance problems.
2. Measuring network performance.
3. System design for better performance.
4. Fast TPDU processing.
5. Protocols for future high-performance networks.

As an aside, we need a generic name for the units exchanged by transport entities. The TCP term, segment, is confusing at best and is never used outside the TCP world in this context. The ATM terms (CS-PDU, SAR-PDU, and CPCS-PDU) are specific to ATM. Packets clearly refer to the network layer, and messages belong to the application layer. For lack of a standard term, we will go back to calling the units exchanged by transport entities TPDUs. When we mean both TPDU and packet together, we will use packet as the collective term, as in "The CPU must be fast enough to process incoming packets in real time." By this we mean both the network layer packet and the TPDU encapsulated in it.

6.6.1 Performance Problems in Computer Networks

Some performance problems, such as congestion, are caused by temporary resource overloads. If more traffic suddenly arrives at a router than the router can handle, congestion will build up and performance will suffer. We studied congestion in detail in the previous chapter.

Performance also degrades when there is a structural resource imbalance. For example, if a gigabit communication line is attached to a low-end PC, the poor CPU will not be able to process the incoming packets fast enough and some will be lost. These packets will eventually be retransmitted, adding delay, wasting bandwidth, and generally reducing performance.

Overloads can also be synchronously triggered. For example, if a TPDU contains a bad parameter (e.g., the port for which it is destined), in many cases the receiver will thoughtfully send back an error notification. Now consider what could happen if a bad TPDU is broadcast to 10,000 machines: each one might send back an error message. The resulting **broadcast storm** could cripple the network. UDP suffered from this problem until the protocol was changed to cause hosts to refrain from responding to errors in UDP TPDUs sent to broadcast addresses.

A second example of synchronous overload is what happens after an electrical power failure. When the power comes back on, all the machines simultaneously jump to their ROMs to start rebooting. A typical reboot sequence might require first going to some (DHCP) server to learn one's true identity, and then to some file server to get a copy of the operating system. If hundreds of machines all do this at once, the server will probably collapse under the load.

Even in the absence of synchronous overloads and the presence of sufficient resources, poor performance can occur due to lack of system tuning. For example, if a machine has plenty of CPU power and memory but not enough of the memory has been allocated for buffer space, overruns will occur and TPDUs will be lost. Similarly, if the scheduling algorithm does not give a high enough priority to processing incoming TPDUs, some of them may be lost.

Another tuning issue is setting timeouts correctly. When a TPDU is sent, a timer is typically set to guard against loss of the TPDU. If the timeout is set too short, unnecessary retransmissions will occur, clogging the wires. If the timeout is set too long, unnecessary delays will occur after a TPDU is lost. Other tunable parameters include how long to wait for data on which to piggyback before sending a separate acknowledgement, and how many retransmissions before giving up.

Gigabit networks bring with them new performance problems. Consider, for example, sending a 64-KB burst of data from San Diego to Boston in order to fill the receiver's 64-KB buffer. Suppose that the link is 1 Gbps and the one-way speed-of-light-in-fiber delay is 20 msec. Initially, at $t = 0$, the pipe is empty, as illustrated in Fig. 6-41(a). Only 500 μsec later, in Fig. 6-41(b), all the TPDUs are out on the fiber. The lead TPDU will now be somewhere in the vicinity of Brawley, still deep in Southern California. However, the transmitter must stop until it gets a window update.

After 20 msec, the lead TPDU hits Boston, as shown in Fig. 6-41(c) and is acknowledged. Finally, 40 msec after starting, the first acknowledgement gets back to the sender and the second burst can be transmitted. Since the transmission line was used for 0.5 msec out of 40, the efficiency is about 1.25 percent. This situation is typical of older protocols running over gigabit lines.

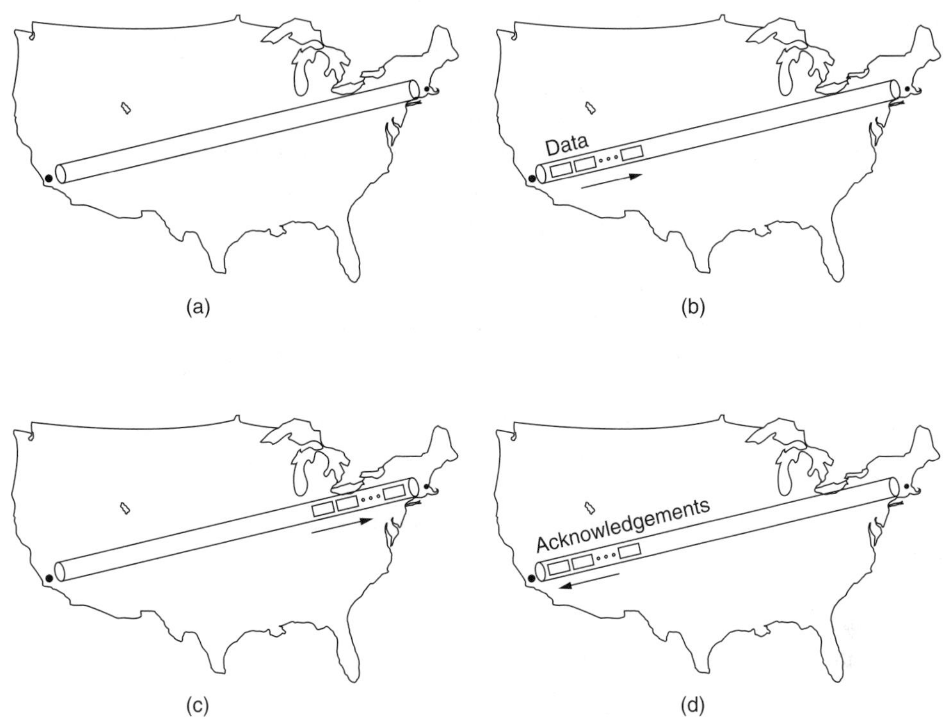

Figure 6-41. The state of transmitting one megabit from San Diego to Boston. (a) At $t = 0$. (b) After 500 μsec. (c) After 20 msec. (d) After 40 msec.

A useful quantity to keep in mind when analyzing network performance is the **bandwidth-delay product**. It is obtained by multiplying the bandwidth (in bits/sec) by the round-trip delay time (in sec). The product is the capacity of the pipe from the sender to the receiver and back (in bits).

For the example of Fig. 6-41 the bandwidth-delay product is 40 million bits. In other words, the sender would have to transmit a burst of 40 million bits to be able to keep going full speed until the first acknowledgement came back. It takes this many bits to fill the pipe (in both directions). This is why a burst of half a million bits only achieves a 1.25 percent efficiency: it is only 1.25 percent of the pipe's capacity.

The conclusion that can be drawn here is that for good performance, the receiver's window must be at least as large as the bandwidth-delay product, preferably somewhat larger since the receiver may not respond instantly. For a transcontinental gigabit line, at least 5 megabytes are required.

If the efficiency is terrible for sending a megabit, imagine what it is like for a short request of a few hundred bytes. Unless some other use can be found for the line while the first client is waiting for its reply, a gigabit line is no better than a megabit line, just more expensive.

Another performance problem that occurs with time-critical applications like audio and video is jitter. Having a short mean transmission time is not enough. A small standard deviation is also required. Achieving a short mean transmission time along with a small standard deviation demands a serious engineering effort.

6.6.2 Network Performance Measurement

When a network performs poorly, its users often complain to the folks running it, demanding improvements. To improve the performance, the operators must first determine exactly what is going on. To find out what is really happening, the operators must make measurements. In this section we will look at network performance measurements. The discussion below is based on the work of Mogul (1993).

The basic loop used to improve network performance contains the following steps:

1. Measure the relevant network parameters and performance.
2. Try to understand what is going on.
3. Change one parameter.

These steps are repeated until the performance is good enough or it is clear that the last drop of improvement has been squeezed out.

Measurements can be made in many ways and at many locations (both physically and in the protocol stack). The most basic kind of measurement is to start a timer when beginning some activity and see how long that activity takes. For example, knowing how long it takes for a TPDU to be acknowledged is a key measurement. Other measurements are made with counters that record how often some event has happened (e.g., number of lost TPDUs). Finally, one is often interested in knowing the amount of something, such as the number of bytes processed in a certain time interval.

Measuring network performance and parameters has many potential pitfalls. Below we list a few of them. Any systematic attempt to measure network performance should be careful to avoid these.

Make Sure That the Sample Size Is Large Enough

Do not measure the time to send one TPDU, but repeat the measurement, say, one million times and take the average. Having a large sample will reduce the uncertainty in the measured mean and standard deviation. This uncertainty can be computed using standard statistical formulas.

Make Sure That the Samples Are Representative

Ideally, the whole sequence of one million measurements should be repeated at different times of the day and the week to see the effect of different system loads on the measured quantity. Measurements of congestion, for example, are of little use if they are made at a moment when there is no congestion. Sometimes the results may be counterintuitive at first, such as heavy congestion at 10, 11, 1, and 2 o'clock, but no congestion at noon (when all the users are away at lunch).

Be Careful When Using a Coarse-Grained Clock

Computer clocks work by incrementing some counter at regular intervals. For example, a millisecond timer adds 1 to a counter every 1 msec. Using such a timer to measure an event that takes less than 1 msec is possible, but requires some care. (Some computers have more accurate clocks, of course.)

To measure the time to send a TPDU, for example, the system clock (say, in milliseconds) should be read out when the transport layer code is entered and again when it is exited. If the true TPDU send time is 300 μsec, the difference between the two readings will be either 0 or 1, both wrong. However, if the measurement is repeated one million times and the total of all measurements added up and divided by one million, the mean time will be accurate to better than 1 μsec.

Be Sure That Nothing Unexpected Is Going On during Your Tests

Making measurements on a university system the day some major lab project has to be turned in may give different results than if made the next day. Likewise, if some researcher has decided to run a video conference over your network during your tests, you may get a biased result. It is best to run tests on an idle system and create the entire workload yourself. Even this approach has pitfalls though. While you might think nobody will be using the network at 3 A.M., that might be precisely when the automatic backup program begins copying all the disks to tape. Furthermore, there might be heavy traffic for your wonderful World Wide Web pages from distant time zones.

Caching Can Wreak Havoc with Measurements

The obvious way to measure file transfer times is to open a large file, read the whole thing, close it, and see how long it takes. Then repeat the measurement many more times to get a good average. The trouble is, the system may cache the file, so only the first measurement actually involves network traffic. The rest are just reads from the local cache. The results from such a measurement are essentially worthless (unless you want to measure cache performance).

Often you can get around caching by simply overflowing the cache. For example, if the cache is 10 MB, the test loop could open, read, and close two 10-

MB files on each pass, in an attempt to force the cache hit rate to 0. Still, caution is advised unless you are absolutely sure you understand the caching algorithm.

Buffering can have a similar effect. One popular TCP/IP performance utility program has been known to report that UDP can achieve a performance substantially higher than the physical line allows. How does this occur? A call to UDP normally returns control as soon as the message has been accepted by the kernel and added to the transmission queue. If there is sufficient buffer space, timing 1000 UDP calls does not mean that all the data have been sent. Most of them may still be in the kernel, but the performance utility thinks they have all been transmitted.

Understand What You Are Measuring

When you measure the time to read a remote file, your measurements depend on the network, the operating systems on both the client and server, the particular hardware interface boards used, their drivers, and other factors. If the measurements are done carefully, you will ultimately discover the file transfer time for the configuration you are using. If your goal is to tune this particular configuration, these measurements are fine.

However, if you are making similar measurements on three different systems in order to choose which network interface board to buy, your results could be thrown off completely by the fact that one of the network drivers is truly awful and is only getting 10 percent of the performance of the board.

Be Careful about Extrapolating the Results

Suppose that you make measurements of something with simulated network loads running from 0 (idle) to 0.4 (40 percent of capacity), as shown by the data points and solid line through them in Fig. 6-42. It may be tempting to extrapolate linearly, as shown by the dotted line. However, many queueing results involve a factor of $1/(1 - \rho)$, where ρ is the load, so the true values may look more like the dashed line, which rises much faster than linearly.

6.6.3 System Design for Better Performance

Measuring and tinkering can often improve performance considerably, but they cannot substitute for good design in the first place. A poorly-designed network can be improved only so much. Beyond that, it has to be redesigned from scratch.

In this section, we will present some rules of thumb based on hard experience with many networks. These rules relate to system design, not just network design, since the software and operating system are often more important than the routers and interface boards. Most of these ideas have been common knowledge to net-

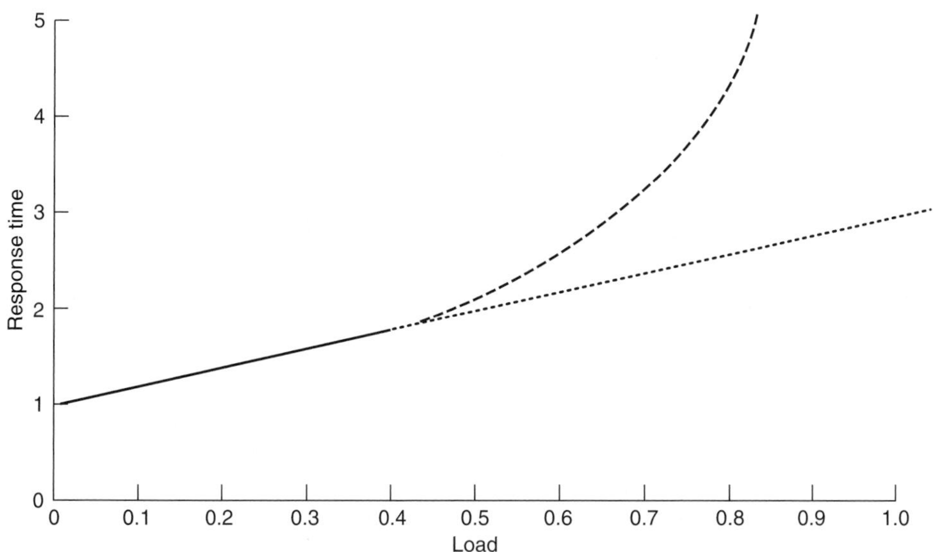

Figure 6-42. Response as a function of load.

work designers for years and have been passed on from generation to generation by word of mouth. They were first stated explicitly by Mogul (1993); our treatment largely follows his. Another relevant source is (Metcalfe, 1993).

Rule #1: CPU Speed Is More Important Than Network Speed

Long experience has shown that in nearly all networks, operating system and protocol overhead dominate actual time on the wire. For example, in theory, the minimum RPC time on an Ethernet is 102 μsec, corresponding to a minimum (64-byte) request followed by a minimum (64-byte) reply. In practice, overcoming the software overhead and getting the RPC time anywhere near there is a substantial achievement.

Similarly, the biggest problem in running at 1 Gbps is getting the bits from the user's buffer out onto the fiber fast enough and having the receiving CPU process them as fast as they come in. In short, if you double the CPU speed, you often can come close to doubling the throughput. Doubling the network capacity often has no effect since the bottleneck is generally in the hosts.

Rule #2: Reduce Packet Count to Reduce Software Overhead

Processing a TPDU has a certain amount of overhead per TPDU (e.g., header processing) and a certain amount of processing per byte (e.g., doing the checksum). When 1 million bytes are being sent, the per-byte overhead is the same no matter what the TPDU size is. However, using 128-byte TPDUs means 32 times as much per-TPDU overhead as using 4-KB TPDUs. This overhead adds up fast.

In addition to the TPDU overhead, there is overhead in the lower layers to consider. Each arriving packet causes an interrupt. On a modern pipelined processor, each interrupt breaks the CPU pipeline, interferes with the cache, requires a change to the memory management context, and forces a substantial number of CPU registers to be saved. An n-fold reduction in TPDUs sent thus reduces the interrupt and packet overhead by a factor of n.

This observation argues for collecting a substantial amount of data before transmission in order to reduce interrupts at the other side. Nagle's algorithm and Clark's solution to the silly window syndrome are attempts to do precisely this.

Rule #3: Minimize Context Switches

Context switches (e.g., from kernel mode to user mode) are deadly. They have the same bad properties as interrupts, the worst being a long series of initial cache misses. Context switches can be reduced by having the library procedure that sends data do internal buffering until it has a substantial amount of them. Similarly, on the receiving side, small incoming TPDUs should be collected together and passed to the user in one fell swoop instead of individually, to minimize context switches.

In the best case, an incoming packet causes a context switch from the current user to the kernel, and then a switch to the receiving process to give it the newly-arrived data. Unfortunately, with many operating systems, additional context switches happen. For example, if the network manager runs as a special process in user space, a packet arrival is likely to cause a context switch from the current user to the kernel, then another one from the kernel to the network manager, followed by another one back to the kernel, and finally one from the kernel to the receiving process. This sequence is shown in Fig. 6-43. All these context switches on each packet are very wasteful of CPU time and will have a devastating effect on network performance.

Rule #4: Minimize Copying

Even worse than multiple context switches are multiple copies. It is not unusual for an incoming packet to be copied three or four times before the TPDU enclosed in it is delivered. After a packet is received by the network interface in a special on-board hardware buffer, it is typically copied to a kernel buffer. From there it is copied to a network layer buffer, then to a transport layer buffer, and finally to the receiving application process.

A clever operating system will copy a word at a time, but it is not unusual to require about five instructions per word (a load, a store, incrementing an index

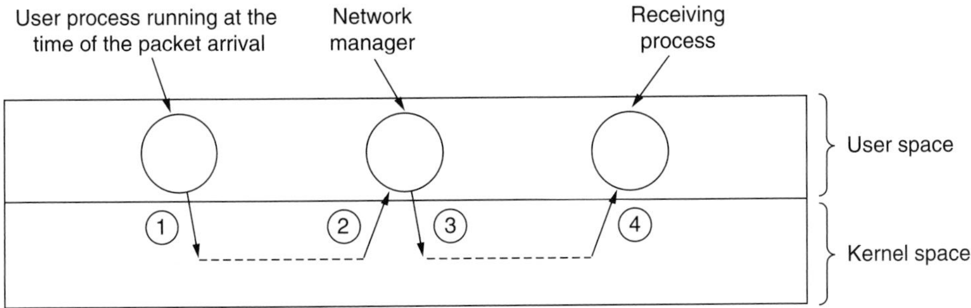

Figure 6-43. Four context switches to handle one packet with a user-space network manager.

register, a test for end-of-data, and a conditional branch). Making three copies of each packet at five instructions per 32-bit word copied requires 15/4 or about four instructions per byte copied. On a 500-MIPS CPU, an instruction takes 2 nsec so each byte needs 8 nsec of processing time or about 1 nsec per bit, giving a maximum rate of about 1 Gbps. When overhead for header processing, interrupt handling, and context switches is factored in, 500 Mbps might be achievable, and we have not even considered the actual processing of the data. Clearly, handling a 10-Gbps Ethernet running at full blast is out of the question.

In fact, probably a 500-Mbps line cannot be handled at full speed either. In the computation above, we have assumed that a 500-MIPS machine can execute any 500 million instructions/sec. In reality, machines can only run at such speeds if they are not referencing memory. Memory operations are often a factor of ten slower than register-register instructions (i.e., 20 nsec/instruction). If 20 percent of the instructions actually reference memory (i.e., are cache misses), which is likely when touching incoming packets, the average instruction execution time is 5.6 nsec ($0.8 \times 2 + 0.2 \times 20$). With four instructions/byte, we need 22.4 nsec/byte, or 2.8 nsec/bit), which gives about 357 Mbps. Factoring in 50 percent overhead gives us 178 Mbps. Note that hardware assistance will not help here. The problem is too much copying by the operating system.

Rule #5: You Can Buy More Bandwidth but Not Lower Delay

The next three rules deal with communication, rather than protocol processing. The first rule states that if you want more bandwidth, you can just buy it. Putting a second fiber next to the first one doubles the bandwidth but does nothing to reduce the delay. Making the delay shorter requires improving the protocol software, the operating system, or the network interface. Even if all of these improvements are made, the delay will not be reduced if the bottleneck is the transmission time.

Rule #6: Avoiding Congestion Is Better Than Recovering from It

The old maxim that an ounce of prevention is worth a pound of cure certainly holds for network congestion. When a network is congested, packets are lost, bandwidth is wasted, useless delays are introduced, and more. Recovering from congestion takes time and patience. Not having it occur in the first place is better. Congestion avoidance is like getting your DTP vaccination: it hurts a little at the time you get it, but it prevents something that would hurt a lot more in the future.

Rule #7: Avoid Timeouts

Timers are necessary in networks, but they should be used sparingly and timeouts should be minimized. When a timer goes off, some action is generally repeated. If it is truly necessary to repeat the action, so be it, but repeating it unnecessarily is wasteful.

The way to avoid extra work is to be careful that timers are set a little bit on the conservative side. A timer that takes too long to expire adds a small amount of extra delay to one connection in the (unlikely) event of a TPDU being lost. A timer that goes off when it should not have uses up scarce CPU time, wastes bandwidth, and puts extra load on perhaps dozens of routers for no good reason.

6.6.4 Fast TPDU Processing

The moral of the story above is that the main obstacle to fast networking is protocol software. In this section we will look at some ways to speed up this software. For more information, see (Clark et al., 1989; and Chase et al., 2001).

TPDU processing overhead has two components: overhead per TPDU and overhead per byte. Both must be attacked. The key to fast TPDU processing is to separate out the normal case (one-way data transfer) and handle it specially. Although a sequence of special TPDUs is needed to get into the *ESTABLISHED* state, once there, TPDU processing is straightforward until one side starts to close the connection.

Let us begin by examining the sending side in the *ESTABLISHED* state when there are data to be transmitted. For the sake of clarity, we assume here that the transport entity is in the kernel, although the same ideas apply if it is a user-space process or a library inside the sending process. In Fig. 6-44, the sending process traps into the kernel to do the SEND. The first thing the transport entity does is test to see if this is the normal case: the state is *ESTABLISHED*, neither side is trying to close the connection, a regular (i.e., not an out-of-band) full TPDU is being sent, and enough window space is available at the receiver. If all conditions are met, no further tests are needed and the fast path through the sending transport entity can be taken. Typically, this path is taken most of the time.

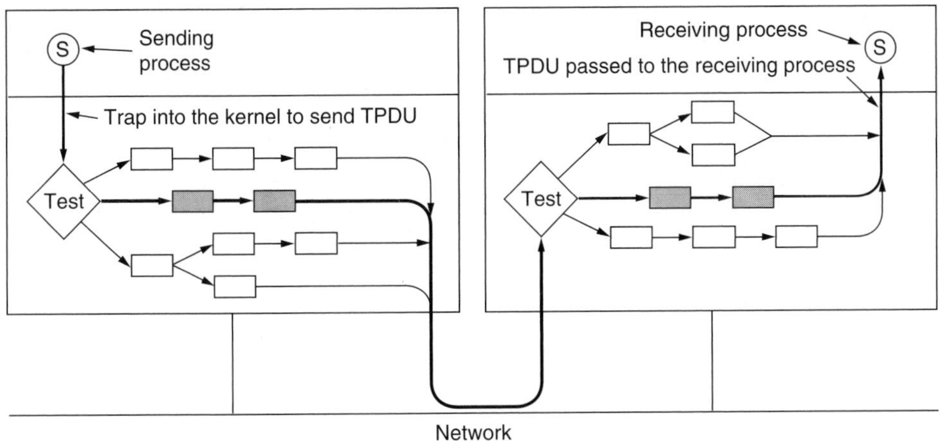

Figure 6-44. The fast path from sender to receiver is shown with a heavy line. The processing steps on this path are shaded.

In the usual case, the headers of consecutive data TPDUs are almost the same. To take advantage of this fact, a prototype header is stored within the transport entity. At the start of the fast path, it is copied as fast as possible to a scratch buffer, word by word. Those fields that change from TPDU to TPDU are then overwritten in the buffer. Frequently, these fields are easily derived from state variables, such as the next sequence number. A pointer to the full TPDU header plus a pointer to the user data are then passed to the network layer. Here the same strategy can be followed (not shown in Fig. 6-44). Finally, the network layer gives the resulting packet to the data link layer for transmission.

As an example of how this principle works in practice, let us consider TCP/IP. Fig. 6-45(a) shows the TCP header. The fields that are the same between consecutive TPDUs on a one-way flow are shaded. All the sending transport entity has to do is copy the five words from the prototype header into the output buffer, fill in the next sequence number (by copying it from a word in memory), compute the checksum, and increment the sequence number in memory. It can then hand the header and data to a special IP procedure for sending a regular, maximum TPDU. IP then copies its five-word prototype header [see Fig. 6-45(b)] into the buffer, fills in the *Identification* field, and computes its checksum. The packet is now ready for transmission.

Now let us look at fast path processing on the receiving side of Fig. 6-44. Step 1 is locating the connection record for the incoming TPDU. For TCP, the connection record can be stored in a hash table for which some simple function of the two IP addresses and two ports is the key. Once the connection record has been located, both addresses and both ports must be compared to verify that the correct record has been found.

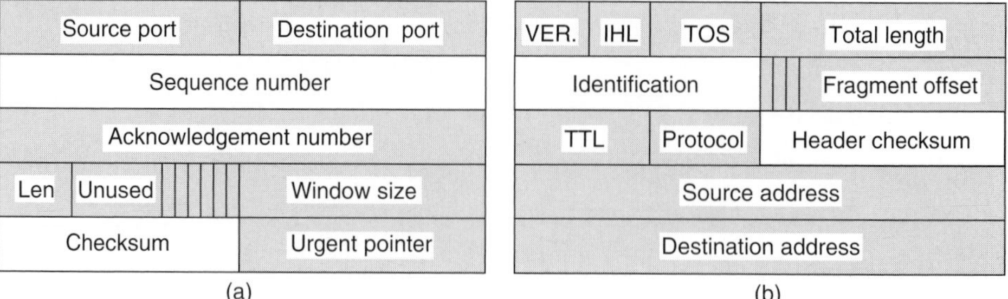

Figure 6-45. (a) TCP header. (b) IP header. In both cases, the shaded fields are taken from the prototype without change.

An optimization that often speeds up connection record lookup even more is to maintain a pointer to the last one used and try that one first. Clark et al. (1989) tried this and observed a hit rate exceeding 90 percent. Other lookup heuristics are described in (McKenney and Dove, 1992).

The TPDU is then checked to see if it is a normal one: the state is *ESTABLISHED*, neither side is trying to close the connection, the TPDU is a full one, no special flags are set, and the sequence number is the one expected. These tests take just a handful of instructions. If all conditions are met, a special fast path TCP procedure is called.

The fast path updates the connection record and copies the data to the user. While it is copying, it also computes the checksum, eliminating an extra pass over the data. If the checksum is correct, the connection record is updated and an acknowledgement is sent back. The general scheme of first making a quick check to see if the header is what is expected and then having a special procedure handle that case is called **header prediction**. Many TCP implementations use it. When this optimization and all the other ones discussed in this chapter are used together, it is possible to get TCP to run at 90 percent of the speed of a local memory-to-memory copy, assuming the network itself is fast enough.

Two other areas where major performance gains are possible are buffer management and timer management. The issue in buffer management is avoiding unnecessary copying, as mentioned above. Timer management is important because nearly all timers set do not expire. They are set to guard against TPDU loss, but most TPDUs arrive correctly and their acknowledgements also arrive correctly. Hence, it is important to optimize timer management for the case of timers rarely expiring.

A common scheme is to use a linked list of timer events sorted by expiration time. The head entry contains a counter telling how many ticks away from expiry it is. Each successive entry contains a counter telling how many ticks after the previous entry it is. Thus, if timers expire in 3, 10, and 12 ticks, respectively, the three counters are 3, 7, and 2, respectively.

At every clock tick, the counter in the head entry is decremented. When it hits zero, its event is processed and the next item on the list becomes the head. Its counter does not have to be changed. In this scheme, inserting and deleting timers are expensive operations, with execution times proportional to the length of the list.

A more efficient approach can be used if the maximum timer interval is bounded and known in advance. Here an array, called a **timing wheel**, can be used, as shown in Fig. 6-46. Each slot corresponds to one clock tick. The current time shown is $T = 4$. Timers are scheduled to expire at 3, 10, and 12 ticks from now. If a new timer suddenly is set to expire in seven ticks, an entry is just made in slot 11. Similarly, if the timer set for $T + 10$ has to be canceled, the list starting in slot 14 has to be searched and the required entry removed. Note that the array of Fig. 6-46 cannot accommodate timers beyond $T + 15$.

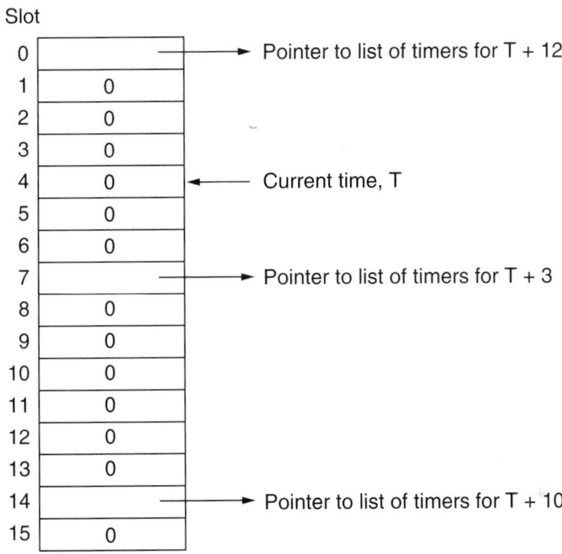

Figure 6-46. A timing wheel.

When the clock ticks, the current time pointer is advanced by one slot (circularly). If the entry now pointed to is nonzero, all of its timers are processed. Many variations on the basic idea are discussed in (Varghese and Lauck, 1987).

6.6.5 Protocols for Gigabit Networks

At the start of the 1990s, gigabit networks began to appear. People's first reaction was to use the old protocols on them, but various problems quickly arose. In this section we will discuss some of these problems and the directions new protocols are taking to solve them as we move toward ever faster networks.

The first problem is that many protocols use 32-bit sequence numbers. When the Internet began, the lines between routers were mostly 56-kbps leased lines, so a host blasting away at full speed took over 1 week to cycle through the sequence numbers. To the TCP designers, 2^{32} was a pretty decent approximation of infinity because there was little danger of old packets still being around a week after they were transmitted. With 10-Mbps Ethernet, the wrap time became 57 minutes, much shorter, but still manageable. With a 1-Gbps Ethernet pouring data out onto the Internet, the wrap time is about 34 seconds, well under the 120 sec maximum packet lifetime on the Internet. All of a sudden, 2^{32} is not nearly as good an approximation to infinity since a sender can cycle through the sequence space while old packets still exist. RFC 1323 provides an escape hatch, though.

The problem is that many protocol designers simply assumed, without stating it, that the time to use up the entire sequence space would greatly exceed the maximum packet lifetime. Consequently, there was no need to even worry about the problem of old duplicates still existing when the sequence numbers wrapped around. At gigabit speeds, that unstated assumption fails.

A second problem is that communication speeds have improved much faster than computing speeds. (Note to computer engineers: Go out and beat those communication engineers! We are counting on you.) In the 1970s, the ARPANET ran at 56 kbps and had computers that ran at about 1 MIPS. Packets were 1008 bits, so the ARPANET was capable of delivering about 56 packets/sec. With almost 18 msec available per packet, a host could afford to spend 18,000 instructions processing a packet. Of course, doing so would soak up the entire CPU, but it could devote 9000 instructions per packet and still have half the CPU left to do real work.

Compare these numbers to 1000-MIPS computers exchanging 1500-byte packets over a gigabit line. Packets can flow in at a rate of over 80,000 per second, so packet processing must be completed in 6.25 μsec if we want to reserve half the CPU for applications. In 6.25 μsec, a 1000-MIPS computer can execute 6250 instructions, only 1/3 of what the ARPANET hosts had available. Furthermore, modern RISC instructions do less per instruction than the old CISC instructions did, so the problem is even worse than it appears. The conclusion is this: there is less time available for protocol processing than there used to be, so protocols must become simpler.

A third problem is that the go back n protocol performs poorly on lines with a large bandwidth-delay product. Consider, for example, a 4000-km line operating at 1 Gbps. The round-trip transmission time is 40 msec, in which time a sender can transmit 5 megabytes. If an error is detected, it will be 40 msec before the sender is told about it. If go back n is used, the sender will have to retransmit not just the bad packet, but also the 5 megabytes worth of packets that came afterward. Clearly, this is a massive waste of resources.

A fourth problem is that gigabit lines are fundamentally different from megabit lines in that long gigabit lines are delay limited rather than bandwidth limited.

In Fig. 6-47 we show the time it takes to transfer a 1-megabit file 4000 km at various transmission speeds. At speeds up to 1 Mbps, the transmission time is dominated by the rate at which the bits can be sent. By 1 Gbps, the 40-msec round-trip delay dominates the 1 msec it takes to put the bits on the fiber. Further increases in bandwidth have hardly any effect at all.

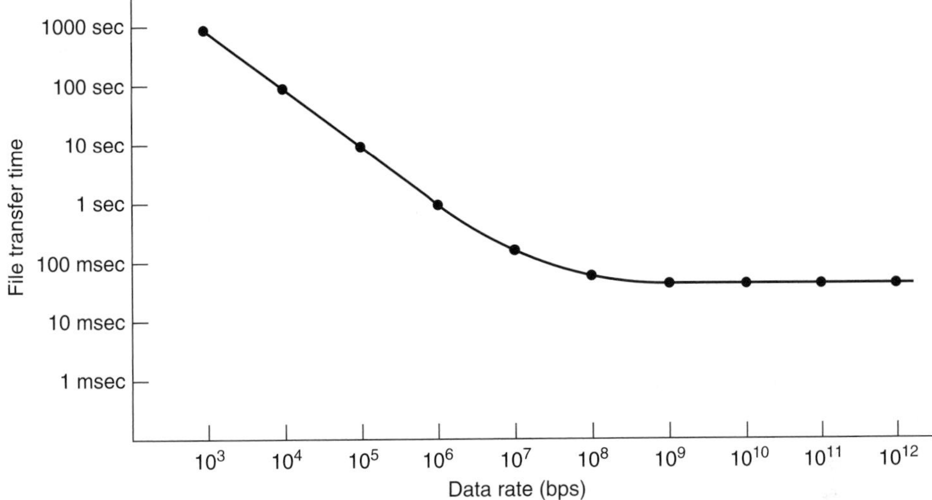

Figure 6-47. Time to transfer and acknowledge a 1-megabit file over a 4000-km line.

Figure 6-47 has unfortunate implications for network protocols. It says that stop-and-wait protocols, such as RPC, have an inherent upper bound on their performance. This limit is dictated by the speed of light. No amount of technological progress in optics will ever improve matters (new laws of physics would help, though).

A fifth problem that is worth mentioning is not a technological or protocol one like the others, but a result of new applications. Simply stated, it is that for many gigabit applications, such as multimedia, the variance in the packet arrival times is as important as the mean delay itself. A slow-but-uniform delivery rate is often preferable to a fast-but-jumpy one.

Let us now turn from the problems to ways of dealing with them. We will first make some general remarks, then look at protocol mechanisms, packet layout, and protocol software.

The basic principle that all gigabit network designers should learn by heart is:

Design for speed, not for bandwidth optimization.

Old protocols were often designed to minimize the number of bits on the wire, frequently by using small fields and packing them together into bytes and words.

Nowadays, there is plenty of bandwidth. Protocol processing is the problem, so protocols should be designed to minimize it. The IPv6 designers clearly understood this principle.

A tempting way to go fast is to build fast network interfaces in hardware. The difficulty with this strategy is that unless the protocol is exceedingly simple, hardware just means a plug-in board with a second CPU and its own program. To make sure the network coprocessor is cheaper than the main CPU, it is often a slower chip. The consequence of this design is that much of the time the main (fast) CPU is idle waiting for the second (slow) CPU to do the critical work. It is a myth to think that the main CPU has other work to do while waiting. Furthermore, when two general-purpose CPUs communicate, race conditions can occur, so elaborate protocols are needed between the two processors to synchronize them correctly. Usually, the best approach is to make the protocols simple and have the main CPU do the work.

Let us now look at the issue of feedback in high-speed protocols. Due to the (relatively) long delay loop, feedback should be avoided: it takes too long for the receiver to signal the sender. One example of feedback is governing the transmission rate by using a sliding window protocol. To avoid the (long) delays inherent in the receiver sending window updates to the sender, it is better to use a rate-based protocol. In such a protocol, the sender can send all it wants to, provided it does not send faster than some rate the sender and receiver have agreed upon in advance.

A second example of feedback is Jacobson's slow start algorithm. This algorithm makes multiple probes to see how much the network can handle. With high-speed networks, making half a dozen or so small probes to see how the network responds wastes a huge amount of bandwidth. A more efficient scheme is to have the sender, receiver, and network all reserve the necessary resources at connection setup time. Reserving resources in advance also has the advantage of making it easier to reduce jitter. In short, going to high speeds inexorably pushes the design toward connection-oriented operation, or something fairly close to it. Of course, if bandwidth becomes so plentiful in the future that nobody cares about wasting lots of it, the design rules will become very different.

Packet layout is an important consideration in gigabit networks. The header should contain as few fields as possible, to reduce processing time, and these fields should be big enough to do the job and be word aligned for ease of processing. In this context, "big enough" means that problems such as sequence numbers wrapping around while old packets still exist, receivers being unable to advertise enough window space because the window field is too small, and so on do not occur.

The header and data should be separately checksummed, for two reasons. First, to make it possible to checksum the header but not the data. Second, to verify that the header is correct before copying the data into user space. It is desirable to do the data checksum at the time the data are copied to user space, but if the header is incorrect, the copy may go to the wrong process. To avoid an incorrect copy but to allow the data checksum to be done during copying, it is essential that the two checksums be separate.

The maximum data size should be large, to permit efficient operation even in the face of long delays. Also, the larger the data block, the smaller the fraction of the total bandwidth devoted to headers. 1500 bytes is too small.

Another valuable feature is the ability to send a normal amount of data along with the connection request. In this way, one round-trip time can be saved.

Finally, a few words about the protocol software are appropriate. A key thought is concentrating on the successful case. Many older protocols tend to emphasize what to do when something goes wrong (e.g., a packet getting lost). To make the protocols run fast, the designer should aim for minimizing processing time when everything goes right. Minimizing processing time when an error occurs is secondary.

A second software issue is minimizing copying time. As we saw earlier, copying data is often the main source of overhead. Ideally, the hardware should dump each incoming packet into memory as a contiguous block of data. The software should then copy this packet to the user buffer with a single block copy. Depending on how the cache works, it may even be desirable to avoid a copy loop. In other words, to copy 1024 words, the fastest way may be to have 1024 back-to-back MOVE instructions (or 1024 load-store pairs). The copy routine is so critical it should be carefully handcrafted in assembly code, unless there is a way to trick the compiler into producing precisely the optimal code.

6.7 SUMMARY

The transport layer is the key to understanding layered protocols. It provides various services, the most important of which is an end-to-end, reliable, connection-oriented byte stream from sender to receiver. It is accessed through service primitives that permit the establishment, use, and release of connections. A common transport layer interface is the one provided by Berkeley sockets.

Transport protocols must be able to do connection management over unreliable networks. Connection establishment is complicated by the existence of delayed duplicate packets that can reappear at inopportune moments. To deal with them, three-way handshakes are needed to establish connections. Releasing a connection is easier than establishing one but is still far from trivial due to the two-army problem.

Even when the network layer is completely reliable, the transport layer has plenty of work to do. It must handle all the service primitives, manage connections and timers, and allocate and utilize credits.

The Internet has two main transport protocols: UDP and TCP. UDP is a connectionless protocol that is mainly a wrapper for IP packets with the additional feature of multiplexing and demultiplexing multiple processes using a single IP address. UDP can be used for client-server interactions, for example, using RPC. It can also be used for building real-time protocols such as RTP.

The main Internet transport protocol is TCP. It provides a reliable bidirectional byte stream. It uses a 20-byte header on all segments. Segments can be fragmented by routers within the Internet, so hosts must be prepared to do reassembly. A great deal of work has gone into optimizing TCP performance, using algorithms from Nagle, Clark, Jacobson, Karn, and others. Wireless links add a variety of complications to TCP. Transactional TCP is an extension to TCP that handles client-server interactions with a reduced number of packets.

Network performance is typically dominated by protocol and TPDU processing overhead, and this situation gets worse at higher speeds. Protocols should be designed to minimize the number of TPDUs, context switches, and times each TPDU is copied. For gigabit networks, simple protocols are called for.

PROBLEMS

1. In our example transport primitives of Fig. 6-2, LISTEN is a blocking call. Is this strictly necessary? If not, explain how a nonblocking primitive could be used. What advantage would this have over the scheme described in the text?

2. In the model underlying Fig. 6-4, it is assumed that packets may be lost by the network layer and thus must be individually acknowledged. Suppose that the network layer is 100 percent reliable and never loses packets. What changes, if any, are needed to Fig. 6-4?

3. In both parts of Fig. 6-6, there is a comment that the value of *SERVER_PORT* must be the same in both client and server. Why is this so important?

4. Suppose that the clock-driven scheme for generating initial sequence numbers is used with a 15-bit wide clock counter. The clock ticks once every 100 msec, and the maximum packet lifetime is 60 sec. How often need resynchronization take place
   (a) in the worst case?
   (b) when the data consumes 240 sequence numbers/min?

5. Why does the maximum packet lifetime, *T*, have to be large enough to ensure that not only the packet but also its acknowledgements have vanished?

6. Imagine that a two-way handshake rather than a three-way handshake were used to set up connections. In other words, the third message was not required. Are deadlocks now possible? Give an example or show that none exist.

7. Imagine a generalized *n*-army problem, in which the agreement of any two of the blue armies is sufficient for victory. Does a protocol exist that allows blue to win?

8. Consider the problem of recovering from host crashes (i.e., Fig. 6-18). If the interval between writing and sending an acknowledgement, or vice versa, can be made relatively small, what are the two best sender-receiver strategies for minimizing the chance of a protocol failure?

9. Are deadlocks possible with the transport entity described in the text (Fig. 6-20)?

10. Out of curiosity, the implementer of the transport entity of Fig. 6-20 has decided to put counters inside the *sleep* procedure to collect statistics about the *conn* array. Among these are the number of connections in each of the seven possible states, n_i $(i = 1, \ldots, 7)$. After writing a massive FORTRAN program to analyze the data, our implementer discovers that the relation $\sum n_i = MAX\_CONN$ appears to always be true. Are there any other invariants involving only these seven variables?

11. What happens when the user of the transport entity given in Fig. 6-20 sends a zero-length message? Discuss the significance of your answer.

12. For each event that can potentially occur in the transport entity of Fig. 6-20, tell whether it is legal when the user is sleeping in *sending* state.

13. Discuss the advantages and disadvantages of credits versus sliding window protocols.

14. Why does UDP exist? Would it not have been enough to just let user processes send raw IP packets?

15. Consider a simple application-level protocol built on top of UDP that allows a client to retrieve a file from a remote server residing at a well-known address. The client first sends a request with file name, and the server responds with a sequence of data packets containing different parts of the requested file. To ensure reliability and sequenced delivery, client and server use a stop-and-wait protocol. Ignoring the obvious performance issue, do you see a problem with this protocol? Think carefully about the possibility of processes crashing.

16. A client sends a 128-byte request to a server located 100 km away over a 1-gigabit optical fiber. What is the efficiency of the line during the remote procedure call?

17. Consider the situation of the previous problem again. Compute the minimum possible response time both for the given 1-Gbps line and for a 1-Mbps line. What conclusion can you draw?

18. Both UDP and TCP use port numbers to identify the destination entity when delivering a message. Give two reasons for why these protocols invented a new abstract ID (port numbers), instead of using process IDs, which already existed when these protocols were designed.

19. What is the total size of the minimum TCP MTU, including TCP and IP overhead but not including data link layer overhead?

20. Datagram fragmentation and reassembly are handled by IP and are invisible to TCP. Does this mean that TCP does not have to worry about data arriving in the wrong order?

21. RTP is used to transmit CD-quality audio, which makes a pair of 16-bit samples 44,100 times/sec, one sample for each of the stereo channels. How many packets per second must RTP transmit?

22. Would it be possible to place the RTP code in the operating system kernel, along with the UDP code? Explain your answer.

23. A process on host 1 has been assigned port p, and a process on host 2 has been assigned port q. Is it possible for there to be two or more TCP connections between these two ports at the same time?

24. In Fig. 6-29 we saw that in addition to the 32-bit *Acknowledgement* field, there is an *ACK* bit in the fourth word. Does this really add anything? Why or why not?

25. The maximum payload of a TCP segment is 65,495 bytes. Why was such a strange number chosen?

26. Describe two ways to get into the *SYN RCVD* state of Fig. 6-33.

27. Give a potential disadvantage when Nagle's algorithm is used on a badly-congested network.

28. Consider the effect of using slow start on a line with a 10-msec round-trip time and no congestion. The receive window is 24 KB and the maximum segment size is 2 KB. How long does it take before the first full window can be sent?

29. Suppose that the TCP congestion window is set to 18 KB and a timeout occurs. How big will the window be if the next four transmission bursts are all successful? Assume that the maximum segment size is 1 KB.

30. If the TCP round-trip time, *RTT*, is currently 30 msec and the following acknowledgements come in after 26, 32, and 24 msec, respectively, what is the new *RTT* estimate using the Jacobson algorithm? Use $\alpha = 0.9$.

31. A TCP machine is sending full windows of 65,535 bytes over a 1-Gbps channel that has a 10-msec one-way delay. What is the maximum throughput achievable? What is the line efficiency?

32. What is the fastest line speed at which a host can blast out 1500-byte TCP payloads with a 120-sec maximum packet lifetime without having the sequence numbers wrap around? Take TCP, IP, and Ethernet overhead into consideration. Assume that Ethernet frames may be sent continuously.

33. In a network that has a maximum TPDU size of 128 bytes, a maximum TPDU lifetime of 30 sec, and an 8-bit sequence number, what is the maximum data rate per connection?

34. Suppose that you are measuring the time to receive a TPDU. When an interrupt occurs, you read out the system clock in milliseconds. When the TPDU is fully processed, you read out the clock again. You measure 0 msec 270,000 times and 1 msec 730,000 times. How long does it take to receive a TPDU?

35. A CPU executes instructions at the rate of 1000 MIPS. Data can be copied 64 bits at a time, with each word copied costing 10 instructions. If an coming packet has to be copied four times, can this system handle a 1-Gbps line? For simplicity, assume that all instructions, even those instructions that read or write memory, run at the full 1000-MIPS rate.

36. To get around the problem of sequence numbers wrapping around while old packets still exist, one could use 64-bit sequence numbers. However, theoretically, an optical fiber can run at 75 Tbps. What maximum packet lifetime is required to make sure that future 75 Tbps networks do not have wraparound problems even with 64-bit sequence numbers? Assume that each byte has its own sequence number, as TCP does.

37. Give one advantage of RPC on UDP over transactional TCP. Give one advantage of T/TCP over RPC.

38. In Fig. 6-40(a), we see that it takes 9 packets to complete the RPC. Are there any circumstances in which it takes exactly 10 packets?

39. In Sec. 6.6.5, we calculated that a gigabit line dumps 80,000 packets/sec on the host, giving it only 6250 instructions to process it and leaving half the CPU time for applications. This calculation assumed a 1500-byte packet. Redo the calculation for an ARPANET-sized packet (128 bytes). In both cases, assume that the packet sizes given include all overhead.

40. For a 1-Gbps network operating over 4000 km, the delay is the limiting factor, not the bandwidth. Consider a MAN with the average source and destination 20 km apart. At what data rate does the round-trip delay due to the speed of light equal the transmission delay for a 1-KB packet?

41. Calculate the bandwidth-delay product for the following networks: (1) T1 (1.5 Mbps), (2) Ethernet (10 Mbps), (3) T3 (45 Mbps), and (4) STS-3 (155 Mbps). Assume an RTT of 100 msec. Recall that a TCP header has 16 bits reserved for Window Size. What are its implications in light of your calculations?

42. What is the bandwidth-delay product for a 50-Mbps channel on a geostationary satellite? If the packets are all 1500 bytes (including overhead), how big should the window be in packets?

43. The file server of Fig. 6-6 is far from perfect and could use a few improvements. Make the following modifications.
(a) Give the client a third argument that specifies a byte range.
(b) Add a client flag –w that allows the file to be written to the server.

44. Modify the program of Fig. 6-20 to do error recovery. Add a new packet type, *reset*, that can arrive after a connection has been opened by both sides but closed by neither. This event, which happens simultaneously on both ends of the connection, means that any packets that were in transit have either been delivered or destroyed, but in either case are no longer in the subnet.

45. Write a program that simulates buffer management in a transport entity, using a sliding window for flow control rather than the credit system of Fig. 6-20. Let higher-layer processes randomly open connections, send data, and close connections. To keep it simple, have all the data travel from machine *A* to machine *B*, and none the other way. Experiment with different buffer allocation strategies at *B*, such as dedicating buffers to specific connections versus a common buffer pool, and measure the total throughput achieved by each one.

46. Design and implement a chat system that allows multiple groups of users to chat. A chat coordinator resides at a well-known network address, uses UDP for communication with chat clients, sets up chat servers for each chat session, and maintains a chat session directory. There is one chat server per chat session. A chat server uses TCP for communication with clients. A chat client allows users to start, join, and leave a chat session. Design and implement the coordinator, server, and client code.

7

THE APPLICATION LAYER

Having finished all the preliminaries, we now come to the layer where all the applications are found. The layers below the application layer are there to provide reliable transport, but they do not do real work for users. In this chapter we will study some real network applications.

However, even in the application layer there is a need for support protocols, to allow the applications to function. Accordingly, we will look at one of these before starting with the applications themselves. The item in question is DNS, which handles naming within the Internet. After that, we will examine three real applications: electronic mail, the World Wide Web, and finally, multimedia.

7.1 DNS—THE DOMAIN NAME SYSTEM

Although programs theoretically could refer to hosts, mailboxes, and other resources by their network (e.g., IP) addresses, these addresses are hard for people to remember. Also, sending e-mail to *tana@128.111.24.41* means that if Tana's ISP or organization moves the mail server to a different machine with a different IP address, her e-mail address has to change. Consequently, ASCII names were introduced to decouple machine names from machine addresses. In this way, Tana's address might be something like *tana@art.ucsb.edu.* Nevertheless, the network itself understands only numerical addresses, so some mechanism is required to convert the ASCII strings to network addresses. In the following sections we will study how this mapping is accomplished in the Internet.

Way back in the ARPANET, there was simply a file, *hosts.txt*, that listed all the hosts and their IP addresses. Every night, all the hosts would fetch it from the site at which it was maintained. For a network of a few hundred large timesharing machines, this approach worked reasonably well.

However, when thousands of minicomputers and PCs were connected to the net, everyone realized that this approach could not continue to work forever. For one thing, the size of the file would become too large. However, even more important, host name conflicts would occur constantly unless names were centrally managed, something unthinkable in a huge international network due to the load and latency. To solve these problems, **DNS** (the **Domain Name System**) was invented.

The essence of DNS is the invention of a hierarchical, domain-based naming scheme and a distributed database system for implementing this naming scheme. It is primarily used for mapping host names and e-mail destinations to IP addresses but can also be used for other purposes. DNS is defined in RFCs 1034 and 1035.

Very briefly, the way DNS is used is as follows. To map a name onto an IP address, an application program calls a library procedure called the **resolver**, passing it the name as a parameter. We saw an example of a resolver, *gethostbyname*, in Fig. 6-6. The resolver sends a UDP packet to a local DNS server, which then looks up the name and returns the IP address to the resolver, which then returns it to the caller. Armed with the IP address, the program can then establish a TCP connection with the destination or send it UDP packets.

7.1.1 The DNS Name Space

Managing a large and constantly changing set of names is a nontrivial problem. In the postal system, name management is done by requiring letters to specify (implicitly or explicitly) the country, state or province, city, and street address of the addressee. By using this kind of hierarchical addressing, there is no confusion between the Marvin Anderson on Main St. in White Plains, N.Y. and the Marvin Anderson on Main St. in Austin, Texas. DNS works the same way.

Conceptually, the Internet is divided into over 200 top-level **domains**, where each domain covers many hosts. Each domain is partitioned into subdomains, and these are further partitioned, and so on. All these domains can be represented by a tree, as shown in Fig. 7-1. The leaves of the tree represent domains that have no subdomains (but do contain machines, of course). A leaf domain may contain a single host, or it may represent a company and contain thousands of hosts.

The top-level domains come in two flavors: generic and countries. The original generic domains were *com (commercial), edu* (educational institutions), *gov* (the U.S. Federal Government), *int* (certain international organizations), *mil* (the U.S. armed forces), *net* (network providers), and *org* (nonprofit organizations). The country domains include one entry for every country, as defined in ISO 3166.

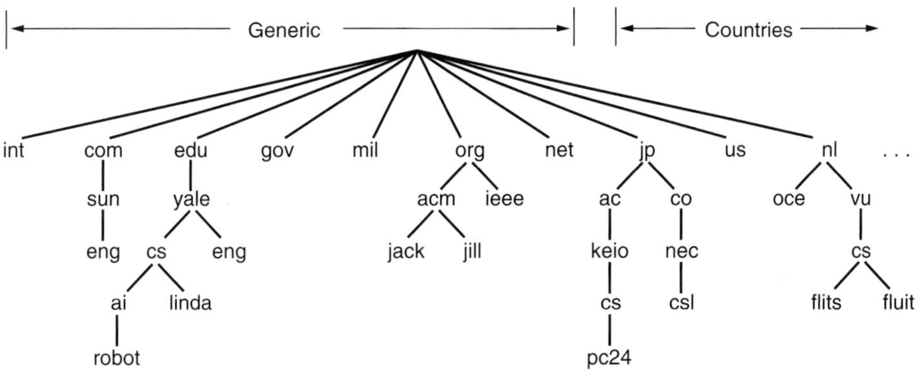

Figure 7-1. A portion of the Internet domain name space.

In November 2000, ICANN approved four new, general-purpose, top-level domains, namely, *biz* (businesses), *info* (information), *name* (people's names), and *pro* (professions, such as doctors and lawyers). In addition, three more specialized top-level domains were introduced at the request of certain industries. These are *aero* (aerospace industry), *coop* (co-operatives), and *museum* (museums). Other top-level domains will be added in the future.

As an aside, as the Internet becomes more commercial, it also becomes more contentious. Take *pro*, for example. It was intended for certified professionals. But who is a professional? And certified by whom? Doctors and lawyers clearly are professionals. But what about freelance photographers, piano teachers, magicians, plumbers, barbers, exterminators, tattoo artists, mercenaries, and prostitutes? Are these occupations professional and thus eligible for *pro* domains? And if so, who certifies the individual practitioners?

In general, getting a second-level domain, such as *name-of-company*.com, is easy. It merely requires going to a registrar for the corresponding top-level domain (*com* in this case) to check if the desired name is available and not somebody else's trademark. If there are no problems, the requester pays a small annual fee and gets the name. By now, virtually every common (English) word has been taken in the *com* domain. Try household articles, animals, plants, body parts, etc. Nearly all are taken.

Each domain is named by the path upward from it to the (unnamed) root. The components are separated by periods (pronounced "dot"). Thus, the engineering department at Sun Microsystems might be *eng.sun.com.*, rather than a UNIX-style name such as */com/sun/eng*. Notice that this hierarchical naming means that *eng.sun.com.* does not conflict with a potential use of *eng* in *eng.yale.edu.*, which might be used by the Yale English department.

Domain names can be either absolute or relative. An absolute domain name always ends with a period (e.g., *eng.sun.com.*), whereas a relative one does not.

Relative names have to be interpreted in some context to uniquely determine their true meaning. In both cases, a named domain refers to a specific node in the tree and all the nodes under it.

Domain names are case insensitive, so *edu*, *Edu*, and *EDU* mean the same thing. Component names can be up to 63 characters long, and full path names must not exceed 255 characters.

In principle, domains can be inserted into the tree in two different ways. For example, *cs.yale.edu* could equally well be listed under the *us* country domain as *cs.yale.ct.us*. In practice, however, most organizations in the United States are under a generic domain, and most outside the United States are under the domain of their country. There is no rule against registering under two top-level domains, but few organizations except multinationals do it (e.g., *sony.com* and *sony.nl*).

Each domain controls how it allocates the domains under it. For example, Japan has domains *ac.jp* and *co.jp* that mirror *edu* and *com*. The Netherlands does not make this distinction and puts all organizations directly under *nl*. Thus, all three of the following are university computer science departments:

1. *cs.yale.edu* (Yale University, in the United States)
2. *cs.vu.nl* (Vrije Universiteit, in The Netherlands)
3. *cs.keio.ac.jp* (Keio University, in Japan)

To create a new domain, permission is required of the domain in which it will be included. For example, if a VLSI group is started at Yale and wants to be known as *vlsi.cs.yale.edu*, it has to get permission from whoever manages *cs.yale.edu*. Similarly, if a new university is chartered, say, the University of Northern South Dakota, it must ask the manager of the *edu* domain to assign it *unsd.edu*. In this way, name conflicts are avoided and each domain can keep track of all its subdomains. Once a new domain has been created and registered, it can create subdomains, such as *cs.unsd.edu*, without getting permission from anybody higher up the tree.

Naming follows organizational boundaries, not physical networks. For example, if the computer science and electrical engineering departments are located in the same building and share the same LAN, they can nevertheless have distinct domains. Similarly, even if computer science is split over Babbage Hall and Turing Hall, the hosts in both buildings will normally belong to the same domain.

7.1.2 Resource Records

Every domain, whether it is a single host or a top-level domain, can have a set of **resource records** associated with it. For a single host, the most common resource record is just its IP address, but many other kinds of resource records also exist. When a resolver gives a domain name to DNS, what it gets back are the resource records associated with that name. Thus, the primary function of DNS is to map domain names onto resource records.

A resource record is a five-tuple. Although they are encoded in binary for efficiency, in most expositions, resource records are presented as ASCII text, one line per resource record. The format we will use is as follows:

Domain_name Time_to_live Class Type Value

The *Domain_name* tells the domain to which this record applies. Normally, many records exist for each domain and each copy of the database holds information about multiple domains. This field is thus the primary search key used to satisfy queries. The order of the records in the database is not significant.

The *Time_to_live* field gives an indication of how stable the record is. Information that is highly stable is assigned a large value, such as 86400 (the number of seconds in 1 day). Information that is highly volatile is assigned a small value, such as 60 (1 minute). We will come back to this point later when we have discussed caching.

The third field of every resource record is the *Class*. For Internet information, it is always *IN*. For non-Internet information, other codes can be used, but in practice, these are rarely seen.

The *Type* field tells what kind of record this is. The most important types are listed in Fig. 7-2.

Type	Meaning	Value
SOA	Start of Authority	Parameters for this zone
A	IP address of a host	32-Bit integer
MX	Mail exchange	Priority, domain willing to accept e-mail
NS	Name Server	Name of a server for this domain
CNAME	Canonical name	Domain name
PTR	Pointer	Alias for an IP address
HINFO	Host description	CPU and OS in ASCII
TXT	Text	Uninterpreted ASCII text

Figure 7-2. The principal DNS resource record types for IPv4.

An *SOA* record provides the name of the primary source of information about the name server's zone (described below), the e-mail address of its administrator, a unique serial number, and various flags and timeouts.

The most important record type is the *A* (Address) record. It holds a 32-bit IP address for some host. Every Internet host must have at least one IP address so that other machines can communicate with it. Some hosts have two or more network connections, in which case they will have one type *A* resource record per network connection (and thus per IP address). DNS can be configured to cycle through these, returning the first record on the first request, the second record on the second request, and so on.

The next most important record type is the *MX* record. It specifies the name of the host prepared to accept e-mail for the specified domain. It is used because not every machine is prepared to accept e-mail. If someone wants to send e-mail to, for example, *bill@microsoft.com*, the sending host needs to find a mail server at *microsoft.com* that is willing to accept e-mail. The *MX* record can provide this information.

The *NS* records specify name servers. For example, every DNS database normally has an *NS* record for each of the top-level domains, so, for example, e-mail can be sent to distant parts of the naming tree. We will come back to this point later.

CNAME records allow aliases to be created. For example, a person familiar with Internet naming in general and wanting to send a message to someone whose login name is *paul* in the computer science department at M.I.T. might guess that *paul@cs.mit.edu* will work. Actually, this address will not work, because the domain for M.I.T.'s computer science department is *lcs.mit.edu*. However, as a service to people who do not know this, M.I.T. could create a *CNAME* entry to point people and programs in the right direction. An entry like this one might do the job:

```
cs.mit.edu    86400    IN    CNAME    lcs.mit.edu
```

Like *CNAME*, *PTR* points to another name. However, unlike *CNAME*, which is really just a macro definition, *PTR* is a regular DNS datatype whose interpretation depends on the context in which it is found. In practice, it is nearly always used to associate a name with an IP address to allow lookups of the IP address and return the name of the corresponding machine. These are called **reverse lookups**.

HINFO records allow people to find out what kind of machine and operating system a domain corresponds to. Finally, *TXT* records allow domains to identify themselves in arbitrary ways. Both of these record types are for user convenience. Neither is required, so programs cannot count on getting them (and probably cannot deal with them if they do get them).

Finally, we have the *Value* field. This field can be a number, a domain name, or an ASCII string. The semantics depend on the record type. A short description of the *Value* fields for each of the principal record types is given in Fig. 7-2.

For an example of the kind of information one might find in the DNS database of a domain, see Fig. 7-3. This figure depicts part of a (semihypothetical) database for the *cs.vu.nl* domain shown in Fig. 7-1. The database contains seven types of resource records.

The first noncomment line of Fig. 7-3 gives some basic information about the domain, which will not concern us further. The next two lines give textual information about where the domain is located. Then come two entries giving the first

```
; Authoritative data for cs.vu.nl
cs.vu.nl.        86400  IN  SOA    star boss (9527,7200,7200,241920,86400)
cs.vu.nl.        86400  IN  TXT    "Divisie Wiskunde en Informatica."
cs.vu.nl.        86400  IN  TXT    "Vrije Universiteit Amsterdam."
cs.vu.nl.        86400  IN  MX     1 zephyr.cs.vu.nl.
cs.vu.nl.        86400  IN  MX     2 top.cs.vu.nl.

flits.cs.vu.nl.  86400  IN  HINFO  Sun Unix
flits.cs.vu.nl.  86400  IN  A      130.37.16.112
flits.cs.vu.nl.  86400  IN  A      192.31.231.165
flits.cs.vu.nl.  86400  IN  MX     1 flits.cs.vu.nl.
flits.cs.vu.nl.  86400  IN  MX     2 zephyr.cs.vu.nl.
flits.cs.vu.nl.  86400  IN  MX     3 top.cs.vu.nl.
www.cs.vu.nl.    86400  IN  CNAME  star.cs.vu.nl
ftp.cs.vu.nl.    86400  IN  CNAME  zephyr.cs.vu.nl

rowboat                 IN  A      130.37.56.201
                        IN  MX     1 rowboat
                        IN  MX     2 zephyr
                        IN  HINFO  Sun Unix

little-sister           IN  A      130.37.62.23
                        IN  HINFO  Mac MacOS

laserjet                IN  A      192.31.231.216
                        IN  HINFO  "HP Laserjet IIISi" Proprietary
```

Figure 7-3. A portion of a possible DNS database for *cs.vu.nl*

and second places to try to deliver e-mail sent to *person@cs.vu.nl*. The *zephyr* (a specific machine) should be tried first. If that fails, the *top* should be tried as the next choice.

After the blank line, added for readability, come lines telling that the *flits* is a Sun workstation running UNIX and giving both of its IP addresses. Then three choices are given for handling e-mail sent to *flits.cs.vu.nl*. First choice is naturally the *flits* itself, but if it is down, the *zephyr* and *top* are the second and third choices. Next comes an alias, *www.cs.vu.nl*, so that this address can be used without designating a specific machine. Creating this alias allows *cs.vu.nl* to change its World Wide Web server without invalidating the address people use to get to it. A similar argument holds for *ftp.cs.vu.nl*.

The next four lines contain a typical entry for a workstation, in this case, *rowboat.cs.vu.nl*. The information provided contains the IP address, the primary and secondary mail drops, and information about the machine. Then comes an entry for a non-UNIX system that is not capable of receiving mail itself, followed by an entry for a laser printer that is connected to the Internet.

What are not shown (and are not in this file) are the IP addresses used to look up the top-level domains. These are needed to look up distant hosts, but since they are not part of the *cs.vu.nl* domain, they are not in this file. They are supplied by the root servers, whose IP addresses are present in a system configuration file and loaded into the DNS cache when the DNS server is booted. There are about a dozen root servers spread around the world, and each one knows the IP addresses of all the top-level domain servers. Thus, if a machine knows the IP address of at least one root server, it can look up any DNS name.

7.1.3 Name Servers

In theory at least, a single name server could contain the entire DNS database and respond to all queries about it. In practice, this server would be so overloaded as to be useless. Furthermore, if it ever went down, the entire Internet would be crippled.

To avoid the problems associated with having only a single source of information, the DNS name space is divided into nonoverlapping **zones**. One possible way to divide the name space of Fig. 7-1 is shown in Fig. 7-4. Each zone contains some part of the tree and also contains name servers holding the information about that zone. Normally, a zone will have one primary name server, which gets its information from a file on its disk, and one or more secondary name servers, which get their information from the primary name server. To improve reliability, some servers for a zone can be located outside the zone.

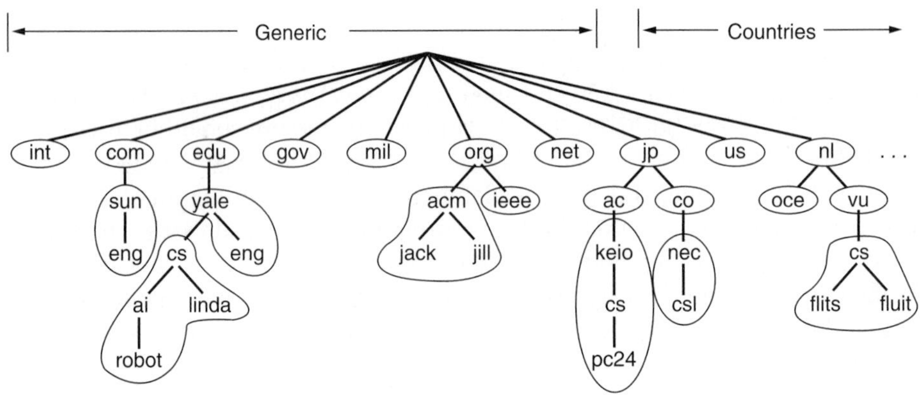

Figure 7-4. Part of the DNS name space showing the division into zones.

Where the zone boundaries are placed within a zone is up to that zone's administrator. This decision is made in large part based on how many name servers are desired, and where. For example, in Fig. 7-4, Yale has a server for *yale.edu* that handles *eng.yale.edu* but not *cs.yale.edu*, which is a separate zone with its own name servers. Such a decision might be made when a department such as English does not wish to run its own name server, but a department such as computer science does. Consequently, *cs.yale.edu* is a separate zone but *eng.yale.edu* is not.

When a resolver has a query about a domain name, it passes the query to one of the local name servers. If the domain being sought falls under the jurisdiction of the name server, such as *ai.cs.yale.edu* falling under *cs.yale.edu*, it returns the authoritative resource records. An **authoritative record** is one that comes from the authority that manages the record and is thus always correct. Authoritative records are in contrast to cached records, which may be out of date.

If, however, the domain is remote and no information about the requested domain is available locally, the name server sends a query message to the top-level name server for the domain requested. To make this process clearer, consider the example of Fig. 7-5. Here, a resolver on *flits.cs.vu.nl* wants to know the IP address of the host *linda.cs.yale.edu*. In step 1, it sends a query to the local name server, *cs.vu.nl*. This query contains the domain name sought, the type (*A*) and the class (*IN*).

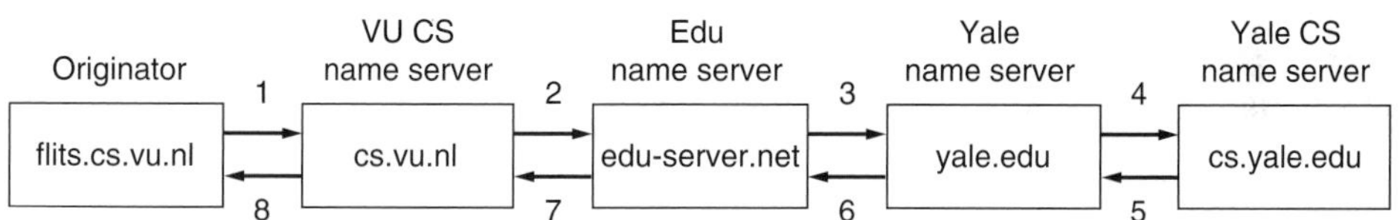

Figure 7-5. How a resolver looks up a remote name in eight steps.

Let us suppose the local name server has never had a query for this domain before and knows nothing about it. It may ask a few other nearby name servers, but if none of them know, it sends a UDP packet to the server for *edu* given in its database (see Fig. 7-5), *edu-server.net*. It is unlikely that this server knows the address of *linda.cs.yale.edu*, and probably does not know *cs.yale.edu* either, but it must know all of its own children, so it forwards the request to the name server for *yale.edu* (step 3). In turn, this one forwards the request to *cs.yale.edu* (step 4), which must have the authoritative resource records. Since each request is from a client to a server, the resource record requested works its way back in steps 5 through 8.

Once these records get back to the *cs.vu.nl* name server, they will be entered into a cache there, in case they are needed later. However, this information is not authoritative, since changes made at *cs.yale.edu* will not be propagated to all the caches in the world that may know about it. For this reason, cache entries should not live too long. This is the reason that the *Time_to_live* field is included in each resource record. It tells remote name servers how long to cache records. If a certain machine has had the same IP address for years, it may be safe to cache that information for 1 day. For more volatile information, it might be safer to purge the records after a few seconds or a minute.

It is worth mentioning that the query method described here is known as a **recursive query**, since each server that does not have the requested information goes and finds it somewhere, then reports back. An alternative form is also possible. In this form, when a query cannot be satisfied locally, the query fails, but the name of the next server along the line to try is returned. Some servers do not implement recursive queries and always return the name of the next server to try.

It is also worth pointing out that when a DNS client fails to get a response before its timer goes off, it normally will try another server next time. The assumption here is that the server is probably down, rather than that the request or reply got lost.

While DNS is extremely important to the correct functioning of the Internet, all it really does is map symbolic names for machines onto their IP addresses. It does not help locate people, resources, services, or objects in general. For locating these things, another directory service has been defined, called **LDAP** (**Lightweight Directory Access Protocol**). It is a simplified version of the OSI X.500 directory service and is described in RFC 2251. It organizes information as a tree and allows searches on different components. It can be regarded as a "white pages" telephone book. We will not discuss it further in this book, but for more information see (Weltman and Dahbura, 2000).

7.2 ELECTRONIC MAIL

Electronic mail, or **e-mail**, as it is known to its many fans, has been around for over two decades. Before 1990, it was mostly used in academia. During the 1990s, it became known to the public at large and grew exponentially to the point where the number of e-mails sent per day now is vastly more than the number of **snail mail** (i.e., paper) letters.

E-mail, like most other forms of communication, has its own conventions and styles. In particular, it is very informal and has a low threshold of use. People who would never dream of calling up or even writing a letter to a Very Important Person do not hesitate for a second to send a sloppily-written e-mail.

E-mail is full of jargon such as BTW (By The Way), ROTFL (Rolling On The Floor Laughing), and IMHO (In My Humble Opinion). Many people also use little ASCII symbols called **smileys** or **emoticons** in their e-mail. A few of the more interesting ones are reproduced in Fig. 7-6. For most, rotating the book 90 degrees clockwise will make them clearer. For a minibook giving over 650 smileys, see (Sanderson and Dougherty, 1993).

The first e-mail systems simply consisted of file transfer protocols, with the convention that the first line of each message (i.e., file) contained the recipient's address. As time went on, the limitations of this approach became more obvious.

<table>
<tr><th>Smiley</th><th>Meaning</th><th>Smiley</th><th>Meaning</th><th>Smiley</th><th>Meaning</th></tr>
<tr><td>:-)</td><td>I'm happy</td><td>=|:-)</td><td>Abe Lincoln</td><td>:+)</td><td>Big nose</td></tr>
<tr><td>:-(</td><td>I'm sad/angry</td><td>=):-)</td><td>Uncle Sam</td><td>:-))</td><td>Double chin</td></tr>
<tr><td>:-|</td><td>I'm apathetic</td><td>*<:-)</td><td>Santa Claus</td><td>:-{)</td><td>Mustache</td></tr>
<tr><td>;-)</td><td>I'm winking</td><td><:-(</td><td>Dunce</td><td>#:-)</td><td>Matted hair</td></tr>
<tr><td>:-(O)</td><td>I'm yelling</td><td>(-:</td><td>Australian</td><td>8-)</td><td>Wears glasses</td></tr>
<tr><td>:-(*)</td><td>I'm vomiting</td><td>:-)X</td><td>Man with bowtie</td><td>C:-)</td><td>Large brain</td></tr>
</table>

Figure 7-6. Some smileys. They will not be on the final exam :-)

Some of the complaints were as follows:

1. Sending a message to a group of people was inconvenient. Managers often need this facility to send memos to all their subordinates.
2. Messages had no internal structure, making computer processing difficult. For example, if a forwarded message was included in the body of another message, extracting the forwarded part from the received message was difficult.
3. The originator (sender) never knew if a message arrived or not.
4. If someone was planning to be away on business for several weeks and wanted all incoming e-mail to be handled by his secretary, this was not easy to arrange.
5. The user interface was poorly integrated with the transmission system requiring users first to edit a file, then leave the editor and invoke the file transfer program.
6. It was not possible to create and send messages containing a mixture of text, drawings, facsimile, and voice.

As experience was gained, more elaborate e-mail systems were proposed. In 1982, the ARPANET e-mail proposals were published as RFC 821 (transmission protocol) and RFC 822 (message format). Minor revisions, RFC 2821 and RFC 2822, have become Internet standards, but everyone still refers to Internet e-mail as RFC 822.

In 1984, CCITT drafted its X.400 recommendation. After two decades of competition, e-mail systems based on RFC 822 are widely used, whereas those based on X.400 have disappeared. How a system hacked together by a handful of computer science graduate students beat an official international standard strongly backed by all the PTTs in the world, many governments, and a substantial part of the computer industry brings to mind the Biblical story of David and Goliath.

The reason for RFC 822's success is not that it is so good, but that X.400 was so poorly designed and so complex that nobody could implement it well. Given a choice between a simple-minded, but working, RFC 822-based e-mail system and a supposedly truly wonderful, but nonworking, X.400 e-mail system, most organizations chose the former. Perhaps there is a lesson lurking in there somewhere. Consequently, our discussion of e-mail will focus on the Internet e-mail system.

7.2.1 Architecture and Services

In this section we will provide an overview of what e-mail systems can do and how they are organized. They normally consist of two subsystems: the **user agents**, which allow people to read and send e-mail, and the **message transfer agents**, which move the messages from the source to the destination. The user agents are local programs that provide a command-based, menu-based, or graphical method for interacting with the e-mail system. The message transfer agents are typically system **daemons**, that is, processes that run in the background. Their job is to move e-mail through the system.

Typically, e-mail systems support five basic functions. Let us take a look at them.

Composition refers to the process of creating messages and answers. Although any text editor can be used for the body of the message, the system itself can provide assistance with addressing and the numerous header fields attached to each message. For example, when answering a message, the e-mail system can extract the originator's address from the incoming e-mail and automatically insert it into the proper place in the reply.

Transfer refers to moving messages from the originator to the recipient. In large part, this requires establishing a connection to the destination or some intermediate machine, outputting the message, and releasing the connection. The e-mail system should do this automatically, without bothering the user.

Reporting has to do with telling the originator what happened to the message. Was it delivered? Was it rejected? Was it lost? Numerous applications exist in which confirmation of delivery is important and may even have legal significance ("Well, Your Honor, my e-mail system is not very reliable, so I guess the electronic subpoena just got lost somewhere").

Displaying incoming messages is needed so people can read their e-mail. Sometimes conversion is required or a special viewer must be invoked, for example, if the message is a PostScript file or digitized voice. Simple conversions and formatting are sometimes attempted as well.

Disposition is the final step and concerns what the recipient does with the message after receiving it. Possibilities include throwing it away before reading, throwing it away after reading, saving it, and so on. It should also be possible to retrieve and reread saved messages, forward them, or process them in other ways.

In addition to these basic services, some e-mail systems, especially internal corporate ones, provide a variety of advanced features. Let us just briefly mention a few of these. When people move or when they are away for some period of time, they may want their e-mail forwarded, so the system should be able to do this automatically.

Most systems allow users to create **mailboxes** to store incoming e-mail. Commands are needed to create and destroy mailboxes, inspect the contents of mailboxes, insert and delete messages from mailboxes, and so on.

Corporate managers often need to send a message to each of their subordinates, customers, or suppliers. This gives rise to the idea of a **mailing list**, which is a list of e-mail addresses. When a message is sent to the mailing list, identical copies are delivered to everyone on the list.

Other advanced features are carbon copies, blind carbon copies, high-priority e-mail, secret (i.e., encrypted) e-mail, alternative recipients if the primary one is not currently available, and the ability for secretaries to read and answer their bosses' e-mail.

E-mail is now widely used within industry for intracompany communication. It allows far-flung employees to cooperate on complex projects, even over many time zones. By eliminating most cues associated with rank, age, and gender, e-mail debates tend to focus on ideas, not on corporate status. With e-mail, a brilliant idea from a summer student can have more impact than a dumb one from an executive vice president.

A key idea in e-mail systems is the distinction between the **envelope** and its contents. The envelope encapsulates the message. It contains all the information needed for transporting the message, such as the destination address, priority, and security level, all of which are distinct from the message itself. The message transport agents use the envelope for routing, just as the post office does.

The message inside the envelope consists of two parts: the **header** and the **body**. The header contains control information for the user agents. The body is entirely for the human recipient. Envelopes and messages are illustrated in Fig. 7-7.

7.2.2 The User Agent

E-mail systems have two basic parts, as we have seen: the user agents and the message transfer agents. In this section we will look at the user agents. A user agent is normally a program (sometimes called a mail reader) that accepts a variety of commands for composing, receiving, and replying to messages, as well as for manipulating mailboxes. Some user agents have a fancy menu- or icon-driven interface that requires a mouse, whereas others expect 1-character commands from the keyboard. Functionally, these are the same. Some systems are menu- or icon-driven but also have keyboard shortcuts.

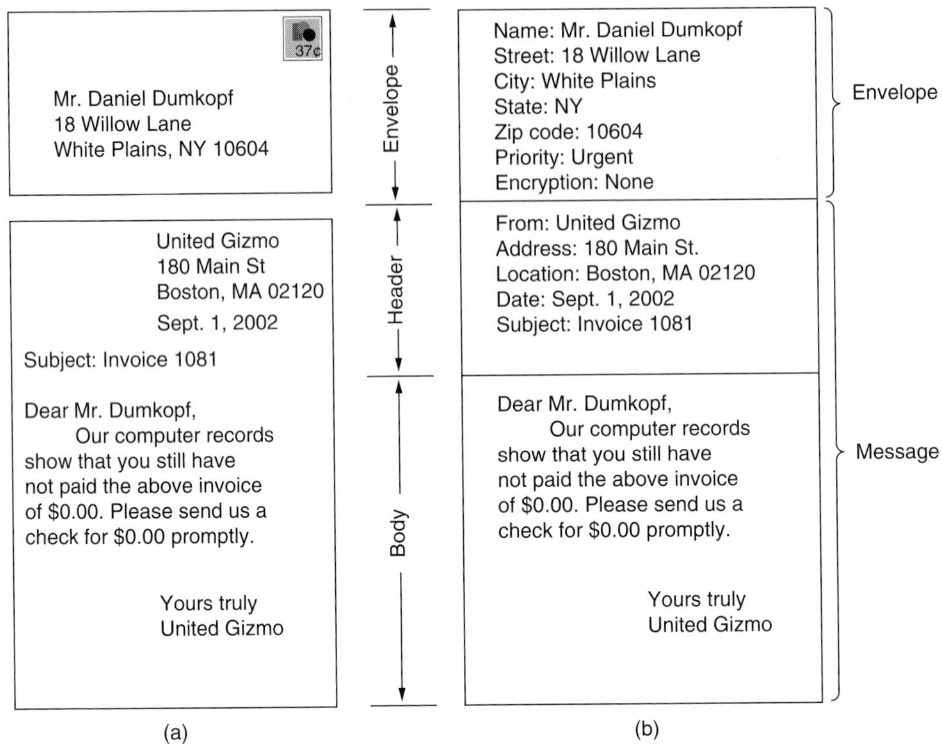

Figure 7-7. Envelopes and messages. (a) Paper mail. (b) Electronic mail.

Sending E-mail

To send an e-mail message, a user must provide the message, the destination address, and possibly some other parameters. The message can be produced with a free-standing text editor, a word processing program, or possibly with a specialized text editor built into the user agent. The destination address must be in a format that the user agent can deal with. Many user agents expect addresses of the form *user@dns-address*. Since we have studied DNS earlier in this chapter, we will not repeat that material here.

However, it is worth noting that other forms of addressing exist. In particular, X.400 addresses look radically different from DNS addresses. They are composed of *attribute* = *value* pairs separated by slashes, for example,

/C=US/ST=MASSACHUSETTS/L=CAMBRIDGE/PA=360 MEMORIAL DR./CN=KEN SMITH/

This address specifies a country, state, locality, personal address and a common name (Ken Smith). Many other attributes are possible, so you can send e-mail to someone whose exact e-mail address you do not know, provided you know enough other attributes (e.g., company and job title). Although X.400 names are considerably less convenient than DNS names, most e-mail systems have aliases (sometimes called nicknames) that allow users to enter or select a person's name and get the correct e-mail address. Consequently, even with X.400 addresses, it is usually not necessary to actually type in these strange strings.

Most e-mail systems support mailing lists, so that a user can send the same message to a list of people with a single command. If the mailing list is maintained locally, the user agent can just send a separate message to each intended recipient. However, if the list is maintained remotely, then messages will be expanded there. For example, if a group of bird watchers has a mailing list called *birders* installed on *meadowlark.arizona.edu*, then any message sent to *birders@meadowlark.arizona.edu* will be routed to the University of Arizona and expanded there into individual messages to all the mailing list members, wherever in the world they may be. Users of this mailing list cannot tell that it is a mailing list. It could just as well be the personal mailbox of Prof. Gabriel O. Birders.

Reading E-mail

Typically, when a user agent is started up, it looks at the user's mailbox for incoming e-mail before displaying anything on the screen. Then it may announce the number of messages in the mailbox or display a one-line summary of each one and wait for a command.

As an example of how a user agent works, let us take a look at a typical mail scenario. After starting up the user agent, the user asks for a summary of his e-mail. A display like that of Fig. 7-8 then appears on the screen. Each line refers to one message. In this example, the mailbox contains eight messages.

#	Flags	Bytes	Sender	Subject
1	K	1030	asw	Changes to MINIX
2	KA	6348	trudy	Not all Trudys are nasty
3	K F	4519	Amy N. Wong	Request for information
4		1236	bal	Bioinformatics
5		104110	kaashoek	Material on peer-to-peer
6		1223	Frank	Re: Will you review a grant proposal
7		3110	guido	Our paper has been accepted
8		1204	dmr	Re: My student's visit

Figure 7-8. An example display of the contents of a mailbox.

Each line of the display contains several fields extracted from the envelope or header of the corresponding message. In a simple e-mail system, the choice of fields displayed is built into the program. In a more sophisticated system, the user can specify which fields are to be displayed by providing a **user profile**, a file describing the display format. In this basic example, the first field is the message number. The second field, *Flags*, can contain a *K*, meaning that the message is not new but was read previously and kept in the mailbox; an *A*, meaning that the message has already been answered; and/or an *F*, meaning that the message has been forwarded to someone else. Other flags are also possible.

The third field tells how long the message is, and the fourth one tells who sent the message. Since this field is simply extracted from the message, this field may contain first names, full names, initials, login names, or whatever else the sender chooses to put there. Finally, the *Subject* field gives a brief summary of what the message is about. People who fail to include a *Subject* field often discover that responses to their e-mail tend not to get the highest priority.

After the headers have been displayed, the user can perform any of several actions, such as displaying a message, deleting a message, and so on. The older systems were text based and typically used one-character commands for performing these tasks, such as T (type message), A (answer message), D (delete message), and F (forward message). An argument specified the message in question. More recent systems use graphical interfaces. Usually, the user selects a message with the mouse and then clicks on an icon to type, answer, delete, or forward it.

E-mail has come a long way from the days when it was just file transfer. Sophisticated user agents make managing a large volume of e-mail possible. For people who receive and send thousands of messages a year, such tools are invaluable.

7.2.3 Message Formats

Let us now turn from the user interface to the format of the e-mail messages themselves. First we will look at basic ASCII e-mail using RFC 822. After that, we will look at multimedia extensions to RFC 822.

RFC 822

Messages consist of a primitive envelope (described in RFC 821), some number of header fields, a blank line, and then the message body. Each header field (logically) consists of a single line of ASCII text containing the field name, a colon, and, for most fields, a value. RFC 822 was designed decades ago and does not clearly distinguish the envelope fields from the header fields. Although it was revised in RFC 2822, completely redoing it was not possible due to its widespread usage. In normal usage, the user agent builds a message and passes it to the message transfer agent, which then uses some of the header fields to construct the actual envelope, a somewhat old-fashioned mixing of message and envelope.

The principal header fields related to message transport are listed in Fig. 7-9. The *To:* field gives the DNS address of the primary recipient. Having multiple recipients is also allowed. The *Cc:* field gives the addresses of any secondary recipients. In terms of delivery, there is no distinction between the primary and secondary recipients. It is entirely a psychological difference that may be important to the people involved but is not important to the mail system. The term *Cc:* (Carbon copy) is a bit dated, since computers do not use carbon paper, but it is well established. The *Bcc:* (Blind carbon copy) field is like the *Cc:* field, except that this line is deleted from all the copies sent to the primary and secondary recipients. This feature allows people to send copies to third parties without the primary and secondary recipients knowing this.

Header	Meaning
To:	E-mail address(es) of primary recipient(s)
Cc:	E-mail address(es) of secondary recipient(s)
Bcc:	E-mail address(es) for blind carbon copies
From:	Person or people who created the message
Sender:	E-mail address of the actual sender
Received:	Line added by each transfer agent along the route
Return-Path:	Can be used to identify a path back to the sender

Figure 7-9. RFC 822 header fields related to message transport.

The next two fields, *From:* and *Sender:*, tell who wrote and sent the message, respectively. These need not be the same. For example, a business executive may write a message, but her secretary may be the one who actually transmits it. In this case, the executive would be listed in the *From:* field and the secretary in the *Sender:* field. The *From:* field is required, but the *Sender:* field may be omitted if it is the same as the *From:* field. These fields are needed in case the message is undeliverable and must be returned to the sender.

A line containing *Received:* is added by each message transfer agent along the way. The line contains the agent's identity, the date and time the message was received, and other information that can be used for finding bugs in the routing system.

The *Return-Path:* field is added by the final message transfer agent and was intended to tell how to get back to the sender. In theory, this information can be gathered from all the *Received:* headers (except for the name of the sender's mailbox), but it is rarely filled in as such and typically just contains the sender's address.

In addition to the fields of Fig. 7-9, RFC 822 messages may also contain a variety of header fields used by the user agents or human recipients. The most common ones are listed in Fig. 7-10. Most of these are self-explanatory, so we will not go into all of them in detail.

The *Reply-To:* field is sometimes used when neither the person composing the message nor the person sending the message wants to see the reply. For example,

Header	Meaning
Date:	The date and time the message was sent
Reply-To:	E-mail address to which replies should be sent
Message-Id:	Unique number for referencing this message later
In-Reply-To:	Message-Id of the message to which this is a reply
References:	Other relevant Message-Ids
Keywords:	User-chosen keywords
Subject:	Short summary of the message for the one-line display

Figure 7-10. Some fields used in the RFC 822 message header.

a marketing manager writes an e-mail message telling customers about a new product. The message is sent by a secretary, but the *Reply-To:* field lists the head of the sales department, who can answer questions and take orders. This field is also useful when the sender has two e-mail accounts and wants the reply to go to the other one.

The RFC 822 document explicitly says that users are allowed to invent new headers for their own private use, provided that these headers start with the string *X-*. It is guaranteed that no future headers will use names starting with *X-*, to avoid conflicts between official and private headers. Sometimes wiseguy undergraduates make up fields like *X-Fruit-of-the-Day:* or *X-Disease-of-the-Week:*, which are legal, although not always illuminating.

After the headers comes the message body. Users can put whatever they want here. Some people terminate their messages with elaborate signatures, including simple ASCII cartoons, quotations from greater and lesser authorities, political statements, and disclaimers of all kinds (e.g., The XYZ Corporation is not responsible for my opinions; in fact, it cannot even comprehend them).

MIME—The Multipurpose Internet Mail Extensions

In the early days of the ARPANET, e-mail consisted exclusively of text messages written in English and expressed in ASCII. For this environment, RFC 822 did the job completely: it specified the headers but left the content entirely up to the users. Nowadays, on the worldwide Internet, this approach is no longer adequate. The problems include sending and receiving

1. Messages in languages with accents (e.g., French and German).
2. Messages in non-Latin alphabets (e.g., Hebrew and Russian).
3. Messages in languages without alphabets (e.g., Chinese and Japanese).
4. Messages not containing text at all (e.g., audio or images).

A solution was proposed in RFC 1341 and updated in RFCs 2045–2049. This solution, called **MIME** (**Multipurpose Internet Mail Extensions**) is now widely used. We will now describe it. For additional information about MIME, see the RFCs.

The basic idea of MIME is to continue to use the RFC 822 format, but to add structure to the message body and define encoding rules for non-ASCII messages. By not deviating from RFC 822, MIME messages can be sent using the existing mail programs and protocols. All that has to be changed are the sending and receiving programs, which users can do for themselves.

MIME defines five new message headers, as shown in Fig. 7-11. The first of these simply tells the user agent receiving the message that it is dealing with a MIME message, and which version of MIME it uses. Any message not containing a *MIME-Version:* header is assumed to be an English plaintext message and is processed as such.

Header	Meaning
MIME-Version:	Identifies the MIME version
Content-Description:	Human-readable string telling what is in the message
Content-Id:	Unique identifier
Content-Transfer-Encoding:	How the body is wrapped for transmission
Content-Type:	Type and format of the content

Figure 7-11. RFC 822 headers added by MIME.

The *Content-Description:* header is an ASCII string telling what is in the message. This header is needed so the recipient will know whether it is worth decoding and reading the message. If the string says: "Photo of Barbara's hamster" and the person getting the message is not a big hamster fan, the message will probably be discarded rather than decoded into a high-resolution color photograph.

The *Content-Id:* header identifies the content. It uses the same format as the standard *Message-Id:* header.

The *Content-Transfer-Encoding:* tells how the body is wrapped for transmission through a network that may object to most characters other than letters, numbers, and punctuation marks. Five schemes (plus an escape to new schemes) are provided. The simplest scheme is just ASCII text. ASCII characters use 7 bits and can be carried directly by the e-mail protocol provided that no line exceeds 1000 characters.

The next simplest scheme is the same thing, but using 8-bit characters, that is, all values from 0 up to and including 255. This encoding scheme violates the (original) Internet e-mail protocol but is used by some parts of the Internet that implement some extensions to the original protocol. While declaring the encoding does not make it legal, having it explicit may at least explain things when something goes wrong. Messages using the 8-bit encoding must still adhere to the standard maximum line length.

Even worse are messages that use binary encoding. These are arbitrary binary files that not only use all 8 bits but also do not even respect the 1000-character line limit. Executable programs fall into this category. No guarantee is given that messages in binary will arrive correctly, but some people try anyway.

The correct way to encode binary messages is to use **base64 encoding**, sometimes called **ASCII armor**. In this scheme, groups of 24 bits are broken up into four 6-bit units, with each unit being sent as a legal ASCII character. The coding is "A" for 0, "B" for 1, and so on, followed by the 26 lower-case letters, the ten digits, and finally + and / for 62 and 63, respectively. The == and = sequences indicate that the last group contained only 8 or 16 bits, respectively. Carriage returns and line feeds are ignored, so they can be inserted at will to keep the lines short enough. Arbitrary binary text can be sent safely using this scheme.

For messages that are almost entirely ASCII but with a few non-ASCII characters, base64 encoding is somewhat inefficient. Instead, an encoding known as **quoted-printable encoding** is used. This is just 7-bit ASCII, with all the characters above 127 encoded as an equal sign followed by the character's value as two hexadecimal digits. Control characters and trailing spaces are also so encoded.

In summary, binary data should be sent encoded in base64 or quoted-printable form. When there are valid reasons not to use one of these schemes, it is possible to specify a user-defined encoding in the *Content-Transfer-Encoding:* header.

The last header shown in Fig. 7-11 is really the most interesting one. It specifies the nature of the message body. Seven types are defined in RFC 2045, each of which has one or more subtypes. The type and subtype are separated by a slash, as in

```
Content-Type: video/mpeg
```

The subtype must be given explicitly in the header; no defaults are provided. The initial list of types and subtypes specified in RFC 2045 is given in Fig. 7-12. Many new ones have been added since then, and additional entries are being added all the time as the need arises.

Let us now go briefly through the list of types. The *text* type is for straight ASCII text. The *text/plain* combination is for ordinary messages that can be displayed as received, with no encoding and no further processing. This option allows ordinary messages to be transported in MIME with only a few extra headers.

The *text/enriched* subtype allows a simple markup language to be included in the text. This language provides a system-independent way to express boldface, italics, smaller and larger point sizes, indentation, justification, sub- and superscripting, and simple page layout. The markup language is based on SGML, the

Type	Subtype	Description
Text	Plain	Unformatted text
	Enriched	Text including simple formatting commands
Image	Gif	Still picture in GIF format
	Jpeg	Still picture in JPEG format
Audio	Basic	Audible sound
Video	Mpeg	Movie in MPEG format
Application	Octet-stream	An uninterpreted byte sequence
	Postscript	A printable document in PostScript
Message	Rfc822	A MIME RFC 822 message
	Partial	Message has been split for transmission
	External-body	Message itself must be fetched over the net
Multipart	Mixed	Independent parts in the specified order
	Alternative	Same message in different formats
	Parallel	Parts must be viewed simultaneously
	Digest	Each part is a complete RFC 822 message

Figure 7-12. The MIME types and subtypes defined in RFC 2045.

Standard Generalized Markup Language also used as the basis for the World Wide Web's HTML. For example, the message

The <bold> time </bold> has come the <italic> walrus </italic> said ...

would be displayed as

The **time** has come the *walrus* said ...

It is up to the receiving system to choose the appropriate rendition. If boldface and italics are available, they can be used; otherwise, colors, blinking, underlining, reverse video, etc., can be used for emphasis. Different systems can, and do, make different choices.

When the Web became popular, a new subtype *text/html* was added (in RFC 2854) to allow Web pages to be sent in RFC 822 e-mail. A subtype for the extensible markup language, *text/xml*, is defined in RFC 3023. We will study HTML and XML later in this chapter.

The next MIME type is *image*, which is used to transmit still pictures. Many formats are widely used for storing and transmitting images nowadays, both with and without compression. Two of these, GIF and JPEG, are built into nearly all browsers, but many others exist as well and have been added to the original list.

The *audio* and *video* types are for sound and moving pictures, respectively. Please note that *video* may include only the visual information, not the sound. If a movie with sound is to be transmitted, the video and audio portions may have to be transmitted separately, depending on the encoding system used. The first video format defined was the one devised by the modestly-named Moving Picture Experts Group (MPEG), but others have been added since. In addition to *audio/basic*, a new audio type, *audio/mpeg* was added in RFC 3003 to allow people to e-mail MP3 audio files.

The *application* type is a catchall for formats that require external processing not covered by one of the other types. An *octet-stream* is just a sequence of uninterpreted bytes. Upon receiving such a stream, a user agent should probably display it by suggesting to the user that it be copied to a file and prompting for a file name. Subsequent processing is then up to the user.

The other defined subtype is *postscript*, which refers to the PostScript language defined by Adobe Systems and widely used for describing printed pages. Many printers have built-in PostScript interpreters. Although a user agent can just call an external PostScript interpreter to display incoming PostScript files, doing so is not without some danger. PostScript is a full-blown programming language. Given enough time, a sufficiently masochistic person could write a C compiler or a database management system in PostScript. Displaying an incoming PostScript message is done by executing the PostScript program contained in it. In addition to displaying some text, this program can read, modify, or delete the user's files, and have other nasty side effects.

The *message* type allows one message to be fully encapsulated inside another. This scheme is useful for forwarding e-mail, for example. When a complete RFC 822 message is encapsulated inside an outer message, the *rfc822* subtype should be used.

The *partial* subtype makes it possible to break an encapsulated message into pieces and send them separately (for example, if the encapsulated message is too long). Parameters make it possible to reassemble all the parts at the destination in the correct order.

Finally, the *external-body* subtype can be used for very long messages (e.g., video films). Instead of including the MPEG file in the message, an FTP address is given and the receiver's user agent can fetch it over the network at the time it is needed. This facility is especially useful when sending a movie to a mailing list of people, only a few of whom are expected to view it (think about electronic junk mail containing advertising videos).

The final type is *multipart*, which allows a message to contain more than one part, with the beginning and end of each part being clearly delimited. The *mixed* subtype allows each part to be different, with no additional structure imposed. Many e-mail programs allow the user to provide one or more attachments to a text message. These attachments are sent using the *multipart* type.

In contrast to *multipart*, the *alternative* subtype, allows the same message to be included multiple times but expressed in two or more different media. For example, a message could be sent in plain ASCII, in enriched text, and in

PostScript. A properly-designed user agent getting such a message would display it in PostScript if possible. Second choice would be enriched text. If neither of these were possible, the flat ASCII text would be displayed. The parts should be ordered from simplest to most complex to help recipients with pre-MIME user agents make some sense of the message (e.g., even a pre-MIME user can read flat ASCII text).

The *alternative* subtype can also be used for multiple languages. In this context, the Rosetta Stone can be thought of as an early *multipart/alternative* message.

A multimedia example is shown in Fig. 7-13. Here a birthday greeting is transmitted both as text and as a song. If the receiver has an audio capability, the user agent there will fetch the sound file, *birthday.snd*, and play it. If not, the lyrics are displayed on the screen in stony silence. The parts are delimited by two hyphens followed by a (software-generated) string specified in the *boundary* parameter.

```
From: elinor@abcd.com
To: carolyn@xyz.com
MIME-Version: 1.0
Message-Id: <0704760941.AA00747@abcd.com>
Content-Type: multipart/alternative; boundary=qwertyuiopasdfghjklzxcvbnm
Subject: Earth orbits sun integral number of times

This is the preamble. The user agent ignores it. Have a nice day.

--qwertyuiopasdfghjklzxcvbnm
Content-Type: text/enriched

Happy birthday to you
Happy birthday to you
Happy birthday dear <bold> Carolyn </bold>
Happy birthday to you

--qwertyuiopasdfghjklzxcvbnm
Content-Type: message/external-body;
      access-type="anon-ftp";
      site="bicycle.abcd.com";
      directory="pub";
      name="birthday.snd"

content-type: audio/basic
content-transfer-encoding: base64
--qwertyuiopasdfghjklzxcvbnm--
```

Figure 7-13. A multipart message containing enriched and audio alternatives.

Note that the *Content-Type* header occurs in three positions within this example. At the top level, it indicates that the message has multiple parts. Within each part, it gives the type and subtype of that part. Finally, within the body of the second part, it is required to tell the user agent what kind of an external file it is to fetch. To indicate this slight difference in usage, we have used lower case letters here, although all headers are case insensitive. The *content-transfer-encoding* is similarly required for any external body that is not encoded as 7-bit ASCII.

Getting back to the subtypes for multipart messages, two more possibilities exist. The *parallel* subtype is used when all parts must be "viewed" simultaneously. For example, movies often have an audio channel and a video channel. Movies are more effective if these two channels are played back in parallel, instead of consecutively.

Finally, the *digest* subtype is used when many messages are packed together into a composite message. For example, some discussion groups on the Internet collect messages from subscribers and then send them out to the group as a single *multipart/digest* message.

7.2.4 Message Transfer

The message transfer system is concerned with relaying messages from the originator to the recipient. The simplest way to do this is to establish a transport connection from the source machine to the destination machine and then just transfer the message. After examining how this is normally done, we will examine some situations in which this does not work and what can be done about them.

SMTP—The Simple Mail Transfer Protocol

Within the Internet, e-mail is delivered by having the source machine establish a TCP connection to port 25 of the destination machine. Listening to this port is an e-mail daemon that speaks **SMTP** (**Simple Mail Transfer Protocol**). This daemon accepts incoming connections and copies messages from them into the appropriate mailboxes. If a message cannot be delivered, an error report containing the first part of the undeliverable message is returned to the sender.

SMTP is a simple ASCII protocol. After establishing the TCP connection to port 25, the sending machine, operating as the client, waits for the receiving machine, operating as the server, to talk first. The server starts by sending a line of text giving its identity and telling whether it is prepared to receive mail. If it is not, the client releases the connection and tries again later.

If the server is willing to accept e-mail, the client announces whom the e-mail is coming from and whom it is going to. If such a recipient exists at the destination, the server gives the client the go-ahead to send the message. Then the client sends the message and the server acknowledges it. No checksums are needed because TCP provides a reliable byte stream. If there is more e-mail, that is now sent. When all the e-mail has been exchanged in both directions, the connection is released. A sample dialog for sending the message of Fig. 7-13, including the numerical codes used by SMTP, is shown in Fig. 7-14. The lines sent by the client are marked *C:*. Those sent by the server are marked *S:*.

A few comments about Fig. 7-14 may be helpful. The first command from the client is indeed *HELO*. Of the various four-character abbreviations for *HELLO*, this one has numerous advantages over its biggest competitor. Why all the commands had to be four characters has been lost in the mists of time.

In Fig. 7-14, the message is sent to only one recipient, so only one *RCPT* command is used. Such commands are allowed to send a single message to multiple receivers. Each one is individually acknowledged or rejected. Even if some recipients are rejected (because they do not exist at the destination), the message can be sent to the other ones.

Finally, although the syntax of the four-character commands from the client is rigidly specified, the syntax of the replies is less rigid. Only the numerical code really counts. Each implementation can put whatever string it wants after the code.

To get a better feel for how SMTP and some of the other protocols described in this chapter work, try them out. In all cases, first go to a machine connected to the Internet. On a UNIX system, in a shell, type

```
telnet mail.isp.com 25
```

substituting the DNS name of your ISP's mail server for *mail.isp.com*. On a Windows system, click on Start, then Run, and type the command in the dialog box. This command will establish a telnet (i.e., TCP) connection to port 25 on that machine. Port 25 is the SMTP port (see Fig. 6-27 for some common ports). You will probably get a response something like this:

```
Trying 192.30.200.66...
Connected to mail.isp.com
Escape character is '^]'.
220 mail.isp.com Smail #74 ready at Thu, 25 Sept 2002 13:26 +0200
```

The first three lines are from telnet telling you what it is doing. The last line is from the SMTP server on the remote machine announcing its willingness to talk to you and accept e-mail. To find out what commands it accepts, type

```
HELP
```

From this point on, a command sequence such as the one in Fig. 7-14 is possible, starting with the client's *HELO* command.

It is worth noting that the use of lines of ASCII text for commands is not an accident. Most Internet protocols work this way. Using ASCII text makes the protocols easy to test and debug. They can be tested by sending commands manually, as we saw above, and dumps of the messages are easy to read.

```
                    S: 220 xyz.com SMTP service ready
C: HELO abcd.com
                    S: 250 xyz.com says hello to abcd.com
C: MAIL FROM: <elinor@abcd.com>
                    S: 250 sender ok
C: RCPT TO: <carolyn@xyz.com>
                    S: 250 recipient ok
C: DATA
                    S: 354 Send mail; end with "." on a line by itself
C: From: elinor@abcd.com
C: To: carolyn@xyz.com
C: MIME-Version: 1.0
C: Message-Id: <0704760941.AA00747@abcd.com>
C: Content-Type: multipart/alternative; boundary=qwertyuiopasdfghjklzxcvbnm
C: Subject: Earth orbits sun integral number of times
C:
C: This is the preamble. The user agent ignores it. Have a nice day.
C:
C: --qwertyuiopasdfghjklzxcvbnm
C: Content-Type: text/enriched
C:
C: Happy birthday to you
C: Happy birthday to you
C: Happy birthday dear <bold> Carolyn </bold>
C: Happy birthday to you
C:
C: --qwertyuiopasdfghjklzxcvbnm
C: Content-Type: message/external-body;
C:        access-type="anon-ftp";
C:        site="bicycle.abcd.com";
C:        directory="pub";
C:        name="birthday.snd"
C:
C: content-type: audio/basic
C: content-transfer-encoding: base64
C: --qwertyuiopasdfghjklzxcvbnm
C: .
                    S: 250 message accepted
C: QUIT
                    S: 221 xyz.com closing connection
```

Figure 7-14. Transferring a message from *elinor@abcd.com* to *carolyn@xyz.com*.

Even though the SMTP protocol is completely well defined, a few problems can still arise. One problem relates to message length. Some older implementations cannot handle messages exceeding 64 KB. Another problem relates to timeouts. If the client and server have different timeouts, one of them may give up while the other is still busy, unexpectedly terminating the connection. Finally, in rare situations, infinite mailstorms can be triggered. For example, if host 1 holds mailing list *A* and host 2 holds mailing list *B* and each list contains an entry for the other one, then a message sent to either list could generate a never-ending amount of e-mail traffic unless somebody checks for it.

To get around some of these problems, extended SMTP (**ESMTP**) has been defined in RFC 2821. Clients wanting to use it should send an *EHLO* message instead of *HELO* initially. If this is rejected, then the server is a regular SMTP server, and the client should proceed in the usual way. If the *EHLO* is accepted, then new commands and parameters are allowed.

7.2.5 Final Delivery

Up until now, we have assumed that all users work on machines that are capable of sending and receiving e-mail. As we saw, e-mail is delivered by having the sender establish a TCP connection to the receiver and then ship the e-mail over it. This model worked fine for decades when all ARPANET (and later Internet) hosts were, in fact, on-line all the time to accept TCP connections.

However, with the advent of people who access the Internet by calling their ISP over a modem, it breaks down. The problem is this: what happens when Elinor wants to send Carolyn e-mail and Carolyn is not currently on-line? Elinor cannot establish a TCP connection to Carolyn and thus cannot run the SMTP protocol.

One solution is to have a message transfer agent on an ISP machine accept e-mail for its customers and store it in their mailboxes on an ISP machine. Since this agent can be on-line all the time, e-mail can be sent to it 24 hours a day.

POP3

Unfortunately, this solution creates another problem: how does the user get the e-mail from the ISP's message transfer agent? The solution to this problem is to create another protocol that allows user transfer agents (on client PCs) to contact the message transfer agent (on the ISP's machine) and allow e-mail to be copied from the ISP to the user. One such protocol is **POP3 (Post Office Protocol Version 3)**, which is described in RFC 1939.

The situation that used to hold (both sender and receiver having a permanent connection to the Internet) is illustrated in Fig. 7-15(a). A situation in which the sender is (currently) on-line but the receiver is not is illustrated in Fig. 7-15(b).

POP3 begins when the user starts the mail reader. The mail reader calls up the ISP (unless there is already a connection) and establishes a TCP connection

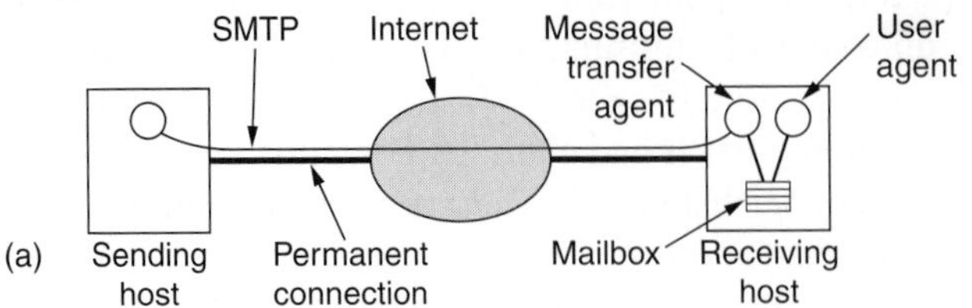

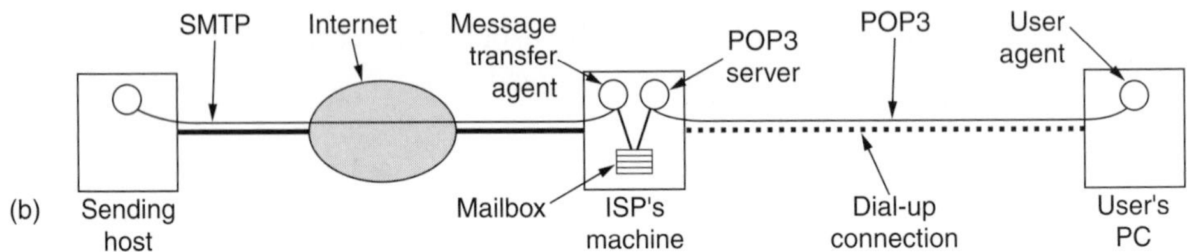

Figure 7-15. (a) Sending and reading mail when the receiver has a permanent Internet connection and the user agent runs on the same machine as the message transfer agent. (b) Reading e-mail when the receiver has a dial-up connection to an ISP.

with the message transfer agent at port 110. Once the connection has been established, the POP3 protocol goes through three states in sequence:

1. Authorization.
2. Transactions.
3. Update.

The authorization state deals with having the user log in. The transaction state deals with the user collecting the e-mails and marking them for deletion from the mailbox. The update state actually causes the e-mails to be deleted.

This behavior can be observed by typing something like:

```
telnet mail.isp.com 110
```

where *mail.isp.com* represents the DNS name of your ISP's mail server. Telnet establishes a TCP connection to port 110, on which the POP3 server listens. Upon accepting the TCP connection, the server sends an ASCII message announcing that it is present. Usually, it begins with +OK followed by a comment. An example scenario is shown in Fig. 7-16 starting after the TCP connection has been established. As before, the lines marked *C:* are from the client (user) and those marked *S:* are from the server (message transfer agent on the ISP's machine).

During the authorization state, the client sends over its user name and then its password. After a successful login, the client can then send over the *LIST* com-

```
            S: +OK POP3 server ready
C: USER carolyn
            S: +OK
C: PASS vegetables
            S: +OK login successful
C: LIST
            S: 1 2505
            S: 2 14302
            S: 3 8122
            S: .
C: RETR 1
            S: (sends message 1)
C: DELE 1
C: RETR 2
            S: (sends message 2)
C: DELE 2
C: RETR 3
            S: (sends message 3)
C: DELE 3
C: QUIT
            S: +OK POP3 server disconnecting
```

Figure 7-16. Using POP3 to fetch three messages.

mand, which causes the server to list the contents of the mailbox, one message per line, giving the length of that message. The list is terminated by a period.

Then the client can retrieve messages using the *RETR* command and mark them for deletion with *DELE*. When all messages have been retrieved (and possibly marked for deletion), the client gives the *QUIT* command to terminate the transaction state and enter the update state. When the server has deleted all the messages, it sends a reply and breaks the TCP connection.

While it is true that the POP3 protocol supports the ability to download a specific message or set of messages and leave them on the server, most e-mail programs just download everything and empty the mailbox. This behavior means that in practice, the only copy is on the user's hard disk. If that crashes, all e-mail may be lost permanently.

Let us now briefly summarize how e-mail works for ISP customers. Elinor creates a message for Carolyn using some e-mail program (i.e., user agent) and clicks on an icon to send it. The e-mail program hands the message over to the message transfer agent on Elinor's host. The message transfer agent sees that it is directed to *carolyn@xyz.com* so it uses DNS to look up the *MX* record for *xyz.com* (where *xyz.com* is Carolyn's ISP). This query returns the DNS name of *xyz.com*'s mail server. The message transfer agent now looks up the IP address of this machine using DNS again, for example, using *gethostbyname*. It then establishes a

TCP connection to the SMTP server on port 25 of this machine. Using an SMTP command sequence analogous to that of Fig. 7-14, it transfers the message to Carolyn's mailbox and breaks the TCP connection.

In due course of time, Carolyn boots up her PC, connects to her ISP, and starts her e-mail program. The e-mail program establishes a TCP connection to the POP3 server at port 110 of the ISP's mail server machine. The DNS name or IP address of this machine is typically configured when the e-mail program is installed or the subscription to the ISP is made. After the TCP connection has been established, Carolyn's e-mail program runs the POP3 protocol to fetch the contents of the mailbox to her hard disk using commands similar to those of Fig. 7-16. Once all the e-mail has been transferred, the TCP connection is released. In fact, the connection to the ISP can also be broken now, since all the e-mail is on Carolyn's hard disk. Of course, to send a reply, the connection to the ISP will be needed again, so it is not generally broken right after fetching the e-mail.

IMAP

For a user with one e-mail account at one ISP that is always accessed from one PC, POP3 works fine and is widely used due to its simplicity and robustness. However, it is a computer-industry truism that as soon as something works well, somebody will start demanding more features (and getting more bugs). That happened with e-mail, too. For example, many people have a single e-mail account at work or school and want to access it from work, from their home PC, from their laptop when on business trips, and from cybercafes when on so-called vacation. While POP3 allows this, since it normally downloads all stored messages at each contact, the result is that the user's e-mail quickly gets spread over multiple machines, more or less at random, some of them not even the user's.

This disadvantage gave rise to an alternative final delivery protocol, **IMAP** (**Internet Message Access Protocol**), which is defined in RFC 2060. Unlike POP3, which basically assumes that the user will clear out the mailbox on every contact and work off-line after that, IMAP assumes that all the e-mail will remain on the server indefinitely in multiple mailboxes. IMAP provides extensive mechanisms for reading messages or even parts of messages, a feature useful when using a slow modem to read the text part of a multipart message with large audio and video attachments. Since the working assumption is that messages will not be transferred to the user's computer for permanent storage, IMAP provides mechanisms for creating, destroying, and manipulating multiple mailboxes on the server. In this way a user can maintain a mailbox for each correspondent and move messages there from the inbox after they have been read.

IMAP has many features, such as the ability to address mail not by arrival number as is done in Fig. 7-8, but by using attributes (e.g., give me the first message from Bobbie). Unlike POP3, IMAP can also accept outgoing e-mail for shipment to the destination as well as deliver incoming e-mail.

The general style of the IMAP protocol is similar to that of POP3 as shown in Fig. 7-16, except that are there dozens of commands. The IMAP server listens to port 143. A comparison of POP3 and IMAP is given in Fig. 7-17. It should be noted, however, that not every ISP supports both protocols and not every e-mail program supports both protocols. Thus, when choosing an e-mail program, it is important to find out which protocol(s) it supports and make sure the ISP supports at least one of them.

Feature	POP3	IMAP
Where is protocol defined	RFC 1939	RFC 2060
TCP port used	110	143
Where is e-mail stored	User's PC	Server
Where is e-mail read	Off-line	On-line
Connect time required	Little	Much
Use of server resources	Minimal	Extensive
Multiple mailboxes	No	Yes
Who backs up mailboxes	User	ISP
Good for mobile users	No	Yes
User control over downloading	Little	Great
Partial message downloads	No	Yes
Are disk quotas a problem	No	Could be in time
Simple to implement	Yes	No
Widespread support	Yes	Growing

Figure 7-17. A comparison of POP3 and IMAP.

Delivery Features

Independently of whether POP3 or IMAP is used, many systems provide hooks for additional processing of incoming e-mail. An especially valuable feature for many e-mail users is the ability to set up **filters**. These are rules that are checked when e-mail comes in or when the user agent is started. Each rule specifies a condition and an action. For example, a rule could say that any message received from the boss goes to mailbox number 1, any message from a select group of friends goes to mailbox number 2, and any message containing certain objectionable words in the Subject line is discarded without comment.

Some ISPs provide a filter that automatically categorizes incoming e-mail as either important or spam (junk e-mail) and stores each message in the corresponding mailbox. Such filters typically work by first checking to see if the source is a known spammer. Then they usually examine the subject line. If hundreds of users have just received a message with the same subject line, it is probably spam. Other techniques are also used for spam detection.

Another delivery feature often provided is the ability to (temporarily) forward incoming e-mail to a different address. This address can even be a computer operated by a commercial paging service, which then pages the user by radio or satellite, displaying the *Subject:* line on his pager.

Still another common feature of final delivery is the ability to install a **vacation daemon**. This is a program that examines each incoming message and sends the sender an insipid reply such as

Hi. I'm on vacation. I'll be back on the 24th of August. Have a nice summer.

Such replies can also specify how to handle urgent matters in the interim, other people to contact for specific problems, etc. Most vacation daemons keep track of whom they have sent canned replies to and refrain from sending the same person a second reply. The good ones also check to see if the incoming message was sent to a mailing list, and if so, do not send a canned reply at all. (People who send messages to large mailing lists during the summer probably do not want to get hundreds of replies detailing everyone's vacation plans.)

The author once ran into an extreme form of delivery processing when he sent an e-mail message to a person who claims to get 600 messages a day. His identity will not be disclosed here, lest half the readers of this book also send him e-mail. Let us call him John.

John has installed an e-mail robot that checks every incoming message to see if it is from a new correspondent. If so, it sends back a canned reply explaining that John can no longer personally read all his e-mail. Instead, he has produced a personal FAQ (Frequently Asked Questions) document that answers many questions he is commonly asked. Normally, newsgroups have FAQs, not people.

John's FAQ gives his address, fax, and telephone numbers and tells how to contact his company. It explains how to get him as a speaker and describes where to get his papers and other documents. It also provides pointers to software he has written, a conference he is running, a standard he is the editor of, and so on. Perhaps this approach is necessary, but maybe a personal FAQ is the ultimate status symbol.

Webmail

One final topic worth mentioning is Webmail. Some Web sites, for example, Hotmail and Yahoo, provide e-mail service to anyone who wants it. They work as follows. They have normal message transfer agents listening to port 25 for incoming SMTP connections. To contact, say, Hotmail, you have to acquire their DNS *MX* record, for example, by typing

```
host –a –v hotmail.com
```

on a UNIX system. Suppose that the mail server is called *mx10.hotmail.com*, then by typing

```
telnet mx10.hotmail.com 25
```

you can establish a TCP connection over which SMTP commands can be sent in the usual way. So far, nothing unusual, except that these big servers are often busy, so it may take several attempts to get a TCP connection accepted.

The interesting part is how e-mail is delivered. Basically, when the user goes to the e-mail Web page, a form is presented in which the user is asked for a login name and password. When the user clicks on Sign In, the login name and password are sent to the server, which then validates them. If the login is successful, the server finds the user's mailbox and builds a listing similar to that of Fig. 7-8, only formatted as a Web page in HTML. The Web page is then sent to the browser for display. Many of the items on the page are clickable, so messages can be read, deleted, and so on.

7.3 THE WORLD WIDE WEB

The World Wide Web is an architectural framework for accessing linked documents spread out over millions of machines all over the Internet. In 10 years, it went from being a way to distribute high-energy physics data to the application that millions of people think of as being "The Internet." Its enormous popularity stems from the fact that it has a colorful graphical interface that is easy for beginners to use, and it provides an enormous wealth of information on almost every conceivable subject, from aardvarks to Zulus.

The Web (also known as **WWW**) began in 1989 at CERN, the European center for nuclear research. CERN has several accelerators at which large teams of scientists from the participating European countries carry out research in particle physics. These teams often have members from half a dozen or more countries. Most experiments are highly complex and require years of advance planning and equipment construction. The Web grew out of the need to have these large teams of internationally dispersed researchers collaborate using a constantly changing collection of reports, blueprints, drawings, photos, and other documents.

The initial proposal for a web of linked documents came from CERN physicist Tim Berners-Lee in March 1989. The first (text-based) prototype was operational 18 months later. In December 1991, a public demonstration was given at the Hypertext '91 conference in San Antonio, Texas.

This demonstration and its attendant publicity caught the attention of other researchers, which led Marc Andreessen at the University of Illinois to start developing the first graphical browser, Mosaic. It was released in February 1993. Mosaic was so popular that a year later, Andreessen left to form a company, Netscape Communications Corp., whose goal was to develop clients, servers, and other Web software. When Netscape went public in 1995, investors, apparently thinking this was the next Microsoft, paid $1.5 billion for the stock. This record was all the more surprising because the company had only one product, was operating deeply in the red, and had announced in its prospectus that it did not expect to make a profit for the foreseeable future. For the next three years, Netscape Navigator and Microsoft's Internet Explorer engaged in a "browser war," each one trying frantically to add more features (and thus more bugs) than the other one. In 1998, America Online bought Netscape Communications Corp. for $4.2 billion, thus ending Netscape's brief life as an independent company.

In 1994, CERN and M.I.T. signed an agreement setting up the **World Wide Web Consortium** (sometimes abbreviated as **W3C**), an organization devoted to further developing the Web, standardizing protocols, and encouraging interoperability between sites. Berners-Lee became the director. Since then, several hundred universities and companies have joined the consortium. Although there are now more books about the Web than you can shake a stick at, the best place to get up-to-date information about the Web is (naturally) on the Web itself. The consortium's home page is at *www.w3.org*. Interested readers are referred there for links to pages covering all of the consortium's numerous documents and activities.

7.3.1 Architectural Overview

From the users' point of view, the Web consists of a vast, worldwide collection of documents or **Web pages**, often just called **pages** for short. Each page may contain links to other pages anywhere in the world. Users can follow a link by clicking on it, which then takes them to the page pointed to. This process can be repeated indefinitely. The idea of having one page point to another, now called **hypertext**, was invented by a visionary M.I.T. professor of electrical engineering, Vannevar Bush, in 1945, long before the Internet was invented.

Pages are viewed with a program called a **browser**, of which Internet Explorer and Netscape Navigator are two popular ones. The browser fetches the page requested, interprets the text and formatting commands on it, and displays the page, properly formatted, on the screen. An example is given in Fig. 7-18(a). Like many Web pages, this one starts with a title, contains some information, and ends with the e-mail address of the page's maintainer. Strings of text that are links to other pages, called **hyperlinks**, are often highlighted, by underlining, displaying them in a special color, or both. To follow a link, the user places the mouse cursor on the highlighted area, which causes the cursor to change, and clicks on it. Although nongraphical browsers, such as Lynx, exist, they are not as popular as graphical browsers, so we will concentrate on the latter. Voice-based browsers are also being developed.

Users who are curious about the Department of Animal Psychology can learn more about it by clicking on its (underlined) name. The browser then fetches the

WELCOME TO THE UNIVERSITY OF EAST PODUNK'S WWW HOME PAGE

- Campus Information
  - □ Admissions information
  - □ Campus map
  - □ Directions to campus
  - □ The UEP student body

- Academic Departments
  - □ Department of Animal Psychology
  - □ Department of Alternative Studies
  - □ Department of Microbiotic Cooking
  - □ Department of Nontraditional Studies
  - □ Department of Traditional Studies

Webmaster@eastpodunk.edu

(a)

THE DEPARTMENT OF ANIMAL PSYCHOLOGY

- Information for prospective majors
- Personnel
  - □ Faculty members
  - □ Graduate students
  - □ Nonacademic staff
- Research Projects
- Positions available
- Our most popular courses
  - □ Dealing with herbivores
  - □ Horse management
  - □ Negotiating with your pet
  - □ User-friendly doghouse construction
- Full list of courses

Webmaster@animalpsyc.eastpodunk.edu

(b)

Figure 7-18. (a) A Web page. (b) The page reached by clicking on Department of Animal Psychology.

page to which the name is linked and displays it, as shown in Fig. 7-18(b). The underlined items here can also be clicked on to fetch other pages, and so on. The new page can be on the same machine as the first one or on a machine halfway around the globe. The user cannot tell. Page fetching is done by the browser, without any help from the user. If the user ever returns to the main page, the links that have already been followed may be shown with a dotted underline (and possibly a different color) to distinguish them from links that have not been followed. Note that clicking on the *Campus Information* line in the main page does nothing. It is not underlined, which means that it is just text and is not linked to another page.

The basic model of how the Web works is shown in Fig. 7-19. Here the browser is displaying a Web page on the client machine. When the user clicks on a line of text that is linked to a page on the *abcd.com* server, the browser follows the hyperlink by sending a message to the *abcd.com* server asking it for the page. When the page arrives, it is displayed. If this page contains a hyperlink to a page on the *xyz.com* server that is clicked on, the browser then sends a request to that machine for the page, and so on indefinitely.

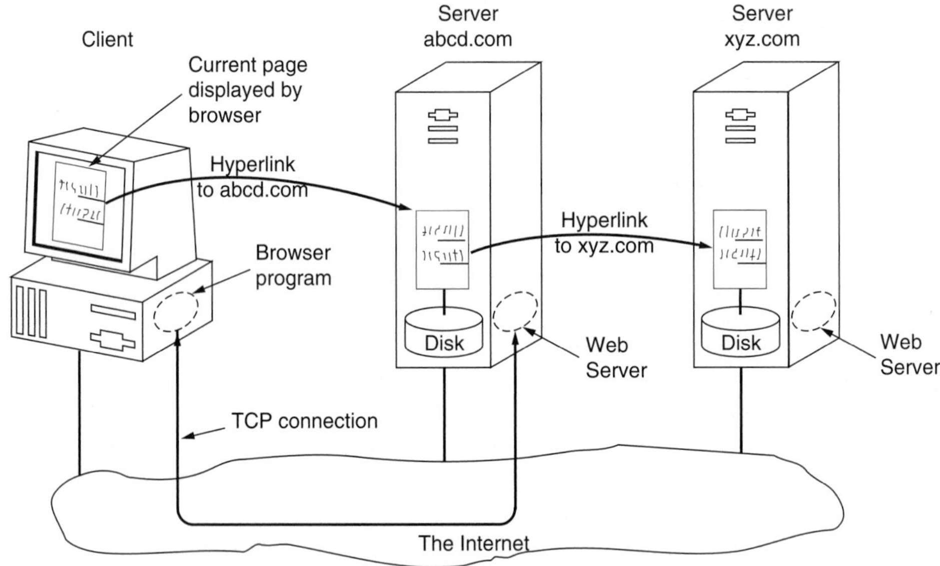

Figure 7-19. The parts of the Web model.

The Client Side

Let us now examine the client side of Fig. 7-19 in more detail. In essence, a browser is a program that can display a Web page and catch mouse clicks to items on the displayed page. When an item is selected, the browser follows the hyperlink and fetches the page selected. Therefore, the embedded hyperlink needs a way to name any other page on the Web. Pages are named using **URLs** (**Uniform Resource Locators**). A typical URL is

http://www.abcd.com/products.html

We will explain URLs later in this chapter. For the moment, it is sufficient to know that a URL has three parts: the name of the protocol (*http*), the DNS name of the machine where the page is located (*www.abcd.com*), and (usually) the name of the file containing the page (*products.html*).

When a user clicks on a hyperlink, the browser carries out a series of steps in order to fetch the page pointed to. Suppose that a user is browsing the Web and finds a link on Internet telephony that points to ITU's home page, which is *http://www.itu.org/home/index.html*. Let us trace the steps that occur when this link is selected.

1. The browser determines the URL (by seeing what was selected).
2. The browser asks DNS for the IP address of *www.itu.org*.
3. DNS replies with 156.106.192.32.
4. The browser makes a TCP connection to port 80 on 156.106.192.32.
5. It then sends over a request asking for file */home/index.html*.
6. The *www.itu.org* server sends the file */home/index.html*.
7. The TCP connection is released.
8. The browser displays all the text in */home/index.html*.
9. The browser fetches and displays all images in this file.

Many browsers display which step they are currently executing in a status line at the bottom of the screen. In this way, when the performance is poor, the user can see if it is due to DNS not responding, the server not responding, or simply network congestion during page transmission.

To be able to display the new page (or any page), the browser has to understand its format. To allow all browsers to understand all Web pages, Web pages are written in a standardized language called HTML, which describes Web pages. We will discuss it in detail later in this chapter.

Although a browser is basically an HTML interpreter, most browsers have numerous buttons and features to make it easier to navigate the Web. Most have a button for going back to the previous page, a button for going forward to the next page (only operative after the user has gone back from it), and a button for going straight to the user's own start page. Most browsers have a button or menu item to set a bookmark on a given page and another one to display the list of bookmarks, making it possible to revisit any of them with only a few mouse clicks. Pages can also be saved to disk or printed. Numerous options are generally available for controlling the screen layout and setting various user preferences.

In addition to having ordinary text (not underlined) and hypertext (underlined), Web pages can also contain icons, line drawings, maps, and photographs. Each of these can (optionally) be linked to another page. Clicking on one of these elements causes the browser to fetch the linked page and display it on the screen, the same as clicking on text. With images such as photos and maps, which page is fetched next may depend on what part of the image was clicked on.

Not all pages contain HTML. A page may consist of a formatted document in PDF format, an icon in GIF format, a photograph in JPEG format, a song in MP3 format, a video in MPEG format, or any one of hundreds of other file types. Since standard HTML pages may link to any of these, the browser has a problem when it encounters a page it cannot interpret.

Rather than making the browsers larger and larger by building in interpreters for a rapidly growing collection of file types, most browsers have chosen a more general solution. When a server returns a page, it also returns some additional information about the page. This information includes the MIME type of the page (see Fig. 7-12). Pages of type *text/html* are just displayed directly, as are pages in a few other built-in types. If the MIME type is not one of the built-in ones, the browser consults its table of MIME types to tell it how to display the page. This table associates a MIME type with a viewer.

There are two possibilities: plug-ins and helper applications. A **plug-in** is a code module that the browser fetches from a special directory on the disk and installs as an extension to itself, as illustrated in Fig. 7-20(a). Because plug-ins run inside the browser, they have access to the current page and can modify its appearance. After the plug-in has done its job (usually after the user has moved to a different Web page), the plug-in is removed from the browser's memory.

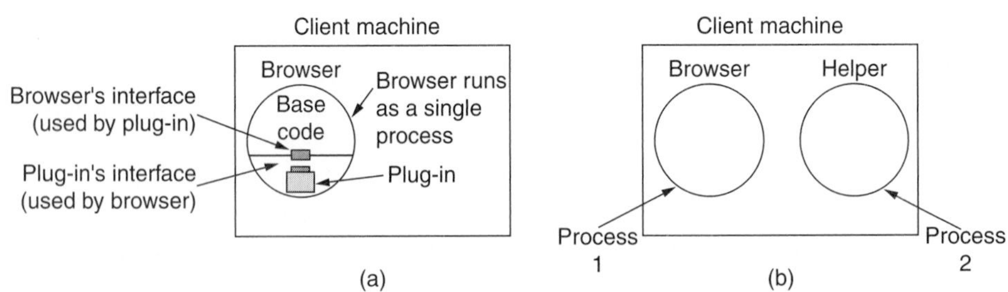

Figure 7-20. (a) A browser plug-in. (b) A helper application.

Each browser has a set of procedures that all plug-ins must implement so the browser can call the plug-in. For example, there is typically a procedure the browser's base code calls to supply the plug-in with data to display. This set of procedures is the plug-in's interface and is browser specific.

In addition, the browser makes a set of its own procedures available to the plug-in, to provide services to plug-ins. Typical procedures in the browser interface are for allocating and freeing memory, displaying a message on the browser's status line, and querying the browser about parameters.

Before a plug-in can be used, it must be installed. The usual installation procedure is for the user to go to the plug-in's Web site and download an installation file. On Windows, this is typically a self-extracting zip file with extension *.exe*. When the zip file is double clicked, a little program attached to the front of the zip file is executed. This program unzips the plug-in and copies it to the browser's plug-in directory. Then it makes the appropriate calls to register the plug-in's MIME type and to associate the plug-in with it. On UNIX, the installer is often a shell script that handles the copying and registration.

The other way to extend a browser is to use a **helper application**. This is a complete program, running as a separate process. It is illustrated in Fig. 7-20(b). Since the helper is a separate program, it offers no interface to the browser and makes no use of browser services. Instead, it usually just accepts the name of a scratch file where the content file has been stored, opens the file, and displays the contents. Typically, helpers are large programs that exist independently of the browser, such as Adobe's Acrobat Reader for displaying PDF files or Microsoft Word. Some programs (such as Acrobat) have a plug-in that invokes the helper itself.

Many helper applications use the MIME type *application*. A considerable number of subtypes have been defined, for example, *application/pdf* for PDF files and *application/msword* for Word files. In this way, a URL can point directly to a PDF or Word file, and when the user clicks on it, Acrobat or Word is automatically started and handed the name of a scratch file containing the content to be displayed. Consequently, browsers can be configured to handle a virtually unlimited number of document types with no changes to the browser. Modern Web servers are often configured with hundreds of type/subtype combinations and new ones are often added every time a new program is installed.

Helper applications are not restricted to using the *application* MIME type. Adobe Photoshop uses *image/x-photoshop* and RealOne Player is capable of handling *audio/mp3*, for example.

On Windows, when a program is installed on the computer, it registers the MIME types it wants to handle. This mechanism leads to conflict when multiple viewers are available for some subtype, such as *video/mpeg*. What happens is that the last program to register overwrites existing (MIME type, helper application) associations, capturing the type for itself. As a consequence, installing a new program may change the way a browser handles existing types.

On UNIX, this registration process is generally not automatic. The user must manually update certain configuration files. This approach leads to more work but fewer surprises.

Browsers can also open local files, rather than fetching them from remote Web servers. Since local files do not have MIME types, the browser needs some way to determine which plug-in or helper to use for types other than its built-in types such as *text/html* and *image/jpeg*. To handle local files, helpers can be associated with a file extension as well as with a MIME type. With the standard configuration, opening *foo.pdf* will open it in Acrobat and opening *bar.doc* will open it in Word. Some browsers use the MIME type, the file extension, and even information taken from the file itself to guess the MIME type. In particular, Internet Explorer relies more heavily on the file extension than on the MIME type when it can.

Here, too, conflicts can arise since many programs are willing, in fact, eager, to handle, say, *.mpg*. During installation, programs intended for professionals often display checkboxes for the MIME types and extensions they are prepared to handle to allow the user to select the appropriate ones and thus not overwrite existing associations by accident. Programs aimed at the consumer market assume that the user does not have a clue what a MIME type is and simply grab everything they can without regard to what previously installed programs have done.

The ability to extend the browser with a large number of new types is convenient but can also lead to trouble. When Internet Explorer fetches a file with extension *exe*, it realizes that this file is an executable program and therefore has no helper. The obvious action is to run the program. However, this could be an enormous security hole. All a malicious Web site has to do is produce a Web page with pictures of, say, movie stars or sports heroes, all of which are linked to a virus. A single click on a picture then causes an unknown and potentially hostile executable program to be fetched and run on the user's machine. To prevent unwanted guests like this, Internet Explorer can be configured to be selective about running unknown programs automatically, but not all users understand how to manage the configuration.

On UNIX an analogous problem can exist with shell scripts, but that requires the user to consciously install the shell as a helper. Fortunately, this installation is sufficiently complicated that nobody could possibly do it by accident (and few people can even do it intentionally).

The Server Side

So much for the client side. Now let us take a look at the server side. As we saw above, when the user types in a URL or clicks on a line of hypertext, the browser parses the URL and interprets the part between *http://* and the next slash as a DNS name to look up. Armed with the IP address of the server, the browser establishes a TCP connection to port 80 on that server. Then it sends over a command containing the rest of the URL, which is the name of a file on that server. The server then returns the file for the browser to display.

To a first approximation, a Web server is similar to the server of Fig. 6-6. That server, like a real Web server, is given the name of a file to look up and return. In both cases, the steps that the server performs in its main loop are:

1. Accept a TCP connection from a client (a browser).
2. Get the name of the file requested.
3. Get the file (from disk).

4. Return the file to the client.

5. Release the TCP connection.

Modern Web servers have more features, but in essence, this is what a Web server does.

A problem with this design is that every request requires making a disk access to get the file. The result is that the Web server cannot serve more requests per second than it can make disk accesses. A high-end SCSI disk has an average access time of around 5 msec, which limits the server to at most 200 requests/sec, less if large files have to be read often. For a major Web site, this figure is too low.

One obvious improvement (used by all Web servers) is to maintain a cache in memory of the n most recently used files. Before going to disk to get a file, the server checks the cache. If the file is there, it can be served directly from memory, thus eliminating the disk access. Although effective caching requires a large amount of main memory and some extra processing time to check the cache and manage its contents, the savings in time are nearly always worth the overhead and expense.

The next step for building a faster server is to make the server multithreaded. In one design, the server consists of a front-end module that accepts all incoming requests and k processing modules, as shown in Fig. 7-21. The $k + 1$ threads all belong to the same process so the processing modules all have access to the cache within the process' address space. When a request comes in, the front end accepts it and builds a short record describing it. It then hands the record to one of the processing modules. In another possible design, the front end is eliminated and each processing module tries to acquire its own requests, but a locking protocol is then required to prevent conflicts.

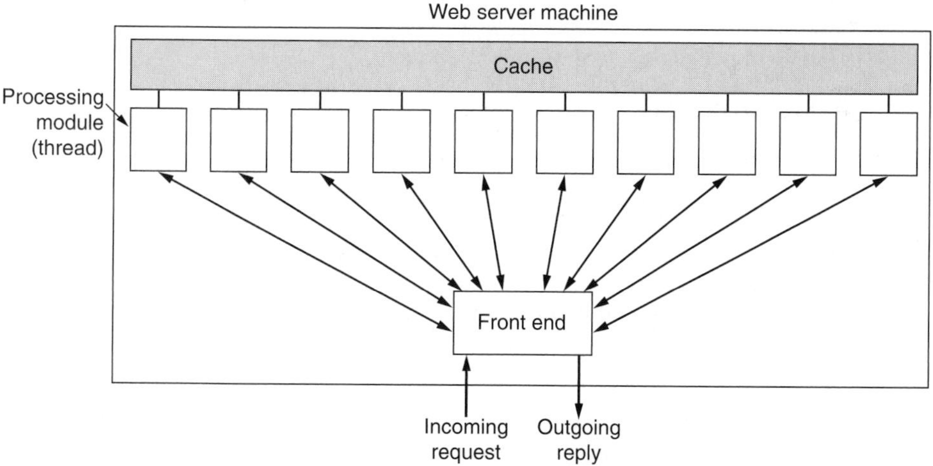

Figure 7-21. A multithreaded Web server with a front end and processing modules.

The processing module first checks the cache to see if the file needed is there. If so, it updates the record to include a pointer to the file in the record. If it is not there, the processing module starts a disk operation to read it into the cache (possibly discarding some other cached files to make room for it). When the file comes in from the disk, it is put in the cache and also sent back to the client.

The advantage of this scheme is that while one or more processing modules are blocked waiting for a disk operation to complete (and thus consuming no CPU time), other modules can be actively working on other requests. Of course, to get any real improvement over the single-threaded model, it is necessary to have multiple disks, so more than one disk can be busy at the same time. With k processing modules and k disks, the throughput can be as much as k times higher than with a single-threaded server and one disk.

In theory, a single-threaded server and k disks could also gain a factor of k, but the code and administration are far more complicated since normal blocking READ system calls cannot be used to access the disk. With a multithreaded server, they can be used since then a READ blocks only the thread that made the call, not the entire process.

Modern Web servers do more than just accept file names and return files. In fact, the actual processing of each request can get quite complicated. For this reason, in many servers each processing module performs a series of steps. The front end passes each incoming request to the first available module, which then carries it out using some subset of the following steps, depending on which ones are needed for that particular request.

1. Resolve the name of the Web page requested.
2. Authenticate the client.
3. Perform access control on the client.
4. Perform access control on the Web page.
5. Check the cache.
6. Fetch the requested page from disk.
7. Determine the MIME type to include in the response.
8. Take care of miscellaneous odds and ends.
9. Return the reply to the client.
10. Make an entry in the server log.

Step 1 is needed because the incoming request may not contain the actual name of the file as a literal string. For example, consider the URL *http://www.cs.vu.nl*, which has an empty file name. It has to be expanded to some default file name. Also, modern browsers can specify the user's default language (e.g., Italian or

English), which makes it possible for the server to select a Web page in that language, if available. In general, name expansion is not quite so trivial as it might at first appear, due to a variety of conventions about file naming.

Step 2 consists of verifying the client's identity. This step is needed for pages that are not available to the general public. We will discuss one way of doing this later in this chapter.

Step 3 checks to see if there are restrictions on whether the request may be satisfied given the client's identity and location. Step 4 checks to see if there are any access restrictions associated with the page itself. If a certain file (e.g., *.htaccess*) is present in the directory where the desired page is located, it may restrict access to the file to particular domains, for example, only users from inside the company.

Steps 5 and 6 involve getting the page. Step 6 needs to be able to handle multiple disk reads at the same time.

Step 7 is about determining the MIME type from the file extension, first few words of the file, a configuration file, and possibly other sources. Step 8 is for a variety of miscellaneous tasks, such as building a user profile or gathering certain statistics.

Step 9 is where the result is sent back and step 10 makes an entry in the system log for administrative purposes. Such logs can later be mined for valuable information about user behavior, for example, the order in which people access the pages.

If too many requests come in each second, the CPU will not be able to handle the processing load, no matter how many disks are used in parallel. The solution is to add more nodes (computers), possibly with replicated disks to avoid having the disks become the next bottleneck. This leads to the **server farm** model of Fig. 7-22. A front end still accepts incoming requests but sprays them over multiple CPUs rather than multiple threads to reduce the load on each computer. The individual machines may themselves be multithreaded and pipelined as before.

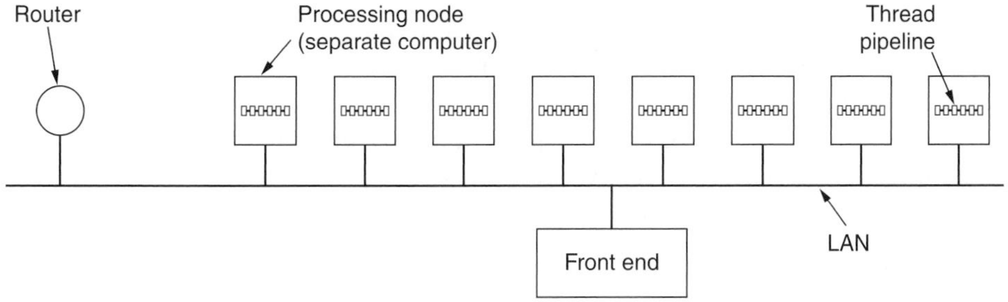

Figure 7-22. A server farm.

One problem with server farms is that there is no longer a shared cache because each processing node has its own memory—unless an expensive shared-memory multiprocessor is used. One way to counter this performance loss is to have a front end keep track of where it sends each request and send subsequent requests for the same page to the same node. Doing this makes each node a specialist in certain pages so that cache space is not wasted by having every file in every cache.

Another problem with server farms is that the client's TCP connection terminates at the front end, so the reply must go through the front end. This situation is depicted in Fig. 7-23(a), where the incoming request (1) and outgoing reply (4) both pass through the front end. Sometimes a trick, called **TCP handoff**, is used to get around this problem. With this trick, the TCP end point is passed to the processing node so it can reply directly to the client, shown as (3) in Fig. 7-23(b). This handoff is done in a way that is transparent to the client.

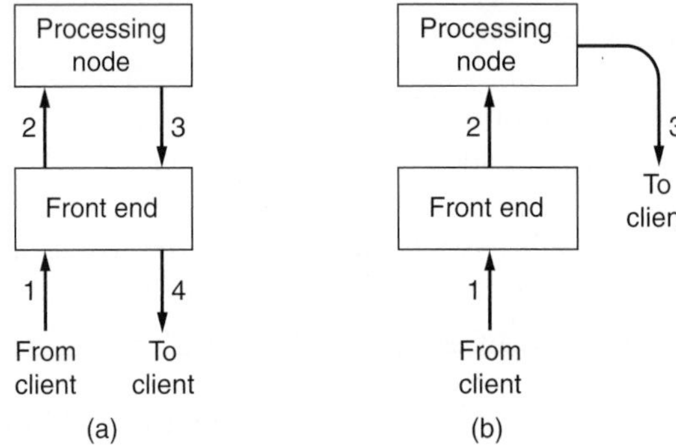

Figure 7-23. (a) Normal request-reply message sequence. (b) Sequence when TCP handoff is used.

URLs—Uniform Resource Locators

We have repeatedly said that Web pages may contain pointers to other Web pages. Now it is time to see in a bit more detail how these pointers are implemented. When the Web was first created, it was immediately apparent that having one page point to another Web page required mechanisms for naming and locating pages. In particular, three questions had to be answered before a selected page could be displayed:

1. What is the page called?
2. Where is the page located?
3. How can the page be accessed?

If every page were somehow assigned a unique name, there would not be any ambiguity in identifying pages. Nevertheless, the problem would not be solved.

Consider a parallel between people and pages. In the United States, almost everyone has a social security number, which is a unique identifier, as no two people are supposed to have the same one. Nevertheless, if you are armed only with a social security number, there is no way to find the owner's address, and certainly no way to tell whether you should write to the person in English, Spanish, or Chinese. The Web has basically the same problems.

The solution chosen identifies pages in a way that solves all three problems at once. Each page is assigned a **URL** (**Uniform Resource Locator**) that effectively serves as the page's worldwide name. URLs have three parts: the protocol (also known as the **scheme**), the DNS name of the machine on which the page is located, and a local name uniquely indicating the specific page (usually just a file name on the machine where it resides). As an example example, the Web site for the author's department contains several videos about the university and the city of Amsterdam. The URL for the video page is

http://www.cs.vu.nl/video/index-en.html

This URL consists of three parts: the protocol (*http*), the DNS name of the host (*www.cs.vu.nl*), and the file name (*video/index-en.html*), with certain punctuation separating the pieces. The file name is a path relative to the default Web directory at *cs.vu.nl*.

Many sites have built-in shortcuts for file names. At many sites, a null file name defaults to the organization's main home page. Typically, when the file named is a directory, this implies a file named *index.html*. Finally, *~user/* might be mapped onto *user*'s WWW directory, and then onto the file *index.html* in that directory. Thus, the author's home page can be reached at

http://www.cs.vu.nl/~ast/

even though the actual file name is *index.html* in a certain default directory.

Now we can see how hypertext works. To make a piece of text clickable, the page writer must provide two items of information: the clickable text to be displayed and the URL of the page to go to if the text is selected. We will explain the command syntax later in this chapter.

When the text is selected, the browser looks up the host name using DNS. Once it knows the host's IP address, the browser establishes a TCP connection to the host. Over that connection, it sends the file name using the specified protocol. Bingo. Back comes the page.

This URL scheme is open-ended in the sense that it is straightforward to have browsers use multiple protocols to get at different kinds of resources. In fact, URLs for various other common protocols have been defined. Slightly simplified forms of the more common ones are listed in Fig. 7-24.

Let us briefly go over the list. The *http* protocol is the Web's native language, the one spoken by Web servers. **HTTP** stands for **HyperText Transfer Protocol**. We will examine it in more detail later in this chapter.

Name	Used for	Example
http	Hypertext (HTML)	http://www.cs.vu.nl/~ast/
ftp	FTP	ftp://ftp.cs.vu.nl/pub/minix/README
file	Local file	file:///usr/suzanne/prog.c
news	Newsgroup	news:comp.os.minix
news	News article	news:AA0134223112@cs.utah.edu
gopher	Gopher	gopher://gopher.tc.umn.edu/11/Libraries
mailto	Sending e-mail	mailto:JohnUser@acm.org
telnet	Remote login	telnet://www.w3.org:80

Figure 7-24. Some common URLs.

The *ftp* protocol is used to access files by FTP, the Internet's file transfer protocol. FTP has been around more than two decades and is well entrenched. Numerous FTP servers all over the world allow people anywhere on the Internet to log in and download whatever files have been placed on the FTP server. The Web does not change this; it just makes obtaining files by FTP easier, as FTP has a somewhat arcane interface (but it is more powerful than HTTP, for example, it allows a user on machine *A* to transfer a file from machine *B* to machine *C*).

It is possible to access a local file as a Web page, either by using the *file* protocol, or more simply, by just naming it. This approach is similar to using FTP but does not require having a server. Of course, it works only for local files, not remote ones.

Long before there was an Internet, there was the USENET news system. It consists of about 30,000 newsgroups in which millions of people discuss a wide variety of topics by posting and reading articles related to the topic of the newsgroup. The *news* protocol can be used to call up a news article as though it were a Web page. This means that a Web browser is simultaneously a news reader. In fact, many browsers have buttons or menu items to make reading USENET news even easier than using standard news readers.

Two formats are supported for the *news* protocol. The first format specifies a newsgroup and can be used to get a list of articles from a preconfigured news site. The second one requires the identifier of a specific news article to be given, in this case *AA0134223112@cs.utah.edu*. The browser then fetches the given article from its preconfigured news site using the **NNTP** (**Network News Transfer Protocol**). We will not study NNTP in this book, but it is loosely based on SMTP and has a similar style.

The *gopher* protocol was used by the Gopher system, which was designed at the University of Minnesota and named after the school's athletic teams, the Golden Gophers (as well as being a slang expression meaning "go for", i.e., go fetch). Gopher predates the Web by several years. It was an information retrieval scheme, conceptually similar to the Web itself, but supporting only text and no images. It is essentially obsolete now and rarely used any more.

The last two protocols do not really have the flavor of fetching Web pages, but are useful anyway. The *mailto* protocol allows users to send e-mail from a Web browser. The way to do this is to click on the OPEN button and specify a URL consisting of *mailto:* followed by the recipient's e-mail address. Most browsers will respond by starting an e-mail program with the address and some of the header fields already filled in.

The telnet protocol is used to establish an on-line connection to a remote machine. It is used the same way as the telnet program, which is not surprising, since most browsers just call the telnet program as a helper application.

In short, the URLs have been designed to not only allow users to navigate the Web, but to deal with FTP, news, Gopher, e-mail, and telnet as well, making all the specialized user interface programs for those other services unnecessary and thus integrating nearly all Internet access into a single program, the Web browser. If it were not for the fact that this idea was thought of by a physics researcher, it could easily pass for the output of some software company's advertising department.

Despite all these nice properties, the growing use of the Web has turned up an inherent weakness in the URL scheme. A URL points to one specific host. For pages that are heavily referenced, it is desirable to have multiple copies far apart, to reduce the network traffic. The trouble is that URLs do not provide any way to reference a page without simultaneously telling where it is. There is no way to say: I want page xyz, but I do not care where you get it. To solve this problem and make it possible to replicate pages, IETF is working on a system of **URN**s (**Universal Resource Names**). A URN can be thought of as a generalized URL. This topic is still the subject of research, although a proposed syntax is given in RFC 2141.

Statelessness and Cookies

As we have seen repeatedly, the Web is basically stateless. There is no concept of a login session. The browser sends a request to a server and gets back a file. Then the server forgets that it has ever seen that particular client.

At first, when the Web was just used for retrieving publicly available documents, this model was perfectly adequate. But as the Web started to acquire other functions, it caused problems. For example, some Web sites require clients to register (and possibly pay money) to use them. This raises the question of how servers can distinguish between requests from registered users and everyone else. A second example is from e-commerce. If a user wanders around an electronic store, tossing items into her shopping cart from time to time, how does the server keep track of the contents of the cart? A third example is customized Web portals such as Yahoo. Users can set up a detailed initial page with only the information they want (e.g., their stocks and their favorite sports teams), but how can the server display the correct page if it does not know who the user is?

At first glance, one might think that servers could track users by observing their IP addresses. However, this idea does not work. First of all, many users work on shared computers, especially at companies, and the IP address merely identifies the computer, not the user. Second, and even worse, many ISPs use NAT, so all outgoing packets from all users bear the same IP address. From the server's point of view, all the ISP's thousands of customers use the same IP address.

To solve this problem, Netscape devised a much-criticized technique called **cookies**. The name derives from ancient programmer slang in which a program calls a procedure and gets something back that it may need to present later to get some work done. In this sense, a UNIX file descriptor or a Windows object handle can be considered as a cookie. Cookies were later formalized in RFC 2109.

When a client requests a Web page, the server can supply additional information along with the requested page. This information may include a cookie, which is a small (at most 4 KB) file (or string). Browsers store offered cookies in a cookie directory on the client's hard disk unless the user has disabled cookies. Cookies are just files or strings, not executable programs. In principle, a cookie could contain a virus, but since cookies are treated as data, there is no official way for the virus to actually run and do damage. However, it is always possible for some hacker to exploit a browser bug to cause activation.

A cookie may contain up to five fields, as shown in Fig. 7-25. The *Domain* tells where the cookie came from. Browsers are supposed to check that servers are not lying about their domain. Each domain may store no more than 20 cookies per client. The *Path* is a path in the server's directory structure that identifies which parts of the server's file tree may use the cookie. It is often /, which means the whole tree.

Domain	Path	Content	Expires	Secure
toms-casino.com	/	CustomerID=497793521	15-10-02 17:00	Yes
joes-store.com	/	Cart=1-00501;1-07031;2-13721	11-10-02 14:22	No
aportal.com	/	Prefs=Stk:SUNW+ORCL;Spt:Jets	31-12-10 23:59	No
sneaky.com	/	UserID=3627239101	31-12-12 23:59	No

Figure 7-25. Some examples of cookies.

The *Content* field takes the form *name* = *value*. Both *name* and *value* can be anything the server wants. This field is where the cookie's content is stored.

The *Expires* field specifies when the cookie expires. If this field is absent, the browser discards the cookie when it exits. Such a cookie is called a **nonpersistent cookie**. If a time and date are supplied, the cookie is said to be **persistent** and is kept until it expires. Expiration times are given in Greenwich Mean Time. To remove a cookie from a client's hard disk, a server just sends it again, but with an expiration time in the past.

Finally, the *Secure* field can be set to indicate that the browser may only return the cookie to a secure server. This feature is used for e-commerce, banking, and other secure applications.

We have now seen how cookies are acquired, but how are they used? Just before a browser sends a request for a page to some Web site, it checks its cookie directory to see if any cookies there were placed by the domain the request is going to. If so, all the cookies placed by that domain are included in the request message. When the server gets them, it can interpret them any way it wants to.

Let us examine some possible uses for cookies. In Fig. 7-25, the first cookie was set by *toms-casino.com* and is used to identify the customer. When the client logs in next week to throw away some more money, the browser sends over the cookie so the server knows who it is. Armed with the customer ID, the server can look up the customer's record in a database and use this information to build an appropriate Web page to display. Depending on the customer's known gambling habits, this page might consist of a poker hand, a listing of today's horse races, or a slot machine.

The second cookie came from *joes-store.com*. The scenario here is that the client is wandering around the store, looking for good things to buy. When she finds a bargain and clicks on it, the server builds a cookie containing the number of items and the product code and sends it back to the client. As the client continues to wander around the store, the cookie is returned on every new page request. As more purchases accumulate, the server adds them to the cookie. In the figure, the cart contains three items, the last of which is desired in duplicate. Finally, when the client clicks on *PROCEED TO CHECKOUT*, the cookie, now containing the full list of purchases, is sent along with the request. In this way the server knows exactly what has been purchased.

The third cookie is for a Web portal. When the customer clicks on a link to the portal, the browser sends over the cookie. This tells the portal to build a page containing the stock prices for Sun Microsystems and Oracle, and the New York Jets football results. Since a cookie can be up to 4 KB, there is plenty of room for more detailed preferences concerning newspaper headlines, local weather, special offers, etc.

Cookies can also be used for the server's own benefit. For example, suppose a server wants to keep track of how many unique visitors it has had and how many pages each one looked at before leaving the site. When the first request comes in, there will be no accompanying cookie, so the server sends back a cookie containing *Counter = 1*. Subsequent clicks on that site will send the cookie back to the server. Each time the counter is incremented and sent back to the client. By keeping track of the counters, the server can see how many people give up after seeing the first page, how many look at two pages, and so on.

Cookies have also been misused. In theory, cookies are only supposed to go back to the originating site, but hackers have exploited numerous bugs in the browsers to capture cookies not intended for them. Since some e-commerce sites put credit card numbers in cookies, the potential for abuse is clear.

A controversial use of cookies is to secretly collect information about users' Web browsing habits. It works like this. An advertising agency, say, Sneaky Ads, contacts major Web sites and places banner ads for its corporate clients' products on their pages, for which it pays the site owners a fee. Instead of giving the site a GIF or JPEG file to place on each page, it gives them a URL to add to each page. Each URL it hands out contains a unique number in the file part, such as

http://www.sneaky.com/382674902342.gif

When a user first visits a page, *P*, containing such an ad, the browser fetches the HTML file. Then the browser inspects the HTML file and sees the link to the image file at *www.sneaky.com*, so it sends a request there for the image. A GIF file containing an ad is returned, along with a cookie containing a unique user ID, 3627239101 in Fig. 7-25. Sneaky records the fact that the user with this ID visited page *P*. This is easy to do since the file requested (*382674902342.gif*) is referenced only on page *P*. Of course, the actual ad may appear on thousands of pages, but each time with a different file name. Sneaky probably collects a couple of pennies from the product manufacturer each time it ships out the ad.

Later, when the user visits another Web page containing any of Sneaky's ads, after the browser has fetched the HTML file from the server, it sees the link to, say, *http://www.sneaky.com/493654919923.gif* and requests that file. Since it already has a cookie from the domain *sneaky.com*, the browser includes Sneaky's cookie containing the user ID. Sneaky now knows a second page the user has visited.

In due course of time, Sneaky can build up a complete profile of the user's browsing habits, even though the user has never clicked on any of the ads. Of course, it does not yet have the user's name (although it does have his IP address, which may be enough to deduce the name from other databases). However, if the user ever supplies his name to any site cooperating with Sneaky, a complete profile along with a name is now available for sale to anyone who wants to buy it. The sale of this information may be profitable enough for Sneaky to place more ads on more Web sites and thus collect more information. The most insidious part of this whole business is that most users are completely unaware of this information collection and may even think they are safe because they do not click on any of the ads.

And if Sneaky wants to be supersneaky, the ad need not be a classical banner ad. An "ad" consisting of a single pixel in the background color (and thus invisible), has exactly the same effect as a banner ad: it requires the browser to go fetch the 1×1-pixel gif image and send it all cookies originating at the pixel's domain.

To maintain some semblance of privacy, some users configure their browsers to reject all cookies. However, this can give problems with legitimate Web sites that use cookies. To solve this problem, users sometimes install cookie-eating software. These are special programs that inspect each incoming cookie upon arrival and accept or discard it depending on choices the user has given it (e.g., about which Web sites can be trusted). This gives the user fine-grained control over which cookies are accepted and which are rejected. Modern browsers, such as Mozilla (*www.mozilla.org*), have elaborate user-controls over cookies built in.

7.3.2 Static Web Documents

The basis of the Web is transferring Web pages from server to client. In the simplest form, Web pages are static, that is, are just files sitting on some server waiting to be retrieved. In this context, even a video is a static Web page because it is just a file. In this section we will look at static Web pages in detail. In the next one, we will examine dynamic content.

HTML—The HyperText Markup Language

Web pages are currently written in a language called **HTML** (**HyperText Markup Language**). HTML allows users to produce Web pages that include text, graphics, and pointers to other Web pages. HTML is a markup language, a language for describing how documents are to be formatted. The term "markup" comes from the old days when copyeditors actually marked up documents to tell the printer—in those days, a human being—which fonts to use, and so on. Markup languages thus contain explicit commands for formatting. For example, in HTML, <b> **means start boldface mode, and** </b> means leave boldface mode. The advantage of a markup language over one with no explicit markup is that writing a browser for it is straightforward: the browser simply has to understand the markup commands. TeX and troff are other well-known examples of markup languages.

By embedding all the markup commands within each HTML file and standardizing them, it becomes possible for any Web browser to read and reformat any Web page. Being able to reformat Web pages after receiving them is crucial because a page may have been produced in a 1600×1200 window with 24-bit color but may have to be displayed in a 640×320 window configured for 8-bit color.

Below we will give a brief introduction to HTML, just to give an idea of what it is like. While it is certainly possible to write HTML documents with any standard editor, and many people do, it is also possible to use special HTML editors or word processors that do most of the work (but correspondingly give the user less control over all the details of the final result).

A Web page consists of a head and a body, each enclosed by <html> and </html> **tags** (formatting commands), although most browsers do not complain if these tags are missing. As can be seen from Fig. 7-26(a), the head is bracketed by the <head> and </head> tags and the body is bracketed by the <body> and </body> tags. The strings inside the tags are called **directives**. Most HTML tags have this format, that is they use, <something> to mark the beginning of something and </something> to mark its end. Most browsers have a menu item VIEW SOURCE or something like that. Selecting this item displays the current page's HTML source, instead of its formatted output.

Tags can be in either lower case or upper case. Thus, <head> and <HEAD> mean the same thing, but newer versions of the standard require lower case only. Actual layout of the HTML document is irrelevant. HTML parsers ignore extra spaces and carriage returns since they have to reformat the text to make it fit the current display area. Consequently, white space can be added at will to make HTML documents more readable, something most of them are badly in need of. As another consequence, blank lines cannot be used to separate paragraphs, as they are simply ignored. An explicit tag is required.

Some tags have (named) parameters, called **attributes**. For example,

```
<img src="abc"  alt="foobar">
```

is a tag, <img>, with parameter *src* set equal to *abc* and parameter *alt* set equal to *foobar*. For each tag, the HTML standard gives a list of what the permitted parameters, if any, are, and what they mean. Because each parameter is named, the order in which the parameters are given is not significant.

Technically, HTML documents are written in the ISO 8859-1 Latin-1 character set, but for users whose keyboards support only ASCII, escape sequences are present for the special characters, such as è. The list of special characters is given in the standard. All of them begin with an ampersand and end with a semicolon. For example,   produces a space, è produces è and é produces é. Since <, >, and & have special meanings, they can be expressed only with their escape sequences, <, >, and &, respectively.

The main item in the head is the title, delimited by <title> and </title>, but certain kinds of meta-information may also be present. The title itself is not displayed on the page. Some browsers use it to label the page's window.

Let us now take a look at some of the other features illustrated in Fig. 7-26. All of the tags used in Fig. 7-26 and some others are shown in Fig. 7-27. Headings are generated by an <h*n*> tag, where *n* is a digit in the range 1 to 6. Thus <h1> is the most important heading; <h6> is the least important one. It is up to the browser to render these appropriately on the screen. Typically the lower numbered headings will be displayed in a larger and heavier font. The browser may also choose to use different colors for each level of heading. Typically <h1> headings are large and boldface with at least one blank line above and below. In contrast, <h2> headings are in a smaller font with less space above and below.

```
<html>
<head> <title> AMALGAMATED WIDGET, INC. </title> </head>
<body> <h1> Welcome to AWI's Home Page </h1>
<img src="http://www.widget.com/images/logo.gif" ALT="AWI Logo"> <br>
We are so happy that you have chosen to visit <b> Amalgamated Widget's</b>
home page. We hope <i> you </i> will find all the information you need here.
<p>Below we have links to information about our many fine products.
You can order electronically (by WWW), by telephone, or by fax. </p>
<hr>
<h2> Product information </h2>
<ul>
  <li> <a href="http://widget.com/products/big"> Big widgets </a>
  <li> <a href="http://widget.com/products/little"> Little widgets </a>
</ul>
<h2> Telephone numbers </h2>
<ul>
  <li> By telephone: 1-800-WIDGETS
  <li> By fax: 1-415-765-4321
</ul>
</body>
</html>
```

(a)

Welcome to AWI's Home Page

We are so happy that you have chosen to visit **Amalgamated Widget's** home page. We hope *you* will find all the information you need here.

Below we have links to information about our many fine products. You can order electronically (by WWW), by telephone, or by FAX.

Product Information

- Big widgets
- Little widgets

Telephone numbers

- 1-800-WIDGETS
- 1-415-765-4321

(b)

Figure 7-26. (a) The HTML for a sample Web page. (b) The formatted page.

The tags <b> and <i> are used to enter boldface and italics mode, respectively. If the browser is not capable of displaying boldface and italics, it must use some other method of rendering them, for example, using a different color for each or perhaps reverse video.

HTML provides various mechanisms for making lists, including nested lists. Lists are started with <ul> or <ol>, with <li> used to mark the start of the items in both cases. The <ul> tag starts an unordered list. The individual items, which are marked with the <li> tag in the source, appear with bullets (•) in front of them. A variant of this mechanism is <ol>, which is for ordered lists. When this tag is used, the <li> items are numbered by the browser. Other than the use of different starting and ending tags, <ul> and <ol> have the same syntax and similar results.

The <br>, <p>, and <hr> tags all indicate a boundary between sections of text. The precise format can be determined by the style sheet (see below) associated with the page. The <br> tag just forces a line break. Typically, browsers do not insert a blank line after <br>. In contrast, <p> starts a paragraph, which might, for example, insert a blank line and possibly some indentation. (Theoretically, </p> exists to mark the end of a paragraph, but it is rarely used; most HTML authors do not even know it exists.) Finally, <hr> forces a break and draws a horizontal line across the screen.

HTML allows images to be included in-line on a Web page. The <img> tag specifies that an image is to be displayed at the current position in the page. It can have several parameters. The *src* parameter gives the URL of the image. The HTML standard does not specify which graphic formats are permitted. In practice, all browsers support GIF amd JPEG files. Browsers are free to support other formats, but this extension is a two-edged sword. If a user is accustomed to a browser that supports, say, BMP files, he may include these in his Web pages and later be surprised when other browsers just ignore all of his wonderful art.

Other parameters of <img> are *align*, which controls the alignment of the image with respect to the text baseline (*top*, *middle*, *bottom*), *alt*, which provides text to use instead of the image when the user has disabled images, and *ismap*, a flag indicating that the image is an active map (i.e., clickable picture).

Finally, we come to hyperlinks, which use the <a> (anchor) and </a> tags. Like <img>, <a> has various parameters, including *href* (the URL) and *name* (the hyperlink's name). The text between the <a> and </a> is displayed. If it is selected, the hyperlink is followed to a new page. It is also permitted to put an <img> image there, in which case clicking on the image also activates the hyperlink.

As an example, consider the following HTML fragment:

```
<a href="http://www.nasa.gov"> NASA's home page </a>
```

When a page with this fragment is displayed, what appears on the screen is

NASA's home page

Tag	Description
<html> ... </html>	Declares the Web page to be written in HTML
<head> ... </head>	Delimits the page's head
<title> ... </title>	Defines the title (not displayed on the page)
<body> ... </body>	Delimits the page's body
<h *n*> ... </h*n*>	Delimits a level *n* heading
<b> ... </b>	Set ... in boldface
<i> ... </i>	Set ... in italics
<center> ... </center>	Center ... on the page horizontally
<ul> ... </ul>	Brackets an unordered (bulleted) list
<ol> ... </ol>	Brackets a numbered list
<li> ... </li>	Brackets an item in an ordered or numbered list
 	Forces a line break here
<p>	Starts a paragraph
<hr>	Inserts a horizontal rule
<img src="...">	Displays an image here
<a href="..."> ... </a>	Defines a hyperlink

Figure 7-27. A selection of common HTML tags. Some can have additional parameters.

If the user subsequently clicks on this text, the browser immediately fetches the page whose URL is *http://www.nasa.gov* and displays it.

As a second example, now consider

```
<a href="http://www.nasa.gov"> <img src="shuttle.gif" alt="NASA"> </a>
```

When displayed, this page shows a picture (e.g., of the space shuttle). Clicking on the picture switches to NASA's home page, just as clicking on the underlined text did in the previous example. If the user has disabled automatic image display, the text NASA will be displayed where the picture belongs.

The <a> tag can take a parameter *name* to plant a hyperlink, to allow a hyperlink to point to the middle of a page. For example, some Web pages start out with a clickable table of contents. By clicking on an item in the table of contents, the user jumps to the corresponding section of the page.

HTML keeps evolving. HTML 1.0 and HTML 2.0 did not have tables, but they were added in HTML 3.0. An HTML table consists of one or more rows, each consisting of one or more **cells**. Cells can contain a wide range of material, including text, figures, icons, photographs, and even other tables. Cells can be merged, so, for example, a heading can span multiple columns. Page authors have limited control over the layout, including alignment, border styles, and cell margins, but the browsers have the final say in rendering tables.

An HTML table definition is listed in Fig. 7-28(a) and a possible rendition is shown in Fig. 7-28(b). This example just shows a few of the basic features of HTML tables. Tables are started by the <table> tag. Additional information can be provided to describe general properties of the table.

The <caption> tag can be used to provide a figure caption. Each row begins with a <tr> (Table Row) tag. The individual cells are marked as <th> (Table Header) or <td> (Table Data). The distinction is made to allow browsers to use different renditions for them, as we have done in the example.

Numerous attributes are also allowed in tables. They include ways to specify horizontal and vertical cell alignments, justification within a cell, borders, grouping of cells, units, and more.

In HTML 4.0, more new features were added. These include accessibility features for handicapped users, object embedding (a generalization of the <img> tag so other objects can also be embedded in pages), support for scripting languages (to allow dynamic content), and more.

When a Web site is complex, consisting of many pages produced by multiple authors working for the same company, it is often desirable to have a way to prevent different pages from having a different appearance. This problem can be solved using **style sheets**. When these are used, individual pages no longer use physical styles, such as boldface and italics. Instead, page authors use logical styles such as <dn> (define), <em> (weak emphasis), <strong> (strong emphasis), and <var> (program variables). The logical styles are defined in the style sheet, which is referred to at the start of each page. In this way all pages have the same style, and if the Webmaster decides to change <strong> from 14-point italics in blue to 18-point boldface in shocking pink, all it requires is changing one definition to convert the entire Web site. A style sheet can be compared to an #include file in a C program: changing one macro definition there changes it in all the program files that include the header.

Forms

HTML 1.0 was basically one-way. Users could call up pages from information providers, but it was difficult to send information back the other way. As more and more commercial organizations began using the Web, there was a large demand for two-way traffic. For example, many companies wanted to be able to take orders for products via their Web pages, software vendors wanted to distribute software via the Web and have customers fill out their registration cards electronically, and companies offering Web searching wanted to have their customers be able to type in search keywords.

These demands led to the inclusion of **forms** starting in HTML 2.0. Forms contain boxes or buttons that allow users to fill in information or make choices and then send the information back to the page's owner. They use the <input> tag for this purpose. It has a variety of parameters for determining the size, nature,

```
<html>
<head> <title> A sample page with a table </title> </head>
<body>
<table border=1 rules=all>
<caption> Some Differences between HTML Versions </caption>
<col align=left>
<col align=center>
<col align=center>
<col align=center>
<col align=center>
<tr> <th>Item  <th>HTML 1.0  <th>HTML 2.0  <th>HTML 3.0 <th>HTML 4.0 </tr>
<tr> <th> Hyperlinks <td> x <td> x <td> x <td> x </tr>
<tr> <th> Images <td> x <td> x <td> x <td> x </tr>
<tr> <th> Lists <td> x <td> x <td> x <td> x </tr>
<tr> <th> Active Maps and Images <td>   <td> x <td> x <td> x </tr>
<tr> <th> Forms <td>   <td> x <td> x <td> x </tr>
<tr> <th> Equations <td>   <td>   <td> x <td> x </tr>
<tr> <th> Toolbars <td>   <td>   <td> x <td> x </tr>
<tr> <th> Tables <td>   <td>   <td> x <td> x </tr>
<tr> <th> Accessibility features <td>   <td>   <td>   <td> x </tr>
<tr> <th> Object embedding <td>   <td>   <td>   <td> x </tr>
<tr> <th> Scripting <td>   <td>   <td>   <td> x </tr>
</table>
</body>
</html>
```

(a)

Some Differences between HTML Versions

Item	**HTML 1.0**	**HTML 2.0**	**HTML 3.0**	**HTML 4.0**
Hyperlinks	x	x	x	x
Images	x	x	x	x
Lists	x	x	x	x
Active Maps and Images		x	x	x
Forms		x	x	x
Equations			x	x
Toolbars			x	x
Tables			x	x
Accessibility features				x
Object embedding				x
Scripting				x

Figure 7-28. (a) An HTML table. (b) A possible rendition of this table.

and usage of the box displayed. The most common forms are blank fields for accepting user text, boxes that can be checked, active maps, and *submit* buttons. The example of Fig. 7-29 illustrates some of these choices.

Let us start our discussion of forms by going over this example. Like all forms, this one is enclosed between the <form> and </form> tags. Text not enclosed in a tag is just displayed. All the usual tags (e.g., <b>) are allowed in a form. Three kinds of input boxes are used in this form.

The first kind of input box follows the text "Name". The box is 46 characters wide and expects the user to type in a string, which is then stored in the variable *customer* for later processing. The <p> tag instructs the browser to display subsequent text and boxes on the next line, even if there is room on the current line. By using <p> and other layout tags, the author of the page can control the look of the form on the screen.

The next line of the form asks for the user's street address, 40 columns wide, also on a line by itself. Then comes a line asking for the city, state, and country. No <p> tags are used between the fields here, so the browser displays them all on one line if they will fit. As far as the browser is concerned, this paragraph just contains six items: three strings alternating with three boxes. It displays them linearly from left to right, going over to a new line whenever the current line cannot hold the next item. Thus, it is conceivable that on a 1600×1200 screen all three strings and their corresponding boxes will appear on the same line, but on a 1024×768 screen they might be split over two lines. In the worst scenario, the word "Country" is at the end of one line and its box is at the beginning of the next line.

The next line asks for the credit card number and expiration date. Transmitting credit card numbers over the Internet should only be done when adequate security measures have been taken. We will discuss some of these in Chap. 8.

Following the expiration date we encounter a new feature: radio buttons. These are used when a choice must be made among two or more alternatives. The intellectual model here is a car radio with half a dozen buttons for choosing stations. The browser displays these boxes in a form that allows the user to select and deselect them by clicking on them (or using the keyboard). Clicking on one of them turns off all the other ones in the same group. The visual presentation is up to the browser. Widget size also uses two radio buttons. The two groups are distinguished by their *name* field, not by static scoping using something like <radiobutton> ... </radiobutton>.

The *value* parameters are used to indicate which radio button was pushed. Depending on which of the credit card options the user has chosen, the variable *cc* will be set to either the string "mastercard" or the string "visacard".

After the two sets of radio buttons, we come to the shipping option, represented by a box of type *checkbox*. It can be either on or off. Unlike radio buttons, where exactly one out of the set must be chosen, each box of type *checkbox* can be on or off, independently of all the others. For example, when ordering a

```
<html>
<head> <title> AWI CUSTOMER ORDERING FORM </title> </head>
<body>
<h1> Widget Order Form </h1>
<form ACTION="http://widget.com/cgi-bin/widgetorder" method=POST>
<p> Name <input name="customer" size=46> </p>
<p> Street Address <input name="address" size=40> </p>
<p> City <input name="city" size=20> State <input name="state" size =4>
Country <input name="country" size=10> </p>
<p> Credit card # <input name="cardno" size=10>
Expires <input name="expires" size=4>
M/C <input name="cc" type=radio value="mastercard">
VISA <input name="cc" type=radio value="visacard"> </p>
<p> Widget size Big <input name="product" type=radio value="expensive">
Little <input name="product" type=radio value="cheap">
Ship by express courier <input name="express" type=checkbox> </p>
<p><input type=submit value="submit order"> </p>
Thank you for ordering an AWI widget, the best widget money can buy!
</form>
</body>
</html>
```

(a)

Widget Order Form

Name

Street address

City State Country

Credit card # Expires M/C Visa

Widget size Big Little Ship by express courier

Submit order

Thank you for ordering an AWI widget, the best widget money can buy!

(b)

Figure 7-29. (a) The HTML for an order form. (b) The formatted page.

pizza via Electropizza's Web page, the user can choose sardines *and* onions *and* pineapple (if she can stand it), but she cannot choose small *and* medium *and* large for the same pizza. The pizza toppings would be represented by three separate boxes of type *checkbox*, whereas the pizza size would be a set of radio buttons.

As an aside, for very long lists from which a choice must be made, radio buttons are somewhat inconvenient. Therefore, the <select> and </select> tags are provided to bracket a list of alternatives, but with the semantics of radio buttons (unless the *multiple* parameter is given, in which case the semantics are those of checkable boxes). Some browsers render the items located between <select> and </select> as a drop-down menu.

We have now seen two of the built-in types for the <input> tag: *radio* and *checkbox*. In fact, we have already seen a third one as well: *text*. Because this type is the default, we did not bother to include the parameter *type* = *text*, but we could have. Two other types are *password* and *textarea*. A *password* box is the same as a *text* box, except that the characters are not displayed as they are typed. A *textarea* box is also the same as a *text* box, except that it can contain multiple lines.

Getting back to the example of Fig. 7-29, we now come across an example of a *submit* button. When this is clicked, the user information on the form is sent back to the machine that provided the form. Like all the other types, *submit* is a reserved word that the browser understands. The *value* string here is the label on the button and is displayed. All boxes can have values; only here we needed that feature. For *text* boxes, the contents of the *value* field are displayed along with the form, but the user can edit or erase it. *checkbox* and *radio* boxes can also be initialized, but with a field called *checked* (because *value* just gives the text, but does not indicate a preferred choice).

When the user clicks the *submit* button, the browser packages the collected information into a single long line and sends it back to the server for processing. The & is used to separate fields and + is used to represent space. For our example form, the line might look like the contents of Fig. 7-30 (broken into three lines here because the page is not wide enough):

```
customer=John+Doe&address=100+Main+St.&city=White+Plains&
state=NY&country=USA&cardno=1234567890&expires=6/98&cc=mastercard&
product=cheap&express=on
```

Figure 7-30. A possible response from the browser to the server with information filled in by the user.

The string would be sent back to the server as one line, not three. If a *checkbox* is not selected, it is omitted from the string. It is up to the server to make sense of this string. We will discuss how this could be done later in this chapter.

XML and XSL

HTML, with or without forms, does not provide any structure to Web pages. It also mixes the content with the formatting. As e-commerce and other applications become more common, there is an increasing need for structuring Web pages and separating the content from the formatting. For example, a program that searches the Web for the best price for some book or CD needs to analyze many Web pages looking for the item's title and price. With Web pages in HTML, it is very difficult for a program to figure out where the title is and where the price is.

For this reason, the W3C has developed an enhancement to HTML to allow Web pages to be structured for automated processing. Two new languages have been developed for this purpose. First, **XML** (**eXtensible Markup Language**) describes Web content in a structured way and second, **XSL** (**eXtensible Style Language**) describes the formatting independently of the content. Both of these are large and complicated topics, so our brief introduction below just scratches the surface, but it should give an idea of how they work.

Consider the example XML document of Fig. 7-31. It defines a structure called book_list, which is a list of books. Each book has three fields, the title, author, and year of publication. These structures are extremely simple. It is permitted to have structures with repeated fields (e.g., multiple authors), optional fields (e.g., title of included CD-ROM), and alternative fields (e.g., URL of a bookstore if it is in print or URL of an auction site if it is out of print).

In this example, each of the three fields is an indivisible entity, but it is also permitted to further subdivide the fields. For example, the author field could have been done as follows to give a finer-grained control over searching and formatting:

```
<author>
  <first_name> Andrew </first_name>
  <last_name> Tanenbaum </last_name>
</author>
```

Each field can be subdivided into subfields and subsubfields arbitrarily deep.

All the file of Fig. 7-31 does is define a book list containing three books. It says nothing about how to display the Web page on the screen. To provide the formatting information, we need a second file, *book_list.xsl*, containing the XSL definition. This file is a style sheet that tells how to display the page. (There are alternatives to style sheets, such as a way to convert XML into HTML, but these alternatives are beyond the scope of this book.)

A sample XSL file for formatting Fig. 7-31 is given in Fig. 7-32. After some necessary declarations, including the URL of the XSL standard, the file contains tags starting with <html> and <body>. These define the start of the Web page, as

```
<?xml version="1.0" ?>
<?xml-stylesheet type="text/xsl" href="book_list.xsl"?>

<book_list>

<book>
  <title> Computer Networks, 4/e </title>
  <author> Andrew S. Tanenbaum </author>
  <year> 2003 </year>
</book>

<book>
  <title> Modern Operating Systems, 2/e </title>
  <author> Andrew S. Tanenbaum </author>
  <year> 2001 </year>
</book>

<book>
  <title> Structured Computer Organization, 4/e </title>
  <author> Andrew S. Tanenbaum </author>
  <year> 1999 </year>
</book>

</book_list>
```

Figure 7-31. A simple Web page in XML.

usual. Then comes a table definition, including the headings for the three columns. Note that in addition to the <th> tags there are </th> tags as well, something we did not bother with so far. The XML and XSL specifications are much stricter than HTML specification. They state that rejecting syntactically incorrect files is mandatory, even if the browser can determine what the Web designer meant. A browser that accepts a syntactically incorrect XML or XSL file and repairs the errors itself is not conformant and will be rejected in a conformance test. Browsers are allowed to pinpoint the error, however. This somewhat draconian measure is needed to deal with the immense number of sloppy Web pages currently out there.

The statement

```
<xsl:for-each select="book_list/book">
```

is analogous to a for statement in C. It causes the browser to iterate the loop body (ended by <xsl:for-each>) one iteration for each book. Each iteration outputs five lines: <tr>, the title, author, and year, and </tr>. After the loop, the closing tags </body> and </html> are output. The result of the browser's interpreting this style sheet is the same as if the Web page contained the table in-line. However, in this

```
<?xml version='1.0'?>
<xsl:stylesheet xmlns:xsl="http://www.w3.org/1999/XSL/Transform" version="1.0">
<xsl:template match="/">

<html>
<body>

<table border="2">
  <tr>
    <th> Title</th>
    <th> Author</th>
    <th> Year </th>
  </tr>

  <xsl:for-each select="book_list/book">
  <tr>
    <td> <xsl:value-of select="title"/> </td>
    <td> <xsl:value-of select="author"/> </td>
    <td> <xsl:value-of select="year"/> </td>
 </tr>
 </xsl:for-each>
</table>

</body>
</html>
</xsl:template>
</xsl:stylesheet>
```

Figure 7-32. A style sheet in XSL.

format, programs can analyze the XML file and easily find books published after 2000, for example. It is worth emphasizing that even though our XSL file contained a kind of a loop, Web pages in XML and XSL are still static since they simply contain instructions to the browser about how to display the page, just as HTML pages do. Of course, to use XML and XSL, the browser has to be able to interpret XML and XSL, but most of them already have this capability. It is not yet clear whether XSL will take over from traditional style sheets.

We have not shown how to do this, but XML allows the Web site designer to make up definition files in which the structures are defined in advance. These definition files can be included, making it possible to use them to build complex Web pages. For additional information on this and the many other features of XML and XSL, see one of the many books on the subject. Two examples are (Livingston, 2002; and Williamson, 2001).

Before ending our discussion of XML and XSL, it is worth commenting on a ideological battle going on within the WWW consortium and the Web designer community. The original goal of HTML was to specify the *structure* of the document, not its *appearance*. For example,

```
<h1> Deborah's Photos </h1>
```

instructs the browser to emphasize the heading, but does not say anything about the typeface, point size, or color. That was left up to the browser, which knows the properties of the display (e.g., how many pixels it has). However, many Web page designers wanted absolute control over how their pages appeared, so new tags were added to HTML to control appearance, such as

```
<font face="helvetica" size="24" color="red"> Deborah's Photos </font>
```

Also, ways were added to control positioning on the screen accurately. The trouble with this approach is that it is not portable. Although a page may render perfectly with the browser it is developed on, with another browser or another release of the same browser or a different screen resolution, it may be a complete mess. XML was in part an attempt to go back to the original goal of specifying just the structure, not the appearance of a document. However, XSL is also provided to manage the appearance. Both formats can be misused, however. You can count on it.

XML can be used for purposes other than describing Web pages. One growing use of it is as a language for communication between application programs. In particular, **SOAP** (**Simple Object Access Protocol**) is a way for performing RPCs between applications in a language- and system-independent way. The client constructs the request as an XML message and sends it to the server, using the HTTP protocol (described below). The server sends back a reply as an XML formatted message. In this way, applications on heterogeneous platforms can communicate.

XHTML—The eXtended HyperText Markup Language

HTML keeps evolving to meet new demands. Many people in the industry feel that in the future, the majority of Web-enabled devices will not be PCs, but wireless, handheld PDA-type devices. These devices have limited memory for large browsers full of heuristics that try to somehow deal with syntactically incorrect Web pages. Thus, the next step after HTML 4 is a language that is Very Picky. It is called **XHTML** (**eXtended HyperText Markup Language**) rather than HTML 5 because it is essentially HTML 4 reformulated in XML. By this we mean that tags such as <h1> have no intrinsic meaning. To get the HTML 4 effect, a definition is needed in the XSL file. XHTML is the new Web standard and should be used for all new Web pages to achieve maximum portability across platforms and browsers.

There are six major differences and a variety of minor differences between XHTML and HTML 4, Let us now go over the major differences. First, XHTML pages and browsers must strictly conform to the standard. No more shoddy Web pages. This property was inherited from XML.

Second, all tags and attributes must be in lower case. Tags like <HTML> are not valid in XHTML. The use of tags like <html> is now mandatory. Similarly, <img SRC="pic001.jpg"> is also forbidden because it contains an upper-case attribute.

Third, closing tags are required, even for </p>. For tags that have no natural closing tag, such as <br>, <hr>, and <img>, a slash must precede the closing ">," for example

```
<img src="pic001.jpg" />
```

Fourth, attributes must be contained within quotation marks. For example,

```
<img SRC="pic001.jpg"  height=500 />
```

is no longer allowed. The 500 has to be enclosed in quotation marks, just like the name of the JPEG file, even though 500 is just a number.

Fifth, tags must nest properly. In the past, proper nesting was not required as long as the final state achieved was correct. For example,

```
<center> <b> Vacation Pictures </center> </b>
```

used to be legal. In XHTML it is not. Tags must be closed in the inverse order that they were opened.

Sixth, every document must specify its document type. We saw this in Fig. 7-32, for example. For a discussion of all the changes, major and minor, see *www.w3.org*.

7.3.3 Dynamic Web Documents

So far, the model we have used is that of Fig. 6-6: the client sends a file name to the server, which then returns the file. In the early days of the Web, all content was, in fact, static like this (just files). However, in recent years, more and more content has become dynamic, that is, generated on demand, rather than stored on disk. Content generation can take place either on the server side or on the client side. Let us now examine each of these cases in turn.

Server-Side Dynamic Web Page Generation

To see why server-side content generation is needed, consider the use of forms, as described earlier. When a user fills in a form and clicks on the *submit* button, a message is sent to the server indicating that it contains the contents of a form, along with the fields the user filled in. This message is not the name of a file to return. What is needed is that the message is given to a program or script to process. Usually, the processing involves using the user-supplied information to look up a record in a database on the server's disk and generate a custom HTML page to send back to the client. For example, in an e-commerce application, after the user clicks on *PROCEED TO CHECKOUT*, the browser returns the cookie containing the contents of the shopping cart, but some program or script on the server has to be invoked to process the cookie and generate an HTML page in response. The HTML page might display a form containing the list of items in the cart and the user's last-known shipping address along with a request to verify the information and to specify the method of payment. The steps required to process the information from an HTML form are illustrated in Fig. 7-33.

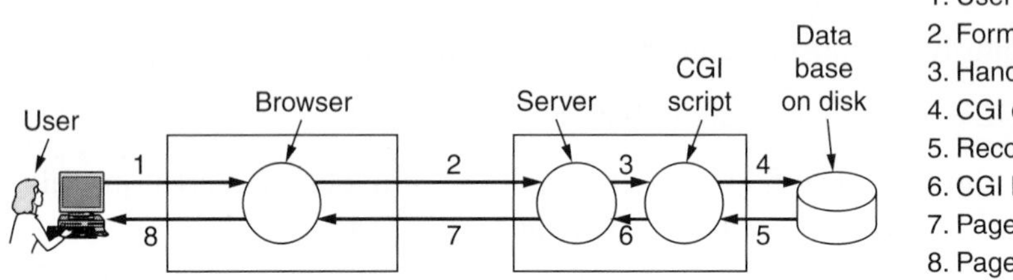

Figure 7-33. Steps in processing the information from an HTML form.

The traditional way to handle forms and other interactive Web pages is a system called the **CGI (Common Gateway Interface)**. It is a standardized interface to allow Web servers to talk to back-end programs and scripts that can accept input (e.g., from forms) and generate HTML pages in response. Usually, these back-ends are scripts written in the Perl scripting language because Perl scripts are easier and faster to write than programs (at least, if you know how to program in Perl). By convention, they live in a directory called *cgi-bin*, which is visible in the URL. Sometimes another scripting language, Python, is used instead of Perl.

As an example of how CGI often works, consider the case of a product from the Truly Great Products Company that comes without a warranty registration card. Instead, the customer is told to go to *www.tgpc.com* to register on-line. On that page, there is a hyperlink that says

Click here to register your product

This link points to a Perl script, say, *www.tgpc.com/cgi-bin/reg.perl.* When this script is invoked with no parameters, it sends back an HTML page containing the registration form. When the user fills in the form and clicks on *submit*, a message is sent back to this script containing the values filled in using the style of Fig. 7-30. The Perl script then parses the parameters, makes an entry in the database for the new customer, and sends back an HTML page providing a registration number and a telephone number for the help desk. This is not the only way to handle forms, but it is a common way. There are many books about making CGI scripts and programming in Perl. A few examples are (Hanegan, 2001; Lash, 2002; and Meltzer and Michalski, 2001).

CGI scripts are not the only way to generate dynamic content on the server side. Another common way is to embed little scripts inside HTML pages and have them be executed by the server itself to generate the page. A popular language for writing these scripts is **PHP** (**PHP: Hypertext Preprocessor**). To use it, the server has to understand PHP (just as a browser has to understand XML to interpret Web pages written in XML). Usually, servers expect Web pages containing PHP to have file extension *php* rather than *html* or *htm*.

A tiny PHP script is illustrated in Fig. 7-34; it should work with any server that has PHP installed. It contains normal HTML, except for the PHP script inside the <?php ... ?> tag. What it does is generate a Web page telling what it knows about the browser invoking it. Browsers normally send over some information along with their request (and any applicable cookies) and this information is put in the variable *HTTP_USER_AGENT*. When this listing is put in a file *test.php* in the WWW directory at the ABCD company, then typing the URL *www.abcd.com/test.php* will produce a Web page telling the user what browser, language, and operating system he is using.

```
<html>
<body>

<h2> This is what I know about you </h2>
<?php echo $HTTP_USER_AGENT ?>

</body>
</html>
```

Figure 7-34. A sample HTML page with embedded PHP.

PHP is especially good at handling forms and is simpler than using a CGI script. As an example of how it works with forms, consider the example of Fig. 7-35(a). This figure contains a normal HTML page with a form in it. The only unusual thing about it is the first line, which specifies that the file *action.php* is to be invoked to handle the parameters after the user has filled in and submitted the form. The page displays two text boxes, one with a request for a name and one with a request for an age. After the two boxes have been filled in and the form submitted, the server parses the Fig. 7-30-type string sent back, putting the name in the *name* variable and the age in the *age* variable. It then starts to process the *action.php* file, shown in Fig. 7-35(b) as a reply. During the processing of this file, the PHP commands are executed. If the user filled in "Barbara" and "24" in the boxes, the HTML file sent back will be the one given in Fig. 7-35(c). Thus, handling forms becomes extremely simple using PHP.

Although PHP is easy to use, it is actually a powerful programming language oriented toward interfacing between the Web and a server database. It has variables, strings, arrays, and most of the control structures found in C, but much more powerful I/O than just *printf*. PHP is open source code and freely available.

```
<html>
<body>
<form action="action.php" method="post">
<p> Please enter your name: <input type="text" name="name"> </p>
<p> Please enter your age: <input type="text" name="age"> </p>
<input type="submit">
</form>
</body>
</html>
```

(a)

```
<html>
<body>
<h1> Reply: </h1>
Hello <?php echo $name; ?>.
Prediction: next year you will be <?php echo $age + 1; ?>
</body>
</html>
```

(b)

```
<html>
<body>
<h1> Reply: </h1>
Hello Barbara.
Prediction: next year you will be 25
</body>
</html>
```

(c)

Figure 7-35. (a) A Web page containing a form. (b) A PHP script for handling the output of the form. (c) Output from the PHP script when the inputs are "Barbara" and 24, respectively.

It was designed specifically to work well with Apache, which is also open source and is the world's most widely used Web server. For more information about PHP, see (Valade, 2002).

We have now seen two different ways to generate dynamic HTML pages: CGI scripts and embedded PHP. There is also a third technique, called **JSP** (**JavaServer Pages**), which is similar to PHP, except that the dynamic part is written in the Java programming language instead of in PHP. Pages using this technique have the file extension *jsp*. A fourth technique, **ASP** (**Active Server Pages**), is Microsoft's version of PHP and JavaServer Pages. It uses Microsoft's proprietary scripting language, Visual Basic Script, for generating the dynamic content. Pages using this technique have extension *asp*. The choice among *PHP*,

JSP, and *ASP* usually has more to do with politics (open source vs. Sun vs. Microsoft) than with technology, since the three languages are roughly comparable.

The collection of technologies for generating content on the fly is sometimes called **dynamic HTML**.

Client-Side Dynamic Web Page Generation

CGI, PHP, JSP, and ASP scripts solve the problem of handling forms and interactions with databases on the server. They can all accept incoming information from forms, look up information in one or more databases, and generate HTML pages with the results. What none of them can do is respond to mouse movements or interact with users directly. For this purpose, it is necessary to have scripts embedded in HTML pages that are executed on the client machine rather than the server machine. Starting with HTML 4.0, such scripts are permitted using the tag <script>. The most popular scripting language for the client side is **JavaScript**, so we will now take a quick look at it.

JavaScript is a scripting language, *very* loosely inspired by some ideas from the Java programming language. It is definitely not Java. Like other scripting languages, it is a very high level language. For example, in a single line of JavaScript it is possible to pop up a dialog box, wait for text input, and store the resulting string in a variable. High-level features like this make JavaScript ideal for designing interactive Web pages. On the other hand, the fact that it is not standardized and is mutating faster than a fruit fly trapped in an X-ray machine makes it extremely difficult to write JavaScript programs that work on all platforms, but maybe some day it will stabilize.

As an example of a program in JavaScript, consider that of Fig. 7-36. Like that of Fig. 7-35(a), it displays a form asking for a name and age, and then predicts how old the person will be next year. The body is almost the same as the PHP example, the main difference being the declaration of the submit button and the assignment statement in it. This assignment statement tells the browser to invoke the *response* script on a button click and pass it the form as a parameter.

What is completely new here is the declaration of the JavaScript function *response* in the head of the HTML file, an area normally reserved for titles, background colors, and so on. This function extracts the value of the *name* field from the form and stores it in the variable *person* as a string. It also extracts the value of the *age* field, converts it to an integer by using the *eval* function, adds 1 to it, and stores the result in *years*. Then it opens a document for output, does four writes to it using the *writeln* method, and closes the document. The document is an HTML file, as can be seen from the various HTML tags in it. The browser then displays the document on the screen.

It is very important to understand that while Fig. 7-35 and Fig. 7-36 look similar, they are processed totally differently. In Fig. 7-35, after the user has clicked on the *submit* button, the browser collects the information into a long string of the

```
<html>
<head>
<script language="javascript" type="text/javascript">
function response(test_form) {
   var person = test_form.name.value;
   var years = eval(test_form.age.value) + 1;
   document.open();
   document.writeln("<html> <body>");
   document.writeln("Hello " + person + ".<br>");
   document.writeln("Prediction: next year you will be " + years + ".");
   document.writeln("</body> </html>");
   document.close();
}
</script>
</head>

<body>
<form>
Please enter your name: <input type="text" name="name">
<p>
Please enter your age: <input type="text" name="age">
<p>
<input type="button" value="submit" onclick="response(this.form)">
</form>
</body>
</html>
```

Figure 7-36. Use of JavaScript for processing a form.

style of Fig. 7-30 and sends it off to the server that sent the page. The server sees the name of the PHP file and executes it. The PHP script produces a new HTML page and that page is sent back to the browser for display. With Fig. 7-36, when the *submit* button is clicked the browser interprets a JavaScript function contained on the page. All the work is done locally, inside the browser. There is no contact with the server. As a consequence, the result is displayed virtually instantaneously, whereas with PHP, there can be a delay of several seconds before the resulting HTML arrives at the client. The difference between server-side scripting and client-side scripting is illustrated in Fig. 7-37, including the steps involved. In both cases, the numbered steps start after the form has been displayed. Step 1 consists of accepting the user input. Then comes the processing of the input, which differs in the two cases.

This difference does not mean that JavaScript is better than PHP. Their uses are completely different. PHP (and, by implication, JSP and ASP) are used when interaction with a remote database is needed. JavaScript is used when the interaction is with the user at the client computer. It is certainly possible (and com-

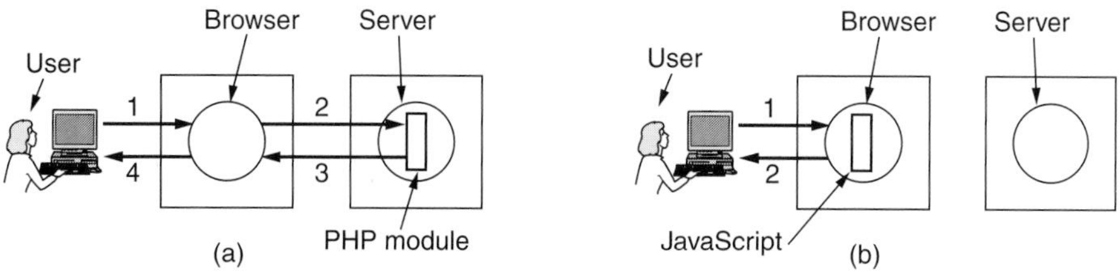

Figure 7-37. (a) Server-side scripting with PHP. (b) Client-side scripting with JavaScript.

mon) to have HTML pages that use both PHP and JavaScript, although they cannot do the same work or own the same button, of course.

JavaScript is a full-blown programming language, with all the power of C or Java. It has variables, strings, arrays, objects, functions, and all the usual control structures. It also has a large number of facilities specific for Web pages, including the ability to manage windows and frames, set and get cookies, deal with forms, and handle hyperlinks. An example of a JavaScript program that uses a recursive function is given in Fig. 7-38.

```
<html>
<head>
<script language="javascript" type="text/javascript">

function response(test_form) {
  function factorial(n) {if (n == 0) return 1; else return n * factorial(n – 1);}
  var r = eval(test_form.number.value);       // r = typed in argument
  document.myform.mytext.value = "Here are the results.\n";
  for (var i = 1; i <= r; i++)                 // print one line from 1 to r
    document.myform.mytext.value += (i + "! = " + factorial(i) + "\n");
}
</script>
</head>

<body>
<form name="myform">
Please enter a number: <input type="text" name="number">
<input type="button" value="compute table of factorials" onclick="response(this.form)">
<p>
<textarea name="mytext" rows=25 cols=50> </textarea>
</form>
</body>
</html>
```

Figure 7-38. A JavaScript program for computing and printing factorials.

JavaScript can also track mouse motion over objects on the screen. Many JavaScript Web pages have the property that when the mouse cursor is moved over some text or image, something happens. Often the image changes or a menu suddenly appears. This kind of behavior is easy to program in JavaScript and leads to lively Web pages. An example is given in Fig. 7-39.

```
<html>
<head>
<script language="javascript" type="text/javascript">
if (!document.myurl) document.myurl = new Array();
document.myurl[0] = "http://www.cs.vu.nl/ ast/im/kitten.jpg";
document.myurl[1] = "http://www.cs.vu.nl/ ast/im/puppy.jpg";
document.myurl[2] = "http://www.cs.vu.nl/ ast/im/bunny.jpg";
function pop(m) {
   var urx = "http://www.cs.vu.nl/ ast/im/cat.jpg";
   popupwin = window.open(document.myurl[m],"mywind","width=250,height=250");
}
</script>
</head>

<body>
<p> <a href="#" onMouseover="pop(0); return false;" > Kitten  </a> </p>
<p> <a href="#" onMouseover="pop(1); return false;" > Puppy  </a> </p>
<p> <a href="#" onMouseover="pop(2); return false;" > Bunny  </a> </p>
</body>
</html>
```

Figure 7-39. An interactive Web page that responds to mouse movement.

JavaScript is not the only way to make Web pages highly interactive. Another popular method is through the use of **applets**. These are small Java programs that have been compiled into machine instructions for a virtual computer called the **JVM** (**Java Virtual Machine**). Applets can be embedded in HTML pages (between <applet> and </applet>) and interpreted by JVM-capable browsers. Because Java applets are interpreted rather than directly executed, the Java interpreter can prevent them from doing Bad Things. At least in theory. In practice, applet writers have found a nearly endless stream of bugs in the Java I/O libraries to exploit.

Microsoft's answer to Sun's Java applets was allowing Web pages to hold **ActiveX controls**, which are programs compiled to Pentium machine language and executed on the bare hardware. This feature makes them vastly faster and more flexible than interpreted Java applets because they can do anything a program can do. When Internet Explorer sees an ActiveX control in a Web page, it downloads it, verifies its identity, and executes it. However, downloading and running foreign programs raises security issues, which we will address in Chap. 8.

Since nearly all browsers can interpret both Java programs and JavaScript, a designer who wants to make a highly-interactive Web page has a choice of at least two techniques, and if portability to multiple platforms is not an issue, ActiveX in addition. As a general rule, JavaScript programs are easier to write, Java applets execute faster, and ActiveX controls run fastest of all. Also, since all browers implement exactly the same JVM but no two browsers implement the same version of JavaScript, Java applets are more portable than JavaScript programs. For more information about JavaScript, there are many books, each with many (often > 1000) pages. A few examples are (Easttom, 2001; Harris, 2001; and McFedries, 2001).

Before leaving the subject of dynamic Web content, let us briefly summarize what we have covered so far. Complete Web pages can be generated on-the-fly by various scripts on the server machine. Once they are received by the browser, they are treated as normal HTML pages and just displayed. The scripts can be written in Perl, PHP, JSP, or ASP, as shown in Fig. 7-40.

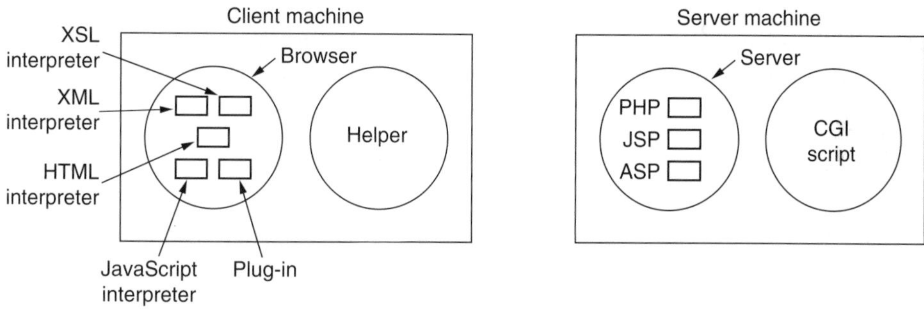

Figure 7-40. The various ways to generate and display content.

Dynamic content generation is also possible on the client side. Web pages can be written in XML and then converted to HTML according to an XSL file. JavaScript programs can perform arbitrary computations. Finally, plug-ins and helper applications can be used to display content in a variety of formats.

7.3.4 HTTP—The HyperText Transfer Protocol

The transfer protocol used throughout the World Wide Web is **HTTP** (**HyperText Transfer Protocol**). It specifies what messages clients may send to servers and what responses they get back in return. Each interaction consists of one ASCII request, followed by one RFC 822 MIME-like response. All clients and all servers must obey this protocol. It is defined in RFC 2616. In this section we will look at some of its more important properties.

Connections

The usual way for a browser to contact a server is to establish a TCP connection to port 80 on the server's machine, although this procedure is not formally required. The value of using TCP is that neither browsers nor servers have to worry about lost messages, duplicate messages, long messages, or acknowledgements. All of these matters are handled by the TCP implementation.

In HTTP 1.0, after the connection was established, a single request was sent over and a single response was sent back. Then the TCP connection was released. In a world in which the typical Web page consisted entirely of HTML text, this method was adequate. Within a few years, the average Web page contained large numbers of icons, images, and other eye candy, so establishing a TCP connection to transport a single icon became a very expensive way to operate.

This observation led to HTTP 1.1, which supports **persistent connections**. With them, it is possible to establish a TCP connection, send a request and get a response, and then send additional requests and get additional responses. By amortizing the TCP setup and release over multiple requests, the relative overhead due to TCP is much less per request. It is also possible to pipeline requests, that is, send request 2 before the response to request 1 has arrived.

Methods

Although HTTP was designed for use in the Web, it has been intentionally made more general than necessary with an eye to future object-oriented applications. For this reason, operations, called **methods**, other than just requesting a Web page are supported. This generality is what permitted SOAP to come into existence. Each request consists of one or more lines of ASCII text, with the first word on the first line being the name of the method requested. The built-in methods are listed in Fig. 7-41. For accessing general objects, additional object-specific methods may also be available. The names are case sensitive, so *GET* is a legal method but *get* is not.

The *GET* method requests the server to send the page (by which we mean object, in the most general case, but in practice normally just a file). The page is suitably encoded in MIME. The vast majority of requests to Web servers are *GET*s. The usual form of *GET* is

```
GET filename HTTP/1.1
```

where *filename* names the resource (file) to be fetched and 1.1 is the protocol version being used.

The *HEAD* method just asks for the message header, without the actual page. This method can be used to get a page's time of last modification, to collect information for indexing purposes, or just to test a URL for validity.

Method	Description
GET	Request to read a Web page
HEAD	Request to read a Web page's header
PUT	Request to store a Web page
POST	Append to a named resource (e.g., a Web page)
DELETE	Remove the Web page
TRACE	Echo the incoming request
CONNECT	Reserved for future use
OPTIONS	Query certain options

Figure 7-41. The built-in HTTP request methods.

The *PUT* method is the reverse of *GET*: instead of reading the page, it writes the page. This method makes it possible to build a collection of Web pages on a remote server. The body of the request contains the page. It may be encoded using MIME, in which case the lines following the *PUT* might include *Content-Type* and authentication headers, to prove that the caller indeed has permission to perform the requested operation.

Somewhat similar to *PUT* is the *POST* method. It, too, bears a URL, but instead of replacing the existing data, the new data is "appended" to it in some generalized sense. Posting a message to a newsgroup or adding a file to a bulletin board system are examples of appending in this context. In practice, neither *PUT* nor *POST* is used very much.

DELETE does what you might expect: it removes the page. As with *PUT*, authentication and permission play a major role here. There is no guarantee that *DELETE* succeeds, since even if the remote HTTP server is willing to delete the page, the underlying file may have a mode that forbids the HTTP server from modifying or removing it.

The *TRACE* method is for debugging. It instructs the server to send back the request. This method is useful when requests are not being processed correctly and the client wants to know what request the server actually got.

The *CONNECT* method is not currently used. It is reserved for future use.

The *OPTIONS* method provides a way for the client to query the server about its properties or those of a specific file.

Every request gets a response consisting of a status line, and possibly additional information (e.g., all or part of a Web page). The status line contains a three-digit status code telling whether the request was satisfied, and if not, why not. The first digit is used to divide the responses into five major groups, as shown in Fig. 7-42. The 1xx codes are rarely used in practice. The 2xx codes mean that the request was handled successfully and the content (if any) is being returned. The 3xx codes tell the client to look elsewhere, either using a different

Code	Meaning	Examples
1xx	Information	100 = server agrees to handle client's request
2xx	Success	200 = request succeeded; 204 = no content present
3xx	Redirection	301 = page moved; 304 = cached page still valid
4xx	Client error	403 = forbidden page; 404 = page not found
5xx	Server error	500 = internal server error; 503 = try again later

Figure 7-42. The status code response groups.

URL or in its own cache (discussed later). The 4xx codes mean the request failed due to a client error such an invalid request or a nonexistent page. Finally, the 5xx errors mean the server itself has a problem, either due to an error in its code or to a temporary overload.

Message Headers

The request line (e.g., the line with the *GET* method) may be followed by additional lines with more information. They are called **request headers**. This information can be compared to the parameters of a procedure call. Responses may also have **response headers**. Some headers can be used in either direction. A selection of the most important ones is given in Fig. 7-43.

The *User-Agent* header allows the client to inform the server about its browser, operating system, and other properties. In Fig. 7-34 we saw that the server magically had this information and could produce it on demand in a PHP script. This header is used by the client to provide the server with the information.

The four *Accept* headers tell the server what the client is willing to accept in the event that it has a limited repertoire of what is acceptable. The first header specifies the MIME types that are welcome (e.g., text/html). The second gives the character set (e.g., ISO-8859-5 or Unicode-1-1). The third deals with compression methods (e.g., gzip). The fourth indicates a natural language (e.g., Spanish) If the server has a choice of pages, it can use this information to supply the one the client is looking for. If it is unable to satisfy the request, an error code is returned and the request fails.

The *Host* header names the server. It is taken from the URL. This header is mandatory. It is used because some IP addresses may serve multiple DNS names and the server needs some way to tell which host to hand the request to.

The *Authorization* header is needed for pages that are protected. In this case, the client may have to prove it has a right to see the page requested. This header is used for that case.

Although cookies are dealt with in RFC 2109 rather than RFC 2616, they also have two headers. The *Cookie* header is used by clients to return to the server a cookie that was previously sent by some machine in the server's domain.

Header	Type	Contents
User-Agent	Request	Information about the browser and its platform
Accept	Request	The type of pages the client can handle
Accept-Charset	Request	The character sets that are acceptable to the client
Accept-Encoding	Request	The page encodings the client can handle
Accept-Language	Request	The natural languages the client can handle
Host	Request	The server's DNS name
Authorization	Request	A list of the client's credentials
Cookie	Request	Sends a previously set cookie back to the server
Date	Both	Date and time the message was sent
Upgrade	Both	The protocol the sender wants to switch to
Server	Response	Information about the server
Content-Encoding	Response	How the content is encoded (e.g., gzip)
Content-Language	Response	The natural language used in the page
Content-Length	Response	The page's length in bytes
Content-Type	Response	The page's MIME type
Last-Modified	Response	Time and date the page was last changed
Location	Response	A command to the client to send its request elsewhere
Accept-Ranges	Response	The server will accept byte range requests
Set-Cookie	Response	The server wants the client to save a cookie

Figure 7-43. Some HTTP message headers.

The *Date* header can be used in both directions and contains the time and date the message was sent. The *Upgrade* header is used to make it easier to make the transition to a future (possibly incompatible) version of the HTTP protocol. It allows the client to announce what it can support and the server to assert what it is using.

Now we come to the headers used exclusively by the server in response to requests. The first one, *Server*, allows the server to tell who it is and some of its properties if it wishes.

The next four headers, all starting with *Content-*, allow the server to describe properties of the page it is sending.

The *Last-Modified* header tells when the page was last modified. This header plays an important role in page caching.

The *Location* header is used by the server to inform the client that it should try a different URL. This can be used if the page has moved or to allow multiple URLs to refer to the same page (possibly on different servers). It is also used for companies that have a main Web page in the *com* domain, but which redirect clients to a national or regional page based on their IP address or preferred language.

If a page is very large, a small client may not want it all at once. Some servers will accept requests for byte ranges, so the page can be fetched in multiple small units. The *Accept-Ranges* header announces the server's willingness to handle this type of partial page request.

The second cookie header, *Set-Cookie*, is how servers send cookies to clients. The client is expected to save the cookie and return it on subsequent requests to the server.

Example HTTP Usage

Because HTTP is an ASCII protocol, it is quite easy for a person at a terminal (as opposed to a browser) to directly talk to Web servers. All that is needed is a TCP connection to port 80 on the server. Readers are encouraged to try this scenario personally (preferably from a UNIX system, because some other systems do not return the connection status). The following command sequence will do it:

```
telnet www.ietf.org 80 >log
GET /rfc.html HTTP/1.1
Host: www.ietf.org

close
```

This sequence of commands starts up a telnet (i.e., TCP) connection to port 80 on IETF's Web server, *www.ietf.org*. The result of the session is redirected to the file *log* for later inspection. Then comes the *GET* command naming the file and the protocol. The next line is the mandatory *Host* header. The blank line is also required. It signals the server that there are no more request headers. The *close* command instructs the telnet program to break the connection.

The *log* can be inspected using any editor. It should start out similarly to the listing in Fig. 7-44, unless IETF has changed it recently.

The first three lines are output from the telnet program, not from the remote site. The line beginning HTTP/1.1 is IETF's response saying that it is willing to talk HTTP/1.1 with you. Then come a number of headers and then the content. We have seen all the headers already except for *ETag* which is a unique page identifier related to caching, and *X-Pad* which is nonstandard and probably a workaround for some buggy browser.

7.3.5 Performance Enhancements

The popularity of the Web has almost been its undoing. Servers, routers, and lines are frequently overloaded. Many people have begun calling the WWW the World Wide Wait. As a consequence of these endless delays, researchers have developed various techniques for improving performance. We will now examine three of them: caching, server replication, and content delivery networks.

```
Trying 4.17.168.6...
Connected to www.ietf.org.
Escape character is '^]'.
HTTP/1.1 200 OK
Date: Wed, 08 May 2002 22:54:22 GMT
Server: Apache/1.3.20 (Unix) mod_ssl/2.8.4 OpenSSL/0.9.5a
Last-Modified: Mon, 11 Sep 2000 13:56:29 GMT
ETag: "2a79d-c8b-39bce48d"
Accept-Ranges: bytes
Content-Length: 3211
Content-Type: text/html
X-Pad: avoid browser bug

<html>
<head>
<title>IETF RFC Page</title>

<script language="javascript">
function url() {
 var x = document.form1.number.value
 if (x.length == 1) {x = "000" + x }
 if (x.length == 2) {x = "00" + x }
 if (x.length == 3) {x = "0" + x }
 document.form1.action = "/rfc/rfc" + x + ".txt"
 document.form1.submit
}
</script>

</head>
```

Figure 7-44. The start of the output of *www.ietf.org/rfc.html*.

Caching

A fairly simple way to improve performance is to save pages that have been requested in case they are used again. This technique is especially effective with pages that are visited a great deal, such as *www.yahoo.com* and *www.cnn.com*. Squirreling away pages for subsequent use is called **caching**. The usual procedure is for some process, called a **proxy**, to maintain the cache. To use caching, a browser can be configured to make all page requests to a proxy instead of to the page's real server. If the proxy has the page, it returns the page immediately. If not, it fetches the page from the server, adds it to the cache for future use, and returns it to the client that requested it.

Two important questions related to caching are as follows:

1. Who should do the caching?
2. How long should pages be cached?

There are several answers to the first question. Individual PCs often run proxies so they can quickly look up pages previously visited. On a company LAN, the proxy is often a machine shared by all the machines on the LAN, so if one user looks at a certain page and then another one on the same LAN wants the same page, it can be fetched from the proxy's cache. Many ISPs also run proxies, in order to speed up access for all their customers. Often all of these caches operate at the same time, so requests first go to the local proxy. If that fails, the local proxy queries the LAN proxy. If that fails, the LAN proxy tries the ISP proxy. The latter must succeed, either from its cache, a higher-level cache, or from the server itself. A scheme involving multiple caches tried in sequence is called **hierarchical caching**. A possible implementation is illustrated in Fig. 7-45.

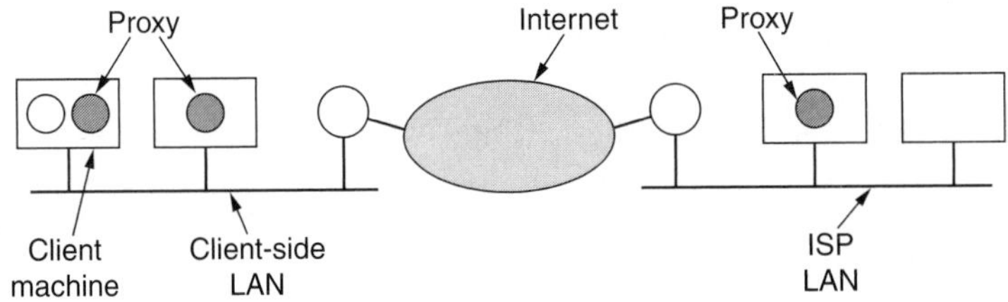

Figure 7-45. Hierarchical caching with three proxies.

How long should pages be cached is a bit trickier. Some pages should not be cached at all. For example, a page containing the prices of the 50 most active stocks changes every second. If it were to be cached, a user getting a copy from the cache would get **stale** (i.e., obsolete) data. On the other hand, once the stock exchange has closed for the day, that page will remain valid for hours or days, until the next trading session starts. Thus, the cacheability of a page may vary wildly over time.

The key issue with determining when to evict a page from the cache is how much staleness users are willing to put up with (since cached pages are kept on disk, the amount of storage consumed is rarely an issue). If a proxy throws out pages quickly, it will rarely return a stale page but it will also not be very effective (i.e., have a low hit rate). If it keeps pages too long, it may have a high hit rate but at the expense of often returning stale pages.

There are two approaches to dealing with this problem. The first one uses a heuristic to guess how long to keep each page. A common one is to base the holding time on the *Last-Modified* header (see Fig. 7-43). If a page was modified an hour ago, it is held in the cache for an hour. If it was modified a year ago, it is obviously a very stable page (say, a list of the gods from Greek and Roman mythology), so it can be cached for a year with a reasonable expectation of it not changing during the year. While this heuristic often works well in practice, it does return stale pages from time to time.

The other approach is more expensive but eliminates the possibility of stale pages by using special features of RFC 2616 that deal with cache management. One of the most useful of these features is the *If-Modified-Since* request header, which a proxy can send to a server. It specifies the page the proxy wants and the time the cached page was last modified (from the *Last-Modified* header). If the page has not been modified since then, the server sends back a short *Not Modified* message (status code 304 in Fig. 7-42), which instructs the proxy to use the cached page. If the page has been modified since then, the new page is returned. While this approach always requires a request message and a reply message, the reply message will be very short when the cache entry is still valid.

These two approaches can easily be combined. For the first ΔT after fetching the page, the proxy just returns it to clients asking for it. After the page has been around for a while, the proxy uses *If-Modified-Since* messages to check on its freshness. Choosing ΔT invariably involves some kind of heuristic, depending on how long ago the page was last modified.

Web pages containing dynamic content (e.g., generated by a PHP script) should never be cached since the parameters may be different next time. To handle this and other cases, there is a general mechanism for a server to instruct all proxies along the path back to the client not to use the current page again without verifying its freshness. This mechanism can also be used for any page expected to change quickly. A variety of other cache control mechanisms are also defined in RFC 2616.

Yet another approach to improving performance is proactive caching. When a proxy fetches a page from a server, it can inspect the page to see if there are any hyperlinks on it. If so, it can issue requests to the relevant servers to preload the cache with the pages pointed to, just in case they are needed. This technique may reduce access time on subsequent requests, but it may also flood the communication lines with pages that are never needed.

Clearly, Web caching is far from trivial. A lot more can be said about it. In fact, entire books have been written about it, for example (Rabinovich and Spatscheck, 2002; and Wessels, 2001); But it is time for us to move on to the next topic.

Server Replication

Caching is a client-side technique for improving performance, but server-side techniques also exist. The most common approach that servers take to improve performance is to replicate their contents at multiple, widely-separated locations. This technique is sometimes called **mirroring**.

A typical use of mirroring is for a company's main Web page to contain a few images along with links for, say, the company's Eastern, Western, Northern, and Southern regional Web sites. The user then clicks on the nearest one to get to that server. From then on, all requests go to the server selected.

Mirrored sites are generally completely static. The company decides where it wants to place the mirrors, arranges for a server in each region, and puts more or less the full content at each location (possibly omitting the snow blowers from the Miami site and the beach blankets from the Anchorage site). The choice of sites generally remains stable for months or years.

Unfortunately, the Web has a phenomenon known as **flash crowds** in which a Web site that was previously an unknown, unvisited, backwater all of a sudden becomes the center of the known universe. For example, until Nov. 6, 2000, the Florida Secretary of State's Web site, *www.dos.state.fl.us*, was quietly providing minutes of the meetings of the Florida State cabinet and instructions on how to become a notary in Florida. But on Nov. 7, 2000, when the U.S. Presidency suddenly hinged on a few thousand disputed votes in a handful of Florida counties, it became one of the top five Web sites in the world. Needless to say, it could not handle the load and nearly died trying.

What is needed is a way for a Web site that suddenly notices a massive increase in traffic to automatically clone itself at as many locations as needed and keep those sites operational until the storm passes, at which time it shuts many or all of them down. To have this ability, a site needs an agreement in advance with some company that owns many hosting sites, saying that it can create replicas on demand and pay for the capacity it actually uses.

An even more flexible strategy is to create dynamic replicas on a per-page basis depending on where the traffic is coming from. Some research on this topic is reported in (Pierre et al., 2001; and Pierre et al., 2002).

Content Delivery Networks

The brilliance of capitalism is that somebody has figured out how to make money from the World Wide Wait. It works like this. Companies called **CDN**s (**Content Delivery Networks**) talk to content providers (music sites, newspapers, and others that want their content easily and rapidly available) and offer to deliver their content to end users efficiently for a fee. After the contract is signed, the content owner gives the CDN the contents of its Web site for preprocessing (discussed shortly) and then distribution.

Then the CDN talks to large numbers of ISPs and offers to pay them well for permission to place a remotely-managed server bulging with valuable content on their LANs. Not only is this a source of income, but it also provides the ISP's customers with excellent response time for getting at the CDN's content, thereby giving the ISP a competitive advantage over other ISPs that have not taken the free money from the CDN. Under these conditions, signing up with a CDN is kind of a no-brainer for the ISP. As a consequence, the largest CDNs have more than 10,000 servers deployed all over the world.

With the content replicated at thousands of sites worldwide, there is clearly great potential for improving performance. However, to make this work, there has to be a way to redirect the client's request to the nearest CDN server, preferably one colocated at the client's ISP. Also, this redirection must be done without modifying DNS or any other part of the Internet's standard infrastructure. A slightly simplified description of how Akamai, the largest CDN, does it follows.

The whole process starts when the content provider hands the CDN its Web site. The CDN then runs each page through a preprocessor that replaces all the URLs with modified ones. The working model behind this strategy is that the content provider's Web site consists of many pages that are tiny (just HTML text), but that these pages often link to large files, such as images, audio, and video. The modified HTML pages are stored on the content provider's server and are fetched in the usual way; it is the images, audio, and video that go on the CDN's servers.

To see how this scheme actually works, consider Furry Video's Web page of Fig. 7-46(a). After preprocessing, it is transformed to Fig. 7-46(b) and placed on Furry Video's server as *www.furryvideo.com/index.html.*

When a user types in the URL *www.furryvideo.com*, DNS returns the IP address of Furry Video's own Web site, allowing the main (HTML) page to be fetched in the normal way. When any of the hyperlinks is clicked on, the browser asks DNS to look up *cdn-server.com*, which it does. The browser then sends an HTTP request to this IP address, expecting to get back an MPEG file.

That does not happen because *cdn-server.com* does not host any content. Instead, it is CDN's fake HTTP server. It examines the file name and server name to find out which page at which content provider is needed. It also examines the IP address of the incoming request and looks it up in its database to determine where the user is likely to be. Armed with this information, it determines which of CDN's content servers can give the user the best service. This decision is difficult because the closest one geographically may not be the closest one in terms of network topology, and the closest one in terms in network topology may be very busy at the moment. After making a choice, *cdn-server.com* sends back a response with status code 301 and a *Location* header giving the file's URL on the CDN content server nearest to the client. For this example, let us assume that URL is *www.CDN-0420.com/furryvideo/bears.mpg*. The browser then processes this URL in the usual way to get the actual MPEG file.

The steps involved are illustrated in Fig. 7-47. The first step is looking up *www.furryvideo.com* to get its IP address. After that, the HTML page can be fetched and displayed in the usual way. The page contains three hyperlinks to *cdn-server* [see Fig. 7-46(b)]. When, say, the first one is selected, its DNS address is looked up (step 5) and returned (step 6). When a request for *bears.mpg* is sent to *cdn-server* (step 7), the client is told to go to *CDN-0420.com* instead (step

```
<html>
<head> <title> Furry Video </title> </head>
<body>
<h1> Furry Video's Product List </h1>
<p> Click below for free samples. </p>

<a href="bears.mpg"> Bears Today </a> <br>
<a href="bunnies.mpg"> Funny Bunnies </a> <br>
<a href="mice.mpg"> Nice Mice </a> <br>
</body>
</html>
```

(a)

```
<html>
<head> <title> Furry Video </title> </head>
<body>
<h1> Furry Video's Product List </h1>
<p> Click below for free samples. </p>

<a href="http://cdn-server.com/furryvideo/bears.mpg"> Bears Today </a> <br>
<a href="http://cdn-server.com/furryvideo/bunnies.mpg"> Funny Bunnies </a> <br>
<a href="http://cdn-server.com/furryvideo/mice.mpg"> Nice Mice </a> <br>
</body>
</html>
```

(b)

Figure 7-46. (a) Original Web page. (b) Same page after transformation.

8). When it does as instructed (step 9), it is given the file from the proxy's cache (step 10). The property that makes this whole mechanism work is step 8, the fake HTTP server redirecting the client to a CDN proxy close to the client.

The CDN server to which the client is redirected is typically a proxy with a large cache preloaded with the most important content. If, however, someone asks for a file not in the cache, it is fetched from the true server and placed in the cache for subsequent use. By making the content server a proxy rather than a complete replica, the CDN has the ability to trade off disk size, preload time, and the various performance parameters.

For more on content delivery networks see (Hull, 2002; and Rabinovich and Spatscheck, 2002).

7.3.6 The Wireless Web

There is considerable interest in small portable devices capable of accessing the Web via a wireless link. In fact, the first tentative steps in that direction have already been taken. No doubt there will be a great deal of change in this area in

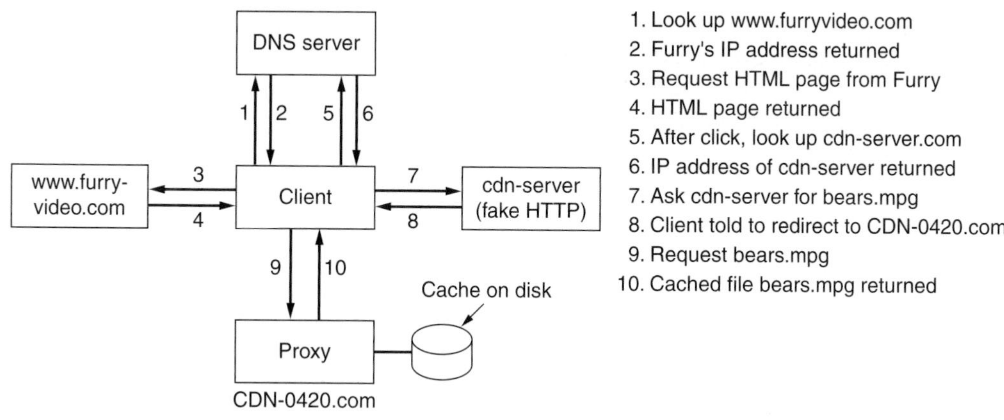
DNS server
1
2
5
6
www.furry-video.com
3
4
Client
7
8
cdn-server (fake HTTP)
9
10
Cache on disk
Proxy
CDN-0420.com
1. Look up www.furryvideo.com
2. Furry's IP address returned
3. Request HTML page from Furry
4. HTML page returned
5. After click, look up cdn-server.com
6. IP address of cdn-server returned
7. Ask cdn-server for bears.mpg
8. Client told to redirect to CDN-0420.com
9. Request bears.mpg
10. Cached file bears.mpg returned

Figure 7-47. Steps in looking up a URL when a CDN is used.

the coming years, but it is still worth examining some of the current ideas relating to the wireless Web to see where we are now and where we might be heading. We will focus on the first two wide area wireless Web systems to hit the market: WAP and i-mode.

WAP—The Wireless Application Protocol

Once the Internet and mobile phones had become commonplace, it did not take long before somebody got the idea to combine them into a mobile phone with a built-in screen for wireless access to e-mail and the Web. The "somebody" in this case was a consortium initially led by Nokia, Ericsson, Motorola, and phone.com (formerly Unwired Planet) and now boasting hundreds of members. The system is called **WAP (Wireless Application Protocol)**.

A WAP device may be an enhanced mobile phone, PDA, or notebook computer without any voice capability. The specification allows all of them and more. The basic idea is to use the existing digital wireless infrastructure. Users can literally call up a WAP gateway over the wireless link and send Web page requests to it. The gateway then checks its cache for the page requested. If present, it sends it; if absent, it fetches it over the wired Internet. In essence, this means that WAP 1.0 is a circuit-switched system with a fairly high per-minute connect charge. To make a long story short, people did not like accessing the Internet on a tiny screen and paying by the minute, so WAP was something of a flop (although there were other problems as well). However, WAP and its competitor, i-mode (discussed below), appear to be converging on a similar technology, so WAP 2.0 may yet be a big success. Since WAP 1.0 was the first attempt at wireless Internet, it is worth describing it at least briefly.

WAP is essentially a protocol stack for accessing the Web, but optimized for low-bandwidth connections using wireless devices having a slow CPU, little memory, and a small screen. These requirements are obviously different from those of the standard desktop PC scenario, which leads to some protocol differences. The layers are shown in Fig. 7-48.

Wireless application environment (WAE)
Wireless session protocol (WSP)
Wireless transaction protocol (WTP)
Wireless transport layer security (WTLS)
Wireless datagram protocol (WDP)
Bearer layer (GSM, CDMA, D-AMPS, GPRS, etc.)

Figure 7-48. The WAP protocol stack.

The lowest layer supports all the existing mobile phone systems, including GSM, D-AMPS, and CDMA. The WAP 1.0 data rate is 9600 bps. On top of this is the datagram protocol, **WDP (Wireless Datagram Protocol)**, which is essentially UDP. Then comes a layer for security, obviously needed in a wireless system. WTLS is a subset of Netscape's SSL, which we will look at in Chap. 8. Above this is a transaction layer, which manages requests and responses, either reliably or unreliably. This layer replaces TCP, which is not used over the air link for efficiency reasons. Then comes a session layer, which is similar to HTTP/1.1 but with some restrictions and extensions for optimization purposes. At the top is a microbrowser (WAE).

Besides cost, the other aspect that no doubt hurt WAP's acceptance is the fact that it does not use HTML. Instead, the WAE layer uses a markup language called **WML (Wireless Markup Language)**, which is an application of XML. As a consequence, in principle, a WAP device can only access those pages that have been converted to WML. However, since this greatly restricts the value of WAP, the architecture calls for an on-the-fly filter from HTML to WML to increase the set of pages available. This architecture is illustrated in Fig. 7-49.

In all fairness, WAP was probably a little ahead of its time. When WAP was first started, XML was hardly known outside W3C and so the press reported its launch as **WAP DOES NOT USE HTML.** A more accurate headline would have been: **WAP ALREADY USES THE NEW HTML STANDARD.** But once the damage was done, it was hard to repair and WAP 1.0 never caught on. We will revisit WAP after first looking at its major competitor.

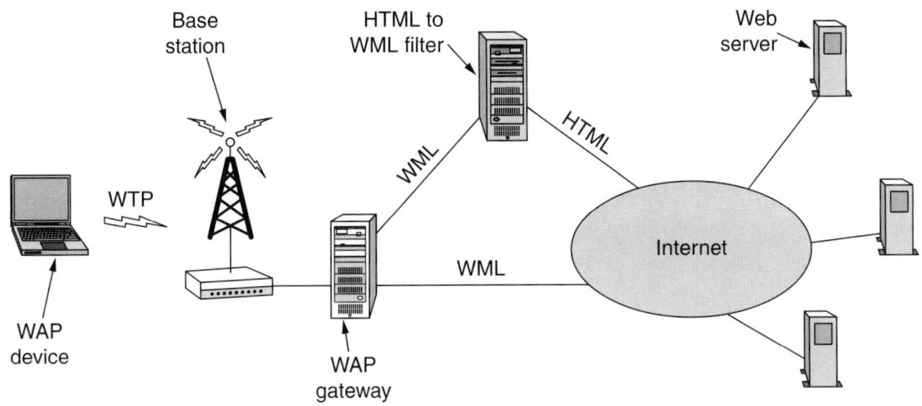

Figure 7-49. The WAP architecture.

I-Mode

While a multi-industry consortium of telecom vendors and computer companies was busy hammering out an open standard using the most advanced version of HTML available, other developments were going on in Japan. There, a Japanese woman, Mari Matsunaga, invented a different approach to the wireless Web called **i-mode** (**information-mode**). She convinced the wireless subsidiary of the former Japanese telephone monopoly that her approach was right, and in Feb. 1999 NTT DoCoMo (literally: Japanese Telephone and Telegraph Company everywhere you go) launched the service in Japan. Within 3 years it had over 35 million Japanese subscribers, who could access over 40,000 special i-mode Web sites. It also had most of the world's telecom companies drooling over its financial success, especially in light of the fact that WAP appeared to be going nowhere. Let us now take a look at what i-mode is and how it works.

The i-mode system has three major components: a new transmission system, a new handset, and a new language for Web page design. The transmission system consists of two separate networks: the existing circuit-switched mobile phone network (somewhat comparable to D-AMPS), and a new packet-switched network constructed specifically for i-mode service. Voice mode uses the circuit switched network and is billed per minute of connection time. I-mode uses the packet-switched network and is always on (like ADSL or cable), so there is no billing for connect time. Instead, there is a charge for each packet sent. It is not currently possible to use both networks at once.

The handsets look like mobile phones, with the addition of a small screen. NTT DoCoMo heavily advertises i-mode devices as better mobile phones rather than wireless Web terminals, even though that is precisely what they are. In fact, probably most customers are not even aware they are on the Internet. They think of their i-mode devices as mobile phones with enhanced services. In keeping with this model of i-mode being a service, the handsets are not user programmable, although they contain the equivalent of a 1995 PC and could probably run Windows 95 or UNIX.

When the i-mode handset is switched on, the user is presented with a list of categories of the officially-approved services. There are well over 1000 services divided into about 20 categories. Each service, which is actually a small i-mode Web site, is run by an independent company. The major categories on the official menu include e-mail, news, weather, sports, games, shopping, maps, horoscopes, entertainment, travel, regional guides, ringing tones, recipes, gambling, home banking, and stock prices. The service is somewhat targeted at teenagers and people in their 20s, who tend to love electronic gadgets, especially if they come in fashionable colors. The mere fact that over 40 companies are selling ringing tones says something. The most popular application is e-mail, which allows up to 500-byte messages, and thus is seen as a big improvement over SMS (Short Message Service) with its 160-byte messages. Games are also popular.

There are also over 40,000 i-mode Web sites, but they have to be accessed by typing in their URL, rather than selecting them from a menu. In a sense, the official list is like an Internet portal that allows other Web sites to be accessed by clicking rather than by typing a URL.

NTT DoCoMo tightly controls the official services. To be allowed on the list, a service must meet a variety of published criteria. For example, a service must not have a bad influence on society, Japanese-English dictionaries must have enough words, services with ringing tones must add new tones frequently, and no site may inflame faddish behavior or reflect badly on NTT DoCoMo (Frengle, 2002). The 40,000 Internet sites can do whatever they want.

The i-mode business model is so different from that of the conventional Internet that it is worth explaining. The basic i-mode subscription fee is a few dollars per month. Since there is a charge for each packet received, the basic subscription includes a small number of packets. Alternatively the customer can choose a subscription with more free packets, with the per-packet charge dropping sharply as you go from 1 MB per month to 10 MB per month. If the free packets are used up halfway through the month, additional packets can be purchased on-line.

To use a service, you have to subscribe to it, something accomplished by just clicking on it and entering your PIN code. Most official services cost around \$1–\$2 per month. NTT DoCoMo adds the charge to the phone bill and passes 91% of it onto the service provider, keeping 9% itself. If an unofficial service has 1 million customers, it has to send out 1 million bills for (about) \$1 each every month. If that service becomes official, NTT DoCoMo handles the billing and just transfers \$910,000 to the service's bank account every month. Not having to handle billing is a huge incentive for a service provider to become official, which generates more revenue for NTT DoCoMo. Also, being official gets you on the initial menu, which makes your site much easier to find. The user's phone bill includes phone calls, i-mode subscription charges, service subscription charges, and extra packets.

Despite its massive success in Japan, it is far from clear whether it will catch on in the U.S. and Europe. In some ways, the Japanese circumstances are different from those in the West. First, most potential customers in the West (e.g., teenagers, college students, and businesspersons) already have a large-screen PC at home, almost assuredly with an Internet connection at a speed of at least 56 kbps, often much more. In Japan, few people have an Internet-connected PC at home, in part due to lack of space, but also due to NTT's exorbitant charges for local telephone services (something like $700 for installing a line and $1.50 per hour for local calls). For most users, i-mode is their only Internet connection.

Second, people in the West are not used to paying $1 a month to access CNN's Web site, $1 a month to access Yahoo's Web site, $1 a month to access Google's Web site, and so on, not to mention a few dollars per MB downloaded. Most Internet providers in the West now charge a fixed monthly fee independent of actual usage, largely in response to customer demand.

Third, for many Japanese people, prime i-mode time is while they are commuting to or from work or school on the train or subway. In Europe, fewer people commute by train than in Japan, and in the U.S. hardly anyone does. Using i-mode at home next to your computer with a 17-inch monitor, a 1-Mbps ADSL connection, and all the free megabytes you want does not make a lot of sense. Nevertheless, nobody predicted the immense popularity of mobile phones at all, so i-mode may yet find a niche in the West.

As we mentioned above, i-mode handsets use the existing circuit-switched network for voice and a new packet-switched network for data. The data network is based on CDMA and transmits 128-byte packets at 9600 bps. A diagram of the network is given in Fig. 7-50. Handsets talk **LTP** (**Lightweight Transport Protocol**) over the air link to a protocol conversion gateway. The gateway has a wideband fiber-optic connection to the i-mode server, which is connected to all the services. When the user selects a service from the official menu, the request is sent to the i-mode server, which caches most of the pages to improve performance. Requests to sites not on the official menu bypass the i-mode server and go directly through the Internet.

Current handsets have CPUs that run at about 100 MHz, several megabytes of flash ROM, perhaps 1 MB of RAM, and a small built-in screen. I-mode requires the screen to be at least 72×94 pixels, but some high-end devices have as many as 120×160 pixels. Screens usually have 8-bit color, which allows 256 colors. This is not enough for photographs but is adequate for line drawings and simple cartoons. Since there is no mouse, on-screen navigation is done with the arrow keys.

The software structure is as shown in Fig. 7-51. The bottom layer consists of a simple real-time operating system for controlling the hardware. Then comes a module for doing network communication, using NTT DoCoMo's proprietary

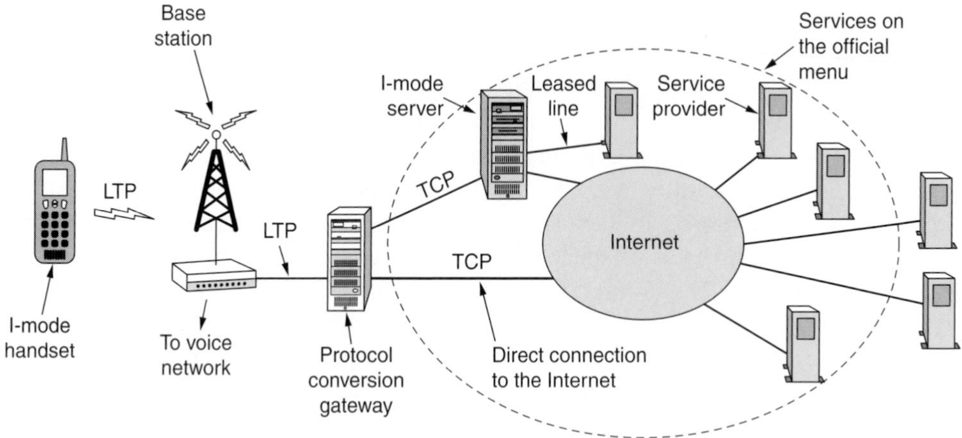

Figure 7-50. Structure of the i-mode data network showing the transport protocols.

LTP protocol. Above that is a simple window manager that handles text and simple graphics (GIF files). With screens having only about 120 × 160 pixels at best, there is not much to manage.

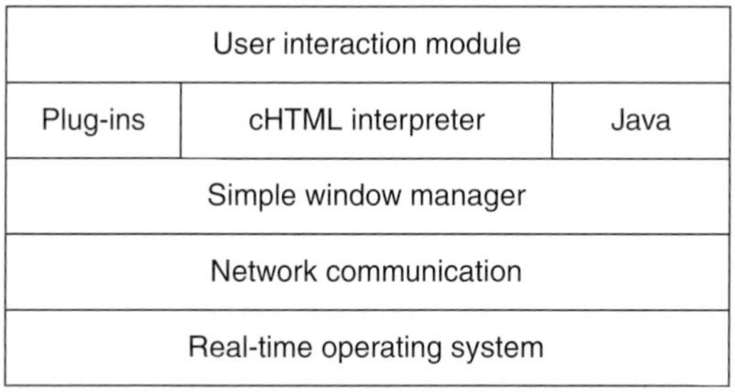

User interaction module		
Plug-ins	cHTML interpreter	Java
Simple window manager		
Network communication		
Real-time operating system		

Figure 7-51. Structure of the i-mode software.

The fourth layer contains the Web page interpreter (i.e., the browser). I-mode does not use full HTML, but a subset of it, called **cHTML** (**compact HTML**), based loosely on HTML 1.0. This layer also allows helper applications and plug-ins, just as PC browsers do. One standard helper application is an interpreter for a slightly modified version of JVM.

At the top is a user interaction module, which manages communication with the user.

Let us now take a closer look at cHTML. As mentioned, it is approximately HTML 1.0, with a few omissions and some extensions for use on a mobile handsets. It was submitted to W3C for standardization, but W3C showed little interest in it, so it is likely to remain a proprietary product.

Most of the basic HTML tags are allowed, including <html>, <head>, <title>, <body>, <h*n*>, <center>, <ul>, <ol>, <menu>, <li>, <br>, <p>, <hr>, <img>, <form>, and <input>. The <b> and <i> tags are not permitted.

The <a> tag is allowed for linking to other pages, but with the additional scheme *tel* for dialing telephone numbers. In a sense *tel* is analogous to *mailto*. When a hyperlink using the *mailto* scheme is selected, the browser pops up a form to send e-mail to the destination named in the link. When a hyperlink using the *tel* scheme is selected, the browser dials the telephone number. For example, an address book could have simple pictures of various people. When selecting one of them, the handset would call him or her. RFC 2806 discusses telephone URLs.

The cHTML browser is limited in other ways. It does not support JavaScript, frames, style sheets, background colors, or background images. It also does not support JPEG images, because they take too much time to decompress. Java applets are allowed, but are (currently) limited to 10 KB due to the slow transmission speed over the air link.

Although NTT DoCoMo removed some HTML tags, it also added some new ones. The <blink> tag makes text turn on and off. While it may seem inconsistent to forbid <b> (on the grounds that Web sites should not handle the appearance) and then add <blink> which relates only to the appearance, this is how they did it. Another new tag is <marquee>, which scrolls its contents on the screen in the manner of a stock ticker.

One new feature is the *align* attribute for the <br> tag. It is needed because with a screen of typically 6 rows of 16 characters, there is a great danger of words being broken in the middle, as shown in Fig. 7-52(a). *Align* helps reduce this problem to make it possible to get something more like Fig. 7-52(b). It is interesting to note that Japanese does not suffer from words being broken over lines. For kanji text, the screen is broken up into a rectangular grid of cells of size 9×10 pixels or 12×12 pixels, depending on the font supported. Each cell holds exactly one kanji character, which is the equivalent of a word in English. Line breaks between words are always allowed in Japanese.

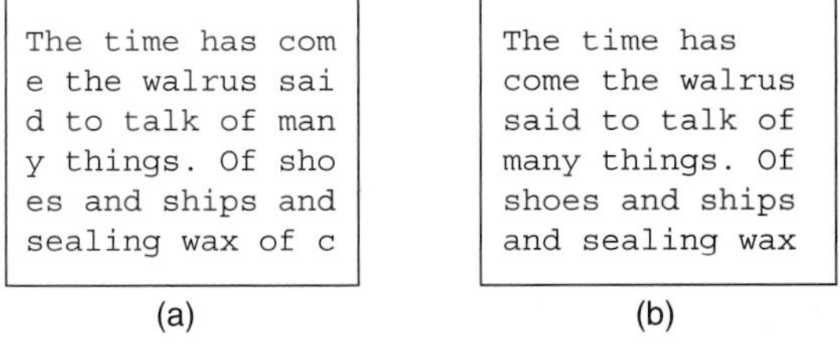

Figure 7-52. Lewis Carroll meets a 16×6 screen.

Although the Japanese language has tens of thousands of kanji, NTT DoCoMo invented 166 brand new ones, called **emoji**, with a higher cuteness factor—essentially pictograms like the smileys of Fig. 7-6. They include symbols for the astrological signs, beer, hamburger, amusement park, birthday, mobile phone, dog, cat, Christmas, broken heart, kiss, mood, sleepy, and, of course, one meaning cute.

Another new attribute is the ability for allowing users to select hyperlinks using the keyboard, clearly an important property on a mouseless computer. An example of how this attribute is used is shown in the cHTML file of Fig. 7-53.

```
<html>
<body>
<h1> Select an option </h1>
<a href="messages.chtml" accesskey="1"> Check voicemail </a> <br>
<a href="mail.chtml" accesskey="2"> Check e-mail </a> <br>
<a href="games.chtml" accesskey="3"> Play a game </a>
</body>
</html>
```

Figure 7-53. An example cHTML file.

Although the client side is somewhat limited, the i-mode server is a full-blown computer, with all the usual bells and whistles. It supports CGI, Perl, PHP, JSP, ASP, and everything else Web servers normally support.

A brief comparison of the WAP and i-mode as actually implemented in the first-generation systems is given in Fig. 7-54. While some of the differences may seem small, often they are important. For example, 15-year-olds do not have credit cards, so being able to buy things via e-commerce and have them charged to the phone bill makes a big difference in their interest in the system.

For additional information about i-mode, see (Frengle, 2002; and Vacca, 2002).

Second-Generation Wireless Web

WAP 1.0, based on recognized international standards, was supposed to be a serious tool for people in business on the move. It failed. I-mode was an electronic toy for Japanese teenagers using proprietary everything. It was a huge success. What happens next? Each side learned something from the first generation of wireless Web. The WAP consortium learned that content matters. Not having a large number of Web sites that speak your markup language is fatal. NTT DoCoMo learned that a closed, proprietary system closely tied to tiny handsets and Japanese culture is not a good export product. The conclusion that both sides drew is that to convince a large number of Web sites to put their content in your format, it is necessary to have an open, stable, markup language that is universally accepted. Format wars are not good for business.

Both services are about to enter the second generation of wireless Web technology. WAP 2.0 came out first, so we will use that as our example. WAP 1.0

Feature	WAP	I-mode
What it is	Protocol stack	Service
Device	Handset, PDA, notebook	Handset
Access	Dial up	Always on
Underlying network	Circuit-switched	Two: circuit + packet
Data rate	9600 bps	9600 bps
Screen	Monochrome	Color
Markup language	WML (XML application)	cHTML
Scripting language	WMLscript	None
Usage charges	Per minute	Per packet
Pay for shopping	Credit card	Phone bill
Pictograms	No	Yes
Standardization	WAP forum open standard	NTT DoCoMo proprietary
Where used	Europe, Japan	Japan
Typical user	Businessman	Young woman

Figure 7-54. A comparison of first-generation WAP and i-mode.

got some things right, and they have been continued. For one thing, WAP can be carried on a variety of different networks. The first generation used circuit-switched networks, but packet-switched networks were always an option and still are. Second-generation systems are likely to use packet switching, for example, GPRS. For another, WAP initially was aimed at supporting a wide variety of devices, from mobile phones to powerful notebook computers, and still is.

WAP 2.0 also has some new features. The most significant ones are:

1. Push model as well as pull model.
2. Support for integrating telephony into applications.
3. Multimedia messaging.
4. Inclusion of 264 pictograms.
5. Interface to a storage device.
6. Support for plug-ins in the browser.

The pull model is well known: the client asks for a page and gets it. The push model supports data arriving without being asked for, such as a continuous feed of stock prices or traffic alerts.

Voice and data are starting to merge, and WAP 2.0 supports them in a variety of ways. We saw one example of this earlier with i-mode's ability to hyperlink an icon or text on the screen to a telephone number to be called. Along with e-mail and telephony, multimedia messaging is supported.

The huge popularity of i-mode's emoji stimulated the WAP consortium to invent 264 of its own emoji. The categories include animals, appliances, dress, emotion, food, human body, gender, maps, music, plants, sports, time, tools, vehicles, weapons, and weather. Interesting enough, the standard just names each pictogram; it does not give the actual bit map, probably out of fear that some culture's representation of "sleepy" or "hug" might be insulting to another culture. I-mode did not have that problem since it was intended for a single country.

Providing for a storage interface does not mean that every WAP 2.0 phone will come with a large hard disk. Flash ROM is also a storage device. A WAP-enabled wireless camera could use the flash ROM for temporary image storage before beaming the best pictures to the Internet.

Finally, plug-ins can extend the browser's capabilities. A scripting language is also provided.

Various technical differences are also present in WAP 2.0. The two biggest ones concern the protocol stack and the markup language. WAP 2.0 continues to support the old protocol stack of Fig. 7-48, but it also supports the standard Internet stack with TCP and HTTP/1.1 as well. However, four minor (but compatible) changes to TCP were made (to simplify the code): (1) Use of a fixed 64-KB window, (2) no slow start, (3) a maximum MTU of 1500 bytes, and (4) a slightly different retransmission algorithm. TLS is the transport-layer security protocol standardized by IETF; we will examine it in Chap. 8. Many initial devices will probably contain both stacks, as shown in Fig. 7-55.

XHTML	
WSP	HTTP
WTP	TLS
WTLS	TCP
WDP	IP
Bearer layer	Bearer layer
WAP 1.0 protocol stack	WAP 2.0 protocol stack

Figure 7-55. WAP 2.0 supports two protocol stacks.

The other technical difference with WAP 1.0 is the markup language. WAP 2.0 supports XHTML Basic, which is intended for small wireless devices. Since NTT DoCoMo has also agreed to support this subset, Web site designers can use this format and know that their pages will work on the fixed Internet and on all wireless devices. These decisions will end the markup language format wars that were impeding growth of the wireless Web industry.

A few words about XHTML Basic are perhaps in order. It is intended for mobile phones, televisions, PDAs, vending machines, pagers, cars, game machines, and even watches. For this reason, it does not support style sheets, scripts, or frames, but most of the standard tags are there. They are grouped into 11 modules. Some are required; some are optional. All are defined in XML. The modules and some example tags are listed in Fig. 7-56. We have not gone over all the example tags, but more information can be found at *www.w3.org*.

Module	Req.?	Function	Example tags
Structure	Yes	Doc. structure	body, head, html, title
Text	Yes	Information	br, code, dfn, em, h*n*, kbd, p, strong
Hypertext	Yes	Hyperlinks	a
List	Yes	Itemized lists	dl, dt, dd, ol, ul, li
Forms	No	Fill-in forms	form, input, label, option, textarea
Tables	No	Rectangular tables	caption, table, td, th, tr
Image	No	Pictures	img
Object	No	Applets, maps, etc.	object, param
Meta-information	No	Extra info	meta
Link	No	Similar to <a>	link
Base	No	URL starting point	base

Figure 7-56. The XHTML Basic modules and tags.

Despite the agreement on the use of XHTML Basic, a threat to WAP and i-mode is lurking in the air: 802.11. The second-generation wireless Web is supposed to run at 384 kbps, far better than the 9600 bps of the first generation, but far worse than the 11 Mbps or 54 Mbps offered by 802.11. Of course, 802.11 is not everywhere, but as more restaurants, hotels, stores, companies, airports, bus stations, museums, universities, hospitals, and other organizations decide to install base stations for their employees and customers, there may be enough coverage in urban areas that people are willing to walk a few blocks to sit down in an 802.11-enabled fast food restaurant for a cup of coffee and an e-mail. Businesses may routinely put 802.11 logos next to the logos that show which credit cards they accept, and for the same reason: to attract customers. City maps (downloadable, naturally) may show covered areas in green and silent areas in red, so people can wander from base station to base station, like nomads trekking from oasis to oasis in the desert.

Although fast food restaurants may be quick to install 802.11 base stations, farmers will probably not, so coverage will be spotty and limited to the downtown areas of cities, due to the limited range of 802.11 (a few hundred meters at best). This may lead to dual-mode wireless devices that use 802.11 if they can pick up a signal and fall back to WAP if they cannot.

7.4 MULTIMEDIA

The wireless Web is an exciting new development, but it is not the only one. For many people, multimedia is the holy grail of networking. When the word is mentioned, both the propeller heads and the suits begin salivating as if on cue. The former see immense technical challenges in providing (interactive) video on demand to every home. The latter see equally immense profits in it. Since multimedia requires high bandwidth, getting it to work over fixed connections is hard enough. Even VHS-quality video over wireless is a few years away, so our treatment will focus on wired systems.

Literally, multimedia is just two or more media. If the publisher of this book wanted to join the current hype about multimedia, it could advertise the book as using multimedia technology. After all, it contains two media: text and graphics (the figures). Nevertheless, when most people refer to multimedia, they generally mean the combination of two or more **continuous media**, that is, media that have to be played during some well-defined time interval, usually with some user interaction. In practice, the two media are normally audio and video, that is, sound plus moving pictures.

However, many people often refer to pure audio, such as Internet telephony or Internet radio as multimedia as well, which it is clearly not. Actually, a better term is **streaming media**, but we will follow the herd and consider real-time audio to be multimedia as well. In the following sections we will examine how computers process audio and video, how they are compressed, and some network applications of these technologies. For a comprehensive (three volume) treatment on networked multimedia, see (Steinmetz and Nahrstedt, 2002; Steinmetz and Nahrstedt, 2003a; and Steinmetz and Nahrstedt, 2003b).

7.4.1 Introduction to Digital Audio

An audio (sound) wave is a one-dimensional acoustic (pressure) wave. When an acoustic wave enters the ear, the eardrum vibrates, causing the tiny bones of the inner ear to vibrate along with it, sending nerve pulses to the brain. These pulses are perceived as sound by the listener. In a similar way, when an acoustic wave strikes a microphone, the microphone generates an electrical signal, representing the sound amplitude as a function of time. The representation, processing, storage, and transmission of such audio signals are a major part of the study of multimedia systems.

The frequency range of the human ear runs from 20 Hz to 20,000 Hz. Some animals, notably dogs, can hear higher frequencies. The ear hears logarithmically, so the ratio of two sounds with power A and B is conventionally expressed in **dB (decibels)** according to the formula

$$\text{dB} = 10 \log_{10}(A/B)$$

If we define the lower limit of audibility (a pressure of about 0.0003 dyne/cm^2) for a 1-kHz sine wave as 0 dB, an ordinary conversation is about 50 dB and the pain threshold is about 120 dB, a dynamic range of a factor of 1 million.

The ear is surprisingly sensitive to sound variations lasting only a few milliseconds. The eye, in contrast, does not notice changes in light level that last only a few milliseconds. The result of this observation is that jitter of only a few milliseconds during a multimedia transmission affects the perceived sound quality more than it affects the perceived image quality.

Audio waves can be converted to digital form by an **ADC** (**Analog Digital Converter**). An ADC takes an electrical voltage as input and generates a binary number as output. In Fig. 7-57(a) we see an example of a sine wave. To represent this signal digitally, we can sample it every ΔT seconds, as shown by the bar heights in Fig. 7-57(b). If a sound wave is not a pure sine wave but a linear superposition of sine waves where the highest frequency component present is f, then the Nyquist theorem (see Chap. 2) states that it is sufficient to make samples at a frequency $2f$. Sampling more often is of no value since the higher frequencies that such sampling could detect are not present.

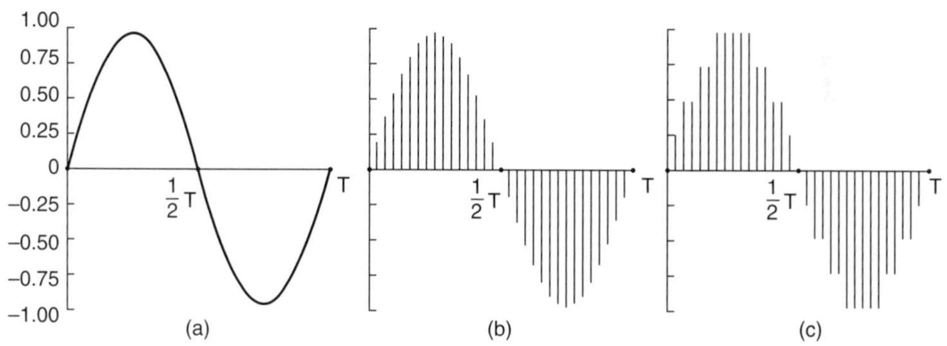

Figure 7-57. (a) A sine wave. (b) Sampling the sine wave. (c) Quantizing the samples to 4 bits.

Digital samples are never exact. The samples of Fig. 7-57(c) allow only nine values, from −1.00 to +1.00 in steps of 0.25. An 8-bit sample would allow 256 distinct values. A 16-bit sample would allow 65,536 distinct values. The error introduced by the finite number of bits per sample is called the **quantization noise**. If it is too large, the ear detects it.

Two well-known examples where sampled sound is used are the telephone and audio compact discs. Pulse code modulation, as used within the telephone system, uses 8-bit samples made 8000 times per second. In North America and Japan, 7 bits are for data and 1 is for control; in Europe all 8 bits are for data. This system gives a data rate of 56,000 bps or 64,000 bps. With only 8000 samples/sec, frequencies above 4 kHz are lost.

Audio CDs are digital with a sampling rate of 44,100 samples/sec, enough to capture frequencies up to 22,050 Hz, which is good enough for people, but bad for canine music lovers. The samples are 16 bits each and are linear over the range of amplitudes. Note that 16-bit samples allow only 65,536 distinct values, even though the dynamic range of the ear is about 1 million when measured in steps of the smallest audible sound. Thus, using only 16 bits per sample introduces some quantization noise (although the full dynamic range is not covered—CDs are not supposed to hurt). With 44,100 samples/sec of 16 bits each, an audio CD needs a bandwidth of 705.6 kbps for monaural and 1.411 Mbps for stereo. While this is lower than what video needs (see below), it still takes almost a full T1 channel to transmit uncompressed CD quality stereo sound in real time.

Digitized sound can be easily processed by computers in software. Dozens of programs exist for personal computers to allow users to record, display, edit, mix, and store sound waves from multiple sources. Virtually all professional sound recording and editing are digital nowadays.

Music, of course, is just a special case of general audio, but an important one. Another important special case is speech. Human speech tends to be in the 600-Hz to 6000-Hz range. Speech is made up of vowels and consonants, which have different properties. Vowels are produced when the vocal tract is unobstructed, producing resonances whose fundamental frequency depends on the size and shape of the vocal system and the position of the speaker's tongue and jaw. These sounds are almost periodic for intervals of about 30 msec. Consonants are produced when the vocal tract is partially blocked. These sounds are less regular than vowels.

Some speech generation and transmission systems make use of models of the vocal system to reduce speech to a few parameters (e.g., the sizes and shapes of various cavities), rather than just sampling the speech waveform. How these vocoders work is beyond the scope of this book, however.

7.4.2 Audio Compression

CD-quality audio requires a transmission bandwidth of 1.411 Mbps, as we just saw. Clearly, substantial compression is needed to make transmission over the Internet practical. For this reason, various audio compression algorithms have been developed. Probably the most popular one is MPEG audio, which has three layers (variants), of which **MP3** (**MPEG audio layer 3**) is the most powerful and best known. Large amounts of music in MP3 format are available on the Internet, not all of it legal, which has resulted in numerous lawsuits from the artists and copyright owners. MP3 belongs to the audio portion of the MPEG video compression standard. We will discuss video compression later in this chapter; let us look at audio compression now.

Audio compression can be done in one of two ways. In **waveform coding** the signal is transformed mathematically by a Fourier transform into its frequency components. Figure 2-1(a) shows an example function of time and its Fourier amplitudes. The amplitude of each component is then encoded in a minimal way. The goal is to reproduce the waveform accurately at the other end in as few bits as possible.

The other way, **perceptual coding**, exploits certain flaws in the human auditory system to encode a signal in such a way that it sounds the same to a human listener, even if it looks quite different on an oscilloscope. Perceptual coding is based on the science of **psychoacoustics**—how people perceive sound. MP3 is based on perceptual coding.

The key property of perceptual coding is that some sounds can **mask** other sounds. Imagine you are broadcasting a live flute concert on a warm summer day. Then all of a sudden, a crew of workmen nearby turn on their jackhammers and start tearing up the street. No one can hear the flute any more. Its sounds have been masked by the jackhammers. For transmission purposes, it is now sufficient to encode just the frequency band used by the jackhammers because the listeners cannot hear the flute anyway. This is called **frequency masking**—the ability of a loud sound in one frequency band to hide a softer sound in another frequency band that would have been audible in the absence of the loud sound. In fact, even after the jackhammers stop, the flute will be inaudible for a short period of time because the ear turns down its gain when they start and it takes a finite time to turn it up again. This effect is called **temporal masking**.

To make these effects more quantitative, imagine experiment 1. A person in a quiet room puts on headphones connected to a computer's sound card. The computer generates a pure sine wave at 100 Hz at low, but gradually increasing power. The person is instructed to strike a key when she hears the tone. The computer records the current power level and then repeats the experiment at 200 Hz, 300 Hz, and all the other frequencies up to the limit of human hearing. When averaged over many people, a log-log graph of how much power it takes for a tone to be audible looks like that of Fig. 7-58(a). A direct consequence of this curve is that it is never necessary to encode any frequencies whose power falls below the threshold of audibility. For example, if the power at 100 Hz were 20 dB in Fig. 7-58(a), it could be omitted from the output with no perceptible loss of quality because 20 dB at 100 Hz falls below the level of audibility.

Now consider Experiment 2. The computer runs experiment 1 again, but this time with a constant-amplitude sine wave at, say, 150 Hz, superimposed on the test frequency. What we discover is that the threshold of audibility for frequencies near 150 Hz is raised, as shown in Fig. 7-58(b).

The consequence of this new observation is that by keeping track of which signals are being masked by more powerful signals in nearby frequency bands, we can omit more and more frequencies in the encoded signal, saving bits. In Fig. 7-58, the 125-Hz signal can be completely omitted from the output and no one will be able to hear the difference. Even after a powerful signal stops in some frequency band, knowledge of its temporal masking properties allow us to continue

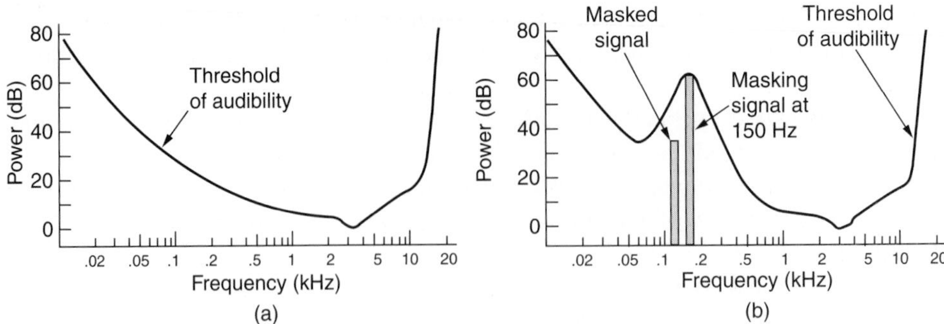

Figure 7-58. (a) The threshold of audibility as a function of frequency. (b) The masking effect.

to omit the masked frequencies for some time interval as the ear recovers. The essence of MP3 is to Fourier-transform the sound to get the power at each frequency and then transmit only the unmasked frequencies, encoding these in as few bits as possible.

With this information as background, we can now see how the encoding is done. The audio compression is done by sampling the waveform at 32 kHz, 44.1 kHz, or 48 kHz. Sampling can be done on one or two channels, in any of four configurations:

1. Monophonic (a single input stream).

2. Dual monophonic (e.g., an English and a Japanese soundtrack).

3. Disjoint stereo (each channel compressed separately).

4. Joint stereo (interchannel redundancy fully exploited).

First, the output bit rate is chosen. MP3 can compress a stereo rock 'n roll CD down to 96 kbps with little perceptible loss in quality, even for rock 'n roll fans with no hearing loss. For a piano concert, at least 128 kbps are needed. These differ because the signal-to-noise ratio for rock 'n roll is much higher than for a piano concert (in an engineering sense, anyway). It is also possible to choose lower output rates and accept some loss in quality.

Then the samples are processed in groups of 1152 (about 26 msec worth). Each group is first passed through 32 digital filters to get 32 frequency bands. At the same time, the input is fed into a psychoacoustic model in order to determine the masked frequencies. Next, each of the 32 frequency bands is further transformed to provide a finer spectral resolution.

In the next phase the available bit budget is divided among the bands, with more bits allocated to the bands with the most unmasked spectral power, fewer bits allocated to unmasked bands with less spectral power, and no bits allocated to masked bands. Finally, the bits are encoded using Huffman encoding, which assigns short codes to numbers that appear frequently and long codes to those that occur infrequently.

There is actually more to the story. Various techniques are also used for noise reduction, antialiasing, and exploiting the interchannel redundancy, if possible, but these are beyond the scope of this book. A more formal mathematical introduction to the process is given in (Pan, 1995).

7.4.3 Streaming Audio

Let us now move from the technology of digital audio to three of its network applications. Our first one is streaming audio, that is, listening to sound over the Internet. This is also called music on demand. In the next two, we will look at Internet radio and voice over IP, respectively.

The Internet is full of music Web sites, many of which list song titles that users can click on to play the songs. Some of these are free sites (e.g., new bands looking for publicity); others require payment in return for music, although these often offer some free samples as well (e.g., the first 15 seconds of a song). The most straightforward way to make the music play is illustrated in Fig. 7-59.

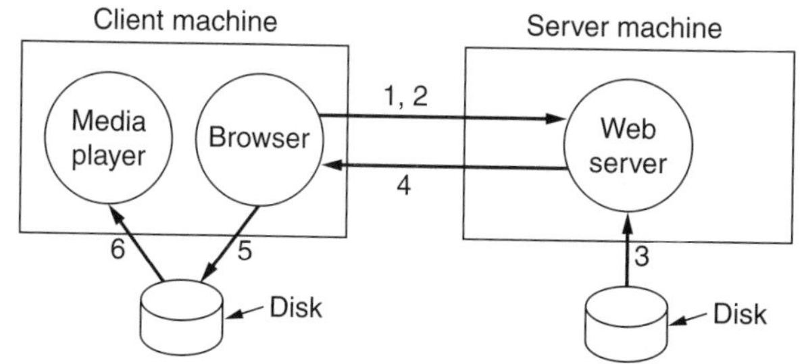

1. Establish TCP connection
2. Send HTTP GET request
3. Server gets file from disk
4. File sent back
5. Browser writes file to disk
6. Media player fetches file block by block and plays it

Figure 7-59. A straightforward way to implement clickable music on a Web page.

The process starts when the user clicks on a song. Then the browser goes into action. Step 1 is for it to establish a TCP connection to the Web server to which the song is hyperlinked. Step 2 is to send over a *GET* request in HTTP to request the song. Next (steps 3 and 4), the server fetches the song (which is just a file in MP3 or some other format) from the disk and sends it back to the browser. If the file is larger than the server's memory, it may fetch and send the music a block at a time.

Using the MIME type, for example, *audio/mp3*, (or the file extension), the browser looks up how it is supposed to display the file. Normally, there will be a helper application such as RealOne Player, Windows Media Player, or Winamp, associated with this type of file. Since the usual way for the browser to communicate with a helper is to write the content to a scratch file, it will save the entire music file as a scratch file on the disk (step 5) first. Then it will start the media player and pass it the name of the scratch file. In step 6, the media player starts fetching and playing the music, block by block.

In principle, this approach is completely correct and will play the music. The only trouble is that the entire song must be transmitted over the network before the music starts. If the song is 4 MB (a typical size for an MP3 song) and the modem is 56 kbps, the user will be greeted by almost 10 minutes of silence while the song is being downloaded. Not all music lovers like this idea. Especially since the next song will also start with 10 minutes of download time, and the one after that as well.

To get around this problem without changing how the browser works, music sites have come up with the following scheme. The file linked to the song title is not the actual music file. Instead, it is what is called a **metafile**, a very short file just naming the music. A typical metafile might be only one line of ASCII text and look like this:

```
rtsp://joes-audio-server/song-0025.mp3
```

When the browser gets the 1-line file, it writes it to disk on a scratch file, starts the media player as a helper, and hands it the name of the scratch file, as usual. The media player then reads the file and sees that it contains a URL. Then it contacts *joes-audio-server* and asks for the song. Note that the browser is not in the loop any more.

In most cases, the server named in the metafile is not the same as the Web server. In fact, it is generally not even an HTTP server, but a specialized media server. In this example, the media server uses **RTSP** (**Real Time Streaming Protocol**), as indicated by the scheme name *rtsp*. It is described in RFC 2326.

The media player has four major jobs to do:

1. Manage the user interface.
2. Handle transmission errors.
3. Decompress the music.
4. Eliminate jitter.

Most media players nowadays have a glitzy user interface, sometimes simulating a stereo unit, with buttons, knobs, sliders, and visual displays. Often there are interchangeable front panels, called **skins**, that the user can drop onto the player. The media player has to manage all this and interact with the user.

Its second job is dealing with errors. Real-time music transmission rarely uses TCP because an error and retransmission might introduce an unacceptably long gap in the music. Instead, the actual transmission is usually done with a protocol like RTP, which we studied in Chap. 6. Like most real-time protocols, RTP is layered on top of UDP, so packets may be lost. It is up to the player to deal with this.

In some cases, the music is interleaved to make error handling easier to do. For example, a packet might contain 220 stereo samples, each containing a pair of 16-bit numbers, normally good for 5 msec of music. But the protocol might send all the odd samples for a 10-msec interval in one packet and all the even samples in the next one. A lost packet then does not represent a 5 msec gap in the music, but loss of every other sample for 10 msec. This loss can be handled easily by having the media player interpolate using the previous and succeeding samples. estimate the missing value.

The use of interleaving to achieve error recovery is illustrated in Fig. 7-60. Here each packet holds the alternate time samples for an interval of 10 msec. Consequently, losing packet 3, as shown, does not create a gap in the music, but only lowers the temporal resolution for some interval. The missing values can be interpolated to provide continuous music. This particular scheme only works with uncompressed sampling, but shows how clever coding can convert a lost packet into lower quality rather than a time gap. However, RFC 3119 gives a scheme that works with compressed audio.

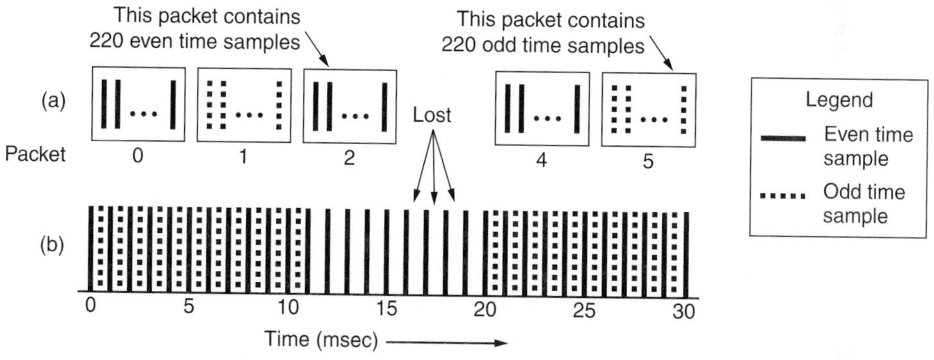

Figure 7-60. When packets carry alternate samples, the loss of a packet reduces the temporal resolution rather than creating a gap in time.

The media player's third job is decompressing the music. Although this task is computationally intensive, it is fairly straightforward.

The fourth job is to eliminate jitter, the bane of all real-time systems. All streaming audio systems start by buffering about 10–15 sec worth of music before starting to play, as shown in Fig. 7-61. Ideally, the server will continue to fill the buffer at the exact rate it is being drained by the media player, but in reality this may not happen, so feedback in the loop may be helpful.

Two approaches can be used to keep the buffer filled. With a **pull server**, as long as there is room in the buffer for another block, the media player just keeps

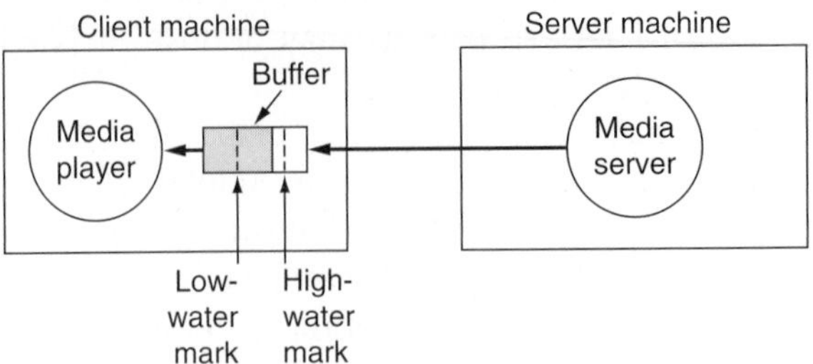

Figure 7-61. The media player buffers input from the media server and plays from the buffer rather than directly from the network.

sending requests for an additional block to the server. Its goal is to keep the buffer as full as possible.

The disadvantage of a pull server is all the unnecessary data requests. The server knows it has sent the whole file, so why have the player keep asking? For this reason, it is rarely used.

With a **push server**, the media player sends a *PLAY* request and the server just keeps pushing data at it. There are two possibilities here: the media server runs at normal playback speed or it runs faster. In both cases, some data is buffered before playback begins. If the server runs at normal playback speed, data arriving from it are appended to the end of the buffer and the player removes data from the front of the buffer for playing. As long as everything works perfectly, the amount of data in the buffer remains constant in time. This scheme is simple because no control messages are required in either direction.

The other push scheme is to have the server pump out data faster than it is needed. The advantage here is that if the server cannot be guaranteed to run at a regular rate, it has the opportunity to catch up if it ever gets behind. A problem here, however, is potential buffer overruns if the server can pump out data faster than it is consumed (and it has to be able to do this to avoid gaps).

The solution is for the media player to define a **low-water mark** and a **high-water mark** in the buffer. Basically, the server just pumps out data until the buffer is filled to the high-water mark. Then the media player tells it to pause. Since data will continue to pour in until the server has gotten the pause request, the distance between the high-water mark and the end of the buffer has to be greater than the bandwidth-delay product of the network. After the server has stopped, the buffer will begin to empty. When it hits the low-water mark, the media player tells the media server to start again. The low-water mark has to be positioned so that buffer underrun does not occur.

To operate a push server, the media player needs a remote control for it. This is what RTSP provides. It is defined in RFC 2326 and provides the mechanism for the player to control the server. It does not provide for the data stream, which is usually RTP. The main commands provided for by RTSP are listed in Fig. 7-62.

Command	Server action
DESCRIBE	List media parameters
SETUP	Establish a logical channel between the player and the server
PLAY	Start sending data to the client
RECORD	Start accepting data from the client
PAUSE	Temporarily stop sending data
TEARDOWN	Release the logical channel

Figure 7-62. RTSP commands from the player to the server.

7.4.4 Internet Radio

Once it became possible to stream audio over the Internet, commercial radio stations got the idea of broadcasting their content over the Internet as well as over the air. Not so long after that, college radio stations started putting their signal out over the Internet. Then college *students* started their own radio stations. With current technology, virtually anyone can start a radio station. The whole area of Internet radio is very new and in a state of flux, but it is worth saying a little bit about.

There are two general approaches to Internet radio. In the first one, the programs are prerecorded and stored on disk. Listeners can connect to the radio station's archives and pull up any program and download it for listening. In fact, this is exactly the same as the streaming audio we just discussed. It is also possible to store each program just after it is broadcast live, so the archive is only running, say, half an hour, or less behind the live feed. The advantages of this approach are that it is easy to do, all the techniques we have discussed work here too, and listeners can pick and choose among all the programs in the archive.

The other approach is to broadcast live over the Internet. Some stations broadcast over the air and over the Internet simultaneously, but there are increasingly many radio stations that are Internet only. Some of the techniques that are applicable to streaming audio are also applicable to live Internet radio, but there are also some key differences.

One point that is the same is the need for buffering on the user side to smooth out jitter. By collecting 10 or 15 seconds worth of radio before starting the playback, the audio can be kept going smoothly even in the face of substantial jitter over the network. As long as all the packets arrive before they are needed, it does not matter when they arrived.

One key difference is that streaming audio can be pushed out at a rate greater than the playback rate since the receiver can stop it when the high-water mark is hit. Potentially, this gives it the time to retransmit lost packets, although this strategy is not commonly used. In contrast, live radio is always broadcast at exactly the rate it is generated and played back.

Another difference is that a live radio station usually has hundreds or thousands of simultaneous listeners whereas streaming audio is point to point. Under these circumstances, Internet radio should use multicasting with the RTP/RTSP protocols. This is clearly the most efficient way to operate.

In current practice, Internet radio does not work like this. What actually happens is that the user establishes a TCP connection to the station and the feed is sent over the TCP connection. Of course, this creates various problems, such as the flow stopping when the window is full, lost packets timing out and being retransmitted, and so on.

The reason TCP unicasting is used instead of RTP multicasting is threefold. First, few ISPs support multicasting, so that is not a practical option. Second, RTP is less well known than TCP and radio stations are often small and have little computer expertise, so it is just easier to use a protocol that is widely understood and supported by all software packages. Third, many people listen to Internet radio at work, which in practice, often means behind a firewall. Most system administrators configure their firewall to protect their LAN from unwelcome visitors. They usually allow TCP connections from remote port 25 (SMTP for e-mail), UDP packets from remote port 53 (DNS), and TCP connections from remote port 80 (HTTP for the Web). Almost everything else may be blocked, including RTP. Thus, the only way to get the radio signal through the firewall is for the Web site to pretend it is an HTTP server, at least to the firewall, and use HTTP servers, which speak TCP. These severe measures, while providing only minimal security. often force multimedia applications into drastically less efficient modes of operation.

Since Internet radio is a new medium, format wars are in full bloom. RealAudio, Windows Media Audio, and MP3 are aggressively competing in this market to become the dominant format for Internet radio. A newcomer is Vorbis, which is technically similar to MP3 but open source and different enough that it does not use the patents MP3 is based on.

A typical Internet radio station has a Web page listing its schedule, information about its DJs and announcers, and many ads. There are also one or more icons listing the audio formats it supports (or just LISTEN NOW if only one format is supported). These icons or LISTEN NOW are linked metafiles of the type we discussed above.

When a user clicks on one of the icons, the short metafile is sent over. The browser uses its MIME type or file extension to determine the appropriate helper (i.e., media player) for the metafile. Then it writes the metafile to a scratch file on disk, starts the media player, and hands it the name of the scratch file. The media player reads the scratch file, sees the URL contained in it (usually with scheme *http* rather than *rtsp* to get around the firewall problem and because some popular multimedia applications work that way), contacts the server, and starts acting like a radio. As an aside, audio has only one stream, so *http* works, but for video, which has at least two streams, *http* fails and something like *rtsp* is really needed.

Another interesting development in the area of Internet radio is an arrangement in which anybody, even a student, can set up and operate a radio station. The main components are illustrated in Fig. 7-63. The basis of the station is an ordinary PC with a sound card and a microphone. The software consists of a media player, such as Winamp or Freeamp, with a plug-in for audio capture and a codec for the selected output format, for example, MP3 or Vorbis.

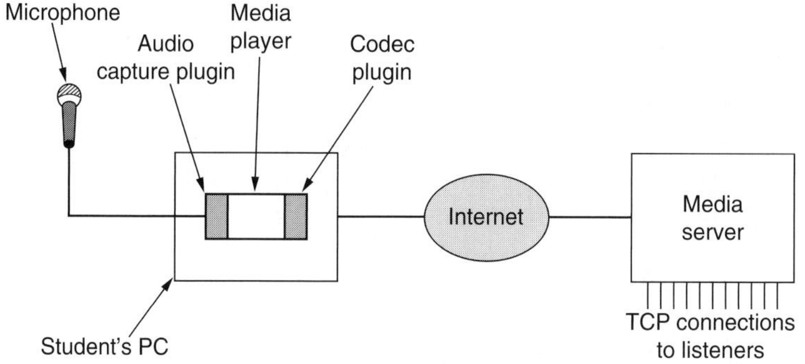

Figure 7-63. A student radio station.

The audio stream generated by the station is then fed over the Internet to a large server, which handles distributing it to large numbers of TCP connections. The server typically supports many small stations. It also maintains a directory of what stations it has and what is currently on the air on each one. Potential listeners go to the server, select a station, and get a TCP feed. There are commercial software packages for managing all the pieces, as well as open source packages such as icecast. There are also servers that are willing to handle the distribution for a fee.

7.4.5 Voice over IP

Once upon a time, the public switched telephone system was primarily used for voice traffic with a little bit of data traffic here and there. But the data traffic grew and grew, and by 1999, the number of data bits moved equaled the number of voice bits (since voice is in PCM on the trunks, it can be measured in bits/sec). By 2002, the volume of data traffic was an order of magnitude more than the volume of voice traffic and still growing exponentially, with voice traffic being almost flat (5% growth per year).

As a consequence of these numbers, many packet-switching network operators suddenly became interested in carrying voice over their data networks. The amount of additional bandwidth required for voice is minuscule since the packet networks are dimensioned for the data traffic. However, the average person's phone bill is probably larger than his Internet bill, so the data network operators saw Internet telephony as a way to earn a large amount of additional money without having to put any new fiber in the ground. Thus **Internet telephony** (also known as **voice over IP**), was born.

H.323

One thing that was clear to everyone from the start was that if each vendor designed its own protocol stack, the system would never work. To avoid this problem, a number of interested parties got together under ITU auspices to work out standards. In 1996 ITU issued recommendation **H.323** entitled "Visual Telephone Systems and Equipment for Local Area Networks Which Provide a Non-Guaranteed Quality of Service." Only the telephone industry would think of such a name. The recommendation was revised in 1998, and this revised H.323 was the basis for the first widespread Internet telephony systems.

H.323 is more of an architectural overview of Internet telephony than a specific protocol. It references a large number of specific protocols for speech coding, call setup, signaling, data transport, and other areas rather than specifying these things itself. The general model is depicted in Fig. 7-64. At the center is a **gateway** that connects the Internet to the telephone network. It speaks the H.323 protocols on the Internet side and the PSTN protocols on the telephone side. The communicating devices are called **terminals**. A LAN may have a **gatekeeper**, which controls the end points under its jurisdiction, called a **zone**.

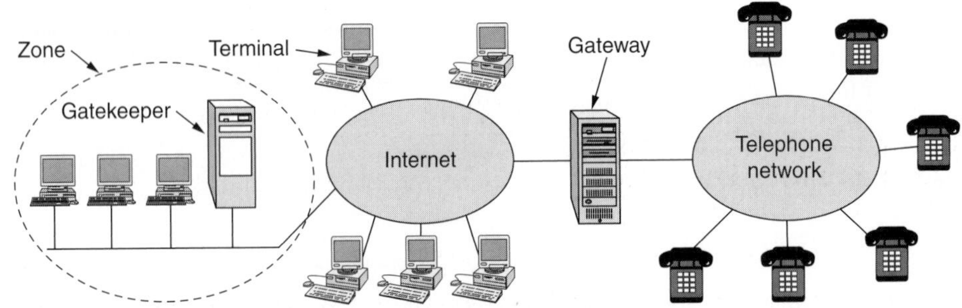

Figure 7-64. The H.323 architectural model for Internet telephony.

A telephone network needs a number of protocols. To start with, there is a protocol for encoding and decoding speech. The PCM system we studied in Chap. 2 is defined in ITU recommendation **G.711**. It encodes a single voice channel by sampling 8000 times per second with an 8-bit sample to give uncompressed speech at 64 kbps. All H.323 systems must support G.711. However, other speech compression protocols are also permitted (but not required). They use different compression algorithms and make different trade-offs between quality and bandwidth. For example, **G.723.1** takes a block of 240 samples (30 msec of speech) and uses predictive coding to reduce it to either 24 bytes or 20 bytes. This algorithm gives an output rate of either 6.4 kbps or 5.3 kbps (compression factors of 10 and 12), respectively, with little loss in perceived quality. Other codecs are also allowed.

Since multiple compression algorithms are permitted, a protocol is needed to allow the terminals to negotiate which one they are going to use. This protocol is called **H.245**. It also negotiates other aspects of the connection such as the bit rate. RTCP is need for the control of the RTP channels. Also required is a protocol for establishing and releasing connections, providing dial tones, making ringing sounds, and the rest of the standard telephony. ITU **Q.931** is used here. The terminals need a protocol for talking to the gatekeeper (if present). For this purpose, **H.225** is used. The PC-to-gatekeeper channel it manages is called the **RAS (Registration/Admission/Status)** channel. This channel allows terminals to join and leave the zone, request and return bandwidth, and provide status updates, among other things. Finally, a protocol is needed for the actual data transmission. RTP is used for this purpose. It is managed by RTCP, as usual. The positioning of all these protocols is shown in Fig. 7-65.

<table>
<tr><td>Speech</td><td colspan="4">Control</td></tr>
<tr><td>G.7xx
RTP</td><td>RTCP</td><td>H.225
(RAS)</td><td>Q.931
(Call
signaling)</td><td>H.245
(Call
control)</td></tr>
<tr><td colspan="3">UDP</td><td colspan="2">TCP</td></tr>
<tr><td colspan="5">IP</td></tr>
<tr><td colspan="5">Data link protocol</td></tr>
<tr><td colspan="5">Physical layer protocol</td></tr>
</table>

Figure 7-65. The H.323 protocol stack.

To see how these protocols fit together, consider the case of a PC terminal on a LAN (with a gatekeeper) calling a remote telephone. The PC first has to discover the gatekeeper, so it broadcasts a UDP gatekeeper discovery packet to port 1718. When the gatekeeper responds, the PC learns the gatekeeper's IP address. Now the PC registers with the gatekeeper by sending it a RAS message in a UDP packet. After it has been accepted, the PC sends the gatekeeper a RAS admission message requesting bandwidth. Only after bandwidth has been granted may call setup begin. The idea of requesting bandwidth in advance is to allow the gatekeeper to limit the number of calls to avoid oversubscribing the outgoing line in order to help provide the necessary quality of service.

The PC now establishes a TCP connection to the gatekeeper to begin call setup. Call setup uses existing telephone network protocols, which are connection oriented, so TCP is needed. In contrast, the telephone system has nothing like RAS to allow telephones to announce their presence, so the H.323 designers were free to use either UDP or TCP for RAS, and they chose the lower-overhead UDP.

Now that it has bandwidth allocated, the PC can send a Q.931 *SETUP* message over the TCP connection. This message specifies the number of the telephone being called (or the IP address and port, if a computer is being called). The gatekeeper responds with a Q.931 *CALL PROCEEDING* message to acknowledge correct receipt of the request. The gatekeeper then forwards the *SETUP* message to the gateway.

The gateway, which is half computer, half telephone switch, then makes an ordinary telephone call to the desired (ordinary) telephone. The end office to which the telephone is attached rings the called telephone and also sends back a Q.931 *ALERT* message to tell the calling PC that ringing has begun. When the person at the other end picks up the telephone, the end office sends back a Q.931 *CONNECT* message to signal the PC that it has a connection.

Once the connection has been established, the gatekeeper is no longer in the loop, although the gateway is, of course. Subsequent packets bypass the gatekeeper and go directly to the gateway's IP address. At this point, we just have a bare tube running between the two parties. This is just a physical layer connection for moving bits, no more. Neither side knows anything about the other one.

The H.245 protocol is now used to negotiate the parameters of the call. It uses the H.245 control channel, which is always open. Each side starts out by announcing its capabilities, for example, whether it can handle video (H.323 can handle video) or conference calls, which codecs it supports, etc. Once each side knows what the other one can handle, two unidirectional data channels are set up and a codec and other parameters assigned to each one. Since each side may have different equipment, it is entirely possible that the codecs on the forward and reverse channels are different. After all negotiations are complete, data flow can begin using RTP. It is managed using RTCP, which plays a role in congestion control. If video is present, RTCP handles the audio/video synchronization. The various channels are shown in Fig. 7-66. When either party hangs up, the Q.931 call signaling channel is used to tear down the connection.

When the call is terminated, the calling PC contacts the gatekeeper again with a RAS message to release the bandwidth it has been assigned. Alternatively, it can make another call.

We have not said anything about quality of service, even though this is essential to making voice over IP a success. The reason is that QoS falls outside the scope of H.323. If the underlying network is capable of producing a stable, jitter-free connection from the calling PC (e.g., using the techniques we discussed in Chap. 5) to the gateway, then the QoS on the call will be good; otherwise it will not be. The telephone part uses PCM and is always jitter free.

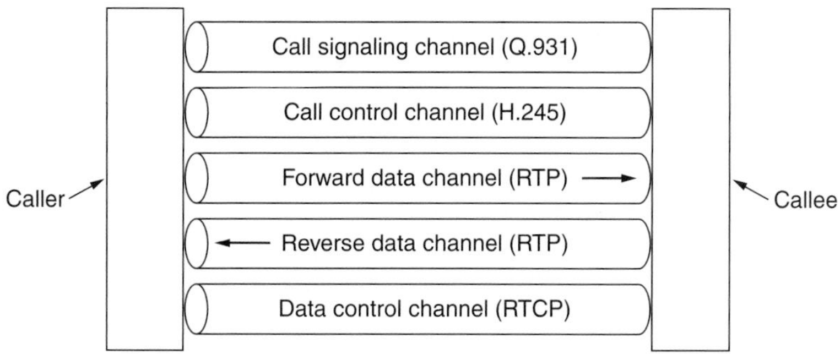

Figure 7-66. Logical channels between the caller and callee during a call.

SIP—The Session Initiation Protocol

H.323 was designed by ITU. Many people in the Internet community saw it as a typical telco product: large, complex, and inflexible. Consequently, IETF set up a committee to design a simpler and more modular way to do voice over IP. The major result to date is the **SIP** (**Session Initiation Protocol**), which is described in RFC 3261. This protocol describes how to set up Internet telephone calls, video conferences, and other multimedia connections. Unlike H.323, which is a complete protocol suite, SIP is a single module, but it has been designed to interwork well with existing Internet applications. For example, it defines telephone numbers as URLs, so that Web pages can contain them, allowing a click on a link to initiate a telephone call (the same way the *mailto* scheme allows a click on a link to bring up a program to send an e-mail message).

SIP can establish two-party sessions (ordinary telephone calls), multiparty sessions (where everyone can hear and speak), and multicast sessions (one sender, many receivers). The sessions may contain audio, video, or data, the latter being useful for multiplayer real-time games, for example. SIP just handles setup, management, and termination of sessions. Other protocols, such as RTP/RTCP, are used for data transport. SIP is an application-layer protocol and can run over UDP or TCP.

SIP supports a variety of services, including locating the callee (who may not be at his home machine) and determining the callee's capabilities, as well as handling the mechanics of call setup and termination. In the simplest case, SIP sets up a session from the caller's computer to the callee's computer, so we will examine that case first.

Telephone numbers in SIP are represented as URLs using the *sip* scheme, for example, *sip:ilse@cs.university.edu* for a user named Ilse at the host specified by the DNS name *cs.university.edu*. SIP URLs may also contain IPv4 addresses, IPv6 address, or actual telephone numbers.

The SIP protocol is a text-based protocol modeled on HTTP. One party sends a message in ASCII text consisting of a method name on the first line, followed by additional lines containing headers for passing parameters. Many of the headers are taken from MIME to allow SIP to interwork with existing Internet applications. The six methods defined by the core specification are listed in Fig. 7-67.

Method	Description
INVITE	Request initiation of a session
ACK	Confirm that a session has been initiated
BYE	Request termination of a session
OPTIONS	Query a host about its capabilities
CANCEL	Cancel a pending request
REGISTER	Inform a redirection server about the user's current location

Figure 7-67. The SIP methods defined in the core specification.

To establish a session, the caller either creates a TCP connection with the callee and sends an *INVITE* message over it or sends the *INVITE* message in a UDP packet. In both cases, the headers on the second and subsequent lines describe the structure of the message body, which contains the caller's capabilities, media types, and formats. If the callee accepts the call, it responds with an HTTP-type reply code (a three-digit number using the groups of Fig. 7-42, 200 for acceptance). Following the reply-code line, the callee also may supply information about its capabilities, media types, and formats.

Connection is done using a three-way handshake, so the caller responds with an *ACK* message to finish the protocol and confirm receipt of the 200 message.

Either party may request termination of a session by sending a message containing the *BYE* method. When the other side acknowledges it, the session is terminated.

The *OPTIONS* method is used to query a machine about its own capabilities. It is typically used before a session is initiated to find out if that machine is even capable of voice over IP or whatever type of session is being contemplated.

The *REGISTER* method relates to SIP's ability to track down and connect to a user who is away from home. This message is sent to a SIP location server that keeps track of who is where. That server can later be queried to find the user's current location. The operation of redirection is illustrated in Fig. 7-68. Here the caller sends the *INVITE* message to a proxy server to hide the possible redirection. The proxy then looks up where the user is and sends the *INVITE* message there. It then acts as a relay for the subsequent messages in the three-way handshake. The *LOOKUP* and *REPLY* messages are not part of SIP; any convenient protocol can be used, depending on what kind of location server is used.

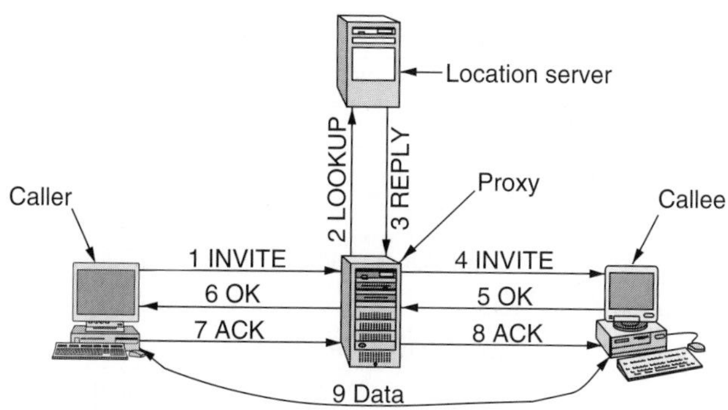

Figure 7-68. Use a proxy and redirection servers with SIP.

SIP has a variety of other features that we will not describe here, including call waiting, call screening, encryption, and authentication. It also has the ability to place calls from a computer to an ordinary telephone, if a suitable gateway between the Internet and telephone system is available.

Comparison of H.323 and SIP

H.323 and SIP have many similarities but also some differences. Both allow two-party and multiparty calls using both computers and telephones as end points. Both support parameter negotiation, encryption, and the RTP/RTCP protocols. A summary of the similarities and differences is given in Fig. 7-69.

Although the feature sets are similar, the two protocols differ widely in philosophy. H.323 is a typical, heavyweight, telephone-industry standard, specifying the complete protocol stack and defining precisely what is allowed and what is forbidden. This approach leads to very well defined protocols in each layer, easing the task of interoperability. The price paid is a large, complex, and rigid standard that is difficult to adapt to future applications.

In contrast, SIP is a typical Internet protocol that works by exchanging short lines of ASCII text. It is a lightweight module that interworks well with other Internet protocols but less well with existing telephone system signaling protocols. Because the IETF model of voice over IP is highly modular, it is flexible and can be adapted to new applications easily. The downside is potential interoperability problems, although these are addressed by frequent meetings where different implementers get together to test their systems.

Voice over IP is an up-and-coming topic. Consequently, there are several books on the subject already. A few examples are (Collins, 2001; Davidson and Peters, 2000; Kumar et al., 2001; and Wright, 2001). The May/June 2002 issue of *Internet Computing* has several articles on this topic.

Item	H.323	SIP
Designed by	ITU	IETF
Compatibility with PSTN	Yes	Largely
Compatibility with Internet	No	Yes
Architecture	Monolithic	Modular
Completeness	Full protocol stack	SIP just handles setup
Parameter negotiation	Yes	Yes
Call signaling	Q.931 over TCP	SIP over TCP or UDP
Message format	Binary	ASCII
Media transport	RTP/RTCP	RTP/RTCP
Multiparty calls	Yes	Yes
Multimedia conferences	Yes	No
Addressing	Host or telephone number	URL
Call termination	Explicit or TCP release	Explicit or timeout
Instant messaging	No	Yes
Encryption	Yes	Yes
Size of standards	1400 pages	250 pages
Implementation	Large and complex	Moderate
Status	Widely deployed	Up and coming

Figure 7-69. Comparison of H.323 and SIP

7.4.6 Introduction to Video

We have discussed the ear at length now; time to move on to the eye (no, this section is not followed by one on the nose). The human eye has the property that when an image appears on the retina, the image is retained for some number of milliseconds before decaying. If a sequence of images is drawn line by line at 50 images/sec, the eye does not notice that it is looking at discrete images. All video (i.e., television) systems exploit this principle to produce moving pictures.

Analog Systems

To understand video, it is best to start with simple, old-fashioned black-and-white television. To represent the two-dimensional image in front of it as a one-dimensional voltage as a function of time, the camera scans an electron beam rapidly across the image and slowly down it, recording the light intensity as it goes. At the end of the scan, called a **frame**, the beam retraces. This intensity as a function of time is broadcast, and receivers repeat the scanning process to reconstruct the image. The scanning pattern used by both the camera and the receiver is shown in Fig. 7-70. (As an aside, CCD cameras integrate rather than scan, but some cameras and all monitors do scan.)

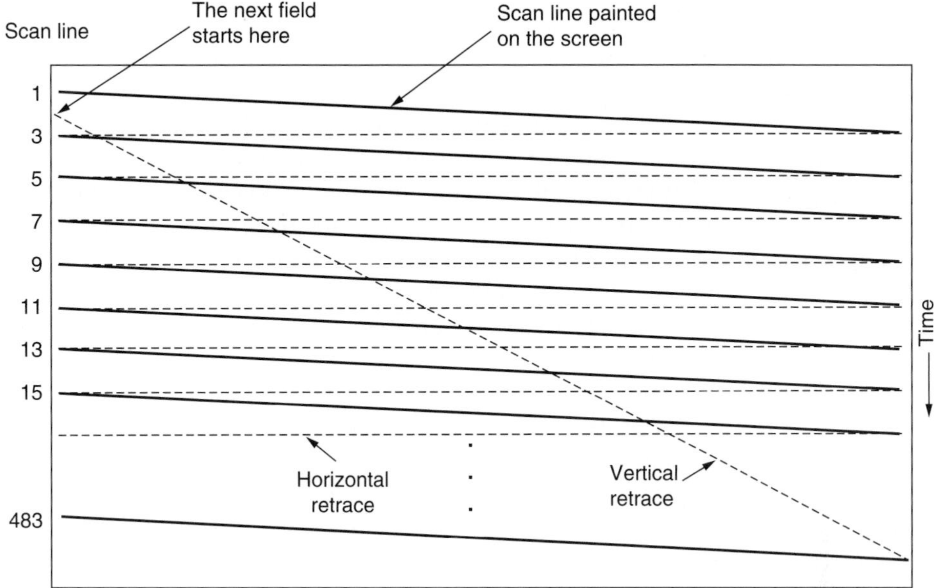

Figure 7-70. The scanning pattern used for NTSC video and television.

The exact scanning parameters vary from country to country. The system used in North and South America and Japan has 525 scan lines, a horizontal-to-vertical aspect ratio of 4:3, and 30 frames/sec. The European system has 625 scan lines, the same aspect ratio of 4:3, and 25 frames/sec. In both systems, the top few and bottom few lines are not displayed (to approximate a rectangular image on the original round CRTs). Only 483 of the 525 NTSC scan lines (and 576 of the 625 PAL/SECAM scan lines) are displayed. The beam is turned off during the vertical retrace, so many stations (especially in Europe) use this time to broadcast TeleText (text pages containing news, weather, sports, stock prices, etc.).

While 25 frames/sec is enough to capture smooth motion, at that frame rate many people, especially older ones, will perceive the image to flicker (because the old image has faded off the retina before the new one appears). Rather than increase the frame rate, which would require using more scarce bandwidth, a different approach is taken. Instead of the scan lines being displayed in order, first all the odd scan lines are displayed, then the even ones are displayed. Each of these half frames is called a **field**. Experiments have shown that although people notice flicker at 25 frames/sec, they do not notice it at 50 fields/sec. This technique is called **interlacing**. Noninterlaced television or video is called **progressive**. Note that movies run at 24 fps, but each frame is fully visible for 1/24 sec.

Color video uses the same scanning pattern as monochrome (black and white), except that instead of displaying the image with one moving beam, it uses three beams moving in unison. One beam is used for each of the three additive primary colors: red, green, and blue (RGB). This technique works because any color can be constructed from a linear superposition of red, green, and blue with the appropriate intensities. However, for transmission on a single channel, the three color signals must be combined into a single **composite** signal.

When color television was invented, various methods for displaying color were technically possible, and different countries made different choices, leading to systems that are still incompatible. (Note that these choices have nothing to do with VHS versus Betamax versus P2000, which are recording methods.) In all countries, a political requirement was that programs transmitted in color had to be receivable on existing black-and-white television sets. Consequently, the simplest scheme, just encoding the RGB signals separately, was not acceptable. RGB is also not the most efficient scheme.

The first color system was standardized in the United States by the **National Television System Committee**, which lent its acronym to the standard: **NTSC**. Color television was introduced in Europe several years later, by which time the technology had improved substantially, leading to systems with greater noise immunity and better colors. These systems are called **SECAM** (**SEquentiel Couleur Avec Memoire**), which is used in France and Eastern Europe, and **PAL** (**Phase Alternating Line**) used in the rest of Europe. The difference in color quality between the NTSC and PAL/SECAM has led to an industry joke that NTSC really stands for Never Twice the Same Color.

To allow color transmissions to be viewed on black-and-white receivers, all three systems linearly combine the RGB signals into a **luminance** (brightness) signal and two **chrominance** (color) signals, although they all use different coefficients for constructing these signals from the RGB signals. Oddly enough, the eye is much more sensitive to the luminance signal than to the chrominance signals, so the latter need not be transmitted as accurately. Consequently, the luminance signal can be broadcast at the same frequency as the old black-and-white signal, so it can be received on black-and-white television sets. The two chrominance signals are broadcast in narrow bands at higher frequencies. Some television sets have controls labeled brightness, hue, and saturation (or brightness, tint, and color) for controlling these three signals separately. Understanding luminance and chrominance is necessary for understanding how video compression works.

In the past few years, there has been considerable interest in **HDTV** (**High Definition TeleVision**), which produces sharper images by roughly doubling the number of scan lines. The United States, Europe, and Japan have all developed HDTV systems, all different and all mutually incompatible. Did you expect otherwise? The basic principles of HDTV in terms of scanning, luminance, chrominance, and so on, are similar to the existing systems. However, all three formats have a common aspect ratio of 16:9 instead of 4:3 to match them better to the format used for movies (which are recorded on 35 mm film, which has an aspect ratio of 3:2).

Digital Systems

The simplest representation of digital video is a sequence of frames, each consisting of a rectangular grid of picture elements, or **pixels**. Each pixel can be a single bit, to represent either black or white. The quality of such a system is similar to what you get by sending a color photograph by fax—awful. (Try it if you can; otherwise photocopy a color photograph on a copying machine that does not rasterize.)

The next step up is to use 8 bits per pixel to represent 256 gray levels. This scheme gives high-quality black-and-white video. For color video, good systems use 8 bits for each of the RGB colors, although nearly all systems mix these into composite video for transmission. While using 24 bits per pixel limits the number of colors to about 16 million, the human eye cannot even distinguish this many colors, let alone more. Digital color images are produced using three scanning beams, one per color. The geometry is the same as for the analog system of Fig. 7-70 except that the continuous scan lines are now replaced by neat rows of discrete pixels.

To produce smooth motion, digital video, like analog video, must display at least 25 frames/sec. However, since good-quality computer monitors often rescan the screen from images stored in memory at 75 times per second or more, interlacing is not needed and consequently is not normally used. Just repainting (i.e., redrawing) the same frame three times in a row is enough to eliminate flicker.

In other words, smoothness of motion is determined by the number of *different* images per second, whereas flicker is determined by the number of times the screen is painted per second. These two parameters are different. A still image painted at 20 frames/sec will not show jerky motion, but it will flicker because one frame will decay from the retina before the next one appears. A movie with 20 different frames per second, each of which is painted four times in a row, will not flicker, but the motion will appear jerky.

The significance of these two parameters becomes clear when we consider the bandwidth required for transmitting digital video over a network. Current computer monitors mostly use the 4:3 aspect ratio so they can use inexpensive, mass-produced picture tubes designed for the consumer television market. Common configurations are 1024×768, 1280×960, and 1600×1200. Even the smallest of these with 24 bits per pixel and 25 frames/sec needs to be fed at 472 Mbps. It would take a SONET OC-12 carrier to manage this, and running an OC-12 SONET carrier into everyone's house is not exactly on the agenda. Doubling this rate to avoid flicker is even less attractive. A better solution is to transmit 25 frames/sec and have the computer store each one and paint it twice. Broadcast television does not use this strategy because television sets do not have memory. And even if they did have memory, analog signals cannot be stored in RAM without conversion to digital form first, which requires extra hardware. As a consequence, interlacing is used for broadcast television but not for digital video.

7.4.7 Video Compression

It should be obvious by now that transmitting uncompressed video is completely out of the question. The only hope is that massive compression is possible. Fortunately, a large body of research over the past few decades has led to many compression techniques and algorithms that make video transmission feasible. In this section we will study how video compression is accomplished.

All compression systems require two algorithms: one for compressing the data at the source, and another for decompressing it at the destination. In the literature, these algorithms are referred to as the **encoding** and **decoding** algorithms, respectively. We will use this terminology here, too.

These algorithms exhibit certain asymmetries that are important to understand. First, for many applications, a multimedia document, say, a movie will only be encoded once (when it is stored on the multimedia server) but will be decoded thousands of times (when it is viewed by customers). This asymmetry means that it is acceptable for the encoding algorithm to be slow and require expensive hardware provided that the decoding algorithm is fast and does not require expensive hardware. After all, the operator of a multimedia server might be quite willing to rent a parallel supercomputer for a few weeks to encode its entire video library, but requiring consumers to rent a supercomputer for 2 hours to view a video is not likely to be a big success. Many practical compression systems go to great lengths to make decoding fast and simple, even at the price of making encoding slow and complicated.

On the other hand, for real-time multimedia, such as video conferencing, slow encoding is unacceptable. Encoding must happen on-the-fly, in real time. Consequently, real-time multimedia uses different algorithms or parameters than storing videos on disk, often with appreciably less compression.

A second asymmetry is that the encode/decode process need not be invertible. That is, when compressing a file, transmitting it, and then decompressing it, the user expects to get the original back, accurate down to the last bit. With multimedia, this requirement does not exist. It is usually acceptable to have the video signal after encoding and then decoding be slightly different from the original. When the decoded output is not exactly equal to the original input, the system is said to be **lossy**. If the input and output are identical, the system is **lossless**. Lossy systems are important because accepting a small amount of information loss can give a huge payoff in terms of the compression ratio possible.

The JPEG Standard

A video is just a sequence of images (plus sound). If we could find a good algorithm for encoding a single image, this algorithm could be applied to each image in succession to achieve video compression. Good still image compression algorithms exist, so let us start our study of video compression there. The **JPEG** (**Joint Photographic Experts Group**) standard for compressing continuous-tone still pictures (e.g., photographs) was developed by photographic experts working under the joint auspices of ITU, ISO, and IEC, another standards body. It is important for multimedia because, to a first approximation, the multimedia standard for moving pictures, MPEG, is just the JPEG encoding of each frame separately, plus some extra features for interframe compression and motion detection. JPEG is defined in International Standard 10918.

JPEG has four modes and many options. It is more like a shopping list than a single algorithm. For our purposes, though, only the lossy sequential mode is relevant, and that one is illustrated in Fig. 7-71. Furthermore, we will concentrate on the way JPEG is normally used to encode 24-bit RGB video images and will leave out some of the minor details for the sake of simplicity.

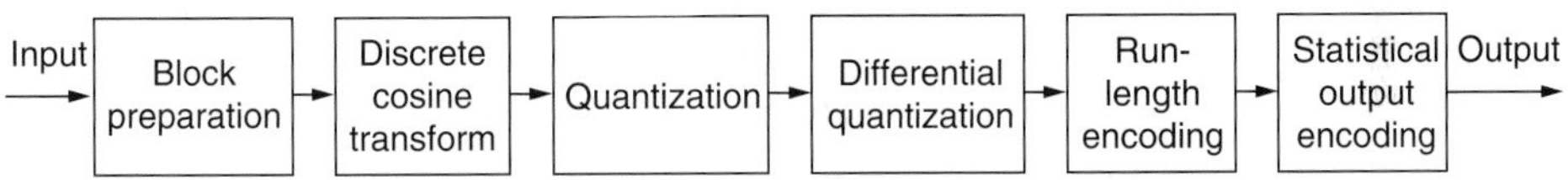

Figure 7-71. The operation of JPEG in lossy sequential mode.

Step 1 of encoding an image with JPEG is block preparation. For the sake of specificity, let us assume that the JPEG input is a 640×480 RGB image with 24 bits/pixel, as shown in Fig. 7-72(a). Since using luminance and chrominance gives better compression, we first compute the luminance, Y, and the two chrominances, I and Q (for NTSC), according to the following formulas:

$$\begin{aligned} Y &= 0.30R + 0.59G + 0.11B \\ I &= 0.60R - 0.28G - 0.32B \\ Q &= 0.21R - 0.52G + 0.31B \end{aligned}$$

For PAL, the chrominances are called U and V and the coefficients are different, but the idea is the same. SECAM is different from both NTSC and PAL.

Separate matrices are constructed for Y, I, and Q, each with elements in the range 0 to 255. Next, square blocks of four pixels are averaged in the I and Q matrices to reduce them to 320×240. This reduction is lossy, but the eye barely notices it since the eye responds to luminance more than to chrominance. Nevertheless, it compresses the total amount of data by a factor of four. Now 128 is subtracted from each element of all three matrices to put 0 in the middle of the

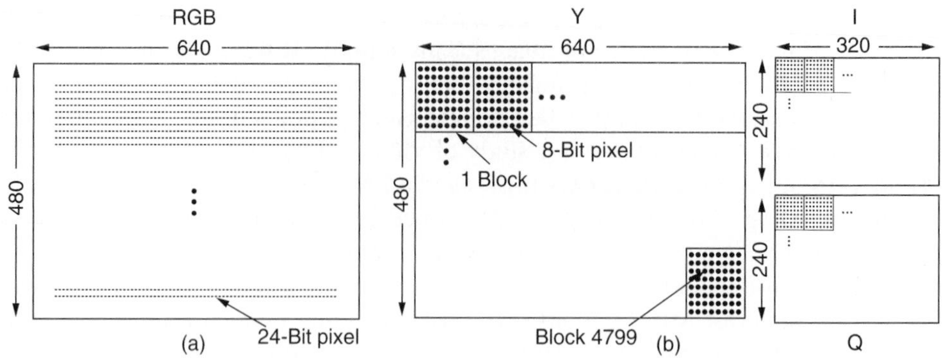

Figure 7-72. (a) RGB input data. (b) After block preparation.

range. Finally, each matrix is divided up into 8×8 blocks. The *Y* matrix has 4800 blocks; the other two have 1200 blocks each, as shown in Fig. 7-72(b).

Step 2 of JPEG is to apply a **DCT** (**Discrete Cosine Transformation**) to each of the 7200 blocks separately. The output of each DCT is an 8×8 matrix of DCT coefficients. DCT element (0, 0) is the average value of the block. The other elements tell how much spectral power is present at each spatial frequency. In theory, a DCT is lossless, but in practice, using floating-point numbers and transcendental functions always introduces some roundoff error that results in a little information loss. Normally, these elements decay rapidly with distance from the origin, (0, 0), as suggested by Fig. 7-73.

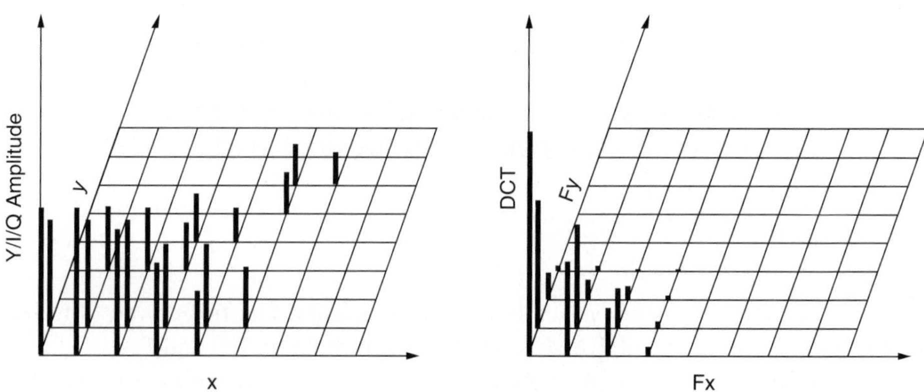

Figure 7-73. (a) One block of the *Y* matrix. (b) The DCT coefficients.

Once the DCT is complete, JPEG moves on to step 3, called **quantization**, in which the less important DCT coefficients are wiped out. This (lossy) transformation is done by dividing each of the coefficients in the 8×8 DCT matrix by a weight taken from a table. If all the weights are 1, the transformation does nothing. However, if the weights increase sharply from the origin, higher spatial frequencies are dropped quickly.

An example of this step is given in Fig. 7-74. Here we see the initial DCT matrix, the quantization table, and the result obtained by dividing each DCT element by the corresponding quantization table element. The values in the quantization table are not part of the JPEG standard. Each application must supply its own, allowing it to control the loss-compression trade-off.

DCT Coefficients

150	80	40	14	4	2	1	0
92	75	36	10	6	1	0	0
52	38	26	8	7	4	0	0
12	8	6	4	2	1	0	0
4	3	2	0	0	0	0	0
2	2	1	1	0	0	0	0
1	1	0	0	0	0	0	0
0	0	0	0	0	0	0	0

Quantization table

1	1	2	4	8	16	32	64
1	1	2	4	8	16	32	64
2	2	2	4	8	16	32	64
4	4	4	4	8	16	32	64
8	8	8	8	8	16	32	64
16	16	16	16	16	16	32	64
32	32	32	32	32	32	32	64
64	64	64	64	64	64	64	64

Quantized coefficients

150	80	20	4	1	0	0	0
92	75	18	3	1	0	0	0
26	19	13	2	1	0	0	0
3	2	2	1	0	0	0	0
1	0	0	0	0	0	0	0
0	0	0	0	0	0	0	0
0	0	0	0	0	0	0	0
0	0	0	0	0	0	0	0

Figure 7-74. Computation of the quantized DCT coefficients.

Step 4 reduces the (0, 0) value of each block (the one in the upper-left corner) by replacing it with the amount it differs from the corresponding element in the previous block. Since these elements are the averages of their respective blocks, they should change slowly, so taking the differential values should reduce most of them to small values. No differentials are computed from the other values. The (0, 0) values are referred to as the DC components; the other values are the AC components.

Step 5 linearizes the 64 elements and applies run-length encoding to the list. Scanning the block from left to right and then top to bottom will not concentrate the zeros together, so a zigzag scanning pattern is used, as shown in Fig. 7-75. In this example, the zig zag pattern produces 38 consecutive 0s at the end of the matrix. This string can be reduced to a single count saying there are 38 zeros, a technique known as **run-length encoding**.

Now we have a list of numbers that represent the image (in transform space). Step 6 Huffman-encodes the numbers for storage or transmission, assigning common numbers shorter codes that uncommon ones.

JPEG may seem complicated, but that is because it *is* complicated. Still, since it often produces a 20:1 compression or better, it is widely used. Decoding a JPEG image requires running the algorithm backward. JPEG is roughly symmetric: decoding takes as long as encoding. This property is not true of all compression algorithms, as we shall now see.

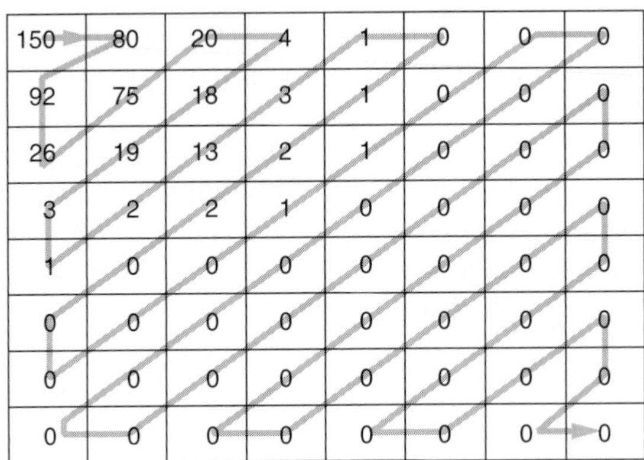

Figure 7-75. The order in which the quantized values are transmitted.

The MPEG Standard

Finally, we come to the heart of the matter: the **MPEG** (**Motion Picture Experts Group**) standards. These are the main algorithms used to compress videos and have been international standards since 1993. Because movies contain both images and sound, MPEG can compress both audio and video. We have already examined audio compression and still image compression, so let us now examine video compression.

The first standard to be finalized was MPEG-1 (International Standard 11172). Its goal was to produce video-recorder-quality output (352×240 for NTSC) using a bit rate of 1.2 Mbps. A 352×240 image with 24 bits/pixel and 25 frames/sec requires 50.7 Mbps, so getting it down to 1.2 Mbps is not entirely trivial. A factor of 40 compression is needed. MPEG-1 can be transmitted over twisted pair transmission lines for modest distances. MPEG-1 is also used for storing movies on CD-ROM.

The next standard in the MPEG family was MPEG-2 (International Standard 13818), which was originally designed for compressing broadcast-quality video into 4 to 6 Mbps, so it could fit in a NTSC or PAL broadcast channel. Later, MPEG-2 was expanded to support higher resolutions, including HDTV. It is very common now, as it forms the basis for DVD and digital satellite television.

The basic principles of MPEG-1 and MPEG-2 are similar, but the details are different. To a first approximation, MPEG-2 is a superset of MPEG-1, with additional features, frame formats, and encoding options. We will first discuss MPEG-1, then MPEG-2.

MPEG-1 has three parts: audio, video, and system, which integrates the other two, as shown in Fig. 7-76. The audio and video encoders work independently, which raises the issue of how the two streams get synchronized at the receiver.

This problem is solved by having a 90-kHz system clock that outputs the current time value to both encoders. These values are 33 bits, to allow films to run for 24 hours without wrapping around. These timestamps are included in the encoded output and propagated all the way to the receiver, which can use them to synchronize the audio and video streams.

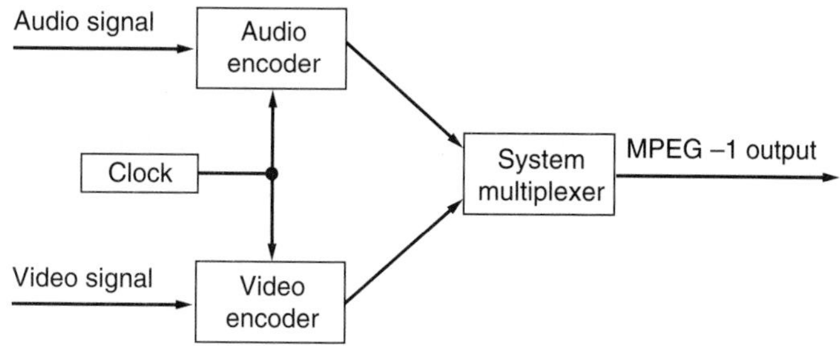

Figure 7-76. Synchronization of the audio and video streams in MPEG-1.

Now let us consider MPEG-1 video compression. Two kinds of redundancies exist in movies: spatial and temporal. MPEG-1 uses both. Spatial redundancy can be utilized by simply coding each frame separately with JPEG. This approach is occasionally used, especially when random access to each frame is needed, as in editing video productions. In this mode, a compressed bandwidth in the 8- to 10-Mbps range is achievable.

Additional compression can be achieved by taking advantage of the fact that consecutive frames are often almost identical. This effect is smaller than it might first appear since many moviemakers cut between scenes every 3 or 4 seconds (time a movie and count the scenes). Nevertheless, even a run of 75 highly similar frames offers the potential of a major reduction over simply encoding each frame separately with JPEG.

For scenes in which the camera and background are stationary and one or two actors are moving around slowly, nearly all the pixels will be identical from frame to frame. Here, just subtracting each frame from the previous one and running JPEG on the difference would do fine. However, for scenes where the camera is panning or zooming, this technique fails badly. What is needed is some way to compensate for this motion. This is precisely what MPEG does; it is the main difference between MPEG and JPEG.

MPEG-1 output consists of four kinds of frames:

1. I (Intracoded) frames: Self-contained JPEG-encoded still pictures.

2. P (Predictive) frames: Block-by-block difference with the last frame.

3. B (Bidirectional) frames: Differences between the last and next frame.

4. D (DC-coded) frames: Block averages used for fast forward.

I-frames are just still pictures coded using a variant of JPEG, also using full-resolution luminance and half-resolution chrominance along each axis. It is necessary to have I-frames appear in the output stream periodically for three reasons. First, MPEG-1 can be used for a multicast transmission, with viewers tuning it at will. If all frames depended on their predecessors going back to the first frame, anybody who missed the first frame could never decode any subsequent frames. Second, if any frame were received in error, no further decoding would be possible. Third, without I-frames, while doing a fast forward or rewind, the decoder would have to calculate every frame passed over so it would know the full value of the one it stopped on. For these reasons, I-frames are inserted into the output once or twice per second.

P-frames, in contrast, code interframe differences. They are based on the idea of **macroblocks**, which cover 16×16 pixels in luminance space and 8×8 pixels in chrominance space. A macroblock is encoded by searching the previous frame for it or something only slightly different from it.

An example of where P-frames would be useful is given in Fig. 7-77. Here we see three consecutive frames that have the same background, but differ in the position of one person. The macroblocks containing the background scene will match exactly, but the macroblocks containing the person will be offset in position by some unknown amount and will have to be tracked down.

Figure 7-77. Three consecutive frames.

The MPEG-1 standard does not specify how to search, how far to search, or how good a match has to be to count. This is up to each implementation. For example, an implementation might search for a macroblock at the current position in the previous frame, and all other positions offset $\pm\Delta x$ in the x direction and $\pm\Delta y$ in the y direction. For each position, the number of matches in the luminance matrix could be computed. The position with the highest score would be declared the winner, provided it was above some predefined threshold. Otherwise, the macroblock would be said to be missing. Much more sophisticated algorithms are also possible, of course.

If a macroblock is found, it is encoded by taking the difference with its value in the previous frame (for luminance and both chrominances). These difference matrices are then subject to the discrete cosine transformation, quantization, run-length encoding, and Huffman encoding, just as with JPEG. The value for the macroblock in the output stream is then the motion vector (how far the macroblock moved from its previous position in each direction), followed by the Huffman-encoded list of numbers. If the macroblock is not located in the previous frame, the current value is encoded with JPEG, just as in an I-frame.

Clearly, this algorithm is highly asymmetric. An implementation is free to try every plausible position in the previous frame if it wants to, in a desperate attempt to locate every last macroblock, no matter where it moved to. This approach will minimize the encoded MPEG-1 stream at the expense of very slow encoding. This approach might be fine for a one-time encoding of a film library but would be terrible for real-time videoconferencing.

Similarly, each implementation is free to decide what constitutes a "found" macroblock. This freedom allows implementers to compete on the quality and speed of their algorithms, but always produce compliant MPEG-1. No matter what search algorithm is used, the final output is either the JPEG encoding of the current macroblock or the JPEG encoding of the difference between the current macroblock and one in the previous frame at a specified offset from the current one.

So far, decoding MPEG-1 is straightforward. Decoding I-frames is the same as decoding JPEG images. Decoding P-frames requires the decoder to buffer the previous frame and then build up the new one in a second buffer based on fully encoded macroblocks and macroblocks containing differences from the previous frame. The new frame is assembled macroblock by macroblock.

B-frames are similar to P-frames, except that they allow the reference macroblock to be in either a previous frame or in a succeeding frame. This additional freedom allows improved motion compensation and is also useful when objects pass in front of, or behind, other objects. To do B-frame encoding, the encoder needs to hold three decoded frames in memory at once: the past one, the current one, and the future one. Although B-frames give the best compression, not all implementations support them.

D-frames are only used to make it possible to display a low-resolution image when doing a rewind or fast forward. Doing the normal MPEG-1 decoding in real time is difficult enough. Expecting the decoder to do it when slewing through the video at ten times normal speed is asking a bit much. Instead, the D-frames are used to produce low-resolution images. Each D-frame entry is just the average value of one block, with no further encoding, making it easy to display in real time. This facility is important to allow people to scan through a video at high speed in search of a particular scene. The D-frames are generally placed just before the corresponding I-frames so if fast forwarding is stopped, it will be possible to start viewing at normal speed.

Having finished our treatment of MPEG-1, let us now move on to MPEG-2. MPEG-2 encoding is fundamentally similar to MPEG-1 encoding, with I-frames, P-frames, and B-frames. D-frames are not supported, however. Also, the discrete cosine transformation uses a 10×10 block instead of a 8×8 block, to give 50 percent more coefficients, hence better quality. Since MPEG-2 is targeted at broadcast television as well as DVD, it supports both progressive and interlaced images, in contrast to MPEG-1, which supports only progressive images. Other minor details also differ between the two standards.

Instead of supporting only one resolution level, MPEG-2 supports four: low (352 × 240), main (720 × 480), high-1440 (1440 × 1152), and high (1920 × 1080). Low resolution is for VCRs and backward compatibility with MPEG-1. Main is the normal one for NTSC broadcasting. The other two are for HDTV. PAL uses different sizes. For high-quality output, MPEG-2 usually runs at 4–8 Mbps.

7.4.8 Video on Demand

Video on demand is sometimes compared to an electronic video rental store. The user (customer) selects any one of a large number of available videos and takes it home to view. Only with video on demand, the selection is made at home using the television set's remote control, and the video starts immediately. No trip to the store is needed. Needless to say, implementing video on demand is a wee bit more complicated than describing it. In this section, we will give an overview of the basic ideas and their implementation.

Is video on demand really like renting a video, or is it more like picking a movie to watch from a 500-channel cable system? The answer has important technical implications. In particular, video rental users are used to the idea of being able to stop a video, make a quick trip to the kitchen or bathroom, and then resume from where the video stopped. Television viewers do not expect to put programs on pause.

If video on demand is going to compete successfully with video rental stores, it may be necessary to allow users to stop, start, and rewind videos at will. Giving users this ability virtually forces the video provider to transmit a separate copy to each one.

On the other hand, if video on demand is seen more as advanced television, then it may be sufficient to have the video provider start each popular video, say, every 10 minutes, and run these nonstop. A user wanting to see a popular video may have to wait up to 10 minutes for it to start. Although pause/resume is not possible here, a viewer returning to the living room after a short break can switch to another channel showing the same video but 10 minutes behind. Some material will be repeated, but nothing will be missed. This scheme is called **near video on demand**. It offers the potential for much lower cost, because the same feed from the video server can go to many users at once. The difference between video on demand and near video on demand is similar to the difference between driving your own car and taking the bus.

Watching movies on (near) demand is but one of a vast array of potential new services possible once wideband networking is available. The general model that many people use is illustrated in Fig. 7-78. Here we see a high-bandwidth (national or international) wide area backbone network at the center of the system. Connected to it are thousands of local distribution networks, such as cable TV or telephone company distribution systems. The local distribution systems reach into people's houses, where they terminate in **set-top boxes**, which are, in fact, powerful, specialized personal computers.

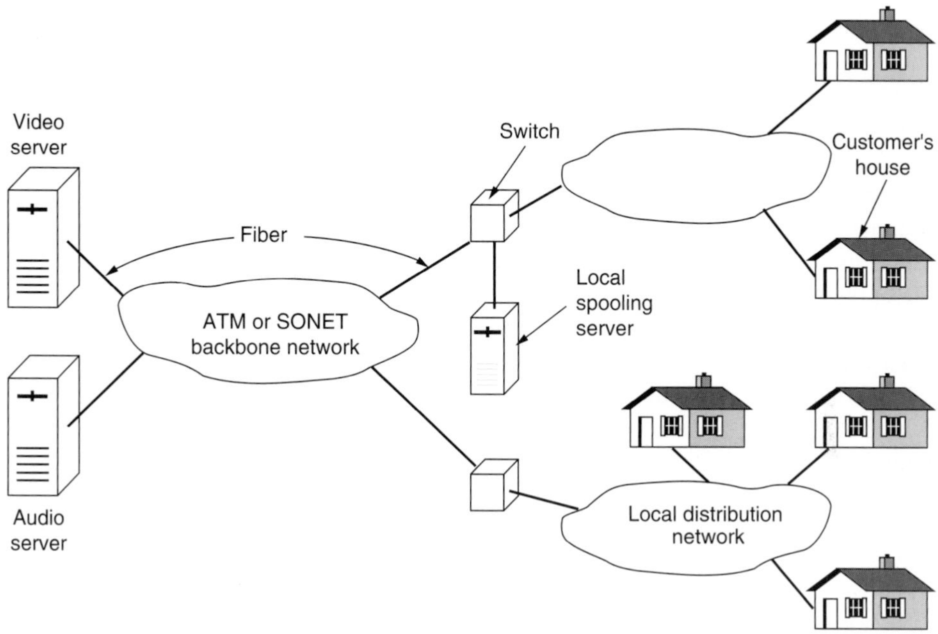

Figure 7-78. Overview of a video-on-demand system.

Attached to the backbone by high-bandwidth optical fibers are numerous information providers. Some of these will offer pay-per-view video or pay-per-hear audio CDs. Others will offer specialized services, such as home shopping (letting viewers rotate a can of soup and zoom in on the list of ingredients or view a video clip on how to drive a gasoline-powered lawn mower). Sports, news, reruns of "I Love Lucy," WWW access, and innumerable other possibilities will no doubt quickly become available.

Also included in the system are local spooling servers that allow videos to be placed closer to the users (in advance), to save bandwidth during peak hours. How these pieces will fit together and who will own what are matters of vigorous debate within the industry. Below we will examine the design of the main pieces of the system: the video servers and the distribution network.

Video Servers

To have (near) video on demand, we need **video servers** capable of storing and outputting a large number of movies simultaneously. The total number of movies ever made is estimated at 65,000 (Minoli, 1995). When compressed in MPEG-2, a normal movie occupies roughly 4 GB of storage, so 65,000 of them would require something like 260 terabytes. Add to this all the old television programs ever made, sports films, newsreels, talking shopping catalogs, etc., and it is clear that we have an industrial-strength storage problem on our hands.

The cheapest way to store large volumes of information is on magnetic tape. This has always been the case and probably always will be. An Ultrium tape can store 200 GB (50 movies) at a cost of about \$1–\$2 per movie. Large mechanical tape servers that hold thousands of tapes and have a robot arm for fetching any tape and inserting it into a tape drive are commercially available now. The problem with these systems is the access time (especially for the 50th movie on a tape), the transfer rate, and the limited number of tape drives (to serve n movies at once, the unit would need n drives).

Fortunately, experience with video rental stores, public libraries, and other such organizations shows that not all items are equally popular. Experimentally, when N movies are available, the fraction of all requests being for the kth most popular one is approximately C/k. Here C is computed to normalize the sum to 1, namely,

$$C = 1/(1 + 1/2 + 1/3 + 1/4 + 1/5 + \cdots + 1/N)$$

Thus, the most popular movie is seven times as popular as the number seven movie. This result is known as **Zipf's law** (Zipf, 1949).

The fact that some movies are much more popular than others suggests a possible solution in the form of a storage hierarchy, as shown in Fig. 7-79. Here, the performance increases as one moves up the hierarchy.

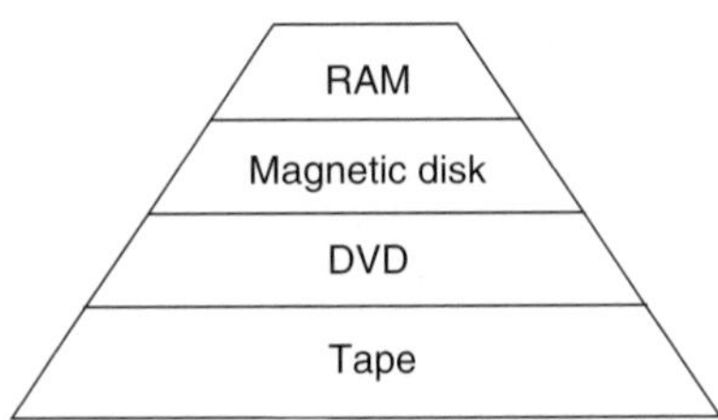

Figure 7-79. A video server storage hierarchy.

An alternative to tape is optical storage. Current DVDs hold 4.7 GB, good for one movie, but the next generation will hold two movies. Although seek times are slow compared to magnetic disks (50 msec versus 5 msec), their low cost and high reliability make optical juke boxes containing thousands of DVDs a good alternative to tape for the more heavily used movies.

Next come magnetic disks. These have short access times (5 msec), high transfer rates (320 MB/sec for SCSI 320), and substantial capacities (> 100 GB), which makes them well suited to holding movies that are actually being transmitted (as opposed to just being stored in case somebody ever wants them). Their main drawback is the high cost for storing movies that are rarely accessed.

At the top of the pyramid of Fig. 7-79 is RAM. RAM is the fastest storage medium, but also the most expensive. When RAM prices drop to $50/GB, a 4-GB movie will occupy $200 worth of RAM, so having 100 movies in RAM will cost $20,000 for the 200 GB of memory. Still, for a video server feeding out 100 movies, just keeping all the movies in RAM is beginning to look feasible. And if the video server has 100 customers but they are collectively watching only 20 different movies, it begins to look not only feasible, but a good design.

Since a video server is really just a massive real-time I/O device, it needs a different hardware and software architecture than a PC or a UNIX workstation. The hardware architecture of a typical video server is illustrated in Fig. 7-80. The server has one or more high-performance CPUs, each with some local memory, a shared main memory, a massive RAM cache for popular movies, a variety of storage devices for holding the movies, and some networking hardware, normally an optical interface to a SONET or ATM backbone at OC-12 or higher. These subsystems are connected by an extremely high speed bus (at least 1 GB/sec).

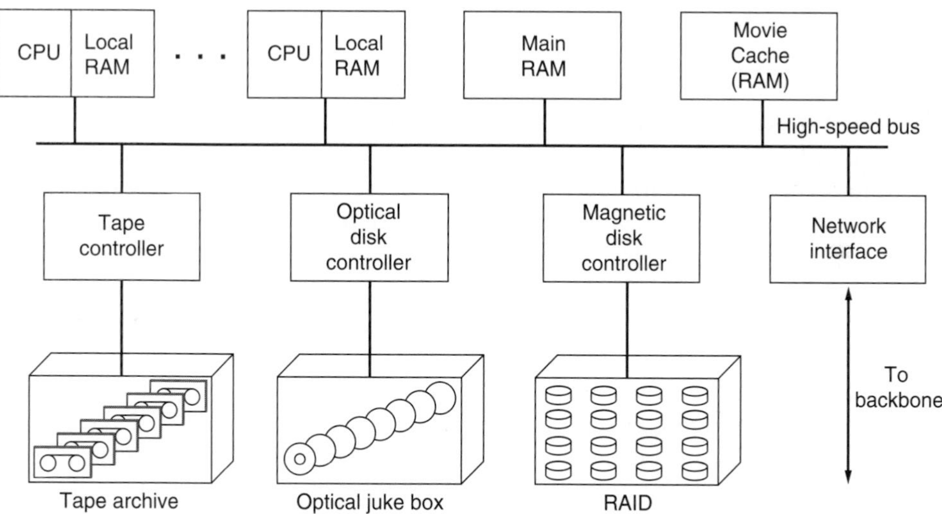

Figure 7-80. The hardware architecture of a typical video server.

Now let us take a brief look at video server software. The CPUs are used for accepting user requests, locating movies, moving data between devices, customer billing, and many other functions. Some of these are not time critical, but many others are, so some, if not all, the CPUs will have to run a real-time operating system, such as a real-time microkernel. These systems normally break work up into small tasks, each with a known deadline. The scheduler can then run an algorithm such as nearest deadline next or the rate monotonic algorithm (Liu and Layland, 1973).

The CPU software also defines the nature of the interface that the server presents to the clients (spooling servers and set-top boxes). Two designs are popular. The first one is a traditional file system, in which the clients can open, read, write, and close files. Other than the complications introduced by the storage hierarchy and real-time considerations, such a server can have a file system modeled after that of UNIX.

The second kind of interface is based on the video recorder model. The commands to the server request it to open, play, pause, fast forward, and rewind files. The difference with the UNIX model is that once a *PLAY* command is given, the server just keeps pumping out data at a constant rate, with no new commands required.

The heart of the video server software is the disk management software. It has two main jobs: placing movies on the magnetic disk when they have to be pulled up from optical or tape storage, and handling disk requests for the many output streams. Movie placement is important because it can greatly affect performance.

Two possible ways of organizing disk storage are the disk farm and the disk array. With the **disk farm**, each drive holds some number of entire movies. For performance and reliability reasons, each movie should be present on at least two drives, maybe more. The other storage organization is the **disk array** or **RAID** (**Redundant Array of Inexpensive Disks**), in which each movie is spread out over multiple drives, for example, block 0 on drive 0, block 1 on drive 1, and so on, with block $n - 1$ on drive $n - 1$. After that, the cycle repeats, with block n on drive 0, and so forth. This organizing is called **striping**.

A striped disk array has several advantages over a disk farm. First, all n drives can be running in parallel, increasing the performance by a factor of n. Second, it can be made redundant by adding an extra drive to each group of n, where the redundant drive contains the block-by-block exclusive OR of the other drives, to allow full data recovery in the event one drive fails. Finally, the problem of load balancing is solved (manual placement is not needed to avoid having all the popular movies on the same drive). On the other hand, the disk array organization is more complicated than the disk farm and highly sensitive to multiple failures. It is also ill-suited to video recorder operations such as rewinding or fast forwarding a movie.

The other job of the disk software is to service all the real-time output streams and meet their timing constraints. Only a few years ago, this required complex disk scheduling algorithms, but with memory prices so low now, a much simpler approach is beginning to be possible. For each stream being served, a buffer of, say, 10 sec worth of video (5 MB) is kept in RAM. It is filled by a disk process and emptied by a network process. With 500 MB of RAM, 100 streams can be fed directly from RAM. Of course, the disk subsystem must have a sustained data rate of 50 MB/sec to keep the buffers full, but a RAID built from high-end SCSI disks can handle this requirement easily.

The Distribution Network

The distribution network is the set of switches and lines between the source and destination. As we saw in Fig. 7-78, it consists of a backbone, connected to a local distribution network. Usually, the backbone is switched and the local distribution network is not.

The main requirement imposed on the backbone is high bandwidth. It used to be that low jitter was also a requirement, but with even the smallest PC now able to buffer 10 sec of high-quality MPEG-2 video, low jitter is not a requirement anymore.

Local distribution is highly chaotic, with different companies trying out different networks in different regions. Telephone companies, cable TV companies, and new entrants, such as power companies, are all convinced that whoever gets there first will be the big winner. Consequently, we are now seeing a proliferation of technologies being installed. In Japan, some sewer companies are in the Internet business, arguing that they have the biggest pipe of all into everyone's house (they run an optical fiber through it, but have to be very careful about precisely where it emerges). The four main local distribution schemes for video on demand go by the acronyms ADSL, FTTC, FTTH, and HFC. We will now explain each of these in turn.

ADSL is the first telephone industry's entrant in the local distribution sweepstakes. We studied ADSL in Chap. 2 and will not repeat that material here. The idea is that virtually every house in the United States, Europe, and Japan already has a copper twisted pair going into it (for analog telephone service). If these wires could be used for video on demand, the telephone companies could clean up.

The problem, of course, is that these wires cannot support even MPEG-1 over their typical 10-km length, let alone MPEG-2. High-resolution, full-color, full motion video needs 4–8 Mbps, depending on the quality desired. ADSL is not really fast enough except for very short local loops.

The second telephone company design is **FTTC** (**Fiber To The Curb**). In FTTC, the telephone company runs optical fiber from the end office into each residential neighborhood, terminating in a device called an **ONU** (**Optical Network Unit**). On the order of 16 copper local loops can terminate in an ONU. These loops are now so short that it is possible to run full-duplex T1 or T2 over them, allowing MPEG-1 and MPEG-2 movies, respectively. In addition, videoconferencing for home workers and small businesses is now possible because FTTC is symmetric.

The third telephone company solution is to run fiber into everyone's house. It is called **FTTH** (**Fiber To The Home**). In this scheme, everyone can have an OC-1, OC-3, or even higher carrier if that is required. FTTH is very expensive and will not happen for years but clearly will open a vast range of new possibilities when it finally happens. In Fig. 7-63 we saw how everybody could operate his or her own radio station. What do you think about each member of the family operating his or her own personal television station? ADSL, FTTC, and FTTH are all point-to-point local distribution networks, which is not surprising given how the current telephone system is organized.

A completely different approach is **HFC** (**Hybrid Fiber Coax**), which is the preferred solution currently being installed by cable TV providers. It is illustrated in Fig. 2-47(a). The story goes something like this. The current 300- to 450-MHz coax cables are being replaced by 750-MHz coax cables, upgrading the capacity from 50 to 75 6-MHz channels to 125 6-MHz channels. Seventy-five of the 125 channels will be used for transmitting analog television.

The 50 new channels will each be modulated using QAM-256, which provides about 40 Mbps per channel, giving a total of 2 Gbps of new bandwidth. The headends will be moved deeper into the neighborhoods so that each cable runs past only 500 houses. Simple division shows that each house can then be allocated a dedicated 4-Mbps channel, which can handle an MPEG-2 movie.

While this sounds wonderful, it does require the cable providers to replace all the existing cables with 750-MHz coax, install new headends, and remove all the one-way amplifiers—in short, replace the entire cable TV system. Consequently, the amount of new infrastructure here is comparable to what the telephone companies need for FTTC. In both cases the local network provider has to run fiber into residential neighborhoods. Again, in both cases, the fiber terminates at an optoelectrical converter. In FTTC, the final segment is a point-to-point local loop using twisted pairs. In HFC, the final segment is a shared coaxial cable. Technically, these two systems are not really as different as their respective proponents often make out.

Nevertheless, there is one real difference that is worth pointing out. HFC uses a shared medium without switching and routing. Any information put onto the cable can be removed by any subscriber without further ado. FTTC, which is fully switched, does not have this property. As a result, HFC operators want video servers to send out encrypted streams so customers who have not paid for a movie cannot see it. FTTC operators do not especially want encryption because it adds complexity, lowers performance, and provides no additional security in their system. From the point of view of the company running a video server, is it a good idea to encrypt or not? A server operated by a telephone company or one of its subsidiaries or partners might intentionally decide not to encrypt its videos, claiming efficiency as the reason but really to cause economic losses to its HFC competitors.

For all these local distribution networks, it is possible that each neighborhood will be outfitted with one or more spooling servers. These are, in fact, just smaller versions of the video servers we discussed above. The big advantage of these local servers is that they move some load off the backbone.

They can be preloaded with movies by reservation. If people tell the provider which movies they want well in advance, they can be downloaded to the local server during off-peak hours. This observation is likely to lead the network operators to lure away airline executives to do their pricing. One can envision tariffs in which movies ordered 24 to 72 hours in advance for viewing on a Tuesday or Thursday evening before 6 P.M, or after 11 P.M. get a 27 percent discount. Movies ordered on the first Sunday of the month before 8 A.M. for viewing on a Wednesday afternoon on a day whose date is a prime number get a 43 percent discount, and so on.

7.4.9 The MBone—The Multicast Backbone

While all these industries are making great—and highly publicized—plans for future (inter)national digital video on demand, the Internet community has been quietly implementing its own digital multimedia system, **MBone** (**Multicast Backbone**). In this section we will give a brief overview of what it is and how it works.

MBone can be thought of as Internet television. Unlike video on demand, where the emphasis is on calling up and viewing precompressed movies stored on a server, MBone is used for broadcasting live video in digital form all over the world via the Internet. It has been operational since early 1992. Many scientific conferences, especially IETF meetings, have been broadcast, as well as newsworthy scientific events, such as space shuttle launches. A Rolling Stones concert was once broadcast over MBone as were portions of the Cannes Film Festival. Whether this qualifies as a newsworthy scientific event is arguable.

Technically, MBone is a virtual overlay network on top of the Internet. It consists of multicast-capable islands connected by tunnels, as shown in Fig. 7-81. In this figure, MBone consists of six islands, *A* through *F*, connected by seven tunnels. Each island (typically a LAN or group of interconnected LANs) supports hardware multicast to its hosts. The tunnels propagate MBone packets between the islands. Some day in the future, when all the routers are capable of handling multicast traffic directly, this superstructure will no longer be needed, but for the moment, it does the job.

Each island contains one or more special routers called **mrouters** (**multicast routers**). Some of these are actually normal routers, but most are just UNIX workstations running special user-level software (but as the root). The mrouters

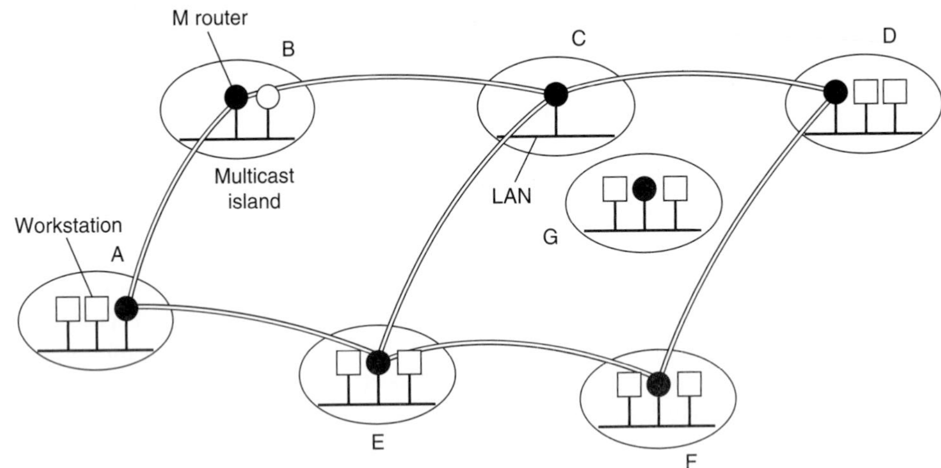

Figure 7-81. MBone consists of multicast islands connected by tunnels.

are logically connected by tunnels. MBone packets are encapsulated within IP packets and sent as regular unicast packets to the destination mrouter's IP address.

Tunnels are configured manually. Usually, a tunnel runs above a path for which a physical connection exists, but this is not a requirement. If, by accident, the physical path underlying a tunnel goes down, the mrouters using the tunnel will not even notice it, since the Internet will automatically reroute all the IP traffic between them via other lines.

When a new island appears and wishes to join MBone, such as *G* in Fig. 7-81, its administrator sends a message announcing its existence to the MBone mailing list. The administrators of nearby sites then contact him to arrange to set up tunnels. Sometimes existing tunnels are reshuffled to take advantage of the new island to optimize the topology. After all, tunnels have no physical existence. They are defined by tables in the mrouters and can be added, deleted, or moved simply by changing these tables. Typically, each country on MBone has a backbone, with regional islands attached to it. Normally, MBone is configured with one or two tunnels crossing the Atlantic and Pacific oceans, making MBone global in scale.

Thus, at any instant, MBone consists of a specific topology consisting of islands and tunnels, independent of the number of multicast addresses currently in use and who is listening to them or watching them. This situation is very similar to a normal (physical) subnet, so the normal routing algorithms apply to it. Consequently, MBone initially used a routing algorithm, **DVMRP** (**Distance Vector Multicast Routing Protocol**) based on the Bellman-Ford distance vector algorithm. For example, in Fig. 7-81, island *C* can route to *A* either via *B* or via *E* (or conceivably via *D*). It makes its choice by taking the values those nodes give it about their respective distances to *A* and then adding its distance to them. In this way, every island determines the best route to every other island. The routes are not actually used in this way, however, as we will see shortly.

Now let us consider how multicasting actually happens. To multicast an audio or video program, a source must first acquire a class D multicast address, which acts like a station frequency or channel number. Class D addresses are reserved by a program that looks in a database for free multicast addresses. Many multicasts may be going on at once, and a host can "tune" to the one it is interested in by listening to the appropriate multicast address.

Periodically, each mrouter sends out an IGMP broadcast packet limited to its island asking who is interested in which channel. Hosts wishing to (continue to) receive one or more channels send another IGMP packet back in response. These responses are staggered in time, to avoid overloading the local LAN. Each mrouter keeps a table of which channels it must put out onto its LAN, to avoid wasting bandwidth by multicasting channels that nobody wants.

Multicasts propagate through MBone as follows. When an audio or video source generates a new packet, it multicasts it to its local island, using the hardware multicast facility. This packet is picked up by the local mrouter, which then copies it into all the tunnels to which it is connected.

Each mrouter getting such a packet via a tunnel then checks to see if the packet came along the best route, that is, the route that its table says to use to reach the source (as if it were a destination). If the packet came along the best route, the mrouter copies the packet to all its other tunnels. If the packet arrived via a suboptimal route, it is discarded. Thus, for example, in Fig. 7-81, if *C*'s tables tell it to use *B* to get to *A*, then when a multicast packet from *A* reaches *C* via *B*, the packet is copied to *D* and *E*. However, when a multicast packet from *A* reaches *C* via *E* (not the best path), it is simply discarded. This algorithm is just the reverse path forwarding algorithm that we saw in Chap. 5. While not perfect, it is fairly good and very simple to implement.

In addition to using reverse path forwarding to prevent flooding the Internet, the IP *Time to live* field is also used to limit the scope of multicasting. Each packet starts out with some value (determined by the source). Each tunnel is assigned a weight. A packet is passed through a tunnel only if it has enough weight. Otherwise it is discarded. For example, transoceanic tunnels are normally configured with a weight of 128, so packets can be limited to the continent of origin by being given an initial *Time to live* of 127 or less. After passing through a tunnel, the *Time to live* field is decremented by the tunnel's weight.

While the MBone routing algorithm works, much research has been devoted to improving it. One proposal keeps the idea of distance vector routing, but makes the algorithm hierarchical by grouping MBone sites into regions and first routing to them (Thyagarajan and Deering, 1995).

Another proposal is to use a modified form of link state routing instead of distance vector routing. In particular, an IETF working group modified OSPF to make it suitable for multicasting within a single autonomous system. The resulting multicast OSPF is called **MOSPF** (Moy, 1994). What the modifications do is have the full map built by MOSPF keep track of multicast islands and tunnels, in addition to the usual routing information. Armed with the complete topology, it is straightforward to compute the best path from every island to every other island using the tunnels. Dijkstra's algorithm can be used, for example.

A second area of research is inter-AS routing. Here an algorithm called **PIM** (**Protocol Independent Multicast**) was developed by another IETF working group. PIM comes in two versions, depending on whether the islands are dense (almost everyone wants to watch) or sparse (almost nobody wants to watch). Both versions use the standard unicast routing tables, instead of creating an overlay topology as DVMRP and MOSPF do.

In PIM-DM (dense mode), the idea is to prune useless paths. Pruning works as follows. When a multicast packet arrives via the "wrong" tunnel, a prune packet is sent back through the tunnel telling the sender to stop sending it packets from the source in question. When a packet arrives via the "right" tunnel, it is copied to all the other tunnels that have not previously pruned themselves. If all the other tunnels have pruned themselves and there is no interest in the channel within the local island, the mrouter sends a prune message back through the "right" channel. In this way, the multicast adapts automatically and only goes where it is wanted.

PIM-SM (spare mode), described in RFC 2362, works differently. The idea here is to prevent saturating the Internet because three people in Berkeley want to hold a conference call over a class D address. PIM-SM works by setting up rendezvous points. Each of the sources in a PIM-SM multicast group send their packets to the rendezvous points. Any site interested in joining up asks one of the rendezvous points to set up a tunnel to it. In this way, all PIM-SM traffic is transported by unicast instead of by multicast. PIM-SM is becoming more popular, and the MBone is migrating toward its use. As PIM-SM becomes more widely used, MOSPF is gradually disappearing. On the other hand, the MBone itself seems to be somewhat stagnant and will probably never catch on in a big way.

Nevertheless, networked multimedia is still an exciting and rapidly moving field, even if the MBone does not become a huge success. New technologies and applications are announced daily. Increasingly, multicasting and quality of service are coming together, as discussed in (Striegel and Manimaran, 2002). Another hot topic is wireless multicast (Gossain et al., 2002). The whole area of multicasting and everything related to it are likely to remain important for years to come.

7.5 SUMMARY

Naming in the Internet uses a hierarchical scheme called the domain name system (DNS). At the top level are the well-known generic domains, including *com* and *edu* as well as about 200 country domains. DNS is implemented as a distributed database system with servers all over the world. DNS holds records with IP addresses, mail exchanges, and other information. By querying a DNS server, a process can map an Internet domain name onto the IP address used to communicate with that domain.

E-mail is one of the two killer apps for the Internet. Everyone from small children to grandparents now use it. Most e-mail systems in the world use the mail system now defined in RFCs 2821 and 2822. Messages sent in this system use system ASCII headers to define message properties. Many kinds of content can be sent using MIME. Messages are sent using SMTP, which works by making a TCP connection from the source host to the destination host and directly delivering the e-mail over the TCP connection.

The other killer app for the Internet is the World Wide Web. The Web is a system for linking hypertext documents. Originally, each document was a page written in HTML with hyperlinks to other documents. Nowadays, XML is gradually starting to take over from HTML. Also, a large amount of content is dynamically generated, using server-side scripts (PHP, JSP, and ASP), as well as client-side scripts (notably JavaScript). A browser can display a document by establishing a TCP connection to its server, asking for the document, and then closing the connection. These request messages contain a variety of headers for providing additional information. Caching, replication, and content delivery networks are widely used to enhance Web performance.

The wireless Web is just getting started. The first systems are WAP and i-mode, each with small screens and limited bandwidth, but the next generation will be more powerful.

Multimedia is also a rising star in the networking firmament. It allows audio and video to be digitized and transported electronically for display. Audio requires less bandwidth, so it is further along. Streaming audio, Internet radio, and voice over IP are a reality now, with new applications coming along all the time. Video on demand is an up-and-coming area in which there is great interest. Finally, the MBone is an experimental, worldwide digital live television service sent over the Internet.

PROBLEMS

1. Many business computers have three distinct and worldwide unique identifiers. What are they?

2. According to the information given in Fig. 7-3, is *little-sister.cs.vu.nl* on a class A, B, or C network?

3. In Fig. 7-3, there is no period after *rowboat*? Why not?

4. Make a guess about what the smiley :-X (sometimes written as :-#) might mean.

5. DNS uses UDP instead of TCP. If a DNS packet is lost, there is no automatic recovery. Does this cause a problem, and if so, how is it solved?

6. In addition to being subject to loss, UDP packets have a maximum length, potentially as low as 576 bytes. What happens when a DNS name to be looked up exceeds this length? Can it be sent in two packets?

7. Can a machine with a single DNS name have multiple IP addresses? How could this occur?

8. Can a computer have two DNS names that fall in different top-level domains? If so, give a plausible example. If not, explain why not.

9. The number of companies with a Web site has grown explosively in recent years. As a result, thousands of companies are registered in the *com* domain, causing a heavy load on the top-level server for this domain. Suggest a way to alleviate this problem without changing the naming scheme (i.e., without introducing new top-level domain names). It is permitted that your solution requires changes to the client code.

10. Some e-mail systems support a header field *Content Return:*. It specifies whether the body of a message is to be returned in the event of nondelivery. Does this field belong to the envelope or to the header?

11. Electronic mail systems need directories so people's e-mail addresses can be looked up. To build such directories, names should be broken up into standard components (e.g., first name, last name) to make searching possible. Discuss some problems that must be solved for a worldwide standard to be acceptable.

12. A person's e-mail address is his or her login name @ the name of a DNS domain with an *MX* record. Login names can be first names, last names, initials, and all kinds of other names. Suppose that a large company decided too much e-mail was getting lost because people did not know the login name of the recipient. Is there a way for them to fix this problem without changing DNS? If so, give a proposal and explain how it works. If not, explain why it is impossible.

13. A binary file is 3072 bytes long. How long will it be if encoded using base64 encoding, with a CR+LF pair inserted after every 80 bytes sent and at the end?

14. Consider the quoted-printable MIME encoding scheme. Mention a problem not discussed in the text and propose a solution.

15. Name five MIME types not listed in the book. You can check your browser or the Internet for information.

16. Suppose that you want to send an MP3 file to a friend, but your friend's ISP limits the amount of incoming mail to 1 MB and the MP3 file is 4 MB. Is there a way to handle this situation by using RFC 822 and MIME?

17. Suppose that someone sets up a vacation daemon and then sends a message just before logging out. Unfortunately, the recipient has been on vacation for a week and also has a vacation daemon in place. What happens next? Will canned replies go back and forth until somebody returns?

18. In any standard, such as RFC 822, a precise grammar of what is allowed is needed so that different implementations can interwork. Even simple items have to be defined carefully. The SMTP headers allow white space between the tokens. Give *two* plausible alternative definitions of white space between tokens.

19. Is the vacation daemon part of the user agent or the message transfer agent? Of course, it is set up using the user agent, but does the user agent actually send the replies? Explain your answer.

20. POP3 allows users to fetch and download e-mail from a remote mailbox. Does this mean that the internal format of mailboxes has to be standardized so any POP3 program on the client side can read the mailbox on any mail server? Discuss your answer.

21. From an ISP's point of view, POP3 and IMAP differ in an important way. POP3 users generally empty their mailboxes every day. IMAP users keep their mail on the server indefinitely. Imagine that you were called in to advise an ISP on which protocol it should support. What considerations would you bring up?

22. Does Webmail use POP3, IMAP, or neither? If one of these, why was that one chosen? If neither, which one is it closer to in spirit?

23. When Web pages are sent out, they are prefixed by MIME headers. Why?

24. When are external viewers needed? How does a browser know which one to use?

25. Is it possible that when a user clicks on a link with Netscape, a particular helper is started, but clicking on the same link in Internet Explorer causes a completely different helper to be started, even though the MIME type returned in both cases is identical? Explain your answer.

26. A multithreaded Web server is organized as shown in Fig. 7-21. It takes 500 μsec to accept a request and check the cache. Half the time the file is found in the cache and returned immediately. The other half of the time the module has to block for 9 msec while its disk request is queued and processed. How many modules should the server have to keep the CPU busy all the time (assuming the disk is not a bottleneck)?

27. The standard *http* URL assumes that the Web server is listening on port 80. However, it is possible for a Web server to listen to some other port. Devise a reasonable syntax for a URL accessing a file on a nonstandard port.

28. Although it was not mentioned in the text, an alternative form for a URL is to use the IP address instead of its DNS name. An example of using an IP address is *http://192.31.231.66/index.html*. How does the browser know whether the name following the scheme is a DNS name or an IP address?

29. Imagine that someone in the CS Department at Stanford has just written a new program that he wants to distribute by FTP. He puts the program in the FTP directory *ftp/pub/freebies/newprog.c*. What is the URL for this program likely to be?

30. In Fig. 7-25, *www.aportal.com* keeps track of user preferences in a cookie. A disadvantage of this scheme is that cookies are limited to 4 KB, so if the preferences are extensive, for example, many stocks, sports teams, types of news stories, weather for multiple cities, specials in numerous product categories, and more, the 4-KB limit may be reached. Design an alternative way to keep track of preferences that does not have this problem.

31. Sloth Bank wants to make on-line banking easy for its lazy customers, so after a customer signs up and is authenticated by a password, the bank returns a cookie containing a customer ID number. In this way, the customer does not have to identify himself or type a password on future visits to the on-line bank. What do you think of this idea? Will it work? Is it a good idea?

32. In Fig. 7-26, the *ALT* parameter is set in the <img> tag. Under what conditions does the browser use it, and how?

33. How do you make an image clickable in HTML? Give an example.

34. Show the <a> tag that is needed to make the string "ACM" be a hyperlink to *http://www.acm.org*.

35. Design a form for a new company, Interburger, that allows hamburgers to be ordered via the Internet. The form should include the customer's name, address, and city, as well as a choice of size (either gigantic or immense) and a cheese option. The burgers are to be paid for in cash upon delivery, so no credit card information is needed.

36. Design a form that requests the user to type in two numbers. When the user clicks on the submit button, the server returns their sum. Write the server side as a PHP script.

37. For each of the following applications, tell whether it would be (1) possible and (2) better to use a PHP script or JavaScript and why.
(a) Displaying a calendar for any requested month since September 1752.
(b) Displaying the schedule of flights from Amsterdam to New York.
(c) Graphing a polynomial from user-supplied coefficients

38. Write a program in JavaScript that accepts an integer greater than 2 and tells whether it is a prime number. Note that JavaScript has if and while statements with the same syntax as C and Java. The modulo operator is %. If you need the square root of x, use *Math.sqrt* (x).

39. An HTML page is as follows:

```
<html> <body>
<a href="www.info-source.com/welcome.html"> Click here for info </a>
</body> </html>
```

If the user clicks on the hyperlink, a TCP connection is opened and a series of lines is sent to the server. List all the lines sent.

40. The *If-Modified-Since* header can be used to check whether a cached page is still valid. Requests can be made for pages containing images, sound, video, and so on, as well as HTML. Do you think the effectiveness of this technique is better or worse for JPEG images as compared to HTML? Think carefully about what "effectiveness" means and explain your answer.

41. On the day of a major sporting event, such as the championship game in some popular sport, many people go to the official Web site. Is this a flash crowd in the same sense as the Florida election in 2000? Why or why not?

42. Does it make sense for a single ISP to function as a CDN? If so, how would that work? If not, what is wrong with the idea?

43. Under what conditions is using a CDN a bad idea?

44. Wireless Web terminals have low bandwidth, which makes efficient coding important. Devise a scheme for transmitting English text efficiently over a wireless link to a WAP device. You may assume that the terminal has several megabytes of ROM and a moderately powerful CPU. *Hint*: think about how you transmit Japanese, in which each symbol is a word.

45. A compact disc holds 650 MB of data. Is compression used for audio CDs? Explain your reasoning.

46. In Fig. 7-57(c) quantization noise occurs due to the use of 4-bit samples to represent nine signal values. The first sample, at 0, is exact, but the next few are not. What is the percent error for the samples at 1/32, 2/32, and 3/32 of the period?

47. Could a psychoacoustic model be used to reduce the bandwidth needed for Internet telephony? If so, what conditions, if any, would have to be met to make it work? If not, why not?

48. An audio streaming server has a one-way distance of 50 msec with a media player. It outputs at 1 Mbps. If the media player has a 1-MB buffer, what can you say about the position of the low-water mark and the high-water mark?

49. The interleaving algorithm of Fig. 7-60 has the advantage of being able to survive an occasional lost packet without introducing a gap in the playback. However, when used for Internet telephony, it also has a small disadvantage. What is it?

50. Does voice over IP have the same problems with firewalls that streaming audio does? Discuss your answer.

51. What is the bit rate for transmitting uncompressed 800×600 pixel color frames with 8 bits/pixel at 40 frames/sec?

52. Can a 1-bit error in an MPEG frame affect more than the frame in which the error occurs? Explain your answer.

53. Consider a 100,000-customer video server, where each customer watches two movies per month. Half the movies are served at 8 P.M. How many movies does the server have to transmit at once during this time period? If each movie requires 4 Mbps, how many OC-12 connections does the server need to the network?

54. Suppose that Zipf's law holds for accesses to a 10,000-movie video server. If the server holds the most popular 1000 movies on magnetic disk and the remaining 9000 on optical disk, give an expression for the fraction of all references that will be to magnetic disk. Write a little program to evaluate this expression numerically.

55. Some cybersquatters have registered domain names that are misspellings of common corporate sites, for example, *www.microsfot.com*. Make a list of at least five such domains.

56. Numerous people have registered DNS names that consist of a *www.word.com* where *word* is a common word. For each of the following categories, list five Web sites and briefly summarize what it is (e.g., *www.stomach.com* is a gastroenterologist on Long Island). Here is the list of categories: animals, foods, household objects, and body parts. For the last category, please stick to body parts above the waist.

57. Design some emoji of your own using a 12×12 bit map. Include boyfriend, girlfriend, professor, and politician.

58. Write a POP3 server that accepts the following commands: *USER*, *PASS*, *LIST*, *RETR*, *DELE*, and *QUIT*.

59. Rewrite the server of Fig. 6-6 as a true Web server using the *GET* command for HTTP 1.1. It should also accept the *Host* message. The server should maintain a cache of files recently fetched from the disk and serve requests from the cache when possible.

8

NETWORK SECURITY

For the first few decades of their existence, computer networks were primarily used by university researchers for sending e-mail and by corporate employees for sharing printers. Under these conditions, security did not get a lot of attention. But now, as millions of ordinary citizens are using networks for banking, shopping, and filing their tax returns, network security is looming on the horizon as a potentially massive problem. In this chapter, we will study network security from several angles, point out numerous pitfalls, and discuss many algorithms and protocols for making networks more secure.

Security is a broad topic and covers a multitude of sins. In its simplest form, it is concerned with making sure that nosy people cannot read, or worse yet, secretly modify messages intended for other recipients. It is concerned with people trying to access remote services that they are not authorized to use. It also deals with ways to tell whether that message purportedly from the IRS saying: Pay by Friday or else is really from the IRS and not from the Mafia. Security also deals with the problems of legitimate messages being captured and replayed, and with people trying to deny that they sent certain messages.

Most security problems are intentionally caused by malicious people trying to gain some benefit, get attention, or to harm someone. A few of the most common perpetrators are listed in Fig. 8-1. It should be clear from this list that making a network secure involves a lot more than just keeping it free of programming errors. It involves outsmarting often intelligent, dedicated, and sometimes well-funded adversaries. It should also be clear that measures that will thwart casual adversaries will have little impact on the serious ones. Police records show that most attacks are not perpetrated by outsiders tapping a phone line but by insiders with a grudge. Consequently, security systems should be designed with this fact in mind.

Adversary	Goal
Student	To have fun snooping on people's e-mail
Cracker	To test out someone's security system; steal data
Sales rep	To claim to represent all of Europe, not just Andorra
Businessman	To discover a competitor's strategic marketing plan
Ex-employee	To get revenge for being fired
Accountant	To embezzle money from a company
Stockbroker	To deny a promise made to a customer by e-mail
Con man	To steal credit card numbers for sale
Spy	To learn an enemy's military or industrial secrets
Terrorist	To steal germ warfare secrets

Figure 8-1. Some people who cause security problems and why.

Network security problems can be divided roughly into four closely intertwined areas: secrecy, authentication, nonrepudiation, and integrity control. Secrecy, also called confidentiality, has to do with keeping information out of the hands of unauthorized users. This is what usually comes to mind when people think about network security. Authentication deals with determining whom you are talking to before revealing sensitive information or entering into a business deal. Nonrepudiation deals with signatures: How do you prove that your customer really placed an electronic order for ten million left-handed doohickeys at 89 cents each when he later claims the price was 69 cents? Or maybe he claims he never placed any order. Finally, how can you be sure that a message you received was really the one sent and not something that a malicious adversary modified in transit or concocted?

All these issues (secrecy, authentication, nonrepudiation, and integrity control) occur in traditional systems, too, but with some significant differences. Integrity and secrecy are achieved by using registered mail and locking documents up. Robbing the mail train is harder now than it was in Jesse James' day.

Also, people can usually tell the difference between an original paper document and a photocopy, and it often matters to them. As a test, make a photocopy of a valid check. Try cashing the original check at your bank on Monday. Now try cashing the photocopy of the check on Tuesday. Observe the difference in the bank's behavior. With electronic checks, the original and the copy are indistinguishable. It may take a while for banks to learn how to handle this.

People authenticate other people by recognizing their faces, voices, and handwriting. Proof of signing is handled by signatures on letterhead paper, raised seals, and so on. Tampering can usually be detected by handwriting, ink, and paper experts. None of these options are available electronically. Clearly, other solutions are needed.

Before getting into the solutions themselves, it is worth spending a few moments considering where in the protocol stack network security belongs. There is probably no one single place. Every layer has something to contribute. In the physical layer, wiretapping can be foiled by enclosing transmission lines in sealed tubes containing gas at high pressure. Any attempt to drill into a tube will release some gas, reducing the pressure and triggering an alarm. Some military systems use this technique.

In the data link layer, packets on a point-to-point line can be encrypted as they leave one machine and decrypted as they enter another. All the details can be handled in the data link layer, with higher layers oblivious to what is going on. This solution breaks down when packets have to traverse multiple routers, however, because packets have to be decrypted at each router, leaving them vulnerable to attacks from within the router. Also, it does not allow some sessions to be protected (e.g., those involving on-line purchases by credit card) and others not. Nevertheless, **link encryption**, as this method is called, can be added to any network easily and is often useful.

In the network layer, firewalls can be installed to keep good packets and bad packets out. IP security also functions in this layer.

In the transport layer, entire connections can be encrypted, end to end, that is, process to process. For maximum security, end-to-end security is required.

Finally, issues such as user authentication and nonrepudiation can only be handled in the application layer.

Since security does not fit neatly into any layer, it does not fit into any chapter of this book. For this reason, it rates its own chapter.

While this chapter is long, technical, and essential, and it is also quasi-irrelevant for the moment. It is well documented that most security failures at banks, for example, are due to incompetent employees, lax security procedures, or insider fraud, rather than clever criminals tapping phone lines and then decoding encrypted messages. If a person can walk into a random branch of a bank with an ATM slip he found on the street claiming to have forgotten his PIN and get a new one on the spot (in the name of good customer relations), all the cryptography in the world will not prevent abuse. In this respect, Ross Anderson's book is a real eye-opener, as it documents hundreds of examples of security failures in numerous industries, nearly all of them due to what might politely be called sloppy business practices or inattention to security (Anderson, 2001). Nevertheless, we are optimistic that as e-commerce becomes more widespread, companies will eventually debug their operational procedures, eliminating this loophole and bringing the technical aspects of security to center stage again.

Except for physical layer security, nearly all security is based on cryptographic principles. For this reason, we will begin our study of security by examining cryptography in some detail. In Sec. 8.1, we will look at some of the basic principles. In Sec. 8-2 through Sec. 8-5, we will examine some of the fundamental algorithms and data structures used in cryptography. Then we will examine in detail how these concepts can be used to achieve security in networks. We will conclude with some brief thoughts about technology and society.

Before starting, one last thought is in order: what is not covered. We have tried to focus on networking issues, rather than operating system and application issues, although the line is often hard to draw. For example, there is nothing here about user authentication using biometrics, password security, buffer overflow attacks, Trojan horses, login spoofing, logic bombs, viruses, worms, and the like. All of these topics are covered at great length in Chap. 9 of *Modern Operating Systems* (Tanenbaum, 2001). The interested reader is referred to that book for the systems aspects of security. Now let us begin our journey.

8.1 CRYPTOGRAPHY

Cryptography comes from the Greek words for "secret writing." It has a long and colorful history going back thousands of years. In this section we will just sketch some of the highlights, as background information for what follows. For a complete history of cryptography, Kahn's (1995) book is recommended reading. For a comprehensive treatment of the current state-of-the-art in security and cryptographic algorithms, protocols, and applications, see (Kaufman et al., 2002). For a more mathematical approach, see (Stinson, 2002). For a less mathematical approach, see (Burnett and Paine, 2001).

Professionals make a distinction between ciphers and codes. A **cipher** is a character-for-character or bit-for-bit transformation, without regard to the linguistic structure of the message. In contrast, a **code** replaces one word with another word or symbol. Codes are not used any more, although they have a glorious history. The most successful code ever devised was used by the U.S. armed forces during World War II in the Pacific. They simply had Navajo Indians talking to each other using specific Navajo words for military terms, for example *chay-da-gahi-nail-tsaidi* (literally: tortoise killer) for antitank weapon. The Navajo language is highly tonal, exceedingly complex, and has no written form. And not a single person in Japan knew anything about it.

In September 1945, the *San Diego Union* described the code by saying "For three years, wherever the Marines landed, the Japanese got an earful of strange gurgling noises interspersed with other sounds resembling the call of a Tibetan monk and the sound of a hot water bottle being emptied." The Japanese never broke the code and many Navajo code talkers were awarded high military honors for extraordinary service and bravery. The fact that the U.S. broke the Japanese code but the Japanese never broke the Navajo code played a crucial role in the American victories in the Pacific.

8.1.1 Introduction to Cryptography

Historically, four groups of people have used and contributed to the art of cryptography: the military, the diplomatic corps, diarists, and lovers. Of these, the military has had the most important role and has shaped the field over the centuries. Within military organizations, the messages to be encrypted have traditionally been given to poorly-paid, low-level code clerks for encryption and transmission. The sheer volume of messages prevented this work from being done by a few elite specialists.

Until the advent of computers, one of the main constraints on cryptography had been the ability of the code clerk to perform the necessary transformations, often on a battlefield with little equipment. An additional constraint has been the difficulty in switching over quickly from one cryptographic method to another one, since this entails retraining a large number of people. However, the danger of a code clerk being captured by the enemy has made it essential to be able to change the cryptographic method instantly if need be. These conflicting requirements have given rise to the model of Fig. 8-2.

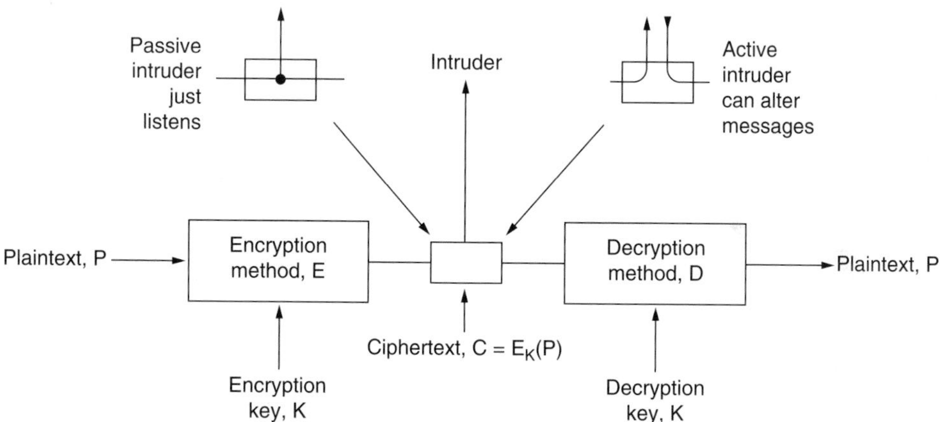

Figure 8-2. The encryption model (for a symmetric-key cipher).

The messages to be encrypted, known as the **plaintext**, are transformed by a function that is parameterized by a **key**. The output of the encryption process, known as the **ciphertext**, is then transmitted, often by messenger or radio. We assume that the enemy, or **intruder**, hears and accurately copies down the complete ciphertext. However, unlike the intended recipient, he does not know what the decryption key is and so cannot decrypt the ciphertext easily. Sometimes the intruder can not only listen to the communication channel (passive intruder) but can also record messages and play them back later, inject his own messages, or modify legitimate messages before they get to the receiver (active intruder). The art of breaking ciphers, called **cryptanalysis**, and the art devising them (cryptography) is collectively known as **cryptology**.

It will often be useful to have a notation for relating plaintext, ciphertext, and keys. We will use $C = E_K(P)$ to mean that the encryption of the plaintext P using key K gives the ciphertext C. Similarly, $P = D_K(C)$ represents the decryption of C to get the plaintext again. It then follows that

$$D_K(E_K(P)) = P$$

This notation suggests that E and D are just mathematical functions, which they are. The only tricky part is that both are functions of two parameters, and we have written one of the parameters (the key) as a subscript, rather than as an argument, to distinguish it from the message.

A fundamental rule of cryptography is that one must assume that the cryptanalyst knows the methods used for encryption and decryption. In other words, the cryptanalyst knows how the encryption method, E, and decryption, D, of Fig. 8-2 work in detail. The amount of effort necessary to invent, test, and install a new algorithm every time the old method is compromised (or thought to be compromised) has always made it impractical to keep the encryption algorithm secret. Thinking it is secret when it is not does more harm than good.

This is where the key enters. The key consists of a (relatively) short string that selects one of many potential encryptions. In contrast to the general method, which may only be changed every few years, the key can be changed as often as required. Thus, our basic model is a stable and publicly-known general method parameterized by a secret and easily changed key. The idea that the cryptanalyst knows the algorithms and that the secrecy lies exclusively in the keys is called **Kerckhoff's principle**, named after the Flemish military cryptographer Auguste Kerckhoff who first stated it in 1883 (Kerckhoff, 1883). Thus, we have:

Kerckhoff's principle: All algorithms must be public; only the keys are secret

The nonsecrecy of the algorithm cannot be emphasized enough. Trying to keep the algorithm secret, known in the trade as **security by obscurity**, never works. Also, by publicizing the algorithm, the cryptographer gets free consulting from a large number of academic cryptologists eager to break the system so they can publish papers demonstrating how smart they are. If many experts have tried to break the algorithm for 5 years after its publication and no one has succeeded, it is probably pretty solid.

Since the real secrecy is in the key, its length is a major design issue. Consider a simple combination lock. The general principle is that you enter digits in sequence. Everyone knows this, but the key is secret. A key length of two digits means that there are 100 possibilities. A key length of three digits means 1000 possibilities, and a key length of six digits means a million. The longer the key, the higher the **work factor** the cryptanalyst has to deal with. The work factor for breaking the system by exhaustive search of the key space is exponential in the key length. Secrecy comes from having a strong (but public) algorithm and a long key. To prevent your kid brother from reading your e-mail, 64-bit keys will do. For routine commercial use, at least 128 bits should be used. To keep major governments at bay, keys of at least 256 bits, preferably more, are needed.

From the cryptanalyst's point of view, the cryptanalysis problem has three principal variations. When he has a quantity of ciphertext and no plaintext, he is confronted with the **ciphertext-only** problem. The cryptograms that appear in the puzzle section of newspapers pose this kind of problem. When the cryptanalyst has some matched ciphertext and plaintext, the problem is called the **known plaintext** problem. Finally, when the cryptanalyst has the ability to encrypt pieces of plaintext of his own choosing, we have the **chosen plaintext** problem. Newspaper cryptograms could be broken trivially if the cryptanalyst were allowed to ask such questions as: What is the encryption of ABCDEFGHIJKL?

Novices in the cryptography business often assume that if a cipher can withstand a ciphertext-only attack, it is secure. This assumption is very naive. In many cases the cryptanalyst can make a good guess at parts of the plaintext. For example, the first thing many computers say when you call them up is login: . Equipped with some matched plaintext-ciphertext pairs, the cryptanalyst's job becomes much easier. To achieve security, the cryptographer should be conservative and make sure that the system is unbreakable even if his opponent can encrypt arbitrary amounts of chosen plaintext.

Encryption methods have historically been divided into two categories: substitution ciphers and transposition ciphers. We will now deal with each of these briefly as background information for modern cryptography.

8.1.2 Substitution Ciphers

In a **substitution cipher** each letter or group of letters is replaced by another letter or group of letters to disguise it. One of the oldest known ciphers is the **Caesar cipher**, attributed to Julius Caesar. In this method, *a* becomes *D*, *b* becomes *E*, *c* becomes *F*, . . . , and *z* becomes *C*. For example, *attack* becomes *DWWDFN*. In examples, plaintext will be given in lower case letters, and ciphertext in upper case letters.

A slight generalization of the Caesar cipher allows the ciphertext alphabet to be shifted by *k* letters, instead of always 3. In this case *k* becomes a key to the general method of circularly shifted alphabets. The Caesar cipher may have fooled Pompey, but it has not fooled anyone since.

The next improvement is to have each of the symbols in the plaintext, say, the 26 letters for simplicity, map onto some other letter. For example,

```
plaintext:    a b c d e f g h i j k l m n o p q r s t u v w x y z
ciphertext:   Q W E R T Y U I O P A S D F G H J K L Z X C V B N M
```

The general system of symbol-for-symbol substitution is called a **monoalphabetic substitution**, with the key being the 26-letter string corresponding to the full alphabet. For the key above, the plaintext *attack* would be transformed into the ciphertext *QZZQEA*.

At first glance this might appear to be a safe system because although the cryptanalyst knows the general system (letter-for-letter substitution), he does not know which of the $26! \approx 4 \times 10^{26}$ possible keys is in use. In contrast with the Caesar cipher, trying all of them is not a promising approach. Even at 1 nsec per solution, a computer would take 10^{10} years to try all the keys.

Nevertheless, given a surprisingly small amount of ciphertext, the cipher can be broken easily. The basic attack takes advantage of the statistical properties of natural languages. In English, for example, *e* is the most common letter, followed by *t*, *o*, *a*, *n*, *i*, etc. The most common two-letter combinations, or **digrams**, are *th*, *in*, *er*, *re*, and *an*. The most common three-letter combinations, or **trigrams**, are *the*, *ing*, *and*, and *ion*.

A cryptanalyst trying to break a monoalphabetic cipher would start out by counting the relative frequencies of all letters in the ciphertext. Then he might tentatively assign the most common one to *e* and the next most common one to *t*. He would then look at trigrams to find a common one of the form *tXe*, which strongly suggests that *X* is *h*. Similarly, if the pattern *thYt* occurs frequently, the *Y* probably stands for *a*. With this information, he can look for a frequently occurring trigram of the form *aZW*, which is most likely *and*. By making guesses at common letters, digrams, and trigrams and knowing about likely patterns of vowels and consonants, the cryptanalyst builds up a tentative plaintext, letter by letter.

Another approach is to guess a probable word or phrase. For example, consider the following ciphertext from an accounting firm (blocked into groups of five characters):

```
CTBMN BYCTC BTJDS QXBNS GSTJC BTSWX CTQTZ CQVUJ
QJSGS TJQZZ MNQJS VLNSX VSZJU JDSTS JQUUS JUBXJ
DSKSU JSNTK BGAQJ ZBGYQ TLCTZ BNYBN QJSW
```

A likely word in a message from an accounting firm is *financial*. Using our knowledge that *financial* has a repeated letter (*i*), with four other letters between their occurrences, we look for repeated letters in the ciphertext at this spacing. We find 12 hits, at positions 6, 15, 27, 31, 42, 48, 56, 66, 70, 71, 76, and 82.

However, only two of these, 31 and 42, have the next letter (corresponding to *n* in the plaintext) repeated in the proper place. Of these two, only 31 also has the *a* correctly positioned, so we know that *financial* begins at position 30. From this point on, deducing the key is easy by using the frequency statistics for English text.

8.1.3 Transposition Ciphers

Substitution ciphers preserve the order of the plaintext symbols but disguise them. **Transposition ciphers**, in contrast, reorder the letters but do not disguise them. Figure 8-3 depicts a common transposition cipher, the columnar transposition. The cipher is keyed by a word or phrase not containing any repeated letters. In this example, MEGABUCK is the key. The purpose of the key is to number the columns, column 1 being under the key letter closest to the start of the alphabet, and so on. The plaintext is written horizontally, in rows, padded to fill the matrix if need be. The ciphertext is read out by columns, starting with the column whose key letter is the lowest.

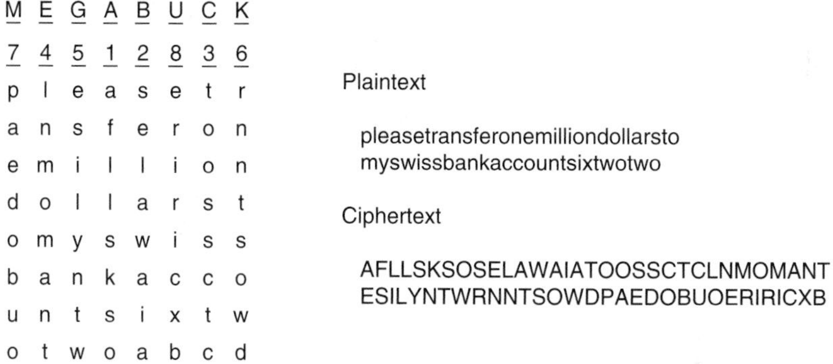

Figure 8-3. A transposition cipher.

To break a transposition cipher, the cryptanalyst must first be aware that he is dealing with a transposition cipher. By looking at the frequency of *E*, *T*, *A*, *O*, *I*, *N*, etc., it is easy to see if they fit the normal pattern for plaintext. If so, the cipher is clearly a transposition cipher, because in such a cipher every letter represents itself, keeping the frequency distribution intact.

The next step is to make a guess at the number of columns. In many cases a probable word or phrase may be guessed at from the context. For example, suppose that our cryptanalyst suspects that the plaintext phrase *milliondollars* occurs somewhere in the message. Observe that digrams *MO*, *IL*, *LL*, *LA*, *IR* and *OS* occur in the ciphertext as a result of this phrase wrapping around. The ciphertext letter *O* follows the ciphertext letter *M* (i.e., they are vertically adjacent in column 4) because they are separated in the probable phrase by a distance equal to the key length. If a key of length seven had been used, the digrams *MD*, *IO*, *LL*, *LL*, *IA*, *OR*, and *NS* would have occurred instead. In fact, for each key length, a different set of digrams is produced in the ciphertext. By hunting for the various possibilities, the cryptanalyst can often easily determine the key length.

The remaining step is to order the columns. When the number of columns, k, is small, each of the $k(k-1)$ column pairs can be examined to see if its digram frequencies match those for English plaintext. The pair with the best match is assumed to be correctly positioned. Now each remaining column is tentatively tried as the successor to this pair. The column whose digram and trigram frequencies give the best match is tentatively assumed to be correct. The predecessor column is found in the same way. The entire process is continued until a potential ordering is found. Chances are that the plaintext will be recognizable at this point (e.g., if *milloin* occurs, it is clear what the error is).

Some transposition ciphers accept a fixed-length block of input and produce a fixed-length block of output. These ciphers can be completely described by giving a list telling the order in which the characters are to be output. For example, the cipher of Fig. 8-3 can be seen as a 64 character block cipher. Its output is 4, 12, 20, 28, 36, 44, 52, 60, 5, 13 , . . . , 62. In other words, the fourth input character, *a*, is the first to be output, followed by the twelfth, *f*, and so on.

8.1.4 One-Time Pads

Constructing an unbreakable cipher is actually quite easy; the technique has been known for decades. First choose a random bit string as the key. Then convert the plaintext into a bit string, for example by using its ASCII representation. Finally, compute the XOR (eXclusive OR) of these two strings, bit by bit. The resulting ciphertext cannot be broken, because in a sufficiently large sample of ciphertext, each letter will occur equally often, as will every digram, every trigram, and so on. This method, known as the **one-time pad**, is immune to all present and future attacks no matter how much computational power the intruder has. The reason derives from information theory: there is simply no information in the message because all possible plaintexts of the given length are equally likely.

An example of how one-time pads are used is given in Fig. 8-4. First, message 1, "I love you." is converted to 7-bit ASCII. Then a one-time pad, pad 1, is chosen and XORed with the message to get the ciphertext. A cryptanalyst could try all possible one-time pads to see what plaintext came out for each one. For example, the one-time pad listed as pad 2 in the figure could be tried, resulting in plaintext 2, "Elvis lives", which may or may not be plausible (a subject beyond the scope of this book). In fact, for every 11-character ASCII plaintext, there is a one-time pad that generates it. That is what we mean by saying there is no information in the ciphertext: you can get any message of the correct length out of it.

Message 1:	1001001 0100000 1101100 1101111 1110110 1100101 0100000 1111001 1101111 1110101 0101110
Pad 1:	1010010 1001011 1110010 1010101 1010010 1100011 0001011 0101010 1010111 1100110 0101011
Ciphertext:	0011011 1101011 0011110 0111010 0100100 0000110 0101011 1010011 0111000 0010011 0000101
Pad 2:	1011110 0000111 1101000 1010011 1010111 0100110 1000111 0111010 1001110 1110110 1110110
Plaintext 2:	1000101 1101100 1110110 1101001 1110011 0100000 1101100 1101001 1110110 1100101 1110011

Figure 8-4. The use of a one-time pad for encryption and the possibility of getting any possible plaintext from the ciphertext by the use of some other pad.

One-time pads are great in theory but have a number of disadvantages in practice. To start with, the key cannot be memorized, so both sender and receiver must carry a written copy with them. If either one is subject to capture, written keys are clearly undesirable. Additionally, the total amount of data that can be transmitted is limited by the amount of key available. If the spy strikes it rich and discovers a wealth of data, he may find himself unable to transmit it back to headquarters because the key has been used up. Another problem is the sensitivity of the method to lost or inserted characters. If the sender and receiver get out of synchronization, all data from then on will appear garbled.

With the advent of computers, the one-time pad might potentially become practical for some applications. The source of the key could be a special DVD that contains several gigabytes of information and if transported in a DVD movie box and prefixed by a few minutes of video, would not even be suspicious. Of course, at gigabit network speeds, having to insert a new DVD every 30 sec could become tedious. And the DVDs must be personally carried from the sender to the receiver before any messages can be sent, which greatly reduces their practical utility.

Quantum Cryptography

Interestingly, there may be a solution to the problem of how to transmit the one-time pad over the network, and it comes from a very unlikely source: quantum mechanics. This area is still experimental, but initial tests are promising. If it can be perfected and be made efficient, virtually all cryptography will eventually be done using one-time pads since they are provably secure. Below we will briefly explain how this method, **quantum cryptography**, works. In particular, we will describe a protocol called **BB84** after its authors and publication year (Bennet and Brassard, 1984).

A user, Alice, wants to establish a one-time pad with a second user, Bob. Alice and Bob are called **principals**, the main characters in our story. For example, Bob is a banker with whom Alice would like to do business. The names

"Alice" and "Bob" have been used for the principals in virtually every paper and book on cryptography in the past decade. Cryptographers love tradition. If we were to use "Andy" and "Barbara" as the principals, no one would believe anything in this chapter. So be it.

If Alice and Bob could establish a one-time pad, they could use it to communicate securely. The question is: How can they establish it without previously exchanging DVDs? We can assume that Alice and Bob are at opposite ends of an optical fiber over which they can send and receive light pulses. However, an intrepid intruder, Trudy, can cut the fiber to splice in an active tap. Trudy can read all the bits in both directions. She can also send false messages in both directions. The situation might seem hopeless for Alice and Bob, but quantum cryptography can shed some new light on the subject.

Quantum cryptography is based on the fact that light comes in little packets called **photons**, which have some peculiar properties. Furthermore, light can be polarized by being passed through a polarizing filter, a fact well known to both sunglasses wearers and photographers. If a beam of light (i.e., a stream of photons) is passed through a polarizing filter, all the photons emerging from it will be polarized in the direction of the filter's axis (e.g., vertical). If the beam is now passed through a second polarizing filter, the intensity of the light emerging from the second filter is proportional to the square of the cosine of the angle between the axes. If the two axes are perpendicular, no photons get through. The absolute orientation of the two filters does not matter; only the angle between their axes counts.

To generate a one-time pad, Alice needs two sets of polarizing filters. Set one consists of a vertical filter and a horizontal filter. This choice is called a **rectilinear basis**. A basis (plural: bases) is just a coordinate system. The second set of filters is the same, except rotated 45 degrees, so one filter runs from the lower left to the upper right and the other filter runs from the upper left to the lower right. This choice is called a **diagonal basis**. Thus, Alice has two bases, which she can rapidly insert into her beam at will. In reality, Alice does not have four separate filters, but a crystal whose polarization can be switched electrically to any of the four allowed directions at great speed. Bob has the same equipment as Alice. The fact that Alice and Bob each have two bases available is essential to quantum cryptography.

For each basis, Alice now assigns one direction as 0 and the other as 1. In the example presented below, we assume she chooses vertical to be 0 and horizontal to be 1. Independently, she also chooses lower left to upper right as 0 and upper left to lower right as 1. She sends these choices to Bob as plaintext.

Now Alice picks a one-time pad, for example based on a random number generator (a complex subject all by itself). She transfers it bit by bit to Bob, choosing one of her two bases at random for each bit. To send a bit, her photon gun emits one photon polarized appropriately for the basis she is using for that bit. For example, she might choose bases of diagonal, rectilinear, rectilinear, diagonal, rectilinear, etc. To send her one-time pad of 1001110010100110 with these bases, she would send the photons shown in Fig. 8-5(a). Given the one-time pad and the sequence of bases, the polarization to use for each bit is uniquely determined. Bits sent one photon at a time are called **qubits**.

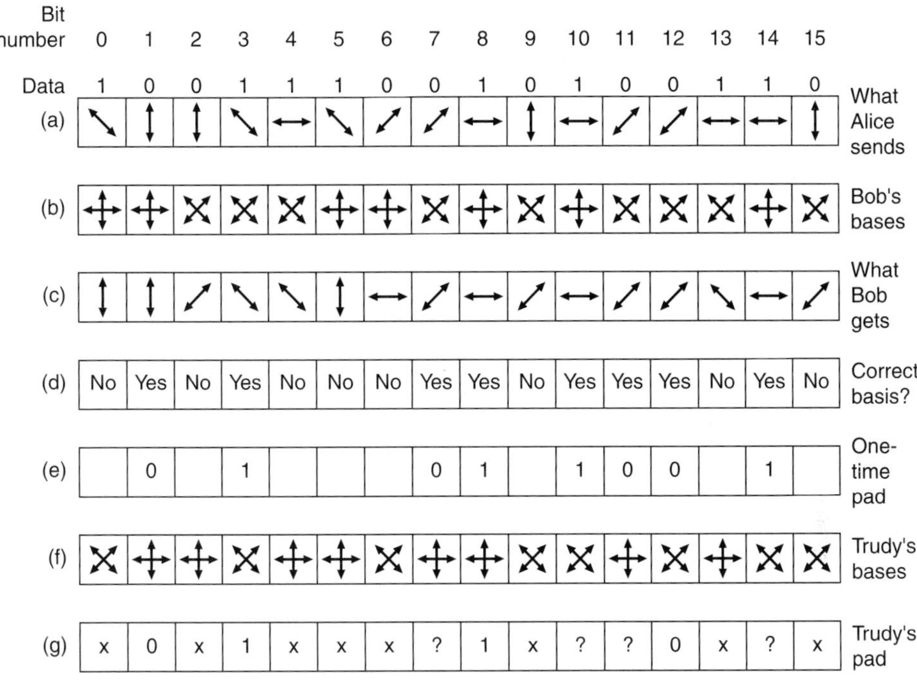

Figure 8-5. An example of quantum cryptography.

Bob does not know which bases to use, so he picks one at random for each arriving photon and just uses it, as shown in Fig. 8-5(b). If he picks the correct basis, he gets the correct bit. If he picks the incorrect basis, he gets a random bit because if a photon hits a filter polarized at 45 degrees to its own polarization, it randomly jumps to the polarization of the filter or to a polarization perpendicular to the filter with equal probability. This property of photons is fundamental to quantum mechanics. Thus, some of the bits are correct and some are random, but Bob does not know which are which. Bob's results are depicted in Fig. 8-5(c).

How does Bob find out which bases he got right and which he got wrong? He simply tells Alice which basis he used for each bit in plaintext and she tells him which are right and which are wrong in plaintext, as shown in Fig. 8-5(d). From this information both of them can build a bit string from the correct guesses, as shown in Fig. 8-5(e). On the average, this bit string will be half the length of the original bit string, but since both parties know it, they can use it as a one-time pad. All Alice has to do is transmit a bit string slightly more than twice the desired length and she and Bob have a one-time pad of the desired length. Problem solved.

But wait a minute. We forgot Trudy. Suppose that she is curious about what Alice has to say and cuts the fiber, inserting her own detector and transmitter. Unfortunately for her, she does not know which basis to use for each photon either. The best she can do is pick one at random for each photon, just as Bob does. An example of her choices is shown in Fig. 8-5(f). When Bob later reports (in plaintext) which bases he used and Alice tells him (in plaintext) which ones are correct, Trudy now knows when she got it right and when she got it wrong. In Fig. 8-5 she got it right for bits 0, 1, 2, 3, 4, 6, 8, 12, and 13. But she knows from Alice's reply in Fig. 8-5(d) that only bits 1, 3, 7, 8, 10, 11, 12, and 14 are part of the one-time pad. For four of these bits (1, 3, 8, and 12), she guessed right and captured the correct bit. For the other four (7, 10, 11, and 14) she guessed wrong and does not know the bit transmitted. Thus, Bob knows the one-time pad starts with 01011001, from Fig. 8-5(e) but all Trudy has is 01?1??0?, from Fig. 8-5(g).

Of course, Alice and Bob are aware that Trudy may have captured part of their one-time pad, so they would like to reduce the information Trudy has. They can do this by performing a transformation on it. For example, they could divide the one-time pad into blocks of 1024 bits and square each one to form a 2048-bit number and use the concatenation of these 2048-bit numbers as the one-time pad. With her partial knowledge of the bit string transmitted, Trudy has no way to generate its square and so has nothing. The transformation from the original one-time pad to a different one that reduces Trudy's knowledge is called **privacy amplification**. In practice, complex transformations in which every output bit depends on every input bit are used instead of squaring.

Poor Trudy. Not only does she have no idea what the one-time pad is, but her presence is not a secret either. After all, she must relay each received bit to Bob to trick him into thinking he is talking to Alice. The trouble is, the best she can do is transmit the qubit she received, using the polarization she used to receive it, and about half the time she will be wrong, causing many errors in Bob's one-time pad.

When Alice finally starts sending data, she encodes it using a heavy forward-error-correcting code. From Bob's point of view, a 1-bit error in the one-time pad is the same as a 1-bit transmission error. Either way, he gets the wrong bit. If there is enough forward error correction, he can recover the original message despite all the errors, but he can easily count how many errors were corrected. If this number is far more than the expected error rate of the equipment, he knows that Trudy has tapped the line and can act accordingly (e.g., tell Alice to switch to a radio channel, call the police, etc.). If Trudy had a way to clone a photon so she had one photon to inspect and an identical photon to send to Bob, she could avoid detection, but at present no way to clone a photon perfectly is known. But even if Trudy could clone photons, the value of quantum cryptography to establish one-time pads would not be reduced.

Although quantum cryptography has been shown to operate over distances of 60 km of fiber, the equipment is complex and expensive. Still, the idea has promise. For more information about quantum cryptography, see (Mullins, 2002).

8.1.5 Two Fundamental Cryptographic Principles

Although we will study many different cryptographic systems in the pages ahead, two principles underlying all of them are important to understand.

Redundancy

The first principle is that all encrypted messages must contain some redundancy, that is, information not needed to understand the message. An example may make it clear why this is needed. Consider a mail-order company, The Couch Potato (TCP), with 60,000 products. Thinking they are being very efficient, TCP's programmers decide that ordering messages should consist of a 16-byte customer name followed by a 3-byte data field (1 byte for the quantity and 2 bytes for the product number). The last 3 bytes are to be encrypted using a very long key known only by the customer and TCP.

At first this might seem secure, and in a sense it is because passive intruders cannot decrypt the messages. Unfortunately, it also has a fatal flaw that renders it useless. Suppose that a recently-fired employee wants to punish TCP for firing her. Just before leaving, she takes the customer list with her. She works through the night writing a program to generate fictitious orders using real customer names. Since she does not have the list of keys, she just puts random numbers in the last 3 bytes, and sends hundreds of orders off to TCP.

When these messages arrive, TCP's computer uses the customer's name to locate the key and decrypt the message. Unfortunately for TCP, almost every 3-byte message is valid, so the computer begins printing out shipping instructions. While it might seem odd for a customer to order 837 sets of children's swings or 540 sandboxes, for all the computer knows, the customer might be planning to open a chain of franchised playgrounds. In this way an active intruder (the ex-employee) can cause a massive amount of trouble, even though she cannot understand the messages her computer is generating.

This problem can be solved by the addition of redundancy to all messages. For example, if order messages are extended to 12 bytes, the first 9 of which must be zeros, then this attack no longer works because the ex-employee can no longer generate a large stream of valid messages. The moral of the story is that all messages must contain considerable redundancy so that active intruders cannot send random junk and have it be interpreted as a valid message.

However, adding redundancy also makes it easier for cryptanalysts to break messages. Suppose that the mail order business is highly competitive, and The Couch Potato's main competitor, The Sofa Tuber, would dearly love to know how many sandboxes TCP is selling. Consequently, they have tapped TCP's telephone line. In the original scheme with 3-byte messages, cryptanalysis was nearly impossible, because after guessing a key, the cryptanalyst had no way of telling whether the guess was right. After all, almost every message is technically legal.

With the new 12-byte scheme, it is easy for the cryptanalyst to tell a valid message from an invalid one. Thus, we have

Cryptographic principle 1: Messages must contain some redundancy

In other words, upon decrypting a message, the recipient must be able to tell whether it is valid by simply inspecting it and perhaps performing a simple computation. This redundancy is needed to prevent active intruders from sending garbage and tricking the receiver into decrypting the garbage and acting on the "plaintext." However, this same redundancy makes it much easier for passive intruders to break the system, so there is some tension here. Furthermore, the redundancy should never be in the form of *n* zeros at the start or end of a message, since running such messages through some cryptographic algorithms gives more predictable results, making the cryptanalysts' job easier. A CRC polynomial is much better than a run of 0s since the receiver can easily verify it, but it generates more work for the cryptanalyst. Even better is to use a cryptographic hash, a concept we will explore later.

Getting back to quantum cryptography for a moment, we can also see how redundancy plays a role there. Due to Trudy's interception of the photons, some bits in Bob's one-time pad will be wrong. Bob needs some redundancy in the incoming messages to determine that errors are present. One very crude form of redundancy is repeating the message two times. If the two copies are not identical, Bob knows that either the fiber is very noisy or someone is tampering with the transmission. Of course, sending everything twice is overkill; a Hamming or Reed-Solomon code is a more efficient way to do error detection and correction. But it should be clear that some redundancy is needed to distinguish a valid message from an invalid message, especially in the face of an active intruder.

Freshness

The second cryptographic principle is that some measures must be taken to ensure that each message received can be verified as being fresh, that is, sent very recently. This measure is needed to prevent active intruders from playing back old messages. If no such measures were taken, our ex-employee could tap TCP's phone line and just keep repeating previously sent valid messages. Restating this idea we get:

Cryptographic principle 2: Some method is needed to foil replay attacks

One such measure is including in every message a timestamp valid only for, say, 10 seconds. The receiver can then just keep messages around for 10 seconds, to compare newly arrived messages to previous ones to filter out duplicates. Messages older than 10 seconds can be thrown out, since any replays sent more than 10 seconds later will be rejected as too old. Measures other than timestamps will be discussed later.

8.2 SYMMETRIC-KEY ALGORITHMS

Modern cryptography uses the same basic ideas as traditional cryptography (transposition and substitution) but its emphasis is different. Traditionally, cryptographers have used simple algorithms. Nowadays the reverse is true: the object is to make the encryption algorithm so complex and involuted that even if the cryptanalyst acquires vast mounds of enciphered text of his own choosing, he will not be able to make any sense of it at all without the key.

The first class of encryption algorithms we will study in this chapter are called **symmetric-key algorithms** because they used the same key for encryption and decryption. Fig. 8-2 illustrates the use of a symmetric-key algorithm. In particular, we will focus on **block ciphers**, which take an n-bit block of plaintext as input and transform it using the key into n-bit block of ciphertext.

Cryptographic algorithms can be implemented in either hardware (for speed) or in software (for flexibility). Although most of our treatment concerns the algorithms and protocols, which are independent of the actual implementation, a few words about building cryptographic hardware may be of interest. Transpositions and substitutions can be implemented with simple electrical circuits. Figure 8-6(a) shows a device, known as a **P-box** (P stands for permutation), used to effect a transposition on an 8-bit input. If the 8 bits are designated from top to bottom as 01234567, the output of this particular P-box is 36071245. By appropriate internal wiring, a P-box can be made to perform any transposition and do it at practically the speed of light since no computation is involved, just signal propagation. This design follows Kerckhoff's principle: the attacker knows that the general method is permuting the bits. What he does not know is which bit goes where, which is the key.

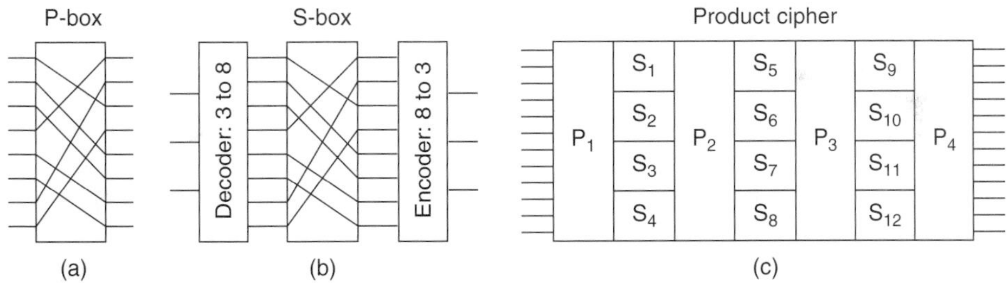

Figure 8-6. Basic elements of product ciphers. (a) P-box. (b) S-box. (c) Product.

Substitutions are performed by **S-boxes**, as shown in Fig. 8-6(b). In this example a 3-bit plaintext is entered and a 3-bit ciphertext is output. The 3-bit input selects one of the eight lines exiting from the first stage and sets it to 1; all the other lines are 0. The second stage is a P-box. The third stage encodes the selected input line in binary again. With the wiring shown, if the eight octal numbers

01234567 were input one after another, the output sequence would be 24506713. In other words, 0 has been replaced by 2, 1 has been replaced by 4, etc. Again, by appropriate wiring of the P-box inside the S-box, any substitution can be accomplished. Furthermore, such a device can be built in hardware and can achieve great speed since encoders and decoders have only one or two (subnanosecond) gate delays and the propagation time across the P-box may well be less than 1 picosecond.

The real power of these basic elements only becomes apparent when we cascade a whole series of boxes to form a **product cipher**, as shown in Fig. 8-6(c). In this example, 12 input lines are transposed (i.e., permuted) by the first stage (P_1). Theoretically, it would be possible to have the second stage be an S-box that mapped a 12-bit number onto another 12-bit number. However, such a device would need $2^{12} = 4096$ crossed wires in its middle stage. Instead, the input is broken up into four groups of 3 bits, each of which is substituted independently of the others. Although this method is less general, it is still powerful. By inclusion of a sufficiently large number of stages in the product cipher, the output can be made to be an exceedingly complicated function of the input.

Product ciphers that operate on k-bit inputs to produce k-bit outputs are very common. Typically, k is 64 to 256. A hardware implementation usually has at least 18 physical stages, instead of just seven as in Fig. 8-6(c). A software implementation is programmed as a loop with at least 8 iterations, each one performing S-box-type substitutions on subblocks of the 64- to 256-bit data block, followed by a permutation that mixes the outputs of the S-boxes. Often there is a special initial permutation and one at the end as well. In the literature, the iterations are called **rounds**.

8.2.1 DES—The Data Encryption Standard

In January 1977, the U.S. Government adopted a product cipher developed by IBM as its official standard for unclassified information. This cipher, **DES** (**Data Encryption Standard**), was widely adopted by the industry for use in security products. It is no longer secure in its original form, but in a modified form it is still useful. We will now explain how DES works.

An outline of DES is shown in Fig. 8-7(a). Plaintext is encrypted in blocks of 64 bits, yielding 64 bits of ciphertext. The algorithm, which is parameterized by a 56-bit key, has 19 distinct stages. The first stage is a key-independent transposition on the 64-bit plaintext. The last stage is the exact inverse of this transposition. The stage prior to the last one exchanges the leftmost 32 bits with the rightmost 32 bits. The remaining 16 stages are functionally identical but are parameterized by different functions of the key. The algorithm has been designed to allow decryption to be done with the same key as encryption, a property needed in any symmetric-key algorithm. The steps are just run in the reverse order.

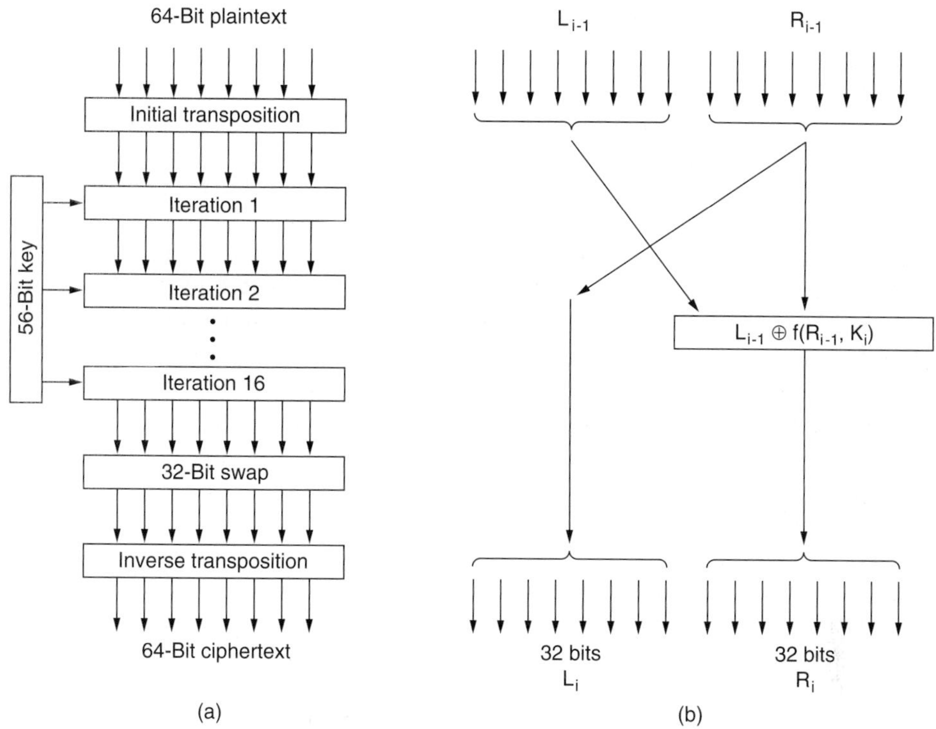

Figure 8-7. The data encryption standard. (a) General outline. (b) Detail of one iteration. The circled + means exclusive OR.

The operation of one of these intermediate stages is illustrated in Fig. 8-7(b). Each stage takes two 32-bit inputs and produces two 32-bit outputs. The left output is simply a copy of the right input. The right output is the bitwise XOR of the left input and a function of the right input and the key for this stage, K_i. All the complexity lies in this function.

The function consists of four steps, carried out in sequence. First, a 48-bit number, E, is constructed by expanding the 32-bit R_{i-1} according to a fixed transposition and duplication rule. Second, E and K_i are XORed together. This output is then partitioned into eight groups of 6 bits each, each of which is fed into a different S-box. Each of the 64 possible inputs to an S-box is mapped onto a 4-bit output. Finally, these 8×4 bits are passed through a P-box.

In each of the 16 iterations, a different key is used. Before the algorithm starts, a 56-bit transposition is applied to the key. Just before each iteration, the key is partitioned into two 28-bit units, each of which is rotated left by a number of bits dependent on the iteration number. K_i is derived from this rotated key by applying yet another 56-bit transposition to it. A different 48-bit subset of the 56 bits is extracted and permuted on each round.

A technique that is sometimes used to make DES stronger is called **whitening**. It consists of XORing a random 64-bit key with each plaintext block before feeding it into DES and then XORing a second 64-bit key with the resulting ciphertext before transmitting it. Whitening can easily be removed by running the reverse operations (if the receiver has the two whitening keys). Since this technique effectively adds more bits to the key length, it makes exhaustive search of the key space much more time consuming. Note that the same whitening key is used for each block (i.e., there is only one whitening key).

DES has been enveloped in controversy since the day it was launched. It was based on a cipher developed and patented by IBM, called Lucifer, except that IBM's cipher used a 128-bit key instead of a 56-bit key. When the U.S. Federal Government wanted to standardize on one cipher for unclassified use, it "invited" IBM to "discuss" the matter with NSA, the U.S. Government's code-breaking arm, which is the world's largest employer of mathematicians and cryptologists. NSA is so secret that an industry joke goes:

Q: What does NSA stand for?
A: No Such Agency.

Actually, NSA stands for National Security Agency.

After these discussions took place, IBM reduced the key from 128 bits to 56 bits and decided to keep secret the process by which DES was designed. Many people suspected that the key length was reduced to make sure that NSA could just break DES, but no organization with a smaller budget could. The point of the secret design was supposedly to hide a back door that could make it even easier for NSA to break DES. When an NSA employee discreetly told IEEE to cancel a planned conference on cryptography, that did not make people any more comfortable. NSA denied everything.

In 1977, two Stanford cryptography researchers, Diffie and Hellman (1977), designed a machine to break DES and estimated that it could be built for 20 million dollars. Given a small piece of plaintext and matched ciphertext, this machine could find the key by exhaustive search of the 2^{56}-entry key space in under 1 day. Nowadays, such a machine would cost well under 1 million dollars.

Triple DES

As early as 1979, IBM realized that the DES key length was too short and devised a way to effectively increase it, using triple encryption (Tuchman, 1979). The method chosen, which has since been incorporated in International Standard 8732, is illustrated in Fig. 8-8. Here two keys and three stages are used. In the first stage, the plaintext is encrypted using DES in the usual way with K_1. In the second stage, DES is run in decryption mode, using K_2 as the key. Finally, another DES encryption is done with K_1.

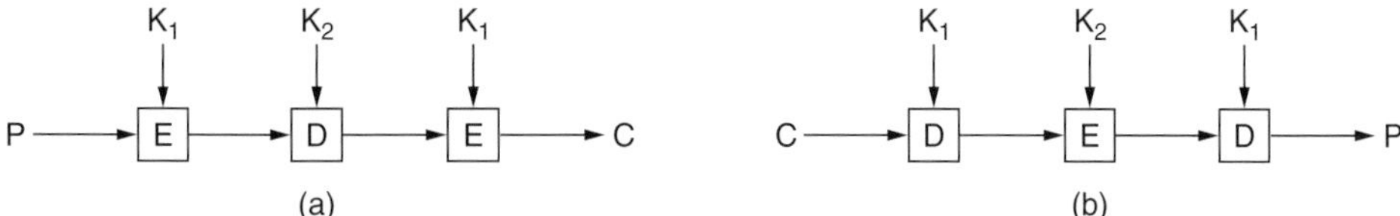

Figure 8-8. (a) Triple encryption using DES. (b) Decryption.

This design immediately gives rise to two questions. First, why are only two keys used, instead of three? Second, why is **EDE** (**Encrypt Decrypt Encrypt**) used, instead of **EEE** (**Encrypt Encrypt Encrypt**)? The reason that two keys are used is that even the most paranoid cryptographers believe that 112 bits is adequate for routine commercial applications for the time being. (And among cryptographers, paranoia is considered a feature, not a bug.) Going to 168 bits would just add the unnecessary overhead of managing and transporting another key for little real gain.

The reason for encrypting, decrypting, and then encrypting again is backward compatibility with existing single-key DES systems. Both the encryption and decryption functions are mappings between sets of 64-bit numbers. From a cryptographic point of view, the two mappings are equally strong. By using EDE, however, instead of EEE, a computer using triple encryption can speak to one using single encryption by just setting $K_1 = K_2$. This property allows triple encryption to be phased in gradually, something of no concern to academic cryptographers, but of considerable importance to IBM and its customers.

8.2.2 AES—The Advanced Encryption Standard

As DES began approaching the end of its useful life, even with triple DES, **NIST** (**National Institute of Standards and Technology**), the agency of the U.S. Dept. of Commerce charged with approving standards for the U.S. Federal Government, decided that the government needed a new cryptographic standard for unclassified use. NIST was keenly aware of all the controversy surrounding DES and well knew that if it just announced a new standard, everyone knowing anything about cryptography would automatically assume that NSA had built a back door into it so NSA could read everything encrypted with it. Under these conditions, probably no one would use the standard and it would most likely die a quiet death.

So NIST took a surprisingly different approach for a government bureaucracy: it sponsored a cryptographic bake-off (contest). In January 1997, researchers from all over the world were invited to submit proposals for a new standard, to be called **AES** (**Advanced Encryption Standard**). The bake-off rules were:

1. The algorithm must be a symmetric block cipher.
2. The full design must be public.
3. Key lengths of 128, 192, and 256 bits must be supported.
4. Both software and hardware implementations must be possible.
5. The algorithm must be public or licensed on nondiscriminatory terms.

Fifteen serious proposals were made, and public conferences were organized in which they were presented and attendees were actively encouraged to find flaws in all of them. In August 1998, NIST selected five finalists primarily on the basis of their security, efficiency, simplicity, flexibility, and memory requirements (important for embedded systems). More conferences were held and more pot-shots taken. A nonbinding vote was taken at the last conference. The finalists and their scores were as follows:

1. Rijndael (from Joan Daemen and Vincent Rijmen, 86 votes).
2. Serpent (from Ross Anderson, Eli Biham, and Lars Knudsen, 59 votes).
3. Twofish (from a team headed by Bruce Schneier, 31 votes).
4. RC6 (from RSA Laboratories, 23 votes).
5. MARS (from IBM, 13 votes).

In October 2000, NIST announced that it, too, voted for Rijndael, and in November 2001 Rijndael became a U.S. Government standard published as Federal Information Processing Standard FIPS 197. Due to the extraordinary openness of the competition, the technical properties of Rijndael, and the fact that the winning team consisted of two young Belgian cryptographers (who are unlikely to have built in a back door just to please NSA), it is expected that Rijndael will become the world's dominant cryptographic standard for at least a decade. The name Rijndael, pronounced Rhine-doll (more or less), is derived from the last names of the authors: Rijmen + Daemen.

Rijndael supports key lengths and block sizes from 128 bits to 256 bits in steps of 32 bits. The key length and block length may be chosen independently. However, AES specifies that the block size must be 128 bits and the key length must be 128, 192, or 256 bits. It is doubtful that anyone will ever use 192-bit keys, so de facto, AES has two variants: a 128-bit block with 128-bit key and a 128-bit block with a 256-bit key.

In our treatment of the algorithm below, we will examine only the 128/128 case because this is likely to become the commercial norm. A 128-bit key gives a key space of $2^{128} \approx 3 \times 10^{38}$ keys. Even if NSA manages to build a machine with 1 billion parallel processors, each being able to evaluate one key per picosecond, it would take such a machine about 10^{10} years to search the key space. By then the sun will have burned out, so the folks then present will have to read the results by candlelight.

Rijndael

From a mathematical perspective, Rijndael is based on Galois field theory, which gives it some provable security properties. However, it can also be viewed as C code, without getting into the mathematics.

Like DES, Rijndael uses substitution and permutations, and it also uses multiple rounds. The number of rounds depends on the key size and block size, being 10 for 128-bit keys with 128-bit blocks and moving up to 14 for the largest key or the largest block. However, unlike DES, all operations involve entire bytes, to allow for efficient implementations in both hardware and software. An outline of the code is given in Fig. 8-9.

```
#define LENGTH 16                                   /* # bytes in data block or key */
#define NROWS 4                                     /* number of rows in state */
#define NCOLS 4                                     /* number of columns in state */
#define ROUNDS 10                                   /* number of iterations */
typedef unsigned char byte;                         /* unsigned 8-bit integer */

rijndael(byte plaintext[LENGTH], byte ciphertext[LENGTH], byte key[LENGTH])
{
  int r;                                            /* loop index */
  byte state[NROWS][NCOLS];                         /* current state */
  struct {byte k[NROWS][NCOLS];} rk[ROUNDS + 1];    /* round keys */

  expand_key(key, rk);                              /* construct the round keys */
  copy_plaintext_to_state(state, plaintext);        /* init current state */
  xor_roundkey_into_state(state, rk[0]);            /* XOR key into state */

  for (r = 1; r <= ROUNDS; r++) {
       substitute(state);                           /* apply S-box to each byte */
       rotate_rows(state);                          /* rotate row i by i bytes */
       if (r < ROUNDS) mix_columns(state);          /* mix function */
       xor_roundkey_into_state(state, rk[r]);       /* XOR key into state */
  }
  copy_state_to_ciphertext(ciphertext, state);      /* return result */
}
```

Figure 8-9. An outline of Rijndael.

The function *rijndael* has three parameters. They are: *plaintext*, an array of 16 bytes containing the input data, *ciphertext*, an array of 16 bytes where the enciphered output will be returned, and *key*, the 16-byte key. During the calculation, the current state of the data is maintained in a byte array, *state*, whose size is *NROWS* $\times$ *NCOLS*. For 128-bit blocks, this array is 4×4 bytes. With 16 bytes, the full 128-bit data block can be stored.

The *state* array is initialized to the plaintext and modified by every step in the computation. In some steps, byte-for-byte substitution is performed. In others, the bytes are permuted within the array. Other transformations are also used. At the end, the contents of the *state* are returned as the ciphertext.

The code starts out by expanding the key into 11 arrays of the same size as the state. They are stored in *rk*, which is an array of structs, each containing a state array. One of these will be used at the start of the calculation and the other 10 will be used during the 10 rounds, one per round. The calculation of the round keys from the encryption key is too complicated for us to get into here. Suffice it to say that the round keys are produced by repeated rotation and XORing of various groups of key bits. For all the details, see (Daemen and Rijmen, 2002).

The next step is to copy the plaintext into the *state* array so it can be processed during the rounds. It is copied in column order, with the first four bytes going into column 0, the next four bytes going into column 1, and so on. Both the columns and the rows are numbered starting at 0, although the rounds are numbered starting at 1. This initial setup of the 12 byte arrays of size 4×4 is illustrated in Fig. 8-10.

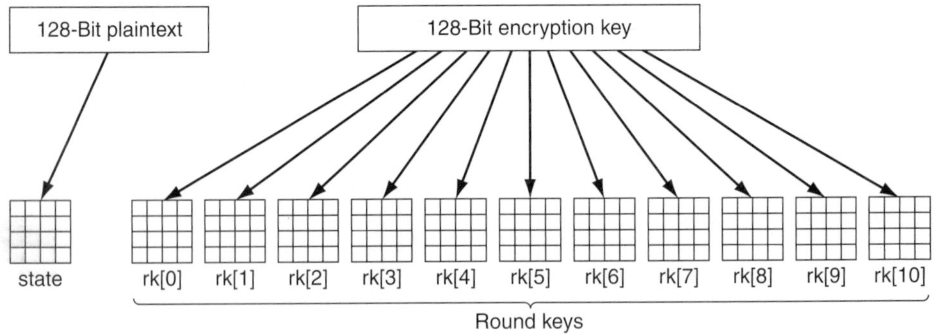

Figure 8-10. Creating of the *state* and *rk* arrays.

There is one more step before the main computation begins: *rk*[0] is XORed into *state* byte for byte. In other words each of the 16 bytes in *state* is replaced by the XOR of itself and the corresponding byte in *rk*[0].

Now it is time for the main attraction. The loop executes 10 iterations, one per round, transforming *state* on each iteration. The contents of each round consist of four steps. Step 1 does a byte-for-byte substitution on *state*. Each byte in turn is used as an index into an S-box to replace its value by the contents of that S-box entry. This step is a straight monoalphabetic substitution cipher. Unlike DES, which has multiple S-boxes, Rijndael has only one S-box.

Step 2 rotates each of the four rows to the left. Row 0 is rotated 0 bytes (i.e., not changed), row 1 is rotated 1 byte, row 2 is rotated 2 bytes, and row 3 is rotated 3 bytes. This step diffuses the contents of the current data around the block, analogous to the permutations of Fig. 8-6.

Step 3 mixes up each column independently of the other ones. The mixing is done using matrix multiplication in which the new column is the product of the old column and a constant matrix, with the multiplication done using the finite Galois field, $GF(2^8)$. Although this may sound complicated, an algorithm exists that allows each element of the new column to be computed using two table lookups and three XORs (Daemen and Rijmen, 2002, Appendix E).

Finally, step 4 XORs the key for this round into the *state* array.

Since every step is reversible, decryption can be done just by running the algorithm backward. However, there is also a trick available in which decryption can be done by running the encryption algorithm, using different tables.

The algorithm has been designed not only for great security, but also for great speed. A good software implementation on a 2-GHz machine should be able to achieve an encryption rate of 700 Mbps, which is fast enough to encrypt over 100 MPEG-2 videos in real time. Hardware implementations are faster still.

8.2.3 Cipher Modes

Despite all this complexity, AES (or DES or any block cipher for that matter) is basically a monoalphabetic substitution cipher using big characters (128-bit characters for AES and 64-bit characters for DES). Whenever the same plaintext block goes in the front end, the same ciphertext block comes out the back end. If you encrypt the plaintext *abcdefgh* 100 times with the same DES key, you get the same ciphertext 100 times. An intruder can exploit this property to help subvert the cipher.

Electronic Code Book Mode

To see how this monoalphabetic substitution cipher property can be used to partially defeat the cipher, we will use (triple) DES because it is easier to depict 64-bit blocks than 128-bit blocks, but AES has exactly the same problem. The straightforward way to use DES to encrypt a long piece of plaintext is to break it up into consecutive 8-byte (64-bit) blocks and encrypt them one after another with the same key. The last piece of plaintext is padded out to 64 bits, if need be. This technique is known as **ECB mode** (**Electronic Code Book mode**) in analogy with old-fashioned code books where each plaintext word was listed, followed by its ciphertext (usually a five-digit decimal number).

In Fig. 8-11 we have the start of a computer file listing the annual bonuses a company has decided to award to its employees. This file consists of consecutive 32-byte records, one per employee, in the format shown: 16 bytes for the name, 8 bytes for the position, and 8 bytes for the bonus. Each of the sixteen 8-byte blocks (numbered from 0 to 15) is encrypted by (triple) DES.

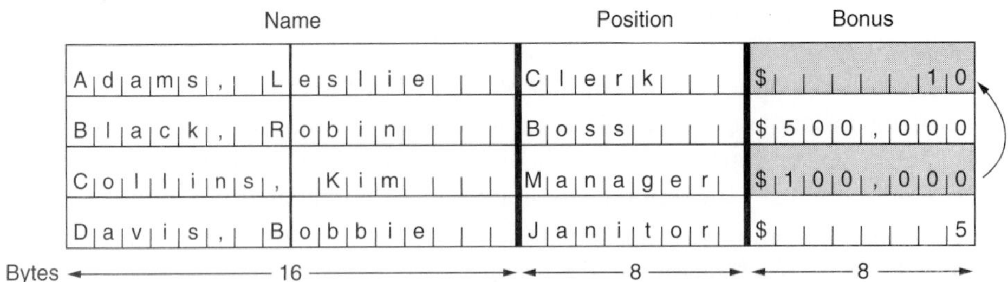

Figure 8-11. The plaintext of a file encrypted as 16 DES blocks.

Leslie just had a fight with the boss and is not expecting much of a bonus. Kim, in contrast, is the boss' favorite, and everyone knows this. Leslie can get access to the file after it is encrypted but before it is sent to the bank. Can Leslie rectify this unfair situation, given only the encrypted file?

No problem at all. All Leslie has to do is make a copy of the 12th ciphertext block (which contains Kim's bonus) and use it to replace the 4th ciphertext block (which contains Leslie's bonus). Even without knowing what the 12th block says, Leslie can expect to have a much merrier Christmas this year. (Copying the 8th ciphertext block is also a possibility, but is more likely to be detected; besides, Leslie is not a greedy person.)

Cipher Block Chaining Mode

To thwart this type of attack, all block ciphers can be chained in various ways so that replacing a block the way Leslie did will cause the plaintext decrypted starting at the replaced block to be garbage. One way of chaining is **cipher block chaining**. In this method, shown in Fig. 8-12, each plaintext block is XORed with the previous ciphertext block before being encrypted. Consequently, the same plaintext block no longer maps onto the same ciphertext block, and the encryption is no longer a big monoalphabetic substitution cipher. The first block is XORed with a randomly chosen **IV** (**Initialization Vector**), which is transmitted (in plaintext) along with the ciphertext.

We can see how cipher block chaining mode works by examining the example of Fig. 8-12. We start out by computing $C_0 = E(P_0 \text{ XOR } IV)$. Then we compute $C_1 = E(P_1 \text{ XOR } C_0)$, and so on. Decryption also uses XOR to reverse the process, with $P_0 = IV \text{ XOR } D(C_0)$, and so on. Note that the encryption of block i is a function of all the plaintext in blocks 0 through $i - 1$, so the same plaintext generates different ciphertext depending on where it occurs. A transformation of the type Leslie made will result in nonsense for two blocks starting at Leslie's bonus field. To an astute security officer, this peculiarity might suggest where to start the ensuing investigation.

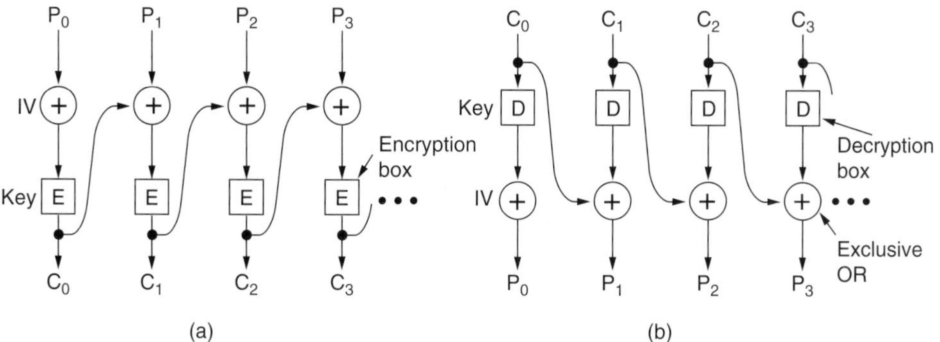

Figure 8-12. Cipher block chaining. (a) Encryption. (b) Decryption.

Cipher block chaining also has the advantage that the same plaintext block will not result in the same ciphertext block, making cryptanalysis more difficult. In fact, this is the main reason it is used.

Cipher Feedback Mode

However, cipher block chaining has the disadvantage of requiring an entire 64-bit block to arrive before decryption can begin. For use with interactive terminals, where people can type lines shorter than eight characters and then stop, waiting for a response, this mode is unsuitable. For byte-by-byte encryption, **cipher feedback mode**, using (triple) DES is used, as shown in Fig. 8-13. For AES the idea is exactly the same, only a 128-bit shift register is used. In this figure, the state of the encryption machine is shown after bytes 0 through 9 have been encrypted and sent. When plaintext byte 10 arrives, as illustrated in Fig. 8-13(a), the DES algorithm operates on the 64-bit shift register to generate a 64-bit ciphertext. The leftmost byte of that ciphertext is extracted and XORed with P_{10}. That byte is transmitted on the transmission line. In addition, the shift register is shifted left 8 bits, causing C_2 to fall off the left end, and C_{10} is inserted in the position just vacated at the right end by C_9. Note that the contents of the shift register depend on the entire previous history of the plaintext, so a pattern that repeats multiple times in the plaintext will be encrypted differently each time in the ciphertext. As with cipher block chaining, an initialization vector is needed to start the ball rolling.

Decryption with cipher feedback mode just does the same thing as encryption. In particular, the content of the shift register is *encrypted*, not *decrypted*, so the selected byte that is XORed with C_{10} to get P_{10} is the same one that was XORed with P_{10} to generate C_{10} in the first place. As long as the two shift registers remain identical, decryption works correctly. It is illustrated in Fig. 8-13(b).

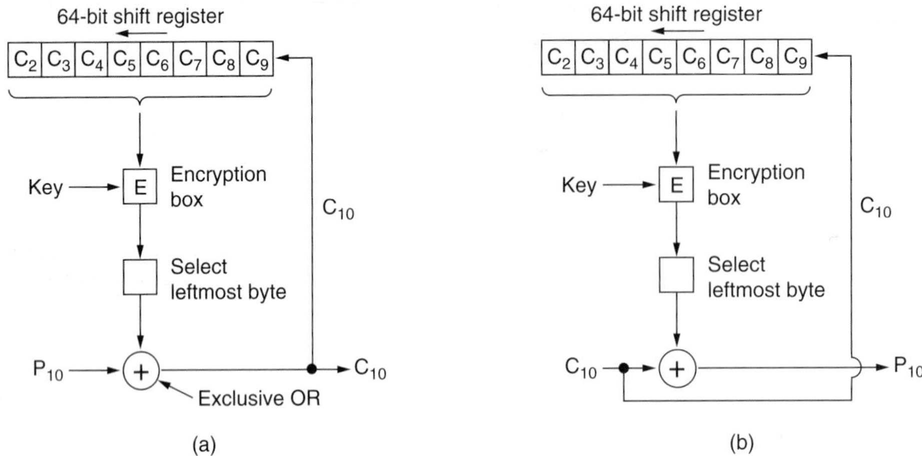

Figure 8-13. Cipher feedback mode. (a) Encryption. (b) Decryption.

A problem with cipher feedback mode is that if one bit of the ciphertext is accidentally inverted during transmission, the 8 bytes that are decrypted while the bad byte is in the shift register will be corrupted. Once the bad byte is pushed out of the shift register, correct plaintext will once again be generated. Thus, the effects of a single inverted bit are relatively localized and do not ruin the rest of the message, but they do ruin as many bits as the shift register is wide.

Stream Cipher Mode

Nevertheless, applications exist in which having a 1-bit transmission error mess up 64 bits of plaintext is too large an effect. For these applications, a fourth option, **stream cipher mode**, exists. It works by encrypting an initialization vector, using a key to get an output block. The output block is then encrypted, using the key to get a second output block. This block is then encrypted to get a third block, and so on. The (arbitrarily large) sequence of output blocks, called the **keystream**, is treated like a one-time pad and XORed with the plaintext to get the ciphertext, as shown in Fig. 8-14(a). Note that the IV is used only on the first step. After that, the output is encrypted. Also note that the keystream is independent of the data, so it can be computed in advance, if need be, and is completely insensitive to transmission errors. Decryption is shown in Fig. 8-14(b).

Decryption occurs by generating the same keystream at the receiving side. Since the keystream depends only on the IV and the key, it is not affected by transmission errors in the ciphertext. Thus, a 1-bit error in the transmitted ciphertext generates only a 1-bit error in the decrypted plaintext.

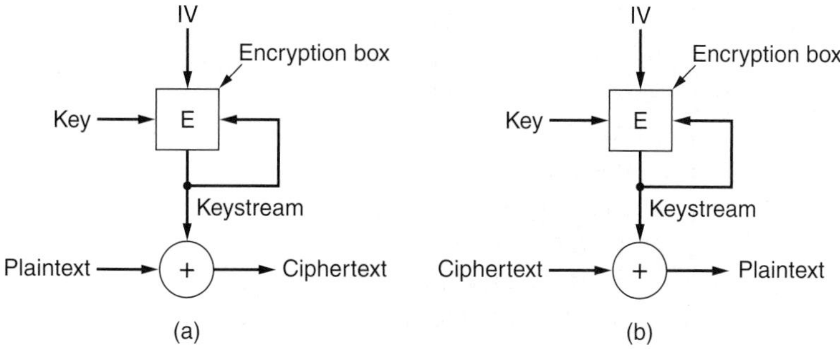

Figure 8-14. A stream cipher. (a) Encryption. (b) Decryption.

It is essential never to use the same (key, IV) pair twice with a stream cipher because doing so will generate the same keystream each time. Using the same keystream twice exposes the ciphertext to a **keystream reuse attack**. Imagine that the plaintext block, P_0, is encrypted with the keystream to get P_0 XOR K_0. Later, a second plaintext block, Q_0, is encrypted with the same keystream to get Q_0 XOR K_0. An intruder who captures both of these ciphertext blocks can simply XOR them together to get P_0 XOR Q_0, which eliminates the key. The intruder now has the XOR of the two plaintext blocks. If one of them is known or can be guessed, the other can also be found. In any event, the XOR of two plaintext streams can be attacked by using statistical properties of the message. For example, for English text, the most common character in the stream will probably be the XOR of two spaces, followed by the XOR of space and the letter "e", etc. In short, equipped with the XOR of two plaintexts, the cryptanalyst has an excellent chance of deducing both of them.

Counter Mode

One problem that all the modes except electronic code book mode have is that random access to encrypted data is impossible. For example, suppose a file is transmitted over a network and then stored on disk in encrypted form. This might be a reasonable way to operate if the receiving computer is a notebook computer that might be stolen. Storing all critical files in encrypted form greatly reduces the damage due to secret information leaking out in the event that the computer falls into the wrong hands.

However, disk files are often accessed in nonsequential order, especially files in databases. With a file encrypted using cipher block chaining, accessing a random block requires first decrypting all the blocks ahead of it, an expensive proposition. For this reason, yet another mode has been invented, **counter mode**, as illustrated in Fig. 8-15. Here the plaintext is not encrypted directly. Instead, the initialization vector plus a constant is encrypted, and the resulting ciphertext XORed with the plaintext. By stepping the initialization vector by 1 for each new block, it is easy to decrypt a block anywhere in the file without first having to decrypt all of its predecessors.

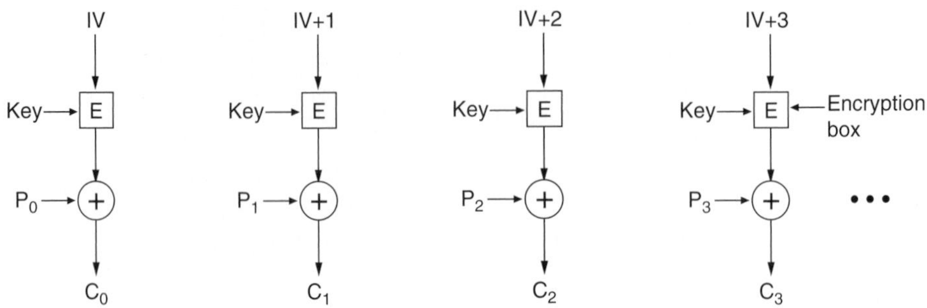

Figure 8-15. Encryption using counter mode.

Although counter mode is useful, it has a weakness that is worth pointing out. Suppose that the same key, *K*, is used again in the future (with a different plaintext but the same IV) and an attacker acquires all the ciphertext from both runs. The keystreams are the same in both cases, exposing the cipher to a keystream reuse attack of the same kind we saw with stream ciphers. All the cryptanalyst has to do is to XOR the two ciphertexts together to eliminate all the cryptographic protection and just get the XOR of the plaintexts. This weakness does not mean counter mode is a bad idea. It just means that both keys and initialization vectors should be chosen independently and at random. Even if the same key is accidentally used twice, if the IV is different each time, the plaintext is safe.

8.2.4 Other Ciphers

DES and Rijndael are the best-known symmetric-key, cryptographic algorithms. However, it is worth mentioning that numerous other symmetric-key ciphers have been devised. Some of these are embedded inside various products. A few of the more common ones are listed in Fig. 8-16.

8.2.5 Cryptanalysis

Before leaving the subject of symmetric-key cryptography, it is worth at least mentioning four developments in cryptanalysis. The first development is **differential cryptanalysis** (Biham and Shamir, 1993). This technique can be used to attack any block cipher. It works by beginning with a pair of plaintext blocks that differ in only a small number of bits and watching carefully what happens on each internal iteration as the encryption proceeds. In many cases, some bit patterns are

Cipher	Author	Key length	Comments
Blowfish	Bruce Schneier	1–448 bits	Old and slow
DES	IBM	56 bits	Too weak to use now
IDEA	Massey and Xuejia	128 bits	Good, but patented
RC4	Ronald Rivest	1–2048 bits	Caution: some keys are weak
RC5	Ronald Rivest	128–256 bits	Good, but patented
Rijndael	Daemen and Rijmen	128–256 bits	Best choice
Serpent	Anderson, Biham, Knudsen	128–256 bits	Very strong
Triple DES	IBM	168 bits	Second best choice
Twofish	Bruce Schneier	128–256 bits	Very strong; widely used

Figure 8-16. Some common symmetric-key cryptographic algorithms.

much more common than other patterns, and this observation leads to a probabilistic attack.

The second development worth noting is **linear cryptanalysis** (Matsui, 1994). It can break DES with only 2^{43} known plaintexts. It works by XORing certain bits in the plaintext and ciphertext together and examining the result for patterns. When this is done repeatedly, half the bits should be 0s and half should be 1s. Often, however, ciphers introduce a bias in one direction or the other, and this bias, however small, can be exploited to reduce the work factor. For the details, see Matsui's paper.

The third development is using analysis of the electrical power consumption to find secret keys. Computers typically use 3 volts to represent a 1 bit and 0 volts to represent a 0 bit. Thus, processing a 1 takes more electrical energy than processing a 0. If a cryptographic algorithm consists of a loop in which the key bits are processed in order, an attacker who replaces the main *n*-GHz clock with a slow (e.g., 100-Hz) clock and puts alligator clips on the CPU's power and ground pins, can precisely monitor the power consumed by each machine instruction. From this data, deducing the key is surprisingly easy. This kind of cryptanalysis can be defeated only by carefully coding the algorithm in assembly language to make sure power consumption is independent of the key and also independent of all the individual round keys.

The fourth development is timing analysis. Cryptographic algorithms are full of if statements that test bits in the round keys. If the then and else parts take different amounts of time, by slowing down the clock and seeing how long various steps take, it may also be possible to deduce the round keys. Once all the round keys are known, the original key can usually be computed. Power and timing analysis can also be employed simultaneously to make the job easier. While power and timing analysis may seem exotic, in reality they are powerful techniques that can break any cipher not specifically designed to resist them.

8.3 PUBLIC-KEY ALGORITHMS

Historically, distributing the keys has always been the weakest link in most cryptosystems. No matter how strong a cryptosystem was, if an intruder could steal the key, the system was worthless. Cryptologists always took for granted that the encryption key and decryption key were the same (or easily derived from one another). But the key had to be distributed to all users of the system. Thus, it seemed as if there was an inherent built-in problem. Keys had to be protected from theft, but they also had to be distributed, so they could not just be locked up in a bank vault.

In 1976, two researchers at Stanford University, Diffie and Hellman (1976), proposed a radically new kind of cryptosystem, one in which the encryption and decryption keys were different, and the decryption key could not feasibly be derived from the encryption key. In their proposal, the (keyed) encryption algorithm, E, and the (keyed) decryption algorithm, D, had to meet three requirements. These requirements can be stated simply as follows:

1. $D(E(P)) = P$.
2. It is exceedingly difficult to deduce D from E.
3. E cannot be broken by a chosen plaintext attack.

The first requirement says that if we apply D to an encrypted message, $E(P)$, we get the original plaintext message, P, back. Without this property, the legitimate receiver could not decrypt the ciphertext. The second requirement speaks for itself. The third requirement is needed because, as we shall see in a moment, intruders may experiment with the algorithm to their hearts' content. Under these conditions, there is no reason that the encryption key cannot be made public.

The method works like this. A person, say, Alice, wanting to receive secret messages, first devises two algorithms meeting the above requirements. The encryption algorithm and Alice's key are then made public, hence the name **public-key cryptography**. Alice might put her public key on her home page on the Web, for example. We will use the notation E_A to mean the encryption algorithm parameterized by Alice's public key. Similarly, the (secret) decryption algorithm parameterized by Alice's private key is D_A. Bob does the same thing, publicizing E_B but keeping D_B secret.

Now let us see if we can solve the problem of establishing a secure channel between Alice and Bob, who have never had any previous contact. Both Alice's encryption key, E_A, and Bob's encryption key, E_B, are assumed to be in publicly readable files. Now Alice takes her first message, P, computes $E_B(P)$, and sends it to Bob. Bob then decrypts it by applying his secret key D_B [i.e., he computes $D_B(E_B(P)) = P$]. No one else can read the encrypted message, $E_B(P)$, because the encryption system is assumed strong and because it is too difficult to derive

D_B from the publicly known E_B. To send a reply, R, Bob transmits $E_A(R)$. Alice and Bob can now communicate securely.

A note on terminology is perhaps useful here. Public-key cryptography requires each user to have two keys: a public key, used by the entire world for encrypting messages to be sent to that user, and a private key, which the user needs for decrypting messages. We will consistently refer to these keys as the *public* and *private* keys, respectively, and distinguish them from the *secret* keys used for conventional symmetric-key cryptography.

8.3.1 RSA

The only catch is that we need to find algorithms that indeed satisfy all three requirements. Due to the potential advantages of public-key cryptography, many researchers are hard at work, and some algorithms have already been published. One good method was discovered by a group at M.I.T. (Rivest et al., 1978). It is known by the initials of the three discoverers (Rivest, Shamir, Adleman): **RSA**. It has survived all attempts to break it for more than a quarter of a century and is considered very strong. Much practical security is based on it. Its major disadvantage is that it requires keys of at least 1024 bits for good security (versus 128 bits for symmetric-key algorithms), which makes it quite slow.

The RSA method is based on some principles from number theory. We will now summarize how to use the method; for details, consult the paper.

1. Choose two large primes, p and q (typically 1024 bits).
2. Compute $n = p \times q$ and $z = (p - 1) \times (q - 1)$.
3. Choose a number relatively prime to z and call it d.
4. Find e such that $e \times d = 1 \; mod \; z$.

With these parameters computed in advance, we are ready to begin encryption. Divide the plaintext (regarded as a bit string) into blocks, so that each plaintext message, P, falls in the interval $0 \le P < n$. Do that by grouping the plaintext into blocks of k bits, where k is the largest integer for which $2^k < n$ is true.

To encrypt a message, P, compute $C = P^e$ (mod n). To decrypt C, compute $P = C^d$ (mod n). It can be proven that for all P in the specified range, the encryption and decryption functions are inverses. To perform the encryption, you need e and n. To perform the decryption, you need d and n. Therefore, the public key consists of the pair (e, n), and the private key consists of (d, n).

The security of the method is based on the difficulty of factoring large numbers. If the cryptanalyst could factor the (publicly known) n, he could then find p and q, and from these z. Equipped with knowledge of z and e, d can be found using Euclid's algorithm. Fortunately, mathematicians have been trying to factor large numbers for at least 300 years, and the accumulated evidence suggests that it is an exceedingly difficult problem.

According to Rivest and colleagues, factoring a 500-digit number requires 10^{25} years using brute force. In both cases, they assume the best known algorithm and a computer with a 1–μsec instruction time. Even if computers continue to get faster by an order of magnitude per decade, it will be centuries before factoring a 500-digit number becomes feasible, at which time our descendants can simply choose p and q still larger.

A trivial pedagogical example of how the RSA algorithm works is given in Fig. 8-17. For this example we have chosen $p = 3$ and $q = 11$, giving $n = 33$ and $z = 20$. A suitable value for d is $d = 7$, since 7 and 20 have no common factors. With these choices, e can be found by solving the equation $7e = 1 \pmod{20}$, which yields $e = 3$. The ciphertext, C, for a plaintext message, P, is given by $C = P^3 \pmod{33}$. The ciphertext is decrypted by the receiver by making use of the rule $P = C^7 \pmod{33}$. The figure shows the encryption of the plaintext "SUZANNE" as an example.

Plaintext (P)			Ciphertext (C)		After decryption	
Symbolic	Numeric	P^3	P^3 (mod 33)	C^7	C^7 (mod 33)	Symbolic
S	19	6859	28	13492928512	19	S
U	21	9261	21	1801088541	21	U
Z	26	17576	20	1280000000	26	Z
A	01	1	1	1	01	A
N	14	2744	5	78125	14	N
N	14	2744	5	78125	14	N
E	05	125	26	8031810176	05	E

Sender's computation (Plaintext through P^3 (mod 33)); Receiver's computation (P^3 (mod 33) through Symbolic)

Figure 8-17. An example of the RSA algorithm.

Because the primes chosen for this example are so small, P must be less than 33, so each plaintext block can contain only a single character. The result is a monoalphabetic substitution cipher, not very impressive. If instead we had chosen p and $q \approx 2^{512}$, we would have $n \approx 2^{1024}$, so each block could be up to 1024 bits or 128 eight-bit characters, versus 8 characters for DES and 16 characters for AES.

It should be pointed out that using RSA as we have described is similar to using a symmetric algorithm in ECB mode—the same input block gives the same output block. Therefore, some form of chaining is needed for data encryption. However, in practice, most RSA-based systems use public-key cryptography primarily for distributing one-time session keys for use with some symmetric-key algorithm such as AES or triple DES. RSA is too slow for actually encrypting large volumes of data but is widely used for key distribution.

8.3.2 Other Public-Key Algorithms

Although RSA is widely used, it is by no means the only public-key algorithm known. The first public-key algorithm was the knapsack algorithm (Merkle and Hellman, 1978). The idea here is that someone owns a large number of objects, each with a different weight. The owner encodes the message by secretly selecting a subset of the objects and placing them in the knapsack. The total weight of the objects in the knapsack is made public, as is the list of all possible objects. The list of objects in the knapsack is kept secret. With certain additional restrictions, the problem of figuring out a possible list of objects with the given weight was thought to be computationally infeasible and formed the basis of the public-key algorithm.

The algorithm's inventor, Ralph Merkle, was quite sure that this algorithm could not be broken, so he offered a $100 reward to anyone who could break it. Adi Shamir (the "S" in RSA) promptly broke it and collected the reward. Undeterred, Merkle strengthened the algorithm and offered a $1000 reward to anyone who could break the new one. Ronald Rivest (the "R" in RSA) promptly broke the new one and collected the reward. Merkle did not dare offer $10,000 for the next version, so "A" (Leonard Adleman) was out of luck. Nevertheless, the knapsack algorithm is not considered secure and is not used in practice any more.

Other public-key schemes are based on the difficulty of computing discrete logarithms. Algorithms that use this principle have been invented by El Gamal (1985) and Schnorr (1991).

A few other schemes exist, such as those based on elliptic curves (Menezes and Vanstone, 1993), but the two major categories are those based on the difficulty of factoring large numbers and computing discrete logarithms modulo a large prime. These problems are thought to be genuinely difficult to solve—mathematicians have been working on them for many years without any great breakthroughs.

8.4 DIGITAL SIGNATURES

The authenticity of many legal, financial, and other documents is determined by the presence or absence of an authorized handwritten signature. And photocopies do not count. For computerized message systems to replace the physical transport of paper and ink documents, a method must be found to allow documents to be signed in an unforgeable way.

The problem of devising a replacement for handwritten signatures is a difficult one. Basically, what is needed is a system by which one party can send a signed message to another party in such a way that the following conditions hold:

1. The receiver can verify the claimed identity of the sender.
2. The sender cannot later repudiate the contents of the message.
3. The receiver cannot possibly have concocted the message himself.

The first requirement is needed, for example, in financial systems. When a customer's computer orders a bank's computer to buy a ton of gold, the bank's computer needs to be able to make sure that the computer giving the order really belongs to the company whose account is to be debited. In other words, the bank has to authenticate the customer (and the customer has to authenticate the bank).

The second requirement is needed to protect the bank against fraud. Suppose that the bank buys the ton of gold, and immediately thereafter the price of gold drops sharply. A dishonest customer might sue the bank, claiming that he never issued any order to buy gold. When the bank produces the message in court, the customer denies having sent it. The property that no party to a contract can later deny having signed it is called **nonrepudiation**. The digital signature schemes that we will now study help provide it.

The third requirement is needed to protect the customer in the event that the price of gold shoots up and the bank tries to construct a signed message in which the customer asked for one bar of gold instead of one ton. In this fraud scenario, the bank just keeps the rest of the gold for itself.

8.4.1 Symmetric-Key Signatures

One approach to digital signatures is to have a central authority that knows everything and whom everyone trusts, say Big Brother (*BB*). Each user then chooses a secret key and carries it by hand to *BB*'s office. Thus, only Alice and *BB* know Alice's secret key, K_A, and so on.

When Alice wants to send a signed plaintext message, P, to her banker, Bob, she generates $K_A(B, R_A, t, P)$, where B is Bob's identity, R_A is a random number chosen by Alice, t is a timestamp to ensure freshness, and $K_A(B, R_A, t, P)$ is the message encrypted with her key, K_A. Then she sends it as depicted in Fig. 8-18. *BB* sees that the message is from Alice, decrypts it, and sends a message to Bob as shown. The message to Bob contains the plaintext of Alice's message and also the signed message $K_{BB}(A, t, P)$. Bob now carries out Alice's request.

What happens if Alice later denies sending the message? Step 1 is that everyone sues everyone (at least, in the United States). Finally, when the case comes to court and Alice vigorously denies sending Bob the disputed message, the judge will ask Bob how he can be sure that the disputed message came from Alice and not from Trudy. Bob first points out that *BB* will not accept a message from Alice unless it is encrypted with K_A, so there is no possibility of Trudy sending *BB* a false message from Alice without BB detecting it immediately.

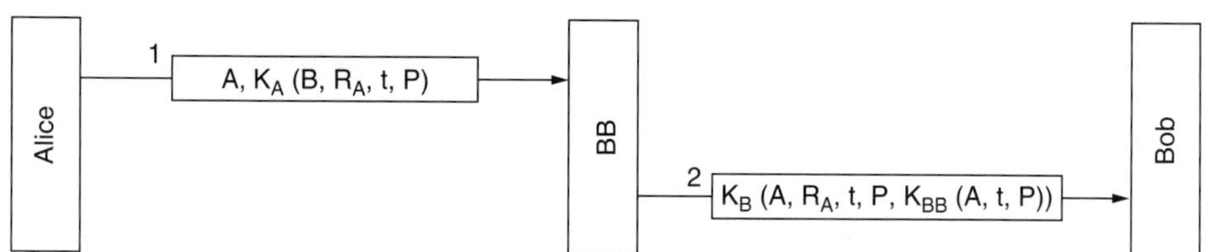

Figure 8-18. Digital signatures with Big Brother.

Bob then dramatically produces Exhibit A: $K_{BB}(A,\ t,\ P)$. Bob says that this is a message signed by *BB* which proves Alice sent *P* to Bob. The judge then asks *BB* (whom everyone trusts) to decrypt Exhibit A. When *BB* testifies that Bob is telling the truth, the judge decides in favor of Bob. Case dismissed.

One potential problem with the signature protocol of Fig. 8-18 is Trudy replaying either message. To minimize this problem, timestamps are used throughout. Furthermore, Bob can check all recent messages to see if R_A was used in any of them. If so, the message is discarded as a replay. Note that based on the timestamp, Bob will reject very old messages. To guard against instant replay attacks, Bob just checks the R_A of every incoming message to see if such a message has been received from Alice in the past hour. If not, Bob can safely assume this is a new request.

8.4.2 Public-Key Signatures

A structural problem with using symmetric-key cryptography for digital signatures is that everyone has to agree to trust Big Brother. Furthermore, Big Brother gets to read all signed messages. The most logical candidates for running the Big Brother server are the government, the banks, the accountants, and the lawyers. Unfortunately, none of these organizations inspire total confidence in all citizens. Hence, it would be nice if signing documents did not require a trusted authority.

Fortunately, public-key cryptography can make an important contribution in this area. Let us assume that the public-key encryption and decryption algorithms have the property that $E(D(P)) = P$ in addition, of course, to the usual property that $D(E(P)) = P$. (RSA has this property, so the assumption is not unreasonable.) Assuming that this is the case, Alice can send a signed plaintext message, P, to Bob by transmitting $E_B(D_A(P))$. Note carefully that Alice knows her own (private) key, D_A, as well as Bob's public key, E_B, so constructing this message is something Alice can do.

When Bob receives the message, he transforms it using his private key, as usual, yielding $D_A(P)$, as shown in Fig. 8-19. He stores this text in a safe place and then applies E_A to get the original plaintext.

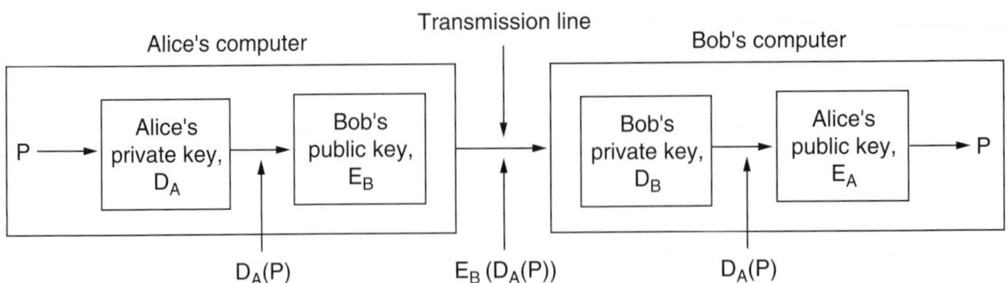

Figure 8-19. Digital signatures using public-key cryptography.

To see how the signature property works, suppose that Alice subsequently denies having sent the message P to Bob. When the case comes up in court, Bob can produce both P and $D_A(P)$. The judge can easily verify that Bob indeed has a valid message encrypted by D_A by simply applying E_A to it. Since Bob does not know what Alice's private key is, the only way Bob could have acquired a message encrypted by it is if Alice did indeed send it. While in jail for perjury and fraud, Alice will have plenty of time to devise interesting new public-key algorithms.

Although using public-key cryptography for digital signatures is an elegant scheme, there are problems that are related to the environment in which they operate rather than with the basic algorithm. For one thing, Bob can prove that a message was sent by Alice only as long as D_A remains secret. If Alice discloses her secret key, the argument no longer holds, because anyone could have sent the message, including Bob himself.

The problem might arise, for example, if Bob is Alice's stockbroker. Alice tells Bob to buy a certain stock or bond. Immediately thereafter, the price drops sharply. To repudiate her message to Bob, Alice runs to the police claiming that her home was burglarized and the PC holding her key was stolen. Depending on the laws in her state or country, she may or may not be legally liable, especially if she claims not to have discovered the break-in until getting home from work, several hours later.

Another problem with the signature scheme is what happens if Alice decides to change her key. Doing so is clearly legal, and it is probably a good idea to do so periodically. If a court case later arises, as described above, the judge will apply the *current* E_A to $D_A(P)$ and discover that it does not produce P. Bob will look pretty stupid at this point.

In principle, any public-key algorithm can be used for digital signatures. The de facto industry standard is the RSA algorithm. Many security products use it. However, in 1991, NIST proposed using a variant of the El Gamal public-key algorithm for their new **Digital Signature Standard** (**DSS**). El Gamal gets its security from the difficulty of computing discrete logarithms, rather than from the difficulty of factoring large numbers.

As usual when the government tries to dictate cryptographic standards, there was an uproar. DSS was criticized for being

1. Too secret (NSA designed the protocol for using El Gamal).
2. Too slow (10 to 40 times slower than RSA for checking signatures).
3. Too new (El Gamal had not yet been thoroughly analyzed).
4. Too insecure (fixed 512-bit key).

In a subsequent revision, the fourth point was rendered moot when keys up to 1024 bits were allowed. Nevertheless, the first two points remain valid.

8.4.3 Message Digests

One criticism of signature methods is that they often couple two distinct functions: authentication and secrecy. Often, authentication is needed but secrecy is not. Also, getting an export license is often easier if the system in question provides only authentication but not secrecy. Below we will describe an authentication scheme that does not require encrypting the entire message.

This scheme is based on the idea of a one-way hash function that takes an arbitrarily long piece of plaintext and from it computes a fixed-length bit string. This hash function, *MD*, often called a **message digest**, has four important properties:

1. Given P, it is easy to compute $MD(P)$.
2. Given $MD(P)$, it is effectively impossible to find P.
3. Given P no one can find P' such that $MD(P') = MD(P)$.
4. A change to the input of even 1 bit produces a very different output.

To meet criterion 3, the hash should be at least 128 bits long, preferably more. To meet criterion 4, the hash must mangle the bits very thoroughly, not unlike the symmetric-key encryption algorithms we have seen.

Computing a message digest from a piece of plaintext is much faster than encrypting that plaintext with a public-key algorithm, so message digests can be used to speed up digital signature algorithms. To see how this works, consider the signature protocol of Fig. 8-18 again. Instead of signing P with $K_{BB}(A, t, P)$, *BB* now computes the message digest by applying *MD* to P, yielding $MD(P)$. BB then encloses $K_{BB}(A, t, MD(P))$ as the fifth item in the list encrypted with K_B that is sent to Bob, instead of $K_{BB}(A, t, P)$.

If a dispute arises, Bob can produce both P and $K_{BB}(A, t, MD(P))$. After Big Brother has decrypted it for the judge, Bob has $MD(P)$, which is guaranteed to be genuine, and the alleged *P*. However, since it is effectively impossible for Bob to find any other message that gives this hash, the judge will easily be convinced that Bob is telling the truth. Using message digests in this way saves both encryption time and message transport costs.

Message digests work in public-key cryptosystems, too, as shown in Fig. 8-20. Here, Alice first computes the message digest of her plaintext. She then signs the message digest and sends both the signed digest and the plaintext to Bob. If Trudy replaces *P* underway, Bob will see this when he computes $MD(P)$ himself.

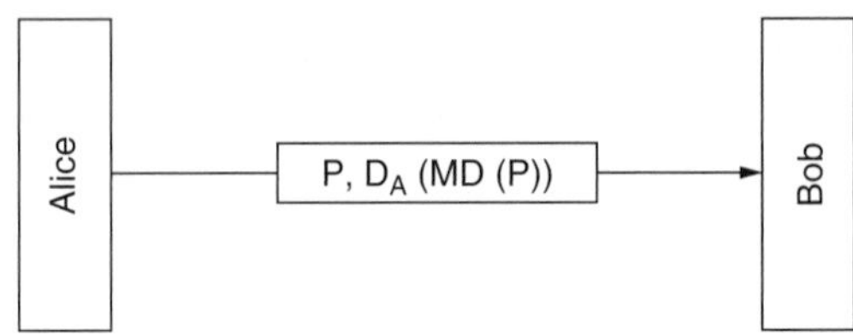

Figure 8-20. Digital signatures using message digests.

MD5

A variety of message digest functions have been proposed. The most widely used ones are MD5 (Rivest, 1992) and SHA-1 (NIST, 1993). **MD5** is the fifth in a series of message digests designed by Ronald Rivest. It operates by mangling bits in a sufficiently complicated way that every output bit is affected by every input bit. Very briefly, it starts out by padding the message to a length of 448 bits (modulo 512). Then the original length of the message is appended as a 64-bit integer to give a total input whose length is a multiple of 512 bits. The last precomputation step is initializing a 128-bit buffer to a fixed value.

Now the computation starts. Each round takes a 512-bit block of input and mixes it thoroughly with the 128-bit buffer. For good measure, a table constructed from the sine function is also thrown in. The point of using a known function like the sine is not because it is more random than a random number generator, but to avoid any suspicion that the designer built in a clever back door through which only he can enter. Remember that IBM's refusal to disclose the principles behind the design of the S-boxes in DES led to a great deal of speculation about back doors. Rivest wanted to avoid this suspicion. Four rounds are performed per input block. This process continues until all the input blocks have been consumed. The contents of the 128-bit buffer form the message digest.

MD5 has been around for over a decade now, and many people have attacked it. Some vulnerabilities have been found, but certain internal steps prevent it from being broken. However, if the remaining barriers within MD5 fall, it may eventually fail. Nevertheless, at the time of this writing, it was still standing.

SHA-1

The other major message digest function is **SHA-1 (Secure Hash Algorithm 1)**, developed by NSA and blessed by NIST in FIPS 180-1. Like MD5, SHA-1 processes input data in 512-bit blocks, only unlike MD5, it generates a 160-bit message digest. A typical way for Alice to send a nonsecret but signed message to Bob is illustrated in Fig. 8-21. Here her plaintext message is fed into the SHA-1 algorithm to get a 160-bit SHA-1 hash. Alice then signs the hash with her RSA private key and sends both the plaintext message and the signed hash to Bob.

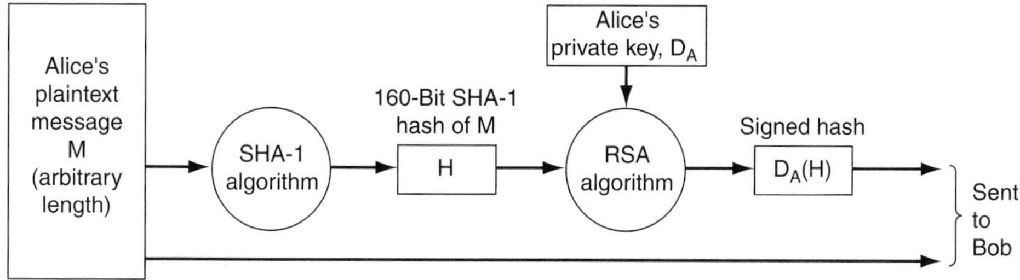

Figure 8-21. Use of SHA-1 and RSA for signing nonsecret messages.

After receving the message, Bob computes the SHA-1 hash himself and also applies Alice's public key to the signed hash to get the original hash, *H*. If the two agree, the message is considered valid. Since there is no way for Trudy to modify the (plaintext) message while its is in transit and produce a new one that hashes to *H*, Bob can easily detect any changes Trudy has made to the message. For messages whose integrity is important but whose contents are not secret, the scheme of Fig. 8-21 is widely used. For a relatively small cost in computation, it guarantees that any modifications made to the plaintext message in transit can be detected with very high probability.

Now let us briefly see how SHA-1 works. It starts out by padding the message by adding a 1 bit to the end, followed by as many 0 bits as are needed to make the length a multiple of 512 bits. Then a 64-bit number containing the message length before padding is ORed into the low-order 64 bits. In Fig. 8-22, the message is shown with padding on the right because English text and figures go from left to right (i.e., the lower right is generally perceived as the end of the figure). With computers, this orientation corresponds to big-endian machines such as the SPARC, but SHA-1 always pads the end of the message, no matter which endian machine is used.

During the computation, SHA-1 maintains five 32-bit variables, H_0 through H_4, where the hash accumulates. These are shown in Fig. 8-22(b). They are initialized to constants specified in the standard.

Each of the blocks M_0 through M_{n-1} is now processed in turn. For the current block, the 16 words are first copied into the start of an auxiliary 80-word

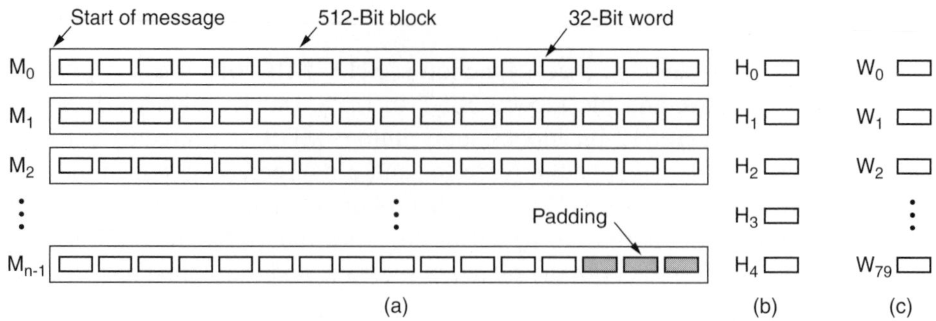

Figure 8-22. (a) A message padded out to a multiple of 512 bits. (b) The output variables. (c) The word array.

array, W, as shown in Fig. 8-22(c). Then the other 64 words in W are filled in using the formula

$$W_i = S^1(W_{i-3} \text{ XOR } W_{i-8} \text{ XOR } W_{i-14} \text{ XOR } W_{i-16}) \quad (16 \le i \le 79)$$

where $S^b(W)$ represents the left circular rotation of the 32-bit word, W, by b bits. Now five scratch variables, A through E are initialized from H_0 through H_4, respectively.

The actual calculation can be expressed in pseudo-C as

```
for (i = 0; i < 80; i++) {
    temp = S^5(A) + f_i (B, C, D) + E + W_i + K_i;
    E = D;  D = C;  C = S^30(B);  B = A;  A = temp;
}
```

where the K_i constants are defined in the standard. The mixing functions f_i are defined as

$$f_i(B,C,D) = (B \text{ AND } C) \text{ OR } (\text{NOT } B \text{ AND } D) \quad (0 \le i \le 19)$$
$$f_i(B,C,D) = B \text{ XOR } C \text{ XOR } D \quad (20 \le i \le 39)$$
$$f_i(B,C,D) = (B \text{ AND } C) \text{ OR } (B \text{ AND } D) \text{ OR } (C \text{ AND } D) \quad (40 \le i \le 59)$$
$$f_i(B,C,D) = B \text{ XOR } C \text{ XOR } D \quad (60 \le i \le 79)$$

When all 80 iterations of the loop are completed, A through E are added to H_0 through H_4, respectively.

Now that the first 512-bit block has been processed, the next one is started. The W array is reinitialized from the new block, but H is left as it was. When this block is finished, the next one is started, and so on, until all the 512-bit message blocks have been tossed into the soup. When the last block has been finished, the five 32-bit words in the H array are output as the 160-bit cryptographic hash. The complete C code for SHA-1 is given in RFC 3174.

New versions of SHA-1 are under development for hashes of 256, 384, and 512 bits, respectively.

8.4.4 The Birthday Attack

In the world of crypto, nothing is ever what it seems to be. One might think that it would take on the order of 2^m operations to subvert an m-bit message digest. In fact, $2^{m/2}$ operations will often do using the **birthday attack,** an approach published by Yuval (1979) in his now-classic paper "How to Swindle Rabin."

The idea for this attack comes from a technique that math professors often use in their probability courses. The question is: How many students do you need in a class before the probability of having two people with the same birthday exceeds 1/2? Most students expect the answer to be way over 100. In fact, probability theory says it is just 23. Without giving a rigorous analysis, intuitively, with 23 people, we can form $(23 \times 22)/2 = 253$ different pairs, each of which has a probability of 1/365 of being a hit. In this light, it is not really so surprising any more.

More generally, if there is some mapping between inputs and outputs with n inputs (people, messages, etc.) and k possible outputs (birthdays, message digests, etc.), there are $n(n-1)/2$ input pairs. If $n(n-1)/2 > k$, the chance of having at least one match is pretty good. Thus, approximately, a match is likely for $n > \sqrt{k}$. This result means that a 64-bit message digest can probably be broken by generating about 2^{32} messages and looking for two with the same message digest.

Let us look at a practical example. The Department of Computer Science at State University has one position for a tenured faculty member and two candidates, Tom and Dick. Tom was hired two years before Dick, so he goes up for review first. If he gets it, Dick is out of luck. Tom knows that the department chairperson, Marilyn, thinks highly of his work, so he asks her to write him a letter of recommendation to the Dean, who will decide on Tom's case. Once sent, all letters become confidential.

Marilyn tells her secretary, Ellen, to write the Dean a letter, outlining what she wants in it. When it is ready, Marilyn will review it, compute and sign the 64-bit digest, and send it to the Dean. Ellen can send the letter later by e-mail.

Unfortunately for Tom, Ellen is romantically involved with Dick and would like to do Tom in, so she writes the letter below with the 32 bracketed options.

Dear Dean Smith,

This [*letter* | *message*] is to give my [*honest* | *frank*] opinion of Prof. Tom Wilson, who is [*a candidate* | *up*] for tenure [*now* | *this year*]. I have [*known* | *worked with*] Prof. Wilson for [*about* | *almost*] six years. He is an [*outstanding* | *excellent*] researcher of great [*talent* | *ability*] known [*worldwide* | *internationally*] for his [*brilliant* | *creative*] insights into [*many* | *a wide variety of*] [*difficult* | *challenging*] problems.

He is also a [*highly* | *greatly*] [*respected* | *admired*] [*teacher* | *educator*]. His students give his [*classes* | *courses*] [*rave* | *spectacular*] reviews. He is [*our* | *the Department's*] [*most popular* | *best-loved*] [*teacher* | *instructor*].

[*In addition* | *Additionally*] Prof. Wilson is a [*gifted* | *effective*] fund raiser. His [*grants* | *contracts*] have brought a [*large* | *substantial*] amount of money into [*the* | *our*] Department. [*This money has* | *These funds have*] [*enabled* | *permitted*] us to [*pursue* | *carry out*] many [*special* | *important*] programs, [*such as* | *for example*] your State 2000 program. Without these funds we would [*be unable* | *not be able*] to continue this program, which is so [*important* | *essential*] to both of us. I strongly urge you to grant him tenure.

Unfortunately for Tom, as soon as Ellen finishes composing and typing in this letter, she also writes a second one:

Dear Dean Smith,

This [*letter* | *message*] is to give my [*honest* | *frank*] opinion of Prof. Tom Wilson, who is [*a candidate* | *up*] for tenure [*now* | *this year*]. I have [*known* | *worked with*] Tom for [*about* | *almost*] six years. He is a [*poor* | *weak*] researcher not well known in his [*field* | *area*]. His research [*hardly ever* | *rarely*] shows [*insight in* | *understanding of*] the [*key* | *major*] problems of [*the* | *our*] day.

Furthermore, he is not a [*respected* | *admired*] [*teacher* | *educator*]. His students give his [*classes* | *courses*] [*poor* | *bad*] reviews. He is [*our* | *the Department's*] least popular [*teacher* | *instructor*], known [*mostly* | *primarily*] within [*the* | *our*] Department for his [*tendency* | *propensity*] to [*ridicule* | *embarrass*] students [*foolish* | *imprudent*] enough to ask questions in his classes.

[*In addition* | *Additionally*] Tom is a [*poor* | *marginal*] fund raiser. His [*grants* | *contracts*] have brought only a [*meager* | *insignificant*] amount of money into [*the* | *our*] Department. Unless new [*money is* | *funds are*] quickly located, we may have to cancel some essential programs, such as your State 2000 program. Unfortunately, under these [*conditions* | *circumstances*] I cannot in good [*conscience* | *faith*] recommend him to you for [*tenure* | *a permanent position*].

Now Ellen programs her computer to compute the 2^{32} message digests of each letter overnight. Chances are, one digest of the first letter will match one digest of the second letter. If not, she can add a few more options and try again during the weekend. Suppose that she finds a match. Call the "good" letter *A* and the "bad" one *B*.

Ellen now e-mails letter *A* to Marilyn for her approval. Letter *B* she keeps completely secret, showing it to no one. Marilyn, of course, approves, computes her 64-bit message digest, signs the digest, and e-mails the signed digest off to Dean Smith. Independently, Ellen e-mails letter *B* to the Dean (not letter *A*, as she is supposed to).

After getting the letter and signed message digest, the Dean runs the message digest algorithm on letter *B*, sees that it agrees with what Marilyn sent him, and fires Tom. The Dean does not realize that Ellen managed to generate two letters with the same message digest and sent her a different one than Marilyn saw and approved. (Optional ending: Ellen tells Dick what she did. Dick is appalled and breaks off with her. Ellen is furious and confesses to Marilyn. Marilyn calls the Dean. Tom gets tenure after all.) With MD5 the birthday attack is difficult because even at 1 billion digests per second, it would take over 500 years to compute all 2^{64} digests of two letters with 64 variants each, and even then a match is not guaranteed. Of course, with 5000 computers working in parallel, 500 years becomes 5 weeks. SHA-1 is better (because it is longer).

8.5 MANAGEMENT OF PUBLIC KEYS

Public-key cryptography makes it possible for people who do not share a common key to communicate securely. It also makes signing messages possible without the presence of a trusted third party. Finally, signed message digests make it possible to verify the integrity of received messages easily.

However, there is one problem that we have glossed over a bit too quickly: if Alice and Bob do not know each other, how do they get each other's public keys to start the communication process? The obvious solution—put your public key on your Web site—does not work for the following reason. Suppose that Alice wants to look up Bob's public key on his Web site. How does she do it? She starts by typing in Bob's URL. Her browser then looks up the DNS address of Bob's home page and sends it a *GET* request, as shown in Fig. 8-23. Unfortunately, Trudy intercepts the request and replies with a fake home page, probably a copy of Bob's home page except for the replacement of Bob's public key with Trudy's public key. When Alice now encrypts her first message with E_T, Trudy decrypts it, reads it, reencrypts it with Bob's public key, and sends it to Bob, who is none the wiser that Trudy is reading his incoming messages. Worse yet, Trudy could modify the messages before reencrypting them for Bob. Clearly, some mechanism is needed to make sure that public keys can be exchanged securely.

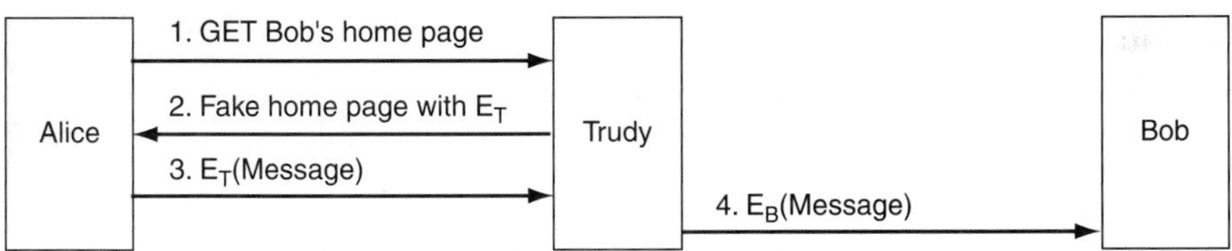

Figure 8-23. A way for Trudy to subvert public-key encryption.

8.5.1 Certificates

As a first attempt at distributing public keys securely, we could imagine a key distribution center available on-line 24 hours a day to provide public keys on demand. One of the many problems with this solution is that it is not scalable, and the key distribution center would rapidly become a bottleneck. Also, if it ever went down, Internet security would suddenly grind to a halt.

For these reasons, people have developed a different solution, one that does not require the key distribution center to be on-line all the time. In fact, it does not have to be on-line at all. Instead, what it does is certify the public keys belonging to people, companies, and other organizations. An organization that certifies public keys is now called a **CA** (**Certification Authority**).

As an example, suppose that Bob wants to allow Alice and other people to communicate with him securely. He can go to the CA with his public key along with his passport or driver's license and ask to be certified. The CA then issues a certificate similar to the one in Fig. 8-24 and signs its SHA-1 hash with the CA's private key. Bob then pays the CA's fee and gets a floppy disk containing the certificate and its signed hash.

```
I hereby certify that the public key
    19836A8B03030CF83737E3837837FC3s87092827262643FFA82710382828282A
belongs to
    Robert John Smith
    12345 University Avenue
    Berkeley, CA 94702
    Birthday: July 4, 1958
    Email: bob@superdupernet.com

SHA-1 hash of the above certificate signed with the CA's private key
```

Figure 8-24. A possible certificate and its signed hash.

The fundamental job of a certificate is to bind a public key to the name of a principal (individual, company, etc.). Certificates themselves are not secret or protected. Bob might, for example, decide to put his new certificate on his Web site, with a link on the main page saying: Click here for my public-key certificate. The resulting click would return both the certificate and the signature block (the signed SHA-1 hash of the certificate).

Now let us run through the scenario of Fig. 8-23 again. When Trudy intercepts Alice's request for Bob's home page, what can she do? She can put her own certificate and signature block on the fake page, but when Alice reads the certificate she will immediately see that she is not talking to Bob because Bob's name is not in it. Trudy can modify Bob's home page on-the-fly, replacing Bob's public key with her own. However, when Alice runs the SHA-1 algorithm on the certificate, she will get a hash that does not agree with the one she gets when she applies the CA's well-known public key to the signature block. Since Trudy does not have the CA's private key, she has no way of generating a signature block that contains the hash of the modified Web page with her public key on it. In this way, Alice can be sure she has Bob's public key and not Trudy's or someone else's. And as we promised, this scheme does not require the CA to be on-line for verification, thus eliminating a potential bottleneck.

While the standard function of a certificate is to bind a public key to a principal, a certificate can also be used to bind a public key to an **attribute**. For example, a certificate could say: This public key belongs to someone over 18. It could be used to prove that the owner of the private key was not a minor and thus allowed to access material not suitable for children, and so on, but without disclosing the owner's identity. Typically, the person holding the certificate would send it to the Web site, principal, or process that cared about age. That site, principal, or process would then generate a random number and encrypt it with the public key in the certificate. If the owner were able to decrypt it and send it back, that would be proof that the owner indeed had the attribute stated in the certificate. Alternatively, the random number could be used to generate a session key for the ensuing conversation.

Another example of where a certificate might contain an attribute is in an object-oriented distributed system. Each object normally has multiple methods. The owner of the object could provide each customer with a certificate giving a bit map of which methods the customer is allowed to invoke and binding the bit map to a public key using a signed certificate. Again here, if the certificate holder can prove possession of the corresponding private key, he will be allowed to perform the methods in the bit map. It has the property that the owner's identity need not be known, a property useful in situations where privacy is important.

8.5.2 X.509

If everybody who wanted something signed went to the CA with a different kind of certificate, managing all the different formats would soon become a problem. To solve this problem, a standard for certificates has been devised and approved by ITU. The standard is called **X.509** and is in widespread use on the Internet. It has gone through three versions since the initial standardization in 1988. We will discuss V3.

X.509 has been heavily influenced by the OSI world, borrowing some of its worst features (e.g., naming and encoding). Surprisingly, IETF went along with X.509, even though in nearly every other area, from machine addresses to transport protocols to e-mail formats, IETF generally ignored OSI and tried to do it right. The IETF version of X.509 is described in RFC 3280.

At its core, X.509 is a way to describe certificates. The primary fields in a certificate are listed in Fig. 8-25. The descriptions given there should provide a general idea of what the fields do. For additional information, please consult the standard itself or RFC 2459.

For example, if Bob works in the loan department of the Money Bank, his X.500 address might be:

```
/C=US/O=MoneyBank/OU=Loan/CN=Bob/
```

where *C* is for country, *O* is for organization, *OU* is for organizational unit, and *CN* is for common name. CAs and other entities are named in a similar way. A

Field	Meaning
Version	Which version of X.509
Serial number	This number plus the CA's name uniquely identifies the certificate
Signature algorithm	The algorithm used to sign the certificate
Issuer	X.500 name of the CA
Validity period	The starting and ending times of the validity period
Subject name	The entity whose key is being certified
Public key	The subject's public key and the ID of the algorithm using it
Issuer ID	An optional ID uniquely identifying the certificate's issuer
Subject ID	An optional ID uniquely identifying the certificate's subject
Extensions	Many extensions have been defined
Signature	The certificate's signature (signed by the CA's private key)

Figure 8-25. The basic fields of an X.509 certificate.

substantial problem with X.500 names is that if Alice is trying to contact *bob@moneybank.com* and is given a certificate with an X.500 name, it may not be obvious to her that the certificate refers to the Bob she wants. Fortunately, starting with version 3, DNS names are now permitted instead of X.500 names, so this problem may eventually vanish.

Certificates are encoded using the OSI **ASN.1** (**Abstract Syntax Notation 1**), which can be thought of as being like a struct in C, except with a very peculiar and verbose notation. More information about X.509 can be found in (Ford and Baum, 2000).

8.5.3 Public Key Infrastructures

Having a single CA to issue all the world's certificates obviously would not work. It would collapse under the load and be a central point of failure as well. A possible solution might be to have multiple CAs, all run by the same organization and all using the same private key to sign certificates. While this would solve the load and failure problems, it introduces a new problem: key leakage. If there were dozens of servers spread around the world, all holding the CA's private key, the chance of the private key being stolen or otherwise leaking out would be greatly increased. Since the compromise of this key would ruin the world's electronic security infrastructure, having a single central CA is very risky.

In addition, which organization would operate the CA? It is hard to imagine any authority that would be accepted worldwide as legitimate and trustworthy. In some countries people would insist that it be a government, while in other countries they would insist that it not be a government.

For these reasons, a different way for certifying public keys has evolved. It goes under the general name of **PKI** (**Public Key Infrastructure**). In this section we will summarize how it works in general, although there have been many proposals so the details will probably evolve in time.

A PKI has multiple components, including users, CAs, certificates, and directories. What the PKI does is provide a way of structuring these components and define standards for the various documents and protocols. A particularly simple form of PKI is a hierarchy of CAs, as depicted in Fig. 8-26. In this example we have shown three levels, but in practice there might be fewer or more. The top-level CA, the root, certifies second-level CAs, which we call **RA**s (**Regional Authorities**) because they might cover some geographic region, such as a country or continent. This term is not standard, though; in fact, no term is really standard for the different levels of the tree. These in turn certify the real CAs, which issue the X.509 certificates to organizations and individuals. When the root authorizes a new RA, it generates an X.509 certificate stating that it has approved the RA, includes the new RA's public key in it, signs it, and hands it to the RA. Similarly, when an RA approves a new CA, it produces and signs a certificate stating its approval and containing the CA's public key.

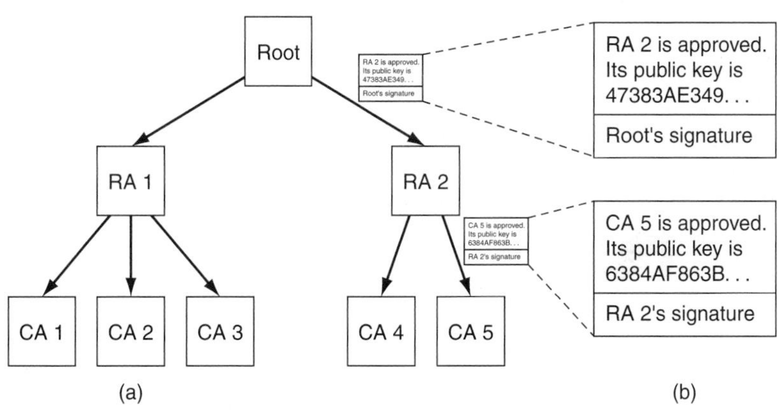

Figure 8-26. (a) A hierarchical PKI. (b) A chain of certificates.

Our PKI works like this. Suppose that Alice needs Bob's public key in order to communicate with him, so she looks for and finds a certificate containing it, signed by CA 5. But Alice has never heard of CA 5. For all she knows, CA 5 might be Bob's 10-year-old daughter. She could go to CA 5 and say: Prove your legitimacy. CA 5 responds with the certificate it got from RA 2, which contains CA 5's public key. Now armed with CA 5's public key, she can verify that Bob's certificate was indeed signed by CA 5 and is thus legal.

Unless RA 2 is Bob's 12-year-old son. So the next step is for her to ask RA 2 to prove it is legitimate. The response to her query is a certificate signed by the root and containing RA 2's public key. Now Alice is sure she has Bob's public key.

But how does Alice find the root's public key? Magic. It is assumed that everyone knows the root's public key. For example, her browser might have been shipped with the root's public key built in.

Bob is a friendly sort of guy and does not want to cause Alice a lot of work. He knows that she is going to have to check out CA 5 and RA 2, so to save her some trouble, he collects the two needed certificates and gives her the two certificates along with his. Now she can use her own knowledge of the root's public key to verify the top-level certificate and the public key contained therein to verify the second one. In this way, Alice does not need to contact anyone to do the verification. Because the certificates are all signed, she can easily detect any attempts to tamper with their contents. A chain of certificates going back to the root like this is sometimes called a **chain of trust** or a **certification path**. The technique is widely used in practice.

Of course, we still have the problem of who is going to run the root. The solution is not to have a single root, but to have many roots, each with its own RAs and CAs. In fact, modern browsers come preloaded with the public keys for over 100 roots, sometimes referred to as **trust anchors**. In this way, having a single worldwide trusted authority can be avoided.

But there is now the issue of how the browser vendor decides which purported trust anchors are reliable and which are sleazy. It all comes down to the user trusting the browser vendor to make wise choices and not simply approve all trust anchors willing to pay its inclusion fee. Most browsers allow users to inspect the root keys (usually in the form of certificates signed by the root) and delete any that seem shady.

Directories

Another issue for any PKI is where certificates (and their chains back to some known trust anchor) are stored. One possibility is to have each user store his or her own certificates. While doing this is safe (i.e., there is no way for users to tamper with signed certificates without detection), it is also inconvenient. One alternative that has been proposed is to use DNS as a certificate directory. Before contacting Bob, Alice probably has to look up his IP address using DNS, so why not have DNS return Bob's entire certificate chain along with his IP address?

Some people think this is the way to go, but others would prefer dedicated directory servers whose only job is managing X.509 certificates. Such directories could provide lookup services by using properties of the X.500 names. For example, in theory such a directory service could answer a query such as: "Give me a list of all people named Alice who work in sales departments anywhere in the U.S. or Canada." LDAP might be a candidate for holding such information.

Revocation

The real world is full of certificates, too, such as passports and drivers' licenses. Sometimes these certificates can be revoked, for example, drivers' licenses can be revoked for drunken driving and other driving offenses. The same problem occurs in the digital world: the grantor of a certificate may decide to revoke it because the person or organization holding it has abused it in some way. It can also be revoked if the subject's private key has been exposed, or worse yet, the CA's private key has been compromised. Thus, a PKI needs to deal with the issue of revocation.

A first step in this direction is to have each CA periodically issue a **CRL** (**Certificate Revocation List**) giving the serial numbers of all certificates that it has revoked. Since certificates contain expiry times, the CRL need only contain the serial numbers of certificates that have not yet expired. Once its expiry time has passed, a certificate is automatically invalid, so no distinction is needed between those that just timed out and those that were actually revoked. In both cases, they cannot be used any more.

Unfortunately, introducing CRLs means that a user who is about to use a certificate must now acquire the CRL to see if the certificate has been revoked. If it has been, it should not be used. However, even if the certificate is not on the list, it might have been revoked just after the list was published. Thus, the only way to really be sure is to ask the CA. And on the next use of the same certificate, the CA has to be asked again, since the certificate might have been revoked a few seconds ago.

Another complication is that a revoked certificate could conceivably be reinstated, for example, if it was revoked for nonpayment of some fee that has since been paid. Having to deal with revocation (and possibly reinstatement) eliminates one of the best properties of certificates, namely, that they can be used without having to contact a CA.

Where should CRLs be stored? A good place would be the same place the certificates themselves are stored. One strategy is for the CA to actively push out CRLs periodically and have the directories process them by simply removing the revoked certificates. If directories are not used for storing certificates, the CRLs can be cached at various convenient places around the network. Since a CRL is itself a signed document, if it is tampered with, that tampering can be easily detected.

If certificates have long lifetimes, the CRLs will be long, too. For example, if credit cards are valid for 5 years, the number of revocations outstanding will be much longer than if new cards are issued every 3 months. A standard way to deal with long CRLs is to issue a master list infrequently, but issue updates to it more often. Doing this reduces the bandwidth needed for distributing the CRLs.

8.6 COMMUNICATION SECURITY

We have now finished our study of the tools of the trade. Most of the important techniques and protocols have been covered. The rest of the chapter is about how these techniques are applied in practice to provide network security, plus some thoughts about the social aspects of security at the end of the chapter.

In the following four sections, we will look at communication security, that is, how to get the bits secretly and without modification from source to destination and how to keep unwanted bits outside the door. These are by no means the only security issues in networking, but they are certainly among the most important ones, making this a good place to start.

8.6.1 IPsec

IETF has known for years that security was lacking in the Internet. Adding it was not easy because a war broke out about where to put it. Most security experts believe that to be really secure, encryption and integrity checks have to be end to end (i.e., in the application layer). That is, the source process encrypts and/or integrity protects the data and sends that to the destination process where it is decrypted and/or verified. Any tampering done in between these two processes, including within either operating system, can then be detected. The trouble with this approach is that it requires changing all the applications to make them security aware. In this view, the next best approach is putting encryption in the transport layer or in a new layer between the application layer and the transport layer, making it still end to end but not requiring applications to be changed.

The opposite view is that users do not understand security and will not be capable of using it correctly and nobody wants to modify existing programs in any way, so the network layer should authenticate and/or encrypt packets without the users being involved. After years of pitched battles, this view won enough support that a network layer security standard was defined. In part the argument was that having network layer encryption does not prevent security-aware users from doing it right and it does help security-unaware users to some extent.

The result of this war was a design called **IPsec** (**IP security**), which is described in RFCs 2401, 2402, and 2406, among others. Not all users want encryption (because it is computationally expensive). Rather than make it optional, it was decided to require encryption all the time but permit the use of a null algorithm. The null algorithm is described and praised for its simplicity, ease of implementation, and great speed in RFC 2410.

The complete IPsec design is a framework for multiple services, algorithms and granularities. The reason for multiple services is that not everyone wants to pay the price for having all the services all the time, so the services are available a la carte. The major services are secrecy, data integrity, and protection from replay attacks (intruder replays a conversation). All of these are based on symmetric-key cryptography because high performance is crucial.

The reason for having multiple algorithms is that an algorithm that is now thought to be secure may be broken in the future. By making IPsec algorithm-independent, the framework can survive even if some particular algorithm is later broken.

The reason for having multiple granularities is to make it possible to protect a single TCP connection, all traffic between a pair of hosts, or all traffic between a pair of secure routers, among other possibilities.

One slightly surprising aspect of IPsec is that even though it is in the IP layer, it is connection oriented. Actually, that is not so surprising because to have any security, a key must be established and used for some period of time—in essence, a kind of connection. Also connections amortize the setup costs over many packets. A "connection" in the context of IPsec is called an **SA** (**security association**). An SA is a simplex connection between two end points and has a security identifier associated with it. If secure traffic is needed in both directions, two security associations are required. Security identifiers are carried in packets traveling on these secure connections and are used to look up keys and other relevant information when a secure packet arrives.

Technically, IPsec has two principal parts. The first part describes two new headers that can be added to packets to carry the security identifier, integrity control data, and other information. The other part, **ISAKMP** (**Internet Security Association and Key Management Protocol**) deals with establishing keys. We will not deal with ISAKMP further because (1) it is extremely complex and (2) its main protocol, **IKE** (**Internet Key Exchange**), is deeply flawed and needs to be replaced (Perlman and Kaufman, 2000).

IPsec can be used in either of two modes. In **transport mode**, the IPsec header is inserted just after the IP header. The *Protocol* field in the IP header is changed to indicate that an IPsec header follows the normal IP header (before the TCP header). The IPsec header contains security information, primarily the SA identifier, a new sequence number, and possibly an integrity check of the payload.

In **tunnel mode**, the entire IP packet, header and all, is encapsulated in the body of a new IP packet with a completely new IP header. Tunnel mode is useful when the tunnel ends at a location other than the final destination. In some cases, the end of the tunnel is a security gateway machine, for example, a company firewall. In this mode, the firewall encapsulates and decapsulates packets as they pass though the firewall. By terminating the tunnel at this secure machine, the machines on the company LAN do not have to be aware of IPsec. Only the firewall has to know about it.

Tunnel mode is also useful when a bundle of TCP connections is aggregated and handled as one encrypted stream because it prevents an intruder from seeing who is sending how many packets to whom. Sometimes just knowing how much traffic is going where is valuable information. For example, if during a military crisis, the amount of traffic flowing between the Pentagon and the White House drops sharply, but the amount of traffic between the Pentagon and some military installation deep in the Colorado Rocky Mountains increases by the same amount, an intruder might be able to deduce some useful information from this data. Studying the flow patterns of packets, even if they are encrypted, is called **traffic analysis**. Tunnel mode provides a way to foil it to some extent. The disadvantage of tunnel mode is that it adds an extra IP header, thus increasing packet size substantially. In contrast, transport mode does not affect packet size as much.

The first new header is **AH** (**Authentication Header**). It provides integrity checking and antireplay security, but not secrecy (i.e., no data encryption). The use of AH in transport mode is illustrated in Fig. 8-27. In IPv4 it is interposed between the IP header (including any options) and the TCP header. In IPv6 it is just another extension header and treated as such. In fact, the format is close to that of a standard IPv6 extension header. The payload may have to be padded out to some particular length for the authentication algorithm, as shown.

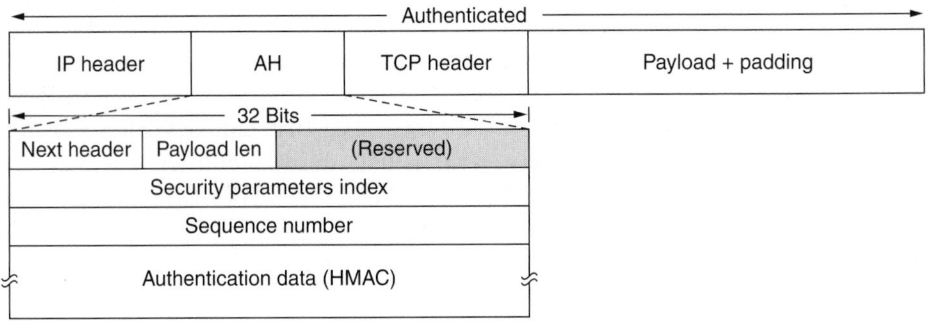

Figure 8-27. The IPsec authentication header in transport mode for IPv4.

Let us now examine the AH header. The *Next header field* is used to store the previous value that the IP *Protocol* field had before it was replaced with 51 to indicate that an AH header follows. In most cases, the code for TCP (6) will go here. The *Payload length* is the number of 32-bit words in the AH header minus 2.

The *Security parameters index* is the connection identifier. It is inserted by the sender to indicate a particular record in the receiver's database. This record contains the shared key used on this connection and other information about the connection. If this protocol had been invented by ITU rather than IETF, this field would have been called *Virtual circuit number*.

The *Sequence number* field is used to number all the packets sent on an SA. Every packet gets a unique number, even retransmissions. In other words, the retransmission of a packet gets a different number here than the original (even though its TCP sequence number is the same). The purpose of this field is to detect replay attacks. These sequence numbers may not wrap around. If all 2^{32} are exhausted, a new SA must be established to continue communication.

Finally, we come to the *Authentication data*, which is a variable-length field that contains the payload's digital signature. When the SA is established, the two sides negotiate which signature algorithm they are going to use. Normally, public-key cryptography is not used here because packets must be processed extremely rapidly and all known public-key algorithms are too slow. Since IPsec is based on symmetric-key cryptography and the sender and receiver negotiate a shared key before setting up an SA, the shared key is used in the signature computation. One simple way is to compute the hash over the packet plus the shared key. The shared key is not transmitted, of course. A scheme like this is called an **HMAC (Hashed Message Authentication Code)**. It is much faster to compute than first running SHA-1 and then running RSA on the result.

The AH header does not allow encryption of the data, so it is mostly useful when integrity checking is needed but secrecy is not needed. One noteworthy feature of AH is that the integrity check covers some of the fields in the IP header, namely, those that do not change as the packet moves from router to router. The *Time to live* field changes on each hop, for example, so it cannot be included in the integrity check. However, the IP source address is included in the check, making it impossible for an intruder to falsify the origin of a packet.

The alternative IPsec header is **ESP (Encapsulating Security Payload)**. Its use for both transport mode and tunnel mode is shown in Fig. 8-28.

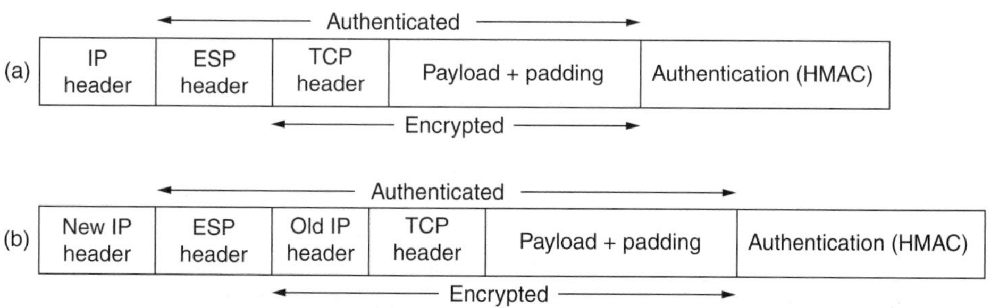

Figure 8-28. (a) ESP in transport mode. (b) ESP in tunnel mode.

The ESP header consists of two 32-bit words. They are the *Security parameters index* and *Sequence number* fields that we saw in AH. A third word that generally follows them (but is technically not part of the header) is the *Initialization vector* used for the data encryption, unless null encryption is used, in which case it is omitted.

ESP also provides for HMAC integrity checks, as does AH, but rather than being included in the header, they come after the payload, as shown in Fig. 8-28. Putting the HMAC at the end has an advantage in a hardware implementation. The HMAC can be calculated as the bits are going out over the network interface and appended to the end. This is why Ethernet and other LANs have their CRCs in a trailer, rather than in a header. With AH, the packet has to be buffered and the signature computed before the packet can be sent, potentially reducing the number of packets/sec that can be sent.

Given that ESP can do everything AH can do and more and is more efficient to boot, the question arises: Why bother having AH at all? The answer is mostly historical. Originally, AH handled only integrity and ESP handled only secrecy. Later, integrity was added to ESP, but the people who designed AH did not want to let it die after all that work. Their only real argument, however, is that AH checks part of the IP header, which ESP does not, but it is a weak argument. Another weak argument is that a product supporting AH but not ESP might have less trouble getting an export license because it cannot do encryption. AH is likely to be phased out in the future.

8.6.2 Firewalls

The ability to connect any computer, anywhere, to any other computer, anywhere, is a mixed blessing. For individuals at home, wandering around the Internet is lots of fun. For corporate security managers, it is a nightmare. Most companies have large amounts of confidential information on-line—trade secrets, product development plans, marketing strategies, financial analyses, etc. Disclosure of this information to a competitor could have dire consequences.

In addition to the danger of information leaking out, there is also a danger of information leaking in. In particular, viruses, worms, and other digital pests can breach security, destroy valuable data, and waste large amounts of administrators' time trying to clean up the mess they leave. Often they are imported by careless employees who want to play some nifty new game.

Consequently, mechanisms are needed to keep "good" bits in and "bad" bits out. One method is to use IPsec. This approach protects data in transit between secure sites. However, IPsec does nothing to keep digital pests and intruders from getting onto the company LAN. To see how to accomplish this goal, we need to look at firewalls.

Firewalls are just a modern adaptation of that old medieval security standby: digging a deep moat around your castle. This design forced everyone entering or leaving the castle to pass over a single drawbridge, where they could be inspected by the I/O police. With networks, the same trick is possible: a company can have many LANs connected in arbitrary ways, but all traffic to or from the company is forced through an electronic drawbridge (firewall), as shown in Fig. 8-29.

The firewall in this configuration has two components: two routers that do packet filtering and an application gateway. Simpler configurations also exist, but the advantage of this design is that every packet must transit two filters and an application gateway to go in or out. No other route exists. Readers who think that one security checkpoint is enough clearly have not made an international flight on a scheduled airline recently.

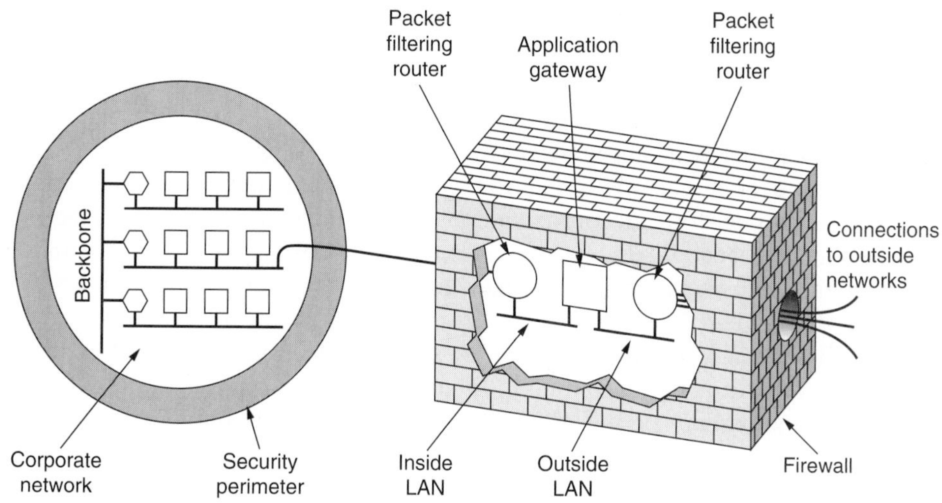

Figure 8-29. A firewall consisting of two packet filters and an application gateway.

Each **packet filter** is a standard router equipped with some extra functionality. The extra functionality allows every incoming or outgoing packet to be inspected. Packets meeting some criterion are forwarded normally. Those that fail the test are dropped.

In Fig. 8-29, most likely the packet filter on the inside LAN checks outgoing packets and the one on the outside LAN checks incoming packets. Packets crossing the first hurdle go to the application gateway for further examination. The point of putting the two packet filters on different LANs is to ensure that no packet gets in or out without having to pass through the application gateway: there is no path around it.

Packet filters are typically driven by tables configured by the system administrator. These tables list sources and destinations that are acceptable, sources and destinations that are blocked, and default rules about what to do with packets coming from or going to other machines.

In the common case of a TCP/IP setting, a source or destination consists of an IP address and a port. Ports indicate which service is desired. For example, TCP port 23 is for telnet, TCP port 79 is for finger, and TCP port 119 is for USENET news. A company could block incoming packets for all IP addresses combined with one of these ports. In this way, no one outside the company could log in via telnet or look up people by using the Finger daemon. Furthermore, the company would be spared from having employees spend all day reading USENET news.

Blocking outgoing packets is trickier because although most sites stick to the standard port numbering conventions, they are not forced to do so. Furthermore, for some important services, such as FTP (File Transfer Protocol), port numbers are assigned dynamically. In addition, although blocking TCP connections is difficult, blocking UDP packets is even harder because so little is known a priori about what they will do. Many packet filters are configured to simply ban UDP traffic altogether.

The second half of the firewall is the **application gateway**. Rather than just looking at raw packets, the gateway operates at the application level. A mail gateway, for example, can be set up to examine each message going in or coming out. For each one, the gateway decides whether to transmit or discard the message based on header fields, message size, or even the content (e.g., at a military installation, the presence of words like "nuclear" or "bomb" might cause some special action to be taken).

Installations are free to set up one or more application gateways for specific applications, but it is not uncommon for suspicious organizations to permit e-mail in and out, and perhaps permit use of the World Wide Web, but to ban everything else as too dicey. Combined with encryption and packet filtering, this arrangement offers a limited amount of security at the cost of some inconvenience.

Even if the firewall is perfectly configured, plenty of security problems still exist. For example, if a firewall is configured to allow in packets from only specific networks (e.g., the company's other plants), an intruder outside the firewall can put in false source addresses to bypass this check. If an insider wants to ship out secret documents, he can encrypt them or even photograph them and ship the photos as JPEG files, which bypasses any word filters. And we have not even discussed the fact that 70% of all attacks come from inside the firewall, for example, from disgruntled employees (Schneier, 2000).

In addition, there is a whole other class of attacks that firewalls cannot deal with. The basic idea of a firewall is to prevent intruders from getting in and secret data from getting out. Unfortunately, there are people who have nothing better to do than try to bring certain sites down. They do this by sending legitimate packets at the target in great numbers until it collapses under the load. For example, to cripple a Web site, an intruder can send a TCP *SYN* packet to establish a connection. The site will then allocate a table slot for the connection and send a *SYN* + *ACK* packet in reply. If the intruder does not respond, the table slot will be tied up for a few seconds until it times out. If the intruder sends thousands of connection requests, all the table slots will fill up and no legitimate connections will be able to get through. Attacks in which the intruder's goal is to shut down the target rather than steal data are called **DoS** (**Denial of Service**) attacks. Usually, the request packets have false source addresses so the intruder cannot be traced easily.

An even worse variant is one in which the intruder has already broken into hundreds of computers elsewhere in the world, and then commands all of them to attack the same target at the same time. Not only does this approach increase the intruder's firepower, it also reduces his chance of detection, since the packets are coming from a large number of machines belonging to unsuspecting users. Such an attack is called a **DDoS** (**Distributed Denial of Service**) attack. This attack is difficult to defend against. Even if the attacked machine can quickly recognize a bogus request, it does take some time to process and discard the request, and if enough requests per second arrive, the CPU will spend all its time dealing with them.

8.6.3 Virtual Private Networks

Many companies have offices and plants scattered over many cities, sometimes over multiple countries. In the olden days, before public data networks, it was common for such companies to lease lines from the telephone company between some or all pairs of locations. Some companies still do this. A network built up from company computers and leased telephone lines is called a **private network**. An example private network connecting three locations is shown in Fig. 8-30(a).

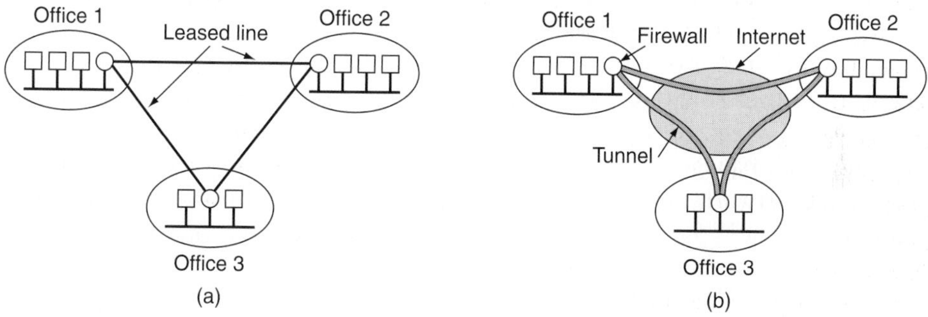

Figure 8-30. (a) A leased-line private network. (b) A virtual private network.

Private networks work fine and are very secure. If the only lines available are the leased lines, no traffic can leak out of company locations and intruders have to physically wiretap the lines to break in, which is not easy to do. The problem with private networks is that leasing a single T1 line costs thousands of dollars a month and T3 lines are many times more expensive. When public data networks and later the Internet appeared, many companies wanted to move their data (and possibly voice) traffic to the public network, but without giving up the security of the private network.

This demand soon led to the invention of **VPNs** (**Virtual Private Networks**), which are overlay networks on top of public networks but with most of the properties of private networks. They are called "virtual" because they are merely an illusion, just as virtual circuits are not real circuits and virtual memory is not real memory.

Although VPNs can be implemented on top of ATM (or frame relay), an increasingly popular approach is to build VPNs directly over the Internet. A common design is to equip each office with a firewall and create tunnels through the Internet between all pairs of offices, as illustrated in Fig. 8-30(b). If IPsec is used for the tunneling, then it is possible to aggregate all traffic between any two pairs of offices onto a single authenticated, encrypted SA, thus providing integrity control, secrecy, and even considerable immunity to traffic analysis.

When the system is brought up, each pair of firewalls has to negotiate the parameters of its SA, including the services, modes, algorithms, and keys. Many firewalls have VPN capabilities built in, although some ordinary routers can do this as well. But since firewalls are primarily in the security business, it is natural to have the tunnels begin and end at the firewalls, providing a clear separation between the company and the Internet. Thus, firewalls, VPNs, and IPsec with ESP in tunnel mode are a natural combination and widely used in practice.

Once the SAs have been established, traffic can begin flowing. To a router within the Internet, a packet traveling along a VPN tunnel is just an ordinary packet. The only thing unusual about it is the presence of the IPsec header after the IP header, but since these extra headers have no effect on the forwarding process, the routers do not care about this extra header.

A key advantage of organizing a VPN this way is that it is completely transparent to all user software. The firewalls set up and manage the SAs. The only person who is even aware of this setup is the system administrator who has to configure and manage the firewalls. To everyone else, it is like having a leased-line private network again. For more about VPNs, see (Brown, 1999; and Izzo, 2000).

8.6.4 Wireless Security

It is surprisingly easy to design a system that is logically completely secure by using VPNs and firewalls, but that, in practice, leaks like a sieve. This situation can occur if some of the machines are wireless and use radio communication, which passes right over the firewall in both directions. The range of 802.11 networks is often a few hundred meters, so anyone who wants to spy on a company can simply drive into the employee parking lot in the morning, leave an 802.11-enabled notebook computer in the car to record everything it hears, and take off for the day. By late afternoon, the hard disk will be full of valuable goodies. Theoretically, this leakage is not supposed to happen. Theoretically, people are not supposed to rob banks, either.

Much of the security problem can be traced to the manufacturers of wireless base stations (access points) trying to make their products user friendly. Usually, if the user takes the device out of the box and plugs it into the electrical power socket, it begins operating immediately—nearly always with no security at all, blurting secrets to everyone within radio range. If it is then plugged into an Ethernet, all the Ethernet traffic suddenly appears in the parking lot as well. Wireless is a snooper's dream come true: free data without having to do any work. It therefore goes without saying that security is even more important for wireless systems than for wired ones. In this section, we will look at some ways wireless networks handle security. Some additional information can be found in (Nichols and Lekkas, 2002).

802.11 Security

The 802.11 standard prescribes a data link-level security protocol called **WEP (Wired Equivalent Privacy)**, which is designed to make the security of a wireless LAN as good as that of a wired LAN. Since the default for wired LANs is no security at all, this goal is easy to achieve, and WEP achieves it, as we shall see.

When 802.11 security is enabled, each station has a secret key shared with the base station. How the keys are distributed is not specified by the standard. They could be preloaded by the manufacturer. They could be exchanged in advance over the wired network. Finally, either the base station or user machine could pick a random key and send it to the other one over the air encrypted with the other one's public key. Once established, keys generally remain stable for months or years.

WEP encryption uses a stream cipher based on the RC4 algorithm. RC4 was designed by Ronald Rivest and kept secret until it leaked out and was posted to the Internet in 1994. As we have pointed out before, it is nearly impossible to keep algorithms secret, even when the goal is guarding intellectual property (as it was in this case) rather than security by obscurity (which was not the goal with RC4). In WEP, RC4 generates a keystream that is XORed with the plaintext to form the ciphertext.

Each packet payload is encrypted using the method of Fig. 8-31. First the payload is checksummed using the CRC-32 polynomial and the checksum appended to the payload to form the plaintext for the encryption algorithm. Then this plaintext is XORed with a chunk of keystream its own size. The result is the ciphertext. The IV used to start RC4 is sent along with the ciphertext. When the receiver gets the packet, it extracts the encrypted payload from it, generates the keystream from the shared secret key and the IV it just got, and XORs the keystream with the payload to recover the plaintext. It can then verify the checksum to see if the packet has been tampered with.

While this approach looks good at first glance, a method for breaking it has already been published (Borisov et al., 2001). Below we will summarize their results. First of all, surprisingly many installations use the same shared key for all users, in which case each user can read all the other users' traffic. This is certainly equivalent to Ethernet, but it is not very secure.

But even if each user has a distinct key, WEP can still be attacked. Since keys are generally stable for long periods of time, the WEP standard recommends (but does not mandate) that IV be changed on every packet to avoid the keystream

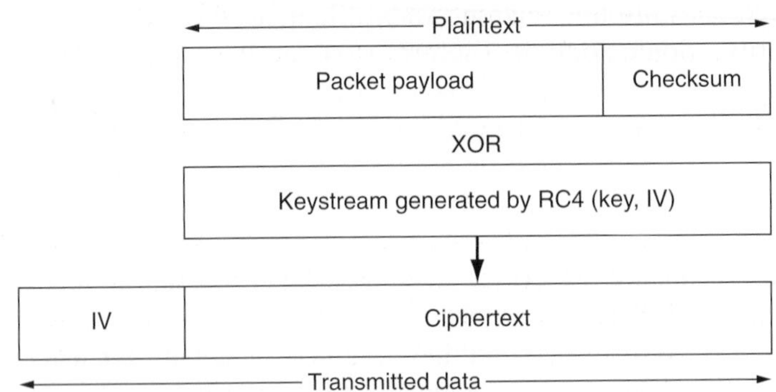

Figure 8-31. Packet encryption using WEP.

reuse attack we discussed in Sec. 8.2.3. Unfortunately, many 802.11 cards for notebook computers reset IV to 0 when the card is inserted into the computer, and increment it by one on each packet sent. Since people often remove and reinsert these cards, packets with low IV values are common. If Trudy can collect several packets sent by the same user with the same IV value (which is itself sent in plaintext along with each packet), she can compute the XOR of two plaintext values and probably break the cipher that way.

But even if the 802.11 card picks a random IV for each packet, the IVs are only 24 bits, so after 2^{24} packets have been sent, they have to be reused. Worse yet, with randomly chosen IVs, the expected number of packets that have to be sent before the same one is used twice is about 5000, due to the birthday attack described in Sec. 8.4.4. Thus, if Trudy listens for a few minutes, she is almost sure to capture two packets with the same IV and same key. By XORing the ciphertexts she is able to obtain the XOR of the plaintexts. This bit sequence can be attacked in various ways to recover the plaintexts. With some more work, the keystream for that IV can also be obtained. Trudy can continue working like this for a while and compile a dictionary of keystreams for various IVs. Once an IV has been broken, all the packets sent with it in the future (but also in the past) can be fully decrypted.

Furthermore, since IVs are used at random, once Trudy has determined a valid (IV, keystream) pair, she can use it to generate all the packets she wants to using it and thus actively interfere with communication. Theoretically, a receiver could notice that large numbers of packets suddenly all have the same IV, but (1) WEP allows this, and (2) nobody checks for this anyway.

Finally, the CRC is not worth much, since it is possible for Trudy to change the payload and make the corresponding change to the CRC, without even having to remove the encryption In short, breaking 802.11's security is fairly straightforward, and we have not even listed all the attacks Borisov et al. found.

In August 2001, a month after the Borisov et al. paper was presented, another devastating attack on WEP was published (Fluhrer et al., 2001). This one found cryptographic weaknesses in RC4 itself. Fluhrer et al. discovered that many of the keys have the property that it is possible to derive some key bits from the keystream. If this attack is performed repeatedly, it is possible to derive the entire key with a modest amount of effort. Being somewhat theoretically inclined, Fluhrer et al. did not actually try to break any 802.11 LANs.

In contrast, when a summer student and two researchers at AT&T Labs learned about the Fluhrer et al. attack, they decided to try it out for real (Stubblefield et al., 2002). Within a week they had broken their first 128-bit key on a production 802.11 LAN, and most of the week was actually devoted to looking for the cheapest 802.11 card they could find, getting permission to buy it, installing it, and testing it. The programming took only two hours.

When they announced their results, CNN ran a story entitled "Off-the-Shelf Hack Breaks Wireless Encryption," in which some industry gurus tried to pooh-pooh their results by saying what they had done was trivial, given the Fluhrer et al. results. While that remark is technically true, the fact remains that the combined efforts of these two teams demonstrated a fatal flaw in WEP and 802.11.

On September 7, 2001, IEEE responded to the fact that WEP was now completely broken by issuing a short statement making six points that can be roughly summarized as follows:

1. We told you that WEP security was no better than Ethernet's.
2. A much bigger threat is forgetting to enable security at all.
3. Try using some other security (e.g., transport layer security).
4. The next version, 802.11i, will have better security.
5. Future certification will mandate the use of 802.11i.
6. We will try to figure out what to do until 802.11i arrives.

We have gone through this story in some detail to make the point that getting security right is not easy, even for experts.

Bluetooth Security

Bluetooth has a considerably shorter range than 802.11, so it cannot be attacked from the parking lot, but security is still an issue here. For example, imagine that Alice's computer is equipped with a wireless Bluetooth keyboard. In the absence of security, if Trudy happened to be in the adjacent office, she could read everything Alice typed in, including all her outgoing e-mail. She could also capture everything Alice's computer sent to the Bluetooth printer sitting next to it (e.g., incoming e-mail and confidential reports). Fortunately, Bluetooth has an elaborate security scheme to try to foil the world's Trudies. We will now summarize the main features of it below.

Bluetooth has three security modes, ranging from nothing at all to full data encryption and integrity control. As with 802.11, if security is disabled (the default), there is no security. Most users have security turned off until a serious breach has occurred; then they turn it on. In the agricultural world, this approach is known as locking the barn door after the horse has escaped.

Bluetooth provides security in multiple layers. In the physical layer, frequency hopping provides a tiny bit of security, but since any Bluetooth device that moves into a piconet has to be told the frequency hopping sequence, this sequence is obviously not a secret. The real security starts when the newly-arrived slave asks for a channel with the master. The two devices are assumed to share a secret key set up in advance. In some cases, both are hardwired by the manufacturer (e.g., for a headset and mobile phone sold as a unit). In other cases, one device (e.g., the headset) has a hardwired key and the user has to enter that key into the other device (e.g., the mobile phone) as a decimal number. These shared keys are called **passkeys**.

To establish a channel, the slave and master each check to see if the other one knows the passkey. If so, they negotiate whether that channel will be encrypted, integrity controlled, or both. Then they select a random 128-bit session key, some of whose bits may be public. The point of allowing this key weakening is to comply with government restrictions in various countries designed to prevent the export or use of keys longer than the government can break.

Encryption uses a stream cipher called $\mathbf{E_0}$; integrity control uses **SAFER+**. Both are traditional symmetric-key block ciphers. SAFER+ was submitted to the AES bake-off, but was eliminated in the first round because it was slower than the other candidates. Bluetooth was finalized before the AES cipher was chosen; otherwise it would most likely have used Rijndael.

The actual encryption using the stream cipher is shown in Fig. 8-14, with the plaintext XORed with the keystream to generate the ciphertext. Unfortunately, E_0 itself (like RC4) may have fatal weaknesses (Jakobsson and Wetzel, 2001). While it was not broken at the time of this writing, its similarities to the A5/1 cipher, whose spectacular failure compromises all GSM telephone traffic, are cause for concern (Biryukov et al., 2000). It sometimes amazes people (including the author), that in the perennial cat-and-mouse game between cryptographers and cryptanalysts, the cryptanalysts are so often on the winning side.

Another security issue is that Bluetooth authenticates only devices, not users, so theft of a Bluetooth device may give the thief access to the user's financial and other accounts. However, Bluetooth also implements security in the upper layers, so even in the event of a breach of link-level security, some security may remain, especially for applications that require a PIN code to be entered manually from some kind of keyboard to complete the transaction.

WAP 2.0 Security

For the most part, the WAP Forum learned its lesson from having a nonstandard protocol stack in WAP 1.0. WAP 2.0 largely uses standard protocols in all layers. Security is no exception. Since it is IP based, it supports full use of IPsec in the network layer. In the transport layer, TCP connections can be protected by TLS, an IETF standard we will study later in this chapter. Higher still, it uses HTTP client authentication, as defined in RFC 2617. Application-layer crypto libraries provide for integrity control and nonrepudiation. All in all, since WAP 2.0 is based on well-known standards, there is a chance that its security services, in particular, privacy, authentication, integrity control, and nonrepudiation may fare better than 802.11 and Bluetooth security.

8.7 AUTHENTICATION PROTOCOLS

Authentication is the technique by which a process verifies that its communication partner is who it is supposed to be and not an imposter. Verifying the identity of a remote process in the face of a malicious, active intruder is surprisingly difficult and requires complex protocols based on cryptography. In this section, we will study some of the many authentication protocols that are used on insecure computer networks.

As an aside, some people confuse authorization with authentication. Authentication deals with the question of whether you are actually communicating with a specific process. Authorization is concerned with what that process is permitted to do. For example, a client process contacts a file server and says: I am Scott's process and I want to delete the file *cookbook.old*. From the file server's point of view, two questions must be answered:

1. Is this actually Scott's process (authentication)?
2. Is Scott allowed to delete *cookbook.old* (authorization)?

Only after both of these questions have been unambiguously answered in the affirmative can the requested action take place. The former question is really the key one. Once the file server knows to whom it is talking, checking authorization is just a matter of looking up entries in local tables or databases. For this reason, we will concentrate on authentication in this section.

The general model that all authentication protocols use is this. Alice starts out by sending a message either to Bob or to a trusted **KDC** (**Key Distribution Center**), which is expected to be honest. Several other message exchanges follow in various directions. As these messages are being sent Trudy may intercept, modify, or replay them in order to trick Alice and Bob or just to gum up the works.

Nevertheless, when the protocol has been completed, Alice is sure she is talking to Bob and Bob is sure he is talking to Alice. Furthermore, in most of the protocols, the two of them will also have established a secret **session key** for use in the upcoming conversation. In practice, for performance reasons, all data traffic is encrypted using symmetric-key cryptography (typically AES or triple DES), although public-key cryptography is widely used for the authentication protocols themselves and for establishing the session key.

The point of using a new, randomly-chosen session key for each new connection is to minimize the amount of traffic that gets sent with the users' secret keys or public keys, to reduce the amount of ciphertext an intruder can obtain, and to minimize the damage done if a process crashes and its core dump falls into the wrong hands. Hopefully, the only key present then will be the session key. All the permanent keys should have been carefully zeroed out after the session was established.

8.7.1 Authentication Based on a Shared Secret Key

For our first authentication protocol, we will assume that Alice and Bob already share a secret key, K_{AB}. This shared key might have been agreed upon on the telephone or in person, but, in any event, not on the (insecure) network.

This protocol is based on a principle found in many authentication protocols: one party sends a random number to the other, who then transforms it in a special way and then returns the result. Such protocols are called **challenge-response** protocols. In this and subsequent authentication protocols, the following notation will be used:

A, B are the identities of Alice and Bob.
R_i's are the challenges, where the subscript identifies the challenger.
K_i are keys, where i indicates the owner.
K_S is the session key.

The message sequence for our first shared-key authentication protocol is illustrated in Fig. 8-32. In message 1, Alice sends her identity, A, to Bob in a way that Bob understands. Bob, of course, has no way of knowing whether this message came from Alice or from Trudy, so he chooses a challenge, a large random number, R_B, and sends it back to "Alice" as message 2, in plaintext. Random numbers used just once in challenge-response protocols like this one are called **nonces**. Alice then encrypts the message with the key she shares with Bob and sends the ciphertext, $K_{AB}(R_B)$, back in message 3. When Bob sees this message, he immediately knows that it came from Alice because Trudy does not know K_{AB} and thus could not have generated it. Furthermore, since R_B was chosen randomly from a large space (say, 128-bit random numbers), it is very unlikely that Trudy would have seen R_B and its response from an earlier session. It is equally unlikely that she could guess the correct response to any challenge.

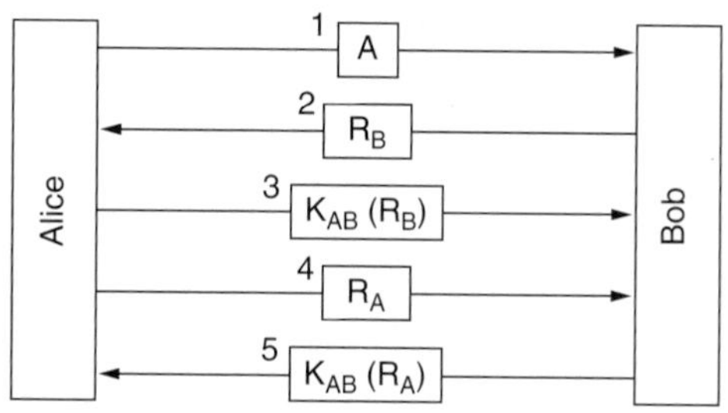

Figure 8-32. Two-way authentication using a challenge-response protocol.

At this point, Bob is sure he is talking to Alice, but Alice is not sure of anything. For all Alice knows, Trudy might have intercepted message 1 and sent back R_B in response. Maybe Bob died last night. To find out to whom she is talking, Alice picks a random number, R_A and sends it to Bob as plaintext, in message 4. When Bob responds with $K_{AB}(R_A)$, Alice knows she is talking to Bob. If they wish to establish a session key now, Alice can pick one, K_S, and send it to Bob encrypted with K_{AB}.

The protocol of Fig. 8-32 contains five messages. Let us see if we can be clever and eliminate some of them. One approach is illustrated in Fig. 8-33. Here Alice initiates the challenge-response protocol instead of waiting for Bob to do it. Similarly, while he is responding to Alice's challenge, Bob sends his own. The entire protocol can be reduced to three messages instead of five.

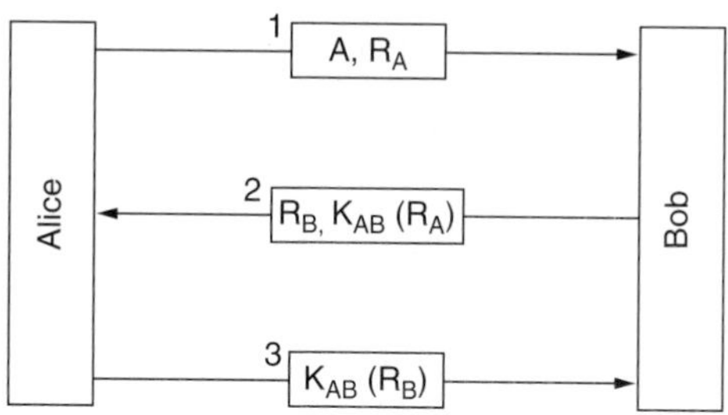

Figure 8-33. A shortened two-way authentication protocol.

Is this new protocol an improvement over the original one? In one sense it is: it is shorter. Unfortunately, it is also wrong. Under certain circumstances, Trudy can defeat this protocol by using what is known as a **reflection attack**. In particular, Trudy can break it if it is possible to open multiple sessions with Bob at once. This situation would be true, for example, if Bob is a bank and is prepared to accept many simultaneous connections from teller machines at once.

Trudy's reflection attack is shown in Fig. 8-34. It starts out with Trudy claiming she is Alice and sending R_T. Bob responds, as usual, with his own challenge, R_B. Now Trudy is stuck. What can she do? She does not know $K_{AB}(R_B)$.

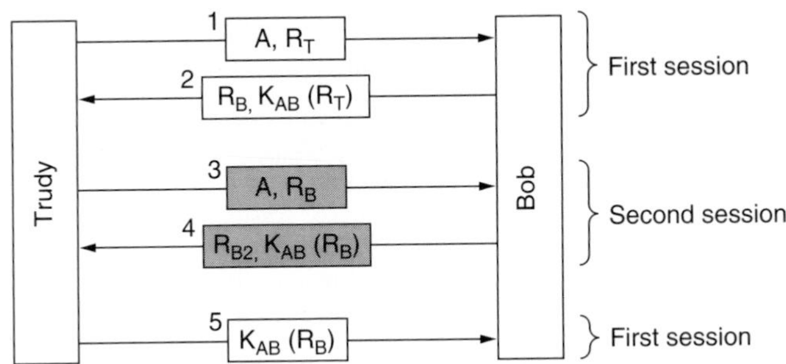

Figure 8-34. The reflection attack.

She can open a second session with message 3, supplying the R_B taken from message 2 as her challenge. Bob calmly encrypts it and sends back $K_{AB}(R_B)$ in message 4. We have shaded the messages on the second session to make them stand out. Now Trudy has the missing information, so she can complete the first session and abort the second one. Bob is now convinced that Trudy is Alice, so when she asks for her bank account balance, he gives it to her without question. Then when she asks him to transfer it all to a secret bank account in Switzerland, he does so without a moment's hesitation.

The moral of this story is:

Designing a correct authentication protocol is harder than it looks.

The following four general rules often help:

1. Have the initiator prove who she is before the responder has to. In this case, Bob gives away valuable information before Trudy has to give any evidence of who she is.

2. Have the initiator and responder use different keys for proof, even if this means having two shared keys, K_{AB} and K'_{AB}.

3. Have the initiator and responder draw their challenges from different sets. For example, the initiator must use even numbers and the responder must use odd numbers.

4. Make the protocol resistant to attacks involving a second parallel session in which information obtained in one session is used in a different one.

If even one of these rules is violated, the protocol can frequently be broken. Here, all four rules were violated, with disastrous consequences.

Now let us go back and take a closer look at Fig. 8-32. Surely that protocol is not subject to a reflection attack? Well, it depends. It is quite subtle. Trudy was able to defeat our protocol by using a reflection attack because it was possible to open a second session with Bob and trick him into answering his own questions. What would happen if Alice were a general-purpose computer that also accepted multiple sessions, rather than a person at a computer? Let us take a look what Trudy can do.

To see how Trudy's attack works, see Fig. 8-35. Alice starts out by announcing her identity in message 1. Trudy intercepts this message and begins her own session with message 2, claiming to be Bob. Again we have shaded the session 2 messages. Alice responds to message 2 by saying: You claim to be Bob? Prove it. in message 3. At this point Trudy is stuck because she cannot prove she is Bob.

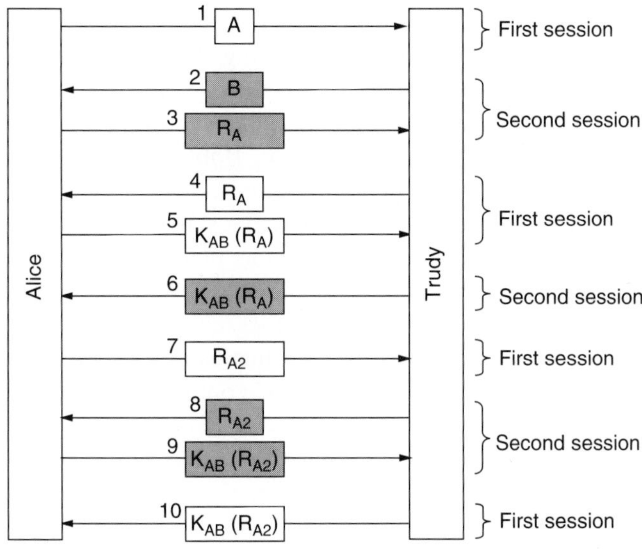

Figure 8-35. A reflection attack on the protocol of Fig. 8-32.

What does Trudy do now? She goes back to the first session, where it is her turn to send a challenge, and sends the R_A she got in message 3. Alice kindly responds to it in message 5, thus supplying Trudy with the information she needs to send message 6 in session 2. At this point, Trudy is basically home free because she has successfully responded to Alice's challenge in session 2. She can now cancel session 1, send over any old number for the rest of session 2, and she will have an authenticated session with Alice in session 2.

But Trudy is nasty, and she really wants to rub it in. Instead of sending any old number over to complete session 2, she waits until Alice sends message 7, Alice's challenge for session 1. Of course, Trudy does not know how to respond, so she uses the reflection attack again, sending back R_{A2} as message 8. Alice conveniently encrypts R_{A2} in message 9. Trudy now switches back to session 1 and sends Alice the number she wants in message 10, conveniently copied from what Alice sent in message 9. At this point Trudy has two fully authenticated sessions with Alice.

This attack has a somewhat different result than the attack on the three-message protocol shown in Fig. 8-34. This time, Trudy has two authenticated connections with Alice. In the previous example, she had one authenticated connection with Bob. Again here, if we had applied all the general authentication protocol rules discussed above, this attack could have been stopped. A detailed discussion of these kind of attacks and how to thwart them is given in (Bird et al., 1993). They also show how it is possible to systematically construct protocols that are provably correct. The simplest such protocol is nevertheless a bit complicated, so we will now show a different class of protocol that also works.

The new authentication protocol is shown in Fig. 8-36 (Bird et al., 1993). It uses an HMAC of the type we saw when studying IPsec. Alice starts out by sending Bob a nonce, R_A as message 1. Bob responds by selecting his own nonce, R_B, and sending it back along with an HMAC. The HMAC is formed to building a data structure consisting of the Alice's nonce, Bob's nonce, their identities, and the shared secret key, K_{AB}. This data structured is then hashed into the HMAC, for example using SHA-1. When Alice receives message 2, she now has R_A (which she picked herself), R_B, which arrives as plaintext, the two identities, and the secret key, K_{AB}, which has known all along, so she can compute the HMAC herself. If it agrees with the HMAC in the message, she knows she is talking to Bob because Trudy does not know K_{AB} and thus cannot figure out which HMAC to send. Alice responds to Bob with an HMAC containing just the two nonces.

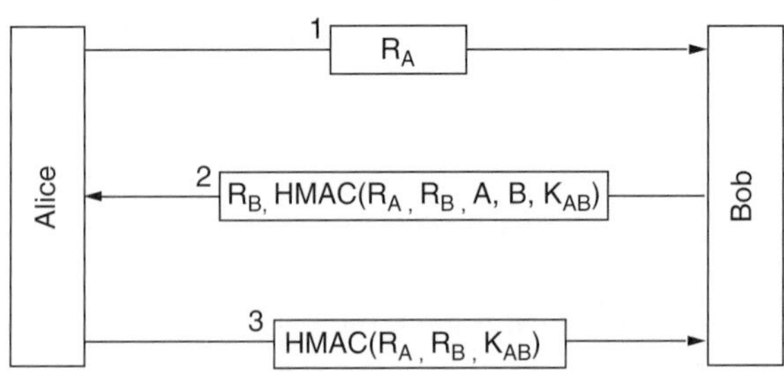

Figure 8-36. Authentication using HMACs.

Can Trudy somehow subvert this protocol? No, because she cannot force either party to encrypt or hash a value of her choice, as happened in Fig. 8-34 and Fig. 8-(Fo. Both HMACs include values chosen by the sending party, something which Trudy cannot control.

Using HMACs is not the only way to use this idea. An alternative scheme that is often used instead of computing the HMAC over a series of items is to encrypt the items sequentially using cipher block chaining.

8.7.2 Establishing a Shared Key: The Diffie-Hellman Key Exchange

So far we have assumed that Alice and Bob share a secret key. Suppose that they do not (because so far there is no universally accepted PKI for signing and distributing certificates). How can they establish one? One way would be for Alice to call Bob and give him her key on the phone, but he would probably start out by saying: How do I know you are Alice and not Trudy? They could try to arrange a meeting, with each one bringing a passport, a drivers' license, and three major credit cards, but being busy people, they might not be able to find a mutually acceptable date for months. Fortunately, incredible as it may sound, there is a way for total strangers to establish a shared secret key in broad daylight, even with Trudy carefully recording every message.

The protocol that allows strangers to establish a shared secret key is called the **Diffie-Hellman key exchange** (Diffie and Hellman, 1976) and works as follows. Alice and Bob have to agree on two large numbers, n and g, where n is a prime, $(n - 1)/2$ is also a prime and certain conditions apply to g. These numbers may be public, so either one of them can just pick n and g and tell the other openly. Now Alice picks a large (say, 512-bit) number, x, and keeps it secret. Similarly, Bob picks a large secret number, y.

Alice initiates the key exchange protocol by sending Bob a message containing $(n, g, g^x \bmod n)$, as shown in Fig. 8-37. Bob responds by sending Alice a message containing $g^y \bmod n$. Now Alice raises the number Bob sent her to the xth power modulo n to get $(g^y \bmod n)^x$ *mod n*. Bob performs a similar operation to get $(g^x \bmod n)^y$ *mod n*. By the laws of modular arithmetic, both calculations yield $g^{xy} \bmod n$. Lo and behold, Alice and Bob suddenly share a secret key, $g^{xy} \bmod n$.

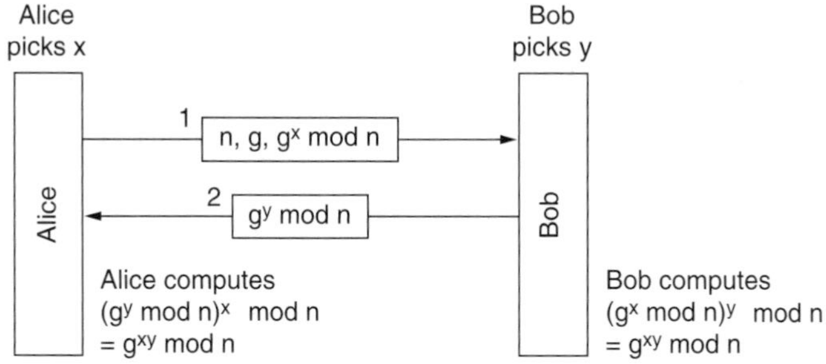

Figure 8-37. The Diffie-Hellman key exchange.

Trudy, of course, has seen both messages. She knows g and n from message 1. If she could compute x and y, she could figure out the secret key. The trouble is, given only $g^x \bmod n$, she cannot find x. No practical algorithm for computing discrete logarithms modulo a very large prime number is known.

To make the above example more concrete, we will use the (completely unrealistic) values of $n = 47$ and $g = 3$. Alice picks $x = 8$ and Bob picks $y = 10$. Both of these are kept secret. Alice's message to Bob is (47, 3, 28) because 3^8 mod 47 is 28. Bob's message to Alice is (17). Alice computes 17^8 mod 47, which is 4. Bob computes 28^{10} mod 47, which is 4. Alice and Bob have independently determined that the secret key is now 4. Trudy has to solve the equation 3^x mod $47 = 28$, which can be done by exhaustive search for small numbers like this, but not when all the numbers are hundreds of bits long. All currently-known algorithms simply take too long, even on massively parallel supercomputers.

Despite the elegance of the Diffie-Hellman algorithm, there is a problem: when Bob gets the triple (47, 3, 28), how does he know it is from Alice and not from Trudy? There is no way he can know. Unfortunately, Trudy can exploit this fact to deceive both Alice and Bob, as illustrated in Fig. 8-38. Here, while Alice and Bob are choosing x and y, respectively, Trudy picks her own random number, z. Alice sends message 1 intended for Bob. Trudy intercepts it and sends message 2 to Bob, using the correct g and n (which are public anyway) but with her own z instead of x. She also sends message 3 back to Alice. Later Bob sends message 4 to Alice, which Trudy again intercepts and keeps.

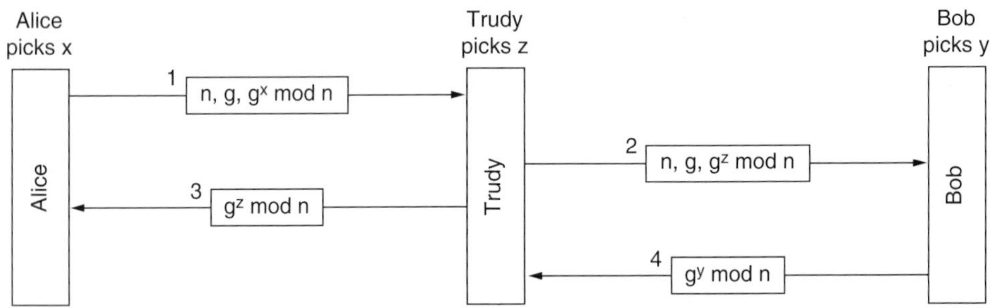

Figure 8-38. The bucket brigade or man-in-the-middle attack.

Now everybody does the modular arithmetic. Alice computes the secret key as g^{xz} mod n, and so does Trudy (for messages to Alice). Bob computes g^{yz} mod n and so does Trudy (for messages to Bob). Alice thinks she is talking to Bob so she establishes a session key (with Trudy). So does Bob. Every message that Alice sends on the encrypted session is captured by Trudy, stored, modified if desired, and then (optionally) passed on to Bob. Similarly, in the other direction. Trudy sees everything and can modify all messages at will, while both Alice and Bob are under the illusion that they have a secure channel to one another. This attack is known as the **bucket brigade attack**, because it vaguely resembles an old-time volunteer fire department passing buckets along the line from the fire truck to the fire. It is also called the **man-in-the-middle attack**.

8.7.3 Authentication Using a Key Distribution Center

Setting up a shared secret with a stranger almost worked, but not quite. On the other hand, it probably was not worth doing in the first place (sour grapes attack). To talk to n people this way, you would need n keys. For popular people, key management would become a real burden, especially if each key had to be stored on a separate plastic chip card.

A different approach is to introduce a trusted key distribution center (KDC). In this model, each user has a single key shared with the KDC. Authentication and session key management now goes through the KDC. The simplest known KDC authentication protocol involving two parties and a trusted KDC is depicted in Fig. 8-39.

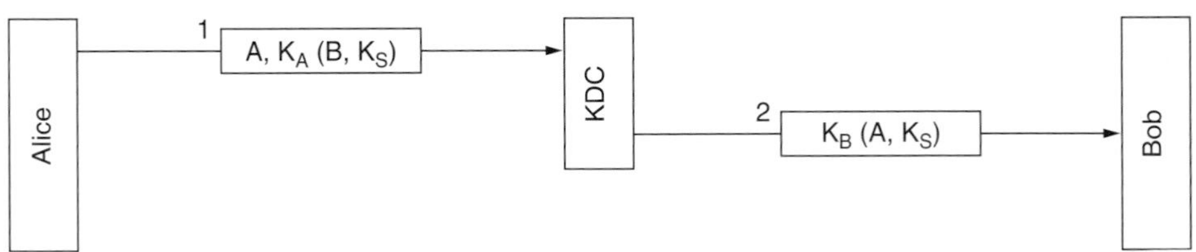

Figure 8-39. A first attempt at an authentication protocol using a KDC.

The idea behind this protocol is simple: Alice picks a session key, K_S, and tells the KDC that she wants to talk to Bob using K_S. This message is encrypted with the secret key Alice shares (only) with the KDC, K_A. The KDC decrypts this message, extracting Bob's identity and the session key. It then constructs a new message containing Alice's identity and the session key and sends this message to Bob. This encryption is done with K_B, the secret key Bob shares with the KDC. When Bob decrypts the message, he learns that Alice wants to talk to him and which key she wants to use.

The authentication here happens for free. The KDC knows that message 1 must have come from Alice, since no one else would have been able to encrypt it with Alice's secret key. Similarly, Bob knows that message 2 must have come from the KDC, whom he trusts, since no one else knows his secret key.

Unfortunately, this protocol has a serious flaw. Trudy needs some money, so she figures out some legitimate service she can perform for Alice, makes an attractive offer, and gets the job. After doing the work, Trudy then politely requests Alice to pay by bank transfer. Alice then establishes a session key with her banker, Bob. Then she sends Bob a message requesting money to be transferred to Trudy's account.

Meanwhile, Trudy is back to her old ways, snooping on the network. She copies both message 2 in Fig. 8-39 and the money-transfer request that follows it.

Later, she replays both of them to Bob. Bob gets them and thinks: Alice must have hired Trudy again. She clearly does good work. Bob then transfers an equal amount of money from Alice's account to Trudy's. Some time after the 50th message pair, Bob runs out of the office to find Trudy to offer her a big loan so she can expand her obviously successful business. This problem is called the **replay attack**.

Several solutions to the replay attack are possible. The first one is to include a timestamp in each message. Then if anyone receives an obsolete message, it can be discarded. The trouble with this approach is that clocks are never exactly synchronized over a network, so there has to be some interval during which a timestamp is valid. Trudy can replay the message during this interval and get away with it.

The second solution is to put a nonce in each message. Each party then has to remember all previous nonces and reject any message containing a previously-used nonce. But nonces have to be remembered forever, lest Trudy try replaying a 5-year-old message. Also, if some machine crashes and it loses its nonce list, it is again vulnerable to a replay attack. Timestamps and nonces can be combined to limit how long nonces have to be remembered, but clearly the protocol is going to get a lot more complicated.

A more sophisticated approach to mutual authentication is to use a multiway challenge-response protocol. A well-known example of such a protocol is the **Needham-Schroeder authentication** protocol (Needham and Schroeder, 1978), one variant of which is shown in Fig. 8-40.

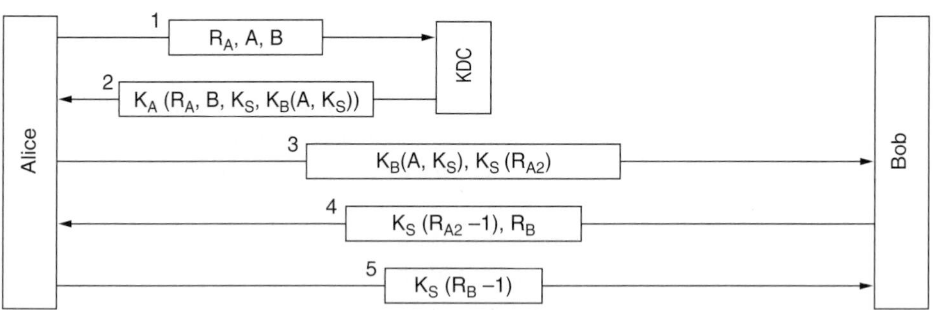

Figure 8-40. The Needham-Schroeder authentication protocol.

The protocol begins with Alice telling the KDC that she wants to talk to Bob. This message contains a large random number, R_A, as a nonce. The KDC sends back message 2 containing Alice's random number, a session key, and a ticket that she can send to Bob. The point of the random number, R_A, is to assure Alice that message 2 is fresh, and not a replay. Bob's identity is also enclosed in case Trudy gets any funny ideas about replacing B in message 1 with her own identity so the KDC will encrypt the ticket at the end of message 2 with K_T instead of K_B. The ticket encrypted with K_B is included inside the encrypted message to prevent Trudy from replacing it with something else on the way back to Alice.

Alice now sends the ticket to Bob, along with a new random number, R_{A2}, encrypted with the session key, K_S. In message 4, Bob sends back $K_S(R_{A2} - 1)$ to prove to Alice that she is talking to the real Bob. Sending back $K_S(R_{A2})$ would not have worked, since Trudy could just have stolen it from message 3.

After receiving message 4, Alice is now convinced that she is talking to Bob and that no replays could have been used so far. After all, she just generated R_{A2} a few milliseconds ago. The purpose of message 5 is to convince Bob that it is indeed Alice he is talking to, and no replays are being used here either. By having each party both generate a challenge and respond to one, the possibility of any kind of replay attack is eliminated.

Although this protocol seems pretty solid, it does have a slight weakness. If Trudy ever manages to obtain an old session key in plaintext, she can initiate a new session with Bob by replaying the message 3 corresponding to the compromised key and convince him that she is Alice (Denning and Sacco, 1981). This time she can plunder Alice's bank account without having to perform the legitimate service even once.

Needham and Schroeder later published a protocol that corrects this problem (Needham and Schroeder, 1987). In the same issue of the same journal, Otway and Rees (1987) also published a protocol that solves the problem in a shorter way. Figure 8-41 shows a slightly modified Otway-Rees protocol.

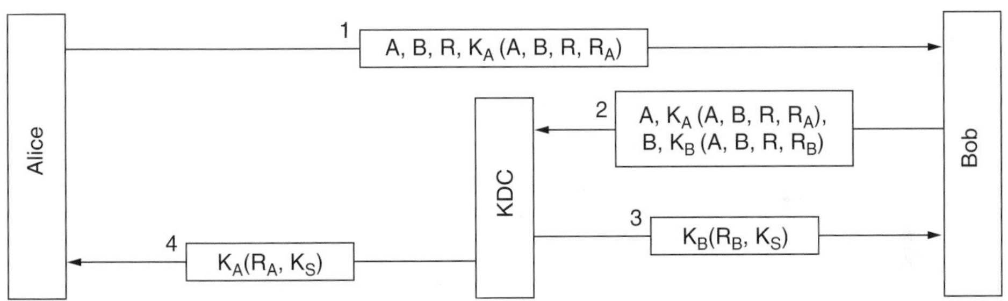

Figure 8-41. The Otway-Rees authentication protocol (slightly simplified).

In the Otway-Rees protocol, Alice starts out by generating a pair of random numbers, R, which will be used as a common identifier, and R_A, which Alice will use to challenge Bob. When Bob gets this message, he constructs a new message from the encrypted part of Alice's message and an analogous one of his own. Both the parts encrypted with K_A and K_B identify Alice and Bob, contain the common identifier, and contain a challenge.

The KDC checks to see if the R in both parts is the same. It might not be because Trudy tampered with R in message 1 or replaced part of message 2. If the two Rs match, the KDC believes that the request message from Bob is valid. It then generates a session key and encrypts it twice, once for Alice and once for Bob. Each message contains the receiver's random number, as proof that the KDC, and not Trudy, generated the message. At this point both Alice and Bob are in possession of the same session key and can start communicating. The first time they exchange data messages, each one can see that the other one has an identical copy of K_S, so the authentication is then complete.

8.7.4 Authentication Using Kerberos

An authentication protocol used in many real systems (including Windows 2000) is **Kerberos**, which is based on a variant of Needham-Schroeder. It is named for a multiheaded dog in Greek mythology that used to guard the entrance to Hades (presumably to keep undesirables out). Kerberos was designed at M.I.T. to allow workstation users to access network resources in a secure way. Its biggest difference from Needham-Schroeder is its assumption that all clocks are fairly well synchronized. The protocol has gone through several iterations. V4 is the version most widely used in industry, so we will describe it. Afterward, we will say a few words about its successor, V5. For more information, see (Steiner et al., 1988).

Kerberos involves three servers in addition to Alice (a client workstation):

Authentication Server (AS): verifies users during login
Ticket-Granting Server (TGS): issues "proof of identity tickets"
Bob the server: actually does the work Alice wants performed

AS is similar to a KDC in that it shares a secret password with every user. The TGS's job is to issue tickets that can convince the real servers that the bearer of a TGS ticket really is who he or she claims to be.

To start a session, Alice sits down at an arbitrary public workstation and types her name. The workstation sends her name to the AS in plaintext, as shown in Fig. 8-42. What comes back is a session key and a ticket, $K_{TGS}(A, K_S)$, intended for the TGS. These items are packaged together and encrypted using Alice's secret key, so that only Alice can decrypt them. Only when message 2 arrives does the workstation ask for Alice's password. The password is then used to generate K_A in order to decrypt message 2 and obtain the session key and TGS ticket inside it. At this point, the workstation overwrites Alice's password to make sure that it is only inside the workstation for a few milliseconds at most. If Trudy tries logging in as Alice, the password she types will be wrong and the workstation will detect this because the standard part of message 2 will be incorrect.

After she logs in, Alice may tell the workstation that she wants to contact Bob the file server. The workstation then sends message 3 to the TGS asking for a ticket to use with Bob. The key element in this request is $K_{TGS}(A, K_S)$, which is encrypted with the TGS's secret key and used as proof that the sender really is

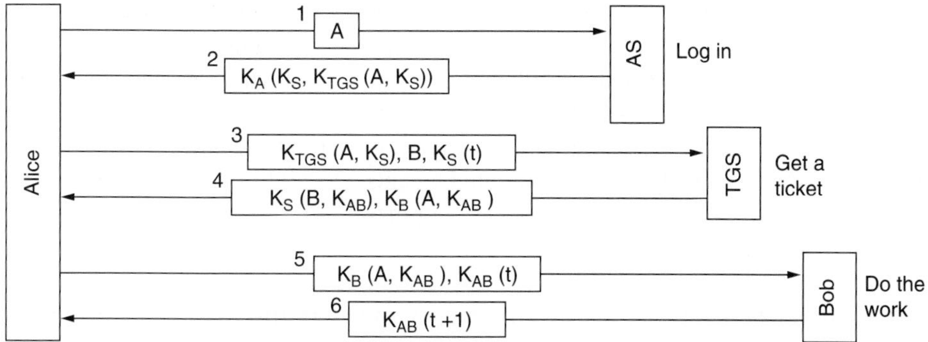

Figure 8-42. The operation of Kerberos V4.

Alice. The TGS responds by creating a session key, K_{AB}, for Alice to use with Bob. Two versions of it are sent back. The first is encrypted with only K_S, so Alice can read it. The second is encrypted with Bob's key, K_B, so Bob can read it.

Trudy can copy message 3 and try to use it again, but she will be foiled by the encrypted timestamp, *t*, sent along with it. Trudy cannot replace the timestamp with a more recent one, because she does not know K_S, the session key Alice uses to talk to the TGS. Even if Trudy replays message 3 quickly, all she will get is another copy of message 4, which she could not decrypt the first time and will not be able to decrypt the second time either.

Now Alice can send K_{AB} to Bob to establish a session with him. This exchange is also timestamped. The response is proof to Alice that she is actually talking to Bob, not to Trudy.

After this series of exchanges, Alice can communicate with Bob under cover of K_{AB}. If she later decides she needs to talk to another server, Carol, she just repeats message 3 to the TGS, only now specifying *C* instead of *B*. The TGS will promptly respond with a ticket encrypted with K_C that Alice can send to Carol and that Carol will accept as proof that it came from Alice.

The point of all this work is that now Alice can access servers all over the network in a secure way and her password never has to go over the network. In fact, it only had to be in her own workstation for a few milliseconds. However, note that each server does its own authorization. When Alice presents her ticket to Bob, this merely proves to Bob who sent it. Precisely what Alice is allowed to do is up to Bob.

Since the Kerberos designers did not expect the entire world to trust a single authentication server, they made provision for having multiple **realms**, each with its own AS and TGS. To get a ticket for a server in a distant realm, Alice would ask her own TGS for a ticket accepted by the TGS in the distant realm. If the distant TGS has registered with the local TGS (the same way local servers do), the local TGS will give Alice a ticket valid at the distant TGS. She can then do business over there, such as getting tickets for servers in that realm. Note, however, that for parties in two realms to do business, each one must trust the other's TGS.

Kerberos V5 is fancier than V4 and has more overhead. It also uses OSI ASN.1 (Abstract Syntax Notation 1) for describing data types and has small changes in the protocols. Furthermore, it has longer ticket lifetimes, allows tickets to be renewed, and will issue postdated tickets. In addition, at least in theory, it is not DES dependent, as V4 is, and supports multiple realms by delegating ticket generation to multiple ticket servers.

8.7.5 Authentication Using Public-Key Cryptography

Mutual authentication can also be done using public-key cryptography. To start with, Alice needs to get Bob's public key. If a PKI exists with a directory server that hands out certificates for public keys, Alice can ask for Bob's, as shown in Fig. 8-43 as message 1. The reply, in message 2, is an X.509 certificate containing Bob's public key. When Alice verifies that the signature is correct, she sends Bob a message containing her identity and a nonce.

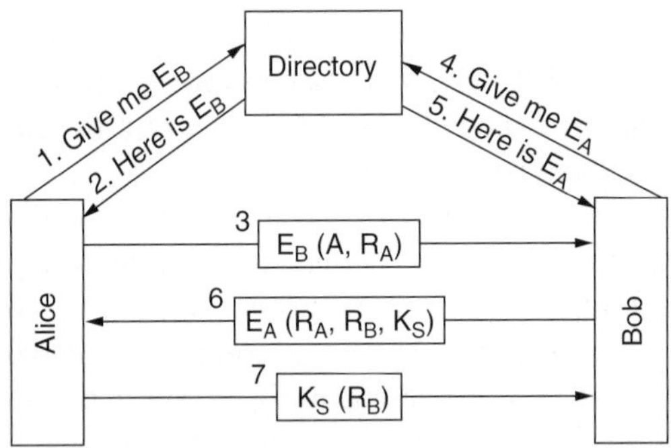

Figure 8-43. Mutual authentication using public-key cryptography.

When Bob receives this message, he has no idea whether it came from Alice or from Trudy, but he plays along and asks the directory server for Alice's public key (message 4) which he soon gets (message 5). He then sends Alice a message containing Alice's R_A, his own nonce, R_B, and a proposed session key, K_S, as message 6.

When Alice gets message 6, she decrypts it using her private key. She sees R_A in it, which gives her a warm feeling inside. The message must have come from Bob, since Trudy has no way of determining R_A. Furthermore, it must be fresh and not a replay, since she just sent Bob R_A. Alice agrees to the session by sending back message 7. When Bob sees R_B encrypted with the session key he just generated, he knows Alice got message 6 and verified R_A.

What can Trudy do to try to subvert this protocol? She can fabricate message 3 and trick Bob into probing Alice, but Alice will see an R_A that she did not send and will not proceed further. Trudy cannot forge message 7 back to Bob because she does not know R_B or K_S and cannot determine them without Alice's private key. She is out of luck.

8.8 E-MAIL SECURITY

When an e-mail message is sent between two distant sites, it will generally transit dozens of machines on the way. Any of these can read and record the message for future use. In practice, privacy is nonexistent, despite what many people think. Nevertheless, many people would like to be able to send e-mail that can be read by the intended recipient and no one else: not their boss and not even their government. This desire has stimulated several people and groups to apply the cryptographic principles we studied earlier to e-mail to produce secure e-mail. In the following sections we will study a widely-used secure e-mail system, PGP, and then briefly mention two others, PEM and S/MIME. For additional information about secure e-mail, see (Kaufman et al., 2002; and Schneier, 1995).

8.8.1 PGP—Pretty Good Privacy

Our first example, **PGP** (**Pretty Good Privacy**) is essentially the brainchild of one person, Phil Zimmermann (Zimmermann, 1995a, 1995b). Zimmermann is a privacy advocate whose motto is: If privacy is outlawed, only outlaws will have privacy. Released in 1991, PGP is a complete e-mail security package that provides privacy, authentication, digital signatures, and compression, all in an easy-to-use form. Furthermore, the complete package, including all the source code, is distributed free of charge via the Internet. Due to its quality, price (zero), and easy availability on UNIX, Linux, Windows, and Mac OS platforms, it is widely used today.

PGP encrypts data by using a block cipher called **IDEA** (**International Data Encryption Algorithm**), which uses 128-bit keys. It was devised in Switzerland at a time when DES was seen as tainted and AES had not yet been invented. Conceptually, IDEA is similar to DES and AES: it mixes up the bits in a series of rounds, but the details of the mixing functions are different from DES and AES. Key management uses RSA and data integrity uses MD5, topics that we have already discussed.

PGP has also been embroiled in controversy since day 1 (Levy, 1993). Because Zimmermann did nothing to stop other people from placing PGP on the Internet, where people all over the world could get it, the U.S. Government claimed that Zimmermann had violated U.S. laws prohibiting the export of munitions. The U.S. Government's investigation of Zimmermann went on for 5 years, but was eventually dropped, probably for two reasons. First, Zimmermann did not place PGP on the Internet himself, so his lawyer claimed that *he* never exported anything (and then there is the little matter of whether creating a Web site constitutes export at all). Second, the government eventually came to realize that winning a trial meant convincing a jury that a Web site containing a downloadable privacy program was covered by the arms-trafficking law prohibiting the export of war materiel such as tanks, submarines, military aircraft, and nuclear weapons. Years of negative publicity probably did not help much, either.

As an aside, the export rules are bizarre, to put it mildly. The government considered putting code on a Web site to be an illegal export and harassed Zimmermann for 5 years about it. On the other hand, when someone published the complete PGP source code, in C, as a book (in a large font with a checksum on each page to make scanning it in easy) and then exported the book, that was fine with the government because books are not classified as munitions. The sword is mightier than the pen, at least for Uncle Sam.

Another problem PGP ran into involved patent infringement. The company holding the RSA patent, RSA Security, Inc., alleged that PGP's use of the RSA algorithm infringed on its patent, but that problem was settled with releases starting at 2.6. Furthermore, PGP uses another patented encryption algorithm, IDEA, whose use caused some problems at first.

Since PGP is open source, various people and groups have modified it and produced a number of versions. Some of these were designed to get around the munitions laws, others were focused on avoiding the use of patented algorithms, and still others wanted to turn it into a closed-source commercial product. Although the munitions laws have now been slightly liberalized (otherwise products using AES would not have been exportable from the U.S.), and the RSA patent expired in September 2000, the legacy of all these problems is that several incompatible versions of PGP are in circulation, under various names. The discussion below focuses on classic PGP, which is the oldest and simplest version. Another popular version, Open PGP, is described in RFC 2440. Yet another is the GNU Privacy Guard.

PGP intentionally uses existing cryptographic algorithms rather than inventing new ones. It is largely based on algorithms that have withstood extensive peer review and were not designed or influenced by any government agency trying to weaken them. For people who tend to distrust government, this property is a big plus.

PGP supports text compression, secrecy, and digital signatures and also provides extensive key management facilities, but oddly enough, not e-mail facilities. It is more of a preprocessor that takes plaintext as input and produces signed ciphertext in base64 as output. This output can then be e-mailed, of course. Some PGP implementations call a user agent as the final step to actually send the message.

To see how PGP works, let us consider the example of Fig. 8-44. Here, Alice wants to send a signed plaintext message, *P*, to Bob in a secure way. Both Alice and Bob have private (D_X) and public (E_X) RSA keys. Let us assume that each one knows the other's public key; we will cover PGP key management shortly.

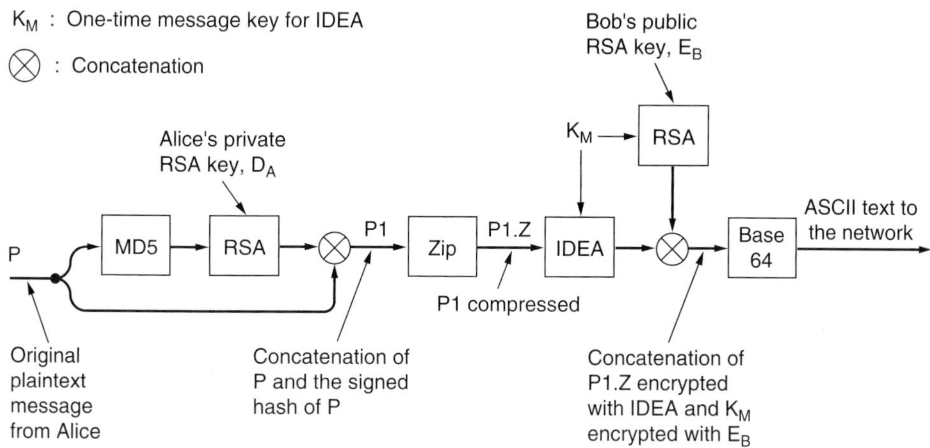

Figure 8-44. PGP in operation for sending a message.

Alice starts out by invoking the PGP program on her computer. PGP first hashes her message, *P*, using MD5, and then encrypts the resulting hash using her private RSA key, D_A. When Bob eventually gets the message, he can decrypt the hash with Alice's public key and verify that the hash is correct. Even if someone else (e.g., Trudy) could acquire the hash at this stage and decrypt it with Alice's known public key, the strength of MD5 guarantees that it would be computationally infeasible to produce another message with the same MD5 hash.

The encrypted hash and the original message are now concatenated into a single message, *P1*, and compressed using the ZIP program, which uses the Ziv-Lempel algorithm (Ziv and Lempel, 1977). Call the output of this step *P1.Z*.

Next, PGP prompts Alice for some random input. Both the content and the typing speed are used to generate a 128-bit IDEA message key, K_M (called a session key in the PGP literature, but this is really a misnomer since there is no session). K_M is now used to encrypt *P1.Z* with IDEA in cipher feedback mode. In addition, K_M is encrypted with Bob's public key, E_B. These two components are then concatenated and converted to base64, as we discussed in the section on MIME in Chap. 7. The resulting message then contains only letters, digits, and the symbols +, /, and =, which means it can be put into an RFC 822 body and be expected to arrive unmodified.

When Bob gets the message, he reverses the base64 encoding and decrypts the IDEA key using his private RSA key. Using this key, he decrypts the message to get *P1.Z.* After decompressing it, Bob separates the plaintext from the encrypted hash and decrypts the hash using Alice's public key. If the plaintext hash agrees with his own MD5 computation, he knows that *P* is the correct message and that it came from Alice.

It is worth noting that RSA is only used in two places here: to encrypt the 128-bit MD5 hash and to encrypt the 128-bit IDEA key. Although RSA is slow, it has to encrypt only 256 bits, not a large volume of data. Furthermore, all 256 plaintext bits are exceedingly random, so a considerable amount of work will be required on Trudy's part just to determine if a guessed key is correct. The heavy-duty encryption is done by IDEA, which is orders of magnitude faster than RSA. Thus, PGP provides security, compression, and a digital signature and does so in a much more efficient way than the scheme illustrated in Fig. 8-19.

PGP supports four RSA key lengths. It is up to the user to select the one that is most appropriate. The lengths are

1. Casual (384 bits): can be broken easily today.
2. Commercial (512 bits): breakable by three-letter organizations.
3. Military (1024 bits): Not breakable by anyone on earth.
4. Alien (2048 bits): Not breakable by anyone on other planets, either.

Since RSA is only used for two small computations, everyone should use alien strength keys all the time.

The format of a classic PGP message is shown in Fig. 8-45. Numerous other formats are also in use. The message has three parts, containing the IDEA key, the signature, and the message, respectively. The key part contains not only the key, but also a key identifier, since users are permitted to have multiple public keys.

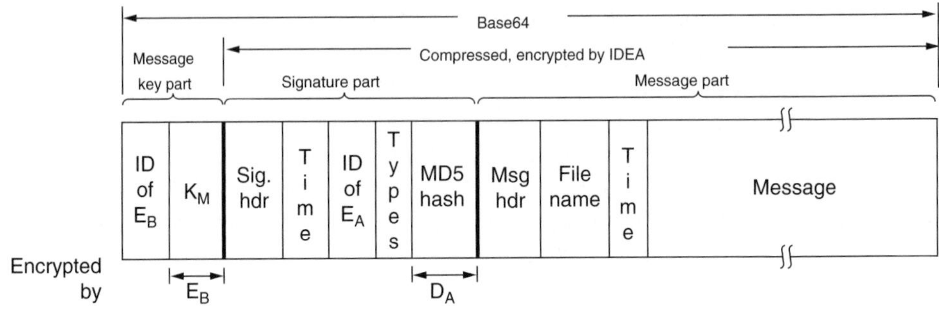

Figure 8-45. A PGP message.

The signature part contains a header, which will not concern us here. The header is followed by a timestamp, the identifier for the sender's public key that can be used to decrypt the signature hash, some type information that identifies the algorithms used (to allow MD6 and RSA2 to be used when they are invented), and the encrypted hash itself.

The message part also contains a header, the default name of the file to be used if the receiver writes the file to the disk, a message creation timestamp, and, finally, the message itself.

Key management has received a large amount of attention in PGP as it is the Achilles heel of all security systems. Key management works as follows. Each user maintains two data structures locally: a private key ring and a public key ring. The **private key ring** contains one or more personal private-public key pairs. The reason for supporting multiple pairs per user is to permit users to change their public keys periodically or when one is thought to have been compromised, without invalidating messages currently in preparation or in transit. Each pair has an identifier associated with it so that a message sender can tell the recipient which public key was used to encrypt it. Message identifiers consist of the low-order 64 bits of the public key. Users are responsible for avoiding conflicts in their public key identifiers. The private keys on disk are encrypted using a special (arbitrarily long) password to protect them against sneak attacks.

The **public key ring** contains public keys of the user's correspondents. These are needed to encrypt the message keys associated with each message. Each entry on the public key ring contains not only the public key, but also its 64-bit identifier and an indication of how strongly the user trusts the key.

The problem being tackled here is the following. Suppose that public keys are maintained on bulletin boards. One way for Trudy to read Bob's secret e-mail is to attack the bulletin board and replace Bob's public key with one of her choice. When Alice later fetches the key allegedly belonging to Bob, Trudy can mount a bucket brigade attack on Bob.

To prevent such attacks, or at least minimize the consequences of them, Alice needs to know how much to trust the item called "Bob's key" on her public key ring. If she knows that Bob personally handed her a floppy disk containing the key, she can set the trust value to the highest value. It is this decentralized, user-controlled approach to public-key management that sets PGP apart from centralized PKI schemes.

Nevertheless, people do sometimes obtain public keys by querying a trusted key server. For this reason, after X.509 was standardized, PGP supported these certificates as well as the traditional PGP public key ring mechanism. All current versions of PGP have X.509 support.

8.8.2 PEM—Privacy Enhanced Mail

In contrast to PGP, which was initially a one-man show, our second example, **PEM (Privacy Enhanced Mail)**, developed in the late 1980s, is an official Internet standard and described in four RFCs: RFC 1421 through RFC 1424. Very roughly, PEM covers the same territory as PGP: privacy and authentication for RFC 822-based e-mail systems. Nevertheless, it also has some differences from PGP in approach and technology.

Messages sent using PEM are first converted to a canonical form so they all have the same conventions about white space (e.g., tabs, trailing spaces). Next, a message hash is computed using MD2 or MD5. Then the concatenation of the hash and the message is encrypted using DES. In light of the known weakness of a 56-bit key, this choice is certainly suspect. The encrypted message can then be encoded with base64 coding and transmitted to the recipient.

As in PGP, each message is encrypted with a one-time key that is enclosed along with the message. The key can be protected either with RSA or with triple DES using EDE.

Key management is more structured than in PGP. Keys are certified by X.509 certificates issued by CAs, which are arranged in a rigid hierarchy starting at a single root. The advantage of this scheme is that certificate revocation is possible by having the root issue CRLs periodically.

The only problem with PEM is that nobody ever used it and it has long-since gone to that big bit bin in the sky. The problem was largely political: who would operate the root and under what conditions? There was no shortage of candidates, but many people were afraid to trust any one company with the security of the whole system. The most serious candidate, RSA Security, Inc., wanted to charge per certificate issued. However, some organizations balked at this idea. In particular, the U.S. Government is allowed to use all U.S. patents for free, and companies outside the U.S. had become accustomed to using the RSA algorithm for free (the company forgot to patent it outside the U.S.). Neither was enthusiastic about suddenly having to pay RSA Security, Inc., for doing something that they had always done for free. In the end, no root could be found and PEM collapsed.

8.8.3 S/MIME

IETF's next venture into e-mail security, called **S/MIME** (**Secure/MIME**), is described in RFCs 2632 through 2643. Like PEM, it provides authentication, data integrity, secrecy, and nonrepudiation. It also is quite flexible, supporting a variety of cryptographic algorithms. Not surprisingly, given the name, S/MIME integrates well with MIME, allowing all kinds of messages to be protected. A variety of new MIME headers are defined, for example, for holding digital signatures.

IETF definitely learned something from the PEM experience. S/MIME does not have a rigid certificate hierarchy beginning at a single root. Instead, users can have multiple trust anchors. As long as a certificate can be traced back to some trust anchor the user believes in, it is considered valid. S/MIME uses the standard algorithms and protocols we have been examining so far, so we will not discuss it any further here. For the details, please consult the RFCs.

8.9 WEB SECURITY

We have just studied two important areas where security is needed: communications and e-mail. You can think of these as the soup and appetizer. Now it is time for the main course: Web security. The Web is where most of the Trudies hang out nowadays and do their dirty work. In the following sections we will look at some of the problems and issues relating to Web security.

Web security can be roughly divided into three parts. First, how are objects and resources named securely? Second, how can secure, authenticated connections be established? Third, what happens when a Web site sends a client a piece of executable code? After looking at some threats, we will examine all these issues.

8.9.1 Threats

One reads about Web site security problems in the newspaper almost weekly. The situation is really pretty grim. Let us look at a few examples of what has already happened. First, the home page of numerous organizations has been attacked and replaced by a new home page of the crackers' choosing. (The popular press calls people who break into computers "hackers," but many programmers reserve that term for great programmers. We prefer to call these people "crackers.") Sites that have been cracked include Yahoo, the U.S. Army, the CIA, NASA, and the New York Times. In most cases, the crackers just put up some funny text and the sites were repaired within a few hours.

Now let us look at some much more serious cases. Numerous sites have been brought down by denial-of-service attacks, in which the cracker floods the site with traffic, rendering it unable to respond to legitimate queries. Often the attack is mounted from a large number of machines that the cracker has already broken into (DDoS atacks). These attacks are so common that they do not even make the news any more, but they can cost the attacked site thousands of dollars in lost business.

In 1999, a Swedish cracker broke into Microsoft's Hotmail Web site and created a mirror site that allowed anyone to type in the name of a Hotmail user and then read all of the person's current and archived e-mail.

In another case, a 19-year-old Russian cracker named Maxim broke into an e-commerce Web site and stole 300,000 credit card numbers. Then he approached the site owners and told them that if they did not pay him $100,000, he would post all the credit card numbers to the Internet. They did not give in to his blackmail, and he indeed posted the credit card numbers, inflicting great damage to many innocent victims.

In a different vein, a 23-year-old California student e-mailed a press release to a news agency falsely stating that the Emulex Corporation was going to post a large quarterly loss and that the C.E.O. was resigning immediately. Within hours, the company's stock dropped by 60%, causing stockholders to lose over $2 billion. The perpetrator made a quarter of a million dollars by selling the stock short just before sending the announcement. While this event was not a Web site break-in, it is clear that putting such an announcement on the home page of any big corporation would have a similar effect.

We could (unfortunately) go on like this for many pages. But it is now time to examine some of the technical issues related to Web security. For more information about security problems of all kinds, see (Anderson, 2001; Garfinkel with Spafford, 2002; and Schneier, 2000). Searching the Internet will also turn up vast numbers of specific cases.

8.9.2 Secure Naming

Let us start with something very basic: Alice wants to visit Bob's Web site. She types Bob's URL into her browser and a few seconds later, a Web page appears. But is it Bob's? Maybe yes and maybe no. Trudy might be up to her old tricks again. For example, she might be intercepting all of Alice's outgoing packets and examining them. When she captures an HTTP *GET* request headed to Bob's Web site, she could go to Bob's Web site herself to get the page, modify it as she wishes, and return the fake page to Alice. Alice would be none the wiser. Worse yet, Trudy could slash the prices at Bob's e-store to make his goods look very attractive, thereby tricking Alice into sending her credit card number to "Bob" to buy some merchandise.

One disadvantage to this classic man-in-the-middle attack is that Trudy has to be in a position to intercept Alice's outgoing traffic and forge her incoming traffic. In practice, she has to tap either Alice's phone line or Bob's, since tapping the fiber backbone is fairly difficult. While active wiretapping is certainly possible, it is a certain amount of work, and while Trudy is clever, she is also lazy. Besides, there are easier ways to trick Alice.

DNS Spoofing

For example, suppose Trudy is able to crack the DNS system, maybe just the DNS cache at Alice's ISP, and replace Bob's IP address (say, 36.1.2.3) with her (Trudy's) IP address (say, 42.9.9.9). That leads to the following attack. The way it is supposed to work is illustrated in Fig. 8-46(a). Here (1) Alice asks DNS for Bob's IP address, (2) gets it, (3) asks Bob for his home page, and (4) gets that, too. After Trudy has modified Bob's DNS record to contain her own IP address instead of Bob's, we get the situation of Fig. 8-46(b). Here, when Alice looks up Bob's IP address, she gets Trudy's, so all her traffic intended for Bob goes to Trudy. Trudy can now mount a man-in-the-middle attack without having to go to the trouble of tapping any phone lines. Instead, she has to break into a DNS server and change one record, a much easier proposition.

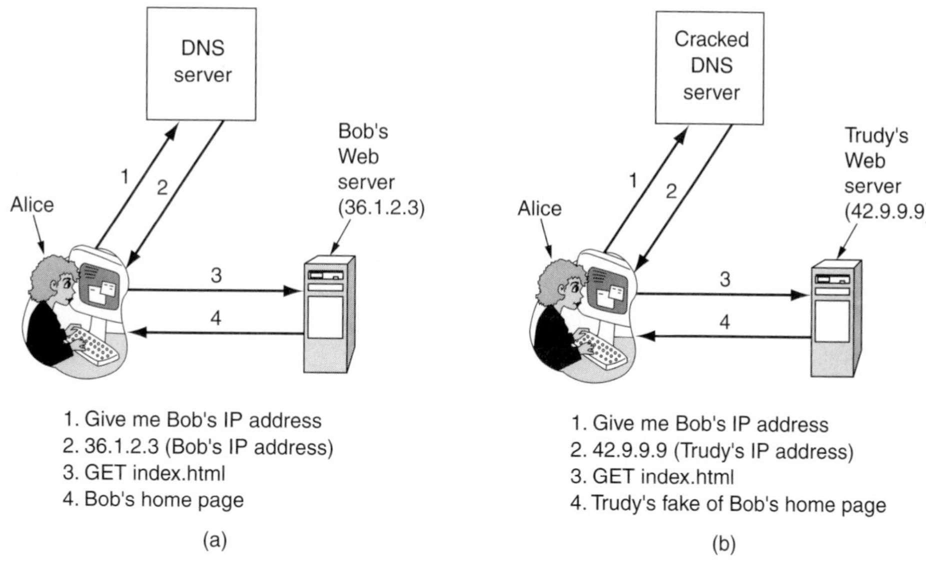

Figure 8-46. (a) Normal situation. (b) An attack based on breaking into DNS and modifying Bob's record.

How might Trudy fool DNS? It turns out to be relatively easy. Briefly summarized, Trudy can trick the DNS server at Alice's ISP into sending out a query to look up Bob's address. Unfortunately, since DNS uses UDP, the DNS server has no real way of checking who supplied the answer. Trudy can exploit this property by forging the expected reply and thus injecting a false IP address into the DNS server's cache. For simplicity, we will assume that Alice's ISP does not initially have an entry for Bob's Web site, *bob.com*. If it does, Trudy can wait until it times out and try later (or use other tricks).

Trudy starts the attack by sending a lookup request to Alice's ISP asking for the IP address of *bob.com*. Since there is no entry for this DNS name, the cache server queries the top-level server for the *com* domain to get one. However, Trudy beats the *com* server to the punch and sends back a false reply saying: "*bob.com* is 42.9.9.9," where that IP address is hers. If her false reply gets back to Alice's ISP first, that one will be cached and the real reply will be rejected as an unsolicited reply to a query no longer outstanding. Tricking a DNS server into installing a false IP address is called **DNS spoofing**. A cache that holds an intentionally false IP address like this is called a **poisoned cache**.

Actually, things are not quite that simple. First, Alice's ISP checks to see that the reply bears the correct IP source address of the top-level server. But since Trudy can put anything she wants in that IP field, she can defeat that test easily since the IP addresses of the top-level servers have to be public.

Second, to allow DNS servers to tell which reply goes with which request, all requests carry a sequence number. To spoof Alice's ISP, Trudy has to know its current sequence number. The easiest way to learn the current sequence number is for Trudy to register a domain herself, say, *trudy-the-intruder.com*. Let us assume its IP address is also 42.9.9.9. She also creates a DNS server for her newly-hatched domain, *dns.trudy-the-intruder.com*. It, too, uses Trudy's 42.9.9.9 IP address, since Trudy has only one computer. Now she has to make Alice's ISP aware of her DNS server. That is easy to do. All she has to do is ask Alice's ISP for *foobar.trudy-the-intruder.com*, which will cause Alice's ISP to find out who serves Trudy's new domain by asking the top-level *com* server.

With *dns.trudy-the-intruder.com* safely in the cache at Alice's ISP, the real attack can start. Trudy now queries Alice's ISP for *www.trudy-the-intruder.com*. The ISP naturally sends Trudy's DNS server a query asking for it. This query bears the sequence number that Trudy is looking for. Quick like a bunny, Trudy asks Alice's ISP to look up Bob. She immediately answers her own question by sending the ISP a forged reply, allegedly from the top-level *com* server saying: "*bob.com* is 42.9.9.9". This forged reply carries a sequence number one higher than the one she just received. While she is at it, she can also send a second forgery with a sequence number two higher, and maybe a dozen more with increasing sequence numbers. One of them is bound to match. The rest will just be thrown out. When Alice's forged reply arrives, it is cached; when the real reply comes in later, it is rejected since no query is then outstanding.

Now when Alice looks up *bob.com*, she is told to use 42.9.9.9, Trudy's address. Trudy has mounted a successful man-in-the-middle attack from the comfort of her own living room. The various steps to this attack are illustrated in Fig. 8-47. To make matters worse, this is not the only way to spoof DNS. There are many other ways as well.

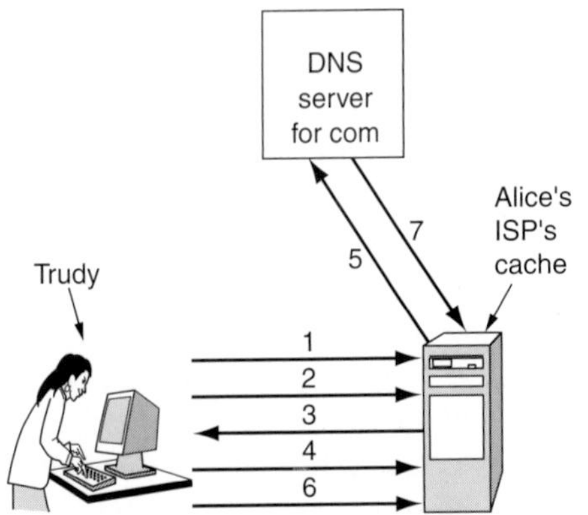

1. Look up foobar.trudy-the-intruder.com
   (to force it into the ISP's cache)
2. Look up www.trudy-the-intruder.com
   (to get the ISP's next sequence number)
3. Request for www.trudy-the-intruder.com
   (Carrying the ISP's next sequence number, n)
4. Quick like a bunny, look up bob.com
   (to force the ISP to query the com server in step 5)
5. Legitimate query for bob.com with seq = n+1
6. Trudy's forged answer: Bob is 42.9.9.9, seq = n+1
7. Real answer (rejected, too late)

Figure 8-47. How Trudy spoofs Alice's ISP.

Secure DNS

This one specific attack can be foiled by having DNS servers use random IDs in their queries rather than just counting, but it seems that every time one hole is plugged, another one turns up. The real problem is that DNS was designed at a time when the Internet was a research facility for a few hundred universities and neither Alice, nor Bob, nor Trudy was invited to the party. Security was not an issue then; making the Internet work at all was the issue. The environment has changed radically over the years, so in 1994 IETF set up a working group to make DNS fundamentally secure. This project is known as **DNSsec** (**DNS security**); its output is presented in RFC 2535. Unfortunately, DNSsec has not been fully deployed yet, so numerous DNS servers are still vulnerable to spoofing attacks.

DNSsec is conceptually extremely simple. It is based on public-key cryptography. Every DNS zone (in the sense of Fig. 7-4) has a public/private key pair. All information sent by a DNS server is signed with the originating zone's private key, so the receiver can verify its authenticity.

DNSsec offers three fundamental services:

1. Proof of where the data originated.
2. Public key distribution.
3. Transaction and request authentication.

The main service is the first one, which verifies that the data being returned has been approved by the zone's owner. The second one is useful for storing and retrieving public keys securely. The third one is needed to guard against playback and spoofing attacks. Note that secrecy is not an offered service since all the information in DNS is considered public. Since phasing in DNSsec is expected to take several years, the ability for security-aware servers to interwork with security-ignorant servers is essential, which implies that the protocol cannot be changed. Let us now look at some of the details.

DNS records are grouped into sets called **RRSets** (**Resource Record Sets**), with all the records having the same name, class and type being lumped together in a set. An RRSet may contain multiple *A* records, for example, if a DNS name resolves to a primary IP address and a secondary IP address. The RRSets are extended with several new record types (discussed below). Each RRSet is cryptographically hashed (e.g., using MD5 or SHA-1). The hash is signed by the zone's private key (e.g., using RSA). The unit of transmission to clients is the signed RRSet. Upon receipt of a signed RRSet, the client can verify whether it was signed by the private key of the originating zone. If the signature agrees, the data are accepted. Since each RRSet contains its own signature, RRSets can be cached anywhere, even at untrustworthy servers, without endangering the security.

DNSsec introduces several new record types. The first of these is the *KEY* record. This records holds the public key of a zone, user, host, or other principal, the cryptographic algorithm used for signing, the protocol used for transmission, and a few other bits. The public key is stored naked. X.509 certificates are not used due to their bulk. The algorithm field holds a 1 for MD5/RSA signatures (the preferred choice), and other values for other combinations. The protocol field can indicate the use of IPsec or other security protocols, if any.

The second new record type is the *SIG* record. It holds the signed hash according to the algorithm specified in the *KEY* record The signature applies to all the records in the RRSet, including any *KEY* records present, but excluding itself. It also holds the times when the signature begins its period of validity and when it expires, as well as the signer's name and a few other items.

The DNSsec design is such that a zone's private key can be kept off-line. Once or twice a day, the contents of a zone's database can be manually transported (e.g., on CD-ROM) to a disconnected machine on which the private key is located. All the RRSets can be signed there and the *SIG* records thus produced can be conveyed back to the zone's primary server on CD-ROM. In this way, the private key can be stored on a CD-ROM locked in a safe except when it is inserted into the disconnected machine for signing the day's new RRSets. After signing is completed, all copies of the key are erased from memory and the disk and the CD-ROM are returned to the safe. This procedure reduces electronic security to physical security, something people understand how to deal with.

This method of presigning RRSets greatly speeds up the process of answering queries since no cryptography has to be done on the fly. The trade-off is that a large amount of disk space is needed to store all the keys and signatures in the DNS databases. Some records will increase tenfold in size due to the signature.

When a client process gets a signed RRSet, it must apply the originating zone's public key to decrypt the hash, compute the hash itself, and compare the two values. If they agree, the data are considered valid. However, this procedure begs the question of how the client gets the zone's public key. One way is to acquire it from a trusted server, using a secure connection (e.g., using IPsec).

However, in practice, it is expected that clients will be preconfigured with the public keys of all the top-level domains. If Alice now wants to visit Bob's Web site, she can ask DNS for the RRSet of *bob.com*, which will contain his IP address and a *KEY* record containing Bob's public key. This RRSet will be signed by the top-level *com* domain, so Alice can easily verify its validity. An example of what this RRSet might contain is shown in Fig. 8-48.

Now armed with a verified copy of Bob's public key, Alice can ask Bob's DNS server (run by Bob) for the IP address of *www.bob.com*. This RRSet will be signed by Bob's private key, so Alice can verify the signature on the RRSet Bob returns. If Trudy somehow manages to inject a false RRSet into any of the caches, Alice can easily detect its lack of authenticity because the *SIG* record contained in it will be incorrect.

However, DNSsec also provides a cryptographic mechanism to bind a response to a specific query, to prevent the kind of spoof Trudy managed to pull off

Domain name	Time to live	Class	Type	Value
bob.com.	86400	IN	A	36.1.2.3
bob.com.	86400	IN	KEY	3682793A7B73F731029CE2737D...
bob.com.	86400	IN	SIG	86947503A8B848F5272E53930C...

Figure 8-48. An example RRSet for *bob.com*. The *KEY* record is Bob's public key. The *SIG* record is the top-level *com* server's signed hash of the *A* and *KEY* records to verify their authenticity.

in Fig. 8-47. This (optional) antispoofing measure adds to the response a hash of the query message signed with the respondent's private key. Since Trudy does not know the private key of the top-level *com* server, she cannot forge a response to a query Alice's ISP sent there. She can certainly get her response back first, but it will be rejected due to its invalid signature over the hashed query.

DNSsec also supports a few other record types. For example, the *CERT* record can be used for storing (e.g., X.509) certificates. This record has been provided because some people want to turn DNS into a PKI. Whether this actually happens remains to be seen. We will stop our discussion of DNSsec here. For more details, please consult RFC 2535.

Self-Certifying Names

Secure DNS is not the only possibility for securing names. A completely different approach is used in the **Secure File System** (Mazières et al., 1999). In this project, the authors designed a secure, scalable, worldwide file system, without modifying (standard) DNS and without using certificates or assuming the existence of a PKI. In this section we will show how their ideas could be applied to the Web. Accordingly, in the description below, we will use Web terminology rather than the file system terminology used in the paper. But to avoid any possible confusion, while this scheme *could* be applied to the Web to achieve high security, it is not currently in use and would require substantial software changes to introduce it.

We start out by assuming that each Web server has a public/private key pair. The essence of the idea is that each URL contains a cryptographic hash of the server's name and public key as part of the URL. For example, in Fig. 8-49 we see the URL for Bob's photo. It starts out with the usual *http* scheme followed by the DNS name of the server (*www.bob.com*). Then comes a colon and 32-character hash. At the end is the name of the file, again as usual. Except for the hash, this is a standard URL. With the hash, it is a **self-certifying URL**.

The obvious question is: What is the hash for? The hash is computed by concatenating the DNS name of the server with the server's public key and running

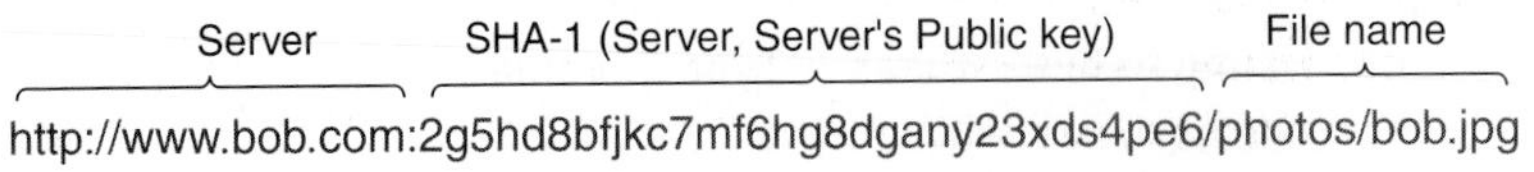

Figure 8-49. A self-certifying URL containing a hash of server's name and public key.

the result through the SHA-1 function to get a 160-bit hash. In this scheme, the hash is represented as a sequence of 32 digits and lower-case letters, with the exception of the letters "l" and "o" and the digits "1" and "0", to avoid confusion. This leaves 32 digits and letters over. With 32 characters available, each one can encode a 5-bit string. A string of 32 characters can hold the 160-bit SHA-1 hash. Actually, it is not necessary to use a hash; the key itself could be used. The advantage of the hash is to reduce the length of the name.

In the simplest (but least convenient) way to see Bob's photo, Alice just types the string of Fig. 8-49 to her browser. The browser sends a message to Bob's Web site asking him for his public key. When Bob's public key arrives, the browser concatenates the server name and public key and runs the hash algorithm. If the result agrees with the 32-character hash in the secure URL, the browser is sure it has Bob's public key. After all, due to the properties of SHA-1, even if Trudy intercepts the request and forges the reply, she has no way to find a public key that gives the expected hash. Any interference from her will thus be detected. Bob's public key can be cached for future use.

Now Alice has to verify that Bob has the corresponding private key. She constructs a message containing a proposed AES session key, a nonce, and a timestamp. She then encrypts the message with Bob's public key and sends it to him. Since only Bob has the corresponding private key, only Bob is able to decrypt the message and send back the nonce encrypted with the AES key. Upon receiving the correct AES-encrypted nonce, Alice knows she is talking to Bob. Also, Alice and Bob now have an AES session key for subsequent *GET* requests and replies.

Once Alice has Bob's photo (or any Web page), she can bookmark it, so she does not have to type in the full URL again. Furthermore, the URLs embedded in Web pages can also be self certifying, so they can be used by just clicking on them, but with the additional security of knowing that the page returned is the correct one. Other ways to avoid the initial typing of the self-certifying URLs are to get them over a secure connection to a trusted server or have them present in X.509 certificates signed by CAs.

Another way to get self-certifying URLs would be to connect to a trusted search engine by typing in its self-certifying URL (the first time) and going through the same protocol as described above, leading to a secure, authenticated connection to the trusted search engine. The search engine could then be queried, with the results appearing on a signed page full of self-certifying URLs that could be clicked on without having to type in long strings.

Let us now see how well this approach stands up to Trudy's DNS spoofing. If Trudy manages to poison the cache of Alice's ISP, Alice's request may be falsely delivered to Trudy rather than to Bob. But the protocol now requires the recipient of an initial message (i.e., Trudy) to return a public key that produces the correct hash. If Trudy returns her own public key, Alice will detect it immediately because the SHA-1 hash will not match the self-certifying URL. If Trudy returns Bob's public key, Alice will not detect the attack, but Alice will encrypt her next message, using Bob's key. Trudy will get the message, but she will have no way to decrypt it to extract the AES key and nonce. Either way, all spoofing DNS can do is provide a denial-of-service attack.

8.9.3 SSL—The Secure Sockets Layer

Secure naming is a good start, but there is much more to Web security. The next step is secure connections. We will now look at how secure connections can be achieved.

When the Web burst into public view, it was initially used for just distributing static pages. However, before long, some companies got the idea of using it for financial transactions, such as purchasing merchandise by credit card, on-line banking, and electronic stock trading. These applications created a demand for secure connections. In 1995, Netscape Communications Corp, the then-dominant browser vendor, responded by introducing a security package called **SSL** (**Secure Sockets Layer**) to meet this demand. This software and its protocol is now widely used, also by Internet Explorer, so it is worth examining in some detail.

SSL builds a secure connection between two sockets, including

1. Parameter negotiation between client and server.
2. Mutual authentication of client and server.
3. Secret communication.
4. Data integrity protection.

We have seen these items before, so there is no need to elaborate on them.

The positioning of SSL in the usual protocol stack is illustrated in Fig. 8-50. Effectively, it is a new layer interposed between the application layer and the transport layer, accepting requests from the browser and sending them down to TCP for transmission to the server. Once the secure connection has been established, SSL's main job is handling compression and encryption. When HTTP is used over SSL, it is called **HTTPS** (**Secure HTTP**), even though it is the standard HTTP protocol. Sometimes it is available at a new port (443) instead of the standard port (80), though. As an aside, SSL is not restricted to being used only with Web browsers, but that is its most common application.

The SSL protocol has gone through several versions. Below we will discuss only version 3, which is the most widely used version. SSL supports a variety of different algorithms and options. These options include the presence or absence

Application (HTTP)
Security (SSL)
Transport (TCP)
Network (IP)
Data link (PPP)
Physical (modem, ADSL, cable TV)

Figure 8-50. Layers (and protocols) for a home user browsing with SSL.

of compression, the cryptographic algorithms to be used, and some matters relating to export restrictions on cryptography. The last is mainly intended to make sure that serious cryptography is used only when both ends of the connection are in the United States. In other cases, keys are limited to 40 bits, which cryptographers regard as something of a joke. Netscape was forced to put in this restriction in order to get an export license from the U.S. Government.

SSL consists of two subprotocols, one for establishing a secure connection and one for using it. Let us start out by seeing how secure connections are established. The connection establishment subprotocol is shown in Fig. 8-51. It starts out with message 1 when Alice sends a request to Bob to establish a connection. The request specifies the SSL version Alice has and her preferences with respect to compression and cryptographic algorithms. It also contains a nonce, R_A, to be used later.

Now it is Bob's turn. In message 2, Bob makes a choice among the various algorithms that Alice can support and sends his own nonce, R_B. Then in message 3, he sends a certificate containing his public key. If this certificate is not signed by some well-known authority, he also sends a chain of certificates that can be followed back to one. All browsers, including Alice's, come preloaded with about 100 public keys, so if Bob can establish a chain anchored at one of these, Alice will be able to verify Bob's public key. At this point Bob may send some other messages (such as a request for Alice's public-key certificate). When Bob is done, he sends message 4 to tell Alice it is her turn.

Alice responds by choosing a random 384-bit **premaster key** and sending it to Bob encrypted with his public key (message 5). The actual session key used for encrypting data is derived from the premaster key combined with both nonces in a complex way. After message 5 has been received, both Alice and Bob are able to compute the session key. For this reason, Alice tells Bob to switch to the new cipher (message 6) and also that she is finished with the establishment subprotocol (message 7). Bob then acknowledges her (messages 8 and 9).

However, although Alice knows who Bob is, Bob does not know who Alice is (unless Alice has a public key and a corresponding certificate for it, an unlikely situation for an individual). Therefore, Bob's first message may well be a request for Alice to log in using a previously established login name and password. The

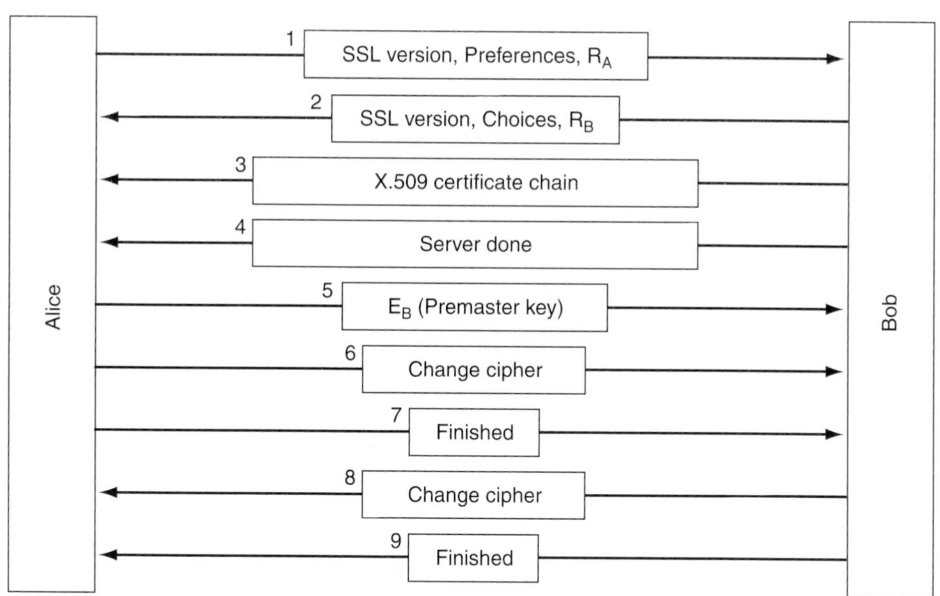

Figure 8-51. A simplified version of the SSL connection establishment subprotocol.

login protocol, however, is outside the scope of SSL. Once it has been accomplished, by whatever means, data transport can begin.

As mentioned above, SSL supports multiple cryptographic algorithms. The strongest one uses triple DES with three separate keys for encryption and SHA-1 for message integrity. This combination is relatively slow, so it is mostly used for banking and other applications in which the highest security is required. For ordinary e-commerce applications, RC4 is used with a 128-bit key for encryption and MD5 is used for message authentication. RC4 takes the 128-bit key as a seed and expands it to a much larger number for internal use. Then it uses this internal number to generate a keystream. The keystream is XORed with the plaintext to provide a classical stream cipher, as we saw in Fig. 8-14. The export versions also use RC4 with 128-bit keys, but 88 of the bits are made public to make the cipher easy to break.

For actual transport, a second subprotocol is used, as shown in Fig. 8-52. Messages from the browser are first broken into units of up to 16 KB. If compression is enabled, each unit is then separately compressed. After that, a secret key derived from the two nonces and premaster key is concatenated with the compressed text and the result hashed with the agreed-on hashing algorithm (usually MD5). This hash is appended to each fragment as the MAC. The compressed fragment plus MAC is then encrypted with the agreed-on symmetric encryption algorithm (usually by XORing it with the RC4 keystream). Finally, a fragment header is attached and the fragment is transmitted over the TCP connection.

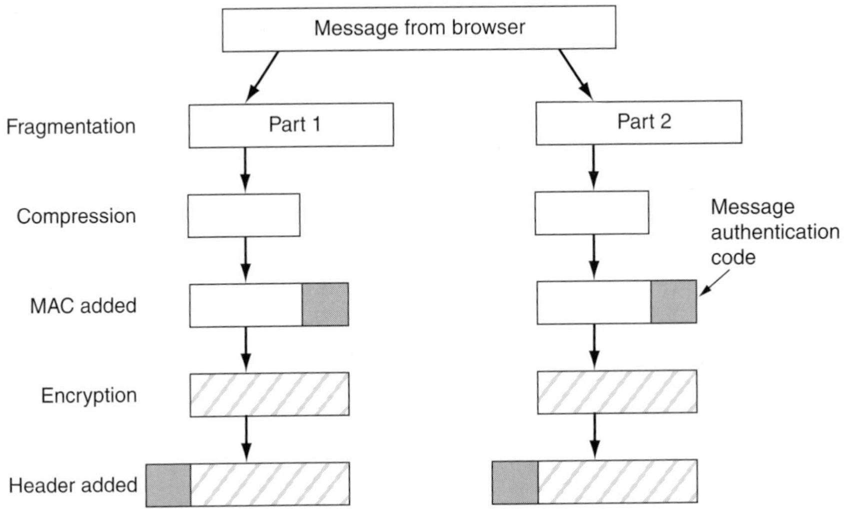

Figure 8-52. Data transmission using SSL.

A word of caution is in order, however. Since it has been shown that RC4 has some weak keys that can be easily cryptanalyzed, the security of SSL using RC4 is on shaky ground (Fluhrer et al., 2001). Browsers that allow the user to choose the cipher suite should be configured to use triple DES with 168-bit keys and SHA-1 all the time, even though this combination is slower than RC4 and MD5.

Another problem with SSL is that the principals may not have certificates and even if they do, they do not always verify that the keys being used match them.

In 1996, Netscape Communications Corp. turned SSL over to IETF for standardization. The result was **TLS** (**Transport Layer Security**). It is described in RFC 2246.

The changes made to SSL were relatively small, but just enough that SSL version 3 and TLS cannot interoperate. For example, the way the session key is derived from the premaster key and nonces was changed to make the key stronger (i.e., harder to cryptanalyze). The TLS version is also known as SSL version 3.1. The first implementations appeared in 1999, but it is not clear yet whether TLS will replace SSL in practice, even though it is slightly stronger. The problem with weak RC4 keys remains, however.

8.9.4 Mobile Code Security

Naming and connections are two areas of concern related to Web security. But there are more. In the early days, when Web pages were just static HTML files, they did not contain executable code. Now they often contain small programs, including Java applets, ActiveX controls, and JavaScripts. Downloading and executing such **mobile code** is obviously a massive security risk, so various methods have been devised to minimize it. We will now take a quick peek at some of the issues raised by mobile code and some approaches to dealing with it.

Java Applet Security

Java applets are small Java programs compiled to a stack-oriented machine language called **JVM (Java Virtual Machine)**. They can be placed on a Web page for downloading along with the page. After the page is loaded, the applets are inserted into a JVM interpreter inside the browser, as illustrated in Fig. 8-53.

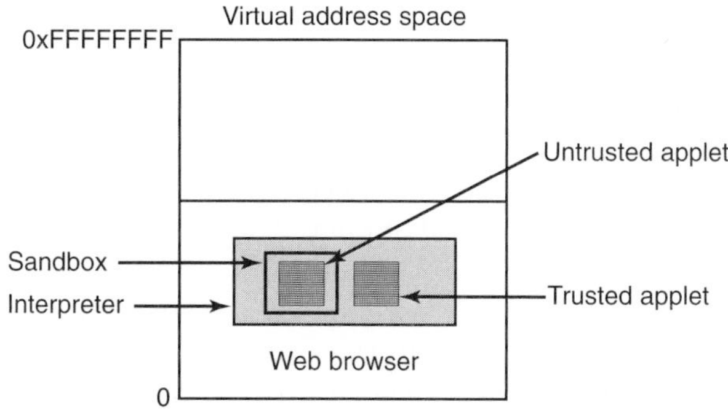

Figure 8-53. Applets can be interpreted by a Web browser.

The advantage of running interpreted code over compiled code is that every instruction is examined by the interpreter before being executed. This gives the interpreter the opportunity to check whether the instruction's address is valid. In addition, system calls are also caught and interpreted. How these calls are handled is a matter of the security policy. For example, if an applet is trusted (e.g., it came from the local disk), its system calls could be carried out without question. However, if an applet is not trusted (e.g., it came in over the Internet), it could be encapsulated in what is called a **sandbox** to restrict its behavior and trap its attempts to use system resources.

When an applet tries to use a system resource, its call is passed to a security monitor for approval. The monitor examines the call in light of the local security policy and then makes a decision to allow or reject it. In this way, it is possible to give applets access to some resources but not all. Unfortunately, the reality is that the security model works badly and that bugs in it crop up all the time.

ActiveX

ActiveX controls are Pentium binary programs that can be embedded in Web pages. When one of them is encountered, a check is made to see if it should be executed, and it if passes the test, it is executed. It is not interpreted or sandboxed in any way, so it has as much power as any other user program and can potentially do great harm. Thus, all the security is in the decision whether to run the ActiveX control.

The method that Microsoft chose for making this decision is based on the idea of **code signing**. Each ActiveX control is accompanied by a digital signature—a hash of the code that is signed by its creator using public key cryptography. When an ActiveX control shows up, the browser first verifies the signature to make sure it has not been tampered with in transit. If the signature is correct, the browser then checks its internal tables to see if the program's creator is trusted or there is a chain of trust back to a trusted creator. If the creator is trusted, the program is executed; otherwise, it is not. The Microsoft system for verifying ActiveX controls is called **Authenticode**.

It is useful to contrast the Java and ActiveX approaches. With the Java approach, no attempt is made to determine who wrote the applet. Instead, a run-time interpreter makes sure it does not do things the machine owner has said applets may not do. In contrast, with code signing, there is no attempt to monitor the mobile code's run-time behavior. If it came from a trusted source and has not been modified in transit, it just runs. No attempt is made to see whether the code is malicious or not. If the original programmer *intended* the code to format the hard disk and then erase the flash ROM so the computer can never again be booted, and if the programmer has been certified as trusted, the code will be run and destroy the computer (unless ActiveX controls have been disabled in the browser).

Many people feel that trusting an unknown software company is scary. To demonstrate the problem, a programmer in Seattle formed a software company and got it certified as trustworthy, which is easy to do. He then wrote an ActiveX control that did a clean shutdown of the machine and distributed his ActiveX control widely. It shut down many machines, but they could just be rebooted, so no harm was done. He was just trying to expose the problem to the world. The official response was to revoke the certificate for this specific ActiveX control, which ended a short episode of acute embarrassment, but the underlying problem is still there for an evil programmer to exploit (Garfinkel with Spafford, 2002). Since there is no way to police thousands of software companies that might write mobile code, the technique of code signing is a disaster waiting to happen.

JavaScript

JavaScript does not have any formal security model, but it does have a long history of leaky implementations. Each vendor handles security in a different way. For example, Netscape Navigator version 2 used something akin to the Java model, but by version 4 that had been abandoned for a code signing model.

The fundamental problem is that letting foreign code run on your machine is asking for trouble. From a security standpoint, it is like inviting a burglar into your house and then trying to watch him carefully so he cannot escape from the kitchen into the living room. If something unexpected happens and you are distracted for a moment, bad things can happen. The tension here is that mobile code allows flashy graphics and fast interaction, and many Web site designers think that this is much more important than security, especially when it is somebody else's machine at risk.

Viruses

Viruses are another form of mobile code. Only unlike the examples above, viruses are not invited in at all. The difference between a virus and ordinary mobile code is that viruses are written to reproduce themselves. When a virus arrives, either via a Web page, an e-mail attachment, or some other way, it usually starts out by infecting executable programs on the disk. When one of these programs is run, control is transferred to the virus, which usually tries to spread itself to other machines, for example, by e-mailing copies of itself to everyone in the victim's e-mail address book. Some viruses infect the boot sector of the hard disk, so when the machine is booted, the virus gets to run. Viruses have become a huge problem on the Internet and have caused billions of dollars worth of damage. There is no obvious solution. Perhaps a whole new generation of operating systems based on secure microkernels and tight compartmentalization of users, processes, and resources might help.

8.10 SOCIAL ISSUES

The Internet and its security technology is an area where social issues, public policy, and technology meet head on, often with huge consequences. Below we will just briefly examine three areas: privacy, freedom of speech, and copyright. Needless to say, we can only scratch the surface here. For additional reading, see (Anderson, 2001; Garfinkel with Spafford, 2002; and Schneier, 2000). The Internet is also full of material. Just type words such as "privacy," "censorship," and "copyright" into any search engine. Also, see this book's Web site for some links.

8.10.1 Privacy

Do people have a right to privacy? Good question. The Fourth Amendment to the U.S. Constitution prohibits the government from searching people's houses, papers, and effects without good reason, and goes on to restrict the circumstances under which search warrants shall be issued. Thus, privacy has been on the public agenda for over 200 years, at least in the U.S.

What has changed in the past decade is both the ease with which governments can spy on their citizens and the ease with which the citizens can prevent such spying. In the 18th century, for the government to search a citizen's papers, it had to send out a policeman on a horse to go to the citizen's farm demanding to see certain documents. It was a cumbersome procedure. Nowadays, telephone companies and Internet providers readily provide wiretaps when presented with search warrants. It makes life much easier for the policeman and there is no danger of falling off the horse.

Cryptography changes all that. Anybody who goes to the trouble of downloading and installing PGP and who uses a well-guarded alien-strength key can be fairly sure that nobody in the known universe can read his e-mail, search warrant or no search warrant. Governments well understand this and do not like it. Real privacy means it is much harder for them to spy on criminals of all stripes, but it is also much harder to spy on journalists and political opponents. Consequently, some governments restrict or forbid the use or export of cryptography. In France, for example, prior to 1999, all cryptography was banned unless the government was given the keys.

France was not alone. In April 1993, the U.S. Government announced its intention to make a hardware cryptoprocessor, the **clipper chip**, the standard for all networked communication. In this way, it was said, citizens' privacy would be guaranteed. It also mentioned that the chip provided the government with the ability to decrypt all traffic via a scheme called **key escrow**, which allowed the government access to all the keys. However, it promised only to snoop when it had a valid search warrant. Needless to say, a huge furor ensued, with privacy advocates denouncing the whole plan and law enforcement officials praising it. Eventually, the government backed down and dropped the idea.

A large amount of information about electronic privacy is available at the Electronic Frontier Foundation's Web site, *www.eff.org*.

Anonymous Remailers

PGP, SSL, and other technologies make it possible for two parties to establish secure, authenticated communication, free from third-party surveillance and interference. However, sometimes privacy is best served by *not* having authentication, in fact by making communication anonymous. The anonymity may be desired for point-to-point messages, newsgroups, or both.

Let us consider some examples. First, political dissidents living under authoritarian regimes often wish to communicate anonymously to escape being jailed or killed. Second, wrongdoing in many corporate, educational, governmental, and other organizations has often been exposed by whistleblowers, who frequently prefer to remain anonymously to avoid retribution. Third, people with unpopular social, political, or religious views may wish to communicate with each other via e-mail or newsgroups without exposing themselves. Fourth, people may wish to discuss alcoholism, mental illness, sexual harassment, child abuse, or being a member of a persecuted minority in a newsgroup without having to go public. Numerous other examples exist, of course.

Let us consider a specific example. In the 1990s, some critics of a nontraditional religious group posted their views to a USENET newsgroup via an **anonymous remailer**. This server allowed users to create pseudonyms and send e-mail to the server, which then re-mailed or re-posted them using the pseudonym, so no one could tell where the message really came from. Some postings revealed what the religious group claimed were trade secrets and copyrighted documents. The religious group responded by telling local authorities that its trade secrets had been disclosed and its copyright infringed, both of which were crimes where the server was located. A court case followed and the server operator was compelled to turn over the mapping information which revealed the true identities of the persons who had made the postings. (Incidentally, this was not the first time that a religion was unhappy when someone leaked its secrets: William Tyndale was burned at the stake in 1536 for translating the Bible into English).

A substantial segment of the Internet community was outraged by this breach of confidentiality. The conclusion that everyone drew is that an anonymous remailer that stores a mapping between real e-mail addresses and pseudonyms (called a type 1 remailer) is not worth much. This case stimulated various people into designing anonymous remailers that could withstand subpoena attacks.

These new remailers, often called **cypherpunk remailers**, work as follows. The user produces an e-mail message, complete with RFC 822 headers (except *From:*, of course), encrypts it with the remailer's public key, and sends it to the remailer. There the outer RFC 822 headers are stripped off, the content is decrypted and the message is remailed. The remailer has no accounts and maintains no logs, so even if the server is later confiscated, it retains no trace of messages that have passed through it.

Many users who wish anonymity chain their requests through multiple anonymous remailers, as shown in Fig. 8-54. Here, Alice wants to send Bob a really, really, really anonymous Valentine's Day card, so she uses three remailers. She composes the message, M, and puts a header on it containing Bob's e-mail address. Then she encrypts the whole thing with remailer 3's public key, E_3. (indicated by horizontal hatching). To this she prepends a header with remailer 3's e-mail address in plaintext. This is the message shown between remailers 2 and 3 in the figure.

Then she encrypts this message with remailer 2's public key, E_2 (indicated by vertical hatching) and prepends a plaintext header containing remailer 2's e-mail address. This message is shown between 1 and 2 in Fig. 8-54. Finally, she encrypts the entire message with remailer 1's public key, E_1, and prepends a plaintext header with remailer 1's e-mail address. This is the message shown to the right of Alice in the figure and this is the message she actually transmits.

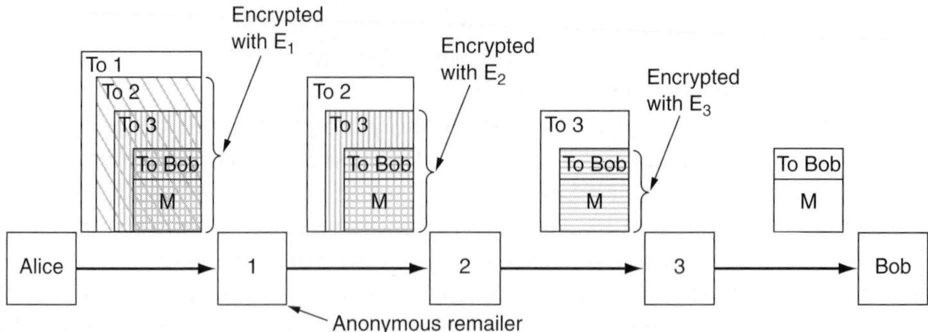

Figure 8-54. How Alice uses 3 remailers to send Bob a message.

When the message hits remailer 1, the outer header is stripped off. The body is decrypted and then e-mailed to remailer 2. Similar steps occur at the other two remailers.

Although it is extremely difficult for anyone to trace the final message back to Alice, many remailers take additional safety precautions. For example, they may hold messages for a random time, add or remove junk at the end of a message, and reorder messages, all to make it harder for anyone to tell which message output by a remailer corresponds to which input, in order to thwart traffic analysis. For a description of a system that represents the state of the art in anonymous e-mail, see (Mazières and Kaashoek, 1998).

Anonymity is not restricted to e-mail. Services also exist that allow anonymous Web surfing. The user configures his browser to use the anonymizer as a proxy. Henceforth, all HTTP requests go to the anonymizer, which requests the page and sends it back. The Web site sees the anonymizer as the source of the request, not the user. As long as the anonymizer refrains from keeping a log, after the fact no one can determine who requested which page.

8.10.2 Freedom of Speech

Privacy relates to individuals wanting to restrict what other people can see about them. A second key social issue is freedom of speech, and its opposite, censorship, which is about governments wanting to restrict what individuals can read and publish. With the Web containing millions and millions of pages, it has become a censor's paradise. Depending on the nature and ideology of the regime, banned material may include Web sites containing any of the following:

1. Material inappropriate for children or teenagers.
2. Hate aimed at various ethnic, religious, sexual or other groups.
3. Information about democracy and democratic values.

4. Accounts of historical events contradicting the government's version.

5. Manuals for picking locks, building weapons, encrypting messages, etc.

The usual response is to ban the bad sites.

Sometimes the results are unexpected. For example, some public libraries have installed Web filters on their computers to make them child friendly by blocking pornography sites. The filters veto sites on their blacklists but also check pages for dirty words before displaying them. In one case in Loudoun County, Virginia, the filter blocked a patron's search for information on breast cancer because the filter saw the word "breast." The library patron sued Loudoun county. However, in Livermore, California, a parent sued the public library for *not* installing a filter after her 12-year-old son was caught viewing pornography there. What's a library to do?

It has escaped many people that the World Wide Web is a Worldwide Web. It covers the whole world. Not all countries agree on what should be allowed on the Web. For example, in November 2000, a French court ordered Yahoo, a California Corporation, to block French users from viewing auctions of Nazi memorabilia on Yahoo's Web site because owning such material violates French law. Yahoo appealed to a U.S. court, which sided with it, but the issue of whose laws apply where is far from settled.

Just imagine. What would happen if some court in Utah instructed France to block Web sites dealing with wine because they do not comply with Utah's much stricter laws about alcohol? Suppose that China demanded that all Web sites dealing with democracy be banned as not in the interest of the State. Do Iranian laws on religion apply to more liberal Sweden? Can Saudi Arabia block Web sites dealing with women's rights? The whole issue is a veritable Pandora's box.

A relevant comment from John Gilmore is: "The net interprets censorship as damage and routes around it." For a concrete implementation, consider the **eternity service** (Anderson, 1996). Its goal is make sure published information cannot be depublished or rewritten, as was common in the Soviet Union during Josef Stalin's reign. To use the eternity service, the user specifies how long the material is to be preserved, pays a fee proportional to its duration and size, and uploads it. Thereafter, no one can remove or edit it, not even the uploader.

How could such a service be implemented? The simplest model is to use a peer-to-peer system in which stored documents would be placed on dozens of participating servers, each of which gets a fraction of the fee, and thus an incentive to join the system. The servers should be spread over many legal jurisdictions for maximum resilience. Lists of 10 randomly-selected servers would be stored securely in multiple places, so that if some were compromised, others would still exist. An authority bent on destroying the document could never be sure it had found all copies. The system could also be made self-repairing in the sense that if it became known that some copies had been destroyed, the remaining sites would attempt to find new repositories to replace them.

The eternity service was the first proposal for a censorship-resistant system. Since then, others have been proposed and, in some cases, implemented. Various new features have been added, such as encryption, anonymity, and fault tolerance. Often the files to be stored are broken up into multiple fragments, with each fragment stored on many servers. Some of these systems are Freenet (Clarke et al., 2002), PASIS (Wylie et al., 2000), and Publius (Waldman et al., 2000). Other work is reported in (Serjantov, 2002).

Increasingly, many countries are now trying to regulate the export of intangibles, which often include Web sites, software, scientific papers, e-mail, telephone helpdesks, and more. Even the U.K., which has a centuries-long tradition of freedom of speech, is now seriously considering highly restrictive laws, which would, for example, define technical discussions between a British professor and his foreign student at the University of Cambridge as regulated export needing a government license (Anderson, 2002). Needless to say, such policies are controversial.

Steganography

In countries where censorship abounds, dissidents often try to use technology to evade it. Cryptography allows secret messages to be sent (although possibly not lawfully), but if the government thinks that Alice is a Bad Person, the mere fact that she is communicating with Bob may get him put in this category, too, as repressive governments understand the concept of transitive closure, even if they are short on mathematicians. Anonymous remailers can help, but if they are banned domestically and messages to foreign ones require a government export license, they cannot help much. But the Web can.

People who want to communicate secretly often try to hide the fact that any communication at all is taking place. The science of hiding messages is called **steganography**, from the Greek words for "covered writing." In fact, the ancient Greeks used it themselves. Herodotus wrote of a general who shaved the head of a messenger, tattooed a message to his scalp, and let the hair grow back before sending him off. Modern techniques are conceptually the same, only they have a higher bandwidth and lower latency.

As a case in point, consider Fig. 8-55(a). This photograph, taken by the author in Kenya, contains three zebras contemplating an acacia tree. Fig. 8-55(b) appears to be the same three zebras and acacia tree, but it has an extra added attraction. It contains the complete, unabridged text of five of Shakespeare's plays embedded in it: *Hamlet*, *King Lear*, *Macbeth*, *The Merchant of Venice*, and *Julius Caesar*. Together, these plays total over 700 KB of text.

How does this steganographic channel work? The original color image is 1024×768 pixels. Each pixel consists of three 8-bit numbers, one each for the red, green, and blue intensity of that pixel. The pixel's color is formed by the linear superposition of the three colors. The steganographic encoding method uses the low-order bit of each RGB color value as a covert channel. Thus, each

(a) (b)

Figure 8-55. (a) Three zebras and a tree. (b) Three zebras, a tree, and the complete text of five plays by William Shakespeare.

pixel has room for 3 bits of secret information, one in the red value, one in the green value, and one in the blue value. With an image of this size, up to $1024 \times 768 \times 3$ bits or 294,912 bytes of secret information can be stored in it.

The full text of the five plays and a short notice add up to 734,891 bytes. This text was first compressed to about 274 KB using a standard compression algorithm. The compressed output was then encrypted using IDEA and inserted into the low-order bits of each color value. As can be seen (or actually, cannot be seen), the existence of the information is completely invisible. It is equally invisible in the large, full-color version of the photo. The eye cannot easily distinguish 21-bit color from 24-bit color.

Viewing the two images in black and white with low resolution does not do justice to how powerful the technique is. To get a better feel for how steganography works, the author has prepared a demonstration, including the full-color high-resolution image of Fig. 8-55(b) with the five plays embedded in it. The demonstration, including tools for inserting and extracting text into images, can be found at the book's Web site.

To use steganography for undetected communication, dissidents could create a Web site bursting with politically-correct pictures, such as photographs of the Great Leader, local sports, movie, and television stars, etc. Of course, the pictures would be riddled with steganographic messages. If the messages were first compressed and then encrypted, even someone who suspected their presence would have immense difficulty in distinguishing the messages from white noise. Of course, the images should be fresh scans; copying a picture from the Internet and changing some of the bits is a dead giveaway.

Images are by no means the only carrier for steganographic messages. Audio files also work fine. Video files have a huge steganographic bandwidth. Even the layout and ordering of tags in an HTML file can carry information.

Although we have examined steganography in the context of free speech, it has numerous other uses. One common use is for the owners of images to encode secret messages in them stating their ownership rights. If such an image is stolen and placed on a Web site, the lawful owner can reveal the steganographic message in court to prove whose image it is. This technique is called **watermarking**. It is discussed in (Piva et al., 2002).

For more on steganography, see (Artz, 2001; Johnson and Jajoda, 1998; Katzenbeisser and Petitcolas, 2000; and Wayner, 2002).

8.10.3 Copyright

Privacy and censorship are just two areas where technology meets public policy. A third one is copyright. **Copyright** is the granting to the creators of **IP** (**Intellectual Property**), including writers, artists, composers, musicians, photographers, cinematographers, choreographers, and others, the exclusive right to exploit their IP for some period of time, typically the life of the author plus 50 years or 75 years in the case of corporate ownership. After the copyright of a work expires, it passes into the public domain and anyone can use or sell it as they wish. The Gutenberg Project (*www.promo.net/pg*), for example, has placed thousands of public domain works (e.g., by Shakespeare, Twain, Dickens) on the Web. In 1998, the U.S. Congress extended copyright in the U.S. by another 20 years at the request of Hollywood, which claimed that without an extension nobody would create anything anymore. By way of contrast, patents last for only 20 years and people still invent things.

Copyright came to the forefront when Napster, a music-swapping service, had 50 million members. Although Napster did not actually copy any music, the courts held that its holding a central database of who had which song was contributory infringement, that is, they helped other people infringe. While nobody seriously claims copyright is a bad idea (although many claim that the term is far too long, favoring big corporations over the public), the next generation of music sharing is already raising major ethical issues.

For example, consider a peer-to-peer network in which people share legal files (public domain music, home videos, religious tracts that are not trade secrets, etc.) and perhaps a few that are copyrighted. Assume that everyone is on-line all the time via ADSL or cable. Each machine has an index of what is on the hard disk, plus a list of other members. Someone looking for a specific item can pick a random member and see if he has it. If not, he can check out all the members in that person's list, and all the members in their lists, and so on. Computers are very good at this kind of work. Having found the item, the requester just copies it.

If the work is copyrighted, chances are the requester is infringing (although for international transfers, the question of whose law applies is unclear). But what about the supplier? Is it a crime to keep music you have paid for and legally downloaded on your hard disk where others might find it? If you have an unlocked cabin in the country and a IP thief sneaks in carrying a notebook computer and scanner, copies a copyrighted book, and sneaks out, are *you* guilty of the crime of failing to protect someone else's copyright?

But there is more trouble brewing on the copyright front. There is a huge battle going on now between Hollywood and the computer industry. The former wants stringent protection of all intellectual property and the latter does not want to be Hollywood's policeman. In October 1998, Congress passed the **DMCA** (**Digital Millennium Copyright Act**) which makes it a crime to circumvent any protection mechanism present in a copyrighted work or to tell others how to circumvent it. Similar legislation is being set in place in the European Union. While virtually no one thinks that pirates in the Far East should be allowed to duplicate copyrighted works, many people think that the DMCA completely shifts the balance between the copyright owner's interest and the public interest.

A case in point. In September 2000, a music industry consortium charged with building an unbreakable system for selling music on-line sponsored a contest inviting people to try to break the system (which is precisely the right thing to do with any new security system). A team of security researchers from several universities, led by Prof. Edward Felten of Princeton, took up the challenge and broke the system. They then wrote a paper about their findings and submitted it to a USENIX security conference, where it underwent peer review and was accepted. Before the paper was to be presented, Felten received a letter from the Recording Industry Association of America which threatened to sue the authors under the DMCA if they published the paper.

Their response was to file suit asking a federal court to rule on whether publishing scientific papers on security research was still legal. Fearing a definitive court ruling against them, the industry withdrew its threat and the court dismissed Felten's suit. No doubt the industry was motivated by the weakness of its case: they had invited people to try to break their system and then threatened to sue some of them for accepting their challenge. With the threat withdrawn, the paper was published (Craver et al., 2001). A new confrontation is virtually certain.

A related issue is the extent of the **fair use doctrine**, which has been established by court rulings in various countries. This doctrine says that purchasers of a copyrighted work have certain limited rights to copy the work, including the right to quote parts of it for scientific purposes, use it as teaching material in schools or colleges, and in some cases make backup copies for personal use in case the original medium fails. The tests for what constitutes fair use include (1) whether the use is commercial, (2) what percentage of the whole is being copied, and (3) the effect of the copying on sales of the work. Since the DMCA and similar laws within the European Union prohibit circumvention of copy protection schemes, these laws also prohibit legal fair use. In effect, the DMCA takes away historical rights from users to give content sellers more power. A major showdown is inevitable.

Another development in the works that dwarfs even the DMCA in its shifting of the balance between copyright owners and users is the **TCPA** (**Trusted Computing Platform Alliance**) led by Intel and Microsoft. The idea is to have the CPU chip and operating system carefully monitor user behavior in various ways (e.g., playing pirated music) and prohibit unwanted behavior. The system even allows content owners to remotely manipulate user PCs to change the rules when that is deemed necessary. Needless to say, the social consequences of this scheme are immense. It is nice that the industry is finally paying attention to security, but it is lamentable that it is entirely aimed at enforcing copyright law rather than dealing with viruses, crackers, intruders, and other security issues that most people are concerned about.

In short, the lawmakers and lawyers will be busy balancing the economic interests of copyright owners with the public interest for years to come. Cyberspace is no different from meatspace: it constantly pits one group against another, resulting in power struggles, litigation, and (hopefully) eventually some kind of resolution, at least until some new disruptive technology comes along.

8.11 SUMMARY

Cryptography is a tool that can be used to keep information confidential and to ensure its integrity and authenticity. All modern cryptographic systems are based on Kerckhoff's principle of having a publicly-known algorithm and a secret key. Many cryptographic algorithms use complex transformations involving substitutions and permutations to transform the plaintext into the ciphertext. However, if quantum cryptography can be made practical, the use of one-time pads may provide truly unbreakable cryptosystems.

Cryptographic algorithms can be divided into symmetric-key algorithms and public-key algorithms. Symmetric-key algorithms mangle the bits in a series of rounds parameterized by the key to turn the plaintext into the ciphertext. Triple DES and Rijndael (AES) are the most popular symmetric-key algorithms at present. These algorithms can be used in electronic code book mode, cipher block chaining mode, stream cipher mode, counter mode, and others.

Public-key algorithms have the property that different keys are used for encryption and decryption and that the decryption key cannot be derived from the encryption key. These properties make it possible to publish the public key. The main public-key algorithm is RSA, which derives its strength from the fact that it is very difficult to factor large numbers.

Legal, commercial, and other documents need to be signed. Accordingly, various schemes have been devised for digital signatures, using both symmetric-key and public-key algorithms. Commonly, messages to be signed are hashed using algorithms such as MD5 or SHA-1, and then the hashes are signed rather than the original messages.

Public-key management can be done using certificates, which are documents that bind a principal to a public key. Certificates are signed by a trusted authority or by someone (recursively) approved by a trusted authority. The root of the chain has to be obtained in advance, but browsers generally have many root certificates built into them.

These cryptographic tools can be used to secure network traffic. IPsec operates in the network layer, encrypting packet flows from host to host. Firewalls can screen traffic going into or out of an organization, often based on the protocol and port used. Virtual private networks can simulate an old leased-line network to provide certain desirable security properties. Finally, wireless networks need good security and 802.11's WEP does not provide it, although 802.11i should improve matters considerably.

When two parties establish a session, they have to authenticate each other and if need be, establish a shared session key. Various authentication protocols exist, including some that use a trusted third party, Diffie-Hellman, Kerberos, and public-key cryptography.

E-mail security can be achieved by a combination of the techniques we have studied in this chapter. PGP, for example, compresses messages, then encrypts them using IDEA. It sends the IDEA key encrypted with the receiver's public key. In addition, it also hashes the message and sends the signed hash to verify message integrity.

Web security is also an important topic, starting with secure naming. DNSsec provides a way to prevent DNS spoofing, as do self-certifying names. Most e-commerce Web sites use SSL to establish secure, authenticated sessions between the client and server. Various techniques are used to deal with mobile code, especially sandboxing and code signing.

The Internet raises many issues in which technology interacts strongly with public policy. Some of the areas include privacy, freedom of speech, and copyright.

PROBLEMS

1. Break the following monoalphabetic cipher. The plaintext, consisting of letters only, is a well-known excerpt from a poem by Lewis Carroll.

kfd ktbd fzm eubd kfd pzyiom mztx ku kzyg ur bzha kfthcm
ur mftnm zhx mfudm zhx mdzythc pzq ur ezsszcdm zhx gthcm
zhx pfa kfd mdz tm sutythc fuk zhx pfdkfdi ntcm fzld pthcm

sok pztk z stk kfd uamkdim eitdx sdruid pd fzld uoi efzk
rui mubd ur om zid uok ur sidzkf zhx zyy ur om zid rzk
hu foiia mztx kfd ezindhkdi kfda kfzhgdx ftb boef rui kfzk

2. Break the following columnar transposition cipher. The plaintext is taken from a popular computer textbook, so "computer" is a probable word. The plaintext consists entirely of letters (no spaces). The ciphertext is broken up into blocks of five characters for readability.

aauan cvlre rurnn dltme aeepb ytust iceat npmey iicgo gorch srsoc
nntii imiha oofpa gsivt tpsit lbolr otoex

3. Find a 77-bit one-time pad that generates the text "Donald Duck" from the ciphertext of Fig. 8-4.

4. Quantum cryptography requires having a photon gun that can, on demand, fire a single photon carrying 1 bit. In this problem, calculate how many photons a bit carries on a 100-Gbps fiber link. Assume that the length of a photon is equal to its wavelength, which for purposes of this problem, is 1 micron. The speed of light in fiber is 20 cm/nsec.

5. If Trudy captures and regenerates photons when quantum cryptography is in use, she will get some of them wrong and cause errors to appear in Bob's one-time pad. What fraction of Bob's one-time pad bits will be in error, on average?

6. A fundamental cryptographic principle states that all messages must have redundancy. But we also know that redundancy helps an intruder tell if a guessed key is correct. Consider two forms of redundancy. First, the initial n bits of the plaintext contain a known pattern. Second, the final n bits of the message contain a hash over the message. From a security point of view, are these two equivalent? Discuss your answer.

7. In Fig. 8-6, the P-boxes and S-boxes alternate. Although this arrangement is esthetically pleasing, is it any more secure than first having all the P-boxes and then all the S-boxes?

8. Design an attack on DES based on the knowledge that the plaintext consists exclusively of upper case ASCII letters, plus space, comma, period, semicolon, carriage return, and line feed. Nothing is known about the plaintext parity bits.

9. In the text we computed that a cipher-breaking machine with a billion processors that could analyze a key in 1 picosecond would take only 10^{10} years to break the 128-bit version of AES. However, current machines might have 1024 processors and take 1 msec to analyze a key, so we need a factor of 10^{15} improvement in performance just to obtain the AES-breaking machine. If Moore's law (computing power doubles every 18 months) continues to hold, how many years will it take to even build the machine?

10. AES supports a 256-bit key. How many keys does AES-256 have? See if you can find some number in physics, chemistry, or astronomy of about the same size. Use the Internet to help search for big numbers. Draw a conclusion from your research.

11. Suppose that a message has been encrypted using DES in ciphertext block chaining mode. One bit of ciphertext in block C_i is accidentally transformed from a 0 to a 1 during transmission. How much plaintext will be garbled as a result?

12. Now consider ciphertext block chaining again. Instead of a single 0 bit being transformed into a 1 bit, an extra 0 bit is inserted into the ciphertext stream after block C_i. How much plaintext will be garbled as a result?

13. Compare cipher block chaining with cipher feedback mode in terms of the number of encryption operations needed to transmit a large file. Which one is more efficient and by how much?

14. Using the RSA public key cryptosystem, with $a = 1$, $b = 2$, etc.,
(a) If $p = 7$ and $q = 11$, list five legal values for d.
(b) If $p = 13$, $q = 31$, and $d = 7$, find e.
(c) Using $p = 5$, $q = 11$, and $d = 27$, find e and encrypt "abcdefghij".

15. Suppose a user, Maria, discovers that her private RSA key $(d1, n1)$ is same as the public RSA key $(e2, n2)$ of another user, Frances. In other words, $d1 = e2$ and $n1 = n2$. Should Maria consider changing her public and private keys? Explain your answer.

16. Consider the use of counter mode, as shown in Fig. 8-15, but with $IV = 0$. Does the use of 0 threaten the security of the cipher in general?

17. The signature protocol of Fig. 8-18 has the following weakness. If Bob crashes, he may lose the contents of his RAM. What problems does this cause and what can he do to prevent them?

18. In Fig. 8-20, we see how Alice can send Bob a signed message. If Trudy replaces P, Bob can detect it. But what happens if Trudy replaces both P and the signature?

19. Digital signatures have a potential weakness due to lazy users. In e-commerce transactions, a contract might be drawn up and the user asked to sign its SHA-1 hash. If the user does not actually verify that the contract and hash correspond, the user may inadvertently sign a different contract. Suppose that the Mafia try to exploit this weakness to make some money. They set up a pay Web site (e.g., pornography, gambling, etc.) and ask new customers for a credit card number. Then they send over a contract saying that the customer wishes to use their service and pay by credit card and ask the customer to sign it, knowing that most of them will just sign without verifying that the contract and hash agree. Show how the Mafia can buy diamonds from a legitimate Internet jeweler and charge them to unsuspecting customers.

20. A math class has 20 students. What is the probability that at least two students have the same birthday? Assume that nobody was born on leap day, so there are 365 possible birthdays.

21. After Ellen confessed to Marilyn about tricking her in the matter of Tom's tenure, Marilyn resolved to avoid this problem by dictating the contents of future messages into a dictating machine and having her new secretary just type them in. Marilyn then planned to examine the messages on her terminal after they had been typed in to make sure they contained her exact words. Can the new secretary still use the birthday attack to falsify a message, and if so, how? *Hint*: She can.

22. Consider the failed attempt of Alice to get Bob's public key in Fig. 8-23. Suppose that Bob and Alice already share a secret key, but Alice still wants Bob's public key. Is there now a way to get it securely? If so, how?

23. Alice wants to communicate with Bob, using public-key cryptography. She establishes a connection to someone she hopes is Bob. She asks him for his public key and he sends it to her in plaintext along with an X.509 certificate signed by the root CA. Alice already has the public key of the root CA. What steps does Alice carry out to verify that she is talking to Bob? Assume that Bob does not care who he is talking to (e.g., Bob is some kind of public service).

24. Suppose that a system uses PKI based on a tree-structured hierarchy of CAs. Alice wants to communicate with Bob, and receives a certificate from Bob signed by a CA X after establishing a communication channel with Bob. Suppose Alice has never heard of X. What steps does Alice take to verify that she is talking to Bob?

25. Can IPsec using AH be used in transport mode if one of the machines is behind a NAT box? Explain your answer.

26. Give one advantage of HMACs over using RSA to sign SHA-1 hashes.

27. Give one reason why a firewall might be configured to inspect incoming traffic. Give one reason why it might be configured to inspect outgoing traffic. Do you think the inspections are likely to be successful?

28. The WEP packet format is shown in Fig. 8-31. Suppose that the checksum is 32 bits, computed by XORing all the 32-bit words in the payload together. Also suppose that the problems with RC4 are corrected by replacing it with a stream cipher having no weaknesses and that IV's are extended to 128 bits. Is there any way for an intruder to spy on or interfere with traffic without being detected?

29. Suppose an organization uses VPN to securely connect its sites over the Internet. Is there a need for a user, Jim, in this organization to use encryption or any other security mechanism to communicate with another user Mary in the organization.

30. Change one message in protocol of Fig. 8-34 in a minor way to make it resistant to the reflection attack. Explain why your change works.

31. The Diffie-Hellman key exchange is being used to establish a secret key between Alice and Bob. Alice sends Bob (719, 3, 191). Bob responds with (543). Alice's secret number, x, is 16. What is the secret key?

32. If Alice and Bob have never met, share no secrets, and have no certificates, they can nevertheless establish a shared secret key using the Diffie-Hellman algorithm. Explain why it is very hard to defend against a man-in-the-middle attack.

33. In the protocol of Fig. 8-39, why is A sent in plaintext along with the encrypted session key?

34. In the protocol of Fig. 8-39, we pointed out that starting each plaintext message with 32 zero bits is a security risk. Suppose that each message begins with a per-user random number, effectively a second secret key known only to its user and the KDC. Does this eliminate the known plaintext attack? Why?

35. In the Needham-Schroeder protocol, Alice generates two challenges, R_A and R_{A2}. This seems like overkill. Would one not have done the job?

36. Suppose an organization uses Kerberos for authentication. In terms of security and service availability, what is the effect if AS or TGS goes down?

37. In the public-key authentication protocol of Fig. 8-43, in message 7, R_B is encrypted with K_S. Is this encryption necessary, or would it have been adequate to send it back in plaintext? Explain your answer.

38. Point-of-sale terminals that use magnetic-stripe cards and PIN codes have a fatal flaw: a malicious merchant can modify his card reader to capture and store all the information on the card as well as the PIN code in order to post additional (fake) transactions in the future. The next generation of point-of-sale terminals will use cards with a complete CPU, keyboard, and tiny display on the card. Devise a protocol for this system that malicious merchants cannot break.

39. Give *two* reasons why PGP compresses messages.

40. Assuming that everyone on the Internet used PGP, could a PGP message be sent to an arbitrary Internet address and be decoded correctly by all concerned? Discuss your answer.

41. The attack shown in Fig. 8-47 leaves out one step. The step is not needed for the spoof to work, but including it might reduce potential suspicion after the fact. What is the missing step?

42. It has been proposed to foil DNS spoofing using ID prediction by having the server put in a random ID rather than using a counter. Discuss the security aspects of this approach.

43. The SSL data transport protocol involves two nonces as well as a premaster key. What value, if any, does using the nonces have?

44. The image of Fig. 8-55(b) contains the ASCII text of five plays by Shakespeare. Would it be possible to hide music among the zebras instead of text? If so, how would it work and how much could you hide in this picture? If not, why not?

45. Alice was a heavy user of a type 1 anonymous remailer. She would post many messages to her favorite newsgroup, *alt.fanclub.alice*, and everyone would know they all came from Alice because they all bore the same pseudonym. Assuming that the remailer worked correctly, Trudy could not impersonate Alice. After type 1 remailers werer all shut down, Alice switched to a cypherpunk remailer and started a new thread in her newsgroup. Devise a way for her to prevent Trudy from posting new messages to the newsgroup, impersonating Alice.

46. Search the Internet for an interesting case involving privacy and write a 1-page report on it.

47. Search the Internet for some court case involving copyright versus fair use and write a 1-page report summarizing your findings.

48. Write a program that encrypts its input by XORing it with a keystream. Find or write as good a random number generator as you can to generate the keystream. The program should act as a filter, taking plaintext on standard input and producing ciphertext on standard output (and vice versa). The program should take one parameter, the key that seeds the random number generator.

49. Write a procedure that computes the SHA-1 hash of a block of data. The procedure should have two parameters: a pointer to the input buffer and a pointer to a 20-byte output buffer. To see the exact specification of SHA-1, search the Internet for FIPS 180-1, which is the full specification.

9

READING LIST AND BIBLIOGRAPHY

We have now finished our study of computer networks, but this is only the beginning. Many interesting topics have not been treated in as much detail as they deserve, and others have been omitted altogether for lack of space. In this chapter we provide some suggestions for further reading and a bibliography, for the benefit of readers who wish to continue their study of computer networks.

9.1 SUGGESTIONS FOR FURTHER READING

There is an extensive literature on all aspects of computer networks. Three journals that frequently publish papers in this area are *IEEE Transactions on Communications*, *IEEE Journal on Selected Areas in Communications*, and *Computer Communication Review*. Many other journals also publish occasional papers on the subject.

IEEE also publishes three magazines—*IEEE Internet Computing*, *IEEE Network Magazine*, and *IEEE Communications Magazine*—that contain surveys, tutorials, and case studies on networking. The first two emphasize architecture, standards, and software, and the last tends toward communications technology (fiber optics, satellites, and so on).

In addition, there are a number of annual or biannual conferences that attract numerous papers on networks and distributed systems, in particular, *SIGCOMM*

Annual Conference, *The International Conference on Distributed Computer Systems*. and *The Symposium on Operating Systems Principles*,

Below we list some suggestions for supplementary reading, keyed to the chapters of this book. Most of these are tutorials or surveys on the subject. A few are chapters from textbooks.

9.1.1 Introduction and General Works

Bi et al., "Wireless Mobile Communications at the Start of the 21st Century"

A new century, a new technology. Sounds good. After some history of wireless, the major topics are covered here, including standards, applications, Internet, and technologies.

Comer, *The Internet Book*

Anyone looking for an easy-going introduction to the Internet should look here. Comer describes the history, growth, technology, protocols, and services of the Internet in terms that novices can understand, but so much material is covered that the book is also of interest to more technical readers.

Garber, "Will 3G Really Be the Next Big Wireless Technology?"

Third-generation mobile phones are supposed to combine voice and data and provide data rates up to 2 Mbps. They have been slow to take off. The promises, pitfalls, technology, politics, and economics of using broadband wireless communication are all covered in this easy-to-read article.

IEEE Internet Computing, Jan.-Feb. 2000

The first issue of *IEEE Internet Computing* in the new millennium did exactly what you would expect: ask the people who helped create the Internet in the previous millennium to speculate on where it is going in the next one. The experts are Paul Baran, Lawrence Roberts, Leonard Kleinrock, Stephen Crocker, Danny Cohen, Bob Metcalfe, Bill Gates, Bill Joy, and others. For best results, wait 500 years, *then* read their predictions.

Kipnis, "Beating the System: Abuses of the Standards Adoption Process"

Standards committees try to be fair and vendor neutral in their work, but unfortunately there are companies that try to abuse the system. For example, it has happened repeatedly that a company helps develop a standard and after it is approved, announces that the standard is based on a patent it owns and which it will license to companies that it likes and not to companies that it does not like, and at prices that it alone determines. For a look at the dark side of standardization, this article is an excellent start.

Kyas and Crawford, *ATM Networks*

ATM was once touted as the networking protocol of the future, and is still important within the telephone system. This book is an up-to-date guide to ATM's current status, with detailed information on ATM protocols and how they can integrate with IP-based networks.

Kwok, "A Vision for Residential Broadband Service"

If you want to know what Microsoft thought about delivering video on demand in 1995, read this article. Five years later the vision was hopelessly obsolete. The value of the article is to demonstrate that even highly-knowledgeable and well-motivated people cannot see even five years into the future with any accuracy at all. It should be a lesson for all of us.

Naughton, *A Brief History of the Future*

Who invented the Internet, anyway? Many people have claimed credit. And rightly so, since many people had a hand in it, in different ways. This history of the Internet tells how it all happened, and in a witty and charming way, replete with anecdotes, such as AT&T's repeatedly making clear its belief that digital communication had no future.

Perkins, "Mobile Networking in the Internet"

For a good overview of mobile networking protocol layer by protocol layer, this is the place to look. The physical through transport layers are covered, as well as middleware, security, and ad hoc networking.

Teger and Waks,"End-User Perspectives on Home Networking"

Home networks are not like corporate networks. The applications are different (more multimedia intensive), the equipment comes from a wider range of suppliers, and the users have little technical training and no patience whatsoever for any failures. To find out more, look here.

Varshney and Vetter, "Emerging Mobile and Wireless Networks"

Another introduction to wireless communication. It covers wireless LANs, wireless local loops, and satellites, as well as some of the software and applications.

Wetteroth, *OSI Reference Model for Telecommunications*

Though the OSI protocols themselves are not used any more, the seven-layer model has become very well-known. As well as explaining more about OSI, this book applies the model to telecom (as opposed to computer) networks, showing where common telephony and other voice protocols fit into the networking stack.

9.1.2 The Physical Layer

Abramson, "Internet Access Using VSATs"

Small earth stations are becoming more popular for both rural telephony and corporate Internet access in developed countries. However, the nature of the traffic for these two cases differs dramatically, so different protocols are needed to handle the two cases. In this article, the inventor of the ALOHA system discusses numerous channel allocation methods that can be used for VSAT systems.

Alkhatib et al., "Wireless Data Networks: Reaching the Extra Mile"

For a quick introduction to wireless networking terms and technologies, including spread spectrum, this tutorial paper is a good starting place.

Azzam and Ransom, *Broadband Access Technologies*

The telephone system, fiber, ADSL, cable networks, satellites, even power lines are covered here as network access technologies. Other topics include home networks, services, network performance, and standards. The book concludes with biographies of the major companies in the telecom and network business, but with the rate of change in the industry, this chapter may have a shorter shelf life than the technology chapters.

Bellamy, *Digital Telephony*

Everything you ever wanted to know about the telephone system and more is contained in this authoritative book. Particularly interesting are the chapters on transmission and multiplexing, digital switching, fiber optics, mobile telephony, and DSL.

Berezdivin et al., "Next-Generation Wireless Communications Concepts and Technologies"

These folks are one step ahead of everyone else. The "next generation" in the title refers to fourth-generation wireless networks. These networks are expected to provide IP service everywhere with seamless connectivity to the Internet with high bandwidth and excellent quality of service. These goals are to be achieved through smart spectrum usage, dynamic resource management, and adaptive service. All this sounds visionary now, but mobile telephones sounded pretty visionary back in 1995.

Dutta-Roy, "An Overview of Cable Modem Technology and Market Perspectives"

Cable TV has gone from simple CATV to a complex distribution system for TV, Internet, and telephony. These changes have affected the cable infrastructure considerably. For a discussion of cable plant, standards, and marketing, with an emphasis on DOCSIS, this article is worth reading.

Farserotu and Prasad, "A Survey of Future Broadband Multimedia Satellite Systems, Issues, and Trends"

A variety of data communication satellites are in the sky or on the drawing board, including Astrolink, Cyberstar, Spaceway, Skybridge, Teledesic, and iSky. They use various techniques including bent pipe and satellite switching. For an overview of different satellite systems and techniques, this paper is a good starting place.

Hu and Li, "Satellite-Based Internet: A Tutorial"

Internet access via satellite is different from access via terrestrial lines. Not only is there the issue of delay, but routing and switching are also different. In this paper, the authors examine some of the issues related to using satellites for Internet access.

Joel, "Telecommunications and the IEEE Communications Society"

For a compact, but surprisingly comprehensive, history of telecommunications, starting with the telegraph and ending with 802.11, this article is the place to look. It also covers radio, telephones, analog and digital switching, submarine cables, digital transmission, ATM, television broadcasting, satellites, cable TV, optical communications, mobile phones, packet switching, the ARPANET, and the Internet.

Metcalfe, "Computer/Network Interface Design: Lessons from Arpanet & Ethernet"

Although engineers have been building network interfaces for decades now, one often wonders if they have learned anything from all this experience. In this paper, the designer of the Ethernet tells how to build a network interface and what to do with it once you have built it. He pulls no punches, telling what he did wrong as well as what he did right.

Palais, *Fiber Optic Communication*, 3rd ed.

Books on fiber optic technology tend to be aimed at the specialist, but this one is more accessible than most. It covers waveguides, light sources, light detectors, couplers, modulation, noise, and many other topics.

Pandya, "Emerging Mobile and Personal Communications Systems"

For a short and sweet introduction to hand-held personal communication systems, this article is worth looking at. One of the nine pages contains a list of 70 acronyms used on the other eight pages.

Sarikaya, "Packet Mode in Wireless Networks: Overview of Transition to Third Generation"

The whole idea of third-generation cellular networks is wireless data transmission. To get an overview of how second-generation networks handle data and what the evolution to third generation will be, this is a good place to look. Topics covered include GPRS, IS-95B, WCDMA, and CDMA2000.

9.1.3 The Data Link Layer

Carlson, *PPP Design, Implementation and Debugging*, 2nd ed.
If you are interested in detailed information on all the protocols that make up the PPP suite, including CCP (compression) and ECP (encryption), this book is a good reference. There is a particular focus on ANU PPP-2.3, a popular implementation of PPP.

Gravano, *Introduction to Error Control Codes*
Errors creep into nearly all digital communications, and many types of codes have been developed to detect and correct for them. This book explains some of the most important, from simple linear Hamming codes to more complex Galois fields and convolutional codes. It tries to do so with the minimum algebra necessary, but that is still a lot.

Holzmann, *Design and Validation of Computer Protocols*
Readers interested in the more formal aspects of data link (and similar) protocols should look here. The specification, modeling, correctness, and testing of such protocols are all covered in this book.

Peterson and Davie, *Computer Networks: A Systems Approach*
Chapter 2 contains material about many data link issues, including framing, error detection, stop-and-wait protocols, sliding window protocols, and IEEE 802 LANs.

Stallings, *Data and Computer Communications*
Chapter 7 deals with the data link layer and covers flow control, error detection, and the basic data link protocols, including stop-and-wait and go back n. The HDLC-type protocols are also covered.

9.1.4 The Medium Access Control Sublayer

Bhagwat, "Bluetooth: Technology for Short-Range Wireless Apps"
For a straightforward introduction to the Bluetooth system, this is a good place to start. The core protocols and profiles, radio, piconets, and links are discussed, followed by an introduction to the various protocols.

Bisdikian, "An Overview of the Bluetooth Wireless Technology"
Like the Bhagwat paper (above), this is also a good starting point for learning more about the Bluetooth system. The piconets, the protocol stack, and the profiles are all discussed, among other topics.

Crow et al., "IEEE 802.11 Wireless Local Area Networks"

For a simple introduction to the technology and protocols of 802.11, this is a good place to start. The emphasis is on the MAC sublayer. Both distributed control and centralized control are covered. The paper concludes with some simulation studies of the performance of 802.11 under various conditions.

Eklund et al., "IEEE Standard 802.16: A Technical Overview of the Wireless MAN Air Interface for Broadband Wireless Access"

The wireless local loop standardized by IEEE in 2002 as 802.16 may revolutionize telephone service, bringing broadband to the home. In this overview, the authors explain the main technological issues relating to this standard.

Kapp, "802.11: Leaving the Wire Behind"

This short introduction to 802.11 covers the basics, protocols, and relevant standards.

Kleinrock, "On Some Principles of Nomadic Computing and Multi-Access Communications"

Wireless access over a shared channel is more complex than having wired stations share a channel. Among other issues are dynamic topologies, routing, and power management. These and other issues related to channel access by mobile wireless devices are covered in this article.

Miller and Cummins, *LAN Technologies Explained*

Need to know more about the technologies that can be used in a LAN? This book covers most of them, including FDDI and token ring as well as the ever-popular Ethernet. While new installations of the first two are now rare, many existing networks still use them, and ring networks are still common (e.g., SONET).

Perlman, *Interconnections*, 2nd ed.

For an authoritative, but entertaining, treatment of bridges, routers, and routing in general, Perlman's book is the place to look. The author designed the algorithms used in the IEEE 802 spanning tree bridge and is one of the world's leading authorities on various aspects of networking.

Webb, "Broadband Fixed Wireless Access"

Both the "why" and the "how" of fixed broadband wireless are examined in this paper. The "why" section argues that people do not want a home e-mail address, a work e-mail address, separate telephone numbers for home, work, and mobile, an instant messaging account, and perhaps a fax number or two. They want a single integrated system that works everywhere. The emphasis in the technology section is on the physical layer, including topics such as TDD versus FDD, adaptive versus fixed modulation, and number of carriers.

9.1.5 The Network Layer

Bhatti and Crowcroft, "QoS Sensitive Flows: Issues in IP Packet Handling"

One of the ways to achieve better quality of service in a network is to schedule packet departures from each router carefully. In this paper, a variety of packet scheduling algorithms, as well as related issues, are discussed in some detail.

Chakrabarti, "QoS Issues in Ad Hoc Wireless Networks"

Routing in ad hoc networks of notebook computers that just happen to be near each other is hard enough without having to worry about quality of service as well. Nevertheless, people do care about quality of service, so attention needs to be paid to this topic. The nature of ad hoc networks and some of the issues related to routing and quality of service are discussed in this article.

Comer, *Internetworking with TCP/IP*, Vol. 1, 4th ed.

Comer has written the definitive work on the TCP/IP protocol suite. Chapters 4 through 11 deal with IP and related protocols in the network layer. The other chapters deal primarily with the higher layers and are also worth reading.

Huitema, *Routing in the Internet*

If you want to know everything there is to know about routing in the Internet, this is the book for you. Both pronounceable algorithms (e.g., RIP, CIDR, and MBONE) and unpronounceable algorithms (e.g., OSPF, IGRP, EGP, and BGP) are treated in great detail. New features, such as multicast, mobile IP, and resource reservation, are also here.

Malhotra, *IP Routing*

For a detailed guide to IP routing, this book contains a lot of material. The protocols covered include RIP, RIP-2, IGRP, EIGRP, OSPF, and BGP-4.

Metz, "Differentiated Services"

Quality-of-service guarantees are important for many multimedia applications. Integrated services and differentiated services are two possible approaches to achieving them. Both are discussed here, with the emphasis on differentiated services.

Metz, "IP Routers: New Tool for Gigabit Networking"

Most of the other references for Chap. 5 are about routing algorithms. This one is different: it is about how routers actually work. They have gone through an evolutionary process from being general-purpose workstations to being highly special-purpose routing machines. If you want to know more, this article is a good starting place.

Nemeth et al., *UNIX System Administration Handbook*

For a change of pace, Chap. 13 of this book deals with networking in a more practical way than most of our other references. Rather than just dealing with the abstract concepts, it gives much advice here about what to do if you are actually managing a real network.

Perkins, "Mobile Networking through Mobile IP"

As mobile computing devices become more and more common, Mobile IP is becoming more and more important. This tutorial gives a good introduction to it and related topics.

Perlman, *Interconnections: Bridges and Routers*, 2nd ed.

In Chapters 12 through 15, Perlman describes many of the issues involved in unicast and multicast routing algorithm design, both for WANs and networks of LANs, and their implementation in various protocols. But the best part of the book is Chap. 18, in which the author distills her years of experience about network protocols into an informative and fun chapter.

Puzmanova, *Routing and Switching: Time of Convergence?*

In the late 1990s, some networking equipment vendors began to call everything a switch, while many managers of large networks said that they were switching from routers to switches. As the title implies, this book predicts the future of both routers and switches and asks whether they really are converging.

Royer and Toh, "A Review of Current Routing Protocols for Ad-Hoc Mobile Wireless Networks"

The AODV ad hoc routing algorithm that we discussed in Chap. 5 is not the only one known. A variety of other ones, including DSDV, CGSR, WRP, DSR, TORA, ABR, DRP, and SRP, are discussed here and compared with one another. Clearly, if you are planning to invent a new ad hoc routing protocol, step 1 is to think of a three- or four-letter acronym.

Stevens, *TCP/IP Illustrated*, Vol. 1

Chapters 3-10 provide a comprehensive treatment of IP and related protocols (ARP, RARP, and ICMP) illustrated by examples.

Striegel and Manimaran, "A Survey of QoS Multicasting Issues"

Multicasting and quality of service are two increasing important topics as services such as internet radio and television begin to take off. In this survey paper, the authors discuss how routing algorithms can take both of these issues into account.

Yang and Reddy, "A Taxonomy for Congestion Control Algorithms in Packet Switching Networks"

The authors have devised a taxonomy for congestion control algorithms. The main categories are open loop with source control, open loop with destination control, closed loop with explicit feedback, and closed loop with implicit feedback. They use this taxonomy to describe and classify 23 existing algorithms.

9.1.6 The Transport Layer

Comer, *Internetworking with TCP/IP*, Vol. 1, 4th ed.

As mentioned above, Comer has written the definitive work on the TCP/IP protocol suite. Chap. 12 is about UDP; Chap. 13 is about TCP.

Hall and Cerf, *Internet Core Protocols: The Definitive Guide*

If you like your information straight from the source, this is the place to learn more about TCP. After all, Cerf co-invented it. Chapter 7 is a good reference on TCP, showing how to interpret the information supplied by protocol analysis and network management tools. Other chapters cover UDP, IGMP, ICMP and ARP.

Kurose and Ross, *Computer Networking: A Top-Down Approach Featuring the Internet*

Chapter 3 is about the transport layer and contains a fair amount of material on UDP and TCP. It also discusses the stop-and-wait and go back n protocols we examined in Chap. 3.

Mogul, "IP Network Performance"

Despite the title of this article, it is at least, if not more, about TCP and network performance in general, than about IP performance in particular. It is full of useful guidelines and rules of thumb.

Peterson and Davie, *Computer Networks: A Systems Approach*

Chapter 5 is about UDP, TCP, and a few related protocols. Network performance is also covered briefly.

Stevens, *TCP/IP Illustrated*, Vol. 1

Chapters 17-24 provide a comprehensive treatment of TCP illustrated by examples.

9.1.7 The Application Layer

Bergholz, "Extending Your Markup: An XML Tutorial"

A short and straightforward introduction to XML for beginners.

Cardellini et al., *The State-of-the-Art in Locally Distributed Web-Server Systems"*

As the Web gets more popular, some Web sites need to have large server farms to handle the traffic. The hard part of building a server farm is distributing the load among the machines. This tutorial paper discusses that subject at great length.

Berners-Lee et al., "The World Wide Web"

A perspective on the Web and where it is going by the person who invented it and some of his colleagues at CERN. The article focuses on the Web architecture, URLs, HTTP, and HTML, as well as future directions, and compares it to other distributed information systems.

Choudbury et al., "Copyright Protection for Electronic Publishing on Computer Networks"

Although numerous books and articles describe cryptographic algorithms, few describe how they could be used to prevent users from further distributing documents that they are allowed to decrypt. This paper describes a variety of mechanisms that might help protect authors' copyrights in the electronic era.

Collins, "Carrier Grade Voice over IP"

If you have read the Varshney et al. paper and now want to know all the details about voice over IP using H.323, this is a good place to look. Although the book is long and detailed, it is tutorial in nature and does not require any previous knowledge of telephone engineering.

Davison, "A Web Caching Primer"

As the Web grows, caching is becoming crucial to good performance. For a brief introduction to Web caching, this is a good place to look.

Krishnamurthy and Rexford, *Web Protocols and Practice*

It would be hard to find a more comprehensive book about all aspects of the Web than this one. It covers clients, servers, proxies, and caching, as you might expect. But there are also chapters on Web traffic and measurements as well as chapters on current research and improving the Web.

Rabinovich and Spatscheck, *Web Caching and Replication*

For a comprehensive treatment of Web caching and replication, this is a good bet. Proxies, caches, prefetching, content delivery networks, server selection, and much more are covered in great detail.

Shahabi et al. "Yima: A Second-Generation Continuous Media Server"

Multimedia servers are complex systems that have to manage CPU scheduling, disk file placement, stream synchronization and more. As time has gone on, people have learned how to design them better. An architectural overview of one recent system is presented in this paper.

Tittel et al., *Mastering XHTML*

Two books in one large volume, covering the Web's new standard markup language. First, there's a text describing XHTML, focusing mostly on how it differs from regular HTML. Then there is a comprehensive reference guide to the tags, codes, and special characters used in XHTML 1.0.

Varshney et al., "Voice over IP"

How does voice over IP work and is it going to replace the public switched telephone network? Read and find out.

9.1.8 Network Security

Anderson, "Why Cryptosystems Fail"

According to Anderson, security in banking systems is poor, but not due to clever intruders breaking DES on their PCs. The real problems range from dishonest employees (a bank clerk's changing a customer's mailing address to his own to intercept the bank card and PIN number) to programming errors (giving all customers the same PIN code). What is especially interesting is the arrogant response banks give when confronted with a clear problem: "Our systems are perfect and therefore all errors must be due to customer errors or fraud."

Anderson, *Security Engineering*

To some extent, this book is a 600-page version of "Why Cryptosystems Fail." It is more technical than *Secrets and Lies* but less technical than *Network Security* (see below). After an introduction to the basic security techniques, entire chapters are devoted to various applications, including banking, nuclear command and control, security printing, biometrics, physical security, electronic warfare, telecom security, e-commerce, and copyright protection. The third part of the book is about policy, management, and system evaluation.

Artz, "Digital Steganography"

Steganography goes back to ancient Greece, where the wax was melted off blank tablets so secret messages could be applied to the underlying wood before the wax was reapplied. Nowadays different techniques are used, but the goal is the same. Various modern techniques for hiding information in images, audio, and other carriers are discussed here.

Brands, *Rethinking Public Key Infrastructures and Digital Certificates*

More than a wide-ranging introduction to digital certificates, this is also a powerful work of advocacy. The author believes that current paper-based systems of identity verification are outdated and inefficient, and argues that digital certificates can be used for applications such as electronic voting, digital rights management and even as a replacement for cash. He also warns that without PKI and encryption, the Internet could become a large-scale surveillance tool.

Kaufman et al., *Network Security*, 2nd ed.

This authoritative and witty book is the first place to look for more technical information on network security algorithms and protocols. Secret and public key algorithms and protocols, message hashes, authentication, Kerberos, PKI, IPsec, SSL/TLS, and e-mail security are all explained carefully and at considerable length, with many examples. Chapter 26 on security folklore is a real gem. In security, the devil is in the details. Anyone planning to design a security system that will actually be used will learn a lot from the real-world advice in this chapter.

Pohlmann, *Firewall Systems*

Firewalls are most networks' first (and last) line of defense against attackers. This book explains how they work and what they do, from the simplest software-based firewall designed to protect a single PC to the advanced firewall appliances that sit between a private network and its Internet connection.

Schneier, *Applied Cryptography*, 2nd ed.

This monumental compendium is NSA's worst nightmare: a single book that describes every known cryptographic algorithm. To make it worse (or better, depending on your point of view), the book contains most of the algorithms as runnable programs (in C). Furthermore, over 1600 references to the cryptographic literature are provided. This book is not for beginners, but if you *really* want to keep your files secret, read this book.

Schneier, *Secrets and Lies*

If you read *Applied Cryptography* from cover to cover, you will know everything there is to know about cryptographic algorithms. If you then read *Secrets and Lies* cover to cover (which can be done in a lot less time), you will learn that cryptographic algorithms are not the whole story. Most security weaknesses are not due to faulty algorithms or even keys that are too short, but to flaws in the security environment. Endless examples are presented about threats, attacks, defenses, counterattacks, and much more. For a nontechnical and fascinating discussion of computer security in the broadest sense, this book is the one to read.

Skoudis, *Counter Hack*

The best way to stop a hacker is to think like a hacker. This book shows how hackers see a network, and argues that security should be a function of the entire network's design, not an afterthought based on one specific technology. It covers almost all common attacks, including the "social engineering" types that take advantage of users who are not always familiar with computer security measures.

9.2 ALPHABETICAL BIBLIOGRAPHY

ABRAMSON, N.: "Internet Access Using VSATs," *IEEE Commun. Magazine*, vol. 38, pp. 60-68, July 2000.

ABRAMSON, N.: "Development of the ALOHANET," *IEEE Trans. on Information Theory*, vol. IT-31, pp. 119-123, March 1985.

ADAMS, M., and DULCHINOS, D.: "OpenCable," *IEEE Commun. Magazine*, vol. 39, pp. 98-105, June 2001.

ALKHATIB, H.S., BAILEY, C., GERLA, M., and McRAE, J.: "Wireless Data Networks: Reaching the Extra Mile," *Computer*, vol. 30, pp. 59-62, Dec. 1997.

ANDERSON, R.J.: "Free Speech Online and Office," *Computer*, vol. 25, pp. 28-30, June 2002.

ANDERSON, R.J.: *Security Engineering*, New York: Wiley, 2001.

ANDERSON, R.J.: "The Eternity Service," *Proc. First Int'l Conf. on Theory and Appl. of Cryptology*, CTU Publishing House, 1996.

ANDERSON, R.J.: "Why Cryptosystems Fail," *Commun. of the ACM*, vol. 37, pp. 32-40, Nov. 1994.

ARTZ, D.: "Digital Steganography," *IEEE Internet Computing*, vol. 5, pp. 75-80, 2001.

AZZAM, A.A., and RANSOM, N.: *Broadband Access Technologies*, New York: McGraw-Hill, 1999.

BAKNE, A., and BADRINATH, B.R.: "I-TCP: Indirect TCP for Mobile Hosts," *Proc. 15th Int'l Conf. on Distr. Computer Systems*, IEEE, pp. 136-143, 1995.

BALAKRISHNAN, H., SESHAN, S., and KATZ, R.H.: "Improving Reliable Transport and Handoff Performance in Cellular Wireless Networks," *Proc. ACM Mobile Computing and Networking Conf.*, ACM, pp. 2-11, 1995.

BALLARDIE, T., FRANCIS, P., and CROWCROFT, J.: "Core Based Trees (CBT)," *Proc. SIGCOMM '93 Conf.*, ACM, pp. 85-95, 1993.

BARAKAT, C., ALTMAN, E., and DABBOUS, W.: "On TCP Performance in a Heterogeneous Network: A Survey," *IEEE Commun. Magazine*, vol. 38, pp. 40-46, Jan. 2000.

BELLAMY, J.: *Digital Telephony*, 3rd ed., New York: Wiley, 2000.

BELLMAN, R.E.: *Dynamic Programming*, Princeton, NJ: Princeton University Press, 1957.

BELSNES, D.: "Flow Control in the Packet Switching Networks," *Communications Networks*, Uxbridge, England: Online, pp. 349-361, 1975.

BENNET, C.H., and BRASSARD, G.: "Quantum Cryptography: Public Key Distribution and Coin Tossing," *Int'l Conf. on Computer Systems and Signal Processing*, pp. 175-179, 1984.

BEREZDIVIN, R., BREINIG, R., and TOPP, R.: "Next-Generation Wireless Communication Concepts and Technologies," *IEEE Commun. Magazine*, vol. 40, pp. 108-116, March 2002.

BERGHEL, H.L.: "Cyber Privacy in the New Millennium," *Computer*, vol. 34, pp. 132-134, Jan. 2001.

BERGHOLZ, A.: "Extending Your Markup: An XML Tutorial," *IEEE Internet Computing*, vol. 4, pp. 74-79, July-Aug. 2000.

BERNERS-LEE, T., CAILLIAU, A., LOUTONEN, A., NIELSEN, H.F., and SECRET, A.: "The World Wide Web," *Commun. of the ACM*, vol. 37, pp. 76-82, Aug. 1994.

BERTSEKAS, D., and GALLAGER, R.: *Data Networks*, 2nd ed., Englewood Cliffs, NJ: Prentice Hall, 1992.

BHAGWAT, P.: "Bluetooth: Technology for Short-Range Wireless Apps," *IEEE Internet Computing*, vol. 5, pp. 96-103, May-June 2001.

BHARGHAVAN, V., DEMERS, A., SHENKER, S., and ZHANG, L.: "MACAW: A Media Access Protocol for Wireless LANs," *Proc. SIGCOMM '94 Conf.*, ACM, pp. 212-225, 1994.

BHATTI, S.N., and CROWCROFT, J.: "QoS Sensitive Flows: Issues in IP Packet Handling," *IEEE Internet Computing*, vol. 4, pp. 48-57, July-Aug. 2000.

BI, Q., ZYSMAN, G.I., and MENKES, H.: "Wireless Mobile Communications at the Start of the 21st Century," *IEEE Commun. Magazine*, vol. 39, pp. 110-116, Jan, 2001.

BIHAM, E., and SHAMIR, A.: "Differential Cryptanalysis of the Data Encryption Standard," *Proc. 17th Ann. Int'l Cryptology Conf.*, Berlin: Springer-Verlag LNCS 1294, pp. 513-525, 1997.

BIRD, R., GOPAL, I., HERZBERG, A., JANSON, P.A., KUTTEN, S., MOLVA, R, and YUNG, M.: "Systematic Design of a Family of Attack-Resistant Authentication Protocols," *IEEE J. on Selected Areas in Commun.*, vol. 11, pp. 679-693, June 1993.

BIRRELL, A.D., and NELSON, B.J.: "Implementing Remote Procedure Calls," *ACM Trans. on Computer Systems*, vol. 2, pp. 39-59, Feb. 1984.

BIRYUKOV, A., SHAMIR, A., and WAGNER, D.: "Real Time Cryptanalysis of A5/1 on a PC," *Proc. Seventh Int'l Workshop on Fast Software Encryption*, Berlin: Springer-Verlag LNCS 1978, p. 1, 2000.

BISDIKIAN, C.: "An Overview of the Bluetooth Wireless Technology," *IEEE Commun. Magazine*, vol. 39, pp. 86-94, Dec. 2001.

BLAZE, M.: "Protocol Failure in the Escrowed Encryption Standard," *Proc. Second ACM Conf. on Computer and Commun. Security*, ACM, pp. 59-67, 1994.

BLAZE, M., and BELLOVIN, S.: "Tapping on My Network Door," *Commun. of the ACM*, vol. 43, p. 136 , Oct. 2000.

BOGINENI, K., SIVALINGAM, K.M., and DOWD, P.W.: "Low-Complexity Multiple Access Protocols for Wavelength-Division Multiplexed Photonic Networks," *IEEE Journal on Selected Areas in Commun.*, vol. 11, pp. 590-604, May 1993.

BOLCSKEI, H., PAULRAJ, A.J., HARI, K.V.S., and NABAR, R.U.: "Fixed Broadband Wireless Access: State of the Art, Challenges, and Future Directions," *IEEE Commun. Magazine*, vol. 39, pp. 100-108, Jan. 2001.

BORISOV, N., GOLDBERG, I., and WAGNER, D.: "Intercepting Mobile Communications: The Insecurity of 802.11," *Seventh Int'l Conf. on Mobile Computing and Networking*, ACM, pp. 180-188, 2001.

BRANDS, S.: *Rethinking Public Key Infrastructures and Digital Certificates*, Cambridge, MA: M.I.T. Press, 2000.

BRAY, J., and STURMAN, C.F.: *Bluetooth 1.1: Connect without Cables*, 2nd ed., Upper Saddle River, NJ: Prentice Hall, 2002.

BREYER, R., and RILEY, S.: *Switched, Fast, and Gigabit Ethernet*, Indianapolis, IN: New Riders, 1999.

BROWN, S.: *Implementing Virtual Private Networks*, New York: McGraw-Hill, 1999.

BROWN, L., KWAN, M., PIEPRZYK, J., and SEBERRY, J.: "Improving Resistance to Differential Cryptanalysis and the Redesign of LOKI," *ASIACRYPT '91 Abstracts*, pp. 25-30, 1991.

BURNETT, S., and PAINE, S.: *RSA Security's Official Guide to Cryptography*, Berkeley, CA: Osborne/McGraw-Hill, 2001.

CAPETANAKIS, J.I.: "Tree Algorithms for Packet Broadcast Channels," *IEEE Trans. on Information Theory*, vol. IT-25, pp. 505-515, Sept. 1979.

CARDELLINI, V., CASALICCHIO, E., COLAJANNI, M., and YU, P.S.: *"The State-of-the-Art in Locally Distributed Web-Server Systems," ACM Computing Surveys, vol. 34, pp. 263-311, June 2002.*

CARLSON, J.: *PPP Design, Implementation and Debugging*, 2nd ed., Boston: Addison-Wesley, 2001.

CERF, V., and KAHN, R.: "A Protocol for Packet Network Interconnection," *IEEE Trans. on Commun.*, vol. COM-22, pp. 637-648, May 1974.

CHAKRABARTI, S.: "QoS Issues in Ad Hoc Wireless Networks," *IEEE Commun. Magazine*, vol. 39, pp. 142-148, Feb. 2001.

CHASE, J.S., GALLATIN, A.J., and YOCUM, K.G.: "End System Optimizations for High-Speed TCP," *IEEE Commun. Magazine*, vol. 39, pp. 68-75, April 2001.

CHEN, B., JAMIESON, K., BALAKRISHNAN, H., and MORRIS, R.: "Span: An Energy-Efficient Coordination Algorithm for Topology Maintenance in Ad Hoc Wireless Networks," *ACM Wireless Networks*, vol. 8, Sept. 2002.

CHEN, K.-C.: "Medium Access Control of Wireless LANs for Mobile Computing," *IEEE Network Magazine*, vol. 8, pp. 50-63, Sept./Oct. 1994.

CHOUDBURY, A.K., MAXEMCHUK, N.F., PAUL, S., and SCHULZRINNE, H.G.: "Copyright Protection for Electronic Publishing on Computer Networks," *IEEE Network Magazine*, vol. 9, pp. 12-20, May/June, 1995.

CHU, Y., RAO, S.G., and ZHANG, H.: "A Case for End System Multicast," *Proc. Int'l Conf. on Measurements and Modeling of Computer Syst.*, ACM, pp. 1-12, 2000.

CLARK, D.D.: "The Design Philosophy of the DARPA Internet Protocols," *Proc. SIGCOMM '88 Conf.*, ACM, pp. 106-114, 1988.

CLARK, D.D.: "Window and Acknowledgement Strategy in TCP," RFC 813, July 1982.

CLARK, D.D., DAVIE, B.S., FARBER, D.J., GOPAL, I.S., KADABA, B.K., SINCOSKIE, W.D., SMITH, J.M., and TENNENHOUSE, D.L.: "The Aurora Gigabit Testbed," *Computer Networks and ISDN Systems*, vol. 25, pp. 599-621, Jan. 1993.

CLARK, D.D., JACOBSON, V., ROMKEY, J., and SALWEN, H.: "An Analysis of TCP Processing Overhead," *IEEE Commun. Magazine*, vol. 27, pp. 23-29, June 1989.

CLARK, D.D., LAMBERT, M., and ZHANG, L.: "NETBLT: A High Throughput Transport Protocol," *Proc. SIGCOMM '87 Conf.*, ACM, pp. 353-359, 1987.

CLARKE, A.C.: "Extra-Terrestrial Relays," *Wireless World*, 1945.

CLARKE, I., MILLER, S.G., HONG, T.W., SANDBERG, O., and WILEY, B.: "Protecting Free Expression Online with Freenet," *IEEE Internet Computing*, vol. 6, pp. 40-49, Jan.-Feb. 2002.

COLLINS, D.: *Carrier Grade Voice over IP*, New York: McGraw-Hill, 2001.

COLLINS, D., and SMITH, C.: *3G Wireless Networks*, New York: McGraw-Hill, 2001.

COMER, D.E.: *The Internet Book*, Englewood Cliffs, NJ: Prentice Hall, 1995.

COMER, D.E.: *Internetworking with TCP/IP*, vol. 1, 4th ed., Englewood Cliffs, NJ: Prentice Hall, 2000.

COSTA, L.H.M.K., FDIDA, S., and DUARTE, O.C.M.B.: "Hop by Hop Multicast Routing Protocol," *Proc. 2001 Conf. on Applications, Technologies, Architectures, and Protocols for Computer Commun.*, ACM, pp. 249-259, 2001.

CRAVER, S.A., WU, M., LIU, B., STUBBLEFIELD, A., SWARTZLANDER, B., WALLACH, D.W., DEAN, D., and FELTEN, E.W.: "Reading Between the Lines: Lessons from the SDMI Challenge," *Proc. 10th USENIX Security Symp.*, USENIX, 2001.

CRESPO, P.M., HONIG, M.L., and SALEHI, J.A.: "Spread-Time Code-Division Multiple Access," *IEEE Trans. on Commun.*, vol. 43, pp. 2139-2148, June 1995.

CROW, B.P., WIDJAJA, I, KIM, J.G., and SAKAI, P.T.: "IEEE 802.11 Wireless Local Area Networks," *IEEE Commun. Magazine*, vol. 35, pp. 116-126, Sept. 1997.

CROWCROFT, J., WANG, Z., SMITH, A., and ADAMS, J.: "A Rough Comparison of the IETF and ATM Service Models," *IEEE Network Magazine*, vol. 9, pp. 12-16, Nov./Dec. 1995.

DABEK, F., BRUNSKILL, E., KAASHOEK, M.F., KARGER, D., MORRIS, R., STOICA, R., and BALAKRISHNAN, H.: "Building Peer-to-Peer Systems With Chord, a Distributed Lookup Service," *Proc. 8th Workshop on Hot Topics in Operating Systems*, IEEE, pp. 71-76, 2001a.

DABEK, F., KAASHOEK, M.F., KARGER, D., MORRIS, R., and STOICA, I.: "Wide-Area Cooperative Storage with CFS," *Proc. 18th Symp. on Operating Systems Prin.*, ACM, pp. 202-15 , 2001b.

DAEMEN, J., and RIJMEN, V.: *The Design of Rijndael*, Berlin: Springer-Verlag, 2002.

DANTHINE, A.A.S.: "Protocol Representation with Finite-State Models," *IEEE Trans. on Commun.*, vol. COM-28, pp. 632-643, April 1980.

DAVIDSON, J., and PETERS, J.: *Voice over IP Fundamentals*, Indianapolis, IN: Cisco Press, 2000.

DAVIE, B., and REKHTER, Y.: *MPLS Technology and Applications*, San Francisco: Morgan Kaufmann, 2000.

DAVIS, P.T., and McGUFFIN, C.R.: *Wireless Local Area Networks*, New York: McGraw-Hill, 1995.

DAVISON, B.D.: "A Web Caching Primer," *IEEE Internet Computing*, vol. 5, pp. 38-45, July-Aug. 2001.

DAY, J.D.: "The (Un)Revised OSI Reference Model," *Computer Commun. Rev.*, vol. 25, pp. 39-55, Oct. 1995.

DAY, J.D., and ZIMMERMANN, H.: "The OSI Reference Model," *Proc. of the IEEE*, vol. 71, pp. 1334-1340, Dec. 1983.

DE VRIENDT, J., LAINE, P., LEROUGE, C, and XU, X.: "Mobile Network Evolution: A Revolution on the Move," *IEEE Commun. Magazine*, vol. 40, pp. 104-111, April 2002.

DEERING, S.E.: "SIP: Simple Internet Protocol," *IEEE Network Magazine*, vol. 7, pp. 16-28, May/June 1993.

DEMERS, A., KESHAV, S., and SHENKER, S.: "Analysis and Simulation of a Fair Queueing Algorithm," *Internetwork: Research and Experience*, vol. 1, pp. 3-26, Sept. 1990.

DENNING, D.E., and SACCO, G.M.: "Timestamps in Key Distribution Protocols," *Commun. of the ACM*, vol. 24, pp. 533-536, Aug. 1981.

DIFFIE, W., and HELLMAN, M.E.: "Exhaustive Cryptanalysis of the NBS Data Encryption Standard," *Computer*, vol. 10, pp. 74-84, June 1977.

DIFFIE, W., and HELLMAN, M.E.: "New Directions in Cryptography," *IEEE Trans. on Information Theory*, vol. IT-22, pp. 644-654, Nov. 1976.

DIJKSTRA, E.W.: "A Note on Two Problems in Connexion with Graphs," *Numer. Math.*, vol. 1, pp. 269-271, Oct. 1959.

DOBROWSKI, G., and GRISE, D.: *ATM and SONET Basics*, Fuquay-Varina, NC: APDG Telecom Books, 2001.

DONALDSON, G., and JONES, D.: "Cable Television Broadband Network Architectures," *IEEE Commun. Magazine*, vol. 39, pp. 122-126, June 2001.

DORFMAN, R.: "Detection of Defective Members of a Large Population," *Annals Math. Statistics*, vol. 14, pp. 436-440, 1943.

DOUFEXI, A., ARMOUR, S., BUTLER, M., NIX, A., BULL, D., McGEEHAN, J., and KARLSSON, P.: "A Comparison of the HIPERLAN/2 and IEEE 802.11A Wireless LAN Standards," *IEEE Commun. Magazine*, vol. 40, pp. 172-180, May 2002.

DURAND, A.: "Deploying IPv6," *IEEE Internet Computing*, vol. 5, pp. 79-81, Jan.-Feb. 2001.

DUTCHER, B.: *The NAT Handbook*, New York: Wiley, 2001.

DUTTA-ROY, A.: "An Overview of Cable Modem Technology and Market Perspectives," *IEEE Commun. Magazine*, vol. 39, pp. 81-88, June 2001.

EASTTOM, C.: *Learn JavaScript*, Ashburton, U.K.: Wordware Publishing, 2001.

EL GAMAL, T.: "A Public-Key Cryptosystem and a Signature Scheme Based on Discrete Logarithms," *IEEE Trans. on Information Theory*, vol. IT-31, pp. 469-472, July 1985.

ELHANANY, I., KAHANE, M., and SADOT, D.: "Packet Scheduling in Next-Generation Multiterabit Networks," *Computer*, vol. 34, pp. 104-106, April 2001.

ELMIRGHANI, J.M.H., and MOUFTAH, H.T.: "Technologies and Architectures for Scalable Dynamic Dense WDM Networks," *IEEE Commun. Magazine*, vol. 38, pp. 58-66, Feb. 2000.

FARSEROTU, J., and PRASAD, R.: "A Survey of Future Broadband Multimedia Satellite Systems, Issues, and Trends," *IEEE Commun. Magazine*, vol. 38, pp. 128-133, June 2000.

FIORINI, D., CHIANI, M., TRALLI, V., and SALATI., C.: "Can we Trust HDLC?," *Computer Commun. Rev.*, vol. 24, pp. 61-80, Oct. 1994.

FLOYD, S., and JACOBSON, V.: "Random Early Detection for Congestion Avoidance," *IEEE/ACM Trans. on Networking*, vol. 1, pp. 397-413, Aug. 1993.

FLUHRER, S., MANTIN, I., and SHAMIR, A.: "Weakness in the Key Scheduling Algorithm of RC4," *Proc. Eighth Ann. Workshop on Selected Areas in Cryptography*, 2001.

FORD, L.R., Jr., and FULKERSON, D.R.: *Flows in Networks*, Princeton, NJ: Princeton University Press, 1962.

FORD, W., and BAUM, M.S.: *Secure Electronic Commerce*, Upper Saddle River, NJ: Prentice Hall, 2000.

FORMAN, G.H., and ZAHORJAN, J.: "The Challenges of Mobile Computing," *Computer*, vol. 27, pp. 38-47, April 1994.

FRANCIS, P.: "A Near-Term Architecture for Deploying Pip," *IEEE Network Magazine*, vol. 7, pp. 30-37, May/June 1993.

FRASER, A.G.: "Towards a Universal Data Transport System," in *Advances in Local Area Networks*, Kummerle, K., Tobagi, F., and Limb, J.O. (Eds.), New York: IEEE Press, 1987.

FRENGLE, N.: *I-Mode: A Primer*, New York: Hungry Minds, 2002.

GADECKI, C., and HECKERT, C.: *ATM for Dummies*, New York: Hungry Minds, 1997.

GARBER, L.: "Will 3G Really Be the Next Big Wireless Technology?," *Computer*, vol. 35, pp. 26-32, Jan. 2002.

GARFINKEL, S., with SPAFFORD, G.: *Web Security, Privacy, and Commerce*, Sebastopol, CA: O'Reilly, 2002.

GEIER, J.: *Wireless LANs*, 2nd ed., Indianapolis, IN: Sams, 2002.

GEVROS, P., CROWCROFT, J., KIRSTEIN, P., and BHATTI, S.: "Congestion Control Mechanisms and the Best Effort Service Model," *IEEE Network Magazine*, vol. 15, pp. 16-25, May-June 2001.

GHANI, N., and DIXIT, S.: "TCP/IP Enhancements for Satellite Networks," *IEEE Commun. Magazine*, vol. 37, pp. 64-72, 1999.

GINSBURG, D.: *ATM: Solutions for Enterprise Networking*, Boston: Addison-Wesley, 1996.

GOODMAN, D.J.: "The Wireless Internet: Promises and Challenges," *Computer*, vol. 33, pp. 36-41, July 2000.

GORALSKI, W.J.: *Optical Networking and WDM*, New York: McGraw-Hill, 2001.

GORALSKI, W.J.: *SONET*, 2nd ed., New York: McGraw-Hill, 2000.

GORALSKI, W.J.: *Introduction to ATM Networking*, New York: McGraw-Hill, 1995.

GOSSAIN, H., DE MORAIS CORDEIRO, and AGRAWAL, D.P.: "Multicast: Wired to Wireless," *IEEE Commun. Mag.*, vol. 40, pp. 116-123, June 2002.

GRAVANO, S.: *Introduction to Error Control Codes*, Oxford, U.K.: Oxford University Press, 2001.

GUO, Y., and CHASKAR, H.: "Class-Based Quality of Service over Air Interfaces in 4G Mobile Networks," *IEEE Commun. Magazine*, vol. 40, pp. 132-137, March 2002.

HAARTSEN, J.: "The Bluetooth Radio System," *IEEE Personal Commun. Magazine*, vol. 7, pp. 28-36, Feb. 2000.

HAC, A.: "Wireless and Cellular Architecture and Services," *IEEE Commun. Magazine*, vol. 33, pp. 98-104, Nov. 1995.

HAC, A., and GUO, L.: "A Scalable Mobile Host Protocol for the Internet," *Int'l J. of Network Mgmt*, vol. 10, pp. 115-134, May-June, 2000.

HALL, E., and CERF, V.: *Internet Core Protocols: The Definitive Guide*, Sebastopol, CA: O'Reilly, 2000.

HAMMING, R.W.: "Error Detecting and Error Correcting Codes," *Bell System Tech. J.*, vol. 29, pp. 147-160, April 1950.

HANEGAN, K.: *Custom CGI Scripting with Perl*, New York: Wiley, 2001.

HARRIS, A.: *JavaScript Programming for the Absolute Beginner*, Premier Press, 2001.

HARTE, L., KELLOGG, S., DREHER, R., and SCHAFFNIT, T.: *The Comprehensive Guide to Wireless Technology*, Fuquay-Varina, NC: APDG Publishing, 2000.

HARTE, L., LEVINE, R., and KIKTA, R.: *3G Wireless Demystified*, New York: McGraw-Hill, 2002.

HAWLEY, G.T.: "Historical Perspectives on the U.S. Telephone System," *IEEE Commun. Magazine*, vol. 29, pp. 24-28, March 1991.

HECHT, J.: "Understanding Fiber Optics," Upper Saddle River, NJ: Prentice Hall, 2001.

HEEGARD, C., COFFEY, J.T., GUMMADI, S., MURPHY, P.A., PROVENCIO, R., ROSSIN, E.J., SCHRUM, S., and SHOEMAKER, M.B.: "High-Performance Wireless Ethernet," *IEEE Commun. Magazine*, vol. 39, pp. 64-73, Nov. 2001.

HELD, G.: *The Complete Modem Reference*, 2nd ed., New York: Wiley, 1994.

HELLMAN, M.E.: "A Cryptanalytic Time-Memory Tradeoff," *IEEE Trans. on Information Theory*, vol. IT-26, pp. 401-406, July 1980.

HILLS, A.: "Large-Scale Wireless LAN Design," *IEEE Commun. Magazine*, vol. 39, pp. 98-104, Nov. 2001.

HOLZMANN, G.J.: *Design and Validation of Computer Protocols*, Englewood Cliffs, NJ: Prentice Hall, 1991.

HU, Y., and LI, V.O.K.: "Satellite-Based Internet Access," *IEEE Commun. Magazine*, vol. 39, pp. 155-162, March 2001.

HU, Y.-C., and JOHNSON, D.B.: "Implicit Source Routes for On-Demand Ad Hoc Network Routing," *Proc. ACM Int'l Symp. on Mobile Ad Hoc Networking & Computing*, ACM, pp. 1-10, 2001.

HUANG, V., and ZHUANG, W.: "QoS-Oriented Access Control for 4G Mobile Multimedia CDMA Communications," *IEEE Commun. Magazine*, vol. 40, pp. 118-125, March 2002.

HUBER, J.F., WEILER, D., and BRAND, H.: "UMTS, the Mobile Multimedia Vision for IMT-2000: A Focus on Standardization," *IEEE Commun. Magazine*, vol. 38, pp. 129-136, Sept. 2000. nr u 0

HUI, J.: "A Broadband Packet Switch for Multi-rate Services," *Proc. Int'l Conf. on Commun.*, IEEE, pp. 782-788, 1987.

HUITEMA, C.: *Routing in the Internet*, Englewood Cliffs, NJ: Prentice Hall, 1995.

HULL, S.: *Content Delivery Networks*, Berkeley, CA: Osborne/McGraw-Hill, 2002.

HUMBLET, P.A., RAMASWAMI, R., and SIVARAJAN, K.N.: "An Efficient Communication Protocol for High-Speed Packet-Switched Multichannel Networks," *Proc. SIGCOMM '92 Conf.*, ACM, pp. 2-13, 1992.

HUNTER, D.K., and ANDONOVIC, I.: "Approaches to Optical Internet Packet Switching," *IEEE Commun. Magazine*, vol. 38, pp. 116-122, Sept. 2000.

HUSTON, G.: "TCP in a Wireless World," *IEEE Internet Computing*, vol. 5, pp. 82-84, March-April, 2001.

IBE, O.C.: *Essentials of ATM Networks and Services*, Boston: Addison-Wesley, 1997.

IRMER, T.: "Shaping Future Telecommunications: The Challenge of Global Standardization," *IEEE Commun. Magazine*, vol. 32, pp. 20-28, Jan. 1994.

IZZO, P.: *Gigabit Networks*, New York: Wiley, 2000.

JACOBSON, V.: "Congestion Avoidance and Control," *Proc. SIGCOMM '88 Conf.*, ACM, pp. 314-329, 1988.

JAIN, R.: "Congestion Control and Traffic Management in ATM Networks: Recent Advances and a Survey," *Computer Networks and ISDN Systems*, vol. 27, Nov. 1995.

JAIN, R.: *FDDI Handbook—High-Speed Networking Using Fiber and Other Media*, Boston: Addison-Wesley, 1994.

JAIN, R.: "Congestion Control in Computer Networks: Issues and Trends," *IEEE Network Magazine*, vol. 4, pp. 24-30, May/June 1990.

JAKOBSSON, M., and WETZEL, S.: "Security Weaknesses in Bluetooth," *Topics in Cryptology: CT-RSA 2001*, Berlin: Springer-Verlag LNCS 2020, pp. 176-191, 2001.

JOEL, A.: "Telecommunications and the IEEE Communications Society," *IEEE Commun. Magazine*, 50th Anniversary Issue, pp. 6-14 and 162-167, May 2002.

JOHANSSON, P., KAZANTZIDIS, M., KAPOOR, R., and GERLA, M.: "Bluetooth: An Enabler for Personal Area Networking," *IEEE Network Magazine*, vol. 15, pp. 28-37, Sept.-Oct 2001.

JOHNSON, D.B.: "Scalable Support for Transparent Mobile Host Internetworking," *Wireless Networks*, vol. 1, pp. 311-321, Oct. 1995.

JOHNSON, H.W.: *Fast Ethernet—Dawn of a New Network*, Englewood Cliffs, NJ: Prentice Hall, 1996.

JOHNSON, N.F., and JAJODA, S.: "Exploring Steganography: Seeing the Unseen," *Computer*, vol. 31, pp. 26-34, Feb. 1998.

KAHN, D.: "Cryptology Goes Public," *IEEE Commun. Magazine*, vol. 18, pp. 19-28, March 1980.

KAHN, D.: *The Codebreakers*, 2nd ed., New York: Macmillan, 1995.

KAMOUN, F., and KLEINROCK, L.: "Stochastic Performance Evaluation of Hierarchical Routing for Large Networks," *Computer Networks*, vol. 3, pp. 337-353, Nov. 1979.

KAPP, S.: "802.11: Leaving the Wire Behind," *IEEE Internet Computing*, vol. 6, pp. 82-85, Jan.-Feb. 2002.

KARN, P.: "MACA—A New Channel Access Protocol for Packet Radio," *ARRL/CRRL Amateur Radio Ninth Computer Networking Conf.*, pp. 134-140, 1990.

KARTALOPOULOS, S.: *Introduction to DWDM Technology: Data in a Rainbow*, New York, NY: IEEE Communications Society, 1999.

KASERA, S.K., HJALMTYSSON, G., TOWLSEY, D.F., and KUROSE, J.F.: "Scalable Reliable Multicast Using Multiple Multicast Channels," *IEEE/ACM Trans. on Networking*, vol. 8, pp. 294-310, 2000.

KATZ, D., and FORD, P.S.: "TUBA: Replacing IP with CLNP," *IEEE Network Magazine*, vol. 7, pp. 38-47, May/June 1993.

KATZENBEISSER, S., and PETITCOLAS, F.A.P.: *Information Hiding Techniques for Steganography and Digital Watermarking*, London, Artech House, 2000.

KAUFMAN, C., PERLMAN, R., and SPECINER, M.: *Network Security*, 2nd ed., Englewood Cliffs, NJ: Prentice Hall, 2002.

KELLERER, W., VOGEL, H.-J., and STEINBERG, K.-E.: "A Communication Gateway for Infrastructure-Independent 4G Wireless Access," *IEEE Commun. Magazine*, vol. 40, pp. 126-131, March 2002.

KERCKHOFF, A.: "La Cryptographie Militaire," *J. des Sciences Militaires*, vol. 9, pp. 5-38, Jan. 1883 and pp. 161-191, Feb. 1883.

KIM, J.B., SUDA, T., and YOSHIMURA, M.: "International Standardization of B-ISDN," *Computer Networks and ISDN Systems*, vol. 27, pp. 5-27, Oct. 1994.

KIPNIS, J.: "Beating the System: Abuses of the Standards Adoptions Process," *IEEE Commun. Magazine*, vol. 38, pp. 102-105, July 2000.

KLEINROCK, L.: "On Some Principles of Nomadic Computing and Multi-Access Communications," *IEEE Commun. Magazine*, vol. 38, pp. 46-50, July 2000.

KLEINROCK, L., and TOBAGI, F.: "Random Access Techniques for Data Transmission over Packet-Switched Radio Channels," *Proc. Nat. Computer Conf.*, pp. 187-201, 1975.

KRISHNAMURTHY, B., and REXFORD, J.: *Web Protocols and Practice*, Boston: Addison-Wesley, 2001.

KUMAR, V., KORPI, M., and SENGODAN, S.: *IP Telephony with H.323*, New York: Wiley, 2001.

KUROSE, J.F., and ROSS, K.W.: *Computer Networking: A Top-Down Approach Featuring the Internet*, Boston: Addison-Wesley, 2001.

KWOK, T.: "A Vision for Residential Broadband Service: ATM to the Home," *IEEE Network Magazine*, vol. 9, pp. 14-28, Sept./Oct. 1995.

KYAS, O., and CRAWFORD, G.: *ATM Networks*, Upper Saddle River, NJ: Prentice Hall, 2002.

LAM, C.K.M., and TAN, B.C.Y.: "The Internet Is Changing the Music Industry," *Commun. of the ACM*, vol. 44, pp. 62-66, Aug. 2001.

LANSFORD, J., STEPHENS, A, and NEVO, R.: "Wi-Fi (802.11b) and Bluetooth: Enabling Coexistence," *IEEE Network Magazine*, vol. 15, pp. 20-27, Sept.-Oct 2001.

LASH, D.A.: *The Web Wizard's Guide to Perl and CGI*, Boston: Addison-Wesley, 2002.

LAUBACH, M.E., FARBER, D.J., and DUKES, S.D.: *Delivering Internet Connections over Cable*, New York: Wiley, 2001.

LEE, J.S., and MILLER, L.E.: *CDMA Systems Engineering Handbook*, London: Artech House, 1998.

LEEPER, D.G.: "A Long-Term View of Short-Range Wireless," *Computer*, vol. 34, pp. 39-44, June 2001.

LEINER, B.M., COLE, R., POSTEL, J., and MILLS, D.: "The DARPA Internet Protocol Suite," *IEEE Commun. Magazine*, vol. 23, pp. 29-34, March 1985.

LEVINE, D.A., and AKYILDIZ, I.A.: "PROTON: A Media Access Control Protocol for Optical Networks with Star Topology," *IEEE/ACM Trans. on Networking*, vol. 3, pp. 158-168, April 1995.

LEVY, S.: "Crypto Rebels," *Wired*, pp. 54-61, May/June 1993.

LI, J., BLAKE, C., DE COUTO, D.S.J., LEE, H.I., and MORRIS, R.: "Capacity of Ad Hoc Wireless Networks," *Proc. 7th Int'l Conf. on Mobile Computing and Networking*, ACM, pp. 61-69, 2001.

LIN, F., CHU, P., and LIU, M.: "Protocol Verification Using Reachability Analysis: The State Space Explosion Problem and Relief Strategies," *Proc. SIGCOMM '87 Conf.*, ACM, pp. 126-135, 1987.

LIN, Y.-D., HSU, N.-B., and HWANG, R.-H.: "QoS Routing Granularity in MPLS Networks" , *IEEE Commun. Magazine*, vol. 40, pp. 58-65, June 2002.

LISTANI, M., ERAMO, V., and SABELLA, R.: "Architectural and Technological Issues for Future Optical Internet Networks," *IEEE Commun. Magazine*, vol. 38, pp. 82-92, Sept. 2000.

LIU, C.L., and LAYLAND, J.W.: "Scheduling Algorithms for Multiprogramming in a Hard Real-Time Environment," *Journal of the ACM*, vol. 20, pp. 46-61, Jan. 1973.

LIVINGSTON, D.: *Essential XML for Web Professionals*, Upper Saddle River, NJ: Prentice Hall, 2002.

LOSHIN, P.: *IPv6 Clearly Explained*, San Francisco: Morgan Kaufmann, 1999.

LOUIS, P.J.: *Broadband Crash Course*, New York: McGraw-Hill, 2002.

LU, W.: *Broadband Wireless Mobile: 3G and Beyond*, New York: Wiley, 2002.

MACEDONIA, M.R.: "Distributed File Sharing," *Computer*, vol. 33, pp. 99-101, 2000.

MADRUGA, E.L., and GARCIA-LUNA-ACEVES, J.J.: "Scalable Multicasting: the Core-Assisted Mesh Protocol," *Mobile Networks and Applications*, vol. 6, pp. 151-165, April 2001.

MALHOTRA, R.: *IP Routing*, Sebastopol, CA: O'Reilly, 2002.

MATSUI, M.: "Linear Cryptanalysis Method for DES Cipher," *Advances in Cryptology—Eurocrypt '93 Proceedings*, Berlin: Springer-Verlag LNCS 765, pp. 386-397, 1994.

MAUFER, T.A.: *IP Fundamentals*, Upper Saddle River, NJ: Prentice Hall, 1999.

MAZIERES, D., and KAASHOEK, M.F.: "The Design, Implementation, and Operation of an Email Pseudonym Server," *Proc. Fifth Conf. on Computer and Commun. Security*, ACM, pp. 27-36, 1998.

MAZIERES, D., KAMINSKY, M., KAASHOEK, M.F., and WITCHEL, E.: "Separating Key Management from File System Security," *Proc. 17th Symp. on Operating Systems Prin.*, ACM, pp. 124-139, Dec. 1999.

McFEDRIES, P: *Using JavaScript*, Indianapolis, IN: Que, 2001.

McKENNEY, P.E., and DOVE, K.F.: "Efficient Demultiplexing of Incoming TCP Packets," *Proc. SIGCOMM '92 Conf.*, ACM, pp. 269-279, 1992.

MELTZER, K., and MICHALSKI, B.: *Writing CGI Applications with Perl*, Boston: Addison-Wesley, 2001.

MENEZES, A.J., and VANSTONE, S.A.: "Elliptic Curve Cryptosystems and Their Implementation," *Journal of Cryptology*, vol. 6, pp. 209-224, 1993.

MERKLE, R.C.: "Fast Software Encryption Functions," *Advances in Cryptology—CRYPTO '90 Proceedings*, Berlin: Springer-Verlag LNCS 473, pp. 476-501, 1991.

MERKLE, R.C., and HELLMAN, M.: "On the Security of Multiple Encryption," *Commun. of the ACM*, vol. 24, pp. 465-467, July 1981.

MERKLE, R.C., and HELLMAN, M.: "Hiding and Signatures in Trapdoor Knapsacks," *IEEE Trans. on Information Theory*, vol. IT-24, pp. 525-530, Sept. 1978.

METCALFE, R.M.: "On Mobile Computing," *Byte*, vol. 20, p. 110, Sept. 1995.

METCALFE, R.M.: "Computer/Network Interface Design: Lessons from Arpanet and Ethernet," *IEEE Journal on Selected Areas in Commun.*, vol. 11, pp. 173-179, Feb. 1993.

METCALFE, R.M., and BOGGS, D.R.: "Ethernet: Distributed Packet Switching for Local Computer Networks," *Commun. of the ACM*, vol. 19, pp. 395-404, July 1976.

METZ, C: "Interconnecting ISP Networks," *IEEE Internet Computing*, vol. 5, pp. 74-80, March-April 2001.

METZ, C.: "Differentiated Services," *IEEE Multimedia Magazine*, vol. 7, pp. 84-90, July-Sept. 2000.

METZ, C.: "IP Routers: New Tool for Gigabit Networking," *IEEE Internet Computing*, vol. 2, pp. 14-18, Nov.-Dec. 1998.

MILLER, B.A., and BISDIKIAN, C.,: *Bluetooth Revealed*, Upper Saddle River, NJ: Prentice Hall, 2001.

MILLER, P., and CUMMINS, M.: *LAN Technologies Explained*, Woburn, MA: Butterworth-Heinemann, 2000.

MINOLI, D.: *Video Dialtone Technology*, New York: McGraw-Hill, 1995.

MINOLI, D., and VITELLA, M.: *ATM & Cell Relay for Corporate Environments*, New York: McGraw-Hill, 1994.

MISHRA, P.P., and KANAKIA, H.: "A Hop by Hop Rate-Based Congestion Control Scheme," *Proc. SIGCOMM '92 Conf.*, ACM, pp. 112-123, 1992.

MISRA, A., DAS, S., DUTTA, A., McAULEY, A., and DAS, S.: "IDMP-Based Fast Handoffs and Paging in IP-Based 4G Mobile Networks," *IEEE Commun. Magazine*, vol. 40, pp. 138-145, March 2002.

MOGUL, J.C.: "IP Network Performance," in *Internet System Handbook*, Lynch, D.C. and Rose, M.T. (eds.), Boston: Addison-Wesley, pp. 575-675, 1993.

MOK, A.K., and WARD, S.A.: "Distributed Broadcast Channel Access," *Computer Networks*, vol. 3, pp. 327-335, Nov. 1979.

MOY, J.: "Multicast Routing Extensions," *Commun. of the ACM*, vol. 37, pp. 61-66, AUg. 1994.

MULLINS, J.: "Making Unbreakable Code," *IEEE Spectrum*, pp. 40-45, May 2002.

NAGLE, J.: "On Packet Switches with Infinite Storage," *IEEE Trans. on Commun.*, vol. COM-35, pp. 435-438, April 1987.

NAGLE, J.: "Congestion Control in TCP/IP Internetworks," *Computer Commun. Rev.*, vol. 14, pp. 11-17, Oct. 1984.

NARAYANASWAMI, C., KAMIJOH, N., RAGHUNATH, M., INOUE, T., CIPOLLA, T., SANFORD, J., SCHLIG, E., VENTKITESWARAN, S., GUNIGUNTALA, D., KULKARNI, V., and YAMAZAKI, K.: "IBM's Linux Watch: The Challenge of Miniaturization," *Computer*, vol. 35, pp. 33-41, Jan. 2002.

NAUGHTON, J.: "A Brief History of the Future," Woodstock, NY: Overlook Press, 2000.

NEEDHAM, R.M., and SCHROEDER, M.D.: "Authentication Revisited," *Operating Systems Rev.*, vol. 21, p. 7, Jan. 1987.

NEEDHAM, R.M., and SCHROEDER, M.D.: "Using Encryption for Authentication in Large Networks of Computers," *Commun. of the ACM*, vol. 21, pp. 993-999, Dec. 1978.

NELAKUDITI, S., and ZHANG, Z.-L.: "A Localized Adaptive Proportioning Approach to QoS Routing," *IEEE Commun. Magazine* vol. 40, pp. 66-71, June 2002.

NEMETH, E., SNYDER, G., SEEBASS, S., and HEIN, T.R.: *UNIX System Administration Handbook*, 3rd ed., Englewood Cliffs, NJ: Prentice Hall, 2000.

NICHOLS, R.K., and LEKKAS, P.C.: *Wireless Security*, New York: McGraw-Hill, 2002.

NIST: "Secure Hash Algorithm," U.S. Government Federal Information Processing Standard 180, 1993.

O'HARA, B., and PETRICK, A.: *802.11 Handbook: A Designer's Companion*, New York: IEEE Press, 1999.

OTWAY, D., and REES, O.: "Efficient and Timely Mutual Authentication," *Operating Systems Rev.*, pp. 8-10, Jan. 1987.

OVADIA, S.: *Broadband Cable TV Access Networks: from Technologies to Applications*, Upper Saddle River, NJ: Prentice Hall, 2001.

PALAIS, J.C.: *Fiber Optic Commun.*, 3rd ed., Englewood Cliffs, NJ: Prentice Hall, 1992.

PAN, D.: "A Tutorial on MPEG/Audio Compression," *IEEE Multimedia Magazine*, vol. 2, pp.60-74, Summer 1995.

PANDYA, R.: "Emerging Mobile and Personal Communication Systems," *IEEE Commun. Magazine*, vol. 33, pp. 44-52, June 1995.

PARAMESWARAN, M., SUSARLA, A., and WHINSTON, A.B.: "P2P Networking: An Information-Sharing Alternative," *Computer*, vol. 34, pp. 31-38, July 2001.

PARK, J.S., and SANDHU, R.: "Secure Cookies on the Web," *IEEE Internet Computing*, vol. 4, pp. 36-44, July-Aug. 2000.

PARTRIDGE, C., HUGHES, J., and STONE, J.: "Performance of Checksums and CRCs over Real Data," *Proc. SIGCOMM '95 Conf.*, ACM, pp. 68-76, 1995.

PAXSON, V.: "Growth Trends in Wide-Area TCP Connections," *IEEE Network Magazine*, vol. 8, pp. 8-17, July/Aug. 1994.

PAXSON, V., and FLOYD, S.: "Wide-Area Traffic: The Failure of Poisson Modeling," *Proc. SIGCOMM '94 Conf.*, ACM, pp. 257-268, 1995.

PEPELNJAK, I., and GUICHARD, J.: *MPLS and VPN Architectures*, Indianapolis, IN: Cisco Press, 2001.

PERKINS, C.E.: *RTP: Audio and Video for the Internet*, Boston: Addison-Wesley, 2002.

PERKINS, C.E. (ed.): *Ad Hoc Networking*, Boston: Addison-Wesley, 2001.

PERKINS, C.E.: *Mobile IP Design Principles and Practices*, Upper Saddle River, NJ: Prentice Hall, 1998a.

PERKINS, C.E.: "Mobile Networking in the Internet," *Mobile Networks and Applications*, vol. 3, pp. 319-334, 1998b.

PERKINS, C.E.: "Mobile Networking through Mobile IP," *IEEE Internet Computing*, vol. 2, pp. 58-69, Jan.-Feb. 1998c.

PERKINS, C.E., and ROYER, E.: "The Ad Hoc On-Demand Distance-Vector Protocol," in *Ad Hoc Networking*, edited by C. Perkins, Boston: Addison-Wesley, 2001.

PERKINS, C.E., and ROYER, E.: "Ad-hoc On-Demand Distance Vector Routing," *Proc. Second Ann. IEEE Workshop on Mobile Computing Systems and Applications*, IEEE, pp. 90-100, 1999.

PERLMAN, R.: *Interconnections*, 2nd ed., Boston: Addison-Wesley, 2000.

PERLMAN, R.: *Network Layer Protocols with Byzantine Robustness*, Ph.D. thesis, M.I.T., 1988.

PERLMAN, R., and KAUFMAN, C.: "Key Exchange in IPsec," *IEEE Internet Computing*, vol. 4, pp. 50-56, Nov.-Dec. 2000.

PETERSON, L.L., and DAVIE, B.S.: *Computer Networks: A Systems Approach*, San Francisco: Morgan Kaufmann, 2000.

PETERSON, W.W., and BROWN, D.T.: "Cyclic Codes for Error Detection," *Proc. IRE*, vol. 49, pp. 228-235, Jan. 1961.

PICKHOLTZ, R.L., SCHILLING, D.L., and MILSTEIN, L.B.: "Theory of Spread Spectrum Communication—A Tutorial," *IEEE Trans. on Commun.*, vol. COM-30, pp. 855-884, May 1982.

PIERRE, G., KUZ, I., VAN STEEN, M., TANENBAUM, A.S.: "Differentiated Strategies for Replicating Web Documents," *Computer Commun.*, vol. 24, pp. 232-240, Feb. 2001.

PIERRE, G., VAN STEEN, M., and TANENBAUM, A.S.: "Dynamically Selecting Optimal Distribution Strategies for Web Documents," *IEEE Trans. on Computers*, vol. 51, pp., June 2002.

PISCITELLO, D.M., and CHAPIN, A.L.: *Open Systems Networking: TCP/IP and OSI*, Boston: Addison-Wesley, 1993.

PITT, D.A.: "Bridging—The Double Standard," *IEEE Network Magazine*, vol. 2, pp. 94-95, Jan. 1988.

PIVA, A., BARTOLINI, F., and BARNI, M.: "Managing Copyrights in Open Networks," *IEEE Internet Computing*, vol. 6, pp. 18-26, May-June 2002.

POHLMANN, N.: *Firewall Systems*, Bonn, Germany: MITP-Verlag, 2001.

PUZMANOVA, R.: *Routing and Switching: Time of Convergence?*, London: Addison-Wesley, 2002.

RABINOVICH, M., and SPATSCHECK, O,: *Web Caching and Replication*, Boston: Addison-Wesley, 2002.

RAJU, J., and GARCIA-LUNA-ACEVES, J.J.: "Scenario-based Comparison of Source-Tracing and Dynamic Source Routing Protocols for Ad-Hoc Networks," *ACM Computer Communications Review*, vol. 31, October 2001.

RAMANATHAN, R., and REDI, J.: "A Brief Overview of Ad Hoc Networks: Challenges and Directions," *IEEE Commun. Magazine*, 50th Anniversary Issue, pp. 20-22, May 2002.

RATNASAMY, S., FRANCIS, P., HANDLEY, M., KARP, R., and SHENKER, S.: "A Scalable Content-Addressable Network," *Proc. SIGCOMM '01 Conf.*, ACM, pp. 1161-172, 2001.

RIVEST, R.L.: "The MD5 Message-Digest Algorithm," RFC 1320, April 1992.

RIVEST, R.L., and SHAMIR, A.: "How to Expose an Eavesdropper," *Commun. of the ACM*, vol. 27, pp. 393-395, April 1984.

RIVEST, R.L., SHAMIR, A., and ADLEMAN, L.: "On a Method for Obtaining Digital Signatures and Public Key Cryptosystems," *Commun. of the ACM*, vol. 21, pp. 120-126, Feb. 1978.

ROBERTS, L.G.: "Dynamic Allocation of Satellite Capacity through Packet Reservation," *Proc. NCC*, AFIPS, pp. 711-716, 1973.

ROBERTS, L.G.: "Extensions of Packet Communication Technology to a Hand Held Personal Terminal," *Proc. Spring Joint Computer Conference*, AFIPS, pp. 295-298, 1972.

ROBERTS, L.G.: "Multiple Computer Networks and Intercomputer Communication," *Proc. First Symp. on Operating Systems Prin.*, ACM, 1967.

ROSE, M.T.: *The Simple Book*, Englewood Cliffs, NJ: Prentice Hall, 1994.

ROSE, M.T.: *The Internet Message*, Englewood Cliffs, NJ: Prentice Hall, 1993.

ROSE, M.T., and McCLOGHRIE, K.: *How to Manage Your Network Using SNMP*, Englewood Cliffs, NJ: Prentice Hall, 1995.

ROWSTRON, A., and DRUSCHEL, P.: "Storage Management and Caching in PAST, a Large-Scale, Persistent Peer-to-Peer Storage Utility," *Proc. 18th Symp. on Operating Systems Prin.*, ACM, pp. 188-201, 2001a.

ROWSTRON, A., and DRUSCHEL, P.: "Pastry: Scalable, Distributed Object Location and Routing for Large-Scale Peer-to-Peer Storage Utility," *Proc. 18th Int'l Conf. on Distributed Systems Platforms*, ACM/IFIP, 2001b.

ROYER, E.M., and TOH, C.-K.: "A Review of Current Routing Protocols for Ad-Hoc Mobile Wireless Networks," *IEEE Personal Commun. Magazine*, vol. 6, pp. 46-55, April 1999.

RUIZ-SANCHEZ, M.A., BIERSACK, E.W., and DABBOUS, W.: "Survey and Taxonomy of IP Address Lookup Algorithms," *IEEE Network Magazine*, vol. 15, pp. 8-23, March-April 2001.

SAIRAM, K.V.S.S.S.S., GUNASEKARAN, N., and REDDY, S.R.: "Bluetooth in Wireless Communication," *IEEE Commun. Mag.*, vol. 40, pp. 90-96, June 2002.

SALTZER, J.H., REED, D.P., and CLARK, D.D.: "End-to-End Arguments in System Design," *ACM Trans. on Computer Systems*, vol. 2, pp. 277-288, Nov. 1984.

SANDERSON, D.W., and DOUGHERTY, D.: *Smileys*, Sebastopol, CA: O'Reilly, 1993.

SARI, H., VANHAVERBEKE, F., and MOENECLAEY, M.: "Extending the Capacity of Multiple Access Channels," *IEEE Commun. Magazine*, vol. 38, pp. 74-82, Jan. 2000.

SARIKAYA, B.: "Packet Mode in Wireless Networks: Overview of Transition to Third Generation," *IEEE Commun. Magazine*, vol. 38, pp. 164-172, Sept. 2000.

SCHNEIER, B.: *Secrets and Lies*, New York: Wiley, 2000.

SCHNEIER, B.: *Applied Cryptography*, 2nd ed., New York: Wiley, 1996.

SCHNEIER, B.: *E-Mail Security*, New York: Wiley, 1995.

SCHNEIER, B.: "Description of a New Variable-Length Key, 64-Bit Block Cipher [Blowfish]," *Proc. of the Cambridge Security Workshop*, Berlin: Springer-Verlag LNCS 809, pp. 191-204, 1994.

SCHNORR, C.P.: "Efficient Signature Generation for Smart Cards," *Journal of Cryptology*, vol. 4, pp. 161-174, 1991.

SCHOLTZ, R.A.: "The Origins of Spread-Spectrum Communications," *IEEE Trans. on Commun.*, vol. COM-30, pp. 822-854, May 1982.

SCOTT, R.: "Wide Open Encryption Design Offers Flexible Implementations," *Cryptologia*, vol. 9, pp. 75-90, Jan. 1985.

SEIFERT, R.: *The Switch Book*, Boston: Addison-Wesley, 2000.

SEIFERT, R.: *Gigabit Ethernet*, Boston: Addison-Wesley, 1998.

SENN, J.A.: "The Emergence of M-Commerce," *Computer*, vol. 33, pp. 148-150, Dec. 2000.

SERJANTOV, A.: "Anonymizing Censorship Resistant Systems," *Proc. First Int'l Workshop on Peer-to-Peer Systems*, Berlin: Springer-Verlag LNCS, 2002.

SEVERANCE, C.: "IEEE 802.11: Wireless Is Coming Home," *Computer*, vol. 32, pp. 126-127, Nov. 1999.

SHAHABI, C., ZIMMERMANN, R., FU, K., and YAO, S.-Y.D.: "YIMA: A Second-Generation Continuous Media Server," *Computer*, vol. 35, pp. 56-64, June 2002.

SHANNON, C.: "A Mathematical Theory of Communication," *Bell System Tech. J.*, vol. 27, pp. 379-423, July 1948; and pp. 623-656, Oct. 1948.

SHEPARD, S.: *SONET/SDH Demystified*, New York: McGraw-Hill, 2001.

SHREEDHAR, M., and VARGHESE, G.: "Efficient Fair Queueing Using Deficit Round Robin," *Proc. SIGCOMM '95 Conf.*, ACM, pp. 231-243, 1995.

SKOUDIS, E.: *Counter Hack*, Upper Saddle River, NJ: Prentice Hall, 2002.

SMITH, D.K., and ALEXANDER, R.C.: *Fumbling the Future*, New York: William Morrow, 1988.

SMITH, R.W.: *Broadband Internet Connections*, Boston: Addison Wesley, 2002.

SNOEREN, A.C., and BALAKRISHNAN, H.: "An End-to-End Approach to Host Mobility," *Int'l Conf. on Mobile Computing and Networking* , ACM, pp. 155-166, 2000.

SOBEL, D.L.: "Will Carnivore Devour Online Privacy," *Computer*, vol. 34, pp. 87-88, May 2001.

SOLOMON, J.D.: *Mobile IP: The Internet Unplugged*, Upper Saddle River, NJ: Prentice Hall, 1998.

SPOHN, M., and GARCIA-LUNA-ACEVES, J.J.: "Neighborhood Aware Source Routing," *Proc. ACM MobiHoc 2001*, ACM, pp. 2001.

SPURGEON, C.E.: *Ethernet: The Definitive Guide*, Sebastopol, CA: O'Reilly, 2000.

STALLINGS, W.: *Data and Computer Communications*, 6th ed., Upper Saddle River, NJ: Prentice Hall, 2000.

STEINMETZ, R., and NAHRSTEDT, K.: *Multimedia Fundamentals. Vol. 1: Media Coding and Content Processing*, Upper Saddle River, NJ: Prentice Hall, 2002.

STEINMETZ, R., and NAHRSTEDT, K.: *Multimedia Fundamentals. Vol. 2: Media Processing and Communications*, Upper Saddle River, NJ: Prentice Hall, 2003a.

STEINMETZ, R., and NAHRSTEDT, K.: *Multimedia Fundamentals. Vol. 3: Documents, Security, and Applications*, Upper Saddle River, NJ: Prentice Hall, 2003b.

STEINER, J.G., NEUMAN, B.C., and SCHILLER, J.I.: "Kerberos: An Authentication Service for Open Network Systems," *Proc. Winter USENIX Conf.*, USENIX, pp. 191-201, 1988.

STEVENS, W.R.: *UNIX Network Programming, Volume 1: Networking APIs - Sockets and XTI*, Upper Saddle River, NJ: Prentice Hall, 1997.

STEVENS, W.R.: *TCP/IP Illustrated*, Vol. 1, Boston: Addison-Wesley, 1994.

STEWART, R., and METZ, C.: "SCTP: New Transport Protocol for TCP/IP," *IEEE Internet Computing*, vol. 5, pp. 64-69, Nov.-Dec. 2001.

STINSON, D.R.: *Cryptography Theory and Practice*, 2nd ed., Boca Raton, FL: CRC Press, 2002.

STOICA, I., MORRIS, R., KARGER, D., KAASHOEK, M.F., and BALAKRISHNAN, H.: "Chord: A Scalable Peer-to-Peer Lookup Service for Internet Applications," *Proc. SIGCOMM '01 Conf.*, ACM, pp. 149-160, 2001.

STRIEGEL, A., and MANIMARAN, G.: "A Survey of QoS Multicasting Issues," *IEEE Commun. Mag.*, vol. 40, pp. 82-87, June 2002.

STUBBLEFIELD, A., IOANNIDIS, J., and RUBIN, A.D.: "Using the Fluhrer, Mantin, and Shamir Attack to Break WEP," *Proc Network and Distributed Systems Security Symp.*, ISOC, pp. 1-11, 2002.

SUMMERS, C.K.: *ADSL: Standards, Implementation, and Architecture*, Boca Raton, FL: CRC Press, 1999.

SUNSHINE, C.A., and DALAL, Y.K.: "Connection Management in Transport Protocols," *Computer Networks*, vol. 2, pp. 454-473, 1978.

TANENBAUM, A.S.: *Modern Operating Systems*, Upper Saddle River, NJ: Prentice Hall, 2001.

TANENBAUM, A.S., and VAN STEEN, M.: *Distributed Systems: Principles and Paradigms*, Upper Saddle River, NJ: Prentice Hall, 2002.

TEGER, S., and WAKS, D.J.: "End-User Perspectives on Home Networking," *IEEE Commun. Magazine*, vol. 40, pp. 114-119, April 2002.

THYAGARAJAN, A.S., and DEERING, S.E.: "Hierarchical Distance-Vector Multicast Routing for the MBone," *Proc. SIGCOMM '95 Conf.*, ACM, pp. 60-66, 1995.

TITTEL, E., VALENTINE, C., BURMEISTER, M., and DYKES, L.: *Mastering XHTML*, Alameda, CA: Sybex, 2001.

TOKORO, M., and TAMARU, K.: "Acknowledging Ethernet," *Compcon*, IEEE, pp. 320-325, Fall 1977.

TOMLINSON, R.S.: "Selecting Sequence Numbers," *Proc. SIGCOMM/SIGOPS Interprocess Commun. Workshop*, ACM, pp. 11-23, 1975.

TSENG, Y.-C., WU, S.-L., LIAO, W.-H., and CHAO, C.-M.: "Location Awareness in Ad Hoc Wireless Mobile Networks," *Computer*, vol. 34, pp. 46-51, 2001.

TUCHMAN, W.: "Hellman Presents No Shortcut Solutions to DES," *IEEE Spectrum*, vol. 16, pp. 40-41, July 1979.

TURNER, J.S.: "New Directions in Communications (or Which Way to the Information Age)," *IEEE Commun. Magazine*, vol. 24, pp. 8-15, Oct. 1986.

VACCA, J.R.: *I-Mode Crash Course*, New York: McGraw-Hill, 2002.

VALADE, J.,: *PHP & MySQL for Dummies*, New York: Hungry Minds, 2002.

VARGHESE, G., and LAUCK, T.: "Hashed and Hierarchical Timing Wheels: Data Structures for the Efficient Implementation of a Timer Facility," *Proc. 11th Symp. on Operating Systems Prin.*, ACM, pp. 25-38, 1987.

VARSHNEY, U., SNOW, A., McGIVERN, M., and HOWARD, C.: "Voice over IP," *Commun. of the ACM*, vol. 45, pp. 89-96, 2002.

VARSHNEY, U., and VETTER, R.: "Emerging Mobile and Wireless Networks," *Commun. of the ACM*, vol. 43, pp. 73-81, June 2000.

VETTER, P., GODERIS, D., VERPOOTEN, L., and GRANGER, A.: "Systems Aspects of APON/VDSL Deployment," *IEEE Commun. Magazine*, vol. 38, pp. 66-72, May 2000.

WADDINGTON, D.G., and CHANG, F.: "Realizing the Transition to IPv6," *IEEE Commun. Mag.*, vol. 40, pp. 138-148, June 2002.

WALDMAN, M., RUBIN, A.D., and CRANOR, L.F.: "Publius: A Robust, Tamper-Evident, Censorship-Resistant, Web Publishing System," *Proc. Ninth USENIX Security Symp.*, USENIX, pp. 59-72, 2000.

WANG, Y., and CHEN, W.: "Supporting IP Multicast for Mobile Hosts," *Mobile Networks and Applications*, vol. 6, pp. 57-66, Jan.-Feb. 2001.

WANG, Z.: *Internet QoS*, San Francisco: Morgan Kaufmann, 2001.

WARNEKE, B., LAST, M., LIEBOWITZ, B., and PISTER, K.S.J.: "Smart Dust: Communicating with a Cubic Millimeter Computer," *Computer*, vol. 34, pp. 44-51, Jan. 2001.

WAYNER, P.: *Disappearing Cryptography: Information Hiding, Steganography, and Watermarking*, 2nd ed., San Francisco: Morgan Kaufmann, 2002.

WEBB, W.: "Broadband Fixed Wireless Access as a Key Component of the Future Integrated Communications Environment," *IEEE Commun. Magazine*, vol. 39, pp. 115-121, Sept. 2001.

WEISER, M.: "Whatever Happened to the Next Generation Internet?," *Commun. of the ACM*, vol. 44, pp. 61-68, Sept. 2001.

WELTMAN, R., and DAHBURA, T.: *LDAP Programming with Java*, Boston: Addison-Wesley, 2000.

WESSELS, D.: *Web Caching*, Sebastopol, CA: O'Reilly, 2001.

WETTEROTH, D.: *OSI Reference Model for Telecommunications*, New York: McGraw-Hill, 2001.

WILJAKKA, J.: "Transition to Ipv6 in GPRS and WCDMA Mobile Networks," *IEEE Commun. Magazine*, vol. 40, pp. 134-140, April 2002.

WILLIAMSON, H.: *XML: The Complete Reference*, New York: McGraw-Hill, 2001.

WILLINGER, W., TAQQU, M.S., SHERMAN, R., and WILSON, D.V.: "Self-Similarity through High Variability: Statistical Analysis of Ethernet LAN Traffic at the Source Level," *Proc. SIGCOMM '95 Conf.*, ACM, pp. 100-113, 1995.

WRIGHT, D.J.: *Voice over Packet Networks*, New York: Wiley, 2001.

WYLIE, J., BIGRIGG, M.W., STRUNK, J.D., GANGER, G.R., KILICCOTE, H., and KHOSLA, P.K.: "Survivable Information Storage Systems," *Computer*, vol. 33, pp. 61-68, Aug. 2000.

XYLOMENOS, G., POLYZOS, G.C., MAHONEN, P., and SAARANEN, M.: "TCP Performance Issues over Wireless Links" , *IEEE Commun. Magazine*, vol. 39, pp. 52-58, April 2001.

YANG, C.-Q., and REDDY, A.V.S.: "A Taxonomy for Congestion Control Algorithms in Packet Switching Networks," *IEEE Network Magazine*, vol. 9, pp. 34-45, July/Aug. 1995.

YUVAL, G.: "How to Swindle Rabin," *Cryptologia*, vol. 3, pp. 187-190, July 1979.

ZACKS, M.: "Antiterrorist Legislation Expands Electronic Snooping," *IEEE Internet Computing*, vol. 5, pp. 8-9, Nov.-Dec. 2001.

ZADEH, A.N., JABBARI, B., PICKHOLTZ, R., and VOJCIC, B.: "Self-Organizing Packet Radio Ad Hoc Networks with Overlay (SOPRANO)," *IEEE Commun. Mag.*, vol. 40, pp. 149-157, June 2002.

ZHANG, L.: "Comparison of Two Bridge Routing Approaches," *IEEE Network Magazine*, vol. 2, pp. 44-48, Jan./Feb. 1988.

ZHANG, L.: "RSVP: A New Resource ReSerVation Protocol," *IEEE Network Magazine*, vol. 7, pp. 8-18, Sept./Oct. 1993.

ZHANG, Y., and RYU, B.: "Mobile and Multicast IP Services in PACS: System Architecture, Prototype, and Performance," *Mobile Networks and Applications*, vol. 6, pp. 81-94, Jan.-Feb. 2001.

ZIMMERMANN, P.R.: *The Official PGP User's Guide*, Cambridge, MA: M.I.T. Press, 1995a.

ZIMMERMANN, P.R.: *PGP: Source Code and Internals*, Cambridge, MA: M.I.T. Press, 1995b.

ZIPF, G.K.: *Human Behavior and the Principle of Least Effort: An Introduction to Human Ecology*, Boston: Addison-Wesley, 1949.

ZIV, J., and LEMPEL, Z.: "A Universal Algorithm for Sequential Data Compression," *IEEE Trans. on Information Theory*, vol. IT-23, pp. 337-343, May 1977.

INDEX

Numbers

A

B

C

D

E

F

G

H

I

J

K

L

M

N

O

P

Q

R

S

T

U

V

W

X

Z

ABOUT THE AUTHOR

Andrew S. Tanenbaum has an S.B. degree from M.I.T. and a Ph.D. from the University of California at Berkeley. He is currently a Professor of Computer Science at the Vrije Universiteit in Amsterdam, The Netherlands, where he heads the Computer Systems Group. He is also Dean of the Advanced School for Computing and Imaging, an interuniversity graduate school doing research on advanced parallel, distributed, and imaging systems. Nevertheless, he is trying very hard to avoid turning into a bureaucrat.

In the past, he has done research on compilers, operating systems, networking, and local-area distributed systems. His current research focuses primarily on the design and implementation of wide-area distributed systems that scales to a billion users. This research, being done together with Prof. Maarten van Steen, is described at *www.cs.vu.nl/globe*. Together, all these research projects have led to over 100 refereed papers in journals and conference proceedings and five books.

Prof. Tanenbaum has also produced a considerable volume of software. He was the principal architect of the Amsterdam Compiler Kit, a widely-used toolkit for writing portable compilers, as well as of MINIX, a small UNIX clone intended for use in student programming labs. This system provided the inspiration and base on which Linux was developed. Together with his Ph.D. students and programmers, he helped design the Amoeba distributed operating system, a high-performance microkernel-based distributed operating system. The MINIX and Amoeba systems are now available for free via the Internet.

His Ph.D. students have gone on to greater glory after getting their degrees. He is very proud of them. In this respect he resembles a mother hen.

Prof. Tanenbaum is a Fellow of the ACM, a Fellow of the the IEEE, and a member of the Royal Netherlands Academy of Arts and Sciences. He is also winner of the 1994 ACM Karl V. Karlstrom Outstanding Educator Award, winner of the 1997 ACM/SIGCSE Award for Outstanding Contributions to Computer Science Education, and winner of the 2002 Texty award for excellence in textbooks. He is also listed in *Who's Who in the World*. His home page on the World Wide Web can be found at URL *http://www.cs.vu.nl/~ast/* .